# Les Routiers
# BRITAIN
## AND IRELAND 1996

*food and accommodation*
## RECOMMENDED
*for Quality and Value*

IN
ASSOCIATION
WITH

First published in the United Kingdom in 1996
Routiers Ltd.
25 Vanston Place
London SW6 IAZ

ISBN 1-85733-141-9

Les Routiers inspectors visit each new establishment anonymously and settle their bill before revealing their identity. Complimentary meals and/or accommodation are not accepted.

Les Routiers, 25 Vanston Place, London SW6 1AZ

For reservations and further information, phone - *Les Routiers FreeCall 0500 700456* (Mon-Fri 9-6pm) *Club Bon Viveur:* 0171 385 6644
*Partnership Protection Insurance*: 01734 660955

| | |
|---|---|
| Managing Editor: | Martin Barton-Smith |
| Editor: | Malcolm Morris |
| Typeset and design: | Multi Media Services Ltd.<br>31 Lancaster Mews, Bayswater<br>London W2 3QE, UK<br>Tel: 0171 706 0011    Fax: 0171 262 1434 |
| Digital Cartography: | European Map Graphics Ltd.<br>Finchampstead, Berkshire, UK |
| Production, Marketing & Distribution: | Kuperard (London) Ltd.<br>32-34 Gordon House Road<br>London NW5 ILP, UK<br>Tel: 0171 424 0554.    Fax: 0171 424 9556 |
| Printed in Great Britain by: | The Bath Press, Bath, Avon |

# CONTENTS

# See Why Our Members Prefer Us

# We Offer You the Choice

## Road Rescue -
## What price peace of mind?
## Answer -
## Less than you'd think!

For thirteen years, Britannia Rescue has been providing a fast, efficient breakdown and recovery service, originally exclusively for members of the CSMA. But now, this excellent service is offered to buyers of the Les Routiers Guides to Britain and France. Britain's leading consumer testing magazine in their April 1992 issue, voted Britannia Rescue as their 'Best Buy' with an average callout time of 34 minutes, well ahead of the AA, RAC and Green Flag.

## What services can you have?

All of our services are tailored to meet the needs of the individual driver. At Britannia Rescue, we continue to have a growing number of members. Members who know that a call to us means just a short wait until they are on their way again. Women who appreciate the priority care we give them and drivers who depend on their cars for business and need to rely on our serivce to keep operations running smoothly. Each service is detailed below:

## Rescue Plus - roadside assistance and local recovery service from £30.00 per year or £2.70 per month*

Designed to offer protection against minor breakdowns away from your home. If your problem can't be solved at the roadside we will transport you, your vehicle and up to five passengers to a nearby garage. We will also reimburse you up to £12 towards the cost of a taxi or other alternative transport.

## Standard Cover - roadside assistance and recovery to a nearby garage or home or to an onward destination from £57.25 per year or £5.75 per month*

Cover offers protection from every breakdown situation while away from the vicinity of your home, both for your car and for you. We will endeavour to fix any minor problems on the spot as quickly as possible. If, however, this is not possible, our agent will tranpsort you, your vehicle and up to five passengers home or to the destination of your choice.

## Comprehensive Cover - roadside assistance, recovery, attendance at home from £75.70 per year or £7.60 per month*

This cover gives you complete peace of mind. We cater for annoying non-start problems such as flat batteries and damp engines to roadside breakdowns and accident recovery. We also include Housecall, covering you at home or within a half a mile radius of home. It should be noted that Housecall is not intended as a home maintenance service and we would not expect to attend recurring faults.

## Deluxe Cover - roadside assistance, recovery, attendance at home, free car hire or hotel accommodation from £92.50 per year or £9.25 per month*

As the name suggests, this is the highest level of cover. You and your vehicle are not only catered for both at home and on the road, but if your car cannot be repaired the same day you can choose between a free replacement car (for up to 48 hours), or assistance with overnight hotel accommodation. Please note that car hire is subject to the terms and conditions of Britannia Rescue's car companies, minimum age of drivers must be 23 years.

## Personal Cover - £19.50 per year or £1.95 per month*

Whichever Britannia Rescue cover you choose, for just £19.50 we will extend the cover to include any car you or your spouse/domestic partner may drive.

## *Monthly Premiums

Monthly premiums are available on all four levels of service - Rescue Plus, Standard, Comprehensive and DeLuxe - when paying by Direct Debit, or Continuous Credit Card Authority.

# All Part of Our Service

## Legal advice and defence

We offer every member a 24 hour legal advice service. We can also provide representation in magistrates' courts.

## Assistance after theft and vandalism

In the case of vehicle immobilization, we will provide roadside repair or transport to a local garage or on to your destination.

## Relief driver

Britannia Rescue will arrange a relief driver to assist you in case of illness, injury or severe mental distress.

## Tyres and windscreens

We assist on less serious, but often annoying occasions, such as punctures, shattered windscreens, lack of fuel or even locking your keys in the car.

**BRITANNIA RESCUE**

## Caravans and trailers

These are covered free of charge (excluding Housecall).

# Why choose Britannia Rescue?

- Dedicated to providing every member with a fast, caring road rescue service

- 34 minutes average callout time

- Over 3,000 trained personnel on call 24 hours a day, 365 days a year

- A BSI registered firm committed to consistent service quality

- Value for money prices with easy payment methods

- Recommended by Britain's leading consumer watchdog as 'Best Buy'

# How to apply for Britannia Rescue membership

To join immediately call us FREE on **0800 591 563** and quote your credit card number or complete and return the application form and direct debit mandate near the back of this book.

# Travelling abroad

Available to anyone, whether covered by Britannia Rescue in the UK or not, Britannia Continental is a superb emergency breakdown service, competitively priced, and designed to cover any mishap while travelling abroad. There are two types of cover, one for travel with a vehicle in Europe, and the other for travel anywhere in the world. Personal Insurance includes medical repatriation by air ambulance. **For further details and a brochure, ring 01484 514 848.**

# NOTES

# BRITAIN AND IRELAND

## KEY TO MAP PAGES

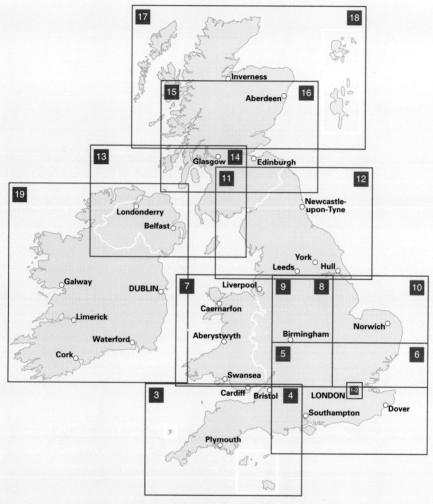

## KEY TO MAP SYMBOLS

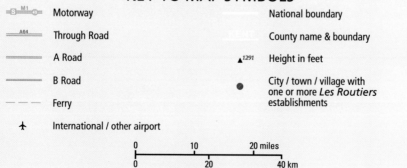

| | |
|---|---|
| Motorway | National boundary |
| Through Road | County name & boundary |
| A Road | ▲1291 Height in feet |
| B Road | City / town / village with one or more *Les Routiers* establishments |
| Ferry | |
| ✈ International / other airport | |

```
0          10          20 miles
0          20          40 km
```

Scale applies to maps 3–16 only
For maps 1–2, 17–18 and 19, see separate scale bars

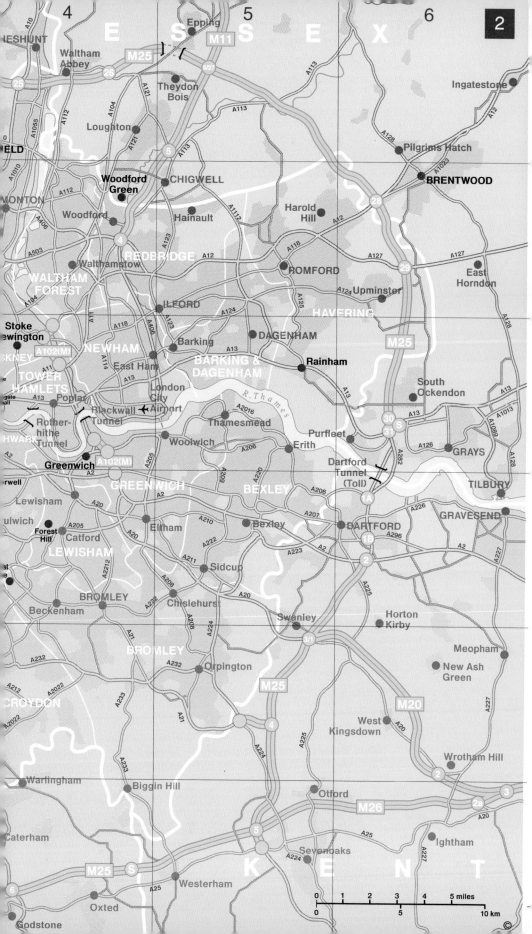

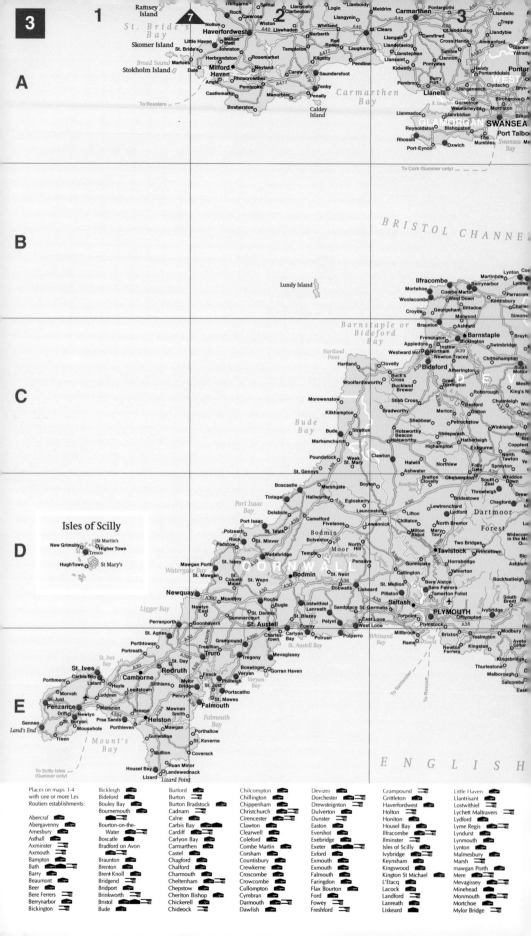

**6**

*Les Routiers* establishments within the M25 are located on maps 1-2

| 7 | 1 | 14 | 2 | 3 |

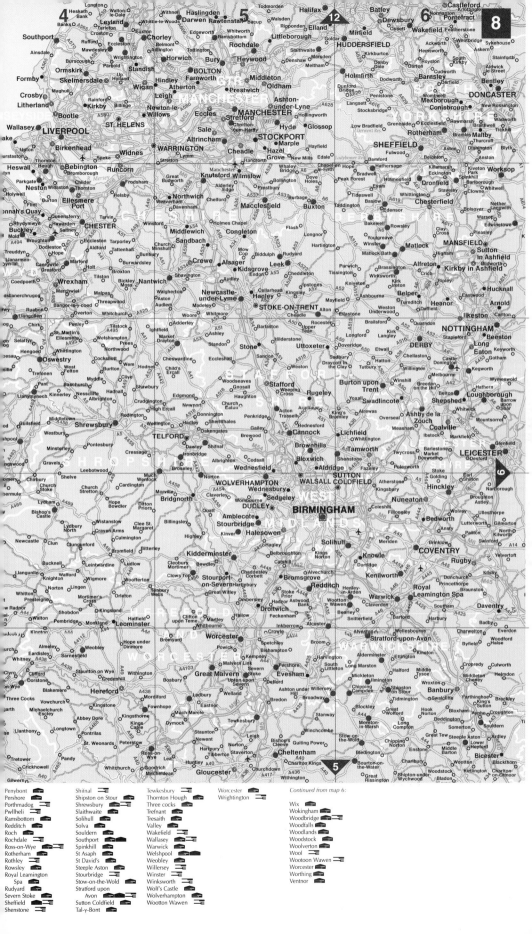

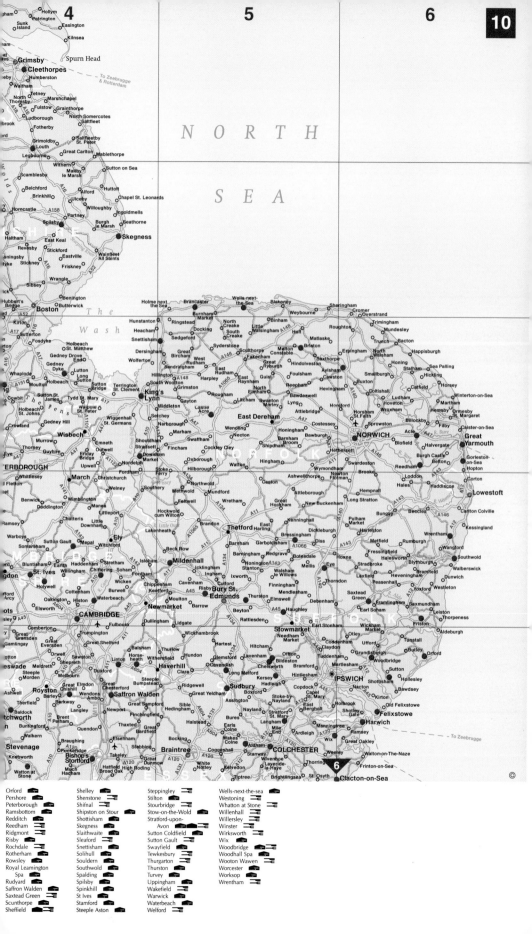

NORTH SEA

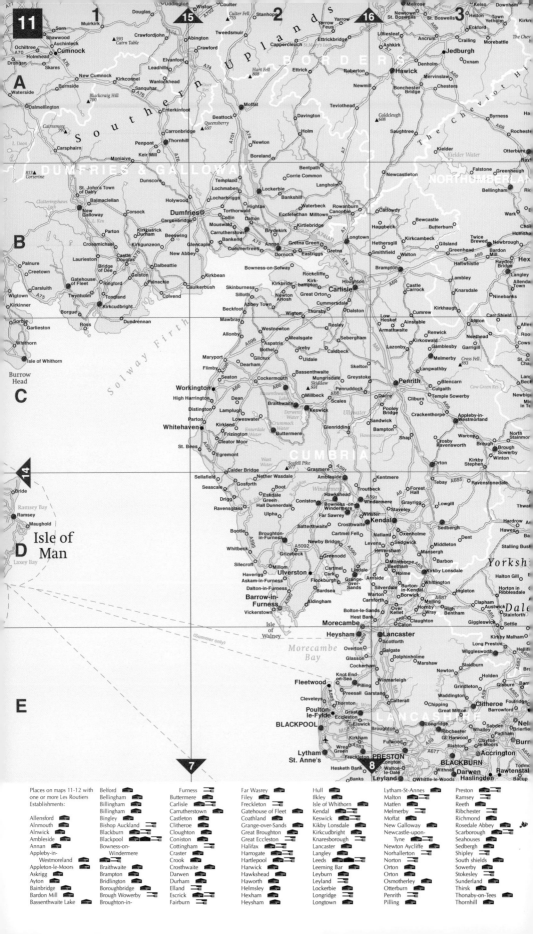

**Places on maps 11-12 with one or more Les Routiers Establishments:**

Allensford
Alnmouth
Alnwick
Ambleside
Annan
Appleby-in-Westmoreland
Appleton-le-Moors
Askrigg
Ayton
Bainbridge
Bardon Mill
Bassenthwaite Lake

Belford
Bellingham
Billingham
Billingham
Bingley
Bishop Auckland
Blackburn
Blackpool
Bowness-on-Windermere
Braithwaite
Brampton
Bridlington
Boroughbridge
Brough Wowerby
Broughton-in-

Furness
Buttermere
Carlisle
Carrutherstown
Castleton
Clitheroe
Cloughton
Coniston
Cottingham
Craster
Crook
Crosthwaite
Darwen
Durham
Elland
Escrick
Fairburn

Far Wasrey
Filey
Freckleton
Gatehouse of Fleet
Coathland
Grange-over-Sands
Great Broughton
Great Eccleston
Halifax
Harrogate
Hartlepool
Harwick
Hawkshead
Haworth
Helmsley
Hexham
Heysham

Hull
Ilkley
Isle of Whithorn
Kendal
Keswick
Kikby Lonsdale
Kirkcudbright
Knaresborough
Lancaster
Langley
Leeds
Leeming Bar
Leyburn
Leyland
Lockerbie
Longridge
Longtown

Lytham-St-Annes
Malton
Matfen
Melmerby
Moffat
New Galloway
Newcastle-upon-Tyne
Newton Aycliffe
Norhallerton
Norton
Orton
Orton
Osmotherley
Otterburn
Penrith
Pilling

Preston
Ramsey
Reeth
Ribchester
Richmond
Rosedale Abbey
Scarborough
Seahouses
Sedbergh
Shipley
South shields
Sowerby
Stokesley
Sunderland
Thirsk
Thonaby-on-Tees
Thornhill

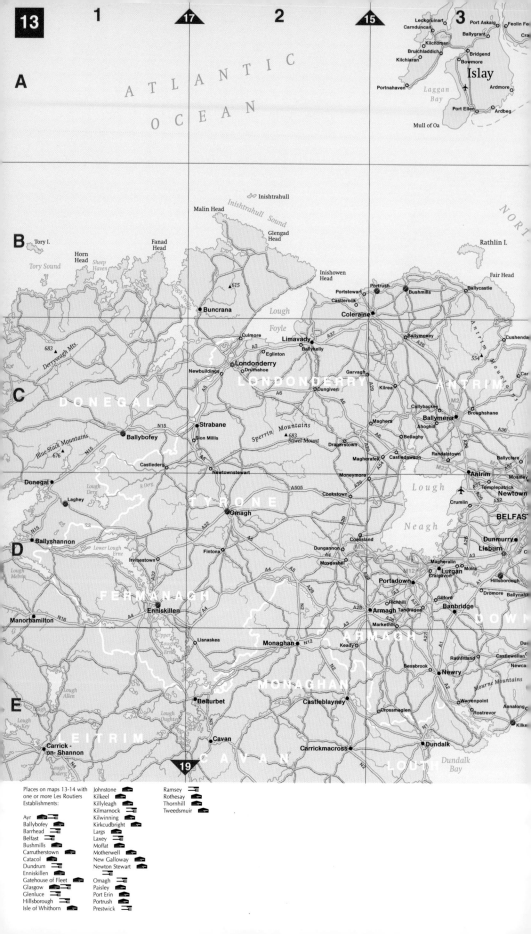

# 13

**1** ▲ **17** **2** ▲ **15** **3**

## ATLANTIC OCEAN

### A

ATLANTIC
OCEAN

Leckgruinart
Carnduncan
Port Askaig
Feolin Fe
Kilchoman
Ballygrant
Cra
Bruichladdich
Bridgend
Kilchiaran
Bowmore
Portnahaven
**Islay**
Ardmore
Laggan
Bay
Port Ellen
Ardbeg
Mull of Oa

### B

Tory I.
Rathlin I.
Horn
Head
Fanad
Head
Fair Head
NOR
Tory Sound
Sheep
Haven
Inishtrahull
Inishtrahull Sound
Malin Head
Glengad
Head
Inishowen
Head
▲615
Portrush
Portstewart
Bushmills
Ballycastle
Castlerock
Coleraine

### C

683 ▲
Derryveagh Mts.
Buncrana
Lough
Foyle
Culmore
Limavady
Ballymoney
Cushenda
A2
Ballykelly
Car
Eglinton
Londonderry
Drumahoe
A37
A26
554
Newbuildings
A5
Garvagh
Kilrea
ANTRIM
DONEGAL
LONDONDERRY
A6
Dungiven
A29
Cullybackey
M2
Broughshane
Strabane
Maghera
Ahoghill
Ballymena
Sion Mills
Sperrin Mountains
Bellaghy
A6
A36
Ballybofey
683 ▲
Sawel Mount
Draperstown
Magherafelt
Castledawson
Randalstown
Ballyclare
Blue Stack Mountains
Castlederg
Moneymore
A54
Mosele
676 ▲
Newtownstewart
Cookstown
A29
Crumlin
Templepatrick
A52

### D

Donegal
Laghey
TYRONE
Omagh
A505
A5
Lough
Neagh
Antrim
Newtown
A6
BELFAS
Ballyshannon
Fintona
Dungannon
Coalisland
Dunmurry
Lisburn
Lower Lough
Erne
A4
Moygashel
Magheralin
Moira
Irvinestown
A32
A4
A5
A4
Portadown
Craigavon
M12
Lurgan
A3
Hillsborough
Lough
Melvin
FERMANAGH
Enniskillen
Richhill
Gilford
Dromore
Ballynah
Manorhamilton
A4
A26
Armagh
Tandragee
Banbridge
A1
N16
Upper Lough
Erne
Markethill
A28
A3
DOW

### E

Lisnaskea
Monaghan
N12
Keady
Rathfriland
Castlewellan
Newca
ARMAGH
Bessbrook
Newry
Warrenpoint
Mourne Mountains
Annalong
MONAGHAN
Castleblayney
Crossmaglen
Rostrevor
LEITRIM
Belturbet
Kilke
Carrick-
on-Shannon
Cavan
Carrickmacross
Dundalk
Lough
Allen
Lough
Key
CAVAN
LOUTH
Dundalk
Bay
Lough
Oughter
▲ **19**

---

**Places on maps 13-14 with one or more Les Routiers Establishments:**

Ayr
Ballybofey
Barrhead
Belfast
Bushmills
Carrutherstown
Catacol
Dundrum
Enniskillen
Gatehouse of Fleet
Glasgow
Glenluce
Hillsborough
Isle of Whithorn

Johnstone
Kilkeel
Killyleagh
Kilmarnock
Kilwinning
Kirkcudbright
Largs
Laxey
Moffat
Motherwell
New Galloway
Newton Stewart
Omagh
Paisley
Port Erin
Portrush
Prestwick

Ramsey
Rothesay
Thornhill
Tweedsmuir

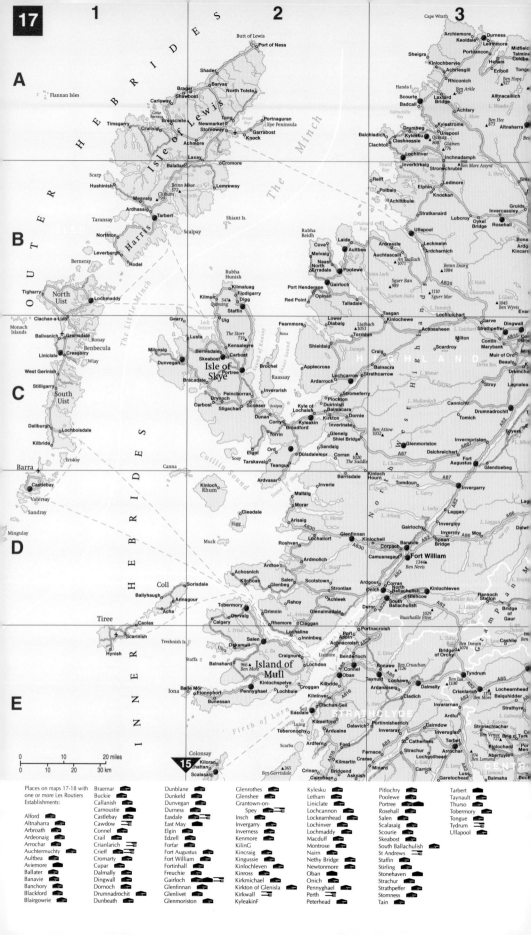

Places on maps 17-18 with one or more Les Routiers Establishments:

| | | | | |
|---|---|---|---|---|
| Alford | Braemar | Dunblane | Glenrothes | Kylesku | Pitlochry | Tarbert |
| Altnaharra | Buckie | Dunkeld | Glenshee | Letham | Poolewe | Taynault |
| Arbroath | Callanish | Dunvegan | Grantown-on-Spey | Liniclate | Portree | Thurso |
| Ardeonaig | Carnoustie | Durness | | Lochcannon | Rosehall | Tobermory |
| Arrochar | Castlebay | Easdale | Insch | Lockearnhead | Salen | Tongue |
| Auchtermuchty | Cawdow | East May | Invergarry | Lochinver | Scalasaig | Tydrum |
| Aultbea | Connel | Elgin | Inverness | Lochmaddy | Scourie | Ullapool |
| Aviemore | Crail | Edzell | Kenmore | Macduff | Skeabost | |
| Ballater | Crianlarich | Forfar | KilinG | Montrose | South Ballachulish | |
| Banavie | Crieff | Fort Augustus | Kincraig | Nairn | St Andrews | |
| Banchory | Cromarty | Fort William | Kingussie | Nethy Bridge | Staffin | |
| Blackford | Cupar | Fortinhall | Kinlochleven | Newtonmore | Stirling | |
| Blairgowrie | Dalmally | Freuchie | Kinross | Oban | Stonehaven | |
| | Dingwall | Gairloch | Kirkmichael | Onich | Strachur | |
| | Dornoch | Glenfinnan | Kirkton of Glenisla | Pennyghael | Strathpeffer | |
| | Drumnadrochit | Glenlivet | Kirkwall | Perth | Stomness | |
| | Dunbeath | Glenmoriston | KyleakinF | Peterhead | Tain | |

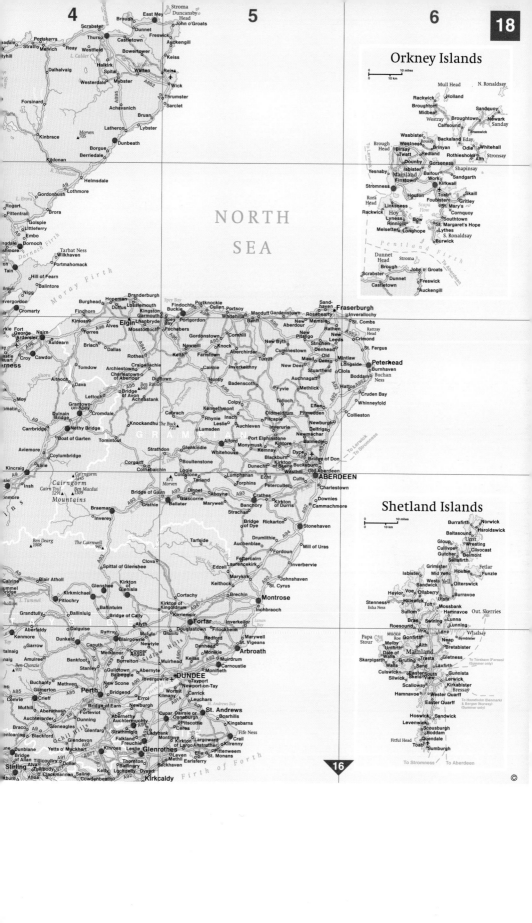

## Orkney Islands

0    10 miles
0    10 km

Mull Head    N. Ronaldsay
Rackwick   Holland
Broughton    Sandquoy
Midbea   Westray    Broughton   Newark   Sanday
Calfsound    Braeswick
Wasbister    Backaland   Eday
Brough   Westness   Brinyan   Odie   Whitehall
Head   Birsay   Rousay   Rothiesholm   Stronsay
Twatt   Redland   Gorseness
Dounby   Isbister   Shapinsay
Yesnaby   Mainland   Balfour   Sandgarth
Finstown   Work   Kirkwall
Stromness    Houton   Toab   Skaill
Rora    Foubister   Gritley
Head   Linksness   Cornquoy
Rackwick   Hoy   Scapa   St. Mary's   Southtown
Lyness   Flow   Bow   St. Margaret's Hope
Rinnigill   Lythes
Melsetter   Longhope   S. Ronaldsay
Dunnet    Burwick
Head   Stroma
Scrabster   John o' Groats   Freswick
Dunnet   Auckengill
Castletown

## NORTH

## SEA

## Shetland Islands

0    10 miles
0    10 km

Burrafirth   Norwick
Baltasound   Haroldswick
Gloup   Unst   Wresting
Cullivoe   Clivocast
Gutcher   Belmont
Sellafirth
Grimister   Fetlar
Mid Yell   Houbie   Funzie
Isbister   West   Yell   Otterswick
Sandwick
Heylor   Voe   Ollaberry   Ulsta   Burravoe
Stenness   Toft
Esha Ness   Nibbswick   Out. Skerries
Sullom   Swining   Lunna
Roesound   Brae   Lunning
Whalsay
Papa   Muckle   Gonfirth   Symbister
Stour   Roe   Melby   Neap
Unifirth   Bretabister
Skarpigarth   Dale of   Tresta   Gletness
Walls   Gruting   Sand   Laxfirth   To Torshavn (Faroes)
Culswick   Easter   South   Lerwick   (Summer only)
Silwick   Skeld   Vee   Kirkabister
Scalloway   Bressay
Hamnavoe   Wester Quarff
Easter Quarff   To Hanstholm (Denmark)
& Bergen (Norway)
Hoswick   (Summer only)
Levenwick
Scousburg
Fitful Head   Boddam
Toab   Sandwick
Quendale
Sumburgh

To Stromness    To Aberdeen

Scrabster   East Me   Duncansby   Stroma
Brough   Head   John o'Groats
Portskerra   Dunnet   Freswick
Strathy   Melvich   Reay   Thurso   Castletown   Auckengill
Westfield   Bowertower   Keiss
Dalhalvaig   Halkirk   Watten   Reiss
Spital   Mybster   Wick
Westerdale   Thrumster
Forsinard   Achavanich   Sarclet
Bruan
Morven   Latheron   Lybster
Kinbrace   705
Borgue   Dunbeath
Berriedale
Kildonan
Helmsdale
Gordonbush   Lothmore
Rogart   Brora
Pittentrail   Golspie
Littleferry
Embo
Dornoch   Tarbat Ness
Tain   Wilkhaven
Portmahomack
Hill of Fearn
Nigg   Balintore
Cromarty
Moray Firth
Branderburgh   Hopeman   Spey Bay   Findochty   Portknockie   Cullen   Portsoy   Macduff   Gardenstown   Sand-   haven   Fraserburgh
Burghead   Lossiemouth   Buckie   Whitehills   Banff   Inverallochy
Duffus   Garmouth   Spey   Portgordon   St. Combs
Findhorn   Elgin   Lhanbryde   Fochabers   New   Memsie   Rattray
Kinloss   Alves   Mosstodloch   Aberdour   New Leeds   Crimond
Forres   Newmill   Keith   Gordonstown   Cornhill   New Byth   New   Rathen   St. Fergus
Nairn   Briach   Dallas   Rothes   Knock   Aberchirder   Pitsligo   Strichen   Denhead
Auldearn   Craigellachie   Farmtown   Turriff   Maud   Old   Mintlaw   Peterhead
Croy   Cawdor   Tomdow   Charlestown   Cairnie   Inverkeithny   New Deer   Deer   Longside   Burnhaven
Aitnoch   Dava   of Aberlour   Huntly   Cuminestown   Stuartfield   Clola   Buchan Ness
Moy   Dufftown   Badenscoth   Auchnagatt   Boddam
Grantown-   Bridge   Fyvie   Methlick   Hatton   Cruden Bay
Dulnain   on-Spey   of Avon   Knockandhu   Cabrach   Colpy   Tolloch   Ellon   Whinnyfold
Bridge   Achnastank   Rhynie   Insch   Oldmeldrum   Pitmedden   Collieston
Carrbridge   Cromdale   The Buck   Leslie   Auchleven   Pitcaple   Newburgh
Nethy Bridge   Tomintoul   721   Lumsden   Inverurie   Delfrigs
Boat of Garten   Port   Newmachar
Aviemore   Strathdon   Glenkindie   Alford   Monymusk   Elphinstone   Balmedie
Coylumbridge   Corgarff   Whitehouse   Kemnay   Kirkton   Dyce   To Lerwick
Kincraig   Colnabaichin   Boultenstone   Blackburn   of Skene   Bridge of Don   To Stromness
Alvie   Cairngorm   871   Coldstone   Dunecht   Wasthill   Old Aberdeen
Insh   1245   Morven   Lumphanan   Echt   Cults   ABERDEEN
Cairn Toul   Ben Macdui   Tarland   Torphins   Peterculter   Charlestown
1291   1309   Dinnet   Aboyne   Crathes   Downies
Mountains   Bridge of Gairn   Glascorrie   Kirkton   Cammachmore
Braemar   Crathie   Ballater   Marywell   Banchory   of Durris
Inverey   Strachan
Ben Dearg   Bridge   Rickarton   Stonehaven
1008   The Cairnwell   of Dye
941   Drumlithie   Mill of Uras
Tarfside   Auchenblae   Fordoun   Inverbervie
Blair Atholl   Clova   Fettercairn   Johnshaven
Spittal of Glenshee   Edzell   Laurencekirk   St. Cyrus
Ben Chonzie   Marykirk
931   Kirkmichael   Keithock   Brechin   Montrose
Glenshee   Kirkton of   Cortachy   Inchbraoch
Pitlochry   Kirkton   Kingoldrum   Logan
Grandtully   of Glenisla   Kirriemuir
Ballinluig   Balintuim   Forfar   Inverkeilor
Aberfeldy   Bridge of Cally   Alyth   Douglastown   Friockheim
Kenmore   Rattray   Blairgowrie   Newtyle   Redford   Marywell
Garrow   Dunkeld   Cupar   Denhead   St. Vigeans
Amulree   Caputh   Meikleour   Angus   Kellas   Monikie   Arbroath
Buchanty   Bankfoot   Burrelton   Muirhead   Muirdrum
Methven   Stanley   Guildtown   Abernyte   Monifieth
Gilmerton   Balbeggie   Invergowrie   Carnoustie
Comrie   New Scone   DUNDEE
Crieff   Perth   Bridgend   Tayport
Muthill   Errol   Newport-on-Tay
Abernethv   Wormit   Carrick
Auchterarder   Bridge of Earn   Kilmany   Leuchars
Braco   Fortevoit   Newburgh   St. Andrews Bay
Gleneagles   Dunning   Cupar   Dairsie or   St. Andrews
Blackford   Abernethy   Osnaburgh   Boarhills
Dunblane   Auchtermuchty   Pitscottie   Kingsbarns
Yetts o' Muckhart   Strathmiglo   Ladybank   Ceres
Bridge   Falkland   Craigrothie   Fife Ness
of Allan   Glendevon   Glenfarg   Kirkton   Largoward   Crail
Stirling   Alva   Dollar   Kinross   Leslie   of Largo   Pittenweem
Tullibody   Glenrothes   Leven   Elie   St. Monans
Clackmannan   Saline   Thornton   Methil   Earlsferry
Ballingry   Lochgelly   Buckhaven
Kelty   Dysart
Cowdenbeath   Kirkcaldy

Firth of Forth

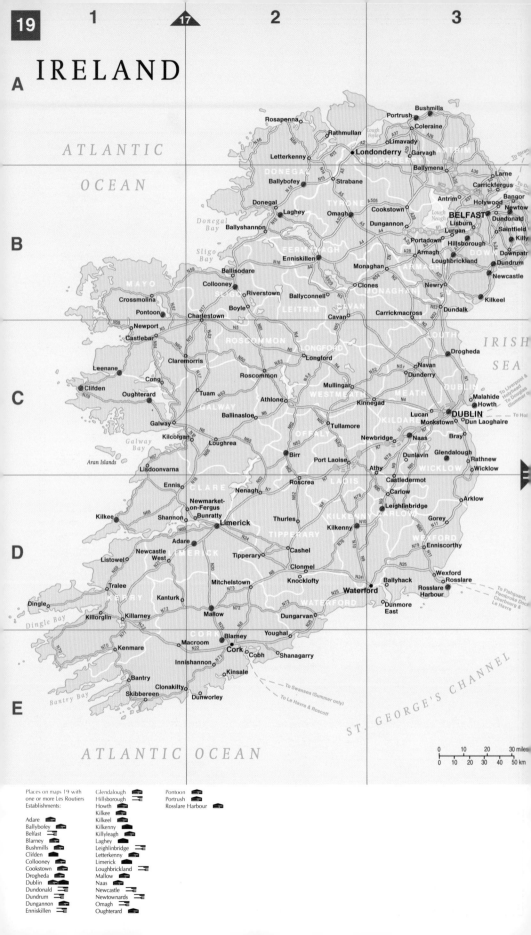

# Les Routiers Welcomes You

A personal introduction from Gordon Wilson, Managing Director of Les Routiers (UK) Ltd.

Welcome to the 1996 edition of the Les Routiers Guide to Britain and Ireland; Les Routiers' 25th edition of its now famous Guide to both the Quality and Value to be found in hotels, guest houses, inns and restaurants throughout Britain and Ireland. Regular users of the Guide will see that in this 25th anniversary edition there are even more illustrations. Their addition will help you to find that special hotel or restaurant and makes travelling or dining an even greater pleasure.

## HOTEL, GUEST HOUSES, INNS AND RESTAURANT INSPECTIONS

Before being able to display the famous red and blue Les Routiers' symbol, every hotel and restaurant undergoes a detailed inspection. Not just when they apply to join, but each year they remain a member. Payment for membership is only accepted after this detailed inspection confirms that the hotel or restaurant meet the wide range of criteria set by Les Routiers. These cover decor, cleanliness, service, comfort, and of course the key criteria of Quality and Value as related to the type and style of hotel and restaurant and the prices charged. These inspections include the all important areas to which you the public do not have access.

## ANNUAL INSPECTIONS MAINTAIN STANDARDS

At least once a year each Les Routiers appointed hotel or restaurant receives a visit from a Les Routiers' inspector. This enables Les Routiers to ensure that standards are maintained and the traveller continues to receive the very best in Quality and Value. If standards are found to be slipping, then the hotel or restaurant concerned will be asked to take whatever action may be necessary to meet the Quality and Value criteria of Les Routiers. If this is not achieved, Les Routiers membership is suspended or terminated. And, in the case of establishments that continue to display the Les Routiers symbol without a valid membership certificate, legal proceedings are instigated. In many cases this is done in conjuction with the appropriate local Standards Trading Officer.

## HOTEL, GUEST HOUSES, INNS AND RESTAURANT BENEFITS THAT PROVIDE YOU WITH GREATER QUALITY AND BETTER VALUE

As someone who travels on pleasure or business, you're no doubt aware of the comments made in the press, as well as on television, about publishers who charge for their guide entries. Guides that do this are thought not to be impartial in regard to their recommendations. Well, members of Les Routiers do pay an annual fee; but it's paid to cover a number of services that Les Routiers provides to its members. These include business generation programmes, discount buying directory and specially negotiated business insurance rates. Members are also provided with advertising and public relations support together with specially created promotions. All these services enable the owners of Les Routiers appointed establishments to offer you greater Quality and Value. And yes, part of their fee does go to cover the production and distribution costs of this Guide.

## YOU - THE CONSUMER -
## ARE THE BEST JUDGE OF QUALITY AND VALUE

As good as this or any other guide might be, it's you, the consumer, that's the final judge of Quality and Value. So if you think any hotel or restaurant displaying a valid membership certificate doesn't deserve a Les Routiers accreditation, please let me know. I'd also welcome letters detailing paticularly good experiences. Your comments, both good and bad, will be shared with the appropriate Les Routiers member. * *There is a form at the back of the guide for your comments or recommendations.*

## QUALITY, VALUE AND A WARM WELCOME

As you can see, Les Routiers aim is to get together a collection of establishments that offer not only good quality, good service and good value, but a warm welcome that makes travelling a real pleasure. And in this Guide you'll find the hotels and restaurants throughout Britain and Ireland that do just that. And they're all waiting to welcome you.

Yours sincerely,

GORDON WILSON
MANAGING DIRECTOR

PS: For more information about Les Routiers, or for a hotel booking, just call Les Routiers Free on 0500 700 456. This Helpline is open from 9.30 a.m. to 5.30 p.m., from Monday until Friday, excluding England's National Holidays.

# SUPER SAVINGS WITH LES ROUTIERS AND

# P&O

## European Ferries

By purchasing this guide you are now eligible to join *Les Routiers* **Discovery Club.** This club enables you to benefit from some of the best ferry deals around when you book P&O European Ferries through the Club and make all-year-round savings of **up to 50%** on crossings to France, Spain, Northern Ireland and Scotland with Britain's No. 1 Ferry Company.

Membership of the Club is **FREE**, with the compliments of *Les Routiers*. To receive your membership card and pack, simply complete the box below and send it to: *Les Routiers* **Discovery Club, Greenleaf House, Darkes Lane, Potters Bar, Herts EN6 1AE.**

By return you will receive your personal membership card, showing the Channel crossing discount hotline number and regular updates of exclusive opportunities for *Les Routiers* **Discovery Club** members. Please allow 21 days for delivery. You must quote the unique number shown on your membership card each time you book.

---

## LES ROUTIERS DISCOVERY CLUB

Title (Mr/Mrs/Ms/Miss)............................... Initials.................................................

Surname.................................................................................................................

Address..................................................................................................................

..............................................................................................................................

..........................................................................Postcode.....................................

Telephone (day)..................................................(evening)...........................................

**FOR OFFICE USE ONLY-LR**

# YOUR LES ROUTIERS GUIDE

## DISCOVER EXCELLENT CUISINE

This guide enables you to choose from hundreds of specially selected places, where menus have been carefully chosen to balance colour, taste and texture in a mouthwatering combination of dishes. In kitchens everywhere, talented chefs are being more adventurous than ever before, by cleverly combining unusual new foods and vegetables from all corners of the globe with their own inventive creations. Not only can you sample some of the best British cuisine, but many outstanding examples of Greek, Indian, Chinese, Italian, even Mongolian, as well as deliciously flavoured regional dishes, prepared from traditional revived recipes, accompanied by fine wines and real ales.

Nature's all-year-round harvest allows many exciting seasonal specialities to be enjoyed from January to December. Ward off the cold in winter with rich, full-flavoured, warming soups and dark, steaming puddings spiced with nutmeg and ginger. The arrival of Spring breathes new life into the kitchen, bringing with it an abundance of crisp, tender vegetables and fresh herbs. In high summer, the tangled hedgerows provide nuts and soft, ripe, melting fruits for jams, trifles, sorbets and as a refreshing accompaniment to long cool drinks. From the seashore comes fresh fish and seafood. And as the Autumn tints change from gold to purple and game comes into season, there will be traditional favourites such as wood pigeon, hare and partridge served with delicious home-made pickles, chutney and tipsy sauces. The 'icing on the cake', as the saying goes (excuse our pun), is improved menus offering constantly changing selections of more appetizing, interesting and unusual dishes to suit all tastes and ages.

## RELAX IN COMFORTABLE ACCOMMODATION

No two Les Routiers establishments are alike, and in this guide you will find a superb range of comfortable accommodation to suit any occasion. Some are basic, some luxurious, but whether you favour a grand 4-poster in an isolated hunting lodge in the Scottish Isles or a contemporary suite in a London town house, all are clean and homely. After all, if we could only offer you one style of accommodation, this would be a rather tedious guide, don't you agree? Unlike many convenience hotels, each and every Les Routiers establishment offers the same traditional values: a warm and friendly welcome, good food and drink, and quality and value for money.

## A WARM WELCOME AWAITS

However impressive an establishment may appear, unless the host can offer guests a spontaneous greeting, the staff are polite and friendly, the service is efficient and the atmosphere warm and inviting - we simply wouldn't want to know ... would you?

# HOW TO USE THIS GUIDE

To ensure this guide is reader-friendly, we have kept everything as simple as possible to help you locate the perfect Les Routiers of your choice, quickly and easily.

## REGIONAL SECTIONS
For your convenience, we have divided the guide into nine regional sections:

London

South-East England and East Anglia

South-West England

The Channel Islands

Central England

Northern England and the Isle of Man

Wales

Scotland

Ireland

## ENTRIES LISTED BY COUNTY
Within each regional section, individual establishments are grouped in county order and listed alphabetically by town name. Each detailed entry gives a clear, concise description of the establishment, its cuisine, accommodation, facilities, prices for food and/or accommodation, opening hours, directions and lots more, including a map reference.

## COLOUR MAPS
Near the front of the book are full-colour regional maps of Great Britain and Ireland. As well as providing a useful touring guide, the maps show the location of all towns and villages where there is a Les Routiers establishment. An alphabetical list below each map tells you where you can find a Les Routiers-recommended member offering food, accommodation or both.

## INDEX
At the back of this guide there is an A-Z index of towns and villages in which there are Les Routiers establishments. A second index lists establishments by name.

☎ What could be simpler? But if you do have difficulty locating a particular Les Routiers, please don't hesitate to call our **Information & Bookings line** on FREECALL 0500 700 456.

# READING AN ENTRY

## PRICE GUIDE
Full details of food and accommodaton prices are given on page 41

## MAP REFERENCE
Each entry has its own map reference number, keyed to the full-colour regional maps near the front of the map.

### AYR • map 14B5

**FOUTERS BISTRO**
**25 Academy Street, KA7 1HS**
*Authentic cellar restaurant serving interesting French and British dishes using the best of local produce. Fouters Bistro is renowned for the high quality of its cuisine, steak and seafood specialities. Personally run by the proprietors. On-street parking opposite Town Hall.*
FOOD: from £20 to £25 ⌒◯◠ CLUB
**Hours:** lunch 12 noon-2pm, dinner 6.30pm-10.30pm, Sunday 7pm-10pm, closed 4 days over Christmas and 4 days over New Year.
**Cuisine:** SCOTTISH/FRENCH - fine Scottish produce cooked in the French style. Vegetarians welcomed and special diets catered for.
**Cards:** Visa, Acess, Diners, AmEx.
**Other points:** children welcome.
**Directions:** opposite Town Hall, in a cobbled stone lane.
FRAN & LAURIE BLACK
☎ (0171) 283 4363   Fax (0171) 283 4897

## SYMBOLS
Some of these symbols represent 'special achievement' by the establishment. Refer to page 40 for details of all the symbols.

# HOW WE CHOOSE SUITABLE ESTABLISHMENTS

As well as receiving personal recommendations from readers of this guide, many establishments eager to receive the Les Routiers recommendation approach us directly, and we have a nationwide team who visit each establishment anonymously, before sending us a detailed and comprehensive report which determines whether or not they meet our exacting standards.

One simple but successful formula we use to recognise a potential Les Routiers is to put ourselves in your shoes . . . if it's good enough for you - then it's good enough for us!

## WHO DON'T WE INCLUDE?
There are, of course, many establishments who do not meet our required standards by being either uncongenial and inferior in appearance, and others where the choice of cuisine is poorly presented and greatly overpriced. These we can certainly do without.

## WHAT STANDARDS DO WE SET?
Good food and accommodation, value for money and a warm and friendly welcome towards guests have always been the criteria for selecting suitable establishments for the Les Routiers guide, and we are delighted to say that these basic but well-tested standards have met with constant customer approval for over 25 years.

## MAINTAINING STANDARDS
All the establishments we have recommended in this guide are regularly re-inspected to ensure that the correct standards are being maintained. Only when we are completely satisfied do we permit an establishment to display the coveted red and blue Les Routiers sign.

## THE LES ROUTIERS SIGN
The Les Routiers sign is a recognised and reliable standard of achievement in all types of cuisine and comfortable accommodation at hotels, restaurants, guest houses and inns throughout Britain and the north of Ireland. It is displayed by all members demonstrating their commitment to providing quality and value for their customers. However, an establishment can only claim to be a current member if it has a current certificate with the correct proprietor's or manager's name.

Every year, there are establishments which close down or change ownership, or occasionally places which allow their standards to fall and have to be withdrawn. Unfortunately, despite our efforts, there are establishments which continue to display the sign when they are no longer members. If you know of a Les Routiers establishment which you do not consider worthy of the sign, or which is displaying a sign without a current certificate, please let us know.

# HELPING US TO HELP YOU!

Every year more and more people are discovering the pleasures of dining or staying at *Les Routiers*-recommended establishments. We know this from all the complimentary letters and comments we receive from users of our guide, and also from their recommendations to include new establishments that we didn't previously know about.

This feedback is invaluable and helps us to maintain the high standards of which we are justifiably proud. At the back of this guide we have included some space for you to record your own comments, and to propose any establishments which you feel are worthy of the *Les Routiers* 'recommendation' and a possible place in next year's guide.

# SYMBOLS USED IN THIS GUIDE

As you browse through this guide you will see that some of the entries have the following symbols. Look out for them!

These symbols are for 'special achievement' by an establishment, signifying that it has received one or more of our prestigious annual awards for outstanding and consistent presentation of food, wine or cheeseboards.

### Casserole Award
The Les Routiers Casserole is awarded to any establishment that has consistently offered outstanding service and an impressive ability to present above-average cuisine to its customers. Refer to pages 50 - 54 for a complete list of Casserole Award holders.

### Cheeseboard
This symbol indicates a Les Routiers establishment where you have the opportunity to sample a superb selection of well-chosen and prepared cheeses, including regional and less common varieties. Refer to pages 55 - 57 for a complete list of Cheeseboard Award holders.

### Wine - Les Routiers 'Corps D'Elite'
Awarded to Les Routiers establishments who offer interesting, carefully selected wines, with a list which can be easily read and understood. Refer to pages 58 - 62 for a complete list of Wine Award holders.

There is also one other symbol you will see against certain entries. This is to inform you that the establishment is offering YOU a very special scheme;

### Club Bon Viveur - The Ultimate Dining Scheme
Entries showing this sign offer - on less busy nights of the week - exceptional discounts to Club Bon Viveur members.

To find out how you can join, refer to pages 65.

## OTHER SYMBOLS
 Telephone

 Fax facilities available

 Establishments with accommodation

 Restaurants

 Establishments with accommodation and dining facilities

# QUALITY AND VALUE FOR MONEY

If you are still can't believe that Les Routiers establishments really do offer quality and value for money, we can tell you that all their prices and services form the basis of consistent and accurate market research by ourselves to bring you, the customer, precisely that. There are also many places that exceed our expectations by consistently offering outstanding quality of service and above average cuisine. These are rewarded with a Les Routiers Casserole Award (see page 50 ).

Every establishment listed in this guide includes a carefully researched estimate of cost, so that all customers know what to expect.

**FOOD**
Prices are based on a 3-course evening meal taken from the table d'hôte menu, excluding wine and service.

up to £15 per person
between £15 and £20 per person
between £20 and £25 per person
between £25 and £30 per person

**ACCOMMODATION** ( *Breakfast is included in the prices given below* )

Prices given for **double accommodation** are **per person**, assuming two people sharing a double room. (Prices given in italics within brackets are for **single accommodation**).

up to £20 (£25) per person
from £20 to £30 (£25 to £35) per person
from £30 to £40 (£35 to £45) per person
from £40 to £50 (£45 to £55) per person
over £50 (£55) per person

**Please Note:** These price bands indicate the range of meals and accommodation available and reflect regional price variations. However, an establishment may have accommodation available at a higher or lower rate according to season and availability.

**Single accommodation:** Guests staying at an establishment whose accommodation rating is 'from £25 to £35 per person' can in most instances expect to pay up to, but not more than, £35 per room.

**Double accommodation:** Guests staying at an establishment whose accommodation rating is 'from £30 to £40 per person' can in most instances expect to pay up to, but not more than, £40 per person per room.

**All prices are based on information supplied to us by the establishment, and although the prices quoted are correct at the time of going to press, they cannot be guaranteed.**

# LES ROUTIERS AWARDS 1996

All establishments listed in this guide have attained the prestigious Les Routiers recommendation only by meeting our exacting standards, providing **quality, value for money, and a warm welcome**. There are some, however, whose efforts have far exceeded these standards, and our expectations, by making a concerted effort towards achieving **total customer satisfaction**, offering that something extra. In recognition of their achievements, each year we present a number of awards.

## Restaurant of the Year
A restaurant or bistro which offers a full and varied menu with imaginative, mouthwatering dishes served by knowledgeable, efficient, friendly staff.

## Hotel of the Year
A hotel where you start to relax the minute you arrive. Rooms should be inviting, clean and comfortable, with special touches like fresh flower arrangements, visitor information and for the ladies the humble hair dryer - a welcome addition, especially if they have forgotten to pack their own. Little extras such as these clearly demonstrate further consideration towards the guest. Exceptional food and welcoming hospitality are two other important ingredients of an award-winning hotel.

## Guest House of the Year
Guest houses may not offer the same comprehensive facilities as hotels and restaurants, but they certainly provide comfortable accommodation, quality and value, and the warmest welcome you'll find anywhere. This is just one reason why we created this award last year to recognize those that offer all these qualities (and more!), leaving guests with lasting memories of a thoroughly enjoyable stay.

## Inn of the Year
An establishment that echoes the true traditions of the English inn. Essential factors are a cheerful, friendly greeting, relaxed informality, a welcome for families, and the promise of traditional, wholesome food and carefully selected ales.

## Newcomer of the Year
Any hotel, guest house, restaurant or inn that is being featured in the Les Routiers guide for the very first time, and is clearly already offering an outstanding level of service. Nominations for this award are usually instantly recognizable from the glowing report which follows their inspection. Les Routiers establishments in Ireland have their own Newcomer of the Year Award.

## Cheeseboard of the Year
Awarded for the most exceptional cheeseboard at a Les Routiers establishment. Cheese is a serious business at this establishment, and the proprietor and staff will be able to provide customers with expert knowledge of the varieties of cheeses which they are offering.

# LES ROUTIERS AWARDS 1996

### Prix D'Elite (Wine of the Year)

The award for the most exceptional wine at a Les Routiers establishment. Like the Cheeseboard winner, wine plays a very important role in the daily programme. Although the establishment may specialize in certain varieties and vintages, the customer will find the wine list informative and easy to read and will be able to receive sound advice on the perfect selection.

### Symbol of Excellence

Not an annual award, but given to an establishment that has been recommended by Les Routiers for at least a decade. Over this time it will have consistently provided its customers with outstanding service.

### Highly Commended

A new award introduced this year, for full details see page 62.

As well as having their normal full entries in the main regional listings, this year's · award-winners are also specially featured in the following pages . . .

# Restaurant of the Year

## THE MOAT HOUSE
### Acton Trussell, Staffordshire

The Moat House at Acton Trussell has proved to be outstanding in all aspects - a beautiful setting, impeccable service and exceptional menu's.

Steeped in character and history, it is set amidst six acres of beautifully landscaped grounds where the moat flanks one of the suites and the restaurant overlooks the Staffordshire & Worcestershire Canal with its abundance of narrowboats and waterfowl.

As well as having its own purpose-built seminar and conference centre, this 13th century manor house provides the perfect setting for a wide range of private functions. The Colin Lewis Suite is an original oak-beamed room and, with its own bar it makes the ideal venue for an evening reception of up to 66 guests. The Trussell Room and Restaurant is an ornate Victorian conservatory with a maximum capacity of 86.

The cuisine, like most things at The Moat House, is exceptional including the home-made bread and petit fours. Main-course dishes may include, half a lobster and prawns in a brandy cream sauce served in the shell, breast of chicken filled with a Mousseline of chicken and apricots drenched in brandy sliced on to a fresh peach sauce, or possibly escalopes of veal with coconut, pan fried in butter set on a pool of fresh redcurrants. The huge range of desserts is equally as tempting; chocolate roulade filled with raspberries and cream, home-made apple strudel with a warm butterscotch sauce, and meringue nest filled with seasonal berries, to name just three. Even the Sunday lunch menu offers a splendid choice of starters, main courses and desserts.

The Moat House management team can arrange overnight accommodation with two fine hotels situated just minutes away, and transport is provided for conference delegates at no extra cost.

# Hotel of the Year

## POWDERMILLS
### Battle, East Sussex

Powdermills is a stunning 18th century listed country house hotel, nestling in 150 acres of parks and woodland, just outside the historic town of Battle, in the heart of 1066 Country. It takes its name from the Gunpowder Mills which thrived here in the grounds from 1676-1874, helping to win some of the most famous victories in history.

Privately owned and run by Douglas and Julie Cowpland, Powdermills offers visitors the highest standards of personal care and attention.

Richly furnished with antiques, the entrance hall, drawing room and library all have wonderful log fires burning on cooler days, where guests can relax and enjoy reading the many books that line the shelves. The bedrooms, two of which have four-poster beds, are all individually furnished and decorated and each has its own luxury en suite bathroom.

The Orangery Restaurant has received many accolades for its imaginative and exciting cuisine, and is open to both resident's and non-resident's who can enjoy the finest country house classical cooking in the south-east of England. In the summer months, lunch and dinner may be taken on the terrace overlooking the swimming pool and grounds. Alternatively, morning coffees, light lunches and bar snacks are available in the Georgian library.

Powdermills provides the perfect setting for those wanting to return to nature. There are endless peaceful walks to be enjoyed through the woodland trails. Wild geese, swans, ducks, kingfishers and herons abound, whilst on the woodland banks are the Soay, a rare breed of primitive sheep from the Scottish Hebrides. A delightful seven acre specimen fishing lake and three smaller lakes stocked with trout are available for guests use.

The proprietors and staff are always on hand to greet visitors and to make them feel completely at home in warm and friendly surroundings. This is the Powdermills Hotel.

# Guesthouse of the Year

## BROMPTON HOUSE
### Bath, Avon

Brompton House is beautifully situated in the secluded surroundings of a prize-winning garden, just a few minutes walk from Bath's historic city centre.

A former Georgian rectory, built in 1777 and Grade II listed, it has been tastefully converted and extended with exquisite care and attention to detail. Although modernized, the house is decorated with oil paintings, furniture and other fittings of the Georgian era. All rooms have been furnished with guests' comfort in mind, including the 18 luxurious en suite bedrooms - one a four poster - and all are extremely well-appointed and equipped with colour television, radio, telephone, tea and coffee-making facilities. Residents have their own lounge and have access to the garden.

Breakfast is a delightful choice of Traditional English, Continental or Wholefood. Guests need not worry about lunch and dinner as there are many good restaurants within easy walking distance.

To find accommodation in such beautiful grounds so near to the centre of a heritage city is really unique. Brompton House has its own parking, allowing guests the opportunity to discover Bath on foot. The city itself boasts many historic and architectural gems - the Abbey, the Pump Room and Roman Baths, the Royal and Landsdown Crescent, as well as modern centres such as the University and the American Museum. Bath is alo a convenient centre from which to tour the Cotswolds, Salisbury and Wells Cathedral cities, Stonehenge and Glastonbury.

Proprietors, David and Susan Selby and their helpful staff assure a friendly and courteous welcome to all guests amidst a relaxed, informal atmosphere.

The Les Routiers Guest House of the Year Award was introduced only last year.

# Inn of the Year

## THE WHITE HART
### Ford, Chippenham, Wiltshire

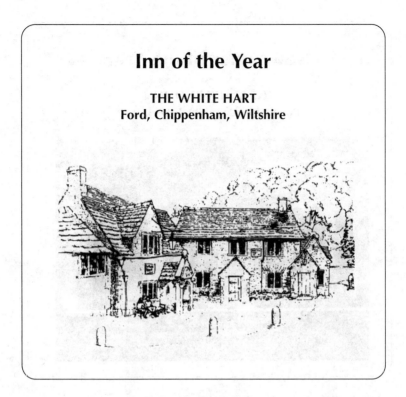

"The old inn by the trout stream" as it is often referred to, is a worthy winner of this award for its combination of good food, warmth and friendliness, courtesy of mine hosts, Chris and Jenny Phillips.

Reputedly built in 1533 and listed as being of architectural and historical interest, this attractive, beamed, West Country inn was featured in the film "Dr Doolittle". As well as its olde-world charm, it has a proud reputation for good food and ale, at value-for-money prices.

In Spring and Summer, the terrace overlooking the Bybrook River is an ideal spot to eat and drink and contemplate the abundance of nature. In the Riverside Restaurant, guests can choose from an extensive à la carte menu with English and French dishes ranging from venison and wild boar sausages with wild mushrooms through to salmon, steaks and poultry. The more informal bar menu offers home-made soup, scampi, steak-and kidney pie and a full range of sandwiches, ploughman's and salads, including vegetarian choices. A good choice of desserts may include tasty treats, such as hot toffee pudding, or possibly blackberry and vanilla ice cream. Customers can indulge in a bottle of wine from a comprehensive list, or sample traditional real beers. Guest beers are served straight from the cellar and include Wadsworth 6X, Bass, Badger Best Bitter, London Pride, Tanglefoot, Marston's Pedigree and many others. Traditional "scrumpy" cider is also available and makes a refreshing long drink for a summer's day beside the river.

The inn provides comfortable accommodation with all en suite rooms furnished to a very high standard, some with half tester and four poster beds. The latter are popular with honeymooners, but business travellers are also adequately catered for and can expect a trouser press and writing desin in their room. The Bybrook valley is a perfect backdrop for The White Hart, affording many quiet, country walks, either beside the river or along the winding lanes.

# Newcomer of the Year

### THE BLACK BULL INN
### Boroughbridge, North Yorkshire

The Black Bull Inn perfectly illustrates the Les Routiers philosophy of 'quality, value and a warm welcome' with that something special, and the reason why they were chosen as our Newcomer of the Year for 1996.

This pretty, market town hotel in St. James Square is Grade II listed and exceptionally well-maintained. The interior, like the four comfortable bedrooms, is beautifully-appointed and complements the relaxed, warm, friendly atmosphere of this delightful 13th century hostelry.

Food is served in the bar and also the restaurant which is open to both guests and non-residents. The á la carte menu offers an outstanding range of Cosmopolitan dishes, and there is also a daily specials board featuring fresh seafood, game and selectively prepared vegetarian choices. Country-farmed venison with a stem ginger and tangy plum sauce, dressed with crispy pot pourri scented won tons, or loin of English lamb sautéed in garlic wrapped in spinach and a lattice of flaky pastry on a rich minted pan gravy, are just two of the mouthwatering main course choices.

All dishes use only the freshest of produce and are prepared with the pride, care and attention one would expect of an award winning establishment. To complement the fine cuisine, there is a wide variety of wines from around the world, and a nice selection of cheeses. A special three-course menu is offered for Sunday lunch, and a selection of tailored menu's can be provided for parties of up to 60 people.

The location of the hotel, just off the A1(M) and north of the A59 junction, makes it ideal for exploring the 'Dales' and for visiting Harrogate and York or the east coast.

# Hotel of the Year: Ireland

**PONTOON BRIDGE HOTEL**
**Pontoon, Co.**

For those who really want to get-away-from-it-all, the Pontoon Bridge Hotel on the sandy shores of Lough Conn and Cullin, with panoramic surroundings, is the place to come. This is an locality unspoilt by industrialisation, housing schemes and intensive farming. Near the hotel is an old oak wood, still growing the oldest oak trees in the country, and pine martens and squirrels are plentiful. Also nearby is a designated wildlife sanctuary.

In its setting of unparalleled beauty, the hotel offers excellent, fresh, home-cooked international cuisine, including vegetarian choices and good-value wine in the Lakeside Restaurant. Expect dishes, such as Chef's oak-smoked wild Irish salmon, roast stuffed Mayo lamb with mint sauce, and roast stuffed turkey with orange glazed gammon. There are two bars, one with its own patio balcony overlooking the lake and its beautiful sunsets.

In addition to nightly entertainment, the hotel is Ireland's number one angling centre for trout and salmon fishing, with guides, boats, rod and tackle hire. The School of Fly Fishing was established in the grounds in 1987 and caters for the experienced angler as well as the novice. Two and four-day fly-fishing schools are available, as well as landscape-painting and cookery, all with professional tuition.

The hotel - which was featured on the BBC's 'Holiday Programme' provides comfortably furnished en suite accommodation, conference and sport's facilities and pets and children are both welcome.

A wealth of activities are available locally, including pony trekking, golf, sea angling and wind surfing off the dramatic beaches. Across Lough Cullin is the village of Straide which has a historical folk museum, and at Belderrig an outdoor archaeological museum of educational interest.

# THE 1996 CASSEROLE AWARDS

The Casserole, the Les Routiers mark of excellence, represents the finest culinary traditions. It is awarded annually to our members who offer that little something extra.

Whatever dish you order, it will have that extra-thoughtful finishing touch, allowing you to experience an exciting new world of wonderful sensations through clever use of herbs and aromatic spices, combinations of carefully matched colours and varying textures, all immaculately prepared and professionally presented. To qualify for the Casserole Award, an establishment must demonstrate that they have maintained the required standards for a minimum period of one year. Each year a select handful of new establishments join our list of past winners, who are allowed to display a prestigious certificate and receive a Casserole Award symbol against their full entry in this guide.

Look for the 🍲 symbol throughout the main regional section for full entries on the establishments listed below and overleaf.

## CASSEROLE AWARDS

**• Avon**
**BATH**
- The Abbey Hotel
- Brompton House
- The Canary Restaurant
- Dorian House
- The Old Malt House Hotel
- Rajpoot
- Rascals Bistro
- The Wife Of Bath Restaurant

**BRISTOL**
- Arches Hotel

**FRESHFORD**
- Inn At Freshford

**RANGEWORTHY**
- Rangeworthy Court Hotel

**WESTON-SUPER-MARE**
- The Commodore Hotel

**• Bedfordshire**
**BEDFORD**
- Edwardian House Hotel
- The Knife & Cleaver
- The Laws Hotel
- Three Cranes

**BIGGLESWADE**
- La Cachette

**• Berkshire**
**READING**
- Calcot Hotel

**WINDSOR**
- Christopher Hotel

**• Borders**
**BURNMOUTH**
- The Flemington Inn

**GALASHIELS**
- Abbotsford Arms Hotel

**HAWICK**
- Kirklands Hotel

**PEEBLES**
- Cringletie House Hotel

- Park Hotel
- Peebles Hotel Hydro

**• Buckinghamshire**
**BEACONSFIELD**
- The Royal Standard Of England

**PRINCES RISBOROUGH**
- King William Iv Freehouse & Restaurant

**• Cambridgeshire**
**ELY**
- The Anchor Inn

**STILTON**
- Bell Inn Hotel

**• Central**
**CRIANLARICH**
- The Rod & Reel

**DUNBLANE**
- Stirling Arms Hotel

**• Channel Islands**
**ALDERNEY**
- Inchalla Hotel
- Rose & Crown

**GUERNSEY**
- Imperial Hotel, Bars & Restaurant
- La Grande Mare

**ISLAND OF SARK**
- Dixcart Hotel

**JERSEY**
- Bryn-y-mor
- Waters Edge Hotel

**• Cheshire**
**CHESTER**
- Francs Restaurant
- Redland Hotel

**PARKGATE**
- The Boathouse
- Parkgate Hotel

**• Clwyd**
**COLWYN BAY**
    🍽 Cafe Nicoise
    🍽 Edelweiss Hotel
**LLANGOLLEN**
    🍽 Gales
**MOLD**
    🍽 Chez Colette

**• Co. Antrim**
**BUSHMILLS**
    🍽 Hillcrest Country House & Restaurant

**• Co. Cork**
**MALLOW**
    🍽 Springfort Hall

**• Co. Limerick**
**ADARE**
    🍽 Woodlands House Hotel

**• Cornwall**
**LOOE**
    🍽 Allhays Country House
**LOSTWITHIEL**
    🍽 Trewithen Restaurant
**MEVAGISSEY**
    🍽 Sharksfin Hotel & Restaurant
**PHILLEIGH**
    🍽 Smugglers Cottage Of Tolverne
**PILLATON**
    🍽 The Weary Friar Inn
**PORT ISAAC**
    🍽 Old School Hotel
**ST IVES**
    🍽 Chy-an-gwedhen
    🍽 Pedn-olva Hotel & Restaurant
**TREGONY**
    🍽 Kea House Restaurant

**• County Durham**
**DURHAM**
    🍽 Hallgarth Manor Hotel
    🍽 Ramside Hall Hotel

**• Cumbria**
**BASSENTHWAITE LAKE**
    🍽 The Pheasant Inn
**BOWNESS-ON-WINDERMERE**
    🍽 Blenheim Lodge
    🍽 Quinn's Restaurant
**GRANGE-OVER-SANDS**
    🍽 Netherwood Hotel
**HAWKSHEAD**
    🍽 Grizedale Lodge Hotel & Restaurant
**LONGTOWN**
    🍽 The Sportsman's Restaurant & March Bank Hotel
**MELMERBY**
    🍽 Shepherds Inn
**WINDERMERE**
    🍽 The Hideaway Hotel

**• Derbyshire**
**KEGWORTH**
    🍽 Kegworth Hotel
**MATLOCK**
    🍽 The Tavern At Tansley
**WIRKSWORTH**
    🍽 Le Bistro

**• Devon**
**BAMPTON**
    🍽 The Swan Hotel
**BOVEY TRACEY**
    🍽 The Edgemoor Hotel
**EXETER**
    🍽 The Old Thatch Inn
**ILFRACOMBE**
    🍽 Upstairs Restaurant

**LYNMOUTH**
    🍽 Rising Sun Hotel
**LYNTON**
    🍽 Millslade Country House Hotel
    🍽 Rockvale Hotel
**PLYMOUTH**
    🍽 Trattoria Pescatore
**SOUTH MOLTON**
    🍽 Stumbles Hotel & Restaurant
**TORQUAY**
    🍽 Jingle's Restaurant
    🍽 Livermead Cliff Hotel

**• Dorset**
**BOURNEMOUTH**
    🍽 The Bear Cross
    🍽 Hotel Mon Bijou
**CHRISTCHURCH**
    🍽 The Amberwood
    🍽 The Fisherman's Haunt Hotel
    🍽 Le Petit St Tropez
**DORCHESTER**
    🍽 Judge Jeffreys Restaurant
**LONGHAM**
    🍽 Angel Inn
**POOLE**
    🍽 Allans Seafood Restaurant
**TRENT**
    🍽 The Rose & Crown
**WEYMOUTH**
    🍽 Alessandria Hotel And Italian Restaurant
    🍽 The Chatsworth
    🍽 Sea Cow Restaurant
**WIMBORNE**
    🍽 The World's End

**• Dumfries & Galloway**
**LOCKERBIE**
    🍽 Lockerbie Manor Country Hotel

**• Dyfed**
**CARDIGAN**
    🍽 Skippers
**HAVERFORDWEST**
    🍽 Wolfscastle Country Hotel
**NEWCASTLE EMLYN**
    🍽 Maes-y-derw Guest House & Restaurant
**ST DAVID'S**
    🍽 Ramsey House
    🍽 Y Glennydd Guest House
**TENBY**
    🍽 Atlantic Hotel

**• Essex**
**CHELMSFORD**
    🍽 Miami Hotel
**CLACTON-ON-SEA**
    🍽 The Robin Hood
**COLCHESTER**
    🍽 The Old Queen's Head
    🍽 Rose & Crown Hotel
    🍽 The Warehouse Brasserie

**• Fife**
**BURNTISLAND**
    🍽 Kingswood Hotel
**CRAIL**
    🍽 Marine Hotel
**FREUCHIE**
    🍽 The Lomond Hills Hotel
**GLENROTHES**
    🍽 Town House Hotel
**ST ANDREWS**
    🍽 The Pancake Place

**• Glamorgan Mid**
**BRIDGEND**
    🍽 Ashoka Tandoori

**• Glamorgan South**
**CARDIFF**
Benedicto's

**• Gloucestershire**
**BOURTON-ON-THE-WATER**
The Old Manse Hotel
**CHIPPING CAMPDEN**
Noel Arms Hotel
**CLEARWELL**
Wyndham Arms
**STOW-ON-THE-WOLD**
Grapevine Hotel

**• Grampian**
**BALLATER**
Alexandra Hotel
Auld Kirk Hotel
**BANCHORY**
Banchory Lodge Hotel
**BRAEMAR**
Callater Lodge Hotel

**• Greater Manchester**
**ALTRINCHAM**
Woodland Park Hotel
**BOLTON**
Georgian House Hotel
**BURY**
The Bolholt
Rosco's Eating House
**MANCHESTER**
That Cafe
**ROCHDALE**
After Eight Restaurant

**• Gwent**
**CHEPSTOW**
The Huntsman Hotel
**CWMBRAN**
The Parkway Hotel & Conference Centre
**MONMOUTH**
The Crown At Whitebrook
**NEWPORT**
Villa Dino Restaurant
**TINTERN**
The Fountain Inn

**• Gwynedd**
**ABERSOCH**
The White House Hotel
**BALA**
Palê Hall Country House
**BETWS-Y-COED**
Ty Gwyn Hotel
**CRICCIETH**
The Moelwyn Restaurant With Rooms
**DOLGELLAU**
Clifton House Hotel
**LLANBEDROG**
Ship Inn
**LLANDUDNO**
Dunoon Hotel
Empire Hotel
Imperial Hotel
Sandringham Hotel
**PORTHMADOG**
Blossoms Restaurant
**PWLLHELI**
Twnti Seafood Restaurant
**TAL-Y-BONT**
The Lodge Hotel

**• Hampshire**
**BROCKENHURST**
The Cloud Hotel
**FORDINGBRIDGE**
Lions Court Restaurant & Hotel
**ODIHAM**
La Foret

**PORTSMOUTH**
Beaufort Hotel
Pride of Bilbao
Pride of Le Havre
Pride of Portsmouth
**RINGWOOD**
The Old Cottage Restaurant
**ROCKBOURNE**
Rose & Thistle
**SOUTHAMPTON**
Langley's Bistro
**WOODFALLS**
The Woodfalls Inn

**• Hereford & Worcester**
**HAY-ON-WYE**
The Old Black Lion
**PERSHORE**
Chequers Inn
**REDDITCH**
Hotel Montville & Granny's Restaurant

**• Hertfordshire**
**WATFORD**
The White House Hotel

**• Highlands**
**CROMARTY**
Royal Hotel
**FORT AUGUSTUS**
The Brae Hotel
**GLENFINNAN**
The Princes House
**GLENMORISTON**
Cluanie Inn
**GRANTOWN-ON-SPEY**
Ravenscourt House Hotel
**INVERNESS**
Culduthel Lodge
**ISLE OF SKYE**
Flodigarry Country House Hotel
Kinloch Lodge
Skeabost House Hotel
**KYLESKU**
Newton Lodge
**NAIRN**
Ramleh Hotel & Fingal's Restaurant
**TONGUE**
Ben Loyal Hotel
**ULLAPOOL**
The Harbour Lights Hotel

**• Humberside**
**HULL**
Kingstown Hotel
**SCUNTHORPE**
Briggate Lodge Inn

**• Isle Of Man**
**DOUGLAS**
Inglewood Hotel
La Brasserie
Sefton Hotel
**LAXEY**
Brown's Cafe & Tea Rooms
**RAMSEY**
Harbour Bistro

**• Isle Of Wight**
**SEAVIEW**
Seaview Hotel & Restaurant

**• Kent**
**BIRCHINGTON**
Smugglers Restaurant
**EDENBRIDGE**
Castle Inn
**MAIDSTONE**
The Limetree Restaurant And Hotel

**RAMSGATE**
🍽 Morton's Fork
**WHITSTABLE**
🍽 Giovanni's Restaurant

• **Lancashire**
**BLACKBURN**
🍽 May House Restaurant
**BLACKPOOL**
🍽 White Tower Restaurant
**CHORLEY**
🍽 Shaw Hill Hotel, Golf & Country Club
**ECCLESTON**
🍽 The Original Farmers Arms
**LANCASTER**
🍽 Springfield House Hotel & Restaurant
**LEYLAND**
🍽 Runshaw College School Of Catering
**LONGRIDGE**
🍽 Corporation Arms
**LYTHAM ST-ANNES**
🍽 Bedford Hotel
🍽 Fernlea Hotel & Leisure Complex
**PRESTON**
🍽 The Bushell's Arms
🍽 Ye Horn's Inn

• **Leicestershire**
**BOTTESFORD**
🍽 The Rutland Arms
**BURTON ON THE WOLDS**
🍽 Greyhound Inn
**CASTLE DONINGTON**
🍽 Donington Manor Hotel
🍽 Le Chevalier
**LOUGHBOROUGH**
🍽 The George Hotel
**OLD DALBY**
🍽 The Crown Inn

• **Lincolnshire**
**GRANTHAM**
🍽 The Royal Oak Inn
**SPALDING**
🍽 The Red Lion Hotel
**STAMFORD**
🍽 Candlesticks Hotel & Restaurant

• **London**
**BATTERSEA**
🍽 Buchan's
**BLOOMSBURY**
🍽 Academy Hotel
**CLAPHAM**
🍽 Windmill On The Common
**EALING**
🍽 Anne-marie At The 'taste Of The Taj'
**FOREST HILL**
🍽 Babur Brasserie
**FULHAM**
🍽 La Terraza
**HARROW**
🍽 Cumberland Hotel
🍽 Fiddler's Restaurant
🍽 The Harrow Hotel
**KEW**
🍽 Pissarro's Wine Bar
**PUTNEY**
🍽 Gavin's Restaurant
**TEDDINGTON**
🍽 The Italian Place Brasserie
**WEST END**
🍽 Don Pepe Restaurant
**WESTMINSTER**
🍽 Hanover Square Wine Bar & Grill

• **Lothian**
**EDINBURGH**
🍽 The Howard
🍽 Lancers Brasserie

🍽 The Old Bordeaux
🍽 The Tattler
🍽 The Town House
🍽 Verandah Tandoori Restaurant
**LEADBURN**
🍽 The Leadburn Inn
**ROSLIN**
🍽 Old Original Rosslyn Inn

• **Merseyside**
**LIVERPOOL**
🍽 Del Secolo
🍽 La Bouffe
**THORNTON HOUGH**
🍽 Thornton Hall Hotel
**WALLASEY**
🍽 Grove House Hotel & Restaurant
🍽 Leasowe Castle

• **Norfolk**
**CASTLE ACRE**
🍽 The Ostrich Inn
**DOWNHAM MARKET**
🍽 The Crown Hotel
**GREAT YARMOUTH**
🍽 The Cliff Hotel
**SNETTISHAM**
🍽 The Rose & Crown Freehouse
**WELLS-NEXT-THE-SEA**
🍽 Crown Hotel & Restaurant

• **Northumberland**
**ALNMOUTH**
🍽 Famous Schooner Hotel
**BELFORD**
🍽 Blue Bell
**BELLINGHAM**
🍽 Riverdale Hall Hotel
**HADRIAN'S WALL**
🍽 Vallum Lodge
**HEXHAM**
🍽 County Hotel
🍽 Langley Castle Hotel
**WARKWORTH**
🍽 The Jackdaw Restaurant

• **Orkney & Shetland Islands**
**KIRKWALL**
🍽 Albert Hotel

• **Oxfordshire**
**OXFORD**
🍽 Belfry Hotel
**SOULDERN**
🍽 Fox Inn
**WITNEY**
🍽 The Country Pie

• **Powys**
**LLANWDDYN**
🍽 Lake Vyrnwy Hotel

• **Shropshire**
**LLANYMYNECH**
🍽 Bradford Arms & Restaurant
**NORTON**
🍽 Hundred House Hotel, Restaurant & Inn
**OSWESTRY**
🍽 Restaurant Sebastian

• **Somerset**
**BRENT KNOLL**
🍽 Battleborough Grange Country Hotel
**CREWKERNE**
🍽 The Manor Arms
**DUNSTER**
🍽 The Tea Shoppe
**EXEBRIDGE**
🍽 Anchor Inn Hotel

**RODE**
 The Bell Inn
**TAUNTON**
 The Corner House
**WELLS**
 Crossways Inn
 Fountain Inn & Boxers Restaurant
**WINCANTON**
 Holbrook House Hotel

**• Staffordshire**
**BURTON UPON TRENT**
 The Horseshoe Inn
**STAFFORD**
 The Moat House Restaurant

**• Strathclyde**
**AYR**
 Fouters Bistro
**GLASGOW**
 Ewington Hotel
 La Fiorentina
**KILWINNING**
 Montgreenan Mansion House Hotel
**MOTHERWELL**
 The Moorings House Hotel
**OBAN**
 Foxholes Hotel

**• Suffolk**
**BILDESTON**
 The Crown Hotel
**BURY ST EDMUNDS**
 The Grange Hotel
 The White Horse
**HAUGHLEY**
 The Old Counting House Restaurant
**KERSEY**
 The Bell Inn
**SOUTHWOLD**
 Sutherland House Restaurant
**WOODBRIDGE**
 Captain's Table
**WRENTHAM**
 Quiggins Restaurant

**• Surrey**
**COBHAM**
 Woodlands Park Hotel

**• Sussex East**
**BATTLE**
 Powdermills Hotel
**FLETCHING**
 The Rose & Crown

**• Sussex West**
**CHICHESTER**
 Platters Restaurant

**• Tayside**
**KINROSS**
 Balgedie Toll Tavern
**PITLOCHRY**
 Green Park Hotel

**• Western Isles**
**ISLE OF BENBECULA**
 Dark Island Hotel

**• Wiltshire**
**BRADFORD ON AVON**
 Gongoozler Restaurant
 Widbrook Grange
**CHIPPENHAM**
 The Old House At Home
 The Three Crowns
**FORD**
 White Hart Hotel

**SALISBURY**
 Antrobus Arms Hotel
 Finders Keepers
**SHERSTON**
 Rattlebone Inn
**WARMINSTER**
 Old Bell Hotel
**WILTON**
 Pembroke Arms Hotel

**• Yorkshire North**
**APPLETON-LE-MOORS**
 Appleton Hall Country House Hotel
**ASKRIGG**
 King's Arms Hotel & Clubroom Restaurant
**HARROGATE**
 Grundy's Restaurant
 Studley Hotel
**HELMSLEY**
 The Feversham Arms Hotel
 Pheasant Hotel
**LEEMING BAR**
 Motel Leeming
**MALTON**
 Cornucopia
**NORTHALLERTON**
 Duke Of Wellington Inn
**RICHMOND**
 Peat Gate Head
**ROSEDALE ABBEY**
 The Milburn Arms Hotel
**SCARBOROUGH**
 The Falcon Inn
**STOKESLEY**
 Millers Restaurant
 The Wainstones Hotel
**THIRSK**
 Nag's Head Hotel & Restaurant
 Sheppard's Hotel, Restaurant & Bistro
**WHITBY**
 The Magpie Cafe
**WIGGLESWORTH**
 The Plough Inn
**YORK**
 Mount Royale
 Red Lion Motel & Country Inn

**• Yorkshire South**
**DONCASTER**
 The Regent Hotel, Parade Bar & Restaurant
**SHEFFIELD**
 The Old Sidings

**• Yorkshire West**
**HALIFAX**
 Imperial Crown Hotel
 Rock Inn Hotel & Churchill's
**HUDDERSFIELD**
 Huddersfield Hotel & Rosemary Lane Bistro
 The White House
**LEEDS**
 The Butlers Hotel

# LES ROUTIERS
# CHEESEBOARD AWARDS 1996

The variety of cheeses now generally available in the UK is wider and more unusual than ever before. However, it is not just the selection or variety that makes a good cheeseboard. There are many important factors. We put ourselves in the customer's shoes and looked for taste through expert selection. We looked for variety, with an imaginative choice of traditional, new and local cheeses. Presentation requires not only good use of colour, texture and shape to bring out a tempting display, but careful handling and storage to bring out the best in the cheese. And finally, we looked for knowledge of the cheeses offered. We hope you will discover that cheese is fun, and that in this guide there is a vast range of establishments offering an infinite and delicious choice of cheeses, from English, Scottish and Welsh cheeses to European varieties and many interesting regional specialities, complemented by well matched vintage wines. After careful consideration, the establishments listed below and overleaf have all been judged worthy of inclusion in the Les Routiers Cheeseboard Honours List. From this list, one establishment has been selected as the overall winner and receives the prestigious Les Routiers Cheeseboard of the Year Award 1996 .

Look for the ⌐ Symbol throughout the main regional section for full entries on the establishments listed below and overleaf.

## CHEESEBOARD

• **Bedfordshire**
**BEDFORD**
⌐ The Knife & Cleaver
**BIGGLESWADE**
⌐ La Cachette

• **Berkshire**
**MAIDENHEAD**
⌐ Chauntry House Hotel

• **Buckinghamshire**
**PRINCES RISBOROUGH**
⌐ King William Iv Freehouse & Restaurant

• **Cambridgeshire**
**ELY**
⌐ The Anchor Inn

• **Channel Islands**
**ALDERNEY**
⌐ Inchalla Hotel
**GUERNSEY**
⌐ La Grande Mare
**JERSEY**
⌐ Waters Edge Hotel

• **Cheshire**
**CHESTER**

⌐ The Blue Bell Restaurant
⌐ Francs Restaurant

• **Co. Antrim**
**PORTRUSH**
⌐ Causeway Coast Hotel & Conference Centre

• **Co. Down**
**HILLSBOROUGH**
⌐ The Plough Inn

• **Cornwall**
**FALMOUTH**
⌐ Green Lawns Hotel
**LOOE**
⌐ Allhays Country House

• **Cumbria**
**BROUGHTON-IN-FURNESS**
⌐ Beswicks Restaurant
**MELMERBY**
⌐ Shepherds Inn

• **Devon**
**TORQUAY**
⌐ Livermead Cliff Hotel

• **Dorset**
**TRENT**

The Rose & Crown

• **Dyfed**
**CARDIGAN**
Skippers
**HAVERFORDWEST**
Wolfscastle Country Hotel

• **Grampian**
**BALLATER**
Alexandra Hotel

• **Gwent**
**MONMOUTH**
The Crown at Whitebrook

• **Hampshire**
**PORTSMOUTH**
Pride of Bilbao
Pride of Le Havre
Pride of Portsmouth

• **Highlands**
**NAIRN**
Ramleh Hotel & Fingal's Restaurant

• **Humberside**
**HULL**
Pearson Park Hotel

• **Lancashire**
**CLITHEROE**
The Inn At Whitewell
**LEYLAND**
Runshaw College School of Catering
(Fox Holes Restaurant)

• **Lincolnshire**
**LEADENHAM**
George Hotel

• **London**
**COVENT GARDEN**
Le Cafe Des Amis Du Vin

• **Northumberland**
**ALNWICK**
The Cottage Inn Hotel

• **Nottinghamshire**
**NEWARK-ON-TRENT**
New Ferry Restaurant

• **Shropshire**
**LLANYMYNECH**
Bradford Arms & Restaurant
**SHREWSBURY**
Sydney House Hotel

• **Somerset**
**WELLS**
Fountain Inn & Boxers Restaurant

• **Strathclyde**
**AYR**
Fouters Bistro
**JOHNSTONE**
Lynnhurst Hotel

• **Suffolk**
**HAUGHLEY**
The Old Counting House Restaurant

• **Western Isles**
**NORTH UIST**
Lochmaddy Hotel

• **Yorkshire North**
**HELMSLEY**
The Feversham Arms Hotel
**LEEMING BAR**
Motel Leeming

• **Yorkshire West**
**HUDDERSFIELD**
The Lodge Hotel
**LEEDS**
Pinewood Private Hotel

# Cheeseboard of the Year
### BRADFORD ARMS & RESTAURANT
### Llanymynech, Shropshire

# The Bradford Arms and Restaurant

A member of Les Routiers since 1987, this fine old coaching inn, situated on the main road in Llanymynech has a widespread reputation for its excellent cuisine and warm hospitality, but notably for its superb farmhouse cheeses which has won them the coveted title of Les Routiers Cheeseboard of the Year 1996.

The Bradford Arms was 'Victorianized' in 1902, and although traditionally furnished with soft lighting, a marble fireplace and a mahogany bar, such features do not detract from the overall comfort of this friendly, welcoming establishment. The cheeseboard is outstanding and offers an diverse selection of reasonably priced small farm 'real' cheeses; Ticklemore - a hand-pressed goat's cheese with a smooth flavour made in Totnes, Dunsyre - a full-flavoured semi-soft blue made from the milk of Ayrshire cows, and Lady Lanover - a ewe's milk cheese, saffron washed with a distinctive flavour.

As well as cheeses from the UK, customers can enjoy an equally interesting selection of foreign varieties; Reblechon - a French, fruity, rind washed cheese with a creamy, nutty flavour, Mountain Gorgonzola - an Italian, creamy, spicy, sharp tasting blue cheese, and Pyrenees - a mild, creamy, mountain cheese from the hills of Spain, to name just three. Many of the excellent cheeses available are thoughtfully reflected throughout the main menu of modern English dishes as imaginative sauces and dressings; Tagliatelle with walnut and blue cheese dressing, mushrooms Trapanese with a grilled goat's cheese, and chicken in Stilton chive sauce. All dishes are home-made, using only fresh vegetables, and there is also a selection of home-made desserts and an excellent wine list. "The cheeseboard at the Bradford Arms & Restaurant continues to reflect their high standards and is one of the best I have seen," said our inspector when he visited.

# LES ROUTIERS CORPS D'ELITE
# (WINE AWARDS) 1996

Although the emphasis and care taken by both chef and proprietor over food purchase, preparation and presentation may seem ponderously slow and pedantic to the casual diner, it generally takes only one small taste of a good wine to justify the attention to detail. Choosing a bottle of wine is a matter of personal taste, the food it is to be served with and the amount you want to spend. However, finding out about wines from different countries will make that selection so much easier. As the consumption of wine in the UK continues to enjoy tremendous growth, so too does the demand for more adventurous selections. A well-balanced wine list should offer an interesting selection of different wines with varying tastes to suit all palates and at good value for money. Equally important is an easy-to-read wine list which is free of jargon, the provision of half-bottles throughout the range, and the enthusiasm displayed by the proprietor in giving advice on selection. When visiting Les Routiers establishments you will be able to choose from an extensive range of imaginative wines from the UK and Europe, as well as from many other countries around the globe. From Australia, full-flavoured Cabernet Sauvignons have long been popular for their powerful blackcurranty taste, whilst New Zealand produces a good range of full-flavoured wines, some of which have a slightly perfumed aroma. Other countries where the wine industry has been greatly modernized in the past decade, which are currently producing some remarkable-tasting wines, include Chile, Japan, California, South Africa, China, Albania and even Romania. Be adventurous in your selections and you will not be disappointed. The judges found all the essential qualities of a good wine list at the establishments listed opposite. From the shortlist, one establishment has been selected for the most outstanding wine list of all, and receives the coveted Les Routiers Prix D'Elite Award for 1996 (see page 62).

**Look for the ⇌ symbol throughout the main regional section for full entries on the establishments listed opposite.**

## CORPS D'ELITE

• **Avon**
**FRESHFORD**
⇌ Inn At Freshford

• **Bedfordshire**
**BEDFORD**
⇌ The Knife & Cleaver
⇌ Three Cranes
**BIGGLESWADE**
⇌ La Cachette

• **Buckinghamshire**
**PRINCES RISBOROUGH**
⇌ King William Iv Freehouse & Restaurant

• **Cambridgeshire**
**CAMBRIDGE**

⇌ Ancient Shepherds
**ELY**
⇌ The Anchor Inn

• **Channel Islands**
**GUERNSEY**
⇌ La Grande Mare
**JERSEY**
⇌ Millbrook House

• **Clwyd**
**COLWYN BAY**
⇌ Cafe Nicoise
**LLANGOLLEN**
⇌ Gales

• **Co. Antrim**
**BUSHMILLS**
⇌ Hillcrest Country House & Restaurant

- **Co. Tyrone**
**OMAGH**
- The Mellon Country Inn

- **Cornwall**
**FALMOUTH**
- Green Lawns Hotel
**NEWQUAY**
- The Headland Hotel
**PORT ISAAC**
- The Cornish Arms

- **Cumbria**
**BOWNESS-ON-WINDERMERE**
- Blenheim Lodge
**BROUGH SOWERBY**
- The Black Bull Inn
**BROUGHTON-IN-FURNESS**
- Beswicks Restaurant
**BUTTERMERE**
- Bridge Hotel
**WINDERMERE**
- The Hideaway Hotel

- **Devon**
**CLAWTON**
- Court Barn Country House Hotel

- **Dorset**
**DORCHESTER**
- The Manor Hotel
**WEYMOUTH**
- Sea Cow Restaurant

- **Dyfed**
**ST DAVID'S**
- Ramsey House

- **Essex**
**BILLERICAY**
- Duke Of York
**COLCHESTER**
- The Warehouse Brasserie

- **Grampian**
**BANCHORY**
- Banchory Lodge Hotel

- **Greater Manchester**
**ALTRINCHAM**
- Woodland Park Hotel
**BOLTON**
- Georgian House Hotel
**MANCHESTER**
- Elm Grange Hotel
**ROCHDALE**
- After Eight Restaurant

- **Gwent**
**MONMOUTH**
- The Crown At Whitebrook

- **Gwynedd**
**HARLECH**
- Castle Cottage Hotel & Restaurant
**LLANDUDNO**
- Imperial Hotel

- **Hampshire**
**PORTSMOUTH**
- Pride of Bilbao
- Pride of Le Havre
- Pride of Portsmouth

- **Hereford & Worcester**
**HAY-ON-WYE**
- The Old Black Lion
**WEOBLEY**
- Ye Olde Salutation Inn

- **Highlands**
**ISLE OF SKYE**
- Hotel Eilean Iarmain
- Kinloch Lodge
**NAIRN**
- Ramleh Hotel & Fingal's Restaurant

- **Humberside**
**SCUNTHORPE**
- Briggate Lodge Inn

- **Isle Of Man**
**RAMSEY**
- Harbour Bistro

- **Isle Of Wight**
**CHALE**
- Clarendon Hotel & Wight Mouse Inn

- **Kent**
**EDENBRIDGE**
- Castle Inn
**MAIDSTONE**
- The Limetree Restaurant And Hotel

- **Lancashire**
**BLACKBURN**
- May House Restaurant
**BLACKPOOL**
- White Tower Restaurant
**CHORLEY**
- Shaw Hill Hotel, Golf & Country Club
**LANCASTER**
- Springfield House Hotel & Restaurant
**LYTHAM ST-ANNES**
- Bedford Hotel
- Fernlea Hotel & Leisure Complex
**PRESTON**
- The Bushell's Arms
- Ye Horn's Inn

- **London**
**BISHOPSGATE**
- City Limits Restaurant & Wine Bar

**KEW**
 ☰ Pissarro's Wine Bar
**WEST HAMPSTEAD**
 ☰ No. 77 Wine Bar
**WESTMINSTER**
 ☰ Hanover Square Wine Bar & Grill

• **Merseyside**
**LIVERPOOL**
 ☰ Del Secolo
 ☰ La Bouffe
**THORNTON HOUGH**
 ☰ Thornton Hall Hotel
**WALLASEY**
 ☰ Grove House Hotel & Restaurant
 ☰ Leasowe Castle

• **Norfolk**
**BRANCASTER STAITHE**
 ☰ The Jolly Sailors
**GREAT YARMOUTH**
 ☰ The Cliff Hotel
 ☰ Imperial Hotel
**WELLS-NEXT-THE-SEA**
 ☰ Crown Hotel & Restaurant

• **Northumberland**
**BELLINGHAM**
 ☰ Riverdale Hall Hotel
**HEXHAM**
 ☰ Langley Castle Hotel

• **Nottinghamshire**
**NEWARK-ON-TRENT**
 ☰ New Ferry Restaurant

• **Oxfordshire**
**SHIPTON-UNDER-WYCHWOOD**
 ☰ The Shaven Crown Hotel

• **Shropshire**
**LLANYMYNECH**
 ☰ Bradford Arms & Restaurant
**SHREWSBURY**
 ☰ Sydney House Hotel

• **Strathclyde**
**AYR**
 ☰ Fouters Bistro
**GLASGOW**
 ☰ Ewington Hotel
**OBAN**
 ☰ Foxholes Hotel

• **Suffolk**
**HAUGHLEY**
 ☰ The Old Counting House Restaurant
**WOODBRIDGE**
 ☰ Captain's Table
**WRENTHAM**
 ☰ Quiggins Restaurant

• **Surrey**

**COBHAM**
 ☰ Woodlands Park Hotel

• **Sussex East**
**FLETCHING**
 ☰ The Rose & Crown

• **Sussex West**
**CHICHESTER**
 ☰ Platters Restaurant
**WEST WITTERING**
 ☰ The Lamb Inn West Wittering

• **Wiltshire**
**PEWSEY**
 ☰ Woodbridge Inn
**SHERSTON**
 ☰ Rattlebone Inn

• **Yorkshire North**
**CLAPHAM**
 ☰ New Inn Hotel
**HARROGATE**
 ☰ Studley Hotel
**HELMSLEY**
 ☰ The Feversham Arms Hotel
**LEEMING BAR**
 ☰ Motel Leeming
**THIRSK**
 ☰ Sheppard's Hotel, Restaurant & Bistro
**WIGGLESWORTH**
 ☰ The Plough Inn

• **Yorkshire West**
**HALIFAX**
 ☰ Imperial Crown Hotel
 ☰ Rock Inn Hotel & Churchill's
**HUDDERSFIELD**
 ☰ Huddersfield Hotel & Rosemary
  Lane Bistro
 ☰ The Lodge Hotel

# Prix D'Elite: Wine of the Year
## THE LODGE HOTEL
### Birkby, Huddersfield, West Yorkshire

In a closely contested final, The Lodge Hotel at Birkby was chosen as the overall winner of the 1996 Prix D'Elite: Wine of the Year Awards.

This fine Victorian gentlemans' residence, sympathetically restored as Huddersfield's first country house hotel, is set in two acres of mature gardens. As well as its elegant reception rooms, the beautiful 50-cover restaurant offers excellent and innovative cuisine using fresh seasonal foods and, of course, an exceptional wine list. The list features not only classic European but popular new world wines selected from around the globe, reflecting the multiplicity of flavours, textures and styles available. Although prices may vary, all have one thing in common - they are all of high quality.

From Australia comes a 1985 Black Label Cabernet Sauvignon/Merlot, an elegant combination of only the very best grapes from prime areas of South Australia. The Black Label is a strictly limited release each year. From Chile, a 1988 Chevalier Vedrines, Roger Joanne is a well-balanced claret with bags of fruit. From Russia, Krasny Reserve from the Krikova Winery, Moldova 1986 is a truly unique red wine, deeply coloured, raisiny with a very gentle, slightly sweet chocolate edge. A range of Californian wines, includes a 1987 Chardonnay from the Napa Valley, made from organically-grown grapes producing a luscious berry, cedar and cinnamon-spice flavoured wine. And from Washington State, a 1992 Sauvignon Blanc with the aroma of citrus and pear. As well as a wide choice of rich, smooth, fruity reds and crisply dry, fragrant white wines from France, the list includes varieties from Germany, Italy, Spain, New Zealand, Chile, Lebanon, and South Africa. Even England is represented on the list with two excellent white wines from leading winerys in Hastings and Kent.

The excellent presentation of the list shows consideration for both the connoisseur and the general consumer as it is informative without being intimidating. All visitors to The Lodge Hotel can be assured of finding the ideal wine for their taste and pocket.

# HIGHLY COMMENDED

Selecting major award-winners each year is always difficult due to the excellent standards our Area Managers encounter on their regular field visits. To reflect this, we have introduced a special "Highly Commended" category so that recognition can be given to members who have achieved consistently high standards of accommodation, food, wine and cheeseboard, and who symbolize the Les Routiers philosophy of quality, value and a warm welcome. Each establishment receives a certificate of commendation.

**LONDON**
BOISDALE RESTAURANT Belgravia, London
OAK LODGE HOTEL Enfield, Greater London
BEAUCHAMP'S RESTAURANT Leadenhall, London

**SOUTH-EAST ENGLAND (SOUTH)**
THE ROSE & CROWN Fletching, East Sussex
THE LIME TREES RESTAURANT AND HOTEL Lenham, Kent
THE CASTLE Chiddingstone, Kent

**SOUTH-EAST ENGLAND (NORTH)**
THE CLIFF HOTEL Gt. Yarmouth, Norfolk
TATTIES Cambridge Cambridgeshire
THE WHITE HORSE Bury St. Edmunds, Suffolk

**SOUTH-WEST ENGLAND (EAST)**
UPLAND PARK HOTEL Portsmouth, Hampshire
WESSEX ROYALE HOTEL Dorchester, Dorset
HAVENHURST HOTEL Swanage, Dorset

**SOUTH-WEST ENGLAND (CENTRAL)**
BROMPTON HOUSE Bath, Avon
THE WIFE OF BATH RESTAURANT Bath, Avon
BATTLEBOROUGH GRANGE COUNTRY HOTEL Brent Knoll, Somerset

**SOUTH-WEST ENGLAND (WEST)**
CHY-AN-GWEDHEN St. Ives, Cornwall
COWICK BARTON INN Exeter, Devon
LA GRANDE MARE Guernsey, Channel Islands

**CENTRAL ENGLAND (SOUTH)**
THE OLD MANSE HOTEL Bourton-on-the-Water, Gloucestershire
GRAPEVINE HOTEL Stow-on-the-Wold, Gloucestershire
THE MOON AND SIXPENCE Banbury, Oxfordshire

**CENTRAL ENGLAND (NORTH)**
ASHFORD HOTEL AND RESTAURANT Bakewell, Derbyshire
BRACKENBOROUGH ARMS HOTEL Louth, Lincolnshire
TERRACE RESTAURANT Brownhills, West Midlands

**NORTHERN ENGLAND (EAST)**
THE JACKDAW RESTAURANT Warkworth, Northumberland
THE FEVERSHAM ARMS HOTEL Helmsley, North Yorkshire
VALLUM LODGE Hadrian's Wall, Northumberland

**NORTHERN ENGLAND (WEST)**
M & J's Windermere, Cumbria
BROWN'S CAFE Laxey, Isle of Man
ROCK INN HOTEL & CHURCHILL'S RESTAURANT Halifax, W. Yorks

**WALES (NORTH)**
CAFE NICOISE Colwyn Bay, Clwyd
EMPIRE HOTEL Llandudno, Gwynedd
WHITE COURT HOTEL Llandudno, Gwynedd

**WALES (SOUTH)**
TREHERNE ARMS Culverhouse Cross
MARLBOROUGH GUEST HOUSE Cardiff, South Glamorgan
WOLFCASTLE COUNTRY HOTEL Haverfordwest, Dyfed

**SCOTLAND (SOUTH)**
HOWARD HOTEL Edinburgh, Lothian
THE TOWN HOUSE Edinburgh, Lothian
THE MAGNUM Edinburgh, Lothian

**SCOTLAND (NORTH)**
BANCHORY LODGE HOTEL Banchory, Grampian
CULLEN BAY HOTEL Cullen, Grampian
NEWTON LODGE Kylesku, Highlands

# Symbol of Excellence

## CRINGLETIE HOUSE HOTEL
### Peebles, Borders

In recognition of consistently high standards over the past ten years, and as a holder of the Les Routiers Casserole - our mark of excellence - since 1987, we have enormous pleasure in presenting this special award to the Cringletie House Hotel in Peebles.

Cringletie - a distinguished mansion house, set well back in 28 acres of peaceful gardens and woodlands - has retained the warm atmosphere of a private country house. Designed by David Bryce, the renowned Scottish architect, it was built for the Wolfe Murray family in 1861. Colonel Alexander Murray from Cringletie accepted the surrender of Quebec after General Wolfe was killed.

Today, the resident proprietors provide interesting and imaginative, freshly-cooked food, with fruit and vegetables in season from the hotel's own extensive, two-acres walled kitchen garden which is featured in the "The Gourmet Garden" by Geraldene Holt. The menus change daily to ensure maximum variety for both long and short-stay guests. It is complemented by an extensive, well-chosen wine list.

All rooms are tastefully decorated, and furnished to a high standard of comfort. There are magnificent views from all rooms. As well as its own hard tennis court, croquet lawn and putting green, there are pleasant walks in the grounds and surrounding countryside.

There is an attractive 18-hole golf course, and several other courses within half-an-hour's drive. Trout and salmon fishing are available by permit on the nearby River Tweed, and the area is rich in history with many notable houses which are open to the public.

For consistently maintaining such impeccable standards and for continuing to delight the Les Routiers Inspectors for over a decade, Les Routiers has voted the Cringletie House Hotel a most worthy winner of the Symbol of Excellence Award for 1996.

# OFFICIAL UK TOURIST BOARDS

**ENGLISH TOURIST BOARD**
Thames Tower, Black's Road,
Hammersmith, London W6 9EL
☎ 0181 846 9000

**CUMBRIA TOURIST BOARD**
Ashleigh, Holly Road,
Windermere LA23 2AQ
☎ 015394 44444

**EAST ANGLIA TOURIST BOARD**
Toppesfield Hall, Hadleigh,
Suffolk IP7 7DN
☎ 01473 822922

**EAST MIDLANDS TOURIST BOARD**
Exchequergate, Lincoln LN2 IPZ
☎ 01522 531521

**HEART OF ENGLAND TOURIST
BOARD**
Larkhill Road, Worcester WR5 2EF
☎ 01905 763436

**LONDON TOURIST BOARD**
25 Grosvenor Gardens,
London SWlW ODU
☎ 0171 730 34S0

**NORTHUMBRIA TOURIST BOARD**
Aykley Heads, Durham DH1 5UX
☎ 0191 384 6905

**SOUTHERN TOURIST BOARD**
40 Chamberlayne Road, Eastleigh,
Hants S05 5JH
☎ 01703 620006

**SOUTH EAST ENGLAND TOURIST
BOARD**
The Old Brew House, Warwick Park,
Tunbridge Wells, Kent TN2 5TU
☎ 01892 540766

**WEST COUNTRY TOURIST BOARD**
60 St. David's Hill, Exeter EX4 4SY
☎ 01392 76351

**YORKSHIRE & HUMBERSIDE
TOURIST BOARD**
312 Tadcaster Road, York YO2 2HF
☎ 01904 707961

**NORTHERN IRELAND TOURIST
BOARD**
St. Anne's Court, 59 North Street,
Belfast BT1 lNB
☎ 01232 231221/246609

**NORTHERN IRELAND TOURIST
BOARD (LONDON)**
11 Berkeley Street, London WlX 5AD
☎ 0171 493 0601

**DUBLIN TOURISM**
☎ 01 2844768

**SCOTTISH TOURIST BOARD**
23 Ravelston Terrace,
Edinburgh EH4 3EU
☎ 0131 332 2433

**SC0TTISH TOURIST BOARD
(LONDON)**
19 Cockspur Street, London SWlY 5BL
☎ 0171 930 8661

**WALES TOURIST BQARD**
Brunel House, 2 Fitzalan Road,
Cardiff CF2 1UY
☎ 01222 499909

**WALES TOURIST BOARD (LONDON)**
12 Lower Regent Street,
London SW1A 4PQ
☎ 0171 409 0969

**JERSEY TOURISM**
Liberation Square, St. Helier,
Jersey JE1 1BB, Channel Islands
☎ 01534 500700

**STATE OF GUERNSEY TOURIST
BOARD**
PO Box 23, White Rock, St. Peter Port,
Guernsey, Channel Islands
☎ 01481 726611

**ISLE OF MAN DEPARTMENT OF
TOURISM & LEISURE**
Sea Terminal Building, Douglas,
Isle of Man
☎ 01624 686760

# HALF-PRICE
# MEMBERSHIP!
## to the ultimate Dining Scheme!

**CLUB BON VIVEUR** is an exciting British nationwide scheme for diners, operated by *Les Routiers*, through which you are invited to rediscover the *Joie de Vivre* in hundreds of restaurants throughout Britain, offering more than 23 types of international cuisine!

As a *Club Bon Viveur* cardholder, you are entitled to a range of substantial discounts and benefits, including reductions of up to 50% on food bills (subject to individual restaurants' restrictions), when dining with one or more guests. You can use your card as often as you wish, in any of the establishments listed in the *Joie de Vivre* Directory. The Directory will be sent to you with your Members' Pack, when you join.

Membership of *Club Bon Viveur* is just £15 per annum, which can very quickly be recouped through discounts.

**MEMBERSHIP BENEFITS INCLUDE:**

- Discounted food prices when dining out
- The *Joie de Vivre* Directory for easy reference
- Discounts on purchases of Les Routiers guidebooks and publications
- Other promotional offers

To apply for your *Club Bon Viveur* membership, simply complete the application form on page 69 and return it with your payment of £15 to:

**The Club Secretary**
**CLUB BON VIVEUR,**
**25 Vanston Place, London SW6 1AZ**

---

**For Reservations & Special Offers FreeCall 0500 700 456**

# SAMPLE THE PLEASURES OF CLUB BON VIVEUR BY USING EACH OF THESE 8 FREE VOUCHERS FOR A MEAL AT A PARTICIPATING LES ROUTIERS HOTEL.

## How to use your Club Bon Viveur vouchers.

1. Each voucher entitles you to a discounted meal at any of the restaurants in the 1996 Guide to Britain and Ireland displaying the CLUB symbol.

2. Discounts are as follows: 2 people dining, 50% off the price of the meal, 3 people dining, 33.3% off the price and 4 people dining 25% off. Prices apply to food only and do not include beverages or tobacco.

3. Please telephone the restaurant of your choice IN ADVANCE to make a reservation, also to establish the days and times at which club terms are offered. These times vary from restaurant to restaurant and MUST be confirmed before starting your journey. This will ensure that you are not disappointed.

4. Take the guide with you - do NOT detach the vouchers. When settling your bill, sign a voucher on the reverse to validate it and hand it to the restaurant as proof of your entitlement to the advertised discounts. Restaurants can decline to accept vouchers if they are not tendered in a manner which does not clearly show that they are an integral part of the 1996 Guide to Britain and Ireland.

### Terms and Conditions:
(1) The Club BON Viveur 1st Dine voucher entitles you to the special terms offered by participating restaurants. (2) Restaurants are entitled to decline to give the advertised discounts if diners fail to comply with any of these terms and conditions. (3) Select a restaurant from the Guide showing the symbol [CLUB] and telephone to make sure it is offering Club BON Viveur discounts on the day and the time you wish to dine. (4) You MUST make a table reservation by telephone stating that your wish to use your Club BON Viveur 1st Dine voucher. (5) Club BON Viveur 1st Dine participating restaurants will offer one or more of the following discounts when you dine with at least one guest: Voucher holder plus one guest: 50%, plus two guests: 33.3%, plus three guests: 25%. (6) Discounts are granted on the basis of availability. This means reservations will be accepted until the restaurant expects to be fully booked. (7) Validate your voucher by signing in ink. (8) Show your voucher before you take your table and surrender it when settling your bill. Please take into account the full price of your bill when deciding your gratuity. (9) Vouchers may not be used in conjunction with any other promotional offer, saving or discount scheme that may be available at the restaurant. (10) A minimum of one voucher is accepted per party of up to four people. Larger parties should confirm with the restaurant if they will accept more than one voucher and if so, what the overall discount would be. (11) Restaurants are also entitled to refuse admission to guests that may disturb or upset other guests in the restaurant. (12) Whilst Club BON Viveur will take all reasonable steps to ensure the accuracy of all information, it cannot accept liability for any inaccurate information.

For Reservations & Special Offers FreeCall 0500 700 456

## TERMS AND CONDITIONS
### for the use of Club BON Viveur 1st Dine Voucher

(1) The Club BON Viveur 1st Dine voucher entitles you to the special terms offered by participating restaurants. (2) Restaurants are entitled to decline to give the advertised discounts if diners fail to comply with any of these terms and conditions. (3) Select a restaurant from the Guide showing the symbol [CLUB] and telephone to make sure it is offering Club BON Viveur discounts on the day and the time you wish to dine. (4) You MUST make a table reservation by telephone stating that your wish to use your Club BON Viveur 1st Dine voucher. (5) Club BON Viveur 1st Dine participating restaurants will offer one or more of the following discounts when you dine with at least one guest: Voucher holder plus one guest: 50%, plus two guests: 33.3%, plus three guests: 25%. (6) Discounts are granted on the basis of availability. This means reservations will be accepted until the restaurant expects to be fully booked. (7) Validate your voucher by signing in ink. (8) Show your voucher before you take your table and surrender it when settling your bill. Please take into account the full price of your bill when deciding your gratuity. (9) Vouchers may not be used in conjunction with any other promotional offer, saving or discount scheme that may be available at the restaurant. (10) A minimum of one voucher is accepted per party of up to four people. Larger parties should confirm with the restaurant if they will accept more than one voucher and if so, what the overall discount would be. (11) Restaurants are also entitled to refuse admission to guests that may disturb or upset other guests in the restaurant. (12) Whilst Club BON Viveur will take all reasonable steps to ensure the accuracy of all information, it cannot accept liability for any inaccurate information.

Signature: ..........................................................

## TERMS AND CONDITIONS
### for the use of Club BON Viveur 1st Dine Voucher

(1) The Club BON Viveur 1st Dine voucher entitles you to the special terms offered by participating restaurants. (2) Restaurants are entitled to decline to give the advertised discounts if diners fail to comply with any of these terms and conditions. (3) Select a restaurant from the Guide showing the symbol [CLUB] and telephone to make sure it is offering Club BON Viveur discounts on the day and the time you wish to dine. (4) You MUST make a table reservation by telephone stating that your wish to use your Club BON Viveur 1st Dine voucher. (5) Club BON Viveur 1st Dine participating restaurants will offer one or more of the following discounts when you dine with at least one guest: Voucher holder plus one guest: 50%, plus two guests: 33.3%, plus three guests: 25%. (6) Discounts are granted on the basis of availability. This means reservations will be accepted until the restaurant expects to be fully booked. (7) Validate your voucher by signing in ink. (8) Show your voucher before you take your table and surrender it when settling your bill. Please take into account the full price of your bill when deciding your gratuity. (9) Vouchers may not be used in conjunction with any other promotional offer, saving or discount scheme that may be available at the restaurant. (10) A minimum of one voucher is accepted per party of up to four people. Larger parties should confirm with the restaurant if they will accept more than one voucher and if so, what the overall discount would be. (11) Restaurants are also entitled to refuse admission to guests that may disturb or upset other guests in the restaurant. (12) Whilst Club BON Viveur will take all reasonable steps to ensure the accuracy of all information, it cannot accept liability for any inaccurate information.

Signature: ..........................................................

## TERMS AND CONDITIONS
### for the use of Club BON Viveur 1st Dine Voucher

(1) The Club BON Viveur 1st Dine voucher entitles you to the special terms offered by participating restaurants. (2) Restaurants are entitled to decline to give the advertised discounts if diners fail to comply with any of these terms and conditions. (3) Select a restaurant from the Guide showing the symbol [CLUB] and telephone to make sure it is offering Club BON Viveur discounts on the day and the time you wish to dine. (4) You MUST make a table reservation by telephone stating that your wish to use your Club BON Viveur 1st Dine voucher. (5) Club BON Viveur 1st Dine participating restaurants will offer one or more of the following discounts when you dine with at least one guest: Voucher holder plus one guest: 50%, plus two guests: 33.3%, plus three guests: 25%. (6) Discounts are granted on the basis of availability. This means reservations will be accepted until the restaurant expects to be fully booked. (7) Validate your voucher by signing in ink. (8) Show your voucher before you take your table and surrender it when settling your bill. Please take into account the full price of your bill when deciding your gratuity. (9) Vouchers may not be used in conjunction with any other promotional offer, saving or discount scheme that may be available at the restaurant. (10) A minimum of one voucher is accepted per party of up to four people. Larger parties should confirm with the restaurant if they will accept more than one voucher and if so, what the overall discount would be. (11) Restaurants are also entitled to refuse admission to guests that may disturb or upset other guests in the restaurant. (12) Whilst Club BON Viveur will take all reasonable steps to ensure the accuracy of all information, it cannot accept liability for any inaccurate information.

Signature: ..........................................................

## TERMS AND CONDITIONS
### for the use of Club BON Viveur 1st Dine Voucher

(1) The Club BON Viveur 1st Dine voucher entitles you to the special terms offered by participating restaurants. (2) Restaurants are entitled to decline to give the advertised discounts if diners fail to comply with any of these terms and conditions. (3) Select a restaurant from the Guide showing the symbol [CLUB] and telephone to make sure it is offering Club BON Viveur discounts on the day and the time you wish to dine. (4) You MUST make a table reservation by telephone stating that your wish to use your Club BON Viveur 1st Dine voucher. (5) Club BON Viveur 1st Dine participating restaurants will offer one or more of the following discounts when you dine with at least one guest: Voucher holder plus one guest: 50%, plus two guests: 33.3%, plus three guests: 25%. (6) Discounts are granted on the basis of availability. This means reservations will be accepted until the restaurant expects to be fully booked. (7) Validate your voucher by signing in ink. (8) Show your voucher before you take your table and surrender it when settling your bill. Please take into account the full price of your bill when deciding your gratuity. (9) Vouchers may not be used in conjunction with any other promotional offer, saving or discount scheme that may be available at the restaurant. (10) A minimum of one voucher is accepted per party of up to four people. Larger parties should confirm with the restaurant if they will accept more than one voucher and if so, what the overall discount would be. (11) Restaurants are also entitled to refuse admission to guests that may disturb or upset other guests in the restaurant. (12) Whilst Club BON Viveur will take all reasonable steps to ensure the accuracy of all information, it cannot accept liability for any inaccurate information.

Signature: ..........................................................

## TERMS AND CONDITIONS
### for the use of Club BON Viveur 1st Dine Voucher

(1) The Club BON Viveur 1st Dine voucher entitles you to the special terms offered by participating restaurants. (2) Restaurants are entitled to decline to give the advertised discounts if diners fail to comply with any of these terms and conditions. (3) Select a restaurant from the Guide showing the symbol [CLUB] and telephone to make sure it is offering Club BON Viveur discounts on the day and the time you wish to dine. (4) You MUST make a table reservation by telephone stating that your wish to use your Club BON Viveur 1st Dine voucher. (5) Club BON Viveur 1st Dine participating restaurants will offer one or more of the following discounts when you dine with at least one guest: Voucher holder plus one guest: 50%, plus two guests: 33.3%, plus three guests: 25%. (6) Discounts are granted on the basis of availability. This means reservations will be accepted until the restaurant expects to be fully booked. (7) Validate your voucher by signing in ink. (8) Show your voucher before you take your table and surrender it when settling your bill. Please take into account the full price of your bill when deciding your gratuity. (9) Vouchers may not be used in conjunction with any other promotional offer, saving or discount scheme that may be available at the restaurant. (10) A minimum of one voucher is accepted per party of up to four people. Larger parties should confirm with the restaurant if they will accept more than one voucher and if so, what the overall discount would be. (11) Restaurants are also entitled to refuse admission to guests that may disturb or upset other guests in the restaurant. (12) Whilst Club BON Viveur will take all reasonable steps to ensure the accuracy of all information, it cannot accept liability for any inaccurate information.

Signature: ..........................................................

## TERMS AND CONDITIONS
### for the use of Club BON Viveur 1st Dine Voucher

(1) The Club BON Viveur 1st Dine voucher entitles you to the special terms offered by participating restaurants. (2) Restaurants are entitled to decline to give the advertised discounts if diners fail to comply with any of these terms and conditions. (3) Select a restaurant from the Guide showing the symbol [CLUB] and telephone to make sure it is offering Club BON Viveur discounts on the day and the time you wish to dine. (4) You MUST make a table reservation by telephone stating that your wish to use your Club BON Viveur 1st Dine voucher. (5) Club BON Viveur 1st Dine participating restaurants will offer one or more of the following discounts when you dine with at least one guest: Voucher holder plus one guest: 50%, plus two guests: 33.3%, plus three guests: 25%. (6) Discounts are granted on the basis of availability. This means reservations will be accepted until the restaurant expects to be fully booked. (7) Validate your voucher by signing in ink. (8) Show your voucher before you take your table and surrender it when settling your bill. Please take into account the full price of your bill when deciding your gratuity. (9) Vouchers may not be used in conjunction with any other promotional offer, saving or discount scheme that may be available at the restaurant. (10) A minimum of one voucher is accepted per party of up to four people. Larger parties should confirm with the restaurant if they will accept more than one voucher and if so, what the overall discount would be. (11) Restaurants are also entitled to refuse admission to guests that may disturb or upset other guests in the restaurant. (12) Whilst Club BON Viveur will take all reasonable steps to ensure the accuracy of all information, it cannot accept liability for any inaccurate information.

Signature: ..........................................................

# Your personal invitation . . .

*To Club Bon Viveur*
*25 Vanston Place, London SW6 1AZ*
*Telephone: 0171 385 6644  Fax: 0171 385 7136*

*Please enrol me in the Club Bon Viveur National Dining Scheme, at an annual subscription of £15.00*
**PLEASE COMPLETE IN BLOCK CAPITALS**

*Mr/Mrs/Ms/Miss* . . . . . . . . . . . . . . . . . . . . . . . . . . . . . . . . .

*Forename* . . . . . . . . . . . . . . . . . . . . . . . . . . . . . . . . . . . . .

*Surname* . . . . . . . . . . . . . . . . . . . . . . . . . . . . . . . . . . . . . .

*Address* . . . . . . . . . . . . . . . . . . . . . . . . . . . . . . . . . . . . . .

. . . . . . . . . . . . . . . . . . . . . . . . . . . . . . . . . . . . . . . . . . .

*Postcode* . . . . . . . . . . . . . . . . . . . . . . . . . . . . . . . . . . . . .

*Telephone:* . . . . . . . . . . . . . . . . . . . . . . . . . . . . . . . . . . . .

*Profession* . . . . . . . . . . . . . . . . . . . . . . . . . . . . . . . . . . . .

*THE ABOVE INFORMATION WILL BE KEPT IN THE STRICTEST CONFIDENCE AND USED FOR INTERNAL PURPOSES ONLY.*

*I enclose my cheque for £15.00 made payable to*
*Club Bon Viveur*
*Or*
*Charge my Access/Visa/Mastercard/Amex No.*

*Expiry Date* _____ / _____ / _____

**IF YOU ARE INTRODUCING A NEW MEMBER, PLEASE COMPLETE YOUR DETAILS BELOW**

*Restaurant Name* . . . . . . . . . . . . . . . . . . . . . . . . . . . . . . . .

*Postcode* . . . . . . . . . . . . . . . . . . . . . . . . . . . . . . . . . . . . .

*Or*

*Cardmember Name* . . . . . . . . . . . . . . . . . . . . . . . . . . . . . . .

*Membership No.* . . . . . . . . . . . . . . . . . . . . . . . . . . . . . . . . .

*Postcode* . . . . . . . . . . . . . . . . . . . . . . . . . . . . . . . . . . . . .

# ESTABLISHMENTS

# LISTED

# BY REGION

# LONDON REGION

As one of the most exciting and vibrant cities in the world, London offers the traveller, the tourist and the casual visitor a world of adventure in places to see, places to eat and places to stay!

Scattered amongst its historical landmarks, world-famous department stores, colourful Cockney markets and quiet leafy lanes is the most extensive and diverse selection of Les Routiers establishments you will find anywhere. Here you can eat and drink you way around the world in a week, savouring fine food and wine of the highest quality that would cost a fortune in many other restaurants. Any absence of regional dishes is made up for by good, hearty English cooking using only the best and freshest ingredients, hand-picked from the daily markets.

After a busy day touring the capital, there is simply no better way to relax than with a drink in one of *Les Routiers'* Olde Worlde inns. There is also a superb choice of wine bars and bistros serving a wide range of delicious gastronomic snacks, prepared by first-class chefs who are not egocentrically out to dazzle customers and tickle their fancies.

# *LONDON*

## BATTERSEA • map ID3

### BUCHAN'S
62-4 Battersea Bridge Road, SW11 3AU
*An attractive shop-fronted restaurant/wine-bar which serves outstanding French cuisine in a bustling, friendly atmosphere. The service is welcoming and efficient. Although the cuisine is French, Buchan's also offers Scottish specialities such as Arbroath smokie mousse, Scotch fillet steak flambéed in whisky, and a Scottish-based cheeseboard.*
FOOD: from £16 to £20
Hours: lunch 12noon-2.45pm, dinner 6pm-10.45pm, open bank holidays.
Cuisine: FRENCH - specialities include some Scottish dishes. Menu changes weekly. Master chef: Alain Jeannon.
Cards: Visa, Access, Diners, AmEx.
Other points: licensed, Sunday lunch, children welcome, pets allowed.
Directions: 200 yards from Battersea bridge, on the south side of River Thames.
JEREMY BOLAM ☎(0171) 228 0888 Fax(0171) 924 1718

## BAYSWATER • map IC3

### GARDEN COURT HOTEL
30-31 Kensington Garden Square, W2 4BG
*Situated in a calm, leafy Victorian garden square in central London, the Garden Court, built in 1870, is a family-run hotel within walking distance of many of the city's finest tourist attractions, including Kensington Palace and Portobello antique market. Its location allows easy access to buses and the tube.*
DOUBLE ROOM: from £31 to £40
SINGLE ROOM: from £31 to £40
Hours: breakfast 7.30am-9.30am, open all year.
Cuisine: BREAKFAST - full English breakfast, a selection of fruits and yoghurts.
Cards: Visa, Mastercard.
Other points: children welcome, open bank holidays.
Rooms: 13 single rooms, 7 double rooms, 8 twin rooms, 1 triple room, 1 family room. All with TV, radio, tea/coffee-making facilities, hair dryer, cots.
Directions: 4-minute walk from Bayswater tube, 6 minutes from Queensway tube.
MR E. CONNOLLY ☎(0171) 229 2553 Fax(0171) 727 2749

## BELGRAVIA • map IC3

### BOISDALE
15 Eccleston Street, SW1W 9LX
*A warm and intimate Belgravia restaurant a few minutes walk from Victoria and with an excellent reputation for its food. Everything is prepared on the premises and cooked to order. There are over 140 carefully chosen wines listed and a cosy clubbable bar where locals congregate to gentle 1930's jazz. The garden in the summer is a major attraction. The staff are informed and welcoming.*
FOOD: from £20 to £25

**Hours:** lunch 12noon-2.30pm, dinner 7pm-10.30pm. Closed bank holidays.
**Cuisine:** a good balance of wine and food. French and Scottish specialities. Fixed-price set menus offered at £11 and £15. Comprehensive wine list.
**Cards:** Access, Visa, AmEx, Diners, Switch
**Directions:** in Belgravia very close to Victoria station.
MR RANALD MACDONALD ☎(0171) 7306922 Fax(0171) 7300548

  **NAG'S HEAD**
53 Kinnerton Street, SW1X 8ED
*Built in 1780, this has been called the smallest pub in London and is thought to be a former gaol. In 1921 it was sold for £11 7s 6d - almost the price of a couple of rounds of drinks today. The Nag's Head, the village pub in Belgravia, is now a free house in the real sense. Since December 1992 the pub has become an independent, one of the very few in the heart of London.*
FOOD: up to £15
**Hours:** meals all day 12noon-10pm.
**Cuisine:** ENGLISH - traditional home-cooked pub food with daily specials and daily roasts: Irish stew, various curries, chilli con carne, home-made pies.
**Other points:** licensed, open-air dining, Sunday lunch, no smoking area, children welcome.
**Directions:** near to Hyde Park Corner tube, Kinnerton Street is off Wilton Road.
KEVIN MORAN ☎(0171) 235 1135

**TOPHAMS EBURY COURT**
24-32 Ebury Court, SW1W 0LV

*Superbly located three minutes from Victoria station, the hotel evokes the charm of an English Country House and yet is situated in the heart of Belgravia, one of the most exclusive residential areas in London. Owned and run by three generations of the same family, Tophams has a worldwide reputation for caring for their guests, who return year after year. An intimate, friendly atmosphere greets you instantly upon entering the hotel.*
DOUBLE ROOM: from £57
SINGLE ROOM: from £70
FOOD: from £16 to £20   CLUB
**Hours:** breakfast 7.30am-9.30am, lunch 12noon-2.30pm, dinner 6pm-9.30pm.
**Cuisine:** BRITISH - a constantly changing traditional

à la carte menu.
**Cards:** Visa, Access, Diners, AmEx.
**Other points:** children welcome, pets allowed by prior arrangement, conference facilities, residents' sitting rooms, vegetarian meals, afternoon teas.
**Rooms:** 16 single rooms, 15 double rooms, 10 twin rooms, 1 triple room. 21 bedrooms en suite. All with TV, telephone, hair dryer.
**Directions:** close to Victoria train, tube and bus stations.
NICHOLAS & MARIANNE KINGSFORD ☎(0171) 730 8147 Fax(0171) 823 5966

**CITY LIMITS RESTAURANT & WINE BAR**
16-18 Brushfield Street, E1 6AN
*A buzzing, ground-floor wine bar with restaurant downstairs, which doubles as an evening private function room. Situated between the market and offices, with good car-parking facilities very close by.*
FOOD: from £15 to £20
**Hours:** bar meals 11.30am-2.30pm, lunch 12noon-3pm, bar meals 5pm-8pm, closed Saturday and Sunday.
**Cuisine:** INTERNATIONAL - varied international foods; speciality starters, fresh fish, excellent gateaux. Imaginative wine list, international and unusual beers (non-draught).
**Cards:** Visa, Access, AmEx.
**Other points:** children welcome, parking.
**Directions:** situated in Spitalfields, near the Bishopsgate Institution.
DAVID HUGHES ☎(0171) 377 9877

**BLOOMSBURY • map 1C3**

**ACADEMY HOTEL**
17-21 Gower Street, WC1E 6HG
*The Academy Hotel is a beautifully appointed hotel set in a listed building, providing comfort and personal service for tourists and business travellers. Ideally situated for theatreland and many historical places of interest, including the British Museum, Jewish Museum and Covent Garden. Conference facilities are available for 6 to 40 people.*
DOUBLE ROOM: over £50
SINGLE ROOM: over £50
FOOD: up to £15
**Hours:** breakfast 7am-10.30am, lunch 12noon-2.30pm, dinner 6.30pm-12midnight.
**Cuisine:** ENGLISH - own club/restaurant, GHQ, with Les Routiers Golden Casserole award-winning cuisine, predominantly European/English dishes. Good, reasonably priced wine list.
**Cards:** Visa, Access, Diners, AmEx.
**Other points:** licensed, children welcome, afternoon tea, garden, conferences, library.
**Directions:** Nearest tube: Goodge Street, Tottenham Court Road or Russell Square.
METTE DOESSING ☎(0171) 631 4115 Fax(0171) 636 3442

### ARRAN HOUSE HOTEL
77-79 Gower Street, WC1 6HJ

A small English family-run hotel offering warmth and hospitality, which has brought back the same dedicated clientele for many years. A 200-year-old Georgian building in the centre of `Literary Bloomsbury', it offers guests a wide range of modern facilities to ensure a comfortable stay. Within walking distance of the British Museum, Piccadilly Circus, Oxford Street and London's theatreland.

DOUBLE ROOM: from £20 to £30
SINGLE ROOM: from £30
**Hours:** breakfast 7.30am-9am, Sunday 8am-9.30am.
**Cuisine:** ENGLISH - breakfast included, other meals to order.
**Rooms:** 30 bedrooms. Some en suite.
**Directions:** situated in Gower Street, between Chenies Street and Torrington Place.
MR J. RICHARDS ☎(0171) 637 1140/636 2186
Fax(0171) 436 5328

### THE BONNINGTON IN BLOOMSBURY
Southampton Row, WC1B 4BH

Owned and run by the Frame family since its construction in 1911, the Bonnington, with its Edwardian facade, offers up-to-the-minute standards of comfort at value-for-money prices. With 200 comfortable bedrooms, imposing lounges and a splendid dining room, an 80-year tradition of friendly service and hospitality awaits. The hotel offers eight flexibly designed function rooms and provides the ideal venue for anything from a small committee meeting to a major conference or luncheon. Its central location makes it ideal for visitors to London.

DOUBLE ROOM: from £40 to £50
SINGLE ROOM: from £60
FOOD: from £15 to £20  CLUB
**Hours:** breakfast 7am-10am, lunch 12noon-2pm, bar snacks 12noon-2.30pm, dinner 5.30pm-10.30pm, bar snacks 5pm-9.30pm, restaurant closed Saturday and Sunday lunch.
**Cuisine:** INTERNATIONAL - à la carte and table d'hôte menus.
**Cards:** Visa, Access, Diners, AmEx.
**Other points:** children welcome, open bank holidays, no-smoking rooms, afternoon tea, disabled access, pets allowed, residents' lounge, vegetarian meals, conferences, functions, foreign exchange, 24hr reception, residents' bar, baby-listening device, baby-sitting, cots.
**Rooms:** 108 single rooms, 43 double rooms, 44 twin rooms, 20 family rooms. All with TV, radio, telephone, tea/coffee-making facilities, hair dryer, trouser-press.
**Directions:** in the heart of London, just minutes from Holborn tube station.
BONNINGTON HOTELS LTD ☎(0171) 242 2828
Fax(0171) 831 9170

### EURO & GEORGE HOTELS
51-53 Cartwright Gardens, WC1H 9EL

The Euro and George Hotels are situated in a quiet crescent of historically-listed buildings. Both provide a high standard of service and comfort at good-value prices. Their central position offers easy access to the West End and local attractions such as the British Museum.

DOUBLE ROOM: from £21 to £30
SINGLE ROOM: from £31 to £40
**Hours:** breakfast 7.30am-9am.
**Cuisine:** BREAKFAST
**Cards:** Visa, Access, AmEx, Switch.
**Other points:** children welcome, residents' lounge, garden, in-house films, tennis, garden, cots.
**Rooms:** 23 single rooms, 10 double rooms, 10 twin rooms, 26 triple rooms, 6 quad rooms. All with TV, radio, alarm, direct dial telephone, tea/coffe making facilities.
**Directions:** close to King's Cross, Euston and Russell Square tube stations.
MR PETER EVANS ☎(0171) 387 8777/387 6789
Fax(0171) 383 5044

## CHELSEA • map 1C3

### LA CARRETA
163b Draycott Avenue, SW3 3AJ

An attractive basement restaurant with pavement dining area available in summer months. A well stocked cocktail bar, which stays open until late, offers a wide range of exotic drinks. The grilled meat is of an exceptional standard, and provides the main emphasis of the menu, complemented by interesting starters and a good wine selection including wines from Argentina.

FOOD: up to £20  CLUB
**Hours:** dinner 7pm-1am Monday-Saturday.
**Cuisine:** outstanding charcoal grilled Argentinian beef steaks, beef brought over chilled from Argentina.
**Cards:** Visa, AmEx, Mastercard, Switch.
**Other points:** live Latin American music every night, Monday night Tango night. Private parties catered for.
**Directions:** South Kensington tube, up Pelham Street parallel to Sloane Avenue 30 yards from Brompton Road.
MR CARLOS NAVARRO ☎(0171) 584 7496 / 4715

## CHISWICK • map 1C2

### CHISWICK HOTEL
73 Chiswick High Road, W4 2LS

A well-appointed, luxuriously furnished Victorian hotel offering an ideal base for families visiting London. Under the same ownership for 19 years, it has a warm and welcoming atmosphere and has been steadily improved to an extremely high standard with many modern facilities. Special weekend rates are available on request.

DOUBLE ROOM: from £40 to £50
SINGLE ROOM: over £60
FOOD: up to £20
**Cuisine:** ENGLISH
**Cards:** Visa, Access, Diners, AmEx, Switch.
**Other points:** parking, children welcome, open

bank holidays, pets allowed, residents' lounge, vegetarian meals, garden.
**Rooms:** 16 single rooms, 3 double rooms, 14 twin rooms.
**Directions:** turn north on Chiswick Lane from A4, between M4 and Hammersmith at Hogarth roundabout. The hotel is at the junction with Chiswick High Road. Nearest tube Turnham Green (District Line). 30 minutes to Heathrow Airport.
BRYN DREW ☎(0181) 994 1712 Fax (0181) 742 2585

## CLAPHAM • map 1D3

### ☞ HORNIMAN'S RESTAURANT
69 Clapham Common Southside, SW4 9DA

*Attractive, well maintained restaurant with cane furniture, wooden floors, candles and interesting artwork adorning the walls. The relaxed atmosphere attracts a wide clientele of all ages. Wimbledon Lawn Tennis Museum is nearby.*
FOOD: from £10 to £15
**Hours:** lunch and bar meals 11.30am-4pm, dinner and bar meals 4pm-11pm, open bank holidays.
**Cuisine:** Sunday roasts.
**Cards:** Visa, Access.
**Other points:** patio area.
**Directions:** follow A24 out of London to Clapham Common, close to South Circular.
☎(0181) 673 9162

### ☞ WINDMILL ON THE COMMON
Southside, Clapham Common, SW4 9DE

*First mentioned in local records in 1729, the Windmill retains much of its Victorian character and charm. Prize-winning traditional beers are complemented by modern hotel accommodation offering peace and tranquility. An ideal venue for meetings, luncheons, wedding receptions and cocktail parties. Clapham Common is nearby.*
DOUBLE ROOM: from £30 to £40
SINGLE ROOM: from £60 to £80
FOOD: up to £15 ☞ CLUB
**Hours:** breakfast 7am-10am, bar snacks 12noon-2.30pm, dinner 7pm-10pm, bar snacks 7pm-10pm.
**Cuisine:** BRITISH
**Cards:**
Visa,Access,Diners,AmEx,Switch,MasterCard,Delta
**Other points:** parking, children welcome (please check for free accommodation with parents), no-smoking area, disabled access, pets by prior arrangement, garden, vegetarian meals, open-air dining.
**Rooms:** 9 twin rooms, 20 double rooms.
**Directions:** follow South Circular to where it crosses A24, turn towards central London on A24; .25 mile along on Common side.
MR J. & MRS R. WATTS ☎(0181) 673 4578 Fax (0181) 675 1486

## CLERKENWELL • map 2C4

### ☞ THE HELLENIK RESTAURANT
86 St John Street, Smithfield, EC1M 4EH

*A family-run, fully licensed Greek/Cypriot restaurant for good authentic food at reasonable prices. Situated near Smithfield and the Barbican, it is ideal for business and pre- or post-theatre meals.*
FOOD: up to £15
**Hours:** lunch 12noon-3pm, dinner 6pm-11pm, closed in August for three weeks, closed Sunday and bank holidays.
**Cuisine:** GREEK / CYPRIOT - kleftico, moussaka, meze, souvlaki. Special lunch meze: over 12 hot/cold starters, charcoal grills, pitta and salad for £8.50 per person (min. 2 people).
**Cards:** Visa, Access, AmEx.
**Other points:** children welcome, street parking.
**Directions:** 500 yards from Smithfield market. Farringdon and Barbican tube stations.
MR P. & MRS A. KRASE ☎(0171) 253 0754

## COVENT GARDEN • map 1C3

### ☞ FOOD FOR THOUGHT
31 Neal Street, WC2 9PA

*Ideal for the hungry traveller, this lively vegetarian restaurant provides a warm welcome and quick, friendly service. Menu changed twice a day. Take-away meals and snacks also available.*
FOOD: up to £15
**Hours:** meals all day 9.30am-8pm, Sunday 10.30am-4.00pm, closed Christmas and New Year.
**Cuisine:** VEGETARIAN - wide range of imaginative vegetarian dishes, all prepared on premises from fresh produce; daily specials. 3 course meal at £7 inc.
**Cards:** None
**Other points:** no-smoking area, children welcome, parking, outside seating in summer, regular art exhibitions.
**Directions:** close to Covent Garden tube. NCP car park in St Martin's Lane.
MARK MCGLYNN & MARTIN WIFFEN ☎(0171) 836 9072/836 0239 Fax (0171) 379 1249

### ☞ FUNG-SHING
15 Lisle Street, WC2 7BE

*Fung-Shing is situated in a converted Victorian warehouse. Customers can enjoy a wide variety of competently served Cantonese dishes.*
FOOD: up to £15
**Hours:** meals all day 12noon-11.30pm.
**Cuisine:** CANTONESE - crispy duck, sizzling prawns.
**Cards:** Visa, Access, Diners, AmEx.
**Other points:** licensed, Sunday lunch, private dining.
**Directions:** in Chinatown.
JIMMY CHIM ☎(0171) 437 1539

## LE CAFE DES AMIS DU VIN
12 Hanover Place (off Long Acre),
WC2E 9JP

*This restaurant offers good value for money in that the food is well prepared, cooked and served, the service is friendly and you can enjoy your meal amidst pleasant surroundings. Popular basement wine bar for theatre-goers. Adjacent to the Royal Opera House. Les Routiers Cheeseboard Award 1991, 1992, 1993, 1994 and 1995.*

FOOD: up to £20    CLUB   ⌂

**Hours:** meals all day 11.30am-11.30pm.
**Cuisine:** FRENCH - charcuterie, plats du jour. French cheese and wines.
**Cards:** Visa, Access, Diners, AmEx, Switch.
**Other points:** open-air dining, children welcome.
**Directions:** nearest tube Covent Garden, on the Piccadilly Line.
CAFE DES AMIS LIMITED ☎(0171) 379 3444
Fax(0171) 379 9124

### CROUCH END • map 1B3

## L'AMICO ITALIAN RESTAURANT
12 Crouch End Hill, N8 8AA

*A bright and cheerful Italian restaurant, appropriately furnished with paintings and artefacts and serving a wide range of fresh, well-prepared dishes.*

FOOD: up to £15
**Hours:** lunch 12noon-2.30pm, dinner 6pm-11.30pm. Closed Christmas day.
**Cuisine:** modern European and Italian menu, offering an extensive choice of dishes supplemented by an excellent wine list. Vegetarian meals available. Fixed price 3-course menu offered 7 days a week, lunch and dinner.
**Cards:**
Access,Visa,AmEx,Diners,Switch,Electrom,JCB.
**Other points:** licensed, Sunday lunch, no smoking area, children catered for (please check for age limits).
**Directions:** at the bottom of Crouch End Hill in the centre of Crouch End.
☎(0181) 340 5143

### CROYDON • map 1E3

## BRIARLEY HOTEL
8 Outram Road, CR0 6XE

*A Victorian exterior, but inside, everything you expect from a hotel in the 1990s, including colour TV, tea facilities and direct-dial telephone. Quietly situated but excellent for public transport. Private car park. Launderette.*

DOUBLE ROOM: from £25 to £32
SINGLE ROOM: from £50 to £54
FOOD: up to £15    CLUB

**Hours:** Sunday lunch 12noon-1.30pm, dinner (except Sunday) 6.30pm-10pm.
**Cuisine:** ENGLISH - traditional home-made food with soups, steaks, Briarley burger and fresh vegetables, and all the usual favourites associated with the à la carte menu.

**Cards:** Visa, Access, Diners, AmEx.
**Other points:** licensed, Sunday lunch, children welcome, baby-listening device, cots, bar, lounge, central heating.
**Rooms:** 18 single rooms, 7 double rooms, 8 twin rooms, 5 family rooms. All with TV, radio intercom, telephone, tea/coffee-making facilities.
**Directions:** Outram Road runs between the A232 and A222, near East Croydon station.
MRS S.P. MILLS ☎(0181) 654 1000 Fax(0181) 656 6084

## MARKINGTON HOTEL
9 Haling Park Road, CR2 6NG

*This comfortable, friendly hotel is situated in a quiet area, yet is very close to the commercial centre of Croydon. After a day's shopping in the covered shopping centre, you can relax in the bar lounge.*

DOUBLE ROOM: from £20 to £30
SINGLE ROOM: from £35 to £45
FOOD: up to £15
**Hours:** breakfast 7am-9am, dinner 6.30pm-8.30pm.
**Cuisine:** ENGLISH
**Cards:** Visa, Access, AmEx, JCB.
**Other points:** children welcome, vegetarian meals, parking, residents' lounge, bar.
**Rooms:** 9 single rooms, 10 double rooms, 3 twin rooms, 1 family room. All with TV, radio, telephone, tea/coffee-making facilities, hair dryer, video, trouser-press.
**Directions:** just off A235 to Brighton, opposite Croydon bus garage.
MR & MRS MICKELBURGH ☎(0181) 681 6494
Fax(0181) 688 6530

### CRYSTAL PALACE • map 2D4

## JOANNA'S
56 Westow Hill, SE19 1RX

*Situated in the heart of Crystal Palace, this popular bistro is convenient for Dulwich Picture Gallery, Horniman Museum and the National Sports Centre. There is a distinct North American influence, with wall-mounted pictures, posters and celebrity photographs throughout. The atmosphere is lively and is reminiscent of a true American restaurant.*

FOOD: up to £15
**Hours:** lunch 12noon-2.30pm, dinner 6pm-11.30pm, meals all day Saturday and Sunday 12noon-11.30pm.
**Cuisine:** AMERICAN - freshly prepared American and Oriental dishes. Features special low-cost menus as well as a good à la carte menu.
**Cards:** Visa, Access, AmEx, Switch.
**Other points:** parking, children welcome, no-smoking area, open-air dining, vegetarian meals.
**Directions:** 1 mile south of Dulwich village on the A214. Close to Crystal Palace Sports Centre.
JOHN & CHRIS ELLNER ☎(0181) 670 4052
Fax(0181) 670 8306

## EALING • map IC2

### ANNE-MARIE AT THE 'TASTE OF THE TAJ'
4 Norbreck Parade, Hanger Lane, NW10 7HR

*The warmth and efficiency of the staff here make this a pleasant and enjoyable place to spend an evening, sampling cuisine of a high quality. The proprietor, Anne-Marie, is pleased to guide you through the many different dishes, which are offered at varying levels of hotness. The service is friendly and efficient and the atmosphere calm and welcoming.*

FOOD: up to £15

**Hours:** lunch Monday-Friday 12noon-2.30pm, dinner everyday 6pm-11.30pm except Friday-Saturday 6pm-12midnight, closed for lunch Saturday and Sunday, closed Christmas.
**Cuisine:** INDIAN - comprehensive choice of fine Indian-style cuisine.
**Cards:** Visa, Access, Diners, AmEx.
**Other points:** licensed, children welcome, disabled access, vegetarian meals, open bank holidays, street parking.
**Directions:** on Hanger Lane gyratory system - telephone for directions, which are essential.
ANNE-MARIE DUBREIL ☎(0181) 991 5366/991 5209 Fax(0181) 5668060

## EALING COMMON • map IC2

### CARNARVON HOTEL
Ealing Common, W5 3HN

*A modern, well-appointed hotel overlooking Ealing Common, offering both the business visitor and tourist a convenient and comfortable base just 15 minutes from central London. Spacious and comfortable lounges with a well-stocked bar. The Gunnersby and Creffield suites are ideal for meetings and training seminars. Ideally located for quick and easy access to motorways, airport and tube stations.*

DOUBLE ROOM: over £50
SINGLE ROOM: over £50
FOOD: from £16 to £20  CLUB
**Hours:** breakfast 7am-9.30am, lunch 12.30am-2.30pm, bar snacks 9am-10pm, dinner 6.30pm-9.30pm.
**Cuisine:** ENGLISH - à la carte and snack menus available.
**Cards:** Visa, Diners, AmEx, MasterCard, JCB.
**Other points:** licensed.
**Rooms:** 145 bedrooms.
**Directions:** located at the junction of the A406 North Circular and Uxbridge Road A4020, overlooking Ealing Common.
CARNARVON HOTELS LTD ☎(0181) 992 5399 Fax(0181) 992 7082

### CHARLOTTE'S PLACE
16 St Matthews Road, Ealing Common, W5 3JT

*A small, cosy restaurant providing imaginative French/English cuisine. Candlelit tables, nostalgic music and friendly staff add to the overall ambience.*

FOOD: from £20 to £25  CLUB
**Hours:** lunch 12.30am-2pm, dinner 7.30pm-10pm, closed Saturday lunch and Sunday.
**Cuisine:** FRENCH / ENGLISH - complemented by a comprehensive wine list. Fixed-price lunch menu.
**Cards:** Visa, Access, Diners, AmEx.
**Other points:** licensed, children welcome, vegetarian meals.
**Directions:** just off Uxbridge Road, overlooking Ealing Common.
JOHN & CHARLOTTE KEARNS ☎(0181) 567 7541 Fax(0181) 567 0346

## EARLS COURT • map IC3

### AMSTERDAM HOTEL
7 Trebovir Road, SW5 9LS

*Situated close to Earls Court Exhibition Centre, catering for tourists and business people alike. Recently modernised and refurbished, the Amsterdam offers a refreshingly clean and bright environment with a pleasing atmosphere. Ideal for visiting South Kensington's museums.*

DOUBLE ROOM: from £28 to £32
SINGLE ROOM: from £45 to £52
**Hours:** Open all year
**Cards:** Visa, Access, AmEx, Eurocard, JCB.
**Other points:** no restaurant, children welcome, open bank holidays, garden.
**Rooms:** 20 bedrooms. All en suite with TV, telephone, tea/coffee-making facilities.
**Directions:** The hotel is close to Earls Court tube station and is readily visible from the junction with Earls Court Road
MR AHMED JAJBHAY ☎(0171) 3702814 Fax(0171) 2447608

### KENSINGTON INTERNATIONAL HOTEL
4 Templeton Place, SW5 9LZ

*A delightful Victorian hotel, recently renovated to a high standard. An inventive decorating scheme means every floor follows a different theme; Art Deco, Chinese, Tudor. Imaginative lunch and dinner scheme involving local restaurants. Extremely friendly, helpful staff. Altogether outstanding value for money.*

DOUBLE ROOM: from £40 to £50
SINGLE ROOM: from £65
FOOD: up to £15
**Hours:** bar meals 6pm-11pm, breakfast 8am-10am.
**Cuisine:** ENGLISH / CONTINENTAL - substantial continental or English breakfast. Lunch and dinner provided by local Chinese, Italian or Indian restaurants using hotel voucher.
**Cards:** Visa, Access, Diners, AmEx.
**Other points:** room service, conservatory, residents' bar, children welcome, residents' lounge, garden, cots, 24hr reception, left luggage, vegetarian meals.
**Rooms:** 15 single rooms, 15 double rooms, 24 twin rooms, 2 triple rooms. All with TV, telephone, tea/coffee-making facilities.
**Directions:** close to Earl's Court tube, between Warwick Road and Earls Court Road.
DENZIL RATNAM ☎(0171) 370 4333 Fax(0171) 244 7873

## ENFIELD • map 2A4

### OAK LODGE HOTEL
80 Village Road, Bush Hill Park, EN1 2EU

*An exclusive country-style hotel set in secluded gardens, offering a personal atmosphere and service. English Tourist Board 3-Crown `Highly Commended', it has a reputation as the `Director's Choice'. Favoured at weekends by visiting family wedding guests or newlyweds who are attracted by the romantic atmosphere. Luxurious and well-appointed with a unique personal charm.*

DOUBLE ROOM: from £30 to £40
SINGLE ROOM: from £55
FOOD: from £15 to £20      CLUB
**Hours:** breakfast 7am-10am, dinner 7pm-10pm.
**Cards:** Visa, Access, Diners, AmEx.
**Other points:** civil marriage ceremonies performed, Club Bon Viveur and meals residents only, licensed, Sunday lunch, children welcome, pets by prior arrangement, parking, residents' lounge, garden, honeymoon suite, functions.
**Rooms:** 5 bedrooms.
**Directions:** 1 mile from A10. Turn right at seventh set of lights from exit 25 of M25.
JOHN BROWN ☎(0181) 360 7082

---

**Join the Les Routiers Discovery Club FREE and enjoy year round savings up to 50% on P&O European Ferries fares.**
**See page 34 for details.**

---

### THE ROYAL CHACE HOTEL
The Ridgeway, EN28AR

*Set in a unique position on the edge of London, overlooking rolling fields and woodland this comfortable hotel enjoys easy access to the motorway network and is just 35 minutes from central London by underground. Equally popular for social functions or business meetings, the Royal Chace offers all the amenities expected of a modern hotel. The helpful staff will help guests with London theatre and restaurant reservations.*

DOUBLE ROOM: from £40
SINGLE ROOM: from £59
FOOD: from £15 to £20
**Hours:** breakfast 7am-9.30am, lunch (restaurant) 12.30pm-1.45pm, dinner 7pm-9.45pm, bar snacks 11am-3pm & 5pm-11pm. Closed over Christmas, re-open for New Year's eve.
**Cuisine:** house specialities include forerib of beef in madeira sauce, stir-fried oriental chicken, parcels of quail with wild rice and port and redcurrant sauce, steak, kidney and mushroom pudding. Vegetarian dishes available. Extensive wine list.
**Cards:** Access, Visa, AmEx, Diners, Switch
**Other points:** parking, children welcome, swimming pool, conference facilities, residents' garden, vegetarian meals, traditional Sunday lunch.
**Rooms:** 46 twin rooms & 46 double rooms, all en suite with tea/coffee maker, SkyTV, telephone, radio, alarm, hair dryer, trouser press, baby listening device.
**Directions:** from junction 24 of M25 3 miles along the A1005 (The Ridgeway) towards Enfield.
MR RAYMOND NICHOLAS ☎(0181) 366 6500 Fax(0181) 367 7191

## FINCHLEY • map 1B3

### RANI VEGETARIAN RESTAURANT
7 Long Lane, Finchley Central, N3 2PR

*A high-class and well-known speciality restaurant, offering an extensive choice of Indian vegetarian dishes. All produce is freshly prepared by family chefs. Bright and welcoming, with a warm and friendly atmosphere.*

FOOD: up to £15      CLUB
**Hours:** lunch 12.15am-4pm, dinner 6pm-12midnight, closed lunchtime Monday, Saturday and Christmas day.
**Cuisine:** INDIAN VEGETARIAN
**Cards:** Visa, Access, AmEx.
**Other points:** children welcome, Sunday lunch, open bank holidays, no-smoking area, disabled access.

**Directions:** 5-minute walk from Finchley Central tube.
JYOTINDRA PATTNI ☎(0181) 349 4386 **Fax**(0181) 349 4386

## FOREST HILL • map 2D4

### BABUR BRASSERIE
119 Brockley Rise, SE23 1JP
*A stylish, upmarket restaurant providing comfortable dining in smart surroundings. The Moghul-style menu spoils you for choice, ranging from the tasty appetizers through the Tandoori selection, to fish, prawn and vegetable dishes. Babur specialities: Shugati Masala (chicken in spices and a masala sauce enriched with coconut and poppy seeds) and Babur-e-Bhojan (a selection of Murgh Tikka, Boti Kebab, Sali Jardaloo and Makhani, with nan and basmati rice). Although not listed separately, the chef will prepare any traditional dishes, such as Rogan Josh, Dupeaza or Dhansak at your request.*
FOOD: up to £15 🍲
**Hours:** lunch 12noon-2.30pm, dinner 6pm-11.30pm, closed Christmas day and Boxing day.
**Cuisine:** MOGHUL
**Cards:** Visa, Access, Diners, AmEx.
**Other points:** licensed, Sunday buffet lunch, children welcome.
**Directions:** Brockley Rise is off the South Circular-Stansted Road.
BABUR LTD ☎(0181) 291 2400/291 4881

## FULHAM • map 1D3

### CASA CARLO
32 Vanston Place, SW6
*A popular restaurant with locals, Casa Carlo has a warm and friendly atmosphere and is busy at mid-day and lively in the evenings. This inviting and relaxed restaurant has its own bar and serves a variety of Italian dishes and traditional Italian pizzas cooked to order.*
FOOD: from £15
**Hours:** food 12noon-12 midnight, open 7 days a week including bank holidays.
**Cuisine:** Italian pizzas, pasta dishes and salads.
**Cards:** Visa, Access, AmEx.
**Other points:** licensed, vegetarian meals, children welcome, disabled access.
**Directions:** just off North End Road, close to Fulham Broadway Tube station.
☎(0171) 3813782 **Fax**(0171) 3859125

### LA TERRAZA
53 Fulham Broadway, SW6 1AE
*A light, bright and airy Spanish restaurant, decorated with plants and paintings to create comfortable, authentic surroundings. All dishes from the large, varied menu are fresh and the servings are plentiful. The newly opened La Terraza is a welcome addition for local residents and business people. It is also popular with visitors to the Fulham area.*

FOOD: up to £15 🍲 **CLUB**
**Hours:** lunch 12noon-3pm, dinner 6pm-10.30pm.
**Cuisine:** SPANISH - typical Spanish dishes, with both à la carte and Tapas menus available.
**Cards:** Visa, Access.
**Other points:** children welcome, no-smoking area, vegetarian meals.
**Directions:** situated 100 yards from Fulham Broadway tube station.
ARTHUR & TONY ROSA ☎(0171) 385 9272

## GREENWICH • map 2C4

### SPREAD EAGLE RESTAURANT
1&2 Stockwell Street, SE10 9JN
*A tavern since before the 1650s and later a thriving coaching inn and hostelry. Situated right opposite the Greenwich Theatre, the Spread Eagle has strong 19th century music hall connections and is a truly fascinating place steeped in history, much of it still visible. Provides business lunches, bar snacks and pre-theatre suppers. Three dining areas. Private party facilities. A visit is highly recommended.*
FOOD: from £15 to £25
**Hours:** lunch 12noon-3pm, dinner 6.30pm-10.30pm (last orders). Booking advisable
**Cuisine:** FRENCH - a constantly changing menu. Lunch menu available from £10. All foods fresh from London markets.
**Other points:** children welcome, disabled access, vegetarian meals.
**Directions:** situated just off the A2 and A206, opposite the Greenwich Theatre.
MR R. MOY ☎(0181) 853 2333 **Fax**(0181) 305 1666

## HAMMERSMITH • map 1C3

### "103" FRENCH BISTRO
Black Lion Lane, W6 9BG
*Sample the delights of a typical French bistro - in London! Flickering candles, red and white tablecloths, low ceilings, French poster adorning the walls, music and first class service. The intimacy and ambience of this restaurant will have you imagining that when you finish your excellent meal you will step outside into Paris!*
FOOD: from £20 to £25
**Hours:** open Monday to Saturday evenings only 6pm-11pm. Pre and post-theatre bookings welcome.
**Cuisine:** offering a range of imaginative, traditional French dishes. Blackboard menu changes regularly.
**Cards:** Visa, Access, Diners, AmEx
**Other points:** complimentary Kir and canapes. All main dishes served with a selection of fresh vegetables. Vegetarian meals available. Private parties catered for.
**Directions:** off King Street near Stamford Brook tube station.
☎(0181) 748 9070

### DALMACIA HOUSE
71 Shepherd's Bush Road, W6 7LS

*This recently refurbished Victorian terraced house offers en suite facilities in clean, comfortable and value-for-money accommodation. The family who run the hotel speak French and Serbo-Croat. The Apollo, Hammersmith, Kensington Olympia Exhibition Halls and the Bottom Line Club Shepherds Bush are all nearby. Brochures available. Please book early to avoid disappointment.*

**DOUBLE ROOM:** from £20 to £25
**SINGLE ROOM:** from £25 to £30
**Hours:** breakfast 7am-9.30am, dinner 6pm-8.30pm.
**Cuisine:** ENGLISH/CONTINENTAL BREAKFAST
**Cards:** Visa, Access, Diners, AmEx, Switch, Delta, JCB.
**Other points:** children welcome, cots, left luggage.
**Rooms:** 3 single rooms, 3 double rooms, 6 twin rooms, 4 triple rooms. All with satellite TV, telephone, hair dryer, tea/coffee-making facilities, European electrical sockets.
**Directions:** 450 metres north of Hammersmith tube or 700 metres north of Hammersmith exit from A(M)4.
GEORGE KRIVOSIC ☎(0171) 603 2887 Fax(0171) 602 9226

## HARROW • map 1B2

### CRESCENT LODGE HOTEL
58-62 Welldon Crescent, HA1 1QR

*A modern hotel which still manages to retain a friendly family atmosphere. Conveniently situated in the heart of Harrow, central London is easily accessible by tube with the station only 5 minutes walk away. After visiting the exciting attractions of the capital, one can leave the hustle and bustle behind and return and relax in a comfortable and carefree atmosphere where nothing is too much trouble and a warm welcome is extended to all visitors.*

**DOUBLE ROOM:** from £30 to £40
**FOOD:** up to £15
**Hours:** breakfast 7.30am-9am.
**Cuisine:** ENGLISH - varied menu, including vegetarian. Dishes may include venison in red wine, nut Wellington provençal, chicken satay with noodles, steaks.
**Cards:** Visa, Access, AmEx.
**Other points:** children welcome, open bank holidays, conferences, secretary available, children welcome, baby-listening device, cots, 24hr reception, foreign exchange, left luggage, vegetarian meals, residents' bar, residents' lounge.
**Rooms:** 9 single rooms, 3 double rooms, 7 twin rooms, 1 triple room, 1 quad room. All with satellite TV, radio, telephone, tea/coffee-making facilities, refrigerator.
**Directions:** off Headstone Road, onto Hindes Road, then Welldon Crescent.
ZENNIE & SHIRAZ JIVRAJ ☎(0181) 863 5491 Fax(0181) 427 5965

### CUMBERLAND HOTEL
St John's Road, HA1 2EF

*Relax in the unrushed, peaceful atmosphere of this long-established hotel. The restaurant offers generous portions of freshly prepared food to suit all tastes. Every care is taken by the attentive staff to make all visitors feel relaxed and welcome. Highly recommended. When booking, please quote `Les Routiers'.*

**DOUBLE ROOM:** from £30 to £40
**SINGLE ROOM:** from £30 to £40
**FOOD:** from £15 to £20 🍽CLUB
**Hours:** breakfast 7am-9am, lunch 12noon-2pm, dinner 7pm-9pm.
**Cuisine:** FRENCH / CONTINENTAL - dishes are mainly French on the à la carte menu, with vegetarian and healthy option meals available. Also a speciality children's menu. Les Routiers Casserole Award winner.
**Cards:** Visa, Access, Diners, AmEx.
**Other points:** Sunday lunch, no-smoking area, conferences, gym facilities, sauna, children welcome, baby-listening device, cots, 24hr reception, parking, disabled access.
**Rooms:** 31 single rooms, 28 double rooms, 16 twin rooms, 5 family rooms, all en suite with satellite TV, radio, telephone, tea/coffee-making facilities, trouser-press.
**Directions:** leave M4 at exit 3. Follow the A312 to Harrow.
GARY JONES ☎(0181) 863 4111 Fax(0181) 861 5668

### FIDDLER'S RESTAURANT
221-225 High Road, Harrow Weald, HA3 5EE

*Part of a 1930s row of shops, Fiddler's has a black and white mock-Tudor frontage. Inside, Tudor decor, bric-a-brac and mirrors create warm, attractive surroundings in which to enjoy the excellent food. All dishes are well cooked and well presented. Everything is done to ensure that customers enjoy their meal, and the service and atmosphere is warm and welcoming.*

**FOOD:** up to £15 🍽CLUB
**Hours:** lunch 12noon-2.30pm, dinner 7pm-1am (7pm-2am Fri, Sat).
**Cuisine:** ITALIAN / FRENCH - wide selection of Italian and French cuisine such as duck with orange sauce; beef al pepe (with a crushed pepper, brandy and cream sauce); calamari fritti.
**Cards:** Visa, Access, Diners, AmEx, MasterCard.
**Other points:** licensed, Sunday lunch, no-smoking area, children welcome, entertainment, conferences, functions, air-conditioned.
**Directions:** on A409, between Harrow Wealdstone station and Uxbridge Road roundabout.
ANTONIO BRANCA ☎(0181) 863 6066/427 1931 Fax(0181) 861 2807

### THE HARROW HOTEL
Roxborough Bridge, 12-22 Pinner Road,
HA1 4HZ

*Situated within easy travelling distance of Wembley Stadium and Conference Centre and the heart of London, The Harrow Hotel is popular with business people and tourists alike. Warm and courteous service is displayed at all times, whether relaxing in the luxurious lounge and bar or dining in the superb restaurant. A pleasant stay is assured.*
DOUBLE ROOM: from £30 to £40
SINGLE ROOM: from £55
FOOD: from £15 to £20
**Hours:** breakfast 7am-9.30am, lunch 12noon-2pm, dinner 6pm-9.45pm.
**Cuisine:** ENGLISH
**Cards:** Visa, Access, Diners, AmEx.
**Other points:** parking, children welcome, no-smoking bedrooms, disabled access, garden, vegetarian meals.
**Rooms:** 58 bedrooms. All with en suite, TV, radio, telephone, tea/coffee-making facilities, hair dryer.
**Directions:** at the junction of the A404 and A312 at the Harrow Town end of Pinner Road.
MRS REBECCA FLASH ☎(0181) 427 3435
Fax(0181) 861 1370

### OLD ETONIAN RESTAURANT
38 High Street, Harrow on the Hill,
HA1 3LL
*An 18th century French bistro-style restaurant, situated in the town centre near the famous Harrow Public School, combining the qualities of excellent food and service with comfortable and relaxed surroundings.*
FOOD: up to £15
**Hours:** lunch 12noon-2.30pm, dinner 7pm-11pm, closed Saturday lunch, Sunday evening and bank holidays.
**Cuisine:** FRENCH - featuring seafood pancake, steak dijon, roast duck in orange sauce with guava, chocolate mousse, creme brulée.
**Cards:** Visa, Access, Diners, AmEx.
**Other points:** licensed, children welcome, parking.
**Directions:** off Uxbridge road, in the town centre, near the school.
MR PELAEZ ☎(0181) 422 8482 Fax(0181) 4231225

### HODGSON'S RESTAURANT
115 Chancery Lane, WC2A 1PP
*This attractive restaurant, once the legal book depository for Sotheby's, serves beautifully presented food in generous portions. The à la carte menu is changed every 6 weeks, and there is a daily table d'hôte lunch menu offering a choice of three starters, main courses and desserts, representing excellent value-for-money. For dinner, a two course table d'hôte menu is offered at £9.95, three courses £12.95. The Hodgson's Wine Bar offers a new menu each day with a wide choice of hot and cold dishes at reasonable prices.*
FOOD: from £15 to £20
**Hours:** lunch 12noon-2.30pm, bar meals 11am-11pm, dinner 5pm-11pm, closed Saturday and Sunday.
**Cuisine:** MODERN BRITISH - à la carte and table d'hôte menus. Includes fillet of sea bass with crispy asparagus, chive butter and anchovy fritters, seared tuna steak, medallion of wild venison with leek and celeriac crumble, wild mushroom gateau with stilton and walnut butter sauce.
**Cards:** Visa, Access, Diners, AmEx.
**Other points:** children welcome.
**Directions:** off Fleet Street.
DENISE SOLLIS ☎(0171) 242 2836 Fax(0171) 831 9637

### HOLLAND PARK HOTEL
6 Ladbroke Terrace, W11 3PG
*Situated in a quiet tree-lined area close to Kensington Palace, this Victorian town house provides fine accommodation in relaxed and comfortable surroundings. There is an elegant sitting room and a beautiful garden. Close to shops and restaurants, with major train, bus and tube services just minutes away.*
DOUBLE ROOM: from £20 to £25
SINGLE ROOM: from £37 to £49
**Cuisine:** BREAKFAST - continental breakfast.
**Cards:** Visa, Access, Diners, AmEx.
**Other points:** licensed, children welcome, residents' lounge, garden, cots, 24hr reception.
**Rooms:** 11 single rooms, 7 double rooms, 5 twin rooms, 2 triple rooms.
**Directions:** situated north of Holland Park Road, near Holland Park tube station.
ROBERT BELLHOUSE ☎(0171) 792 0216
Fax(0171) 727 8166

### ABCONE HOTEL
10 Ashburn Gardens, SW7 4DG
*Located in a quiet street in the heart of Kensington, the Abcone is ideal for business or pleasure. All rooms are equipped with many modern facilities, including in-house video and satellite movies. Full*

secretarial services are available to all business clients. Just a short walk away from Hyde Park, the Natural History and Victoria & Albert Museums, and the world-famous Harrods. The hotel has its own tapas bar.

DOUBLE ROOM: from £30 to £40
SINGLE ROOM: from £40 to £75
FOOD: up to £15
**Hours:** breakfast 7.30am-9.30am, dinner (Tapas bar) 7pm-11pm.
**Cuisine:** SPANISH - à la carte menu plus other dishes.
**Cards:** Visa, Access, Diners, AmEx, JCB.
**Other points:** residents' lounge, children welcome.
**Rooms:** 17 single rooms, 14 double rooms, 4 twin rooms.
**Directions:** off Cromwell Road, turn on to Ashburn Gardens.
MR A.A. SADDUDDIN ☎(0171) 370 3383
Fax(0171) 373 3082

### ATLAS HOTEL
24-30 Lexham Gardens, W8 5JE
This well-maintained Victorian terraced hotel is situated in a desirable part of Kensington, close to Earls Court and Olympia exhibition centres, Natural History Museum, Victoria & Albert Museum, Science Museum, Kensington Gardens and Hyde Park. Recently refurbished to provide tasteful and comfortable accommodation, the Atlas Hotel is an ideal place to stay when visiting London on business or pleasure.
DOUBLE ROOM: from £30 to £40
SINGLE ROOM: over £50
**Hours:** breakfast 7.30am-9.15am.
**Cards:** Visa, Access, Diners, AmEx, JCB, Delta, Connect.
**Other points:** children welcome, residents' lounge, residents' bar, conference room.
**Rooms:** 12 single rooms, 6 double rooms, 18 twin rooms, 9 triple rooms. All en suite and with TV, telephone, radio.
**Directions:** off Cromwell Road (A4), first turn on left after Cromwell Hospital. Within easy walking distance of High Street Kensington, Gloucester Road and Earls Court tube stations.
KEITH FENTON ☎(0171) 835 1155 Fax(0171) 370 4853

### IL PORTICO
277 Kensington High Street, W8 6SA
A popular high street restaurant, offering a good selection of Italian-style cuisine. The atmosphere is warm and friendly, attracting a regular, mostly local clientele. Ideally situated for visiting the famous Albert Hall, Hyde Park and many other London tourist attractions.
FOOD: from £20 to £25
**Hours:** lunch 12noon-3pm, dinner 6pm-11.30pm.
**Cuisine:** ITALIAN - à la carte menu, offering a wide range of Italian-style cuisine. Vegetarian dishes available.
**Cards:** Visa, Access, AmEx.

**Other points:** no-smoking area, children welcome, vegetarian meals.
**Directions:** easy to locate - situated almost opposite the Commonwealth Institute.
ANNA & PINO CHIAVARINI ☎(0171) 602 6262

### LA SALA ROMANA
1st Floor, 117 Gloucester Road, SW7 4ST
Newly decorated, La Sala Romana offers diners a cosy, relaxed atmosphere in which to enjoy the freshly prepared Italian dishes. Close to the museums and the many hotels in the area, the restaurant is not only frequented by locals but also by tourists of all nationalities.
FOOD: from £20 to £25  CLUB
**Hours:** lunch 12noon-2.30pm, dinner 6.30pm-9.30pm, closed Christmas eve, Christmas day and Boxing day.
**Cuisine:** ITALIAN - freshly prepared Italian dishes from an extensive à la carte menu.
**Cards:** Visa, Access, Diners, AmEx.
**Other points:** children welcome, vegetarian meals.
**Directions:** located near Gloucester Road tube station.
MATTHEW NELSON ☎(0171) 373 5703 Fax(0171) 370 1316

### SCOFFS EATING HOUSE
267 Kensington High Street, W8 6NA
The decor of this popular `eating house' is reminiscent of North Italian restaurants, with brick floors, white plaster walls and wooden beams. The food is made from fresh produce, and the good-sized portions are served by pleasant, efficient staff.
FOOD: up to £15
**Hours:** meals all day 8am-12midnight everyday.
**Cuisine:** ITALIAN - breakfast from £3, lunch from £5, dinner from £8-£15.
**Cards:** Visa, Access, Diners, AmEx.
**Other points:** children welcome.
**Directions:** next to the Odeon Cinema in Kensington High Street.
MR L. SBUTTONI AND MS P. MANCINI ☎(0171) 602 6777

## KEW • map 1D2

### JASPER'S BUN IN THE OVEN
11 Kew Green, TW9 3AA
French/English cuisine is served in this charming Georgian house overlooking Kew Green. Jasper's offers winter dining in front of log fires and summer dining in the courtyard. Great-value set-price menu, extensive à la carte menu and special Sunday menu. Open for lunch and dinner except Sunday evening. Extensive wine list. Private room available for business lunches/dinners. Parties and weddings catered for.
FOOD: from £15 to £20
**Hours:** lunch 12.30am-3pm, dinner 7pm-11pm, closed Sunday evening, Good Friday, Christmas eve, Christmas day and Boxing day.
**Cuisine:** FRENCH / ENGLISH - complemented by

an extensive wine list.
**Cards:** Visa, Access, Diners, AmEx.
**Other points:** licensed, garden, children welcome, vegetarian meals, private rooms available.
**Directions:** situated on Kew Green.
PAUL & PENNY CARVOSSO ☎(0181) 940 3987
Fax(0181) 940 6387

### PISSARRO'S WINE BAR
1 Kew Green, Richmond, TW9 3AA
*A roaring open fire, oak beams, a host of antique curios, some 50 wines and a delicious selection of home-made foods are all there to welcome and tempt you. Pissarro once painted the buildings where this enchanting wine bar now stands.*
FOOD: up to £15
**Hours:** bar 11.30am-11pm, Sunday 12noon-10.30pm, closed Easter Sunday and Christmas.
**Cuisine:** ENGLISH - home-made country pies, delicious soups, fresh vegetables, a hearty selection of cheeses, plus a daily cold buffet with special slimmers' salads, mouthwatering desserts and a traditional Sunday lunch.
**Cards:** Visa, Access.
**Other points:** licensed, Sunday lunch, disabled access, no children.
**Directions:** on the A205 (South Circular), south of Kew Bridge, just off Kew Green.
PAUL & PENNY CARVOSSO ☎(0181) 940 3987

## KING'S CROSS • map 1C3

### THE GREAT NORTHERN HOTEL
N1 9AN
*Opened in 1854, The Great Northern Hotel is situated between King's Cross and St Pancras main line stations. The atmosphere is of a warm and friendly modern establishment. In response to demand the main menu in The Coffee House features light meals and is complemented by a breakfast menu before 10am, and dishes of the day lunchtime menu. The comfortable Northern Bar was refurbished in 1995. The hotel also has 13 meeting and conference rooms, and private catering arrangements with seating for up to 100.*
DOUBLE ROOM: from £40 to £50
SINGLE ROOM: from £80
FOOD: from £15 to £20        CLUB
**Hours:** open daily 7am-10pm (9pm Sunday), closed Christmas eve until Boxing day.
**Cuisine:** ENGLISH
**Cards:** Visa, Access, Diners, AmEx.
**Other points:** parking, children welcome, afternoon teas, vegetarian meals, residents' lounge, residents' bar.
**Rooms:** 13 single rooms, 28 double rooms, 32 twin rooms, 16 family rooms. All with satellite TV, telephone, tea/coffee-making facilities.
**Directions:** access from Pancras Road.
MICHAEL DAVIES ☎(0171) 837 5454 Fax(0171) 278 5270

## KINGSTON-UPON-THAMES • map 1D2

### CHASE LODGE HOTEL
10 Park Road, Hampton Wick, KT1 4AS
*Set on a quiet residential street in Hampton Wick, this tranquil hotel is a real gem. Tastefully furnished with a conservatory and a well-tended garden, it strives to provide personal service and attention to detail, and offers a welcome retreat in a busy world.*
DOUBLE ROOM: from £20 to £40
SINGLE ROOM: from £25 to £48
FOOD: up to £15
**Hours:** breakfast 7am-9am, dinner 7pm-9.30pm.
**Cuisine:** ENGLISH - traditional English cuisine with imaginative sauces. Prepared to a high standard. Good selection of wines.
**Cards:** Visa, Access, AmEx.
**Other points:** no-smoking area, parking, residents' lounge, garden, vegetarian meals, Sunday dinner.
**Rooms:** 1 single room, 6 double rooms, 3 twin rooms.
**Directions:** Kingston-upon-Thames, near Hampton Court.
MR & MRS STAFFORD HAWORTH ☎(0181) 943 1862 Fax(0181) 943 9363

## LEADENHALL • map 2C4

### BEAUCHAMPS RESTAURANT
25 Leadenhall Market, EC3V 1LR
*A turn-of-the-century city restaurant, tastefully furnished in dark wood and brass, situated within the confines of Leadenhall Market. A range of quality fish speciality dishes are available. The restaurant is unique in London by owning its own fishmonger, `Ashdown,' with live holding-tanks for shellfish. Attractions nearby include Lloyds, Stock Exchange and Bank of England. Evening parties welcome by appointment.*
FOOD: from £20 to £25
**Hours:** morning coffee 9.30am-11.30am, meals all day 11.30am-3.30pm, closed bank holidays, Saturdays and Sundays.
**Cuisine:** SEAFOOD - excellent selection of fish speciality dishes, including lobster with ginger and spring onion, halibut steak with thyme, parsley and cream. Often two or three daily specials.
**Cards:** Visa, Access, Diners, AmEx, Air Miles.
**Other points:** licensed, children welcome (not under 6), vegetarian meals, hard to park.
**Directions:** take either the Bank or Monument tube. Just off Leadenhall Street.
ANDREA FOKI ☎(0171) 621 1331 Fax(0171) 626 5889

## LEICESTER SQUARE • map 1C3

### MARCHE RESTAURANT - THE SWISS CENTRE
1 Swiss Court, WIV 1FJ
*Continental café meets outdoor market. Choose the ingredients for your meal from diverse stations, then watch it being cooked before your eyes. An unusual set-up, but the cheerful, café-type decor and helpful*

*service make for an interesting, enjoyable meal.*
FOOD: up to £15    CLUB
**Hours:** breakfast 8am-11am(bank holidays from
9am), meals all day 11am-12midnight, closed
Christmas day.
**Cuisine:** INTERNATIONAL (MAINLY SWISS) - Fresh
ingredients, varied menu changing daily at
reasonable prices.
**Cards:** Visa, Access, Diners, AmEx.
**Other points:** licensed, Sunday lunch, no-smoking
area, children welcome, open bank holidays.
**Directions:** closest tube stations Piccadilly Circus
and Leicester Square.
DERK JOLLES ☎(0171) 494 0498 Fax (0171) 494
2180

## MARBLE ARCH • map 1C3

### ■ EDWARD LEAR HOTEL
28-30 Seymour Street, W1H 5WD
*Formerly the home of the famous Victorian painter
and poet Edward Lear. The hotel offers cheerful
rooms with all the usual facilities and is in the
perfect location, just minutes away from Hyde Park,
Speakers' Corner and Oxford Street.*
DOUBLE ROOM: from £20 to £30
SINGLE ROOM: from £31 to £40
**Hours:** breakfast 7.30am-9.15am.
**Cuisine:** BREAKFAST
**Cards:** Visa, Access, Diners.
**Other points:** children welcome, in-house films,
baby-listening device, cots, residents' lounge.
**Rooms:** 14 single rooms, 2 double rooms, 11 twin
rooms, 4 family rooms, all with satellite TV, radio,
telephone, tea/coffee-making facilities.
**Directions:** close to Marble Arch tube and a
minute's walk from Oxford Street.
JOHM MCLAREN ☎(0171) 402 5401 Fax (0171)
706 3766

### ■ LINCOLN HOUSE HOTEL
33 Gloucester Place, W1H 3PD
*An attractively refurbished hotel in a Georgian
terrace, centrally located close to Oxford Street.
Good value accommodation, with most bedrooms
offering en suite facilities. Car parking close by.*
DOUBLE ROOM: from £30 to £40
SINGLE ROOM: from £40 to £50
**Hours:** breakfast 8am-10am.
**Cards:** Access,Visa,AmEx,Diners,Switch,JCB.
**Other points:** hot and cold beverages 24 hour
service. Fax and photocopying facilities, 24 hour
access, NCP parking nearby, centrally situated.
**Rooms:** 6 single rooms, 8 double rooms, 4 twin
rooms and 4 family rooms, all en suite.
**Directions:** exit Marble Arch tube station into
Oxford Street. Take second left which is Portman
Street which runs into Gloucester Place. Hotel on
left.
MR JOSEPH SHERIFF ☎(0171) 486 7630
Fax (0171) 486 0166

### ■ PARKWOOD HOTEL
4 Stanhope Place, W2 2HB

*An attractive town house situated in a quiet,
residential street, but just one minute from Oxford
Street, Marble Arch and Hyde Park. The Parkwood
is under excellent management, offering spotlessly
clean and airy bedrooms serviced by friendly and
efficient staff.*
DOUBLE ROOM: from £20 to £30
SINGLE ROOM: from £45 to £55
**Hours:** breakfast 7.30am-9.15am.
**Cuisine:** BREAKFAST
**Cards:** Visa, Access.
**Other points:** children welcome, in-house films,
baby-listening device, cots, hairdryers, satellite TV.
**Rooms:** 5 single rooms, 2 double rooms, 7 twin
rooms, 4 family rooms. All with TV, radio, alarm,
telephone, tea/coffee-making facilities.
**Directions:** a minute's walk from Marble Arch tube
station.
PETER EVANS ☎(0171) 402 2241 Fax (0171) 402
1574

## MAYFAIR • map 1C3

### ⇶ DINO'S (MAYFAIR)
33 North Audley Street, W1Y 1WG
*Forming part of an attractive Edwardian terrace,
Dino's is divided into three sections and decorated
accordingly: coffee bar, trattoria and restaurant. It
offers a typical Italian menu and the atmosphere is
lively, with an upmarket clientele.*
FOOD: up to £15    CLUB
**Hours:** meals all day 8am-11.30pm.
**Cuisine:** ITALIAN
**Cards:** Visa, Access, Diners, AmEx.
**Other points:** children welcome, afternoon teas,
disabled access, vegetarian meals.
**Directions:** situated just off Oxford Street, close to
Selfridges and minutes from the tube.
☎(0171) 629 7070 Fax (0171) 370 1316

## MUSWELL HILL • map 1B3

### ⇔ RAGLAN HALL HOTEL
8-12 Queens Avenue, N10 3NR
*Situated in an elegant tree-lined avenue in north
London, the Raglan Hall exudes an air of calm
competence throughout. Ideally situated for
business and pleasure travellers alike, all the major
sight-seeing attractions in central London can be
reached within 15 minutes by underground. Local*

attractions include Alexandra Palace and park, Kenwood House, Highgate and Hampstead villages. Excellent dining, bar and accommodation standards.
DOUBLE ROOM: over £50
SINGLE ROOM: over £50
FOOD: up to £15
**Hours:** breakfast 7.30am-9.30am (8am-10am Saturday/Sunday), dinner 7pm-9.45pm. Open all year.
**Cuisine:** prix fixe and table d'hôte menus including such items as calamari and crab risotto, poached sea trout with dill butter sauce, jumbo asparagus served on baked avocado and deep fried brie, roast saddle of Welsh lamb studded with stem ginger. Bar snacks available.
**Cards:** Access, Visa, AmEx, Diners
**Other points:** parking, residents' lounge, secluded garden with outdoor dining, Raglan's Bar with military memorabilia, air conditioned conference suite.
**Rooms:** 14 single rooms, 13 twin rooms, 14 double rooms, 7 family rooms, all en suite with tea/coffee maker, TV, telephone, radio, alarm, hair dryer, baby listening device, trouser press (on request).
**Directions:** from either direction turn off the North Circular Road junction sign for Muswell Hill (B550). Follow Colney Hatch Lane to roundabout at Muswell Hill Broadway. Last exit is Queens Avenue, hotel is 75 yards on right.
MR M J BENNETT ☎(0181) 883 9836 Fax(0181) 883 5002

## PADDINGTON • map 1C3

### ASHLEY HOTEL
15 Norfolk Square, W2 1RU
The Ashley Hotel is flanked by its sister hotels, the Tregaron and the Oasis; all three adjoin one another and are interconnected. Very centrally situated in a pretty garden square, a few minutes' bus ride from Oxford Street and close to Paddington station. The Norfolk gardens were redesigned in 1990 to re-create the Victorian era. A lovely and quiet place to sit and take your ease.
DOUBLE ROOM: from £24 to £30
SINGLE ROOM: from £28 to £39
**Hours:** breakfast 7.30am-9am, closed Christmas.
**Cuisine:** BREAKFAST - full English breakfast.
**Cards:** Visa, Access.
**Other points:** central heating, children welcome, no evening meal, residents' lounge, left luggage.
**Rooms:** 12 single rooms, 14 double rooms, 14 twin rooms, 1 triple room, 5 family rooms. All with TV, radio, tea/coffee-making facilities. Most rooms are en suite.
**Directions:** situated between Praed Street and Sussex Gardens. 3 minutes from Paddington station.
MR W.J. & MR D.E. GEORGE ☎(0171) 723 3375 Fax(0171) 723 0173

### MITRE HOUSE HOTEL
178-184 Sussex Gardens, W2 1TU
The Mitre House Hotel has been run by the same family for over 30 years, and this is reflected in its comfortable atmosphere and ambience. Ideally located on the north side of Hyde Park. Central London is easily accessible, and should you require a hired car or a sightseeing tour, the helpful staff will be happy to assist.
DOUBLE ROOM: from £30 to £40
SINGLE ROOM: from £50 to £60
**Hours:** breakfast 7.30am-9am.
**Cards:** Visa, Access, Diners, AmEx.
**Other points:** children welcome.
**Rooms:** 6 single rooms, 27 double rooms, 27 twin rooms, 7 family rooms, 3 junior suites. All with TV, radio, telephone. Suites also have trouser-press, fridge, Jacuzzi bath.
**Directions:** south of Paddington tube, parallel to Praed Street.
ANDREW & MICHAEL CHRIS ☎(0171) 723 8040 Fax(0171) 402 0990

## PIMLICO • map 1C3

### THE BLUE JADE
44 Hugh Street, SW1V 4EP
Considered to be one of the best and most reasonably priced Thai restaurants in London. Extensive menu with imaginative specialities. Close to Buckingham Palace and the Houses of Parliament.
FOOD: from £15 to £20
**Hours:** lunch 12noon-3pm Monday to Friday, dinner 6pm-11pm Monday to Saturday, closed bank holidays.
**Cuisine:** crispy fried boneless trout, topped with shredded pork, spring onions and mushrooms; chicken in red curry with coconut cream, red chilies and Thai herbs; mussamun beef curry.
**Cards:** Visa, Access, Diners, AmEx.
**Other points:** private room and wine bar.
**Directions:** 5 minutes from Victoria rail and coach stations.
☎(0171) 8280321

## PINNER • map 1B2

### FRIENDS RESTAURANT
11 High Street, HA5 5PJ

Situated in the heart of picturesque Pinner High street, Friends Restaurant is a charming 400-year-

old building with oak beams, open fireplaces and lots of character. The weekly changing set menu and the seasonally changing à la carte menu offer superb meals made from fresh local produce.
FOOD: from £15 to £20 [CLUB]
Hours: lunch 12noon-2.30pm, dinner 6.30pm-10pm, closed Sunday evening, Christmas day and Boxing day.
Cuisine: MODERN ENGLISH / FRENCH - innovative dishes professionally presented.
Cards: Visa, Access, Diners, AmEx.
Other points: children welcome, conference facilities, no-smoking area, vegetarian meals, traditional Sunday lunch.
Directions: follow A404 from Harrow; in the centre of Pinner.
TERRY FARR ☎(0181) 866 0286

## PUTNEY • map ID3

### GAVIN'S RESTAURANT
5 Lacy Road, SW15 1NH
This lively Putney restaurant has an interesting menu with imaginative brasserie-style dishes and an excellent choice of fresh pasta with a wide selection of sauces, all complemented by a well-selected wine list. It has a great atmosphere and a well-established local reputation.
FOOD: up to £15
Hours: lunch 12noon-3.30pm, dinner 6pm-11pm.
Cuisine: ECLECTIC CONTINENTAL - à la carte menu specializing in brasserie and fresh pasta dishes.
Cards: Visa, Access, Diners, AmEx.
Other points: Sunday lunch, children welcome.
Directions: Lacy Road runs off Putney High Street, opposite Marks & Spencer.
NEIL GILMOUR ☎(0181) 785 9151 Fax(0181) 788 1703

### THE LODGE HOTEL
52-54 Upper Richmond Road, SW15 2RN
A family-owned and managed hotel which offers excellent value accommodation and dining within easy reach of London's West End by rail or underground, yet close to the motorway network for those touring by car. The Turf Club restaurant includes a magnificent conservatory and patio overlooking its own private garden, and the Sportsman Bar offers a wide selection of imported beers. First-rate accommodation at sensible prices.
DOUBLE ROOM: from £30 to £40
SINGLE ROOM: from £60
FOOD: up to £15
Hours: breakfast 6.30am-9am, dinner 6.30pm-9pm. Bar snacks available all day. Open all year.
Cuisine: inexpensive à la carte menu and chef's special daily menu. Comprehensive wine list.
Cards: Access,Visa,AmEx
Other points: parking, residents' lounge, garden, conference and banqueting facilities.
Rooms: 66 rooms, 1 single and 2 twin not en suite, 10 single, 23 twin, 8 double, 4 family and 18 triple

rooms all en suite with tea/coffe maker, TV, telephone, radio. 1 room designed for disabled.
Directions: on Upper Richmond Road between Putney and Wandsworth.
MR ANTHONY HIRSCHFELD ☎(0181) 874 1598 Fax(0181) 8740910

### MYRA RESTAURANT
240 Upper Richmond Road, SW15 6TG
This cosy, Victorian-fronted restaurant is situated close to the junction with Putney High Street and welcomes family groups to complement its strong local patronage. Theme nights are a popular `speciality', so book ahead to avoid disappointment! Traditional English fayre, all home-cooked by Myra, and a warm welcome guarantee satisfaction.
FOOD: from £15 to £20 [CLUB]
Hours: lunch 12noon-2.30pm, Sunday 12.30am-4pm, dinner 6.30pm-11pm.
Cuisine: ENGLISH - à la carte, fixed price three-course menu, lunch £5.50, dinner £9.95 including coffee. Mon-Sat.
Cards: Visa, Access, Diners, AmEx.
Other points: licensed, open-air dining, Sunday lunch, children welcome, garden.
Directions: on South Circular, near Putney Bridge.
MISS MOLONY ☎(0181) 788 9450 Fax(0181) 788 9450

## RICHMOND • map ID2

### CAFFÉ MAMMA
24 Hill Street, TW9 1TW
Decorated in the style of a Neapolitan café with typical Italian ambience. Situated in the main shopping area of Richmond, not far from the river. Caffé Mamma enjoys a good reputation in the area and is popular with all ages.
FOOD: up to £15
Hours: meals all day 12noon-12midnight, closed Christmas day and New Year's day.
Cuisine: ITALIAN - Italian, specializing in pasta dishes.
Cards: Visa, Access, AmEx, Switch, Luncheon Vouchers.
Other points: Sunday lunch, children welcome.
Directions: in the centre of Richmond, near Odeon Cinema.
TIM DIXON-NUTTALL ☎(0181) 940 1625 Fax(0181) 948 7330

### THE NAKED TURTLE
505-507 Upper Richmond Road West, SW14
A popular brasserie-style restaurant offering a most interesting menu with something for everyone. Prompt and courteous service adds to the dining pleasure. Evenings are especially popular and the 'fun' atmosphere is complemented by live jazz every night and Sunday lunchtime.
FOOD: from £15 to £20 [CLUB]
Hours: meals available from 12noon to 12midnight.

Open all year.

**Cuisine:** a well presented ë very inventive menu including such items as mille feuille of chicken ë crab roulade, blackened swordfish steak with clementine chutney, rack of lamb crepinette with chicken ë basil mousse. For those of an adventurous nature, dishes of ostrich, kangaroo or crocodile are offered. Also 3 course fixed price luch menu available.

**Cards:** Visa, Access, AmEx, Switch.

**Other points:** parking in nearby side streets, outdoor dining in garden/patio area.

**Directions:** the brasserie is beyond Sheen centre on the Richmond side of the South Circular road.
MR SAMMY BASHLAWI ☎(0181) 8781995
Fax(0181) 3921388

## RUISLIP • map IBI

### ⊨ RUISLIP TANDOORI
115 High Street, HA4 8JW
*A 60-seater Tandoori restaurant serving Nepalese cuisine. The atmosphere is set by subdued lighting and soft background music. Well patronized by the locals. Established since 1980.*

**FOOD:** up to £15

**Hours:** lunch 12noon-2.30pm, dinner 6pm-11.30pm, closed Christmas day.

**Cuisine:** NEPALESE - chicken zhal frazi, chicken gurkhali, butter chicken, chicken Nepal, chicken chili massala. Karai dishes and Kathmandu dishes. Set Nepalese Thali and set dinner. Special Sunday lunch buffet: 12 dishes to choose from at £6.95 for adults and £3.50 for children.

**Cards:** Visa, Access, Diners, AmEx.

**Other points:** Sunday lunch, children catered for (please check for age limit), no service charge.

**Directions:** situated centrally on Ruislip High Street.
K.B. RAICHHETRI ☎(01895) 632859/674890

## SHEPHERD'S BUSH • map IC3

### ⊨ BALZAC BISTRO
4 Wood Lane, W12 7DT
*A typical bistro-style restaurant offering regional French cuisine of a high quality. A pleasant, warm and friendly atmosphere abounds. Metered parking during the day.*

**FOOD:** from £15 to £20

**Hours:** lunch, 12noon-2.30pm, dinner 7pm-11pm, closed Saturday lunchtime and Sunday, closed bank holidays.

**Cuisine:** FRENCH

**Cards:** Visa, Access, Diners, AmEx.

**Other points:** children welcome, vegetarian meals.

**Directions:** corner of Shepherd's Bush Green and Wood Lane.
MR P. TARELLI ☎(0181) 743 6787

## SHEPPERTON-ON-THAMES • map IEI

### WARREN LODGE & ANCHOR HOTELS
Church Square, TW17 9JZ
*Warren Lodge backs onto the river Thames and has*

*a delightful riverside terrace. Just across the square, the Anchor hotel is an attractive wood-panelled inn. Both establishments are well-maintained and provide a mix of comfortable accommodation and generous servings of modern British cuisine. Hampton Court is nearby.*

DOUBLE ROOM: from £60
SINGLE ROOM: from £30 to £40
FOOD: up to £15

**Hours:** breakfast 7am-9.30am (Sundays 8am-10am), lunch 12noon-2pm, dinner 7pm-10pm, open bank holidays.

**Cuisine:** interesting, inventive menus.

**Cards:** Visa, Access, Diners, AmEx.

**Other points:** licensed, parking, baby-listening device, room service.

**Rooms:** 38 single rooms, 33 double rooms, 4 twin rooms, 2 triple rooms. All en suite, with TV, radio, telephone, alarm, tea/coffee making facilities and hairdryers.

**Directions:** Exit M25 at junction 11 towards Chertsey, take the B375 to Shepperton, turn right into Church Sqaure, just beyond the main shopping area.
SHEPPERTON HOTELS LTD ☎(01932) 242972
Fax(01931) 253883

## SOUTH CROYDON • map IE3

### ▬ HAYESTHORPE HOTEL
48-52 St Augustine's Avenue, CR2 6JJ
*Located in a quiet, residential area close to East Croydon station and easily accessible to Gatwick airport. The 25 newly-refurbished rooms all have en suite facilities. Conference facilities are available, including lunch and tea.*

DOUBLE ROOM: from £20 to £30
SINGLE ROOM: from £40 to £50

**Hours:** breakfast 7am-9am, dinner(restaurant)7pm-8.30pm.

**Cards:** Access, Visa, AmEx, Diners, Switch, JAC.

**Other points:** licensed, dining room overlooking conservatory lounge and mature gardens, conference facilities, parking.

**Rooms:** 25 rooms, 10 single, 6 twin, 3 triple, 6 family - all en suite. Tea/coffee makers, TV, telephone, alarm, baby listening, room service, trouser press (in most), hair dryer (on request).

**Directions:** on west side of main Brighton road (A 235) in South Croydon. Half way down St Augustine's Avenue.
MR MICHAEL CULLEY AND BRUNO INZANI
☎(0181) 688 8120 Fax(0181) 6888120

## STAINES • map IDI

### ▬ THE ANGEL INN
24 High Street, TW18 4EE
*The coaching inn was originally built in 1685. It was carefully rebuilt at the turn of the century and has recently been refurbished and redecorated to a very good standard. All the bedrooms are comfortable and well furnished. The brasserie-style restaurant offers freshly prepared food and caters for all tastes.*

DOUBLE ROOM: from £40 to £50
SINGLE ROOM: from £26 to £30
FOOD: up to £15
**Hours:** breakfast 7am-9am, lunch 12noon-2.30pm, dinner 5.30pm-9.45pm, bar meals 11am-10pm.
**Cuisine:** INTERNATIONAL - a brasserie-style menu with a good selection of English, French and Eastern dishes.
**Cards:** Visa, Access, AmEx.
**Other points:** traditional ales, parking, children welcome, pets allowed by arrangement, no-smoking area, garden, open-air dining, vegetarian meals, afternoon teas, traditional Sunday lunch.
**Rooms:** 3 single rooms, 3 double rooms, 6 twin rooms. All with TV, tea/coffee-making facilities. Some en suite.
**Directions:** on the main High Street, opposite Debenhams, close to river Thames.
GALLEON TAVERNS LTD ☎(01784) 452509
Fax(01784) 458336

## STOKE NEWINGTON • map 2B4

### THE FOX REFORMED
176 Stoke Newington Church Street, N16 0JL
*Formerly a restaurant, The Fox Reformed is now a popular wine bar and brasserie, offering a good selection from the well-stocked bar, tasty meals amd courteous, friendly service. In the warmer months, the patio to the rear of the restaurant allows for pleasant outdoor dining.*
FOOD: from £15 to £20
**Hours:** lunch 12noon-2.30pm, dinner 6.30pm-10.30pm.
**Cuisine:** FRENCH / INTERNATIONAL - delicious home-made dishes. The ice cream is a must!
**Cards:** Visa, Access, Switch.
**Other points:** children welcome, garden, open-air dining, vegetarian meals.
**Directions:** just off A10, at junction with Stoke Newington High Street.
ROBBIE & CAROL RICHARDS ☎(0171) 254 5975

## SUTTON • map 1E3

### ASHLING TARA HOTEL
44-50 Rosehill, SM1 3EU
*A family-run hotel with a friendly and welcoming atmosphere, situated within easy walking distance of Sutton town centre and directly opposite the Rose Hill tennis centre and sports complex. With the comfort of her guests in mind, Mrs Harold has succeeded in offering a combination of tasty home-cooked meals to complement comfortable, attractive accommodation. A pleasure to visit.*
DOUBLE ROOM: over £50
SINGLE ROOM: over £50
FOOD: up to £15
**Hours:** breakfast 7.30am-8.45am, dinner 7pm-9pm.
**Cuisine:** ENGLISH
**Cards:** Visa, Access, Diners, AmEx.
**Other points:** children welcome, open bank holidays, residents' lounge, bar, restaurant, patio and garden, launderette, fax, wedding/conference

facilities.
**Rooms:** 4 single rooms, 5 double rooms, 5 twin rooms, 2 family rooms. All with TV, radio, bar, telephone, trouser-press, tea/coffee-making facilities.
**Directions:** near Angel Hill.
CATHERINE HAROLD ☎(0181) 641 6142
Fax(0181) 644 7872

### THATCHED HOUSE HOTEL
135 Cheam Road, SM1 2BN
*Situated a short walk from Sutton centre and Cheam village, this lovely thatched cottage has been completely modernized and offers good food, comfortable accommodation and a friendly welcome. Close proximity to Epsom Downs, Wimbledon Tennis, Hampton Court, Windsor Castle and RHS Gardens at Wisley. Golf can be arranged at Banstead Downs only a mile from the hotel.*
DOUBLE ROOM: from £20 to £30
FOOD: up to £15
**Hours:** breakfast 7.30am-9am, dinner 7pm-9pm.
**Cuisine:** ENGLISH - chef's specials daily.
**Cards:** Visa, Access, MasterCard, JCB.
**Other points:** licensed, children welcome, afternoon tea, functions, conferences, garden.
**Rooms:** 5 single rooms, 11 double rooms, 10 twin rooms, 2 four-poster rooms. All with TV, telephone, tea/coffee-making facilities.
**Directions:** on the A232, opposite Sutton cricket and squash club.
MR J. JEFFS ☎(0181) 642 3131 Fax(0181) 770 0684

## TEDDINGTON • map 1D2

### THE CLARENCE HOTEL
Park Road, TW11 0AB
*The hotel is conveniently situated just 5 miles from Heathrow Airport and very close to Hampton Court, Bushey Park and the River Thames. Within its attractive listed Victorian exterior are 20 recently refurbished en suite bedrooms, a Victorian-style bar and Parisian-style restaurant, all offering good value for money.*
DOUBLE ROOM: from £30 to £40
SINGLE ROOM: from £25
FOOD: up to £15
**Hours:** breakfast 7am-9am, lunch 12noon-3pm, dinner 6pm-9.45pm.
**Cuisine:** ENGLISH - family steakhouse menu with home-cooked daily specials.
**Cards:** Visa, Access, Diners, AmEx.
**Other points:** parking, children welcome, pets allowed by arrangement, open-air dining, vegetarian meals, afternoon teas, traditional Sunday lunch.
**Rooms:** 7 single rooms, 7 double rooms, 3 twin rooms. All with en suite, TV, telephone, radio, alarm, hair dryer, trouser-press, tea/coffee-making facilities.
**Directions:** over Kingston Bridge and follow A310 past Bushey Park. The hotel is opposite the police station.

GALLEON TAVERNS LTD ☎(0181) 977 8025
Fax (0181) 977 8698

### THE ITALIAN PLACE BRASSERIE
38 High Street, TW11 8EW
*An excellent Italian restaurant in the centre of
Teddington. The menu offers an extensive choice of
authentic and creative Italian dishes at very
reasonable prices, with all meals freshly cooked and
well presented. Highly recommended for the
excellent food and welcoming service in a lively yet
relaxed atmosphere.*
FOOD: from £15 to £20   CLUB
Hours: lunch 12noon-2.30pm, Sunday 12noon-
3pm, dinner 6.30pm-11pm, Sunday 7pm-10.30pm,
open bank holidays.
Cuisine: ITALIAN - dishes may include polenta con
funghi, fettuccine Federico, manzo alla mostarda,
insalata marinara. Specials change daily.
Cards: Visa, Access, Diners, AmEx, Switch, Delta.
Other points: licensed, Sunday lunch, no-smoking
area.
Directions: on Teddington High Street.
FEDERICO SECOLA ☎(0181) 943 2433 Fax (0181)
943 2616

## TWICKENHAM · map ID2

### CAFE DE BONHEUR
55 Church Street, TW1 3NR
*A French-style bistro/brasserie situated in an
historical and picturesque part of Twickenham,
close to the River Thames. There are three seating
areas: the light and airy ground-floor level, a more
intimate dining area upstairs as well as the outside
patio area.*
FOOD: up to £15    CLUB
Hours: meals all day 10am-11pm.
Cuisine: FRENCH
Cards: Visa, Access, AmEx.
Other points: parking adjacent, children welcome,
no-smoking area, disabled access, vegetarian meals,
open-air dining.
Directions: off the junction of King Street and York
Street in Twickenham.
IAN STANTON ☎(0181) 891 6338

## VICTORIA · map IC3

### MARCHÉ MÔVENPICK
Portland House, Stag Place, SW1E 5BH
*Visit the new Marché restaurant and experience a
brand new way way of eating. With freshness and
fun as the key points of their philosophy, Marché
provides a delightful environment which makes
eating there a novel experience. Dishes change
daily to make use of the best products available,
and the key to the Marché concept is a collection of
market stalls or "stations" where the food is prepared
to order and cooked before your eyes.*
FOOD: up to £15
Hours: breakfast 7.30am-11.30am, lunch 11.30am-
5pm, dinner 5pm-12midnight. Open bank holidays.

Closed 24th, 25th and 26th December.
Cuisine: daily specials are prepared and cooked
before your eyes at a number of market stalls or
'stations'.
Cards: Visa, Access, Diners, AmEx.
Directions: 5 minutes walk from Victoria Station, off
Victoria Street.
MOVENPICK LTD ☎(0171) 630 1733 Fax (0171)
630 5198

## WANDSWORTH · map ID3

### CALICO CAFE BAR RESTAURANT
573 Garratt Lane, Earlsfield, SW18
*A local neighbourhood bar and restaurant with a
bustling yet relaxed atmosphere, with a large patio
for alfresco dining in summer and an open fire for
cosy winter visits. Traditional Sunday lunch is very
popular with families - children are genuinely
welcome. Calico offer excellent-value two- and
three-course menus as well as imaginative brasserie
cooking, with an extensive, reasonably priced wine
list.*
FOOD: up to £15
Hours: open for lunch and dinner 7 days, open all
day Saturday and Sunday.
Cuisine: CONTINENTAL
Cards: Visa, Access, Diners, AmEx.
Other points: children welcome, open-air dining,
vegetarian meals, traditional Sunday lunch.
Directions: 300 yards from Earlsfield station.
ELAINE O'REILLY ☎(0181) 947 9616 Fax (0181)
944 5704

## WEST END · map IC3

### BICKENHALL HOTEL
119 Gloucester Place, W1H 3PJ
*This spacious and elegant hotel in the heart of
London provides guests with comfortable, well-
appointed accommodation of a very good standard.
Popular with business people and holiday-makers,
the hotel has an atmosphere similar to that of a
small country house hotel. It is conveniently located
for Madame Tussaud's, the Planetarium and the
Wallace Collection.*
DOUBLE ROOM: from £30 to £40
SINGLE ROOM: from £35 to £55
Hours: breakfast 7.30am-10am.
Cards: Visa, Access, Diners, AmEx.
Other points: children welcome, pets allowed,
residents' lounge.
Rooms: 5 single rooms, 3 double rooms, 2 twin
rooms, 8 triple rooms, 2 family rooms. All with
satellite TV, telephone, radio, alarm, hair dryer,
tea/coffee-making facilities, trouser press.
Directions: at top end of Gloucester Place, close to
Marylebone Road. Nearest tube Baker Street.
IRENE AGHABEGIAN ☎(0171) 935 3401
Fax (0171) 224 0614

## CAFE IN THE CRYPT
St Martin-In-The-Fields, WC2N 4JS

*A unique café, situated immediately underneath the famous church of St Martin-In-The-Fields, Trafalgar Square. Generous portions of wholesome food are offered at outstanding value for money. Meals can be enjoyed beneath the vaulted ceilings in what must be one of the most unusual eating places in London. Centrally situated and very close to the National Gallery.*

**FOOD:** up to £15
**Hours:** meals all day 10am-8pm, 7 days a week.
**Cuisine:** ENGLISH - English home-cooking. Self-service. Menu changes daily.
**Cards:** Luncheon vouchers only.
**Other points:** licensed, Sunday lunch, children welcome, afternoon tea.
**Directions:** nearest tubes Leicester Square and Charing Cross. Entrance: Duncannon Street.
ALLYSON HARGREAVES ☎(0171) 839 4342
Fax (0171) 839 5163

## DON PEPE RESTAURANT
99 Frampton Street, NW8 8NA

*Founded by the present owner 20 years ago, this was one of London's first Tapas bars. Today it is undoubtedly one of the capital's premier Spanish restaurants, offering a wide range of excellent Spanish cuisine. This popular restaurant offers live music and alfresco dining in summertime. Ideal for Lord's cricket ground and Little Venice canal.*

**FOOD:** up to £15 🍷
**Hours:** lunch 12noon-3pm, dinner 7pm-1am, closed Sunday and Christmas day.
**Cuisine:** SPANISH
**Cards:** All major.
**Other points:** children welcome, vegetarian meals, open bank holidays.
**Directions:** just off Edgware Road, between Lisson Grove and Edgware Road itself.
☎(0171) 262 3834/723 9749 Fax (0171) 724 8305

## GARTH HOTEL
69 Gower Street, WC1E 6HJ

*A privately-owned Georgian terrace hotel in the heart of London, offering guests a friendly, peaceful atmosphere with clean and comfortable rooms. The Garth is centrally located and very reasonably priced for central London.*

DOUBLE ROOM: up to £22.50
SINGLE ROOM: from £30 to £38
**Hours:** breakfast 7.30am-8.45am.
**Cards:** Visa, Access, AmEx, MasterCard, EuroCard, Switch.
**Other points:** children welcome.
**Rooms:** 3 single rooms, 4 double rooms, 5 twin rooms, 3 triple rooms, 2 family rooms. All with TV.
**Directions:** situated in Gower Street, between Oxford Street and Euston Road, opposite London University.
JOEY CRUZ ☎(0171) 636 5761 Fax (0171) 637 4854

## LA MADELEINE
5 Vigo Street, W1X 1AH

*For a great selection of French meals or snacks, superbly cooked and attractively presented, look no further than La Madeleine. Situated in the heart of the West End, it is conveniently accessible from theatreland and all the West End attractions. The delectable pastries are a must!*

**FOOD:** up to £15
**Hours:** open Monday to Saturday 8am-7pm, closed Sundays. Party room available every evening and Sundays for private functions.
**Cuisine:** FRENCH - a delicious and varied à la carte menu. The pastries are marvellous and the fish soup is highly recommended.
**Cards:** Visa, Access, Switch.
**Other points:** children welcome, no-smoking area, vegetarian meals, afternoon teas, private function room available evenings (including Sunday).
**Directions:** located off Regent Street between Piccadilly and Oxford Street.
JOEL CARRERAS & CORINNE VANDERHAEGEN ☎(0171) 734 8353 Fax (0171) 287 9554

## LONDON CONTINENTAL HOTEL
88 Gloucester Place, Baker Street, W1H 3HN

*This centrally located hotel offers guests comfortable accommodation in newly decorated and furnished surroundings. The bedrooms are coordinated in soothing pastel tones to a very high standard. With a cheery and bright atmosphere, this is a highly recommended hotel, suitable for business people and holidaymakers alike.*

DOUBLE ROOM: from £25 to £35
SINGLE ROOM: from £50 to £55
**FOOD:** CONTINENTAL BREAKFAST
**Cards:** Visa, Diners, AmEx, Mastercard, JAC, Switch, Eurocard.
**Other points:** children welcome, residents' lounge, no-smoking area.
**Rooms:** 8 single rooms, 8 double rooms, 4 twin rooms, 2 triple rooms, 3 quad rooms. All with satellite TV, telephone, radio, alarm, hair dryer, tea/coffee-making facilities. All rooms are en suite.
**Directions:** 5 minutes from Baker Street tube station.
AZHAR AHMED KHAN ☎(0171) 486 8670
Fax (0171) 486 8671

## PICCADILLY RESTAURANT
31 Great Windmill Street, W1V 7PG

*Centrally situated in the heart of theatreland and on the fringes of Soho. The restaurant is on two levels, and both have a cosy, informal atmosphere. Excellent for eating either before or after the theatre.*

**FOOD:** from £15 to £20
**Hours:** lunch Monday-Saturday 12noon-2.30pm, dinner Monday-Saturday 5.30pm-11.15pm, open Sunday 12.30pm-8.30pm. Open bank holidays from 1pm-8.30pm.
**Cuisine:** ITALIAN - Italian cuisine.
**Cards:** Visa, Access, Diners, AmEx, JCB.

**Other points:** children welcome, guide dogs.
**Directions:** nearest tube Piccadilly Circus.
CLAUDIO MUSSI ☎(0171) 734 4956 Fax(0171) 287 9683

---

 **ST GILES HOTEL**
Bedford Avenue, Wc1 3AS

*A modern international 3-star hotel of 600 bedrooms, located at the eastern end of Oxford Street. Just 50 yards from Tottenham Court Road tube station, it is within easy walking distance of all the West End shops and theatres. All the bedrooms have been recently refurbished, and guests have free access to the pool and leisure facilities situated in the same building. Café Bagatelle, the hotel's street café on Tottenham Court Road, features English and Continental cuisine at reasonable prices. The Clock Bar offers a large selection of drinks and pub food throughout the day.*

DOUBLE ROOM: over £50
SINGLE ROOM: over £55
FOOD: from £15 to £20
**Hours:** breakfast 7am-10.30am, meals or snacks all day.
**Cuisine:** ENGLISH/INTERNATIONAL
**Rooms:** 600 bedrooms
**Cards:** Visa, Access, Diners, AmEx.
**Other points:** open bank holidays, residents' lounge, vegetarian meals.
**Directions:** situated on the corner of Tottenham Court Road and Bedford Avenue
MR D TAYLOR ☎(0171) 636 8616 Fax(0171) 631 1031

---

 **TOPO GIGIO**
46 Brewer Street, W1R 3HN

*A busy, popular Italian restaurant in the basement of a modern development close to Berwick Street market with NCP parking close by. Excellent a la carte menu offers classical Italian dishes served by efficient, cheerful staff. Good, well-described selection of Italian regional wines.*

FOOD: from £15 to £20
**Hours:** open 12noon-11.15pm (last orders), closed Sundays, open bank holidays.
**Cuisine:** a la carte menu, classical Italian dishes. Good selection of regional Italian wines.
**Cards:** Visa, Access, Diners, AmEx, Switch.
**Other points:** licensed.
**Directions:** from Piccadilly Circus tube station, take the East exit up Sherwood Street, then turning right onto Brewer Street. Near Berwick Street market.
MR L. BOSI ☎(0171) 437 8516

---

## WEST HAMPSTEAD • map IC3

 **CHARLOTTE RESTAURANT & GUEST HOUSE**
221 West End Land, NW6 1UX

*An old-established restaurant and guest house, 2 minutes from West Hampstead tube (Jubilee Line) and direct British Rail link to Gatwick and Luton Airports. A free London Travel Card is issued to guests staying one week or more. The restaurant is tastefully decorated and the ample portions are served by cheerful staff. The accommodation is unbeatable value and comfortable.*

DOUBLE ROOM: up to £20
SINGLE ROOM: up to £20
FOOD: up to £15
**Hours:** breakfast 7.30am-11.30am, lunch 12noon-4pm, dinner 6pm-11pm, closed Sunday.
**Cuisine:** ENGLISH / CONTINENTAL - from liver Bavaria and debreziner sausages to stir-fried vegetables with rice and prawn, and poussin à la diable.
**Other points:** children welcome.
**Rooms:** 12 single rooms, 24 double rooms. All with TV.
**Directions:** 2 minutes from West Hampstead tube (Jubilee Line).
MR L KOCH ☎(0171) 794 6476 Fax(0171) 431 3584

---

 **NO. 77 WINE BAR**
77 Mill Lane, NW6 1NB

*A popular wine bar decorated in pine with old film bills on the walls. International theme evenings such as Burns Night, July 4th, Greek Evening. The in-house club sails and plays cricket, rugby and golf tournaments.*

FOOD: from £15 to £20
**Hours:** lunch 12noon-3pm, dinner 6pm-11pm, closed bank holidays, Good Friday and Christmas.
**Cuisine:** ENGLISH - home-made soups, lamb Shrewsbury.
**Cards:** Visa, Access.
**Other points:** children welcome, street parking.
**Directions:** Mill Lane is off the Edgware Road between Kilburn and Cricklewood.
DAVID BLAKEMORE ☎(0171) 435 7787

---

## WESTMINSTER • map IC3

 **BUMBLES RESTAURANT**
16 Buckingham Palace Road, SW1W 0QP

*Friendly English restaurant with cartoons and old prints lining the walls, padded bench-style seating set in alcoves, and a spacious basement which is also air-conditioned. Private room available for functions. Places of interest nearby include Buckingham Palace, Westminster Abbey and local theatres.*

FOOD: from £15 to £20    CLUB
**Hours:** lunch 12noon-2.15pm, dinner 6pm-10.45pm, closed Saturday lunch and Sunday, closed bank holidays.
**Cuisine:** ENGLISH / INTERNATIONAL - fresh fish, lamb, duck, game in season, home-made pies. Super puddings. Extensive wine list.
**Cards:** Visa, Access, Diners, AmEx.
**Other points:** children welcome, functions.
**Directions:** 200 yards from Victoria station going towards Buckingham Palace.
PHILIP BARNETT ☎(0171) 828 2903 Fax(0171) 828 9220

---

### HANOVER SQUARE WINE BAR & GRILL
25 Hanover Square, W1

*Don Hewitson's spacious and stylish addition to the Mayfair eating-and-drinking scene. Award-winning wine bar food where the `South of France meets California', plus an ever-changing selection of charcoal grills. A full-service restaurant, `Don's Room', at lunch. The wine list features the `200 Wines From All Around The World' made famous at the Cork and Bottle - many, including champagne, available by the glass. An excellent central London venue for evening events (private room for parties up to 60). The entire place is available at weekends (parties up to 150).*

FOOD: from £15 to £20

**Hours:** lunch 12noon-4pm, dinner 6pm-10.30pm, bar meals 12noon-11pm.
**Cuisine:** CALIFORNIAN / SOUTHERN FRENCH
**Cards:** Visa, Access, AmEx.
**Other points:** vegetarian meals.
**Directions:** nearest tubes Oxford Circus, Bond Street.
DON & NOELENE HEWITSON ☎(0171) 408 0935
Fax(0171) 483 2230

## WIMBLEDON • map 1D3

### GOURMET RESTAURANT
2a King's Road, SW19 8QN

*A modern-style restaurant situated just off Wimbledon Broadway and close to the theatre, offering an excellent mix of French cuisine with continental influence. The spacious and comfortable interior is attractively decorated around a large central chimney feature, amidst subtle lighting and gentle background music, providing a perfect setting for diners. The staff are friendly and efficient, and in summer alfresco dining on pavement tables is an additional attraction.*

FOOD: up to £15  CLUB

**Hours:** lunch from 11.30am, dinner 5.30pm-11.30pm.
**Cuisine:** ITALIAN / FRENCH - vegetarian food a speciality. 3 course set lunch £10.95, 3 course set dinner £11.95, half price children menu, free cocktail. Traditional Sunday set lunch £7.95.
**Cards:** Visa, Access, Diners, AmEx.
**Other points:** children welcome, Sunday lunch, open bank holidays, vegetarian meals.
**Directions:** just off Wimbledon Broadway.

ABDOULLAH SHIRAZI ☎(0181) 540 5710/543 6416

### VILLAGIO ITALIANO
25 High Street, SW19 5DX

*Recently completely refurbished, this light and airy restaurant offers traditional dishes and daily specials. The staff are friendly and courteous and the relaxed atmosphere appeals to diners of all ages.*

FOOD: up to £15

**Hours:** closed Christmas day,Boxing day and New Years day. Lunch 12noon-3pm, dinner 6.30pm-11.30pm.Sunday 12noon-10.30pm.
**Cuisine:** daily specials.
**Cards:** Access,Visa,Mastercard,Switch.
**Directions:** in the centre of Wimbledon Village close to the common.
MR TIM DIXON-NUTTALL ☎(0181) 946 7779
Fax(0181) 948 7330

## WOODFORD GREEN • map 2B4

### PACKFORD'S HOTEL
16 Snakes Lane, IG8 0BS

*A turn of the century house where the proprietors have imaginatively retained the original Victorian features whilst at the same time incorporating discreet innovations. The hotel provides a well organised wedding banqueting and conference service and is now licensed for wedding ceremonies on the premises. Situated within easy reach of the unspoilt Epping Forest, Packford's Hotel is just a 30 minute trip from the heart of London.*

DOUBLE ROOM: from £50 to £65
SINGLE ROOM: from £40 to £50
FOOD: from £15 to £20

**Hours:** breakfast 7.30am-8.30am, dinner 6.30pm-8pm.
**Cuisine:** ENGLISH
**Cards:** Visa, Access, AmEx, Switch, Delta.
**Other points:** parking, children welcome, pets allowed, conference facilities, banqueting, residents' lounge, garden, vegetarian meals.
**Rooms:** 11 bedrooms. All with en suite, TV, telephone, iron, baby-listening device, tea/coffee-making facilities.
**Directions:** exit junction 26 on M25, follow signs to Woodford.
SIMON & DEBRA PACKFORD ☎(0181) 504 2642
Fax(0181) 505 5778

# SOUTH EAST ENGLAND & EAST ANGLIA

However long your stay, you will not exhaust the pleasures and hearty welcome offered by these beautiful regions, from the wide open skies of East Anglia to the rolling North and South Downs, from the charming chocolate-box villages of the Thames and Chilterns to the famous South-East holiday coastline.

This is an area where the opportunities to sample really fine food have increased immensely over the past few years. It is rich in quality restaurants run by a new generation of chefs who have successfully created a new Anglo-French cuisine with a greener, leaner image.

There are endless comfortable inns in which to spend a relaxing evening enjoying good home-cooked treats and the very best of ethnic cuisine, with a first-class choice for vegetarians. The Essex coastline, in particular, is world-famous for its fresh fish and seafood, notably Colchester oysters, which have been farmed here since Roman times. Look out also for Staithe mussels, Aylesbury duckling and Norfolk crab, country pies, toasted savouries, traditional roasts and succulent steaks, all complemented by a mouthwatering selection of market-fresh vegetables.

The following counties are included in this chapter:

BEDFORDSHIRE
BUCKINGHAMSHIRE
CAMBRIDGESHIRE
ESSEX
(Other Essex entries appear in the preceding chapter)

HERTFORDSHIRE
KENT
NORFOLK
SUFFOLK
SURREY
(Other Surrey entries appear in the preceding chapter
SUSSEX (EAST)
SUSSEX (WEST)

# BEDFORDSHIRE

## BEDFORD • map 9E3

 **EDWARDIAN HOUSE HOTEL**
Shakespeare Road, MK40 2DZ
*On a beautiful tree-lined road in the poets area of Bedford, just a few minutes from the town centre, this charming, family-run hotel offers modern facilities, excellent service and a friendly atmosphere. The hotel is very tastefully decorated and the accommodation is of a high standard. Enjoy good, freshly prepared food in the restaurant and relax in the hotel's bar and lounge.*
DOUBLE ROOM: from £19 to £25
SINGLE ROOM: from £29 to £42
FOOD: up to £15
**Hours:** breakfast 7.30am-9am, bar meals 6.30pm-8.45pm.
**Cuisine:** ENGLISH

**Cards:** Visa, Access, AmEx, MasterCard.
**Other points:** children welcome, conferences, vegetarian meals.
**Rooms:** 11 single rooms, 5 double rooms, 2 twin rooms, 1 family room. All with TV, telephone, tea/coffee-making facilities, alarm, heating.
**Directions:** centrally located in Bedford, a few minutes from railway station.
GRAEME A. WOOD ☎(01234) 211156 Fax(01234) 262492

**THE KNIFE & CLEAVER**
The Grove, Houghton Conquest, MK45 3LA
*In a prominent position opposite the medieval church in Houghton Conquest. The restaurant is an airy Victorian-style conservatory, and the innovative*

menu, which changes monthly, incorporates seasonal specialities made from the finest fresh produce. Fresh shellfish, lobster and vegetarian dishes. List of 100 well-chosen wines, over 20 by the glass. Flowery terrace and other open-air dining areas. Within easy reach of Woburn Abbey and Luton Airport.

DOUBLE ROOM: from £22.50 to £35
SINGLE ROOM: from £40 to £55
FOOD: from £17.50 to £25 🍽 🍴 ≡

**Hours:** breakfast 7.30am, weekends 8.30am, lunch 12noon-2.30pm, bar meals 12noon-2.30pm, dinner 7pm-9.30pm, bar meals 7pm-9.30pm; both hotel and restaurant are closed on Sunday evening, but arrangements can be made in advance for accommodation

**Cuisine:** MODERN ENGLISH / FRENCH - specialising in fresh fish, including oysters and lobster.

**Cards:** Visa, Access, Diners, AmEx.

**Other points:** licensed, Sunday lunch, children welcome, pets allowed, open bank holidays, functions.

**Rooms:** 4 double rooms, 5 twin rooms. All with en suite, TV, radio, tea/coffee-making facilities, alarm, refrigerators, power showers.

**Directions:** between A6 and B530, 5 miles south of Bedford and 2 miles north of Ampthill.

DAVID & PAULINE LOOM ☎(01234) 740387
Fax(01234) 740900

---

🛏 **THE LAWS HOTEL**
High Street, Turvey, MK43 8DB

Situated in the pleasant village of Turvey, north-west of Bedford, this hotel offers attractive and comfortable accommodation. The restaurant serves well-presented meals and provides excellent service in a light and relaxed atmosphere. Close to Woburn Abbey and Whipsnade Park Zoo.

DOUBLE ROOM: from £20 to £30
FOOD: from £15 to £20 🍽

**Hours:** breakfast 7am-8.30am, lunch 12noon-2pm, dinner 7pm-9.45pm.

**Cuisine:** ENGLISH / SEAFOOD - a wide selection of dishes on the à la carte menu, plus a table d'hôte menu featuring specials: fillet steak and lobster tail, queen scallops, Dover sole.

**Cards:** Visa, Access, AmEx.

**Other points:** licensed, open-air dining, Sunday lunch, children welcome, afternoon tea, pets allowed, residents' lounge, residents' bar.

**Rooms:** 2 single rooms, 17 double rooms. All with TV, radio, alarm, telephone, tea/coffee-making facilities, hair dryer, trouser-press.

**Directions:** follow A6, take exit for A428 to Bedford. Continue to Turvey.

JEROME & FRANCESCA MACK ☎(01234) 881213
Fax(01234) 888864

---

🛏 **THREE CRANES**
High Street, Turvey, MK43 8EP

Set in the centre of the attractive village of Turvey, next to the ancient Turvey church, the Three Cranes offers very good food, a welcoming atmosphere and excellent service. All meals are well-cooked and presented, served by friendly and efficient staff. The Three Cranes is a very popular pub and well worth a visit.

DOUBLE ROOM: from £20
SINGLE ROOM: from £30
FOOD: up to £15 🍽 ≡

**Hours:** breakfast 7.30am-9.30am; bar meals lunchtime Monday-Saturday 12noon-2pm, evening Monday-Wednesday 6.30pm-9.30pm, Thursday-Saturday 6.30pm-10pm, Sunday 12noon-2.30pm and 7pm-9.30pm.

**Cuisine:** ENGLISH - wide choice of dishes such as Crane's mixed grill, salads, steaks. Blackboard specials including fresh fish dishes, especially at the weekend.

**Cards:** Visa, Access, Switch.

**Other points:** licensed, open-air dining, Sunday lunch, beer garden.

**Rooms:** 2 single rooms, 1 double room, 2 twin rooms.

**Directions:** on A428, midway between Bedford and Northampton.

DAVID & SANDRA ALEXANDER ☎(01234) 881305

---

## BIGGLESWADE • map 10E4

🍽 **LA CACHETTE**
61 Hitchin Street, SG18 8BE

A welcoming restaurant offering an imaginative menu and excellently cooked, fresh food. A separate menu caters for vegetarian guests and provides an equally good choice and high standard of cuisine. With a warm atmosphere and excellent service, La Cachette is definitely worth a visit.

FOOD: from £15 to £20 🍽 🍴 ≡

**Hours:** dinner 7pm-10pm, closed Sunday and Monday.

**Cuisine:** FRENCH / CONTINENTAL - imaginative cuisine which also features specialities from around the world. Dishes may include wild sea trout stuffed with prawns and mushrooms, loin of lamb with orange and redcurrant sauce, shank of pork. Set price menu which changes regularly.

**Cards:** Visa, AmEx, Mastercard.

**Other points:** licensed, children welcome, street parking.

**Directions:** From the A1M, follow signs to the town centre. Two minutes' walk from market square.

RICHARD & MARGARET POOL ☎(01767) 313508

---

## DUNSTABLE • map 9E3

🏠 **BELLOWS MILL**
Bellows Mill, Eaton Bray, LU6 1QZ

For a truly memorable break, this delightful mill, set in its own grounds and dating back to the Domesday Book, is idyllic. The accent is on highly personal attention to your needs, and facilities include an all-weather tennis court, pool table, and even fishing by arrangement. Bellows Mill is also ideal for private receptions and small conferences (marquee for larger functions). Children and pets are

*welcome by prior arrangement.*
DOUBLE ROOM: from £25
SINGLE ROOM: from £30 to £45
FOOD: up to £15
**Hours:** breakfast 7am-10.30am, dinner 7pm-9pm, open all year.
**Cuisine:** HOME COOKING - fixed-price menu. Dishes may include pheasant normande, chicken in lemon and coriander (Indian-style), and lamb noisettes. Dinner by arrangement.
**Cards:** Visa, Access.
**Other points:** licensed, residents' lounge, garden, disabled access, parking, children welcome, pets by prior arrangement, open bank holidays.
**Rooms:** 5 double rooms, 1 family room. All with TV, telephone, tea/coffee-making facilities.
**Directions:** follow signs for zoo, and at Plough Pub take road to Eaton Bray off B489; Bellows Mill is 3rd on the left.
RACHAEL HODGE ☎(01525) 220548 **Fax**(01525) 222754

## LUTON • map 9E3

### LEASIDE HOTEL
72 New Bedford Road, LU3 1BT
*A Victorian hotel, set in its own well-tended gardens with large patio. Pleasantly decorated with comfortable furnishings and serving well-cooked food, attractively presented from a comprehensive menu. The light, pleasant atmosphere attracts tourists and business persons alike.*
DOUBLE ROOM: from £20 to £30
SINGLE ROOM: from £35 to £45
FOOD: from £15 to £20
**Hours:** breakfast 7am-9am, lunch 12noon-2pm, dinner 7pm-9.30pm, closed Christmas day and Boxing day.
**Cuisine:** ENGLISH - à la carte menu, fixed-price three-course menu, bar meals/snacks and vegetarian meals available.
**Cards:** Visa, Access, Diners, AmEx.
**Other points:** licensed, Sunday lunch, children welcome, garden.
**Rooms:** 11 single rooms, 2 double rooms, 1 twin room, 1 family room.
**Directions:** on A6 near Moor Park.
MRS C.A. GILLIES ☎(01582) 417643 **Fax**(01582) 34961

## RIDGMONT • map 5A3

### THE ROSE & CROWN
89 High Street, MK43 0TY
*A 300-year-old country pub with a prize-winning large garden. Patio for barbecues. Games room, conference and private party facilities. Recommended for its traditional ales; also offers an extensive wine list. 20 years in the Good Beer Guide. The pub has its own camping and caravanning site.*
FOOD: up to £15
**Hours:** dinner 6.30pm-10pm, lunch 12noon-2pm.
**Cuisine:** ENGLISH - bar: a comprehensive menu including specials of the day, e.g., tarragon lamb,

lemon chicken, beef olives, etc.
**Cards:** Visa, Access, Diners, AmEx.
**Other points:** open-air dining, Sunday lunch.
**Directions:** on the main street in Ridgmont (A507), 2 miles from junction 13 of M1.
NEIL & ELIZABETH MCGREGOR ☎(01525) 280245 **Fax**(01525) 280279

## STEPPINGLEY • map 5A3

### THE FRENCH HORN
Rectory Road, MK45 5AU
*This beautiful old-world inn, restored to its original character, has gained a proud reputation in and around the picturesque village of Steppingley, near Woburn Abbey, for its imaginative, freshly prepared menus and friendly hospitality. The intimate, candlelit restaurant and timber-beamed bars with roaring fires are warm and inviting. A range of real ales and fine wines available.*
FOOD: from £15 to £20
**Hours:** lunch 12noon-3.30pm, bar meals 12noon-3.30pm, dinner 7pm-10.30pm, bar meals 6pm-10pm.
**Cuisine:** ENGLISH - traditional fare with a flair for fresh fish and game.
**Cards:** Visa, Access, AmEx.
**Other points:** parking, children welcome, pets allowed, no-smoking area, open-air dining, vegetarian meals, traditional Sunday lunch.
**Directions:** Take junction 12 off M1 through Toddington and Flitwick. Restaurant is on left opposite Bury Lawn School.
OLD ENGLISH PUB COMPANY ☎(01525) 712051

## WESTONING • map 5A3

### THE CHEQUERS
Park Road, MK45 5LA
*A 17th century thatched inn, retaining all of its original character. The stables have been tastefully redecorated to form an outstanding restaurant offering good value for money. Very highly recommended.*
FOOD: up to £15
**Hours:** Monday to Saturday 11am-11pm, Sunday 12noon-10.30pm, meals all day.
**Cuisine:** ENGLISH / INTERNATIONAL - fixed-price menu. English cuisine. Dishes include char-grilled steaks, lamb steaks, Cajun chicken. Extensive bar food menu. Daily specials on blackboards.
**Cards:** Visa, Access, Diners, AmEx, Switch.
**Other points:** children welcome, courtyard, Sunday lunch.
**Directions:** off junction 12 on the M1, on A5120, in centre of village.
PAUL WALLMAN ☎(01525) 713125 **Fax**(01525) 716702

# BUCKINGHAMSHIRE

## AMERSHAM • map 5B3

### THE CHEQUERS INN
London Road, HP7 9DA

*These 17th century converted barns are now a popular local inn attracting custom from local residents and travellers of all ages. The lunchtime food trade in the bar is busy, and the tasty à la carte menu is supplemented by daily blackboard specials. 3 en suite double bedrooms are available, together with one single.*

DOUBLE ROOM: up to £20
SINGLE ROOM: up to £20
FOOD: up to £10
**Hours:** breakfast 7.30am-10am, lunch 12noon-2.30pm. Open bank holidays.
**Cuisine:** roast beef, T bone steak, home-made steak and kidney pie and a wide range of bar snacks, salads and sandwiches.
**Other points:** car parking on site.
**Rooms:** 1 single room, 2 twin rooms, 1 triple room. Most en suite. All with TV, radio, tea/coffee-making facilities.
**Directions:** on A413 London road in Amersham.
MR JAMES RYAN ☎(01494) 727866

## BEACONSFIELD • map 5B3

### THE ROYAL STANDARD OF ENGLAND
Forty Green, HP9 1XT

*Famous old English pub boasting a beautiful country atmosphere, in character with its surroundings. Reputed to be one of the oldest public houses in England. English and continental draught beers.*

FOOD: up to £15
**Hours:** open 11am-3pm, 5.30pm-11pm, (Mon-Sat), 12noon-3pm, 7pm-10.30pm (Sun). Food available 12noon-2.30pm and 7pm-10.30pm (Mon-Sat), 12noon-2.30pm and 7pm-10pm (Sun).
**Cuisine:** TRADITIONAL BRITISH / INTERNATIONAL
**Cards:** Visa, Mastercard.
**Other points:** licensed, open-air dining, Sunday lunch, childrens' licence.
**Directions:** Forty Green is 1.5 miles from Beaconsfield, off the Beaconsfield-Penn road.
MR P.W. ELDRIDGE ☎(01494) 673382 Fax(01494) 523332

## CHESHAM • map 5B3

### THE ROSE & CROWN
The Vale, Hawridge Common, HP5 2UQ

*Situated in the Vale of Chesham, this 17th century inn is full of character, with open log fires and a raised candlelit restaurant area offering excellent home-cooked meals, using only the finest produce. It has a fine selection of real ales. A beautiful garden with views across the valley.*

FOOD: from £7 to £15
**Hours:** lunch 12.30am-2.30pm, bar meals 12noon-2.30pm, dinner 7pm-10pm, bar meals 6pm-10pm.
**Cuisine:** ENGLISH cuisine with daily and seasonal specials.
**Cards:** Visa, Access, AmEx, Switch.
**Other points:** parking, children welcome, pets allowed, open-air dining, vegetarian meals, traditional Sunday lunch.
**Directions:** The Vale, between Chesham and Cholesbury.
KAREN ☎(01494) 758386

## GREAT MISSENDEN • map 5B3

### THE GEORGE
94 High Street, HP16 OBG

*Many-levelled, old-beamed and tastefully furnished pub, which offers excellent food, competent service and a pleasant atmosphere at very good value.*

DOUBLE ROOM: from £20 to £30
FOOD: up to £15   CLUB
**Hours:** lunch 12noon-2pm, dinner 7pm-11.30pm, last orders 9.45pm, bar snacks all day.
**Cuisine:** ENGLISH / CONTINENTAL - steaks, pasta and vegetarian selections.
**Cards:** Visa.
**Other points:** licensed, open-air dining, Sunday lunch, children welcome.
**Rooms:** 4 double rooms, 6 twin rooms, 2 family rooms.
**Directions:** .25 mile from A413, between Amersham and Wendover. In town's main street.
GUY & SALLY SMITH ☎(01494) 862084
Fax(01494) 865622

## HIGH WYCOMBE • map 5B3

### DRAKE COURT HOTEL
141 London Road, HP11 1BT

*A small, friendly hotel situated close to the centre of historic High Wycombe. The staff are welcoming and efficient. Convenient for the M40 London-Oxford motorway and for touring the Thames Valley, Oxford and the Cotswolds.*

DOUBLE ROOM: up to £20
SINGLE ROOM: up to £25
FOOD: up to £15
**Hours:** breakfast 7.30am-8.30am, dinner 7pm-9.30pm.
**Cuisine:** ENGLISH / CONTINENTAL - traditional English and continental cuisine.
**Cards:** Visa, Access, Diners, AmEx.
**Other points:** licensed, children welcome, open bank holidays, residents' lounge, swimming pool.
**Directions:** On A40 London Road, close to High Wycombe. Approximately 1 mile from M40 motorway.
☎(01494) 523639 Fax(01494) 472696

## LEDBURN • map 5B3

### THE HARE & HOUNDS
Near Leighton Buzzard, LU7 0QB

*A large country inn steeped with unique character, situated in open countryside. It caters for the discerning diner, with freshly prepared home-cooked meals, and the real-ale enthusiast. The delightful restaurant and bar are enhanced by an impressive open fire.*

**FOOD:** up to £15

**Hours:** lunch 12noon-3pm, dinner 6.30pm-10pm.

**Cuisine:** ENGLISH - featuring char grilled meat and fish seasonal specialities.

**Cards:** Visa, Access, AmEx.

**Other points:** parking, children welcome, garden, open-air dining, vegetarian meals, traditional Sunday lunch.

**Directions:** out of Leighton Buzzard on the A418, turn left onto B4032, then left to Ledburn.

MR & MRS KEVIN BLUNDELL ☎(01525) 373484

## MILTON KEYNES • map 5A3

### OLD GREEN MAN
Watling Street, Little Brickhill, MK17 9LU

*This elegant country inn has become a major feature of the village, with its tasteful exterior and outstanding floral displays, and the old-world ambience of the restaurant with its beamed bars and inglenook fireplace. Good home-cooked locally-produced fare is always available. The range of real ales, fine wines and friendly hospitality is second to none.*

**FOOD:** up to £15

**Hours:** lunch 12noon-2.30pm, dinner 6.30pm-11pm.

**Cuisine:** ENGLISH - imaginative traditional cuisine with daily specials.

**Cards:** Visa, Access, AmEx.

**Other points:** parking, children welcome, vegetarian meals, traditional Sunday lunch.

**Directions:** off A5 to Little Brickhill, turn right at roundabout, 500 yards on the right.

OLD ENGLISH PUB COMPANY ☎(01525) 261253

## NEWPORT PAGNELL • map 5A3

### MYSORE INDIAN CUISINE
97-101 High Street, MK16 8EN

*The Mysore restaurant offers a wide range of high-quality traditional Indian and Persian cuisine, with take-away menu also available. For special occasions a Mysore table of Murgh Masala or Kurzi Lamb can be ordered for four or more people at 48 hours' notice. On Sundays a special hot buffet lunch is available for a very reasonable set price. Best in Britain Award Top 30 1994 by Real Curry Restaurant guide, Patak's Restaurant of the Year 1993/1994, second in Curry Club 1994.*

**FOOD:** up to £15

**Hours:** lunch 12noon-2.30pm, dinner 6pm-11.30pm, closed Christmas, bank holidays.

**Cuisine:** INDIAN - Tandoori specialities.

**Cards:** Visa, Access, AmEx.

**Other points:** licensed, Sunday lunch, no-smoking area, children welcome.

**Directions:** Take M1 junction 14. Situated in centre of Newport Pagnell.

MR ODUD ☎(01908) 216426 Fax(01908) 216726

### THE OLD SWAN
Main Road, Astwood, MK16 9JS

*Visit this 17th century thatched inn, situated in the heart of the pretty village of Astwood, and step back in time. It boasts an open fire, low timbered beams, flagstone floors and that old-world ambience. Sample home-cooked local produce in the intimate, candlelit restaurant, or relax with one of their real ales by a roaring fire.*

**FOOD:** up to £15 ☜

**Hours:** lunch 12noon-2.30pm, dinner 6pm-9.30pm.

**Cuisine:** ENGLISH

**Cards:** Visa, Access.

**Other points:** parking, children welcome, open-air dining, vegetarian meals, traditional Sunday lunch.

**Directions:** just off A422 Newport Pagnell road.

PHIL & KAREN STRINGER ☎(01234) 391351

## PENN • map 5B3

### THE OLD QUEEN'S HEAD
Hammersley Lane, Tylers Green, HP10 8EV

*This impressive, heavily beamed country inn is situated at Penn in the heart of the beautiful Buckinghamshire countryside. It boasts excellent food, an old English cheese counter, real ales and fine wines, with an old-charm ambience of its own. The warm, candlelit bars and restaurant make this the perfect venue for any occasion.*

**FOOD:** from £15 to £20

**Hours:** bar meals 12noon-2.30pm, dinner 7pm-9.30pm, bar meals 6pm-9.30pm, bar 11am-11pm.

**Cuisine:** ENGLISH - bar: traditional and creative bar snacks. Restaurant: full à la carte and daily specials board.

**Cards:** Visa, Access, AmEx, Switch.

**Other points:** parking, children welcome, garden, open-air dining, vegetarian meals, traditional Sunday lunch.

**Directions:** junction 3 off M40, head for High Wycombe on A40, turn right into Hammersley Lane. At the top of the road on the right.

OLD ENGLISH PUB COMPANY ☎(01494) 813371

## PRINCES RISBOROUGH • map 5B3

### KING WILLIAM IV FREEHOUSE & RESTAURANT
Hampden Road, Speen, HP27 0RU

*A Grade II listed building, originally an old farmhouse dating from 1668, offering a combination of good food and unobtrusive expert service. The fresh flowers on every table are an additional bonus. Ideally situated for visiting Hughenden*

*Manor and the Home of Rest for Horses*
FOOD: from £15 to £20
**Hours:** lunch 12noon-3pm, dinner 7pm-11pm, last orders 9.30pm, closed Sunday evening.
**Cuisine:** ENGLISH - two types of dining offered using all fresh ingredients. A full menu with a choice of starters, main courses, and sweet selection at an average of £17.50 (3 courses). Also a more relaxed menu offering single courses such as steak and kidney "pot" pie, minute steak grill, coronation chicken and seafood hors d'oeuvre. Prices from £4.50 to £8. Always daily specials available on the blackboard.
**Cards:** Visa, Access, Switch.
**Other points:** licensed, open-air dining, Sunday lunch, children welcome, parking, open bank holidays, all dining areas non-smoking.
**Directions:** from High Wycombe, take Hughenden Valley road (A4128).
GEOFFREY & SANDRA CARTER ☎(01494) 488329 **Fax**(01494) 488301

## STONY STRATFORD • map 5A3

### COCK HOTEL
High Street, MK11 1AH
*The Cock Hotel has stood on Watling Street for almost 600 years. A disastrous fire destroyed the original building in 1742 resulting in the present impressive facade. The old traditions of inn-keeping have been retained by Christopher Helliar, and today a comfortable mix of local residents and conference delegates benefit from the good food and comfortable bedrooms. 5 minutes from central Milton Keynes and convenient for Woburn Abbey.*
DOUBLE ROOM: from £20 to £30
SINGLE ROOM: from £45 to £55
FOOD: up to £15 **CLUB**
**Hours:** breakfast 7am-10am, lunch (restaurant and bar) 12noon-2pm, dinner (restaurant and bar) 7pm-10pm. Open 7 days a week.
**Cuisine:** wide ranging bar and brasserie menu together with à la carte and table d'hôte in the restaurant. Vegetarian specialities also available.
**Cards:** Visa, Access, AmEx, Diners
**Other points:** car parking on site, conference and party facilities for up to 200, garden, lounge bars.
**Rooms:** 10 single rooms, 7 twin rooms, 10 double rooms, 1 family room. All en suite with tea/coffee-maker, TV, telephone, radio, alarm, hair dryer, trouser press.
**Directions:** on the old A5 (Watling Street), 5

minutes from central Milton Keynes.
CHRISTOPHER HELLIAR ☎(01908) 567733
**Fax**(01908) 562109

## TRING • map 5B3

### THE WHITE LION
Startops End, Marsworth, HP12 4LJ
*This 15th century inn is idyllically situated on the Grand Union Canal at Marsworth Lock, an ideal stop for longboats, walkers and fishermen. Its unique character, with open fires, low beams, real ales and home-cooked food using only fresh local produce, makes this inn well worth a visit.*
FOOD: from £15 to £20
**Hours:** meals all day 12noon-11pm.
**Cuisine:** ENGLISH - bar meals and à la carte restaurant menu. Daily seasonal specials.
**Cards:** Visa, Access, AmEx.
**Other points:** parking, children welcome, pets allowed, vegetarian meals, traditional Sunday lunch, large patio overlooking canal.
**Directions:** 1 mile out of Tring on Grand Union Canal, B489.
GLEN & WENDY SMITH ☎(01442) 822325

## WEST WYCOMBE • map 5B3

### THE GEORGE & DRAGON
High Street, HP14 3AB
*This charming country inn is situated in a National Trust village, with several tourist attractions within walking distance. Renowned for traditional English home-cooking, the George & Dragon offers superior accommodation for that special stay. Private room available for functions.*
DOUBLE ROOM: from £20 to £30
SINGLE ROOM: from £40 to £46
FOOD: up to £15
**Hours:** lunch 12noon-2pm, dinner 6pm-9.30pm. Sundays, lunch 12noon-3pm, dinner 7pm-9pm.
**Cuisine:** ENGLISH - home-cooking, local game in season.
**Cards:** Visa, Access, Diners, AmEx, Switch.
**Other points:** licensed, open-air dining, Sunday lunch, children's room.
**Directions:** on the A40 in West Wycombe village, 3 miles west of High Wycombe.
PHILIP TODD ☎(01494) 464414 **Fax**(01494) 462432

# CAMBRIDGESHIRE

## CAMBRIDGE • map 10D4

### ANCIENT SHEPHERDS
High Street, Fen Ditton, CB5 8ST
*A very friendly country inn, c.1540, serving well-cooked and presented food. Very pleasant atmosphere, with a good cross-section of business people, students and locals.*

FOOD: from £15 to £20
**Hours:** lunch 12noon-2.15pm; bar meals 12noon-2.15pm, 6.30pm-9.30pm; dinner Monday to Thursday 6.30pm-9.30pm, Friday and Saturday 6.30pm-10pm; closed Sunday night and for one week at Christmas.
**Cuisine:** ENGLISH / CONTINENTAL - varied à la carte menu, including moules marinière and fresh

fish. Bar meals include chicken ancient shepherds (chicken with apricots, brandy and cream).
**Cards:** Visa, Access.
**Other points:** children catered for (please check for age limits), pets allowed, garden, open bank holidays.
**Directions:** 2 miles from the centre of Cambridge, off Newmarket Road. B1047 off A14 east.
HILTON ROSE ☎(01223) 293280

### ARUNDEL HOUSE HOTEL
Chesterton Road, CB4 3AN
*Overlooking the River Cam and Jesus Green, the Arundel House Hotel is one of the few privately-owned hotels in Cambridge. Within easy walking distance of the city centre and university colleges. An elegant conversion of fine Victorian terraced houses, with a reputation for some of the best food in the area.*
DOUBLE ROOM: from £27 to £39
SINGLE ROOM: from £37 to £57
FOOD: up to £15
**Hours:** lunch 12.15am-1.45pm, dinner 6.30pm-9.30pm.
**Cuisine:** FRENCH / ENGLISH - predominantly French and English but with a variety of other international styles. Restaurant offering à la carte, table d'hôte, vegetarian and children's menu. Plus a large new conservatory open all day (9.30am-10pm) offering a range of alternative dishes, cream teas etc.
**Cards:** Visa, Access, Diners, AmEx.
**Other points:** licensed, Sunday lunch, children welcome, limited disabled access.
**Rooms:** 42 single rooms, 33 double rooms, 24 twin rooms, 6 family rooms. All with TV, radio, telephone, tea/coffee-making facilities, hair dryer. Nearly all rooms are en suite.
**Directions:** on the A1303. Exit junction 13 on M11.
MR R.J.C. NORFOLK ☎(01223) 367701
Fax(01223) 367721

### BRIDGE HOTEL
Clayhithe, near Waterbeach, CB5 9NZ
*The historic Bridge Hotel is not only one of the most popular luncheon and dinner rendezvous in the area, but is internationally famous as a riverside hotel. The riverside restaurant offers you excellent service and personal attention, and a delicious full à la carte menu is always available. Sited beside the River Cam, with a lawn sweeping down to the water's edge. Residents have fishing rights on the river from the garden.*
DOUBLE ROOM: from £20 to £30
FOOD: up to £15
**Hours:** breakfast 7.30am-9am, bar meals 12noon-2pm, dinner 7pm-9pm, bar meals 6.30pm-9.30pm.
**Cuisine:** ENGLISH
**Cards:** Visa, Access, AmEx.
**Other points:** parking, children welcome, pets allowed, no-smoking area, vegetarian meals, open-air dining, traditional Sunday lunch.
**Rooms:** 6 single rooms, 10 double rooms, 10 twin

rooms, 2 family rooms. All with en suite, TV, telephone, tea/coffee-making facilities.
**Directions:** 4 miles north of Cambridge off A10, pass through Waterbeach. The hotel is on the left.
MARGARET MANSON ☎(01223) 860252
Fax(01223) 440448

### THE PANOS HOTEL & RESTAURANT
154-156 Hills Road, CB2 2PB
*The Panos is small and intimate which ensures a friendly, personal service. It is a family hotel run by the owner Geneviève who does everything possible to make her guests feel welcome. The bedrooms are very well appointed, and the central location makes this an ideal base to explore the beautiful attractions of Cambridge.*
DOUBLE ROOM: from £35
SINGLE ROOM: from £45 to £50
FOOD: from £15 to £20
**Hours:** breakfast 7.30am-9.30am, lunch and bar meals 12noon-3pm, dinner and bar meals 6.30pm-10pm.
**Cuisine:** delicious Greek and French specialities including Mezze (a mixed hors d'oeuvre), Xifias (marinated and grilled sword-fish kebabs) and lamb Souvlaki. Comprehensive wine list including Greek varieties.
**Cards:** Visa, Access, Diners, AmEx.
**Other points:** licensed, sauna, parking.
**Rooms:** 1 single room, 1 twin room, 4 double rooms, all en suite. All with TV, radio, alarm, telephone, hair dryer, room service, tea/coffee-making facilities, mini bars.
**Directions:** going into Cambridge on the A604, the hotel is on the left, near the railway station.
MRS GENEVIEVE KRETZ ☎(01223) 212958
Fax(01223) 210980

### THE REGENT HOTEL
41 Regent Street, CB2 1AB
*The Regent Hotel is a fine, listed building, situated in the heart of Cambridge. The location offers easy access to various business amenities and cultural attractions, and provides superb views over the famous Parkers Piece. Recently refurbished, the hotel maintains the tradition of friendly service, sumptuous meals in an elegant and luxurious environment and reasonably priced, quality accommodation.*
DOUBLE ROOM: from £30 to £40
SINGLE ROOM: up to £60
FOOD: up to £15
**Hours:** breakfast 7.30am-9.30am, lunch 12noon-2pm, dinner 6pm-10pm, closed 24th December until 2nd January.
**Cuisine:** CONTINENTAL / ITALIAN - with a menu to suit all tastes, the hotel has an excellent reputation for superb cuisine.
**Cards:** Visa, Access, Diners, AmEx, Switch.
**Other points:** children welcome, conference facilities, residents' lounge, no-smoking area, vegetarian meals, afternoon teas.
**Rooms:** 6 single rooms, 17 double/twin rooms, 2

family rooms. All with en suite, TV, telephone, radio, alarm, hair dryer, trouser-press, room service, baby-listening device, tea/coffee-making facilities.
**Directions:** situated in the centre of Cambridge.
PAOLO PASCHALIS ☎(01223) 351470 Fax(01223) 566562

 **THE SUFFOLK HOUSE**
69 Milton Road, CB4 1XA
*A spacious 1930s gable-fronted detached house, set in a large secluded garden. A high standard of comfort and cleanliness is maintained by Mary and Michael Cuthbert, who extend a warm welcome to their guests. Less than 20 minutes' walk from the city centre.*
DOUBLE ROOM: from £25 to £32.50
SINGLE ROOM: from £38 to £50
**Hours:** breakfast weekdays 8am-8.45am, weekends 8.30am-9.15am.
**Cuisine:** BREAKFAST
**Cards:** Visa, Access, AmEx, JCB.
**Other points:** central heating, children welcome, garden.
**Rooms:** 4 double rooms, 2 twin rooms, 5 family rooms. All with TV.
**Directions:** situated on the A1309 - leave the A14 at A10 Ely and A1309 junction.
MR & MRS CUTHBERT ☎(01223) 352016
Fax(01223) 566816

 **TATTIES**
26-28 Regent Street, CB2 1DB
*Tatties has been completely refurbished and enlarged, whilst still retaining its original character. Decorated with a wealth of traditional metal advertising signs (1890-1930), antique cooking utensils, garden tools, market barrows and other interesting items of a bygone era. The restaurant also has a large roof garden, overlooking the grounds of Downing College. It is conveniently located in the centre of the city and is a popular venue for undergraduates and tourists.*
FOOD: up to £15
**Hours:** breakfast 10am-11.30am, meals all day 10.00am-10.30pm, open 7 days.
**Cuisine:** ENGLISH - specializing in baked potatoes: here the jacket spud is plucked from its humble roots and transformed into a mouth-watering meal in its own right! Charcoal-grilled chicken, fish and steaks, salads and pasta dishes also available.
**Cards:** Visa, Access, Diners, Mastercard, JCB
**Other points:** licensed, children welcome, disabled facilities, guide dogs welcome, open-air dining, vegetarian meals.
**Directions:** located in the centre of Cambridge next to Downing College.
BARRY PAIN & MIKE LAMBOURN-BROWN
☎(01223) 358478 Fax(01223) 359703

**THE WHITE HORSE INN**
1 Market Street, Swavesey, CB4 5QG
*Situated in the centre of an attractive village with*

easy parking on the adjacent square, this 17th century pub offers a comprehensive home-cooked bar and restaurant menu and has won prizes in national competitions for both its steak and kidney pies and curries. Well worth a visit.
FOOD: up to £15
**Hours:** lunch 12noon-2pm (bar and restaurant), dinner 7pm-9.30pm (last orders)(bar and restaurant).
**Cuisine:** HOME COOKED ENGLISH PLUS ETHNIC, most dishes are made using locally produced meat and vegetables. Pies are a speciality, and the White Horse's steak-and-kidney recently won an award in a national competition. Choice of 4 authentic curries made with individual spices always available.
**Cards:** Access, Visa
**Other points:** parking close by, vegetarian meals, theme nights (programme available on request), conference and private dining facilities available.
**Directions:** in the village of Swavesey which lies 2 miles off the A14 between Cambridge and St Ives.
ANTHONY & MARLENE STOCKBRIDGE
☎(01954) 230239 Fax(01954) 206031

## CHITTERING • map 10D4

 **TRAVELLERS REST**
Ely Road, CB5 9PH
*A 300-year-old beamed public house with its own restaurant, decorated throughout with a cottage theme, providing a perfect atmosphere for families and caravanners. Carvery offering 3-course meals. Ideal location for visiting Anglesey Abbey and Wicken Fen, or for touring Cambridge, Bury St Edmunds and Newmarket.*
FOOD: up to £15
**Hours:** lunch Monday-Saturday 12noon-2.30pm, dinner Monday-Saturday 6pm-9.30pm, Sunday open 12noon-9pm.
**Cuisine:** ENGLISH / CONTINENTAL - quality à la carte.
**Cards:** Visa, Access, AmEx.
**Other points:** parking, children welcome, no-smoking area, disabled access, vegetarian meals, open-air dining, caravan and camp site.
**Directions:** on A10, exactly halfway between Ely and Cambridge (8 miles each way).
KEITH & ALEXANDRA RICHARDSON ☎(01223) 860751

## ELY • map 10D4

**THE ANCHOR INN**
Sutton Gault, Sutton, CB6 2BD

A traditional Fen riverside inn, approximately 350 years old, lit by gas lamps and with old beams, scrubbed wooden tables and chairs. Frequented by locals and tourists alike, the atmosphere is homely and welcoming, and the service is very efficient. Recognized in all the guides. Ideal base for visiting Ely Cathedral, the Ouse Washes, Welney Wildfowl Reserve and for exploring the real Fen country. Cambridge and Newmarket within easy reach.
DOUBLE ROOM: from £21 to £30
SINGLE ROOM: from £45
FOOD: from £15 to £20
Hours: lunch, 12noon-2.00pm, dinner 7pm-11pm, last orders 9pm, every day.
Cuisine: ENGLISH / CONTINENTAL - à la carte menu, offering an extensive range of imaginative dishes, changes daily. Set lunch also available.
Cards: Visa, Access, AmEx.
Other points: licensed, open-air dining, Sunday lunch, large no-smoking area, children catered for (please check for age limits), open bank holidays.
Rooms: 1 twin room en suite, 1 suite (double room, sitting room and bath).
Directions: signposted to Sutton Gault, just south of Sutton Village (B1381). 7 miles west of Ely.
HEATHER & ROBIN MOORE ☎(01353) 778537
Fax (01353) 776180

## GREAT CHISHILL • map 10E4

 **THE PHEASANT**
24 Heydon Road, near Royston, SG8 8JH
This charming country inn, situated in the beautiful village of Great Chishill, has been tastefully refurbished with character and features an impressive inglenook fireplace, flagstone floors and candlelit restaurant, giving a warm and cosy atmosphere with excellent home-cooked food and real ales. It has a large raised garden with panoramic views across the countryside.
FOOD: up to £15
Hours: lunch 12noon-2pm, dinner 7pm-9.30pm.
Cuisine: ENGLISH - from simple bar food to haute cuisine.
Cards: Visa, Access, AmEx, Mastercard.
Other points: parking, children welcome, open-air dining, vegetarian meals, traditional Sunday lunch.
Directions: Barley/Barkway turning off A505, heading east out of Royston; at 'T' junction after about 2 to 3 miles, turn right into village.
NICK CLARKE & JOANNA WOOD ☎(01763) 838535

## HORSEHEATH • map 10E4

**THE OLD RED LION**
Linton Road, CB1 6QF
This beautiful 17th century country inn is situated on the A604 close to Cambridge, offering good food, real ales and fine wines. Totally refurbished with flagstone floors, open fire and timber beams and a wealth of character. It boasts elegantly furnished en suite letting rooms. Close by is Chilford Hall Vineyard and Linton Zoo.
DOUBLE ROOM: from £30 to £40

FOOD: up to £15
Hours: breakfast 7.30am-9.30am, meals all day 11am-10.30pm.
Cuisine: ENGLISH - traditional cuisine with European and international influences. Daily specials.
Cards: Visa, Access, AmEx.
Other points: parking, children welcome, pets allowed, conference facilities, garden, open-air dining, vegetarian meals, traditional Sunday lunch.
Rooms: 14 bedrooms. All with TV, telephone, radio, alarm, hair dryer, trouser-press, tea/coffee-making facilities.
Directions: on the main A604 between Linton and Haverhill, 14 miles outside Cambridge.
JOHN & ANGELA ERA ☎(01223) 892909
Fax (01223) 894217

## HUNTINGDON • map 10D4

 **THE OLD FERRY BOAT INN**
Holywell, St Ives, PE17 3TG
This charming thatched riverside inn claims to be the oldest in England, with the spirit of over a thousand years of good hospitality. Judging by the number of visitors, this reputation is still upheld. One sad spirit still exists: the ghost of young Juliette, whose gravestone forms part of the ancient floor in the bar.
DOUBLE ROOM: from £20 to £35
SINGLE ROOM: from £40 to £49.50
FOOD: up to £15
Hours: breakfast 7.30am-10am, lunch 12noon-2pm, dinner 6.30pm-10pm, Sunday 7pm-9.30pm.
Cuisine: INTERNATIONAL - including traditional English. Daily specials, extensive choice of bar meals and weekend specials. Real ales available.
Cards: Visa, Access, Switch.
Other points: children welcome, parking, disabled access, vegetarian meals.
Rooms: 7 bedrooms. All ensuite.
Directions: from the A141, take the B1090 towards St Ives, followed by the A1123. At Needingworth, take the road on the right to Holywell.
RICHARD & SHELLEY JEFFREY ☎(01480) 463227
Fax (01480) 494885

## LINTON • map 10E4

**THE CROWN INN**
High Street, CB1 6HS
A lime-washed Georgian pub, situated in the centre of the pleasant village of Linton, offering a choice of tasty bar meals or an interesting à la carte menu in their restaurant. Excellent service, and a very warm welcome typical of a charming village pub, make a visit here well worthwhile.
DOUBLE ROOM: up to £20
FOOD: up to £15
Hours: lunch 12noon-2pm, dinner 7pm-9.45pm, bar 12noon-2.30pm and 5.30pm-11pm, no food Sunday evenings.
Cuisine: INTERNATIONAL - home-cooked food using fresh ingredients.
Cards: Visa, Access.

**Other points:** licensed, open-air dining, Sunday lunch, children welcome.
**Rooms:** 1 double room, 3 twin rooms. All with en suite, TV, tea-making facilities.
**Directions:** 100 yards off A604, on the main High Street.
JOEL PALMER ☎(01223) 891759

## PETERBOROUGH • map 9D3

### THE BLACK HORSE
Nassington, PE8 6QU
*A listed, 15th century coaching inn with a warm, welcoming atmosphere serving a good choice of food, accompanied by speciality sauces, home-made sweets and some excellent wines. Regular theme-evenings are popular and feature live entertainment from talented musicians and singers from around the world. Close to Nene Valley Railway and Rutland Water.*
FOOD: from £15 to £20
**Hours:** lunch 12noon-1.45pm (3pm bar), dinner 7pm-9.45pm (restaurant), 7pm-11pm (bar). Sundays 12noon-1.45pm (restaurant) 3pm (bar), 7pm-11pm (bar).
**Cuisine:** extremely varied menus featuring home-made sweets and sauces. Regular theme evenings offer music and a national menu with a wide range of dishes. Details available 4 weeks in advance and booking is recommended.
**Cards:** Access,Visa,AmEx
**Other points:** beer garden, vegetarian meals, Sunday roasts, parking.
**Directions:** turn off A1 northbound at Wansford. Drive through Yarwell to Nassington. Black Horse is on the right hand side.
THE OLD ENGLISH PUB CO ☎(01780) 782324

### THE SIBSON INN
Sibson, PE8 6ND
*Once the haunt of famous highwayman, Dick Turpin, this beautiful old farmhouse attracts a wide clientele who come from afar to enjoy the wholesome, traditional fare such as steak-and-kidney pie. Ideal stop-off when visiting nearby Nene Valley Railway or Rutland Water.*
DOUBLE ROOM: from £22
SINGLE ROOM: from £40
FOOD: from £15 to £20
**Hours:** breakfast 7.30am-9am, lunch 12noon-3pm, dinner 6pm-9.30pm.
**Cuisine:** steak and kidney pie, speciality fish dishes, game in seasons, traditional sponge puddings.
**Cards:** Access,Visa,AmEx
**Other points:** parking, outdoor dining, sauna, mini gym, meeting rooms, golf and fishing breaks available.
**Rooms:** 3 twin rooms, 13 double rooms, 1 family room all en suite with tea/coffee-maker, TV, telephone, radio, alarm, trouser press, room service. Hair dryer on request.
**Directions:** on A1 northbound 5 miles past Norman

Cross roundabout on left hand side of the road. 6 miles south of Stamford.
THE OLD ENGLISH PUB CO ☎(01780) 782227

## ST IVES • map 10D4

### THE DOLPHIN HOTEL
Bridge Foot, London Road, PE17 4EP
*The Dolphin is a family-owned hotel on the banks of the Great Ouse in the old market town of St Ives. Guests enjoy good food, friendly but efficient service and panoramic views of the river and surrounding meadows. The large riverside terrace is the perfect setting for a refreshing drink or a light meal served in a relaxed atmosphere. For the convenience of the guests, there is a large car park and mooring for 20 boats.*
DOUBLE ROOM: from £30 to £40
SINGLE ROOM: over £50
FOOD: from £15 to £20
**Hours:** breakfast 7.30am-9.30am, lunch 12noon-2pm, dinner 7pm-9.30pm.
**Cuisine:** ENGLISH / CONTINENTAL - with a good selection of wines from an extensive list. Special carvery Sunday lunch.
**Cards:** Visa, Access, Diners, AmEx.
**Other points:** fully licensed.
**Rooms:** 2 single rooms, 13 double rooms (2 have been adapted for disabled persons), 31 twin rooms, 2 family rooms. All with TV, radio, telephone, tea/coffee-making facilities, hair dryer.
**Directions:** from A14 take A1096 towards St Ives, left at first roundabout, then immediately right; the Dolphin is about 800 yards, by the old river bridge.
H.R. WADSWORTH ☎(01480) 466966
Fax (01480) 495597

## STILTON • map 9D3

### BELL INN HOTEL
Great North Road, PE7 3RA
*This hotel has been built around the courtyard of an ancient inn. It offers old-world charm, relaxing comfort and modern facilities. The inn dates from 1500 and is a dream for history lovers.*
DOUBLE ROOM: from £30 to £40
SINGLE ROOM: from £40
FOOD: from £15 to £20
**Hours:** breakfast 7am-9am, lunch 12noon-2pm, dinner 7pm-9.30pm.
**Cuisine:** ENGLISH - à la carte. Dishes include Byron fillet of beef, wild salmon dumpling, vegetable filo parcels.
**Cards:** Visa, Access, AmEx, Switch.
**Other points:** open-air dining, Sunday lunch, no-smoking area, garden, conferences.
**Rooms:** 2 single rooms, 13 double rooms, 3 twin rooms, 1 family room.
**Directions:** .5 mile off A1 northbound; 5 miles south of Peterborough.
MR & MRS MCGIVERN ☎(01733) 241066

# ESSEX

## BILLERICAY • map 6B5

### DUKE OF YORK
Southend Road, South Green, CM11 2PR
*A pub and restaurant offering good-value meals and efficient, friendly service. The Duke of York was a beer house in 1868, and the restaurant has since been sympathetically added to complement the original building. Customers will find a warm, cosy atmosphere in which to enjoy their meal.*
FOOD: from £20 to £25
Hours: lunch and bar snacks 12noon-2pm, dinner and bar snacks 7pm-10pm, no food Sunday evenings.
Cuisine: FRENCH / ENGLISH - choice of menus - set menu at £16. Large choice of bar snacks. Hot and cold bar food Sunday lunchtime as well as a traditional Sunday roast (£4.65). Very extensive vegetarian menu.
Cards: Visa, Access, Diners, AmEx.
Other points: licensed, children welcome.
Directions: On A129 Billericay to Wickford road, 1 mile from Billericay High Street.
MRS EDNA WHITE, KEITH WHITE, DAVID WHITE
☎(01277) 651403

## BRENTWOOD • map 6B4

### THE BLACK HORSE
Ongar Road, Pilgrims Hatch, CM15 9JN
*Dating back to the 14th century, this delightful converted farmhouse retains its rustic charm and atmosphere. Warm and friendly staff make guests welcome. Substantial, well-prepared meals are complemented by a good range of beers.*
FOOD: up to £15
Hours: meals Monday-Saturday from 11am to 11pm (last orders 10pm), Sunday 12noon-9.30pm.
Cuisine: ENGLISH - traditional English steak-and-ale pie, mixed grills, fresh fish, steaks.
Cards: Visa, Access, Delta, Switch.
Other points: licensed, children catered for (please check for age limits), garden, parking, disabled access.
Directions: in the village of Pilgrim's Hatch on A128, 4 miles from Brentwood.
JOHN & LINDA SWAIL ☎(01277) 372337

## CHELMSFORD • map 6B5

### MIAMI HOTEL
Princes Road, CM2 9AJ
*The Miami Hotel has been a family-run business for the past 30 years, with three generations working in the hotel. 55 bedrooms, all twin/double size, but let as single if required. All rooms have colour television, Sky TV, trouser-press and tea-making facilities. Easy access from all main routes, M25, A12 and A1016. Close to all major airports for the international traveller. The Miami Hotel offers value, comfort and hospitality.*
DOUBLE ROOM: from £31 to £40
FOOD: from £16 to £20 CLUB
Hours: breakfast 7.30am-9am, dinner 6.30pm-9.30pm, lunch 12noon-2.30pm.
Cuisine: CONTINENTAL - filet mignon, steak au poivre, beef stroganoff.
Cards: Visa, Diners, AmEx, MasterCard.
Other points: Sunday lunch, children welcome.
Rooms: 16 double rooms, 39 twin rooms. All with TV, tea/coffee-making facilities.
Directions: by the A1016 Billericay roundabout.
MR C. NEWCOMBE ☎(01245) 269603/264848
Fax(01245) 259860

### SOUTH LODGE HOTEL
196 New London Road, CM2 0AR
*A busy commercial hotel close to the town centre and County Cricket Ground. South Lodge is a converted Victorian residence standing in its own mature gardens. Full conference, function and leisure facilities available.*
DOUBLE ROOM: from £20 to £35
SINGLE ROOM: from £45 to £60
FOOD: up to £15
Hours: breakfast 7.30am-9.30am, lunch 12.30am-2.30pm, dinner 7pm-10pm.
Cuisine: ENGLISH / INTERNATIONAL - international and new English cuisine.
Cards: Visa, Access, Diners, AmEx.
Other points: licensed, Sunday lunch, no-smoking area, children welcome, cots.
Rooms: 20 single rooms, 11 double rooms, 10 twin rooms. All with TV, telephone, tea/coffee-making facilities.
Directions: off the A12, close to the town centre.
THE PROPRIETOR ☎(01245) 264564 Fax(01245) 492827

## CLACTON-ON-SEA • map 6B6

### THE ROBIN HOOD
221 London Road, CO15 4ED
*Originally a farmhouse, this delightful pub has retained its rustic charm. Hot, home-style meals at affordable prices and friendly staff will make you feel at home. There is a family atmosphere and children are welcome when dining.*
FOOD: up to £15
Hours: meals all day from 11am to 10pm.
Cuisine: ENGLISH - good selection of pub-style food. Blackboard specials daily. Children's menu. Generous portions at extremely reasonable prices.
Cards: Visa, Access, Switch.
Other points: licensed, children catered for (please check for age limits), open bank holidays.
Directions: on A133, follow signs to Clacton town centre. The Robin Hood is on the right.
MR & MRS CALDER ☎(01255) 421519

---

## COLCHESTER • map 6A5

### JACKLINS RESTAURANT
147 High Street, CO1 1PG

*A first-floor restaurant, situated in the town centre on the site of the pottery shops of Roman Colchester. Delightful oak-panelled rooms, where breakfasts, lunches and afternoon teas are served. Also specialist shop downstairs for tobacco products, teas and confectionery.*

FOOD: up to £15    CLUB

**Hours:** meals all day 9.15am-5pm, closed Sunday and bank holidays.

**Cuisine:** ENGLISH - breakfasts, lunches, light meals and afternoon teas.

**Cards:** Visa, Access, AmEx.

**Other points:** children welcome, parking.

**Directions:** 100 yards west of the town hall in the high street.

MR S.H. JACKLIN ☎(01206) 572157

### THE OLD QUEEN'S HEAD
Ford Street, Aldham, CO6 3PH

*Following a major refurbishment, this traditional 17th century inn now boasts an abundance of charm and character with open fires, timber beams and flagstone floors, specializing in good food, real ales and fine wines in warm and friendly surroundings. A main feature of this pub is a beautiful 150-seater canopied patio.*

FOOD: up to £15

**Hours:** lunch 12noon-2pm, dinner 6pm-10pm.

**Cuisine:** ENGLISH - traditional home-cooked fare. Local and seasonal specialities.

**Cards:** Visa, Access, AmEx.

**Other points:** parking, children welcome, open-air dining, vegetarian meals, traditional Sunday lunch.

**Directions:** on A604, off A12.

OLD ENGLISH PUB COMPANY ☎(01206) 241584

### ROSE & CROWN HOTEL
East Street, CO1 2TZ

*The original style of this Tudor building has been carefully retained, while extensively refurbished inside, and is the oldest inn in Britain's oldest recorded town. The restaurant has a cosy cocktail bar and offers fresh home-made food every day of the year. A delightful place for lovers of history. Easy access to all town amenities.*

DOUBLE ROOM: from £29

SINGLE ROOM: from £58

FOOD: up to £15

**Hours:** breakfast 7am-9.30am, lunch 12noon-2pm, dinner 7pm-10pm.

**Cuisine:** FRENCH / ENGLISH - à la carte, fixed-price menu.

**Cards:** Visa, Access, Diners, AmEx.

**Other points:** licensed, children welcome, conferences, residents' lounge, residents' bar, off-street parking.

**Rooms:** 13 single rooms, 11 double rooms, 2 twin rooms, 4 family rooms. All with TV, telephone, tea/coffee-making facilities.

**Directions:** in town centre off A12. Follow signs for university/Rollerworld.

MR BAGHERZADEH ☎(01206) 866677

Fax (01206) 866616

### THE SHEPHERD & DOG
Moor Road, Langham, CO4 5NR

*Set in a small village near Colchester, this pub offers tasty meals presented with care. As this is a free-house, there is a good selection of beers. Booking recommended, as restaurant can be busy.*

FOOD: up to £15    CLUB

**Hours:** lunch 11am-3pm, dinner 6pm-12midnight, last orders 10pm, bar meals 11am-2.30pm, bar meals 6pm-11pm.

**Cuisine:** ENGLISH / CONTINENTAL - bar and restaurant meals with the emphasis on local produce.

**Cards:** Visa, Access, Diners, AmEx.

**Other points:** licensed, open-air dining, Sunday lunch, children welcome, open bank holidays, pets allowed.

**Directions:** first exit off A12 north of Colchester (sign-posted to Langham).

MR PAUL BARNES & MISS JANE GRAHAM ☎(01206) 272711

### THE WAREHOUSE BRASSERIE
12 Chapel Street North, CO2 7AT

*A converted chapel with a unique layout, the Brasserie is an enticingly different restaurant to any other in the area. The menu combines the best of traditional English, provincial French and Mediterranean dishes, presented simply but attractively. This is a very well-known and popular restaurant.*

FOOD: from £15 to £20

**Hours:** lunch 12noon-2pm, dinner 7pm-10pm, closed Sunday evening.

**Cuisine:** ENGLISH / FRENCH - 2-course lunch £8.25.

**Cards:** Visa, Access, Diners, AmEx, Switch.

**Other points:** children welcome, no-smoking area, disabled access, vegetarian meals, air-conditioned, no music.

**Directions:** Located off St John's Street, which can be found at the junctions of Butt Road and Head Street in Colchester town centre.

MR M. BURLEY & MR A. BROOKS ☎(01206) 765656

## HARWICH • map 6A6

### CLIFF HOTEL
Marine Parade, Dovercourt, CO12 3RE

*Overlooking the seafront, this large Victorian hotel is decorated and furnished in keeping with the character of the building. Attractively presented meals are served by friendly, competent staff, and the accommodation is very comfortable. Ideally located on the seafront for holiday-makers.*

DOUBLE ROOM: from £20 to £30

SINGLE ROOM: from £45 to £55

**FOOD:** up to £15
**Hours:** breakfast 7.30am-9.30am, lunch 12.30am-2pm, dinner 6.30pm-9pm, bar meals 12noon-2pm, 6pm-9pm.
**Cuisine:** ENGLISH - wide choice of dishes including fresh fish.
**Cards:** Visa, Access, Diners, AmEx.
**Other points:** licensed, Sunday lunch, children welcome, open bank holidays, afternoon tea.
**Rooms:** 2 single rooms, 11 double rooms, 10 twin rooms, 5 family rooms.
**Directions:** on seafront at Dovercourt.
D. BALAAM & A. LOFTS ☎(01255) 503345
Fax (01255) 240358

### NEW FARM HOUSE
Spinnel's Lane, Wix, CO11 2UJ
*A large modern farmhouse, set in its own well-tended gardens situated on the outskirts of the quiet village of Wix. Comfortable, clean bedrooms complemented by a relaxing and friendly atmosphere.*
**DOUBLE ROOM:** from £20 to £30
**SINGLE ROOM:** up to £25
**FOOD:** up to £15
**Hours:** breakfast 8am-10am, dinner 6.30pm-7pm.
**Cuisine:** ENGLISH
**Cards:** Visa, Access, AmEx.
**Other points:** children welcome, playland, pets allowed, vegetarian meals.
**Rooms:** 2 single rooms, 1 double room, 3 twin rooms, 5 family rooms. All with TV, tea/coffee-making facilities.
**Directions:** follow A120 from Colchester to Harwich. Turn into Wix village, turn left at crossroads and right at the top of the hill.
THE MITCHELL FAMILY ☎(01255) 870365
Fax (01255) 870837

### TOWER HOTEL
Main Road, Dovercourt, CO12 3PJ
*Built in 1885, the main feature of the building is a tower in the north-east corner. Inside, it retains many original architectural features with friezes, cornices and architraves. The Pattrick Suite is a magnificent function room, which is available for private hire.*
**DOUBLE ROOM:** from £20 to £30
**FOOD:** up to £15
**Hours:** breakfast 8am-9.30am, lunch 12noon-2pm, dinner 6.30pm-9.30pm.
**Cuisine:** ENGLISH / SEAFOOD - fresh local lobster and Dover sole.
**Cards:** Visa, Access, Diners, AmEx.
**Other points:** licensed, Sunday lunch, children welcome.
**Rooms:** 2 single rooms, 8 double rooms, 2 twin rooms, 2 family rooms.
**Directions:** on the left side of A136 (Harwich bound) near Dovercourt station.
DOUGLAS HUTCHINS ☎(01255) 504952

## SAFFRON WALDEN • map 6B4

### THE BLUEBELL
Hempstead, CB10 2PD
*A beautiful 300-year-old country inn set in a quiet village, close to the Essex/Suffolk border. The Bluebell is the birthplace of the notorious outlaw Dick Turpin, who ran a butcher's shop from what is now the bar. Nearby places to visit include Duxford Air Museum and Cambridge.*
**FOOD:** from £15 to £20
**Hours:** lunch and bar meals 12noon-2pm, and 6.30-9.30pm, open bank holidays.
**Cuisine:** game and seasonal specialities.
**Cards:** Visa, Access, AmEx.
**Other points:** extensive bar, patio, beer garden, large car park.
**Directions:** situated halfway between Saffron Walden and Steeple Bumpstead, on the B1054.
OLD ENGLISH PUB COMPANY PLC. ☎(01799) 599486

## SOUTHEND-ON-SEA • map 6B5

### LA POUBELLE
50A Hamlet Court Road, Westcliff, SS0 7LX
*A small, friendly, family-run restaurant with an emphasis on good, honest, fresh food in comfortable surroundings. An informal atmosphere provides the ideal ambience for pleasant dining. Very popular locally, so booking is advised.*
**FOOD:** up to £15
**Hours:** Sunday lunch 12.30am-2.15pm, dinner 7pm (last orders 10.30pm), closed Sunday evening and Monday.
**Cuisine:** INTERNATIONAL - paella, chicken breast in Stilton sauce, braised lamb fillet, home-smoked produce. All dishes home-prepared and cooked. Set-price menus from £7.50. Menu changes monthly
**Cards:** Visa, Access.
**Other points:** licensed, Sunday lunch, children welcome.
**Directions:** on shopping street near Westcliff railway station, 5 minutes from seafront, Cliffs Pavilion and Palace Theatre.
MR & MRS R.C. BERNER ☎(01702) 351894

### ROSLIN HOTEL
Thorpe Esplanade, Thorpe Bay, SS1 3BG
*Situated on the seafront, the Roslin Hotel boasts one of the finest views of the Thames estuary in residential Thorpe Bay. Facilities for golfing, sailing, tennis, bowling, horse-riding, ten-pin bowling. Weekend bargain breaks. Temporary membership of local leisure centre for residents.*
**DOUBLE ROOM:** from £30 to £40
**SINGLE ROOM:** from £35 to £45
**FOOD:** up to £15
**Hours:** lunch 12.30am-2pm, dinner 6.30pm-9.30pm.
**Cuisine:** ENGLISH - noisette of lamb gascoigne,

veal milanese, local trout with chestnut and cucumber. Sunday lunches. Vegetarian menu. A la carte and table d'hôte menus.
**Cards:** Visa, Access, Diners, AmEx.
**Other points:** Sunday lunch, children welcome, residents' lounge, residents' bar, disabled access.
**Rooms:** 18 single rooms, 20 double/twin rooms. All with satellite TV, radio, alarm, telephone, tea/coffee-making facilities, hair dryer.
**Directions:** close to the seafront.
MR K.G. OLIVER ☎(01702) 586375

### TOWER HOTEL AND RESTAURANT
146 Alexandra Road, SS1 1HE
*Built in 1901 as a unique gentleman's residence, Taranaki, it first became a hotel in 1923. Fully renovated and restored in the elegant ambience of the era, it combines every modern convenience and luxury. The `tower' rooms afford views of the Thames estuary and the Kentish coastline. To complement a comfortable stay in luxurious accomodation, a superb English breakfast is served daily. Just a few minutes' walk from the town's finest amenities.*
DOUBLE ROOM: from £20 to £30
SINGLE ROOM: from £29 to £45
FOOD: up to £15
**Hours:** breakfast weekdays 7am-9am, weekends 8am-10am; dinner 6.30pm-9.30pm; bar snacks 6.30pm-11pm; closed Sunday evening.
**Cuisine:** ENGLISH
**Cards:** Visa, Access, Diners, AmEx.
**Other points:** children welcome, Sunday lunch, disabled access, pets allowed, residents' lounge, vegetarian meals.
**Rooms:** 13 single rooms, 10 double rooms, 6 twin rooms, 3 family rooms.
**Directions:** phone hotel for verbal or faxed directions.
MR M. TAYLOR ☎(01702) 348635 Fax(01702) 433044

## WOODFORD GREEN
See London Region

# HERTFORDSHIRE

## BALDOCK • map 6A4

### THE JESTER HOTEL
116 Station Road, Odsey, SG7 5RS
*Set in pleasant gardens, The Jester Hotel offers comfortable accommodation and well-presented meals at value-for-money prices. Popular with locals, the hotel enjoys a relaxed atmosphere.*
DOUBLE ROOM: from £20 to £30
SINGLE ROOM: from £35 to £45
FOOD: up to £15
**Hours:** breakfast 7am-10am, lunch 12noon-3pm, dinner 7pm-10pm, bar meals 11.30am-2.30pm, 6.30pm-10pm.
**Cuisine:** ENGLISH - serving bar snacks, table d'hôte and full à la carte menu. Home-made pies and puddings, choice of fresh fish plus blackboard specials.
**Cards:** Visa, Access, Diners, AmEx, Switch.
**Other points:** licensed, open-air dining, Sunday lunch, no-smoking area, no-smoking conservatory, children welcome, garden, wedding and function specialists.
**Rooms:** 3 single rooms, 8 double rooms, 3 twin rooms.
**Directions:** just off A505 between Royston and Baldock. Turn off Steeple Morden. Opposite Ashwell and Morden station.
DEN & PAM MILDENHALL-CLARKE ☎(01462) 742011 Fax(01462) 742011

## BISHOP'S STORTFORD • map 6B4

### PEARSE HOUSE
Parsonage Lane, CM23 5BQ
*Pearse House is an established management training and conference centre, offering residential conference facilities of the highest standard. It is easily accessible by road, rail and air and just one hour from London. All rooms are equipped with the most modern business facilities. The attractive modern bedrooms offer comfortable accommodation, and leisure facilities are also available on site and close by.*
DOUBLE ROOM: from £20 to £30
SINGLE ROOM: from £35 to £45
FOOD: from £15 to £20
**Hours:** breakfast 7.30am-9am, lunch 12noon-2pm, dinner 6.30pm-9pm, bar snacks 3pm-10.30pm.
**Cuisine:** BRITISH - there is a good selection of fine wines to accompany your meal.
**Cards:** Visa, Access, AmEx.
**Other points:** parking, children welcome, limited disabled access, residents' lounge, vegetarian meals, conferences.
**Rooms:** 23 single rooms, 8 double rooms.
**Directions:** situated in Parsonage Lane off Dunmow Road (B1250), which leads from town centre to M11. From motorway (M11), 2 minutes' drive following signs to Bishop's Stortford; or follow signs from Stansted Road (B1184). Ten minutes from Stansted Airport.
VALERIE MCGREGOR ☎(01279) 757400
Fax(01279) 506591

## HEMEL HEMPSTEAD • map 5B3

### THE SWAN INN BOXMOOR
London Road, Boxmoor, HP1 2RA
*A 300-year-old Georgian inn, recently converted into a delightful air-conditioned restaurant/bistro with private dining facility offering a mix of*

traditional English, French and ethnic dishes in generous portions served by efficient, friendly staff. Sunday traditional roasts a speciality. Unobtrusive atmosphere.
**FOOD:** up to £15
**Hours:** lunch (Monday to Saturday) 12noon-2.30pm, dinner (Monday to Saturday) 6pm-10.30pm, Sunday brunch from 9.30am, Sunday lunches 12noon-9.30pm.
**Cuisine:** TRADITIONAL ENGLISH/FRENCH/ETHNIC roasts.
**Cards:** Visa, Access, Switch.
**Other points:** car park, children welcome, no smoking area, conference facilities, vegetarian meals, afternoon teas, traditional Sunday lunch.
**Directions:** proceed towards Berkhamsted on A4251 past BR station. 1st pub on road.
MR JAMES MUNDY ☎(01442) 253521 Fax(01442) 216862

## HERTFORD • map 6B4

 **SALISBURY ARMS HOTEL**
Fore Street, SG14 1BZ
*Hertford's oldest hostelry, offering guests the opportunity to enjoy excellent food, traditional ales and a warm welcome in surroundings that retain all the character and charm of a bygone age. The oak-beamed and wood panelled restaurant offers exceptional cuisine, and the well-appointed bedrooms are furnished in a blend of subtle pastel shades, complementing the cottage atmosphere.*
DOUBLE ROOM: from £30
SINGLE ROOM: from £45
FOOD: from £15 to £20
**Hours:** breakfast 7am-9am, lunch 12noon-2pm, dinner 7pm-10pm.
**Cuisine:** INTERNATIONAL
**Cards:** Visa, Access, Diners, AmEx.
**Other points:** licensed.
**Rooms:** 29 bedrooms.
**Directions:** A414 to Hertford from A10.
MRS O'REGAN ☎(01992) 583091 Fax(01992) 552510

## HITCHIN • map 6A4

 **REDCOATS FARMHOUSE HOTEL**
Redcoats Green, SG4 7JR
*A 15th century farmhouse set in beautiful grounds amid the rolling Hertfordshire countryside near Little Wymondley village, yet only minutes from the A1. Full of English charm, with its beamed and comfortable interior, bar and lounge, the intimate quiet of the dining rooms and individual character of the bedrooms, Redcoats exudes an air of peace and tranquility. Excellent food and efficient service. Ideally situated for visiting Knebworth and Woburn parks. Bargain-break weekends available.*
DOUBLE ROOM: from £25 to £46
SINGLE ROOM: from £39 to £75 (en suite)
FOOD: from £20 to £28
**Hours:** breakfast 7am-9am, club lunch 12noon-2pm, club supper from 7pm, dinner, 7pm-9.30pm, lunch 12noon-1.30pm.

**Cuisine:** ENGLISH / FRENCH
**Cards:** Visa, Access, Diners, AmEx.
**Other points:** parking, children welcome, no-smoking area, residents' lounge, vegetarian meals, open-air dining.
**Rooms:** 1 single room, 10 double rooms, 3 twin rooms.
**Directions:** junction 8 on A1M. South of Little Wymondley. Follow signs for Todds Green, then Redcoats Green.
PETER BUTTERFIELD & JACKIE GAINSFORD ☎(01438) 729500 Fax(01438) 723322

## ROYSTON • map 6A4

 **BRITISH RAJ BANGLADESHI RESTAURANT**
55 High Street, SG8 9AW
*Reputed to be one of East Anglia's best Indian restaurants and one of the top 100 curry houses. In a varied menu, dishes may include such specialities as shooting bird bhuna, fixed bayonet poussin, crab rezalla, meat jaljalae chicken silsila and the latest, all the Balti dishes. Silver Award winner in Best Menu category, Top 30 in Best in Britain category, listed in Real Curry Restaurant guide amongst others. Highly recommended.*
FOOD: up to £15   CLUB
**Hours:** lunch 12noon-3pm, dinner 6pm-12midnight.
**Cuisine:** BANGLADESHI-INDIAN - lamb masala: a whole leg of lamb cooked for four. Tandoori, royal, karai dishes. English menu also available. Thalia dishes including wedding feast. Weekday business lunch and Saturday/Sunday buffet lunch.
**Cards:** Visa, Access, Diners, AmEx.
**Other points:** children welcome.
**Directions:** situated in Royston, on the A10.
NAZIR UDDIN CHOUDHURY ☎(01763) 241471

**THE FOX & DUCK**
The Green, Therfield, SG8 9PN
*This former Victorian hotel, now a delightful country inn with a friendly atmosphere is situated on the edge of an attractive village green. The menu offers a wide range of choices from a full meal to a light snack. Ideal for visiting Duxford Air Museum and the university city of Cambridge.*
FOOD: from £15 to £20
**Hours:** lunch 12noon-2.30pm (bar 3pm.), dinner from 6pm.
**Cuisine:** wide variety of seasonal dishes.
**Cards:** Access,Visa,AmEx
**Other points:** garden, patio, parking.
**Directions:** 1 mile south of Royston off the A505.
JOHN & LIZ MANN ☎(01763) 287246

## WATFORD • map 5B3

**UPTON LODGE**
Upton Road, WD1 2EL
*Upton Lodge is owned by the same family-run company that operates The White House Hotel,*

situated directly across the road. This cosy lodge is well designed and appointed to a high level of comfort. Although the reception is at The White House Hotel, guests receive their own key to the front door of the Lodge and are most welcome to use the facilities of the main hotel.
DOUBLE ROOM: from £20 to £30
SINGLE ROOM: from £31 to £40
FOOD: from £15 to £20
**Hours:** breakfast 7.30am-10am, lunch 12noon-2pm, dinner 6.30pm-9.45pm.
**Cuisine:** ENGLISH / INTERNATIONAL - all food taken at The White House opposite.
**Cards:** Visa, Diners, AmEx, Switch, MasterCard.
**Other points:** parking, children welcome, pets allowed, no-smoking areas, garden.
**Rooms:** 22 bedrooms. All with TV, telephone, tea/coffee-making facilities, trouser press. No-smoking rooms available.
**Directions:** just off the ring road at the junction with Cassio Road, near Watford town centre.
MR I.F. HARTOG ☎(01923) 237316 Fax(01923) 233109

### THE WHITE HOUSE HOTEL
Upton Road, WD1 2EL
Privately-owned and run by a professional, caring staff, The White House is popular with both discerning business executives and well-travelled tourists. A high standard prevails throughout this well-appointed hotel, which offers luxury three-star accommodation and superb international cuisine. (See also UPTON LODGE)
DOUBLE ROOM: from £30 to £40
SINGLE ROOM: from £55
FOOD: from £15 to £20 ☜CLUB
**Hours:** breakfast 7.30am-10am, lunch 12noon-2pm, dinner 6.30pm-9.45pm.

**Cuisine:** BRITISH / INTERNATIONAL
**Cards:** Visa, Access, Diners, AmEx.
**Other points:** children welcome, parking.
**Rooms:** 58 bedrooms. All with TV, telephone, radio, hair dryer, trouser-press, tea/coffee-making facilities. No-smoking rooms available.
**Directions:** Just off the ring road at the junction of Cassio Road, near the town centre.
MR I.F. HARTOG ☎(01923) 237316 Fax(01923) 233109

## WATTON-AT-STONE • map 6B4

### THE GEORGE & DRAGON
High Street, SG14 3TA
An attractive 16th century extended village pub with patio and car park at the rear. The welcoming, comfortable interior gives it a warm glow and the traditional bar meals and comprehensive à la carte menu are complemented by the delicious home-made sweets. Large garden at rear.
FOOD: up to £15
**Hours:** lunch (restaurant and bar) 12noon-2pm, dinner 7pm-10pm. Restaurant closed Sunday night. Closed Christmas day.
**Cuisine:** an imaginative menu includes medallions of venison in port and juniper berry sauce, lamb's liver cooked au poivre, half a fresh lobster with fresh mussels and darne of fresh salmon baked in whisky and fresh lemon juice. Good selection of home-made puddings and bar meals.
**Cards:** Access, AmEx, Visa, Diners, Switch
**Other points:** parking, residents' lounge and garden, outdoor dining, vegetarian meals, traditional Sunday lunch, children catered for (please check for age limits).
**Directions:** in centre of the village on A602 between Hertford and Stevenage.
MR AND MRS DINNIN ☎(01920) 830285

# KENT

## ASHFORD • map 6C5

### THE ROYAL STANDARD
Ashford Road, Bethersden, TN26 3LF
A popular free-house with a warm and friendly atmosphere, offering a very good selection of meals at reasonable prices. Dine in the restaurant or the bar, beside the warmth of log fires in winter or in the large garden during summer. A visit at any time of the year is memorable.
FOOD: up to £15
**Hours:** lunch 12noon-2pm, dinner 7pm-9.30pm, open every day including bank holidays.
**Cuisine:** ENGLISH - traditional, featuring home-made dishes including a vegetarian selection. Large no-smoking area in the restaurant.
**Cards:** Visa, Eurocard, MasterCard.
**Other points:** parking, garden, patio, play area, no-smoking area.
**Directions:** On A28, 1 mile west of Bethersden.
ROGER HAMBERG ☎(01233) 820280

## BIRCHINGTON • map 6C6

### SMUGGLERS RESTAURANT
212 Canterbury Road, CT7 9AB
A comfortable, welcoming restaurant, which offers a very extensive choice of well-cooked food. The cuisine is predominantly French, with dishes ranging from salmon with a prawn-and-dill sauce to fillet steak cooked in brandy and French mustard. All dishes are made from fresh ingredients and attractively presented. The quality of the food is complemented by excellent service.
FOOD: up to £20 ☜
**Hours:** lunch 12noon-2pm, dinner 7pm-10pm, closed Monday lunch.
**Cuisine:** FRENCH / ENGLISH - table d'hôte menus and extensive à la carte menu. Duckling aux cerises, châteaubriand, fish dishes.
**Cards:** Visa, Access, Diners, AmEx.
**Other points:** licensed, open-air dining, Sunday lunch, children welcome, functions.
**Directions:** on road to Margate from Thanet Way,

just past Birchington roundabout.
BOB & SUE SHERMAN ☎(01843) 841185

## BROADSTAIRS • map 6C6

### THE TARTAR FRIGATE
Harbour Street, CT10 1EU
*An attractive 17th century flint pub with superb views over Broadstairs harbour. The first-floor seafood restaurant is beautifully appointed, and the menu is a culinary delight, with many unique dishes. With the restaurant being so close to the harbour, you may feel inclined to walk a delicious meal off along the seafront.*
FOOD: from £15 to £20
Hours: lunch 12noon-2.30pm, dinner 7pm-9.45pm.
Cuisine: SEAFOOD - à la carte and table d'hôte menu, freshly cooked dishes in generous portions, children's menu available.
Cards: All cards except AmEx.
Other points: parking, children welcome, vegetarian meals, traditional Sunday lunch.
Directions: opposite picturesque Broadstairs harbour.
THORLEY TAVERNS ☎(01843) 862013
Fax(01843) 230231

## CANTERBURY • map 6C5

 THE GREEN MAN
Shatterling, near Wingham, CT3 1JR
*Old English country inn with garden, set in an area known for its hop-growing and vine culture. Two `bat & trap pitches'. Ideal for golfing breaks with 6 major golf courses nearby. Easy access to Dover and Ramsgate ports with Canterbury a mere 7 miles away.*
DOUBLE ROOM: from £30 to £40
SINGLE ROOM: up to £20
FOOD: up to £15
Hours: breakfast 7.45am-9am, lunch 12noon-2pm, dinner 7pm-8.45pm (last orders), closed Sunday evening except for residents.
Cuisine: ENGLISH - genuine English home-cooking with a range of à la carte food. Bar meals are also available.
Cards: Visa, Access.
Other points: open-air dining, Sunday lunch, children welcome at owners discretion, special rates available for family room.
Rooms: 3 twin rooms, 1 family room en suite. All with TV, tea/coffee-making facilities.
Directions: on the A257 between Wingham and Ash.
MR FERNE & MR GREENWOOD ☎(01304) 812525

### THE THREE TUNS INN
Staple, near Canterbury, CT3 1LN
*A family-run free-house situated 9 miles from Canturbury and 5 miles from the historic town of Sandwich. Here you can enjoy good home-cooked meals in a friendly atmosphere or stay in the new,*

tastefully furnished chalet accommodation, whilst visiting this beautiful part of England.*
DOUBLE ROOM: from £25 to £30
SINGLE ROOM: from £35
FOOD: from £15
Hours: breakfast, lunch and dinner served daily.
Cuisine: BRITISH - steaks, fresh fish, vegetable dishes: good, wholesome traditional meals.
Cards: Visa, Access, AmEx.
Other points: parking, children welcome, conference facilities, garden, open-air dining, vegetarian meals, traditional Sunday lunch, payphone available.
Rooms: 8 bedrooms. All en suite with TV, tea/coffee-making facilities. Radio, alarm, hairdryer available on request.
Directions: take the A2 to Barham, followed by the B2046 to Wingham. The Three Tuns Inn may be found by following signs towards Staple.
RICHARD GUNNER ☎(01304) 812317
Fax(01304) 812317

## EDENBRIDGE • map 6C4

### CASTLE INN
Chiddingstone, TN8 7AH
*The Castle Inn is a delightful oak-beamed pub in the centre of one of Kent's most unspoilt villages. Enjoy traditional English bar food from the comfort of the Saloon Bar or in the pretty cottage garden during summertime. There is a separate restaurant with formal waiter service and an ever-changing menu. Extensive list of over 150 wines and three hand-pumped draught beers.*
FOOD: from £15 to £20
Hours: lunch 12noon-2pm, dinner 7.30pm-9.30pm.
Cuisine: ENGLISH / CONTINENTAL - mainly British with European overtones. Roast rib beef, roast rack of lamb, local game, fresh fish, fresh vegetables.
Cards: Visa, Access, Diners, AmEx.
Other points: licensed, Sunday lunch, children welcome.
Directions: 1.5 miles south of the B2027 Edenbridge to Tonbridge road.
NIGEL D. LUCAS ☎(01892) 870247 Fax(01892) 870808

### THE VILLAGE TEA SHOP
3 The Village, Chiddingstone, TN8 7AH
*The Village Tea Shop in the Old Coach House helps to set the scene in the picturesque historic village of Chiddingstone. Inside this lovely restaurant, the aroma of freshly-made coffee and home-baked scones will entice you to relax over morning coffee, afternoon tea or enjoy a tasty lunch, before continuing on your expedition around this beautiful village.*
FOOD: up to £15
Hours: lunch 11am-3pm, afternoon tea until 5.30pm.
Cuisine: ENGLISH - hearty traditional meals with a vegetarian selection. Lunch menu from £2.95.
Other points: children welcome, no-smoking area, disabled access.

**Directions:** off B2027 between Tonbridge and Edenbridge, within the National Trust village of Chiddingstone.
MR D. AITCHISON ☎(01892) 870326 Fax (01892) 870326

## ICKHAM • map 6C5

### THE DUKE WILLIAM
The Street, CT3 1QP

*A 16th century free house in a picturesque village surrounded by farmlands. There is a lovely garden to the rear, with ponds, a fountain and flowers, as well as swings for the children. Situated only ten minutes from Canterbury, Ickham is central for Kent's many tourist attractions.*
**FOOD:** from £20 to £25
**Hours:** open every day 11am-2.30pm and 6pm-10.30pm - food available during these hours in both bar and restaurant.
**Cuisine:** ENGLISH / INTERNATIONAL - extensive seafood menu, beef, lamb, poultry, veal. In the bar: omelettes, fish, home-made soup, chilli, home-baked bread. Exciting bar meals.
**Cards:** Visa, Access, Diners, AmEx.
**Other points:** air-conditioned restaurants, no-smoking conservatory, licensed, open-air dining, Sunday lunch, children welcome, pets allowed, conservatory, garden.
**Directions:** in the centre of Ickham, which is signposted from the A257.
MR A. ROBIN & MRS C.A. MCNEILL ☎(01227) 721308

## MAIDSTONE • map 6C5

### THE LIMETREE RESTAURANT AND HOTEL

The Limes, The Square, Lenham, ME17 2PQ

*Situated in the picturesque old Kentish village of Lenham, this family-run establishment is steeped in history, boasting timber frames dating back to the 14th century. Sympathetically renovated and refurbished, the hotel still retains many traditional features of a 600-year-old building. The seven en suite bedrooms are all comfortably furnished, and the restaurant specializes in classic French and continental cuisine. The atmosphere is relaxed and informal. Small weddings and parties can be catered for. Ideally located for motorway and channel ports, with the beautiful Leeds Castle just five miles away.*
**DOUBLE ROOM:** from £20 to £30

**SINGLE ROOM:** from £35 to £45
**FOOD:** up to £30 🍽 🍴
**Hours:** breakfast 7am-9am, lunch 12noon-2.30pm, bar snacks 12noon-2.30pm, dinner 7pm-10.30pm, bar snacks 7pm-10.30pm.
**Cuisine:** ENGLISH / FRENCH - an extensive à la carte menu and set menu Monday to Sunday.
**Other points:** parking, children welcome, Sunday lunch, open bank holidays, no-smoking area, afternoon tea, vegetarian meals, open-air dining, garden, licensed.
**Rooms:** 2 double rooms, 3 twin rooms, 1 family room, 1 four-poster room. All with TV, telephone, tea/coffee-making facilities.
**Directions:** situated in the square just off the A20.
MUSA KIVRAK ☎(01622) 859509 Fax (01622) 850096

## MARGATE • map 6C6

### IVYSIDE HOTEL
25 Sea Road, Westgate-on-Sea, CT8 8SB

*The Ivyside overlooks the sea, standing in its own grounds. Tourists, conference delegates and families blend well to make an excellent atmosphere. Good value, open 24 hours, with super sports complex and swimming pools.*
**DOUBLE ROOM:** from £24 to £27
**SINGLE ROOM:** from £28 to £32
**FOOD:** up to £15
**Hours:** breakfast 7am-10am, lunch 12.30am-2.30pm, bar meals 12noon-2pm & 6pm-10pm, dinner 6.30pm-9pm.
**Cuisine:** TRADITIONAL ENGLISH - à la carte and vegetarian, junior menu.
**Cards:** Visa, Access, AmEx.
**Other points:** indoor swimming pool, spa pool, paddling pool, outdoor swimming pool, steam room, sauna, massage, squash, children welcome, family suites, baby-listening, entertainment.
**Rooms:** 75 bedrooms. All en suite.
**Directions:** A28 from Canterbury or A299 from M2. Close to Canterbury and Ramsgate.
MICHAEL WISEMAN ☎(01843) 831082 Fax (01843) 831082

### KINGSDOWN HOTEL
59-61 Harold Road, Cliftonville, CT9 2HS

*A Victorian hotel, situated near the main shopping area and seafront, offering pleasantly decorated and spotlessly clean accommodation. The warm and courteous service and welcoming atmosphere attracts business people and tourists alike.*
**DOUBLE ROOM:** up to £20

SINGLE ROOM: up to £25
FOOD: up to £15
**Hours:** breakfast 9am-9.30am, bar snacks 12.30am-2pm, dinner 6pm.
**Cuisine:** ENGLISH - winner of Thanet Clean Food Award and Kent Heart Beat Award. Highly commended.
**Cards:** Visa, Access, AmEx.
**Other points:** free phone 0500 543262, children welcome, afternoon tea, parking.
**Rooms:** 4 single rooms, 5 double room, 10 twin rooms. Some en suite.
**Directions:** follow A28 to Margate or follow the Isle of Thanet signs.
MR JAMES WILLIAMS ☎(01843) 221672

## PENSHURST • map 6C4

### THE SPOTTED DOG
Smarts Hill, TN11 8EE
*Originally established in 1520, having started life as a row of cottages. The pub sign was intended to represent the coat of arms of the Sydney family who resided at Penshurst Place. A short-sighted painter mistook the leopard on the family crest for a spotted hunting dog, since when the pub has been known as The Spotted Dog. A typical Kentish pub with good food and a warm, hearty welcome. A large garden and terraced area complements the warm atmosphere inside.*
FOOD: up to £15
**Hours:** bar meals 12noon-2.15pm, bar meals 7pm-9.45pm, dinner 7.15pm-10pm.
**Cuisine:** ENGLISH / FRENCH - traditional English and French, complemented by a fine wine list. Dishes may include roast half-rack of lamb and monkfish, king prawn and scallop ragout. Wide choice of vegetarian dishes, fresh fish in abundance.
**Cards:** Visa, Access, Diners, AmEx, Switch.
**Other points:** licensed, open-air dining, Sunday lunch, children welcome, parking, vegetarian meals.
**Directions:** B2176 and B2110. Through Penshurst village, third turning on the right.
ANDY & NIKKI TUCKER ☎(01892) 870253
Fax(01892) 870107

## PLUCKLEY • map 6C5

### THE DERING ARMS
Station Road, near Ashford, TN27 0RR
*Originally built as a hunting lodge for the Dering family, the inn has some unusual features such as the curved Dutch gables and the windows. Visitors to The Dering Arms are assured of a varied choice of real ales and fine wines. Good home-made food is served seven days a week, and comfortable accommodation is available throughout the year. Friendly and welcoming.*
DOUBLE ROOM: up to £20
SINGLE ROOM: from £25 to £35
FOOD: from £15 to £20
**Hours:** dinner 6.30pm-11pm, last orders 2pm and 10pm, lunch (Monday-Saturday) 12noon-3pm, Sundays 12noon-2pm.

**Cuisine:** ENGLISH - continually changing menu: seafood specials and daily specials. Restaurant and bar menus.
**Cards:** Visa, Access, AmEx.
**Other points:** licensed, Sunday lunch, garden.
**Rooms:** 2 double rooms, 1 twin room.
**Directions:** on Bethersden Road, 100 yards from Pluckley railway station.
MR JAMES BUSS ☎(01233) 840371 Fax(01233) 840498

## RAMSGATE • map 6C6

### MORTON'S FORK
42 Station Road, Minster, CT12 4BZ
*A charming 17th century restaurant and wine bar, situated in a quiet, historical village, only 5 miles from Ramsgate. Charming ambience with a menu that offers good regional and imaginative dishes. The guest rooms have been attractively refurbished, retaining character yet providing modern conveniences.*
DOUBLE ROOM: from £20 to £30
SINGLE ROOM: from £35 to £45
FOOD: from £15 to £20 CLUB
**Hours:** lunch 11.30am-2pm, dinner 6.30pm-10pm.
**Cuisine:** BRITISH / CONTINENTAL - including salmon parcel and chicken stuffed with crab. Good vegetarian dishes available. Also good wholesome bar meals available.
**Cards:** Visa, Access, Diners, AmEx.
**Other points:** Sunday lunch, children welcome, parking, vegetarian meals, residents' bar, disabled access.
**Rooms:** 3 double rooms. All with TV, telephone, tea/coffee-making facilities.
**Directions:** follow the A28, exit onto A253. Turn left for Minster village.
MR DAVID J. SWORDER ☎(01843) 823000
Fax(01843) 821224

## ROYAL TUNBRIDGE WELLS • map 6D4

### PORTOVINO'S RESTAURANT
Church Road, TN4 0XY
*An attractive Edwardian-style house, with a delightfully furnished green and white interior and fresh flowers. Comfortable, clean and very efficiently run, offering fine food and wine in a restful and pleasing atmosphere.*
FOOD: from £15 to £20 CLUB
**Hours:** lunch 12noon-2.30pm, dinner 7pm-10pm; closed Sunday evening and Monday.
**Cuisine:** ENGLISH / CONTINENTAL - à la carte and table d'hôte menus, offering an extensive selection of dishes, complemented by a fine wine list. Vegetarian meals also available.
**Cards:** Visa, Access, AmEx.
**Other points:** licensed, Sunday lunch, children welcome, parking.
**Directions:** off Southborough Common on A26 between Tunbridge and Tunbridge Wells.
ANDREW BOND ☎(01892) 513161 Fax(01892) 513161

### RUSSELL HOTEL
80 London Road, TN1 1DZ

*The Russell Hotel is a large Victorian house furnished to a high standard. It is situated facing the common and is only a few minutes' walk from the town centre. This hotel offers generous portions of appetizing meals, cooked from local fresh produce. The staff are welcoming and helpful, making a stay here very comfortable. Residents' lounge in annexe.*
DOUBLE ROOM: from £40 to £50
SINGLE ROOM: from £68
FOOD: from £15 to £20    CLUB
**Hours:** breakfast 7am-9.30am, Sunday 8am-10am, dinner 7pm-9.30pm, Sunday 7pm-9pm.
**Cuisine:** MODERN ENGLISH - à la carte menu, fixed three-course menu, bar snacks. Dishes include stuffed mushrooms, veal cooked in marsala and cream, and grilled steak in mustard sauce.
**Cards:** Visa, Access, Diners, AmEx, JCB.
**Other points:** children welcome, foreign exchange, residents' lounge, residents' bar, vegetarian meals, parking.
**Rooms:** 2 single rooms, 11 double rooms, 13 twin rooms. All with TV, telephone, tea/coffee-making facilities, hair dryer. Some no-smoking rooms.
**Directions:** take M25 exit 5. Follow A21 south and join A26. On A26 near A264 junction.
MR & MRS K.A. WILKINSON ☎(01892) 544833
Fax(01892) 515846

## SEVENOAKS • map 6C4

### MOORINGS HOTEL
97 Hitchen Hatch Lane, TN13 3BE

*A small, friendly family hotel offering a high standard of accommodation for tourists and business travellers. One especially pleasant feature is the range of garden patio bedrooms, which are arranged like a small motel around a secluded lawn. Sevenoaks is a pleasant Kentish market town within easy reach of many places of historical interest. The newly refurbished restaurant opened January 1994.*
DOUBLE ROOM: from £20 to £30
SINGLE ROOM: from £25 to £42
FOOD: up to £15    CLUB
**Hours:** breakfast weekdays 7.30am-9am, weekends 8am-9am, dinner 7pm-9pm.
**Cuisine:** INTERNATIONAL
**Cards:** Visa, Access, AmEx, JCB.
**Other points:** children welcome, no-smoking area, vegetarian meals, garden, residents' bar, residents' lounge, parking.
**Rooms:** 24 bedrooms.
**Directions:** situated on the A224, two minutes from the M25. 200 yards from Sevenoaks BR station.
FIONA & TIM RYAN ☎(01732) 452589
Fax(01732) 456462

### SEVENOAKS PARK HOTEL
Seal Hollow Road, TN13 3SH

*The Sevenoaks Park Hotel is a charming building standing in 3 acres of Elizabethan gardens overlooking superb views of Knole Park. Offering*

*well-cooked and presented cuisine and attractive comfortable accommodation, the hotel provides guests with a pleasant and welcoming atmosphere. An ideal base for touring areas of interest such as Royal Tunbridge Wells and Leeds Castle.*
DOUBLE ROOM: up to £20
SINGLE ROOM: from £30
FOOD: up to £15
**Hours:** breakfast 7am-9.30am, dinner 7pm-9.30pm.
**Cuisine:** MODERN ENGLISH - à la carte, table d'hôte: dishes include poached salmon served in lemon and mustard sauce, breast of duck fried and served with strawberry and blackcurrant.
**Cards:** Visa, Access, Diners, AmEx.
**Other points:** licensed, open-air dining, Sunday lunch, children welcome, afternoon tea, swimming pool.
**Rooms:** 2 single rooms, 10 double rooms, 20 twin rooms, 1 family room. All with TV, radio, telephone.
**Directions:** off A225.
MR NOBLE & MR HUNTLEY ☎(01732) 454245
Fax(01732) 457468

## SITTINGBOURNE • map 6C5

### CONISTON HOTEL
70 London Road, ME10 1NT

*The hotel is very well placed for visiting Kent's many sights and attractions. The ballroom can seat 160 people and is available for private hire.*
DOUBLE ROOM: from £20 to £30
SINGLE ROOM: from £49
FOOD: from £15 to £25
**Hours:** breakfast 7.30am-9.30am, lunch 12noon-2.30pm, dinner 7pm-10pm, open 7 days.
**Cuisine:** ENGLISH / SEAFOOD - speciality: Dover sole.
**Cards:** Visa, Access, Diners, AmEx.
**Other points:** traditional Sunday lunch, children welcome, coaches by prior arrangement, charge for pets.
**Rooms:** 16 single rooms, 14 double rooms, 16 twin rooms, 5 family rooms. All with TV, telephone, tea/coffee-making facilities.
**Directions:** on the A2, .5 mile from the town centre.
MR S. KLECZKOWSKI ☎(01795) 472131/427907
Fax(01795) 428056

## TONBRIDGE • map 6C4

### THE CHASER INN
Stumble Hill, Shipbourne, TN11 9PE

*Built in the 1880s, The Chaser Inn is an attractive colonial-style building. An extensive and imaginative range of food is offered in the bars and*

a creative set menu can be enjoyed in the restaurant, which features a beamed vaulted ceiling and panelled walls. Only minutes from the M25, M20 and M26 motorway networks, The Chaser Inn is well placed to greet travellers.
DOUBLE ROOM: from £20 to £30
SINGLE ROOM: from £45 to £55
FOOD: from £20 to £25
**Hours:** breakfast 7.30am-9.30am, lunch 12.30am-2pm, dinner 7.30pm-9.30pm, bar meals 12noon-2pm, 7pm-9.30pm.
**Cuisine:** ENGLISH / FRENCH - table d'hôte menu in restaurant. Dishes may include lamb fillet on a raspberry and mint sauce, lemon sole. Also bar snacks.
**Cards:** Visa, Access, AmEx.
**Other points:** licensed, open-air dining, Sunday lunch, children welcome, functions, baby-listening device, cots, 24hr reception, residents' bar, vegetarian meals, parking, residents' lounge, disabled access.
**Rooms:** 5 single rooms, 6 double rooms, 4 twin rooms. All with TV, telephone, tea/coffee-making facilities.
**Directions:** On A227, north of Tonbridge. Next to Shipbourne church and opposite green.
MICHAEL AND VIVIEN NIX ☎(01732) 810360
Fax(01732) 810941

#### ☲ THE OFFICE WINE BAR
163 High Street, TN9 1BX
A 16th century half-brick timbered building in Tonbridge High Street, offering a very warm and friendly bistro-style atmosphere. The menu and wine list are extensive, the service polite and efficient. An ideal stop-off for tourists who wish to visit Tonbridge Castle, Penshurst Place, Tunbridge Wells, and the beautiful Kent countryside.
FOOD: up to £15
**Hours:** lunch 12noon-2pm, dinner 7pm-9.30pm, bar 10.30am-2.30pm, bar 6pm-11pm, closed Sunday and bank holidays.
**Cuisine:** ENGLISH - bistro-style menu, with an added touch of French. Wide choice of dishes, nicely presented. Vegetarian dishes also available.
**Cards:** Visa, Access, Diners, AmEx.
**Other points:** licensed, children welcome.
**Directions:** situated at north end of the High Street, near Tonbridge School.
JERRY HALFHIDE ☎(01732) 353660

### WHITSTABLE • map 6C5

#### ☲ GIOVANNI'S RESTAURANT
49-55 Canterbury Road, CT5 4HH
This fully air-conditioned cocktail bar and restaurant is very popular and booking is recommended. Established in 1968, Giovanni's is owner-managed, with an enthusiastic continental staff.
FOOD: from £15 to £20 ☜
**Hours:** lunch 12noon-2.30pm, dinner 6pm-10.30pm, closed Sunday evening and all day Monday.
**Cuisine:** ITALIAN / FRENCH
**Cards:** Visa, Access, Diners, AmEx.
**Other points:** licensed, Sunday lunch, children welcome.
**Directions:** on the A290 near the railway bridge.
GIOVANNI FERRARI ☎(01227) 273034
Fax(01227) 771160

# NORFOLK

### ACLE • map 10C6

#### ☷ MANNINGS HOTEL & RESTAURANT
South Walsham Road, NR13 3ES
A small family-run hotel, set in peaceful landscaped gardens. All rooms are elegantly furnished and comfortable. The licensed restaurant is open to non-residents, offering cuisine which is believed to be the best in the area. Centrally situated for touring the Norfolk Broads and for exploring the beautiful Norfolk countryside.
DOUBLE ROOM: from £40
FOOD: up to £15
**Hours:** breakfast 7.30am-9am, lunch 12noon-2pm, bar meals 12noon-2pm, dinner 7pm-9.30pm.
**Cuisine:** ENGLISH - full à la carte and table d'hôte menus offering a very high standard of catering, using only the freshest of produce.
**Cards:** Visa, Access, AmEx.
**Other points:** licensed, open-air dining, Sunday lunch, children welcome, pets allowed, parking, garden, vegetarian meals.
**Rooms:** 3 single rooms, 4 double rooms, 3 twin rooms. All with TV, radio, telephone, tea/coffee-making facilities.
**Directions:** midway between Great Yarmouth (9 miles) and Norwich (11 miles).
ROBERT MANNING ☎(01493) 750377
Fax(01493) 751220

### AYLSHAM • map 10C6

#### ☷ AYLSHAM MOTEL & THE BARN FREEHOUSE
Norwich Road, NR11 6JH
Situated on the outskirts of the thriving, market town of Aylsham in peaceful countryside. There is an extensive bar and à la carte menu and 15 comfortable, en suite bedrooms. A large Function Room with its own private bar and dance floor caters for up to 150 people. Many National Trust properties and other attractions to visit nearby.
DOUBLE ROOM: from £20 to £30
SINGLE ROOM: from £25 to £35
FOOD: up to £15
**Hours:** breakfast 7.30am-9.30am, lunch 12noon-2pm, dinner 7pm-9.30pm. Open all year.
**Cuisine:** extensive bar and à la carte menus which

can be taken in the bar or no smoking room.
**Cards:** Visa, Access, Switch.
**Other points:** parking, no smoking area, pets allowed, licensed, residents' lounge, tv lounge, central heating, garden, children welcome.
**Rooms:** 10 twin rooms, 3 double rooms, 2 family rooms all en suite and with tea/coffee-maker, TV, telephone, alarm, room service. Hair dryer and trouser press available on request.
**Directions:** on the A140 Norwich to Cromer road. From Norwich straight over roundabout on edge of Aylsham. Hotel is first building on the right.
MR AND MRS SPRINGALL ☎(01263) 734851
Fax (01263) 734851

## BRANCASTER STAITHE • map 10C5

### THE JOLLY SAILORS
Brancaster Staithe, PE13 8BJ
*Records of The Jolly Sailors date back to 1789 - a popular haunt with locals, where beer is still drawn by hand pumps. It is ideally situated for good beaches, sailing, bird reserves and many places of interest, including Sandringham House and Holkham Hall. Award-winning wine list.*
FOOD: up to £15  CLUB
**Hours:** lunch 12noon-2pm, dinner 7pm-9pm (later at weekends), meals all day July and August, closed Christmas day. Bar open all legal hours in July and August, lunchtime and evenings rest of the year.
**Cuisine:** ENGLISH - Staithe mussels, lasagne, game casserole. All food prepared and cooked on the premises. Bar food and restaurant meals available.
**Cards:** Visa, Access.
**Other points:** licensed, open-air dining, Sunday lunch, pets allowed, children welcome, log fire, no music, playland, tennis court.
**Rooms:** no rooms on premises but good contacts with local bed and breakfast establishments.
**Directions:** on A149 coast road, halfway between Hunstanton and Wells-Next-The-Sea.
ALISTER BORTHWICK ☎(01485) 210314
Fax (01485) 210158

## BRESSINGHAM • map 10D5

### THE OLD GARDEN HOUSE
Thetford Road, IP22 2AG
*This charming, heavily-beamed, thatched inn has a cosy, warm ambience of its own. The imaginative home-cooked food, selection of real ales and excellent wines, coupled with roaring fires and flagstone floors, make this the ideal setting for any occasion. It is situated opposite the Bressingham Steam Railway Museum and Blooms Garden Centre.*
FOOD: from £15 to £20
**Hours:** lunch 12noon-2.30pm, dinner 7pm-9pm.
**Cuisine:** ENGLISH / CONTINENTAL - local and seasonal dishes.
**Cards:** Visa, AmEx, MasterCard.
**Other points:** parking, children welcome, no-smoking area, open-air dining, vegetarian meals, traditional Sunday lunch.
**Directions:** on the main Thetford-Diss road,

opposite Bressingham Church.
KEN & FRANKIE HORN ☎(01379) 687405

## BRISTON • map 10C5

### THE JOHN H. STRACEY
West End, near Melton Constable, NR24 2JA
*Professional and friendly staff take special care to make guests feel at home. Mr Fox is at present offering Bargain Breaks. With the good food and relaxing surroundings, this promises to be a popular bargain indeed.*
DOUBLE ROOM: up to £20
SINGLE ROOM: up to £20
FOOD: from £15 to £20  CLUB
**Hours:** lunch 12noon-2.15pm, bar meals 12noon-2.15pm, dinner 7pm-9.30pm, bar meals 7pm-10pm.
**Cuisine:** INTERNATIONAL - comprehensive menu including salmon à la Stracey (fresh salmon steaks, poached in white wine, with prawns and parsley).
**Cards:** Visa.
**Other points:** licensed, Sunday lunch, children welcome, vegetarian meals, afternoon tea.
**Rooms:** 2 double rooms, 1 twin room. All with TV.
**Directions:** on B1354 close to Melton Constable and en route to Aylsham and Fakenham.
MR & MRS R.E. FOX ☎(01263) 860891

## CASTLE ACRE • map 10C5

### THE OSTRICH INN
Stocks Green, near King's Lynn, PE32 2AE
*Large 16th century coaching inn with two big open fires in the lounge bar. On the A1065 in a typical, small Norfolk village which has the Peddars Way running through it. Many National Trust attractions nearby.*
DOUBLE ROOM: up to £20
FOOD: up to £15
**Hours:** bar meals 12noon-2pm, bar meals 7.30pm-10.30pm, closed Christmas.
**Cuisine:** INTERNATIONAL - bar meals ranging from sausages to caviar, cockles to T-bone steaks. Daily specials from all over the world, cooked by the chef/proprietor.
**Cards:** None.
**Other points:** licensed, Sunday lunch, children welcome, children welcome, coaches by prior arrangement.
**Rooms:** 2 twin rooms.
**Directions:** on the A1065 between Swaffham and Fakenham, on the village green.
RAYMOND H. WAKELEN ☎(01760) 755398

## DOWNHAM MARKET • map 10C4

### THE CROWN HOTEL
Bridge Street, PE38 9DH
*This impressive old coaching inn, dating back to the 17th century, is situated in the centre of Downham Market. It has recently been restored to its former glory, with log fires and flagstone floors, boasting*

ten letting rooms, restaurant, stables bar, locals bar and function room. The hotel has all the facilities, together with its warm and friendly atmosphere, to offer something for everyone.
DOUBLE ROOM: £39.50
SINGLE ROOM: from £29.50
FOOD: from £10 to £15
**Hours:** breakfast 7.30am-10am, lunch 12noon-2.30pm, dinner 7pm-10pm.
**Cuisine:** ENGLISH
**Cards:** Visa, Access, AmEx.
**Other points:** parking, children welcome, pets allowed, conference facilities, residents' lounge, vegetarian meals, traditional Sunday lunch.
**Rooms:** 10 bedrooms. All with TV, telephone, tea/coffee-making facilities.
**Directions:** 2 miles off A10 London to King's Lynn road, 9 miles from King's Lynn.
TIM & KATH SMITH ☎(01366) 382322
Fax(01366) 386194

## GREAT YARMOUTH • map 10C6

### THE CLIFF HOTEL
Cliff Hill, Gorleston-on-Sea, NR31 6DH

A welcoming business and holiday hotel overlooking the harbour on the quieter side of Great Yarmouth. The chefs and their staff provide a large selection of English dishes, offering the opportunity to sample the best from the produce of Norfolk farms and market gardens.
DOUBLE ROOM: from £40 to £50
SINGLE ROOM: from £62
FOOD: from £15 to £20
**Hours:** breakfast 7.30am-9.45am, lunch 12.30am-2pm, dinner 7pm-9.30pm, open all year.
**Cuisine:** ENGLISH - traditional roasts.
**Cards:** Visa, Access, Diners, AmEx.
**Other points:** Sunday lunch, children welcome.
**Rooms:** 39 bedrooms.
**Directions:** overlooking the harbour at Gorleston-on-Sea, the quieter side of Great Yarmouth
MR R.W. SCOTT ☎(01493) 662179/653617

### THE FERRY INN
Riverside, Stokesby, NR29 3EX
Beautifully situated by the river Bure, this inn offers a traditional Norfolk welcome for travellers and sailors alike. Generous helpings of good, honest pub food washed down with draught ales will satisfy the keenest of appetites. Children are not neglected, and as well as children's dishes, there is a large and well-appointed family room. Well recommended.

FOOD: up to £15
**Hours:** lunch 11am-2.30pm, dinner 6pm-9pm, open bank holidays.
**Cuisine:** there is a comprehensive basic daily menu with chef's specials on the blackboard. Adnams and Flowers bitter on draught.
**Other points:** parking, children welcome, (special menus), outdoor dining.
**Directions:** from Great Yarmouth take the A1064 through Caister and turn left at Filby. Follow the signs through Runham to Stokesby.
MR ROGER SCOTT-PHILLIPS ☎(01493) 751096
Fax(01493) 751460

### THE GALLON POT
Market Place, NR30 1NB
A traditional town-centre public house, which has built up a fine reputation for good-quality bar food at very reasonable prices. Popular with locals of all ages, the pub also appeals to seasonal holiday-makers. A relaxed and comfortable atmosphere.
FOOD: up to £10
**Hours:** bar 10am-11pm, lunch 11.30am-2.30pm, Sunday lunch 12noon-2.30pm, dinner 6.30pm-10pm, Sunday dinner 7pm-9.30pm, snacks served throughout afternoon Monday to Saturday.
**Cuisine:** ENGLISH - traditional pub food. Special weekend and lunchtime menus.
**Cards:** none.
**Other points:** licensed, open-air dining, two function rooms, children welcome, parking.
**Directions:** in town centre, in open market square. Next to large public car park.
MICHAEL & MARIA SPALDING ☎(01493) 842230

### IMPERIAL HOTEL
North Drive, NR30 1EQ

For many years the Imperial has enjoyed an outstanding reputation for its quality of food and wine. The Rambouillet, with its quiet intimacy, offers a wide range of dishes to appeal to both the gourmet and traditional diner. The excellently appointed rooms are equipped with all modern facilities, and many have glorious sea views. A perfect base for touring East Anglia.
DOUBLE ROOM: from £35
SINGLE ROOM: from £55
FOOD: from £15 to £20
**Hours:** breakfast 7.30am-9.30am, lunch 12.30am-2.30pm, dinner 7pm-10pm, open all year.
**Cuisine:** ENGLISH / FRENCH - regional English and French cuisine of the highest quality, complemented

by a superb wine list. Special gastronomic weekends are held each year.
**Other points:** licensed, Sunday lunch, children catered for (please check for age limits), afternoon tea, residents' lounge, pets allowed, conferences.
**Rooms:** 4 single rooms, 23 double rooms, 12 twin rooms. All with satellite TV, radio, telephone, tea/coffee-making facilities, hair dryer, trouser-press.
**Directions:** on seafront, opposite the Waterways.
NICHOLAS MOBBS ☎(01493) 851113 Fax(01493) 852229

### REGENCY HOTEL
5 North Drive, NR30 1ED
*A modern seaside hotel offering comfortable accommodation in a good seafront location. Guests only can choose from table d'hôte or à la carte menus at dinner, and there is a good choice at breakfast. The Regency Hotel is popular with holiday-makers and business people alike.*
DOUBLE ROOM: from £20 to £30
SINGLE ROOM: from £25 to £35
**Cards:** Visa, Access, Diners, AmEx, Switch.
**Other points:** licensed.
**Rooms:** 3 single rooms, 9 double rooms, 1 family room. All en suite.
**Directions:** on the seafront in Great Yarmouth.
J. BARNETT ☎(01493) 843759 Fax(01493) 330411

### KING'S LYNN • map 10C4

### GUANOCK HOTEL
Southgates, PE30 5JG
*Close to the historic Southgates and adjacent to Jubilee Gardens. Just a few minutes from the town centre in a pleasant area of town.*
DOUBLE ROOM: up to £20
SINGLE ROOM: up to £25
FOOD: up to £15
**Hours:** breakfast 7am-8.30am, dinner 6pm-7pm.
**Cuisine:** BREAKFAST - full English, or your choice from a large selection.
**Cards:** Visa, Access, AmEx.
**Other points:** central heating, children welcome, residents' lounge, roof patio garden, pool room.
**Rooms:** 5 single rooms, 4 double rooms, 3 twin rooms, 5 family rooms. All with TV, radio, tea/coffee-making facilities, iron, hair dryer.
**Directions:** on the London road, enter King's Lynn via Southgates.
TERRY PARCHMENT ☎(01553) 772959 Fax(01553) 772959

### NORWICH • map 10C6

### GRANGE HOTEL
230 Thorpe Road, NR1 1TJ
*Formerly an old manor house and now tastefully restored, the Grange Hotel provides comfortable accommodation to the casual visitor and businessman alike. The comfortable bar is an ideal spot in which to spend a relaxing evening or enjoy*

a pre-dinner drink. Sauna and solarium. Available for special and private function hire. Ideal for touring Norfolk.
DOUBLE ROOM: from £20 to £30
SINGLE ROOM: from £30 to £40
FOOD: up to £20
**Hours:** breakfast 7.30am-9am, dinner 6.30pm-9.30pm, closed Christmas until New Year.
**Cuisine:** ENGLISH - à la carte and table d'hôte. Dishes may include roast Aylesbury duckling, lamb cutlets Marchale, supreme of chicken, darne of salmon rouge. Vegetarian.
**Cards:** Visa, Access, Diners, AmEx.
**Other points:** licensed, no-smoking area, children welcome, parking, residents' lounge, disabled access, children welcome, cots, functions, vegetarian meals, residents' bar.
**Rooms:** 16 single rooms, 12 double rooms, 6 twin rooms, 1 quad room. All with TV, telephone, tea/coffee-making facilities, alarm.
**Directions:** 1 mile from Norwich station, travelling towards Great Yarmouth.
ROBERT HARGREAVES ☎(01603) 34734 Fax(01603) 34734

### REEDHAM • map 10C6

### REEDHAM FERRY & INN
Near Norwich, NR13 3HH
*Situated on the River Yare, adjacent to the ferry crossing, this popular old inn provides a pleasant stop for locals and tourists alike. Well-presented, well-served, good-value meals and welcoming family atmosphere. Riverside tables and chairs with garden. Adjoining the Inn is the Reedham Ferry Camping & Caravan Park, four acres of landscaped grounds and modern facilities next to the river Yare.*
FOOD: up to £15
**Hours:** lunch 12noon-2.15pm, dinner 7pm-10pm.
**Cuisine:** ENGLISH - a changing seasonal menu using only fresh produce, with prime meat from local butchers and hand-picked fish from Lowestoft Market. Chef's own daily specials, vegetarian and diet-conscious dishes. A selection of salads, fresh filled rolls and sandwiches.
**Cards:** Visa, Access, Diners, Switch.
**Other points:** open-air dining, Sunday lunch, children welcome, pets allowed.
**Directions:** just off the B1140 in Reedham on the north side of the ferry.
MR D.N. ARCHER ☎(01493) 700429 Fax(01493) 700999

### SNETTISHAM • map 10C5

 THE ROSE & CROWN FREEHOUSE
Old Church Road, PE31 7LX
*Situated just off the A149, this 14th century pub offers good food, real ales and a friendly, welcoming atmosphere. Log fires and live jazz during the winter. Walled garden with children's play area and family bar, children and families welcome.*
DOUBLE ROOM: up to £25
SINGLE ROOM: up to £35

FOOD: up to £15 🍽
Hours: dinner 6.30pm-10.30pm, lunch 12noon-2pm.
Cuisine: ENGLISH - rare roast beef, quality steaks, good selection of vegetarian dishes, dish of the day: good home-cooking.
Cards: Visa, Access.
Other points: open-air dining, Sunday lunch, children welcome, coaches by prior arrangement, enclosed garden.
Rooms: 2 double rooms, 1 twin room.
Directions: from King's Lynn, take A149 north for 10 miles; follow signs for Snettisham.
MR A. GOODRICH ☎(01485) 541382 Fax (01485) 543172

## WELLS-NEXT-THE-SEA • map 10B4

CROWN HOTEL & RESTAURANT
The Buttlands, NR23 1EX
*The hotel is ideally situated for visiting historic*
churches, priories and stately homes, including Holkham Hall and Sandringham. Both table d'hôte and à la carte menus are available in the restaurant.
DOUBLE ROOM: from £30 to £40
SINGLE ROOM: from £35 to £55
FOOD: up to £15 🍽 ▤
Hours: lunch 12noon-2pm, dinner 7pm-9.30pm.
Cuisine: ENGLISH / FRENCH - sea and shellfish, steak-and-kidney pie, home-made soups, pâté and French specialities. Local produce used where possible.
Cards: Visa, Access, Diners, AmEx.
Other points: licensed, Sunday lunch, children welcome.
Rooms: 1 single room, 5 double rooms, 5 twin rooms, 1 family room.
Directions: The Buttlands is a tree-lined square in the centre of town.
MR & MRS W. FOYERS ☎(01328) 710209 Fax (01328) 711432

# SUFFOLK

THE CROWN HOTEL
104 High Street, IP7 7EB

*A 15th century coaching inn in the heart of the Suffolk countryside. Along with excellent food and accommodation, The Crown Hotel offers guests the chance to spot one of its several ghosts!*
DOUBLE ROOM: from £20 to £30
FOOD: up to £15 🍽 CLUB
Hours: breakfast 7.30am-10am, lunch 12noon-2pm, Sunday 12.30am-2.30pm, dinner 7pm-9.30pm.
Cuisine: ENGLISH - traditional English. Victorian diable mixed meats in a spicy sauce is a speciality.
Cards: Visa, Access.
Other points: licensed, open-air dining, Sunday lunch, children welcome, garden, afternoon tea, residents' bar, baby-listening device, baby-sitting.
Rooms: 1 single room, 8 double rooms, 5 twin rooms, 1 triple room. All with TV.
Directions: in the village on the B1115.
MR HENDERSON ☎(01449) 740510 Fax (01449) 740224

## BURY ST EDMUNDS • map 10D5

THE GRANGE HOTEL
Thurston, IP31 3PQ
*The Grange is an attractive Tudor style country house hotel, family run for three generations. The hotel is set in its own secluded gardens amidst open countryside and within easy reach of nearby places of interest - Newmarket 20 minutes, Cambridge 40 minutes and Bury St Edmunds with its wealth of historic buildings, only 4 miles away. The Grange provides the ideal setting for a relaxing break or a base to explore East Anglia for business or pleasure.*
DOUBLE ROOM: from £20 to £30
SINGLE ROOM: from £30 to £40
FOOD: from £15 to £20 🍽
Hours: breakfast 7am-9.30am, lunch 12noon-2.30pm, bar meals 12noon-2.30pm, dinner 7pm-10pm, bar meals 7pm-10pm.
Cuisine: ENGLISH / FRENCH - wherever possible local produce is used, to ensure that meat, fish and vegetables are all fresh and of a high standard.
Cards: Visa, Access.
Other points: licensed, traditional Sunday lunch, children welcome, pets allowed, open bank holidays, bargain breaks.
Rooms: 8 double rooms, 4 twin rooms, 2 family rooms. All with TV, telephone, hair dryer, tea/coffee-making facilities.
Directions: A14 (was A45) to Bury St Edmunds, exit at Bury Central and follow A143 to Great Barton and Thurston.
MR & MRS E.G. WAGSTAFF ☎(01359) 231260 Fax (01359) 231260

THE WHITE HORSE
Old Newmarket Road, Risby, IP28 6NJ
*A 17th century inn offering good home-cooked food and real ales in a very romantic atmosphere with a candlelit dining room, open fire and soft background music. The inn is well worth a visit.*
DOUBLE ROOM: from £20 to £30
FOOD: up to £15 🍽
Hours: lunch 12noon-2pm, dinner 7pm-10.30pm.

---

For Reservations & Special Offers FreeCall 0500 700 456

**Cuisine:** ENGLISH - with daily and seasonal specials.
**Cards:** Visa, Access, AmEx.
**Other points:** parking, children welcome, pets allowed, open-air dining, vegetarian meals, traditional Sunday lunch.
**Directions:** Risby turn-off on A14, 10 miles east of Newmarket.
DAVID MEARS & GEORGINA SMITH ☎(01284) 810686

## CHELSWORTH • map 10E5

 **THE PEACOCK INN**
The Street, IP7 7HV
*A genuine 14th century oak-timbered inn with inglenook fireplaces and unique character. It is a prominent feature of the picturesque village of Chelsworth, opposite the River Brett. The Peacock prides itself on imaginative home-cooked meals with a selection of real ales and fine wines, coupled with quaint letting rooms. The village inn is the ideal traveller's rest.*
DOUBLE ROOM: from £20 to £30
FOOD: up to £15
**Hours:** breakfast 9am-10am, lunch 12noon-2pm, dinner 7pm-9.30pm.
**Cuisine:** ENGLISH / MEDITERRANEAN
**Cards:** Visa, Access, AmEx.
**Other points:** children welcome, pets allowed, open-air dining, traditional Sunday lunch.
**Rooms:** 4 bedrooms. All with TV, tea/coffee-making facilities.
**Directions:** on the A1115 between Stowmarket and Lavenham.
NIGEL & CAROL RAMSBOTTOM ☎(01449) 740758

## EYE • map 10D5

**THE FOUR HORSESHOES**
Thornham Magna, IP23 7DH
*An ancient, thatched farmhouse, circa. 1150 situated in the beautiful Suffolk village of Thornham Magna. Traditional English fare is served, including speciality pies. Has a quaint, olde-worlde ambience with an interesting well in the bar. Ideal base when touring this beautiful county with its wide skies.*
DOUBLE ROOM: from £40 to £50
SINGLE ROOM: from £30 to £40
FOOD: up to £15
**Hours:** breakfast 7-9.30am, lunch 12noon-2.30pm (3pm bar), dinner 6.45pm-10pm. Open all year.
**Cuisine:** TRADITIONAL ENGLISH home-made pies and seasonal specialities.
**Cards:** Visa, Access, AmEx
**Other points:** parking.
**Rooms:** 3 single rooms, 1 twin room, 4 double rooms, 1 family room en suite, 1 double not en suite, all with tea/coffee-making facilities, TV, telephone, alarm, hair dryer, room service.
**Directions:** turn off A140 to Thornham Magna 12 miles south of A14.
THE OLD ENGLISH PUB CO ☎(01379) 678777

## FELIXSTOWE • map 6A6

**THE WAVERLEY HOTEL**
Wolsey Gardens, IP11 7DF
*The Waverley is a beautiful, recently refurbished Victorian-style hotel standing high on the cliff, offering spectacular views of the sea and promenade. Wolsey's Restaurant provides an excellent à la carte menu as well as specially priced, changing daily menus. There is always a selection of fresh fish and seafood, game, poultry and meat dishes available. Lighter meals available in Gladstones Bar and Brasserie, where a selection of real ales is always available with guest beers changing monthly.*
DOUBLE ROOM: from £20 to £30
SINGLE ROOM: from £45 to £55
FOOD: up to £15
**Hours:** lunch 12noon-2pm, dinner 7pm-9.30pm.
**Cuisine:** ENGLISH / CONTINENTAL - varied à la carte menu in the restaurant. Bar meals include steaks, fresh fish, chilli, lasagne, salads and home-made pies, with daily changing specials.
**Cards:** Visa, Access, Diners, AmEx.
**Other points:** Sunday lunch, children welcome, weekend breaks, Christmas packages, functions.
**Rooms:** 4 single rooms, 9 double rooms, 6 twin rooms, 1 family room. All with en suite, satellite TV, telephone, tea/coffee-making facilities, radio, hair dryer, trouser-press. Most rooms have sea views; some have lovely balconies.
**Directions:** above Under Cliff Road, one minute from main high street.
MR KEVIN AVERY ☎(01394) 282811 Fax(01394) 670185

## FRAMLINGHAM • map 10D6

**THE OLD MILL HOUSE**
Saxtead Green, IP13 9QE
*This delightful pub has been beautifully restored with open fires, flagstone floors and timber beams. It offers an excellent menu, a special lunchtime buffet, coupled with a range of fine cask ales. Families welcome. The garden has a large fishpond and is situated on the village green, opposite the famous windmill. A must for connoisseurs of good food, ales and wines.*
FOOD: from £15 to £20
**Hours:** lunch 12noon-2pm, dinner 7pm-9pm.
**Cuisine:** ENGLISH / CONTINENTAL - with daily and seasonal specials.
**Cards:** Visa, Access, AmEx, MasterCard.
**Other points:** parking, children welcome, no-smoking area, open-air dining, vegetarian meals, traditional Sunday lunch.
**Directions:** situated on the village green at Saxtead Green, on B1119.
NICK BARLOW & RUTH SHEPHERD ☎(01728) 685064

## HAUGHLEY • map 10D5

### THE OLD COUNTING HOUSE RESTAURANT
Near Stowmarket, IP14 3NR

*Typical Suffolk timber-framed house dating back to the 1500s when it was a bank. Now you may dine at tables set with damask linen, fine glassware and classic cutlery.*

FOOD: from £12 to £22

**Hours:** lunch (Monday to Friday) 12noon-2pm, dinner (Monday to Saturday) 7.15pm-9.30pm, closed Sunday.
**Cuisine:** ENGLISH / FRENCH - lunch: two- or three-course table d'hôte plus bistro menu. Dinner: four-course table d'hôte, six choices for each course, changed every three weeks. Also bistro menu available for lunch and dinner.
**Cards:** Visa, Access, Diners, AmEx.
**Other points:** licensed, children welcome.
**Directions:** 3 miles west of Stowmarket, 1.5 miles from A14. At Haughley centre.
MR & MRS P. WOODS ☎(01449) 673617
Fax(01449) 673617

## KERSEY • map 10E5

### THE BELL INN
The Street, near Ipswich, IP7 6DY

*Built in 1320, this timber-framed inn is situated in one of the prettiest villages in Suffolk. The beautiful inn with its restaurant and two bars offers a friendly, informal atmosphere in delightful surroundings. It is the perfect venue for a romantic dinner for two, private parties or a relaxing evening, sampling the excellent selection of real ales and fine wines.*

FOOD: from £15 to £20

**Hours:** lunch 12noon-2.30pm, dinner 7pm-9.30pm.
**Cuisine:** ENGLISH / CONTINENTAL - creative cuisine with lobster a speciality.
**Cards:** Visa, Access, AmEx.
**Other points:** parking, children welcome, pets allowed, no-smoking area, open-air dining, vegetarian meals, traditional Sunday lunch.
**Directions:** north of A1071 (Hadleigh to Lavenham).
DOUGLAS & LESLEY HAMILTON-DICK ☎(01473) 823229

## LONG MELFORD • map 10E5

### THE COCK & BELL INN
Hall Street, CO10 9JR

*This beautiful Grade II listed coaching inn is situated in the centre of Long Melford, well-known for its antiques. It offers a wealth of English charm with a quiet, intimate restaurant, ideal for families, and with letting rooms, making this the perfect destination for tourists.*

DOUBLE ROOM: up to £20
FOOD: from £15 to £20

**Hours:** breakfast 8.30am-10am, lunch 12noon-3pm, dinner 6pm-10pm.
**Cuisine:** ENGLISH
**Cards:** Visa, Access, AmEx.

**Other points:** parking, children welcome, pets allowed, no-smoking area, conference facilities, vegetarian meals, traditional Sunday lunch.
**Rooms:** 2 bedrooms. Both with TV, tea/coffee-making facilities, vanity unit.
**Directions:** from Sudbury, follow signs off Bury Road, on A134.
MARK BELLERBY & KAREN BROWN ☎(01787) 379807 Fax(01787) 375464

### CROWN INN HOTEL
Hall Street, CO10 9JL

*This historic family-run inn, originally built in 1610, still retains many of its interesting architectural features. The warm and friendly hospitality of the inn prevails throughout, whether relaxing in the comfortable bar or enjoying a home-cooked meal in the intimate restaurant. The lovely Suffolk countryside provides many enjoyable walks and popular attractions nearby.*

DOUBLE ROOM: from £20 to £30
SINGLE ROOM: from £30
FOOD: up to £15

**Hours:** breakfast 8am-9.30am, lunch 12noon-2pm, bar snacks 12noon-2pm, dinner 7pm-9pm, bar snacks 7pm-9pm.
**Cuisine:** ENGLISH / EUROPEAN
**Cards:** Visa, Access.
**Other points:** parking, children welcome, no-smoking area, residents' lounge, garden, open-air dining, vegetarian meals, traditional Sunday lunch.
**Rooms:** 11 bedrooms. All with TV, direct dial telephone, tea/coffee-making facilities.
**Directions:** located in the centre of Long Melford.
MR & MRS QUINCEY ☎(01787) 377666
Fax(01787) 379005

## MILDENHALL • map 10D5

### THE DRAGON HOUSE
4 & 5 Police Station Square, IP28 7ER

*Situated in a Grade II listed building in the town centre, the Dragon House offers a wide range of traditional dishes in a comfortable and relaxed atmosphere. Popular with local diners, a takeaway service is also offered together with set meals and `feasts' recommended by the chef.*

FOOD: up to £15

**Hours:** lunch 12noon-2pm, dinner 5pm-11.30pm.
**Cuisine:** wide range of specialities.
**Cards:** Visa, Access, Switch
**Other points:** licensed, children welcome, parking, vegetarian meals.
**Directions:** in the centre of Mildenhall
MR DAVID LI ☎(01638) 712087

### THE SMOKE HOUSE
Beck Row, IP28 8DH

*Tony and Inez Warin extend a warm welcome to this atmospheric 16th century establishment, set in the heart of the East Anglian countryside. It has an established reputation for its friendly staff and caring attitude, good food and accommodation. Ideal for*

the country lover and sportsman, offering fishing,
shooting, riding, and horse-racing at nearby
Newmarket. Ten golf courses nearby.
DOUBLE ROOM: from £40 to £50
SINGLE ROOM: from £60
FOOD: from £15 to £20  `CLUB`
**Hours:** breakfast 7am-9.30am, lunch 12noon-2pm,
dinner 5pm-10pm, bar meals 11am-2.30pm, bar
meals 5pm-11pm, open all year.
**Cuisine:** ENGLISH - à la carte and table d'hôte,
offering a wide range of traditional English dishes.
**Cards:** Visa, Access, Diners, AmEx, Switch.
**Other points:** licensed, Sunday lunch, no-smoking
area, children welcome, afternoon tea, residents'
lounge, garden, parking, baby-listening device, 24hr
reception, foreign exchange.
**Rooms:** 18 double rooms, 83 twin rooms. All with
TV, radio, alarm, telephone, tea/coffee-making
facilities.
**Directions:** 4 miles from A11 Barton Mills
roundabout on A1101, near Mildenhall.
TONY & INEZ WARIN ☎(01638) 713223
`Fax`(01638) 712202

## SAXMUNDHAM • map 10D6

### THE OLD CHEQUERS
Aldeburgh Road, Friston, IP17 1NP
*This ever-popular, attractive country inn has
established an excellent reputation for its fine
cuisine, specializing in local fresh fish and game.
The delightful decor of the restaurant and bar have
been tastefully refurbished to create a warm and
friendly atmosphere. Situated just a few miles from
Aldeburgh on the Suffolk coast, it is well worth a
visit.*
FOOD: from £15 to £20
**Hours:** lunch 12noon-2pm, dinner from 7pm.
**Cuisine:** ENGLISH / EUROPEAN - local and
seasonal dishes a speciality.
**Cards:** Visa, Access, AmEx.
**Other points:** parking, children welcome, open-air
dining, covered patio, vegetarian meals, traditional
Sunday lunch.
**Directions:** 3 miles off A12 on the way to
Aldeburgh.
OLD ENGLISH PUB COMPANY ☎(01728) 688270

## SOUTHWOLD • map 10D6

### SUTHERLAND HOUSE RESTAURANT
56 High Street, IP18 6DN
*Built in the 16th century, Sutherland House was
once the headquarters of an admiral who became
King of England, James II. Today it carefully
preserves its historic past and specializes in good
food and refreshment of high quality. You can be
assured of welcoming service, well-presented, fresh
home-*
DOUBLE ROOM: from £20 to £30
FOOD: up to £15
**Hours:** breakfast 9am-10am, Sunday lunch 12noon-
2pm, dinner 7pm-9pm, open for dinner 6 days in
summer (closed Sundays).
**Cuisine:** ENGLISH - a daily menu featuring all fresh,

home-cooked local produce. Fresh, local fish dishes
are a speciality. Informal brasserie-style cuisine.
**Cards:** Visa, Access.
**Other points:** licensed, Sunday lunch, no smoking
in bedrooms.
**Rooms:** 3 double rooms. All with TV, tea/coffee-
making facilities.
**Directions:** 4 miles from A12, on High Street in the
centre of Southwold.
PAUL & MARGARET SAMAIN ☎(01502) 722260

## SUDBURY • map 10E5

### RED ONION BISTRO
57 Ballingdon Street, CO10 6DA
*A warm and friendly bistro style restaurant offering
a wide variety of delicious and interesting dishes
which offer exceptional value for money. You may
visit the wine cellars to make your own selection, or
settle for the house wine which is good and
reasonable! Highly recommended.*
FOOD: up to £15
**Hours:** lunch 12noon-2pm, dinner 6.30pm-9.30pm
**Cuisine:** EUROPEAN - excellent value table d'hôte
dinner menu at £9.75 with house wines at £5.95.
Lunchtime light specials for every taste, including
vegetarians.
**Cards:** Visa, MasterCard, Switch.
**Other points:** licensed, vegetarian meals, parking.
**Directions:** on the outskirts of Sudbury on A131.
MR & MRS FORD ☎(01787) 376777

## WOODBRIDGE • map 10E6

### BULL HOTEL
Market Hill, IP12 4LR

*A 16th century coaching inn on the A12 in the
centre of town. Facilities for conferences, private
hire and receptions.*
DOUBLE ROOM: from £20 to £30
FOOD: up to £15
**Hours:** breakfast 7.30am-9.30am, lunch 12noon-
2pm, dinner 7pm-10pm.
**Cuisine:** ENGLISH - home-made soup, steaks, bar
snacks.
**Cards:** Visa, Access, Diners, AmEx.
**Other points:** Sunday lunch, no-smoking area,
children welcome, residents' lounge, residents' bar.
**Rooms:** 4 single rooms, 10 double rooms, 7 twin
rooms, 2 triple rooms, 1 family room. All with TV,
telephone, tea/coffee-making facilities.
**Directions:** on A12 in town centre.
NEVILLE & ANNE ALLEN ☎(01394) 382089
`Fax`(01394) 384902

### CAPTAIN'S TABLE
3 Quay Street, IR12 1BX

*This fish and seafood restaurant has a timbered interior with a distinct nautical flavour to the decor. Very close to the river and the town centre.*

**FOOD:** from £15 to £25 ⌣ ⍟

**Hours:** lunch 12noon-2pm, dinner 6.30pm-9.30pm, closed Monday and Sunday.

**Cuisine:** SEAFOOD - local seafood.

**Cards:** Visa, Access, Diners, AmEx.

**Other points:** open-air dining, no-smoking area, children welcome.

**Directions:** close to the quayside and town centre.

MR A.J. PRENTICE ☎(01394) 383145


### WOOD HALL HOTEL & COUNTRY CLUB
Shottisham, IP12 3EG

*Set in ten acres of magnificent grounds, this imposing Elizabethan manor house has been completely refurbished to a luxurious standard. The hotel offers individually decorated, luxury bedrooms, three intimate candlelit restaurants, an elegant lounge with a real log fire, a superb banqueting suite, its own exclusive leisure club and `Woodies' unique night-club.*

**DOUBLE ROOM:** from £32

**SINGLE ROOM:** from £45 to £55

**FOOD:** from £16 to £20     CLUB

**Hours:** breakfast 7.30am-9.30am, lunch 12noon-3pm, dinner 7pm-10pm, bar snacks 12noon-3pm.

**Cuisine:** MODERN ENGLISH / FRENCH - all dishes are carefully prepared with special attention to detail.

**Cards:** Visa, Access, Diners, AmEx.

**Other points:** parking, children welcome, no-smoking area, disabled access, vegetarian meals.

**Rooms:** 15 bedrooms. All en suite.

**Directions:** take the A12 north through Woodbridge to the A1152 junction. Turn right towards Melton and after two miles take the B1083 south to Shottisham.

DAVID HARRINGTON ☎(01394) 411283
Fax(01394) 410007

## WRENTHAM • map 10D6

### QUIGGINS RESTAURANT
2 High Street, near Beccles, NR34 7HB

*An elegant yet comfortable and relaxing, beamed restaurant, decorated with plants, family pictures and knick-knacks to create a homely atmosphere. The food is well-cooked and presented. A choice of main course may include filet au fromage, Brigit's plum duck and prawn creole, among others. Warm and courteous service. Wide range of wines with emphasis on New World varieties. Quiggins adhere to the BTA's `Restaurant Customers Charter'.*

**FOOD:** from £21 to £25 ⌣ CLUB   ⍟

**Hours:** lunch 11.30am-2pm, dinner 7pm-10pm, closed Sunday evening and Monday.

**Cuisine:** ENGLISH / INTERNATIONAL - all made from fresh ingredients, including English puddings. Established reputation for quality seafood.

**Cards:** Visa, Access, AmEx, Switch, Delta, JCB, Electron.

**Other points:** licensed, open-air dining, Sunday lunch, no-smoking area, children welcome, close to beach.

**Rooms:** Quiggins Cottage now available for rent. Various `packages' available on request.

**Directions:** situated on crossroads in centre of Wrentham. On the A12.

DUDLEY & JILL MCNALLY ☎(01502) 675397


# SURREY

## BLETCHINGLEY • map 6C4

### WILLIAM IV
Little Common Lane, RH1 4QG

*A traditional, unspoilt British village pub situated down a quiet leafy lane with compact bars and an old English garden. The pub offers an extensive à la carte and bar-meals menu, with dishes ranging from shellfish to rack of lamb and home-made pies and curries. Friendly, efficient service complements the warm, bustling atmosphere of the pub. Ideally situated for walks over the North Downs and Tillgates Gardens.*

**FOOD:** up to £15

**Hours:** lunch 12noon-2pm, dinner 7pm-9.15pm.

**Cuisine:** ENGLISH / INTERNATIONAL - extensive menu including grills, home-made pies, curries, pizzas, fish dishes and extensive vegetarian menu. Daily specials and bar meals. Dining room (booking advisable).

**Cards:** Visa, Access.

**Other points:** licensed, open-air dining, children welcome, beer garden, pets allowed (under control).

**Directions:** Little Common Lane is located at the top of Bletchingley High Street (A25).

BRIAN & SANDRA STRANGE ☎(01883) 743278

## CHARLWOOD • map 6C4

### RUSS HILL HOTEL
Russ Hill, near Gatwick, RH6 0EL

*Built in the late 1800s as a fine country manor house, this hotel is rich in Victorian charm and elegance, enjoying panoramic views of Surrey's hills. All 150 air-conditioned bedrooms feature the most modern facilities, with furnishings of the highest standard. Superb health and leisure centre, conference and banqueting facilities are also available. Ideal for Gatwick Airport and many nearby places of interest. A courtesy coach to Gatwick Airport is available to guests.*

**DOUBLE ROOM:** from £20 to £30

**SINGLE ROOM:** from £40

**FOOD:** up to £20     CLUB

**Hours:** bar snacks 12noon-12midnight, breakfast 6.30am-10am, dinner 7pm-10pm.
**Cuisine:** INTERNATIONAL
**Other points:** parking, children catered for (please check for age limits), open bank holidays, Sunday dinner, disabled access, pets allowed, vegetarian meals, conferences, garden, leisure club.
**Rooms:** 19 single rooms, 96 double rooms, 25 twin rooms, 12 family rooms.
**Directions:** from A23 follow signs to Charlwood. At the end of the village turn left into Rectory Lane: the hotel is at the top of the hill. Close to Gatwick Zoo.
MR HILLBECK ☎(01293) 862171 Fax (01293) 862390

## COBHAM • map 5C3

### WOODLANDS PARK HOTEL
Woodlands Lane, Stoke D'Abernon, KT11 3QB
*The Woodlands Park Hotel is a magnificent Victorian mansion, pleasantly set in its own landscaped grounds. At the turn of the century, the then Prince of Wales and the famous actress Lillie Langtry were frequent visitors. Today the hotel is ideally located for touring the picturesque Surrey and Berkshire countryside, the great gardens and stately homes.*
DOUBLE ROOM: from £70
SINGLE ROOM: from £110
FOOD: from £15 to £20 ☜ ☴
**Hours:** breakfast 7am-9.30am, lunch 12.30am-2.30pm, dinner 7pm-9.30pm, brasserie 11am-11pm, closed 24th December until 31st December.
**Cuisine:** ENGLISH / FRENCH
**Cards:** Visa, Access, Diners, AmEx.
**Other points:** parking, children welcome, open-air dining, conference facilities, vegetarian meals.
**Rooms:** 5 single rooms, 35 double rooms, 13 twin rooms, 5 suites. All with tea-making facilities, TV, telephone, radio, hair dryer, trouser-press, room service.
**Directions:** on A245, junction 10 off M25, or Cobham off A3.
MR M. DICKSON ☎(01372) 843933 Fax (01372) 842704

## CRANLEIGH • map 5D3

### BRICKS RESTAURANT
Smithbrook Kilns, GU6 8JJ
*Situated in a multi-workshop craft centre in an old brickworks. Self-service from kitchen counter with table service for drinks, desserts and coffee. Waitress service in evenings.*
FOOD: up to £15
**Hours:** lunch 12noon-2pm, dinner 7.30pm-9.45pm, closed 25th December until 27th December and New Year's day.
**Cuisine:** INTERNATIONAL - menus change daily, offering a selection of casseroles with hot potatoes, salads, French bread and butter. All desserts are made on the premises.
**Cards:** Visa, Access.
**Other points:** open-air dining, Sunday lunch,

children welcome, coaches by prior arrangement
**Directions:** on A281, just north of crossroads with B2127.
MRS H. RUSSELL-DAVIS ☎(01483) 276780

### LA SCALA RESTAURANT
High Street, GU6 8RF
*A well-established and popular restaurant under the current ownership for over 20 years. Situated on the first floor above a jeweller's shop on the high street. The menu offers an interesting selection of Italian favourites and regional cuisine.*
FOOD: up to £15    CLUB
**Hours:** lunch 12noon-2pm, dinner 6.30pm, closed Sunday and Monday.
**Cuisine:** ITALIAN - veal escalopa a la crema, sole Isoladoro, fettucini crema, mussels.
**Cards:** Visa, Access, AmEx.
**Other points:** open-air dining, children welcome.
**Directions:** on A281 Guildford to Horsham road.
ROSARIO MAZZOTTA ☎(01483) 274900

## CROYDON
See London

## EPSOM DOWN • map 6C4

### LE RAJ
211 Firtree Road, KT17 3LB
*A truly outstanding restaurant which has won numerous awards over the years. Innovation is an important policy of Le Raj, and "Le Raj Avion" offers you the chance of a 2 hour flight over London whilst being served a memorable Indian banquet complete with free champagne and a running commentary!*
FOOD: from £15 to £20
**Hours:** lunch 12noon-2.30pm, dinner 5.30-11pm, open bank holidays, closed Christmas day and Boxing day.
**Cuisine:** BANGLADESHI superb award-winning cuisine. International Indian chef of the year 1992 and Restaurant of the Year 1993.
**Cards:** Visa, Access, Diners, AmEx.
**Other points:** parking nearby, vegetarian meals.
**Directions:** at junction of Fir Tree road and Reigate road (B291) close to Driftbridge Hotel.
E. ALI ☎(01737) 833931 Fax (0181) 335 3510

## ESHER • map 1E2

### ALBERT ARMS
82 High Street, KT10 9QS
*Situated close to Hampton Court and to Sandown Park and Kempton race courses, The Albert Arms is a traditional pub with a restaurant extension.*
FOOD: from £15 to £20
**Hours:** breakfast 10.30am-12noon, lunch 12noon-3pm, dinner 7.30pm-10pm, bar meals 11am-3pm, 7.30pm-10pm.
**Cuisine:** ENGLISH - wide range of dishes including grills, salads, fish, steaks, pies, casseroles and home-made desserts.

**Cards:** Visa, Access, Diners, AmEx.
**Other points:** function rooms, licensed, Sunday lunch, children welcome.
**Directions:** off the A3 London-Guildford road, on the A304 in Esher.
JEAN & BRUCE MONTGOMERY ☎(01372) 465290 Fax(01372) 469217

### THE HAVEN HOTEL
Portsmouth Road, KT10 9AR

*The hotel, which has established an enviable reputation for its good food and service at sensible prices, boasts all the character and charm of a true Edwardian house. Additionally it provides an ideal setting for private functions, business meetings and conferences and is a perfect base for visiting Hampton Court, Sandown Park or exploring along the Thames.*
DOUBLE ROOM: from £30 to £40
SINGLE ROOM: over £55
FOOD: from £15 to £20 CLUB
**Hours:** breakfast 7am-9am, lunch (bar area) 12noon-2.30pm, dinner (restaurant) 7pm-9.30pm, (bar area) 7pm-10pm.
**Cuisine:** ENGLISH/INTERNATIONAL menu changes daily
**Cards:** Visa, Access, Diners, AmEx, Switch.
**Other points:** parking, children welcome, conference facilities, residents' lounge, vegetarian meals, special diets by arrangement.
**Rooms:** 6 single rooms, 4 twin rooms, 7 double rooms all en suite with tea/coffee-maker, satellite TV, radio, alarm, hair dryer, trouser press, baby listening device, iron, room service 11am-11pm.
**Directions:** on the A307 near its intersection with the A309 at the Scilly Isles junction.
MR DHANANI ☎(0181) 398 0023 Fax(0181) 398 9463

### FARNHAM • map 5C3

### SEVENS WINE BAR & BISTRO
7 The Borough, GU9 7NA

*An 18th century beamed black-and-white restaurant situated in the centre of Farnham, serving tasty, well-prepared food. In summer you can dine in the garden, but whatever the month and setting the food is always good and the service excellent. The friendly, welcoming staff and relaxing, informal atmosphere makes this bistro a pleasure to visit. Fully air-conditioned.*
FOOD: up to £15
**Hours:** morning coffee 9.30am-12noon, lunch 12noon-2.30pm, afternoon tea 2.30pm-6.30pm, dinner 6.30pm-11pm, closed Sunday.
**Cuisine:** FRENCH - French-style bistro, including home-made dishes, home-made sweets. Menus change monthly and blackboard specials daily.
**Cards:** Visa, Access.
**Other points:** licensed, children welcome, garden, afternoon tea, barbecues.
**Directions:** in the centre of Farnham, very close to Castle Street and market.

MR A.C. GREEN ☎(01252) 715345 Fax(01252) 717895

### GODALMING • map 5C3

### THE MONGOLIAN
10-14 Wharf Street, GU7 1NQ

*Discover the unique style of eating which exemplifies an age-old tradition from the homelands of Mongolia. Fill your bowl with a selection of meat or fish, then your choice of vegetables and noodles. Add to this a mixture of delicious marinades and sauces, aromatic herbs and spices and watch your meal being barbecued on the large, curved hotplate in the centre of the restaurant. Fun, friendly and enthusiastic crowd. There is a baby changing-room with full changing facilities, bottle-warmers, etc., and special offers throughout the year for children, including special childrens menu option.*
FOOD: up to £15
**Hours:** dinner from 6pm, open all day Sunday from 12.30am, closed Christmas day and New Year's day.
**Cuisine:** MONGOLIAN - barbecue-style cuisine, enhanced with aromatic spices and seasonings.
**Cards:** Visa, Access, AmEx.
**Other points:** licensed, Sunday lunch, children welcome.
**Directions:** on junction of B3001 and B2130, opposite the police station.
GLENN & CLARE WATERFALL ☎(01483) 414155

### GUILDFORD • map 5C3

### KINGS SHADE COFFEE HOUSE
20 Tunsgate, GU1 3QS

*Well situated between the famous Guildhall clock and the superb Castle gardens. Kings Shade Coffee House is open all day and is a very popular venue in which to enjoy a meal or snack. The menu is extensive, the atmosphere bustling and the service friendly and efficient. The home-made sweets are particularly recommended.*
FOOD: up to £15    CLUB
**Hours:** meals all day 8.30am-6pm, closed Sunday.
**Cuisine:** ENGLISH - house specialities include steak-and-kidney pie, chicken and spinach gratin, lasagne. Salads, toasted savouries, stuffed baked potatoes, sandwiches. Morning coffee, lunch, light meals and clotted cream teas are also available.
**Other points:** vegetarian selection, licensed, air-conditioned.
**Directions:** off the high street, opposite the Guildhall.
DAVID GOLDSBY ☎(01483) 576718

### KEW / KINGSTON UPON THAMES
See London

### LEATHERHEAD • map 6C4

### THE STAR
Kingston Road, KT22 0DP

*In a convenient position close to Chessington World*

of Adventures and the M25, The Star serves good-quality bar meals. A very popular, busy pub.
FOOD: up to £15
Hours: lunch 12noon-2pm, dinner Sunday-Thursday 5.30pm-10pm, dinner Friday-Saturday 5.30pm-10.30pm.
Cuisine: ENGLISH - house speciality: fresh Scottish beef steaks cooked over charcoal.
Cards: Visa, Access, Switch.
Other points: licensed, open-air dining, Sunday lunch, coaches by prior arrangement
Directions: on the A243 one mile from Leatherhead. Close to Chessington and M25.
COLIN & IRENE SUCKLING ☎(01372) 842416 Fax(01372) 843914

## REIGATE • map 6C4

### CRANLEIGH HOTEL
41 West Street, RH2 9BL
The Cranleigh Hotel is set in one of the last unspoilt towns fringing the magnificent forested North Downs, famous for its pilgrims, Romans and spring-waters. Owned and managed by the Bussandri family for over 20 years, who have in this time achieved an unsurpassable reputation for friendliness, care and quality hospitality. The house has been carefully restored to include luxurious bedrooms, fine public rooms and a grand conservatory, leading on to their pride: a garden and orchard, overlooking a swimming pool and tennis courts.
DOUBLE ROOM: from £30 to £40
SINGLE ROOM: from £40 to £55
FOOD: from £16 to £20    CLUB
Hours: breakfast 7.30am-9.30am, dinner 7pm-9pm, closed 24th December until 26th December (inclusive).

Cuisine: INTERNATIONAL
Cards: Access.
Other points: parking, children welcome, residents' lounge, garden, vegetarian meals, open-air dining.
Rooms: 9 bedrooms.
Directions: on A25, at end of Reigate High Street going west.
MR G. BUSSANDRI ☎(01737) 223417 Fax(01737) 223734

### THE MARKET HOTEL
High Street, RH2 9AY
Situated in the centre of Reigate, this lively pub does much to justify its continuing popularity. A good selection of real ales, bottled and continental lagers make the perfect complement to well-cooked food, all at reasonable prices.
FOOD: up to £15
Hours: meals all day 12noon-9.30pm, open all year including bank holidays.
Cuisine: ENGLISH - traditional English pub food, prepared to a high standard. Generous portions complemented by a fine selection of wines, ales and lagers.
Cards: Visa, Access.
Other points: licensed, open-air dining, Sunday lunch, no-smoking area, children welcome, morning tea, afternoon tea, garden.
Directions: at centre of town, by clocktower.
MARKET TAVERNS LIMITED ☎(01737) 240492 Fax(01737) 226221

## RICHMOND / SUTTON
see London

# EAST SUSSEX

## ALFRISTON • map 6D4

### DRUSILLAS PARK
Alfriston, BN26 5QS
The attractive Toucans thatched restaurant forms part of a leisure park that includes a zoo, known as the best small zoo in the south. Set in large well-kept grounds, it was established in 1924 and is still a family-run business. Toucans was Egon Ronay's Family Restaurant of the Year 1991. Toy boxes and play equipment available.
FOOD: up to £15
Hours: lunch 12noon-6pm, closed evenings.
Cuisine: INTERNATIONAL - family menu in Toucans Restaurant. Pub food in Inn at the Zoo.
Cards: Visa, Access.
Other points: licensed, Sunday lunch, children welcome, zoo, playland.
Directions: off the A27 between Lewes and Polegate.
MR M. ANN ☎(01323) 870656 Fax(01323) 870846

## BATTLE • map 6D5

### HOTEL OF THE YEAR 1996
### POWDERMILLS HOTEL
Powdermill Lane, TN33 0SP
Set in 150 acres of park-like grounds and with fishing lakes and woodlands, this Georgian country house hotel is ideal for those wanting to return to nature. The Orangery Restaurant offers imaginative and exciting meals, and the hotel accommodation is of a very high standard. Highly recommended.
DOUBLE ROOM: from £32.50 to £60
SINGLE ROOM: from £45 to £55
FOOD: from £20 to £25
Hours: breakfast 7.30am-9.30am, lunch 12noon-2pm, dinner 7pm-9pm.
Cuisine: ENGLISH - full à la carte menu, table d'hôte and bar snacks. Vegetarian menu.
Cards: Visa, Access, Diners, AmEx.
Other points: licensed, open-air dining, Sunday lunch, children welcome, morning tea, afternoon tea, swimming pool, golf nearby, riding, dogs

allowed, disabled access, vegetarian meals, residents' lounge, residents' bar.
**Rooms:** 13 double rooms, 12 twin rooms. All with TV, telephone.
**Directions:** through Battle towards Hastings, first right turn into Powdermill Lane.
D. & J. COWPLAND ☎(01424) 775511
Fax(01424) 774540

### THE SQUIRREL INN
North Trade Road, TN33 9LJ
*A free-house with its own restaurant serving traditional fare, including bar snacks. Close to Battle Abbey, Bodiam Castle, Drusillas Zoo and many other attractions.*
FOOD: up to £15
**Hours:** lunch 12noon-2.30pm, dinner (Mon-Sat) 6pm-9.30pm, Sunday 7pm-9.30pm, closed Sunday night and Mondays in winter.
**Cuisine:** ENGLISH
**Cards:** Visa, Access, AmEx.
**Other points:** parking, children welcome, Sunday lunch, open bank holidays, no-smoking area, disabled access, pets allowed, vegetarian meals, open-air dining, licensed. 9 real ales available, also in C.A.M.R.A. Good Beer guide.
**Directions:** located on A271, just before approaching A2100 and Battle.
BOB & KATH BRITT ☎(01424) 772717

## BEXHILL-ON-SEA • map 6D5

### THE NORTHERN HOTEL
72-78 Sea Road, TN40 1JN
*Adjacent to the seafront, the hotel is just one minute's walk from the sea. Comfortable accommodation, decorated and furnished to a high standard. The Georgian-style restaurant serves well-prepared, well-presented food at very good value for money. Quiet and relaxing atmosphere, as is the tradition of a family-run hotel.*
DOUBLE ROOM: from £30 to £40
SINGLE ROOM: from £35 to £45
FOOD: up to £15
**Hours:** breakfast 8am-9.30am, lunch 12noon-2pm, dinner 6pm-8pm.
**Cuisine:** ENGLISH - varied high-quality selection on table d'hôte, à la carte and bar snack menu. Vegetarians catered for.
**Cards:** Visa, Access, AmEx.
**Other points:** licensed, children welcome, afternoon tea, pets allowed, disabled access.
**Rooms:** 6 single rooms, 7 double rooms, 21 twin rooms, 1 family room.
**Directions:** off the A259.
THE SIMS FAMILY ☎(01424) 212836 Fax(01424) 213036

## BRIGHTON & HOVE • map 6E5

### BRIGHTON MARINA HOUSE HOTEL AND NO 21 HOTEL
8 and 21 Charlotte Street, off Marine

Parade, BN2 1AG
*Two cosy, well furnished, family run hotels, in a quiet street in the heart of Regency Brighton, close to the beach. Both hotels provide a range of charmingly decorated bedrooms, some with four-poster beds. Guests are made to feel very welcome and at home from the moment they arrive.*
DOUBLE ROOM: from £17 to £35
SINGLE ROOM: from £15 to £50
FOOD: from £15 to £20
**Hours:** breakfast 7.30am-10am.
**Cuisine:** COSMOPOLITAN - English, Chinese, Indian, vegetarian, vegan, kosher, halal.
**Cards:** Visa, Access, Diners, AmEx, MasterCard, JCB.
**Other points:** children welcome, residents' lounge, conference facilities.
**Rooms:** 15 double rooms, 3 twin rooms, 1 triple room, 6 family rooms. Most en suite. All with TV, telephone, radio, alarm, hair dryer, tea/coffee-making facilities.
**Directions:** just off Marine Parade, fourteenth street on left .5 mile from roundabout facing Palace Pier.
MR S. JUNG ☎(01273) 605349/679484/686450
Fax(01273) 605349/695560

### COSMOPOLITAN HOTEL
31 New Steine, Marine Parade, BN2 1PD
*Overlooking the beach and Palace Pier, the Cosmopolitan Hotel is a friendly, comfortable place to stay and popular with holiday-makers and business visitors alike. There is a cosy residential licensed bar, and the hotel is very central for shopping, entertainments and conference centres.*
DOUBLE ROOM: from £20 to £30
SINGLE ROOM: from £25 to £35
**Hours:** breakfast 8am-9am.
**Cuisine:** BREAKFAST
**Cards:** Visa, Access, Diners, AmEx.
**Other points:** children welcome, TV lounge, residents' bar.
**Rooms:** 10 single rooms, 1 double room, 4 twin rooms, 9 family rooms. All with TV, radio, telephone, tea/coffee-making facilities, alarm, heating. Many rooms are en suite.
**Directions:** A23 to Brighton seafront, turn left onto A259 Marine Parade - .25 mile.
C. NICHOLAS ☎(01273) 682461 Fax(01273) 622311

### DONATELLO RESTAURANT
3 Brighton Place, The Lanes, BN1 1HJ
*A popular and well-run Italian restaurant specializing in pasta and pizzas. The menu offers an extensive choice of dishes at good value for money. A lively restaurant with friendly service and a warm, relaxed atmosphere.*
FOOD: up to £15    CLUB
**Hours:** meals all day 11.30am-11.30pm.
**Cuisine:** ITALIAN - extensive menu of Italian dishes including pasta, pizzas, fish and meat dishes.
**Cards:** Visa, Access, Diners, AmEx, Switch.
**Other points:** licensed, Sunday lunch, children

welcome.
**Directions:** in centre of Brighton's Lanes.
MR PIETRO ADDIS ☎(01273) 775477 Fax (01273)
677659

### ENGLISH'S OYSTER BAR & SEAFOOD RESTAURANT
29-31 East Street, BN1 1HL
*The restaurant is housed in three fishermen's cottages on the edge of Brighton's historic Lanes. For more than 200 years, English's Oyster Bar has been a family business, selling oysters and fish without a break in tradition. Enjoy the pleasures of dining alfresco on the outside terrace, where a full menu and barbeque are served.*
FOOD: up to £15
**Hours:** meals all day 12noon-10.15pm, Sunday 12.30am-9.30pm, closed Christmas eve, Christmas day, Boxing day and New Year's day.
**Cuisine:** SEAFOOD - seafood, including oysters, Dover sole, plaice, monkfish, mussels, fresh crab and lobsters. Special two course menu for £6.95, three course menu £10.95. Daily specialities.
**Cards:** Visa, Access, Diners, AmEx, Switch.
**Other points:** Sunday lunch, no-smoking area, children welcome, open bank holidays.
**Directions:** in the heart of Brighton's Lanes, 2 minutes' walk from the Royal Pavilion.
MRS P.M. LEIGH-JONES ☎(01273) 327980/325661 Fax (01273) 329754

### KEMPTON HOUSE HOTEL
33-34 Marine Parade, BN2 1TR
*A friendly, family-run hotel situated opposite the beach and the famous Palace Pier and within minutes of all amenities. Mr and Mrs Swaine assure a warm welcome and real `home from home' atmosphere. With a high standard of accommodation, a patio overlooking the seafront, residential bar and comfortable surroundings, an enjoyable stay is guaranteed.*
DOUBLE ROOM: from £20 to £30
SINGLE ROOM: from £35 to £45
**Hours:** breakfast 8.30am-9am, dinner 6pm.
**Cuisine:** ENGLISH
**Cards:** Visa, Access, AmEx.
**Other points:** children welcome, pets allowed, residents' bar lounge, garden, vegetarian meals, street parking.
**Rooms:** 7 double rooms, 2 twin rooms, 3 family rooms. All with en suite, satellite TV, radio, alarm, telephone, trouser-press, tea/coffee-making facilities.
**Directions:** A23 London Road until Palace Pier roundabout. Left onto A259. 200 yards on left.
PHILIP & VALERIE SWAINE ☎(01273) 570248
Fax (01273) 570248

### KIMBERLEY HOTEL
17 Atlingworth Street, BN2 1PL
*A friendly, family hotel with clean, comfortable rooms, a residents' lounge and bar facilities. Centrally situated, being only two minutes from the*
seafront, with the Royal Pavilion, Palace Pier and marina nearby.
DOUBLE ROOM: up to £20
SINGLE ROOM: up to £25
**Hours:** breakfast - weekdays 8am-9am, weekends 8.30am-9.30am.
**Cuisine:** BREAKFAST
**Cards:** Visa, Access, Diners, AmEx.
**Other points:** children catered for (please check for age limits), open bank holidays, residents' lounge.
**Rooms:** 3 single rooms, 2 double rooms, 7 twin rooms, 3 family rooms. All with TV, tea/coffee-making facilities.
**Directions:** situated between Brighton Marina and Palace Pier off the A259.
MRS M. ROLAND ☎(01273) 603504 Fax (01273) 603504

### MELFORD HALL HOTEL
41 Marine Parade, BN2 1PE
*A seafront hotel on a corner position of a garden square and close to all main amenities. Melford Hall also overlooks the beach. The accommodation is en suite, and ground-floor rooms and four-poster bedrooms are available. Under the personal supervision of the resident proprietors.*
DOUBLE ROOM: from £22 to £27
SINGLE ROOM: from £30 to £34
**Hours:** breakfast 8am-9am.
**Cuisine:** BREAKFAST
**Cards:** Visa, Access, Diners, AmEx.
**Other points:** children catered for (please check for age limits), residents' lounge.
**Rooms:** 2 single rooms, 11 double rooms, 11 twin rooms, 1 quad room. All with TV, direct dial telephone, radio, alarm, tea/coffee-making facilities, hair dryer.
**Directions:** A259 Newhaven to Brighton road, on Marine Parade, close to Palace Pier.
IAN DIXON ☎(01273) 681435 Fax (01273) 624186

### NEW STEINE HOTEL
12A New Steine, BN2 1PB
*A Grade II listed building in a Regency square, within easy walking distance of the town centre, conference centre and the famous Royal Pavilion. Pleasantly decorated and comfortably furnished. An enjoyable stay is assured.*
DOUBLE ROOM: up to £21
**Hours:** breakfast 8am-9am.
**Cuisine:** BREAKFAST
**Other points:** children catered for (please check for age limits), pets allowed, central heating, residents' lounge, street parking.
**Rooms:** 3 single rooms, 6 double rooms, 2 twin rooms. All with TV, tea/coffee-making facilities.
**Directions:** in a Regency square just off the main promenade.
MR SHAW & MR MILLS ☎(01273) 681546

## PINOCCHIO
22 New Road, BN1 1UF

*A traditional Italian meal at a reasonable price in pleasant, unpretentious and relaxed surroundings. This is a very popular restaurant with travellers and locals alike. It is also a regular haunt for theatre-goers and actors - you will often spot a famous face.*
FOOD: up to £15   CLUB
**Hours:** dinner weekdays 5pm-11.30pm, lunch weekdays 11.30am-2.30pm, meals all day, weekends 11.30am-11.30pm.
**Cuisine:** ITALIAN / CONTINENTAL - pizza and pasta. Selection of chicken, veal and fish dishes.
**Cards:** Visa, Access, Diners, AmEx, Switch.
**Other points:** Sunday lunch, children welcome.
**Directions:** easily located opposite the Pavilion Theatre.
MR PIETRO ADDIS ☎(01273) 677676 Fax(01273) 677659

## REGENCY RESTAURANT
131 King's Road, BN1 2HH

*A friendly, relaxed restaurant with welcoming staff where good food can be enjoyed throughout the day. The restaurant specializes in locally caught fresh fish, with a wide choice of other dishes, including roasts, grills and steaks. All food is well cooked and offers good value for money. In fine weather, tables are available outside on the seafront.*
FOOD: up to £15
**Hours:** meals all day 10am-11pm, closed Christmas 23rd December until 10th January.
**Cuisine:** SEAFOOD / ENGLISH - a wide range of meals, with locally caught fresh fish a speciality.
**Cards:** Visa, Access, Diners.
**Other points:** licensed, Sunday lunch, children welcome, morning tea, afternoon tea, parking.
**Directions:** On A259, opposite West Pier on Brighton seafront.
ROVERTOS & EMILIO SAVVIDES ☎(01273) 325014

## ST CATHERINE'S LODGE HOTEL
Seafront, Kingsway, BN3 2RZ

*A 150-year-old Victorian gabled hotel, centrally situated on the seafront, with full accommodation facilities. Good food at value-for-money prices is served by well-trained attentive staff in attractive surroundings. Located nearby is the King Alfred Leisure Centre with swimming pools, waterslides and ten-pin bowling.*
DOUBLE ROOM: from £30 to £40
SINGLE ROOM: from £45 to £55
FOOD: up to £15   CLUB
**Hours:** breakfast 7.45am-9.30am, lunch 12.30am-2pm, dinner 7pm-9pm.
**Cuisine:** ENGLISH - extensive à la carte. Dishes include roast carved at the table.
**Cards:** Visa, Access, Diners, AmEx.
**Other points:** Sunday lunch, children welcome, garden, games room, residents' lounge, afternoon tea, conferences, functions, residents' bar,

vegetarian meals, parking, foreign exchange.
**Rooms:** 10 single rooms, 22 double rooms, 12 twin rooms, 4 family rooms, 2 suites. All with TV, telephone.
**Directions:** hotel is on A259 coast road, on the seafront in the centre of Hove. Near King Alfred Leisure Centre.
JOHN HOULTON ☎(01273) 778181 Fax(01273) 774949

## TROUVILLE HOTEL
11 New Steine, BN2 1PB

*A Regency Grade II listed town-house tastefully restored and furnished, enhanced with window boxes, conveniently situated in a seafront square. The town centre, marina, Pavilion, Lanes and conference centre are all within easy walking distance.*
DOUBLE ROOM: from £21 to £25
SINGLE ROOM: up to £25
**Hours:** breakfast weekdays 8.15am-9am, weekends 8.45am-9.15am.
**Cuisine:** BREAKFAST
**Cards:** Visa, AmEx, MasterCard.
**Other points:** central heating, children welcome, residents' lounge.
**Rooms:** 2 single rooms, 4 double rooms, 2 twin rooms, 1 family room, all with TV, tea/coffee-making facilities. Four poster room available.
**Directions:** just off the seafront, 300 yards east of Palace Pier, off A259.
MR & MRS J.P. HANSELL ☎(01273) 697384

### BURWASH • map 6D4

## THE TUDOR HOUSE RESTAURANT
High Street, TN19 7ET

*A tile hung, timber-framed house dating from 1540 and a good example of a typical Tudor building of the Weald. Centrally located in Burwash, Tudor House offers the very best in home-cooking with deliciously varied table d'hôte menus available on Friday, Saturday and Sunday.*
FOOD: from £15 to £20
**Hours:** lunch 12.15pm-2.30pm, Sunday only, dinner 7.15pm-10pm, Friday & Saturday only (including bank holidays).
**Cuisine:** English/French fixed-price table d'hôte menus for lunch and dinner, personally prepared by Joan Feltham using fresh local ingredients where possible. Main courses featured include stilton stuffed pork chop baked with pears and cream,

aromatic chicken on a mattress of Bulgar wheat, fillet of sole stuffed with smoked salmon and avocado with hollandaise sauce. Range of home-made desserts to tempt even the most dedicated slimmers!

**Cards:** Visa, Access, Mastercard
**Other points:** public parking opposite the restaurant, children welcome, vegetarian meals, traditional Sunday lunch.
**Directions:** situated in the centre of Burwash on the A265 midway between Heathfield & Hurst Green.
SIMON & JOAN FELTHAM ☎(01435) 882258

## CROWBOROUGH • map 6D4

### WHITE HART & VINEYARD RESTAURANT
1 Chapel Green, Crowborough Hill, TN6 2LB

*An impressive, half-timbered pub and restaurant dedicated to satisfying the needs of the most demanding diner. All dishes are produced on the premises using ingredients from local suppliers with a high regard for the 'correct' methods of cooking. The bar menu is equally comprehensive with daily-changing blackboard specials, including childrens and vegetarian dishes. Impressive world wine list including over 18 English wines.*
FOOD: from £15 to £20
**Hours:** breakfast 9am-11.30am, lunch 11am-2.30pm, dinner 6pm-10pm (restaurant), 5pm-10pm (bar). Sundays 12noon-3pm. Bar food served all day Saturday and Sunday.
**Cuisine:** venison cutlets with plum and wine sauce, beef Wellington, Sussex country platter, baked plait of fresh salmon tail, children's menu and vegetarian.
**Cards:** Visa, Access, AmEx, Diners, Switch, JCB
**Other points:** children welcome.
**Directions:** A26 to Crowborough Cross, then B2100 towards Rotherfield. Restaurant is on Crowborough Hill.
CARL & JUDITH MARTIN ☎(01892) 652367

## EASTBOURNE • map 6D4

### THE CHATSWORTH HOTEL
Grand Parade, BN21 3YR
*The Chatsworth Hotel is a traditional English hotel in an elegant Edwardian building. It is ideally situated on the Grand Parade only a minute away from the beach and promenade. With the staff always ready to help in any way, the Chatsworth is a very comfortable three-star hotel.*
DOUBLE ROOM: from £30 to £45

SINGLE ROOM: from £35 to £50
FOOD: from £10 to £15  [CLUB]
**Hours:** breakfast 8am-9.30am, lunch 12.30pm-2.15pm, Sunday lunch 12.30pm-2.15pm, dinner 7pm-8.30pm.
**Cuisine:** ENGLISH - a wide range of food with well cooked English dishes from the best local suppliers. Traditional roasts, excellent local fish and our own home-made sweets and pastries.
**Cards:** Visa, Access, Diners, AmEx.
**Other points:** licensed, Sunday lunch, children welcome, pets allowed, conferences, cots.
**Rooms:** 11 single rooms, 10 double rooms, 27 twin rooms, 2 family rooms. All with TV, radio, telephone, hospitality trays.
**Directions:** on corner of the Grand Parade and Hartington Place, very near the bandstand.
PETER HAWLEY ☎(01323) 411016 Fax(01323) 643270

### WEST ROCKS HOTEL
Grand Parade, BN21 4DL
*A friendly, family-owned/managed hotel, occupying one of Eastbourne's finest seafront locations. Three elegant and spacious lounges afford magnificent views over the parades and the Channel. The 50 comfortable bedrooms - the majority with sea views - are all en suite, and there is also a passenger lift. As one of the sunniest resorts in Great Britain, Eastbourne is the ideal place for your summer holiday.*
DOUBLE ROOM: from £20 to £30
SINGLE ROOM: from £25 to £35
FOOD: up to £15
**Hours:** breakfast 8am-9.30am, bar snacks 12noon-2pm, dinner 6.45pm-8pm, closed mid-November until mid-March.
**Cuisine:** ENGLISH / CONTINENTAL
**Cards:** Visa, Access, Diners, AmEx.
**Other points:** children catered for (please check for age limits), no-smoking area, residents' lounge, vegetarian meals, residents' bar, wheelchair ramp.
**Rooms:** 6 single rooms, 17 double rooms, 24 twin rooms, 3 family rooms. All en suite with TV, telephone, tea/coffee-making facilities.
**Directions:** at western end past the bandstand.
MR K.B. SAYERS ☎(01323) 725217 Fax(01323) 720421

## FLETCHING • map 6D4

### THE ROSE & CROWN
High Street, near Uckfield, TN22 3ST
*This 16th century country inn, with a charm all of its own, offers diners a good choice of delicious meals from the à la carte, table d'hôte and bar menus. With a good selection of wines and ales and courteous service, The Rose & Crown is popular with locals and with visitors to the many nearby tourist attractions.*
FOOD: up to £15
**Hours:** lunch 12noon-2pm, dinner 7pm-9.30pm.
**Cuisine:** ENGLISH - fresh, home-made dishes. Children's menu available.

Cards: Visa, Access, AmEx.
Other points: parking, children welcome, no-smoking area, open-air dining, vegetarian meals, traditional Sunday lunch. Awarded the "Heartbeat" award 1995.
Directions: Fletching is situated off A272, between Uckfield and Haywards Heath.
ROGER & SHEILA HAYWOOD ☎(01825) 722039

## HALLAND • map 6D4

### 🛏 HALLAND FORGE HOTEL & RESTAURANT
Halland, near Uckfield, BN8 6PW

*This charming 3 star hotel in the heart of Sussex is adjacent to unspoilt woodland and has a large car park. The Forge restaurant, with its intimate atmosphere, is renowned for the excellent à la carte and table d'hôte menus complemented by an excellent wine list and friendly service. The location close to the Sussex downs makes it an ideal base for exploring the beautiful Sussex countrside and nearby coastal resorts.*
DOUBLE ROOM: from £30 to £40
SINGLE ROOM: from £44 to £54
FOOD: up to £20    CLUB
Hours: breakfast 7.30am-10am, lunch 12noon-2pm, dinner 7pm-9.30pm.
Cuisine: ENGLISH / FRENCH / ITALIAN - only fresh ingredients. Both à la carte and table d'hôte menus in the restaurant. Carvery/coffee shop is self-service.
Cards: Visa, Access, Diners, AmEx.
Other points: Sunday lunch, fully licensed lounge bar.
Rooms: 11 double rooms, 9 twin rooms. All with TV, radio, telephone, tea/coffee-making facilities, heating, trouser press, hair dryer
Directions: at the junction of the A22 and B2192, 4 miles south of Uckfield.
MR & MRS J.M. HOWELL ☎(01825) 840456
Fax(01825) 840773

## HASTINGS • map 6D5

### 🍽 RESTAURANT TWENTY SEVEN
27 George Street, Hastings Old Town, TN34 3EA
*Attractive French restaurant set in the old part of town near the seafront. All food is freshly prepared for each customer and, with its Impressionist paintings and soft Gallic-style music, the atmosphere is both intimate and relaxing.*
FOOD: from £15 to £20
Hours: dinner 7pm-10.30pm, closed Monday.
Cuisine: FRENCH - French dishes including salad

maconnaise, seafood croustade, filet de porc dijonaise, magret de canard, steak au poivre. Traditional Sunday lunch.
Cards: Visa, Access, AmEx.
Other points: licensed, Sunday lunch.
Directions: east end of the seafront, in pedestrianized area of the old town.
P. ATTRILL & E. GIBBS ☎(01424) 420060

## LEWES • map 6D4

### 🍽 LA CUCINA RESTAURANT
13 Station Street, BN7 2DA
*Outstanding food and excellent service can be found at this Italian restaurant in the centre of Lewes. The menu offers an extensive choice of authentic Italian dishes, superbly cooked and served in generous portions. Highly recommended for the high standard of cuisine and service within an atmosphere of peace and calm.*
FOOD: up to £15
Hours: closed Sunday/bank holidays, dinner Monday to Saturday 6.30pm-10.30pm, lunch Thursday to Saturday 12noon-2pm.
Cuisine: ITALIAN - seasonal specialities may include fresh mussels marinara, pesce misto marinara, pollo alla cacciatora, Sussex lamb, strawberries and cream or maraschino, fagiano, brill, venison.
Cards: Visa, Access, AmEx.
Other points: licensed, children welcome, parking.
Directions: 200 metres from station towards the high street.
JOSE VILAS MAYO ☎(01273) 476707

### 🛏 WHITE HART HOTEL
High Street, BN7 1XE
*A historic 16th century coaching house with a modern extension, tastefully blended to the original architecture. Well placed for exploring the Sussex coast, the hotel offers comfort, good food and warm hospitality.*
DOUBLE ROOM: from £30 to £40
SINGLE ROOM: from £45 to £55
FOOD: up to £15
Hours: breakfast 8am-9.30am, lunch 12.30am-2pm, dinner 7pm-10.15pm.
Cuisine: ENGLISH / FRENCH - à la carte, English and French. Carvery (set price), with fish or vegetarian option.
Cards: Visa, Access, Diners, AmEx, Switch.
Other points: licensed, Sunday lunch, children welcome, pets allowed, conferences, afternoon tea, leisure centre with heated pool, solarium, sauna, fully equipped gym.
Rooms: 50 bedrooms.
Directions: 7 miles from Brighton on A27.
MR AYRIS ☎(01273) 476694 Fax(01273) 476695

---

**Join Les Routiers Discovery Club
FREE!  See page 34 for details.**

---

For Reservations & Special Offers FreeCall 0500 700 456

## RYE • map 6D5

### ⋵ LANDGATE BISTRO
5-6 Landgate, TN34 7LH

*This Grade II listed building in the historic town of
Rye offers unpretentious yet comfortable
surroundings in which to enjoy a fine meal from the
good selection available. The comprehensive wine
list and the relaxed, informal atmosphere ensure an
enjoyable meal out.*
**FOOD:** from £15 to £20
**Hours:** dinner 7pm-9.30pm, closed Sunday and
Monday.
**Cuisine:** BRITISH - modern cuisine made with the
freshest produce.
**Cards:** Visa, Access, Diners, AmEx.
**Other points:** children welcome, licensed.
**Directions:** situated 50 yards below Landgate Arch.
NICK PARKIN & TONI FERGUSON-LEES
☎(01797) 222829

### ⊟ THE SHIP INN
Strand Quay, TN31 7AY

*An attractive 16th century inn, set amongst the
historic Strand Quay warehouses, where confiscated
contraband was once stored by revenue men, as
records show. All bedrooms are equipped with
modern facilities for maximum comfort, and the inn
provides guests with details of where to visit and
what to see in the area. Special breaks are available
throughout the year.*
**DOUBLE ROOM:** from £20 to £30
**SINGLE ROOM:** from £30 to £40

**FOOD:** from £16 to £20
**Hours:** breakfast 8am-9.45am, lunch 12noon-
2.30pm, dinner 7.30pm-9.35pm, bar snacks
12noon-3pm, 6.30pm-9.30pm.
**Cuisine:** SPONTANÉE BISTRO
**Cards:** Visa, Access, Switch.
**Other points:** parking, children welcome,
vegetarian meals, party bookings.
**Rooms:** 1 single room, 6 double rooms, 4 twin
rooms, 1 triple room.
**Directions:** among 18th century warehouses on
Strand Quay, at foot of Mermaid Street.
MR GATWARD ☎(01797) 222233 ▣(01797)
223892

## SEAFORD • map 6D4

### ⋵ THE OLD PLOUGH
20 Church Street, BN25 1HG

*A delightful 17th century coaching inn situated in
the town, which is set in the beautiful East Sussex
Downs, bordering Newhaven. The inn is extremely
popular with tourists who are attracted to the area,
which is steeped in history as a result of the
Norman Conquests. The nearby Heritage Centre is
well worth a visit.*
**FOOD:** up to £15
**Hours:** lunch 12noon-2.30pm, dinner 7pm-10pm,
open all year.
**Cuisine:** ENGLISH - traditional home-style cooking,
offering an extensive selection of dishes, including
speciality home-made pies and steamed puddings.
Carvery, grill, cut-to-order steaks, fresh fish, luxury
desserts.
**Cards:** Visa, Access, Switch.
**Other points:** licensed, Sunday lunch, no-smoking
area, children catered for (please check for age
limits), children's certificate, parking, garden
terrace.
**Directions:** situated off A259 in Seaford, adjoining
the parish church.
JOHN BOOTS ☎(01323) 892379 ▣(01323)
897980

# WEST SUSSEX

## ARUNDEL • map 5D3

### ⊟ SWAN HOTEL
27-29 High Street, BN18 9AG

*Situated in the heart of historic Arundel, the Swan
Hotel has been been lovingly restored to its former
Victorian splendour. Many of the hotel's original
features, including English oak flooring and wall
panelling, are still very much in evidence, creating
a wonderful ambience in the hotel's bar and lounge
areas. The Grade II listed building offers luxurious
accommodation, combining traditional comforts
with modern facilities. The hotel is close to
Arundel's 12th century castle, the River Arun,
cathedral and parks.*
**DOUBLE ROOM:** from £20 to £30
**SINGLE ROOM:** from £45 to £55

**FOOD:** from £15 to £20
**Hours:** breakfast 6.30am-10.30am, lunch 12noon-
2.30pm, dinner 6.30pm-9.30pm.
**Cuisine:** ENGLISH - locally acclaimed chef Michael
Collis has created a range of succulent dishes to suit
all tastes, with seasonal and local produce used
extensively throughout the à la carte and table
d'hôte menus. Wines can be selected from the
original 200-year-old cellar, which stocks a wide
choice of quality wines from around the world.
Local traditional ales complement delicious hot and
cold food served in the hotel's popular bar.
**Cards:** Visa, Access, Diners, AmEx.
**Other points:** vegetarian meals, afternoon teas,
traditional Sunday lunch.
**Rooms:** 15 bedrooms. All with en suite, TV,
telephone, hair dryer, tea/coffee-making facilities,

room service.
**Directions:** Arundel is just off the A27, midway between Chichester and Worthing. The hotel is located on the High Street.
JOHN RYAN ☎(01903) 882314 Fax(01903) 733381

## BOGNOR REGIS • map 5D3

### THE ROYAL HOTEL
The Esplanade, PU21 I52
*A Victorian hotel situated only yards from the sea, with unimpeded views from the restaurant, bars and coffee shop.*
DOUBLE ROOM: from £20 to £30
SINGLE ROOM: from £25 to £35
FOOD: up to £15 CLUB
**Hours:** breakfast 7.30am-9.30am, lunch 12noon-2.30pm, bar meals 11.30am-10.30am, dinner 6pm-10.30pm.
**Cuisine:** ENGLISH / CONTINENTAL - prawns, pasta, lobster.
**Cards:** Visa, Access, Diners, AmEx, Switch.
**Other points:** licensed, Sunday lunch, children welcome, coaches by prior arrangement
**Directions:** on Bognor Regis seafront, 50 yards west of the pier.
DAVID M. COOMBS ☎(01243) 864665/864666 Fax(01243) 863175

## CHICHESTER • map 5D3

### ANGLESEY ARMS
Halnaker, PO18 0NQ
*A small, friendly, traditional pub serving real ales. The single bar and attractive garden are both very popular. Only two miles from Goodwood Racecourse and four miles from Chichester harbour. There is a separate restaurant area.*
FOOD: up to £15
**Hours:** lunch 12noon-2pm, dinner 7.30pm-12midnight, last orders 10pm, closed Christmas day and New Year's day.
**Cuisine:** ENGLISH - peppered fillet steak, fresh Selsey lobster and crab, locally smoked salmon and ham, traditional roast Sunday lunch.
**Cards:** Visa, Access, Diners, AmEx, Switch.
**Other points:** licensed, children welcome.
**Directions:** close to the A27. Take the A285 to Halnaker and Petworth. The pub is one mile up on the right, just after Halnaker cross-roads.
CHRISTOPHER & TESSA HOUSEMAN ☎(01243) 773474 Fax(01243) 530034

### BULL'S HEAD AND SUSSEX BARN
Main Road, Fishbourne, PO19 3JP
*This 17th century pub, in the small village of Fishbourne on the outskirts of Chichester, offers a very attractive bar and good home-cooked food. A wide selection of first-class pub food is available daily for lunch and dinner, served by the friendly, efficient staff, under the supervision of Roger & Julie Jackson. Close to the coast, the pub is within easy*

*travelling distance of Portsmouth and Hayling Island. Near to Fishbourne Roman villa and 100 metres from the sea.*
FOOD: up to £15
**Hours:** lunch 12noon-3pm, dinner 7pm-10.30pm, bar snacks also available.
**Cuisine:** ENGLISH - fresh food is used in preparing all meals. Includes cheeses all hand made with several unpasteurised cheeses.
**Cards:** Visa, Access, AmEx.
**Other points:** children welcome, parking, vegetarian meals.
**Directions:** located on the A259, off the A27 Chichester to Portsmouth Road.
ROGER & JULIE JACKSON ☎(01243) 785707 Fax(01243) 786961

### EARL OF MARCH
Mid Lavant, PO18 0BQ
*Excellent service by well-trained staff will make this a good stop for those travelling in the area. Comfortable surroundings and good food can be found here.*
FOOD: up to £15
**Hours:** lunch 12.30am-2pm, dinner 6pm-10pm, last orders 10pm, Sunday 7pm-9.30pm.
**Cuisine:** ENGLISH - varied selection of traditional cuisine. Special vegetarian dishes. Bar food.
**Cards:** Visa, Access.
**Other points:** licensed, open-air dining, Sunday lunch, children welcome, pets allowed.
**Directions:** 2 miles from Chichester on the A286.
MR A.L. LAURIN ☎(01243) 774751

### EASTON HOUSE
Chidham Lane, Chidham, PO18 8TF
*A former 16th century farmhouse situated on the Chidham peninsula. Within easy reach of Goodwood, Chichester, Portsmouth and the New Forest. Uncrowded and peaceful waterside walks within 5 minutes of the house. The bedrooms overlook either farmland, the harbour or the garden.*
DOUBLE ROOM: up to £20
**Hours:** breakfast 8am-9am.
**Cuisine:** BREAKFAST
**Other points:** central heating, no evening meal, children welcome, residents' lounge, garden.
**Rooms:** 1 double room, 1 twin room.
**Directions:** 1 mile south of the A259.
MRS C.M. HARTLEY ☎(01243) 572514

### THE GRIBBLE INN
Oring, PO20 6BP
*A very attractive, well-preserved 17th century thatched building retaining many original features. A varied menu offers English and Continental dishes and a range of specialities. Spacious interior with characteristic log fires. Has its own brewery serving original ales, such as Gribble Ale, Reg's Tipple and Wobbler.*
FOOD: up to £15
**Hours:** lunch and bar meals 12noon-2pm, dinner

and bar meals 6.30pm-9.30pm, open bank holidays.

**Cuisine:** home-cooked food includes fish, grills, specialities, vegetarian and children's menus. Home brewed beers and country wines.

**Cards:** Access, Visa, AmEx

**Other points:** children welcome, pets allowed, no-smoking area, open-air dining, large beer garden, conference facilities, parking.

**Directions:** turn off A27 onto A259 Bognor road, left at signpost to Oving.

MR AND MRS MAY ☎(01243) 786893

### THE HORSE & GROOM
East Ashling, PO18 9AX

*Situated at the foot of the South Downs, this 17th century inn offers superb home cooking and a fine selection of real ales in a relaxed atmosphere. Five tastefully decorated en suite bedrooms in the converted flint barn provide comfortable accommodation with delightful views over the gardens and the South Downs beyond. An ideal centre for walking, cycling, riding and sailing at Bosham. Close to Chichester with its handsome cathedral and renowned festival theatre.*

DOUBLE ROOM: from £20 to £30

SINGLE ROOM: from £38

FOOD: from £15 to £20

**Hours:** breakfast 8am-9.30am, lunch 12noon-2.30pm, dinner 7pm-9.30pm. Open bank holidays.

**Cuisine:** specialities include rack of lamb and lobster. Restaurant menu changed on a regular basis.

**Cards:** Visa, Access, MasterCard, Eurocard.

**Other points:** real log fires in winter, real ales, large garden with rural outlook. Goodwood close by, children welcome, parking.

**Rooms:** 1 double room, 4 twin rooms. All en suite with radio, alarm, tea/coffee-making facilities. TV on request.

**Directions:** A27 from Brighton or Portsmouth to Chichester. Turn north onto B2178 signposted to Funtington.

MICHAEL MARTELL ☎(01243) 575339

### MICAWBER'S RESTAURANT
13 South Street, PO19 1EH

*Situated just south of the Cross, this popular restaurant has a provincial French character. The fruits de mer are cooked by the chef directly after he gets them from the local fishermen.*

FOOD: up to £15　CLUB

**Hours:** closed Sunday, dinner 6pm-10.30pm, lunch 11.30am-2.30pm.

**Cuisine:** FRENCH / ENGLISH - wide selection of fish dishes and shellfish, fresh meat and vegetables, all from local markets.

**Cards:** Visa, Access, Diners, AmEx.

**Other points:** children welcome, French spoken.

**Directions:** situated just south of the Cross at Chichester.

PHILIP COTTERILL & THIERRY BOISHU ☎(01243) 786989

### PLATTERS RESTAURANT
15 Southgate, PO19 1ES

*A sumptuous meal in this Mediterranean-style restaurant is assured, with very personal attention from the friendly staff. House specialities change from day to day, and you may even be treated to an explanation of the more interesting ingredients, such as local wild mushrooms. Chefs enjoying a break from their own restaurants are known to dine here - high praise indeed.*

FOOD: from £15 to £20

**Hours:** lunch 12noon-2pm, dinner 7pm, closed Sunday and Tuesday.

**Cuisine:** MEDITERRANEAN - à la carte and table d'hôte offering a range of imaginative dishes with daily changes. Vegetarian dishes always available.

**Cards:** Visa, Access.

**Other points:** licensed, open-air dining, children welcome, street parking.

**Directions:** 100 yards north of railway and bus station, opposite magistrates' court.

NIK WESTACOTT ☎(01243) 530430

## FERNHURST • map 5D3

### THE RED LION
The Green, GU27 3HY

*One of the oldest buildings in the village, The Red Lion is an attractive stone-built inn overlooking the village green. With exposed beams and open log fires to add to the cosy atmosphere, you will find the good food and Brenda Heath's hospitality hard to pass by. This free-house offers real ales and an extensive wine list.*

FOOD: up to £15

**Hours:** lunch everyday 12noon-2.30pm, dinner Monday-Saturday 5.30pm-10.30pm, dinner Sunday 7pm-10pm.

**Cuisine:** ENGLISH / CONTINENTAL - including Carribean chicken with fresh limes and root ginger, fresh tuna steak with peppercorns in a port wine sauce and delicious home-made sauce.

**Cards:** Visa, Access, AmEx, Switch.

**Other points:** licensed, Sunday lunch, 2 no-smoking areas, children welcome, large attractive garden.

**Directions:** On the village green in Fernhurst which is 3 miles south of Haslemere Surrey on the A286 to Midhurst.

MRS BRENDA HEATH ☎(01428) 643112/653304 Fax (01428) 661120

## HAYWARDS HEATH • map 6D4

### INN THE PRIORY
Syresham Gardens, RH16 3LB

*A lovely restaurant set in the surroundings of a Victorian priory chapel, with stained-glass windows, ornate wood carvings and a turret clock. Offers a freshly prepared carvery menu of high quality and good value. Conference facilities available. National Trust gardens and Bluebell steam railway located nearby.*

FOOD: from £15 to £20　CLUB

**Hours:** lunch 12noon-3pm, Sunday 11.45am-4pm,

dinner 7pm-11.30pm.
**Cuisine:** ENGLISH - traditional English carvery. Fish and vegetarian menus available.
**Cards:** Visa, Access, Diners, AmEx.
**Other points:** licensed, Sunday lunch, children welcome.
**Directions:** take Caxton Way off Sussex Square roundabout on South Road.
DAVID & MARTINA WHITE ☎(01444) 459533
Fax(01444) 459340

### ◥ THE SLOOP INN
Freshfield Lock, RH17 7NP

This attractive public house offers good-quality bar meals in comfortable surroundings. The service is warm and courteous and the pub enjoys a friendly, welcoming atmosphere.
FOOD. up to £15
**Hours:** lunch 12noon-2pm, dinner 7pm-9.30pm (Sunday to Thursday), 7pm-10pm (Friday and Saturday) .
**Cuisine:** ENGLISH - extensive menu displayed on blackboards: changes daily.
**Cards:** Visa, Access, Diners, AmEx, Switch.
**Other points:** licensed, open-air dining, children welcome, pets allowed, 3 beer gardens, games room.
**Directions:** Off the A272 at Scaynes Hill near Haywards Heath. Approximately 1.5 miles down Church Lane.
MR & MRS MILLS ☎(01444) 831219

## HENFIELD • map 6D4

### ◥ SHEPHERD & DOG INN
Fulking, BN5 9LU
A 400-year-old country pub nestling on the South Downs in this most attractive Sussex village. The atmosphere is extremely warm and welcoming, and the low beamed ceilings and wooden tables and settles all contribute to creating the sort of 'feel' that encourages visitors to return time after time. Both cheese and wine selections on the blackboard carry helpful descriptions. Good home-cooking and an à la carte menu which can be enjoyed outside if you wish.
FOOD: up to £15
**Hours:** lunch 12noon-2pm, dinner 7pm-9.30pm. Open all year.
**Cuisine:** MODERN/TRADITIONAL/INTERNATIONAL - home-made pies.
**Cards:** Visa, Access, AmEx, Switch, MasterCard.
**Other points:** parking, pets allowed, vegetarian meals, garden dining.

**Directions:** on the main street at the end of the village. Fulking is north of Brighton between the A23 and A2037.
JESSICA ANNE BRADLEY-HOLE ☎(01273) 857382

## HORSHAM • map 5D3

### ◥ COUNTRYMAN INN
Shipley, RH13 8PZ
A traditional old country pub with a very friendly atmosphere, set in 3,000 acres of Sussex farmland. Customers can enjoy delicious home-cooked meals, especially the deep-dish pies, which are made with fresh meat from the local farm. A very popular pub with the local community and country walkers. Places of interest nearby include Knepp Castle and Shipley Mill.
FOOD: up to £15
**Hours:** lunch 12noon-2pm, bar meals 12noon-2pm, dinner 7pm-9.30pm, bar meals 7pm-9pm.
**Cuisine:** ENGLISH - rural English cuisine, including speciality deep-dish pies and fresh fish. Good wine list.
**Cards:** Visa, Access, AmEx, Switch.
**Other points:** open-air dining, Sunday lunch, children welcome, open bank holidays, functions.
**Directions:** follow A24 to Worthing, then A272 signs to Billingshurst. Second turn left, then 1 mile to bottom of lane.
ALAN VAUGHAN ☎(01403) 741383

### ■ PARK HOUSE
Stane Street, Slinfold, RH13 7QX
A warm, friendly guest house equipped to a very high standard offering comfortable, good value accommodation to business people and tourists. Breakfast is served in your room.
DOUBLE ROOM: from £20 to £30
SINGLE ROOM: from £25 to £35
**Cards:** Visa, Access
**Other points:** breakfast served in bedrooms, no-smoking area, parking.
**Rooms:** 4 bedrooms all en suite with tea/coffee maker, TV, telephone, radio alarm. 1 room with trouser press.
**Directions:** on A29 at Slinfold, west of Horsham.
MRS P. ROWLAND ☎(01403) 790723
Fax(01403) 790812

## LINDFIELD • map 6D4

### ◢ BENT ARMS
98 High Street, RH16 2HP
The Bent Arms is part of a 16th century coaching inn, which sits in a typical English village with half-timbered houses, a lake and swans. It is popular with locals and has a friendly and relaxed atmosphere.
DOUBLE ROOM: from £20 to £30
SINGLE ROOM: from £25 to £35
FOOD: up to £15
**Hours:** breakfast 7.30am, lunch 12noon-2.15pm, dinner 6.15pm-10.15pm. Open all day for bar food.

**Cuisine:** ENGLISH - à la carte, bar meals/snacks. The speciality is spit-roast beef in the bar - sliced to order, hot.
**Cards:** Visa, Access, Diners, AmEx.
**Other points:** licensed, open-air dining, Sunday lunch, children welcome, garden, pets allowed. Renowned for a wide selection of real ales.
**Rooms:** 9 bedrooms. All en suite, TV, telephone, tea/coffee-making facilities.
**Directions:** 2 miles outside Haywards Heath in centre of Lindfield village.
MR P. HOYLE ☎(01444) 483146 [Fax](01444) 483455

## RUSPER • map 6DA

### 🏠 GHYLL MANOR COUNTRY CLUB
High Street, RH12 4PX

A delightful country hotel formed from a 350 year old manor house with the addition of a converted barn and more modern extensions. The house retains its original features such as beamed ceilings and open log fires, and is furnished with a tasteful mix of period antiques and modern features to make your stay as comfortable as possible. The Benedictine restaurant serves a wide selection of gourmet dishes, and the splendid grounds offer croquet and tennis for guests with an ornamental lake, Golf and horse riding available nearby.
DOUBLE ROOM: over £50
SINGLE ROOM: over £55
FOOD: from £15 to £20
**Hours:** breakfast 7am-9.30am (Monday to Friday), 8am-10am (Saturday and Sunday). Lunch (restaurant) 12noon-2pm, (bar) 11am-2pm. Dinner 7pm-9.30pm. Open bank holidays.
**Cuisine:** very good value table d'hôte menus complemented by an extensive à la carte selection. New wine list in preparation.
**Cards:** Visa, Access, Diners, AmEx, MasterCard, Switch.
**Other points:** tennis court, croquet lawn, two separate cottages available, open terraces, Library Lounge, function and conference facilities, licensed, Sunday lunch, afternoon teas, parking.
**Rooms:** 2 single rooms, 1 twin room, 21 double rooms, all en suite. All with TV, radio, telephone, trouser press, and tea/coffee-making facilities.
**Directions:** Approach from either A264 or A24, follow signs to Rusper. Hotel is in the centre of the village.
CSMA LEISURE LTD. ☎(01293) 871571 [Fax](01293) 871419

## STEYNING • map 5D3

### 🏠 OLD TOLLGATE RESTAURANT & HOTEL
The Street, Bramber, BN44 3WE
Travellers passing through Bramber were, at one time, obliged to interrupt their journey to pay a few pence at a tollgate for the right to continue on their way. Today many still stop there, but only to enjoy the good food and hospitality offered by this establishment, which stands on the original site. Ideal for touring, or for visiting the ruins of nearby Bramber Castle.
DOUBLE ROOM: from £30 to £40
SINGLE ROOM: from £55
FOOD: from £15 to £20
**Hours:** breakfast 7.30am-9.30am, lunch 12noon-2pm, bar meals 12noon-2pm, dinner 7pm-9.30pm, open all year.
**Cuisine:** ENGLISH - traditional old-English cuisine, including shellfish, meats and salads, roasts, casseroles, poultry and savoury pies. Special Christmas menu.
**Cards:** Visa, Access, Diners, AmEx.
**Other points:** licensed, Sunday lunch, children welcome, residents' lounge, garden, parking, functions, conferences, residents' bar, disabled access, vegetarian meals.
**Rooms:** 31 bedrooms en suite. All with satellite TV, telephone, tea/coffee-making facilities, hair dryer, trouser-press.
**Directions:** on A283; situated in Bramber village, 4 miles from Shoreham-by-Sea.
PETER SARGENT ☎(01903) 879494 [Fax](01903) 813399

### ▪ SPRINGWELLS HOTEL
9 High Street, BN44 3GG
A delightful 17th century Georgian hotel situated on the High Street of this picturesque market town and under the personal supervision of the owner. The bedrooms are individually furnished and include two with four-poster beds. The bar and adjoining conservatory lead to a patio and walled garden with heated outdoor swimming pool. At the front of the hotel there is a sunny dining room and elegant lounge.
DOUBLE ROOM: from £22 to £35
SINGLE ROOM: from £26 to £34
**Hours:** breakfast 7.15am-10am.
**Cuisine:** BREAKFAST
**Cards:** Visa, Access, Diners, AmEx.
**Other points:** children welcome, outdoor swimming pool, residents' lounge, garden, vegetarian meals.
**Rooms:** 11 bedrooms. 5 double rooms, 2 single rooms, 2 twin rooms (adaptable to King size), 2 four-poster rooms. 9 rooms en suite, all with tea/coffee-making facilities, TV, telephone, baby listening.
**Directions:** off A283.
MRS J. HESELGRAVE ☎(01903) 812446/812043 [Fax](01903) 879823

## WEST MARDEN • map 5D3

### VICTORIA INN
Near Chichester, PO18 9EN

*A deservedly popular pub in the heart of the Sussex countryside. The inn is family-run and enjoys a friendly atmosphere. Well-cooked and presented meals are served in the bar and in the small restaurant, and the emphasis is on home-cooked dishes. Vegetarian dishes on request. The inn has a well-appointed garden and terrace. Draught beers, including Gibbs Mews, Bishops Tipple and Theakston XB.*

**FOOD:** from £15 to £20

**Hours:** lunch 12noon-2pm, dinner 7pm-9.30pm, Sunday 7pm-9pm.

**Cuisine:** EUROPEAN - all dishes home-cooked. Daily blackboard menu served in both bar and restaurant.

**Cards:** Visa, Access, AmEx.

**Other points:** licensed, Sunday lunch, beer garden, open bank holidays, children catered for (please check for age limits).

**Directions:** on the B2146 road between the coast and Petersfield, situated nine miles west of Chichester.

JAMES NEVILLE ☎(01705) 631330

## WEST WITTERING • map 5D3

### THE LAMB INN WEST WITTERING
Chichester Road, PO20 8QA

*This traditional Sussex country freehouse specializes in real ales and home-cooking; the pies and toasted sandwiches are particularly recommended. The evening menu also features a range of local fresh fish, and during summer months (weather permitting) food is available in the pretty pub garden. With its good value and warm welcome, The Lamb Inn is popular with locals, visiting sailors and windsurfers.*

**FOOD:** up to £15

**Hours:** lunch 12noon-2pm, dinner 7pm-9pm, bar 11am-2.30pm and 6pm-11pm, Sunday 12noon-3pm and 7pm-10.30pm.

**Cuisine:** ENGLISH - home-made food including pies and fresh fish (evenings).

**Cards:** Visa, Access.

**Other points:** licensed, open-air dining, limited Sunday lunch menu, no-smoking area, open bank holidays, dogs allowed (on lead), parking, vegetarian meals.

**Directions:** on B2179, 500 yards beyond Itchenor turn. Sign opposite pub.

MR NIGEL CARTER ☎(01243) 511105

## WORTHING • map 5D3

### THE COURT HOUSE
Sea Lane, Goring-by-Sea, BN12 4NY

*Goring is just west of Worthing town. The Court House is an historic listed building within walking distance of the sea. There are train and bus services to the town centre, Sussex and London. Local attractions include yachting and windsurfing, the National Bowls Centre and other sports facilities.*

**DOUBLE ROOM:** up to £20

**SINGLE ROOM:** up to £25

**Hours:** breakfast 8.15am-9am.

**Cuisine:** BREAKFAST

**Cards:** Visa, Access, Eurocard, MasterCard.

**Other points:** children welcome, pets allowed, residents' lounge, garden, German spoken, French spoken, Dutch spoken.

**Rooms:** 1 single room, 4 twin rooms, 2 family rooms.

**Directions:** A259 from Worthing, 2 miles.

MRS I. GOMME ☎(01903) 248473

### THE HORSE & GROOM
Arundel Road, Patching, BN13 3UQ

*A fine pub/restaurant and steakhouse, serving a wide and varied menu of English and continental dishes. There is a wonderful spacious restaurant and attractively furnished bar area. Outside is a play-area for children and space for dining. Mine host, Stephen Earp extends a warm, friendly welcome to all visitors. Nearby places of interest, include Arundel Castle, Goodwood, Worthing, Littlehampton and Chichester.*

**FOOD:** up to £15

**Hours:** lunch and bar meals 12noon-2.30pm, dinner and bar meals 6.30-9.30pm, open bank holidays.

**Cards:** Access,Visa,AmEx,Diners,Switch

**Other points:** children welcome, pets allowed, no-smoking area, open-air dining, afternoon teas, summer barbeque hire, weddings catered for, vegetarian meals, parking.

**Directions:** half way between Arundel and Worthing, just off A27/A280 roundabout.

RICHARD SVAGERS ☎(01903) 871346

---

**Club Bon Viveur. Take advantage of the
8 FREE vouchers on Page 67.
Join up for a year at only £15. See page 65.**

---

# SOUTH WEST ENGLAND

The counties of the South-West that make up England's most popular holiday areas offer the traveller or tourist a constantly changing choice of magnificent scenery, as well as first-class food complemented by fine wines and traditional cask ales. The undulating coastline, with its secret coves and windswept, grassy cliffs, firm, sandy beaches and picturesque fishing villages, yields an abundance of locally-caught fish and seafood specialities.

Travel further inland through picture-book villages with cottage gardens full of old-fashioned sweet-scented flowers to discover hearty, home-made cooking, prepared from old recipes passed down from generation to generation and served in bounteous proportions to satisfy the most insatiable of appetites. Round it off perhaps with a Devonshire cream tea or a medley of the region's excellent farmhouse cheeses.

Whether you opt for a traditional steak-and-kidney pudding or dine continental, it will be a gourmet experience you'll never forget. And if your stay is for a day or longer, you'll find it hard to ignore the warm, friendly hospitality of your hosts in the true Les Routiers spirit.

The following counties are included in this chapter:

| | |
|---|---|
| AVON | DORSET |
| BERKSHIRE | HAMPSHIRE |
| CORNWALL & | ISLE OF WIGHT |
| THE SCILLY ISLES | SOMERSET |
| DEVON | WILTSHIRE |

# *AVON*

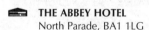

## BATH • map 4B5

### THE ABBEY HOTEL
North Parade, BA1 1LG

*Originally built as a wealthy merchant's house in the 1740s, The Abbey Hotel reopened in May 1990 after a complete refurbishment. Just a minute's walk from the Abbey, Roman baths and Pump Room, it offers comfortable accommodation with many luxuries, including Sky TV. Wedgwood's restaurant, bar and lounge make ideal meeting places while you are exploring the European Heritage City of Bath. The Fernley and Orchard rooms are available for meetings and for conference hire.*
DOUBLE ROOM: from £42

SINGLE ROOM: from £55
FOOD: from £15 to £20
**Hours:** breakfast 7.15am-9.30am, bar snacks 10am-6pm, lunch 12noon-2pm, dinner 7.15pm-9.15pm.
**Cuisine:** ENGLISH
**Cards:** Visa, Access, Diners, AmEx.
**Other points:** children welcome, no-smoking area, afternoon teas, disabled access, residents' lounge, vegetarian meals available.
**Rooms:** 12 single rooms, 25 double rooms, 11 twin rooms, 5 triple rooms, 1 family room, 2 double divan rooms (4 persons).
**Directions:** right in the city centre, 300 metres from Bath Spa station.
COMPASS HOTELS ☎(01225) 461603
Fax (01225) 447758

### APSLEY HOUSE HOTEL
141 Newbridge Hill, BA1 3PP
*Built in 1830, reputedly for the Duke of Wellington, the family-run Apsley House Hotel rates among Britain's finest small hotels. The interior is tastefully decorated with antiques and oil paintings, providing an atmosphere more like a country home than a*

hotel.
DOUBLE ROOM: from £30 to £40
SINGLE ROOM: from £35 to £45
**Hours:** breakfast 8am-9am, light snacks available on request, open all year.
**Cards:** Visa, Access, MasterCard.
**Other points:** parking, children welcome, no-smoking area, residents' lounge, garden.
**Rooms:** 5 double rooms, 2 twin rooms. All with en suite, TV, telephone, alarm, hair dryer, trouser-press.
**Directions:** 1 mile from Bath city centre on A4 to Bristol, proceed along Upper Bristol Road to second set of traffic lights, turn right into Newbridge Hill.
MR AND MRS C. AND A. BAKER ☎(01225) 336966 **Fax**(01225) 425462

### BROMPTON HOUSE
### GUEST HOUSE OF THE YEAR 1996
St Johns Road, BA2 6PT
*A former Georgian rectory of 1777, now converted and extended, it is set amidst a prize-winning garden. All rooms have been tastefully furnished to an extremely high standard with guests' comfort in mind, and although remodernized, the building still retains the Georgian era, with oil paintings, furniture and fittings of the period. A very friendly and courteous welcome is assured from both the management and helpful staff in the relaxing, informal atmosphere.*
DOUBLE ROOM: from £27.50 to £38
SINGLE ROOM: from £32 to £45
**Hours:** breakfast 8.15am-9.15am, closed 23rd December until 2nd January.
**Cuisine:** BREAKFAST ☞
**Cards:** Visa, Access, AmEx, MasterCard, Eurocard, JCB.
**Other points:** parking, children welcome, open bank holidays, no-smoking area, residents' lounge, vegetarian meals, garden.
**Rooms:** 2 single rooms, 11 double rooms, 4 twin rooms, 1 family room. All with TV, radio, telephone, tea/coffee-making facilities.
**Directions:** exit 17 or 18 off M4 to A4, Bath Road. At traffic lights take A35, Warminster Road, crossing Cleveland bridge first right. Brompton House is on left next to church.
DAVID, SUSAN, BELINDA & TIMOTHY SELBY
☎(01225) 420972 **Fax**(01225) 420505

### THE CANARY RESTAURANT
3 Queen Street, BA1 1HE
*The Canary Restaurant has become one of Bath's most popular and well-established restaurants. The chefs produce an array of international dishes to suit all tastes and times of the day. Tea time is a speciality, and the Canary was winner of the Tea Council's Top Tea Place Award of the Year in 1989 and awards for excellence 1988-90 and 1994. Over 40 different types of tea are served, with an impressive selection of patisserie.*
FOOD: up to £15 ☞
**Hours:** meals all day from 9am to 8pm (Sundays 11am to 6pm), closed Christmas day, Boxing day, New Year's day.

**Cuisine:** INTERNATIONAL - varied and interesting range of international cuisine, with award-winning speciality teas and delicious cakes and pastries. 3 course menu from £4.95.
**Cards:** Visa, Access, AmEx.
**Other points:** children catered for (please check for age limits), parking.
**Directions:** on A4, 9 miles off M4 on A46.
MR DAVIES ☎(01225) 424846

### CHESTERFIELD HOTEL
11 Great Pulteney Street, BA2 4BR
*A Grade 1 listed hotel, built in 1793 and offering comfortable en suite bed and breakfast accommodation right in the heart of this fascinating city. Furnished in the period style, the exterior retains its original elegance and will provide a comfortable and memorable base from which to explore Bath and the surrounding area. Well recommended.*
DOUBLE ROOM: from £20 to £30
SINGLE ROOM: from £32 to £50
**Hours:** breakfast 8.30am-9.30am. Closed Christmas day.
**Cards:** Access, Visa, AmEx, Diners, Mastercard
**Other points:** parking, garage parking available on request.
**Rooms:** 4 single rooms, 1 twin room, 9 double rooms, 3 family rooms, 3 four poster suites all with en suite facilities, tea/coffee maker, TV, telephone.
**Directions:** in central Bath by Pulteney bridge via Argyle Street.
PHILLIP & ANN HANSOM ☎(01225) 460953 **Fax**(01225) 448770

### COURT HOTEL
Emborough, Chilcompton, BA3 4SA
*An attractive Victorian stone manor house, this recently refurbished hotel is set in the beautiful countryside of Avon. Tastefully decorated, the rooms are light and airy with good views. Superb food is served in the tranquil dining room. Conference facilities.*
DOUBLE ROOM: from £30 to £40
FOOD: up to £15
**Hours:** breakfast 6.45am-9.30am, lunch 12.15am-2.15pm, dinner 7.30pm-9.30pm.
**Cuisine:** ENGLISH - mainly traditional English and French cuisine. Imaginative cooking. Good selection of wines.
**Cards:** Visa, Access, AmEx.

**Other points:** licensed, open-air dining, Sunday lunch, children welcome, open bank holidays, afternoon tea, residents' lounge, garden.
**Rooms:** 3 single rooms, 5 double rooms, 3 twin rooms, 1 family room. All with TV, tea/coffee-making facilities.
**Directions:** take A367 from Bath to Radstock, then Wells Road.
MISS COLLINS ☎(01761) 232237 **Fax**(01761) 233730

### CROSS KEYS INN
Midford Road, Combe Down, BA2 5RZ
*An attractive olde-worlde pub with a friendly, welcoming atmosphere. The food is well cooked and offers variety and good value for money. The B3110 is a scenic alternative to the main A36 and is worth taking even if only to visit the Cross Keys for its good food, warm welcome and friendly service. In the garden there is an interesting, well-stocked aviary.*
FOOD: up to £15
**Hours:** lunch 12noon-1.50pm, dinner 7pm-9.50pm (for last orders).
**Cuisine:** ENGLISH - bar meals including a large selection of home-made foods.
**Cards:** None.
**Other points:** licensed, Sunday lunch, children welcome, garden, pets allowed.
**Directions:** on B3110 overlooking Bath. Near St Martin's Hospital.
MARK & CAROLINE PALMER ☎(01225) 832002

### DORIAN HOUSE
1 Upper Oldfield Park, BA2 3JX
*A gracious Victorian home with free parking. Situated on the southern slopes overlooking Bath, yet only ten minutes' stroll to the city centre. There are eight charming bedrooms, all en suite. The lounge and small licensed bar provide a pleasant atmosphere for friends to meet. There is a full English breakfast menu and a warm welcome for all guests.*
DOUBLE ROOM: from £30 to £40
SINGLE ROOM: from £35 to £48
**Hours:** breakfast 8am-9.30am, dinner by prior arrangement.
**Cuisine:** BREAKFAST - dinner by prior arrangement.
**Cards:** Visa, Access, Diners, AmEx.
**Other points:** children welcome, residents' lounge, garden, vegetarian meals, parking.
**Rooms:** 1 single room, 3 double rooms, 2 four-poster rooms, 2 family rooms. All en suite with TV, radio, alarm, telephone, tea/coffee-making facilities.
**Directions:** up A367 Wells Road for 250 metres to left-hand bend. First right, then third house on left.
JANE & BRIAN TAYLOR ☎(01225) 426336 **Fax**(01225) 444699

### THE OLD MALT HOUSE HOTEL
Radford, Timsbury, BA3 1QF
*Only 6 miles from Bath, the hotel is an excellent*
base to explore the West Country, and guests are welcome at the farm run by the same family, with its famous Shire horses. The comfortable, relaxed no-smoking restaurant is renowned for its excellent English food. Full English breakfast is included in all B&B rates.
DOUBLE ROOM: from £30 to £40
SINGLE ROOM: from £32.50 to £38
FOOD: from £15 to £20
**Hours:** breakfast 7.45am-9am, lunch 12noon-2pm, dinner 7pm-8.30pm, closed 25th December to 28th December.
**Cuisine:** ENGLISH - traditional English, including pheasant, duck, venison, steak, rabbit and vegetarian dishes.
**Cards:** Visa, Access, Diners, AmEx.
**Other points:** licensed, open-air dining, parking, children by arrangement, afternoon tea, residents' lounge, garden, disabled access, vegetarian meals, residents' bar, conference facilities, pets by arrangement.
**Rooms:** 1 single room, 4 double rooms, 3 twin rooms, 2 triple rooms. All en suite with tea/coffee-making facilities, TV, radio/alarm, telephone, hair dryer.
**Directions:** off A367, take B3115. Follow the `Radford Farm' signs.
MICHAEL & MARGUERITE HORLER ☎(01761) 470106 **Fax**(01761) 472726

### RAJPOOT
Rajpoot House, 4 Argyle Street, BA2 4BA
*A very highly regarded restaurant situated in a listed Georgian building in the centre of Bath. An intimate atmosphere is created by subdued lighting and candlelit tables. Winner of many awards, the Rajpoot makes every effort to persuade you that you are dining in India itself. Attentive staff and excellent traditional food ensure a memorable evening. The food is complemented by an extensive wine list including some memorable Burgundies.*
FOOD: from £15 to £25
**Hours:** lunch 12noon-2.30pm, dinner Monday-Thursday & Sunday 6pm-11pm, dinner Friday-Saturday 6pm-11.30pm.
**Cuisine:** wide range of dishes including Tandoori, Mughlai and Bengali. Extensive wine list including an Indian white.
**Cards:** Visa, Diners, AmEx, MasterCard
**Other points:** parking in multi-storey approximately 100 yards. Entrance by stairs to restaurant in cellar, fully air-conditioned, disabled access by arrangement.
**Directions:** situated in the centre of Bath. Over Pulteney bridge and right into Argyle Street.
MR CHOWDHURY ☎(01225) 466833 **Fax**(01225) 442462

### RASCALS BISTRO
8 Pierrepont Place, BA1 1JX
*Rascals is situated in a listed building in converted cellars and is entered via a main staircase. Its original stone walls give it a warm, intimate*

atmosphere, where you can sample imaginative international cuisine and an excellent wine list. The friendly staff and the emphasis on value for money make for a relaxed and informal ambience. Definitely not to be missed!

FOOD: up to £15 🍽 CLUB

**Hours:** bar snacks 11.30am-2.30pm, lunch 11.30am-2.30pm, dinner weekdays 6pm-10.30pm, weekends 5.30pm-11pm, closed Sunday lunch.

**Cuisine:** INTERNATIONAL - all meals are prepared on the premises and all ingredients are bought fresh each day.

**Cards:** Visa, MasterCard, Switch.

**Other points:** children welcome, open bank holidays, no-smoking area, pets allowed, vegetarian meals.

**Directions:** near Pulteney Bridge off Pierrepont Street, through stone pillars behind Compass Hotel.

NICK ANDERSON & NIGEL MANNING-MORTON ☎(01225) 330201 Fax(01225) 330201

### 🛏 THE ROOKERY
Wells Road, Radstock, BA3 3RS

Set amidst a pleasant garden with flowers and shrubs, this 200-year-old country house is now a homely guest house offering every comfort, good food, personal attention, a happy and friendly atmosphere and olde-worlde charm. Separate guest lounge is available for small conferences. Ideal location for touring the West Country.

DOUBLE ROOM: from £20 to £30
SINGLE ROOM: from £25 to £35
FOOD: up to £15 CLUB

**Hours:** breakfast 7.30am-9.30am, lunch 12noon-2pm, dinner 7pm-9.30pm, bar snacks 12noon-2pm, bar snacks 7pm-9.30pm, closed Christmas day (to non-residents).

**Cuisine:** ENGLISH

**Cards:** Visa, Access, Diners, AmEx.

**Other points:** parking, children welcome, open bank holidays, no-smoking area, afternoon tea, disabled access, pets allowed, residents' lounge, vegetarian meals, garden, licensed.

**Rooms:** 4 double rooms, 3 twin rooms, 3 family rooms. All with TV, telephone, tea/coffee-making facilities, iron.

**Directions:** take A367 from Bath to Radstock, approximately 8 miles to The Rookery.

ANN & ROGER SIMS ☎(01761) 432626 Fax(01761) 432626

### 🍽 THE WIFE OF BATH RESTAURANT
12 Pierrepont Street, BA1 1LA

This well-established bistro-style restaurant is close to Bath Abbey and the famous Pump Rooms. A series of Georgian cellars of great character open onto a walled garden. The atmosphere is informal and staff are welcoming and friendly. The good food is complemented by an interesting wine list. Attractive decor, with quarry-tiled floors, stone walls and Provençal printed fabrics.

FOOD: up to £15 🍽

**Hours:** lunch 12noon-2.15pm, dinner 5.30pm-11pm, closed Sunday lunch.

**Cuisine:** ENGLISH - casseroles, stuffed peppers, steaks, fresh fish, daily specials, toasted sandwiches at lunchtime.

**Cards:** Visa, Access, AmEx.

**Other points:** licensed, open-air dining, children welcome, vegetarian meals, garden, no-smoking area.

**Directions:** situated close to Bath Abbey.

DICK & AINSLIE ENSOM ☎(01225) 461745

## BRISTOL • map 4B5

### 🍽 51 PARK STREET
51 Park Street, BS1 5NT

Prominently positioned in Bristol's shopping area, 51 Park Street is well-decorated and offers a wide variety of dishes at value-for-money prices. Frequented by holiday-makers and locals alike, and of appeal to all age groups.

FOOD: from £15 to £20

**Hours:** closed Christmas day and New Year's day, meals all day Monday-Saturday 7am-11pm (last orders) (continental breakfast 7am-12noon), Sunday 12noon-10pm.

**Cuisine:** INTERNATIONAL - mainly English with French and Asiatic influences. Specialities include modern American dishes and European brasserie food. Sunday carvery.

**Cards:** Visa, Access, Diners, AmEx.

**Other points:** licensed, open-air dining, Sunday lunch, no-smoking area, children welcome, afternoon tea.

**Directions:** from city centre follow route to Bristol University.

MRS H.L. TIMMONS ☎(0117) 926 8016 Fax(01179) 215266

### 🛏 ARCHES HOTEL
132 Cotham Brow, BS6 6AE

This early-Victorian house hotel offers comfortable accommodation and a warm welcome to Les Routiers visitors. Situated just off the A38, it is convenient for the central stations, theatres, waterfront, exhibition and shopping centres, and is located in an area renowned for its diverse restaurants. 🍽

DOUBLE ROOM: from £20 to £30
SINGLE ROOM: up to £31

**Hours:** breakfast weekdays 7.15am-8.30am, Saturday 8am-9am, Sunday 8.30am-9.30am, closed Christmas and New Year.

**Cuisine:** BREAKFAST - choice of continental or 6 cooked breakfasts, with traditional, vegetarian and vegan tastes catered for.

**Cards:** Visa, Diners, AmEx, MasterCard.

**Other points:** no-smoking areas, children welcome, pets allowed, open bank holidays.

**Rooms:** 3 single rooms, 4 double rooms, 1 twin room, 2 family rooms. All with TV, tea/coffee-making facilities. 2 rooms with private showers.

**Directions:** .5 mile from bus station, north on A38, turn left at first mini-roundabout, 100 yards on the left.

MR & MRS D. LAMBERT ☎(0117) 924 7398
Fax (0117) 924 7398

### ⤙ THE GANGES
368 Gloucester Road, Horfield, BS7 8TP

*A friendly restaurant, tastefully decorated in Indian style, with intimate alcoves for romantic dining. The service is courteous and efficient, and the menu includes some lesser-known Indian dishes.*

FOOD: from £10 to £20
**Hours:** lunch 12noon-2.30pm, dinner 6pm-11.30pm, closed Christmas day and Boxing Day.
**Cuisine:** INDIAN - north Indian.
**Cards:** Visa, Access, Diners, AmEx.
**Other points:** licensed, Sunday lunch, children welcome, fully air-conditioned.
**Directions:** on the A38 Gloucester road.
MR CHOWDHURY ☎(0117) 942 8505/924 5234

### 🛏 GRASMERE COURT HOTEL
22-24 Bath Road, Keynsham, BS18 1SN

*Situated approximately halfway between Bath and Bristol city centre, this hotel has recently been renovated and modernized to provide a compact `country-style' hotel with a friendly atmosphere. The hotel offers a haven of peace in which to relax in comfort after a strenuous day exploring the nearby Mendip Hills, shopping or sightseeing.*

DOUBLE ROOM: from £21 to £30
SINGLE ROOM: from £34 to £52
FOOD: up to £15
**Hours:** breakfast 7.30am-9.30am, dinner 6pm-7.30pm, bar snacks 12noon-2pm, 6pm-9.30pm.
**Cuisine:** ENGLISH / COSMOPOLITAN - attractively presented, home-style meals.
**Cards:** Visa, Access, AmEx, Mastercard, JCB.
**Other points:** parking, children welcome, open bank holidays, no-smoking rooms, afternoon tea, residents' lounge, vegetarian meals, garden.
**Rooms:** 1 single room, 12 double rooms, 3 twin rooms.
**Directions:** on main road between Bristol and Bath.
JOHN BARRINGTON LLEWELLIN & M. LLEWELLIN
☎(0117) 986 2662 Fax (0117) 986 2762

### ⤙ THE HALF MOON
Badminton Road, Coalpit Heath, BS17 2QJ

*Although a fairly modern building, the interior is immaculately furnished in olde-worlde style with wooden beams, oak panelling, pictures and artefacts. An extensive menu offers traditional dishes, including Scottish steaks and children's specials. The prevailing intimate atmosphere makes this a perfect location for weddings and private parties in the large function room.*

FOOD: up to £15
**Hours:** lunch (restaurant) 12noon-2pm, (bar) 12noon-2.30pm, 3pm Sundays. Dinner (restaurant) 6pm-10pm, (bar) 6pm-11pm. Closed Christmas day.
**Cuisine:** TRADITIONAL ENGLISH/INTERNATIONAL - good selection of steaks and a generous `house'

mixed grill. Traditional Sunday roasts of beef, lamb or chicken. Vegetarian dishes available.
**Other points:** parking, children welcome
**Directions:** situated on A432 4.5 miles from Mangotsfield and 2 miles from Yate.
MR TIMOTHY HANHAM ☎(01454) 772132

### ⤙ HENRY AFRICA'S HOTHOUSE
65 Whiteladies Road, Clifton, B28 2LY

*This lively restaurant and bar with its extensive cocktail list, busy happy hour and Cajun and Tex-Mex specialities is extremely popular, whether for snacks and drinks at the bar, or for a full meal in the attractive upstairs restaurant.*

FOOD: from £15 to £20
**Hours:** meals served all day 12noon-11pm, Friday-Saturday 12noon-12midnight.
**Cuisine:** CAJUN / TEX-MEX - constant set price menu (£6.95) plus grills, barbecue, Cajun and Tex-Mex specialities. Magnificent selection of cocktails, wines and beers, including a choice of non-alcoholic drinks.
**Cards:** Visa, Access, AmEx, Switch.
**Other points:** licensed, Sunday lunch, no-smoking area, children welcome, afternoon tea, open bank holidays.
**Directions:** just north of the BBC on Whiteladies Road, Clifton, Bristol.
CRAIG COLLINS ☎(0117) 923 8300 Fax (0117) 946 7893

### 🛏 JUBILEE INN
Flax Bourton, BS19 3QX

*An olde-worlde stone-built inn, covered by creepers and hanging baskets. Fresh produce is used to provide well-cooked meals, and all dishes offer good value for money. Traditional English dishes are cooked with an imaginative touch. For warmer days there is an attractive garden for customers' use.*

DOUBLE ROOM: from £20 to £30
SINGLE ROOM: from £25 to £30
FOOD: up to £15
**Hours:** breakfast 8am-9.15am, lunch 12noon-2pm, dinner 7.30pm-10pm.
**Cuisine:** ENGLISH - traditional English home-made dishes. Specialities include the special seafood pie (fresh salmon, white fish and prawns, topped with potato).
**Other points:** licensed, Sunday lunch, garden, pets allowed.
**Rooms:** 3 bedrooms.
**Directions:** between Bristol and Weston-Super-Mare.
BRIAN HAYDOCK ☎(01275) 462741

### 🛏 LINDEN HOTEL
51-59 High Street, Kingswood, BS15 4AD

*A deceptively large hotel offering first-class accommodation, excellent food and luxurious reception rooms, the Linden Hotel is conveniently situated close to Bristol. The helpful and courteous staff are always on hand to ensure that all guests*

requirements are provided for.
DOUBLE ROOM: from £20 to £30
SINGLE ROOM: from £36
FOOD: up to £15
**Hours:** breakfast 7am-9.30am, lunch 12noon-2pm,
dinner 6.30pm-9pm.
**Cuisine:** ENGLISH
**Cards:** Visa, Access, Diners, AmEx, Switch.
**Other points:** parking, children welcome, pets
allowed, no-smoking area, vegetarian meals.
**Rooms:** 5 single rooms, 10 double rooms, 10 twin
rooms, 3 triple rooms, 3 family rooms.
**Directions:** 4 miles east of Bristol city centre on the
north side of the A420 Bristol-Chippenham road.
☎(0117) 967 4331 Fax(0117) 961 5871

### NATRAJ TANDOORI (NEPALESE & INDIAN CUISINE)
185 Gloucester Road, Bishopston,
BS7 8BG
*Natraj offers an excellent mix of traditional Tandoori
with more unusual Nepalese dishes. Try Momocha
(spiced minced lamb in pastry served withNepalese
pickle) as one of the many Nepalese specialities on
offer, or one of the set menus. Friendly, helpful staff
will help you choose from the extensive menu.
Generous helping of food in comfortable, oriental
surroundings.*
FOOD: to £15
**Hours:** lunch (Fri-Sat 12noon to 2pm) dinner (Mon-
Thur) 6pm to midnight Friday and Saturday 6pm to
00.30am, Sunday 6pm to midnight
**Cuisine:** NEPALESE/INDIAN - specialities include
gurkha chick, momocha, murgi mussalam, thuckpa.
Continental dishes and à la carte or special buffet.
**Cards:** Visa,Access,Diners,AmEx
**Other points:** licensed, no smoking area, children
welcome, functions
**Directions:** A38, north of city centre. Opposite
Bristol North swimming baths.
MR D. KARKI ☎(0117) 9248145

### RAINBOW CAFE
9-10 Waterloo Street, Clifton, BS8 4BT
*The combination of home-made meat and
vegetarian dishes on offer has made this small
restaurant very popular. Quality second-hand books
on sale and monthly exhibitions of work by local
artists.*
FOOD: up to £15
**Hours:** snacks 10am-5.30pm, lunch 12noon-
2.30pm, closed Sunday, bank holidays and
Christmas until New Year.
**Cuisine:** ENGLISH / VEGETARIAN - fish and meat
dishes. The lunch menu varies daily and all food is
fresh each day.
**Other points:** licensed, no-smoking area, children
welcome.
**Directions:** from Bristol city centre, follow Clifton
signs. Off Princess Street.
ALISON MOORE & TIM ANSELL ☎(0117) 973
8937

## CLEVEDON • map 4B5

### CASA TOMAS RISTORANTE
Millcross, Southern Way, BS21 5HX
*For a true taste of Italy, one need go no further than
this lively restaurant in the heart of Clevedon.
Warm, friendly service and a vibrant atmosphere
complement the first-class Italian food.*
FOOD: from £15 to £20
**Hours:** dinner 7.30pm-10.30pm, closed Sunday.
**Cuisine:** ITALIAN - distinctive Italian cuisine, with
vegetarian meals also provided.
**Cards:** Visa, Access.
**Other points:** children welcome.
**Directions:** .5 mile off junction 20 of M5.
TOMAS MEDINA ☎(01275) 343578

## FRESHFORD • map 4B5

### INN AT FRESHFORD
Freshford Village, BA3 6EG
*Updated yet retaining all its original charm, this fine
example of an old coaching inn is decorated
throughout in an olde-worlde style, providing an
enchanting atmosphere in which to enjoy a fine
meal. Stephen Turner and his helpful staff have
worked hard to achieve the enviable reputation they
now hold for superb food and an award-winning
wine list.*
FOOD: from £2.95 to £8.95 ☜ ≋
**Hours:** lunch 12noon-2pm, Sunday 12noon-
2.15pm, dinner 6pm-10pm, Sunday 7pm-9.30pm.
**Cuisine:** ENGLISH / FRENCH - a blackboard menu
and an extensive à la carte selection, both at
reasonable prices.
**Cards:** Visa, Access.
**Other points:** parking, children welcome, no-
smoking area, garden, open-air dining, vegetarian
meals, traditional Sunday lunch.
**Directions:** off A36, 5 miles south of Bath between
Limpley Stoke and Bradford on Avon.
STEPHEN TURNER ☎(01225) 722250

## NAILSEA • map 4B5

### THE OLD FARMHOUSE
Trendlewood Way, BS19 2PF
*This Grade II listed, converted farm house retains all
of its original features, including high-pitched roof.
Traditional English and continental cuisine is served
by warm, friendly staff. The building's interesting
interior features stone floors, open fires and walls
adorned with farming implements. Picturesque
setting.*
FOOD: up to £15
**Hours:** bar meals 12noon-2pm, and 7pm-10pm,
open bank holidays.
**Cuisine:** traditional English farmhouse dishes, daily
specials, carvery.
**Cards:** Access,Visa,Switch,Delta
**Other points:** children welcome, open-air dining,
traditional Sunday lunch, vegetarian meals, parking.
**Directions:** Off Trendlewood Way, north of

Blackwell railway station.
MR RICHARD CRAWFORD ☎(01275) 851889

## RANGEWORTHY • map 4A5

### RANGEWORTHY COURT HOTEL
Church Lane, Wotton Road, BS17 5ND

*An attractive, historic country house set in its own grounds beside the church. Inside, the lounges have log fires and candles in winter, flowers all year and a relaxing atmosphere. Food is considered an important feature of the hotel, and the restaurant has a strong local following. Enjoy welcoming service, well-cooked food and the peace and quiet of this country house. (See special feature on page 11.)*
DOUBLE ROOM: from £31 to £40
SINGLE ROOM: from £45 to £55
FOOD: from £16 to £20 🍷 CLUB
**Hours:** breakfast 7.15am-9.30am, lunch 12noon-2pm, dinner 7pm-9pm.
**Cuisine:** ENGLISH - dishes may include devilled crab, lamb steak in Madeira and rosemary sauce, fresh salmon, turbot. Vegetarian and vegan dishes.
**Cards:** Visa, Access, Diners, AmEx.
**Other points:** licensed, Sunday lunch, garden, pets allowed, functions, conferences, children welcome, baby-listening device, cots, residents' bar, residents' lounge, vegetarian meals, parking, swimming pool.
**Rooms:** 3 single rooms, 7 double rooms, 4 triple rooms. All with TV, radio, telephone, tea/coffee-making facilities.
**Directions:** from Bristol, M32 exit 1, then B4058 to Rangeworthy.
MERVYN & LUCIA GILLETT ☎(01454) 228347
Fax(01454) 228945

## WESTON-SUPER-MARE • map 4B5

 **CARRINGTON HOTEL**
28 Knightstone Road, BS23 2AN
*A Victorian terraced house overlooking the beach and the pier, with a patio to the front laid with tables and umbrellas for alfresco dining in summer. Situated near to the Winter Gardens, and with all the facilities of a British seaside town on the doorstep.*
DOUBLE ROOM: from £20 to £30
FOOD: up to £15
**Hours:** breakfast 8.30am-9.30am, lunch 11.30am-3pm, dinner 6pm-9.30pm, bar meals 11am-9.30pm.
**Cuisine:** ENGLISH - in the restaurant, steaks, grills, salads, omelettes, fish. In the bar, home-made steak-and-kidney pie, cottage pie, home-made sweets.

**Cards:** Access.
**Other points:** licensed, open-air dining, Sunday lunch, no-smoking area, children welcome.
**Directions:** on the seafront between the Grand Pier and Marine Lake.
MR & MRS ARNAOUTI ☎(01934) 626621

 **THE COMMODORE HOTEL**
Beach Road, Sand Bay, BS22 9UZ
*On the seafront at Sand Bay, with extensive views across the Bristol Channel and the local countryside. Good access to West Country attractions and several National Trust walks. Golfing discounts and riding can be arranged.*
DOUBLE ROOM: from £30 to £40
SINGLE ROOM: from £45 to £55
FOOD: from £15 to £20 🍷
**Hours:** breakfast weekdays 7.30am-9.30am, weekends 8am-10am, lunch 12noon-2pm, dinner 6.30pm-9.30pm.
**Cuisine:** MODERN ENGLISH - lounge buffet-carvery and à la carte restaurant with international and modern English cuisine.
**Cards:** Visa, Access, Diners, AmEx.
**Other points:** licensed, Sunday lunch, disabled access, children welcome, functions, conferences.
**Rooms:** 18 bedrooms.
**Directions:** overlooking beach in Sand Bay, 1.5 miles north of Weston on Toll Road.
JOHN STOAKES ☎(01934) 415778 Fax(01934) 636483

 **THE FULL QUART**
Hewish, BS24 6RT
*A 200-year-old Wayside inn and a typical Somerset levels building with an interesting interior with a host of features. The traditional English cuisine, includes home-made soups, casseroles, pate and puddings. Staff are very helpful and friendly. Cheddar Gorge is nearby.*
FOOD: up to £15
**Hours:** bar meals 12noon-2pm and 6.30pm-10pm, open bank holidays.
**Cuisine:** TRADITIONAL ENGLISH - home-made soups, pate, casseroles and puddings, using fresh local produce.
**Cards:** Access,Visa,Switch,Delta
**Other points:** children welcome, open-air dining, no-smoking area, traditional Sunday lunch, limited vegetarian meals, parking.
**Directions:** A370, 2 miles east of junction 21 of M5.
MR A J ROUD ☎(01934) 833077

 **PEARL DE MARE CHINESE CUISINE**
15-18 Alexandra Parade, BS23 1QT
*An opportunity to sample excellent cuisine in delightful surroundings. The restaurant is tastefully furnished and comfortable, with pleasant, restful background music. Service is highly efficient and courteous. Executive business lunches available. Situated within easy reach of many major tourist*

attractions, from the seafront to the beautiful surrounding countryside.
FOOD: up to £15
Hours: lunch 12noon-2pm, dinner 6pm-11.30pm, closed Sunday lunch.
Cuisine: CHINESE - Cantonese and Peking cuisine of an extremely high standard and beautifully presented. Fixed-price executive lunches available.
Cards: Visa, Access, Diners, AmEx.
Other points: licensed, children welcome, disabled access, vegetarian meals, street parking.
Directions: situated in the town centre, opposite the Odeon cinemas.
MR CHIM (`JIM') ☎(01934) 621307/626104

# BERKSHIRE

## ETON • map 5C3

### CHRISTOPHER HOTEL
110 High Street, Eton, SL4 6AN

A former coaching inn situated in Eton High Street, close to the famous school and within walking distance of Windsor Castle. The restaurant serves an excellent selection of home-cooked meals.
DOUBLE ROOM: from £41 to £50
SINGLE ROOM: from £55
FOOD: from £15 to £20
Hours: breakfast 7.30am-9.30am, lunch 12noon-2.30pm, dinner weekends 7pm-10pm, weekdays 6.30pm-9.30pm.
Cuisine: ENGLISH / FRENCH - traditional cuisine.
Cards: Visa, Access, Diners, AmEx.
Other points: open-air dining, children welcome, pets allowed, baby-listening device, cots, left luggage.
Rooms: 8 single rooms, 17 double rooms, 5 twin rooms, 3 family rooms. All with TV, telephone, tea/coffee-making facilities.
Directions: 2 miles off M4. 10 miles from M25/Heathrow Airport.
MRS MARTIN ☎(01753) 852359/857091

## MAIDENHEAD • map 5C3

### ANTONIA'S BAR BISTRO
11 Bridge Street, SL6 8LR
This cosy intimate bistro is relaxed and informal

with candlelit tables. The River Thames and Boulters Lock are just two of the many nearby points of interest to visit and explore.
FOOD: from £15 to £20
Hours: lunch 12noon-2.30pm, dinner 7pm-10.30pm, closed Sunday.
Cuisine: CONTINENTAL - freshly prepared food, extensive tapas menu in the bar, classic French dishes in the bistro. Specialities include paella a la salenciana, bouillabaisse.
Cards: Visa, Access.
Other points: licensed, open-air dining, no-smoking area, open bank holidays, parking.
Directions: situated off the A4.
LILIAS MACDONALD ☎(01628) 23670

### BOULTERS LOCK HOTEL
Boulters Island, SL6 8PE
Originally built as a millers house in 1726, this beautifully situated hotel offers tastefully furnished accommodation and gourmet dining in two restaurants with panoramic views over the Thames. Ideally situated for Windsor Castle, Eton, Ascot, Kew gardens and Cliveden.
DOUBLE ROOM: over £50
SINGLE ROOM: over £50
FOOD: up to £15
Hours: breakfast 7am-9.30am, lunch 12noon-3pm, dinner 7pm-10.30pm. Bar snacks available 12noon-10.30pm.
Cuisine: MODERN ENGLISH/FRENCH, ALSO EUROPEAN BISTRO - extensive à la carte and table d'hôte menu served in the Riverside restaurant with panoramic views of the Thames. Supervised by chef Murdo MacSween, chairman of the Master Chefs of Great Britain and member of the Acadamie Culinaire de France. Bistro menu available in Terrace Bar. Comprehensive wine list.
Cards: Access, Visa, AmEx, Diners
Other points: parking, children welcome, conference facilities, vegetarian meals, afternoon teas, traditional Sunday lunch, room service.
Directions: take exit 7 from M4. A4 to Maidenhead, over bridge and turn right onto A4094.
MR J. SMITH ☎(01628) 21291 Fax(01628) 26048

**CHAUNTRY HOUSE HOTEL**
Bray-on-Thames, SL6 2AB

*An outstanding 18th century country-house hotel situated in a delightful village close to Windsor and Heathrow Airport. No visitor can fail to be impressed by the friendly and relaxed atmosphere in this intimate restaurant.*

DOUBLE ROOM: from £40 to £50
SINGLE ROOM: from £55
FOOD: from £15 to £20

**Hours:** breakfast 7.30am-9.30am, lunch 12noon-2pm, dinner 7.30pm-9.30pm.
**Cuisine:** ENGLISH - imaginative English cuisine. Menu changes seasonally.
**Cards:** Visa, Access, Diners, AmEx.
**Other points:** licensed, open-air dining, conferences, functions.
**Rooms:** 2 single rooms, 9 double rooms, 5 twin rooms. All with en suite, satellite TV, telephone, radio, alarm, tea/coffee-making facilities, baby-listening device.
**Directions:** M4 junction 8 or 9, A308 to Windsor, B3028 to Bray. Last building on right.
RAY HAND ☎(01628) 73991 Fax (01628) 773089

 **THAMES RIVIERA HOTEL**
Bridge Road, SL6 8DW

*Edwardian in origin, the Thames Riviera Hotel is situated at one of the most picturesque points on the River Thames. There are 53 luxurious en suite bedrooms situated in two buildings, most of the rooms having river views. There is a superb ground floor opening onto a riverside terrace, comprising a piano bar, à la carte restaurant and separate coffee shop, collectively known as `Jerome's'. Sample the riverside hospitality.*

DOUBLE ROOM: over £50
SINGLE ROOM: from £60
FOOD: from £21 to £25

**Hours:** breakfast 6.30am-8.30am, lunch 12noon-2pm, dinner 7pm-10pm, bar meals 12noon-5pm, closed 26th December until 30th December.
**Cuisine:** ENGLISH / FRENCH - all meals are freshly prepared from quality produce. Plus a more casual coffee shop, open 9am-5pm for snacks etc.
**Cards:** Visa, Access, Diners, AmEx, Switch.
**Other points:** parking, children welcome, conference facilities, garden, open-air dining, vegetarian meals, traditional Sunday lunch, afternoon teas.
**Rooms:** 53 bedrooms. All with satellite TV, telephone, alarm, hair dryer, trouser-press, tea/coffee-making facilities.
**Directions:** situated on the bank of the Thames on A4, off junction 7 of M4.
GALLEON TAVERNS LTD - SALLY WINGROVE
☎(01628) 74057 Fax (01628) 776586

## NEWBURY • map 5C2

 **THE BLACKBIRD**
Bagnor, RG20 8AQ

*A charming mock Tudor building, full of olde-worlde charm with plates and horse brasses adorning the walls and log fires for winter. There is a comprehensive menu and a good wine list which attracts a wide clientele who make good use of the outside tables in good weather. Warm and friendly atmosphere.*

FOOD: from £15 to £20

**Hours:** lunch 12noon-2pm, dinner(restaurant) 6pm-9.30pm, dinner(bar area) 6pm-10pm, open bank holidays, closed Christmas day.
**Cuisine:** TRADITIONAL ENGLISH/INTERNATIONAL - home-made fare, such as steak-and-kidney and chicken pies, currys and pasta dishes.
**Cards:** Visa, Access, AmEx.
**Other points:** licensed, parking, children welcome, large beer garden.
**Directions:** from the M4 or A4, take the Oxford Road, turn onto Grove Road, then right towards Bagnor.
MR JOHN NEWBROOK ☎(01635) 40638
Fax (01635) 40638

## READING • map 5C3

**CALCOT HOTEL**
98-100 Bath Road, Calcot, RG3 5QN

*The recently extended and refurbished Calcot Hotel offers 78 well-appointed bedrooms,informal lively restaurants, traditional bars, well-equipped conference rooms and popular banqueting facilities. In addition to being an ideal venue for the business traveller, the Calcot's location brings many popular sights and attractions within easy reach.*

DOUBLE ROOM: from £41 to £50
SINGLE ROOM: from £41 to £50
FOOD: up to £15

**Hours:** breakfast 7am-9am, lunch 12.15am-2pm, dinner 7pm-10pm.
**Cuisine:** ENGLISH - a range of modern and imaginative dishes freshly prepared. A traditional carvery roast is available on Sunday.
**Cards:** Visa, Access, Diners, AmEx, Switch.
**Other points:** parking, children welcome, no-smoking area, disabled access, residents' lounge, vegetarian meals, open-air dining, garden.
**Rooms:** 78 bedrooms.
**Directions:** situated on the A4 Bath road, 4 miles east of Reading.
JOHN CALCOT ☎(01734) 416423 Fax (01734) 451223

**THE GATEHOUSE HOTEL**
54 Bath Road, RG1 6PG

*A country house style hotel in its own grounds, conveniently located for Windsor Castle and easily accessible from Heathrow airport along the M4 corridor. The public areas and bedrooms are professionally designed and decorated with wall murals giving a bright, modern aura. A pleasant cottage style restaurant offers traditional English à la carte and table d'hôte throughout the day.*

DOUBLE ROOM: from £17.50 to £25
SINGLE ROOM: from £25
FOOD: up to £15

**Hours:** breakfast 7.15am-9am, lunch 12noon-2pm,

dinner 6.30pm-9pm.
**Cuisine:** ENGLISH
**Cards:** Access,Visa,AmEx,Diners
**Other points:** licensed, room service, residents'
lounge, central heating, night porter, children
welcome, parking, meeting room, garden.
**Rooms:** 6 single rooms plus 1 single room en suite.
2 twin rooms plus 6 twin rooms en suite. 1 double
room plus 4 double rooms en suite. 1 family room
plus 1 family room en suite. All with tea/coffee-
maker, TV, telephone, alarm, baby listening device.
**Directions:** from M4 junction 12, 3.5 miles along
A4 (Bath Road) towards Reading.
MR IAN HOLLAND ☎(01734) 572019 Fax(01734)
503203

### HONG HONG RESTAURANT
14 West Street, RG1 1TT
*A friendly, traditional Chinese restaurant serving an*
*interesting selection of regional Chinese specialities,*
*wines and liqueurs.*
**FOOD:** up to £15
**Hours:** meals all day (Monday-Thursday) 12noon-
11.30pm, Friday 12noon-12midnight, Saturday
12noon-12midnight, Sunday 12noon-11.30pm.
**Cuisine:** CHINESE - Peking, Cantonese and
Szechuan food: crispy aromatic duck, Peking-style
imperial hors d'oeuvres, Cantonese-style spicy
Szechuan prawn. Special business lunch 3 courses
£3.80.
**Cards:** Visa, Access, Diners, AmEx.
**Other points:** licensed, Sunday lunch, children
welcome, functions.
**Directions:** in the town centre opposite the Co-op,
next to Prontaprint.
NGAU CHAN & GENEVIEVE ONG ☎(01734)
585372/507472

### WOKINGHAM • map 5C3

### CANTLEY HOUSE HOTEL &
### MARYLINE'S BAR BISTRO &
### RESTAURANT
Milton Road, RG40 5QG
*A spacious independent Victorian country house*
*hotel set amid picturesque private gardens and open*
parklands. Maryline's Bar Bistro and Restaurant are
*situated across a secluded courtyard from the main*
*hotel. Maryline's Restaurant, now gaining national*
*recognition for its fine English food, provides the*
*elegant surroundings associated with a beamed 17th*
*century barn. Alongside, the bar and bistro provide*
*informal dining with a chalked menu.*
DOUBLE ROOM: from £30 to £45
SINGLE ROOM: from £55
FOOD: from £15 to £23
**Hours:** breakfast 7.30am-10am, lunch 12noon-2pm.
**Cuisine:** MODERN ENGLISH - fine modern English
cuisine.
**Cards:** Visa, Access, Diners, AmEx.
**Other points:** Sunday lunch, pets allowed, children
welcome.
**Rooms:** 15 single rooms, 12 double rooms, 2 twin
rooms.
**Directions:** from M4 junction 10, follow signs to
Wokingham. Off A321 towards Henley.
MR MAURICE MONK ☎(01734) 789912
Fax(01734) 774294

### THE HANSOM CABINN
Lower Wokingham Road, Crowthorne,
RG11 3NG
*The Hansom Cabinn is an attractive cabin-like*
*restaurant surrounded by roses. Inside, you will find*
*pine panelling and pictorial reference to hansom*
*cabs. Fresh ingredients are used imaginatively to*
*produce well-cooked meals, simply and*
*thoughtfully presented. Good, welcoming service*
*and a happy and relaxed atmosphere prevails.*
FOOD: up to £15
**Hours:** lunch 12noon-2pm, dinner 7pm-12.30am,
Sunday 7pm-9.30pm, last orders 9.30pm, closed
Saturday lunch and Sunday lunch.
**Cuisine:** ENGLISH - starters range from sliced
smoked trout, fresh soup or prawns. House
specialities are duck or salmon en croute. Desserts
include home-made ice creams.
**Cards:** Visa, Access.
**Other points:** licensed.
**Directions:** alongside A321.
MR JOHN HANSOM ☎(01344) 772450

# CORNWALL

### BODMIN • map 3D2

### ASTERISK RESTAURANT WITH ROOMS
A30 Mount Pleasant, Roche, PL26 8LH
*Situated west of Bodmin, this is an ideal spot from*
*which to visit Land's End and many other*
*fascinating places of interest. Offering good home-*
*cooking, dishes may include beef fillet, duck*
*chartreuse, pork fillet oriental, turbot coriander, Thai*
*beef. Tasty desserts.*
DOUBLE ROOM: up to £27.50
SINGLE ROOM: £30
FOOD: up to £20
**Hours:** breakfast as required, dinner 7pm-10pm.
**Cuisine:** ENGLISH / INTERNATIONAL
**Cards:** Visa, Access, AmEx.
**Other points:** parking, children welcome, open
bank holidays, Sunday dinner, pets allowed,
residents' lounge, vegetarian meals, garden.
**Rooms:** 7 rooms.
**Directions:** on A30 two miles due west of Bodmin
roundabout.
MR F. ZOLA ☎(01726) 890863 Fax(01726)
890863

## BOSCASTLE • map 3D2

 **HALLAGATHER FARMHOUSE**
Crackington Haven, EX23 0LA
*Steeped in history, parts of the farm date from early medieval times. The fascinating interior boasts oak beams, granite arches, slate flagstones and a superb spiral staircase. Breakfasts are enormous and will satisfy the largest of appetites! Ideally situated for exploring the surrounding Heritage coast. Excellent value for money.*
DOUBLE ROOM: from £15 to £20
SINGLE ROOM: from £15 to £20
**Hours:** breakfast 7.30am-9.15am. Closed December & January.
**Cards:** Eurocheques.
**Other points:** car park on site, vegetarian meals on request.
**Rooms:** 1 single room, 1 double room en suite, 1 family room en suite all with tea/coffee maker. Various items available on loan without charge.
**Directions:** take B3263 north from Boscastle for 3.5 miles. Turn left at Tresparett Post, then left signposted Hallagather.
MR & MRS ANTHONY ☎(01840) 230276

## BUDE • map 3C2

 **COOMBE BARTON INN**
Crackington Haven, EX23 0JG
*Recently refurbished, the inn is charmingly decorated throughout. The warm and friendly service complements the high standard of food and accommodation on offer. A wide variety of freshly prepared and cooked meals is served every lunchtime and evening in the public bar or the bar/restaurant.*
DOUBLE ROOM: from £20
SINGLE ROOM: from £17.50
FOOD: up to £15
**Hours:** breakfast 8.45am -9.30am, bar snacks 11am-3pm, dinner 6pm-10pm, bar snacks 6pm-10pm.
**Cuisine:** ENGLISH - large and comprehensive menu, with fresh fish being the speciality.
**Cards:** Visa, Access, Diners.
**Other points:** parking, children welcome, no-smoking area, pets allowed, residents' lounge, vegetarian meals, open-air dining.
**Rooms:** 1 single room, 6 double rooms.
**Directions:** turn off the A39 at Wainhouse Corner towards Crackington Haven.
JOHN COOPER ☎(01840) 230345 Fax(01840) 230788

 **THE FALCON HOTEL**
Breakwater Road, EX23 8SD
*Character hotel in unique position overlooking the historic Bude Canal and yet only a short stroll from the sandy beaches and shops. Renowned for the quality of the food, whether for the high-class menu in the Candlelit Restaurant, or from the extensive bar snack menu in the Coachmans Bar.*
DOUBLE ROOM: from £31 to £40
SINGLE ROOM: from £31 to £40
FOOD: from £15 to £20
**Hours:** breakfast 8am-9.30am, lunch 12noon-2pm, dinner 7pm-9pm, closed Christmas day.
**Cuisine:** ENGLISH / FRENCH / INTERNATIONAL - à la carte and table d'hôte menus of an English and French style are served in the restaurant. An international menu of great variety is available in the bar.
**Cards:** Visa, Access, Diners, AmEx.
**Other points:** licensed, children welcome, pets allowed, garden, car park.
**Rooms:** 4 single rooms, 13 double rooms, 5 twin rooms. All with SkyTV, tea/coffee-making facilities.
**Directions:** on western side of Bude, easily seen from the main road.
TIM & DOROTHY BROWNING ☎(01288) 352005 Fax(01288) 356359

 **MAER LODGE HOTEL**
Crooklets Beach, EX23 8NG
*Maer Lodge Hotel serves excellent and extremely varied home-cooked food. The quality of the ingredients and the care in preparation and presentation are paramount. A friendly, family hotel with first-class personal service.*
DOUBLE ROOM: from £22 to £27
SINGLE ROOM: from £25 to £30
FOOD: up to £15 CLUB
**Hours:** breakfast 8.30am-9.15am, lunch 12.30am-1.30pm, dinner 7pm-7.45pm.
**Cuisine:** ENGLISH / CONTINENTAL
**Cards:** Visa, Access, Diners, AmEx.
**Other points:** pets allowed, children welcome, baby-listening device, baby-sitting, cots, 18hr reception, foreign exchange, left luggage, residents' lounge, residents' bar.
**Rooms:** 2 single rooms, 7 double rooms, 5 twin rooms, 4 family rooms. All with TV, radio, alarm, telephone, tea/coffee-making facilities.
**Directions:** overlooking golf course and close to the beach.
MR & MRS STANLEY ☎(01288) 353306 Fax(01288) 353306

**MORNISH HOTEL**
20 Summerleaze Crescent, EX23 8HL
*The Mornish Hotel offers magnificent views from a prime location in Bude overlooking the beach. Centrally situated, with shops, golf course and beach nearby.*
DOUBLE ROOM: up to £20
SINGLE ROOM: up to £25
FOOD: up to £15
**Hours:** breakfast 8.30am-9am, dinner 6.30pm-7pm to be ordered by 5.30pm, closed November to February.
**Cuisine:** ENGLISH - B&B includes a full English breakfast. Dinner: home-cooking to a very high standard (£8.50 for five courses - if you can manage them!).
**Cards:** Visa, Access, Diners, AmEx.
**Other points:** central heating, children welcome,

residents' lounge, vegetarian meals.
**Rooms:** 5 double rooms, 2 twin rooms, 3 family rooms. All with en suite, TV, tea/coffee-making facilities.
**Directions:** from town centre, turn left at post office corner, towards sea.
JOHN & JULIA HILDER ☎(01288) 352972

## CARLYON BAY • map 3E2

 **PORTH AVALLEN HOTEL**
Sea Road, PL25 3SG

*Situated in several acres of gardens with panoramic views over Carlyon Bay and its rugged coastline, this well-appointed hotel offers perfect peace and quiet. The oak-panelled residents' lounge opens onto the terrace, and is a cosy retreat during the winter months. The 40-seater restaurant maintains a very high standard, as does the accommodation. Ideal base for touring.*
DOUBLE ROOM: from £40 to £50
SINGLE ROOM: from £50 to £60
FOOD: from £15 to £20
**Hours:** breakfast 7.30am-9.30am, lunch 12noon-2pm, dinner 7pm-9pm, closed Christmas day until 2nd January.
**Cuisine:** BRITISH - with a touch of French. Dishes may include: magret of duck, roast rack of lamb, Scottish fillet steak and Dover sole. Vegetarian dishes.
**Cards:** Visa, Access, AmEx, Switch.
**Other points:** licensed, Sunday lunch, children welcome, afternoon tea, residents' lounge, garden, parking, functions, conferences.
**Rooms:** 3 single room, 10 double rooms, 6 twin rooms, 5 family rooms. All with TV, radio, tea/coffee-making facilities, hair dryer, trouser-press.
**Directions:** from Plymouth, take A390 - 45 minutes. On outskirts of St Austell.
N. & M. PERRETT & G. & K. SIM ☎(01726) 812802 Fax(01726) 817097

## COVERACK • map 3E2

 **THE BAY HOTEL**
Near Helston, TR12 6TF
*Set in the unspoilt Cornish countryside of the beautiful Lizard peninsular, providing the perfect location for that away-from-it-all feeling. Furnished to an extremely high standard, most rooms have wonderful sea views. Cornish proprietors Lorraine and David Goldworthy have succeeded in providing a comfortable and friendly atmosphere.*
DOUBLE ROOM: from £20 to £30

SINGLE ROOM: from £20 to £30
FOOD: up to £15
**Hours:** breakfast 8.30am-9.30am, bar snacks 12noon-2pm, dinner 6.30pm-8.30pm, closed November until February, open Christmas and New Year.
**Cuisine:** ENGLISH / CONTINENTAL - all meals are cooked to order with fresh local produce.
**Cards:** Visa, Access.
**Other points:** parking, Sunday lunch, open bank holidays, disabled access, pets allowed, residents' lounge, vegetarian meals, garden, licensed, central heating, children catered for (please check age limits).
**Rooms:** 1 single room, 10 double rooms, 3 twin rooms. All with TV, tea/coffee-making facilities.
**Directions:** from Helston take B3292 to St Keverne; Coverack is signed.
LORRAINE & DAVID GOLDSWORTHY ☎(01326) 280464 Fax(01326) 280464

## FALMOUTH • map 3E2

 **GREEN LAWNS HOTEL**
Western Terrace, TR11 4QJ

*An elegant château-style hotel situated midway between town and beaches. Renowned à la carte restaurant and full banqueting/conference facilities available. The hotel's `Garras Leisure Complex' consists of indoor heated swimming pool, Jacuzzi, sauna, solarium and gymnasium. Honeymoon and Executives suites available.*
DOUBLE ROOM: from £30 to £40
SINGLE ROOM: from £41 to £50
FOOD: from £15 to £20
**Hours:** breakfast 7am-9.30am, lunch 12noon-2pm, dinner 6.45pm-10pm.
**Cuisine:** MODERN ENGLISH - fresh local seafood and speciality steaks.
**Cards:** Visa, Access, Diners, AmEx.
**Other points:** licensed, Sunday lunch, children welcome, coaches by prior arrangement, honeymoon suite, children welcome, baby-listening device, baby-sitting, cots, 24hr reception.
**Rooms:** 6 single rooms, 11 double rooms, 23 twin rooms. All with TV, radio, alarm, telephone, tea/coffee-making facilities.
**Directions:** on the main road into Falmouth heading towards the main beaches.
☎(01326) 312734 Fax(01326) 211427

---

**For Reservations & Special Offers FreeCall 0500 700 456**

## THE GROVE HOTEL
Grove Place, TR11 4AU

Overlooking the harbour, close to shops, quays, railway station and ideally situated for exploring the Cornish coastline, the Grove Hotel was established in 1946. Although the building itself has been changed, you will still find the same relaxed and friendly atmosphere under the second generation of the Corks.
DOUBLE ROOM: from £20 to £30
SINGLE ROOM: from £20 to £25
FOOD: up to £15    CLUB
**Hours:** breakfast 8am-9am, dinner 7pm-9pm.
**Cuisine:** ENGLISH / INTERNATIONAL - vegetarian meals.
**Cards:** Visa, Access, Diners, AmEx.
**Other points:** central heating, children welcome, residents' lounge, street parking.
**Rooms:** 2 single rooms, 5 double rooms, 4 twin rooms, 4 family rooms. All with en suite, TV, tea/coffee-making facilities.
**Directions:** off the A39. Take harbour road to Grove Place near the dinghy hard.
PETER & JANET CORK ☎(01326) 319577
Fax (01326) 319577

## GYLLYNGVASE HOUSE HOTEL
Gyllyngvase Road, TR11 4DJ
Personally supervised by the owners, this is a small hotel which extends the warmest of welcomes to all its guests. The fine cuisine includes seafood specialities, and even special diets and picnic lunches can be arranged. There is an attractive lounge bar and garden terrace, and comfortably furnished rooms in colour co-ordinated schemes. Gyllyngvase is Falmouth's main beach, a wide sweep of golden sands, making it an ideal location for a family holiday.
DOUBLE ROOM: from £20 to £30
SINGLE ROOM: from £19 to £25
FOOD: up to £15
**Hours:** breakfast 8.30am-9am, dinner 6.30pm-7pm, closed November-April.
**Cuisine:** ENGLISH
**Other points:** children welcome, no-smoking area, vegetarian meals, afternoon teas, pets, residents' lounge, garden, parking.
**Rooms:** 3 single rooms, 7 double rooms, 3 twin rooms, 2 family rooms.
**Directions:** from Truro take A3078 to traffic lights, go straight on to Melville Road. Hotel on right.
MR C. LE MAITRE ☎(01326) 312956

## FOWEY • map 3E2

## MARINA HOTEL
Esplanade, PL23 1HY
A beautifully situated hotel with river views from most bedrooms. The restaurant also has magnificent views and there is a large patio for enjoying summer drinks. The small passenger ferry to Polruan is close by, and this is just one of the attractions of this most scenic part of Cornwall. A friendly, comfortable cottage style hotel highly recommended for a relaxing holiday.
DOUBLE ROOM: from £26 to £44
FOOD: from £15 to £20
**Hours:** breakfast 8.30am-9.30am, dinner from 7pm, last orders 8.30pm, open bank holidays, closed January and February.
**Cuisine:** ANGLO /FRENCH - specialising in seafood plus comprehensive table d'hôte and à la carte menus covering all requirements including vegetarian.
**Cards:** Visa, Access, AmEx.
**Other points:** car parking nearby, pets allowed, licensed, residents' lounge, central heating, 24 hour reception, night porter, ironing facilities, guests' garden. Fishing, golfing, beach and water sports nearby.
**Rooms:** 5 twin rooms, 5 double rooms, all en suite. All with TV, telephone, tea/coffee-making facilities.
**Directions:** continue down the hill into Fowey, turn right into The Esplanade, the hotel is on the left.
MR JOHN ROBERTS ☎(01726) 833315
Fax (01726) 832779

## GRAMPOUND • map 3E2

## EASTERN PROMISE CHINESE RESTAURANT
1 Moorview, TR2 4RT
Attractive and roomy, beautifully decorated with matching furnishings, flowers on the tables, and comfortable chairs. Excellent cuisine, efficient and personal service, and a quiet, friendly atmosphere all adds to the overall ambience of this professional restaurant.
FOOD: from £15 to £20
**Hours:** closed Wednesday.
**Cuisine:** CHINESE - à la carte and table d'hôte menus, offering dishes of the highest quality of China's most famous regional cuisine, such as Cantonese, Peking and Szechuan, complemented by an extensive wine list. Vegetarian meals available.
**Cards:** Visa, Access, Diners, AmEx.
**Other points:** licensed, children catered for (minimum age 3 years), vegetarian meals, parking, open bank holidays.
**Directions:** between Truro and St Austell.
PHILIP & LISA TSE ☎(01726) 883033

**Join Les Routiers Discovery Club FREE! See page 34 for details.**

## ISLES OF SCILLY • map 3D1

 **THE NEW INN**
Tresco, TR24 0QQ

*Situated in the heart of the beautiful island of Tresco, the New Inn boasts a happy, friendly atmosphere, comfortable bedrooms and good food, particularly fresh fish. The island is world-famous for its sub-tropical gardens, and any stay here will be an experience to cherish.*
DOUBLE ROOM: from £41 to £50
SINGLE ROOM: over £50
FOOD: from £15 to £20
**Hours:** breakfast 8.30am-9.30am, lunch (bar area) 12noon-2pm, dinner (restaurant) 7.30pm-8.30pm, dinner (bar area) 6.30pm-9pm, open bank holidays.
**Cuisine:** ENGLISH/FRENCH - various sea food specialities.
**Cards:** Visa, Access.
**Other points:** licensed.
**Rooms:** 2 single rooms, 10 twin rooms. All with TV, radio, telephone, tea/coffee making facilities and hairdryers.
**Directions:** Daily ferry from Penzance Harbour, helicopter flights from Penzance Heliport, aeroplane flights from Lands End Airfield. Inn situated in New Grimsby.
☎(01720) 422844 ▣(01720) 423200

## LAND'S END • map 3E1

 **OLD SUCCESS INN HOTEL**
Sennen Cove, TR19 7DG

*With excellent views of the coast and sea, this spacious 17th century inn is the perfect place to relax. In the restaurant you can expect the presentation of the food and the food itself to be first-class. The comfortable bedrooms, including two bridal suites, are all of a very high standard, and the service throughout is warm and friendly, but, most importantly, it is genuine.*
DOUBLE ROOM: from £30 to £40
SINGLE ROOM: up to £25
FOOD: up to £15
**Hours:** breakfast 8.30am-9.30am, lunch 12noon-2.30pm, dinner 7pm-9.30pm.
**Cuisine:** ENGLISH - house specialities are carvery and seafood - particularly Newlyn fish.
**Cards:** Visa, Access, Eurocard, MasterCard.
**Other points:** children welcome, parking, residents' lounge, vegetarian meals, no-smoking area.
**Rooms:** 2 single rooms, 7 double rooms, 2 twin rooms, 1 family room.
**Directions:** A30 towards Land's End, turn right at Sennen Cove sign.
MARTIN BROOKES ☎(01736) 871232 ▣(01736) 871457

## LISKEARD • map 3D2

 **THE OLD RECTORY COUNTRY HOUSE HOTEL**
St Keyne Village, PL14 4RL

*A lovely, 150-year-old rambling country house hotel set in its own woody glade amidst lawns and mature trees. Peaceful and unspoilt atmosphere, the bedrooms and public areas are furnished with a tasteful mix of antique and classic modern furniture. Excellent traditional dishes are prepared and served by Mr and Mrs Minifie and their staff. Highly recommended for those seeking solitude in this lovely part of England.*
DOUBLE ROOM: from £20 to £30
SINGLE ROOM: from £20 to £30
**Hours:** breakfast 8.30am-9.30am, dinner 7pm-8pm. Closed December and January.
**Cuisine:** ENGLISH/CONTINENTAL - full English breakfast, à la carte dinner menu features fine English cooking and the adventure of Continental cuisine. All food home prepared.
**Cards:** Access, Visa, AmEx
**Other points:** parking, non smoking area, children catered for (please check for age limits), pets allowed, licensed, residents' lounge and garden, TV lounge, central heating, real log fires, ironing facilities.
**Rooms:** 1 single room, 7 double rooms, all en suite with tea/coffee maker, TV, electric over blankets. 2 rooms available with four poster beds. 1 ground floor room suitable for disabled.
**Directions:** from A38 take the B3254 signposted St Keyne and Duloe. Hotel is on the left.
JOHN & PAT MINIFIE ☎(01579) 342617

## LOOE • map 3D2

**ALLHAYS COUNTRY HOUSE**
Talland Bay, PL13 2JB

*Allhays is a period country house standing in `an English country garden' with spectacular views over to Talland Bay. A Victorian-style conservatory extends the dining room into the garden for dining alfresco whatever the weather. Allhays has an enviable reputation for its food, and most particularly for its impressive and daily-changing cheeseboard.*
DOUBLE ROOM: from £30 to £40
SINGLE ROOM: from £28
FOOD: up to £15
**Hours:** breakfast 8.30am-9am, dinner 7pm.
**Cuisine:** MODERN ENGLISH - new English cuisine using the finest local and home-grown produce, freshly prepared and cooked in the Aga by chef/patronne Lynda Spring. British cheeses.
**Cards:** Visa, Access, Diners, AmEx.
**Other points:** pets allowed, children welcome (from 10 years old), vegetarian meals, parking, residents' bar, residents' lounge, disabled access.
**Rooms:** 4 double rooms, 3 twin rooms. All with TV, radio, telephone, tea/coffee-making facilities, alarm, hair dryer.
**Directions:** turn left 2.5 miles from Looe on A387. Follow hotel signposts.
BRIAN & LYNDA SPRING ☎(01503) 272434 ▣(01503) 272929

### PUNCHBOWL INN
Lanreath, near Looe, PL13 2NX

*This oak-beamed inn is over 400 years old and has served as the court house, a coaching inn and smugglers' distribution house in its time! It now offers visitors a chance to enjoy traditional hospitality within its historic walls. Set in the heart of the Cornish Riviera in the "picture postcard" village of Lanreath*

DOUBLE ROOM: from £25 to £30

FOOD: up to £15

**Hours:** breakfast 8.30am-9.30am, lunch 12noon-2pm, dinner 6pm-10pm.

**Cuisine:** ENGLISH - à la carte. Traditional English, seasonal fish menu and ice cream specialities. Bar snack menu.

**Cards:** Visa, Access, MasterCard, Eurocard.

**Other points:** licensed, Sunday lunch, no-smoking area, children welcome, beer garden, vegetarian meals, residents' bar, residents' lounge, parking.

**Rooms:** 18 bedrooms (12 en suite). All with TV, tea/coffee-making facilities.

**Directions:** off the B3359 in the centre of Lanreath village.

MR & MRS HADDOW ☎(01503) 220218
Fax(01503) 220218

## LOSTWITHIEL • map 3D2

### TREWITHEN RESTAURANT
3 Fore Street, PL2 0AD

*A personally-run restaurant with a cottage atmosphere, where all the food is home-cooked. The cuisine reflects the proprietors' international background and offers both à la carte and blackboard menus. Situated next door to the Duchy Palace, with Restormel Castle, Lanhydroch House and Bodmin all close by.*

FOOD: from £20 to £25 ☞

**Hours:** dinner 7pm-9.30pm (last orders), closed Sunday and Monday.

**Cuisine:** INTERNATIONAL - including summer seafood, lobster and winter game.

**Cards:** Visa, Access, Diners.

**Other points:** children welcome, no pets, disabled access, vegetarian meals.

**Directions:** A390, halfway between Liskeard and St Austell, 5 miles south of Bodmin.

B.F. & L.J. ROLLS ☎(01208) 872373

## MEVAGISSEY • map 3E2

### MR BISTRO
East Quay, PL26 6QH

*This restaurant is situated facing the harbour in a town with a long-established fishing history. The menu, needless to say, specializes in fish dishes. The `Dish of the Day' depends on the fishermen's catch of the day!*

FOOD: up to £20

**Hours:** lunch 12noon-3pm, dinner 7pm-10pm, closed November until January.

**Cuisine:** ENGLISH / SEAFOOD - fresh fish and shellfish, sweet trolley.

**Cards:** Visa, Access, Diners, AmEx.

**Other points:** children welcome.

**Directions:** on the harbour front.

MRS S. DONOVAN ☎(01726) 842432

### SHARKSFIN HOTEL & RESTAURANT
The Quay, PL26 6QU

*The Sharksfin Hotel and Restaurant occupies a commanding position on the quay, overlooking this quaint and busy fishing harbour. The bar and restaurant provide a warm welcome with a high standard of decor and friendly service. Most of the 11 well-equipped bedrooms have views of the harbour and sea. The location makes the hotel an ideal place from which to tour Cornwall and the many nearby places of interest. For golfers, no Cornish course is more than one hour away and play-as-you-please golf can be arranged to suit all individual requirements.*

DOUBLE ROOM: from £28 to £33

SINGLE ROOM: from £28 to £30

FOOD: from £16 to £20 ☞

**Hours:** breakfast from 8am, lunch 12noon-2.30pm, dinner 7pm-9.30pm, closed January and February.

**Cuisine:** ENGLISH / FRENCH - the head chef offers the best of French and English cuisine using fresh local fish, shellfish and West Country produce. Full à la carte and daily specials.

**Cards:** Visa, Access, Diners, AmEx.

**Other points:** children welcome, afternoon teas, vegetarian meals, residents' lounge.

**Rooms:** 2 single rooms, 8 double rooms, 1 family room. All with TV, radio, telephone, tea/coffee-making facilities.

**Directions:** Sharksfin Hotel is an old historic building situated right on the quay in the picturesque fishing village of Mevagissey, accessed by the B3273.

J. & A. GOODHEW ☎(01726) 843241 Fax(01726) 842552

## MYLOR BRIDGE • map 3E2

### THE PANDORA INN
Restronguet Creek, near Falmouth, TR11 5ST

*A beautiful 13th century thatched inn reputedly owned by Captain Edwards of Bounty mutiny fame. Flagstone floors, low, beamed ceilings and gleaming brasswork complete the picturebook setting. Come by car or by boat (yachts may be moored on the 140ft pontoon at the front) and enjoy the famous, fine cuisine.*

FOOD: up to £20

**Hours:** bar meals 12noon-2.15pm, dinner 7pm-12midnight, last orders 10pm, bar meals 6.30pm-10pm.

**Cuisine:** ENGLISH - local fresh fish and fresh produce. Cornish specialities. Afternoon teas.

**Cards:** Visa, Access, AmEx.

**Other points:** licensed, open-air dining, Sunday lunch, disabled access, pets allowed, afternoon tea, vegetarian meals, open all day in summer and weekends in winter.

**Directions:** from A39 in Falmouth take Mylor turn, then downhill to Pandora.
MRS R. HOUGH ☎(01326) 372678

## NEWLYN • map 3E1

 **THE SMUGGLERS RESTAURANT**
12-14 Fore Street, Newlyn Harbour, TR18 5JN
*A 300 year old building overlooking Newlyn Harbour is home to this exceptional restaurant catering for all lovers of seafood. Its quality can be judged from the numerous complimentary comments on show, and the fact that many locals are numbered amongst its clientele. Louise and Spike Searle and their friendly staff will ensure you have a memorable meal in quiet and restful surroundings. Children are genuinely welcome and a treasure hunt is arranged by the staff.*
**FOOD:** up to £15
**Hours:** dinner 7pm-9.30pm, open bank holidays.
**Cuisine:** SEAFOOD - à la carte and table d'hôte menus offering delicious fresh seafood and a wide choice of meals for meat lovers and vegetarians. Comprehensive wine list, also very good value red and white house wines.
**Cards:** Visa, Access, Mastercard.
**Directions:** take the coast road from Penzance towards Mousehole. In Newlyn go past the fish market and the restaurant is on the right at the top of the harbour. LOUSIE & SPIKE SEARLE
☎(01736) 331501

## NEWQUAY • map 3D2

▱ **CORISANDE MANOR HOTEL**
Riverside Avenue, Pentire, TR7 1PL
*Built in 1900 of Austrian design, standing in three acres of grounds with private foreshore. The Painters have owned and run the hotel since 1968 and they offer many facilities, such as rowing boats, a putting green, crocquet and giant outdoor chess. Advance booking is strongly recommended.*
DOUBLE ROOM: from £21 to £30
SINGLE ROOM: from £21 to £30
FOOD: up to £15
**Hours:** breakfast 8.30am-9.30am, bar meals 12.30am-1.30pm, dinner 7pm-7.30pm, closed 15th October until 4th May 1996.
**Cuisine:** ENGLISH
**Cards:** Visa, Access.
**Other points:** central heating, children catered for (minimum age 3 years), residents' lounge, garden.
**Rooms:** 5 single rooms, 8 double rooms, 3 twin rooms, 3 triple rooms. All with TV, radio, tea/coffee-making facilities. Most rooms are en suite.
**Directions:** located off the B3282 on the Gannel estuary.
DAVID PAINTER ☎(01637) 872042

 **GLEN COURT HOTEL**
Mellanvrane Lane, TR7 2LB
*This excellent family-run hotel offering*

*exceptionally good value is situated in a quiet area of Newquay with boating lake, leisure centre and the beautiful Trenance gardens close by. Personally supervised by Mr and Mrs Witchell, all guests are assured of a warm and friendly atmosphere and superb home-cooking.*
DOUBLE ROOM: from £15 to £20
SINGLE ROOM: from £15 to £20
**Hours:** closed November-February (inclusive). Breakfast 8.30am-9am, dinner from 6.30pm.
**Other points:** separate bar, parking, packed lunches and evening snacks, senior citizens welcome, residents' lounge, vegetarian meals.
**Rooms:** 1 single room, 1 twin room, 6 double rooms with tea/coffee maker, TV. 2 family rooms with tea/coffee maker, TV.
**Directions:** from A30 to Newquay take A392, turn right at Safeway then 5th turn left - hotel facing end.
MRS BRENDA WITCHELL ☎(01637) 874848

▱ **THE GREAT WESTERN HOTEL**
Cliff Road, TR7 2PT
*An imposing cream building perched on the cliff above Great Western Beach, offering magnificent seaviews. The hotel comprises a lawned garden, indoor swimming pool and Jacuzzi, and serves traditional English food with warm hospitality.*
DOUBLE ROOM: from £20 to £30
SINGLE ROOM: from £25 to £35
FOOD: up to £15
**Hours:** breakfast 8am-9.30am, lunch 12noon-2pm, bar meals 12noon-2pm, dinner 7pm-8.30pm, bar meals 6pm-8.30pm.
**Cuisine:** ENGLISH - home-made dishes.
**Cards:** Visa, Access, Diners, AmEx.
**Other points:** licensed, Sunday lunch, coaches by prior arrangement, children welcome, baby-listening device, cots, foreign exchange, residents' lounge, residents' bar, swimming pool.
**Rooms:** 12 single rooms, 21 double rooms, 18 twin rooms, 18 triple rooms, 3 quad rooms. All with TV, radio, alarm, telephone, tea/coffee-making facilities.
**Directions:** on the cliff road near the railway station.
MR J. FITTER ☎(01637) 872010 Fax(01637) 874435

▱ **THE HEADLAND HOTEL**
Fistrol Bay, TR7 1EW

*The `Great British Holiday' revisited at one of the UK's most outstanding locations: 10 acres of private headland with the sea on three sides. Enjoy old-*

fashioned service provided by friendly staff, good Cornish food and excellent-value wines.
DOUBLE ROOM: from £35 to £49
SINGLE ROOM: from £37 to £55
FOOD: from £15 to £20 ▰
**Hours:** lunch 12.30am-2pm, dinner 7.30pm-9pm, early supper available for young children from 5.30pm. Closed early December to mid February (except New Year).
**Cuisine:** ENGLISH - including local crab and lobster. Table d'hôte and à la carte. Snacks, home-made cakes and scones served in coffee shop.
**Cards:** Visa, Access, Diners, AmEx.
**Other points:** children welcome (babies and toddlers not allowed in main restaurant for dinner-see special supper times), pets allowed, residents' lounge, residents' bar, garden, swimming pool, tennis, billiards, putting green, licensed, afternoon tea.
**Rooms:** 100 bedrooms. All with en suite, TV, telephone and tea/coffee-making facilities. Most with superb sea views.
**Directions:** follow directions to Fistral Beach.
MR & MRS ARMSTRONG ☎(01637) 872211
Fax(01637) 872212

### KILBIRNIE HOTEL
Narrowcliffe, TR7 2RS
*Mrs Cobley and her staff are delighted to welcome you to this extremely comfortable and well equipped hotel right on the seafront. Every amenity is provided for a pleasant stay including indoor and outdoor swimming pools, snooker table, table tennis, games room and sauna. Nearby activities include pony trekking, golf, fishing and, of course, the fabulous Newquay beaches.*
DOUBLE ROOM: from £30 to £40
SINGLE ROOM: from £30 to £40
FOOD: up to £15
**Hours:** breakfast 8.30am-9.30am, lunch (bar area) 12.30pm-1.30pm, dinner (restaurant) 7.30pm-8.30pm, open bank holidays.
**Cuisine:** TRADITIONAL ENGLISH - comprehensive à la carte and table d'hôte menus featuring all fresh produce. Excellent cheeseboard and wine list.
**Cards:** Visa, Access.
**Other points:** disabled facilities, children welcome, 24 hour reception, 24 hour laundry/valet service, hairdressing salon, leisure facilities, sun patio.
**Rooms:** 10 single rooms, 25 double rooms, 25 twin rooms, 3 family rooms. All en suite, with satellite TV, radio, telephone, hair dryer, trouser press and tea/coffee-making facilities.
**Directions:** on main road (sea-front) into Newquay, A3058. Hotel is on the left.
MRS B. J. COBLEY ☎(01637) 875155

### TREGURRIAN HOTEL
Watergate Bay, TR8 4AB
*A modern hotel overlooking the surf beach of Watergate Bay. Offering comfortable accommodation, there are excellent facilities for holidays and breaks, with heated swimming pool,*

games room, laundry room, etc. A wide range of bar meals are available. Only 100 yards from the beach, it is suitable for all ages and offers excellent surfing conditions. Central location for all of Cornwall.
DOUBLE ROOM: from £20 to £30
SINGLE ROOM: up to £25
FOOD: up to £15
**Hours:** breakfast 8.30am-9.15am, lunch 12.30am-1.30pm, dinner 6.45pm-7.30pm.
**Cuisine:** ENGLISH
**Cards:** Visa, Access.
**Other points:** children welcome, garden, afternoon tea, pets allowed.
**Rooms:** 4 single rooms, 11 double rooms, 5 twin rooms, 7 family rooms.
**Directions:** 3 miles from Newquay, on the B3276.
MR & MRS MOLLOY ☎(01637) 860280

### WATERGATE BAY HOTEL
Watergate Bay,, TR8 4AA
*Set in countryside-by-the-sea, this family-owned and run hotel has grounds that include a sandy beach and the famous coastal path. Watergate is a magical place away from the bustle of the town, with a wonderful range of indoor/outdoor leisure facilities, good food and friendly service in a happy, relaxed atmosphere.*
DOUBLE ROOM: from £20 to £30
SINGLE ROOM: from £21 to £30
FOOD: up to £15
**Hours:** breakfast 8.30am-9.45am, lunch 12.30am-1.45pm, bar meals 10.30am-6pm, dinner 7pm-8.30pm, closed mid-November until March.
**Cuisine:** ENGLISH - a good selection of traditional and modern English cuisine with vegetarian and continental dishes.
**Cards:** Visa, Access.
**Other points:** children welcome (minimum age in restaurant for dinner, 8 years), traditional Sunday lunch, surfing, heated indoor swimming pool, heated outdoor swimming pool, sports hall, badminton, squash, tennis, skittles, snooker, sauna, solarium, spa bath, live music, dancing, entertainment, pets allowed, parking, special golf rates.
**Rooms:** 8 single rooms, 20 double rooms, 4 twin rooms, 7 triple rooms, 18 family rooms/family suites. All with en suite, TV, telephone, radio, baby-listening device, tea/coffee-making facilities.
**Directions:** from A30 after Bodmin, follow A3059 to airport, then B3276 to Watergate Bay.
JOHN & MARY ASHWORTH ☎(01637) 860543
Fax(01637) 860333

### WHIPSIDERRY HOTEL
Trevelgue Road, Porth, TR7 3LY
*The Whipsiderry commands a superb position overlooking Porth beach and bay, with breathtaking views of both sea and country. Whether exploring the rugged Cornish coastline or venturing inland, the hotel provides a friendly retreat. On fine summer evenings enjoy a barbecue on the terrace,*

*and at night, watch the badgers feed and play only a few feet away.*

DOUBLE ROOM: from £20 to £40

FOOD: up to £15

**Hours:** breakfast 8.30am-9am, lunch 12noon-2pm, dinner 6.30pm-8pm, closed November until March, open Christmas.

**Cuisine:** ENGLISH - varied table d'hôte menu changes daily.

**Cards:** Visa, Access.

**Other points:** licensed, central heating, children welcome, pets allowed, swimming pool, sauna, pool room, bar snacks, launderette.

**Rooms:** 14 double rooms, 3 twin rooms, 4 family rooms, 2 suites. All with TV, radio, tea/coffee-making facilities, baby-listening device, hair dryers.

**Directions:** Trevelgue Road leads off Watergate Road (the seafront).

RICHARD & ANN DRACKFORD ☎(01637) 874777

---

### WHITE LODGE HOTEL
Mawgan Porth, TR8 4BN

*Family-owned and run, the hotel is beautifully situated in an elevated position, just 100 yards from the golden sands of Mawgan Porth. Excellent views of the sea and cliffs from the dining room, bar and most of the bedrooms. Comments from recent visitors highly praise the White Lodge and commend the comfortable accommodation, good food and welcoming, friendly service.*

DOUBLE ROOM: from £22 to £32

SINGLE ROOM: up to £26

FOOD: up to £15

**Hours:** breakfast 8am-9am, bar snacks 12noon-2pm, dinner 6pm-7.30pm, closed November until February.

**Cuisine:** ENGLISH

**Cards:** Visa, Access, AmEx, Switch, Delta, JCB.

**Other points:** children welcome, afternoon tea, pets allowed, residents' lounge, picnic lunches, vegetarian meals, games room, garden.

**Rooms:** 1 single room, 4 double rooms, 7 twin rooms, 6 family rooms. All with TV, tea/coffee-making facilities, heating, baby-listening device.

**Directions:** B3276 coast road between Newquay and Padstow. 5 miles from Newquay.

JOHN & DIANE PARRY ☎(01637) 860512

---

## PENZANCE • map 3EI

### CARNSON HOUSE HOTEL
East Terrace, TR18 2TD

*This small, comfortable, private hotel enjoys one of Penzance's most central positions. Close to harbour and beaches, it is an ideal base for touring the Land's End peninsula with its dramatic scenery of coves and cliffs. Tourist information and excursion booking service available. French and German spoken.*

DOUBLE ROOM: up to £20

SINGLE ROOM: up to £20

FOOD: up to £15

**Hours:** breakfast 8am-8.30am, dinner 6.15pm -

orders to be made by 4pm.

**Cuisine:** ENGLISH

**Cards:** Visa, Access, Diners, AmEx.

**Other points:** central heating, residents' lounge, garden, residents' licence, children welcome (over 12).

**Rooms:** 3 single rooms, 3 double rooms, 2 twin rooms. All with TV, tea/coffee-making facilities. Some en suite.

**Directions:** on the right side of main road entering Penzance from the A30 east.

RICHARD & TRISHA HILDER ☎(01736) 65589

---

### LYNWOOD GUEST HOUSE
41 Morrab Road, TR18 4EX

*A comfortable, well-appointed family guest house built in Victorian times. Situated between the promenade and the town centre, Lynwood is convenient for all amenities and close to the sub-tropical gardens. An ideal base for visiting Land's End and the Lizard peninsula, St Michael's Mount and the Isles of Scilly.*

DOUBLE ROOM: up to £20

**Hours:** breakfast 8am-8.45am.

**Cuisine:** BREAKFAST

**Cards:** Visa, Access, Diners, AmEx.

**Other points:** central heating, children welcome, no evening meal, residents' lounge.

**Rooms:** 1 single room, 1 double room, 2 twin rooms, 3 family rooms. All with TV, radio, alarm, tea/coffee-making facilities.

**Directions:** Morrab Road is a turning off the seafront.

MRS STACEY ☎(01736) 65871

---

 ### PRAH SANDS HOTEL
Praa Sands, TR20 9SY

*The hotel is situated at the base of a sheltered valley overlooking the beautiful beach at Praa Sands. The panoramic coastal views are outstanding, and guests may enjoy the attractive grounds which offer a tennis court and a 45 ft. heated outdoor pool. An outstanding location to soak up the warm and friendly atmosphere and enjoy a relaxing holiday.*

DOUBLE ROOM: from £30 to £45

SINGLE ROOM: from £275 to £35

FOOD: up to £15

**Hours:** breakfast 7am, lunch bar 12noon-3pm, dinner bar 6.30pm-10pm, dinner restaurant 7pm-9.30pm. Open bank holidays.

**Cuisine:** ENGLISH TRADITIONAL - comprehensive table d'hôte menu with 3 or 4 choices per course. Menu changes daily. Good wine list and wines available by the glass.

**Cards:** Visa, Access.

**Other points:** tennis court, heated outdoor pool, resident's lounges, bar, sun patio, snooker table, parking.

**Rooms:** 3 single rooms, 12 double rooms, 3 twin rooms, 3 family rooms, all en suite. All with TV, radio, alarm, tea/coffee-making facilities.

**Directions:** 2 miles outside Penzance on A30 turn left on A394 towards Helston. Praa Sands turning is

---

4 miles along A394 on the right.
ROY & JANE KETTLE ☎(01736) 762438

### UNION HOTEL
Chapel Street, TR18 4AL

*Steeped in history, the hotel dates back to the 17th century. It was here that news of Nelson's victory and death at the Battle of Trafalgar was first announced. Today, well-cooked and presented meals are served in a cosy atmosphere, and the accommodation is comfortable. Log fires in winter add to the warm welcome extended to all guests.*
DOUBLE ROOM: from £26 to £30
SINGLE ROOM: from £26 to £30
FOOD: up to £15
**Hours:** breakfast 8am-9.30am, bar meals 12noon-2pm, dinner 6pm-9.30pm, bar meals 6pm-9pm.
**Cuisine:** ENGLISH - full à la carte menu, table d'hôte and bar snacks.
**Cards:** Visa, Access, Diners, AmEx.
**Other points:** licensed, Sunday lunch, children welcome, covered parking.
**Rooms:** 28 bedrooms. All en suite with TV, tea/coffee-making facilities. Several with sea views.
**Directions:** take the A30 or A394 to Penzance. Follow town centre one-way system.
☎(01736) 62319

## PERRANPORTH • map 3D1

### BEACH DUNES HOTEL
Ramoth Way, Reen Sands, TR6 0BY

*Roomy, comfortably furnished hotel, with colour-coordinated decor and pleasant, cheerful atmosphere. The hotel is situated in the sand dunes above the beach, and adjoins the golf course.*
DOUBLE ROOM: from £25 to £30
FOOD: up to £15
**Hours:** breakfast 8.15am-9.30am, bar meals 12noon-2pm, dinner 6pm-8pm, closed November and December.
**Cuisine:** ENGLISH - traditional English home-cooked food. Fixed menu which changes daily. Vegetarian food available.
**Cards:** Visa, Access, AmEx, Switch, Delta.
**Other points:** no-smoking area, children catered for (please check for age limits), afternoon tea, parking, residents' lounge, garden, indoor swimming pool, squash.
**Rooms:** 4 double rooms, 2 twin rooms, 2 quad rooms. All with TV, radio, telephone, tea/coffee-making facilities.
**Directions:** B3285. Situated along a private road, 400 metres from main road.
KEITH WOOLDRIDGE ☎(01872) 572263
Fax(01872) 573824

### THE GALLEON RESTAURANT
St Pirrans Road, TR6 0BJ

*Excellent service in spacious surroundings makes this a highly popular restaurant with business people, locals and tourists alike. Although there are many delious alternatives all prepared from the freshest produce available, locally caught seafood is a prevailing feature of The Galleon.*
FOOD: up to £15
**Hours:** lunch 12noon-2pm, dinner 6.30pm-9.30pm.
**Cuisine:** ENGLISH - fresh fish and steaks are the specialities from the good selection of home-cooked meals.
**Cards:** Visa, Access, Diners, Eurocard, Switch.
**Directions:** located in Perranporth High Street.
MR & MRS T. & V. SUTTON ☎(01872) 572066

## PHILLEIGH • map 3E2

### SMUGGLERS COTTAGE OF TOLVERNE
Near Truro, TR2 5NG

*This 500-year-old thatched cottage has been run by the Newman family for over 60 years. It is situated on the banks of the River Fal, near the King Harry car ferry on the Roseland Peninsula, with own landing stage and moorings. Smugglers Cottage offers a selection of over 100 different malt whiskies.*
FOOD: from £15 to £20
**Hours:** morning coffee 10.30am, lunch 12noon-2pm, cream teas 3pm-5.30pm, dinner 7.30pm-9pm.
**Cuisine:** ENGLISH - daily changing menu of home-cooked dishes using fresh local produce, particularly fish and seafood. Daily buffet.
**Cards:** Visa, Access.
**Other points:** open-air dining, children catered for (please check for age limits), Friday and Saturday evening barbecues in high season.
**Directions:** near King Harry car ferry on Roseland peninsula.
ELIZABETH & PETER NEWMAN ☎(01872) 580309
Fax(01872) 580216

## PILLATON • map 3D3

### THE WEARY FRIAR INN
Near Saltash, PL12 6QS

*A famous old 12th century inn situated next to the church of St Odolphus, where you will find true character and atmosphere. Today The Weary Friar welcomes you to imaginative food of a high standard, superb surroundings and comfortable accommodation. Highly recommended for its high-quality food and the excellent combination of modern comforts with 12th century character.*
DOUBLE ROOM: from £22.50
SINGLE ROOM: from £35
FOOD: up to £15
**Hours:** breakfast 8am-9am, lunch 12noon-2pm, dinner 7pm-9.30pm.
**Cuisine:** MODERN ENGLISH - dishes may include fillets of sole champagne, honey roast saddle of lamb, smokey carpetbag steak (with oysters), vegetable and nut salousie.
**Cards:** Visa, Access.
**Other points:** licensed, open-air dining, Sunday lunch, children welcome, afternoon tea, residents' lounge.
**Rooms:** 13 bedrooms. All en suite.

**Directions:** between Saltash and Callington, two miles west of A388. Near St Mellion.
SUE & ROGER SHARMAN ☎(01579) 50238

## POLPERRO • map 3E2

 **NELSON'S RESTAURANT**
Big Green, PL13 2QT
*A large, olde-worlde restaurant with a distinct nautical flavour, reflecting the proprietor's long connection with the sea. The table d'hôte menu changes with the availability of fresh produce. An intimate restaurant with a friendly atmosphere.*
FOOD: up to £15
**Hours:** lunch 11.45am-2pm, dinner 7pm-10pm, closed Saturday lunch and Monday, closed mid-January until mid-February.
**Cuisine:** ENGLISH / FRENCH / SEAFOOD - fresh seafood, roasts, grills, game.
**Cards:** Visa, Access, Diners, AmEx.
**Other points:** licensed, Sunday lunch, children welcome, pets by prior arrangement.
**Directions:** on the Saxon bridge in Polperro.
PETER NELSON ☎(01503) 272366 Fax(01503) 273098

## PORT ISAAC • map 3D2

 **THE CORNISH ARMS**
Pendoggett, PL30 3HH
*This typical Cornish 16th century coaching inn, located in the heart of the small village of Pendoggett, is indeed charming. The excellent cuisine is served in a relaxed and friendly atmosphere, and the choice of fresh seafood, from the local fishing villages, makes it well worth a visit!*
DOUBLE ROOM: £24.50
SINGLE ROOM: £35
FOOD: up to £15 CLUB
**Hours:** breakfast 8.30am-9.30am, lunch 12.30am-2pm, dinner 7.15pm-12midnight, last orders 9.30pm.
**Cuisine:** ENGLISH / SEAFOOD - à la carte and bar menu. Fresh local lobster, crab, lemon sole and fillet steak filled with sautéed mushrooms and smoked oysters, specialities.
**Cards:** Visa, Access, Diners, AmEx, Switch.
**Other points:** licensed, open-air dining, Sunday lunch, no-smoking area, pets allowed, children welcome, disabled access, residents' lounge, residents' bar, vegetarian meals.
**Rooms:** 3 double rooms, 4 twin rooms. All with TV, telephone, tea/coffee-making facilities.
**Directions:** off A30, follow A395 until A39 T-junction. Left, then first right onto B3314.
JOHN ROBINSON & MERVYN GILMOUR ☎(01208) 880263 Fax(01208) 880335

**OLD SCHOOL HOTEL**
Fore Street, PL29 3RB
*The Old School dates from 1875 and stands sentinel on the cliff top overlooking the harbour and out to sea. The accommodation is excellent, tastefully*
furnished to provide a high standard of comfort yet retaining the original character of the building. The restaurant specializes in local fish and seafood. Deep-sea fishing, riding, golf and sailing are all available nearby.
DOUBLE ROOM: from £20 to £30
FOOD: up to £15
**Hours:** breakfast 8am-11am, lunch 11am-3pm, bar snacks 11am-9.30pm, dinner 7pm-9.30pm, open all year.
**Cuisine:** SEAFOOD - restaurant specializes in fish and seafood dishes such as whole grilled lemon sole, lobster Thermidor, mariner's fish pie. Bar meals.
**Cards:** Visa, Access.
**Other points:** licensed, open-air dining, Sunday lunch, children welcome, afternoon tea, residents' lounge, pets allowed, garden, barbecues, medieval banquets.
**Rooms:** 6 double rooms, 1 twin room, 3 family rooms, 3 suites. All with TV.
**Directions:** 9 miles north of Wadebridge on B3314 until left turn on B3267.
MICHAEL WARNER ☎(01208) 880721

## ROCK • map 3D2

**ROSKARNON HOUSE HOTEL**
Rock, near Wadebridge, PL27 6LD
*By the golden sands of Rock and the open sea of the Camel estuary, the Roskarnon House Hotel is an ideal place in which to enjoy the delights of a holiday in Cornwall. This small, unpretentious hotel offers all the essentials and amenities to make your stay a happy one. Simple, home-cooked food.*
DOUBLE ROOM: from £20 to £40
SINGLE ROOM: up to £35
FOOD: up to £15
**Hours:** breakfast 8.30am-9.30am, dinner 7pm-8pm, lunch 12noon-1.30pm.
**Cuisine:** ENGLISH - dishes include vegetarian lasagne, roast chicken and poached salmon with butter sauce.
**Cards:** AmEx.
**Other points:** children welcome, garden, afternoon tea.
**Rooms:** 12 bedrooms. Most rooms are en suite.
**Directions:** overlooking Camel estuary. Off A39 and B3314.
IAN VEALL ☎(01208) 862329

## ST AGNES • map 3E1

 **PENKERRIS**
Penwinnick Road, TR5 OPA

*Enchanting Edwardian residence with garden and large lawn in an unspoilt Cornish village. Dramatic cliff walks, beaches, swimming and surfing all nearby. Superb home-cooking: traditional roasts, home-made fruit tarts with local fresh produce. Touches of the exotic with excellent curries, pastas and vegetable dishes.*
DOUBLE ROOM: up to £20
SINGLE ROOM: up to £20
FOOD: up to £15
**Hours:** breakfast 8.30am, dinner 6.30pm.
**Cuisine:** ENGLISH / INTERNATIONAL
**Cards:** Visa, Access, MasterCard, Eurocard.
**Other points:** central heating, children welcome, residents' lounge, garden, piano, log fire, video.
**Rooms:** 1 single room, 2 double rooms, 2 twin rooms, 2 family rooms - 2 rooms en suite. All with TV, radio, tea/coffee-making facilities. 2 large bathrooms and large shower room
**Directions:** take B3277 off A30 at Chiverton roundabout. 3 miles into village.
DOROTHY GILL-CAREY ☎(01872) 552262

## ST IVES • map 3E1

 **BOSKERRIS HOTEL**
Carbis Bay, TR26 2RU
*A family-run hotel, set in private gardens with a heated swimming pool, noted for its fine wines and good food. Overlooks Carbis Bay, with magnificent views across to St Ives harbour on one side and Godrevy Head on the other.*
DOUBLE ROOM: from £32
FOOD: up to £20
**Hours:** breakfast 8.30am-9.30am, bar meals 12.30am-1.30pm, dinner 7pm-8.30pm.
**Cuisine:** INTERNATIONAL - including table d'hôte four course meal (£17.50).
**Cards:** Visa, Access, Diners, AmEx.
**Other points:** free phone 0500 121491, children welcome, pets allowed, afternoon tea, open bank holidays, special breaks.
**Rooms:** 2 single rooms, 9 double rooms, 4 twin rooms, 4 family rooms.
**Directions:** along A30 to St Ives. Third turning on right as you enter Carbis Bay.
MR & MRS MONK ☎(01736) 795295 Fax(01736) 798632

 **CHY-AN-DOUR HOTEL**
Trelyon Avenue, TR26 2AD
*This 19th century former sea captain's home has been extended to form a most attractive hotel with superb panoramic views over St Ives Bay and harbour. All bedrooms are en suite, most with breathtaking views.*
DOUBLE ROOM: from £31 to £40
FOOD: from £15 to £20
**Hours:** breakfast 8.30am-9.30am, dinner 7pm-8pmbar meals 12noon-2pm, .
**Cuisine:** ENGLISH - six-course table d'hôte dinner menu. Main-course dishes include a choice of meat, fish, salad and vegetarian.
**Cards:** Visa, Access.
**Other points:** licensed, no-smoking area, children catered for (please check for age limits), residents' lounge, garden, residents' bar, baby-listening device, baby-sitting, cots.
**Rooms:** 10 double rooms, 10 twin rooms, 3 family rooms. All with TV, radio, telephone, tea/coffee-making facilities.
**Directions:** A3074, on main road into St Ives.
DAVID & RENEE WATSON ☎(01736) 796436 Fax(01736) 795772

**CHY-AN-GWEDHEN**
St Ives Road, Carbis Bay, TR26 2PN
*This delightful, welcoming guest house, a haven for non-smokers, is exceptionally decorated throughout and offers splendid views of St Ives Bay. The superb bedrooms are outstanding in design and offer many facilities for that comfortable home-away-from-home feeling. Located in St Ives, adjacent to the coastal footpath, it is ideal for visiting St Ives' Tate Gallery or Land's End, or relaxing on one of the magnificent beaches nearby, or just walking the wonderful coastline. Watersports, golf, riding close by.*
DOUBLE ROOM: up to £20
SINGLE ROOM: up to £25
FOOD: up to £15
**Hours:** breakfast 7am-9am, dinner at 6.30pm, open Christmas and New Year with bookings only.
**Cuisine:** ENGLISH - Excellent selection of traditional, vegetarian and continental breakfasts. Locally oak-smoked fish.
**Cards:** Visa, Access, AmEx, Eurocard, MasterCard, JCB.
**Other points:** parking, central heating, no™smoking area, patio, garden, sun loungers, telephone available.
**Rooms:** 3 double rooms, 2 twin rooms. All with en suite, TV, hair dryer, tea/coffee-making facilities, clock/radio/alarm.
**Directions:** from A30 take A3074, the main road into St Ives. The guest house is on the right, 500 yards before the Cornish Arms Inn.
LESLIE & MARY HART ☎(01736) 798684

**DEAN COURT HOTEL**
Trelyon Avenue, TR26 2AD
*The Dean Court private hotel is situated in its own*

grounds with ample parking overlooking Porthminster Beach and St. Ives Harbour. Its comfortable rooms are complemented by the private bar, lounge and restaurant, and a delightful terraced garden.

DOUBLE ROOM: from £28 to £35
SINGLE ROOM: from £28 to £35
FOOD: up to £15
**Hours:** breakfast 8.30am-9am, dinner 6.30pm-7pm, open bank holidays, closed from 1st November to 1st March.
**Cuisine:** ENGLISH - excellent set menus, with house specialities of sea foods and roasts.
**Cards:** Access, Visa, JCB
**Other points:** parking, central heating, residents' lounge, bar and private restaurant, children catered for (please check for age limits).
**Rooms:** 2 single rooms, 8 double rooms, 2 twin rooms, all en suite. All with TV, hair dryer, tea/coffee-making facilities.
**Directions:** situated on A3074 - Trelyon Avenue, overlooking Porthminster beach.
IAN D E ALFORD ☎(01736) 796023 Fax (01736) 796233

### HUNTERS RESTAURANT
St Andrews Street, TR26 1AH
Under the personal supervision of the proprietor and the chef, this excellent restaurant offers a wide range of dishes with the accent very much on local seafood, although meat eaters and vegetarians are not neglected. Situated in a 400 year old terraced building, the atmosphere, decor and comfortable seting all contribute to a memorable meal. Well recommended.
FOOD: from £15 to £20
**Hours:** dinner 6pm-10pm, open bank holidays. No children under 10 in restaurant.
**Cuisine:** ENGLISH - seafood specialities using fresh locally caught fish.
**Cards:** Visa, Access, AmEx.
**Other points:** book to avoid disappointment, car parking close by in station or council car parks, children catered for (please check for age limits).
**Directions:** 100 yards from St Ives church.
MR GRAHAM NORTH ☎(01736) 797074

### PEDN-OLVA HOTEL & RESTAURANT
Porthminster Beach, TR26 2EA
`Pedn-Olva' means `look-out on the headland', and this hotel, built with its series of towers, is situated on a rocky promontory overlooking the ancient town, the harbour and bay. Beautifully presented and served, the quality of food and wine offered here only just surpasses the restaurant's seascape view. Attractive balcony bedrooms provide guests with a relaxing holiday setting.
DOUBLE ROOM: from £40 to £50
FOOD: from £15 to £20 ☜
**Hours:** breakfast 8am-9.15am, lunch 12noon-2pm, dinner 6.30pm-9.30pm.
**Cuisine:** ENGLISH - wide selection of table d'hôte or à la carte menu, using fresh quality produce,

including seafood specialities.
**Cards:** Visa, Access.
**Other points:** licensed, Sunday lunch, children welcome, afternoon tea, swimming pool, residents' lounge, pets allowed.
**Directions:** on A3074 - the hotel overlooks the town, harbour and bay.
KENNETH GEORGE EVANS ☎(01736) 796222

### THE ST UNY HOTEL
Carbis Bay, TR26 2NQ
Superb position overlooking the bay, with excellent views from most rooms. Originally a private mansion, now a throroughly refurbished hotel with an atmosphere of calm and relaxation. Standing in two acres of sheltered gardens with semi-tropical trees and shrubs.
DOUBLE ROOM: from £30 to £40
SINGLE ROOM: from £25 to £35
FOOD: from £15 to £20
**Hours:** breakfast 8.45am-9.30am, bar snacks 12noon-2pm, dinner 7pm-8pm. Open Easter-Oct
**Cuisine:** ENGLISH
**Cards:** Visa, Access.
**Other points:** Sunday lunch, children welcome, parking, afternoon tea.
**Rooms:** 30 bedrooms.
**Directions:** from A30 take the A3074; the hotel Is close to Carbis Bay station.
T. & B.C. CARROLL ☎(01736) 795011

## ST JUST • map 3E1

### WELLINGTON HOTEL
Market Square, TR19 7HD
In the centre of St Just, the Wellington Hotel is well located to explore Cornwall. Extensively modernized in recent years, this comfortable, family-run hotel is noted for its excellent food. All room bookings include a full English breakfast, and a menu with daily specials is available for non-residents at lunch and dinner times. Ideal centre for walking, climbing, water sports and relaxing holidays, golf and beaches.
DOUBLE ROOM: up to £20
SINGLE ROOM: from £25 to £35
FOOD: up to £15
**Hours:** breakfast 8am-8.30am, lunch 12noon-2pm, dinner 6pm-8.30pm, open all year.
**Cuisine:** ENGLISH - cuisine for all the family, pub-style, including traditional Sunday lunch and children's menu. Vegetarians also catered for. Fresh local fish and crab, steaks, etc.
**Cards:** Visa, Access, Diners, AmEx.
**Other points:** licensed, open-air dining, Sunday lunch, children welcome, open bank holidays, pets allowed.
**Rooms:** 13 double rooms. Some with TV, telephone.
**Directions:** take A3071 from Penzance to St Just (6 miles).
RODERICK & JENNIFER GRAY ☎(01736) 787319/787906

## ST MAWES • map 3E2

 **ELERKEY HOUSE HOTEL**
Veryan, TR2 5QA

*Situated in this charming village with its picturesque round houses, Elerkey House offers a tranquil setting for a peaceful break supported by excellent home cooking. The public rooms are comfortably furnished and the gardens and great tree make a colourful focal point in the centre of the village. Golf, coastal walks and splendid beaches close by. Highly recommended.*
DOUBLE ROOM: from £21 to £30
SINGLE ROOM: from £21 to £30
FOOD: from £16 to £20
**Hours:** breakfast 8am-9am, lunch 12noon-2pm, dinner 7pm-8pm, open bank holidays.
**Cuisine:** ENGLISH HOOME COOKING - freshly caught fish and local farm produce.
**Cards:** Visa, Access.
**Other points:** smoking confined to bar and bar lounge, licensed, parking, garden, children catered for (please check for age limits), pets allowed by prior arrangement.
**Rooms:** 2 single rooms, 2 double rooms, 2 twin room, 1 family room. All en suite and with TV, telephone and tea/coffee making facilities.
**Directions:** from A390 take B3287 then A3078 and follow signs to Veryan. Hotel is in the centre of the village.
ROGER & DOREEN PRIDDLE ☎(01872) 501261

 **PENDOWER BEACH HOUSE HOTEL**
Gerrans Bay, Ruan High Lanes,
Portscatho, TR2 5LW

*The hotel occupies a prime position on the beautiful Roseland Peninsula. It boasts extensive grounds where peacocks and ducks roam freely. The choice of cuisine is excellent, specializing in local fresh fish served in a relaxing atmosphere.*
DOUBLE ROOM: from £50
FOOD: from £15 to £20
**Hours:** breakfast 8.45am-9.15am, lunch 12noon-2pm, dinner 7.30pm-9pm.
**Cuisine:** ENGLISH - à la carte, fixed five-course menu or light lunches available.
**Cards:** Visa, Access.
**Other points:** licensed, open-air dining, no-smoking area, children welcome, afternoon tea, garden, pets allowed.
**Rooms:** 7 double rooms, 4 twin rooms, 1 family room.
**Directions:** A3078, turning 6 miles north of St Mawes. End of lane to `Pink Hotel', on the beach.
PETER & CAROL BEETHAM ☎(01872) 501241
Fax(01872) 501868

## THE LIZARD • map 3E2

 **HOUSEL BAY HOTEL**
Housel Bay, TR12 7PG

*An elegant Victorian hotel in a spectacular clifftop position, with a secluded sandy cove and extensive grounds. Offers well-equipped, comfortable rooms and value-for-money food. Kynance Cove, the Lizard and Goonhilly Downs all nearby.*
DOUBLE ROOM: from £21 to £30
SINGLE ROOM: from £21 to £30
FOOD: from £15 to £20
**Hours:** breakfast 8.30am-10am, bar meals 12noon-1.45pm, dinner 7.30pm-9.30pm, bar meals 7.30pm-8.45pm. Open all year.
**Cuisine:** ENGLISH - traditional English cuisine, including fresh fish and seafood.
**Cards:** Visa, Access, AmEx.
**Other points:** Sunday lunch, no-smoking area, children welcome, pets allowed, afternoon tea, open bank holidays, disabled access, residents' lounge, residents' bar.
**Rooms:** 4 single rooms, 9 double rooms, 8 twin rooms. All with TV, radio, alarm, telephone, tea/coffee-making facilities.
**Directions:** at The Lizard town signpost, take the left fork, following hotel signs.
FREDA & DEREK OSWALD ☎(01326) 290417
Fax(01326) 290359

## TINTAGEL • map 3D2

 **THE PORT WILLIAM**
Trebarwith Strand, PL34 0HB

*Beautifully situated on top of the cliffs at Trebarwith, overlooking the bay, this cheerful 19th century pub provides good food and a vibrant atmosphere in which to enjoy it. An excellent selection of home-cooked food and seafood at reasonable prices. Live music in the evenings.*
DOUBLE ROOM: from £20
SINGLE ROOM: from £21 to £30
FOOD: up to £15
**Hours:** lunch 12noon-2.30pm, dinner 6pm-9.30pm, closed Christmas day.
**Cuisine:** ENGLISH - à la carte menu offering traditional home-style cooking. Speciality dishes include shellfish and seafood, with daily changing blackboard specials.
**Cards:** Visa, Access.
**Other points:** licensed, bar open all day all year, open-air dining, Sunday lunch, children welcome, pets allowed, parking, afternoon tea, open bank holidays, disabled access.
**Rooms:** 2 single rooms, 3 double rooms, 2 double/family rooms. All en suite with TV, tea/coffee-making facilities.
**Directions:** follow the B3263, off the Tintagel/Camelford road (3 miles).
PETER HALE ☎(01840) 770230

## TREGONY • map 3E2

 **KEA HOUSE RESTAURANT**
69 Fore Street, TR2 5RW

*A two-storey stone building facing the main street, tastefully decorated with a warm, welcoming atmosphere. Excellent cuisine with seafood and fish specialities (in season), and special selection of malt whiskies.*

FOOD: from £16 to £20

**Hours:** summer (Easter to Sept 30th) lunches and teas 11am-4.30pm, dinner from 7pm. onwards, closed Sunday. From October 1st, dinner only. Closed all November and Sunday and Monday for the remainder of winter season.

**Cuisine:** ENGLISH - chicken with fresh herbs and spices fried in filo pastry served in plum sauce; also fish and cheeseboard.

**Cards:** Visa, Access, AmEx, JCB.

**Other points:** licensed, disabled access.

**Directions:** on the B3287, west of Truro.

ANN & ALEX NIXON ☎(01872) 530642

## TRURO • map 3E2

### THE GANGES RESTAURANT
St Clement Street, TR1 1EQ

*The Ganges is close to the city centre, with a large car park opposite. The restaurant is beautifully set out and decorated in traditional Indian style. Seating for 78 persons in comfort and calm atmosphere. Discreet lighting adds to the delicate aroma of Indian spices and sauces. A most pleasant and relaxing restaurant, with happy and attentive staff. Prices are very reasonable and meals can be taken in an unhurried and peaceful ambience.*

FOOD: up to £15

**Hours:** lunch 12noon-2.15pm, dinner 6pm-11.15pm, Friday and Saturday 11.45pm.

**Cuisine:** INDIAN - fresh ingredients used, all meals prepared daily and cooked to order.

**Cards:** Visa, Access, AmEx, MasterCard, Switch.

**Other points:** children welcome, no-smoking area, vegetarian meals.

**Directions:** off A39, close to Truro police station.

BAHAR UDDIN ☎(01872) 42535

 **MARCORRIE**
20 Falmouth Road, TR1 2HX

*A Victorian family-run hotel in a conservation area, 5 minutes' walk from the city centre and cathedral. Centrally situated for touring Cornwall and for visiting the nearby country houses, gardens and coast.*

DOUBLE ROOM: from £20 to £30
SINGLE ROOM: up to £35
FOOD: up to £15

**Hours:** breakfast 7.30am-8.45am, dinner 7pm.

**Cuisine:** ENGLISH - home-cooking.

**Cards:** Visa, Access, Diners, AmEx.

**Other points:** parking, children welcome, conference facilities, pets allowed, residents' lounge, no-smoking area, garden, swimming pool.

**Rooms:** 2 single rooms, 3 double rooms, 4 twin rooms, 1 triple room, 2 family rooms.

**Directions:** located on Falmouth Road, about 500 yards south of Truro city centre.

MRS P. TRESEDER ☎(01872) 77374 Fax(01872) 41666

### THE ROYAL HOTEL
Lemon Street, TR7 1QB

*A 200 year old coaching inn situated in the centre of the beautiful cathedral city of Truro. This historic hotel makes an ideal base for both the business traveller and leisure guest. The high standards of comfort and service and the friendly management and staff ensure that a warm welcome awaits you at The Royal Hotel. With old, original arches and large windows, the exterior sets off the impressive and recently decorated interior and our inspector had nothing but praise following his visit.*

DOUBLE ROOM: from £25 to £35
SINGLE ROOM: from £32 to £49
FOOD: from £15 to £20

**Hours:** breakfast Monday to Saturday 7.30am-9.30am, Sunday 8.30am-9.30am, meals served all day 10am-10pm, open bank holidays, closed Christmas and Boxing day.

**Cuisine:** BRASSERIE - steaks plus a supplementary list of daily special dishes.

**Cards:** Visa, Access, AmEx.

**Other points:** licensed, residents' and television lounges, 24 hour reception, night porter, laundry/valet service, ironing facilities, French and German spoken.

**Rooms:** 11 single, 6 twin, 14 double, 2 family and 2 executive rooms, all en suite. All with satellite TV, radio, telephone, hair dryer, and tea/coffee making facilities.

**Directions:** in Truro city centre at the junction of Lemon Street and Lemon Quay.

☎(01872) 70345 Fax(01872) 42453

## WADEBRIDGE • map 3D2

### THE MOLESWORTH ARMS HOTEL
Molesworth Street, PL27 7DP

*True Cornish hospitality can be found at this 16th century coaching inn. The traditional furnishings and old, beamed ceilings retain the character and olde-worlde elegance of the inn while providing comfortable surroundings in which to enjoy the best in fresh local produce and the friendly, caring atmosphere.*

DOUBLE ROOM: from £20 to £30
SINGLE ROOM: £29.50
FOOD: from £16 to £20

**Hours:** breakfast 8am-10am, bar meals 12noon-2.30pm, dinner 7pm-9.30pm, bar meals 6.30pm-9.30pm.

**Cuisine:** ENGLISH - traditional English cuisine using local produce. Cornish produce includes local shell fish, salmon and speciality steaks.

**Cards:** Visa, Access, AmEx.

**Other points:** licensed, open-air dining, Sunday lunch, children welcome, afternoon tea, pets allowed, residents' lounge, conferences.

**Rooms:** 3 single rooms, 11 twin or double rooms, 2 family rooms. All with TV, tea/coffee-making facilities.

**Directions:** A30 to Bodmin, A389 to Wadebridge. Left over bridge. Parking at rear.

NIGEL CASSIDY ☎(01208) 812055 Fax(01208) 814254

# DEVON

## AXMINSTER • map 4C4

 **THE NEW COMMERCIAL INN**
Trinity Square, EX13 5AN
*This restaurant is found in a natural stone Victorian building in the centre of Axminster and offers excellent service and menu variety, including a special children's menu. The value for money is outstanding.*
FOOD: up to £15
**Hours:** breakfast 7.30am-12noon, lunch 12noon-2pm, afternoon tea 2pm-5.30pm, dinner 6pm-10.30pm.
**Cuisine:** ENGLISH / INTERNATIONAL - hot meals served all day from 7.30am. Children's menu. Dishes include trout, burgers, cod, plaice, steak, gammon and vegetarian options along with home-made soups and desserts.
**Cards:** Visa, Diners, AmEx, Switch, MasterCard, JCB.
**Other points:** licensed, children welcome, afternoon tea, street parking, bread shop.
**Directions:** In the main square in Axminster.
THE WALDEN FAMILY ☎(01297) 33225/35412

## AXMOUTH • map 4D4

 **THE SHIP INN**
Near Seaton, EX12 4AF
*A small, popular pub on the road from Seaton serving an extensive range of lunchtime and evening meals in both bars and the garden. Real ales.*
FOOD: up to £15
**Hours:** lunch 12noon-2pm, dinner 7.30pm-9pm.
**Cuisine:** ENGLISH - deep sea surprise, baked plaice with seafood stuffing, accent on local game and seafood in season. Home-grown fruit, vegetables and herbs.
**Cards:** Visa, Access, Switch, MasterCard.
**Other points:** children welcome, garden, games room.
**Directions:** 1 mile south of the A3052 Lyme Regis-Exeter road towards Seaton.
MR & MRS C. CHAPMAN ☎(01297) 21838

## BAMPTON • map 4C4

 **THE COURTYARD HOTEL**
19 Fore Street
*Situated close to the edge of Exmoor with its splendid variety of scenery, The Courtyard Hotel offers a warm and friendly atmosphere backed up by excellent cuisine to ensure you enjoy your stay. Mr and Mrs Tanner and their staff take great pains to extend to guests the sort of welcome that makes the difference between an adequate hotel and a special one. Highly recommended.*
DOUBLE ROOM: up to £20
SINGLE ROOM: up to £25
FOOD: up to £15
**Hours:** breakfast 8am-9am, lunch and bar meals 12noon-2pm, dinner and bar meals 7pm-9.30pm, open bank holidays.
**Cuisine:** ENGLISH - traditional fare including a selection of Vegetarian dishes.
**Cards:** Visa, Access.
**Other points:** private parties catered for, licensed, parking.
**Rooms:** 1 single room, 1 twin room en suite, 3 double rooms (2 en suite), 1 family room. All with TV, tea/coffee-making facilities.
**Directions:** Take A361 and B3227 to Bampton. Hotel is in the centre of the village.
☎(01398) 331536

 **THE SWAN HOTEL**
Station Road, EX16 9NG
*A 15th century building which retains its old charm and character. Originally, The Swan housed the stone masons who built the nearby church. Close to Exmoor, Bickley Mill and Wimbleball Lake.*
DOUBLE ROOM: up to £20
SINGLE ROOM: up to £20
FOOD: up to £15
**Hours:** breakfast 8am-9.30am, lunch 12noon-2pm, bar meals 12noon-2pm, dinner 7pm-10pm, bar meals 6pm-10pm.
**Cuisine:** ENGLISH - home-style traditional cooking, using fresh produce such as local trout and fresh vegetables.
**Cards:** Visa, Access, Diners.
**Other points:** licensed, Sunday lunch, open bank holidays, children welcome, pets allowed, afternoon tea.
**Rooms:** 1 single room, 1 twin room, 3 double rooms (2 en suite), 1 family room.
**Directions:** on main Barnstable-Taunton road on B3227. Close to public car park.
BRIAN & PAM DUNESBY ☎(01398) 331257

## BEER • map 4D4

 **GARLANDS**
Stovar Long Lane, EX12 3EA
*An Edwardian character house set in an acre of ground on the main coast road between Seaton and Beer. There are superb views from the house both of the sea and the Devon countryside; the beach is within easy walking distance. Fishing trips can be arranged - and your catch cooked for supper.*
DOUBLE ROOM: up to £20
SINGLE ROOM: up to £25
FOOD: up to £15
**Hours:** breakfast 8.30am-9.30am, dinner 7pm to be ordered by 12noon.
**Cuisine:** ENGLISH - traditional English cooking.
**Cards:** Visa, Access.
**Other points:** central heating, children welcome, residents' lounge, with sky TY.

**Rooms:** 2 double rooms, 1 twin room, 3 family rooms. All with en suite, satellite TV, tea/coffee-making facilities.
**Directions:** turn south off A3052 at Hangmans Stone onto B3174. The hotel is signposted.
ANN & NIGEL HARDING ☎(01297) 20958
Fax(01297) 23869

## BICKINGTON • map 3C3

 **THE DARTMOOR HALFWAY**
Near Newton Abbot, TQ12 6JW
*A charming pub, aptly named, half-way between Ashburton and Newton Abbot. The Dartmoor Halfway offers first-class food and service.*
FOOD: up to £15
**Hours:** breakfast 7.30am-11am, full restaurant menu, specialities and bar meals 11am-10.30pm, closed Christmas day.
**Cuisine:** ENGLISH - home-cooking.
**Cards:** Visa, Access, Diners, AmEx.
**Other points:** licensed, Sunday lunch, children welcome, caravan facilities.
**Directions:** on the A383, half-way between Ashburton and Newton Abbot.
MR B.R. & MRS M.D. HUGGINS ☎(01626) 821270 Fax(01626) 821280

## BIDEFORD • map 3C3

 **RIVERSFORD HOTEL**
Limers Lane, EX39 2RG
*A country house hotel in 3 acres of gardens, affording magnificent views of the River Torridge. Ideal touring centre for beaches and countryside or for discovering the hidden charms of Devon and Exmoor.*
DOUBLE ROOM: from £30 to £40
SINGLE ROOM: from £37 to £40
FOOD: up to £15          CLUB
**Hours:** open all year.
**Cuisine:** ENGLISH - home-made country fare, home-made sweets, Devonshire cream teas and interesting wines. Traditional Sunday lunch. Extensive à la catre menu, fresh local fish a speciality.
**Cards:** Visa, Access, Diners, AmEx.
**Other points:** licensed, open-air dining, Sunday lunch, children welcome.
**Rooms:** 13 bedrooms all en suite. Some four-poster beds.
**Directions:** Limers Lane is on the right, 1 mile north of Bideford on the A386.
MAURICE & MERRILYN JARRAD ☎(01237) 474239/470381 Fax(01237) 421661

## BOVEY TRACEY • map 4D4

**THE EDGEMOOR HOTEL**
Lowerdown Cross, Haytor Road, TQ13 9LE
*A 19th century country house, surrounded by extensive well-tended lawns and gardens, lovingly*

*decorated and comfortably furnished in keeping with the era. Offering good-quality food, excellently cooked and presented, complemented by a distinguished wine list and attentive, well-trained staff. A delightful establishment, not to be missed. Highly recommended.*
DOUBLE ROOM: from £40 to £50
SINGLE ROOM: from £35 to £45
FOOD: from £15 to £20 ☜
**Hours:** breakfast 8am-9.30am, lunch 12noon-2pm, dinner 7.30pm-9pm.
**Cuisine:** FRENCH / ENGLISH - dishes include curried cream prawns in a filo pastry croustade, roast duck glazed with orange and Cointreau, roast sirloin of beef with red wine and mushrooms.
**Cards:** Visa, Access, Diners, AmEx.
**Other points:** licensed, Sunday lunch, children catered for (please check for age limits), garden, afternoon tea, pets allowed.
**Rooms:** 3 single rooms, 6 double rooms, 12 twin rooms, 1 family room.
**Directions:** 7 minutes from A38, 1 mile from Bovey Tracey.
ROD & PATRICIA DAY ☎(01626) 832466
Fax(01626) 834760

## BRAUNTON • map 3C3

 **PRESTON HOUSE HOTEL**
Saunton, EX33 1LG
*A grand Victorian country house overlooking the 10-mile sweep of Barnstaple's sandy bay. Built in 1895, the stained-glass windows, moulded ceilings, period furnishings, paintings and ornaments all re-create the glory of the period. Golf, riding, fishing and water sports are all available nearby, and the hotel has its own heated outdoor swimming pool.*
DOUBLE ROOM: from £30 to £40
SINGLE ROOM: from £25 to £35
FOOD: up to £15
**Hours:** breakfast 8.30am-9.30am, lunch 12noon-2pm, dinner 7pm-8.30pm.
**Cuisine:** ENGLISH - table d'hôte menu changes daily. All dishes prepared and cooked on the premises.
**Cards:** Visa, Access.
**Other points:** licensed, Sunday lunch, solarium, sauna, spa bath, residents' lounge, garden, conservatory, residents' bar, swimming pool.
**Rooms:** 2 single rooms, 5 double rooms, 7 twin rooms. All with TV, radio, alarm, telephone, tea/coffee-making facilities.
**Directions:** take the A361 to Braunton. Follow signposts to Saunton.
ANN COOK ☎(01271) 890472 Fax(01271) 890555

## CHAGFORD • map 3D3

**RING O'BELLS**
44 The Square, TQ13 8AH
*A 400 year old coaching inn situated in the centre of an historic Devon Stannary town. The Ring O'Bells has a large open fireplace and comfortable*

dining area. The welcome is warm and friendly, and nothing is too much trouble for Mrs Pool and her staff. Planning permission has been sought for the addition of 5 letting bedrooms in early 1996.
FOOD: up to £15
**Hours:** breakfasts from 10am, lunch from 11am-3pm (bar and dining room). Dinner 6pm-9.15pm (bar and restaurant). Open bank holidays.
**Cuisine:** TRADITIONAL ENGLISH - full à la carte menu which changes on a daily basis.
**Cards:** Access, Visa, Switch, Delta.
**Other points:** freehouse with open fireplace and interesting artefacts, easy parking, bar snacks, dining room and attractive lawned walled garden at the rear.
**Directions:** take A382 to Chagford, Ring O' Bells is in the village square.
JUDITH POOL ☎(01647) 432466

### THE THREE CROWNS HOTEL
Dartmoor, TQ13 5AJ
*Situated in the pretty village of Chagford, within the Dartmoor National Park, this 13th century inn retains an olde-worlde charm with its open fires and four-poster beds.*
DOUBLE ROOM: from £20 to £30
SINGLE ROOM: from £25 to £35
FOOD: from £15 to £20
**Hours:** breakfast 8.30am-9.30am, lunch 12noon-2pm, dinner 7pm-9.30pm.
**Cuisine:** ENGLISH - bar menu, e.g., home-made steak-and-kidney pie, ploughman's, seafood; special vegetarian meals and table d'hôte menus.
**Cards:** Visa, Access, AmEx.
**Other points:** Sunday lunch, children welcome.
**Rooms:** 18 bedrooms.
**Directions:** 3 miles off A382 (B3206). Situated within the village.
MR & MRS J. GILES ☎(01647) 433444 Fax(01647) 433117

### CLAWTON • map 3C3

### COURT BARN COUNTRY HOUSE HOTEL
Near Holsworthy, EX22 6PS
*A country house of great character and charm, with antiques, pictures and flowers throughout, Court Barn is the perfect touring hotel for Dartmoor, Bodmin and Exmoor. Les Routiers/Mercier Wine List of the Year 1989 & 1993, Corps d'Elite 1990, 1991, 1992 and 1994. Tea Council `Best Teas in Britain' 1987 and 1989. National Awards for cuisine. Devon's `Hotel of Distinction'.*
DOUBLE ROOM: from £25 to £35
SINGLE ROOM: from £30 to £40
FOOD: from £16 to £20 CLUB
**Hours:** morning coffee 10am-12noon, lunch 12noon-2pm, afternoon tea 3pm-5pm, dinner 7.30pm-9pm, closed 1st January until 7th January.
**Cuisine:** ENGLISH / FRENCH - Cordon Bleu cuisine. Five-course candlelit dinners. Fresh local produce. Vegetarian dishes. Menu changes daily. Award-winning cream teas and restaurant awards.

**Cards:** Visa, Access, Diners, AmEx.
**Other points:** licensed, traditional Sunday lunch, children welcome, pets allowed, garden, tennis, croquet, residents' lounge, library, residents' bar.
**Rooms:** 1 single room, 4 double rooms, 3 twin rooms. All with TV, telephone, tea/coffee-making facilities.
**Directions:** 3 miles south of Holsworthy, off A388. Next to 12th century church.
ROBERT & SUSAN WOOD ☎(01409) 271219 Fax(01409) 271309

### COMBE MARTIN • map 3B3

### SANDY COVE HOTEL
Berrynarbor, EX34 9SR
*The hotel stands in 20 acres of gardens featuring woods, cliffs and coves. Other facilities include indoor swimming pool, sauna and whirlpool.*
DOUBLE ROOM: from £30 to £50
SINGLE ROOM: from £30 to £50
FOOD: up to £15 CLUB
**Hours:** breakfast 8.30am-9.30am, bar 11am-11pm, lunch 12.30am-2.30pm, afternoon tea 3pm-5pm, dinner 7pm-9.30pm.
**Cuisine:** INTERNATIONAL - fondue, kebabs, five variations of lobster. Large à la carte menu.
**Other points:** licensed, Sunday lunch, children welcome, coaches by prior arrangement, vegetarian meals, disabled access, swimming pool, residents' bar.
**Rooms:** 2 single rooms, 15 double rooms, 5 twin rooms, 11 family rooms. All with TV, telephone, tea/coffee-making facilities.
**Directions:** on the A399 (coast road), 1 mile from Combe Martin.
MR & MRS GILSON ☎(01271) 882243/882888 Fax(01271) 883830

### CULLOMPTON • map 4C4

### MANOR HOUSE HOTEL
Fore Street, EX15 1JL
*Built in 1603, the Manor House has a particularly elegant timbered facade and has been carefully restored to its former glory. The Manor boasts a delightfully intimate restaurant where you can expect a top-class meal, a splendid character bar and, most importantly, excellent, well-appointed accommodation.*
DOUBLE ROOM: from £25 to £30
SINGLE ROOM: from £40
FOOD: up to £15
**Hours:** breakfast 7.15am-9am, lunch 12.15am-1.45pm, dinner 7pm-9pm.
**Cuisine:** ENGLISH / FRENCH - a very wide choice of dishes, freshly prepared, to suit all tastes.
**Cards:** Visa, Access, AmEx.
**Other points:** parking, children welcome, pets allowed, conference facilities, residents' lounge, vegetarian meals, traditional Sunday lunch.
**Rooms:** 1 single room, 4 double rooms, 3 twin rooms, 1 family room, 1 four-poster room. All with en suite, TV, telephone, radio, alarm, hair dryer,

trouser-press, tea/coffee-making facilities.
**Directions:** junction 28 off M5; turn to Cullompton and continue to T-junction; turn left and hotel is 400 yards on the right.
MALCOLM & BREDA POWELL ☎(01884) 32281
**Fax** (01884) 38344

## DARTMOUTH • map 4E4

 **SLOPING DECK RESTAURANT**
The Butterwalk, TP6 9PZ
*The Sloping Deck consists of a bakery on the ground floor and a restaurant on the first floor, both offering quality food at very good value. Situated in one of Dartmouth's most famous historic buildings.*
FOOD: up to £15
**Hours:** meals all day 9am-5.30pm.
**Cuisine:** ENGLISH - home-cooking, including fresh fish and steak-and-kidney pie.
**Cards:** Visa, Access.
**Other points:** licensed, Sunday lunch, no-smoking area, children welcome, pets allowed, afternoon tea.
**Directions:** a historic building at centre of town, in The Butterwalk.
MR & MRS BARNES ☎(01803) 832758

 **STOKE LODGE HOTEL**
Stoke Fleming, TQ6 ORA
*Situated on the scenic coastal road between historic Dartmouth and Kingsbridge, this charming hotel is very popular locally and offers first-class service and comfort with fresh local food, 3 acres of grounds with large gardens, and every facility for a truly relaxing holiday.*
DOUBLE ROOM: from £30 to £40
SINGLE ROOM: from £40 to £50
FOOD: from £15 to £20   **CLUB**
**Cuisine:** ENGLISH / FRENCH - a large variety of English and French cuisine using only the best local fresh ingredients, e.g., poached salmon with hollandaise sauce.
**Cards:** Visa, Access.
**Other points:** licensed, outdoor swimming pool, indoor swimming pool, Jacuzzi, tennis, sauna, river trips, bird-watching, garden, pets allowed, children welcome, baby-listening, reduced golf green fees.
**Rooms:** 3 single rooms, 9 double rooms, 8 twin rooms, 4 triple rooms, 3 suites. All with en suite, TV, radio, alarm, telephone, tea/coffee-making facilities.
**Directions:** on A379, 2 miles south of Dartmouth.
STEVEN MAYER ☎(01803) 770523 **Fax** (01803) 770851

## DAWLISH • map 4D4

**LANGSTONE CLIFF HOTEL**
Mount Pleasant Road, Dawlish Warren, EX7 ONA
*Set in 19 acres of wooded grounds and only 500 yards from the beach, this hotel offers the warmest of welcomes and the best in friendly service, with*

*special consideration for families and children. Superbly decorated, the hotel provides a high standard of food and accommodation, and there is a host of activities for all ages to enjoy. Set in an area of outstanding beauty.*
DOUBLE ROOM: from £30 to £40
SINGLE ROOM: from £30 to £40
FOOD: up to £15
**Hours:** breakfast 7.30am-10am, lunch 12.30am-2pm, dinner 7pm-9pm.
**Cuisine:** ENGLISH - traditional English cuisine. Table d'hôte dinner menu and carvery. Coffee shop offering light refreshments.
**Cards:** Visa, Access, Diners, AmEx.
**Other points:** licensed, Sunday lunch, children welcome, games room, tennis, swimming pool, dinner dances, conferences, children welcome, baby-listening device, baby-sitting, cots, 24hr reception, residents' lounge, residents' bar.
**Rooms:** 6 single rooms, 21 double rooms, 25 triple rooms, 16 quad rooms. All with TV, radio, telephone, tea/coffee-making facilities, alarm.
**Directions:** 1 mile off the A379; 1 mile north of Dawlish.
GEOFFREY ROGERS ☎(01626) 865155
**Fax** (01626) 867166

## EXETER • map 4D4

**THE ANGLER'S REST**
Fingle Bridge, Drewsteignton, EX6 6PW
*A family-run restaurant and lounge bar with riverside terraces. Adjoining Fingle Bridge on the banks of the River Teign deep in Fingle Gorge, The Angler's Rest provides a starting point for miles of walks, fishing and birdwatching.*
FOOD: up to £15
**Hours:** lunch summer 11am-5.30pm, winter 11am-2.30pm; dinner summer 7pm-9pm, winter (Saturday only) 7pm-9pm.
**Cuisine:** ENGLISH / INTERNATIONAL - steak-and-kidney pie, Devon steaks, salmon, trout. Bar meals. Devonshire cream teas. Vegetarian dishes. Home-made speciality curries and pasta dishes.
**Cards:** Visa, Access.
**Other points:** open-air dining, Sunday lunch, children catered for (please check for age limits), functions.
**Directions:** next to Fingle Bridge in Drewsteignton.
THE PRICE FAMILY ☎(01647) 281287

**COWICK BARTON INN**
Cowick Lane, St Thomas, EX2 9JG
*A medieval country inn and restaurant within the city of Exeter, where you will discover some of the charm and tranquility which only a much loved ancient building can radiate. Unlatch the four-foot-wide door and prepare to be impressed by the amazing interior! But it is not only the superb surroundings you will be impressed by: dining and wining at the Cowick Barton is an extremely pleasant experience, and the Uphills are proud of the reputation they have achieved, with the help of their head chef David Williams, for the high*

*standard of their cuisine.*
FOOD: up to £15　CLUB
**Hours:** lunch 12noon-2pm, bar meals 12noon-2pm, dinner 7.30pm-10pm, bar meals 7pm-9.30pm.
**Cuisine:** ENGLISH - delicious country fare.
**Cards:** Visa, Access, AmEx.
**Other points:** parking, children welcome, no-smoking area, conference facilities, open-air dining, vegetarian meals, traditional Sunday lunch.
**Directions:** take Exeter junction off A30, turn left at first traffic lights into Cowick Lane, follow signs to Exwick, 500 yards on right.
PETER UPHILL ☎(01392) 70411 Fax (01392) 211736

### THE HEART OF OAK
34 Main Road, Pinhoe, EX4 8HS
*A very popular, 300-year-old former coaching inn offering an extensive menu with good English traditional fare and grills. The interior is clean and spacious and the atmosphere warm and friendly.*
FOOD: up to £15
**Hours:** bar meals 12noon-2.15pm and 6.30pm-10pm, open bank holidays.
**Cuisine:** TRADITIONAL/ENGLISH - daily blackboard specials, steaks, grills, children's and vegetarian options.
**Cards:** Access, Visa
**Other points:** children welcome, open-air dining, traditional Sunday lunch, vegetarian meals, parking.
**Directions:** north of Exeter city centre on B3181 to Cullompton.
MR JOHN KEIGHTLY ☎(01392) 467329

### LAMB'S
Under the Iron Bridge, 15 Lower North Street, EX4 3ET
*A Grade II listed building approximately 200 years old, providing modern English food in a delightful, friendly setting. The restaurant has a courtyard at the rear alongside the original Roman city wall. The restaurant's city centre location makes it very convenient for visitors to Exeter.*
FOOD: from £15 to £20　CLUB
**Hours:** lunch (Tuesday-Friday) 12noon-2.30pm, dinner (Tuesday-Saturday) 6pm-12midnight.
**Cuisine:** ENGLISH/MODERN
**Cards:** Visa, Access, MasterCard, Switch, Delta.
**Other points:** vegetarian meals.
**Directions:** 100 yards from the Harlequin and Mary Arches Street car parks, under the Iron Bridge.
IAN & ALISON ALDRIDGE ☎(01392) 54269
Fax (01392) 431145

### THE OLD THATCH INN
Cheriton Bishop, EX6 6HJ
*Traditional 16th century thatched free house, originally built as a coaching house. Just 10 miles from Exeter and inside the eastern border of Dartmoor National Park. Les Routiers of the Year 1985.*
DOUBLE ROOM: from £20 to £30

SINGLE ROOM: from £25 to £35
FOOD: up to £15 ☜
**Hours:** lunch 12noon-2.15pm, dinner 6.30pm-9.30pm, Sunday 7pm-9pm.
**Cuisine:** ENGLISH - home-made food using traditional recipes. Dishes may include steak-and-kidney pudding, Thatch mixed grill, leek and aubergine bake, fish rolls with sesame sauce.
**Cards:** Visa, Access, Eurocard.
**Other points:** licensed, traditional Sunday lunch, no young children (please check for age limits).
**Rooms:** 3 double rooms. All en suite with TV, radio, alarm, tea/coffee-making facilities.
**Directions:** from the A30, 10 miles west of Exeter, take Cheriton Bishop road.
BRIAN & HAZEL BRYON-EDMOND ☎(01647) 24204 Fax (01647) 24584

### PARK VIEW HOTEL
8 Howell Road, EX4 4LG
*A popular hotel in the centre of Exeter, which offers comfortable accommodation and excellent full breakfasts. Attractively decorated, Park View Hotel provides a comfortable, welcoming base from which to visit Exeter, whether on business or for pleasure. Very close to the university and station.*
DOUBLE ROOM: up to £20
SINGLE ROOM: up to £20
**Hours:** breakfast 7.30am-9am, breakfast Sunday 8.30am-9.30am, closed Christmas week.
**Cuisine:** BREAKFAST
**Cards:** Visa, Access, AmEx.
**Other points:** children welcome, residents' lounge, beautifully maintained garden with pond.
**Rooms:** 4 single rooms, 9 double/twin rooms, 2 family rooms. All with TV, telephone, tea/coffee-making facilities, heating. Most rooms are en suite.
**Directions:** from M5 (junction 30), first roundabout fourth exit, second roundabout first exit (signposted Park & Ride), third roundabout second exit (signposted B3183 city centre), straight on for 3 miles until the Clock Tower roundabout, third exit (Elm Grove Road), at end of road turn left into Howell Road, Park View Hotel is 100 metres on the right.
MR & MRS BATHO ☎(01392) 71772 Fax (01392) 53047

### THE PROSPECT
The Quay, EX2 4EB
*A delightful, century-old riverside inn, offering a wide choice of excellent English cuisine, seafood and grills. The interior is spacious with ample seating and has a warm, friendly atmosphere and staff for whom nothing is too much trouble. Has lovely riverside views.*
FOOD: up to £15
**Hours:** bar meals 12noon-2.15pm and 7pm-9pm, open bank holidays.
**Cuisine:** ENGLISH - offers a wide range of dishes including seafood and grills.
**Cards:** Access, Visa
**Other points:** children catered for (please check for

age limits), open-air dining, vegetarian meals.
**Directions:** city centre location, on the quayside, by the River Exe.
MR R MADDEX ☎(01392) 73152

 **WHITE HART HOTEL**
66 South Street, EX1 1EE
*This appealing 600-year-old coaching inn has an attractive listed exterior, large courtyard, wine patio and garden, and ancient protected doorways. The interior of the hotel is extremely old and beautifully kept, the original fireplace still stands, and many artefacts, dating back centuries, adorn the public areas. The accommodation is of an excellent standard, as is the fine food available in the comfortable restaurant.*
**DOUBLE ROOM:** from £30 to £40
**FOOD:** up to £15
**Hours:** breakfast 7.30am-9.30am, lunch 12noon-2pm, dinner 7pm-10pm.
**Cuisine:** ENGLISH - traditional fare.
**Cards:** Visa, Access, Diners, AmEx, Switch.
**Other points:** parking, children welcome, conference facilities, residents' lounge, open-air dining, vegetarian meals, traditional Sunday lunch.
**Rooms:** 18 single rooms, 40 double rooms. All with en suite, TV, radio, alarm, trouser-press.
**Directions:** the White Hart Hotel may be found in Exeter city centre, just within the city walls.
GRAHAM STONE ☎(01392) 79897 Fax(01392) 79897

**EXMOUTH** • map 4D4

 **BALCOMBE HOUSE HOTEL**
Stevenstone Road, EX8 2EP
*This is an oasis of peace and tranquility with over half an acre of pretty gardens. Just a short distance away from the seafront, with 2 miles of golden sands and a wealth of leisure activities. The town centre and River Exe nature reserve are both close at hand. Very comfortably furnished to a high standard, with a warm and homely atmosphere. The hotel has a well-stocked bar in a sunny lounge overlooking the garden, and a second no-smoking lounge. The extended hours of service allow guests to dine early or late, choosing from the many varied dishes on offer. The hotel is affiliated to the nearby Cranford Sports Club, where guests can enjoy the facilities free of charge all year round. The hotel offers a special Christmas programme.*
**DOUBLE ROOM:** from £25 to £30
**SINGLE ROOM:** from £30 to £40
**FOOD:** up to £15
**Hours:** breakfast 8am-9.30am, lunch 12noon-2pm, dinner 6.30pm-9pm, open all year.
**Cuisine:** ENGLISH
**Cards:** Visa, Diners, AmEx, MasterCard.
**Other points:** parking, no-smoking area, afternoon teas, disabled access, residents' lounge, garden, vegetarian meals, functions, sports facilities, children catered for (please check for age limits).
**Rooms:** 2 single rooms, 4 double rooms, 4 twin rooms, 2 family rooms. All with en suite, TV, radio,

alarm, tea/coffee-making facilities, hair dryer.
**Directions:** follow road to Sandy Bay, bear right at Littleham Cross, third turn on left.
MR O. SMALDON ☎(01395) 266349

**HONITON** • map 4C4

**THE FLINTLOCK INN**
Marsh, near Honiton, EX14 9AJ
*A charming inn offering value-for-money food, good service and standards. All set in a rural traditional theme. The menus are created to use fresh products whenever possible and are largely home-made.*
**FOOD:** from £15 to £20, bar food up to £15
CLUB
**Hours:** lunch (bar) 12noon-2pm, dinner 7pm-9.45pm, closed Christmas day evening and Boxing day.
**Cuisine:** ENGLISH / EUROPEAN - wide choice of dishes catering for all tastes. The à la carte menu changes periodically. The good-sized portions are always attractively presented. Vegetarian meals available.
**Cards:** Visa, Access, Switch.
**Other points:** parking, no-smoking area, vegetarian meals, traditional Sunday lunch.
**Directions:** situated off the A303 between Honiton and Ilminster.
JOHN & MAGGIE WARDELL ☎(01460) 234403

**THE HEATHFIELD**
Walnut Road, EX14 8UG
*This 16th century traditional thatched Devon longhouse was once a farmhouse. Retaining many of its original features, it is now a busy free house with accommodation. The Heathfield offers an excellent à la carte menu, and a large selection of wines, real ales and spirits is available from the bar. The luxurious bedrooms have all been furnished to a five-star standard.*
**DOUBLE ROOM:** from £20 to £30
**SINGLE ROOM:** from £25 to £35
**FOOD:** up to £15
**Hours:** breakfast 8am-9am, bar meals 12noon-2pm, dinner 7pm-10pm (Friday and Saturday), bar meals 7pm-10pm.
**Cuisine:** ENGLISH / VEGETARIAN
**Cards:** Visa, Access, AmEx.
**Other points:** parking, children welcome, vegetarian meals, conference facilities, residents' garden, open-air dining.
**Rooms:** 2 double rooms, 3 twin rooms. All with tea/coffee-making facilities, TV, telephone, radio, trouser-press.
**Directions:** from the A30 London-Exeter Road, take the A375 towards Sidmouth. The Heathfield is well signposted from the mini-roundabout after the railway bridge.
ANDREW FORD ☎(01404) 45321 Fax(01404) 45321

---

## ILFRACOMBE • map 3B3

 **DEDES HOTEL & WHEEL INN, PUB & RESTAURANT**
1-3 The Promenade, EX34 9BD
*Situated on the Victorian promenade overlooking the sea, incorporating the wheel room. A delightful character restaurant and bar featuring exposed stonework, beams and old coaching wheels.*
DOUBLE ROOM: from £18 to £23
SINGLE ROOM: from £20
FOOD: up to £15
**Hours:** breakfast 8am-10am, lunch 12noon-2pm, dinner 6pm-9pm.
**Cuisine:** MODERN ENGLISH - quality steaks and fresh, local seafood in season, including fresh lobster.
**Cards:** Visa, Access, Diners, AmEx.
**Other points:** Sunday lunch, disabled access, children welcome, cots.
**Rooms:** 5 single rooms, 3 double rooms, 3 twin rooms, 4 triple rooms, 2 quad rooms. All with TV, tea/coffee-making facilities.
**Directions:** A361 to Ilfracombe, situated on the promenade.
MR & MRS C.I. CAWTHORNE ☎(01271) 862545
Fax(01271) 862234

**EPCHRIS HOTEL**
Torrs Park, EX34 8AZ
*A small, friendly family hotel, offering good accommodation and delicious home-cooked meals. All the bedrooms are large and airy, and there is an outdoor swimming pool and two acres of gardens. Conveniently located for Exmoor and the wonders of the Devon coast, and within walking distance of Ilfracombe's attractions.*
DOUBLE ROOM: up to £20
SINGLE ROOM: up to £25
FOOD: up to £15
**Hours:** breakfast 9am, dinner 6.30pm, closed January.
**Cuisine:** ENGLISH - home-cooking.
**Cards:** Visa, Access, Eurocard.
**Other points:** licensed, parking, children welcome, no-smoking area, swimming pool, garden, residents' lounge, bar, vegetarian meals.
**Rooms:** 1 single room, 8 family rooms. All rooms have TV, tea/coffee-making facilities. Most rooms are en suite.
**Directions:** from Barnstaple take A361 to Ilfracombe town centre, turn left at signs for seafront, turn left again. Torrs Park is ahead and the hotel is on the left.
ANN BARLEYCORN ☎(01271) 862751

**HEADLANDS HOTEL**
7 Capstone Crescent, EX34 9BT
*A 100-year-old terraced hotel set in its own cliff garden in a popular holiday resort. Offering good wholesome food, nothing is too much trouble for the proprietors, whose aim is to please. Older,*

*retired clientele. Near to harbour.*
DOUBLE ROOM: up to £20
SINGLE ROOM: up to £20
FOOD: up to £15
**Hours:** breakfast 8.30am, dinner 6.15pm.
**Other points:** licensed, children catered for (please check for age limits).
**Rooms:** 19 bedrooms.
**Directions:** in the harbour area, near Britannia public hotel.
MR & MRS ANGOLD ☎(01271) 862887

**THE ILFRACOMBE CARLTON**
Runnacleave Road, EX34 8AR

*Situated in a central location adjacent to the beach, this hotel offers fresh, well-cooked food in pleasant surroundings. The accommodation is comfortable and the service friendly and attentive. Ilfracombe offers its visitors a choice of recreational and sporting activities, a spectacular coastline and secluded bays.*
DOUBLE ROOM: from £20 to £30
SINGLE ROOM: from £25 to £35
FOOD: up to £15 CLUB
**Hours:** breakfast 8.30am-9.30am, lunch 12noon-2pm, dinner 7pm-8.30pm.
**Cuisine:** ENGLISH - traditional English food.
**Cards:** Visa, Access, Diners, AmEx.
**Other points:** children welcome, afternoon tea, baby-listening device, cots, 24hr reception, residents' lounge, residents' bar.
**Rooms:** 8 single rooms, 15 double rooms, 17 twin rooms, 8 family room. All with TV, radio, alarm, telephone, tea/coffee-making facilities.
**Directions:** off the A361, close to the seafront.
DAWN MARSHALL ☎(01271) 862446 Fax(01271) 865379

**ST BRANNOCKS HOUSE HOTEL**
St Brannocks Road, EX34 8EQ
*A detached Victorian hotel set in its own grounds and close to the beautiful Bicclescombe Park, Cairn Nature Reserve, town centre and seafront. The cosy, well-stocked bar is an ideal place to relax and socialize, and the dining room offers generous portions of good home-cooked food and a selection of table wines. An ideal place for a perfect family holiday, special break or business trip.*
DOUBLE ROOM: up to £20
SINGLE ROOM: up to £25
FOOD: up to £15
**Hours:** breakfast 8.30am-9am, dinner 6.30pm.

**Cuisine:** ENGLISH
**Cards:** Visa, Access, AmEx.
**Other points:** children welcome, pets welcome, residents' lounge, garden, parking, special diets catered for.
**Rooms:** 16 bedrooms. All with TV, radio, tea/coffee-making facilities. Many rooms are en suite.
**Directions:** approach from Barnstaple on A361. Hotel is on left side heading into town.
MRS B. CLARKE ☎(01271) 863873

### TORRS HOTEL
Torrs Park, EX34 8AY
*This hotel is in a commanding position at the end of the Torrs Walk, which follows the cliff along the coast. The hotel has lovely views of the surrounding countryside.*
DOUBLE ROOM: up to £20
SINGLE ROOM: up to £20
FOOD: up to £15
**Hours:** breakfast 8.30am-9.30am, dinner 6.30pm-7.30pm, closed November until February.
**Cuisine:** ENGLISH - roasts, grills, home-cooked dishes.
**Cards:** Visa, Access, Diners, AmEx.
**Other points:** licensed, open-air dining, Sunday lunch, special diets, children catered for (please check for age limits)
**Rooms:** 15 bedrooms. All en suite.
**Directions:** off the A399 or A361 at the end of the Torrs Walk.
MR R.I. COOK ☎(01271) 862334

### TRAFALGAR HOTEL
Larkstone Terrace, Hillsborough Road, EX34 9NU
*A Victorian hotel, retaining many of its original features and furnished to a high standard. Offering excellent sea and woodland views from comfortable rooms, a pleasant, relaxing stay is assured.*
DOUBLE ROOM: from £20 to £30
SINGLE ROOM: from £25 to £35
FOOD: up to £15 CLUB
**Hours:** breakfast 8.30am-9.30am, bar snacks 12noon-2pm, dinner 6.30pm-8pm, bar snacks 6pm-9pm.
**Cuisine:** ENGLISH
**Cards:** Visa, Access, Diners, AmEx.
**Other points:** parking, children welcome, afternoon teas, residents' lounge, vegetarian meals.
**Rooms:** 4 single rooms, 10 double rooms, 11 twin rooms.
**Directions:** continuation of High Street from A361 direction.
TONY & JUNE WHITE ☎(01271) 862145/863745

### UPSTAIRS RESTAURANT
Mullacott Cross, EX34 8AY
*High above Ilfracombe with unrestricted views to Lundy Island, the Welsh coast and Exmoor.*
FOOD: up to £15 ☜
**Hours:** dinner 6pm-10pm, closed October until

Easter.
**Cuisine:** MODERN ENGLISH - carvery with best-quality steaks. Children's menu.
**Cards:** Visa, Access, Diners, AmEx.
**Other points:** open-air dining, Sunday lunch, children welcome.
**Directions:** found on the A361 Mullacott roundabout.
MR D. WRIGHT ☎(01271) 863780/865500

## IVYBRIDGE • map 3D3

### IMPERIAL INN
28 Western Road, PL21 9AR
*A charming olde-worlde village pub adorned with window boxes, with a large, welcoming open fire and a warm welcome to match. There is a large beer garden and a separate children's play area with playground equipment.*
FOOD: up to £15
**Hours:** lunch 12noon-2pm, dinner 6pm-10pm.
**Cuisine:** MODERN ENGLISH - many daily specials, from home-cooked meals to hot beef curry, with a variety of local fresh fish including fresh Avon mussels in wine and cream sauce, and from sautéed lamb's kidneys to chicken marengo - and much more.
**Other points:** open-air dining, Sunday lunch, children welcome, coaches by prior arrangement.
**Directions:** follow the A38 from Plymouth (7 miles).
PHILIP GRIMES ☎(01752) 892269

## KINGSBRIDGE • map 3E3

### THE ASHBURTON ARMS
West Charleton, TQ7 2AH
*A very friendly pub, serving excellent home-made food at good value for money. The steaks are particularly good, served on hot stones so they continue to cook at the table, and there is a good wine list. The pub is set on a main tourist route, in an area of outstanding natural beauty. Well worth visiting.*
DOUBLE ROOM: up to £20
SINGLE ROOM: up to £25
FOOD: up to £15
**Hours:** lunch 12noon-1.45pm, dinner 6.30pm-9pm.
**Cuisine:** ENGLISH - dishes include speciality `steak on the rocks', served on hot stones. Vegetarian dish of the day. Desserts such as pavlova and treacle tart. All home-made. Fresh fish always on the menu. No-smoking area in the restaurant.
**Cards:** Visa, Access.
**Other points:** Sunday lunch, no-smoking area in restaurant, no-smoking in the bedrooms, children catered for (please check for age limits).
**Rooms:** 2 single rooms, 2 double rooms. All with TV, radio, tea/coffee-making facilities, alarm.
**Directions:** on A379, 1.5 miles east of Kingsbridge on the Torcross road.
BRIAN & ELIZABETH SAUNDERS ☎(01548) 531242 Fax(01548) 531189

---

**WHITE HOUSE HOTEL**
Chillington, TQ7 2JX

*The White House Hotel is a lovely Georgian house set in an acre of lawned and terraced gardens and is just two miles from the coast. It offers excellent food and friendly service in peaceful and relaxed surroundings.*

DOUBLE ROOM: from £32 to £42
SINGLE ROOM: from £40 to £44
FOOD: up to £15
**Hours:** breakfast 8.30am-9.30am, dinner 7pm-8.05pm.
**Cuisine:** ENGLISH - All dishes are home-made, with constant change of fixed menu, e.g., roast rack of lamb, fresh lemon sole. The wine list is interesting and most reasonably priced.
**Cards:** Visa, Access, AmEx.
**Other points:** licensed, children catered for (please check for age limits), pets by prior arrangement, residents' lounge, newly built Garden Room restaurant with lovely views.
**Rooms:** 7 bedrooms. All with TV, tea/coffee-making facilities, telephone.
**Directions:** on A379 between Kingsbridge and Dartmouth.
MICHAEL ROBERTS & DAVID ALFORD ☎(01548) 580580 Fax (01548) 581124

## LYDFORD • map 3D3

 **THE CASTLE INN AND HOTEL**
Near Okehampton, EX20 4BH

*A delightful 16th century free house, overlooked by Lydford Castle, and set in one of the loveliest parts of Devon. Featured in the film The Hound of the Baskervilles, The Castle Inn is a traditional West Country inn, offering good food, fine ales, comfortable accommodation and a very warm welcome. Nearby visitor attractions include Lydford Gorge and the beautiful wild moors.*

DOUBLE ROOM: from £20 to £30
SINGLE ROOM: from £28 to £40
FOOD: up to £15
**Hours:** breakfast 8am-9am, dinner 7pm-9.30pm, bar meals 12noon-2.30pm, bar meals 6.30pm-9.30pm.
**Cuisine:** ENGLISH - à la carte and table d'hôte menus, using freshly cooked food and local produce. Dishes may include whiskied steak, local venison in blackberry and juniper berry sauce and salmon cutlets in champagne and lemon thyme sauce.
**Cards:** Visa, Access, Diners, AmEx.
**Other points:** licensed, open-air dining, Sunday lunch, no-smoking area, children catered for (please check for age limits), pets allowed, parking, garden, disabled access, residents' lounge, vegetarian meals, cots, left luggage.
**Rooms:** 6 double rooms, 2 twin rooms. All with TV, radio, tea/coffee-making facilities.
**Directions:** take the Lydford turning off A386 between Okehampton and Tavistock.
CLIVE & MO WALKER ☎(0182282) 242 Fax (01822882) 454

## LYNMOUTH • map 3B3

 **THE BATH HOTEL**
Lynmouth Street, EX35 6EL

*Centrally located by picturesque Lynmouth harbour, the hotel has a relaxed atmosphere in an ideal position for exploring Exmoor and many local attractions. The hotel has been in the same family for over 40 years and guarantees a warm welcome, friendly service and, above all, value for money with appetising menus - all guaranteed to provide a relaxed stay.*

DOUBLE ROOM: from £27 to £37
SINGLE ROOM: from £27 to £37
FOOD: from £15 to £20
**Hours:** breakfast 8.30am-9.30am, lunch 12.30am-2pm, bar meals 12noon-2.15pm, dinner 7pm-8.30pm, closed November until mid-March.
**Cuisine:** EUROPEAN - daily changing varied menu to include seafood, game and fresh local produce. Wild salmon caught in the hotel's own weir and lobster are a speciality.
**Cards:** Visa, Access, Diners, AmEx.
**Other points:** licensed, Sunday lunch, no-smoking area, children welcome, afternoon tea, pets allowed, parking.
**Rooms:** 1 single room, 11 double rooms, 8 twin rooms, 4 family rooms. All with en suite, tea/coffee-making facilities, TV, telephone, baby-listening device, radio/alarm.
**Directions:** situated on the A39 at Lynmouth.
MRS DALGARNO ☎(01598) 752238 Fax (01598) 752544

 **CORNER HOUSE**
Riverside Road, EX35 6EH

*A pleasant and comfortable establishment with a large restaurant, spacious, airy rooms and a garden with attractive shrubs and flowers, overlooking the rivers and Lyn Valley. Ideal for visiting Exmoor, the Valley of Rocks and Watersmeet. Outside paved area for alfresco dining at umbrella tables.*

DOUBLE ROOM: from £20 to £30
FOOD: up to £15
**Hours:** breakfast 8.30am-9.30am, bar snacks 11.30am-5pm, dinner 6pm until late, last orders 9pm, closed November until February.
**Cuisine:** ENGLISH - cream teas available during the afternoon.
**Cards:** Visa, Access, Switch.
**Other points:** residents' parking, Sunday lunch, open bank holidays, afternoon tea, vegetarian meals, open-air dining, licensed.
**Rooms:** 3 double rooms. All with en suite, TV, tea/coffee-making facilities, views.
**Directions:** follow A39; on entry into Lynmouth you will see the black and white umbrellas along the river.
ROBERT & PENELOPE WHITWELL ☎(01598) 753300

## RISING SUN HOTEL
Harbourside, EX35 6EQ

*A lovely 14th century thatched smugglers' inn overlooking a small picturesque harbour and Lynmouth Bay. The hotel offers free salmon-fishing for residents. The buildings were once smugglers' cottages, with a wealth of intriguing staircases and narrow passages.*

DOUBLE ROOM: from £39
SINGLE ROOM: from £35 to £45
FOOD: from £20 to £25
**Hours:** breakfast 8.30am-9.30am, lunch 12.30am-2pm, dinner 7pm-9pm, open all year.
**Cuisine:** ENGLISH - seafood, game in season.
**Cards:** Visa, Access, AmEx.
**Other points:** licensed, Sunday lunch, coaches by prior arrangement, baby-listening device, cots, residents' bar, residents' lounge, vegetarian meals, children catered for (please check for age limits).
**Rooms:** 1 single room, 11 double rooms, 3 twin rooms, 1 suite. All with TV, radio, alarm, telephone, tea/coffee-making facilities.
**Directions:** exit 23 on the M5, then A39 to Lynmouth. Opposite sea harbour.
MR F. ST H. JEUNE ☎(01598) 53223 Fax(01598) 53480

## SHELLEYS COTTAGE HOTEL
Watersmeet Road, EX35 6EP

*A quiet, peaceful hotel and restaurant set in its own shrub gardens in a beautiful Devon village. The proprietors personally supervise the day to day running of the hotel, ensuring that every guest's need is catered for. Ideal base from which to explore the Valley of Rocks, Glen Lyn gorge and the Devon countryside.*

DOUBLE ROOM: up to £25
SINGLE ROOM: up to £20
FOOD: from £20 to £25
**Hours:** breakfast 8.30am-9.30am, dinner 7pm-9pm, closed November until March.
**Cards:** Visa, Access, AmEx.
**Other points:** children welcome, no-smoking area, pets allowed, residents' lounge, vegetarian meals, garden.
**Rooms:** 1 single room, 2 twin rooms, 6 double rooms. All with TV, radio, tea/coffee-making facilities.
**Directions:** A39, end of Watersmeet Road, bottom of Lynmouth Hill.
MRS & MR PRIDEAUX ☎(01598) 753219

## LYNTON • map 3B3

## THE EXMOOR SANDPIPER INN
Countisbury, EX35 6NE

*A long, white 13th century building of considerable charm and character at the top of Countisbury hill, with stunning views over Exmoor. The area is distinctly rural, with sheep roaming the grounds, but the food and accommodation are sophisticated yet homely. An excellent base for walkers.*

DOUBLE ROOM: from £30 to £40
SINGLE ROOM: from £25 to £45
FOOD: from £15 to £20   CLUB
**Hours:** breakfast 8.30am-9.30am, lunch 12noon-2.30pm, dinner 7pm-9.30pm, bar 11am-11pm.
**Cuisine:** ENGLISH - large selection of table d'hôte evening meals, including garlic prawns, local venison in red wine, steaks, lobster, cold seafood platter, home-made soups.
**Other points:** licensed, open-air dining, Sunday lunch, children welcome, pets by prior arrangement, parking, residents' lounge, residents' bar.
**Rooms:** 12 double rooms, 2 twin rooms, 2 family rooms. All with TV, radio, tea/coffee-making facilities.
**Directions:** on the A39 at the top of Countisbury hill, outside Lynton.
PERSONALLY RUN HOTELS LTD ☎(01598) 741263 Fax(01598) 741358

## MILLSLADE COUNTRY HOUSE HOTEL
Brendon, EX35 6PS

*An 18th century country house set in 9 acres of grounds in a quiet spot on the edge of Brendon village, surrounded by the forest and River Lynn. The hotel has fishing rights (salmon and trout) for their guests to enjoy, and there are plenty of local attractions, including Doone Valley, Barnstaple and Minehead.*

DOUBLE ROOM: from £20 to £30
SINGLE ROOM: from £30
FOOD: from £15 to £20
**Hours:** breakfast 8.30am-9.30am, dinner 7pm-9.30pm, lunch 12noon-2.30pm.
**Cards:** Visa.
**Other points:** licensed, Sunday lunch, children catered for (please check for age limits), pets allowed, afternoon tea, open bank holidays, residents' lounge, garden.
**Rooms:** 6 double rooms, 1 twin room - 5 en suite. Also 3 four-poster suites available. All with tea/coffee maker, TV.
**Directions:** two miles from Lynton, just off the A39.
E.M. FREWER ☎(01598) 741322

## ROCKVALE HOTEL
Lee Road, EX35 6HW

*The hotel stands in its own grounds in a delightfully sunny and quiet, yet central, position and enjoys extensive views over Lynton village and the surrounding hills to Exmoor and Countisbury. Judith and David offer their guests comfortable accommodation, an excellent range of freshly cooked meals, and extremely friendly hospitality in a pleasant atmosphere.*

DOUBLE ROOM: from £20 to £30
SINGLE ROOM: up to £20
FOOD: up to £15
**Hours:** closed November until February.
**Cuisine:** ENGLISH - traditional up-market home-cooking.
**Cards:** Visa, Access.
**Other points:** non-smoking hotel, parking, children catered for (please check for age limits), residents'

lounge, vegetarian meals.

**Rooms:** 1 single room, 5 double rooms, 1 triple room, 1 family room. All with en suite, TV, telephone, radio, alarm, tea/coffee-making facilities.

**Directions:** on a private road left of the Town Hall in the centre of Lynton.

JUDITH & DAVID WOODLAND ☎(01598) 752279/753343

## MORTEHOE • map 3B3

### LUNDY HOUSE HOTEL
Chapel Hill, Woolacombe, EX34 7DZ

*Spectacularly situated on the cliff-side opposite a secluded beach, with magnificent sea views over Morte Bay to Lundy Island. Terraced gardens, à la carte restaurant, comfortable licensed lounge bar, separate colour TV, video and satellite TV lounges. Traditional `home from home' cooking. Vegetarian and special diets catered for.*

DOUBLE ROOM: up to £20

SINGLE ROOM: up to £25

FOOD: up to £15

**Hours:** breakfast 8.30am-9.30am, table d'hôte dinner 7.30pm, Nadines à la carte 7pm-9pm, closed November until January.

**Cuisine:** ENGLISH - superb home produced cuisine with personal service. Vegetarian and special diets catered for.

**Other points:** pets allowed, special breaks.

**Rooms:** 10 bedrooms.

**Directions:** situated between Woolacombe and Mortehoe off the A361 on the B3343.

ROGER & DENA SELLS ☎(01271) 870372

## NEWTON ABBOT • map 4D4

### THE CHURCH HOUSE INN
Stokeightonhead, TQ12 4QA

*Dating back some 450 years, this large, old thatched house is very attractive both inside and out. Spacious and pleasantly decorated, it has a warm, friendly atmosphere in which to enjoy traditional English cuisine and fine wines.*

FOOD: up to £15

**Hours:** bar meals 12noon-3pm and 6.30pm-10pm, open bank holidays.

**Cuisine:** TRADITIONAL ENGLISH - a varied selection of dishes using fresh local produce, including vegetarian meals and traditional Sunday lunch.

**Cards:** Access,Visa

**Other points:** children welcome, open-air dining, parking.

**Directions:** off the A379, between Newton Abbot and Babbacombe Bay.

JIM & CORINNA WILSON ☎(01626) 872475

### THE TWO MILE OAK
Abbotskerswell, TQ12 6DE

*An ancient, former coach house of real character, boasting original ceilings and beams on several levels. Inside the atmosphere is warm and friendly*

and there is ample seating on which to enjoy an excellent range of traditional English dishes using local produce.

FOOD: up to £15

**Hours:** bar meals 12noon-2.15pm and 6.30pm-10pm, open bank holidays.

**Cuisine:** varied dishes using fresh local produce, vegetarian meals and traditional Sunday lunch.

**Cards:** Access,Visa

**Other points:** children welcome, parking.

**Directions:** A381, on the Newton Abbot - Totnes road.

MR MARK WARRENER ☎(01803) 812411

## PAIGNTON • map 4D4

### CHANNEL VIEW
8 Marine Parade, TQ3 2NU

*A small, modernised hotel offering exceptional value. The emphasis is on enjoyment and the hotel is furnished and equipped to a high standard. A large new conservatory to the front of the hotel provides additional seating areas, and there is a large terrace for relaxing outside. Being only 15 yards from the beach the hotel has a magnificent sea view covering almost all of Torbay. Well recommended for a comfortable and relaxing holiday in a central location.*

DOUBLE ROOM: from £20 to £30

SINGLE ROOM: from £25 to £35

FOOD: up to £10

**Hours:** breakfast from 9am, dinner 6pm only. Open all year.

**Cuisine:** TRADITIONAL ENGLISH - roast beef and roast lamb.

**Cards:** Access, Visa

**Other points:** parking, non smoking area, licensed, residents' lounge, TV lounge, central heating, children welcome.

**Rooms:** 1 single room, 2 twin rooms, 6 triple rooms, 4 family rooms, all en suite with tea/coffee maker, TV, radio, hair dryer, trouser press. Ironing facilities in some rooms.

**Directions:** off A380 Paignton ring road turn left to Preston at Preston Down roundabout. Follow to traffic lights, straight across and under railway bridge, turn left into Marine Parade.

DAVE & MARGARET TEAGUE ☎(01803) 522432 Fax(01803) 528376

### THE INN ON THE GREEN
Seafront, TQ4 6BG

*A holiday complex set in 2 acres right on the seafront, yet within a 2-minute walk from shops, theatre and other attractions. The menu is very extensive, offering a wide range of dishes, well-cooked and presented, and the apartments are very comfortable. An ideal place for family holidays, as children are well catered for, with sandpits, a Wendy House and their own discos.*

DOUBLE ROOM: up to £20

SINGLE ROOM: up to £20

FOOD: up to £15 CLUB

**Hours:** lunch 12noon-3pm, dinner 6.30pm-

12midnight, Sunday 7pm-10.30pm.
**Cuisine:** INTERNATIONAL - very extensive menu, including traditional English, Indian and Italian dishes. Children's own menu. Desserts include olde-English puddings.
**Cards:** Visa, Diners, MasterCard, Eurocard, Delta.
**Other points:** Sunday lunch, children welcome, pets allowed, garden, playland, swimming pool, launderette, games room.
**Rooms:** self-catering apartments for 2 to 6 persons.
**Directions:** end of M5 to Torbay. Directly on seafront opposite the pier.
BRIAN SHONE ☎(01803) 557841 Fax (01803) 550344

### REDCLIFFE HOTEL
Marine Drive, TQ3 2NL
*Superbly situated in 3 acres of attractive grounds directly adjoining the beach in the centre of the "English Riviera".*
DOUBLE ROOM: from £40 to £50
SINGLE ROOM: from £35 to £45
FOOD: up to £15
**Hours:** breakfast 8am-9.30am, bar snacks 12noon-2pm, Sunday lunch 12.45am-2pm, dinner 7pm-8.30pm.
**Cuisine:** ENGLISH/FRENCH
**Cards:** Visa, Access.
**Other points:** parking, children welcome, afternoon teas, residents' lounge, vegetarian meals, garden, leisure centre, indoor pool.
**Rooms:** 12 single rooms, 23 double rooms, 23 twin rooms.
**Directions:** take the A385 or A380 and head for Paignton seafront. The hotel is at the Torquay end of Paignton Green.
MR`S. TWIGGER ☎(01803) 526397 Fax (01803) 528030

### ROSSLYN HOTEL
16 Colin Road, TQ3 2NR
*This comfortably furnished, privately-owned hotel is situated just off the seafront and is convenient for visiting Torquay and Brixham. The hotel offers many homely attributes, which serve to enhance the general feeling of welcome.*
DOUBLE ROOM: up to £20
SINGLE ROOM: up to £25
FOOD: up to £15
**Hours:** breakfast 8.30am-9am, dinner 6pm-7pm, bar snacks all day.
**Cuisine:** ENGLISH - table d'hôte menu.
**Other points:** parking, children welcome, no-smoking area, residents' lounge, vegetarian meals.
**Rooms:** 1 single room, 5 double rooms, 1 twin room, 3 family rooms.
**Directions:** just off the seafront.
VALERIE ADAMS ☎(01803) 525578

### SOUTH SANDS HOTEL
12 Alta Vista Road, TQ4 6BZ
*South Sands Hotel, situated close to Goodrington*

*Sands, enjoys outstanding views of the bay. Under the personal supervision of the proprietors, visitors are assured of a warm welcome, comfortable, well-equipped bedrooms and superb, freshly prepared food. Very good value for money. Ideally located for the beach, town centre and water adventure park. Free car park.*
DOUBLE ROOM: from £20 to £30
SINGLE ROOM: up to £25
FOOD: up to £15
**Hours:** breakfast 8am-9am, dinner 6pm-7pm.
**Cuisine:** ENGLISH / CONTINENTAL
**Cards:** Visa, MasterCard.
**Other points:** children welcome, vegetarian meals, afternoon tea, pets allowed, garden, residents' lounge, children welcome, baby-listening device, baby-sitting, cots, left luggage.
**Rooms:** 2 single rooms, 3 double rooms, 6 twin rooms, 8 family rooms. All with TV, radio, alarm, tea/coffee-making facilities.
**Directions:** keep Paignton harbour on left, go over top of hill. First hotel on right.
TONY & CECILE CAHILL ☎(01803) 557231/529947 Fax (01803) 551871

## PLYMOUTH • map 3D3

### SMEATONS TOWER HOTEL
40-44 Grand Parade, The Hoe, PL1 3DJ
*This family hotel has been completely refurbished and redecorated to a high standard. New furniture in the public areas and bedrooms means that this centrally located establishment offers families and businessmen alike good food and accommodation at realistic prices.*
DOUBLE ROOM: from £15 to £20
SINGLE ROOM: from £20 to £25
FOOD: up to £15
**Hours:** breakfast 7am-9am, dinner 6.30pm-8.30pm, open bank holidays.
**Cuisine:** ENGLISH - locally caught fish.
**Cards:** Visa, Access.
**Other points:** licensed, residents' and television lounges, children welcome.
**Rooms:** 12 double rooms, 6 twin rooms (4 en suite), 6 family rooms (4 en suite), All with TV, radio, telephone, ironing facilities, tea/coffee making facilities.
**Directions:** from A38 follow signs to Plymouth, the city centre and The Hoe.
ANTHONY & JUNE PARSONS
☎(01752) 221007 Fax (01752) 221664

### THE SPORTSMAN'S INN
Exeter Road, Ivybridge, PL21 0BQ
*This attractive, long, old coaching inn has recently been refurbished throughout to very attractive standards. With an extensive selection of well-cooked dishes, complemented by a wide range of wines, the inn has justifiably proved to be very popular with locals and travellers alike.*
DOUBLE ROOM: from £20 to £30
SINGLE ROOM: from £25 to £40
FOOD: up to £15

**Hours:** breakfast 7.30am-9am, meals all day 11.30am-9.30pm, open every day.
**Cuisine:** ENGLISH - wide choice of traditional dishes.
**Cards:** Visa, Access, AmEx, Eurocard, MasterCard, Switch,
**Other points:** parking, children welcome, pets allowed, no-smoking area, vegetarian meals, traditional Sunday lunch.
**Rooms:** 2 single rooms, 7 double rooms, 1 twin room, 1 family room. All with satellite TV, telephone, radio, alarm, hair dryer, tea/coffee-making facilities. Doubles can be used as singles.
**Directions:** just off the A38 Plymouth-Exeter road.
MS DONNA O. HIBBERT ☎(01752) 892280 Fax (01752) 690714

### TRATTORIA PESCATORE
36 Admiralty Street, Stonehouse, PL1 3RU
*A small Italian restaurant situated in an old Victorian building. Hand-painted murals on the walls add to the truly Italian atmosphere of the restaurant. All food is freshly cooked to order, and seafood is the house speciality. Delicious food and friendly, efficient service. Highly recommended.*
FOOD: from £15 to £20 ☞
**Hours:** lunch 12noon-2pm, dinner 7pm-11pm, closed Saturday lunch, Sunday and bank holidays.
**Cuisine:** ITALIAN - the traditional Italian cuisine selection includes giant prawns tossed in garlic butter, and special vegetarian pastas. Also, chef's specials available from the blackboard.
**Cards:** Visa, Access.
**Other points:** licensed, open-air dining, children welcome.
**Directions:** approximately 1 mile from city centre, near Plymouth to Roscoff ferry port.
GIAN PIERO CALIGARI & RITA ATKINSON ☎(01752) 600201

## SHALDON • map 4D4

### THE NESS HOUSE HOTEL
Marine Parade, near Teignmouth, TQ14 0HP
*Formerly a private country house, the hotel sits in beautiful gardens and enjoys wonderful views of the coast and the Teign Estuary. A friendly hotel serving good food.*
DOUBLE ROOM: from £30 to £40
SINGLE ROOM: from £40 to £55
FOOD: from £15 to £20
**Hours:** breakfast 8am-10am, lunch 12noon-2pm, dinner 7pm-10pm, bar meals 12noon-2pm, bar meals 6.30pm-10pm.
**Cuisine:** FRENCH - a large choice of traditional French dishes. Coquilles Saint-Jacques au saffran, mignon de veau aux fraises.
**Cards:** Visa, Access, AmEx.
**Other points:** licensed, open-air dining, Sunday lunch, children welcome, afternoon tea, garden, residents' bar, residents' lounge.
**Rooms:** 10 double rooms, 2 family rooms. All with telephone, tea/coffee-making facilities, heating,

satellite TV. The rooms are of varying standards and prices; all can be used as singles when required.
**Directions:** on A379 (Teignmouth-Torquay road) in Shaldon, set in parkland.
PETER REYNOLDS ☎(01626) 873480 Fax (01626) 873486

## SIDFORD • map 4D4

### THE BLUE BALL INN
Near Sidmouth, EX10 9QL
*Dating back to 1385, The Blue Ball Inn is thatched and made of cob and flint. Fresh flowers add to the tasteful decor of the building, and outside customers can enjoy barbecues in the garden during summer. Run by the same family since 1912, the pub provides well-cooked food in a busy but relaxed atmosphere. Excellent, friendly service.*
DOUBLE ROOM: from £20 to £30
SINGLE ROOM: £22
FOOD: up to £15
**Hours:** breakfast 8.30am-10am, lunch 10.30am-2pm, dinner 6.30pm-10pm.
**Cuisine:** ENGLISH - home-made specialities include steak-and-kidney pie, chicken mornay, chilli con carne, and local fish.
**Cards:** Visa, Access.
**Other points:** licensed, open-air dining, Sunday lunch, children welcome, garden, barbecues, pets allowed, functions.
**Rooms:** 3 twin rooms.
**Directions:** on the A3052, located just outside Sidmouth.
MR ROGER NEWTON ☎(01395) 514062

## SIDMOUTH • map 4D4

### FORTFIELD HOTEL
Station Road, EX10 8NU

*Privately-owned country house-style hotel, stunning sea views, lovely grounds with putting green and private parking. Indoor heated pool, sauna, solarium and beauty treatments. All rooms en suite, passenger lift, superb traditional English cuisine, old-fashioned quality service assured. Open all year.*
DOUBLE ROOM: from £20 to £30
SINGLE ROOM: from £25 to £35
FOOD: up to £15
**Hours:** breakfast 8am-9.30am, lunch 12noon-2pm, dinner 6.30pm-8.30pm.
**Cuisine:** ENGLISH - prawn and apple cocktail, deep-fried mushroom rossini, pork fillet cider and apple sauce, escalope of veal Italian, traditional

steak-and-kidney pudding.
**Cards:** Visa, Access, Diners, AmEx, Switch.
**Other points:** licensed, open-air dining, Sunday lunch, no-smoking restaurant, children welcome, beauty therapy, afternoon tea.
**Rooms:** 6 single rooms, 11 double rooms, 33 twin rooms, 5 family rooms. All with TV, radio, telephone, tea/coffee-making facilities.
**Directions:** from Exeter take A3052. Turn right at Bowd Inn. Hotel on right just before seafront.
ANDREW TORJUSSEN ☎(01395) 512403
Fax(01395) 512403

 **KINGSWOOD HOTEL**
Esplanade, EX10 8AX
*An excellent family-run establishment on the seafront with an award-winning and colourful, terraced garden. Fully modernized, the interior is spacious, and many of the rooms look out over the Devon coast. Personally supervised by the proprietors, the food and service are excellent. The Kingswood is fully licensed, with a good selection of reasonably priced wines*
DOUBLE ROOM: from £20 to £30
SINGLE ROOM: from £26 to £30
FOOD: up to £15
**Hours:** breakfast 8.15am-9.15am, lunch 12.30pm-1.30am, dinner 6.45pm-7.30pm.
**Cuisine:** ENGLISH
**Cards:** Visa, MasterCard, Eurocard.
**Other points:** central heating, children welcome, pets allowed, residents' lounge, baby-listening device, picnic lunches.
**Rooms:** 8 single rooms, 6 double rooms, 7 twin rooms, 5 family rooms. All with TV, telephone, tea/coffee-making facilities.
**Directions:** on the seafront at the centre of the esplanade.
JOY, COLIN, MARK & JOANNA SEWARD
☎(01395) 516367/513185 Fax(01395) 513185

## SOUTH MOLTON • map 3C3

 **STUMBLES HOTEL & RESTAURANT**
131-134 East Street, EX36 3BU
*Stumbles is situated on the edge of Exmoor in a bustling market town, with many fine antique shops and historic buildings. The attractive and spacious 30-seater restaurant, with its secluded tables and soft lighting, offers fresh food daily. Stumbles have their own hotel offering very comfortable accommodation, all en suite. The bar and courtyard are open for morning coffees and lunches, with barbecues in summmer.*
DOUBLE ROOM: from £20 to £30
SINGLE ROOM: from £35
FOOD: from £15 to £20
**Hours:** breakfast 8am-9am, lunch 12.30am-2pm, dinner 7pm-9.30pm, restaurant closed Sunday.
**Cuisine:** ENGLISH/FRENCH - fresh produce used for the daily changing menu.
**Cards:** Visa, Access.
**Other points:** fully licensed, parking, children welcome, children's license, no-smoking area,

disabled access, pets, residents' lounge, garden, vegetarian meals, open-air dining, satellite TV.
**Rooms:** 3 single rooms, 5 double rooms, 3 twin rooms. All with TV, telephone, tea/coffee-making facilities, hair dryer.
**Directions:** in town centre, just off the square.
MR & MRS M. POTTER ☎(01769) 574145
Fax(01769) 572558

## TAVISTOCK • map 3D3

**THE OLD PLOUGH INN**
Bere Ferrers, near Yelverton, PL20 7JL
*A 16th century inn, situated beside the River Tavy in the scenic village of Bere Ferrers, in an unspoilt area of outstanding beauty. A wide range of home-made food and ales is offered in the bar, restaurant or beer garden. Open log fires in winter.*
FOOD: up to £15
**Hours:** lunch 12noon-3pm, dinner 7.30pm-10.30pm, closed Christmas evening only.
**Cuisine:** ENGLISH - menus change daily, including, when available, fresh fish and 'Maggies Monster' home-made pies. Locally grown vegetables. All dishes home-made.
**Cards:** Visa, Access, AmEx.
**Other points:** licensed, open-air dining, Sunday lunch.
**Directions:** from Plymouth, take A386, following signs for Bere Alston and Bere Ferrers.
ADRIAN & MARGARET HOOPER ☎(01822) 840358

## TEIGNMOUTH • map 4D4

**RATHLIN HOUSE HOTEL**
Upper Hermosa Road, TQ14 9JW
*A beautiful Victorian villa, built in 1892, standing in its own enclosed gardens with a large terrace. Located in a quiet residential area, this is a small private hotel with the atmosphere of a large family home. The hotel is ten minutes' walk from the town centre, the harbour and the seafront.*
DOUBLE ROOM: up to £20
SINGLE ROOM: up to £25
FOOD: up to £15
**Hours:** breakfast 8.15am-9am, dinner 6.30pm, closed November until March.
**Cuisine:** ENGLISH - traditional dishes; gluten-free diets and vegetarians catered for.
**Other points:** parking, children welcome, residents, lounge, garden, vegetarian meals.
**Rooms:** 2 double rooms, 1 twin room, 4 family rooms. All with en suite, TV, tea/coffee-making facilities.
**Directions:** M5, A38, A380, B3192; continue down the hill in Teignmouth, then turn right into Yannom Drive.
TERENCE FALLON ☎(01626) 774473

**Join Les Routiers Discovery Club FREE! See page 34 for details.**

## THROWLEIGH • map 3D3

 **WELL FARM**
Near Okehampton, EX20 2JQ
*Relax in beautiful and peaceful surroundings at Well Farm, a Grade II listed medieval Dartmoor longhouse. It is a working family-run dairy and outdoor pig farm, with peacocks, ornamental pheasants and free-range poultry. Fresh produce is served in a relaxed, family atmosphere.*
DOUBLE ROOM: up to £20
SINGLE ROOM: up to £20
FOOD: up to £15
**Hours:** breakfast 9am, dinner 8pm-9pm, closed Christmas.
**Cuisine:** ENGLISH
**Cards:** AmEx.
**Other points:** children welcome, residents' lounge, vegetarian meals, working farm.
**Rooms:** 1 twin room, 2 family rooms. All with en suite, tea/coffee-making facilities, heating.
**Directions:** 1.5 miles from the A30 in the Dartmoor National Park.
MRS SHEELAGH KNOX ☎(01647) 231294
Fax (01647) 231561

## TIVERTON • map 4C4

 **BICKLEIGH COTTAGE COUNTRY HOTEL**
Bickleigh Bridge, EX16 8RJ
*Situated on the bank of the River Exe near Bickleigh Bridge, a landmark famous for its scenic beauty, Bickleigh Cottage Country Hotel - built circa 1640 - has been privately owned by the Cochrane family since 1933. This partly thatched cottage still retains its low-beamed ceilings and genuine old fireplaces, while providing comfortable, beautifully decorated bedrooms and excellent fresh cuisine in a wonderful, homely atmosphere.*
DOUBLE ROOM: from £20 to £30
SINGLE ROOM: from £25 to £35
FOOD: up to £15
**Hours:** breakfast 8.30am-9.15am, dinner 7pm, closed November until March.
**Cuisine:** ENGLISH - the daily-chosen menus are announced at breakfast.
**Cards:** Visa, Access.
**Other points:** parking, no-smoking area, residents' lounge, garden, children catered for (please check for age limits).
**Rooms:** 2 single rooms, 4 double rooms, 3 twin rooms. All with en suite, tea/coffee-making facilities.
**Directions:** 4 miles south of Tiverton, 10 miles north of Exeter on the A396.
STUART & PAULINE COCHRANE ☎(01884) 855230

 **THE HARTNOLL COUNTRY HOUSE HOTEL**
Bolham Road, Bolham, EX16 7RA
*This lovely Georgian hotel has a cosy and intimate atmosphere, which is very welcome after an active*
*day prowling through the surrounding Devon countryside. A mill-stream runs through the hotel grounds, giving you a delightful feeling of `getting away from it all'. Friendly and courteous staff help make your stay memorable.*
DOUBLE ROOM: from £20 to £30
SINGLE ROOM: from £35 to £45
FOOD: from £15 to £20
**Hours:** breakfast 7.30am-10am, dinner 7pm-9pm, lunch 12noon-2pm.
**Cuisine:** ENGLISH / FRENCH - mixture of traditional English and French cuisine. Regular à la carte.
**Cards:** Visa, Access.
**Other points:** licensed, open-air dining, Sunday lunch, children welcome, pets allowed, open bank holidays, residents' lounge, residents' bar, vegetarian meals, parking, disabled access.
**Directions:** after junction 27 on the M5, take the first roundabout (6 miles). The A396 is the third exit right.
SALLY PRICE AND MAGDI SOLIMAN ☎(01884) 252777

 **THE MERRIEMEADE HOTEL**
1 Lower Town, Sampford Peverell, EX16 7BJ

*Formerly a Georgian-style gentleman's residence, The Merriemeade Hotel overlooks the Blackdown Hills. This hotel caters for all ages, with a children's play area in the rear garden. Its food is both varied and excellently cooked. The rooms are also of high standard. Great value for money.*
DOUBLE ROOM: from £20 to £30
SINGLE ROOM: from £25 to £35
FOOD: up to £15
**Hours:** breakfast 7.30am-9am, lunch 11.30am-2pm, Sunday 12noon-2.30pm, dinner 6.45pm-9pm, Sunday 7pm-9.30pm.
**Cuisine:** ENGLISH / FRENCH - à la carte menu, bar meals and snacks.
**Cards:** Visa, Access, AmEx.
**Other points:** licensed, open-air dining, Sunday lunch, children welcome, pets by arrangement.
**Rooms:** 1 single room, 1 double room, 1 twin room, 2 family rooms.
**Directions:** 1 mile from junction 27 of the M5 and North Devon link road. On A373.
MR L.J. AFFLECK & MR P.J.P. COURT ☎(01884) 820270 Fax (01884) 821614

**PARKWAY HOUSE HOTEL**
Lower Town, Sampford Peverell, EX16 7BJ
*A family hotel and restaurant with a friendly and*

informal atmosphere under the personal supervision of Phyl and George Davenport. Parkway House is well situated close to the motorway network and offers 10 comfortable bedrooms and a range of meeting and conference rooms to accommodate a wide range of social and commercial functions. The Conservatory restaurant has been newly styled and the patio-gardens overlook the Culm Valley.
DOUBLE ROOM: from £20 to £30
SINGLE ROOM: from £35 to £45
FOOD: up to £15
**Hours:** breakfast 7.30am-9.30am, lunch and bar meals 12noon-2pm, dinner and bar meals 7pm-9.30pm, open bank holidays.
**Cuisine:** ENGLISH / CONTINENTLA - an excellent and varied menu featuring à la carte, table d'hôte, bar snack and carvery selections. Vegetarian choices available - fish dishes a speciality.
**Cards:** Visa, Access, Switch.
**Other points:** conservatory restaurant, function rooms, dining room for private use, meeting room, licensed, parking.
**Rooms:** 4 single rooms, 1 twin room, 3 double rooms, 2 family rooms, all en suite. All with TV, telephone, trouser press and tea/coffee-making facilities.
**Directions:** from junction 27 on the M5 take the A361 Sampford Peverell road. Hotel is close to Parkway station.
PHYL & GEORGE DAVENPORT
☎(01884) 820255 Fax(01884) 820780

## TOPSHAM • map 4D4

### THE LIGHTER INN
The Quay, EX3 0HZ
A popular, 200-year-old riverside inn with a warm, happy atmosphere that attracts a mixed crowd of locals and holiday-makers. A comprehensive choice of English dishes are offered, including grills and seafood.
FOOD: up to £15
**Hours:** bar meals 12noon-2.15pm, and 6.30pm-10pm, open bank holidays.
**Cuisine:** comprehensive choice of grills and seafood. Vegetarian meals and traditional Sunday lunch.
**Cards:** Access,Visa
**Other points:** children welcome, open-air dining, afternoon teas, parking.
**Directions:** off the A376, through the Old Town, to the quayside.
MR JOHN SCOTT ☎(01392) 875439

## TORQUAY • map 4D4

### THE DEVONSHIRE HOTEL
Parkhill Road, TQ1 2DY
A large, luxurious and quiet 100-year-old hotel where guests are warmly welcomed with porter service. Distinctive features are the original doors and high, corniced ceilings, leading to the beautiful dining rooms and bar lounges, which have been decorated in restful colours. Convenient for theatre

visits and boat excursions.
DOUBLE ROOM: from £32 to £46
SINGLE ROOM: from £20 to £35
FOOD: up to £15
**Hours:** bar snacks 12noon-2.30pm, dinner 7pm-8.45pm, bar snacks 6.30pm-8.45pm.
**Cuisine:** ENGLISH - traditional cuisine and grill options.
**Cards:** Visa, Access, Diners.
**Other points:** parking, children welcome, open bank holidays, afternoon teas, disabled access, pets allowed, residents' lounge, vegetarian meals, garden, residents' bar, swimming pool.
**Rooms:** 8 single rooms, 14 double rooms, 40 twin rooms, 9 family rooms. All with TV, telephone, tea/coffee-making facilities.
**Directions:** at the harbour clock, turn right along the harbour side and proceed up the hill towards Meadfoot Beach. The hotel is at the crest of the hill.
THE DEVONSHIRE HOTEL (TORQUAY) LTD - MR TREWERN ☎(01803) 291123 Fax(01803) 291710

### INGOLDSBY HOTEL
Chelston Road, TQ2 6PT
A truly delightful hotel where you can relax in the attractive garden or take a short stroll to the seafront or into Cockington village. The spacious dining room overlooks the garden, and there are comfortable bedrooms and a quiet television room. An ideal base for a family hotel or seasonal break.
DOUBLE ROOM: up to £20
**Hours:** breakfast 8.45am-9.30am, bar snacks all day, dinner 6pm-7pm.
**Cuisine:** ENGLISH
**Cards:** Visa, Access.
**Other points:** parking, children welcome, open bank holidays, disabled access, residents' lounge, vegetarian meals, garden.
**Directions:** from seafront, turn right by Grand Hotel, first left, then right at crossroads.
MR R. WELLS ☎(01803) 607497

### JINGLE'S RESTAURANT
34 Torwood Street, TQ1 1EB
A Mexican-American themed restaurant offering a good variety of very well-cooked dishes to suit all tastes. The choice includes char-grilled steaks, hamburgers and vegetarian meals. House specialities are Mexican dishes such as sizzling fajita, a traditional Mexican style of cooking. The good food is complemented by generous portions and welcoming service. International beers.
FOOD: up to £15
**Hours:** dinner 5pm-11pm, happy hour 5pm-6pm.
**Cuisine:** AMERICAN / MEXICAN - wide choice of dishes including char-grilled steaks, Cajun dishes, Mexican dishes, vegetarian meals, hamburgers and deep-pan pizzas.
**Cards:** Visa, Access, AmEx.
**Other points:** licensed, children welcome, parking nearby.
**Directions:** 100 yards from clock tower on harbourside.
JOHN & PAT GOLDER ☎(01803) 293340

**LIVERMEAD CLIFF HOTEL**
Sea Front, TQ2 6RQ

*A comfortable family hotel situated on the seafront at the water's edge, yet only a few minutes' level walk from the centre of town and the English Riviera Centre. The hotel is tastefully decorated and offers a high standard of comfort, which is complemented by the friendly and efficient service. All meals are cooked on the premises using fresh ingredients.*

DOUBLE ROOM: from £30 to £40
SINGLE ROOM: from £30 to £40
FOOD: up to £15
**Hours:** lunch 1pm-2pm, bar meals 12noon-2pm, 6.30pm-8.30pm, dinner 7pm-8.30pm, open all year.
**Cuisine:** ENGLISH / CONTINENTAL - locally caught fish, Devon meats and poultry.
**Cards:** Visa, Access, Diners, AmEx, Switch.
**Other points:** licensed, Sunday lunch, children welcome, afternoon tea, swimming pool, solarium, garden, conferences, baby-listening device, cots, baby-sitting, vegetarian meals, parking, residents' bar, residents' lounge.
**Rooms:** 64 bedrooms. All with TV, radio, alarm, telephone, tea/coffee-making facilities.
**Directions:** from M5, exit onto A380 to Torquay, right at seafront, 600 yards.
MR LEE POWELL ☎(01803) 299666 **Fax**(01803) 294496

### TOTNES • map 4D4

 **OLD CHURCH HOUSE INN**
Torbryan, Ipplepen, TQ12 5UR

*Many kings of England have wined and dined at this inn, which is steeped in history. Recognized as one of the most haunted inns in the West Country, it offers comfortable accommodation in individually heated rooms and good traditional English cuisine. The Locals Bar is well known for the quality of its beer and wide range of spirits and liqueurs. Filmed for numerous television and radio programmes.*

DOUBLE ROOM: from £20 to £30
FOOD: up to £15
**Hours:** breakfast 8.30am-10am, lunch 12noon-3pm, dinner 7pm-10.30pm, open all year.
**Cuisine:** ENGLISH
**Cards:** Visa, Access.
**Other points:** licensed.
**Directions:** turn off the A381 Newton Abbot to Totnes road towards Ipplepen. Go through the village to Orley Common, and then follow signs to the inn.
MR E.G. PIMM ☎(01803) 812372

### WOOLACOMBE • map 3B3

 **BAYCLIFFE HOTEL**
Chapel Hill, Mortehoe, EX34 7AZ

*Small, family-run hotel offering good service, comfortable rooms and superb views of the bay. Beaches are just a few minutes away, and places of interest include an 11th century church. Also, being adjacent to National Trust land, walkers will find this an ideal spot.*

DOUBLE ROOM: from £20 to £30
SINGLE ROOM: up to £20
FOOD: up to £10
**Hours:** breakfast 9am-10am, dinner 7pm-8pm.
**Cuisine:** ENGLISH / CARRIBEAN
**Other points:** licensed, special bargain breaks, children catered for (please check for age limits).
**Rooms:** 10 bedrooms. Including four poster, double en suite and single.
**Directions:** B3343 to Mortehoe village.
MR & MRS MCFARLANE ☎(01271) 870393

# DORSET

### BLANDFORD FORUM • map 4C6

 **ANVIL HOTEL AND RESTAURANT**
Salisbury Road, Pimperne, DT11 8UQ

*Situated in the pretty Dorset village of Pimperne, this beautifully maintained 16th century thatched hotel, just two minutes from Blandford, is steeped in history. The well-appointed restaurant, with log fire and beams, offers a mouthwatering menu with delicious desserts, prepared by a Savoy-trained chef and personally supervised by Carolann Palmer. Very comprehensive tasty bar meals are served in the Forge Bar. Ideally situated for touring Dorset and the surrounding counties of Wiltshire, Hampshire, Somerset and Devon. Enquire about clay pigeon tuition.*

DOUBLE ROOM: from £37 to £50
SINGLE ROOM: from £47 to £50
FOOD: from £15 to £20
**Hours:** breakfast 7.30am-9.30am, lunch 12noon-2pm, bar snacks 12noon-2.15pm, dinner 7pm-9.45pm, bar snacks 7pm-10pm.
**Cuisine:** ENGLISH / CONTINENTAL - varied menu, freshly prepared. Bar snacks also available.
**Cards:** Visa, Access, Diners, AmEx, Switch.
**Other points:** parking, children welcome, open bank holidays, disabled access, pets allowed, vegetarian meals, garden, cots.
**Rooms:** 2 single room, 5 double rooms, 2 twin rooms, 1 family room. All with TV, telephone, tea/coffee-making facilities.
**Directions:** 2 miles out of Blandford on A354 road to Salisbury.
CAROLANN PALMER ☎(01258) 453431/480182
**Fax**(01258) 480182

### BOURNEMOUTH • map 4D6

 **BAY VIEW COURT HOTEL**
35 East Overcliff Drive, East Cliff, BH1 3AH

*A 64-bedroom hotel, completely refurbished*

recently, situated in its own delightful garden with breathtaking views across the bay. This hotel offers the highest standards for business customers, conference delegates and holiday-makers, all of whom can enjoy the indoor pool, snooker room, games room and bars. The hotel is family-run, and a warm welcome with excellent food and service are guaranteed.

DOUBLE ROOM: from £30 to £40
SINGLE ROOM: from £32 to £42
FOOD: from £15 to £20 CLUB
**Hours:** breakfast 8am-9.30am, dinner 6.30pm-8.30pm, bar snacks 12noon-2pm, 6.30pm-8.30pm.
**Cuisine:** ENGLISH / CONTINENTAL - very high quality. Vegetarian meals available on request.
**Cards:** Visa, Access, Diners, AmEx, Switch
**Other points:** parking, children welcome, Sunday lunch, open bank holidays, no-smoking area, vegetarian meals, indoor swimming pool, jacuzzi, live entertainment.
**Rooms:** 9 single rooms, 28 double rooms, 16 twin rooms, 11 family rooms.
**Directions:** from A338 Bournemouth ring road (Wessex Way) take A35 turning at St Pauls roundabout near Central Station to Christchurch Road. Turn left to Manor Road and continue to East Overcliff Drive, overlooking the sea.
MR L. COX ☎(01202) 294449 Fax(01202) 292883

### THE BEAR CROSS
Bear Cross, BH11 9LU
A very comfortable pub/restaurant, set in attractive surroundings conveniently located on the road to Wimborne Minster and the Poole area.
A varied menu is available, offering good value-for-money food including vegetarian, and efficient service. A warm, friendly atmosphere prevails.
FOOD: up to £15
**Hours:** lunch and bar meals 12noon-2.30pm, restaurant and bar meals 7pm-10pm, open bank holidays, all day opening May to September including Sunday.
**Cuisine:** wide selection of traditional dishes, including home-made specials.
**Cards:** Access,Visa,AmEx,Diners
**Other points:** children welcome, no-smoking area, traditional Sunday lunch, vegetarian meals, parking.
**Directions:** from A31 Ringwood, take A348 at Ferndown to Poole. The Bear Cross is on traffic island at Magno Road junction.
MR AND MRS DERBYSHIRE ☎(01202) 574413

### BRAMCOTE HALL HOTEL
1 Glen Road, Boscombe, BH5 1HR
The house was built in 1894 for Lady Jane Shelley, daughter-in-law of the famous poet, and became a hotel in 1926. Great improvements have since been made, but many delightful aspects have remained unchanged. Children are particularly well catered for, with games provided and a special children's menu. The hotel is very close to Boscombe Pier and beach.
DOUBLE ROOM: up to £20

SINGLE ROOM: up to £20
FOOD: up to £15
**Hours:** breakfast 8.30am-9am, dinner 6pm-7pm, refreshments served to order throughout the day.
**Cuisine:** ENGLISH - all meals are freshly cooked to order; even the bread is baked on the premises.
**Cards:** Visa, Access, Diners, AmEx.
**Other points:** parking, children catered for (please check for age limits), pets allowed, vegetarian meals.
**Rooms:** 3 single rooms, 4 double rooms, 1 twin room, 4 triple rooms, 2 family rooms. All with TV, radio, tea/coffee-making facilities.
**Directions:** from Boscombe shopping area, take road signposted Boscombe Pier and Percy Road; the hotel is the first in Glen Road.
JILL & ALLAN DALE ☎(01202) 395555

### BURLEY COURT HOTEL
Bath Road, BH1 2NP
A well-known hotel, in the same family for over 40 years, where the continuing aims are good-quality food, courteous service and a high standard of cleanliness. The hotel is large enough to offer every luxury, yet not too large to be personally supervised throughout. A friendly, comfortable hotel. Children are most welcome, and accommodation is free when sharing with two adults. There is a beach hut on the main promenade for guests' use.
DOUBLE ROOM: from £30 to £40
SINGLE ROOM: from £30 to £40
FOOD: up to £15
**Hours:** breakfast 8am-9.30am, bar meals 12noon-2.30pm, dinner 6.30pm-8.30pm.
**Cuisine:** ENGLISH - traditional English dishes. Snack lunches available in lounge bar or by the pool. Vegetarian meals by arrangement.
**Cards:** Visa, Access, Switch, Connect.
**Other points:** licensed, Sunday lunch, children welcome, afternoon tea, pets allowed, residents' lounge, lift, games room, swimming pool, solarium.
**Rooms:** 5 single rooms, 12 double rooms, 12 twin rooms, 9 family rooms.
**Directions:** East Cliff, near Bournemouth railway station.
MASLYN & JAN HASKER ☎(01202) 552824
Fax(01202) 298514

### CHINE HOTEL
25 Boscombe Spa Road, BH5 1AX
Constructed during 1874 on Sir Henry Drummond-Wolff's estate, the Chine overlooks Poole Bay and the beautifully landscaped Boscombe Chine Gardens. Excellent service and old-world charm combine to create a warm, friendly atmosphere. The Bay Restaurant enjoys sea views and offers a high standard of freshly prepared meals for guests and non-residents.
DOUBLE ROOM: from £40 to £50
FOOD: from £15 to £20
**Hours:** breakfast 8am-9.45am, lunch 12.30pm-2pm, dinner 7pm-8.30pm.
**Cuisine:** ENGLISH / INTERNATIONAL - lunchtime

cold buffet and carvery.
**Cards:** Visa, Access, Diners, AmEx.
**Other points:** licensed, Sunday lunch, children welcome, garden, afternoon tea.
**Rooms:** 9 single rooms, 29 double rooms, 39 twin rooms, 19 family rooms.
**Directions:** M3, M27 to A31 and Wessex Way, Bournemouth ring road, turn at St Paul's roundabout to Christchurch Road and Boscombe Spa Road. Hotel overlooks the sea and Poole Bay to the south.
MR J.G.J. BUTTERWORTH ☎(01202) 396234
Fax (01202) 391737

### 🏠 CHINEHURST HOTEL
Studland Road, Alum Chine, BH4 8JA
*A family-run hotel overlooking the beautiful Alum Chine. Tastefully decorated throughout, this is a medium-sized establishment with all the facilities of a large hotel. Close to the sea and shops on the West Cliff. Entertainment weekly. Separate special Italian restaurant: `Mr Macaws'.*
DOUBLE ROOM: from £20 to £30
SINGLE ROOM: from £20 to £30
FOOD: up to £15 CLUB
**Hours:** breakfast 7.30am-9.30am, lunch 12noon-2.30pm, bar meals 12noon-1.45pm, dinner 6.30pm-10.30pm.
**Cuisine:** ENGLISH / CONTINENTAL - wide selection table d'hôte menu changes daily: roasts, steaks. A la carte menu also available.
**Cards:** Visa, Access, Diners, AmEx.
**Other points:** licensed, Sunday lunch, no-smoking area, children welcome, pets by prior arrangement, afternoon tea, garden, barbecues, residents' lounge, residents' bar, tropical bird gardens.
**Rooms:** 2 single rooms, 15 double rooms, 6 twin rooms, 6 family rooms. All with TV, radio, telephone, tea/coffee-making facilities, heating, baby-listening device, hair dryer.
**Directions:** west of the pier overlooking Alum Chine, close to the seafront.
MR C.K. GRIFFIN & MRS A.E. GRIFFIN ☎(01202) 764583 Fax (01202) 765854

### 🏠 THE CLIFFESIDE HOTEL
East Overcliff Drive, BH1 3AQ
*The Cliffeside Hotel, overlooking the sea, is suitable for all ages. Well-cooked food and friendly, efficient service are complemented by the comfortable furnishings throughout. In an excellent position, close to shops, theatres, the BIC, and with plenty of activities: golf, wind-surfing, tennis and pony-trekking to name a few. Complimentary membership to Queensbury Leisure Club.*
DOUBLE ROOM: from £40 To £50
SINGLE ROOM: from £40 to £50
FOOD: from £15 to £20 CLUB
**Hours:** breakfast 8am-9.30am, lunch 12.45am-2pm, Sunday 12.30am-2pm, dinner 6.45pm-8.30pm.
**Cuisine:** ENGLISH - dishes include grilled lamb cutlet garni and grilled whole dover sole maître

d'hôtel. Cold buffet.
**Cards:** Visa, Access, Diners, AmEx, Switch.
**Other points:** licensed, parking, vegetarian meals, Sunday lunch, no-smoking area, children welcome, pets by prior arrangement, afternoon tea, swimming pool, games room, conferences, seasonal rates available.
**Rooms:** 61 bedrooms.
**Directions:** from M3, M27 to A31 and A338 Wessex Way, Bournemouth Ring Road to East Overcliff Drive.
DAVID A. YOUNG ☎(01202) 555724

### 🍴 CORIANDER RESTAURANT
14 Richmond Hill, BH2 6EJ
*Bournemouth's most famous Mexican restaurant, serving a wide selection of dishes including an excellent vegetarian selection. Open all day, full menu always available, as well as drinks from Mexican beer to Sangria. Lively atmosphere and friendly staff, all adds up to a great meal.*
FOOD: up to £15
**Hours:** open all day, Monday-Saturday 12noon-10.30pm, Sunday 5pm-10.30pm.
**Cuisine:** MEXICAN / INTERNATIONAL - authentic Mexican dishes, including vegetarian and Gringo. Special daytime menu, children's menu, specials and home-made sweets.
**Cards:** Visa, Access, Switch, Delta.
**Other points:** children welcome (children's menu up to age 12), no-smoking area, coaches by prior arrangement
**Directions:** in the heart of Bournemouth.
CHRISTINE MILLS ☎(01202) 552202 Fax (01202) 780322

### 🏠 CUMBERLAND HOTEL
East Overcliff Drive, BH1 3AF
*A purpose-built hotel providing luxurious accommodation and facilities. Situated on the famous East Cliff, there are superb sea views, from the Purbeck Hills to the Isle of Wight. The elegant oak-panelled restaurant offers a varied menu, carefully selected wine list and efficient, courteous service. A family-run hotel which provides excellent standards. Guests have use of the nearby Queensbury Leisure Club.*
DOUBLE ROOM: from £30 to £40
SINGLE ROOM: from £35 to £45
FOOD: from £15 to £20
**Hours:** breakfast 8am-9.30am, lunch 12.30am-1.45pm, bar meals 12.30am-2pm, dinner 7pm-8.30pm, bar meals 7pm-8.30pm.
**Cuisine:** MODERN ENGLISH - four-course table d'hôte menu. Dishes may include poached fillet of sole, medallions of pork tenderloin with a Calvados cream sauce. Bar snacks and coffee shop.
**Cards:** Visa, Access, Diners, AmEx.
**Other points:** licensed, Sunday lunch, no-smoking area, children welcome, large residents' lounge, swimming pool, garden, conferences, parking, vegetarian meals, residents' bar.
**Rooms:** 12 single rooms, 32 double rooms, 44 twin

rooms, 8 triple rooms, 4 quad rooms. 28 bedrooms with sea view and balcony. All with TV, radio, alarm, telephone, hair dryer, tea/coffee-making facilities.
**Directions:** M3, then M27, follow Wessex Way to East Cliff.
MR TONY WILSON ☎(01202) 290722 Fax (01202) 311394

### DEAN PARK HOTEL
41 Wimborne Road, BH2 6NB

*A privately-owned hotel situated close to the town centre, Dean Park Cricket Ground, West Hants Tennis Club, Meyrick Golf Club and Bournemouth Conference Centre. The atmosphere is relaxed and friendly, the food is well prepared and the comfortable accommodation is of a very good standard.*
DOUBLE ROOM: from £40 to £50
SINGLE ROOM: from £50 to £60
FOOD: up to £15
**Hours:** breakfast 8am-10am, dinner 7pm-9.30pm.
**Cuisine:** ENGLISH - à la carte and table d'hôte menus.
**Cards:** Visa, Access, Diners, AmEx.
**Other points:** parking, children welcome, conference facilities, pets allowed, residents' lounge, games room, residents' bar, central heating.
**Rooms:** 6 single rooms, 12 twin rooms. All with TV, radio, telephone, tea-making facilities.
**Directions:** from Wessex Way (Bournemouth by-pass, A338), turn off at Richmond roundabout and follow Wimborne Road, A337, to Number 41. The hotel is on the right.
MR BRIAN THOMPSON ☎(01202) 552941 Fax (01202) 556400

### GRANGE HOTEL
Southbourne Overcliffe Drive, Southbourne, BH6 3NL

*Situated in a premier position by the sea overlooking beautiful Bournemouth Bay, with scenic views from the Isle of Wight in the east to the Isle of Purbeck in the west. Offering quality accommodation and service, many rooms have balconies with excellent sea views. A passenger lift (wheelchair-friendly) serves all floors. The sun terrace and barbecue area are open during the summer season.*
DOUBLE ROOM: from £30 to £40
SINGLE ROOM: from £25 to £35
FOOD: up to £15  CLUB
**Hours:** breakfast 8am-9.30am, Sunday lunch 12noon-2.30pm, dinner 6.30pm-8.30pm, bar snacks 6pm-11pm.
**Cuisine:** ENGLISH / CONTINENTAL
**Cards:** Visa, Eurocard, MasterCard, Switch.
**Other points:** children welcome, parking, no-smoking area, afternoon teas, disabled access, pets, residents' lounge, vegetarian meals.
**Rooms:** 6 single rooms, 16 double rooms, 6 twin rooms, 3 family rooms.
**Directions:** on seafront between Christchurch and

Boscombe (Fisherman's Walk).
GORDON & KAY BLAKEY ☎(01202) 433093/433094 Fax (01202) 424228

### HOTEL MON BIJOU
47 Manor Road, East Cliff, BH1 3EU

*Formerly a Victorian coach house set in a lovely tree lined avenue which has been skilfully converted to provide a luxurious small hotel. Access to the cliff top and beach is only 25 metres away with Bournemouth pier and shopping centre only 2 minutes drive. Also within easy reach are Poole Harbour, Wimborne Minster, Ringwood, Beaulieu Motor Museum and Compton Acres.*
DOUBLE ROOM: from £20 to £30
SINGLE ROOM: from £27 to £35
FOOD: up to £15  CLUB
**Hours:** breakfast 8am-9am, lunch 12.30am-2pm, dinner 6.30pm-7.30pm, à la carte dinner 7.30pm-9pm.
**Cuisine:** ENGLISH - classic dishes.
**Cards:** Visa, Access, Diners, AmEx.
**Other points:** parking, children welcome, afternoon teas, disabled access, pets allowed, residents' lounge, vegetarian meals, open-air dining, garden.
**Rooms:** 7 bedrooms.
**Directions:** from Bournemouth town centre, take the town bypass along Wessex Way on the A338. The hotel is on Manor Road, adjacent to Eastcliff.
SYLVIA & VIC SHEARS ☎(01202) 551389

### MAE-MAR HOTEL
91-93 Westhill Road, West Cliff, BH2 5PQ

*An attractive hotel situated in the heart of the Westcliff area. Within walking distance of both beach and town, the Mae-Mar provides a friendly family retreat at the end of the day.*
DOUBLE ROOM: up to £20
**Hours:** breakfast 8am-9.15am, dinner 6pm-6.30pm, last orders 4.30pm, open all year.
**Cuisine:** BREAKFAST
**Cards:** Visa, Access.
**Other points:** central heating, children welcome, pets by prior arrangement, residents' lounge, lift.
**Rooms:** 9 single rooms, 12 double rooms, 1 twin room, 6 family rooms. All with TV, tea/coffee-making facilities, video.
**Directions:** A31 to Bournemouth; situated in Westcliff area.
MRS JANET CLEAVER ☎(01202) 553167 Fax (01202) 311919

### OAK HALL HOTEL
9 Wilfred Road, Boscombe Manor, BH5 1ND

*A comfortable, family-run hotel with a homely atmosphere, which has been thoroughly refurbished and modernized while retaining many of its old-world features. Resident proprietors Margaret and Joe McDonnell and their staff extend a warm, hearty welcome to all. Oak Hall is adjacent to Shelley Park* with its bowls and tennis courts and is just a short walk away from the seafront.

DOUBLE ROOM: from £20 to £30

FOOD: up to £15

**Hours:** breakfast 9am-10am, dinner 6pm-7pm, closed New Year.

**Cuisine:** ENGLISH

**Cards:** Visa, Access, AmEx.

**Other points:** parking, children welcome, pets, residents' lounge, vegetarian meals, garden.

**Rooms:** 2 single rooms, 5 double rooms, 13 twin rooms, 6 family rooms.

**Directions:** A35 Christchurch road into Bournemouth or Bournemouth ring road (Wessex Way); observe signpost for Boscombe and Boscombe Pier.

J. & M. MCDONNELL ☎(01202) 395062

### THE QUEEN'S HOTEL
Meyrick Road, East Cliff, BH1 3DL

*A comfortable family-run hotel, which caters for every taste, offering full à la carte, table d'hôte and bar menus. Situated on the East Cliff, a minute's walk from the town centre and a host of local amenities. Other attractions like Lulworth Cove and Brownsea Island are also within easy reach. New leisure club, including indoor pool, sauna, Jacuzzi and steam room.*

DOUBLE ROOM: from £30 to £40

SINGLE ROOM: from £35 to £45

FOOD: from £15 to £20    `CLUB`

**Hours:** breakfast 7.30am-9.45am, lunch 12.45am-1.45pm, dinner 7pm-9pm, bar meals 12noon-3pm, 6pm-10pm.

**Cuisine:** ENGLISH / FRENCH

**Cards:** Visa, Access.

**Other points:** licensed, Sunday lunch, children welcome, pets allowed, open bank holidays, conferences.

**Rooms:** 14 single rooms, 36 double rooms, 42 twin rooms, 12 family rooms, 6 suites. All with TV, radio, telephone, tea/coffee-making facilities, hair dryer.

**Directions:** A338 Wessex Way into Bournemouth, then follow signs to East Cliff.

DAVID BURR ☎(01202) 554415 Fax(01202) 294810

### TROUVILLE HOTEL
Priory Road, West Cliff, BH2 5DH

*Centrally situated within walking distance of all the main amenities in Bournemouth, the Trouville provides high standards of food and accommodation. The restaurant overlooks the town and offers first-class table d'hôte cuisine, excellently presented and served in pleasant and relaxed surroundings. The leisure facilities include a sauna, trymnasium, spa pool, indoor swimming pool and solarium.*

DOUBLE ROOM: from £40 to £43

SINGLE ROOM: from £40 to £43

FOOD: from £15 to £20    `CLUB`

**Hours:** breakfast 7.30am-9.15am, lunch 12.15am-1.45pm, dinner 7pm-8.30pm.

**Cuisine:** ENGLISH - dishes may include cubes of salmon, monkfish and scampi in tarragon cream and a flaky pastry case, braised Scotch steak, roast loin of pork.

**Cards:** Visa, Access, Diners, AmEx.

**Other points:** licensed, Sunday lunch, no-smoking area, children welcome, afternoon tea, residents' lounge, pets allowed, leisure centre, conferences, 24hr reception, baby-listening device, baby-sitting, cots, residents' bar.

**Rooms:** 10 single rooms, 21 double rooms, 24 twin rooms, 23 family rooms, 1 suite. All with TV, telephone, tea/coffee-making facilities, hair dryer.

**Directions:** adjacent to Bournemouth International Centre. Very central.

JOHN C. HARPER ☎(01202) 552262 Fax(01202) 293324

## BRIDPORT • map 4D5

### BRITMEAD HOUSE
West Bay Road, DT6 4EG

*A small licensed hotel in the heart of West Dorset with a reputation for friendliness, hospitality and high standards. The spacious south-west facing dining room and lounge overlook an attractive garden with views of the Dorset Coastal Path. The creative menu which uses local fresh produce where possible and changes daily, is complemented by a carefully selected range of well-priced wines.*

DOUBLE ROOM: from £20 to £30

SINGLE ROOM: from £25 to £30

FOOD: up to £15

**Hours:** breakfast 8.15am-9.15am, dinner 7pm.

**Cuisine:** daily, varied menus

**Cards:** Visa, Access, Diners, AmEx.

**Other points:** licensed, parking, private restaurant, children catered for (please check for age limits).

**Rooms:** 7 double rooms. All en suite, with TV, radio, tea/coffee making facilities and hairdryers.

**Directions:** From the A35 south of Bridport, turn off at the Crown Inn roundabout, going south towards West Bay, Britmead House on right.

ANN & DAN WALKER ☎(01308) 422941

### THE GEORGE INN
Chideock, DT6 6JD

*A 16th century thatched inn offering an extensive menu with daily extras and prices to suit all pockets. Restaurant, beer garden, family room with pool, darts and skittles. A true local welcome is assured in this very popular Dorset pub. Reservations are advisable.*

FOOD: up to £15

**Hours:** lunch 12noon-2pm, dinner 6.45pm-9.30pm, open all year.

**Cuisine:** ENGLISH - specialities: omelettes with various fillings, steaks including massive mixed grill, salads, fish, gammon, pasta dishes, vegetarian menu. Daily specials, e.g., venison, lamb, trout. Popular 'sizzler' meals. Heartbeat Award. Good Beer Guide, Good Pub Guide.

**Cards:** Visa, Access, Switch, MasterCard, Delta.

**Other points:** licensed, open-air dining, Sunday

lunch, children catered for (please check for age limits), pets allowed.
**Directions:** on the A35, 2 miles west of Bridport in the east of Chideock.
MIKE & MARILYN TUCK ☎(01297) 489419

 **HADDON HOUSE HOTEL**
West Bay, DT6 4EL
*Regency-style 3-star country house hotel with a reputation for fine cuisine. Situated approximately 300 yards from the picturesque harbour and coast of West Bay, overlooking Dorset's beautiful countryside. Amenities available to visitors include deep-sea fishing, riding, tennis and 18-hole golf course opposite hotel. Ideally situated for touring Dorset, Devon and Somerset.*
DOUBLE ROOM: from £25 to £33
FOOD: from £10 to £20
**Hours:** breakfast 7.45am-9.15am, lunch 12noon-1.30pm, dinner 7pm-9pm.
**Cuisine:** ENGLISH - fresh local fish, grills, own-lable wines.
**Cards:** Visa, Access, Diners, AmEx.
**Other points:** Sunday lunch, children welcome, coaches by prior arrangement, residents' bar.
**Rooms:** 2 single rooms, 6 double rooms, 3 twin rooms, 2 family rooms. All with TV, radio, alarm, telephone, tea/coffee making facilities, heating, hair dryer, trouser-press.
**Directions:** .5 mile south of main A35 at Bridport. Follow signs to West Bay.
PAUL & HELEN LOUD ☎(01308) 423626/425323
Fax(01308) 427348

## CHARMOUTH • map 4D5

 **HENSLEIGH HOTEL**
Lower Sea Lane, DT6 6LW
*A comfortable, well-equipped, family-run hotel in a quiet position. A friendly, homely atmosphere is complemented by good home-cooking using local produce. The rolling hills of Dorset and stunning cliff walks are on the doorstep.*
DOUBLE ROOM: from £21 to £30
SINGLE ROOM: from £21 to £30
FOOD: up to £15
**Hours:** breakfast 8am-9am, lunch 12noon-2pm, dinner 6.30pm-7.45pm, closed November until February.
**Cuisine:** ENGLISH
**Cards:** Visa, AmEx, MasterCard
**Other points:** central heating, children catered for (please check for age limits), pets allowed, residents' lounge.
**Rooms:** 2 single rooms, 3 double rooms, 4 twin rooms, 2 family rooms. All with en suite, TV, tea/coffee-making facilities.
**Directions:** midway between the village and beach, off the A35.
MALCOLM & MARY MACNAIR ☎(01297) 560830

 **NEWLANDS HOUSE**
Stonebarrow Lane, DT6 6RA
*A former 16th century farmhouse, family-run and situated in approximately 2 acres of garden and old orchard at the foot of Stonebarrow Hill, which is part of the National Trust Golden Cap Estate. Newlands House makes an ideal centre for walking and touring and is just minutes away from the famous fossil cliffs and beaches of Lyme Bay. Six miles east of Axminster. No smoking except in the bar lounge. Ample off-road parking for cars.*
DOUBLE ROOM: from £20 to £30
SINGLE ROOM: from £23
FOOD: up to £15
**Hours:** breakfast 8.30am-9.15am, dinner 7pm-7.30pm, open March to October.
**Cuisine:** ENGLISH / CONTINENTAL - home-produced dishes.
**Other points:** licensed, no-smoking areas, children catered for (please check for age limits), residents' lounges, garden.
**Rooms:** 3 single rooms, 4 double rooms, 3 twin rooms, 2 family rooms. All with TV, tea/coffee-making facilities.
**Directions:** via A35, 7 miles west of Bridport at foot of Stonebarrow Lane.
ANNE & VERNON VEAR ☎(01297) 560212

## CHIDEOCK • map 4D5

**CHIDEOCK HOUSE HOTEL**
Main Street, DT6 6JN
*This historic Tudor built house occupies a prime position in the centre of this charming village with its many nearby attractions. Now a privately run, licensed hotel, the en-suite rooms are furnished and decorated to a high standard. The attractive beamed bar and restaurant are open to non-residents and Anna and George Dunn and their staff will ensure that visitors' every need is well catered for. Highly recommended.*
DOUBLE ROOM: from £30 to £40
SINGLE ROOM: from £25 to £35
FOOD: from £15 to £20
**Hours:** breakfast 8am-9am, dinner 7pm-9pm, open bank holidays.
**Cuisine:** ENGLISH/FRENCH - excellent range of home-prepared dishes using fresh ingredients. Try the spinach and cheese soufflé as a starter! Wide choice of good wines with sensibly priced red and white house wine.
**Cards:** Visa, Access, Switch.
**Other points:** licensed, pets welcome (by arrangement), private parties, weddings and special occasions catered for, parking.
**Rooms:** 9 double rooms en suite. All with TV and tea/coffee-making facilities.
**Directions:** on the A35 road between Bridport and Lyme Regis.
ANNA & GEORGE DUNN ☎(01297) 489242
Fax(01297) 489184

## CHRISTCHURCH • map 5E2

### THE AMBERWOOD
154 Ringwood Road, Walkford,
BH23 5RQ
*A warm welcome is guaranteed at the Amberwood, a well-maintained and highly-recommended traditional pub/restaurant serving a wide and varied menu of home-cooked food. Speciality dishes include Lamb Wellington and localy-caught, fresh fish, Yvonne and David Anderson are superb hosts and extend a warm welcome to all visitors. Ideal when visiting the New Forest, Christchurch, Beaulieu Motor Museum and other nearby attractions.*
FOOD: up to £15
**Hours:** lunch 12noon-2.30pm, dinner 7pm-9.30pm, open bank holidays.
**Cuisine:** ENGLISH/CONTINENTAL
**Cards:** Access,Visa
**Other points:** children welcome, pets allowed, no-smoking area, open-air dining, traditional Sunday lunch, children's menu, afternoon teas, vegetarian meals, parking.
**Directions:** situated off the A35 Lyndhurst to Christchurch road, right into Ringwood Road by Cat and Fiddle pub.
MR AND MRS ANDERSON ☎(014562) 72627
Fax(01425) 274632

### THE COPPER SKILLET
17 Church Street, BH23 1BW
*A licensed steak house and family restaurant situated in the old part of Christchurch, close to the town quay, priory and castle ruins.*
FOOD: up to £15
**Hours:** meals all day 9am-9pm, closed Christmas day and Boxing Day.
**Cuisine:** ENGLISH - steaks and grills, weekly fresh fish and vegetarian specialities.
**Cards:** Visa, Access.
**Other points:** Sunday lunch, children welcome, coaches by prior arrangement
**Directions:** off main A35 into Christchurch High Street; take Church Street towards priory.
MICHAEL DEVALL ☎(01202) 485485 Fax(01202) 475866

### THE FISHERMAN'S HAUNT HOTEL
Salisbury Road, Winkton, BH23 7AS
*Superior 2-star/4-crowns country house hotel on the banks of the River Avon. The restaurant overlooks the river, and there is an attractive beer garden with children's play area. Situated on the edge of the New Forest. A freehouse serving real ales.*
DOUBLE ROOM: from £30 to £40
SINGLE ROOM: from £35 to £45
FOOD: from £15 to £20
**Hours:** breakfast 7.30am-9.30am, Sunday 8am-9.30am; lunch 12noon-2pm; dinner 7pm-10pm; bar 10am-2.30pm, 6pm-11pm, Sunday 12noon-3pm, 7pm-10.30pm; closed Christmas day.

**Cuisine:** ENGLISH - fresh Christchurch salmon, Avon trout, steak-and-kidney pie.
**Cards:** Visa, Access, Diners, AmEx.
**Other points:** licensed, open-air dining, Sunday lunch, children welcome.
**Rooms:** 20 bedrooms.
**Directions:** on the B3347 between Christchurch and Ringwood.
MR J. BOCHAN ☎(01202) 477283

### LE PETIT ST TROPEZ
3 Bridge Street, BH23 1DY
*The ambience, cuisine and service at Le Petit St Tropez combine to make dining here a special experience. This genuine French family-run restaurant has a choice of fixed-price or à la carte menu, including their own seasonal specialities.*
FOOD: up to £15
**Hours:** lunch 12noon, dinner 7pm.
**Cuisine:** FRENCH - traditional French from Provence. Seasonal specialities.
**Cards:** Visa, Access, AmEx.
**Other points:** open-air dining, children welcome, open bank holidays, functions.
**Directions:** between the two bridges, 100 metres from the civic offices.
MARCEL & DEBORAH DUVAL ☎(01202) 482522
Fax(01202) 470048

## DORCHESTER • map 4D5

### THE ACORN INN HOTEL
28 Fore Street, Evershot, DT2 0JW

*Dating from the 16th century, The Acorn Inn Hotel nestles in an unspoilt and peaceful village, set in the heart of Thomas Hardy's Dorset. A warm welcome awaits you from the resident owners and their friendly staff in this totally refurbished establishment. An imaginative à la carte menu is available, from plain and simple cooking to the diverse, using local produce when in season.*
DOUBLE ROOM: from £30 to £40
FOOD: up to £15
**Hours:** breakfast 8am-9.30am, lunch 12noon-2pm, dinner 6.30pm-9.45pm, open all year.
**Cuisine:** ENGLISH - dishes may include game bordeaux, pork Wellington, and duck with orange and Grand Marnier. Speciality main course changes daily. Excellent wine selection.
**Cards:** Visa, Access.
**Other points:** licensed, open-air dining, traditional Sunday lunch, no-smoking area, children welcome, residents' lounge, garden, pets allowed.

**Directions:** off A37 towards Evershot, in main street before church.
DENISE MORLEY ☎(01935) 83228

## JUDGE JEFFREYS RESTAURANT
6 High West Street, DT1 1UJ

*In 1685 the notorious Judge Jeffreys lodged at this famous Dorchester House during the time of `The Bloody Assize'. Today the original beamed building houses a restaurant, which provides very good food and polite, friendly service. Highly recommended for its warm welcome, good food and value-for-money prices.*

**FOOD:** up to £15
**Hours:** morning coffee 9.30am-12noon, lunch 12noon-2.30pm, afternoon tea 2.30pm-5pm, dinner 7pm-9.30pm.
**Cuisine:** ENGLISH - wide range of lunchtime specials, which change daily. Evening à la carte menu. Morning coffee and afternoon teas.
**Cards:** Visa, Access.
**Other points:** licensed, no-smoking area, children welcome, pets allowed, afternoon tea.
**Directions:** in centre of town on main road. Public car parks nearby.
IAN & PAT MCLELLAN ☎(01305) 264369

## THE MANOR HOTEL
Beach Road, West Bexington, DT2 9DF

*17th century manor house 500 yards from Chesil Beach. Panoramic views from most bedrooms of unspoilt Dorset coastline. Three real ales served in character cellar bar. Log fires. Private dining room for up to 40. Facilities for conferences, buffets, receptions.*

**DOUBLE ROOM:** from £30 to £40
**SINGLE ROOM:** from £35 to £45
**FOOD:** from £15 to £20
**Hours:** breakfast 8.30am-9.30am, lunch 12noon-2pm, dinner 7pm-10pm.
**Cuisine:** ENGLISH / SEAFOOD - local seafood and imaginative dishes.
**Cards:** Visa, Access, Diners, AmEx.
**Other points:** licensed, Sunday lunch, children welcome, parking.
**Rooms:** 1 single room, 9 double rooms, 3 twin rooms. All with TV, radio, telephone, tea/coffee-making facilities.
**Directions:** on the B3157 Bridport to Weymouth coast road.
RICHARD & JAYNE A. CHILDS ☎(01308) 897616
Fax (01308) 897035

## NEW INN
West Knighton, DT2 8PE

*Attractive old pub with hanging baskets and jasmine creeper. Cheerful, relaxed atmosphere. Efficient service provided by friendly staff.*

**FOOD:** up to £15
**Hours:** lunch 12noon-2pm, dinner 7pm-9pm, open all year.
**Cuisine:** ENGLISH - well-cooked traditional pub

food. Wide selection. Sunday lunches and sizzling dishes a speciality. Extensive specials board. Vegetarian menu.
**Cards:** Visa, Access.
**Other points:** licensed, open-air dining, Sunday lunch, children welcome, pets allowed.
**Directions:** situated off the A352 Wareham road at West Knighton.
ROGER & JULIA GILBEY ☎(01305) 852349

## THE RED LION
Winfrith, DT2 8LE

*A fully-licensed country hotel combining charm with modern comforts. A superb and varied menu is available in the restaurant and bar meals are also available. All rooms are comfortable and well-equipped with most facilities. There is a children's play area and a large function room for private parties. Many tourist attractions nearby.*

**DOUBLE ROOM:** from £20 to £30
**FOOD:** up to £15
**Hours:** breakfast 7am-9.30am, lunch and bar meals 12noon-2pm, dinner and bar meals 6.30pm-9.30pm, open all year including Sunday.
**Cuisine:** ENGLISH - a superb varied menu offering everything from a sandwich to an a la carte restaurant meal, including home-made dishes, daily specials and Sunday roasts.
**Cards:** Access,Visa,AmEx,Diners
**Other points:** children welcome, no-smoking area, traditional Sunday lunch, vegetarian meals, afternoon teas, beer garden, childrens play area with swings, satellite television in public bar, parking.
**Rooms:** 1 double room, 1 twin room, 2 family rooms (1 en suite). All with TV and tea/coffee-making facilities.
**Directions:** A352 Wareham to Dorchester road, just beyond Winfrith.
MR AND MRS ROBBBINS ☎(01305) 852814

## WESSEX ROYALE HOTEL
32 High Street, DT1 1UP

*Dating back to the 1600s, the hotel was originally built as a town house for the Earl of Ilchester. The hotel has been substantially refurbished to provide a friendly, relaxing atmosphere. The generously proportioned rooms have feature fireplaces. Bedrooms are attractively furnished with many modern facilities, and the restaurant offers a high standard of continental and English cuisine. A conservatory is available for banquets and weddings for up to 100 people. Ideal location for the leisure traveller exploring Dorset.*

**DOUBLE ROOM:** from £20 to £30
**SINGLE ROOM:** up to £25
**FOOD:** up to £15
**Hours:** breakfast 7.30am-9.30am, dinner 6.30pm-9.30pm.
**Cuisine:** ENGLISH / CONTINENTAL
**Cards:** Visa, Access, Diners, AmEx, MasterCard, Switch, Delta.
**Other points:** children welcome, no-smoking area,

residents' lounge, garden, pets, vegetarian meals, open bank holidays.
**Rooms:** 2 single rooms, 16 double rooms, 5 twin rooms.
**Directions:** on main road in centre of Dorchester. MR M. BOWLEY ☎(01305) 262660 Fax (01305) 251941

## HAMWORTHY • map 4D6

### THE YACHTSMAN
Lake Road, BH15 4LN
*A traditional inn/restaurant, situated one mile from the historical town of Poole. An interesting and varied menu offering fresh food is available daily. Children are welcome and a large play area is provided. David and Julie extend a warm, friendly welcome to all visitors.*
**FOOD:** up to £15
**Hours:** lunch and bar meals 12noon-2.30pm, dinner and bar meals 7-10pm, open bank holidays, all day opening including Sunday.
**Cuisine:** ENGLISH/CONTINENTAL - steaks, fish and meat dishes, vegetarian and children's choices, speciality coffees, traditional Sunday roast.
**Cards:** Access,Visa,AmEx,Diners
**Other points:** children welcome, no-smoking area, open-air dining, afternoon teas, traditional Sunday lunch, vegetarian meals, parking.
**Directions:** A350 Blandford road, follow signs for Hockley Park Holiday Centre, near Harmworthy Beach.
MR & MRS WOODROFFE ☎(01202) 674568

## LONGHAM • map 4C6

### ANGEL INN
Near Wimborne, BH22 9AD
*Situated on the busy A438 road from Ferndown to Poole or Wimborne Minster. The menu is varied and quite extensive, with the emphasis on fresh, well-cooked, generous portions of food. The inn offers a large beer garden at the rear, a children's play area with an additional area for children to eat, and plenty of car parking where you are welcome to park your car while enjoying one of the many interesting walks nearby.*
**FOOD:** up to £15
**Hours:** lunch 12noon-2pm, dinner 6pm-9.30pm.
**Cuisine:** ENGLISH - Dorset pâté, steak-and-kidney pie, steaks, daily specials.
**Cards:** Visa, Access.
**Other points:** Sunday lunch, children welcome, garden, playland.
**Directions:** on the A348 road from Ferndown to Poole, or approach from the A31 Southampton to Poole road.
MR B. SIMS ☎(01202) 873778

**Join Les Routiers Discovery Club FREE! See page 34 for details.**

## LULWORTH COVE • map 4D6

### MILL HOUSE HOTEL & BISHOP'S COTTAGE
West Lulworth, Wareham, BH20 5RQ

*At one time the Bishop of Salisbury's home, the house stands in its own grounds on the edge of the Cove and is sheltered by Bindon Hill. The grounds have direct access to coastal heritage cliffs and the Cove.*
DOUBLE ROOM: from £20 to £30
SINGLE ROOM: from £20
**FOOD:** up to £15
**Hours:** bar meals 12noon-2.30pm, bar meals 6pm-10pm, breakfast 8am-9.30am, dinner, 6pm-10pm, lunch 12noon-2.30pm, open all year.
**Cuisine:** SEAFOOD - seafood, local fish, vegetarian dishes.
**Cards:** Visa, Access, MasterCard.
**Other points:** licensed, Sunday lunch, children welcome, swimming pool, pets allowed.
**Rooms:** 3 single rooms, 21 double rooms, 2 family rooms. All with TV, radio, telephone, tea/coffee-making facilities, baby-listening device.
**Directions:** overlooking Lulworth Cove.
MRS SUSAN FIRMSTONE ☎(01929) 400261/400404

## LYME REGIS • map 4D5

### BELL CLIFF RESTAURANT
5-6 Broad Street, DT 3QD
*A small, homely restaurant, slightly Dickensian in appearance, with excellent service, quality and ambience. The building dates from the 16th century and was used in the film The French Lieutenant's Woman as the `Old Fossil Depot'. Well placed in the centre of town and popular with both locals and holidaymakers.*
**FOOD:** up to £15
**Hours:** meals all day: summer 8.30am-6pm, winter 9am-5pm.
**Cuisine:** ENGLISH - home-cooking: specialities include home-made sweets and cakes.
**Other points:** licensed, Sunday lunch, children welcome, disabled access, pets allowed, afternoon tea, parking.
**Directions:** off A35 on A3052 or A3070. At sea end of main thoroughfare (A3052).
RICHARD & AUDREY EVANS ☎(01297) 442459

**HOTEL BUENA VISTA**
Pound Street, DT7 3HZ
*A Regency style house, situated in its own grounds in a superb position on a beautiful stretch of coastline. There is a distinct country house atmosphere and guests can relax in a choice of lounges or their own cosy bar. Interestingly, the hotel looks straight onto the Cobb; featured so prominently in the film "The French Lieutenant's Woman."*
DOUBLE ROOM: from £31 to £45
SINGLE ROOM: from £35 to £40
FOOD: up to £20
**Hours:** breakfast 8.30am-9.30am, dinner 7pm-8pm, open bank holidays.
**Cuisine:** ENGLISH - daily menus offering a wide range of dishes.
**Cards:** Visa, Access, Diners, AmEx, Switch.
**Other points:** licensed, parking, room service available.
**Rooms:** 4 single rooms, 9 double rooms, 4 twin rooms, 1 family room. All en suite, with TV, radio, telephone, tea/coffee making facilities.
**Directions:** take the A3052 leading out of Lyme Regis towards Exeter, on the edge of the town.
MR & MRS GORDON FORSYTH, MR & MRS FRANK MEADOWS ☎(01297) 442494

 **KERSBROOK HOTEL & RESTAURANT**
Pound Road, DT7 3HX
*A thatched 18th century listed house, set in its own gardens overlooking Lyme Bay. Carefully modernized to retain the original character of the building and to offer a high level of comfort and convenience. The food is of a good standard, and the restaurant boasts an extensive wine list for every occasion.*
DOUBLE ROOM: from £30 to £40
SINGLE ROOM: from £45 to £55
FOOD: from £15 to £20 **CLUB**
**Hours:** breakfast 8.30am-9.30am, lunch 12.15am-2.15pm, dinner 7.30pm-9pm.
**Cuisine:** ENGLISH / CONTINENTAL - full à la carte menu and table d'hôte.
**Cards:** Visa, Access, AmEx, Switch.
**Other points:** licensed, residents' lounge, garden.
**Rooms:** 10 bedrooms.
**Directions:** from main Lyme Regis-Exeter road, turn right opposite main car park.
ERIC HALL STEPHENSON ☎(01297) 442596
**Fax**(01297) 442596

 **ROYAL LION HOTEL**
Broad Street, DT7 3QF

*A 17th century coaching inn with 30 en suite bedrooms, indoor heated pool and central parking. Apart from being the home town of many writers, artists and artisans, Lyme Regis is famous as the location of United Artists' The French Lieutenant's Woman.*
SINGLE ROOM: from £30 to £40
FOOD: up to £15
**Hours:** breakfast 8.30am-9.30am, lunch 12noon-2pm, dinner 6.30pm-9.30pm.
**Cuisine:** TRADITIONAL - table d'hôte and à la carte.
**Cards:** Visa, Access, Diners, AmEx, Switch.
**Other points:** children welcome, coaches by prior arrangement, large games room.
**Rooms:** 30 bedrooms. All ensuite with TV, telephone, tea/coffee-making facilities.
**Directions:** in the centre of Lyme Regis.
MR & MRS B.A. SIENESI ☎(01297) 445622/442014

## POOLE • map 4D6

 **ALLANS SEAFOOD RESTAURANT**
8 Bournemouth Road, BH14 OES
*A small seafood restaurant offering extremely fresh, perfectly prepared seafood of all types. The exterior is unpretentious and the interior has the feel of a French rural restaurant, in keeping with the very helpful, friendly service. Considering the high cost of seafood, this restaurant offers excellent value for money. Highly recommended.*
FOOD: from £15 to £20 ☞
**Hours:** lunch 12noon-2pm, dinner 6.30pm till late.
**Cuisine:** SEAFOOD - fresh local fish, fresh lobster and crab, all year. Alternative dishes include steaks, veal, duck and chicken. Special lunch menu.
**Cards:** Visa, Access, Switch.
**Other points:** licensed, street parking, upstairs bar, patio.
**Directions:** main Bournemouth-Poole road (A35).
A.D. TOMLINSON ☎(01202) 741489

 **CORKERS CAFE BAR & RESTAURANT**
1 High Street, The Quay, BH15 1AB
*Adjacent to and overlooking Poole harbour and quay, the ground floor is a bistro and café-bar, the first floor a licensed restaurant and the second floor bed & breakfast accommodation.*
DOUBLE ROOM: up to £25
FOOD: from £15 to £20
**Hours:** lunch 12noon-2pm, dinner 7pm-11pm, café-bar 8am-12midnight, café-bar Sunday 8am-10.30pm.
**Cuisine:** ENGLISH / SEAFOOD - seafood a speciality.
**Cards:** Visa, Access, Diners, AmEx.
**Other points:** disabled access, children welcome.
**Rooms:** 5 double rooms.
**Directions:** adjacent to quayside, with good views of the waterfront and sea-going vessels.
ANTONIO OPPO ☎(01202) 681393 **Fax**(01202) 667393

### THE DARBY'S CORNER
Waterloo Road, BH17 7LD

*Situated on the main Wimborne to Poole road, this is a most attractive pub/restaurant offering a varied choice of English and continental cuisine.One feature of the spacious, attractively furnished interior is an interesting Library room for non-smokers, full of shelves and shelves of books. Attracts a wide clientele.*

**FOOD:** up to £15
**Hours:** lunch and bar meals 12noon-3pm, dinner 7pm-10pm, bar meals 6pm-9.30pm, open all year including Sunday.
**Cuisine:** ENGLISH / CONTINENTAL - good selection of steaks, double platters, vegetarian and vegan choices, sweets and puddings, breakfast menu.
**Cards:** Access,Visa,AmEx,Diners
**Other points:** children welcome, no-smoking area, open-air dining, traditional Sunday lunch, parking.
**Directions:** situated on the A349 main Wimborne road from Poole.
MR AND MRS COLLINS ☎(01202) 693780

### THE GREENRIDGE
1 Dorchester Road, Upton, BH16 5NJ

*The Greenridge is a large, well-run pub/restaurant located on the old road from Poole to Dorchester and an ideal stop-off for travellers and holiday-makers. The restaurant offers a varied menu of well-cooked and presented English and continental dishes at excellent value for money. There is a good, spacious bar and the dining room is also tastefully furnished.*

**FOOD:** up to £15
**Hours:** lunch and bar meals 12noon-3pm, dinner and bar meals 6.30pm-10pm, open all year including Sunday.
**Cuisine:** ENGLISH / CONTINENTAL - popular home-made dishes, vegetarian and children's menus, interesting wine list.
**Cards:** Access,Visa,AmEx,Diners
**Other points:** children welcome, no-smoking area, open-air dining, traditional Sunday lunch, parking.
**Directions:** A350 Poole to Blandford road, situated by roundabout at Upton crossroads.
MR AND MRS HODGES ☎(01202) 622325

### HAVEN HOTEL
Banks Road, Sandbanks, BH13 7QL

*An attractive hotel standing on the seafront, with magnificent views across to the Purbeck Hills and*

*Poole Harbour. Like its sister hotels, the Sandbanks and Chine, an informal atmosphere reigns despite its size and sophistication. The Haven Hotel has a purpose-built sports and leisure centre, and a self-contained business centre complex.*

**DOUBLE ROOM:** from £60
**SINGLE ROOM:** from £60
**FOOD:** from £20 to £25
**Hours:** breakfast 8am-9.45am, brasserie 10am-6pm, lunch 12.30am-2pm, dinner 7pm-9.30pm..
**Cuisine:** ENGLISH / INTERNATIONAL - traditional and international cuisine. `La Roche', the hotel's gourmet restaurant, is open 6 days a week (dinner only).
**Cards:** Visa, Access, Diners, AmEx, Switch.
**Other points:** licensed, Sunday lunch, vegetarian meals, residents' lounge, residents' bar, leisure club.
**Rooms:** 18 single rooms, 39 double rooms, 32 twin rooms, 3 quad rooms, 2 family rooms. All with satellite TV, telephone, tea/coffee-making facilities, hair dryer, trouser-press.
**Directions:** from Bournemouth and Poole, follow Sandbanks signs. The hotel is adjacent to the ferry in the Sandbanks area of Poole.
J. BUTTERWORTH ☎(01202) 707333 Fax(01202) 708796

### THE KINGS HEAD
High Street, BH15 1BP

*A traditional 17th century inn, set in a historical area close to Poole quayside. A high standard of English and continental dishes are available, including a large selection of locally-caught fresh fish. The atmosphere is extremely welcoming which makes this a popular venue with both locals and holiday-makers alike.*

**FOOD:** up to £15
**Hours:** lunch and bar meals 12noon-3pm, dinner and bar meals 7pm-10pm, open bank holidays, all day opening May to September including Sunday.
**Cuisine:** ENGLISH / CONTINENTAL - daily home-made specials, traditional Sunday roast, summer barbeques, fish specialities.
**Cards:** Access,Visa,AmEx,Diners
**Other points:** children welcome, no-smoking area, open-air dining, vegetarian meals, senior citizen's special lunch menu.
**Directions:** situated at the end of Poole high street, on the quay.
MR AND MRS POLLARD ☎(01202) 674919

### THE ROSE & CROWN
Wareham Road, Lytchett Matravers, BH16 6DT

*Situated in the centre of the village, this traditional pub has a true country atmosphere and a menu to match. Freshly-cooked, wholesome food, including old favourites, such as steak-and-kidney pie, all prepared on the premises. Bar snacks are also available throughout the day. Situated within easy reach of endless tourist attractions and places to visit.*

**FOOD:** up to £15 🔗 CLUB

**Hours:** lunch and bar meals 12noon-2pm, dinner and bar meals 7pm-9.30pm, open bank holidays, all day opening including Sunday.
**Cuisine:** TRADITIONAL ENGLISH - wholesome fare, Sunday carvery includes beef, pork, lamb, or chicken, Bombay curry nights, blackboard specials.
**Cards:** Access, Visa, AmEx, Diners
**Other points:** children welcome, traditional Sunday lunch/carvery, vegetarian meals, parking.
**Directions:** A35 Dorchester road, left at traffic island, onto A350 Blandford road, turn left for Lytchett Minster.
MR AND MRS FORREST ☎(01202) 625325

### SANDBANKS HOTEL
15 Banks Road, Sandbanks, BH13 7PS
*Sandbanks Hotel occupies a superb position right on the award winning beach, with lovely views of the sea and Poole harbour. A large, fully-equipped hotel with the atmosphere and charm of a smaller establishment.*
DOUBLE ROOM: from £40 to £50
SINGLE ROOM: from £40 to £50
FOOD: from £15 to £20 CLUB
**Hours:** breakfast 8am-9.45am, lunch 12.30am-2pm, brasserie (seasonal) 10am-6pm, dinner 7pm-9pm.
**Cuisine:** ENGLISH - table d'hôte menu changes daily: steaks, game, fish dishes. A la carte restaurant also available.
**Cards:** Visa, Access, Diners, AmEx.
**Other points:** licensed, Sunday lunch, children welcome, garden.
**Rooms:** 105 bedrooms.
**Directions:** from Bournemouth, follow signs to Sandbanks ferry. On the seafront.
JOHN R. BELK ☎(01202) 707377 Fax(01202) 708885

### WATMOUGH'S RESTAURANT
5 Albert Road, Upper Parkstone, BH12 2BT
*This attractive, charming and comfortable restaurant offers a wide choice of cuisine for both lunch and dinner. All food is prepared to order using fresh produce, including locally caught fish and vegetarian meals are always available.*
FOOD: from £15 to £20
**Hours:** lunch Tuesday to Friday 11.30am-2pm, dinner Monday to Saturday from 7.30pm.
**Cuisine:** ENGLISH / FRENCH - varying menus offer a wide selection of dishes, including vegetarian choices, with daily blackboard specials. Dishes may include steak with stilton, port and mushroom sauce, filled spicy tortillas and seafoods.
**Cards:** Visa, Access, Diners, AmEx, Switch.
**Other points:** parties welcome for private funtions, buffets or gourmet dinners, vegetarian meals.
**Directions:** the restaurant is on Albert Road, off Ashley Road, Upper Parkstone Poole Key and Purbeck Hill.
PHILIP AND JANE WATMOUGH
☎(01202) 741207

### THE BENETT ARMS
Semley, SP7 9AS
*Built in the 17th century, The Benett Arms overlooks the village green. A choice of freshly cooked, interesting meals and knowledgeable advice on wine make this traditional pub extremely popular with both locals and many foreign travellers. In summer, you can enjoy a barbecue on the common itself. Special events such as steam rallies, jazz bands, etc. are sometimes organized.*
DOUBLE ROOM: from £20 to £30
SINGLE ROOM: from £25 to £35
FOOD: from £15 to £20 CLUB
**Hours:** breakfast 8.30am-9.30am, lunch 12noon-2pm, dinner 7pm-10pm.
**Cuisine:** ENGLISH / CONTINENTAL - dishes in the restaurant may include steaks, chicken trois frères, traditional bar meals in the bar.
**Cards:** Visa, Access, Diners, AmEx.
**Other points:** licensed, Sunday lunch, children welcome, garden, pets allowed, vegetarian meals, parking, residents' bar, disabled access, residents' lounge.
**Rooms:** 1 twin room, 4 double rooms. All with TV, telephone, tea/coffee-making facilities.
**Directions:** 2 miles off the A350, north of Shaftesbury. Turn right to Semley (1 mile).
J.C.M. DUTHIE ☎(01747) 830221 Fax(01747) 830152

### THE WHITE HORSE
Shaston Road, DT11 8TA
*Situated in a very attractive Dorset village on a main route to Shaftesbury, The White Horse is well known and respected for well-prepared, fresh country food. The menu is varied and is complemented by a good wine list. A warm welcome awaits everyone calling at this public house for a full meal, a snack or just a drink.*
DOUBLE ROOM: from £20 to £30
SINGLE ROOM: up to £20
FOOD: up to £15
**Hours:** lunch 12noon-2pm, dinner 7pm-10pm.
**Cuisine:** ENGLISH - all dishes on the varied menu are prepared to a very high standard.
**Other points:** children welcome, pets allowed, no-smoking area, garden, open-air dining, vegetarian meals, traditional Sunday lunch.
**Rooms:** 1 double room, 1 twin room.
**Directions:** located on the A350 between Blandford Forum and Shaftesbury.
JOHN & MARILYN HURLOW ☎(01258) 453535

### FAIRFIELDS HOTEL
Swanage Road, BH19 3AE
*This family-run and fully-renovated hotel is situated in a most scenic part of Dorset and is well situated*

*to visit Corfe Castle, Swanage and Poole and Bournemouth via the Sandbanks car ferry (3 miles). The 10 comfortable bedrooms are well furnished and some have superb views of the surrounding countryside and coastline. Good home-cooking using vegetables and herbs from the garden ensures that you will have a memorable stay at a very reasonable price.*

DOUBLE ROOM: from £20 to £30
SINGLE ROOM: from £20 to £30
FOOD: up to £15
**Hours:** breakfast 8am-9am, dinner 7pm-7.30pm. Closed during January and February.
**Cuisine:** excellent 4-course table d'hôte dinners featuring home-grown vegatables and herbs. Menu changed regularly.
**Cards:** Access, Visa,
**Other points:** parking, licenced, packed lunches prepared to order, children welcome, garden.
**Rooms:** 2 single rooms, 4 double rooms, 4 family rooms, all en suite with tea/coffee maker, some with sea views.
**Directions:** at entrance to Studland village on B3351 from Swanage or Corfe Castle. 3 miles from Sandbanks car ferry.
MATT & NIKI PARSONS ☎(01929) 450224

### THE MANOR HOUSE
Beach Road, Studland Bay, BH19 3AU

*An 18th century Gothic manor in 20 acres of secluded, mature grounds with two tennis courts, overlooking the sea and 3 miles of sandy beach. The house has been in the Rose family since 1950 and has been fully modernized whilst retaining the original features and character. Wonderful coastal walks.*

DOUBLE ROOM: from £30 to £40
SINGLE ROOM: from £35 to £45
FOOD: from £15 to £20   CLUB
**Hours:** breakfast 8.30am-9.30am, lunch 12noon-2pm, dinner 7pm-8.30pm, closed 15th December until 28th December.
**Cuisine:** ENGLISH - local venison, duckling and fresh local seafood. There is a large terrace outside where bar meals may be served - weather permitting.
**Cards:** Visa, Access.
**Other points:** Sunday lunch, children catered for (please check for age limits), golf nearby, tennis, residents' lounge, residents' bar.
**Rooms:** 6 double rooms, 6 twin rooms, 2 triple rooms, 6 quad rooms. All with TV, radio, telephone, tea/coffee-making facilities.
**Directions:** 3 miles from Swanage, 3 miles from Sandbanks ferry.

MR RICHARD ROSE ☎(01929) 450288
Fax (01929) 450288

### HAVENHURST HOTEL
Cranborne Road, BH19 1EA
*A comfortable hotel standing in its own grounds, just a short stroll from the shops, the safe, sandy beach and all other amenities. With good home-cooked food, a comfortable lounge bar and a spacious colour TV lounge, Havenhurst also offers a high standard of accommodation. The proprietors extend a warm and friendly welcome to all guests.*
DOUBLE ROOM: from £20 to £30
SINGLE ROOM: from £20 to £35
FOOD: up to £15
**Hours:** breakfast 8.30am-9.15am, bar meals 12noon-2pm, dinner 7pm.
**Cuisine:** ENGLISH
**Other points:** children welcome, garden, afternoon tea, TV lounge, hair dryers.
**Rooms:** 3 single rooms, 8 double rooms, 4 twin rooms, 2 family rooms. All with TV, tea/coffee-making facilities.
**Directions:** close to the beach, off Rempstone Road.
MRS P.M. CHERRETT & MRS N.J. ROBSON
☎(01929) 424224

### MOWLEM RESTAURANT
Shore Road, BH19 1DD
*Situated on the beach road, with views over the beach and bay. Very popular with families, as it has a special children's menu, and everyone can enjoy watching their meals being prepared in front of them.*
FOOD: from £15 to £20
**Hours:** lunch 12noon-2pm, dinner 7pm-10pm, open Christmas day.
**Cuisine:** ENGLISH - seafood, steaks, salads, children's menu.
**Cards:** Visa, Access.
**Other points:** Sunday lunch, children welcome, coaches by prior arrangement
**Directions:** on the beach road.
MICHAEL POLLARD ☎(01929) 422496

### THE ROSE & CROWN
Near Sherborne, DT9 4SL
*A 16th century part-thatched freehouse, which could have been plucked from a picture postcard. There are three open fires and stone floors - a traditional atmosphere in which to sample fine ales and cider and tasty home-cooked food, without the intrusion of juke-boxes or fruit machines. Won national awards for cuisine in 1989 and 1990. Children are especially welcome here - there is a children's room where food is available and a playground at the rear of the premises.*
FOOD: up to £15
**Hours:** lunch 12noon-1.45pm, bar meals 12noon-

2pm, dinner 7pm-9pm, bar meals 7pm-9.30pm, closed Christmas day.
**Cuisine:** INTERNATIONAL - fish and game, using local ingredients. The menu changes weekly. Specialities: Cajun and Creole cuisine from Louisiana.
**Cards:** Visa, Access, AmEx.
**Other points:** licensed, open-air dining, Sunday lunch, children welcome, children's room, play area, pets allowed, no-smoking area.
**Directions:** A30 between Sherborne and Yeovil, take Trent turn, approximately 1-2 miles.
MR C.F. MARION-CRAWFORD ☎(01935) 850776

## WEST LULWORTH • map 4D6

### THE CASTLE INN
Main Street, BH20 5RN
*A charming thatched building dating back to the 1600s and close to the famous Lulworth Cove. The large garden is very popular - barbecues are held in summer.*
DOUBLE ROOM: from £20 to £30
SINGLE ROOM: from £20 to £30
FOOD: up to £15
**Hours:** breakfast 8am-9.30am, lunch 12noon-2.30pm, dinner 7.30pm-10pm, bar meals 11am-2.30pm, 7pm 10.30pm.
**Cuisine:** ENGLISH - home-made raised pies, fillet Stilton, spicy lamb, pork in whisky.
**Cards:** Visa, Access, Diners, AmEx.
**Other points:** licensed, open-air dining, Sunday lunch, children welcome, coaches by prior arrangement.
**Rooms:** 2 single rooms, 10 double rooms, 3 twin rooms, 1 family room.
**Directions:** on the B3070 road from Wareham, in the centre of West Lulworth.
GRAHAM & PATRICIA HALLIDAY ☎(01929) 400311

## WEYMOUTH • map 4D5

### ALESSANDRIA HOTEL AND ITALIAN RESTAURANT
71 Wakeham, Easton, Portland, DT5 1HW
*An excellent family-run hotel and Italian restaurant, ideally situated to explore Portland's historic interests. yet close to the beach and shopping centre of Weymouth and the beautiful Dorset coast. Accommodation is of a very high standard, and the à la carte menu offers a wide range of traditional Italian, English and French dishes.*
DOUBLE ROOM: from £20 to £30
SINGLE ROOM: from £25 to £35
FOOD: from £15 to £20 ⌙CLUB
**Hours:** breakfast 7.30am-9.30am, dinner 7pm-9pm.
**Cuisine:** CONTINENTAL / ENGLISH - all fresh produce, cooked to order by Giovanni, chef and proprietor for 30 years, with 5-star experience. Most salads and vegetables from their own garden.
**Cards:** Visa, Access, Diners, AmEx.
**Other points:** parking, children welcome, open

bank holidays, disabled access, residents' lounge, vegetarian meals, residents' bar.
**Rooms:** 4 single rooms, 7 double rooms, 3 twin rooms, 3 family rooms. All with TV, tea/coffee-making facilities.
**Directions:** from Weymouth, take the A354 main road for Portland.
GIOVANNI BISOGNO ☎(01305) 822270/820108
Fax(01305) 820561

### THE CHATSWORTH
14 The Esplanade, DT4 8EB
*An attractive Georgian building with excellent views over Weymouth Bay, the sands to the front, and the picturesque harbour to the rear. The Chatsworth offers a friendly and comfortable base for short breaks and family holidays. All the amenities of an English seaside town are nearby, and it is an ideal centre from which to tour Hardy's Dorset.*
DOUBLE ROOM: from £20
SINGLE ROOM: up to £30
FOOD: up to £15 ⌙
**Hours:** breakfast 8am-9am, dinner 6pm-7pm, closed Christmas.
**Cuisine:** ENGLISH
**Cards:** Visa, Access, AmEx.
**Other points:** central heating, children welcome, pets allowed, residents' lounge, garden.
**Rooms:** 9 bedrooms.
**Directions:** situated on The Esplanade, opposite Alexandra Gardens.
JACKIE & STAN ROBERTS ☎(01305) 785012
Fax(01305) 766342

### MOONFLEET MANOR
Moonfleet, DT3 4ED
*A complete resort hotel set in 5 acres of countryside by the sea. Many sports facilities including indoor pool, gymnasium, 4-rink indoor bowls hall, 9-pin automatic skittles, 2 tennis courts, 1 squash court, 2 snooker tables, children's indoor and outdoor play areas.*
DOUBLE ROOM: from £30 to £40
SINGLE ROOM: from £25 to £35
FOOD: up to £15
**Hours:** bar snacks 12noon-2pm, dinner 7pm-9pm.
**Cuisine:** ENGLISH - Trenchards: carvery, buffet, Sunday roasts, table d'hôte.
**Cards:** Visa, Access, Diners, AmEx.
**Other points:** licensed, Sunday lunch, no-smoking area, children welcome, vegetarian meals, parking, residents' bar, residents' lounge, disabled access.
**Rooms:** 38 bedrooms.
**Directions:** take the B3157 to Weymouth, turn towards sea at Chickerell.
JAN HEMINGWAY ☎(01305) 786948 Fax(01305) 774395

### SEA COW RESTAURANT
7 Custom House Quay, DT4 8BE
*With a prominent quayside position, this restaurant*

specializes in fresh fish and also offers a wide variety of meat, poultry and game. Very popular with visitors to this picturesque town.
FOOD: up to £20
Hours: lunch 12noon-2pm, dinner 7pm-10.15pm, fully licensed bar serving light meals and local seafood during lunch. A la carte dinner in the evenings.
Cuisine: ENGLISH - fresh mussels and scallops in season, fresh local lobster, oysters, skate, lemon sole. Game in season. Emphasis on local seafood.
Cards: Visa, Access, Eurocard, MasterCard.
Other points: Sunday lunch, children welcome, street parking, vegetarian meals, function facilities.
Directions: on the quayside.
MR & MRS T.M. WOOLCOCK ☎(01305) 783524

### THE SHIP INN RESTAURANT
Custom House Quay, DT4 8BE
Overlooking the harbour, this traditional quayside pub has an upstairs restaurant offering food at excellent value for money. There is also a children's menu and a wide range of home-cooked bar snacks.
FOOD: up to £15
Hours: lunch 12noon-2.30pm, Sunday 12noon-2.30pm, dinner 7pm-10pm. Open all day everyday for drinks.
Cuisine: ENGLISH / SEAFOOD - fresh local seafood when available.
Cards: Visa, Access, Diners, AmEx.
Other points: Sunday lunch, children welcome, large parties catered for.
Directions: on the quayside.
R. BALL ☎(01305) 773879

### SOU'WEST LODGE HOTEL
Rodwell Road, DT4 8QT
An extremely pleasant, well-kept hotel with first-class furnishings throughout. A warm, friendly atmosphere has been created by Michael and June Moxham, who will endeavour to make your stay enjoyable. There is a cosy, intimate bar to relax in at the end of the day.
DOUBLE ROOM: from £20 to £25
FOOD: up to £15
Hours: breakfast 7.30am-8.30am, dinner 6pm, last orders 3pm, closed Christmas.
Cuisine: ENGLISH
Other points: children welcome (children's rates), pets allowed, residents' lounge, patio.
Rooms: 5 double rooms, 1 twin room, 2 family rooms. All with en suite, TV, tea/coffee-making facilities.
Directions: situated off harbour road to Portland, over Boot Hill.
MICHAEL & JUNE MOXHAM ☎(01305) 783749

### SUNNINGDALE HOTEL
Preston Road, Preston, DT3 6QD
Set in one and half acres of grounds, with all bedrooms enjoying fine views over the gardens or fields. Only 600 yards from the sea, yet the heated outdoor swimming pool is always popular, especially with small children.
DOUBLE ROOM: from £20 to £30
SINGLE ROOM: from £20 to £30
FOOD: up to £15
Hours: breakfast 8.15am-9.15am, dinner 6.15pm-7.15pm, closed mid-October until March.
Cuisine: ENGLISH
Cards: Visa, Access, Diners.
Other points: children welcome, residents' lounge, garden, swimming pool, putting green, games room, pets allowed.
Rooms: 1 single room, 8 double rooms, 6 twin rooms, 5 family rooms. All with radio, tea/coffee-making facilities.
Directions: off the A353, through Preston village towards the sea.
MR & MRS TONY FLUX ☎(01305) 832179
Fax(01305) 832179

## WIMBORNE • map 4C6

### THE WORLD'S END
Almer, DT11 9EW
This attractive period restaurant is not only popular with most visitors to Dorset, but also locals from miles around who come to enjoy the superb English and continental fare and hearty, warm atmosphere. The area is rich in places to visit, such as Bovingdon Tank Museum and numerous pretty villages.
FOOD: up to £15
Hours: lunch and bar meals 12noon-2.30pm, dinner and bar meals 7pm-10.30pm, open bank holidays, all day opening May to September including Sunday.
Cuisine: ENGLISH / CONTINENTAL - lamb chops in honey and mint; scrumpy pork; braised beef in ale and mushrooms. Sweets include vanilla meringue with blackcurrants and cream; toffee cheesecake with chocolate fudge topping.
Cards: Access, Visa, AmEx, Diners
Other points: children welcome, no smoking area, open-air dining, traditional Sunday lunch, afternoon teas, vegetarian meals, parking.
Directions: on the A131 half way between Wimbourne Minster and Bere Regis.
MR AND MRS WALKEY ☎(01929) 45671

## WINTERBORNE ZELSTON • map 6C4

### THE BOTANY BAY INNE
DT11 9ET
A traditional 200-year-old inn where drinking and dining can be enjoyed on the large patio and seating area which looks out across open countryside at the rear. Children are always welcome. Frequented by locals, business people and holiday-makers of all ages.
FOOD: up to £15
Hours: lunch 12noon-2.30pm, dinner 6pm-10pm, open bank holidays, closed Christmas day.
Cuisine: varied menu available, including

vegetarian dishes.
**Cards:** Visa, Access, Diners, AmEx.
**Other points:** licensed, open-air dining.
**Directions:** A31 between Wimbourne Minster and Dorchester.
BADGER INNS ☎(01929) 459227

## WOOL • map 5E1

 **THE SHIP INN**
Dorchester Road, BH20 6EQ
*A delightful country inn of immense charm, situated close to beautiful countryside near Lulworth Cove within easy reach of the coast and Weymouth. The restaurant offers a wide choice of English and continental dishes, including bar meals. There is a large, children's play area at the rear and outdoor*

dining during the summer months.
FOOD: up to £15
**Hours:** lunch and bar meals 12noon-2.30pm, dinner and bar meals 6pm-10pm, open all year every day.
**Cuisine:** ENGLISH / CONTINENTAL - home-made dishes, grills and steaks, including poached bream with a white wine sauce and garnished with grapes, beef steak marinated in ale. Vegetarian and light bites menus. Home-made sweets.
**Cards:** Access,Visa,AmEx,Diners
**Other points:** children welcome, no-smoking area, open-air dining, traditional Sunday lunch, vegetarian meals, afternoon teas, parking.
**Directions:** A352, Wareham to Weymouth main coast road. Situated before Winfrith, after level crossing.
MR HAYES ☎(01929) 462247

# HAMPSHIRE

## ANDOVER • map 5C2

 **WHITE HART**
Bridge Street, SP10 1BH
*Centrally located in the town centre, this delightful family-run hotel dates back to the 15th century. It is comfortably furnished and decorated, with a spacious bar and reception area. The hotel offers the finest quality cuisine and well-furnished, homely bedrooms. Well located for journeys throughout Hampshire, including Stonehenge, Salisbury and Winchester.*
DOUBLE ROOM: from £30 to £40
SINGLE ROOM: from £55
FOOD: up to £15
**Hours:** breakfast 7am-9am, lunch 12.30am-2.30pm, dinner 6.30pm-10pm.
**Cuisine:** ENGLISH / CONTINENTAL
**Cards:** Visa, Access, Diners, AmEx.
**Other points:** parking, children welcome, pets allowed, conference facilities, vegetarian meals, traditional Sunday lunch, afternoon teas.
**Rooms:** 2 single rooms, 12 double rooms, 6 twin rooms. All with en suite, telephone, radio, hair dryer, trouser-press, tea/coffee-making facilities.
**Directions:** M3 junction 8 onto A303, second exit onto A3057. Follow signs for town centre: Bridge Street runs along the bottom of High Street.
SIMON HUGHES ☎(01264) 352266 Fax(01264) 323767

## BROCKENHURST • map 5D2

**THE CLOUD HOTEL**
Meerut Road, SO42 7TD
*A superbly-run hotel in a delightful situation on the very edge of the beautiful New Forest. Most bedrooms enjoy breathtaking views. Excellent and varied cuisine is served in the panoramic restaurant, and in winter log fires warm the comfortable lounges. Mrs Owton and her staff will ensure that*

you have a memorable stay. Well recommended.
DOUBLE ROOM: from £30 to £40
SINGLE ROOM: from £40 to £50
FOOD: from £15 to £20
**Hours:** breakfast 8am-9.30am, lunch (restaurant and bar) 12noon-2.30pm, dinner (restaurant and bar) 7pm-8.30pm.
**Cuisine:** full table d'hôte menu with a wide variety of dishes including haunch of venison with brandy and redcurrant sauce,h ome-made fisherman's pie, fillet of salmon in sauce Duglere and daily roasts.
**Cards:** Access,Visa
**Other points:** licensed, parking, children welcome, pets allowed (management's discretion), outdoor dining, special activity breaks, rooms with forest view.
**Rooms:** 3 single rooms, 4 twin rooms, 8 double rooms, 1 family room, all en suite.
**Directions:** take A337 from Lyndhurst to Lymington. Meerut Road is on the right just before you enter Brockenhurst village.
AVRIL OWTON ☎(01590) 622165 Fax(01590) 622165

**THE WATERSPLASH HOTEL**
The Rise, SO42 7ZP
*A family-run Victorian country house hotel set in 2 acres of secluded gardens. The hotel is noted for good food, friendly service and comfortable accommodation. The menu offers imaginative, well-cooked food. Situated in the centre of the New Forest.*
DOUBLE ROOM: from £25 to £40
SINGLE ROOM: from £40 to £50
FOOD: from £15 to £20 CLUB
**Hours:** bar meals 12noon-2pm, lunch 1pm-2pm, dinner 7.30pm-8.30pm.
**Cuisine:** ENGLISH - specialities include pot roast haunch of New Forest venison.
**Cards:** Visa, Access.
**Other points:** licensed, open-air dining, Sunday lunch, no-smoking area, children welcome, garden,

pets allowed, afternoon tea.
**Directions:** off A337 south of Lyndhurst. Turning to
The Rise opposite Shell garage.
ROBIN & JUDY FOSTER ☎(01590) 622344

## BURLEY • map 5D2

 **THE WHITE BUCK INN**
Bisterne Close, BH24 4AT

*Completely refurbished to a very high standard, the
White Buck is situated in the very heart of the New
Forest, close to Burley Golf Club. The bedrooms are
furnished to a very high standard and equipped with
en suite facilities and Sky television. A warm,
friendly atmosphere prevails in the bar and
restaurant and visitors are assured of a memorable
stay in this lovely part of the country.*
DOUBLE ROOM: from £20 to £30
FOOD: up to £15
**Hours:** breakfast 8.30am-9.30am, lunch (restaurant
and bar) 12noon-2pm, dinner (restaurant and bar)
7pm-10pm. Open all year.
**Cards:** Access,Visa
**Other points:** parking, children welcome (special
children's room), 3.5 acre garden, patio, golf course
nearby, edge of New Forest.
**Rooms:** 9 rooms all en suite with tea/coffee maker,
Sky TV, telephone, radio, trouser press, baby
listening device.
**Directions:** 1 mile from centre of Burley village on
the Brockenhurst to Lyndhurst road. Look for sign
on left to Bisterne Close.
MR AND MRS WATTS ☎(01425) 402264
Fax(01425) 403588

## CADNAM • map 5D2

 **THE WHITE HART**
Old Romsey Road, SO40
*A superb family-run pub/restaurant, extensively
refurbished recently to a very high standard, yet
retaining a warm and welcoming atmosphere. The
bar and restaurant are spacious, and there is a
delightful garden to the rear to be enjoyed in the
warmer months. All food is freshly prepared daily
by family members, and a varied menu is provided
for both lunch and dinner.*
FOOD: up to £15
**Hours:** lunch 11am-2pm, Sunday 12noon-2pm,
dinner 6pm-9.30pm, Sunday 7pm-9pm.
**Cuisine:** ENGLISH - a varied menu with a wide
choice to suit all tastes, all freshly prepared.
**Cards:** Visa, Access.
**Other points:** parking, children welcome, pets

allowed, no-smoking area, garden, vegetarian
meals, traditional Sunday lunch.
**Directions:** from exit 1 of M27 take Lyndhurst sign
to Cadnam roundabout; turn left to A31 and The
White Hart is immediately on the left.
SUE & NICK EMBERLEY ☎(01703) 812277
Fax(01703) 814632

## DROXFORD • map 5D2

 **HURDLES PUB AND RESTAURANT**
Station Road, SO3 1QU
*The Hurdles is a warm and cosy pub/restaurant,
superbly run by the proprietors, Pam and Paul
Mulle. Open fires in winter, red velvet-style
benches, a long bar with open-plan restaurant and a
wide variety of delicious meals all help to maintain
its popularity. A warm welcome awaits all. Well
worth a visit. Runner-up 1995 Calor Gas "Pie and
Pint" award.*
FOOD: up to £15
**Hours:** lunch 12noon-2pm, dinner 7pm-10pm.
**Cuisine:** ENGLISH - a varied menu using fresh
produce.
**Other points:** parking, vegetarian meals, children
catered for (please check for age limits).
**Directions:** from A32 Alton to Fareham road, take
B2150 just north of Droxford. Positioned on the
right immediately after old railway bridge.
PAUL & PAM MULLE ☎(01489) 877451

## EMSWORTH • map 5D3

**JINGLES**
77 Horndean Road, PO10 7PU
*A homely Victorian building flanked by open
countryside. All bedrooms are individually
decorated and provide comfortable
accommodation. Under the personal supervision of
Kit and Angela Chapman. The atmosphere and
service are welcoming and friendly. Weekend rates
available.*
DOUBLE ROOM: from £20 to £30
SINGLE ROOM: from £23
FOOD: up to £15
**Hours:** breakfast 7am-9am, dinner 7pm-9pm, lunch
Sunday 12noon-2pm.
**Cuisine:** ENGLISH / INTERNATIONAL
**Cards:** Visa, Access.
**Other points:** children welcome, central heating,
residents' lounge, pets allowed, garden, swimming
pool, afternoon tea, vegetarian meals, disabled
access, parking, residents' bar.
**Rooms:** 4 single rooms, 5 double rooms, 2 twin
rooms, 1 family room. All with TV, tea/coffee-
making facilities.
**Directions:** follow the A259 to Emsworth. Proceed
north from village onto B2148.
KIT & ANGELA CHAPMAN ☎(01243) 373755
Fax(01243) 373755

## FAREHAM • map 5D2

### THE OSBORNE VIEW

Hillhead Road, Hillhead, PO14 3JY

*A popular and spacious pub/restaurant, offering an extensive choice of English cuisine with continental overtones. Its location in an unspoilt area facing Cowes makes it an ideal base for watching passing liners and other ships in the Western Channel.*

FOOD: up to £15

**Hours:** bar meals 12noon-2.30pm, and 6pm-9.30pm, open bank holidays.

**Cuisine:** ENGLISH/CONTINENTAL - selection of home-made dishes, including country haddock goujons, blazing red fish, steak-and-kidney and guinness pie. Sweets such as home-baked lemon meringue, orange sorbet and creme caramel. Good wine list.

**Cards:** Access,Visa,AmEx,Switch

**Other points:** children welcome, pets allowed, no-smoking area, open-air dining, traditional Sunday lunch, vegetarian meals, parking.

**Directions:** from M27 take A27 towards Stubbington. Pub overlooks the sea at Hillhead.

MR AND MRS READMAN ☎(01329) 664623

---

## FORDINGBRIDGE • map 5D1

### LIONS COURT RESTAURANT & HOTEL

29-31 High Street, SP6 1AS

*Set on the edge of the New Forest with all its amenities and rural pursuits. The delightful sleepy town of Fordingbridge is ideally centered for the cathedral city of Salisbury, Bournemouth, Stonehenge and many places of interest. The Lions Court is a charming 17th century family hotel with six en suite bedrooms and one 4-poster. The à la carte restaurant has a reputation for excellent cuisine in a relaxed, intimate atmosphere. A classic English setting with gardens extending to the River Avon. Fishing, golf, horse-riding available locally.*

DOUBLE ROOM: from £20 to £40

SINGLE ROOM: from £38

FOOD: up to £20

**Hours:** breakfast 7.30am-9.30am, lunch 12noon-2.30pm, dinner 6.30pm-9.30pm.

**Cuisine:** ENGLISH / CONTINENTAL - a varied menu favouring fresh local produce. Specialities include salad of smoked venison, grilled calf's liver with a bacon and mushroom concasse flavoured with basil. Unusual fish and many vegetarian dishes. Reservations are advised. Chef: Danny Wilson.

**Cards:** Visa, Access, AmEx.

**Other points:** parking, children welcome, pets allowed, vegetarian meals, traditional Sunday lunch.

**Rooms:** 2 single rooms, 3 double rooms, 1 twin room, 1 family apartment (3-4 people). All with en suite, TV, tea/coffee-making facilities.

**Directions:** half-way between Salisbury and Ringwood on the A338.

MICHAEL & JENNY EASTICK ☎(01425) 652006 Fax(01425) 657946

---

## GOSPORT • map 5D2

### BELLE VUE HOTEL

39 Marine Parade East, Lee on the Solent, PO13 9BW

*Situated on the seafront, overlooking the Solent, this modern yet traditional hotel offers comfortable accommodation for a wide range of visitors. The food in the restaurant can be enjoyed in relaxed surroundings.*

DOUBLE ROOM: from £30 to £40

SINGLE ROOM: from £45 to £65

FOOD: up to £20

**Hours:** breakfast 7.15am-9.15am, lunch 12noon-2pm, bar meals 12noon-2.30pm, dinner 7pm-9.45pm, open bank holidays, closed Christmas Day and Boxing Day.

**Cuisine:** ENGLISH - menu includes a good selection of fish, meat, grills and vegetarian dishes and may feature whole red mullet, pan fried entrecôte steak, roasted magret of Barbary duck.

**Cards:** Visa, Access, AmEx, Switch.

**Other points:** licensed, open-air dining, Sunday lunch, no-smoking area, children welcome, patio, entertainment.

**Rooms:** 4 single rooms, 19 double rooms 27 twin rooms.

**Directions:** M27 junction 8 or 11 to Fareham; to Lee on the Solent takes approximately 8 minutes.

MR A.J. BELLASIS ☎(01705) 550258 Fax(01705) 552624

---

## HAVANT • map 5D3

### OLD MILL GUEST HOUSE

Mill Lane, Old Bedhampton, PO9 3JH

*This is an outstanding family-run Georgian guest house of immense charm and interest, with a lake and large grounds housing wild life, fish and water fowl. A place for complete relaxation and with most comfortable, spacious accommodation. John Keats rested here while finishing his poem Eve of St Agnes.*

DOUBLE ROOM: up to £20

SINGLE ROOM: up to £25

FOOD: up to £15

**Hours:** breakfast 7am-9am, evening snacks available on request.

**Cuisine:** BREAKFAST - English breakfast, cooked to order. Picnic snacks can be prepared if requested.

**Other points:** children welcome, residents' lounge, garden, seasonal swimming pool.

**Rooms:** 1 twin room, 4 family rooms.

**Directions:** From A3(M) take the A27 and follow signs for Havant and Bedhampton.

MR & MRS D. & J. KELLY ☎(01705) 454948 Fax(01705) 499677

---

## HAYLING ISLAND • map 5D3

### NEWTOWN HOUSE HOTEL

Manor Road, West Town, PO11 0QR

*An 18th century converted farmhouse set in its own large gardens, Newtown House Hotel provides a cosy bar and lounge, an à la carte restaurant, comfortable accommodation and an indoor leisure*

---

complex. Well suited to families, this hotel is an ideal place to stay throughout the year, due to its location near the sea and the indoor leisure complex.

DOUBLE ROOM: from £20 to £30
SINGLE ROOM: from £35 to £50
FOOD: from £15 to £20
**Hours:** breakfast 7.30am-10am, lunch 12noon-2pm, dinner 7pm-9.45pm.
**Cuisine:** FRENCH / ENGLISH - predominantly French cuisine. Specialities include filet de boeuf Diane, tournedos Rossini, rack of lamb roasted with honey and garlic. Bar meals available.
**Cards:** Visa, Access, Diners, AmEx.
**Other points:** licensed, Sunday lunch, pets allowed, garden, afternoon tea, leisure centre, swimming pool, Jacuzzi, gym facilities, steam room, sauna, tennis, children welcome, baby-listening device, cots.
**Rooms:** 7 single rooms, 13 double rooms, 4 twin rooms, 2 family rooms. All with TV, radio, alarm, telephone, tea/coffee-making facilities.
**Directions:** take the A3023 into South Hayling. Close to shops and shore.
VALLANT ENTERPRISES - MR WITKOWSI
☎(01705) 466131 Fax(01705) 461366

## LYMINGTON • map 5E2

 **PEELERS BISTRO**
Gosport Street, SO41 9BE
Built in 1700 as a police station, Peelers no longer dishes out law and order but rather serves a wide range of delicious food, with a well-deserved reputation for its fish. This is an extremely popular restaurant, especially in the evenings. It is situated close to the Isle of Wight ferry, in a mainly cobbled road. It was acclaimed as `Restaurant of the Year' in 1992 by Where to eat in Hants/Wilts.
DOUBLE ROOM: up to £20
SINGLE ROOM: up to £25
FOOD: from £15 to £20
**Hours:** breakfast 8.30am-9am, lunch 12noon-1.45pm, dinner 7pm-10.15pm (July-September 6.30pm-10.30pm).
**Cuisine:** MODERN ENGLISH - fresh fish and pasta.
**Cards:** Visa, Access, Diners, AmEx.
**Other points:** licensed, open-air dining, children welcome.
**Rooms:** 2 double/twin rooms. All with TV.
**Directions:** at bottom of Lymington High Street, turn left into Gosport Street, Peelers is 100 yards along on the left-hand side.
MR & MRS W.J. SMITH ☎(01590) 676165

 **THE WHITE ROSE HOTEL**
Village Centre, Sway, SO41 6BA
A family-run hotel of immense charm, offering accommodation and food of the finest quality. The hotel is situated in the New Forest village of Sway, close to the coast and with many places of interest to visit nearby. Southampton and Bournemouth are within easy travelling distance, as are such wonderful New Forest locations as Beaulieu,

Brockenhurst, Lyndhurst and Lymington. Standing in 5 acres of gardens with a swimming pool, the hotel is an ideal spot to stay when visiting or touring Hampshire.

DOUBLE ROOM: from £30 to £40
SINGLE ROOM: from £40 to £50
FOOD: up to £15
**Hours:** breakfast 8am-9.30am, lunch 12noon-2pm, dinner 7pm-9pm, bar snacks available.
**Cuisine:** ENGLISH / CONTINENTAL - a varied menu of home-made meals.
**Cards:** Visa, Access, AmEx.
**Other points:** parking, children welcome, pets allowed, no-smoking area, residents' lounge, garden, swimming pool, open-air dining, vegetarian meals, traditional Sunday lunch.
**Rooms:** 7 double rooms, 3 twin rooms, 2 family rooms. All with TV, telephone, radio, tea/coffee-making facilities. Most rooms are en suite.
**Directions:** from junction 1 (M27), follow A337 to Lyndhurst and Brokenhurst and turn right onto B3055 to Sway (centre of village).
PAUL & ANNE WINCHCOMBE ☎(01590) 682754

## LYNDHURST • map 5D2

 **THE PENNY FARTHING HOTEL**
Village Centre, SO43 7AA
This attractive family-run guest house, situated 150 yards from the centre of the village, provides comfortable en suite rooms with remote colour TV and tea/coffee facilities. Lyndhurst is the New Forest capital and offers the main visitor centre and museum, as well as a charming selection of shops, inns and restaurants. The hotel also provides a comfortable bar with satellite TV for guests and a large car park to the rear.
DOUBLE ROOM: from £25 to £35
SINGLE ROOM: from £25 to £35
FOOD: up to £15
**Hours:** breakfast 8am-9.30am, closed Christmas day and Boxing day.
**Cuisine:** ENGLISH - although only breakfast was available at the time of going to press, further selections are planned: please check with the hotel for details of additional meals.
**Cards:** Visa, Access.
**Other points:** parking, children welcome, pets allowed, no-smoking areas, residents' lounge.
**Rooms:** 1 single room, 7 double rooms, 2 twin rooms, 1 family room. All with TV, tea/coffee-making facilities.
**Directions:** from M27, take the A337 Romsey Road. The Penny Farthing can be found on the left just as you enter the village.
JANE & MIKE ☎(01703) 284422 Fax(01703) 284488

## NEW MILTON • map 5E2

 **THE SPECKLED TROUT**
Station Road, BH25 6JR
Located next to the railway station, this large, century-old traditional inn is very popular with rail

passengers. *Serves wholesome English cuisine amidst a welcoming, pub-style atmosphere.*
**FOOD:** up to £15
**Hours:** breakfast 8am-11.30am, bar meals 11.30am-2.30pm, and 6pm-9.30pm, open bank holidays.
**Cuisine:** home-made specials, grills and vegetarian dishes.
**Cards:** Access,Visa,AmEx
**Other points:** children welcome, pets allowed, open-air dining, traditional Sunday lunch, vegetarian meals, conference facilities, parking.
**Directions:** A337 Christchurch to Lyminton road, or A35 from Southampton. Located in the centre of New Milton, beside railway station.
MR BARRY SNODGRASS ☎(01425) 638208

## ODIHAM • map 5C3

### LA FORET
High Street, RG29 1LB
*This intimate French restaurant, situated on the main street of the delightful country town of Odiham, provides excellently cooked French cuisine in attractive, comfortable surroundings. Using an imaginative menu which has obviously been devised by a creative and caring chef, you will find that excellent service and candlelit surroundings complement your gastronomic delights.*
**FOOD:** from £20 to £25 ☜
**Hours:** lunch 12.30am-2pm, dinner 7pm-9.45pm.
**Cuisine:** FRENCH - classic French cuisine, including extensive selection of fish specialities.
**Cards:** Visa, Access, Diners, AmEx, Switch.
**Other points:** licensed, Sunday lunch, children welcome, supervised creche on Sundays.
**Directions:** on the main street in Odiham.
MR & MRS HOULKER ☎(01256) 702697
Fax(01256) 710339

## PORTSMOUTH • map 5D2

### BEAUFORT HOTEL
71 Festing Road, Southsea, PO4 0NQ
*The Beaufort Hotel has achieved an outstanding reputation for comfort and excellence. You can relax in the warm and friendly atmosphere, where the emphasis is on service and quality, confident that your stay will be an enjoyable and memorable one. The hotel is situated in a beautiful part of Southsea, overlooking the canoe lake and the colourful rose garden, with the seafront and promenade just a short stroll away.*
**DOUBLE ROOM:** from £30 to £40
**SINGLE ROOM:** from £35 to £45
**FOOD:** up to £15 ☜ CLUB
**Hours:** dinner 6.30pm-8.30pm.
**Cuisine:** TRADITIONAL ENGLISH
**Cards:** Visa, Access, Amex, Switch, MasterCard.
**Other points:** 24 hour access, licensed.
**Rooms:** 20 bedrooms.
**Directions:** Festing Road is a quiet road 250 yards from the seafront.

PENNY & TONY FREEMANTLE ☎(01705) 823707
Fax(01705) 870270

### PRIDE OF BILBAO, PRIDE OF LE HAVRE, PRIDE OF PORTSMOUTH
Peninsular House, Wharf Road, PO2 8TA
*These three super "Cruiseferries" operate regular sailings between Portsmouth and Le Havre/Cherbourg/Bilbao. Your holiday commences from the moment you step on board, and the range and quality of the catering facilities are absolutely first class. For more details see the special P&O introduction on page 31. Telephone 0990 980 980 for reservations and sailing details. (Purchasers of this Guide to France may obtain a free bottle of house wine when dining in the Goodwood, Deauville or Bacchus Restaurants. For your wine voucher and details of the offer see page 197 of this guide). For details of the Les Routiers/P&O Discovery club see page34.*
**FOOD:** up to £20 ☜
**Hours:** breakfast 8am-10am, lunch 11.30am-1pm, dinner 4pm-12midnight. Bar snacks available all day. For ferry sailing times, see P & O brochures.
**Cuisine:** main restaurants, self-service restaurants, snack bars and breakfast restaurants cater for every possible taste. Children and vegetarians specially catered for.
**Cards:** Visa, Access, Diners, AmEx.
**Other points:** purpose built facilities for the disabled, children's facilities and entertainment(on longer cruises), business traveller facilities including Fax and photocopying, baby changing rooms, indoor pool, jacuzzi, sauna (during daylight hours), Club Class available with private bar and steward service.
**Directions:** take M27 to Portsmouth, and M275 spur into Portsmouth centre. Follow road signs for cross channel ferries.
☎(01705) 772000 Fax(01705) 772134

### SEAFARER STEAK HOUSE & FISH RESTAURANT
177-185 Elm Grove, Southsea, PO5 1LU
*A steak-house-style restaurant, situated 5 minutes by car from the continental ferry port near the central shopping centre, offering good grills, interesting fish dishes and a daily market-produce board. Friendly and efficient service and a welcoming pre-dinner bar.*
**FOOD:** up to £15    CLUB
**Hours:** Monday to Friday 7pm-10pm, Saturday 6pm-11pm, closed Sunday.
**Cuisine:** ENGLISH - English, with strong European influence, using fresh daily market produce.
**Cards:** Visa, Access.
**Other points:** children welcome.
**Directions:** M275 to Portsmouth; first exit at roundabout, over 3 roundabouts, restaurant on right.
TIM HUNT ☎(01705) 827188

### UPLAND PARK HOTEL
Garrison Hill, Droxford, SO3 1QL

*Set in the heart of the beautiful Meon Valley, this superb hotel and excellent restaurant is a gem of a place to stay in, offering guests a welcoming atmosphere in which to enjoy the quality accommodation, spacious dining room, and cosy bar with homely log fire in winter. For summer visitors there is a large pool, and space to relax or explore the lovely surrounding countryside.*

DOUBLE ROOM: from £30 to £40
SINGLE ROOM: from £25 to £35
FOOD: up to £15 **CLUB**
**Hours:** breakfast 7am-10am, lunch 12noon-2.30pm, dinner 7pm-10pm, bar meals all day.
**Cuisine:** ENGLISH / CONTINENTAL - a varied menu including a good selection of fresh fish dishes.
**Cards:** Visa, Access, Diners, AmEx.
**Other points:** parking, pets allowed, conference facilities, no-smoking area, swimming pool, garden, open-air dining, vegetarian meals, afternoon teas, traditional Sunday lunch.
**Rooms:** 3 single rooms, 9 double rooms, 3 twin rooms, 2 family rooms. All with en suite, TV, telephone, trouser-press, tea/coffee-making facilities.
**Directions:** situated on the A32 Alton to Fareham road at Droxford, south of Alton.
BRIAN LAY ☎(01489) 878507 **Fax**(01489) 877853

## RINGWOOD • map 5D1

### THE OLD COTTAGE RESTAURANT
14 West Street, BH24 1DZ

*A unique and beautiful 14th century thatched restaurant, reported to be the oldest building in the area. Retaining many historical features, it offers excellent English and continental cuisine in an atmosphere of olde-worlde charm. The proprietors personally supervise the day to day running of this extremely popular restaurant in a beautiful part of England.*

FOOD: from £15 to £20 **CLUB**
**Hours:** lunch 12noon-2.30pm, dinner 7pm-10.30pm, closed Boxing day.
**Cuisine:** ENGLISH / CONTINENTAL
**Cards:** Visa, Access, AmEx.
**Other points:** parking, children welcome, Sunday lunch, open bank holidays, no-smoking area, disabled access, vegetarian meals, open-air dining.
**Directions:** A31 across New Forest towards Bournemouth, turn off at A31 Ringwood roundabout and proceed to the High Street. West Street is a continuation of High Street.
TRICIA & PAUL HARPER ☎(01425) 474283

## ROCKBOURNE • map 5D1

### ROSE & THISTLE
Rockbourne, near Fordingbridge, SP6 3NL

*A beautiful 16th century thatched roof inn, situated in a picture-postcard village in the New Forest. A popular haunt of locals, tourists and walkers who are drawn by the warm, homely atmosphere and the olde-worlde interior, which offers log fires, oak beams and low ceilings. Fine-quality, imaginative fresh food, with excellent wines and real ales available daily.*

FOOD: from £15 to £20
**Hours:** lunch 12noon-2.30pm last orders, dinner 7pm-9.30pm last orders, open all year.
**Cuisine:** BRITISH - house specialities: duck breast on spinach with an apricot and brandy sauce, medallions of beef fillet with a port and Stilton sauce plus a wide selection of fresh fish dishes including Dover sole.
**Cards:** Visa, Access, Delta, Switch.
**Other points:** licensed, open-air dining, Sunday lunch, children welcome, disabled access, pets allowed.
**Directions:** from Fordingbridge A3078, at Sandleheath look for the sign to the Rockbourne Roman Villa.
TIM NORFOLK ☎(017253) 236

## ROMSEY • map 5D2

### COBWEB TEA ROOMS
49 The Hundred, SO51 8GE

*Situated in the town centre of Romsey, this friendly tea room has a restful atmosphere with a soft green colour scheme inside and an attractive tea garden. Broadlands and Romsey Abbey are nearby places of interest to visit.*

FOOD: up to £15
**Hours:** morning coffee 10am-12noon, lunch 12noon-2pm, afternoon tea 2pm-5.30pm, closed Sunday and Monday, open bank holidays. Closed 2 weeks end of September and 1 week at Christmas.
**Cuisine:** ENGLISH - home-made cakes and sweets. Toasted sandwiches. Light lunches.
**Other points:** open-air dining, children welcome, limited disabled access, all non-smoking.
**Directions:** in the main street in Romsey on the A27, 100 yards from Broadlands estate.
MISS ANGELA WEBLEY ☎(01794) 516434

### SOUTH GARDEN CANTONESE & PEKINESE CUISINE
9 Bell Street, SO5 8GY

*An elegant restaurant in the centre of Romsey, offering excellent food in comfortable surroundings. All dishes are cooked from fresh ingredients and beautifully presented. Cantonese cuisine is based on freshness and stir-fry cooking, while Pekinese cuisine is more spicy and aromatic. The wine list includes Chinese wines. Excellent, welcoming service.*

FOOD: up to £15
**Hours:** lunch (Thursday-Sunday) 12.15am-2.15pm, dinner 6pm-11.30pm.
**Cuisine:** CANTONESE / PEKINESE - including sizzling dishes and a wide choice of seafood dishes. Extensive menu. Set dinners and English dishes also available.
**Cards:** Visa, Access, AmEx.
**Other points:** licensed, Sunday lunch, no-smoking

# EVEN MORE VALUE
# FROM
# LES ROUTIERS
# AND

## P&O European Ferries

By purchasing this guide, you are not only eligible to make substantial fare savings through *Les Routiers* **Discovery Club** (see page 34) but, IN ADDITION the attached voucher entitles you to a free bottle of red or white house wine when a minimum of 2 people dine in the Goodwood, Deauville or Bacchus restaurants onboard *Pride of Portsmouth, Pride of Le Havre*, and *Pride of Bilbao*. Take this guide with you when you dine, and the restaurant staff will detach the voucher and present you with your free bottle of wine.

It's as simple as that!

---

## LES ROUTIERS DISCOVERY CLUB
## FREE WINE VOUCHER

*I claim my free bottle of red
or white house wine!*

---

area, children welcome, parking.
**Directions:** in centre of Romsey, approximately 200 yards from Romsey Abbey. Behind town hall.
JASON MAN ☎(01794) 514428

## SOUTHAMPTON • map 5D2

### AVENUE HOTEL
Lodge Road, SO2 0QR
*Privately owned, the Avenue Hotel is situated in a tree-lined avenue. A friendly welcome awaits you at this modern, comfortably furnished hotel. The restaurant offers fine food and wine served in a convivial ambience, so providing an excellent venue to entertain and in which to be entertained. Conveniently located, with direct access from motorways to the city centre.*
DOUBLE ROOM: from £20 to £30
SINGLE ROOM: from £35
FOOD: up to £15
**Hours:** breakfast 7am-9.30am, lunch 12noon-2.30pm, Sunday 12noon-3pm, dinner 6.30pm-10pm, Sunday 6.30pm-9.30pm.
**Cuisine:** ENGLISH - à la carte and table d'hôte menus. All dishes are home-made.
**Cards:** Visa, Access, AmEx, Switch.
**Other points:** licensed, Sunday lunch, no-smoking area, children welcome, afternoon tea, pets allowed, conferences, functions.
**Rooms:** 48 bedrooms. All en suite with satellite TV.
**Directions:** off the A33.
A. WYLIE ☎(01703) 229023 Fax(01703) 334569

### THE JOLLY SAILOR
Lands End Road, Old Bursledon, SO31 8DN
*A unique, waterfront pub/restaurant on the banks of the River Hamble. It boasts its own private jetty and a large dining area with river views. The food is superb and the two resident chefs provide a wide range of home-cooked food including locally-caught fresh fish and vegetarian dishes. A wonderful place to spend a family day out.*
FOOD: up to £15
**Hours:** bar meals 12noon-2pm weekdays, until 2.30pm weekends, dinner 7pm-9.30pm, bar meals 6.30pm-9.30pm, open bank holidays.
**Cuisine:** ENGLISH / CONTINENTAL - english home-cooked fare with an international flavour, using fresh produce. Old English mushrooms with stilton, bacon and onions in white wine sauce; Burlesdon barbeque chargrill; Chateaubriand Royale.
**Cards:** Access,Visa,AmEx,Diners,Switch,Eurocard
**Other points:** children welcome, pets allowed (on leads), no-smoking area, open-air dining, traditional Sunday lunch, vegetarian meals.
**Directions:** junction 8 of M27, follow signs to Bursledon. Old Bursledon is signposted.
MR & MRS HOUSLEY ☎(01703) 405557

### LA MARGHERITA RESTAURANT
6 Commercial Road, SO1 0GE
*A busy, friendly bistro-type restaurant near the Mayflower Theatre. Popular with theatre-goers and TV stars. Repartee and good humour flow as fast as the Italian red wine.*
FOOD: up to £15
**Hours:** dinner 6.30pm-11.30pm, lunch 12noon-2.30pm, open bank holidays.
**Cuisine:** CONTINENTAL - langostinos, steak Diane, freshly-made pizzas and home-made lasagne. Desserts include crême caramel.
**Cards:** Visa, Access, Diners, AmEx.
**Other points:** disabled access, children welcome.
**Directions:** from main BR station, turn right at traffic lights into Commercial Road.
ANTONIO CENTOLA ☎(01703) 333390
Fax(01703) 630100

### LANGLEY'S BISTRO
10-11 Bedford Place, SO1 2DB
*Situated in a busy area, this is a popular city-centre bistro offering fine English and continental dishes to a sophisticated business clientele whilst also being very popular with locals. Spacious, air-conditioned, with an attractive bar and furnishings, and a comfortable atmosphere prevails.*
FOOD: up to £15 ☜
**Hours:** lunch Monday-Friday 12noon-2pm, dinner Monday-Friday 6.30pm-10.30pm. Closed all Sundays. Open bank holidays Monday-Friday evenings only.
**Cuisine:** ENGLISH / CONTINENTAL
**Cards:** Visa, Access, AmEx, Switch.
**Other points:** children welcome, open bank holidays evenings only, disabled access, vegetarian meals.
**Directions:** via Winchester, from M3 motorway take A33 to Southampton.
MR TUCKER ☎(01703) 224551

### THE TALISMAN
Bridge Road, Park Gate, SO31 7GD
*A traditional inn and pub/restaurant offering a wide choice of freshly prepared home-cooked food. There is a comfortable restaurant and a bar serving snacks, including vegetarian choices. Has its own space at the rear for outside dining in Summer. A warm, friendly atmosphere prevails.*
FOOD: up to £15
**Hours:** bar meals Monday-Friday 12noon-2.30pm, dinner and bar meals Monday-Friday 6pm-10pm, Saturday-Sunday food served 12noon-10pm, open bank holidays.
**Cuisine:** ENGLISH / INTERNATIONAL - tiger king prawns in filo pastry, old english steak, chicken and smoked bacon fusilli, filled baguettes. Sweets include home-made fruits of the forest pancake and jam roly-poly.
**Cards:** Visa, Access, Diners, AmEx, Switch, Delta.
**Other points:** children welcome, pets allowed (on leads), no-smoking area, open-air dining, traditional Sunday lunch, vegetarian meals, afternoon teas,

parking.
**Directions:** exit M27 junction 9, onto A27 towards Southampton.
MR JENKINS & MISS COSENS ☎(01489) 572614

 **THE VICTORIA PARK HOTEL**
75 Station Road, Netley Abbey,
SO31 5AE
*A delightful, family-run hotel with warm and comfortable accommodation and an attractive dining room and bar offering an imaginative choice of daily dishes. Close to Southampton water and the Hamble river, it is ideally situated for exploring the New Forest, visiting Beaulieu Motor Museum, Royal Victoria park and the remains of Netley Abbey. Highly-recommended*
DOUBLE ROOM: from £30 to £40
SINGLE ROOM: from £30 to £40
FOOD: up to £15
**Hours:** breakfast 6.30am-9.30am, lunch bar snacks only, dinner 7.30pm-10pm. Open all year.
**Cuisine:** ENGLISH / CONTINENTAL - the chef prepares an imaginative variety of daily dishes including items such as grilled rib-eye steak, poached salmon, vegetable grillades, home-made steak-and-kidney puddings, curried dishes, salmon en croute.
**Cards:** Access, Visa, AmEx, Diners.
**Other points:** parking, additional parking opposite, complete laundry service, pets allowed, licensed, residents' lounge, central heating.
**Rooms:** 7 twin rooms, 11 double rooms, all with en suite facilities, tea/coffee maker, TV, telephone, radio, trouser press.
**Directions:** take exit 8 from M27 and take road at side of Tesco superstore signposted Netley and Hamble Village (B3397). Past garden centre and right into Hound Road which leads to Netley station and Station Road.
MR AND MRS CLARKE ☎(01703) 453480
Fax(01703) 452228

 **STOCKBRIDGE • map 5D2**

 **THE GAME LARDER RESTAURANT**
New Street, SO20 6HG
*Situated close to the city of Winchester, Romsey, Andover and Salisbury, this beautiful 18th century converted malthouse has a wealth of oak beams, an enormous open log fire, and a minstrel's gallery which overlooks the main restaurant. There is on offer a wide and interesting menu, complemented by a wine list of 72 bins. This is the ideal setting for a romantic dinner for two, a family party or a quiet business meal, and is perfect also for wedding receptions. A very warm welcome awaits you from Terry and Kerry Jayne and their friendly, efficient staff.*
FOOD: from £20 to £25    CLUB
**Hours:** lunch 12noon-2pm, dinner 7pm-10pm, closed Sunday dinner and Monday.
**Cuisine:** ENGLISH - good à la carte menu with dishes made from fresh local produce. Game in season.

**Cards:** Visa, Access, Diners, AmEx.
**Other points:** parking, children welcome, vegetarian meals, traditional Sunday lunch.
**Directions:** on the A30, 7 miles south of Andover. The Game Larder can be found just off the High Street in Stockbridge.
TERRY & KERRY JAYNE ☎(01264) 810414
Fax(01264) 810480

 **THE GREYHOUND HOTEL**
High Street, SO20 6EY
*This small hotel situated in a delightful, small Hampshire town has log fires and oak beams, and the restaurant offers a wide selection of dishes, including game and seafood specialities, crêpes, fruits de mer and smoked trout. The hotel has its own stretch of the famous River Test (day tickets available). Golf day fees can also be arranged, along with clay pigeon shooting.*
DOUBLE ROOM: from £30 to £40
SINGLE ROOM: from £30
FOOD: up to £15
**Hours:** breakfast 7.30am-9.30am, lunch 12noon-2pm, dinner 6pm-9.30pm.
**Cuisine:** ENGLISH / CONTINENTAL - à la carte including a range of seafood, crêpes, and ploughman's.
**Cards:** Visa, Access, AmEx.
**Other points:** licensed, open-air dining, Sunday lunch, children catered for (please check for age limits), garden, pets allowed.
**Rooms:** 6 bedrooms. All en suite with TV, tea/coffee-making facilites.
**Directions:** Stockbridge is located at the intersection of the A30 and A3057.
MR GUMBRELL ☎(01264) 810833

**WINCHESTER • map 5D2**

 **THE ABBEY BAR & COURTYARD CAFE**
The Guildhall, The Broadway, SO22 6EN
*Situated within the delightful Victorian building of Winchester Guildhall, this is an ideal place to stop, meet and visit. Winchester Guildhall is a perfect venue for banqueting, promotions and conferences. Good food is provided in comfortable, friendly surroundings.*
FOOD: up to £15    CLUB
**Hours:** morning coffee 10am-12noon, lunch 12noon-2pm, open bank holidays.
**Cuisine:** ENGLISH - serving morning coffee, bar meals, salad bar and carvery. Afternoon tea in the Café.
**Other points:** Sunday lunch, no-smoking area, parking nearby.
**Directions:** approximately 75 yards from King Alfred statue in city centre and 200 yards from Winchester Cathedral.
MRS SHIRLEY MORRISSEY ☎(01962) 848368
Fax(01962) 878458

**CATHEDRAL VIEW GUEST HOUSE**
9A Magdalen Hill, SO23 8HJ

*Cathedral View is a small guest house of a very high standard. A good-quality, home-cooked breakfast can be enjoyed in the residents' dining room, and the tastefully decorated bedrooms ensure a comfortable night's rest. The guest house is well sited for the City of Winchester, Salisbury, Stonehenge, New Forest and many other places of interest.*

DOUBLE ROOM: from £25
SINGLE ROOM: up to £35
**Hours:** breakfast 7.45am-8.45am.
**Cuisine:** ENGLISH - a good-quality breakfast can be enjoyed in the residents' dining room.
**Other points:** parking, children welcome, garden.
**Rooms:** 3 double rooms, 1 twin room, 1 family room.
**Directions:** on entering Winchester from the east along the B3404, the guest house is situated on the right-hand side, just before entering the city centre.
MR & MRS CRONAN ☎(01962) 863802

 **HARESTOCK LODGE HOTEL & RESTAURANT**
Harestock Road, SO22 6NX

*One of the few remaining family-run hotels in the locality where a warm welcome is assured by the Bishop family. Situated on the outskirts of Winchester, the hotel is tastefully decorated and comfortably furnished. The licensed restaurant has a reputation for good food served, with a choice from table d'hôte, à la carte and vegetarian menus. All the food is freshly prepared and cooked to order.*

DOUBLE ROOM: from £25 to £35
SINGLE ROOM: from £40 to £50
FOOD: up to £15
**Hours:** breakfast 7.30am-9am, dinner 6.30pm-10pm, lunch 12noon-2.30pm.
**Cuisine:** ENGLISH / FRENCH / ITALIAN
**Cards:** Visa, Access, AmEx.
**Other points:** parking, children welcome, afternoon teas, disabled access, pets, residents' lounge, garden, vegetarian meals, open-air dining.
**Directions:** 1 mile north of Winchester, just off A34 to Newbury and the A272 to Salisbury
PETER & NICK BISHOP ☎(01962) 881870/880038
Fax(01962) 886959

 **THE ROYAL HOTEL**
St Peter Street, SO23 8BS

*Formally a bishop's residence, The Royal Hotel was built in the 16th century and has been a hotel for about 150 years. The restaurant offers well-cooked, imaginative dishes using predominantly fresh local produce. The hotel is furnished and decorated to a very high standard, providing attractive surroundings and comfortable accommodation. Two minutes from main shopping street.*

DOUBLE ROOM: from £30 to £40
SINGLE ROOM: from £69
FOOD: from £15 to £25
**Hours:** breakfast weekdays 7am-9.30am, weekends 8am-10am, bar meals 12noon-2.30pm, dinner Sunday 7pm-9.30pm.
**Cuisine:** MODERN ENGLISH - à la carte and table d'hôte menus. Dishes may include baked local pink trout, navarin of spring lamb, medallions of beef cooked in a green peppercorn sauce.
**Cards:** Visa, Access, Diners, AmEx.
**Other points:** licensed, open-air dining, Sunday lunch, afternoon tea, residents' lounge, special breaks, children welcome, residents' bar, vegetarian meals, parking, disabled access.
**Rooms:** 75 bedrooms. All en suite.
**Directions:** from the M3, take exit 9. Follow the one-way system to St George's Street, then turn right.
TONY & PAMELA SMITH ☎(01962) 840840
Fax(01962) 841582

## WOODFALLS • map 5D2

 **THE WOODFALLS INN**
The Ridge, SO5 2LN

*Nestling on the northeren edge of the New Forest on an old road from Salisbury, this award winning 1995/96 regional inn of the year has provided hospitality to travellers seeking rest and refreshment since 1870. An ideal base for the New Forest, Stonehenge and south coast ferry ports. All bedrooms are tastefully decorated with en-suite facilities, and some have four poster beds. Prize winning restaurant, bar food and real ales.*

DOUBLE ROOM: from £25 to £40
SINGLE ROOM: from £40 to £50
FOOD: up to £15 CLUB
**Hours:** breakfast 7.30am-11.45am, lunch 12noon-3pm, bar meals 11.30am-3pm, dinner 6.30pm-9.30pm, bar meals 6.30pm-10pm.
**Cuisine:** ENGLISH - traditional and wholesome English cooking. Frequently changing menus to suit every palate, using a wide variety of fresh, locally grown produce. Kiddies corner menu.
**Cards:** Visa, Access.
**Other points:** licensed, open all day, open-air dining, Sunday lunch, no-smoking area, children welcome, pets allowed, afternoon tea, parking, residents' lounge, residents' bar, disabled access, vegetarian meals.
**Rooms:** 4 double rooms, 6 twin rooms, 2 suites.
**Directions:** exit from M27 at junction 1. Take the B3079 to Brook, then B3078 to Telegraph Corner, then B3080 to Woodfalls.
MR M. ELVIS ☎(01725) 513222 Fax(01725) 513220

# ISLE OF WIGHT

## CHALE • map 5E2

### CLARENDON HOTEL & WIGHT MOUSE INN
St Catherine's Down, PO38 2HA

A charming 17th century inn overlooking Chale Bay in the south of the island, a few minutes from Blackgang Chine. The hotel enjoys a fine reputation for good food, wine, comfort and hospitality. With over 365 whiskies, 6 real ales and open fires, a warm, friendly atmosphere is assured! Children are most welcome.
DOUBLE ROOM: from £20 to £30
SINGLE ROOM: from £25 to £35
FOOD: up to £15  CLUB
Hours: open all day (Monday-Saturday) 11am until late, Sunday 12noon-3pm and 7pm-10.30pm, open all year round.
Cuisine: INTERNATIONAL - Wight Mouse Inn: island steaks, local fish, crab, home-made pizzas, curries, lasagne, chilli, daily specials etc., all home-made. Clarendon Hotel: fresh vegetables, fresh local fish, meat and vegetarian menu.
Cards: Visa, Access, MasterCard, Switch.
Other points: open-air dining, Sunday lunch, entertainment every night, children welcome, baby-listening device, cots, vegetarian meals, parking, residents' bar, residents' lounge.
Rooms: 3 double rooms, 5 quad rooms, 2 suites. All with TV, radio, alarm, hair dryer, baby-listening device, tea/coffee-making facilities.
Directions: on B3399, 50 yards from the Military Road, B3055, in Chale.
JOHN & JEAN BRADSHAW ☎(01983) 730431
Fax(01983) 730431

## NEWPORT • map 5E2

### THE BARN BISTRO
Arreton, near Newport, PO30 3AA
For a good country bistro-style meal and a great atmosphere in appealing country surroundings, look no further than The Barn Bistro and pub. This attractive old farm building is located in the centre of a popular craft centre. Here you can enjoy home-cooked meals made from fresh local produce at excellent value-for-money prices. Live jazz-style music at weekends.
FOOD: up to £15

Hours: lunch 12noon-2.30pm, dinner 7pm-11pm (last orders 9.45pm), bar is open all day.
Cuisine: FRENCH / ENGLISH - speciality sauces. Fresh local duck, chicken, fish, freshly made pizza.
Cards: Visa, Access, AmEx.
Other points: parking, children welcome, no-smoking area, open-air dining, Sunday lunch, afternoon teas.
Directions: on A3056 Sandown to Newport road, at Arreton country craft village.
JENNIFER HOWARD ☎(01983) 825950
Fax(01983) 528004

## SANDOWN • map 5E2

### THE OAKLANDS HOTEL
Yarbridge, PO36 0AB
A friendly, family-run licensed hotel at the foot of the Brading Downs, offering cheerful, efficient service. Local activities include fishing, swimming, golf and sailing. Ideal for walking holidays. The pool is heated to at least 82 degrees Fahrenheit from June to September.
DOUBLE ROOM: from £20 to £30
SINGLE ROOM: from £20 to £30
FOOD: up to £15
Hours: breakfast 8.30am-9am, dinner (low season) 6.30pm-7pm, bar meals (high season) 9pm-10.30pm.
Cuisine: ENGLISH
Cards: Visa, Access, AmEx.
Other points: children catered for (please check for age limits), garden, pets allowed, swimming pool, floodlit boules, aerospa, vegetarian meals, parking.
Rooms: 9 bedrooms including 2 four-poster (all non-smoking). All ensuite with TV, video, hair dryer, radio, tea/coffee-making facilities, trouser-press.
Directions: on Ryde-Sandown road, 1 mile from Sandown in direction of Brading.
JOAN RAWLINGS & FAMILY ☎(01983) 406197
Fax(01983) 406197

## SEAVIEW • map 5E2

### SEAVIEW HOTEL & RESTAURANT
High Street, PO34 5EX
This Victorian hotel is situated in the heart of the pretty sailing village of Seaview. It is possible to while away many hours looking at the unique collection of prints of old ships and liners that once passed the hotel. Frequented by local characters and the visiting yachtsmen. Les Routiers Restaurant of the Year 1989.
DOUBLE ROOM: from £30 to £40
FOOD: from £15 to £20  CLUB
Hours: breakfast 7am-9.30am, lunch 12noon-2pm, dinner 7.30pm-9.45pm.
Cuisine: EUROPEAN - local produce, seafood and game, home-grown vegetables and herbs, island asparagus, garlic, lobster and local wine.
Cards: Visa, Access, Diners, AmEx.

**Other points:** open-air dining, traditional Sunday lunch, children catered for (please check for age limits), residents' lounges, no-smoking area, residents' bar, vegetarian meals, parking.
**Rooms:** 4 double rooms, 10 twin rooms, 2 suites. All with en suite, TV, telephone, room service. Some with sea view.
**Directions:** take B3330 to Seaview. At Nettlestone Green turn left into village. Continue down to sea: hotel on left.
MR & MRS NICHOLAS HAYWARD ☎(01983) 612711 Fax(01983) 613729

## SHANKLIN • map 5E2

### BRAEMAR HOTEL
1 Grange Road, PO37 6NN
*The Braemar is tucked away in Shanklin's old village. Probably the island's most attractive corner, it is ideally placed for the beach, chine, shops and countryside. All bedrooms are tastefully decorated, providing a cosy, relaxing retreat. A large sunbathing balcony is available to all guests, and at mealtimes, individual tables with waitress service make dining here a real pleasure. Entertainment is provided in the comfortable surroundings of the Olde Worlde Thatched bar, which also has its own dance floor. A happy, friendly atmosphere prevails.*
DOUBLE ROOM: up to £20
FOOD: up to £15
**Hours:** breakfast 8.45am, dinner 6pm.
**Cuisine:** ENGLISH - with a touch of continental style.
**Cards:** Visa, Access, AmEx.
**Other points:** parking, children welcome, no-smoking area, pets, vegetarian meals.
**Directions:** Grange Road is directly off Shanklin High Street.
MRS P. WILSON ☎(01983) 863172

### BURLINGTON HOTEL
6 Chine Avenue, PO37 6AG
*An attractive stone building, constructed in the reign of Queen Victoria as a gentleman's residence. Standing in its own grounds overlooking the sea, it is a comfortable family hotel for those seeking the customary seaside holiday. Traditional home-cooking, with a pleasant lounge bar and residents' lounge with sea views.*
DOUBLE ROOM: from £20 to £30
**Other points:** parking, children welcome, residents' lounge, vegetarian meals, garden, residents' bar, cots.
**Rooms:** 3 single rooms, 4 double rooms, 1 twin room, 5 family rooms. All with TV, tea/coffee-making facilities.
**Directions:** follow the B3328 to Chine Avenue, then turn right.
MR J.W. ELLYATT ☎(01983) 862090

### THE HAMBLEDON HOTEL
11 Queens Road, PO37 6AW
*A detached family-run hotel surrounded by well-kept gardens. Tastefully decorated in a traditional*

*style to a high standard, the accommodation is very comfortable. This is an ideal place to stay if you have young children, as there are special provisions for very young children, including baby-sitting: Mrs Birch is a trained nursery nurse.*
DOUBLE ROOM: up to £20
SINGLE ROOM: up to £25
**Hours:** breakfast 8.30am-9am, dinner 6.30pm.
**Cuisine:** BREAKFAST
**Cards:** Visa, Access.
**Other points:** children welcome, garden, nursery, special diets.
**Rooms:** 1 single room, 6 double rooms, 1 twin room, 3 family rooms. All with TV, radio, telephone, hair dryer.
**Directions:** from Fishbourne ferry, take A3055 to Shanklin. Near Cliff Top lift.
NORMAN & BERYL BIRCH ☎(01983) 862403 Fax(01983) 867894

### QUEENSMEAD HOTEL
Queen's Road, PO37 6AN
*Positioned close to the famous Keats' Green area of Shanklin, just minutes from the sea, town and old village. An elegant Victorian villa with modern additions, the hotel has a large, heated outdoor swimming pool and a sheltered rose arbour in the garden. The dining room is also open to non-residents, space permitting. Guaranteed personal all-day service.*
DOUBLE ROOM: from £30 to £40
SINGLE ROOM: from £35 to £45
FOOD: up to £20
**Hours:** breakfast 8.30am-9am, lunch 12noon-2.30pm, dinner 6.30pm, closed December until end of February, open Christmas.
**Cuisine:** ENGLISH
**Cards:** Visa, Access, Mastercard, Amex.
**Other points:** children catered for (please check for age limits), vegetarian meals, garden, residents' lounge.
**Rooms:** 2 single rooms, 12 double rooms, 10 twin rooms, 6 family rooms. All en suite with TV, tea/coffee-making facilities.
**Directions:** opposite the church of St Saviour (very tall spire) on the cliff.
MR & MRS CHAPMAN & MR JULIAN CHAPMAN ☎(01983) 862342

### WEST COOMBE HOTEL
West Hill Road, PO37 6PT
*Situated in a delightful secluded garden at the end of a tree-lined drive on the edge of Shanklin's old village. The tranquility of the gardens is reflected by the mood and decor of the hotel, making for a quiet, relaxing stay. With a cosy bar and restaurant opening out onto the sun terrace, dining is a double pleasure. West Coombe has an enviable reputation for a quality menu, with service to match.*
DOUBLE ROOM: up to £20
FOOD: up to £15
**Hours:** breakfast 8.30am-9am, dinner 6.15pm-7pm, closed November until February.

**Cuisine:** ENGLISH / CONTINENTAL
**Cards:** Visa, Access, AmEx.
**Other points:** parking, no-smoking area, residents' lounge, bar lounge, vegetarian meals, garden, no children.
**Rooms:** 4 single rooms, 8 double rooms, 6 twin rooms. All with en suite, TV, tea/coffee-making facilities.
**Directions:** turn off Victoria Avenue at the sign for the cricket club.
MRS B. STARKEY ☎(01983) 866323

## ST HELEN'S • map 5E2

### ST HELEN'S RESTAURANT
Lower Green Road, PO33 1TS
*This cosy English restaurant, which has a big log fire in winter, has a cheerful, relaxed atmosphere and overlooks the largest green in England. The home-cooking is excellent value and tastes delicious!*
FOOD: from £15 to £20    CLUB
**Hours:** lunch 12noon-2pm, dinner 6.30pm-0.30am, last orders 10pm, closed Monday.
**Cuisine:** ENGLISH - à la carte menu, fixed three-course menu. Mainly traditional English with vegetarian choice.
**Cards:** Visa, Access.
**Other points:** licensed, Sunday lunch, children welcome.
**Directions:** B3330 to St Helen's, right onto Lower Green.
FRANK & ROSEMARY BALDRY ☎(01983) 872303

## TOTLAND BAY • map 5E2

### SENTRY MEAD HOTEL
Madeira Road, PO39 0BJ
*An imposing Victorian country house on the west-coast headland, within two minutes' walk from the beach, providing good-quality, comfortable accommodation in attractive, pleasant surroundings. You can be assured of a warm welcome from resident proprietors Mike and Julie Hodgson. This makes an ideal base for countryside and coastal walking. Freephone 0500 131277 for reservations.*
DOUBLE ROOM: from £20 to £30
SINGLE ROOM: from £20 to £30
FOOD: up to £15
**Hours:** breakfast 8.30am-9.15am, lunch 12noon-2pm, dinner 7pm-8pm.
**Cuisine:** ENGLISH - fixed-price menu. Imaginative home-style cooking. Dishes may include turkey breast in a cream and brandy sauce, lemon sole and lamb Maroc.
**Cards:** Visa, Access, AmEx.
**Other points:** children welcome, garden, pets allowed.
**Rooms:** 2 single rooms, 5 double rooms, 3 twin rooms, 3 triple rooms, 1 family room. All with TV, radio, tea/coffee-making facilities.
**Directions:** situated on the headland, opposite Turf Walk.
MIKE & JULIE HODGSON ☎(01983) 753212/Freephone (0500) 131277 Fax(01983) 753212

## VENTNOR • map 5E2

### OLD PARK HOTEL
St Lawrence, PO38 1XS

*Games room, under-fives supper between 4.30pm and 5.30pm, sauna, solarium, swimming pool, and no danger from traffic - all this plus comfortable accommodation, good food and a friendly atmosphere, adds up to a fantastic family holiday. Mr Thornton has created a fun safe-haven for children, while providing all the qualities of a good hotel.*
DOUBLE ROOM: from £20 to £30
SINGLE ROOM: from £20 to £30
FOOD: up to £15
**Hours:** breakfast 8.30am-9.30am, bar meals 12noon-2pm, dinner 7.30pm-8.30pm.
**Cuisine:** ENGLISH - extensive fixed-price five-course menu (pies, pasties - traditional English).
**Cards:** Visa, Access.
**Other points:** licensed, children welcome, garden, afternoon tea, pets allowed, sauna, solarium, swimming pool, special breaks, residents' lounge, residents' bar, foreign exchange.
**Rooms:** 1 single room, 6 double rooms, 4 twin rooms, 3 family rooms, 20 suites. All with TV, tea/coffee-making facilities.
**Directions:** A3055 to St Lawrence.
MR R.W. THORNTON ☎(01983) 852583
Fax(01983) 854920

### ST MAUR HOTEL
Castle Road, PO38 1LG
*St Maur is beautifully situated on a level with the town, only minutes from Ventnor beach and Steephill cove. All bedrooms have views over the hotel gardens, and some have sea views.*
DOUBLE ROOM: up to £20
SINGLE ROOM: up to £25
FOOD: up to £15
**Hours:** breakfast 8.30am-9am, dinner 6.30pm-7pm, closed December until February.
**Cuisine:** ENGLISH
**Cards:** Visa, Access, Diners, AmEx.
**Other points:** children catered for (please check for age limits).
**Directions:** west of Ventnor, St Maur is 100 yards up Castle Road at end of Park Avenue (A3055).
D.J. GROOCOCK ☎(01983) 852570 Fax(01983) 852306

# SOMERSET

## BRENT KNOLL • map 4B4

### BATTLEBOROUGH GRANGE COUNTRY HOTEL
Bristol Road, TA9 4HJ

This hotel and restaurant nestles in its own grounds at the foot of the historic Iron Age fort known as Brent Knoll. Both the restaurant and bar offer imaginative, well-presented home-made food. The proprietors and their staff ensure that each guest enjoys their visit.

DOUBLE ROOM: from £15 to £30
SINGLE ROOM: from £15 to £50
FOOD: from £15 to £20

**Hours:** breakfast 7.30am-9.30am, lunch 12noon-2pm, bar meals 12noon-2pm, dinner 7pm-9pm.
**Cuisine:** MODERN ENGLISH - Peking prawns, Guiness Pie, Grange fillet steak.
**Cards:** Visa, Access, Diners, AmEx.
**Other points:** licensed, open-air dining, Sunday lunch, afternoon tea.
**Rooms:** 18 bedrooms. Including four poster rooms and executive rooms with spa baths. All with CTV, direct dial telephone.
**Directions:** 1 mile from M5 junction 22, on A38.
TONY & CAROL WILKINS ☎(01278) 760208

## BRIDGWATER • map 4C4

### WALNUT TREE HOTEL
North Petherton, TA6 6QA

Set in the heart of Somerset, this fully modernized 18th century coaching inn makes an ideal touring centre for many attractions. Two popular restaurants, friendly bar, spacious decorated luxury bedrooms, including a four-poster and suites. Quietly located, the Walnut Tree offers everything for a touring holiday base or restful short break. Ample parking.

DOUBLE ROOM: from £20 to £30
SINGLE ROOM: from £25 to £35
FOOD: from £15 to £20

**Hours:** lunch 12noon-2pm, dinner 7pm-10pm.
**Cuisine:** ENGLISH - local produce, fresh meat, duck, local dishes.
**Cards:** Visa, Access, Diners, AmEx.
**Other points:** Sunday lunch, children welcome, baby-listening device, baby-sitting, cots, disabled access, 24hr reception, foreign exchange, residents' bar, residents' lounge, central heating, vegetarian meals, parking.
**Rooms:** 2 single rooms, 22 double rooms, 8 twin rooms. All with TV, radio, alarm, telephone, tea/coffee-making facilities.
**Directions:** exit 24 of M5 to Taunton .25 mile. Follow signs to North Petherton. On A38.
RICHARD & HILARY GOULDEN ☎(01278) 662255 Fax(01278) 663946

## CREWKERNE • map 4C5

### THE GEORGE HOTEL & RESTAURANT
Market Square, TA18 7LP

An interesting building with a fascinating history dating back to the 17th century. With an excellent function room, restaurant and accommodation of the highest standard, it provides an ideal base for touring the counties of Somerset, Dorset and the Devon coastline. Also a good area for walking, cycling, golf, horse-riding, etc.

DOUBLE ROOM: from £24 to £35
SINGLE ROOM: from £24 to £38
FOOD: up to £15

**Hours:** breakfast 7.30am-9.30am, lunch 12noon-2pm, dinner 6.30pm-9.30pm.
**Cuisine:** ENGLISH / CONTINENTAL
**Cards:** Visa, Access, Diners, AmEx, MasterCard, Eurocard.
**Other points:** children welcome, Sunday lunch, residents' lounge, vegetarian meals.
**Rooms:** 3 single rooms, 4 double rooms, 5 twin rooms, 1 suite. All with TV, tea/coffee-making facilities. Bridal suite with Jacuzzi.
**Directions:** half-way between Yeovil and Chard.
FRANK & LINA JOYCE ☎(01460) 73650
Fax(01460) 72974

### THE MANOR ARMS
North Perrott, TA18 7SG

The Manor Arms is a 16th century Grade II listed building, which has been lovingly restored and refurbished. It is full of olde-worlde charm and character, with its exposed stone, inglenook fireplace and original oak beams. The restaurant and bar menu offer only home-made dishes, and comfortable accommodation is available in the adjacent Olde Coach House quietly situated in the garden behind the inn.

DOUBLE ROOM: from £20 to £30
SINGLE ROOM: from £25 to £35
FOOD: up to £15

**Hours:** breakfast 7.30am-9am, lunch 12noon-1.45pm, dinner 7pm-9pm.
**Cuisine:** ENGLISH / FRENCH - à la carte and bar menus available.
**Cards:** Visa, Access.
**Other points:** parking, children welcome, no-smoking area, conference facilities, garden, open-air dining, vegetarian meals, traditional Sunday lunch.
**Rooms:** 3 double rooms, 2 twin rooms. All with TV, tea/coffee-making facilities.
**Directions:** from A30 take A3066, signposted for Bridport. North Perrott is 1.5 miles along this road.
REX & JANE GILMORE ☎(01460) 72901

## DULVERTON • map 4C4

### THE LION HOTEL
Bank Square, TA22 9BU

*Set in the heart of the Exmoor National Park, the Lion is an ideal base for exploring this beautiful, unspoilt corner of England. It offers a warm welcome, comfortable accommodation and good food at excellent value for money. The wide range of holiday breaks cater for every interest, including those who fancy a trip in a hot air balloon.*

DOUBLE ROOM: from £26
SINGLE ROOM: from £26
FOOD: from £15 to £20
**Hours:** breakfast 8.30am-9.30am, lunch 12noon-2pm, dinner 6.30pm-9pm, Sunday 7pm-9pm.
**Cuisine:** ENGLISH - fresh Exmoor produce including salmon, trout, game birds and venison, traditionally cooked and available in the restaurants and bars.
**Other points:** Sunday lunch, children welcome, pets allowed. Shooting, hunting, fishing in the area.
**Rooms:** 4 single rooms, 4 double rooms, 4 twin rooms, 1 family room. All with TV, telephone, tea/coffee-making facilities.
**Directions:** junction 27 off M5. Then off A396, between Tiverton and Minehead.
DUNCAN & JACKIE MACKINNON (MANAGERS)
☎(01398) 323444 Fax(01398) 323980

## DUNSTER • map 4B4

### THE TEA SHOPPE
3 High Street, TA24 6SF

*15th century tea rooms in lovely medieval village close to National Trust castle. Norman and Pam can boast 32 years' experience and specialize in home-cooking. A well-presented tea room offering all sorts of unusual teas, jams, coffees, etc.*

FOOD: up to £15 🍽
**Cuisine:** ENGLISH - home-made soups and traditional recipes. Delicious puddings and home-made cakes.
**Cards:** Visa, Access.
**Other points:** licensed, traditional Sunday lunch, no-smoking area, children welcome, pets allowed.
**Directions:** situated in the town's main road at the end nearest the castle.
NORMAN & PAM GOLDSACK ☎(01643) 821304

### YARN MARKET HOTEL
27 High Street, TA24 6SF

*A Grade II listed building detached building situated next to the Olde Yarn Market in the centre of Dunster. A quiet hotel with a friendly atmosphere. Dunster Castle and Exmoor National Park close by.*

DOUBLE ROOM: from £20 to £30
SINGLE ROOM: from £20 to £30
FOOD: up to £15
**Hours:** open all year, including bank holidays.
**Cuisine:** TRADITIONAL ENGLISH - vegetarian meals available.
**Cards:** Visa, Access, AmEx.

**Other points:** private restaurant, parking.
**Rooms:** 4 bedrooms, all en suite. All with TV, radio, alarm and tea/coffee-making facilities, hair dryer on request. Family and four-poster rooms available
**Directions:** Exit M5 junction 25, A358 to Minehead, follow signs to Dunster.
MRS SARAH ASHMAN☎(01643) 821425
Fax(01643) 821425

## EXEBRIDGE • map 4C4

### ANCHOR INN HOTEL
Near Dulverton, TA22 9AZ

*A 300-year-old residential inn on the banks of the River Exe, with fishing from the hotel grounds. Standing in an acre of grounds, the Anchor Inn provides a high standard of comfort and tranquility. The restaurant is set in a converted stable block overlooking the lawned garden and river. Excellent à la carte menu includes trout from the River Exe. Ideal base for exploring Exmoor.*

DOUBLE ROOM: from £30 to £40
FOOD: from £15 to £20 🍽
**Hours:** breakfast 8.30am-9.30am, lunch 12noon-2pm, dinner 7pm-9pm, open all year.
**Cuisine:** MODERN ENGLISH - good home-cooking with local produce used where possible; the chef bakes his own bread and makes home-made desserts.
**Cards:** Visa, Access.
**Other points:** open-air dining, beer garden, reservations, children welcome, playland.
**Rooms:** 3 double rooms, 6 twin rooms.
**Directions:** on the B3222, just off the A396, north-east of Bampton.
JOHN & JUDY PHRIPP ☎(01398) 323433

## EXFORD • map 4B4

### THE EXMOOR WHITE HORSE INN
Near Minehead, TA24 7PY

*Your dream of an olde-worlde inn with log fires comes true before your eyes, standing on the green by the side of a trickling stream in one of Exmoor's most beautiful villages. Horses all around, the blacksmith busy over the road, and rolling moors await you at the edge of the village.*

DOUBLE ROOM: from £25 to £30
SINGLE ROOM: from £45 to £55
FOOD: from £15 to £20    CLUB
**Hours:** breakfast 8.30am-9.30am, lunch 12noon-2.30pm, dinner 7pm-9.30pm.
**Cuisine:** ENGLISH - steaks, seafood, venison and extensive bar snacks.
**Other points:** licensed, Sunday lunch, children welcome, garden, vegetarian meals, residents' lounge, residents' bar, parking, disabled access.
**Rooms:** 12 double rooms, 3 twin rooms, 3 family rooms. All with TV, radio, tea/coffee-making facilities, heating.
**Directions:** from Taunton take the A358, then the B224 to Exford.
MR & MRS P. HENDRIE ☎(01643) 831229
Fax(01643) 831246

## EXMOOR • map 4C4

### THE ROYAL OAK INN
Withypool, TA24 7QP
*Set in the beautiful village of Withypool in the middle of Exmoor, this is an ideal base from which to ride, hunt, shoot, fish or simply take a leisurely walk. All bedrooms are individually furnished, with their own character, and the two bars with their beamed ceilings are everything you would expect of an old country inn. R.D. Blackmore stayed here while writing his famous novel Lorna Doone.*
DOUBLE ROOM: from £30 to £40
SINGLE ROOM: from £35 to £45
FOOD: from £15 to £20
**Hours:** breakfast 8.30am-9.30am, bar snacks 12noon-2pm, 6.30pm-9.30pm, dinner 7pm-9pm.
**Cuisine:** ENGLISH / CONTINENTAL
**Cards:** Visa, Access, Diners, AmEx.
**Other points:** parking, children catered for (please check for age limits), pets allowed, residents' lounge, vegetarian meals, open-air dining.
**Rooms:** 7 double rooms, 1 twin room.
**Directions:** leave the M5 at Tiverton and take the A361. Turn left for North Molton and Withypool. The establishment is in the centre of Withypool.
MR M. BRADLEY ☎(0164383) 506/507
Fax(0164383) 659

## EXMOOR NATIONAL PARK • map 4C4

### THE ROYAL OAK INN
Winsford, TA24 7JE
*Nestling in the picturesque village of Winsford on the edge of the Exmoor National Park, the inn dates from the 12th century. Its charming thatched roof, open fireplaces and oak beams have been subtly combined with many modern facilities to ensure guests' comfort. The restaurant prides itself on its freshly cooked cuisine, and the lounges are furnished to a high standard of elegance, as are the bedrooms, which maintain cosiness and charm. This is a superb location for exploring Exmoor and its ancient history. A winner of many outstanding awards, including Les Routiers Accommodation of the Year 1994.*
DOUBLE ROOM: from £40 to £50
SINGLE ROOM: from £55 to £68
FOOD: from £15 to £20
**Hours:** bar 11.30am-2.30pm & 6pm-11pm, open all year.
**Cuisine:** ENGLISH
**Other points:** parking, children welcome, open bank holidays, afternoon teas, pets, residents' lounge, garden dining, vegetarian meals.
**Rooms:** 10 double rooms, 2 twin rooms, 1 family room, 1 suite.
**Directions:** M5 south, turn off at junction 27 onto A396 north.
CHARLES STEVEN ☎(01643) 851455 Fax(01643) 851388

## GLASTONBURY • map 4B5

### THE LION AT PENNARD

Glastonbury Road, West Pennard, BA6 8NH
*Built around 1678, the Red Lion has been sympathetically restored to retain the original flagstone floors, log fires and beam and stone interior. The atmosphere is relaxed and friendly, enhanced by welcoming staff, and provides an ideal setting in which to enjoy the excellent food. All dishes are individually prepared, beautifully presented and in generous portions.*
DOUBLE ROOM: from £30 to £40
FOOD: up to £15
**Hours:** breakfast 8am-9.30am, lunch 12noon-2.30pm, dinner 7pm-9pm.
**Cuisine:** ENGLISH / CONTINENTAL - restaurant menu and bar snacks. Dishes may include breast of duck with cherry sauce, veal Portuguese. All dishes individually prepared.
**Cards:** Visa, Access, AmEx.
**Other points:** licensed, Sunday lunch, children welcome.
**Directions:** A361 between Shepton Mallet and Glastonbury in West Pennard.
BOB BUSKIN, LORRAINE JESSEMEY & PARTNERS ☎(01458) 832941

## HOLTON • map 4C5

### THE OLD INN
Near Wincanton, BA9 8AR
*The Old Inn is a 350-year-old coaching inn with a small, intimate restaurant. The bar has an original flagstone floor and inglenook fireplace. The inn is situated half-way between London and the West Country.*
FOOD: up to £15 CLUB
**Hours:** lunch 12noon-2pm, dinner 7pm-12midnight, last orders 10pm; bar Saturday 11.30am-11pm, Sunday 12noon-3pm, 7pm-10.30pm, weekdays 11.30am-3pm and 5pm-11pm.
**Cuisine:** ENGLISH - à la carte menu, extensive wine list. Four-course Sunday lunch if booked. Wide range of bar meals, from sandwiches to steaks.
**Cards:** Visa, Access.
**Other points:** licensed, open-air dining, Sunday lunch, children catered for (please check for age limits), beer garden, pets allowed, coaches by prior arrangement
**Directions:** just off A303 in centre of Holton, one mile from Wincanton.
MARTIN & LINDA LUPTON ☎(01963) 32002

## ILMINSTER • map 4C5

### THE ROYAL OAK

Over Stratton, South Petherton, TA13 5LQ
*This delightful 600-year-old Grade II listed country inn built from Somerset Ham stone, has a traditional olde-worlde feel, the walls and oak beams festooned with dried flowers. It has a superb reputation for its excellent cuisine - which includes wild boar sausages as a speciality - plus an outstanding wine list. Service is first-class.*

FOOD: from £15 to £20
**Hours:** lunch and bar meals 12noon-2.15pm, dinner and bar meals 6.30pm-10pm, open 7 days a week.
**Cuisine:** INTERNATIONAL - dishes include Thai chicken, crab Mexicana, Oak special kebab, pork and apricot medallions, wild boar sausages. Good range of desserts, and extensive wine list.
**Cards:** Access,Visa,Switch,Delta
**Other points:** children welcome, children's adventure play area, no-smoking area, open-air dining, traditional Sunday lunch, vegetarian and children's menus, parking.
**Directions:** off A303 at the end of Ilminster by-pass, South Petherton roundabout, towards Ilminster. First left after garage, pub .5 to 1 mile on the left.
MR BRIAN ELDERFIELD ☎(01460) 240906
Fax (01460) 242421

## MINEHEAD • map 4B4

### BEACONWOOD HOTEL
Church Road, North Hill, TA24 5SB
*A 16-bedroom Edwardian country house hotel, which stands in over two acres of terraced gardens, with panoramic views over Exmoor and the sea. A warm welcome awaits you, and the quiet, friendly atmosphere guarantees a peaceful and relaxing stay. There is a bar decorated like an old country inn, a spacious dining room serving good food, and the accommodation is of a very high standard.*
DOUBLE ROOM: from £20 to £30
SINGLE ROOM: from £30 to £40
FOOD: up to £15
**Hours:** breakfast 8.30am-9.15am, lunch 12noon-1pm, dinner 6.30pm-8pm.
**Cuisine:** ENGLISH
**Cards:** Visa, Access.
**Other points:** children welcome, garden, pets allowed, special breaks, tennis, swimming pool.
**Rooms:** 1 single room, 6 double rooms, 7 twin rooms, 2 family rooms. All with TV, radio, telephone, tea/coffee-making facilities, alarm, baby-listening device.
**Directions:** close to St Michaels Church, off St Michaels Road.
MR T. ROBERTS ☎(01643) 702032

## PANBOROUGH • map 4B5

### THE PANBOROUGH INN
Near Wells, BA5 1PN
*A late-17th century inn situated in the hamlet of Panborough, and offering a quiet, relaxing atmosphere. The well-maintained frontage with hanging baskets and manicured gardens are a joy in summer. Good, traditional food in delightful surroundings!*
FOOD: up to £15
**Hours:** dinner 6.30pm-10pm, lunch 11.30am-2.30pm, open all year.
**Cuisine:** ENGLISH - à la carte and table d'hôte menus offering a wide range of traditional-style

dishes. Good choice of steaks. Vegetarian dishes also available.
**Cards:** Visa, Access.
**Other points:** licensed, open-air dining, Sunday lunch, children welcome, pets allowed, open bank holidays, disabled access.
**Directions:** situated on the B3139 Burnham-on-Sea/Wedmore/Wells road.
JOHN HALLIWELL & KENNETH HARGREAVES ☎(01934) 712554

## RODE • map 4B5

### THE BELL INN
13 Frome Road, BA3 6PW
*Having undergone thorough modernization, the inn still retains the olde-worlde charm of yesteryear. The cuisine is traditional English and international, but the fish specialities come highly recommended. The superb wine list offers 28 wines from around the world to complement any dish selected. After a sumptuous meal you can relax in the comfortable lounge or bar over a post-dinner drink and take in the warm, friendly atmosphere.*
FOOD: from £15 to £20
**Hours:** lunch 12noon-2.30pm, dinner 6pm-10pm, open all year.
**Cuisine:** INTERNATIONAL - an excellent reputation for speciality fish cuisine, and lobster when available.
**Cards:** Visa, Access, MasterCard, Switch.
**Other points:** parking, children welcome, garden, open-air dining, tradtional Sunday lunch, vegetarian meals.
**Directions:** follow A361 Trowbridge to Frome road for approximately 5 miles. The restaurant is on the right when entering Rode.
MIKE & LEZA PRICE ☎(01373) 830356

## STOKE-SUB-HAMDON • map 4C5

### THE BLACK PIPER
1 High Street, TA14 6PP
*A Grade II listed, converted shop, housing Somerset's premier seafood restaurant. Widely renown for its outstanding range of fresh fish and shellfish dishes, the crab Farci is a must.French and Mediterranean dishes and steaks are also available, along with a good selection of value-for-money house wines. Candlelight dining ensures an intimate, yet warm and friendly atmosphere. Yeovil Naval Air Museum is nearby.*
DOUBLE ROOM: up to £20
FOOD: from £15 to £20    CLUB
**Hours:** lunch by arrangement, dinner from 7pm until late.Open all year.
**Cuisine:** SEAFOOD AND SHELLFISH - table d'hôte and à la carte menus specializing in delicious fresh fish and seafood, although a range of meat dishes are also available. Special 'theme' evenings are presented from time to time.
**Cards:** Access, Visa, AmEx, Mastercard, Switch
**Rooms:** 1 double room, 1 twin room.

**Directions:** 5 miles west of Yeovil on A3088, .5 mile from A303.
JOSEPH, BRIAN & MARJORIE FALLOWS ☎(01935) 822826

## TAUNTON • map 4C4

### THE CAREW ARMS
Crowcombe, TA4 4AD

*Nestling in the Somerset countryside yet conveniently situated for access to the South-West, the Carew Arms is the ideal place to stay when exploring the West Country.*
DOUBLE ROOM: up to £20
FOOD: up to £15
**Hours:** breakfast 8am-9am, dinner 8pm-9pm.
**Cuisine:** ENGLISH
**Cards:** Visa, Access.
**Other points:** children welcome.
**Rooms:** 4 double rooms, 4 twin rooms.
**Directions:** off A358 Taunton to Minehead road. Situated 10 miles from Taunton, 4 miles from Williton.
MRS C. BREMNER ☎(01984) 618631

### THE CORNER HOUSE
Park Street, IA1 4QD

*A Victorian hotel of character, situated close to the centre of Taunton. Lunch and dinner is served in the Parkfield Restaurant, offering food and wine of fine quality, and the staff are efficient and friendly. Close to Exmoor, Dartmoor, the Quantocks, and Yeovilton Air Museum.*
DOUBLE ROOM: from £30 to £40
SINGLE ROOM: over £50
FOOD: from £15 to £20 🍲
**Hours:** breakfast 7.30am-9.30am, lunch 12noon-1.30pm, dinner 7pm-9pm.
**Cuisine:** ENGLISH / FRENCH - including trout served with almonds and Chateaubriand. Good wine list.
**Cards:** Visa, Access, Switch.
**Other points:** licensed, no-smoking area, children welcome, open bank holidays, vegetarian meals, parking, residents' lounge, residents' bar, disabled access.
**Rooms:** 12 single rooms, 12 double/twin rooms, 5 family rooms. All with en suite, TV, radio, telephone, tea/coffee-making facilities, alarm.
**Directions:** A38, on south side of Taunton town centre.
MR R. IRISH ☎(01823) 284683 Fax(01823) 323464

### THE PEN & QUILL
Shuttern, TA1 4ET

*Situated in the centre of Devon's cider-making capital, this delightful 180-year-old inn offers traditional English and continental cuisine and speciality mixed grills against an impressive interior and a friendly atmosphere. Difficult to park nearby, but well worth the walk.*

FOOD: up to £15
**Hours:** bar meals 12noon-2.15pm, and 6.30pm-10pm, open bank holidays.
**Cuisine:** TRADITIONAL ENGLISH / CONTINENTAL - steaks with speciality sauces, salad platters, main dishes include home-made tomato, basil and walnut quiche, broccoli and cream cheese bake, chicken pizzaiola.
**Cards:** Access, Visa
**Other points:** children welcome, traditional Sunday lunch, vegetarian meals.
**Directions:** south of the town centre, the pub is on the A38, by the police station.
CHRIS COLE ☎(01823) 256982

## WATCHET • map 4B4

### WEST SOMERSET HOTEL
Swain Street, TA23 0AB

*A 2-crown town pub situated in the ancient port of Watchet. The hotel can arrange sea, freshwater fishing, clay pigeon shooting, golf and horse-riding. For fossil hunters, the local cliffs are of interest. Also an ideal base for cycling and walking holidays in Somerset and Devon.*
DOUBLE ROOM: up to £20
FOOD: up to £15
**Hours:** breakfast 8.30am-10am, lunch 12noon-2pm, dinner 7pm-10pm.
**Cuisine:** ENGLISH - imaginative cuisine using local produce plus standard back-up menu and daily specials. Wine list includes interesting and excellent locally produced wines.
**Cards:** Visa, Access.
**Other points:** open-air dining, Sunday lunch, children welcome, pets allowed.
**Rooms:** 13 rooms.
**Directions:** from junction 23 of M4 take A39 to Minehead and follow A3191 to Watchet at Williton. Hotel in centre of Watchet.
CLIFFORD & VICTORIA BARBER ☎(01984) 634434 Fax(01984) 634434

## WELLS • map 4B5

### THE BULL TERRIER
Croscombe, BA5 3QJ

*An old stone-built country pub with stone flagged floors, open inglenook fireplace and an attractive garden. With a reputation for good food and value for money, The Bull Terrier has an atmosphere which is warm and inviting to locals and holiday-makers alike.*
DOUBLE ROOM: from £22 to £30
SINGLE ROOM: from £30
FOOD: up to £15
**Hours:** breakfast 8.15am-9am, lunch 12noon-2pm, Sunday 12noon-1.45pm, dinner 7pm-9.30pm, Sunday 7pm-9pm, closed all day Monday, 1st October until 31st March.
**Cuisine:** ENGLISH / CONTINENTAL - dishes include tuna and egg mayonnaise, scampi, turkey cordon bleu, home made paté, selection of home made vegetarian dishes, hot butterscotch and

walnut fudge cake.
**Cards:** Visa, Access.
**Other points:** licensed, Sunday lunch, garden, children catered for (please check for age limits), real ales.
**Rooms:** 1 double room, 2 twin rooms, all with tea/coffee-making facilities.
**Directions:** on A371, in the village of Croscombe, east of Wells.
BARRY & RUTH VIDLER ☎(01749) 343658

### CROSSWAYS INN
North Wootton, BA4 4EU
*Located in the heart of the country, off the A361 and midway between Wells, Glastonbury and Shepton Mallet. Overlooking the historic Vale of Avalon and Glastonbury Tor. Advance booking recommended.*
DOUBLE ROOM: up to £20
SINGLE ROOM: up to £25
FOOD: up to £20 ☜
**Hours:** lunch 12noon-2.30pm, dinner 7pm-10pm.
**Cuisine:** ENGLISH - full à la carte menu plus daily specials in the buffet bar, hot and cold bar meals.
**Cards:** Visa, Access.
**Other points:** Sunday lunch, children welcome, coaches by prior arrangement
**Rooms:** 7 bedrooms. All en suite with TV, telephone, tea/coffee-making facilities.
**Directions:** on the A361 midway between Glastonbury and Shepton Mallet or A39 Wells to Glastonbury.
JOHN KIRKHAM ☎(01749) 890237/890476
Fax(01749) 890476

### THE CROWN AT WELLS
Market Place, BA5 2RP
*A Grade II listed building dating from approximately 1450 and located right in the centre of Wells adjacent to the cathedral. The black and white, timbered, exterior is very imposing and the public areas and bedrooms reflect a high standard of comfort and service. The Penn bar retains its original style and has a blackboard menu to complement the wider choices available in Anton's restaurant. Very well situated for exploring this attractive part of Somerset.*
DOUBLE ROOM: from £20 to £30
SINGLE ROOM: from £45 to £55
FOOD: up to £15
**Hours:** breakfast 7.30am-9.30am, lunch 12noon-2pm, bar meals 11am-3pm and 6pm-8.30pm, dinner 7pm-9.30pm, open bank holidays.
**Cuisine:** choice of à la carte and table d'hôte menus with a wide range of traditional dishes. Good selection of international wines.
**Cards:** Visa, Access, AmEx, Switch.
**Other points:** licensed, residents' lounge, no-smoking area, 24 hour reception, pets allowed, laundry/valet service, Spanish and German spoken, parking.
**Rooms:** 3 single rooms, 3 twin rooms, 5 double

rooms, all en suite, and 4 four-poster rooms. All with TV, radio, alarm, telephone, hair dryer, baby-listening device, room service and tea/coffee-making facilities.
**Directions:** in the central market place of Wells, next to the cathedral.
PETER AXTON & ADRIAN LAWRENCE
☎(01749) 673457 Fax(01749) 679792

### FOUNTAIN INN & BOXERS RESTAURANT
1 St Thomas Street, BA5 2UU
*Georgian-style building, 50 yards from Wells Cathedral, enjoying a local reputation for fine food using the freshest ingredients. Good selection of Spanish wines. Restaurant decorated with pine, local prints and Laura Ashley fabrics.*
FOOD: up to £15 ☜ ⬜
**Hours:** lunch 11.30am-2pm, dinner 6pm-10pm, closed Christmas day and Boxing Day.
**Cuisine:** MODERN ENGLISH - local produce mainly used; lamb with redcurrant and rosemary sauce. Fresh fish daily. Interesting selection of West Country cheeses.
**Cards:** Visa, Access, AmEx.
**Other points:** licensed, Sunday lunch, children welcome, real ales.
**Directions:** in the centre of town behind the cathedral.
ADRIAN LAWRENCE ☎(01749) 672317

## WINCANTON • map 4C5

### HOLBROOK HOUSE HOTEL
Holbrook, BA9 8BS
*A genuine country house hotel, set in 15 acres of its own grounds in unspoilt countryside. Behind the walled garden and dovecote lie the squash and tennis courts. The old orchard provides a delightful setting for the outdoor heated pool. A splendid wine list complements the interesting variety of well-cooked food. A lovely hotel that provides visitors with a relaxing and pleasant atmosphere.*
DOUBLE ROOM: from £30 to £40
SINGLE ROOM: from £35 to £45
FOOD: up to £15 ☜
**Hours:** breakfast 8.15am-9.15am, lunch 1pm-2pm, dinner 7.30pm-8.30pm.
**Cuisine:** ENGLISH - à la carte, table d'hôte, using freshest ingredients available. Dining room open to non-residents for lunch only.
**Cards:** Visa, Access, Diners, AmEx.
**Other points:** licensed, traditional Sunday lunch, pets allowed, tennis, squash, swimming pool, games room, golf, riding, fishing, croquet, residents' lounge, children welcome, baby-listening device, cots, residents' bar, special 2 day breaks available.
**Rooms:** 7 single rooms, 4 double rooms, 5 twin rooms, 2 triple rooms, 2 quad rooms. All with radio, alarm, telephone, tea/coffee-making facilities, heating, baby-listening device, cots.
**Directions:** 1.5 miles outside Wincanton off A303,

on the A371 towards Castle Cary and Shepton Mallet.
MRS J.M. TAYLOR ☎(01963) 32377 Fax(01963) 32681

## WOOLVERTON • map 4B5

### WOOLVERTON HOUSE HOTEL
Near Bath, BA3 6QS

*Woolverton House was built in the eary 19th century as a rectory, and has been sympathetically converted to a splendid hotel. Set in its own 22 - acre grounds with scenic views, it offers all the facilities you woul expect from an elegant country house. Surrounded by beautiful countryside, this is an ideal location for a leisurely break.*
DOUBLE ROOM: from £20 to £30
SINGLE ROOM: from £20 to £45
FOOD: from £15 to £20
**Hours:** breakfast 7.30am - 9am, lunch 12 noon - 2pm, dinner 7pm - 9pm, closed 24th December until 3rd January
**Cuisine:** ENGLISH
**Cards:** Visa, Access, Diners, AmEx.
**Other points:** parking, children welcome, open bank holidays, no-smoking area,disabled access, pets allowed, residents' lounge, vegetarian meals, open-air dining, residents' garden.
**Directions:** 9 miles south of Bath on A36.
VERA WILKES ☎(01373) 830415 Fax(01373) 830415

## YEOVIL • map 4C5

### THE PALL TAVERN
Silver Street, BA20 1HN

*A former medieval tavern, interestingly named after a burial cloth boasts a fascinating history. The intimate interior retains an olde-worlde feel, enhanced by the open fires, stone floors and walls adorned with farming implements. Traditional English cuisine is offered. Nearby attractions include Yeovil Air Museum.*
FOOD: up to £15
**Hours:** lunch and bar meals 12noon-2.15pm, dinner and bar meals 6.30pm-10pm, open bank holidays.
**Cuisine:** TRADITIONAL ENGLISH - steaks, grills, daily blackboard specials, home-made puddings. Children's and vegetarian menus.
**Cards:** Access,Visa,Switch,Delta
**Other points:** children welcome, open-air dining, conference facilities, traditional Sunday lunch.
**Directions:** located in Yeovil town centre.
MR BROWN ☎(01935) 76521

# *WILTSHIRE*

## BRADFORD ON AVON • map 5C1

### GONGOOZLER RESTAURANT
Bradford on Avon Marina, Trowbridge Road, BA15 1UD

*This fully licensed restaurant is situated on the water's edge of Bradford's very own marina. The entire frontage presents a panoramic view of the water and the multi-coloured long-boats bobbing up and down in their berths. The beautiful wood panelling, beams and natural stone blend together in total harmony, creating an air of complete relaxation. A comprehensive wine list complements the good menu, offering great value for money in a spectacular location.*
FOOD: up to £15
**Hours:** lunch 12noon-2.30pm, dinner 7pm-10pm.
**Cuisine:** ENGLISH - a good selection from a varied à la carte menu, using fresh ingredients.
**Cards:** Visa, Access, Diners, AmEx.
**Other points:** parking, children welcome, vegetarian meals, no-smoking area, traditional Sunday lunch.
**Directions:** take the A363 from Trowbridge to Bradford on Avon. The Gongoozler can be found in Widbrook on the right-hand side, 200 yards from

the bottom of the hill.
M. & D.J. GRIGGS ☎(01225) 862004 †
Fax(01225) 862004

### RIVERSIDE INN HOTEL & RESTAURANT
49 St Margaret's Street, BA15 1BE

*Overlooking the Avon River, this charming 17th century inn has a long tradition of hospitality and good service. Well located to serve as a base from which to explore the many nearby attractions, the Riverside offers comfortable accommodation and excellent home-cooking. Their succulent steak-and-kidney pies are renowned.*
DOUBLE ROOM: up to £20
SINGLE ROOM: up to £25
FOOD: up to £15
**Hours:** bar meals 12noon-2.30pm, 6pm-10pm, breakfast 7.30am-9am, dinner 6pm-10pm.
**Cuisine:** ENGLISH - traditional home-made English cuisine. A la carte or table d'hôte menus available. Bar meals also available.
**Cards:** Visa, MasterCard, Switch.
**Other points:** open-air dining, Sunday lunch, children welcome, open bank holidays.
**Rooms:** 4 double rooms, 6 twin rooms, 2 family

rooms.
**Directions:** into town centre and over bridge, first right turn.
MR & MRS STEFANICKI ☎(01225) 863526
Fax(01225) 868082

###  TOLL GATE INN
Ham Green, Holt, BA14 6PX
*An attractive, 18th century, Grade II listed inn on the western edge of Holt village with extensive views over the surrounding countryside. Fast gaining a reputation for good home-made food at reasonable prices, the Toll Gate Inn can also offer comfortable bed and breakfast accommodation in 2 nearby annexes. A wide range of beer is stocked and boules may be enjoyed in gardens. Traditional jazz, first Friday of the month, and Holt's Morris Men visit regularly.*
DOUBLE ROOM: from £15 to £20
SINGLE ROOM: up to £20
FOOD: up to £15
**Hours:** lunch (restaurant and bar) 12noon-2pm, dinner Tuesday-Saturday (restaurant and bar) 7pm-9.30pm.
**Cuisine:** TRADITIONAL ENGLISH/CONTINENTAL - steak-and-kidney pie, pork in cider, tipsy chicken together with a varied menu of other home-made dishes.
**Cards:** Access,Visa,Eurocard,Mastercard
**Other points:** parking, patio garden, log fire in bar, disabled access.
**Rooms:** 5 bedrooms.
**Directions:** on the western edge of Holt on the B3107 Bradford on Avon to Melksham road.
MR & MRS DAVIES ☎(01225) 782326 Fax(01225) 782326

### WIDBROOK GRANGE
Trowbridge Road, BA15 1UH
*An impressive building set in 11 acres, expertly converted to provide luxurious accommodation in both the house and the courtyard rooms while retaining the atmosphere of a traditional English farmhouse. Inside, the decor and furnishings are elegant and provide the best in comfort. Widbrook Grange enjoys a welcoming, gracious atmosphere and is highly recommended as a delightful place to stay or as an elegant conference venue.*
DOUBLE ROOM: from £35 to £45
SINGLE ROOM: over £50
FOOD: from £20 to £25 ☞
**Hours:** breakfast 7.30am-9.45am, dinner 6.30pm-8pm.
**Cuisine:** INTERNATIONAL - an evening meal is available Monday to Thursday. Fresh, local produce is used in preparing the daily changing menu. Orders for dinner are requested by 6pm.
**Cards:** Visa, Access, Diners, AmEx.
**Other points:** children welcome, residents' lounge, garden, conferences, indoor swimming pool.
**Rooms:** 1 single room, 13 double rooms, 4 twin rooms, 2 family room. All with TV, telephone, tea/coffee-making facilities.

**Directions:** 1 mile from town centre, 200 meters past canal towards Trowbridge.
JOHN & PAULINE PRICE ☎(01225) 864750/863173 Fax(01225) 862890

## CHIPPENHAM • map 5CI

### THE BELL HOUSE HOTEL
High Street, Sutton Benger , SN15 4RH
*This delightful 15th century former manor house has been transformed into an excellent hotel combining the best of modern and traditional decor. The bedrooms are beautifully appointed and individually styled, each with en suite facilities for a comfortable stay. The softly-lit restaurant specialises in a wide range of traditional Italian dishes complemented by an extensive wine list.*
DOUBLE ROOM: from £20 to £40
SINGLE ROOM: from £30
FOOD: from £15 to £20  CLUB
**Hours:** breakfast 7am-9.30am, lunch 12noon-2.30pm, dinner 6.30-10.30pm
**Cuisine:** ITALIAN WITH TRADITIONAL AND MODERN ENGLISH - specialities, such as stincotto, paella, frito misto, aubergines alla parmigiana, brasato di cinghiale al Piemontese (braised wild boar) and a full range of pasta dishes.
**Cards:** Visa, Access, Diners, AmEx, Switch, Delta.
**Other points:** no smoking area, pets allowed, licensed, central heating, laundry/valet service, garden, languages spoken (Italian/Spanish/French), vegetarian meals, parking, conference facilities.
**Rooms:** 2 single rooms, 4 twin rooms, 5 double rooms, 3 double deluxe rooms and 1 four poster room (honeymoon suite) all en suite and with tea/coffee maker, TV, telephone, radio, alarm, hair dryer, trouser press.
**Directions:** from junction 17 on the M4 take B4069 signposted Sutton Benger. Go 2.25 miles into the village. Hotel on the right opposite the church.
MR MARCO BERNI ☎(01249) 720401 Fax(01249) 720401

### HIT OR MISS INN
Days Lane, Kington Langley, SN15 1NS
*A 16th century, Grade II listed inn nestlin in a quiet area of an attractive Wiltshire village. It is rapidly gaining a fine reputation for its excellent food at reasonable prices from a wide and varied menu. The staff are extremely friendly and courteous.*
FOOD: up to £15 CLUB
**Hours:** lunch (bar & restaurant) 12 noon-2.30pm, dinner (bar & restaurant) 6.30pm-10pm. Closed Mondays October to mid June. Open Bank Holidays and Christmas.
**Cuisine:** TRADITIONAL ENGLISH/INTERNATIONAL - a wide range of bar snacks are offered including freshly baked white or brown baguettes with fillings. Restaurant à la carte menu includes traditional steaks, duck, lobster, crab, mussels; seafood a speciality. Vegetarian dishes also available.
**Cards:** Access,Visa
**Other points:** barbecues in summer, open log fires in winter.

# THE BELL HOUSE
## HOTEL & RESTAURANT

Situated in a quiet Wiltshire village, The Bell House Hotel and Restaurant is a restful blend of traditional style and modern comfort. Its 14 attractive bedrooms are all en suite; its spacious restaurant and bar offer an imaginative and satisfying menu with an Italian flavour. The village of Sutton Benger is conveniently situated only 2 miles from Junction 17 of the M4.

### SUTTON BENGER, NR. CHIPPENHAM SN15 4RH
## TELEPHONE (01249) 720401

**Directions:** exit junction 17 M4 and take road to Chippenham, at first lights turn left to Kington Lanley. Turn left at church in village down Church Lane to end and turn left. Inn on the right.
JEAN CROWLE ☎(01249) 758830

---

### THE JOLLY HUNTSMAN
Kington St Michael, SN14 6JB
*Originally a village brewery and tap room, this 17th century Grade II listed building is now the highly popular Jolly Huntsman. With a very good reputation, the restaurant provides a good selection of traditional English country cuisine, cooked to the highest standards and presented by the friendly, helpful staff. The oak-panelled Colonial Room is the perfect place to relax over a quiet drink. A wide range of beverages is on offer, featuring up to seven real ales at any one time.*
DOUBLE ROOM: up to £20
FOOD: up to £15
**Hours:** breakfast as required, lunch 12noon-2.30pm, dinner 6.30pm-10pm, open all year.
**Cuisine:** ENGLISH / INTERNATIONAL - 4 seasonal menus, and blackboard menu constantly updated.
**Cards:** Visa, Access.
**Other points:** children welcome, parking, pets allowed, residents' lounge, conference facilities, garden, open-air dining, vegetarian meals, traditional Sunday lunch.
**Rooms:** 1 double room, 1 family room, 1 four-poster room. All with TV, tea/coffee-making facilities,

radio, hair dryer, trouser-press.
**Directions:** from M4, junction 17 toward Chippenham, turn right at first set of traffic lights on dual carriageway, then proceed for .5 mile.
MICHAEL LAWRENCE ☎(01249) 750305
Fax(01249) 758846

---

### THE LYSLEY ARMS
Pewsham, SN15 3RU
*A 16th century, former coaching inn, now a listed building offering the weary traveller an excellent choice of traditional English cuisine, including home-made pies. The interior has an intimate atmosphere and boasts a wealth of original features, including stone walls and an inglenook. Very warm and very friendly.*
FOOD: up to £15
**Hours:** bar meals 12noon-3pm, and 6.30pm-10pm, open bank holidays.
**Cuisine:** TRADITIONAL ENGLISH - home-made cuisine, including children's menu, vegetarian dishes, specials of the day and puddings.
**Cards:** Access,Visa
**Other points:** children welcome, open air dining, traditional Sunday lunch, vegetarian meals, conference facilities, parking.
**Directions:** A4 (east), approximately 2 miles from the centre of Chippenham.
MR AND MRS SKINNER ☎(01249) 652864

---

For Reservations & Special Offers FreeCall 0500 700 456

### THE OLD HOUSE AT HOME
Burton, SN14 7LT

*Originally a 17th century coaching inn built in soft Cotswold stone, with oak beams and leaded windows throughout. Offering good home-cooked English and continental cuisine, for which it has a renowned reputation, this is a truly up-market public house with a loyal clientele.*

FOOD: up to £15 CLUB

**Hours:** lunch 12noon-2pm, dinner 7pm-10pm, Sunday dinner 7pm-9.30pm, closed Christmas day, Boxing day and Tuesday lunch.

**Cuisine:** ENGLISH / CONTINENTAL - good choice of meals cooked fresh daily; vegetarian options are available.

**Cards:** Visa, Access, AmEx.

**Other points:** patio, parking, open bank holidays, no-smoking area, disabled access, vegetarian meals, garden, open-air dining.

**Directions:** off A46 from Bath; or from Bristol, take M4 junction 18 to Acton Turville. Situated on the B4039.

DAVE & SALLY WARBURTON ☎(01454) 218227

### THE THREE CROWNS
Brinkworth, SN15 5AF

*A stone-built 18th century pub situated on the village green. There is an extensive menu with an emphasis on fresh produce. All dishes are cooked to order and served with a minimum of six fresh vegetables. The Three Crowns is justifiably proud of its award-winning cuisine. Good service and a relaxed, friendly atmosphere will add to the enjoyment of your meal.*

FOOD: up to £15

**Hours:** lunch 12noon-2pm, dinner 6pm-9.30pm, Sunday 7pm-9.30pm.

**Cuisine:** ENGLISH - blackboard menu changes daily according to the availability of fresh produce, e.g., locally smoked chicken, rack of lamb, steaks, fresh fish.

**Cards:** Visa, Access, AmEx, Switch.

**Other points:** licensed, Sunday lunch, children welcome, garden, pets allowed (in bar only).

**Directions:** on the B4042, next to the village church in Brinkworth.

MR A. WINDLE ☎(01666) 510366 Fax(01666) 510694

## DEVIZES • map 5C1

### THE BEAR HOTEL
Market Place, SN10 1HS

*A 16th century coaching inn where you will find friendly, helpful service and many historic associations. Within easy reach of Bath, Swindon, Salisbury and a host of stately homes and gardens. Weekend breaks.*

DOUBLE ROOM: from £37 to £40
SINGLE ROOM: from £50
FOOD: from £15 to £20

**Hours:** lunch 12noon-2pm, dinner Monday-Thursday 7pm-9.30pm, dinner Friday-Sunday 7pm-10pm.

**Cuisine:** ENGLISH - Devizes pie, roast joints carved at your table daily, charcoal grills in the Lawrence room.

**Cards:** Visa, Access, Switch.

**Other points:** open-air dining, Sunday lunch, children welcome.

**Directions:** 15 miles off M4, A350 to Melksham, then A365 to Devizes.

MR W.K. DICKENSON ☎(01380) 722444 Fax(01380) 722450

### THE WHEATSHEAF INN
High Street, West Lavington, SN10 4HQ

*This family-owned 16th century coaching inn at the gate to the west of England offers guests comfortable accommodation, a full à la carte restaurant, classic English pub bars with real ales, and a suite designed for conferences and functions. To add to the pleasure of your stay, the inn is tastefully decorated throughout, and the helpful staff will always offer a warm and friendly welcome.*

DOUBLE ROOM: from £20 to £30
SINGLE ROOM: from £25 to £35
FOOD: up to £15

**Hours:** breakfast 7.30am-9.30am, lunch 12noon-3pm, dinner 6.30pm-10.30pm.

**Cuisine:** ENGLISH / INTERNATIONAL - fresh fish and home-made pasta dishes are the house speciality.

**Cards:** Visa, Access, MasterCard, Switch.

**Other points:** parking, pets by arrangement, no-smoking area, residents' lounge, conference facilities, vegetarian meals, traditional Sunday lunch.

**Rooms:** 2 single rooms, 5 double rooms, 1 twin room, 1 family room. All with TV, radio, alarm, tea/coffee-making facilities. Most rooms are en suite.

**Directions:** on A360, 5 miles south of Devizes on the Salisbury Road, in the village of West Lavington.

MAUREEN DOWNS & ANDREA SLEEMAN ☎(01380) 813392 Fax(01380) 818038

## FORD • map 5C1
### INN OF THE YEAR 1996
WHITE HART HOTEL
Near Chippenham, SN14 8RP

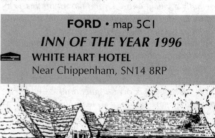

*Reputedly built in 1533 and listed as being of architectural and historical interest, this attractive West Country inn was featured in the film Dr Doolittle. In spring and summer, the terrace*

*overlooking the Bybrook River is an ideal spot to eat, drink and contemplate the abundance of nature. The interior is pleasantly decorated, and there is a wealth of oak beams. The atmosphere lends itself well to the olde-worlde image, and the inn was the Good Pub Guide "Pub of the Year 1995.*

**DOUBLE ROOM:** from £20 to £30
**SINGLE ROOM:** from £35 to £45
**FOOD:** up to £15 🍽
**Hours:** breakfast 7.15am-9.30am, lunch 12noon-2pm, dinner 7pm-9.30pm, open all year.
**Cuisine:** ENGLISH / FRENCH
**Cards:** Visa, Access, Diners, AmEx.
**Other points:** licensed.
**Rooms:** 10 double rooms, 1 twin room.
**Directions:** situated on the A420, exit junction 17 or 18 from Chippenham.
MR & MRS PHILLIPS ☎(01249) 782213
**Fax**(01249) 783075

## LACOCK • map 5C1

### 🏠 CARPENTER'S ARMS
22 Church Street, SN15 2LB

*Originally a 16th century coaching house named the White Hart, the Carpenter's Arms is now a free house and serves many fine real ales. The restaurant offers superb home-made meals, and the bedrooms have been decorated in the style of the 18th century. Situated in the centre of Lacock village. There are many tourist attractions within easy travelling distance.*

**DOUBLE ROOM:** from £20 to £30
**SINGLE ROOM:** from £25 to £35
**FOOD:** from £15 to £20
**Hours:** breakfast 8.30am, lunch 12noon-2pm, dinner 6pm-9.30pm, bar snacks available throughout the day, closed Christmas day.
**Cuisine:** ENGLISH - traditional home-cooking.
**Cards:** Visa, Access, Diners, AmEx.
**Other points:** parking, children catered for (please check for age limits), no-smoking lounge and restaurant, disabled access, residents' lounge, vegetarian meals.
**Rooms:** 3 double rooms.
**Directions:** take A350 from Chippenham towards Melksham. Turn left opposite the Garden Centre and follow signs to Lacock. The Carpenter's Arms can be found by taking the first left after the bridge in the village.
MR F. GALLEY ☎(01249) 730203 **Fax**(01249) 730115

## MALMESBURY • map 5B1

### 🏠 THE WHITE HORSE INN
Station Road, Minety, SN16 9QY

*An imposing, white painted Victorian building with modern extensions and patio dining adjacent to a small lake in the centre of the village. The warm and intimate dining room offers an extensive range of delicious home-produced dishes, also a range of fixed-price party menus which represent very good value.*

**DOUBLE ROOM:** from £15 to £20
**SINGLE ROOM:** from £20 to £30
**FOOD:** from £15 to £20
**Hours:** breakfast 7.30am-10am, lunch 12noon-2pm, dinner 7pm-10pm. Closed at Christmas.
**Cuisine:** ENGLISH HOME COOKING - à la carte menu with fixed-price party menus also available. Dishes may include pork, stilton and bacon pie, home-made fisherman's bake, supreme of chicken flamed in brandy, Cajun lamb or fillet steak Royale.
**Cards:** Access, Visa
**Other points:** parking, separate function room, outdoor dining on patio. Small lake next to inn.
**Rooms:** 2 double rooms en suite with tea/coffee maker, TV, alarm.
**Directions:** from Malmesbury take the B4040 towards Cricklade. The White Horse Inn is in Minety just before the bridge on the right hand side.
MR A GREENWOOD ☎(01666) 860284
**Fax**(01666) 860468

## MERE • map 5D1

### 🏠 THE OLD SHIP HOTEL
Castle Street, BA12 61E

*A delightful and charming hotel dating back to the early 17th century. Many parts of the originl building have been maintained, occupied as a private residence until 1682. The interesting and attractive restaurant, constructed of old ships' timbers, is comfortable and relaxing, serving good, well-prepared food. The large bar area bears the original style of the building, reflecting a hotel full of rustic charm and character, steeped in tradition.*

**DOUBLE ROOM:** from £20 to £25
**SINGLE ROOM:** up to £20
**FOOD:** up to £15
**Hours:** breakfast 8am-9.30am, lunch and bar meals 12noon-2.30pm, dinner 7.30pm-9pm, bar meals 6.30pm-9pm. Open bank holidays.
**Cuisine:** ENGLISH CONTINENTAL - a varied menu featuring such items as salmon and halibut weave, English duck breast with Cointreau sauce and steaks, accompanied by a comprehensive wine list.
**Cards:** Visa, Access, AmEx.
**Other points:** licensed, Hotel Bar & Archway Bar, vegetarian meals, children's menu, parking.
**Rooms:** 5 single rooms (2 ensuite), 5 twin rooms (3 en suite), 12 double rooms (9 en suite). All with TV, radio, alarm, telephone, baby-listening device, tea/coffee making facilities.
**Directions:** Mere is on the B3095 ½ mile from the A303
PAUL HEAD & CAROLINE RIX ☎(01747) 860258
**Fax**(01747) 860258

### 🏠 THE TALBOT HOTEL
The Square, BA12 6DR

*The Talbot Hotel dates from 1580 and is situated in the centre of the delightful Wiltshire country town of Mere, facing the square and the clock tower. Although the hotel has been modernized, it still retains the original features throughout. The stylish restaurant and bar have earned a fine reputation for*

*providing good food at reasonable prices.*
DOUBLE ROOM: from £20 to £30
SINGLE ROOM: from £25 to £35
FOOD: up to £15
**Hours:** breakfast 7.30am-9.30am, Sunday 8am-10am, lunch 12noon-2.30pm, dinner 6.30pm-9.30pm.
**Cuisine:** ENGLISH / INTERNATIONAL - traditional English, continental and Eastern cuisine cooked to a high standard.
**Cards:** Visa, Access, Diners, AmEx, MasterCard.
**Other points:** parking, children welcome, pets by prior arrangement, no-smoking area, conference facilities, residents' lounge, garden, open-air dining, vegetarian meals, traditional Sunday lunch.
**Rooms:** 1 single room, 2 double rooms, 1 twin room, 3 family rooms. All en suite with TV, radio, alarm, tea/coffee-making facilities.
**Directions:** situated in the centre of the village, opposite the clock tower on B3095.
PETER & HELEN AYLETT ☎(01747) 860427

## PEWSEY • map 5C2

 **WOODBRIDGE INN**
North Newnton, SN9 6JZ
*This popular 17th century country riverside inn, located in the tranquil Vale of Pewsey, is unique in offering the best of both worlds. The inn is busy and lively with a friendly atmosphere, yet not rowdy. The award-winning food and drink are imaginatively different and excellent. The rooms are comfortable and well-appointed, and you can really relax. Yet if you want to see the sights, you can make this location your ideal base: Stonehenge 15 minutes, Bath 55 minutes, Avebury 10 minutes, Marlborough 10 minutes, Salisbury 25 minutes, the South Coast 1 hour.*
DOUBLE ROOM: up to £20
SINGLE ROOM: from £25 to £35
FOOD: up to £15    CLUB
**Hours:** meals all day 11am-11pm, Sunday lunch 12noon-3pm, Sunday dinner 7pm-10.30pm.
**Cuisine:** INTERNATIONAL - a wide range of international dishes featuring Cajun, Indonesian, classical French and English, and Mexican specialities such as sizzling fajita, vegetable chimichanga, chicken burrito. Traditional Sunday roasts. Reservations essential to avoid disappointment.
**Cards:** Visa, Access, Diners, AmEx, Switch.
**Other points:** licensed, open-air dining, Sunday lunch, children welcome, beer garden, pétanque pistes, caravan/camping facilities, conferences, cots, trout fishing.
**Rooms:** 2 double room, 1 twin room. All with TV, radio, tea/coffee-making facilities.
**Directions:** 3 miles south of Pewsey on the A345, on the roundabout.
MR L. VERTESSY ☎(01980) 630266 Fax(01980) 630266

## ROWDE • map 4B6

 **THE GEORGE & DRAGON**
High Street, SN10 2PN
*This olde-worlde 17th century village inn has a well-deserved reputation for quality and value for money. Owner Tim Withers prepares the delicious meals, specializing in fresh fish dishes, cooked to order and served in the same informal atmosphere whether in the restaurant, bar or garden.*
FOOD: from £15 to £20
**Hours:** lunch 12noon-2pm, dinner 7pm-10pm, no meals Sunday and Monday, closed Christmas day, Boxing day and New Year's day.
**Cuisine:** INTERNATIONAL - fresh fish and other fresh food cooked to order.
**Cards:** Visa, Access, Switch.
**Other points:** parking, garden, open-air dining.
**Directions:** on A342 Chippenham-Devizes road, 1 mile from Devizes.
TIM & HELEN WITHERS ☎(01380) 723053
Fax(01380) 724738

## SALISBURY • map 5D1

**ANTROBUS ARMS HOTEL**
15 Church Street, Amesbury, SP4 7EY
*Situated on a quiet thoroughfare, the Antrobus Arms Hotel is a traditional hotel offering a warm welcome, good food in both the bar and the renowned Fountain Restaurant, and comfortable accommodation with large public rooms and open fires in winter. There is a large Victorian walled garden with a three-tier fountain in the centre. There is excellent fishing nearby on the River Avon. Also golf and tennis. Stonehenge is only 2 miles from the hotel, and the cathedral city of Salisbury is 6 miles.*
DOUBLE ROOM: from £20 to £30
SINGLE ROOM: from £25 to £35
FOOD: up to £15  CLUB
**Hours:** breakfast 7.30am-9.30am, lunch 12noon-2.30pm, bar meals 12noon-2.30pm, 7pm-9.30pm, dinner 7pm-9.30pm.
**Cuisine:** ENGLISH - serving bar snacks, full à la carte menu and table d'hôte. Vegetarian meals available. Fresh produce and home-grown vegetables.
**Cards:** Visa, Access, Diners, AmEx, MasterCard.
**Other points:** licensed, open-air dining, Sunday lunch, children welcome, afternoon tea, pets allowed.
**Rooms:** 7 single rooms, 6 double rooms, 6 twin rooms, 1 family room. Includes four-poster Garden Room.
**Directions:** 6 miles north of Salisbury A345, .5 mile off the A303, 11 miles west of Andover.
JOHN HALLIDAY ☎(01980) 623163 Fax(01980) 622112

**FINDERS KEEPERS**
Southampton Road, Landford, SP5 2ED
*This cottage-style building is surrounded by well-*

kept grounds, which are lit up at night. It is decorated in a light, attractive colour scheme and comfortably furnished. Serving well-presented and cooked meals, the atmosphere is relaxed and is complemented by the soft tones of music in the background. Excellent value.

**FOOD:** up to £15 ⭕ CLUB

**Hours:** lunch 10.30am-5.30pm, dinner (Tuesday-Saturday) 6.30pm-9.30pm.

**Cuisine:** ENGLISH - a wide variety of traditional fare and local dishes, with the emphasis on fresh produce and all home-made sweets.

**Cards:** Visa, Access, AmEx.

**Other points:** licensed, Sunday lunch, children welcome, garden, afternoon tea.

**Directions:** on A36, on the left travelling west from Southampton.

KIM & SUZANNE SPROAT ☎(01794) 390331

### THE GEORGE & DRAGON
85 Castle Street, SP1 3SP

*A small family pub dating back to the early 16th century, within 5 minutes' walk of the city centre. Real ales, keg bitters, bottled beers and an extensive wine list are offered to complement the variety of meals available. Enjoy the riverside garden - or barbecue your own meal in summer.*

**FOOD:** up to £15     CLUB

**Hours:** lunch 12noon-2.30pm, dinner 6pm-9pm, closed Christmas day.

**Cuisine:** ENGLISH - grills, roasts, fish salads and daily specials. All meals prepared with fresh vegetables and produce wherever possible.

**Cards:** Visa, Access, Diners, AmEx.

**Other points:** open-air dining, Sunday lunch, pets allowed, barbecues.

**Directions:** by the river in Salisbury.

JOHN & WENDY WADDINGTON ☎(01722) 333942

### THE HOOK & GLOVE INN
The Street, Farley, SP5 1AA

*Robin Brown and his staff will ensure you receive a warm, friendly reception at this rural pub which enjoys a fine reputation for good food and wine. The dining room is separate from the bar and discreet wall lighting creates a warm and intimate atmosphere. If you need to work up an appetite you can enjoy a game of boules before dining in the garden!*

**FOOD:** up to £15

**Hours:** lunch (bar and restaurant) 12noon-2pm, dinner (bar and restaurant) 7pm-9.45pm. Closed Christmas day evening and no food served Boxing Day evening.

**Cuisine:** TRADITIONAL ENGLISH WITH CONTINENTAL FLAVOUR - à la carte and blackboard menu (changed twice weekly) featuring game and fresh fish dishes. Bar snacks available, extensive wine list.

**Cards:** Access,Visa,Delta

**Other points:** parking, boules pitch.

**Directions:** leave Salisbury by A30 London road,

after 4 miles turn right to Pitton - through Pitton to Farley, turn left at fork and follow road round.

MR ROBIN KEITH BROWN ☎(01722) 712247

### THE INN
High Post, SP4 6AT

*Privately owned and run by the Sgueglia family who hail from Naples, this excellent hotel, restaurant and leisure complex offers all that is best in accommodation and dining in a beautiful and scenic setting. The leisure club is open to guests, and Enzo's night-club offers entertainment from Wednesday to Saturday. Appealing to all age groups, you will be sure to find that the comfort and relaxation of guests is foremost in the minds of this most hospitable of families.*

**DOUBLE ROOM:** over £50

**SINGLE ROOM:** over £50

**FOOD:** up to £15

**Hours:** breakfast 7am-9.30am, lunch 12noon-2.30pm, dinner 7pm-10pm. Open all year.

**Cuisine:** ITALIAN & TRADITIONAL - excellent traditional Italian dishes - particularly pasta. A special menu blackboard is posted daily with the chef's recommendation of food and wine. A self-service carvery is also offered. Excellent wine list including sparkling and champagne varieties.

**Cards:** Access, Visa, AmEx, Diners

**Other points:** parking, night-club, leisure club with gymnasium, indoor heated pool, jacuzzi and sauna. 18 hole golf course nearby. Banqueting and conference facilities.

**Rooms:** 22 twin rooms, 6 double rooms, 2 triple rooms, all en suite with tea/coffee maker, TV, telephone, trouser press, alarm. Hair dryer on request.

**Directions:** approximately 3 miles from Amesbury on the A345 Amesbury to Salisbury road. On right hand side next to garage.

VINCENZO SGUEGLIA ☎(01722) 782592
Fax (01722) 782630

### THE KINGS ARMS HOTEL
7A-11 St John's Street, SP1 2SB

*Standing in the heart of Salisbury and surrounded by picturebook English countryside, this hotel is full of lovely old oak beams, slanting staircases and sloping floors. Evenings can be spent dining by candlelight in the informal atmosphere of the restaurant. The Snug Bar offers real timeless character, while the bedrooms are individually decorated to a very high standard. Stonehenge and Salisbury Cathedral are nearby.*

**DOUBLE ROOM:** from £30 to £40

**SINGLE ROOM:** from £50

**FOOD:** up to £15

**Hours:** breakfast 7.30am-9am, lunch 12noon-2.30pm, bar snacks 11.30am-3pm, dinner 6pm-10pm, bar snacks 6pm-10pm.

**Cuisine:** ENGLISH / CONTINENTAL

**Cards:** Visa, Access, Diners, AmEx.

**Other points:** parking, children welcome, Sunday lunch, no-smoking area, pets, residents' lounge,

vegetarian meals.
**Rooms:** 1 single room, 3 double rooms, 8 twin rooms, 2 four-poster rooms, 1 family room.
**Directions:** opposite St Anne Gate to the cathedral, in St John's Street.
MR & MRS R. STOKES ☎(01722) 327629
Fax(01722) 414246

 **VICTORIA LODGE GUEST HOUSE**
61 Castle Road, SP1 3RH
*This quiet, warm and friendly guest house is situated only a short riverside walk from Salisbury town centre. Its comfortable accomodation is complemented by traditional food and hospitality.*
DOUBLE ROOM: from £20 to £30
SINGLE ROOM: from £25 to £35
**Hours:** breakfast 7.30am-9am, lunch 12noon-2pm, dinner 6pm-9pm, open bank holidays.
**Cuisine:** full English breakfast, evening bar meals and à la carte menu.
**Other points:** residents' bar, guest lounge, private restaurant, parking.
**Rooms:** 3 single rooms, 2 double rooms, 5 twin rooms, 3 family rooms, all en suite. All with TV and tea/coffee-making facilities.
**Directions:** A345 Amesbury to Salisbury road, turn left before city centre, after traffic lights.
☎(01722) 320586 Fax(01722) 414507

## SHERSTON • map 5B1

 **RATTLEBONE INN**
Church Street, SN16 0LR
*An old Cotswold pub in the time-honoured setting opposite the church. The lounge bar is full of nooks and crannies, while the roof of the dining room is festooned with tankards, water jugs and bottles. The Games Bar walls are covered with boozy cartoons, and the attractive walled garden has a boules pitch.*
FOOD: up to £15
**Hours:** lunch 12noon-2pm, dinner 7pm-9.45pm.
**Cuisine:** ENGLISH - a wide range of meat, fish and vegetarian dishes, together with constantly changing blackboard specials, with fresh vegetables.
**Cards:** Visa, Access, Diners, AmEx.
**Other points:** licensed, Sunday lunch, children welcome, disabled access.
**Directions:** situated 5 miles from Malmesbury on the B4040 heading towards Bristol.
MR I. REES ☎(01666) 840871 Fax by prior arrangement

## TROWBRIDGE • map 5C1

 **EDWARD'S DINING ROOM AT HIGHFIELD HOUSE**
High Street, Semington, BA14 6JN
*This attractive Grade II listed 18th century Georgian farmhouse has been tastefully converted, while maintaining the style of the Georgian era. The*

*restaurant successfully blends old-fashioned hospitality with the very best of modern English cuisine. Conveniently situated for Bath, Bradford on Avon, Devizes and Warminster, it is ideally suited for business entertaining, informal dining, special parties and overnight accommodation.*
DOUBLE ROOM: up to £20
SINGLE ROOM: up to £20
FOOD: from £15 to £20
**Hours:** breakfast everyday 7am-9.30am, lunch Sunday only 12noon-2.30pm, dinner Wednesday-Saturday only 7pm-9.30pm.
**Cuisine:** MODERN ENGLISH - the emphasis is on good food that is well presented and offers great value for money.
**Cards:** Visa, Access, AmEx.
**Other points:** parking, children welcome, residents' lounge, vegetarian meals, open-air dining.
**Rooms:** 1 double room, 1 twin room.
**Directions:** situated on the A350 Chippenham to Westbury road, on the High Street in Semington.
EDWARD STREET ☎(01380) 870554

## WARMINSTER • map 5C1

 **THE FARMERS HOTEL**
1 Silver Street, BA12 8PS
*Centrally located in the town centre, this family-run hotel, whose buildings date back to the 17th century, is comfortably furnished and decorated. The hotel offers good-quality food and accommodation in pleasant surroundings. Ideal for exploring West Country attractions, including Longleat and Stonehenge.*
DOUBLE ROOM: from £20 to £30
SINGLE ROOM: up to £20
FOOD: up to £15
**Hours:** breakfast 7am-9.30am, lunch 12noon-2pm, dinner 6.15pm-12midnight, last orders 10.45am.
**Cuisine:** ENGLISH / CONTINENTAL - English, French and Italian cooking, extensive à la carte and set menus and bar meals. Dishes include fettucine alla carbonara, veal marsala and steak-and-kidney pie.
**Cards:** Visa, Access, Diners, AmEx.
**Other points:** disabled access, children welcome, functions, coaches, parking, vegetarian meals.
**Rooms:** 18 bedrooms. All ensuite with TV, tea/coffee-making facilities.
**Directions:** situated on the A36.
MR G. BRANDANI ☎(01985) 213815/212068

**OLD BELL HOTEL**
42 Market Place, BA12 9AN
*Part of the Old Bell dates from 1483, and much of the character and old-English charm has been retained while adding modern comforts. Enjoy the high standard of English cuisine in the candlelit restaurant, or good bistro and bar meals. On warm days relax in the attractive courtyard, or by the open log fires in winter. Luxury accommodation*

*and excellent, welcoming service.*
DOUBLE ROOM: from £20 to £30
SINGLE ROOM: from £35 to £46
FOOD: up to £15  CLUB
**Hours:** breakfast 7.30am-9.30am, lunch 12noon-2.30pm, bar meals 12noon-2pm, dinner 7pm-10.30pm, bar meals 7pm-9pm, closed Christmas eve until Boxing day inclusive.
**Cuisine:** ENGLISH / INTERNATIONAL - à la carte and bistro menus and bar meals. Mexican, Italian and American. Bistro specialising in pizzas (evening only).
**Cards:** Visa, Access, AmEx.
**Other points:** licensed, Sunday lunch, children welcome, pets allowed, residents' lounge, functions.
**Rooms:** 3 single rooms, 11 double rooms, 4 twin rooms, 2 family rooms. All with TV, telephone, tea/coffee-making facilities.
**Directions:** in the centre of Warminster.
MERVYN PARRISH ☎(01985) 216611 Fax(01985) 217111

DOUBLE ROOM: from £30 to £40
SINGLE ROOM: from £50
FOOD: up to £15
**Hours:** breakfast 7.30am-9.30am, lunch 12noon-2pm.
**Cuisine:** CONTINENTAL - dishes may include beef Wellington, duck à l'orange, scampi provençale, mushroom stroganoff.
**Cards:** Visa, Access, AmEx.
**Other points:** licensed, open-air dining, Sunday lunch, afternoon tea, residents' lounge, garden, children welcome, baby-listening device, cots, vegetarian meals, residents' bar.
**Rooms:** 1 single room, 5 double rooms, 2 twin rooms. All with TV, radio, alarm, telephone, tea/coffee-making facilities.
**Directions:** A36, opposite Wilton House stately home. Approximately 2 miles from the city centre.
SHARON BELL ☎(01722) 743328 Fax(01722) 744886

## WILTON · map 5D1

**PEMBROKE ARMS HOTEL**
Minster Street, SP2 0BH

*A Georgian-style hotel and restaurant, set in an attractive garden complete with a small stream. The accommodation is outstanding, and the restaurant offers very good food at reasonable prices. With welcoming service and a friendly atmosphere, the Pembroke Arms is well worth a visit.*

# THE CHANNEL ISLANDS

For those seeking real solitude, the Channel Islands of Jersey, Guernsey, Alderney and Sark are the perfect location for a relaxing holiday or weekend break.

Guernsey may be very different from Jersey, kut it still has an unmistakeably French atmosphere complemented by excellent cuisine ranging from classical dishes to shellfish and seafood specialities, from the highest standard of international dishes to daily changing selections of traditional English pub food. Vegetarian, vegan and other special diets are all adequately catered for.

For the ultimate peace, tiny Sark - known as the 'Gem of the Channel Islands' - is unspoiled by aircraft or cars. The traditional and leisurely way to travel the island is by horse drawn carriage, although bicycles may be hired for exploring the many superb cliff walks.

The range of accommodation is good too: country manors set in rambling grounds, quaint farmhouses with cobbled courtyards, harbour-side inns, and modern hotels with every convenience. The Channel Islands has it all!

The following counties are included in this chapter:

ALDERNEY                    ISLAND OF SARK
GUERNSEY                    JERSEY

# THE ISLANDS

## ALDERNEY • map 4D5

 **INCHALLA HOTEL**
St Anne's
*A modern hotel with first-class facilities, including sauna and Jacuzzi. A pleasant and relaxing atmosphere in a hotel situated in lovely grounds overlooking the sea.*
DOUBLE ROOM: from £32 to £40
SINGLE ROOM: from £32 to £40
FOOD: up to £20
**Hours:** breakfast 8.30am-9.30am, Sunday lunch 1pm-2pm, dinner 7pm-8.30pm.
**Cuisine:** ENGLISH / FRENCH
**Cards:** Visa, Access, AmEx.
**Other points:** central heating, children welcome, residents' lounge, conservatory restaurant, garden.
**Rooms:** 4 double rooms, 4 twin rooms, 2 family rooms. All with satellite TV, radio, bar, telephone, hair dryer, tea/coffee-making facilities, heating.
**Directions:** at the edge of St Anne's overlooking the sea.
MRS VALERIE WILLS ☎(01481) 823220

 **ROSE & CROWN**
Le Huret, St Anne
*Constructed of Alderney granite around 1770, this hotel is situated in one of the most attractive yet peaceful parts of St Annes. It offers a friendly, homely atmosphere and is tastefully furnished to a very high standard, with added comfort. Picnic lunches are available to those who wish to spend the day walking, exploring or relaxing on the beach. Attractive garden.*
DOUBLE ROOM: from £20 to £30
SINGLE ROOM: from £25 to £35
FOOD: up to £15
**Hours:** breakfast 9am-9.30am, bar meals 12noon-2pm, 6.30pm-9pm.
**Cuisine:** ENGLISH / INTERNATIONAL - traditional English pub cuisine, and a wide choice of international specialities. Daily blackboard specials. Vegetarians catered for.
**Cards:** Visa, Access, AmEx, MasterCard.
**Other points:** licensed, open-air dining, picnic lunches, children welcome, free car hire.
**Rooms:** 6 bedrooms.
**Directions:** situated in the centre of St Anne's in a quiet area.
BASIL BLUMBERG ☎(01481) 823414 Fax(01481) 823615

---

**Join Les Routiers Discovery Club**
**FREE!  See page 34 for details.**

---

## GUERNSEY • map 4E5

### IMPERIAL HOTEL, BARS & RESTAURANT
Pleinmont, Torteval, GY8 0PS

*The Imperial has proved a popular rendezvous with tourists and locals alike for over 100 years, with its unequalled views of the west coast and safe, sandy beaches. The cuisine too is excellent, with seafood specialities and shellfish fresh from the bay. The main restaurant offers superb cuisine for that special dinner with fine wines and friendly service. In the bars, meals are served all year round; in the summer you can enjoy your lunch or supper in the garden or on the terrace.*

DOUBLE ROOM: from £20 to £30
SINGLE ROOM: up to £25
FOOD: up to £15
**Hours:** breakfast 8.15am-9.15am, lunch 12noon-1.30pm, dinner 6.30pm-9pm, bar meals 12noon-2pm, bar meals 7pm-9pm, closed (hotel only) November until March.
**Cuisine:** FRENCH - traditional French haute cuisine with seafood specialities. A la carte, table d'hôte and bar menus.
**Cards:** Visa, Access.
**Other points:** licensed, Sunday lunch, children welcome, disabled access, most rooms have sea views.
**Rooms:** 1 single room, 9 double rooms, 4 twin rooms, 3 family rooms. All en suite with TV, telephone, tea/coffee-making facilities, hair dryer.
**Directions:** at south-western tip of the island, overlooking Rocquaine Bay.
PATRICK & DIANA LINDLEY ☎(01481) 64044
Fax(01481) 66139

### LA GRANDE MARE
Castel, Vazon Bay, GY5 7LL

*La Grande Mare, situated in its own grounds of over 100 acres, enjoys delightful views. Friendly, caring and efficient service complements the high-quality food on offer at this hotel, golf and country club. The restaurant specializes in seafood, shellfish and top-class à la carte cuisine, and an extended wine list. Casserole Award winner 1990, 1991, 1992 and 1993; also Corps D'Elite.*

DOUBLE ROOM: from £50
FOOD: from £20 to £25
**Hours:** lunch 12noon-2pm, dinner 7pm-9.45pm.
**Cuisine:** CONTINENTAL - fresh seafood, shellfish, flambé and the modern interpretation of classical dishes using the best of home-grown and local produce. Extensive wine list. Restaurant of the Year 1992.
**Cards:** Visa, Access, Diners, AmEx.
**Other points:** licensed, Sunday lunch, no-smoking area, children welcome, swimming pool, spa bath, 18 hole golf course and pitch and putt, croquet lawn, fishing.
**Directions:** fronts directly onto Vazon Bay. Only 15 minutes from St Peter Port and 10 minutes from the airport.
MR P.M. VERMEULEN ☎(01481) 56576
Fax(01481) 56532

### LA TRELADE HOTEL
Forest Road, St Martin's, GY4 6UB

*A beautiful, 100-year-old, large detached house set in a country garden with mature trees. No expense has been spared in the spacious, luxuriously furnished bedrooms adorned with historial pictures and documents. The menus offer outstanding cuisine, including seafood specialities. Warm, friendly atmosphere and well-trained, courteous staff.*

DOUBLE ROOM: from £40 to £50
SINGLE ROOM: from £32
FOOD: up to £15
**Hours:** breakfast 7.30am-9.30am, lunch 12noon-2pm, dinner (restaurant) 7pm-9pm, dinner (bar area) 6pm-8.30pm, open bank holidays.
**Cuisine:** ENGLISH / FRENCH - sea foods and vegetarian dishes.
**Cards:** Visa, Access, Diners, AmEx.
**Other points:** licensed, parking.
**Rooms:** 45 bedrooms. All with satellite TV, radio, telephone, tea/coffee making facilities.
**Directions:** from the airport take the main road to St Peterport.
☎(01481) 35454 Fax(01481) 37855

### LE NAUTIQUE RESTAURANT
Quay Steps, St Peter Port

*Black oak beams and whitewashed walls adorned with various fishing items all add up to create a nautical ambience. Meals of the highest quality are served by friendly, efficient staff. Frequented by business people and locals alike, Le Nautique has its fair share of regulars: a tribute to the consistently good food and service. Established for 33 years, 18 of them under Mr Graziani.*

FOOD: from £20 to £25
**Hours:** lunch 12noon, dinner 7pm, closed Sunday, closed 26th December until 15th January, open bank holidays.
**Cuisine:** SEAFOOD - fish dishes a speciality. Dishes may include huitres de sur epinars au currie, turbot grillé au poche-sauce hollandaise.
**Cards:** Visa, Access, Diners, AmEx.
**Other points:** private dining (30 persons), no-smoking in main dining room until after 9pm.
**Directions:** town centre; on seafront overlooking St Peter Port yacht marina.
CARLO GRAZIANI ☎(01481) 721714 Fax(01481) 721786

## ISLAND OF SARK • map 4E5

### DIXCART HOTEL
Sark

*Sark, an ancient, feudal and magical isle, is traffic-free and virtually untouched by the 20th century. Dixcart Hotel has played an important part in Sark's history, and today's visitors will discover the same beauty enjoyed by Victor Hugo and others. Dixcart occupies the original 16th century feudal longhouse of La Jaspellerie Tenement and controls its own extensive acreage of medieval hand-terraced gardens, fields, cliff paths and the densely wooded*

valley of Dixcart. The family-owned hotel is open all year and offers its guests the very best facilities, service and relaxed atmosphere.
DOUBLE ROOM: from £30 to £40
SINGLE ROOM: from £30 to £40
FOOD: up to £15
**Hours:** breakfast 8.30am-10am, lunch 12noon-2pm, dinner 7pm-9pm.
**Cuisine:** LOCAL - Channel Island cuisine, especially fish and crustaceans.
**Cards:** Visa, Access, Diners, AmEx.
**Other points:** children welcome, dogs allowed, garden, bay, residents' lounges, conference facilities, open-air dining, vegetarian meals, afternoon teas, Sunday lunch.
**Rooms:** 3 single rooms, 7 double/twin rooms, 5 family rooms. All with en suite, tea/coffee-making facilities.
**Directions:** sited in the heart of Dixcart Valley on the southern coast of the island.
☎(01481) 832015 Fax(01481) 832164

## JERSEY • map 4E5

### THE ALLANDALE HOTEL
Lower Trinity, JE3 5FH
*An attractive, spacious hotel and restaurant which has been extended over the years to form the present comfortable and welcoming building. The standard of decor and service is exceptional, and Mr Burton and his uniformed and efficient staff will ensure that nothing is too much trouble to make your stay a pleasant one. The excellent restaurant offers a carvery as the house speciality, complemented by a first-class wine list and cheeseboard. Highly recommended.*
DOUBLE ROOM: from £15 to £31
SINGLE ROOM: from£15 to £20
FOOD: up to £15
**Hours:** breakfast 7.30am-9.30am, lunch 12noon-2pm, dinner 6.30pm-9.30pm. Open all year.
**Cuisine:** ENGLISH - excellent choice of menu including carvery. Comprehensive wine list and well presented cheeseboard.
**Cards:** Access,Visa,AmEx
**Other points:** seasonal rates, children catered for (please check for age limits), parking, large open spaces, grass play area, swimming pool.
**Rooms:** 1 single, 6 twin, 12 double, 4 family and 4 double rooms with four poster beds. All en suite with tea/coffee maker, TV, telephone, radio, trouser press.
**Directions:** from the town ring road take the north route on A9. After approximately 1.5 miles, near Sion.
DAVID BURTON ☎(01534) 862744 Fax(01534) 864868

### ANNE PORT BAY HOTEL
Anne Port, St Martin, JE3 6DT
*Situated in the picturesque and unspoilt bay of Anne Port, this small country inn, taking 26 guests, is owned and run by a Jersey family. Over several years, they have built a fine reputation for excellent*

food and a high level of personal service and comfort. The beach is quiet, sandy and safe for bathing. There are many exciting places of interest to visit nearby.
DOUBLE ROOM: from £20 to £30
SINGLE ROOM: from £20 to £30
FOOD: up to £15
**Hours:** breakfast 8.30am-9.15am, bar meals 12noon-1.45pm, dinner 6.30pm-7.15pm, closed November until February.
**Cuisine:** ENGLISH - à la carte and table d'hôte menus, offering home-style cuisine. Vegetarians catered for.
**Cards:** Visa, Access, AmEx.
**Other points:** licensed, children welcome, parking, residents' lounge, baby-listening device, cots, left luggage.
**Rooms:** 2 single rooms, 8 double rooms, 4 twin rooms. All with TV, radio, tea/coffee-making facilities.
**Directions:** first bay north of Gorey on east of Jersey.
MR CHRISTOPHER CAVEY ☎(01534) 852058
Fax(01534) 857887

### ARNEWOOD LODGE GUEST HOUSE
Route des Genets, St Brelade, JE3 8DA
*A small, modern hotel that offers large airy bedrooms and a good restaurant for breakfast and evening meals. Mr and Mrs Brennan and their staff offer you a warm Jersey welcome and are eager to see that all is well for your stay. Very good value and highly-recommended by our inspector.*
DOUBLE ROOM: from £20 to £30
SINGLE ROOM: from £20 to £30
**Hours:** breakfast 8.45am-9am, dinner 6.30pm.
**Cuisine:** ENGLISH/FRENCH - table d'hôte menu offering wide choice of dishes.
**Cards:** Access, Visa, Mastercard, Eurocard
**Other points:** public parking 3 minutes away.
**Rooms:** 2 twin rooms, 9 double rooms, 2 triple rooms, all en suite with tea/coffee facilities. Extra beds available.
**Directions:** take coast road from St Helier to St Brelades (Red Houses). 5 minutes from airport on main bus route.
MR JOHN BRENNAN ☎(01534) 41516
Fax(01534) 490252

### BROMLEY GUEST HOUSE
7 Winchester Street, St Helier, JE2 4TH
*A small family-run hotel offering modern and comfortable accommodation at reasonable prices. Mr and Mrs Schillaci epitomise the Italian approach to hospitality, and the atmosphere at the Bromley Guest House is welcoming and fun. Good value for money and highly recommended.*
DOUBLE ROOM: up to £20
SINGLE ROOM: up to £20
**Hours:** breakfast 8.30am, dinner 6.30pm. Open all year.
**Cuisine:** FRENCH/BRITISH/ITALIAN - table d'hôte menu with good, varied menu. Set menu varies

daily.
**Cards:** Visa, Access, Eurocard, Switch.
**Rooms:** 2 single rooms, 2 twin rooms, 3 double rooms, 1 triple room, 1 family room, all en suite except single rooms, all with tea/coffee maker, TV.
**Directions:** in the old part of the town centre of St Helier.
JOE & MARIA SCHILLACI ☎(01534) 23948
Fax(01534) 69712

### BROOKFIELD GUEST HOUSE
24 Raleigh Avenue, St Helier, JE2 3ZG
*This 100 year old terraced hotel in St helier is undergoing extensive re-modelling of the ground floor ready for the 1996 season. This will provide a new reception and lounge bar together with new decor which will complement the 20 well equipped bedrooms. Mr and Mrs Pass personally oversee the running of the hotel which ensures that guests receive excellent attention and value for money.*
DOUBLE ROOM: up to £20
SINGLE ROOM: up to £25
FOOD: up to £15
**Hours:** breakfast 8.30am, dinner 6.30am, open bank holidays, closed November, December, January.
**Cuisine:** varied menu, vegetarians catered for.
**Cards:** Visa, Access.
**Other points:** licensed, residents' and television lounges, garden, central heating, Jacuzzi, ironing facilities, Portugese spoken, children catered for (please check for age limits).
**Rooms:** 1 single room, 7 twin rooms, 10 double rooms, 2 family rooms, all en suite. All with TV, radio and tea/coffee-making facilities.
**Directions:** Jersey tourist map reference 7J. Past police station, turn right at roundabout, first left and hotel is on the right.
STEPHEN AND ANN PASS
☎(01534) 23168 Fax(01534) 21543

### BRYN-Y-MOR
Route de la Haule, Beaumont, St Aubin's Bay, JE3 8BA
*A large Georgian house, set in well-tended gardens, with a magnificent view of the beautiful bay of St Aubin's. Friendly, attentive service combines with comfortable surroundings and a fine location. Its situation, just 200 yards from 3 miles of golden beach, makes the Bryn-y-Mor a must for all visitors, be it on business or leisure. Open throughout the year.*
DOUBLE ROOM: from £20 to £30
SINGLE ROOM: from £25 to £35
FOOD: up to £15 🍽
**Hours:** breakfast 8.30am-9.30am, dinner 6.30pm-7.30pm.
**Cuisine:** ENGLISH / CONTINENTAL
**Cards:** Visa, Access, Diners, AmEx.
**Other points:** children welcome, TV lounge, picnic lunches, pets allowed.
**Rooms:** 14 bedrooms.
**Directions:** on the A1, situated on the main south

coast road.
MISS M.F. TEMPLETON ☎(01534) 20295
Fax(01534) 24262

### CORNUCOPIA HOTEL
Mont Pinel, St Helier, JE2 4RS
*A privately owned and personally managed hotel on the outskirts of St Helier backing onto beautiful countryside yet only 5 minutes from the main shopping precinct - tranquility without isolation. Open throughout the year, the hotel offers tastefully decorated bedrooms and an intimate restaurant serving a varied selection of dishes.*
DOUBLE ROOM: from £30 to £45
SINGLE ROOM: from £35 to £45
FOOD: from £15 to £20 CLUB
**Hours:** breakfast 7am-9.30am, bar meals 12noon-2pm, dinner 6.30pm-8.30pm, open bank holidays.
**Cuisine:** ENGLISH / SOME FRENCH - fresh seafood and vegetarian.
**Cards:** Visa, Access, Diners, AmEx.
**Other points:** licensed, sauna, solarium, spa bath/jacuzzi, gym, outdoor heated pool, garden for guests' use, no-smoking area, residents' and television lounges, laundry/valet service, ironing facilities, French spoken, parking.
**Rooms:** 2 single rooms, 11 double rooms, 3 triple rooms, all en suite. All with TV, radio alarm, telephone, baby listening device, tea/coffee-making facilities.
**Directions:** use free Jersey tourist map (Perrys), widely available. On St Helier map reference JF No.9.
☎(01534) 32646 Fax(01534) 66199

### COTE DU NORD HOTEL
Côte du Nord, Trinity, JE3 5BN
*Standing in its own grounds on the north-east coast, the Côte du Nord has a spectacular view of the sea and surrounding country, and is within walking distance of the harbour and village of Rozel. The restaurant is known locally for the high standard of cuisine and service it offers.*
DOUBLE ROOM: from £20 to £30
SINGLE ROOM: from £22
FOOD: up to £20
**Hours:** breakfast 8am-9.30am, lunch 12noon-2pm, dinner 7pm-10pm, closed Christmas Day.
**Cuisine:** BRITISH / FRENCH - à la carte, table d'hôte and bar menus. French cuisine: seafood a speciality.
**Cards:** Visa, Access, Diners, AmEx.
**Other points:** licensed, open-air dining, Sunday lunch, children welcome, afternoon tea.
**Rooms:** 2 single rooms, 4 double rooms, 2 twin rooms, 2 family rooms. All with TV, radio, tea/coffee-making facilities.
**Directions:** off the C93, on left towards Rozel.
MR HODSON ☎(01534) 861171/861122
Fax(01534) 865119

**GLENTHORNE HOTEL**
Elizabeth Place, St Helier, JE2 3PN
*A welcoming hotel situated close to the town and beach. The Glenthorne is family-run and offers a friendly, homely atmosphere, good home-cooking and good value for money. The proprietors are always at hand to assist guests and to ensure that your stay in Jersey is enjoyable.*
DOUBLE ROOM: from £20 to £30
SINGLE ROOM: up to £25
FOOD: up to £15
**Hours:** breakfast 8.30am-9am, dinner 6.30pm-7pm, bar 5.45pm-1am.
**Cuisine:** ENGLISH
**Cards:** Visa, Access, Diners, AmEx, Eurocard, Switch.
**Other points:** children catered for (please check for age limits), pets allowed, afternoon tea, residents' lounge, garden, picnic lunches, safe facilities.
**Rooms:** 2 single rooms, 9 double rooms, 4 twin rooms, 3 family rooms. All with TV, radio, alarm, telephone, tea/coffee-making facilities.
**Directions:** 5 minutes' walk to St Helier and beach.
MR & MRS WAYNE & ANN RHODES ☎(01534) 22817 Fax (01534) 58002

**GLOSTER HOUSE**
49 Rouge Bouillon, St Helier

*Set back from the road in a tree lined terrace, Gloster House built in the early 1800's has seen many changes but retains its early elegance with its sweeping staircase and stained glass windows. A pleasant dining room and lounge are complemented by the large airy bedrooms which provide comfortable accommodation with all modern amenities. Outside there is a sheltered garden which offers guests the use of a covered heated swimming pool. Highly recommended.*
DOUBLE ROOM: up to £30
SINGLE ROOM: up to £30
**Hours:** breakfast 8.30am-9am, dinner 6.30pm-6.45pm, open bank holidays, closed from 7th October to 21st May.
**Cuisine:** ENGLISH - varied table d'hôte menu with generous helpings.
**Cards:** Visa, AmEx.
**Other points:** licensed, residents' lounge, garden for guests' use, heated covered swimming pool, pets allowed by arrangement, trips (including travel) can be arranged, French, Italian, Spanish and Portuguese spoken.
**Rooms:** 5 single, 8 twin, 9 double and 2 family rooms, all en suite. All with TV, telephone, radio,

hair dryer and tea/coffee-making facilities.
**Directions:** follow signs for ring road A9 (Rouge Bouillon). Gloster House is set in a tree-lined terrace almost opposite the police station.
☎(01534) 20365 Fax (01534) 69144

**GREENWOOD LODGE HOTEL**
Roseville Street, St Helier, JE2 4PL
*Situated in a quieter part of St Helier, this family-run hotel is decorated to a high standard. The accommodation is bright and airy and more than comfortable. The quality food is prepared under the personal supervision of the proprietors. Staff are helpful and friendly, adding to the hotel's popularity with holiday-makers.*
DOUBLE ROOM: from £20 to £30
SINGLE ROOM: from £20 to £30
FOOD: up to £15
**Hours:** breakfast 8.30am-9.30am, dinner 6.30pm-7.30pm, closed mid-November until end February.
**Cuisine:** ENGLISH - a good selection of traditional English cuisine.
**Cards:** Visa, AmEx, Switch, MasterCard.
**Other points:** children catered for (please check for age limits), pets allowed, vegetarian meals, residents' lounge, open bank holidays, parking.
**Rooms:** 2 single rooms, 15 double rooms, 12 twin rooms, 4 family rooms. All en suite with satellite TV, radio, alarm, telephone, baby-listening device, tea/coffee-making facilities. Some superior no-smoking rooms.
**Directions:** from Weighbridge, go through the tunnel and take second right. Greenwood Lodge Hotel is the first building on the left.
HOWARD & SUE SNOW ☎(01534) 67073 Fax (01534) 67876

**HOTEL LA PLACE**
La Route du Coin, St Brelade, JE3 8BF
*Dating from the early 1640's, this top-class hotel projects all the warmth of a hostelry yet offers every luxury and comfort for a relaxing holiday on this delightful island. Uninterrupted sun-bathing is possible by the swimming pool where snacks are served and the bar faces directly onto the pool. Try a salad La Place accompanied by a crisp white wine alfresco in the south facing old courtyard - delicious. Highly recommended.*
DOUBLE ROOM: over £50
SINGLE ROOM: over £50
FOOD: from £20 to £30
**Hours:** breakfast 7.30am-9.30am, lunch 12.30pm-2pm, bar meals 11.30am-2pm and 6pm-9.30pm, dinner 7.30pm to 9.30pm, open bank holidays.
**Cuisine:** ENGLISH / FRENCH - extensive à la carte menu with flambé dishes a speciality. Vegetarian menu available.
**Cards:** Visa, Access, Diners, AmEx, Switch.
**Other points:** licensed, residents' lounge, 24 hour reception, night porter, laundry/valet service, ironing facilities, French & Italian & Spanish spoken, garden for guests' use, outdoor heated pool, sauna, tennis facilities, children welcome, parking.

**Rooms:** 38 twin rooms, 2 family rooms, all en suite. All with TV, radio, telephone, room service, hair dryer and trouser press, with morning tea/coffee served in the rooms.
**Directions:** from St Helier take the coast road to Saint Aubins, turn up La Haule hill, first left and first right, hotel is on the right.
KARYN BURLEY ☎(01534) 44261
Fax (01534) 45164

### HOTEL MIRAMAR
Mont Gras D'eau, St Brelade, JE3 8ED
*This excellent holiday hotel is well situated within reach of the many attractions Jersey has to offer. Completely modernised and re-decorated, the large open-plan public rooms overlook the garden and swimming pool where you can laze on comfortable furniture without being too close to your neighbour. Morning tea and coffee served in your bedroom in the traditional manner.*
DOUBLE ROOM: from £16 to £30
SINGLE ROOM: up to £30
FOOD: up to £15
**Hours:** breakfast 8am-9.30am, dinner 7pm-8pm, open bank holidays, closed 15th October to 3rd April.
**Cuisine:** ENGLISH - table d'hôte menus changed daily.
**Cards:** Visa, Access, AmEx.
**Other points:** licensed, residents' lounge, garden for guests' use, pets allowed, ironing facilities, French spoken, spa bath/jacuzzi facilities, outdoor heated pool, parking.
**Rooms:** 4 single, 14 twin, 18 double and 2 family rooms, all en suite. All with TV, radio, intercom, morning tea or coffee served in rooms.
**Directions:** situated off the A13, Jersey map reference E.7.
HOTEL MIRAMAR (ST. BRELADES) LTD. ☎(01534) 43831 Fax (01534) 45009

### LA CROIX GUEST HOUSE
Route-De-Millais, St Ouen, JE3 2EJ
*Family run by the owners, this attractive guest house is well situated just 15 minutes from St Helier with buses passing the door en route to St Aubins Bay. The hotel has recently been redecorated to a high standard and the bedrooms provide every comfort. The secluded garden contains a heated swimming pool which is available all day for the use of guests. A well recommended base for exploring this attractive island.*
DOUBLE ROOM: from £20 to £30
**Hours:** breakfast 8am-9am, open bank holidays, closed November to March.
**Cards:** Visa, Access.
**Other points:** residents' lounges, garden for guests' use, children catered for (please check for age limits), outdoor heated swimming pool, no-smoking area, parking.
**Rooms:** 10 twin/double rooms en suite. All with TV, tea/coffee-making facilities.
**Directions:** from airport take the A12, then take the

B34. The guest house is on the left.
PAUL & MAUREEN CARRÉ
☎(01534) 482110 Fax (01534) 481450

### MILLBROOK HOUSE
Rue de Trachy, St Helier, JE3 3JN
*This elegant Georgian residence has been sympathetically modernized and extended to create a hotel of outstanding character. The 10 acres of gardens and park and the stupendous views overlooking St Aubin's Bay give an immediate sense of ease, tranquillity, peace and quiet. Millbrook House is an ideal setting for an away-from-it-all restful holiday. Comprehensive menu, extensive wine list and comfortable accommodation.*
DOUBLE ROOM: from £20 to £30
SINGLE ROOM: from £20 to £30
FOOD: up to £15
**Hours:** breakfast 7.30am-9.30am, dinner 6.30pm-8.30pm.
**Cuisine:** ENGLISH
**Cards:** AmEx.
**Other points:** children catered for (please check for age limits), lift, special diets, vegetarian meals.
**Rooms:** 3 single rooms, 10 double rooms, 9 twin rooms, 2 family rooms. All with en suite, TV, telephone, tea/coffee-making facilities.
**Directions:** off the A1, 1.5 miles west of St Helier.
MR G. PIROUET - G.T.P. (JERSEY) LTD ☎(01534) 33036 Fax (01534) 24317

### MONT MILLAIS HOTEL
Mont Millais, St Helier, JE2 4RA
*Set in own attractive terraced gardens, only 5 minutes away from town centre. Decorated in light shades of welcoming colours and offering accommodation of a high standard. The restaurant enjoys a friendly atmosphere in which you can indulge in a really good meal, made even more enjoyable by the excellent service. Highly recommended.*
DOUBLE ROOM: from £27 to £35
SINGLE ROOM: from £27
FOOD: up to £15
**Hours:** breakfast 8.15am-9.30am, bar meals 12noon-2pm, dinner 7pm-9pm, closed January until April.
**Cuisine:** ENGLISH / CONTINENTAL - home-made soups and sweets. Fresh local fish.
**Cards:** Visa, Access.
**Other points:** licensed, Sunday lunch, children welcome, afternoon tea, coaches by prior arrangement, dry cleaning, picnic lunches.
**Rooms:** 44 bedrooms all en suite.
**Directions:** from Howard Davis Park, approximately 400 metres towards Five Oaks.
COLIN KIRKHAM ☎(01534) 30281 Fax (01534) 66849

### THE STAR & TIPSY TOAD BREWERY
St Peter's village, St Peter Port
*Originally a small Victorian pub and now recently*

refurbished and extended, this is the first pub in Jersey to house its own brewery. Very popular with locals and families alike, and customers can view the brewery at lunchtime or by prior arrangement. Nearby tourist attractions include a German underground hospital, a car museum and an excellent beach for surfing.

FOOD: up to £15

**Hours:** lunch 12noon-2.15pm, dinner 6pm-8.15pm.

**Cuisine:** ENGLISH - extensive menu offering steak, prawn, chicken, fish, salad and pork dishes. Children's menu. Chef's specials. Vegetarian dishes available. Good wine list.

**Cards:** All major cards.

**Other points:** licensed, open-air dining, children welcome, pets allowed, parking, garden, patio, disabled access, playland.

**Directions:** on the A12 in St Peter's village, near airport.

STEVE & SARAH SKINNER ☎(01534) 485556 Fax(01534) 485559

### TWYFORD GUEST HOUSE
La Rocque, St Clement, JE2 6SF

A Jersey house of character and charm, Twyford House is situated close to the small harbour of La Rocque with its sandy beach. Just around the corner is the beautiful Royal Bay of Grouville with fine sandy beaches and a well known golf course. Bed, breakfast and evening meal accommodation is offered at a very reasonable rate, and guests are assured that every effort is made to guarantee them a pleasant stay in this most attractive island.

DOUBLE ROOM: up to £20

SINGLE ROOM: up to £25

**Hours:** breakfast 8.30am, dinner 6.30am, open bank holidays.

**Cuisine:** ENGLISH - vegetarian on request.

**Cards:** Visa, Access, Mastercard, Eurocard.

**Other points:** Residents' and television lounges, garden for guests' use, German and French spoken,

parking, short breaks welcome.

**Rooms:** 3 double rooms, 1 family room. All with tea/coffee-making facilities.

**Directions:** on the coast road at La Rocque. Jersey map reference M8.

DAVID KENNEDY ☎(01534) 853385 Fax(01534) 852070

### WATERS EDGE HOTEL
Les Charrières du Bouley, Bouley Bay, JE3 5AS

Set in its own terraced gardens in a commanding position of outstanding natural beauty. Panoramic windows in nearly all public areas take advantage of the vista afforded by Bouley Bay, the boats and the coast of France. There is outdoor dining in the beautiful terraced gardens, and a swimming pool, heated from April to October.

DOUBLE ROOM: from £42 to £55

SINGLE ROOM: from £47 to £57

FOOD: from £12 to £25 ☜ ⬠

**Hours:** breakfast 8am-9.30am, lunch 12.30am-1.45pm, dinner 7pm-9.45pm, bar snacks 12noon-1.45pm.

**Cuisine:** FRENCH - à la carte and table d'hôte lunch and dinner menus. Wide choice of dishes and local fresh fish specialities. The hotel offers an extensive wine list and a selection of banqueting menus for up to 140 people.

**Cards:** Visa, Access, Diners, AmEx.

**Other points:** children catered for (please check for age limits), pets allowed, afternoon tea, residents' lounge, garden, parking, licensed.

**Rooms:** 7 single rooms, 18 double rooms, 19 twin rooms, 3 family rooms, 3 deluxe suites. All with TV, radio, phone, tea/coffee-making facilities, hair dryer.

**Directions:** take the A8/B31 from St Helier; 500 metres from Trinity Church, turn left.

MR B. OLIVER ☎(01534) 862777 Fax(01534) 863645

---

## Club Bon Viveur. Take advantage of the 8 FREE vouchers on Page 67.
## Join up for a year at only £15. See page 65.

# CENTRAL ENGLAND

No other part of England offers greater variety of countryside, town or village than can be found in the 'Heart of England' - and the food is no exception either!

There are hundreds of places offering an unrivalled choice of excellent cuisine and the heartiest of welcomes. Choose from a superb combination of dishes with an emphasis on fresh produce: Shropshire chicken, Cotswold trout, beef Wellington, smoked quail, rabbit pie, Bakewell pudding, Ashbourne gingerbread, black pudding or pork pies from Melton Mowbray, followed by a tempting home-made dessert.

For those who prefer to eat informally, there is a superb selection of character inns displaying the warmth and comfort of a traditional pub combined with really excellent food for around a pound or two, such as hot pie lunches, filling salads and tangy ploughman's. And if you are 'guest-housing', start your day with a fine British breakfast - still an important part of our culinary heritage.

No visitor to this lovely part of England will have trouble in finding good cooking and a range of comfortable accommodation, with the accent on quality and service.

The following counties are included in this chapter:

| | |
|---|---|
| CHESHIRE | NORTHAMPTONSHIRE |
| DERBYSHIRE | NOTTINGHAMSHIRE |
| GLOUCESTERSHIRE | OXFORDSHIRE |
| HEREFORD & WORCESTER | SHROPSHIRE |
| LEICESTERSHIRE | STAFFORDSHIRE |
| LINCOLNSHIRE | WARWICKSHIRE |
| | WEST MIDLANDS |

# CHESHIRE

## BROUGHTON • map 8B4

### THE SPINNING WHEEL TAVERN
The Old Warren, near Chester, CH4 0EG
*Old roadside pub, attractively furnished and decorated with copper antiques and brass horse artifacts. Freshly prepared traditional meals are served in a convivial, welcoming atmosphere. Friendly staff and efficient service make the meal complete. Good value for money.*
**FOOD:** from £15 to £20
**Hours:** lunch 11.30am-2.30pm, dinner 6pm-10.30pm.
**Cuisine:** ENGLISH / INTERNATIONAL - large selection of meals with over 40 main courses and blackboard specials every day.
**Cards:** Visa, Access, Diners, AmEx.
**Other points:** licensed, Sunday lunch, children welcome, open bank holidays, functions.
**Directions:** on old main road from Broughton to Buckley, 6 miles from Chester.
MIKE & MAGGIE VERNON ☎(01244) 531068/533637

## CHESTER • map 8B4

### ABBOTSFORD COURT HOTEL
17 Victoria Road, CH2 2AX
*A small family run hotel offering extremely good value accommodation in the centre of this most attractive city. Chester lends itself to exploring on foot, and when you return to your hotel you may expect a well cooked dinner complemented by well chosen and reasonable house wine. Very good value for money.*
**DOUBLE ROOM:** from £20 to £30
**SINGLE ROOM:** from £20
**FOOD:** up to £15
**Hours:** breakfast 7.30am-9am, dinner 6.30pm-8pm.
**Cards:** None
**Other points:** children welcome, baby-listening device, on site parking.
**Rooms:** 1 single room, 1 twin room, 5 double rooms (including 1 four-poster), 3 family rooms, all en suite. All with TV, tea/coffee-making facilities.
**Directions:** opposite Northgate Road Arena Leisure Centre.
APOLLONIA MARANO ☎(01244) 390898
Fax (01244) 390898

## THE BLUE BELL RESTAURANT
65 Northgate Street, CH1 2HQ

*The Blue Bell is Chester's oldest surviving domestic structure and the city's only example of a medieval inn. Dating back to the 15th century, the Blue Bell has been beautifully restored as a restaurant and displays a wealth of antique furniture, and a resident ghost. Serving fine English food combining tradition with imagination and noted for its extensive wine list, the Blue Bell offers discreet and efficient service and is the perfect venue for a relaxing lunch or evening meal. Excellent value for money!*

**FOOD:** up to £15
**Hours:** lunch 12noon-2.30pm, dinner 7pm-10pm.
**Cuisine:** ENGLISH / FRENCH
**Cards:** Visa, Access, Switch.
**Other points:** licensed, Sunday lunch and evening meals, no-smoking area, children welcome, garden.
**Directions:** 9 miles south of M53 and M56 intersection.
MRS GLENYS EVANS ☎(01244) 317758
Fax(01244) 317759

## CHESTER COURT HOTEL
48 Hoole Road, CH2 3NL

*An attractive black and white timbered Victorian building of character, family-run and interestingly furnished with many genuine antiques. There is a modern bedroom annexe and a magnificent conservatory dining room. The menu is wide-ranging and supported by an excellent wine list. Boasts a wonderful ambience throughout. Roman city walls, museum, cathedral and racecourse are all nearby.*

**DOUBLE ROOM:** from £20 to £30
**SINGLE ROOM:** from £36 to £38
**FOOD:** up to £15 CLUB
**Hours:** breakfast 7am-9am, lunch (bar area) 12noon-2pm, dinner (restaurant & bar) 6pm-9pm. Closed 24th December to 1st January.
**Cuisine:** ENGLISH/FRENCH - starters include warm watercress,potato and bacon salad, flaked salmon pancakes, fried Somerset brie. Main dishes such as rack of lamb baked with port and rosemary, chicken stuffed with peach stilton, escalope of pork fried with apple, Dijon mustard and cream. Daily blackboard menu.
**Cards:** Access, Visa, AmEx, Diners, Switch, Delta
**Other points:** parking, children welcome, pets

allowed, no smoking area, residents lounge, vegetarian meals, afternoon teas, traditional Sunday lunch.
**Rooms:** 20 bedrooms all with tea/coffee maker, TV, telephone, radio, hair dryer, trouser press, baby listening by arrangement.
**Directions:** take the A56 Hoole Road into Chester from the motorway network. Chester Court is on the right opposite the church.
MS A. WARREN ☎(01244) 320779 Fax(01244) 344795

## CHEYNEY LODGE HOTEL
77-79 Cheyney Road, CH1 4BS

*Half a mile from the city's Roman Wall, Cheyney Lodge was originally three houses. Recently completely refurbished, the hotel is now attractively decorated and provides good quality accommodation, a cosy bar, small dining room and separate lounge. A small, well-furnished hotel with a welcoming atmosphere and tasty home-cooked meals, offering good value for money.*

**DOUBLE ROOM:** up to £20
**SINGLE ROOM:** up to £25
**FOOD:** up to £15
**Hours:** breakfast 08.00 09.00,lunch 12.00 14.00, dinner 18.30 20.00
**Cards:** Visa,Access
**Other points:** children welcome, residents' lounge, ETB - 3 crowns, commended
**Rooms:** 5 Double rooms. 2 Twin rooms. 1 Family room. All with TV, radio, tea/coffee making facilities.
**Directions:** from the city centre take A540 - Hoylake, left into Cheyney Road.
KEVIN DIXON ☎(01244) 381925 Fax(01244) 372440

## FRANCS RESTAURANT
14 Cuppin Street, CH1 2BN

*A 17th century oak-beamed building within the city walls serving top-quality, exclusively French cuisine. Wide choice of dishes, whether you are looking for `un petit morceau' or a whole feast. The wine list has been produced to complement their menus, and there is a wide range of French aperitifs and liqueurs. A friendly, relaxing and informal atmosphere.*

**FOOD:** up to £15
**Hours:** à la carte menu 11am-11pm, plats du jour 11am-7pm.
**Cuisine:** FRENCH - provincial French cuisine. house specialities include traditional French savoury crêpes, boudins and vegetarian dishes.
**Cards:** Visa, Access, AmEx, Switch.
**Other points:** licensed, children welcome, parking, air-conditioned, 3 dining rooms.
**Directions:** off Grosvenor Road, near main North Wales roundabout and police station.
D. JOHNSTON-CREE ☎(01244) 317952 Fax(01244) 661422

---

**For Reservations & Special Offers FreeCall 0500 700 456**

### LA BOHEME
58 Watergate Street, CH1 2LA

*An outstanding French restaurant situated right in the heart of this most historic town. The à la carte and table d'hôte menus offer a true taste of France, and there are special offers for children dining with adults. Incorporating a good selection of vegetarian dishes, the menus are accompanied by an outstanding wine list.*

FOOD: from £15 to £20 [CLUB]
**Hours:** lunch Monday to Saturday 12noon-2.30pm, Sundays 12noon-5pm, dinner Monday to Saturday 6pm-11pm, Sundays 6pm-10.30pm, open bank holidays, closed New Year's Day.
**Cuisine:** FRENCH - excellent table d'hôte and à la carte menus offering the very best of French cooking. Also a worldwide wine list.
**Cards:** Visa, Access, AmEx, Switch.
**Other points:** licensed, children welcome, special Sunday lunch menu with free dining for children.
**Directions:** in the town centre.
STEAK & KEBAB CO. ☎(01244) 313721
[Fax](01244) 346266

### MAMMA MIA
St Werburgh Street, CH1 2DY

*A friendly Italian pizzeria with a lively atmosphere. Diners can watch chefs preparing and cooking pizzas in the traditional way in the open-plan kitchen. Popular with locals and tourists alike.*

FOOD: up to £15
**Hours:** lunch Monday-Saturday 12noon-2.30pm, dinner Monday-Saturday 6pm-11pm, lunch Sunday 12noon-2.30pm, dinner Sunday 6pm-10pm.
**Cuisine:** ITALIAN - authentic Italian dishes: pizzas, pasta, calamari, sirloin.
**Cards:** Visa, Access, Diners, AmEx.
**Other points:** licensed, children welcome.
**Directions:** next to the cathedral.
GIUSEPPE & ANNA LABELLA ☎(01244) 314663
[Fax](01244) 314663

### REDLAND HOTEL
64 Hough Green, CH3 8JY

*An exquisite hotel with a unique Victorian ambience re-created with genuine antiques, tasteful period furnishings and original wood panelling. Each of the rooms has been individually decorated. It has all the facilities of a large hotel but with great character, charm and friendliness. The Redland turns a night away from home into a special*

*experience.*
DOUBLE ROOM: from £30 to £40
SINGLE ROOM: from £45
FOOD: from £25 to £30 🍴
**Hours:** breakfast 7.30am-9.30am.
**Cuisine:** BREAKFAST
**Other points:** children welcome, pets by prior arrangement, residents' lounge, honeymoon suite, garden.
**Rooms:** 11 bedrooms.
**Directions:** on the A5104, 1 mile from the city centre.
MRS THERESA WHITE ☎(01244) 671024
[Fax](01244) 681309

## ELLESMERE PORT • map 8B4

### BROOK MEADOW HOTEL
Heath Lane, Childer Thornton, L66 7NS

*This mock-Tudor country mansion in a green belt area overlooks the hotel's three and half acres of grounds on one side and market gardens on the other. An air of contentment pervades throughout the tastefully decorated, peaceful hotel and restaurant. The general atmosphere and the service are relaxed, informal and very friendly.*

DOUBLE ROOM: up to £20
SINGLE ROOM: from £25
FOOD: up to £15 [CLUB]
**Hours:** breakfast everyday 7.30am-9.30am, lunch Sunday only 12noon-2pm, dinner everyday 7pm-7.30pm, closed Christmas day and Boxing day.
**Cuisine:** CONTINENTAL - à la carte and table d'hôte menus available, also regularly changing specials.
**Other points:** children welcome, parking, no-smoking area, conference facilities, garden, open-air dining, vegetarian meals, Sunday lunch.
**Rooms:** 4 bedrooms. All with TV, tea/coffee-making facilities, radio.
**Directions:** exit M53 at junction 5 and take A41 to A550. Brook Meadow Hotel is located on Heath Lane in Childer Thornton.
MR & MRS JONES ☎(0151) 339 9350

## FRODSHAM • map 8B4

### OLD HALL HOTEL
Main Street, WA6 7AB

*This 15th century house has been beautifully renovated and modernized and is set among other old buildings in the centre of Frodsham. The restaurant serves an imaginative variety of dishes, all of which are beautifully presented and served by friendly, attentive staff.*

DOUBLE ROOM: from £20 to £30
SINGLE ROOM: from £35 to £55
FOOD: from £15 to £20
**Hours:** breakfast 6am-10am, lunch 12noon-2pm, dinner 7pm-10pm.
**Cuisine:** ENGLISH - à la carte menu. Dishes include sea bass champagne, roast duckling cerises.
**Cards:** Visa, Access, Diners, AmEx, Switch.
**Other points:** licensed, open-air dining, Sunday

lunch, children welcome, garden, afternoon tea, pets allowed, parking, residents' lounge, residents' bar.
**Rooms:** 23 twin rooms. All with TV, telephone, tea/coffee-making facilities.
**Directions:** M56, junction 12.
MR & MRS WINFIELD ☎(01928) 732052
Fax(01928) 739046

 ## KNUTSFORD • map 8B5

 ### LONGVIEW HOTEL & RESTAURANT
Manchester Road, WA16 0L6
*A period hotel, recently refurbished to enhance its Victorian splendour. With many antiques, this hotel offers a relaxed and comfortable atmosphere, from its open log fires to the quality of its award-winning restaurant and welcome. Just minutes away from M6 junction 19. Set overlooking the common in this attractive Cheshire market town.*
DOUBLE ROOM: from £28 to £40
SINGLE ROOM: from £37 to £68
FOOD: from £15 to £20
**Cuisine:** BRITISH / CONTINENTAL - an ever-changing menu, which draws on the best of continental foods as well as the rich heritage of British cooking.
**Cards:** Visa, Access, Diners, AmEx.
**Other points:** children welcome, pets allowed, open bank holidays.
**Rooms:** 5 single rooms, 11 double rooms, 7 twin rooms. All with TV, radio, telephone, tea/coffee-making facilities, baby-listening device.
**Directions:** junction 19 off M6, follow A556 towards Chester. Left at lights, left at roundabout.
PAULINE & STEPHEN WEST ☎(01565) 632119
Fax(01565) 652402

## MACCLESFIELD • map 8B5

### SUTTON HALL
Bullocks Lane, Sutton, SK11 0HE
*Once the baronial residence of the Sutton family and more recently a convent, Sutton Hall has been sympathetically restored to create a unique `inn' of distinction, affording the weary traveller superb food, good ales and truly sumptuous accommodation. The fully licensed lounge bar, open to non-residents, boasts a wealth of 16th century oak beams and three open log fires.*
DOUBLE ROOM: from £40 to £50
SINGLE ROOM: over £55
FOOD: from £15 to £20
**Hours:** breakfast 7.30am-10am, lunch 12noon-2.30pm, dinner 7pm-10pm, open all year.
**Cuisine:** INTERNATIONAL - international cuisine: a changing range of fresh seasonal dishes traditionally prepared from the finest fresh ingredients. Fine ales and wines.
**Cards:** Visa, Access.
**Other points:** licensed, open-air dining, Sunday lunch, garden, pets allowed.
**Rooms:** 10 double/twin rooms. All with TV, telephone, tea/coffee-making facilities, trouser-press.

**Directions:** south of Macclesfield via A523, left at Byrons Lane, right at Bullocks Lane.
ROBERT BRADSHAW ☎(01260) 253211
Fax(01260) 252538

## NANTWICH • map 8B5

### THE MALBANK HOTEL
14 Beam Street, CW5 5LL
*Situated close to the heart of Nantwich, this comfortable, well-equipped, family-run hotel is an ideal base for business or pleasure. The Malbank's attractively furnished restaurant has a good reputation for its attentive service, fine food and pleasant ambience. The recently refurbished bars create the atmosphere of a good English pub - an ideal place to meet friends and enjoy fine beers and a wide range of wines and spirits.*
DOUBLE ROOM: from £24
SINGLE ROOM: from £28
FOOD: up to £15
**Hours:** breakfast 7am-10am, food served all day 11am-10pm.
**Cuisine:** ENGLISH - fresh home-made English meals are available in both the restaurant and the bar.
**Cards:** Visa, Access, Diners, AmEx.
**Other points:** children welcome, no-smoking area, afternoon teas, Sunday lunch, vegetarian meals.
**Rooms:** 11 bedrooms. All with en suite, TV, telephone, tea/coffee-making facilities.
**Directions:** located in Nantwich town centre.
CHRISTOPHER EVANS ☎(01270) 626011
Fax(01270) 624435

### ROOKERY HALL HOTEL
Worleston, CW5 6DQ
*Peace and seclusion are guaranteed at Rookery Hall Hotel, with its wonderful outlook over the Cheshire countryside. Set in 200 acres, this luxury country house hotel offers space, elegance and tranquility. All 45 bedrooms are individually designed and overlook the beautiful gardens. Rookery Hall with its growing list of accolades for fine food and service is the perfect setting whatever your requirement.*
DOUBLE ROOM: from £40
SINGLE ROOM: from £65
FOOD: from £12 to £35     CLUB
**Hours:** breakfast 7am-9.30am, lunch 12noon-2pm, dinner 7pm-10pm.
**Cuisine:** MODERN EUROPEAN
**Cards:** Visa, Access, Diners, AmEx, Switch.
**Other points:** children welcome, parking, pets by prior arrangement, conference facilities, residents' lounge, residents' garden, no-smoking area, Sunday lunch, vegetarian meals.
**Rooms:** 45 bedrooms. All with TV, telephone, tea/coffee-making facilities, hair dryer, trouser-press.
**Directions:** from the North, junction 18 off M6, follow A54, A530 and A51, then B5074; Rookery Hall is one mile up the road towards Worleston. From the south, junction 16 off M6, then A5000,

A51, B5074.
MR JEREMY RATA ☎(01270) 610016 Fax(01270) 626017

## PARKGATE • map 8A4

### THE BOATHOUSE
1 The Parade, L64 6RN

*This is an establishment that certainly has a history. First recorded on this site was The Beer House in 1664. Today, The Boathouse has been recently refurbished and pleasantly decorated. Good portions of value-for-money meals are served in a quiet and friendly atmosphere.*

**FOOD:** up to £15 🍴 CLUB

**Hours:** lunch 12noon-2pm, dinner 6.30pm-9.30pm, bar meals 12.30am-2.30pm, open bank holidays.

**Cuisine:** WELSH - classical home-cooking, which has won many awards. Dishes may include Welsh trimmed lamb with elderberry sauce, saddle of hare or barbary duck.

**Cards:** Visa, Access, AmEx, Switch.

**Other points:** licensed, open-air dining, Sunday lunch, children welcome.

**Directions:** 4 miles off M56; off A540.

MR JOHN CLARKE ☎(0151) 336 4187 Fax(0151) 353 0938

### PARKGATE HOTEL
Boathouse Lane, L64 6RD

*This Victorian country-style manor is warm and cosy, not only in its decor but also its ambience. The hotel is decorated to a high standard throughout, with constant attention paid to the appearance and facilities offered. The silver service restaurant is reputed for the excellent quality and value of the meals, made from fresh local produce.*

**DOUBLE ROOM:** from £25 to £35

**SINGLE ROOM:** from £25 to £50

**FOOD:** from £15 to £20 🍴 CLUB

**Hours:** breakfast 7am-10am, lunch 12noon-2.20pm, bar meals 12noon-7.30pm, dinner 7pm-10.30pm.

**Cuisine:** ENGLISH / CONTINENTAL - quality meals at value-for-money prices.

**Cards:** Visa, Access, AmEx.

**Other points:** parking, children welcome, pets allowed, conference facilities, residents' lounge, garden, no-smoking area, vegetarian meals, afternoon teas, traditional Sunday lunch.

**Rooms:** 1 single room, 10 double rooms, 12 twin rooms, 3 family rooms. All with en suite, satellite TV, telephone, radio, alarm, hair dryer, trouser-press, tea/coffee-making facilities.

**Directions:** the hotel is on B5135 off the A540, a few minutes off M53; 10 miles from Chester on the banks of the River Dee.

JOHN & JACQUELINE CAMPBELL ☎(0151) 336 5001 Fax(0151) 336 8504

# DERBYSHIRE

## ASHBOURNE • map 9B2

### THE BENTLEY BROOK INN
Fenny Bentley, DE6 1LF

*This traditional timbered inn, set in 2 acres of well-tended gardens, provides wonderfully cooked food using only the freshest produce - no frozen food here! With a daily changing menu, you will find their tasty main dishes with crispy fresh vegetables and home-made sweets a delight, especially when teamed with their comprehensive list of wines. Good accommodation and welcome.*

**DOUBLE ROOM:** from £20 to £30

**SINGLE ROOM:** up to £30

**FOOD:** up to £15     CLUB

**Hours:** breakfast 7am-10am, meals all day 11am-9.30pm.

**Cuisine:** ENGLISH - dishes include savoury Derbyshire oatcake, prime steaks, selection of home-made sweets.

**Cards:** Visa, Access, Diners, AmEx.

**Other points:** licensed, Sunday lunch, children welcome, garden, pets allowed.

**Rooms:** 1 single room, 8 double rooms, 1 self-catering cottage. All with TV, radio, telephone, tea/coffee-making facilities.

**Directions:** on intersection of the A515 to Buxton and the B5056 to Bakewell.

MR & MRS ALLINGHAM ☎(01335) 350278 Fax(01335) 350422

### STANSHOPE HALL
Stanshope, DE6 2AD

*A 17th century country house with beautiful south-facing views, standing on the brow of a hill above Dovedale in the Peak National Park. The rooms are large and comfortable, featuring unusual decorations such as hand-painted walls. Atmosphere of a country house and family home, combined with the standards and features of a hotel. Also recommended by The Times and The Independent. Ideal for walkers. 30 minutes to Alton Towers.*

**DOUBLE ROOM:** from £20 to £30

**SINGLE ROOM:** from £20 to £30

**FOOD:** from £15 to £20

**Hours:** breakfast 8.30am-9.30am.dinner 7.30pm.

**Cuisine:** ENGLISH - 3-course dinner. Home-cooking and vegetables from the garden. Home-made chocolates served with the coffee. Vegetarians

welcome. Light snacks available.
**Other points:** licensed, children welcome, pets allowed, garden, residents' lounge, payphone.
**Rooms:** 2 double rooms, 1 twin room. All with en suite, TV, tea/coffee-making facilities.
**Directions:** off A515 Ashbourne to Buxton road, in the hamlet of Stanshope between the villages of Alstonefield and Ilam.
NAOMI CHAMBERS & NICK LOURIE ☎(01335) 310278 Fax(01335) 310470

## BAKEWELL • map 9B2

### ASHFORD HOTEL & RESTAURANT
Church Street, Ashford-in-the-Water, DE45 1QB

*An 18th century Grade II listed building with traditional oak beams and open fires. A family-run hotel with a warm welcome and personal service. Good food is beautifully presented in the restaurant, and a wide range of bar meals is also available. Behind the hotel and extending down to the River Wye is a large beer garden, a perfect place to enjoy a snack in summer.*
DOUBLE ROOM: from £30 to £40
SINGLE ROOM: from £50
FOOD: up to £15
**Hours:** breakfast 8am-9.30am, bar meals all day 12noon-9pm.
**Cuisine:** FRENCH - extensive bar menu including vegetarian choices. Party bookings welcome.
**Cards:** All major cards (not JCB), Switch.
**Other points:** licensed, open-air dining, Sunday lunch, children welcome, beer garden, afternoon tea, pets allowed, residents' lounge, morning coffee.
**Rooms:** 1 single room, 3 double rooms, 2 four-poster rooms, 1 twin room, all with en suite facilities, tea/coffee-maker, TV, radio alarm, telephone, trouser press, hair dryer
**Directions:** 2.5 miles outside Bakewell, off the A6 towards Buxton.
JOHN & SUE DAWSON ☎(01629) 812725
Fax(01629) 814749

## BASLOW • map 9B2

### WHEATSHEAF HOTEL
Nether End, DE45 1SR

*A traditional English inn, The Wheatsheaf provides excellent bed and breakfast accommodation. The five bedrooms have been beautifully furnished, and some have en suite facilities.. An extensive range of traditional home cooked food is served in the friendly surroundings of the lounge bar. Family accommodation is enhanced by an extensive children's play area adjoining the inn.*
DOUBLE ROOM: up to £20
SINGLE ROOM: from £25
FOOD: from £15 to £20
**Hours:** breakfast 8am-9am, lunch 11.30am-3.30pm, dinner 5.30pm-9.30pm. Open all year including bank holidays.
**Cuisine:** good range of traditional dishes on à la carte menu supplemented by daily 'blackboard'

specials.Good English puddings a speciality.
**Cards:** Visa, Access, Switch.
**Other points:** parties catered for, children's play area.
**Rooms:** 5 bedrooms. All with TV, tea/coffee-making facilities.
**Directions:** leave M1 at junction 29, through Chesterfield and follow A219, signposted Chatsworth House, into Baslow.
SYLVIA & BARRY FELL ☎(01246) 582240

## BUXTON • map 9B1

### THE HAY-WAY
35 High Street, SK17 6HA

*At first glance this is an appealing restaurant with an attractive water garden right inside. Upon closer inspection, it is cosy and relaxing, offering a warm atmosphere, friendly service and, most importantly, delicious meals and quality wines. Conveniently situated for Buxton Opera House, Baths and Spa, Bakewell, Chatsworth and the Derby Dales.*
FOOD: from £15 to £20   CLUB
**Hours:** lunch 12noon-2.30pm, cream teas (summer only) 1.30pm-4.30pm, dinner 7pm-11pm, closed all day Monday except bank holidays and Wednesday lunch.
**Cuisine:** ENGLISH / FRENCH - a good selection of freshly cooked meals.
**Cards:** Visa, Access, AmEx.
**Other points:** children welcome, no-smoking area, vegetarian meals, traditional Sunday lunch, afternoon teas, pre-theatre and after theatre bookings welcome.
**Directions:** A515 from Ashbourne.
HAYDEN & KATHRYN TAYLOR ☎(01298) 78388

### OLD HALL HOTEL
The Square, SK17 6BB

*This historic hotel dating back to the 16th century has entertained thousands of visitors including Mary Queen of Scots. Overlooking the Pavilion Gardens and Opera House, it is an ideal base for those wishing to visit the theatre. Good food and comfortable accommodation.*
DOUBLE ROOM: from £30 to £40
SINGLE ROOM: from £45
FOOD: from £15 to £20
**Hours:** breakfast 7.30am-9.30am, lunch 12noon-2.30pm, bar meals 6pm-11pm, dinner 6pm-11pm.
**Cuisine:** ENGLISH - serving bar snacks, full à la carte menu and table d'hôte.
**Cards:** Visa, Access, Diners, AmEx.
**Other points:** licensed, open-air dining, Sunday lunch, children welcome, afternoon tea, functions, conferences, foreign exchange, residents' lounge, residents' bar.
**Rooms:** 8 single rooms, 13 double rooms, 12 twin rooms, 4 four-posters. All with TV, telephone, tea/coffee-making facilities.
**Directions:** centre of Buxton, past The Crescent.
MRS LOUISE POTTER ☎(01298) 22841
Fax(01298) 72437

## DERBY • map 9C2

### HOTEL RISTORANTE LA GONDOLA
220 Osmaston Road, DE3 8JX

*The Hotel Ristorante La Gondola is situated 5 minutes from Derby city centre, 15 minutes from the scenic Peak District. The hotel is elegantly decorated and very comfortable. Meals are cooked from fresh produce and served in generous portions, which are enjoyed by locals and holiday-makers alike. Staff are friendly and pleasant, adding to the relaxed atmosphere of the hotel.*

DOUBLE ROOM: over £50
SINGLE ROOM: from £45 to £55
FOOD: from £15 to £20
**Hours:** breakfast 7am-9am, lunch 12.15am-2pm, dinner 7pm-10pm.
**Cuisine:** ENGLISH / CONTINENTAL - traditional English and continental cuisine. Dishes include pork cutlet pizzaiola, rainbow trout, roast duckling.
**Cards:** Visa, Access, Diners, AmEx.
**Other points:** licensed, children welcome, afternoon tea, conferences, baby-listening device, cots, 24hr reception, residents' lounge, residents' bar, parking, vegetarian meals, disabled access.
**Rooms:** 11 double rooms, 2 twin rooms, 7 triple rooms, 1 family room. All with TV, radio, alarm, bar, telephone, tea/coffee-making facilities.
**Directions:** the hotel is located off the A514 dual carriageway into Derby.
MR R. GIOVANNELLI ☎(01332) 332895 Fax(01332) 384512

## HATHERSAGE • map 8B6

### LONGLAND'S EATING HOUSE
Main Road, S30 1BB

*Large country-style café/restaurant with exposed beams and wood floor, offering well-presented, generous portions of good food at excellent value for money. Situated in the main street of an attractive Peak District village.*

FOOD: up to £15
**Hours:** breakfast weekends 9am-11.30am, meals all day 11.30am-5pm, dinner 6.45pm-9.30pm, closed evenings except Saturday.
**Cuisine:** INTERNATIONAL - the menu is half-vegetarian: vegetable and nut risotto, spicy chick peas. Old English beef in ale, steak teriyaki.
**Cards:** Visa, Access.
**Other points:** children welcome, afternoon tea, pets allowed.
**Directions:** on the A625, next to Hathersage services, (Garage 1).
MR P.J.N. LONGLAND ☎(01433) 651978

### THE PLOUGH INN
Leadmill Bridge, S31 1BA

*A 17th century building on the banks of the River Derwent in the midst of the Peak District. The cosy atmosphere, log fires and excellent restaurant ensure its popularity with tourists and visitors to the National Parks area.*

DOUBLE ROOM: from £20 to £30
SINGLE ROOM: from £35
FOOD: from £15 to £20
**Hours:** breakfast 8.30am-9.30am, lunch 11.30am-2.30pm, dinner 6.30pm-9.30pm.
**Cuisine:** ENGLISH - traditional home-cooking.
**Cards:** Visa, Access, Switch.
**Other points:** children welcome, traditional Sunday lunch, vegetarian meals, no pets allowed, parking.
**Rooms:** 7 bedrooms.
**Directions:** situated 1 mile from centre of Hathersage village.
R. W. & C. EMERY ☎(01433) 650319 Fax(01433) 650180

## KEGWORTH • map 9C2

### KEGWORTH HOTEL
Packington Hill, DE74 2DF

*The Kegworth Hotel is situated on the A6 in a quiet village setting, ideally positioned near Loughborough, Nottingham, Derby and Leicester and conveniently located for Alton Towers, Nottingham Castle, Mount St Bernard's Abbey and American Adventure. A warm welcome awaits you at this well-appointed, comfortable hotel, and the helpful staff are always willing to assist you, whether your stay is for a weekend break, a holiday or a business conference.*

DOUBLE ROOM: from £20 to £30
SINGLE ROOM: from £35 to £45
FOOD: up to £15 🍽 CLUB
**Hours:** breakfast 7am-9.30am, lunch 12.30am-2pm, dinner 7pm-9.30pm, bar snacks available all day.
**Cuisine:** ENGLISH / INTERNATIONAL
**Cards:** Visa, Access, AmEx, Switch.
**Other points:** parking, children welcome, disabled access, pets allowed, residents' lounge, vegetarian meals, traditional Sunday lunch, open-air dining, conference facilities, swimming pool, Jacuzzi, solarium, gym, sauna, squash, function suite.
**Rooms:** 8 single rooms, 30 double rooms, 11 twin rooms, 3 family rooms. All en suite with TV, telephone, radio, alarm, hair dryer, tea/coffee-making facilities.
**Directions:** situated on the A6, just south of junction 24 (M1).
JOHN MARSHALL ☎(01509) 672427 Fax(01509) 674664

## MATLOCK • map 9B2

### BOWLING GREEN INN
East Bank, Winster, DE4 2ES

*Situated in a popular and picturesque Derbyshire village, the Bowling Green Inn is thought to be of 15th century origin, with a characteristic fireplace. Along with the resident ghost, Dave and Marilyn Bentley extend a warm and friendly welcome to all. The inn is centrally located when touring nearby attractions, such as Chatsworth House, Haddon Hall, Tissington and Dove Dale.*

FOOD: up to £15
**Hours:** lunch (weekends only) 12noon-2pm. Other

meals every day from 6pm, Sunday from 7pm, bar open all day Saturday.
**Cuisine:** ENGLISH - good selection with fresh daily specials, including vegetarian speciality dishes. Traditional Sunday roast of beef, lamb or pork. Good selection of home-made sweets.
**Cards:** Visa, Access.
**Other points:** open-air dining, Sunday lunch, children welcome, disabled access, parking, open bank holidays, vegetarian meals, garden. Non-smoking restaurant open Friday evenings, Saturday evenings and Sunday lunchtime.
**Directions:** from Matlock, take A6 north for 1.5 miles. Turn left onto B5057 for 2.5 miles.
DAVID & MARILYN BENTLEY ☎(01629) 650219

### THE ELIZABETHAN RESTAURANT
4 Crown Square, DE4 3AT
*This attractive restaurant is located right in the centre of the picturesque town of Matlock on the A6. It offers a warm, friendly welcome and excellent food in idyllic surroundings.*
FOOD: up to £15
**Hours:** morning coffee 10am-12noon, lunch 12noon-3pm, afternoon tea 3pm-5pm, dinner 7.30pm-10pm, open every day.
**Cuisine:** ENGLISH / CONTINENTAL - steak-and-kidney pie, savoury filled pancakes. Home-made continental dishes. Roasts daily.
**Cards:** Visa, Access.
**Other points:** Sunday lunch, children welcome, coaches by prior arrangement
**Directions:** on the A6 in the centre of town.
MR G.E. FAULKNER ☎(01629) 583533

### SUNNYBANK GUEST HOUSE
37 Clifton Road, Matlock Bath, DE4 3PW
*This attractive Victorian house offers guests comfortable accommodation, wonderful home-cooked meals and friendly service in a homely atmosphere. This is an ideal base to discover the many attractions nearby. Local activities include walking, climbing, fishing, sailing, canoeing, caving, horse-riding - the list just goes on and on! Well worth a visit.*
DOUBLE ROOM: from £20 to £30
SINGLE ROOM: up to £30
FOOD: up to £15
**Hours:** breakfast 8.30am (or earlier by arrangement), dinner 7pm (residents only), closed 24th December until 27th December.
**Cuisine:** ENGLISH
**Cards:** Visa, Access, Amex, JCB.
**Other points:** children catered for (please check for age limits), no-smoking area, residents' lounge, garden, vegetarian meals.

**Rooms:** 1 single room, 2 double rooms, 2 twin rooms. All with tea/coffee-making facilities. Some rooms have TV.
**Directions:** from Matlock, travel south along A6 towards Derby. At southern end of Matlock Bath, just before the 40mph speed limit sign turn right into Clifton Road: 250 yards on left.
PETER & DAPHNE WEST ☎(01629) 584621

### THE TAVERN AT TANSLEY
Nottingham Road, Tansley, DE4 5FR
*Situated in the midst of the delightful village of Tansley, this 18th century inn offers guests excellent service, whether enjoying a traditional bar meal in the charming lounge bar or a sumptuous meal in the restaurant. The Tavern At Tansley is an ideal place to use as a base for exploring the Peak District.*
DOUBLE ROOM: from £20 to £30
SINGLE ROOM: from £30
FOOD: up to £20 ☜ CLUB
**Hours:** breakfast 7.30am-9.30am, lunch 12noon-2.30pm, dinner 6.30pm-9.15pm.
**Cuisine:** ENGLISH - varied menu including vegetarian.
**Cards:** Visa, Access.
**Other points:** parking, children welcome, vegetarian meals, traditional Sunday lunch.
**Rooms:** 2 double rooms, 1 twin room. All en suite with TV, tea/coffee-making facilities.
**Directions:** located on the A615 between Matlock and Alfreton.
ERIC & INGEBORG TRAVIS ☎(01629) 57735

## WIRKSWORTH • map 9B2

### LE BISTRO
13 St John Street, DE4 4DR
*Built in 1760, this is a candlelit cellar restaurant approached by a spiral staircase from the reception bar. Situated in the centre of this quaint market town, the freshly prepared, rural French-style cuisine is very popular. The friendly, efficent service complements a wonderful meal. International evenings monthly. Highly recommended.*
FOOD: from £15 to £20 ☜
**Hours:** dinner 6.30pm-9.30pm, closed Sunday.
**Cuisine:** FRENCH - sauce dishes, such as half Norfolk duckling in Grand Marnier and fresh orange sauce, steaks, seafood and an extensive vegetarian menu. Game in season.
**Cards:** Visa, Access, Diners, AmEx.
**Other points:** licensed, reception bar, parking.
**Directions:** in the centre of Wirksworth, opposite Lloyds Bank.
MARK FOX ☎(01629) 823344

---

**A FREE bottle of wine courtesy of P&O!**
**See page adjacent to Portsmouth Hampshire for details.**

---

For Reservations & Special Offers FreeCall 0500 700 456

# GLOUCESTERSHIRE

## AYLBURTON • map 4A5

### THE CROSS
High Street, GL15 6DE

A very attractive traditional 15th century pub, recently extended, offering an extensive à la carte menu which caters for every possible taste. The atmosphere is relaxed and welcoming and the proprietors are very much part of the local community being involved in cricket and darts leagues. Children are not forgotten, there is a special menu for them and family Sunday lunch is a speciality of the house. Forest of Dean steam railway and Lydney gardens are nearby. Well recommended.

FOOD: up to £15

**Hours:** lunch and bar meals 12noon-2.15pm, dinner and bar meals Monday to Saturday 7pm-9.45pm, Sundays 7pm-9.30pm, open bank holidays.

**Cuisine:** steaks, curries, chicken - extensive à la carte menu. Family service Sunday lunch, children's menu also available.

**Cards:** Visa, Access, AmEx.

**Other points:** vegetarian meals, parking, children's play area, outdoor dining,

**Directions:** situated 1 mile outside Lydney on the Gloucester to Chepstow road (A48).

ALAN & KATE YEATES ☎(01594) 842823

## BOURTON-ON-THE-WATER • map 4A6

### BO-PEEP TEA ROOMS
Riverside, GL54 2DP

`Olde worlde' riverside tea rooms and licensed restaurant. The spacious interior has fitted carpets, panelling and exposed Cotswold stone walls. A homely, comfortable atmosphere prevails and the service is efficient and welcoming. All dishes are freshly cooked, well-served and presented. The menu offers a good choice including vegetarian dishes. A beautiful setting. Chosen by the Tea Council as one of the top ten places in Britain for 1992, 1993 and 1994.

FOOD: up to £15

**Hours:** summer 10am-8pm, winter (closed some weekdays) 10am-5.30pm.

**Cuisine:** ENGLISH - home-made. Large Cornish clotted-cream teas.

**Cards:** Visa, Access, Diners, AmEx.

**Other points:** licensed, Sunday lunch, no-smoking area, children welcome, afternoon tea, pets allowed, open bank holidays.

**Directions:** off A429 Fosse Way. Opposite side of river to village green.

JUDY & BOB HISCOKE ☎(01451) 822005

### THE OLD MANSE HOTEL
Victoria Street, GL54 2BX

Built in 1748 as the home of the Reverend Benjamin Beddome, the village's Baptist pastor, this traditional Grade II listed Cotswold stone building stands on the south bank of the River Windrush, which flows leisurely by. A spacious 50-seater restaurant, elegantly decorated and furnished, offers excellent cuisine, using fresh local produce wherever possible, complemented by an extensive wine list. Special dishes can be prepared on request. Places of interest within the village include Birdland, perfumery, motor museum, model village and model railway exhibition.

DOUBLE ROOM: from £20 to £30

SINGLE ROOM: from £30 to £40

FOOD: from £15 to £20

**Hours:** breakfast 8am-9am, Sunday 8.30am-9.30am, Sunday lunch 12noon-2.30pm, bar meals 11.30am-2.30pm, Sunday 11am-2.30pm, dinner and bar meals 6pm-9pm, Sunday 7pm-9pm, bar 11am-11pm, Sunday 11am-3pm, 7pm-10.30pm.

**Cuisine:** ENGLISH / FRENCH

**Cards:** Visa, Access, Diners, AmEx.

**Other points:** children welcome, parking, disabled access, pets, residents' lounge, garden, vegetarian meals, open-air dining.

**Rooms:** 12 bedrooms. All with TV, telephone, tea/coffee-making facilities.

**Directions:** Bourton-on-the-Water is off the A429 (Fosse Way) running between Stow-on-the-Wold and Cirencester. The hotel is located in the conservation area in the centre of the village. It stands on the river bank, overlooking the village green and the high street.

OSWALD & AUDREY DOCKERY ☎(01451) 820082 Fax(01451) 810381

### OLD NEW INN
GL54 2AS

A traditional country inn built in 1709, situated in the heart of the Cotswolds on the banks of the River Windrush and set in attractive gardens. Antique furnishings, warming log fires and traditional home-cooking set the atmosphere. Run by the Morris family for over 60 years.

DOUBLE ROOM: from £27 to £34

SINGLE ROOM: from £25 to £35

FOOD: up to £15

**Hours:** breakfast 8.15am-9.15am, lunch 12.30pm-1.30pm, dinner 7.30pm-8.30pm, closed Christmas day.

**Cuisine:** ENGLISH - traditional home-cooking.

**Cards:** Visa, Access.

**Other points:** open-air dining, Sunday lunch, children welcome, pets allowed.

**Rooms:** 1 single room, 7 double rooms, 4 twin rooms. All en suite with TV, tea/coffee-making facilities.

**Directions:** off the A429. Turn off Fosse Way down to the high street.

PETER MORRIS ☎(01451) 820467 Fax(01451) 810236

## CHELTENHAM • map 4A6

### BELOW STAIRS RESTAURANT
103 Promenade, GL50 1NW

*Situated in the town centre, with front entrance from the Promenade and rear access with evening and weekend parking in Montpellier Street. Cooking is personally supervised by the chef/proprietor.*

FOOD: up to £15  [CLUB]

**Hours:** lunch 12noon, dinner 6pm, closed Sunday, closed bank holidays.

**Cuisine:** ENGLISH / SEAFOOD - fresh seafood is a speciality. Traditional cooking and fresh vegetables. Vegetarian and vegan dishes are available.

**Cards:** Visa, Access, Diners, AmEx.

**Other points:** open-air dining, no-smoking area, children welcome.

**Directions:** in the town centre.

MR J.B. LINTON ☎(01242) 234599

### COTSWOLD GRANGE HOTEL
Pittville Circus Road, GL52 2QH

*Built as the fine country house of a London solicitor, this attractive, mellow, Cotswold-stone building is set in a tree-lined avenue in a pleasant location close to the centre of Cheltenham. The hotel is a friendly, family-run establishment and offers quality food and accommodation at excellent prices.*

DOUBLE ROOM: from £20 to £30

SINGLE ROOM: from £35 to £45

FOOD: up to £15

**Hours:** breakfast 7.15am-9am, lunch 12noon-2pm, dinner 6pm-7.30pm, restaurant closed after breakfast on Sundays, hotel closed Christmas to New Year.

**Cuisine:** ENGLISH

**Cards:** Visa, Access, Diners, AmEx.

**Other points:** licensed, children welcome, connecting rooms, pets welcome, baby-sitting, baby-listening, cots, residents' lounge, residents' bar, parking.

**Rooms:** 9 single rooms, 9 double rooms, 5 twin rooms, 2 family rooms. All with en suite, TV, radio, telephone, tea/coffee-making facilities, alarm, hair dryer.

**Directions:** at roundabout on Prestbury road, take right for Pittville Circus.

MR PAUL WEAVER ☎(01242) 515119 [Fax](01242) 241537

### THE RETREAT
10-11 Suffolk Parade, GL50 2AB

*Lively, friendly bar with fresh food cooked daily on the premises. Its central location and distinctive atmosphere makes The Retreat a popular rendezvous.*

FOOD: up to £15

**Hours:** lunch 12noon-2.15pm, closed Sunday.

**Cuisine:** INTERNATIONAL - prepared in their own kitchen using fresh produce. Wide range of cold meats, salads and fish from servery. Home-made puddings, cheesecakes, tarts. Extensive hot menu with a wide range of vegetarian food.

**Cards:** Visa, Access, Diners, AmEx.

**Other points:** open-air dining, children welcome.

**Directions:** in the centre of Cheltenham's antique area of town.

MIKE DEY ☎(01242) 235436

## CHIPPING CAMPDEN • map 8E6

### NOEL ARMS HOTEL
High Street, GL55 6AT

*This 14th century hotel has been welcoming travellers for more than six centuries. Although the faces have changed, the welcome is still the epitome of traditional hospitality. A freshly prepared meal from the extensive menu may be enjoyed in the delightful and impressive oak-panelled restaurant; or if you simply wish to relax over a quiet drink, the cosy lounge bar with its oak beams and open fire offers a congenial atmosphere.*

DOUBLE ROOM: from £40 to £50

SINGLE ROOM: over £50

FOOD: from £15 to £20 [CLUB]

**Hours:** breakfast 7.30am-9.30am, lunch Monday to Saturday on request, bar meals 12noon-2pm, dinner 7pm-9.30pm.

**Cuisine:** MODERN ENGLISH

**Cards:** Visa, Access, Diners, AmEx, Switch.

**Other points:** parking, children welcome, pets allowed, conference facilities, residents' lounge, traditional Sunday lunch, vegetarian meals.

**Rooms:** 11 double rooms, 13 twin rooms, 2 four-poster rooms. All with TV, telephone, radio, alarm, tea/coffee-making facilities.

**Directions:** located in the centre of Chipping Campden, near the Old Market Hall.

NEIL JOHN ☎(01386) 840317 [Fax](01386) 841136

## CIRENCESTER • map 4A6

### THE CROWN OF CRUCIS HOTEL & RESTAURANT
Ampney Crucis, GL7 5RS

A well-patronized, pleasant hotel and restaurant with good home-cooking. On fine days the tables beside the stream are very popular with families. Facilities for private parties of up to 100 people.
DOUBLE ROOM: from £30 to £40
SINGLE ROOM: from £25 to £35
FOOD: up to £15
**Hours:** dinner 7pm-10pm, lunch 12noon-2.30pm, open all year.
**Cuisine:** ENGLISH - daily specials, home-made desserts, traditional English cooking including award-winning steak-and-kidney pies.
**Cards:** Visa, Access, Diners, AmEx.
**Other points:** licensed, open-air dining, Sunday lunch, parking, garden, children welcome, baby-listening device, baby-sitting, cots, left luggage.
**Rooms:** 8 double rooms, 17 twin rooms. All with TV, radio, telephone, tea/coffee-making facilities.
**Directions:** on the A417 between Cirencester and Fairford.
MR R.K. MILLS ☎(01285) 851806 Fax(01285) 851735

### THE HARE & HOUNDS
Foss Cross, near Chedworth, GL54 4NW
Located in open countryside, the pub dates back to the 17th century, with many original features. They now offer a separate function area. All food is home-made. Registered caravan site for up to 5 vehicles adjacent.
FOOD: up to £15
**Hours:** bar weekdays 11am-3pm, 6pm-11pm, weekends 12noon-3pm, 7pm-10.30pm, bar meals from 7pm, closed Christmas day.
**Cuisine:** ENGLISH - steak-and-kidney with dumplings cooked in ale, grills and a selection of various home-made dishes, including vegetarian.
**Cards:** Visa, Access, Diners, AmEx.
**Other points:** licensed, open-air dining, Sunday lunch, children welcome, coaches by prior arrangement, functions.
**Directions:** half-way between Cirencester and Northleach on A429.
THE TURNER FAMILY ☎(01285) 720288

### HARRY HARE'S RESTAURANT & BRASSERIE
3 Gosditch Street, GL7 2AG
The wide-ranging menu at this restaurant and brasserie caters for all tastes, from those wanting an à la carte lunch or dinner to those seeking a traditional breakfast or just coffee and a cake. The menu changes monthly and includes steaks, pasta, salads, and sautéed king prawns in garlic butter on a julienne of vegetables. All are very fresh, as local suppliers deliver twice daily.
FOOD: up to £15
**Hours:** meals all day 11am-11pm, open for lunch Christmas day.
**Cuisine:** ENGLISH / CONTINENTAL - very varied brasserie-style food including breakfast, brunch and tea.
**Cards:** Visa, Access, AmEx.
**Other points:** licensed, open-air dining, Sunday lunch, children welcome, open bank holidays, afternoon tea.
**Directions:** just off West Market Place, 200 yards from parish church.
MARK R. STEPHENS ☎(01285) 652375 Fax(01285) 641691

### KINGS HEAD HOTEL
Market Place, GL7 2MR

Retaining its old-world charm, this delightful hotel has an inn-keeping tradition that dates back 300 years. Paintings, panelling and high ceilings add atmosphere, while the accommodation has been furnished with attention to comfort
DOUBLE ROOM: from £33 to £40
SINGLE ROOM: from £50 to £63
FOOD: up to £15
**Hours:** breakfast 7.30am-9.15am, Sunday and bank holidays 8.30am-10am, lunch 12.15am-2pm, dinner 7pm-9pm, closed 27th December until 30th December.
**Cuisine:** ENGLISH - appetizing traditional English fare; creative omelettes a house speciality.
**Cards:** Visa, Access, Diners, AmEx.
**Other points:** licensed, Sunday lunch, children welcome, pets allowed, residents' lounge, open bank holidays, baby-listening device, cots, residents' bar.
**Rooms:** 15 single rooms, 20 double rooms, 26 twin rooms, 5 family rooms. All with TV, radio, telephone, tea/coffee-making facilities.

**Directions:** situated in the town centre opposite prominent church tower.
MR & MRS BANNERMAN ☎(01285) 653322
Fax(01285) 655103

### THE VILLAGE PUB
Barnsley, GL7 3EF
*A traditional Cotswold-stone country pub in the centre of Barnsley village. The food is well cooked and presented and served in generous portions. The country-style accommodation boasts low beams, welcoming service and a friendly atmosphere.*
DOUBLE ROOM: from £20 to £30
SINGLE ROOM: from £25 to £35
FOOD: up to £15    CLUB
**Hours:** breakfast 7.30am-9am, lunch 12noon-2pm, dinner 7pm-9.30pm, closed Christmas day.
**Cuisine:** ENGLISH - bar meals and à la carte menu. Dishes include local Bibury trout, deep-fried halibut, gammon steak, bean and vegetable casserole.
**Cards:** Visa, Access, AmEx.
**Other points:** licensed, Sunday lunch, children welcome, garden, pets allowed, afternoon tea.
**Rooms:** 4 double rooms, 1 twin room.
**Directions:** on B4425 in the centre of Barnsley.
MRS S. WARDROP ☎(01285) 740421

## CLEARWELL • map 4A5

### TUDOR FARMHOUSE HOTEL AND RESTAURANT
Near Coleford, GL16 8JS
*Delightful 13th century stone farmhouse in a peaceful village setting. The hotel features an abundance of oak beams, original wall-panelling and a 15th century spiral staircase. Ideal for the Forest of Dean and Wye Valley.*
DOUBLE ROOM: from £20 to £30
SINGLE ROOM: from £40 to £50
FOOD: from £15 to £20
**Hours:** breakfast 7.30am-9.30am, dinner 7pm-9pm.
**Cuisine:** ENGLISH / INTERNATIONAL - à la carte fixed four course menu and vegetarian menu. Comprehensive wine list.
**Cards:** Visa, Access, AmEx, Switch.
**Other points:** licensed, children catered for (please check for age limits), pets allowed, residents' bar, residents' lounge, cots, baby-listening device, 3 ground floor rooms with sitting rooms, parking.
**Rooms:** 7 double rooms, 3 family rooms. All with TV, telephone, tea/coffee-making facilities, alarm.
**Directions:** Clearwell is north of the A48 and east of A466.
DEBORAH & RICHARD FLETCHER ☎(01594) 833046 Fax(01594) 837093

### WYNDHAM ARMS
Near Coleford, GL16 8JT
*Situated within easy reach of Chepstow and Lydney, yet peaceful and secluded, off the main route. The Wyndham Arms has beautifully decorated rooms*

*and offers food of excellent quality. It has been in the Stanford family's competent management since 1973 and deservedly won the Les Routiers Accommodation of the Year Award in 1990.*
DOUBLE ROOM: from £20 to £30
SINGLE ROOM: from £35 to £45
FOOD: up to £15 ☜
**Hours:** lunch 12noon-2pm, dinner 7pm-9.30pm.
**Cuisine:** ENGLISH - fresh food using home-grown fruit and vegetables in season. Fresh Wye and Severn salmon. Home-made puddings.
**Cards:** Visa, Access, Diners, AmEx, JCB.
**Other points:** licensed, Sunday lunch, children stay free in parents' bedroom, pets allowed, 24hr reception, patio, bar meals daily.
**Rooms:** 2 single rooms, 6 double rooms, 9 twin rooms. All with en suite, TV, radio, telephone, tea/coffee-making facilities, alarm, hair dryer, trouser-press, baby-listening device, cots available.
**Directions:** in the centre of Clearwell village, 2 miles from Coleford.
MR J. STANFORD, MRS R. STANFORD, MR R. STANFORD ☎(01594) 833666 Fax(01594) 836450

## COLEFORD • map 4A5

### OREPOOL INN & MOTEL
St Briavels Road, Sling, near Coleford, GL16 8LH
*Charming motel and inn dating from the mid-17th century. Friendly staff ensure a warm welcome. Busy family atmosphere. Conference facilities. Coach parties welcome by prior appointment. C.L. site (five caravans at any one time).*
DOUBLE ROOM: up to £20
SINGLE ROOM: from £30 to £40
FOOD: up to £15
**Hours:** bar snacks 11am-10.30pm, breakfast 7am-10am.
**Cuisine:** ENGLISH - substantial English or continental breakfast. Extensive bar menu and specials board, which changes on a daily basis.
**Cards:** Visa, Access, AmEx.
**Other points:** licensed, open-air dining, Sunday lunch, afternoon tea, children welcome, disabled access.
**Rooms:** 2 single rooms, 4 double rooms, 2 twin rooms, 2 family rooms. All with TV, telephone, tea/coffee-making facilities.
**Directions:** take B4228 Coleford-Chepstow road.
JIM & JOAN WILSON ☎(01594) 833277 Fax(01594) 833785

## GREAT RISSINGTON • map 5B2

### THE LAMB INN
GL54 2LP
*Situated in the heart of the Cotswolds, Great Rissington is popular with tourists. Locally there is the Cotswold Wildlife Park and, slightly further afield, Oxford and Stratford-upon-Avon. Here, at The Lamb Inn, you will find warm hospitality, fine ales and wines, excellent food and comfortable accommodation in rooms with chintz and antique*

*furniture.*
DOUBLE ROOM: from £22 to £38
SINGLE ROOM: from £35 to £45
FOOD: up to £20
**Hours:** breakfast 8.30am-9am, dinner weekdays 7pm-9pm, dinner weekends 7pm-9pm, lunch 12noon-1.45pm.
**Cuisine:** ENGLISH - steaks, Cotswold trout, pâtés, soups, casseroles.
**Cards:** Visa, Access, AmEx.
**Other points:** children welcome, pets allowed, winter breaks available.
**Rooms:** 8 double rooms, 4 suites.
**Directions:** A40 from Oxford to Cheltenham; turn right to the Barringtons and Rissingtons.
MR & MRS CLEVERLY ☎(01451) 820388 Fax(01451) 820724

## MORETON-IN-MARSH • map 8E6

### THE MARSHMALLOW
High Street, GL56 0AT
*This Grade II listed, ivy-clad licensed restaurant offers outstanding, olde-worlde surroundings in which to relax, contemplate life and enjoy a sumptuous meal or light snack. The extensive menu is an indication of Valerie's dedication to providing her valued guests with the very best cuisine and service. Well worth a visit. Tea Council Award of Excellence 1995.*
FOOD: up to £15
**Hours:** meals all day 10am-9.30pm, menu changes at 6pm.
**Cuisine:** ENGLISH / CONTINENTAL - good menu, well-presented dishes using fresh local produce. Candlelit suppers amongst a profusion of hanging baskets on the patio.
**Cards:** Visa, Access.
**Other points:** children welcome, no-smoking area, open-air dining, vegetarian meals, afternoon teas, traditional Sunday lunch.
**Directions:** northern end of the High Street.
VALERIE WEST ☎(01608) 651536

## NYMPSFIELD • map 5B1

### ROSE & CROWN INN
Stonehouse, GL10 3TU
*A 300-year-old coaching inn in an extremely quiet Cotswold village. Close to the Cotswold Way and Nympsfield Gliding Club. A friendly, local inn which is an ideal base for touring, and within easy access of the M4 and M5.*
DOUBLE ROOM: from £20 to £30
SINGLE ROOM: from £25 to £35
FOOD: up to £15
**Hours:** breakfast 8am-9am, lunch 12noon-2pm, bar meals 6.30pm-9.30pm.
**Cuisine:** ENGLISH / INTERNATIONAL - good bar food with sandwiches, salads, steaks, fish meals, spicy dishes. Packed lunch available. Choice of over 65 main meals plus 8 real ales.
**Cards:** Visa, Access, Diners, AmEx.
**Other points:** licensed, Sunday lunch, children

welcome, coaches by prior arrangement
**Rooms:** 4 family rooms. All rooms can be let as twins.
**Directions:** off the B4066 Dursley to Stroud road. Situated in village centre.
BOB & LINDA WOODMAN & NEIL SMITH
☎(01453) 860240 Fax(01453) 860240

## PARKEND • map 4A5

### PARKEND HOUSE HOTEL
Near Lydney, GL15 4HL
*A small country house hotel set in three acres of parkland. Over 200 years old, the house has been tastefully converted to retain its country house atmosphere. The restaurant offers a varied menu of well-cooked dishes at good value for money, served in pleasing surroundings. A welcoming hotel where guests can relax within the peaceful surroundings of the Royal Forest of Dean.*
DOUBLE ROOM: from £20 to £30
SINGLE ROOM: from £25 to £35
FOOD: up to £15
**Hours:** bar meals 12noon-2pm, breakfast 8.30am-9.30am, dinner 7pm-8pm.
**Cuisine:** ENGLISH / CONTINENTAL - table d'hôte menu with a choice of English and continental dishes.
**Cards:** Visa, Access, AmEx.
**Other points:** licensed, children welcome, afternoon tea, pets allowed, residents' lounge, garden, croquet.
**Rooms:** 5 double rooms, 3 twin rooms. All with TV.
**Directions:** A48 Chepstow-Gloucester road to Lydney. In Lydney take B4234 to Parkend.
MRS ROBERTA POOLE ☎(01594) 563666 Fax(01594) 564631

## ROYAL FOREST OF DEAN • map 4A5

### LAMBSQUAY HOUSE HOTEL
Near Coleford, GL16 8QB

*An elegant Georgian country house, full of charm and character, dating back to the 17th century, situated in a pleasant area high up in the Forest of Dean. This friendly, family-run hotel has nine individually decorated comfortable bedrooms and a fine restaurant offering a blend of English and continental food. All meals are prepared using fresh produce, from the hotel garden whenever possible. A warm welcome awaits you, and you will be assured of the best attention throughout your stay.*
DOUBLE ROOM: from £20 to £30

SINGLE ROOM: up to £30
FOOD: up to £15
**Hours:** breakfast weekdays 7am-9am, weekends and bank holidays 7.30am-9.30am, dinner 7pm-8.30pm.
**Cuisine:** ENGLISH - traditional home-cooked dishes.
**Cards:** Visa, Access.
**Other points:** parking, children welcome, pets by arrangement, conference facilities, residents' lounge, garden, vegetarian meals.
**Rooms:** 2 single rooms, 4 double rooms, 2 twin rooms, 1 family room. All with TV, telephone, tea/coffee-making facilities.
**Directions:** 1.5 miles south of Coleford on B4228 Coleford to Chepstow road.
MIKE & LESLEY HARDY ☎(01594) 833127
Fax(01594) 833127

## STOW-ON-THE-WOLD • map 8E6

### GRAPEVINE HOTEL
Sheep Street, GL54 1AU
*Award-winning 17th century hotel in antiques centre. Romantic conservatory restaurant with beautiful furnishings, crowned by magnificent historic vine. Caring staff. Rosette for fine cuisine. Hotel of the Year 1991. Bargain breaks from £47 per person, dinner, bed and breakfast.*
DOUBLE ROOM: from £50
SINGLE ROOM: from £55
FOOD: from £15 to £20  CLUB
**Hours:** breakfast 8.30am-9.45am, bar meals 12noon-2.30pm, dinner 7pm-9.30pm, bar meals 7pm-9.30pm, closed 24th December until 11th January.
**Cuisine:** FRENCH / ENGLISH - bar: delicious selection of unusual dishes. Restaurant: English and French haute cuisine. Changing menu with fresh ingredients. Typically local and national traditional dishes.
**Cards:** Visa, Access, Diners, AmEx.
**Other points:** licensed, open-air dining, Sunday lunch, children welcome, afternoon tea, garden, baby-listening device, cots, left luggage, tennis.
**Rooms:** 1 single room, 9 double rooms, 11 twin room, 2 quad rooms. All with ensuite, TV, alarm, radio, telephone, tea/coffee-making facilities. There are deluxe garden rooms with trouser press and mini-bar available.
**Directions:** from A429, take A436 towards Chipping Norton; 150 yards on right.
MRS SANDRA ELLIOTT ☎(01451) 830344
Fax(01451) 832278

### THE OLD STOCKS HOTEL
The Square, GL54 1AF
*A 17th century Grade II listed hotel, one of the original buildings in the square, and facing the quiet village green on which the original penal stocks still stand. Refurbished to combine modern comforts with original charm and character. Friendly and caring staff make this an ideal base for exploring the beautiful Cotswolds.*

DOUBLE ROOM: from £30 to £40
SINGLE ROOM: from £35 to £45
FOOD: from £15 to £20 CLUB
**Hours:** breakfast 8.15am-9.15am, lunch 12noon-2pm, dinner 7pm-9pm.
**Cuisine:** ENGLISH / VEGETARIAN - extensive table d'hôte and very popular special-value menu, specializing in traditional home-cooked dishes and also catering for the vegetarian.
**Cards:** Visa, Access, MasterCard.
**Other points:** licensed, Sunday lunch, pets allowed, children welcome, garden, patio, disabled access.
**Rooms:** 1 single room, 14 double rooms, 2 twin rooms, 1 family room. All with TV, tea/coffee-making facilities.
**Directions:** take A429 to Stow-on-the-Wold. Hotel in town centre next to the green.
ALAN ROSE ☎(01451) 830666 Fax(01451) 870014

### THE WHITE HART HOTEL
Market Square, GL54 1AF
*A 17th century coaching inn, which still retains much of its old character and ambience. It provides an ideal base for touring the Cotswolds, and the food and service are of a high standard.*
DOUBLE ROOM: from £20 to £30
SINGLE ROOM: from £25 to £30
FOOD: up to £15
**Hours:** breakfast 8.15am-9.15am, lunch 11.45am-2.15pm, dinner 6pm-10pm, Sunday 7pm-9pm.
**Cuisine:** ENGLISH - home-made traditional pies, local grilled trout.
**Cards:** Visa, Access, Diners, AmEx.
**Other points:** Sunday lunch, children welcome.
**Rooms:** 4 double rooms, 4 family rooms. 5 rooms en suite. All with TV, tea/coffee-making facilities, telephone.
**Directions:** off A429. Turn off at town centre sign; on left side of main square.
COLIN & ALISON HEWETT & CLARE PEASTON ☎(01451) 830674 Fax(01451) 830090

## STROUD • map 4A6

### BELL HOTEL & RESTAURANT
Wallbridge, GL5 3JA
*Situated in the town centre of Stroud, this delightful Victorian hotel has 12 newly refurbished bedrooms, a fine restaurant, wine bar and beer garden. The service is welcoming and the general ambience is jovial.*
DOUBLE ROOM: up to £25
SINGLE ROOM: from £25 to £40
FOOD: up to £15
**Hours:** breakfast 7.30am-9am, lunch 12noon-2pm, dinner 7pm-9.30pm.
**Cuisine:** ENGLISH / CONTINENTAL - all meals freshly cooked to order and great value for money.
**Cards:** Visa, Access, Diners, MasterCard.
**Other points:** parking, children welcome, pets allowed, no-smoking area, garden, open-air dining, Sunday lunch, vegetarian meals.
**Rooms:** 1 single room, 7 double rooms (2 with

whirlpool bath), 3 twin rooms, 1 four-poster room.
**Directions:** follow directions to Stroud. The Bell
Hotel & Restaurant is near to the town centre.
MICHAEL & CHRISTINE WILLIAMS ☎(01453)
763556 **Fax**(01453) 758611

### LONDON HOTEL
30-31 London Road, GL5 2AJ
*A very friendly, welcoming hotel situated in the
small industrial town of Stroud, where five valleys
meet in the beautiful Cotswolds. The food in the
candlelit restaurant is of excellent quality, and the
accommodation is very comfortable. Places of
interest nearby include Gatcombe Park, Gloucester
Cathedral and Slimbridge Wild Fowl Trust.*
DOUBLE ROOM: from £15 to £30
SINGLE ROOM: from £25 to £40
FOOD: from £10 to £20 **CLUB**
**Hours:** breakfast 7.30am-9.30am, lunch 12noon-
2pm, dinner 7pm-9.30pm.
**Cuisine:** CONTINENTAL - dishes including sirloin
steak Francaise, Hawaian duck and Romany
chicken. A la carte, table d'hôte and bar meals.
Good wine list.
**Cards:** Visa, Access, AmEx.
**Other points:** licensed, smoking area, children
welcome, open bank holidays, residents' lounge,
afternoon tea, baby-listening device, cots.
**Rooms:** 4 single rooms, 5 double rooms, 3 twin
rooms. All with TV, radio, alarm, telephone,
tea/coffee-making facilities.
**Directions:** from Stroud town centre, take A419
towards Cirencester.
MRS PAGET ☎(01453) 759992
**Fax**(01453) 753363

### GUPSHILL MANOR
Gloucester Road, GL20 5SY
*This is a timbered 15th century manor house and
the site of the 1491 Battle of Tewkesbury. Margaret
of Anjou is rumoured to have watched the battle
from the precarious safety of one of the bedrooms.
The battles are over now, and Gupshill has been
tastefully restored, offering a peaceful setting to
enjoy good food.*
FOOD: from £15 to £20
**Hours:** bar meals 12noon-2.15pm, dinner 7pm-
9.30pm, bar meals 7pm-9.30pm.
**Cuisine:** ENGLISH - all home-cooked. Menu in
carvery changes daily.
**Cards:** Visa, Access, Diners, AmEx.
**Other points:** licensed, open-air dining, Sunday
lunch, children welcome.
**Directions:** situated on the A38 on the edge of
Tewkesbury, only about five minutes from the M5.
MARK & KAY RATCLIFFE ☎(01684) 292278
**Fax**(01684) 290406

# HEREFORD & WORCESTER

### BELL INN
Main Street, Willersey, WR12 7PJ
*A large public house built in traditional Cotswold
stone, the Bell Inn serves excellent food within
comfortable, relaxed surroundings. The food is
made from fresh local produce and is superbly
cooked and presented. Highly recommended for its
welcoming service and excellent food at very good
value for money.*
FOOD: up to £15
**Hours:** lunch 12noon-2pm, dinner 6pm-9.30pm,
Sunday 7pm-9pm.
**Cuisine:** ENGLISH - daily changing menu. Dishes
may include lemon sole, salmon en croute,
traditional game pie, steak au poivre, as well as a
standard menu.
**Cards:** Visa, Access, AmEx, Switch, Delta.
**Other points:** licensed, open-air dining, Sunday
lunch, children welcome, beer garden.
**Directions:** B4632 Broadway (1.5 miles) to
Stratford-upon-Avon. By the duck pond.
WILLIAM MOORE ☎(01386) 858405

 **LEASOW HOUSE**
Laverton Meadows, WR12 7NA
*A most appealing Cotswold stone farmhouse with
superb gardens, this has a very high standard.
Beautifully decorated throughout, it offers guests
accommodation of the highest quality with a warm
and welcoming ambience. Impressed and satisfied
guests keep returning again and again, and this is
surely a high recommendation.*
DOUBLE ROOM: from £20 to £30
**Hours:** breakfast 7am-9am.
**Cards:** Visa, Access, AmEx.
**Other points:** parking, children welcome, pets
allowed, disabled access, no-smoking area,
residents' lounge, garden, vegetarian meals.
**Rooms:** 7 bedrooms. All with en suite, TV,
telephone, radio, alarm, tea/coffee-making facilities.
There is one room for disabled guests.
**Directions:** from Broadway take B4632 to
Cheltenham, and turn right at sign for Wormington
and Dumbleton. First house on the right.
BARBARA MEEKINGS ☎(01386) 584526
**Fax**(01386) 584596

## FOWNHOPE • map 8E4

 **THE GREEN MAN INN**
HR1 4PE

*A 15th century country inn set in the heart of the beautiful Wye Valley, popular for businessmen, families, wedding parties or small functions. Ideal centre for fishing, with some of England's best salmon reaches nearby.*
DOUBLE ROOM: from £20 to £30
SINGLE ROOM: from £30
FOOD: up to £15
**Hours:** breakfast 7am-9am, lunch 12noon-2pm, bar meals 12noon-2pm, dinner 7pm-9pm, bar meals 6pm-10pm.
**Cuisine:** ENGLISH - à la carte and bar food menus. Dishes include beef, mushroom and ale pie.
**Cards:** Visa, Access, AmEx, Switch.
**Other points:** open-air dining, Sunday lunch, children welcome.
**Rooms:** 1 single room, 5 family rooms, 2 twin rooms, 11 double rooms.
**Directions:** on B4224, midway between Ross-on-Wye and Hereford.
ARTHUR & MARGARET WILLIAMS ☎(01432) 860243 **Fax**(01432) 860207

## GREAT MALVERN • map 8E5

 **MOUNT PLEASANT HOTEL**
Belle Vue Terrace, WR14 4PZ

*An attractive early Georgian building and orangery set in one and half acres of mature terraced gardens with lovely views across the town. Close to the theatre and shops yet only seconds from the Malvern Hills rising behind the hotel. An informal hotel with all the facilities of a larger establishment.*
DOUBLE ROOM: from £30 to £40
SINGLE ROOM: from £45
FOOD: up to £15
**Hours:** breakfast 7.45am-9.30am, lunch 12noon-2pm, bar meals 12noon-2pm, dinner 7pm-9.30pm, bar meals 7pm-9pm, coffee shop 10am-6pm, closed Christmas day.
**Cuisine:** INTERNATIONAL - in the restaurant: salmon in plum sauce, paella, gazpacho, guacamole, turkey guajalote and vegetarian menu. Excellent home-cooked bar meals, and table d'hôte menu.
**Cards:** Visa, Access, Diners, AmEx.
**Other points:** licensed, Sunday lunch, children welcome, conferences, functions, cots, left luggage, vegetarian meals, lounge bar, residents' lounge.
**Rooms:** 2 single rooms, 6 double rooms, 6 twin rooms. All with TV, radio, telephone, tea/coffee-making facilities, alarm.
**Directions:** take M5 exit 7, follow A449 to Malvern. Near Priory church in town centre.
SOL & GEOFF PAYNE ☎(01684) 561837 **Fax**(01684) 569968

 **SIDNEY HOUSE**
40 Worcester Road, WR14 4AA

*An attractive, white Georgian listed building standing in an elevated position in Great Malvern, with stunning views over the Severn Valley, towards the Vale of Evesham and the Cotswolds. The town centre, Winter Gardens, Malvern Festival Theatre, Priory Park and the hills are only a few minutes' walk away.*
DOUBLE ROOM: from £20 to £30
SINGLE ROOM: from £20 to £40
FOOD: from £15 to £20
**Hours:** breakfast 8am-9am.
**Cuisine:** BREAKFAST
**Cards:** Visa, Access, AmEx.
**Other points:** central heating, children welcome, pets by prior arrangement, residents' lounge.
**Rooms:** 1 single room, 4 double rooms, 2 twin rooms, 1 family room. All available as singles with TV, hair dryer, radio, alarm, tea/coffee-making facilities, complimentary Malvern Water.
**Directions:** on the A449, 150 yards on right from junction with Church Street.
TOM J.S. & MARGARET E. HAGGETT ☎(01684) 574994

## HAY-ON-WYE • map 8E4

 **THE OLD BLACK LION**
Lion Street, HR3 5AD

*Oliver Cromwell is reputed to have stayed at the Old Black Lion while the Roundheads besieged Hay Castle, which was a Loyalist stronghold. Whether you be Loyalist or Roundhead, this old coaching inn extends a warm welcome to all who visit today by serving delicious country cooking. Hay is the world centre for secondhand books, with over 2 million books in 27 bookshops.*
DOUBLE ROOM: from £20 to £30
SINGLE ROOM: up to £25
FOOD: from £15 to £20
**Hours:** breakfast 8.30am-9.15am, lunch 12noon-2.30pm, dinner 7pm-9pm.
**Cuisine:** INTERNATIONAL - home country cooking with international flair, house specials being steaks, seafood, game and vegetarian. 50 wines from around the world and a choice of 6 malt whiskies.
**Cards:** Visa, Access, AmEx.
**Other points:** licensed, Sunday lunch, children catered for (please check for age limits), pets allowed, fishing, "Gourmet à la carte Breaks" - minimum stay 2 days.

**Rooms:** 1 single room, 4 double rooms, 4 twin rooms, 1 family room. All en suite with TV, radio, telephone, tea/coffee-making facilities.
**Directions:** 50 yards off the B4352 Hereford to Hay road.
JOHN & JOAN COLLINS ☎(01497) 820841

## LEDBURY • map 8E5

### THE VERZONS COUNTRY HOUSE HOTEL
Trumpet, HR8 2PZ

*A most attractive large Georgian country house dating from around 1790, and converted into a comfortable hotel with 9 en suite bedrooms and offering a good range of à la carte dishes in the restaurant. Short break stays are available, and the hotel is very well situated for exploring the Malvern Hills and Hereford with its beautiful cathedral and 3 counties show ground.*
DOUBLE ROOM: from £30 to £40
SINGLE ROOM: from £45
FOOD: from £15 to £20
**Hours:** breakfast 8am-9.30am, lunch bar 12noon-2pm, dinner bar and restaurant 7pm-9.30pm. Open bank holidays, closed 24th-26th December.
**Cuisine:** ENGLISH/FRENCH - steaks, seafood and poultry. Range of vegetarian dishes also offered. Bistro menu up to £15.
**Cards:** Visa, Access.
**Other points:** special breaks, parking, dogs welcome, 4 acres of lawns and grounds, paddocks and stabling available, clay pigeon shoots some Sundays, vintage sports car club meetings last Thursday of each month and New Years day.
**Rooms:** 2 single rooms, 3 double rooms, 2 twin rooms, 2 family rooms. All en suite with TV, radio, tea/coffee-making facilities. 2 ground floor en suite bedrooms being added in 1996 - please ask for details.
**Directions:** 3 miles from Ledbury on A438 Hereford road
FREDERICKE & VIRGINIA COOMBER ☎(01531) 670381 Fax(01531) 670830

**Join Les Routiers Discovery Club FREE! See page 34 for details.**

## PERSHORE • map 8E5

### CHEQUERS INN
Chequers Lane, Fladbury, WR10 2PZ
*Situated at the end of a quiet lane in Fladbury, this old English village inn, parts of which date from the 14th century, offers exceptional accommodation and is renowned for its hospitality and excellent food. Warm and comfortable, there is a traditional country lounge bar with magnificent open fire, cosy restaurant and endless beams. Ideal location for both tourists and business people.*
DOUBLE ROOM: from £25 to £30
SINGLE ROOM: from £40 to £50
FOOD: from £15 to £20
**Hours:** breakfast 7.15am-9.30am, lunch 12noon-2pm, bar snacks 12noon-2pm, dinner 7.30pm-10pm, bar snacks 6pm-10pm.
**Cuisine:** ENGLISH
**Cards:** Visa, Access, AmEx.
**Other points:** parking, children welcome, Sunday lunch, open bank holidays, vegetarian meals, garden.
**Rooms:** 4 double rooms, 4 twin rooms.
**Directions:** between Evesham and Pershore. Off A44 or off B4084.
MR A. & MRS D. CORFIELD ☎(01386) 860276 Fax(01386) 861286

## REDDITCH • map 8D5

### HOTEL MONTVILLE & GRANNY'S RESTAURANT
101 Mount Pleasant, Southcrest, B76 4JE
*A fine 16-bedroomed hotel, offering exceptional quality. The latest addition is Granny's Restaurant, where the majority of guests dine and which is also very popular with the locals. The residents' lounge is comfortably furnished and has a writing desk. The hotel can arrange for guests to play squash, snooker, golf and use a gymnasium.*
DOUBLE ROOM: from £30 to £40
SINGLE ROOM: from £30 to £55
FOOD: up to £20 CLUB
**Hours:** breakfast 7.30am-9.30am, dinner 6.30pm-9.30pm.
**Cuisine:** ENGLISH/INTERNATIONAL - home-cooking using freshly cooked vegetables and salads, with traditional home-made puddings. Vegetarians are also well catered for.
**Cards:** Visa, Access, Diners, AmEx.
**Other points:** no-smoking area, children welcome, pets allowed, residents' lounge, parking.
**Rooms:** 16 bedrooms.
**Directions:** Redditch ring road. Left for Southcrest, turn right into Tunnel Drive, turn right into Parsons Road. Hotel and restaurant at top of the hill on left-hand side.
MARY WARNER ☎(01527) 544411

## ROSS-ON-WYE • map 8E4

 **ARCHES HOTEL**
Walford Road, HR9 5PT

*A small, family-run hotel set in half an acre of lawned gardens only 10 minutes' walk from the town centre. Easy access to many places of interest in the beautiful Wye valley. All bedrooms are decorated and furnished to a high standard and overlook the gardens. Renowned for good food and a warm and friendly atmosphere with personal service.*

DOUBLE ROOM: up to £20
SINGLE ROOM: up to £20
FOOD: up to £15
**Hours:** breakfast 8am-9am, dinner 7pm-8pm, closed Christmas Day and Boxing Day.
**Cuisine:** ENGLISH - dinner is available on request. An excellent and varied menu offers home-cooked dishes using local home-grown produce whenever possible.
**Other points:** central heating, children welcome, residents' lounge, garden, pets by prior arrangement.
**Rooms:** 1 single room, 4 double rooms, 2 twin rooms, 1 family room. All with TV, tea/coffee-making facilities.
**Directions:** A40, then onto B4234.
JEAN JONES ☎(01989) 563348

 **LOUGHPOOL INN**
Sellack, HR9 6LX

*A 17th century pub with oak beams, a large open fireplace and original flagstone flooring. Outside, the inn is set in a large garden, facing a pool surrounded by willows. On the main Hoarwithy road - a popular tourist route.*

FOOD: up to £15
**Hours:** lunch 12noon-2.30pm, dinner 7pm-9.30pm, open all year.
**Cuisine:** ENGLISH / INTERNATIONAL
**Cards:** Visa, Access, MasterCard.
**Other points:** open-air dining, Sunday lunch, garden, restaurant.
**Directions:** turn off the A49, to the Sellack to Hoarwithy road. The Loughpool Inn is midway between Hoarwithy and Ross.
MALCOLM HALL ☎(01989) 730236

**THE OLD COURT HOTEL & RESTAURANT**
Symonds Yat West, HR9 6DA

*This old 16th century manor house is situated in a most beautiful part of the Wye Valley. The carefully selected menus in the Tudor restaurant offer a wide variety of dishes, and the charming Cotswold bar serves a wide choice of hot and cold bar food and a comprehensive selection of ales, lagers and wines. Excellent accommodation and service.*

DOUBLE ROOM: from £20 to £30
SINGLE ROOM: from £35 to £45
FOOD: from £15 to £20
**Hours:** bar meals 12noon-2pm, bar meals 6pm-10pm, dinner 7pm-9.30pm.
**Cuisine:** ENGLISH - à la carte restaurant menu and bar menu.
**Cards:** Visa, Access, Diners, AmEx.
**Other points:** licensed, open-air dining, no-smoking area, children welcome, afternoon tea, pets allowed, swimming pool, conservatory.
**Rooms:** 17 double rooms, 3 twin rooms.
**Directions:** within the Wye valley on A40, 6 miles from end of M50.
JOHN & ELIZABETH SLADE ☎(01600) 890367
Fax (01600) 890964

 **ROCK'S PLACE COUNTRY HOTEL**
Yatton, HR9 7RD

*Recently converted from a 16th century barn into an attractive and comfortable country house hotel retaining many of the original beams in bedrooms and public areas. Rocks Place is an ideal centre from which to explore this beautiful and historic countryside with its many cathedrals, castles and market towns close by. Very easily accessible from the motorway network, only 4.5 miles from the M50.*

DOUBLE ROOM: from £20 to £30
SINGLE ROOM: from £30 to £40
FOOD: from £15 to £20
**Hours:** breakfast to 9.30am, lunch by arrangement only, dinner 7.30pm-9pm.
**Cuisine:** TRADITIONAL ENGLISH - table d'hôte dinner menus and Sunday lunch.
**Cards:** Visa, Access, Diners, AmEx.
**Other points:** parking, golf courses nearby.
**Rooms:** 3 double rooms, 2 twin rooms, 1 triple room, 1 family room. All en suite with TV, radio, alarm, tea/coffee-making facilities.
**Directions:** leave the M50 at exit 4, take A449 to Ledbury and Worcester, then 4th turn to the left, signposted Yatton.
☎(01531) 660218 Fax (01531) 660460

**THE OLD SCHOOL HOUSE**
Severn Stoke, WR8 9JA

*An interesting combination of 17th century farmhouse and Victorian school, overlooking the Severn Valley and Malvern Hills. The popular restaurant specialises in the very best of British cooking, whilst the en-suite bedrooms are decorated in individual styles with all modern facilities. Fast becoming one of the country's most prominent venues for conferences and exhibitions.*

DOUBLE ROOM: from £27 to £37

---

**For Reservations & Special Offers FreeCall 0500 700 456**

SINGLE ROOM: from £38
FOOD: up to £15  CLUB
**Hours:** breakfast weekdays 7.30am-9.30am, weekends 8am-9.30am, lunch and bar meals weekdays 12noon-2pm, until 2.30pm Sundays, dinner Monday to Saturday 7pm-9.30pm, Sunday 8.30pm, open all year.
**Cuisine:** BRITISH - nightly "School Dinner" menu representing the best of British cooking, complemented by a cosmopolitan à la carte menu. Lunchtime snacks served in the headmaster's study. Vegetarian and fish dishes always available - special diets catered for.
**Cards:** Visa, Access, Delta, Switch.
**Other points:** outdoor swimming pool, garden, conference facilities, nearby golf and clay pigeon shoot, short breaks, restaurant boat, riverside walks.
**Rooms:** 2 single rooms, 2 twin rooms, 8 double rooms, 1 family room, 1 four poster room, all en-suite with tea/coffee-making facilities, TV, telephone, radio, alarm.
**Directions:** situated in the village of Severn Stoke on A38 south of Worcester.
MRS LESLIE NEWBROOK ☎(01905) 371368
Fax(01905) 371591

## WEOBLEY • map 8E4

### 🛏 YE OLDE SALUTATION INN
Market Pitch, HR4 8SJ
*Dating back over 500 years, this former Ale & Cider house offers a traditional setting and friendly atmosphere in which to spend a pleasant lunchtime or evening out. A main feature of the comfortable lounge is a large inglenook fireplace, leading into the 40-seater Oak Room Restaurant. The local area offers many activities, including fishing, horse-riding, hiking and golf.*
DOUBLE ROOM: from £20 to £30
SINGLE ROOM: from £25 to £35
FOOD: from £15 to £20   CLUB
**Hours:** breakfast 9am-9.30am (enquire for early breakfast), lunch 12noon-2pm, dinner 7pm-9pm.
**Cuisine:** ENGLISH - traditional English fare of excellent quality, using fresh local produce. All

dishes are cooked to order. Vegetarian dishes also available.
**Cards:** Visa, Access, Diners, AmEx.
**Other points:** licensed, open-air dining, Sunday lunch, no-smoking area, children catered for (please check for age limits), pets allowed, lounge, bar, baby-listening device.
**Rooms:** 3 double rooms, 1 twin room. All with TV, radio, tea/coffee-making facilities, alarm.
**Directions:** situated 8 miles from Leominster on the A4112 Brecon road.
CHRISTOPHER ANTHONY ☎(01544) 318443
Fax(01544) 318216

## WORCESTER • map 8E5

### 🛏 LENCHFORD HOTEL
Shrawley, WR6 6TB
*Stephen and Karen Horn offer you a warm welcome and personal attention in the relaxed atmosphere of this splendid late Georgian house, which still retains many of its original features. Log fires in winter and riverside lawns in summer. The large restaurant offers superb views across the River Severn, which flows gently by. A 100-seater banqueting suite is available for hire.*
DOUBLE ROOM: from £20 to £30
SINGLE ROOM: from £25 to £35
FOOD: from £15 to £20   CLUB
**Hours:** breakfast 7.30am-9am, bar meals 12noon-2pm, dinner 7pm-9.30pm, closed 24th December until 30th December.
**Cuisine:** ENGLISH / CONTINENTAL - extensive à la carte lunch and dinner menus Monday-Saturday. Carvery Sunday lunchtimes. Bar meals available.
**Cards:** Visa, Access, Diners, AmEx.
**Other points:** licensed, open-air dining, Sunday lunch, children catered for (please check for age limits), parking, residents' lounge, garden, vegetarian meals, cots, residents' bar.
**Rooms:** 1 single room, 7 double rooms, 8 twin rooms. All with TV, radio, alarm, telephone, tea/coffee-making facilities.
**Directions:** on the A443-B1496, 6 miles north of Worcester. 7 miles from M5 junctions 5 and 6.
STEPHEN & KAREN HORN ☎(01905) 620229

# LEICESTERSHIRE

## ASHBY DE LA ZOUCH • map 9C2

### 🍴 LA ZOUCH RESTAURANT
2 Kilwardby Street, LE65 2FQ
*A renovated Georgian building, tastefully decorated and furnished and with a walled garden, cottage-style with pebble water feature. There is a small intimate bar with a larger lounge bar upstairs, and private functions and dinner parties can be arranged. The restaurant offers a large selection of English and continental dishes.*
FOOD: from £15 to £20   CLUB
**Hours:** lunch 12noon-2pm, dinner 7pm-10pm, closed Sunday evening, Monday, and from 1st to

15th January and 1st to 14th July.
**Cuisine:** ENGLISH / CONTINENTAL - grilled salmon and cucumber sauce, rump steak and mustard sauce. Home-made sweets. Speciality; Colston Bassett Stilton.
**Cards:** Visa, Access, Diners, AmEx.
**Other points:** licensed, open-air dining, Sunday lunch, children welcome, parking, vegetarian meals.
**Directions:** at the crossroads of the A50 and B5006 in town centre.
GEOFFREY & LYNNE UTTING ☎(01530) 412536

## BOTTESFORD • map 9C3

### THE RUTLAND ARMS
2 High Street, NG13 0AA
*For main entry see Bottesford Nottinghamshire*

## BURTON ON THE WOLDS • map 9C2

### GREYHOUND INN
25 Melton Road, LE12 5AG
*A traditional coaching inn renovated in 1991. All the food is home-cooked and supported by a comprehensive wine list. British Institute of Innkeeping (East Midlands Section) `Pub of the Year' 1988 and 1989. Greenalls Catering `Pub of the Year' 1993.*
FOOD: up to £15
**Hours:** lunch 12noon-2pm, dinner 7pm-10pm.
**Cuisine:** ENGLISH - home-cooked specials. `Big Steak Night' every Thursday.
**Cards:** Visa, Diners, AmEx, Switch, MasterCard, JCB, LV's.
**Other points:** open-air dining, Sunday lunch, children welcome, coaches by prior arrangement
**Directions:** B676 Loughborough to Melton Mowbray road.
PHILIP ASHLEY ☎(01509) 880860 Fax(01509) 881709

## CASTLE DONINGTON • map 9C2

### DONINGTON MANOR HOTEL
High Street, DE74 2PP
*An 18th century Regency coaching inn, refurbished in period style. Donington Manor provides the epitome of traditional British hospitality.*
DOUBLE ROOM: from £30 to £40
SINGLE ROOM: from £49 to £58
FOOD: from £15 to £20
**Hours:** last orders 9.30pm, closed 27th December until 30th December.
**Cuisine:** ANGLO-FRENCH - Melton fillet, fresh duckling, game dishes and fresh fish in season.
**Cards:** Visa, Access, Diners, AmEx.
**Other points:** Sunday lunch, conference facilities.
**Rooms:** 10 single rooms, 15 double rooms, 7 twin rooms, 1 family suite.
**Directions:** off M1 at junction 24, 2 miles along A6 to Derby, turn left at B6540.
MR N. GRIST ☎(01332) 810253 Fax(01332) 850330

### LE CHEVALIER
2 Borough Street, DE74 2LA
*A small, intimate, personally run restaurant with a well-established reputation for its good food and friendly atmosphere. It now has a number of lovely rooms around the rear courtyard and makes an ideal base for exploring the surrounding area, with Donington Park Racetrack, Nottingham, Derby and Alton Towers nearby.*

DOUBLE ROOM: from £32 to £40
FOOD: up to £20
**Hours:** breakfast 7.30am-8.30am, lunch 12noon-2pm, dinner 6.30pm-11pm.
**Cuisine:** FRENCH / CONTINENTAL - specialities including boudin à l'Anglaise and filet de boeuf Chevalier.
**Cards:** Visa, Access, Diners, AmEx.
**Other points:** licensed, children welcome, open bank holidays, garden.
**Rooms:** 2 double rooms, 1 twin room, 1 family room. All with TV, radio, alarm, telephone, tea/coffee-making facilities.
**Directions:** just off B6540 (junction 24 of M1). On main street of Castle Donington.
MR JAD OTAKI & LYNN OTAKI ☎(01332) 812106/812005 Fax(01332) 811372

## LEICESTER • map 9C2

### THE JOHNSCLIFFE HOTEL & RESTAURANT
73 Main Street, LE6 0AF
*The Johnscliffe provides a varied and exciting menu served by friendly and efficient staff. Set in its own wooded grounds, this elegant building has sunlit rooms and a quiet, relaxing atmosphere. Places to visit include Bradgate park (the home of Lady Jane Grey) and Castle Donington race track.*
DOUBLE ROOM: from £20 to £30
SINGLE ROOM: from £40 to £50
FOOD: from £15 to £20
**Hours:** lunch 12noon-2pm, dinner 7pm-9.30pm.
**Cuisine:** ENGLISH / CONTINENTAL - crab, chicken, pheasant, fish and steak in interesting sauces.
**Cards:** Visa, Access, AmEx.
**Other points:** licensed, Sunday lunch, children welcome, pets allowed.
**Rooms:** 2 single rooms, 12 double rooms, 1 twin room, 1 family room.
**Directions:** 5 minutes from junction 22 off the M1.
MR & MRS DEVONPORT ☎(01530) 242228 Fax(01530) 244460

### OLD TUDOR RECTORY
Main Street, Glenfield, LE3 8DG
*A Tudor hotel with Jacobean and Queen Anne additions, set in its own acre of well-tended gardens, offering attractive and comfortable accommodation. The tasteful, well-selected interior adds to the friendly relaxed atmosphere and outstanding hospitality.*
DOUBLE ROOM: from £20 to £30
SINGLE ROOM: from £30 to £40
FOOD: up to £15
**Hours:** breakfast 7.30am-9am, bank holidays 8.30am-9.45am, dinner 7pm-9.30pm, (bookings only).
**Cuisine:** ENGLISH / CONTINENTAL
**Cards:** Visa, Access, Diners, AmEx.
**Other points:** children welcome, garden, pets allowed, beauty therapy, gym facilities, disabled access, parking, vegetarian meals, residents' lounge, residents' bar.

**Rooms:** 3 single rooms, 8 double rooms, 3 twin rooms, 2 family rooms. All with TV, telephone, tea/coffee-making facilities.
**Directions:** leave M1 at exit 22. Take the A50 to Leicester. Opposite Forge Berni Inn.
MR I. PHILLIPS ☎(0116) 2915678 Fax (0116) 2911416

## LOUGHBOROUGH • map 9C2

### THE GEORGE HOTEL
17 Market Place, Belton, LE12 9UH
*This old coaching inn dating back to 1753 is set in the rural village of Belton near the church. It offers a warm welcome and good wholesome food to travellers and locals alike. Near Castle Donnington race track and East Midlands Airport.*
DOUBLE ROOM: from £20 to £30
SINGLE ROOM: from £25 to £35
FOOD: from £20 to £25
**Hours:** breakfast 7.30am-9.30am, lunch 12noon-2.30pm, dinner 7pm-10.30pm, bar meals 12noon-2.30pm, 7pm-10.30pm.
**Cuisine:** ENGLISH - home-made bar meals and very good à la carte menu available.
**Cards:** Visa, Access, Diners, AmEx.
**Other points:** licensed, Sunday lunch, vegetarian meals, children welcome, pets allowed, afternoon tea, disabled access, parking.
**Rooms:** 1 single room, 9 double rooms, 11 twin room, 2 family rooms.
**Directions:** 5 minutes from M1, junction 23 or 24, via A42.
MR HOUSTON ☎(01530) 222426 Fax (01530) 222426

## LYDDINGTON • map 9D3

### OLD WHITE HART COUNTRY INN & RESTAURANT
51 Main Street, LE15 9LS
*Situated in an unspoilt village, this stone building with its walled garden is opposite the village green. Decorated to a high standard, it is furnished with good, solid yet comfortable furniture. In the restaurant you can enjoy quality food, appealingly presented and served in generous portions. The staff are skilled and helpful while the atmosphere is friendly and relaxed. Pétanque (French boules), for 60 persons on site, can be played by all ages. Private parties welcomed (French food and boules).*
FOOD: up to £15
**Hours:** lunch 12noon-2pm, dinner 6.30pm-10pm.
**Cuisine:** ENGLISH - full restaurant and bar menus: most popular dishes are mushrooms Lyddington, chicken in filo pastry with asparagus sauce, and Sussex pond pudding. Menu changes every two months.
**Cards:** Visa, Access.
**Other points:** licensed, Sunday lunch, garden, pets allowed.
**Directions:** 1 mile south of Uppingham, follow `Bede House' signs.
DIANE & BARRY BRIGHT ☎(01572) 821703
Fax (01572) 821965

## MELTON MOWBRAY • map 9C3

### SYSONBY KNOLL HOTEL & RESTAURANT
Asfordby Road, LE13 0HP
*A family-run hotel, set in 2 acres of grounds with river frontage, the Sysonby Knoll has beautifully decorated rooms with quality furnishings. The restaurant offers an imaginative menu, which, our inspector comments, `gives excellent value for money'.*
DOUBLE ROOM: from £20 to £30
SINGLE ROOM: from £35 to £45
FOOD: up to £15
**Hours:** breakfast 7.30am-9.30am, lunch 12noon-2pm, dinner 7pm-9pm.
**Cuisine:** ENGLISH - extensive à la carte menu, which includes a vegetarian selection.
**Cards:** Visa, Access, Diners, AmEx.
**Other points:** Sunday lunch, pets allowed, garden, children welcome, cots, vegetarian meals, parking, residents' lounge, residents' bar, disabled access.
**Rooms:** 6 single rooms, 10 double rooms, 6 twin rooms, 2 triple rooms. All en suite with TV, radio, alarm, telephone, tea/coffee-making facilities.
**Directions:** take A606/607 to Melton Mowbray. Follow A6006; .5 mile from town centre.
STELLA BOOTH ☎(01664) 63563 Fax (01664) 410364

## OLD DALBY • map 9C3

### THE CROWN INN
Debdale Hill, near Melton Mowbray, LE14 3LF
*Tucked away in a corner of the village and approached through the large car park, the Crown Inn offers the facilities of a croquet lawn, large garden and a pétanque pitch. The beer is drawn straight from the wood, and the bar menu is interesting and extensive. Games room, snug and tap room with some no-smoking areas. Routiers Pub of the Year 1991.*
FOOD: from £15 to £20
**Hours:** lunch 12noon-2pm, dinner 6pm-9.30pm.
**Cuisine:** MODERN ENGLISH - fresh, seasonal dishes.
**Other points:** licensed, open-air dining, Sunday lunch, children welcome.
**Directions:** off the A46 and the A606 in Old Dalby.
LYNNE BRYAN & SALVATORE INGUANTA ☎(01664) 823134

## STAPLETON • map 9D2

### WOODSIDE FARM GUEST HOUSE
Ashby Road,, LE9 8JE
*A working farm in a rural and tranquil setting, where Julia Lusher provides a warm welcome for all guests. Comfortable lounge and dining room with traditional farmhouse furniture. Ideally situated for visiting nearby Bosworth Battle Centre, Kirkby Mallory Race Track and Twycross Zoo.*
DOUBLE ROOM: from £20 to £30

SINGLE ROOM: from £25 to £35
FOOD: from £15 to £20
**Hours:** breakfast 7am-9am, dinner 6.30pm-9pm, open all year.
**Cuisine:** ENGLISH - good homely cooking using the freshest of local produce, cooked and served by the proprietor and staff.
**Cards:** Visa, Access, AmEx, Switch, MasterCard, Eurocard.
**Other points:** licensed, open-air dining, Sunday lunch, vegetarian meals, residents' lounge, garden, parking, children welcome, cots.
**Rooms:** 3 single rooms, 3 double rooms, 2 twin rooms, 1 triple room, 1 family/disabled room (4 persons). All en suite with TV, radio, tea/coffee-making facilities.
**Directions:** 3 miles north of Hinckley on left-hand side, past Woodlands Nursery.
JULIA LUSHER ☎(01455) 291929 Fax(01455) 291929/292626

## UPPINGHAM • map 9C3

### FALCON HOTEL
High Street East, LE15 9PY

*Situated in the centre of Uppingham overlooking - the market square, the Falcon is the ideal base from which to explore Rutland. Formerly a renowned coaching inn of great charm and character it has now been transformed into a delightful hotel, offering its guests a warm and relaxed atmosphere and friendly efficient service.*
DOUBLE ROOM: from £30 to £40
SINGLE ROOM: over £50

FOOD: from £15 to £20   CLUB
**Hours:** breakfast 7.30am-9.30am, weekends 8am-10am, lunch 12noon-2pm, dinner 7pm-9.30pm.
**Cuisine:** ENGLISH / INTERNATIONAL - English at heart with an emphasis on fresh seasonal produce. A choice of table d'hôte or à la carte menu is available in the restaurant and in addition the brasserie offers lighter meals and snacks.
**Cards:** Visa, Access, Diners, AmEx.
**Other points:** garden terrace, 2 bars, some ground floor rooms, parking.
**Rooms:** 5 single rooms, 10 double rooms, 2 executive double rooms, 6 twin rooms, 2 suites. All en suite with satellite TV, telephone, radio/alarm, tea/coffee-making facilities, welcome tray.
**Directions:** located just off A47 halfway between Leicester and Peterborough.
KEVIN REID ☎(01572) 823535 Fax(01572) 821620

### THE MONCKTON ARMS
Glaston, LE15 9BP

*An old English hotel offering warm, comfortable accomodation, combined with log fires, a bar serving traditional ales, and a restaurant preparing home-cooked food to order. All complemented by a rich heritage and convivial atmosphere.*
DOUBLE ROOM: from £30 to £40
SINGLE ROOM: from £25 to £35
FOOD: up to £15
**Hours:** breakfast 7.30am-9.30am, lunch and bar meals 12noon-2.30pm, dinner and bar meals 7pm-10pm, open bank holidays.
**Cuisine:** ENGLISH - imaginative traditional cuisine with daily specials, using fresh local produce and including such dishes as Red Mullet, baked avocado, steaks, grills and home-made sweets.
**Cards:** Visa, Access, AmEx.
**Other points:** licensed, real ales, vegetarian meals, log fires, attractive patio, parking.
**Rooms:** 1 single room, 5 double rooms, 4 twin rooms, all en suite. All with TV, telephone, room service and tea/coffee-making facilities.
**Directions:** on A47, between Peterborough and Leicester.
SPENSER ☎(01572) 822326

# LINCOLNSHIRE

## GEDNEY DYKE • map 10C4

### THE CHEQUERS
Near Spalding, PE12 0AJ

*This is a small, homely country freehouse with restaurant. A new conservatory dining room has been added, which overlooks the garden and is non-smoking. The bar has low ceilings with exposed beams and has been attractively furnished. Good food and a friendly, welcoming atmosphere have made this restaurant and freehouse deservedly popular.*

**FOOD:** up to £15
**Hours:** lunch 12noon-1.45pm, dinner 7pm-9.30pm, dinner (Monday-Wednesday) 7pm-9pm, no meals Christmas day and Boxing day, no meals Sunday evenings November to March.
**Cuisine:** ENGLISH - cooked on the premises, with local fresh fish and vegetables, and light meals in the bar. Full à la carte menu in the comfortably furnished restaurant.
**Cards:** Visa, Access, Diners, AmEx.
**Other points:** licensed, open-air dining, Sunday lunch, children welcome, garden.
**Directions:** take B1359 north of the A17 and turn left at the post office.
JUDITH & ROB MARSHALL ☎(01406) 362666
Fax(01406) 362666

## GRANTHAM • map 9C3

### THE ROYAL OAK INN
Swayfield, near Grantham, NG33 4LL

*This traditional stone-built country inn has been excellently maintained and is set amidst the attractive Lincolnshire countryside. Offering well-cooked and presented food, with `special dishes' each day, served by helpful and friendly staff. Outside dining in well-tended beer garden during the summer months. Featured in the Good Beer Guide.*

**DOUBLE ROOM:** up to £20
**SINGLE ROOM:** from £25 to £35
**FOOD:** up to £15
**Hours:** lunch 11.30am-2.30pm, Sunday 12noon-3pm, dinner 6pm-10.30pm, Sunday 7pm-10.30pm.
**Cuisine:** ENGLISH - à la carte with special Sunday lunch menu and special Sunday supper menu. Monday to Friday lunch, three-course table d'hôte and à la carte.
**Cards:** Visa, Access, Diners, AmEx.
**Other points:** licensed, Sunday lunch, children welcome, garden, pets allowed.
**Rooms:** 2 double rooms, 2 twin rooms, 1 family room. All en suite.
**Directions:** A1 south from Grantham. Left at Colsterworth roundabout. 2 miles, follow signs for Swayfield.
DAVID COOKE ☎(01476) 550247 Fax(01476) 550996

## LEADENHAM • map 9B3

### GEORGE HOTEL
High Street, LN5 0PN

*A family-run old coaching inn on the A17. The George is renowned for its well-stocked bar - a whisky-drinkers' delight, with over 500 varieties of whisky and drinks from around the world.*

**DOUBLE ROOM:** up to £20
**SINGLE ROOM:** up to £20
**FOOD:** up to £15
**Hours:** lunch 10.30am-2.30pm, dinner 6pm-11pm, last orders 10pm.
**Cuisine:** ENGLISH - steaks, Lincolnshire duckling à l'orange, Georgian trout.
**Cards:** Visa, Access, Diners, AmEx.
**Other points:** open-air dining, Sunday lunch, children welcome.
**Rooms:** 2 single rooms, 2 double rooms, 3 twin rooms. All with TV, tea/coffee-making facilities.
**Directions:** at the junction of the A17 and the A607, 8 miles from the A1.
MR M.G. WILLGOOSE ☎(01400) 272251
Fax(01400) 272091

## LINCOLN • map 9B3

### HILLCREST HOTEL
15 Lindum Terrace, LN2 5RT

*A former Victorian rectory situated in a quiet avenue, yet only 5 minutes' walk to the cathedral, museums and shops. The Hillcrest offers a chance to relax and enjoy a drink or meal in the wonderful conservatory, with views over the garden and parkland. Non-smoking restaurant and some non-smoking bedrooms.*

**DOUBLE ROOM:** from £30 to £40
**SINGLE ROOM:** from £37 to £47
**FOOD:** up to £15 CLUB
**Hours:** breakfast 7.15am-9am, lunch 12noon-2pm, dinner 7pm-8.45pm, bar meals only Sunday 7pm-9.30pm.
**Cuisine:** MODERN ENGLISH - dishes may include lamb noisettes, gammon in peaches and honey, steaks, vegetarian dishes, pork with honey and apple.
**Cards:** Visa, Access, AmEx, Switch, JCB.
**Other points:** licensed, no-smoking area, children welcome, pets allowed, afternoon tea, baby-listening device, cots, left luggage, vegetarian meals, parking, residents' bar, residents' lounge.
**Rooms:** 6 single rooms, 6 double rooms, 1 twin rooms, 4 family rooms. All with TV, radio, alarm, telephone, tea/coffee-making facilities.
**Directions:** off the A115 Wragby road, close to the cathedral.
JENNIFER BENNETT ☎(01522) 510182 Fax(01522) 510182

## THE PENNY FARTHING INN
15 Station Road, Timberland, LN4 3SA

*Set in the pretty village of Timberland, this cosy, 18th century inn offers a friendly, relaxed atmosphere, excellent food and comfortable accommodation in a country setting. The locality has a wealth of leisure activities and is equally rewarding for those seeking the peace and tranquility of the fens.*

DOUBLE ROOM: from £20 to £30

FOOD: up to £15 `CLUB`

**Hours:** breakfast 7.30am-10am, lunch 12.30pm-1.45pm, bar snacks 12noon-2pm, dinner 7.30pm-9.30pm, bar snacks 7pm-9.45pm, open bank holidays.

**Cuisine:** TRADITIONAL ENGLISH - wholesome pub fare.

**Cards:** Visa, Access, Diners, AmEx.

**Other points:** parking, children welcome, open bank holidays, pets allowed, residents' lounge, vegetarian meals, golf nearby.

**Directions:** on the B1189.

MR M DOBSON ☎(01526) 378359 Fax(01526) 378359

## PORTLAND HOTEL
49-55 Portland Street, LN5 7JZ

*Situated 5 minutes from the city centre and close to the railway and coach stations, this guest house is ideally situated for the passing traveller or for visitors to the city. The reception is friendly and cheerful.*

DOUBLE ROOM: up to £20

SINGLE ROOM: up to £20

**Hours:** breakfast 7.30am-9am, open all year.

**Cuisine:** BREAKFAST

**Cards:** Diners, AmEx.

**Other points:** central heating, no evening meal, children welcome, residents' lounge, games room, bar, garden, parking.

**Rooms:** 7 single rooms, 3 double rooms, 3 twin rooms, 1 family room. All with TV.

**Directions:** off high street, opposite Ritz Theatre.

DAVID HALLGATH ☎(01522) 521098/(01589) 403166

## WASHINGBOROUGH HALL COUNTRY HOUSE HOTEL
Church Hill, Washingborough, LN4 1BE

*Set in 3 acres of lawns and woodland, on the edge of Washingborough village. The bar serves real ales, and the Wedgwood dining room serves an interesting and comprehensive menu as well as an excellent wine list. Outdoor heated swimming pool.*

DOUBLE ROOM: from £36 to £42

SINGLE ROOM: from £52 to £62

FOOD: from £20 to £25 `CLUB`

**Hours:** breakfast 7.30am-9am, dinner 7pm-9pm.

**Cuisine:** ENGLISH - traditional cuisine.

**Cards:** Visa, Access, Diners, AmEx.

**Other points:** licensed, Sunday lunch, no-smoking area, children welcome, pets allowed, afternoon tea, heated swimming pool, residents' lounge, residents' bar, vegetarian meals, parking.

**Rooms:** 6 double rooms, 6 twin rooms.

**Directions:** from Lincoln town centre, take B1190 for Bardney. Turn right after 2 miles, at telephone box up Church Hill.

MARY & BRIAN SHILLAKER ☎(01522) 790340 Fax(01522) 792936

## LOUTH • map 10A4

## BRACKENBOROUGH ARMS HOTEL
Cordeaux Corner, LN11 0SZ

*Set in the heart of the Lincolnshire Wolds, the hotel is situated in pleasant surroundings noted for its natural beauty and within easy reach of all major routes. The bedrooms feature the best in home comforts, with many modern facilities. A beautifully furnished lounge boasts traditional low beams and log fire, and there is a superb dining room offering the finest in fresh cuisine. Nearby are the coastal towns of Mabelthorpe and Skegness, Market Rasen racecourse and Cadwell park, with historical Lincoln just an hour away.*

DOUBLE ROOM: from £20 to £30

SINGLE ROOM: from £45 to £55

FOOD: from £15 to £20

**Hours:** breakfast 7am-10.30am, lunch 12noon-2pm, bar snacks 12noon 2pm, dinner 7pm-10pm, bar snacks 5pm-10pm, closed Christmas day and Boxing day.

**Cuisine:** ENGLISH

**Cards:** Visa, Access, Diners, AmEx, Switch.

**Other points:** children welcome, open-air dining, vegetarian meals, garden, parking, disabled access.

**Rooms:** 18 bedrooms.

**Directions:** A16 Louth to Grimsby, 1 mile outside Louth.

J., D. & A. LIDGARD ☎(01507) 609169 Fax(01507) 609413

## MR CHIPS FISH RESTAURANT
17-21 Aswell Street, LN11 9BA

*A bright and roomy restaurant, which provides excellent value in both quantity and quality. Seating for 300. Self-service.*

FOOD: up to £15

**Hours:** all day 9am-11pm, closed Sunday, closed Christmas, Boxing day and New Year's day, open bank holidays.

**Cuisine:** ENGLISH - fresh North Sea haddock, cod, plaice, scampi with chips and mushy peas. Lincolnshire sausages, Norfolk chicken, vegetarian meals. Selection of sweets.

**Other points:** licensed, no-smoking area, children welcome, parking, air-conditioned, coaches by prior arrangement, baby changing room, disabled access and toilet.

**Directions:** from Market Place, turn into Queen Street, then first right into Aswell Street.

THE HAGAN FAMILY ☎(01507) 603756 Fax(01507) 601255

## SKEGNESS • map 10B4

 **THE CRAWFORD HOTEL**
104 South Parade, PE25 3HR
*A very attractive, well-organized hotel, offering a high standard of service, with comfortable rooms and good food. Mr and Mrs Willis ensure their guests have every satisfaction: a full English breakfast is provided, but vegetarian, continental and any other dietary requirement are catered for on request.*
DOUBLE ROOM: from £20 to £30
SINGLE ROOM: from £28
FOOD: up to £15
**Hours:** breakfast 8.30am-9.15am, lunch 12.30am-1.30pm, dinner 6pm.
**Cuisine:** BREAKFAST
**Cards:** Visa, Access.
**Other points:** children welcome, afternoon tea, residents' lounge, swimming pool, sauna, solarium.
**Rooms:** 3 single rooms, 9 double rooms, 8 family rooms. All with TV, radio, alarm, tea/coffee-making facilities.
**Directions:** A52. Clock tower: right end of parade.
MR & MRS WILLIS ☎(01754) 764215

 **CROWN HOTEL**
Drummond Road, PE25 3AB
*Completely refurbished, the Crown Hotel provides first-class service with an ambience of quiet unobtrusiveness and efficiency in full traditional English style. Enjoy a swim in the hotel pool or a game of golf on one of the many nearby well-known professional courses. Ideally situated for touring the area's many attractions, such as the famous Gibraltar Point nature reserve.*
DOUBLE ROOM: from £30 to £40
SINGLE ROOM: from £45 to £55
FOOD: up to £15
**Hours:** breakfast 7.30am-10am, lunch 12noon-2pm, bar meals 12noon-2pm, dinner 7pm-9.30pm.
**Cuisine:** ENGLISH - à la carte and table d'hôte menus. Dishes may include pork escalope with cider cream and apples, poached salmon steak. Vegetarian and children's dishes.
**Cards:** Visa, Access, Diners, AmEx.
**Other points:** licensed, Sunday lunch, parking, children welcome, residents' lounge, garden, functions, conferences.
**Rooms:** 1 single room, 4 double rooms, 13 twin rooms, 7 family rooms, 1 suite. All with TV, telephone, tea/coffee-making facilities.
**Directions:** A52 to Skegness. Lumley Road. Take last turning right before seafront.
PETER MCGONAGLE ☎(01754) 610760
Fax(01754) 610847

 **STRAND RESTAURANT AND SAVOY HOTEL**
12 North Parade, PE25 2UB
*The Strand Restaurant at The Savoy Hotel is a friendly, family-run business offering a very high standard of cuisine and service provided by warm and courteous staff. An excellent wine list complements the splendid dishes available from the table d'hôte and à la carte menus.*
DOUBLE ROOM: from £20 to £30
SINGLE ROOM: from £20 to £30
FOOD: up to £15    CLUB
**Hours:** breakfast 8am-9.30am, lunch 12noon-2pm.
**Cuisine:** ENGLISH - well-presented home-cooking with fresh local produce.
**Cards:** Visa, Access, Diners.
**Other points:** parking, children welcome, vegetarian meals, no-smoking area.
**Directions:** Situated on the Skegness seafront, close to the pier.
MR & MRS R. UNDERWOOD ☎(01754) 763371
Fax(01754) 761256

## SLEAFORD • map 9B3

 **MILLERS WINE BAR**
Mill Court, Carre Street, NG4 7TR
*A delightful 150-year-old red-brick barn set in the market town of Sleaford, it has been carefully renovated to provide a wine bar of character, with large oak beams and attractive patterned furnishings. Set in a secluded situation, it offers garden dining during the summer months and is extremely popular with people of all ages. Good location for visiting the RAF Museum at Cranwell and Heckington Mill.*
FOOD: up to £15    CLUB
**Hours:** lunch 12noon-2pm, dinner 7pm-12midnight, bookings only on Sunday, closed Christmas day.
**Cuisine:** ENGLISH - healthy, wholesome and delicious. Large choice of vegetarian dishes.
**Cards:** Visa, AmEx, MasterCard, Switch, Delta, JCB.
**Other points:** parking, children welcome, open bank holidays, disabled access, pets allowed, vegetarian meals, open-air dining.
**Directions:** A153 to Skegness into centre of Sleaford, turn right opposite church and right into the carpark.
ROWENA MARY DROWLEY ☎(01529) 413383

## SPALDING • map 10C4

**THE RED LION HOTEL**
Market Place, PE11 1SU
*Empathetically refurbished 18th century town centre hotel offering en suite accommodation, real ales, real food, a warm welcome and value for money. Local facilities include beautiful gardens and nurseries, fishing, clay pigeon shooting and golf.*
DOUBLE ROOM: from £20 to £30
SINGLE ROOM: from £30 to £45
FOOD: up to £15    CLUB
**Hours:** breakfast 7.30am-9.30am, lunch 12noon-2pm, dinner 7pm-9.30pm.
**Cuisine:** ENGLISH / CONTINENTAL
**Cards:** Visa, Access, Diners, AmEx, Switch.
**Other points:** Sunday lunch, children welcome, disabled access.

**Rooms:** 1 single room, 7 double rooms, 7 twin rooms. All en suite with TV, telephone, tea/coffee-making facilities.
**Directions:** centre of Spalding.
MRS J.M. & MR N.J. WILKINS ☎(01775) 722869 Fax(01775) 710074

## SPILSBY • map 10B4

### RED LION INN & LE BARON RESTAURANT
Raithby-by-Spilsby, PE23 4DS

*A pleasant Tudor-style country pub (a listed building), attractively furnished with brick-tiled floor, original beams and comfortable seating. The atmosphere is warm and friendly, as locals and tourists mix together to enjoy good food. Nearby places of interest include Wesley Chapel, Old Bolingbroke Castle and the famous Lincolnshire Wolds.*
DOUBLE ROOM: up to £20
SINGLE ROOM: up to £30
FOOD: up to £15
**Hours:** breakfast 7.30am-10am, lunch by arrangement 12noon-2.30pm, dinner 7.15pm-10.30pm, bar meals every evening 7.15pm-10.30pm, bar meals weekends and bank holidays 12noon-3pm.
**Cuisine:** ENGLISH / FRENCH - with fish and game speciality dishes. Vegetarian meals available. Bistro, balti and pizzeria selection in the bar.
**Cards:** Visa, Access, AmEx.
**Other points:** licensed, open-air dining, Sunday lunch, pets allowed, disabled access, residents' lounge, parking, open bank holidays.
**Rooms:** 2 double rooms, 2 twin rooms.
**Directions:** Lincoln road out of Spilsby; turn right after Hundleby for Raithby.
ROGER & MAGGIE SMITH ☎(01790) 753727

## STAMFORD • map 9C3

### CANDLESTICKS HOTEL & RESTAURANT
1 Church Street, PE9 2JU

*Occupying the corner unit of a stone Victorian building, this hotel has been established for over 18 years. During that time the restaurant has gained a fine reputation for the very high standard of food and for good-value prices. After an enjoyable meal, it is worth taking a walk around the historic stone-built town of Stamford. Highly recommended.*
DOUBLE ROOM: from £30 to £40
SINGLE ROOM: from £20 to £30
FOOD: up to £15
**Hours:** continental breakfast taken in bedroom, lunch 12noon-2pm, dinner 7pm-9.30pm, Sunday 7pm-8.45pm, closed all day Monday and Tuesday morning.
**Cuisine:** FRENCH / CONTINENTAL - specialities include Portuguese dishes. Menu changes monthly.
**Cards:** Visa, Access.
**Other points:** licensed, Sunday lunch, children welcome, no-smoking area, parking, vegetarian meals.

**Rooms:** 2 single rooms, 3 double rooms, 3 twin rooms. All with en suite, satellite TV, telephone, tea/coffee-making facilities, fridge.
**Directions:** opposite St Martins church.
MANUEL PINTO ☎(01780) 64033 Fax(01780) 56071

### THE DOLPHIN INN
60 East Street, PE9 1QD

*The Dolphin is situated in the quaint old stone-built town of Stamford, and is one of the oldest inns in town - the landlords have been traced back to the 18th century. Just two minutes from the town centre, it has an excellent reputation for its fine ales and also for its food, including the Big Steaks. Boasts its own guest house across the road, offering modern bedrooms with every comfort.*
DOUBLE ROOM: from £20 to £30
SINGLE ROOM: from £20 to £25
FOOD: up to £15
**Hours:** breakfast 7am-9am, lunch 12noon-2.30pm, bar snacks 12noon-2.30pm, dinner 6pm-10pm.
**Cuisine:** char-grilled steaks
**Cards:** Access, Visa, Switch, Delta
**Rooms:** 1 single room, 2 en suite double rooms, 3 twin rooms (2 en suite), 2 en suite family rooms. All with hair dryer, radio, television, tea/coffee-making facilities.
**Directions:** 200 yards north of town centre.
MIK & TINA MAKSIMOVIC ☎(01780) 57494/54515 Fax(01780) 55494

## WOODHALL SPA • map 10B4

### EAGLE LODGE HOTEL
The Broadway, LN10 6ST

*Purpose-built as an hotel in 1891, the Eagle Lodge reigned supreme when Woodhall Spa was as well known to high society in London as it now is to the golfing fraternity of the world. As one of the foremost hotels in Lincolnshire, the Eagle offers superb accommodation, a titillating choice of dishes in the Garden Restaurant, lovely garden views to enjoy while taking morning or afternoon tea in the Rose Lounge, and a great atmosphere in the well-stocked Regency Bar.*
DOUBLE ROOM: from £20 to £30
SINGLE ROOM: from £30 to £40
FOOD: up to £15
**Hours:** breakfast 7.30am-9am, lunch 12noon-2pm, dinner 7pm-9.30pm.
**Cuisine:** ENGLISH - daily changing à la carte menu, including local game.
**Cards:** Visa, Access, Diners, AmEx, Switch.
**Other points:** parking, children welcome, pets allowed, conference facilities, residents' lounge, garden, open-air dining, vegetarian meals, traditional Sunday lunch, afternoon teas.
**Rooms:** 23 bedrooms. All en suite, with TV, telephone, radio, alarm, room service, tea/coffee-making facilities.
**Directions:** 45 minutes to A1, 30 miles from East Coast.
MICHAEL ARAM ☎(01526) 353231 Fax(01526) 352797

# NORTHAMPTONSHIRE

## KETTERING • map 9D3

### THE STAR INN
2 Bridge Street, Geddington, NN14 1AD
*Peter and Ann welcome you to The Star Inn, where you will enjoy traditional ales, a good selection of fine wines and home-cooked food. Located in the attractive village of Geddington, this lovely 300-year-old public house and restaurant offers superb surroundings in which to enjoy the friendly atmosphere, whether relaxing over a drink or sampling the delicious cuisine. Log fires in winter.*
FOOD: from £15 to £20    CLUB
**Hours:** lunch weekdays 12noon-2pm, weekends 12noon-3pm, dinner 7pm-10pm, Sunday 6.30pm-8.30pm.
**Cuisine:** ENGLISH - a high standard of freshly prepared meals. Afternoon teas in summer.
**Cards:** Visa, Access, Diners, AmEx.
**Other points:** parking, children welcome, no-smoking area, conference facilities, vegetarian meals, traditional Sunday lunch, afternoon teas.
**Directions:** mid-way between Kettering and Corby on the A43, only minutes from the M1-A1 link (A14).
ANN CAREY & PETER SMART ☎(01536) 742386
Fax(01536) 742386

## NORTHAMPTON • map 9D3

### COACH HOUSE HOTEL
8-10 East Park Parade, Kettering Road, NN1 4LA
*Popular among business people, this charming Victorian hotel offers comfortable accommodation, good food and friendly service at reasonable prices. Close to the centre of town.*
DOUBLE ROOM: from £20 to £30
SINGLE ROOM: from £40 to £50
FOOD: up to £15    CLUB
**Hours:** breakfast 7.30am-9.30am, dinner 7pm-9.30pm.
**Cuisine:** ENGLISH - traditional English cooking. Generous portions at reasonable prices.
**Cards:** Visa, Access, Diners, AmEx.
**Other points:** licensed, children welcome, afternoon tea, pets allowed, residents' lounge, residents' bar, vegetarian meals, parking, satellite TV.
**Rooms:** 29 bedrooms.
**Directions:** .5 mile from town centre on A43 Northampton to Kettering road.
MRS LONG ☎(01604) 250981 Fax(01604) 30940

### RED LION HOTEL
Main Street, East Haddon, NN6 8BU
*Its welcoming old-world atmosphere, comfortable decor and good food has given this establishment a well-deserved reputation as the ideal location for a peaceful weekend break. It is within easy reach of Althorp House and facilities for golf, trout fishing, sailing and horse riding.*
DOUBLE ROOM: up to £30
SINGLE ROOM: from £42
FOOD: from £15 to £20
**Hours:** breakfast 7.30am-9.30am, lunch 12.30am-2pm, dinner 7pm-9.30pm, open all year.
**Cuisine:** ENGLISH - traditional English cooking and more adventurous dishes. Menus might include sautéed escallops of halibut, noisettes of English lamb and a supreme of chicken incorporating stilton, walnuts, bacon and a red wine sauce.
**Cards:** Visa, Access, Diners, AmEx.
**Other points:** licensed, open-air dining, Sunday lunch, children catered for (please check for age limits), residents' lounge, garden.
**Rooms:** 3 single room, 3 double rooms, 2 twin rooms. All en suite with TV, telephone, tea/coffee-making facilities.
**Directions:** off A428 between Northampton and Rugby, 7 miles from junction 18 (M1).
IAN KENNEDY ☎(01604) 770223 Fax(01604) 770767

## WELFORD • map 9D2

### THE SHOULDER OF MUTTON INN
12 High Street, NN6 7HT
*Charming 17th century low-beamed village inn on the A50. There is a large beer garden, and the play area will keep the liveliest children amused! Good home-cooked food served with a ready smile.*
FOOD: up to £15
**Hours:** lunch 12noon-2pm. dinner 7pm-9.30pm.
**Cuisine:** INTERNATIONAL - varied menu to suit all tastes, in addition to daily home-made specials, i.e., Indian curries, beef stroganoff and chicken dishes.
**Cards:** Visa, Access, AmEx.
**Other points:** licensed, open-air dining, Sunday lunch, children welcome, free house.
**Directions:** on the A50, midway between Leicester and Northampton. Near junction 1 of A14 (A1-M1 link).
ARTHUR & JUDY CORLETT ☎(01858) 575375

---

**Join the Les Routiers Discovery Club FREE and enjoy year round savings up to 50% on P&O European Ferries fares.
See page 34 for details.**

# NOTTINGHAMSHIRE

## BOTTESFORD • map 9C3

### THE RUTLAND ARMS
2 High Street, NG13 OAA

*Biult in the early 1900's, this listed building is home to a popular bar and restaurant. the local patrons have opted to congregate here because of its lively atmosphere, good selectin available from the well-stocked bar, and the tasty home-cooked meals on offer. being in such a prominent position, The Rutland Arms is also a highly popular stop for travellers, being only 3 miles from Belvoir Castle.*

FOOD: from £15 to £20
**Hours:** lunch 12noon-2pm, dinner 7pm-9.30pm.
**Cuisine:** ENGLISH - an excellent choice; grills, full à la carte menu, chef's daily specials, freshly baked pizzas to eat in or take away.
**Cards:** Visa, Access, Switch.
**Other Points:** parking, children welcome, no-smoking area, vegetarian meals, traditional Sunday lunch, disabled facilities. Well appointed dining room available for private hire.
**Directions:** main road location off A52 Grantham to Nottingham road.
ANN KATRINA ASHLEY ☎(01949) 81361

## COLSTON BASSETT • map 9C3

### THE MARTINS ARMS INN
School Lane, NG12 3FD

*Housed in an attractive period building, The Martins Arms offers excellent food and and a warm welcome. Only fresh produce is used, and the menu offers a good choice of very well-cooked and presented dishes. During summer, drinks and meals can be enjoyed in the garden. The establishment is under the same ownership as The Crown Inn, Old Dalby, the winner of the Les Routiers Pub of the Year Award 1991.*

DOUBLE ROOM: from £20 to £30
FOOD: from £15 to £20
**Hours:** lunch 12noon-2pm, dinner 6pm-9.30pm.
**Cuisine:** ENGLISH / CONTINENTAL - dishes may include roast rack of English lamb served with a fresh tarragon and cream sauce, freshly-made tagliatelle with spicy chicken pieces.
**Other points:** licensed, open-air dining, Sunday lunch, beer garden, children catered for (please check for age limits).
**Directions:** A46 Bingham roundabout, left on A52, 1 mile, first right for Langar and Colston Bassett.
LYNNE BRYAN & SALVATORE INGUANTA
☎(01949) 81361

## GUNTHORPE • map 9B3

### THE TOLL HOUSE RESTAURANT
Riverside, NG14 7FB

*First-class service is upheld in this small, friendly restaurant. The building itself used to be the toll house to the first Gunthorpe bridge built in 1875.*

FOOD: from £15 to £20
**Hours:** dinner 7pm-10pm, closed Sunday evenings.
**Cuisine:** ENGLISH / FRENCH - moules marinière, salmon and smoked salmon mousse, fish, meat and fresh pasta dishes, with a selection of desserts and cheeses.
**Cards:** Visa, Access.
**Other points:** licensed, Sunday lunch, no-smoking area.
**Directions:** from Nottingham, turn left immediately before Gunthorpe bridge.
MR CLIVE HARRIS ☎(0115) 9663409

## MANSFIELD • map 9B2

### MAID MARIAN RESTAURANT
8 Church Street, Edwinstowe, NG21 9QA

*Legend has it that Maid Marian and Robin Hood were married in the church opposite this restaurant. Still celebrating the occasion, the à la carte menu offers dishes such as Will Scarlett's Feast and Robin's Reward.*

FOOD: up to £15
**Hours:** meals all day 9am-10pm.
**Cuisine:** ENGLISH - extensive grill, snack, table d'hôte and à la carte menus. Excellent choice and good value for money.
**Cards:** Visa, Access, Diners, AmEx.
**Other points:** Sunday lunch, children welcome, coaches by prior arrangement
**Directions:** situated on the B6034 in the heart of Sherwood forest.
MR & MRS C.A. BENNETT ☎(01623) 822266

## NEWARK-ON-TRENT • map 9B3

### NEW FERRY RESTAURANT
Riverside, Farndon, NG24 3SX

*Standing attractively by the River Trent, the New Ferry Restaurant serves generous portions of well-cooked food in a relaxed and friendly atmosphere. The menus offer a wide choice of dishes, and the specialities change three times a week to make use of the best in fresh produce. The high standard of the food is complemented by a good, varied wine list. 1994 Corps d'elite.*

FOOD: from £15 to £20
**Hours:** lunch 12noon-2pm, dinner 7pm-10pm, open bank holidays, closed Monday.
**Cuisine:** MEDITERRANEAN - Mediterranean-influenced cuisine. Dishes may include fresh salmon with a fennel and cream sauce, or rack of lamb with a redcurrant and port sauce. Fresh lobster, shellfish, etc. always available.
**Cards:** Visa, Access, Diners, AmEx.
**Other points:** licensed, open-air dining, Sunday lunch, children welcome.
**Directions:** off A46, Nottingham to Newark road. 5 minutes from Newark. Next to River Trent.
JOSE & PAM GOMES ☎(01636) 76578 Fax(01636) 76578

### THE WILLOW TREE INN

Front Street, Barnby-in-the-Willows,
NG24 2SA

*This delightful 17th century inn was a former stop for drivers on the heavy horse route from Newark to the coast. Retaining its welcoming aspect and atmosphere, this heavily beamed, typical country inn is nestled in the conservation village of Barnby-in-the-Willows and makes a charming resting place for anyone who appreciates good food and good beer. Horse-riding and livery can be arranged locally.*

DOUBLE ROOM: up to £20
SINGLE ROOM: up to £25
FOOD: up to £15
**Hours:** breakfast 7.45am-9am, lunch 12noon-2pm, dinner 7pm-12midnight, last orders 10.30pm, bar meals 7pm-10.30pm, open Christmas day.
**Cuisine:** ENGLISH / FRENCH - everything freshly cooked with a lot of emphasis on fish and traditional English fare.
**Cards:** Visa, Access, AmEx, MasterCard.
**Other points:** licensed, Sunday lunch, children welcome, cots, parking, vegetarian meals, pets allowed.
**Rooms:** 1 single room, 2 double rooms, 2 family rooms. All with TV, clock/radio, tea/coffee-making facilities.
**Directions:** near Newark golf course. Turn off A17 (signposted Barnby).
MR S. O'LEARY ☎(01636) 626613 Fax(01636) 626613

## NOTTINGHAM • map 9C2

### BELL INN

Old Market Square, NG1 6HL

*A 15th century traditional inn, situated in the historic heart of Nottingham, offering well-presented, appetizing English fare complemented by warm and courteous service. Owned and operated by the same family for over 95 years, the Bell Inn, with its original oak beams and ancient flagstones, makes a pleasant lunchtime stop for locals and tourists alike.*

FOOD: up to £15    CLUB
**Hours:** lunch Monday-Saturday 11.30am-2.15pm, lunch Sunday 12noon-2.15pm.
**Cuisine:** ENGLISH - good English fare at reasonable prices.
**Cards:** Visa, Access, Diners, AmEx.
**Other points:** children welcome, pets allowed, street parking.
**Directions:** situated in Old Market Square in the centre of Nottingham.
DAVID R. JACKSON ☎(0115) 9475241 Fax(0115) 9475502

### THE HAVEN

Grantham Road, Whatton, NG13 9EU

*The Haven is a pleasant, homely hotel, situated in 5 acres of grassland in the beautiful Vale of Belvoir. Offers food of fine quality, in generous proportions,*

*at very good value for money.*
DOUBLE ROOM: from £20 to £30
SINGLE ROOM: from £20 to £30
FOOD: up to £15
**Hours:** breakfast 7am-9.30am, lunch 12noon-2.30pm, dinner 6pm-10pm.
**Cuisine:** ENGLISH
**Cards:** Visa, Access, AmEx.
**Other points:** licensed, open-air dining, Sunday lunch, no-smoking area, children catered for (please check for age limits), pets allowed, open bank holidays, afternoon tea.
**Rooms:** 33 bedrooms.
**Directions:** between Nottingham and Grantham. Corner of A52 and road to Belvoir Castle.
LESLIE & BETTY HYDES ☎(01949) 850800 Fax(01949) 851454

### JALLANS

9 Byard Lane, NG1 2GJ

*A Victorian flagged-floor building situated up a small alley in the heart of the city of Nottingham, providing an ideal meeting place for lunch amid a friendly and lively atmosphere. The decor is bright and welcoming, with dried flower arrangements, patterned table cloths and wooden chairs, and the food is well presented, with good use of garnishes. Ideal location for visitors to the city, with Tales of Robin Hood, the Theatre Royal, concert hall and shops all within walking distance.*

FOOD: up to £15    CLUB
**Hours:** meals all day 11am-7pm, closed Christmas day and New Year's day.
**Cuisine:** INTERNATIONAL
**Cards:** Visa, Access, Diners, AmEx.
**Other points:** children welcome, open bank holidays, afternoon tea, disabled access, vegetarian meals, licensed.
**Directions:** situated in the city centre, off Bridlesmith Gate, opposite Paul Smith.
MR ROMER, MR VIGGERS, MR BRADFIELD ☎(0115) 9506684

### THE OLD SHIP

Main Street, Lowdham, NG14 7BE

*This 18th century converted cottage with a nautical theme offers visitors a welcoming atmosphere in which to enjoy a traditional, freshly cooked meal or simply relax with friends over a drink from the well-stocked bar. The Old Ship is popular with locals and travellers of all ages.*

FOOD: up to £15
**Hours:** lunch 12noon-2pm, dinner 6.30pm-10pm.
**Cuisine:** ENGLISH - traditional dishes and chef's daily specials.
**Cards:** Visa, Access.
**Other points:** parking, children welcome, garden, vegetarian meals, traditional Sunday lunch.
**Directions:** centre of Lowdham village.
JAMES RENWICK ☎(0115) 9663049

### WALTON'S HOTEL
North Lodge, The Park, NG7 1AG
*Originally the hunting lodge to the Castle Deer Park, Walton's Hotel is a Regency house furnished with antiques and offering food and accommodation of a very high standard. The atmosphere is pleasant and welcoming, and guests can relax and enjoy the good food and wine in the comfort of the elegant dining room. Within walking distance of the city centre, theatres and castle.*
DOUBLE ROOM: from £75 to £85
SINGLE ROOM: over £55
FOOD: up to £15    CLUB
**Hours:** breakfast 7.30am-10am, dinner 7.30pm-9.30pm, lunch 12.30am-2pm.
**Cuisine:** FRENCH - dishes include scallops in ginger sauce, chicken in hazelnut sauce and a large selection of steaks, but fish is their speciality. Vegetarian restaurant (Thursday-Sunday evenings only).
**Cards:** Visa, Access, Diners, AmEx, Switch.
**Other points:** licensed, open-air dining, Sunday lunch, children welcome, garden, afternoon tea, pets allowed.
**Rooms:** 4 single rooms, 14 double rooms, 3 twin rooms, 1 family room.
**Directions:** A6200. From A52 follow city centre signs. 200 yards from police station.
MRS S. FLANDERS ☎(0115) 9475215 Fax(0115) 9475053

### THURGARTON • map 9B3

### THE RED LION
Southwell Road, NG14 7GP
*An attractive 16th century olde-worlde inn, the tasteful decor in keeping with the period and style of the inn throughout. The food is reputable, the well-stocked bar will quench any thirst, and the service and atmosphere are both very warm and friendly.*
FOOD: up to £15
**Hours:** lunch 12noon-2pm, dinner 7pm-10pm.
**Cuisine:** ENGLISH - traditional à la carte menu; also daily chef's choice.
**Cards:** Visa, Access, Diners, AmEx, Switch, Delta.
**Other points:** parking, children welcome, garden, open-air dining, vegetarian meals, traditional Sunday lunch.
**Directions:** on the main Nottingham to Southwell road.
JAMES RENWICK ☎(01636) 830351

### WHATTON • map 9B3

### THE GRIFFINS HEAD
Grantham Road,, NG13 9EA
*Comfort, quality and value are the main concerns at this popular pub and restaurant, offering good, home-cooked meals and friendly, efficient service. Conveniently situated for Belvoir Castle and Newark.*
FOOD: up to £15
**Hours:** lunch 12noon-2pm, dinner 6.30pm-10pm.
**Cuisine:** ENGLISH - traditional, fresh food.
**Cards:** Visa, Access, Diners, AmEx.
**Other points:** parking, children welcome, garden, vegetarian meals, traditional Sunday lunch.
**Directions:** A52 side of main Nottingham to Grantham road.
JAMES RENWICK ☎(01949) 850214

### WORKSOP • map 9B2

### LION HOTEL
112 Bridge Street, S80 1HT
*A 16th century coaching inn, the Lion Hotel is situated in the centre of Worksop, offering a warm welcome and comfortable accommodation. The restaurant provides well-cooked and presented meals with a good choice of traditional and more imaginative dishes. Bar meals are served in the popular, lively bar adjoining the restaurant. It is close to Sherwood Forest, Clumber Park and Creswell Crags.*
DOUBLE ROOM: from £20 to £30
SINGLE ROOM: from £45 to £55
FOOD: from £20 to £25
**Hours:** breakfast 7am-9.30am, lunch 12noon-2pm, bar meals 11.30am-2.30pm, dinner 7pm-9.45pm, bar meals 7pm-9.30pm.
**Cuisine:** ENGLISH / CONTINENTAL - carte de jour and table d'hôte menus featuring traditional English and more imaginative dishes. Good vegetarian menu available. Traditional Sunday lunch.
**Cards:** Visa, Access, AmEx.
**Other points:** licensed, Sunday lunch, children welcome, pets allowed, residents' lounge, gym facilities, sauna, solarium, functions.
**Rooms:** 32 bedrooms.
**Directions:** Market Square, turn right at Eyres furniture store, then sharp right.
COOPLANDS (DONCASTER) LTD MGR JIM PICKERSGILL ☎(01909) 477925 Fax(01909) 479038

---

**Club Bon Viveur. Take advantage of the
8 FREE vouchers on Page 67.
Join up for a year at only £15. See page 65.**

---

# OXFORDSHIRE

## ABINGDON • map 5B2

### THE DOG HOUSE HOTEL
Frilford Heath, OX13 6QJ

*The Dog House is set in the idyllic countryside of the Vale of the White Horse and is the ideal place to spend a couple of days to get away from it all. There are beautiful panoramic views of the Downs in the distance at all times of the year and always plenty to do in the surrounding area. Each of the comfortable en suite bedrooms is attractively furnished to make your stay as relaxing as possible.*

DOUBLE ROOM: from £20 to £30
SINGLE ROOM: from £30 to £40
FOOD: up to £15
**Hours:** breakfast weekdays 7.30am-9am, weekends 9am-10am, lunch 12noon-2.30pm, dinner 7pm-10pm, Sunday 7pm-9pm.
**Cuisine:** ENGLISH - an excellent range of meals, always with an emphasis on quality and variety.
**Cards:** Visa, Access, Diners, AmEx.
**Other points:** parking, children welcome, pets allowed, conference facilities, garden, vegetarian meals, traditional Sunday lunch.
**Rooms:** 19 bedrooms. All with satellite TV, telephone, radio, alarm, hair dryer, tea/coffee making facilities.
**Directions:** off A34 at Abingdon South junction, onto A415 to Marcham, first right, then approximately 3 miles.
TIM ALLAN ☎(01865) 390830 Fax(01865) 390860

## ASTHALL • map 5B2

### THE MAYTIME INN
Near Burford, OX8 4HW

*Situated in a tiny hamlet, 2.5 miles from Burford, The Maytime Inn has retained much of its centuries-old Cotswold charm. In addition to a spacious bar, there is a dining room seating 80 where one can wine and dine in style and comfort.*

DOUBLE ROOM: from £20 to £30
SINGLE ROOM: from £40 to £50
FOOD: up to £15    CLUB
**Hours:** breakfast 8am-11am, lunch 11am-2.30pm, dinner 7pm-10pm, open bank holidays.
**Cuisine:** ENGLISH / INTERNATIONAL - daily specials, e.g. steak-and-kidney pie, fish pie, half shoulder of lamb, fresh local salmon.
**Cards:** Visa, Access, Diners, AmEx, Switch.
**Other points:** licensed, open-air dining, Sunday lunch, children welcome.
**Rooms:** 3 double rooms, 3 twin rooms.
**Directions:** down a narrow country lane from the A40 between Witney and Burford.
T.M. & M. MORGAN ☎(01993) 822068
Fax(01993) 822635

## BANBURY • map 5A2

### EASINGTON HOUSE & FARMHOUSE RESTAURANT
50 Oxford Road, OX16 9AN

*Malcolm and Gwynneth Hearne ensure that all guests are greeted with warmth and genuine courtesy at this delightful 400-year-old country house hotel. Style and elegance are evident in every room, whether you are relaxing in the intimate lounge, sampling cuisine of a very high standard in the Farmhouse Restaurant or preparing for a restful night in one of the tastefully decorated bedrooms.*

DOUBLE ROOM: from £30 to £40
SINGLE ROOM: from £35 to £48
FOOD: up to £15
**Hours:** breakfast Monday-Friday 7.30am-9am, breakfast Saturday-Sunday 8am-9am (and public holidays), Dinner Monday to Saturday 7pm-8.30pm.
**Cuisine:** ENGLISH / CONTINENTAL - fresh local produce used.
**Cards:** Visa, Access, Diners, AmEx.
**Other points:** parking, pets allowed, conference facilities, residents' lounge, garden, open-air dining, vegetarian meals.
**Rooms:** 12 bedrooms. All with TV, telephone, tea/coffee-making facilities.
**Directions:** 300 yards south of Banbury Cross on B4100.
MALCOLM & GWYNNETH HEARNE ☎(01295) 270181 Fax(01295) 269527

### RED LION INN
High Street, Bloxham, OX15 4LX

*With its good range of first-rate home-cooked bar meals and CAMRA commendation for their excellent selection of beers, there is no cause to doubt the inn's popularity. Paul and Carol provide warm and friendly hospitality and even offer a free mini-bus service (for four or more diners) within a 10-mile radius, so you can relax and enjoy yourself without worring about the ever-present drink/driving problem.*

FOOD: up to £15
**Hours:** lunch 12noon-2pm, dinner 7pm-10pm.
**Cuisine:** ENGLISH - a wide range of grills, home-cooked fare and bar meals.
**Cards:** Visa, Access, AmEx.
**Other points:** parking, children welcome, pets allowed, garden, open-air dining, vegetarian meals, traditional Sunday lunch.
**Directions:** on Main Road, centre of Bloxham Road from Banbury to Chipping Norton.
PAUL COOPER ☎(01295) 720352 Fax(01295) 720007

## DIDCOT • map 5B2

 **THE RED LION**
Nottingham Fee, Blewbury, OX11 9PQ
*A very old, traditional country pub, tucked away in the pretty village of Blewbury. The interior has an olde-worlde appearance and an informal, relaxed atmosphere in which to enjoy the good bar meals.*
FOOD: from £15 to £20
**Hours:** lunch 12noon-2pm, dinner 6pm-9.30pm, Sunday evening 7pm-7.30pm.
**Cuisine:** ENGLISH - meals including daily specials, especially fresh fish.
**Cards:** Visa, Access, Diners, AmEx, Switch, MasterCard.
**Other points:** licensed, Sunday lunch, children welcome, garden, disabled access and toilets.
**Directions:** off the A417. Downhill past the tree on the triangle of grass.
ROGER SMITH ☎(01235) 850403

## FARINGDON • map 5B2

**THE CROWN HOTEL**
Market Square, SN7 7HU
*An outstanding hotel by all accounts, The Crown Hotel offers splendid accommodation, excellent cuisine and superb hospitality to all who dine or stay there. The building surrounds a charming, historic cobbled courtyard where you can sit out and enjoy a meal or snack during the summer months; in the winter you can eat by a log fire in the cosy, panelled Crown Bar. The hotel has a restaurant, a ballroom and conference facilities. Highly recommended.*
DOUBLE ROOM: from £20 to £30
SINGLE ROOM: from £30 to £45
FOOD: from £15 to £20
**Hours:** breakfast 7am-9am, Sunday lunch 12.30am-2.30pm, bar meals 11.30am-2.30pm, dinner 7.30pm-9pm, bar meals 6pm-10.30pm, closed Christmas day and Boxing day.
**Cuisine:** ENGLISH - à la carte restaurant menu and bar meals.
**Cards:** Visa, Access.
**Other points:** parking, children welcome, pets allowed by arrangement only, conference facilities, wedding receptions, garden, open-air dining, vegetarian meals, afternoon teas, traditional Sunday lunch.
**Rooms:** 3 single rooms, 7 double rooms, 1 twin room. All with TV, telephone, television, tea/coffee-making facilities, hair dryer, room service, baby-listening device.
**Directions:** take Faringdon town centre turn from A420 or A417.
ANDREW & BECKY BRYSON ☎(01367) 242744
Fax(01367) 240058

## OXFORD • map 5B2

**BELFRY HOTEL**
Brimpton Grange, Milton Common, OX9 2TN

*Set in the Oxfordshire countryside approximately 10 minutes from Oxford. Decorated and furnished to a high standard and enjoying a friendly atmosphere. Good food and comfortable accommodation. Highly recommended.*
DOUBLE ROOM: from £40 to £50
SINGLE ROOM: over £55
FOOD: from £20 to £25
**Hours:** breakfast weekdays 7.30am-9.30am, weekends 8.30am-9.30am, lunch 12.30am-2pm, bar meals 12.30am-2pm, dinner 7.30pm-9.30pm, closed 24th December until 31st December.
**Cuisine:** ENGLISH / CONTINENTAL - serving bar snacks, full à la carte menu and table d'hôte.
**Cards:** Visa, Access, Diners, AmEx.
**Other points:** licensed, Sunday lunch, children welcome, leisure centre, conferences, baby-sitting, cots, 24hr reception.
**Rooms:** 11 single rooms, 36 double rooms, 30 twin rooms. All with TV, radio, telephone, tea/coffee-making facilities.
**Directions:** situated on the A40 between junctions 7 and 8 of the M40.
MR BARBER ☎(01844) 279381 Fax(01844) 279624

**HOPCROFTS HOLT HOTEL**
Steeple Aston, OX5 3QQ
*A large 15th century coaching inn, which has been extensively refurbished to offer well-appointed bedrooms, good food and a relaxed informal atmosphere. Situated very close to the delightful village of Steeple Aston, the hotel is an ideal base for touring North Oxfordshire and the Northern Cotswolds.*
DOUBLE ROOM: from £40
SINGLE ROOM: from £40
FOOD: from £15 to £20 CLUB
**Hours:** breakfast 7.30am-9.30am, lunch 12noon-2pm, dinner 7pm-9.45pm, Sunday 7pm-8.30pm.
**Cuisine:** MODERN ENGLISH - escalope of salmon and crunchy vegetables with lemon butter, fillet beef with a celery and Stilton jus, poached supreme of chicken and fresh salad.
**Cards:** Visa, Access, Diners, AmEx.
**Other points:** licensed, Sunday lunch, children welcome, garden, afternoon tea, pets allowed, parking, vegetarian meals, residents' lounge, residents' bar, disabled access.
**Rooms:** 88 bedrooms.
**Directions:** midway between Oxford and Banbury on A4260. Close to M40 Oxford.
WENDY MORLEY ☎(01869) 340259 Fax(01869) 340865

**PICKWICKS**
17 London Road, Headington, OX3 7SP
*A comfortable, quiet and efficiently managed hotel with first-class decor and facilities. Large, clean, well-appointed dining room and a comfortable residents' lounge. A welcoming and helpful attitude will be found here.*
DOUBLE ROOM: from £20 to £30

SINGLE ROOM: from £25 to £35
FOOD: up to £15
**Hours:** breakfast 7.30am-9am, Sunday 8am-9am.
**Cuisine:** BREAKFAST
**Cards:** Visa, Access, Diners, AmEx, Switch, MasterCard.
**Other points:** children welcome, garden.
**Rooms:** 15 bedrooms.
**Directions:** .25 mile from Oxford centre on London Road (A420).
G.J. & P. MORRIS ☎(01865) 750487/69413 Fax(01865) 742208

## SHIPTON-UNDER-WYCHWOOD • map 5B2

### THE SHAVEN CROWN HOTEL
Chipping Norton, OX7 6BA
*Built c.1380 as a hospice to Bruern Abbey, The Shaven Crown is now one of the ten oldest inns in England. An attractive building of honey-coloured stone around a medieval courtyard with a fountain, in the heart of the Cotswolds. In fine weather, dine alfresco in the courtyard.*
DOUBLE ROOM: from £30 to £40
SINGLE ROOM: from £30 to £40
FOOD: up to £15
**Hours:** breakfast 8.30am-9.30am, bar meals 12noon-2pm, dinner 7.30pm-9.30pm, Sundays 7.30pm-9pm, bar meals 7pm-9.30pm.
**Cuisine:** ENGLISH - an excellent selection of à la carte and bar meal dishes.
**Cards:** Visa, Access.
**Other points:** licensed, open-air dining, Sunday lunch, children welcome, afternoon tea.
**Rooms:** 9 bedrooms.
**Directions:** 4 miles north of Burford on the A361, opposite the church and green.
TREVOR & MARY BROOKES ☎(01993) 830330

## SOULDERN • map 5A2

### FOX INN
Fox Lane, OX6 9JW
*A traditional 19th century stone-built inn, situated 7 miles north of Bicester off the B4100 in a beautiful Cotswold stone village. Ideal for Oxford, Stratford, the Cotswolds, Warwick and Silverstone motor racing circuit.*
DOUBLE ROOM: up to £20
SINGLE ROOM: up to £28
FOOD: from £15 to £20 CLUB
**Hours:** breakfast 8am-9.30am, lunch 12noon-2pm, bar meals 12noon-2pm, dinner 7pm-12midnight, last orders 9.30pm, bar meals 7pm-9.30pm, no food Sunday evening.
**Cuisine:** EUROPEAN - roast Sunday lunch, table d'hôte and à la carte menu, daily specials in both bar and restaurant.
**Cards:** Visa, Access, AmEx.
**Other points:** open-air dining, Sunday lunch, children welcome, fishing nearby, golf nearby.
**Rooms:** 3 double rooms, 1 twin room. All with TV, tea/coffee-making facilities.

**Directions:** follow Souldern signs off the B4100; situated on left in village, 200 yards past pond. 3 miles from junction 10 of M40.
IAN MACKAY ☎(01869) 345284 Fax(01869) 345667

## STEEPLE ASTON • map 5A2

### THE WHITE HORSE
Duns Tew, Steeple Aston, OX6 4JS
*A 17th century farm house style inn with original stone-flag floors, oak panelling and open fires. Comfortably furnished rooms provide homely accomodation, complimented by varied, freshly prepared foods, choice ales and wines.*
DOUBLE ROOM: from £40 to £50
FOOD: from £15 to £20
**Hours:** breakfast 8am-9.30am, lunch 12noon-2pm, bar meals 12noon-2.30pm, dinner 7.30pm-9.30pm, bar meals 7pm-10pm, open bank holidays.
**Cuisine:** extensive bar and restaurant menus, with game pies and seasonal specialities.
**Cards:** Visa, Access, AmEx.
**Other points:** pets allowed, public telephone, fully licensed, TV and residents' lounges, air conditioning, ironing facilities, open-air dining, vegetarian meals, parking
**Rooms:** 6 double rooms, 7 twin rooms, all en suite. All with TV, telephone, tea/coffee-making facilities.
**Directions:** exit junction 11 from M40, towards Banbury.
OLD ENGLISH PUB COMPANY PLC. ☎(01869) 340272 Fax(01869) 347732

## THAME • map 5B3

### ABINGDON ARMS
21 Cornmarket, OX9 2BL
*A large Victorian public house, which happily caters for families and tourists to the area. There is a large beer garden with children's climbing frame and swing. Barbecues are frequently held in the garden or barn, which is available for private hire, and live bands and discos can be provided. Jazz bands play in the barn on a regular basis.*
DOUBLE ROOM: up to £20
SINGLE ROOM: from £23
FOOD: up to £15
**Hours:** breakfast 8am-10.30am, lunch 12noon-2.30pm, dinner 6pm-9pm.
**Cuisine:** ENGLISH / CONTINENTAL
**Cards:** Visa, Access.
**Other points:** children welcome, parking, real ales, afternoon bar snacks, vegetarian meals, open-air dining, baby changing facilities.
**Rooms:** 5 double rooms.
**Directions:** enter Thame from Oxford direction, in main high street at first zebra crossing and lights: on the right.
WAYNE BONNER ☎(01844) 260116 Fax(01844) 260338

## WATLINGTON • map 5B3

### THE LORD NELSON
Brightwell Baldwin, OX9 5N9

*A 15th century house conversion, the Lord Nelson serves traditional English food, offering extensive a la carte and bar menus and attracting considerable regular custom.*
FOOD: from £15 to £20
**Hours:** lunch 12noon-2pm, dinner 7pm-9.45pm, bar meals 7pm-10pm, open bank holidays.
**Cuisine:** ENGLISH - extensive a la carte and bar menus. Seasonal specialities.
**Cards:** Visa, Access, AmEx.
**Other points:** licensed, attractive gardens, parking.
**Directions:** between Watlington and Benson, off the B4009.
OLD ENGLISH PUB COMPANY PLC. ☎(01491) 612330

## WITNEY • map 5B2

### THE BIRD IN HAND INN
Whiteoak Green, Hailey, OX8 5XP

*A 350-year-old farmhouse and bakery offering good English cuisine amidst a warm, friendly atmosphere. Nearby tourist attractions, include stately Blenheim Palace.*
DOUBLE ROOM: from £20 to £30
SINGLE ROOM: from £40 to £50
FOOD: from £15 to £20
**Hours:** breakfast 7.30am-9.30am, lunch and bar meals 12noon-2pm, dinner and bar meals 7pm-9.30pm, open bank holidays.
**Cuisine:** ENGLISH/MEDITERRANEAN - a wide range of fresh fish from a daily changing chalkboard.
**Cards:** Access,Visa,Switch,Delta
**Other points:** children welcome, no-smoking area, open-air dining, resident's lounge, conference facilities, traditional Sunday lunch, vegetarian meals, parking.
**Rooms:** 10 double rooms, 4 twin rooms and 2 family rooms, all en suite. All with TV, telephone, radio, hair dryer and tea/coffee-making facilities.
**Directions:** midway between Witney and Charlbury, on the B4022.
MR PAUL DAVIDSON ☎(01993) 868321
Fax (01993) 868702

### THE COUNTRY PIE
63 Corn Street, OX8 7DQ

*A 16th century building of Cotswold stone, a short walk from Buttercross. Recent extensive*

*modernization has not detracted from the old-world charm. Here, good food is served in congenial surroundings with an air of calm efficiency.*
FOOD: from £15 to £20 ⌣ CLUB
**Hours:** lunch 12noon-2pm (Tuesday-Sunday), dinner 7pm-9.45pm (Tuesday-Saturday), closed Sunday evening and all day Monday.
**Cuisine:** ENGLISH / CONTINENTAL - traditional English and continental cuisine. Table d'hôte and à la carte menus available.
**Cards:** Visa, Access, Diners, AmEx.
**Other points:** licensed, Sunday lunch, coaches by prior arrangement, children welcome, street parking.
**Directions:** from the A40, follow signs to town centre.
JANET & ALAN DIXEY ☎(01993) 703590

## WOODSTOCK • map 5B2

### THE KINGS HEAD
Chapel Hill, Wootton, OX20 1DX

*A 17th century inn which has been decorated and equipped to a very high standard. Most of the en suite rooms have a fabulous view of the Glyme valley, and the four-poster suite enjoys a private patio in the garden. Excellent fish dishes can be enjoyed in the restaurant, together with lighter snacks in the bar. Blenheim Palace, Oxford and the Cotswolds are all within easy reach.*
DOUBLE ROOM: from £40 to £50
SINGLE ROOM: from £49
FOOD: from £20 to £25      CLUB
**Hours:** breakfast 8am-9.30am, lunch 12noon-2.30pm, dinner 7pm-10pm. Open bank holidays.
**Cuisine:** ENGLISH - extensive à la carte menu featuring many fish specialities.
**Cards:** Visa, Access.
**Other points:** parking.
**Rooms:** 2 double suites, 2 twin rooms. All en suite with TV, alarm, hair dryer, trouser press, tea/coffee-making facilities.
**Directions:** turn right 1 mile north of Woodstock (A44).
MR TONY FAY ☎(01993) 811340

# SHROPSHIRE

## BISHOP'S CASTLE • map 8D4

 **THE BOARS HEAD**
Church Street, SY9 5AE
*A 16th century inn and restaurant in a historic Shropshire market town. The inn has a comfortable restaurant and offers an extensive menu ranging from bar snacks to full à la carte meals. The stable block behind The Boars Head has been converted to provide four comfortable bedrooms. All food is well cooked and provides good value for money. A relaxed, friendly atmosphere prevails.*
DOUBLE ROOM: from £20 to £30
SINGLE ROOM: from £25 to £35
FOOD: from £15 to £20 **CLUB**
**Hours:** breakfast 8am-9am, bar meals 12noon-2pm, dinner 6.30pm-9.30pm, bar meals 6.30pm-9.30pm.
**Cuisine:** ENGLISH - bar snacks and à la carte meals. Predominantly English cuisine.
**Cards:** Visa, Access, Diners, AmEx, Switch, Delta.
**Other points:** licensed, children welcome, pets allowed, cots, parking.
**Rooms:** 1 double room, 2 twin rooms, 1 family room. All with TV, telephone, tea/coffee-making facilities, radio/alarm.
**Directions:** from A488, follow signs to livestock market and continue to car park before crossroads.
GRANT PERRY ☎(01588) 638521 **Fax**(01588) 630126

## LLANYMYNECH • map 8C4

### CHEESEBOARD OF THE YEAR 1996
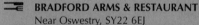 **BRADFORD ARMS & RESTAURANT**
Near Oswestry, SY22 6EJ
*Old coaching inn on A483, which was 'Victorianized' in 1902. Comfortably and traditionally furnished with soft lighting, Victorian marble fireplace and mahogany bar. Sheltered patio area to the side. Large car park to the rear and on-road parking.*
FOOD: up to £20 ☜
**Hours:** Tuesday-Saturday lunch 12noon-2.30pm, dinner 7pm-11pm. Sunday lunch 12 noon-2.30pm, dinner 7pm-10.30pm. Closed Monday excluding bank holidays, closed Christmas, closed for 3 weeks September-October.
**Cuisine:** MODERN ENGLISH - home-made bar meals: soups, bread, filled brioches, mushrooms in port, hot baked avocado and prawns, devilled crab, steak kebabs, salmon and mushroom au gratin. Restaurant: loin of lamb in garlic sauce, vegetarian dishes. Always fresh vegetables and home-made desserts. Large selection of farmhouse cheeses. Menus change monthly.
**Other points:** licensed, open-air dining, children welcome.
**Directions:** on the A483, situated on the main road in Llanymynech between Oswestry and Welshpool.
ANNE & MICHAEL MURPHY ☎(01691) 830582

## MUCH WENLOCK • map 8C5

 **THE WENLOCK EDGE INN**
Hilltop, Wenlock Edge, TF13 6DJ
*Stone-built in the 17th century, this traditional country inn is family-run and provides a delightful rural retreat. The inn is comfortable and the home-cooking is of a high standard. Welcoming service and a relaxed atmosphere ensure an enjoyable meal or stay. Highly recommended.*
DOUBLE ROOM: from £25 to £35
SINGLE ROOM: from £40 to £45
FOOD: up to £15
**Hours:** breakfast 8.30am-9.30am, lunch 12noon-2pm, dinner 7pm-9pm. No meals Mondays except bank holidays.
**Cuisine:** ENGLISH - traditional English cuisine. Pies and puddings are house specialities.
**Cards:** Visa, Access, AmEx.
**Other points:** Sunday lunch, no-smoking area, children catered for (please check for age limits), open bank holidays, pets allowed.
**Rooms:** 3 double rooms, 1 twin room.
**Directions:** from Much Wenlock take B4371. Approximately 4 miles along on left side.
THE WARING FAMILY ☎(01746) 785403

## NORTON • map 8D5

 **HUNDRED HOUSE HOTEL, RESTAURANT & INN**
Bridgnorth Road, near Telford, TF11 9EE
*An award-winning, family-run, country inn with character, charm and a warm atmosphere. It has patchwork-themed bedrooms with antique furnishings and all facilities, and offers superb European and English food. Only 45 minutes from Birmingham International Airport, Conference and Exhibition Centres and an ideal location to explore Ironbridge Gorge museums and the Severn Valley.*
DOUBLE ROOM: from £30 to £40
SINGLE ROOM: over £55
FOOD: from £20 to £25 ☜
**Hours:** breakfast 7.30am-9.30am, lunch 11.30am-2.30pm, dinner 6pm-10pm.
**Cuisine:** ENGLISH / CONTINENTAL - varied menu, which changes frequently: local game, char-grilled meats, traditional roasts, home-made steak-and-kidney pies, lasagne and bruschetta.
**Cards:** Visa, Access, AmEx.
**Other points:** licensed, open-air dining, Sunday lunch, children welcome, garden.
**Rooms:** 10 bedrooms.
**Directions:** situated on the A442 Bridgnorth-Telford road, in Norton village.
HENRY, SYLVIA & DAVID PHILLIPS ☎(01952) 730353 **Fax**(01952) 730355

## OSWESTRY • map 8C4

### RESTAURANT SEBASTIAN

45 Willow Street, SY11 1AQ

*Pleasantly decorated with oak beams and panelling, Restaurant Sebastian enjoys a relaxed atmosphere. The French provincial cuisine is of the highest standard and elegantly presented. A popular restaurant, highly recommended for its outstanding food, welcoming service and attractive surroundings.*

FOOD: from £15 to £25

**Hours:** lunch 12noon-2pm, dinner 6.30pm-10.30pm, closed all day Sunday and Monday, closed Tuesday and Saturday lunch.

**Cuisine:** FRENCH - à la carte menus featuring predominantly French cuisine and a table d' hôte menu at £15.95 (3 course menu with choices). Lunchtime consists of French-style snacks from £2.25.

**Cards:** Visa, Access, AmEx.

**Other points:** licensed.

**Directions:** close to the town centre.

MICHELLE & MARK SEBASTIAN FISHER ☎(01691) 655444 Fax(01691) 653452

### STARLINGS CASTLE

SY10 7NU

*An 18th century sandstone farmhouse, previously a shooting lodge, surrounded by the deep foliage of rhododendrons and conifers and standing within sight of Offa's Dyke, the plain of Shropshire and the hidden valleys and mountains of Berwyn. Ideally situated within reach of many interesting activities: salmon and trout fishing, walking, horse and pony trekking, canoeing, canal cruising and golf. Chirk Castle, Erddig Hall and the medieval flower town of Shrewsbury are all just a short distance away.*

DOUBLE ROOM: up to £20

FOOD: from £15 to £20 CLUB

**Hours:** breakfast 8am-9.30am, Sunday lunch 12.30am-2.30pm, dinner 7.30pm-9.30pm.

**Cuisine:** ECLECTIC

**Cards:** Visa, Access, Diners, AmEx.

**Other points:** parking, children welcome, disabled access, pets, residents' lounge, vegetarian meals, garden, open-air dining.

**Rooms:** 2 single rooms, 4 double rooms, 8 twin rooms.

**Directions:** situated off B4579.

MR A. & MRS J. PITT ☎(01691) 718464 Fax(01691) 718464

## SHREWSBURY • map 8C4

### SHELTON HALL HOTEL

Shelton, SY3 8BH

*A manor house set in three and half acres of beautiful landscaped gardens. Extensive facilities for weddings, parties, meetings and conferences. The*
bedrooms are comfortably furnished with TV, radio, direct-dial telephone and tea/coffee facilities.

DOUBLE ROOM: from £30 to £40

SINGLE ROOM: from £47

FOOD: from £15 to £20

**Hours:** breakfast 7.30am-9.30am, lunch 12.30am-2pm, dinner 7.30pm-8.30pm, closed Boxing day.

**Cuisine:** ENGLISH - fixed-price menus with variety of dishes, e.g., rainbow trout Cleopatra, roast duck Olde Englande, steak chasseur. Popular for Sunday lunch.

**Cards:** Visa, AmEx, Switch, MasterCard, Eurocard, Delta, JCB

**Other points:** Sunday lunch, children welcome.

**Rooms:** 1 single room, 4 double rooms, 2 twin rooms, 2 family rooms. All with TV, radio, telephone, tea/coffee-making facilities.

**Directions:** 1.5 miles north-west of the town on the B4380.

MR GEOFFREY LARKIN ☎(01743) 343982 Fax(01743) 241515

### SYDNEY HOUSE HOTEL

Coton Crescent, Coton Hill, SY1 2LJ

*This Edwardian Hotel is within ten minutes' walk of Shrewsbury's historical town centre. The restaurant boasts an extensive wine list and some excellent ports. You are assured of a warm welcome at the restaurant, as the owners aim to make all guests feel at home.*

DOUBLE ROOM: from £20 to £35

SINGLE ROOM: from £35 to £50

FOOD: up to £15

**Hours:** breakfast 7.30am-9am, dinner 7.30pm-9pm (not Sundays), last orders 8.30pm, closed 1 week over Christmas.

**Cuisine:** ENGLISH - fixed-price menu.

**Cards:** Visa, Access, AmEx.

**Other points:** licensed, no-smoking restaurant, children welcome.

**Rooms:** 2 single rooms, 2 double rooms, 2 twin rooms, 1 family room. All with TV, radio, alarm, telephone, tea/coffee-making facilities. Many rooms are en suite.

**Directions:** at the junction of the A528 and B5067, just outside the town centre.

TERENCE & PAULINE HYDE ☎(01743) 354681/130243 Fax(01743) 354681

# STAFFORDSHIRE

## ALTON • map 8B5

### WILD DUCK INN
New Road, ST10 4AF

*A country house built by Earl John, the Wild Duck Inn is an elegant bar and family restaurant with comfortable and reasonably priced letting bedrooms. Set in Churnet Valley overlooking Alton Towers Leisure Park.*

DOUBLE ROOM: from £20 to £30
FOOD: up to £15
**Hours:** breakfast 8.30am-9.30am, dinner 7pm-9pm.
**Cuisine:** ENGLISH - traditional pub food in the bar. English-style food and snacks in the restaurant.
**Cards:** Visa, Access.
**Other points:** licensed, children welcome, coaches by prior arrangement
**Rooms:** 6 twin rooms, 4 family rooms.
**Directions:** off the B5032. Follow directions for Alton Towers.
MR & MRS KEITH MURDOCH ☎(01538) 702218

## BURTON UPON TRENT • map 8C6

### THE HORSESHOE INN
Main Street, Tatenhill, DE13 9SD

*This attractive country inn, dating back to 1600, stands in its own gardens with a large car park and children's play area. Its traditional cask ales and Sunday roasts are very popular.*

FOOD: up to £15 CLUB
**Hours:** lunch (Monday-Saturday) 12noon-2pm, bar snacks available Saturday 2pm-6pm, Sunday lunch (bookings only) and bar snacks 12noon-2pm, dinner (Monday-Saturday) 6pm-9.30pm.
**Cuisine:** ENGLISH - à la carte menu. Dishes include steaks, salmon steak, duckling and chicken with stilton sauce. Bar snacks include home-made steak-and-kidney pie. Forge grill menu and children's menu.
**Cards:** Visa, Access, MasterCard, Switch, Delta.
**Other points:** children welcome, coaches by appointment, parking, disabled access and toilets, vegetarian meals.
**Directions:** 1 mile from the A38 (Branston exit) signposted Tatenhill. Turn right at crossroads.
MR M. BOULD ☎(01283) 564913 Fax(01283) 511314

## CANNOCK • map 8C5

### SALEEM BAGH
Queens Square, WS11 1EA

*A popular air-conditioned restaurant offering an extensive menu of traditional Indian cuisine with speciality dishes, all freshly prepared. A four-course businessman's lunch is also available.*

FOOD: up to £15
**Hours:** lunch 12noon-2.30pm, dinner 5pm-11pm, closed Sunday, open Christmas day.
**Cuisine:** INDIAN
**Cards:** Visa, Access, Diners, AmEx.
**Other points:** children catered for (please check for age limits), open bank holidays, no-smoking area, disabled access, vegetarian meals.
**Directions:** close to town centre on the ringway (M6 junction 11).
MR N. MIAH ☎(01543) 505089

## LEEK • map 8B5

### THE THREE HORSESHOES INN & RESTAURANT
Buxton Road, Blackshaw Moor, ST13 8TW

*Situated in a lovely country setting with beautiful views towards the moors and Pennines. First-class accommodation in cottage-style bedrooms. Dinner/dance at weekends.*

DOUBLE ROOM: from £20 to £30
SINGLE ROOM: from £40 to £45
FOOD: from £15 to £20
**Hours:** breakfast 7.30am-9.30am, lunch 12noon-2pm, dinner 7pm-9.30pm.
**Cuisine:** ENGLISH - bar carvery at lunch and evening, plus restaurant à la carte and table d'hôte menus in the evening.
**Cards:** Visa, Access.
**Other points:** Sunday lunch, children welcome, garden.
**Rooms:** 4 double rooms, 2 twin rooms. All with TV, radio, alarm, telephone, tea/coffee-making facilities.
**Directions:** located on A53 Leek to Buxton road.
WILLIAM KIRK ☎(01538) 300296 Fax(01538) 300320

## LICHFIELD • map 8C6

### THE BULLS HEAD
Birmingham Road, Shenstone, WS14 0JR

*Having undergone extensive refurbishment throughout, The Bulls Head now offers a relaxed and friendly atmosphere in pleasant surroundings. It is very popular with locals and tourists alike, who come to sample the good, wholesome English cuisine. Close to the famous Belfry Golf Club.*

FOOD: up to £15
**Hours:** meals all day 11am-10pm.
**Cuisine:** ENGLISH - traditional-style menu, offering mixed grill specialities and imaginative desserts. Children's menu. Daily specials. Traditional beers.
**Cards:** Visa, Access, MasterCard.
**Other points:** licensed, open-air dining, Sunday lunch, no-smoking area, children welcome, children's play area, disabled access, parking.
**Directions:** take A5127 off A5 or A38 to Sutton Coldfield. Half a mile on right.
WARREN ASHCROFT ☎(01543) 480214

## NEWCASTLE-UNDER-LYME • map 8B5

### GABLES HOTEL
570-572 Etruria Road, ST5 0SU

*The Gables is a fine Edwardian townhouse set in extensive gardens. Situated next to the New Victoria Theatre and ideal for visitors to Stoke-on-Trent's pottery factories (e.g., Wedgwood, Spode and Royal Doulton) and to Alton Towers.*
DOUBLE ROOM: up to £20
SINGLE ROOM: from £22
**Hours:** breakfast weekdays 7.30am-8.30am, weekends 8.30am-9.30am.
**Other points:** pets allowed, residents' television lounge, garden, parking, children welcome,
**Rooms:** 3 double rooms, 2 twin rooms, 5 family rooms, all with private showers.
**Directions:** on the A53, .5 mile from the town centre, next to New Victoria Theatre.
MS GILL FLETCHER ☎(01782) 619748

### STAFFORD • map 8C5

## RESTAURANT OF THE YEAR 1996
### THE MOAT HOUSE RESTAURANT
Lower Penkridge Road, Acton Trussell, ST17 0RJ

*A 13th century moated manor house set in six acres of landscaped grounds and overlooking the canal, yet only one mile from the M6. The delightful restaurant provides excellent food, with all dishes home-made, including the bread and petit fours. The food is of the highest quality and is beautifully served in generous portions. The Moat House is an outstanding restaurant in every respect.*
FOOD: from £13 to £25 🍲
**Hours:** lunch Monday-Saturday 12noon-2pm, bar meals Monday-Saturday 12noon-2pm, evening bar meals Monday-Friday 7pm-9.30pm, dinner Monday-Saturday 7pm-9.30pm, lunch Sunday 12noon-2pm.
**Cuisine:** ENGLISH - traditional English cuisine. A la carte menu in evenings and table d'hôte luncheon and dinner during the week. Traditional Sunday lunch.
**Cards:** Visa, Access, AmEx, Switch.
**Other points:** licensed, open-air dining, Sunday lunch, no-smoking in dining room, children welcome, patio, disabled access, functions, conservatory.
**Directions:** junction 13, M6. A449 towards Stafford. First right to village. Near church.
JOHN & MARY LEWIS ☎(01785) 712217
Fax(01785) 715364

# WARWICKSHIRE

## ALCESTER • map 9D1

### ROSSINI RESTAURANT
50 Birmingham Road, B49 5EP

*The Rossini is a well-maintained, traditional Italian restaurant, which offers good food and wine in comfortable, friendly surroundings. The 100-year-old Victorian building is pleasantly furnished throughout, and the service is highly efficient. Nearby places of interest include Ragley Hall, Coughton Court, and Stratford-upon-Avon.*
FOOD: from £20   CLUB
**Hours:** lunch 12noon-2pm, dinner 6.30pm-10.30pm.
**Cuisine:** ITALIAN - à la carte and table d'hôte menus. Traditional Italian-style cuisine, including a wide choice of pasta dishes, complemented by a good wine list.
**Cards:** Visa, Access, Diners, AmEx.
**Other points:** licensed, Sunday lunch, children welcome, disabled access, parking.
**Directions:** situated on the main Evesham to Birmingham A435 road.
CARMINE SACCO ☎(01789) 762764

## ALDERMINSTER • map 9E2

### BELL BISTRO
CV37 8NY

*Standing on the A3400, the Bell is an old coaching inn with flagstones, beams and fireplaces. All food is freshly prepared and cooked on the premises, and because of the use of fresh produce, the menu changes daily. Traditional, predominantly English cuisine is imaginatively cooked. A friendly atmosphere prevails.*
FOOD: up to £15
**Hours:** lunch 12noon-2pm, dinner 7pm-9.30pm.
**Cuisine:** ENGLISH - menu written on blackboards: changes daily. Fresh fish and seafood is a speciality.

Low fat and vegetarian dishes always available. All dishes are freshly prepared.
**Cards:** Visa, Access.
**Other points:** licensed, Sunday lunch, no-smoking throughout except entrance bar, children welcome, conference facilities, conservatory and garden with lovely views.
**Directions:** on the A3400, 4 miles south of Stratford-upon-Avon.
KEITH & VANESSA BREWER ☎(01789) 450414
Fax(01789) 450998

## HENLEY-IN-ARDEN • map 9D1

### ARDEN TANDOORI RESTAURANT
137 High Street, B95 5BJ
*Situated right in the centre of the historic town of Henley-in-Arden. The interior has been tastefully decorated with an air of subdued elegance. The Arden offers a warm welcome and excellent food. There is a private room available for parties.*
FOOD: up to £15
**Hours:** lunch 12noon-2.30pm, dinner 5.30pm-11.30pm.
**Cuisine:** INDIAN - kurzi lamb, lamb pasanda nawabi, makhon chicken and balti dishes.
**Cards:** Visa, Access, Diners, AmEx.
**Other points:** open-air dining, Sunday lunch, coaches by prior arrangement, children welcome.
**Directions:** on the A34 between Solihull and Stratford-upon-Avon.
NANU MIAH ☎(01564) 792503

## ILMINGTON • map 9E2

### THE HOWARD ARMS
Lower Green, CV36 4LT
*This tranquil 16th century inn provides a delightful setting in which to sample some delectable English cuisine. Fresh ingredients and an imaginative, constantly changing menu can tempt even the most particular palate.*
DOUBLE ROOM: from £20 to £30
SINGLE ROOM: from £30
FOOD: up to £15
**Hours:** lunch 12noon-2pm, dinner Sunday-Thursday 7pm-9pm, dinner Friday-Saturday 7pm-9.30pm.
**Cuisine:** ENGLISH - classic English cuisine with a regularly changing menu, served in bar, restaurant or garden.
**Cards:** Visa, Access, AmEx, Switch.
**Other points:** licensed, open-air dining, Sunday lunch, children welcome, garden, no smoking room.
**Rooms:** 1 double room, 1 twin room. Both with TV, tea/coffee-making facilities.
**Directions:** from Stratford-upon-Avon on the A3400 Shipston on Stour road after 4 miles take right turn to Ilmington for further 4 miles.
MRS SMART & MR THOMPSON ☎(01608) 682226 Fax(01608) 682226

## KENILWORTH • map 9D2

### CLARENDON ARMS
44 Castle Hill, CV8 1NB
*An olde-worlde inn in a historic, picture-postcard location opposite the entrance to Kenilworth Castle. Dine in the small, intimate bar, or in the larger dining area on the first floor - either way, the cheerful ambience and good home-cooked fare are sure to please.*
FOOD: up to £15
**Hours:** lunch 11am-3pm, Sunday 12noon-3pm, dinner 5.30pm-11pm, Sunday 7pm-10.30pm.
**Cuisine:** ENGLISH / INTERNATIONAL - giant char-grilled steaks, chicken teriyaki, traditional pub meals.
**Cards:** Visa, Access, Diners, AmEx.
**Other points:** licensed, open-air dining, Sunday lunch, children welcome.
**Directions:** opposite the entrance to Kenilworth Castle.
PATRICK MCCOSKER & MAURICE KUTNER ☎(01926) 52017 Fax(01926) 50229

## ROYAL LEAMINGTON SPA • map 9D2

### EATON COURT HOTEL
1-7 St Marks Road, CV32 6DL
*The Eaton family are directly involved in running this comfortable hotel, located in a calm backwater close to the centre of Leamington Spa. The spacious and comfortable bedrooms are furnished to a high standard and provide a convenient base from which to explore the Warwickshire countryside. The superb cuisine uses a wide range of freshly prepared produce, and special diets can be arranged. Ideal for the business traveller, and conferences and weddings can also be catered for. Some rooms are no-smoking.*
DOUBLE ROOM: from £30 to £40
SINGLE ROOM: from £45 to £55
FOOD: up to £15
**Hours:** breakfast 7am-9.30am, lunch by arrangement, dinner 7pm-9pm.
**Cuisine:** ENGLISH / FRENCH
**Cards:** Visa, Access, Diners, AmEx.
**Other points:** parking, children welcome, no-smoking area, pets, residents' lounge, garden, vegetarian meals, open-air dining.
**Rooms:** 36 bedrooms. All en suite.
**Directions:** off A452 Leamington-Warwick road on northern side of Leamington town.
SHAUN GREGORY ☎(01926) 885848 Fax(01926) 885848

## SHIPSTON ON STOUR • map 9E2

### THE HORSESHOE INN
Church Street, CV36 4AP
*This popular inn, situated in the centre of Shipston on Stour, is a favourite with travellers and locals alike. The menu is varied and the service is efficient and friendly. The bedrooms are comfortable and*

clean, the perfect place to rest your weary head after a day's sightseeing in nearby Stratford-upon-Avon, Warwick and Stow-on-the-Wold.
DOUBLE ROOM: up to £20
SINGLE ROOM: up to £25
FOOD: up to £15
**Hours:** breakfast 8am-10.30am, lunch 12noon-3pm, dinner 7pm-10pm.
**Cuisine:** ENGLISH
**Cards:** Visa, Access, Diners, AmEx.
**Other points:** children welcome, parking, disabled access, pets allowed, vegetarian meals, open-air dining.
**Rooms:** 3 twin rooms.
**Directions:** located in the centre of Shipston on Stour.
MRS A. WILLIAMS ☎(01608) 661225 Fax(01608) 663762

## STRATFORD-UPON-AVON • map 8E6

### ◼ ARDEN PARK HOTEL
6 Arden Street, CV37 6PA

This gracious old Victorian house with modern amenities offers comfortable en suite bedroom and breakfast accommodation close to the many attractions of this historic town. Joe and Eileen Morgan offer guests a warm welcome and an assurance of good value-for-money.
DOUBLE ROOM: up to £20
SINGLE ROOM: up to £25
**Hours:** breakfast 7.30am-9.15am. Open all year.
**Cuisine:** BREAKFAST - english, continental and vegetarian breakfasts.
**Cards:** Access,Visa,Mastercard,Eurocard
**Other points:** free parking (disc) opposite hotel.
**Rooms:** 7 rooms en suite with coffee making facilities, TV.
**Directions:** situated 100 metres from the centre of town.
MR JOSEPH MORGAN ☎(01789) 296072
Fax(01789) 296072

### ◼ CRAIG CLEEVE HOUSE
67-69 Shipston Road, CV37 7LW
A licensed private hotel retaining a family atmosphere where the sole aim is to make guests feel comfortable and welcome. Good, friendly service, comfortable rooms of a high standard, and a breakfast where no one is left feeling hungry! Quality, value for money and a warm welcome are

guaranteed. Only 5 minutes' walk from the town centre and within easy reach of the Cotswolds.
DOUBLE ROOM: from £20 to £30
SINGLE ROOM: from £20 to £40
**Hours:** breakfast 7.30am-9am.
**Cuisine:** BREAKFAST
**Cards:** Visa, Access, Diners, AmEx.
**Other points:** children welcome, afternoon tea, pets allowed, residents' lounge, parking, coaches by prior arrangement.
**Rooms:** 2 single rooms, 7 double rooms, 4 twin rooms, 2 family rooms. All with TV, tea/coffee-making facilities.
**Directions:** A3400 Stratford to Oxford Road. Five minutes' walk to town centre.
TERRY & MARGARITA PALMER ☎(01789) 296573 Fax(01789) 299452

### ◲ MARLOWES RESTAURANT
18 High Street, CV37 6AU
Marlowes, originally an Elizabethan town house, is now a first-class restaurant with an enviable clientele, including actors Anthony Quayle, Vanessa Redgrave, Sir John Gielgud, Sir Alec Guinness and many more. It has enjoyed a long association with the Royal Shakespeare Theatre and was once the home of Denny Gilkes, the famous opera singer and actress. Enjoy excellent cuisine, from the charcoal grill to fish, meat and poultry dishes, including vegetarian specials. The restaurant will also cook any speciality or gourmet/party meal, with prior notice.
FOOD: from £15 to £20
**Hours:** lunch 12noon-2.30pm, dinner 5.45pm-10.30pm.
**Cuisine:** ENGLISH
**Cards:** Visa, Access, Diners, AmEx.
**Other points:** Sunday lunch, open bank holidays, vegetarian meals.
**Directions:** centre of Stratford-upon-Avon.
MR GEORGE KRUSZYNSKYJ ☎(01789) 204999 Fax(01789) 204171

### ◼ SEQUOIA HOUSE PRIVATE HOTEL
51 Shipston Road, CV37 7LN
Beautifully appointed, quietly run, private licensed hotel, superbly situated across the River Avon opposite the Royal Shakespeare Theatre. Large private car park. Delightful garden walk to the theatre, riverside gardens and town centre. Fully air-conditioned dining room and conference facility.
DOUBLE ROOM: from £25 to £30
SINGLE ROOM: from £35 to £50
**Hours:** breakfast 7.30am-9am.
**Cuisine:** BREAKFAST
**Cards:** Visa, Access, Diners, AmEx.
**Other points:** central heating, children welcome, residents' lounge, air-conditioned, conferences, vegetarian meals.
**Rooms:** 24 double/twin rooms.
**Directions:** located on A34 approach road from the south, near Clopton bridge.
MR P.L. EVANS ☎(01789) 268852 Fax(01789) 414559

### SWAN HOUSE HOTEL
The Green, Wilmcote, CV37 9XJ

*An attractive listed building overlooking Mary Arden's House. Swan House occupies a rural setting, yet is close enough to Birmingham to be a good centre for business conferences etc.*

DOUBLE ROOM: from £20 to £30
SINGLE ROOM: from £35
FOOD: up to £15
**Hours:** breakfast 7.30am-9.30am, lunch 12noon-2.30pm, dinner 7.30pm-9.30pm, closed 3rd to 6th January.
**Cuisine:** ENGLISH - extensive range of home-made bar meals: steak-and-mushroom pie, lasagne. A la carte: duckling, salmon, peppered sirloin.
**Cards:** Visa, Access, AmEx.
**Other points:** Sunday lunch, children welcome, disabled access.
**Rooms:** 1 single room, 3 double room, 2 twin rooms, 1 family room. All with TV, radio, alarm, tea/coffee-making facilities.
**Directions:** from the A3400, 3 miles north-west of Stratford, take the Wilmcote turn-off.
DIANA SYKES ☎(01789) 267030 Fax(01789) 204875

### THE VINTNER CAFE, WINE BAR
5 Sheep Street, CV37 6ES

*The Vintner's name derives from 1601 when John Smith lived at this address working as a vintner, and the Elizabethan decor reflects this association. An extensive, international wine, beer and spirits list and prompt service make this café/wine bar popular with theatre-goers and locals alike. Open for coffees to three-course meals. Family run.*

FOOD: up to £15
**Hours:** meals all day 10.30am-11.30pm, closed Christmas day and Boxing day.
**Cuisine:** MODERN ENGLISH - wide selection of home-cooked soups, vegetarian dishes, steaks and salads. Superb sweets. Full menu is accompanied by many daily changing chef's specials.
**Cards:** Visa, Access, AmEx.
**Other points:** licensed, Sunday lunch, children welcome, coaches by prior arrangement.
**Directions:** off A34, first right approaching theatre, on waterside near town hall.
MR N. MILLS ☎(01789) 297259

## WARWICK • map 9D2

### TUDOR HOUSE INN
West Street, CV34 6AW

*A privately-owned inn of great charm and character. Dating from 1472, it retains a wealth of timbers, many of which were used in old warships. It is also one of the few buildings to survive the great fire of Warwick in 1694. The inn offers good, plentiful food at reasonable prices in a very friendly and welcoming atmosphere, along with good-value wines.*

DOUBLE ROOM: from £20 to £30
SINGLE ROOM: up to £25
FOOD: up to £15
**Hours:** breakfast 7am-9.30am, lunch 12noon-3pm, dinner 6pm-11pm.
**Cuisine:** ENGLISH/INTERNATIONAL - traditional English and varied international dishes.
**Cards:** Visa, Access, Diners, AmEx, Switch, Delta.
**Other points:** licensed, open-air dining, Sunday lunch, children welcome, afternoon tea, garden, residents' bar.
**Rooms:** 3 single rooms, 4 double rooms, 4 twin rooms. All with TV, telephone, tea/coffee-making facilities. One double room has a four-poster bed.
**Directions:** on the A429, almost opposite the entrance to Warwick Castle.
MR P. MCCOSKER & MR M. KUTNER ☎(01926) 495447 Fax(01926) 492948

# WEST MIDLANDS

## BIRMINGHAM • map 8D5

### AGRA FORT
14-16 Suffolk Street, Queensway, B1 1LT

*A recently opened restaurant with a difference designed for the comfort and pleasure of diners with contemporary and traditional Indian cuisine. The very best dishes from the Indian subcontinent from Bombay to Goa, Delhi to Agra and North Bengal to Southern India are prepared by expert chefs specially brought to the country to ensure your gastronomic pleasure. A lively atmosphere is guaranteed within surroundings which are informal yet gracious.*

FOOD: from £15 to £20
**Hours:** lunch 12noon-2.30pm, dinner 6pm-12midnight, open bank holidays.
**Cuisine:** INDIAN - a wide range of authentic and traditional Indian dishes.
**Cards:** Visa, Access, Diners, AmEx, Switch.
**Directions:** in Birmingham city centre next to the Alexandra Theatre. Near to I.C.C., Copthorne Hotel and Holiday Inn.
JAMEL CHAUDHURI ☎(0121) 643 2230 / 643 9339 Fax(0121) 643 2241

### FOUNTAIN COURT HOTEL
339-343 Hagley Road, B17 8NN

*A friendly, family-run hotel located on a main road about 3 miles west from the city centre. Good location for access to M5 and the International Conference Centre. The hotel is well maintained and has recently been refurbished. Especially popular with business travellers and weekenders.*

DOUBLE ROOM: from £20 to £30
SINGLE ROOM: from £35 to £45
FOOD: up to £15
**Hours:** breakfast 6.45am-9am, dinner 6.30pm-

8.30pm.
**Cuisine:** ENGLISH - table d'hôte menu. Dishes may include roast duck, beef en croute, grilled gammon. Everything is home-made.
**Cards:** Visa, Access, Diners, AmEx.
**Other points:** licensed, children welcome, garden, pets allowed.
**Rooms:** 13 single rooms, 6 double rooms, 6 twin rooms. All with TV, telephone, tea/coffee-making facilities.
**Directions:** A456. Corner of Hagley Road and Fountain Road. (2 miles from junction 3, M5.)
STELLA & RICHARD SMITH ☎(0121) 429 1754 Fax(0121) 429 1209

### HAGLEY COURT HOTEL
229 Hagley Road, Edgbaston, B16 9RP
*A Georgian mansion, set back from the main road leading into the city. The International Conference Centre is only one mile from the hotel, making it an ideal place for delegates to stay. The hotel is renowned for its comfortable and homely accommodation.*
DOUBLE ROOM: from £20 to £30
SINGLE ROOM: from £28 to £45
FOOD: up to £15     CLUB
**Hours:** breakfast 7am-9am, dinner 6pm-9.30pm.
**Cuisine:** FRENCH / ENGLISH - à la carte, table d'hôte and bar menus. Steaks, chicken, fish.
**Cards:** Visa, Diners, AmEx, MasterCard, Switch.
**Other points:** licensed, children welcome, cots, residents' bar, residents' lounge, parking.
**Rooms:** 8 single rooms, 16 double rooms, 3 twin rooms. All en suite with satellite TV, radio, alarm, cots, telephone, tea/coffee-making facilities, heating.
**Directions:** on A456.
CHRISTOPHER PHILIPPIDES ☎(0121) 454 6514 Fax(0121) 456 2722

### HEATH LODGE HOTEL
117 Coleshill Road, Marston Green, B37 7HT
*Family-run hotel, with cosy lounge and coal-effect fire, quietly situated just a short distance away from NEC and Birmingham International Airport. Courtesy car available for airport travellers, and long-term car parking.*
DOUBLE ROOM: up to £25
SINGLE ROOM: up to £40
FOOD: up to £15
**Hours:** dinner 6.30pm-8.30pm.
**Cuisine:** INTERNATIONAL - farmhouse grill, fillet steak, chicken kiev, salmon, halibut.
**Cards:** Visa, Access, Diners, AmEx.
**Other points:** licensed, children welcome, pets allowed, open bank holidays, residents' bar, residents' meals, vegetarian meals, parking.
**Rooms:** 8 single rooms, 4 double rooms, 6 twin rooms. All with TV, telephone, tea/coffee-making facilities.
**Directions:** hotel located 1 mile from entrance to Birmingham Airport.
SIMEON COLLINS ☎(0121) 779 2218 Fax(0121) 779 2218

### LYNDHURST HOTEL
135 Kingsbury Road, Erdington, B24 8QT
*Family-owned and run. Recently refurbished to a high standard, but maintaining a relaxed, family atmosphere. On the route of the 114 and 116 buses, which go to the city centre.*
DOUBLE ROOM: from £20 to £30
FOOD: up to £15
**Hours:** breakfast 7.30am-8.30am, closed Christmas, dinner 6.30pm-8.30pm.
**Cuisine:** ENGLISH
**Cards:** Visa, Access, Diners, AmEx.
**Other points:** central heating, children welcome, residents' lounge, garden, vegetarian meals.
**Rooms:** 8 single rooms, 4 twin rooms, 2 family rooms. All with TV, tea/coffee-making facilities, hair dryer.
**Directions:** off the A5127, .5 mile from M6 turn-off at junction 6.
MR & MRS R. WILLIAMS ☎(0121) 373 5695 Fax(0121) 373 5695

### PINOCCHIO'S RESTAURANT
Chad Square, Hawthorne Road, B15 3TQ
*A traditional Italian decor sets the scene in which to enjoy quality Italian meals generously served. With its warm, friendly and relaxed atmosphere, it is the perfect place for a quiet or romantic dinner. Fresh fish and vegetables are bought daily. Situated just minutes from the city on the Harborne/Edgbaston border, Pinocchio's is a real taste of Italy in Birmingham.*
FOOD: from £20 to £25     CLUB
**Hours:** lunch 12noon-2.30pm, dinner 7pm-11pm, closed Sunday and bank holidays.
**Cuisine:** ITALIAN - extensive menu: dishes may include filetto farfalla, calamari alla livornese, sogliola di Dover grigliata, pollo alla Pinocchio.
**Cards:** Visa, Access, Diners, AmEx.
**Other points:** licensed, children welcome.
**Directions:** opposite White Swan pub, just off Harborne Road. Near Botanical Gardens.
MR SILVIO NOVELLI ☎(0121) 454 8672 Fax(0121) 3539542

### YEW TREE COTTAGE BALTI & TANDOORI RESTAURANT
43 Stoney Lane, Yardley Village, B25 8RE
*Established for over 15 years, the Yew Tree Cottage is a venue of style, character and food beyond compare. A very stylish Indian restaurant, recommended by many good food guides. The genuine and authentic food served here is prepared by chefs who have been acclaimed as experts in the culinary art. The ingredients are bought fresh daily and all meals are cooked to order. For the true taste of India, this is a must!*
FOOD: up to £15     CLUB
**Hours:** dinner 5.30pm-12midnight, closed Christmas day.
**Cuisine:** INDIAN - Northern Indian and Mughal Empire delicacies; unusual North Bengali cuisine.
**Cards:** Visa, Access, Diners, AmEx.

**Other points:** parking, children catered for (please check for age limits), vegetarian meals.
**Directions:** near to NEC, ICC, A45 and M6. A to Z reference 5B 76.
JAMAL CHOUDHURI ☎(0121) 784 0707/786 1814

## BROWNHILLS • map 8C5

### 🍴 TERRACE RESTAURANT
9 Watling Street, Newtown, WS8 6JR
*A superbly appointed restaurant with all modern facilities. Set in award-winning gardens with parking facilities for over 100 cars. Disabled facilities available.*
FOOD: up to £15
**Hours:** lunch 12noon-2.30pm, dinner 7pm-10pm.
**Cuisine:** ENGLISH - traditional English cuisine. Specialities include beef Wellington and fresh fish. Vegetarians also catered for. Advance booking essential on Saturdays and Sundays.
**Cards:** Visa, Access, Diners, AmEx, Switch.
**Other points:** licensed, Sunday lunch, children welcome, functions, conferences.
**Directions:** situated on the main A5 trunk road. 7 miles east of M6. 5 miles north-east of Walsall.
MR ADSHEAD ☎(01543) 378291

## COVENTRY • map 8D6

### 🏨 LADY GODIVA HOTEL
80-90 Holyhead Road, CV1 3AS
*Situated on the main Coventry-Birmingham road, only 11 miles from Birmingham Airport. Good facilities for conferences and private functions of up to 300. Central for the Cotswolds and Shakespeare Country.*
DOUBLE ROOM: from £30 to £40
FOOD: from £15 to £20  CLUB
**Hours:** breakfast 7am-9.30am, lunch 12.30am-2.30pm, dinner 7.30pm-10pm.
**Cuisine:** MODERN ENGLISH - nouvelle cuisine, e.g., salmon with maltaise sauce, mille-feuilles of scampi tomato, garlic, herbs.
**Cards:** Visa, Access, Diners, AmEx.
**Other points:** Sunday lunch, children welcome, coaches by prior arrangement, parking, disabled access, lift.
**Rooms:** 60 single rooms, 9 double rooms, 105 twin rooms.
**Directions:** 10 minutes' walk from city centre; 9 miles from NEC.
MRS ANDREA BURTON (ALL CORRESPONDENCE) ☎(01203) 258585 Fax(01203) 225547

## SOLIHULL • map 8D6

### 🏨 FLEMINGS HOTEL
141 Warwick Road, Olton, B92 7HW
*A patron-run hotel situated only 5.5 miles from the centre of Birmingham. A high standard of comfort and service are provided at reasonable prices, and the restaurant offers both à la carte and table d'hôte menus. All the homely friendliness of a small hotel.*
DOUBLE ROOM: from £30
SINGLE ROOM: from £32
FOOD: up to £20

**Hours:** lunch 12noon-2pm, dinner 6.30pm-9.30pm, Christmas day lunch only.
**Cuisine:** ENGLISH - seafood specials, steaks, beef stroganoff.
**Cards:** Visa, Access, Diners, AmEx, Switch.
**Other points:** licensed, Sunday buffet lunch, open-air dining, children welcome, pets allowed.
**Rooms:** 51 single rooms, 16 double rooms, 7 twin rooms, 4 family rooms. All with TV, radio, alarm, tea/coffee-making facilities, heating, hair dryers.
**Directions:** on A41, 250 yards from Olton station.
W. FLEMING ☎(0121) 706 0371 Fax(0121) 706 4494

## STOURBRIDGE • map 8D5

### 🍴 THE RETREAT
157 Hagley Road, Oldswinford, DY8 2JJ
*A stylish and popular bar and bistro, situated in the village of Oldswinford, serving fine, quality food and drink, six days per week. The brasserie-style menu offers light snacks and full meals, served in an informal atmosphere in pleasant surroundings. Places of interest nearby include Hagley Hall, Harvington Hall and an interesting glassworks.*
FOOD: up to £15
**Hours:** lunch Monday-Saturday 12noon-2.15pm, dinner Monday-Saturday 7pm-11pm, late supper license. Closed Christmas day and Boxing day.
**Cuisine:** ENGLISH / MEDITERRANEAN - full à la carte menu, offering a wide selection of imaginative dishes. Vegetarian meals available. Business lunches and small parties catered for.
**Cards:** Visa, Access, AmEx.
**Other points:** licensed, disabled access, vegetarian meals, open bank holidays, children catered for (please check for age limits).
**Directions:** 1 mile outside the town centre on the left of the A491.
PAT & PETER GULLY ☎(01384) 396290

## SUTTON COLDFIELD • map 8D6

### 🏨 SUTTON COURT HOTEL
60-66 Lichfield Road, near Birmingham, B74  2NA
*Privately owned and convenient for Birmingham International Airport and the NEC. Six golf courses within 15-minutes drive. The restaurant enjoys a fine reputation for its international cuisine. Free car parking.*
DOUBLE ROOM: from £30 to £40
SINGLE ROOM: over £55
FOOD: from £15 to £20 CLUB
**Hours:** breakfast 7.00am - 9.30am, lunch 12 noon - 2pm, diner 7pm-10pm, bar meals 7pm-10pm
**Cuisine:** ENGLISH / ENGLISH - table d'hôte and à la carte menus available, traditional French dishes, vegetarian meals available.
**Cards:** Visa, Access, Diners, AmEx, Switch.
**Other points:** children under 14 get complementary accommodation if sharing with parents (meals extra), airport nearby, baby-sitting available, cots, 24 hr reception, foreign exchange.
**Directions:** off A38 on corner of A5127 and A453.
PETER JOHN BENNETT ☎(0121) 355 6071
Fax  (0121) 355 0083

# NORTHERN ENGLAND & THE ISLE OF MAN

The north of England is a region of tremendous scenic diversity, steeped in history: from the lush, green pastures and rolling fells of Yorkshire and Humberside to the rugged wild countryside of Northumberland with its miles of unspoilt coastline, from the incomparable beauty of the Cumbrian Lakes to the open sweeping moors of Lancashire. Whether you come to climb, hill-walk, cave, sail or simply absorb the breathtaking scenery at your leisure, this region offers endless scope for visitors of all ages.

This is predominantly 'dales' country, where the local folk know the true meaning of a good wholesome feast, and how to marry local ingredients with their own native wit. There is simply no better way to round off the day than with a substantial supper at a sound hostelry. Choose from Westmoreland lamb, Coniston char plucked from the sparkling clear fern-lined waters of a babbling hill-stream that very morning, Cumberland Tattie Pot, Grizedale venison, farmhouse grills - barbecued, flamed or just cold, the choice of excellent cuisine is endless.

For those who enjoy a more vibrant atmosphere, the city centres are the places to visit. Here you will find a superb selection of cafe-bars and bistros serving a wide range of imaginative dishes, tasty beers and colourful, speciality cocktails at great value for money.

The following counties are included in this chapter:

CLEVELAND
COUNTRY DURHAM
CUMBRIA
GREATER MANCHESTER
HUMBERSIDE
ISLE OF MAN

LANCASHIRE
MERSEYSIDE
NORTHUMBERLAND
TYNE & WEAR
YORKSHIRE (NORTH)
YORKSHIRE (SOUTH)
YORKSHIRE (WEST)

# CLEVELAND

## BILLINGHAM • map 12C5

 **BILLINGHAM ARMS HOTEL**
The Causeway, TS23 2HD
*A conveniently located, modern hotel, five minutes from Billingham railway station and ten miles from Teeside Airport. Berties Restaurant is renowned for its good food and friendly service. An ideal hotel for tourists and business-people alike.*
DOUBLE ROOM: from £43 to £64
SINGLE ROOM: from £37 to £49
FOOD: from £15 to £20 CLUB
**Hours:** breakfast 7am-10am, lunch 12noon-2pm, dinner 6pm-11pm.
**Cuisine:** ENGLISH / CONTINENTAL - croissant filled with diced chicken and bacon in a cream cheese and mushroom sauce, strips of beef cooked at your table in a sherry and oyster sauce.
**Cards:** Visa, Access, Diners, AmEx.
**Other points:** licensed, Sunday lunch, pets allowed, coaches by prior arrangement, children welcome, disabled access, residents' lounge, residents' bar, vegetarian meals.
**Rooms:** 17 single rooms, 41 double rooms, 10 twin rooms, 1 suite. All with telephone, tea/coffee-making facilities, satellite TV, trouser-press. Some doubles are available as singles when required.
**Directions:** from A19, in town square next to Forum sports centre and theatre.
MR SNAITH & MR HUGHES ☎(01642) 553661/360880 Fax (01642) 552104

## HARTLEPOOL • map 12C5

### 🛏 GRAND HOTEL
Swainson Street, TS24 8AA

*A Grade II listed Victorian hotel situated in the town centre. Victoria's Lounge Bar serves popular bar food Monday to Saturday lunchtime, while Piper's Restaurant provides table d'hôte and à la carte menus. The food is well cooked and served in generous portions. Excellent, welcoming service adds to the relaxed, friendly atmosphere of the Grand Hotel.*

**DOUBLE ROOM:** from £30 to £40
**SINGLE ROOM:** from £35 to £45
**FOOD:** up to £15 CLUB
**Hours:** breakfast 7.30am-9.30am, lunch 12noon-2pm, dinner 7.30pm-10pm, Sunday 7.30pm-9pm.
**Cuisine:** ENGLISH / CONTINENTAL - table d'hôte and à la carte menu. The specialities are steaks: steak Diane, surf and hoof, etc.
**Cards:** Visa, Access, Diners, AmEx.
**Other points:** licensed, Sunday lunch, children welcome, afternoon tea, pets allowed, conferences, functions, 24hr reception, foreign exchange, residents' bar, residents' lounge, baby-listening device, cots, disabled access.
**Rooms:** 15 single rooms, 15 double rooms, 17 twin rooms. All with TV, radio, alarm, telephone, tea/coffee-making facilities, hair dryer, trouser-press.
**Directions:** town centre by Civic Centre and Cenotaph.
MR IAN DAVIES ☎(01429) 266345 Fax(01429) 265217

### 🍴 KRIMO'S
8 The Front, Seaton Carew, TS25 1BS

*An outstanding restaurant with Mediterranean-style decor, popular with both locals and visitors and offering a relaxed, welcoming atmosphere. The food is well-cooked, well-presented and highly recommended.*

**FOOD:** from £10 to £20
**Hours:** lunch 12noon-1.30pm, dinner 7.30pm-9.30pm, closed Saturday lunch, Sunday and Monday.
**Cuisine:** MEDITERRANEAN - Mediterranean food: steaks, fish.
**Cards:** Visa, Access.
**Other points:** licensed, children welcome, street parking.
**Directions:** on seafront, off A689.
KRIMO BOUABDA ☎(01429) 266120

## THORNABY-ON-TEES • map 12C5

### 🛏 GOLDEN EAGLE HOTEL
Trenchard Avenue, TS17 0DA

*Set in the heart of Teeside's commercial centre, the Golden Eagle is an excellent venue for conferences, yet provides prompt and easy access to the North Yorkshire Moors National Park. The hotel is situated only a few minutes from the A19 and is close to both mainline rail and air communications. There is easy access to the A1 and M1 motorways.*

**DOUBLE ROOM:** from £20 to £30
**SINGLE ROOM:** from £35 to £45
**FOOD:** up to £15 CLUB
**Hours:** breakfast 7am-10am, dinner 7pm-10pm, bar meals 12noon-2pm.
**Cuisine:** ENGLISH
**Cards:** Visa, Access, Diners, AmEx, Switch.
**Other points:** parking, children welcome, disabled access, pets, vegetarian meals, restaurant, bar.
**Rooms:** 15 single rooms, 16 double rooms, 26 twin rooms. All rooms can be double or single occupancy.
**Directions:** leave A19 onto A174, turn left at traffic lights and hotel is .5 mile on the right.
JOHN SNAITH & EDWARD HUGHES ☎(01642) 766511 Fax(01642) 750336

# COUNTY DURHAM

## BISHOP AUCKLAND • map 12C4

### 🍴 BISHOPS BISTRO
17 Cockton Hill Road, DL14 6EN

*Old converted cottages with plenty of character situated in the main street from the town centre. Personally run by the chef/proprietor, there is a restaurant, and a separate bar area where diners may enjoy pre-dinner drinks. Efficient service and well-cooked cuisine in an informal atmosphere.*

**FOOD:** from £15 to £20
**Hours:** lunch 12noon-1.30pm, dinner 7pm-9pm, last orders 9pm, closed Sunday and Monday.
**Cuisine:** ENGLISH / CONTINENTAL - dishes may include honey roast breast of duckling, braised guinea fowl, escalope of veal. Daily specials displayed on blackboard. Choice of vegetarian dishes.
**Cards:** Visa, Access, Diners, AmEx.
**Other points:** licensed, children welcome.
**Directions:** 2 minutes from the new railway station opposite the hospital.
CHARLES & KATE DAVIDSON ☎(01388) 602462

## CONSETT • map 12B4

### 🛏 ROYAL DERWENT HOTEL
Hole Row, Allensford, DH8 9BB

*The Royal Derwent has the ambience and style of a medieval mansion. Timber-beamed bedrooms are furnished with either queen- or king-size beds and equipped with many modern facilities. Enjoy fine cuisine in the Cutlers Restaurant, with its crackling winter log fire, or morning and afternoon teas in the lounge. This hotel is an ideal venue for visiting*

*Hadrian's Wall, Beamish Museum, Durham
Cathedral, the north Pennines and Lake District.*
DOUBLE ROOM: from £30 to £40
SINGLE ROOM: from £45 to £55
FOOD: up to £15 [CLUB]
**Hours:** breakfast 7am-10am, lunch 12noon-2.30pm,
bar meals 12noon-2.45pm, 7pm-9.45pm, dinner
7pm-9.45pm.
**Cuisine:** ENGLISH
**Cards:** Visa, Access, Diners, AmEx.
**Other points:** parking, children welcome, no-
smoking area, afternoon teas, disabled access, pets,
residents' lounge, vegetarian meals, residents' bar.
**Rooms:** 12 double rooms, 31 twin rooms, 2 family
rooms. All en suite with TV, telephone, tea/coffee-
making facilities.
**Directions:** 1 mile north of Castleside.
MISS A. BURGESS ☎(01207) 592000 [Fax](01207)
502472

## DARLINGTON • map 12C4

 **GEORGE HOTEL**
Piercebridge, DL2 3SW
*This 17th century coaching inn is set on the grassy
banks of the River Tees. The restaurant offers
excellent value-for-money dishes, complemented by
a varied selection of good wines. Comfortable
accommodation and friendly, efficient service.*
DOUBLE ROOM: from £20 to £30
**Hours:** breakfast 7.30am-11am, lunch 11.30am-
3pm, dinner 6.30pm-10pm.
**Cuisine:** ENGLISH - à la carte menu and bar meals.
**Cards:** Visa, Access, Diners, AmEx.
**Other points:** licensed, open-air dining, Sunday
lunch, children welcome, garden, afternoon tea,
coaches by prior arrangement, disabled access,
vegetarian meals, residents' lounge, residents' bar.
**Rooms:** 35 bedrooms. All en suite.
**Directions:** follow A1; exit to B6275 to
Piercebridge. Hotel located in village.
MR & MRS WAIN ☎(01325) 374576 [Fax](01325)
374577

## DURHAM • map 12C4

 **HALLGARTH MANOR HOTEL**
Pittington, DH6 1AB
*Located in the small village of Pittington 3.5 miles
from Durham city, this hotel is brightly yet tastefully
decorated. Frequented by all ages, the hotel enjoys
a relaxed atmosphere. First-class food and
accommodation of a high standard.*
DOUBLE ROOM: from £20 to £30
SINGLE ROOM: from £40 to £50
FOOD: from £15 to £20 [CLUB]
**Hours:** breakfast 7.30am-9.30am, lunch 12noon-
2pm, dinner 7pm-9.15pm, bar snacks 12noon-2pm,
5.30pm-9.30pm.
**Cuisine:** ENGLISH - à la carte menu, table d'hôte
and bar snacks.
**Cards:** Visa, Access, Diners, AmEx, MasterCard,
Switch.
**Other points:** licensed, open-air dining, Sunday

lunch, children welcome, afternoon tea, pets
allowed.
**Rooms:** 5 single rooms, 12 double rooms, 6 twin
rooms.
**Directions:** 3.5 miles northeast of Durham city
centre.
MR TERENCE ROBSON ☎(0191) 372 1188
[Fax](0191) 372 1249

 **KENSINGTON HALL HOTEL**
Kensington Terrace, Willington, Crook,
DL15 0PJ
*A delightful old village hall, which has been
tastefully converted to a hotel of a very high
standard. It is widely renowned for its excellent
cuisine. The Regency function suite is available for
private hire. Good base for exploring Durham
Cathedral and Beamish Museum.*
DOUBLE ROOM: from £20 to £30
SINGLE ROOM: from £30 to £35
FOOD: up to £15
**Hours:** lunch 11.30am-2pm, dinner 7pm-9.30pm.
**Cuisine:** ENGLISH
**Cards:** Visa, Access, Diners, AmEx, Switch,
Eurocard,Delta
**Other points:** licensed.
**Rooms:** 10 bedrooms.
**Directions:** on A690, 8 miles from Durham, 2 miles
from Crook.
RON & JOYCE SMEATON ☎(01388) 745071
[Fax](01388) 745800

 **NEVILLE'S CROSS HOTEL**
Darlington Road, Neville's Cross, DH1
4JX
*A small, family-run hotel on the outskirts of
Durham, with open fires which create a warm,
convivial atmosphere.*
DOUBLE ROOM: up to £20
SINGLE ROOM: from £25
FOOD: up to £15
**Hours:** breakfast (except Sunday) 8am-9am, lunch
12noon-2pm, bar meals 12noon-2pm, dinner 7pm-
9pm, bar meals 6.30pm-9.30pm.
**Cuisine:** ENGLISH - home-made steak-and-kidney
pie, steaks grilled in red wine, veal flambé.
**Cards:** Visa, Access, AmEx, MasterCard, JCB, LV.
**Other points:** Sunday lunch, children catered for
(please check for age limits), pets allowed, coaches
by prior arrangement.
**Rooms:** 1 family room, 1 double room, 3 twin
rooms.
**Directions:** on the crossroads of the A167 and
A690.
MR & MRS J.B. HOLLAND ☎(0191) 384 3872
[Fax](0191) 3868250

 **RAMSIDE HALL HOTEL**
Carrville, DH1 1TD
*A country-house-type hotel set in 280 acres of
maturing golf course. Choice of three eating areas,
and musical entertainment seven nights a week. The*

*Ramside Hall Hotel provides an ideal venue for conferences, functions and weddings.*
DOUBLE ROOM: from £40 to £50
SINGLE ROOM: from £75
FOOD: from £15 to £20 🍽
**Hours:** breakfast 7.30am-10.30am, lunch 12noon-2pm, dinner 7pm-9.30pm.
**Cuisine:** ENGLISH - three eating areas: à la carte restaurant (fixed price), carvery, grill room.
**Cards:** Visa, Access, Diners, AmEx.
**Other points:** Sunday lunch, no-smoking area, children welcome, coaches welcome.
**Rooms:** 2 single rooms, 46 double rooms, 30 twin rooms, 2 suites. All with TV, radio, telephone, tea/coffee-making facilities.
**Directions:** on A690, just off the A1 motorway, northeast of Durham.
MR R.J. SMITH ☎(0191) 386 5282 [Fax](0191) 386 0399

🏨 **SEVEN STARS INN**
Shincliffe Village, DH1 2NU
*A 1725 coaching inn set in a charming village, in a conservation area one mile from Durham City. The atmosphere is very relaxed and friendly, the food is well-prepared and served in generous proportions, and the accommodation is very comfortable with all major facilities, plus thoughtful extra touches. Close to Durham Cathedral, castle and museums.*
DOUBLE ROOM: from £20 to £30
SINGLE ROOM: from £29 to £32
FOOD: up to £15
**Hours:** breakfast 8am-9am, lunch 12noon-2pm, bar meals 12noon-2pm, bar meals 7pm-9.30pm.
**Cuisine:** ENGLISH - with traditional roasts, home-made lasagne, pies, and steaks.
**Cards:** Visa.
**Other points:** Sunday lunch, no-smoking area,

children catered for (please check for age limits), open bank holidays, residents' lounge.
**Rooms:** 1 single room, 5 double rooms, 1 twin room. All with TV, radio, alarm, telephone, tea/coffee-making facilities.
**Directions:** from A1 take A177 to Bowburn, then main road into Shincliffe village.
MR A. GARDNER ☎(0191) 384 8454

## NEWTON AYCLIFFE • map 12C4

🏨 **THE GRETNA HOTEL & RESTAURANT**
Great North Road, DL5 7UT
*Situated just a short drive away from Darlington InterCity railway, the Gretna is an ideal place to stay when touring the north-east, with its many interesting attractions. Formerly the Wedding Inn, it has recently undergone extensive refurbishment to provide a high level of comfort. A function room is available for private hire for up to 100 guests.*
DOUBLE ROOM: from £20 to £30
FOOD: up to £15
**Hours:** breakfast 7am-9.30am, lunch 11.30am-2pm, dinner 6.30pm-10pm.
**Cuisine:** ENGLISH / INTERNATIONAL - home-cooked to a high standard.
**Cards:** Visa, Access.
**Other points:** parking, children welcome, Sunday lunch, open bank holidays, afternoon tea, disabled access, pets allowed, vegetarian meals, open-air dining, garden.
**Rooms:** 9 twin rooms. All with TV, telephone, tea/coffee-making facilities, alarm.
**Directions:** A167 junction of A1M, through village of Newton Aycliffe.
MR G. HAMILTON ☎(01325) 300100 [Fax](01325) 300949

# CUMBRIA

## AMBLESIDE • map 11D2

🏨 **COMPSTON HOUSE HOTEL**
Compston Road, LA22 9DJ
*A family-run hotel, beautifully situated opposite park and fells. Ann and Graham Smith offer excellent food and friendly service in cosy surroundings. Most rooms have views of the park, where you may play tennis, croquet and bowls, or test your skills on the putting green. Guided fell-walking, rock-climbing, pony-trekking and riding can be arranged. Excellent water-sports nearby. Guests receive free membership to an exclusive private leisure club with pool.*
DOUBLE ROOM: from £20 to £30
FOOD: from £15 to £20
**Hours:** breakfast 8.30am-9am, dinner 7pm (to be ordered by 5pm).
**Cuisine:** ENGLISH
**Other points:** central heating, children catered for (please check for age limits), lounge, patio,

vegetarian meals, special diets, licensed, residents' bar.
**Rooms:** 6 double rooms, 1 twin room, 1 family room. All with TV, tea/coffee-making facilities.
**Directions:** leave M6 at junction 36. Follow A590/591, bypassing Kendal and Windermere and leading straight on to the centre of Ambleside village. The hotel is situated on the corner, overlooking the park.
ANN & GRAHAM SMITH ☎(015394) 32305

## APPLEBY-IN-WESTMORELAND • map 11C3

🏨 **NEW INN**
Brampton, CA16 6JS
*The New Inn is in fact a very old inn, built around 1730 and charmingly restored with hanging baskets, which enhance its appearance. Inside, low beams, open log fires and flagstone floors take you back to a bygone era. A delightful setting in the Vale of*

Eden, and an ideal stop for the tourist.
DOUBLE ROOM: up to £20
SINGLE ROOM: up to £20
FOOD: up to £15
**Hours:** breakfast 7.30am-9.30am, lunch 12noon-2pm, dinner 7pm-9pm.
**Cuisine:** ENGLISH - steaks, grills, curried nut roast, seafood gratinée, spicy Stroganoff, Westmoreland sweetbake, chocolate fudge cake.
**Other points:** licensed, open-air dining, Sunday lunch, children welcome, beer garden.
**Rooms:** 2 double rooms, 1 twin room. All with TV, tea/coffee-making facilities.
**Directions:** from Appleby, follow signs to Brampton, 1.5 miles away.
ROGER & ANNE CRANSWICK ☎(017683) 51231
Fax(017683) 53130

 **THE WHITE HART HOTEL**
34 Boroughgate, CA16 6XG
*An attractive 350 year old coaching inn situated right in the centre of the historic market town of Appleby. The bar and restaurant attract a wide ranging clientele from the local community which is a reflection that this is a good honest hotel which offers a warm welcome and good service to its customers. 9 bedrooms are available, 4 of them en suite, and there is a twin bedded flat attached to the hotel on the ground floor, also en suite and self-contained.*
DOUBLE ROOM: from £18 to £30
SINGLE ROOM: from £25 to £35
FOOD: up to £15
**Hours:** breakfast 8am-9am (7.30am by request), lunch 12noon-2pm, dinner 6pm-9pm. Open bank holidays.
**Cuisine:** substantial à la carte menu, emphasis on home-made cuisine including lasagne, steak and kidney pies.
**Cards:** Visa, Access, Diners, AmEx, Switch.
**Rooms:** 7 double rooms, 2 twin rooms, separate flat accommodation 2 twin rooms. Most en suite. All with TV, telephone, baby listening device, tea/coffee-making facilities, room service. Iron, hair dryer available.
**Directions:** from Junction 38 (Tebay) on M6 follow signs to Appleby, or take Appleby turnoff from A66. Hotel is half way between church and castle on main street.
MARTIN & CHRISTINE COSGROVE ☎(01768) 351598 Fax(01768) 351598

 **THE PHEASANT INN**
Near Cockermouth, CA13 9YE
*The hotel is an excellent base from which to tour the Lake District, as well as the Roman Wall and Border country, the Eden Valley and Cumbrian coast. It has all the charm and character of a typical old inn and is well known for its excellent English cooking, service and friendliness. Les Routiers Symbol of Excellence award-winner 1993.*
DOUBLE ROOM: from £40 to £50

SINGLE ROOM: from £57
FOOD: from £15 to £20
**Hours:** breakfast 8.30am-9.45am, lunch 12noon-2pm, dinner 7pm-10.30pm, closed Christmas.
**Cuisine:** ENGLISH - roast meats: pheasant, venison (in season), roast duckling with orange sauce, Silloth shrimps.
**Cards:** Visa, Access.
**Other points:** licensed, Sunday lunch, no-smoking area, parking.
**Rooms:** 5 single rooms, 14 double rooms, 20 twin rooms.
**Directions:** just off the A66, 7 miles west of Keswick.
MR W.E. BARRINGTON WILSON ☎(017687) 76234 Fax(017687) 76002

 **BLENHEIM LODGE**
Brantfell Road, LA23 3AE
*A beautiful Lakeland hotel overlooking Lake Windermere, Blenheim Lodge offers peace and quiet, yet is close to the lake and shops. Jacqueline Sanderson is an expert in traditional English cuisine, and guests' admiration for the food has resulted in the Sandersons' own award-winning cookbook. Repeat visits vouch for the warm welcome and quality that are to be found here. Winner of Les Routiers Accommodation of the Year in 1992 and Casserole Award in 1991, 1992, 1993, 1994 and 1995.*
DOUBLE ROOM: from £23 to £35
SINGLE ROOM: from £27 to £30
FOOD: from £16 to £20
**Hours:** breakfast 8.30am-9am, dinner 7pm.
**Cuisine:** ENGLISH - traditional and Victorian dishes. All home-made. Fresh home-grown produce. Extensive vegetarian fare.
**Cards:** Visa, Access, AmEx, MasterCard.
**Other points:** licensed, no-smoking area, children welcome please check for age limits), residents' lounge, coin-operated laundry.
**Rooms:** 3 single rooms, 5 double rooms, 1 twin room, 1 family room.
**Directions:** from M6 turn left off A591 to Windermere. Opposite St Martins church.
FRANK SANDERSON ☎(015394) 45440
Fax(015394) 43440

 **DAMSON DENE HOTEL**
Crosthwaite, Lyth Valley, LA8 8JE
*Lying in the heart of the Lyth Valley in the beautiful Lake District National Park, the Damson Dene is luxury throughout. Log fires in winter, patios and three acres of landscaped gardens to enjoy in summer. Both the restaurant and bar enjoy stunning views across the fields to the fells beyond. Excellent leisure facilities including a swimming pool and squash court, and an entertainment suite with dance floor for special functions. An ideal base for touring the lakes.*

DOUBLE ROOM: from £40 to £50
SINGLE ROOM: from £25 to £35
FOOD: from £15 to £20
**Hours:** breakfast 8am-9.30am, Sunday lunch
12noon-2pm, bar meals 12noon-2pm, dinner 7pm-
9pm.
**Cuisine:** ENGLISH
**Cards:** Visa, Access.
**Other points:** children welcome, Sunday lunch,
parking, no-smoking area, afternoon teas, disabled
access, residents' lounge, garden, vegetarian meals,
garden dining.
**Rooms:** 37 bedrooms all en suite with courtesy
trays.
**Directions:** exit 36 of the M6; take the A590, then
the A5074 for 4.5 miles.
MR PHILIP COULSON ☎(015395) 68676
Fax(015395) 68227

### KNOLL HOTEL
Lake Road, LA23 2JF

A large Victorian country house set in an acre of
gardens and woodland, offering superb views over
Lake Windermere, yet within easy reach of the
shops and the bay.
DOUBLE ROOM: from £20 to £30
SINGLE ROOM: from £25 to £35
FOOD: up to £15
**Hours:** breakfast 8.45am-9.15am, dinner 7pm-
7.30pm.
**Cuisine:** ENGLISH
**Cards:** Visa, Access.
**Other points:** children catered for (please check for
age limits), garden, leisure centre.
**Rooms:** 4 single rooms, 5 double rooms, 1 twin
room, 2 family rooms. All with TV, telephone,
tea/coffee-making facilities. Most rooms are en
suite.
**Directions:** between Windermere station and pier.
MRS BERRY ☎(015394) 43756

### QUINN'S RESTAURANT
Royal Square, LA23 3DB
A corner-site restaurant in Royal Square, on two
floors. Tastefully and simply decorated with cane
furniture and pretty Lakeland pictures. A friendly
atmosphere is created with unobtrusive background
music in which to enjoy well-cooked and well-
presented cuisine.
FOOD: up to £15
**Hours:** lunch 12noon-2.30pm, dinner 6pm-10pm,
closed mid-January until mid-February, open all day

during summer.
**Cuisine:** BRITISH - full à la carte and table d'hôte
menus. Sunday roasts.
**Cards:** Visa, Access, Diners, AmEx.
**Other points:** licensed, children welcome.
**Directions:** in Royal Square in Bowness.
MR & MRS QUINN ☎(015394) 45510

## BRAMPTON • map 11B3

### ABBEY BRIDGE INN
Lanercost, CA8 2HG
This inn is in a superb setting on the banks of the
River Irthing amid the Borders' gently rolling fells.
Proprietor Philip Sayers is an authority on `real ale',
and up to 15 real ales are offered every week. The
rooms in the hotel are attractively furnished in
shades of bright pastel. The excellent cuisine
attracts local and foreign tourists visiting Hadrian's
Wall and the many other nearby attractions.
DOUBLE ROOM: from £20 to £30
SINGLE ROOM: up to £25
FOOD: from £15 to £20
**Hours:** breakfast 8am-9am, lunch 12noon-1.45pm,
dinner 7pm-8.45pm, closed Christmas day.
**Cuisine:** ENGLISH - mainly modern English, but
also includes some international flavour.
**Cards:** Visa, Access, AmEx.
**Other points:** parking, children welcome, no-
smoking area, limited disabled access, pets,
residents' lounge, vegetarian meals, open-air dining,
garden, downstairs room available.
**Rooms:** 1 single room, 4 double rooms, 2 twin
rooms.
**Directions:** 1 mile off A69, north of Brampton.
MR P. SAYERS ☎(016977) 2224 Fax(016977) 2224

## BROUGH SOWERBY • map 11C3

### THE BLACK BULL INN
Near Kirkby Stephen, CA17 4EG
A country inn where the staff are keen to make
guests feel at home, the food is professionally
prepared and the steaks are served in particularly
generous portions. Situated within easy reach of the
Yorkshire Dales and the Lake District National Park.
FOOD: up to £15
**Hours:** bar meals 11.30am-2pm, bar meals 6pm
until late.
**Cuisine:** INTERNATIONAL - barbequed spare ribs,
chicken kiev, lasagne and grills (a speciality). Also
available vegetarian menu and children's menu. All
use local produce.
**Other points:** licensed, Sunday lunch, no-smoking
area, beer garden, afternoon tea, children welcome,
pets allowed outside.
**Directions:** on A685 between Brough and Kirkby
Stephen in the Upper Eden Valley.
MR G. DUTTON ☎(017683) 41413

## BROUGHTON-IN-FURNESS • map 11D2

### BESWICKS RESTAURANT
Langholme House, The Square, LA20 6JF

A traditional Lakeland house facing the square in the village of Broughton, well-decorated and comfortably furnished. The five-course set menu offers a good choice of English/French dishes. The tranquil and unhurried atmosphere, unobtrusive classical music and excellent service ideally complement the high standard of cuisine, with all dishes freshly cooked to order.

**FOOD:** from £15 to £25 [CLUB]
**Hours:** dinner 7.30pm-12midnight, last orders 9.30pm, generally closed Sunday until Tuesday. Lunches by arrangement.
**Cuisine:** ENGLISH / FRENCH - five-course table d'hôte menu with regular changes, also available in individual courses. Main courses may include rack of lamb with Cumberland sauce, roast quail and poached salmon steak.
**Cards:** Visa, Access, Diners, AmEx, Switch, Delta.
**Other points:** licensed, no-smoking area, children welcome.
**Directions:** junction of A595 and A593, in the centre of Broughton-in-Furness.
CHRISTINE ROE ☎(01299) 716285

## BUTTERMERE • map 11C2

### BRIDGE HOTEL
CA13 9UZ

In a beautiful and unspoilt Lakeland valley with easy access to both Buttermere Lake and Crummock Water, this hotel is set in superb unrestricted walking country with wonderful mountain scenery. The home-made food is freshly prepared daily. The comfortable, inviting lounges provide an ideal place in which to relax.

**DOUBLE ROOM:** from £30 to £40
**SINGLE ROOM:** from £25 to £35
**FOOD:** from £15 to £20
**Hours:** bar meals 12noon-9.30pm, open all year.
**Cuisine:** ENGLISH / CUMBRIAN - traditional Cumbrian dishes and English cuisine; Cumberland hot-pot with black pudding, Cumbrian sausages.
**Other points:** Sunday lunch, children welcome, pets allowed, self-catering apartments available.
**Rooms:** 22 bedrooms.
**Directions:** on the B5289 Keswick to Buttermere road.
PETER MCGUIRE ☎(017687) 70252 [Fax](017687) 70252

## CARLISLE • map 11B2

### ANGUS HOTEL & RESTAURANT WITH ALMONDS COFFEE HOUSE & BISTRO
14 Scotland Road, CA3 9DG

At the Angus hotel you will find a warm welcome and an emphasis on making guests feel at home. Good home-cooked food is available from our licenced restaurant, open six evenings per week.

Fresh soup and home-baked bread complement a menu which offers very good value for money. The spotlessly clean and comfortable accommodation offers tea- and coffee-making facilities, radio/alarms and colour TVs in all rooms. En suite rooms have hair dryers too! A friendly place to stay, at very reasonable prices.

**DOUBLE ROOM:** from £20 to £30
**SINGLE ROOM:** from £25 to £35
**FOOD:** up to £15 [CLUB]
**Hours:** breakfast 7.30am-8.45am, dinner 6.30pm-9pm, open all year.
**Cuisine:** BRITISH
**Cards:** Visa, Access, AmEx.
**Other points:** children welcome, pets allowed, vegetarian meals, residents' lounge.
**Rooms:** 2 single rooms, 2 double rooms, 4 twin rooms, 4 family rooms.
**Directions:** leave M6/A74 at junction 44. Hotel at 7th set of lights, on A7.
ELAINE & GEOFF WEBSTER ☎(01228) 23546 [Fax](01228) 31895)

## CONISTON • map 11D2

### CONISTON LODGE HOTEL
Sunny Brow, LA21 8HH

A family-run hotel offering very high standards of comfort, yet retaining a homely feel with country-cottage-style furnishing. The dining room serves excellent home-made cuisine, presented with originality and flair. Comfortable accommodation with beautiful views. The warm welcome and good service is vouched for by the large number of repeat bookings every year.

**DOUBLE ROOM:** from £30 to £40
**FOOD:** from £15 to £20
**Hours:** breakfast 8.30am-9.30am, dinner 7pm-7.30pm, closed Christmas.
**Cuisine:** ENGLISH - traditional English and local dishes such as freshly caught Coniston char. Full Lakeland-style breakfast.
**Cards:** Visa, Access, AmEx.
**Other points:** licensed, no-smoking area, residents' lounge, vegetarian meals.
**Rooms:** 3 double rooms, 3 twin rooms. All with TV, radio, tea/coffee-making facilities.
**Directions:** turn up hill at crossroads by filling station on A593.
ANTHONY & ELIZABETH ROBINSON ☎(015394) 41201

## FAR SAWREY • map 11D2

### THE SAWREY HOTEL
Near Ambleside, LA22 0LQ

This family-run country hotel provides a welcoming and friendly service and excellent home-cooking. Close to Windermere car ferry and Hawkshead; ideally situated for touring the Lake District.

**DOUBLE ROOM:** from £20 to £30
**SINGLE ROOM:** up to £25
**FOOD:** up to £15
**Hours:** lunch 11am-2.30pm, Sunday 12noon-

---

2.30pm, dinner 7pm-8.45pm, closed mid-December until end December.

**Cuisine:** ENGLISH - Windermere char (in season), fresh and smoked Esthwaite trout, home-made soups and gateaux.

**Cards:** Visa, Access, Switch, MasterCard, Eurocard, Delta.

**Other points:** fully licensed, Sunday lunch, children welcome, vegetarian meals to order, special summer and winter breaks.

**Rooms:** 4 single rooms, 10 double rooms, 5 twin rooms, 3 family rooms. All with TV, telephone, tea/coffee-making facilities.

**Directions:** on the B5285 road to Hawkshead, 1 mile from Windermere car ferry.

DAVID D. BRAYSHAW ☎(015394) 43425

## GRANGE-OVER-SANDS • map 11D2

### NETHERWOOD HOTEL
Lindale Road, LA11 6ET

*An imposing hotel enjoying a prime position overlooking Morecambe Bay on the fringe of the Lake District. Inside, the oak panelling and log fires provide an atmosphere of old-world luxury and comfort. In the restaurant, dishes include roast rack of venison Caroline, local venison roasted pink, served on a bed of tagliatelle with wild mushrooms, and a sauce Robert.*

DOUBLE ROOM: from £40 to £50
SINGLE ROOM: from £40 to £50
FOOD: from £15 to £20 ☝

**Hours:** breakfast 7.30am-10am, lunch 12.30pm-2pm, dinner 7pm-8.30pm, open all year.

**Cuisine:** MODERN ENGLISH - imaginative home-cooked dishes using local produce; breast of chicken filled with Cumberland sausagemeat, apples and cranberries, wrapped in puff pastry.

**Cards:** Visa, Access, Switch.

**Other points:** Sunday lunch, children welcome, swimming pool, spa bath, beauty salon, solarium, steam room.

**Rooms:** 4 single rooms, 10 double rooms, 8 twin room, 7 family rooms.

**Directions:** 600 yards from Grange-over-Sands railway station.

MR J.D. & MR M.P. FALLOWFIELD ☎(015395) 32552 Fax(015395) 34121

## HAWKSHEAD • map 11D2

### GRIZEDALE LODGE HOTEL & RESTAURANT
Hawkshead, LA22 0QL

*Situated two miles south of Hawkshead on the Satterthwaite road in the heart of Grizedale Forest, midway between Coniston Water and Lake Windermere. The hotel is approached down a small country road and provides an elegant and relaxing retreat in a superb, peaceful setting. Les Routiers Newcomer of the Year 1986.*

DOUBLE ROOM: from £30 to £40
SINGLE ROOM: from £35 to £45
FOOD: from £15 to £20 ☝

**Hours:** breakfast 8.30am-9.15am, lunch 12.15am-1.45pm, dinner 7pm-8pm, closed January until mid-February.

**Cuisine:** ENGLISH / FRENCH - Cumbrian specialities such as Derwentwater duck, Grizedale venison and Lake Esthwaite trout. Bar lunches available.

**Cards:** Visa, Access.

**Other points:** licensed, residents' lounge, residents' bar.

**Rooms:** 9 double rooms. All with en suite, TV, tea/coffee-making facilities, telephone. All rooms are non-smoking.

**Directions:** on the road to Grizedale visitor centre from Hawkshead.

MR AND MRS R.V. DAWSON ☎(015394) 36532 Fax(015394) 36572

### KINGS ARMS HOTEL
The Square, LA22 0NZ

*Situated in the picturesque village of Hawkshead, close to Beatrix Potter's house, this 16th century pub is ideally positioned for fishing and walking. Fishing holidays arranged at no extra charge*

DOUBLE ROOM: from £20 to £30
SINGLE ROOM: from £29 to £34
FOOD: up to £15    CLUB

**Hours:** lunch 12noon-2.30pm, Sunday 12noon-2.30pm, dinner 6pm-9.30pm, Sunday 7pm-9.30pm, bar open 11am-11pm, bar open Sunday 12noon-10.30pm.

**Cuisine:** ENGLISH - home-cooking, e.g., steak-and-kidney pie, plus other dishes using local fish and game produce.

**Cards:** Visa, Access.

**Other points:** Sunday lunch, children welcome, pets allowed.

**Rooms:** 9 double rooms, 3 twin rooms, 2 family rooms. Also self-catering cottages.

**Directions:** situated within the village of Hawkshead on B5285.

MRS R. JOHNSON ☎(015394) 36372

## KENDAL • map 11D3

### FINKLES RESTAURANT
Yard 34, Finkle Street, LA9 4BW

*A 300-year-old building occupying one of Kendal's famous labyrinthine `yards' behind the main street. A variety of dishes are served by friendly, efficient staff. Seating now available for up to 130 people.*

FOOD: from £15 to £20    CLUB

**Hours:** meals Monday-Saturday all day 9.30am-9.30pm, Sunday 10am-3.30pm.

**Cuisine:** CONTINENTAL - crepes, pizzas, gateaux.

**Cards:** Visa, Access, Switch.

**Other points:** pets allowed, coaches by prior arrangement, children welcome, afternoon tea.

**Directions:** behind the main street in Kendal.

MR & MRS STANWORTH ☎(01539) 727325

### THE KENDAL ARMS HOTEL
72 Milnthorpe Road, PR2 2NL

*A listed building, around 150 years old, serving wholesome good pub food in pleasant surroundings. It is a typical town-style pub, very popular with locals and business people working nearby. Ideal location from which to tour and explore all other Lakeland amenities.*

DOUBLE ROOM: up to £20

FOOD: up to £15  `CLUB`

**Hours:** breakfast 7am-9.30am, lunch 12noon-2pm, dinner 7pm-9pm.

**Cuisine:** ENGLISH - a mixture of classic and modern English cuisine prepared to a high standard.

**Cards:** Visa, Access.

**Other points:** garden, residents' lounge, open bank holidays, pets allowed, licensed.

**Directions:** M5, junction 17 onto A4018. Right at second roundabout, then right at junction.

GEORGE WARDMAN ☎(01539) 720956 `Fax`(01772) 722470

---

## KESWICK • map 11C2

---

### DERWENTWATER HOTEL
Portinscale, CA12 5RE

*Enjoying a breathtaking location on the shores of Lake Derwentwater in the peaceful village of Portinscale, the hotel offers the ultimate in luxury and comfort. The Deer's Leap restaurant is an oasis for lovers of good food and wine, whilst the bedrooms are individually furnished to a very high standard.*

DOUBLE ROOM: from £40 to £50

SINGLE ROOM: from £67

FOOD: from £15 to £20 `CLUB`

**Hours:** breakfast 7.30am-9.30am, lunch bar meals 12noon-2.30pm, dinner 7pm-9.30pm, open bank holidays.

**Cuisine:** speciality dishes and varied menus, using fresh local produce and offering healthy eating options and vegetarian food.

**Cards:** Visa, Access, Diners, AmEx.

**Other points:** conservatory, deluxe suites and four poster bedded rooms, afternoon teas, licensed, children welcome, outdoor play area and games room, self-catering cottages and apartments available.

**Rooms:** 52 bedrooms. All en suite, with TV, radio, telephone, tea/coffee-making facilities, trouser press and hairdryer.

**Directions:** off the A66 in the village of Portinscale, the hotel is by Derwentwater lake.

DIAMENT LTD ☎(017687) 72538 `Fax`(017687) 71002

---

### HIGHFIELD HOTEL
The Heads, CA12 5ER

*Friendly, family-run hotel with superb views of Derwentwater and the mountains. The hotel is opposite the miniature golf course, on a quiet road only minutes from the lake and market square. Bread baked on the premises, and fresh produce used in all dishes.*

DOUBLE ROOM: from £20 to £30

FOOD: up to £15

**Hours:** breakfast 8.30am-9.15am, dinner 6.30pm-7.30pm (to be ordered by 6pm), closed November until March.

**Cuisine:** BRITISH

**Other points:** central heating, children welcome, residents' lounge, garden.

**Rooms:** 5 single room, 8 double rooms, 3 twin rooms, 3 family rooms. Most rooms are en suite.

**Directions:** A66 to Keswick, second entry to Keswick via roundabout, left at T-junction, next right signed Borrowdale, second right after petrol station.

MR & MRS R.M. JORDAN ☎(017687) 72508

---

### IVY HOUSE HOTEL
Braithwaite, CA12 5SY

*Once a 17th century yeoman farmer's house, this beautiful oak-beamed building is tucked away in the corner of a typical Cumbrian village. The restaurant offers an interesting and imaginative menu, and both the proprietors and staff pride themselves in offering a warm welcome and personal service.*

DOUBLE ROOM: from £30 to £40

SINGLE ROOM: from £25 to £35

FOOD: from £15 to £20

**Hours:** breakfast 8.30am-9am, dinner 7pm-7.30pm, closed January.

**Cuisine:** MODERN ENGLISH - chicken stuffed with mango served with a creamy saffron sauce; salmon with ginger and sultanas; haunch of venison with port wine and redcurrant sauce.

**Cards:** Visa, Access, Diners, AmEx.

**Other points:** licensed, no-smoking area, pets by prior arrangement.

**Rooms:** 2 single rooms, 8 double rooms, 2 twin rooms. All en suite with TV, telephone, hair dryer, tea/coffee-making facilities.

**Directions:** north-west from Keswick on A66; Braithwaite is signposted after two miles.

NICK & WENDY SHILL ☎(017687) 78338

---

### THE LEATHES HEAD
Borrowdale, CA12 5UY

*A fine Edwardian country house hotel located in two and a half acres of grounds. It is ideally situated for exploring the Lake District National Park. All the bedrooms have delightful open views of the surrounding fells. A wide range of recreational activities are available locally.*

DOUBLE ROOM: from £30 to £40

SINGLE ROOM: from £30 to £40

FOOD: from £15 to £20  `CLUB`

---

**Cuisine:** local game, salmon and trout.
**Cards:** Visa, MasterCard.
**Other points:** packed lunches on request, central heating, log fires, television lounge, fully licensed.
**Rooms:** 9 bedrooms. All with TV, telephone, radio, hair dryer, baby-listening device and tea/coffee-making facilities.
**Directions:** B5289 Borrowdale road from Keswick.
☎(017687) 77247 **Fax**(017687) 77363

### QUEENS HOTEL
Main Street, CA12 5JF
*An old coaching inn, originally the posting house. The town is on the busy A66 to the north of the Lakes. The hay loft and stables have been converted to provide a cosy bar known as Ye Olde Queens Head.*
DOUBLE ROOM: from £20 to £30
FOOD: up to £15
**Hours:** breakfast 8am-9.30am, lunch 10am-5pm, bar meals 12noon-9pm, dinner 6.30pm-9pm.
**Cuisine:** ENGLISH - traditional British dishes.
**Cards:** Visa, Access, Diners, AmEx.
**Other points:** licensed, Sunday lunch, children welcome, coaches by prior arrangement
**Rooms:** 9 single rooms, 20 double rooms, 8 family rooms.
**Directions:** in the market square in Keswick. Off the A66.
PETER JAMES WILLIAMS ☎(017687) 73333
**Fax**(017687) 71144

### WOODLANDS COUNTRY GUEST HOUSE
Ireby, CA5 1EX
*An elegant Victorian vicarage built of local sandstone, retaining many of the building's original features such as open fires and a grand staircase. Standing in an acre of grounds, Woodlands enjoys magnificent views over the tranquil northern fells and is an excellent base from which to explore the Lakes and attractions of North Cumbria.*
DOUBLE ROOM: from £20 to £30
SINGLE ROOM: up to £25
FOOD: under £15
**Cuisine:** set menus offering freshly prepared home-cooked meals such as local trout pan-fried with Pernod and mushrooms, and incorporating vegetarian selections.
**Cards:** Visa, AmEx, Switch, MasterCard, Eurocard, Delta, Electron.
**Other points:** licensed, central heating, no-smoking establishment, children catered for (please check for age limits), pets welcome, suitable for wheelchair users, vegetarian meals, parking.
**Rooms:** 8 bedrooms, all en suite, 3 on the ground floor. All with TV, alarm, hair dryer, trouser press and tea/coffee making facilities.
☎(016973) 71791 **Fax**(016973) 71482

### THE COPPER KETTLE
3-5 Market Street, LA62 AU
*A 16th century building on the main street of this busy market town. Mr Gamble is a member of the Société Gastronomique Française, evident in the excellent meals produced. Kirkby Lonsdale is a charming market town, and a good base for touring the Lakes and the Yorkshire Dales.*
DOUBLE ROOM: up to £20
SINGLE ROOM: up to £25
FOOD: up to £15    CLUB
**Hours:** meals all day 12noon-9pm, lunch 12noon-3pm, high tea 3pm-6.30pm, dinner 6.30pm-9pm.
**Cuisine:** ENGLISH - roasts, steaks and dishes cooked in wine.
**Cards:** All cards.
**Other points:** licensed, Sunday lunch, children welcome.
**Rooms:** 4 bedrooms. All with TV, tea/coffee-making facilities.
**Directions:** from M6 junction 36, follow signs to Kirkby Lonsdale; Market Street is on left.
MR & MRS GAMBLE ☎(015242) 71714

### THE SPORTSMAN'S RESTAURANT & MARCH BANK HOTEL
Scotsdyke, CA6 5XP
*The `Last Hotel in England' is an old country house with beautiful views over the River Esk. Personally run by the Moore family, you are assured of a warm welcome and excellent service in both the hotel and restaurant. The food is of a very high standard, yet offers excellent value for money. Highly recommended. Fishing available. A Les Routiers Casserole Award winner for four years running.*
DOUBLE ROOM: from £20 to £30
SINGLE ROOM: from £25 to £35
FOOD: from £15 to £20
**Hours:** breakfast 8am-9am, lunch 12noon-2pm, dinner 6pm-8.45pm.
**Cuisine:** BRITISH - specialities include locally smoked salmon, wild salmon, trout, steaks, game.
**Cards:** Visa, Access, AmEx.
**Other points:** licensed, Sunday lunch, no-smoking area, children welcome, private salmon fishing, 3 acres of grounds.
**Rooms:** 1 single room, 3 double rooms. All with TV, tea/coffee-making facilities.
**Directions:** 3 miles north of Longtown on the A7. 9 miles from M6, junction 44.
THE MOORE FAMILY ☎(01228) 791325

### SHEPHERDS INN
Near Penrith, CH10 1HF
*An 18th century pub, built of traditional Cumberland stone, nestling at the foot of Hartside Pass in the northern Pennines. Serves fine traditional*

beers and extensive, original, home-prepared meals. Winner of the 1990 Les Routiers Cheeseboard Award for their outstanding cheese selection. Casserole Award winner 1991, 1992, 1993, 1994 and 1995. 1993 Publican Catering Pub of the Year. Holiday cottages available in village - brochure on request.
FOOD: up to £15 🍽 📖
Hours: lunch 11am-2.30pm, Sunday 12noon-2.30pm, dinner 6pm-10pm, Sunday 7pm-10pm, closed Christmas day.
Cuisine: INTERNATIONAL - many home-made dishes such as spare ribs, chicken Leoni, rogan gosht. Choice of 26 different cheeses for ploughmans, and a range of exotic pickles.
Cards: Visa, Access, Diners, AmEx, Switch.
Other points: open-air dining, Sunday lunch, children welcome.
Directions: on the A686 in Melmerby.
MARTIN & CHRISTINE BAUCUTT ☎(01768) 881217

## PENRITH • map 11C3

### YANWATH GATE INN
Yanwath, CA10 2LF
A lovely olde-worlde inn of 300 years, providing all patrons with a warm welcome, excellent service and a homely atmosphere - not forgetting the superb, home-cooked meals on offer. Situated in the village of Yanwath, the inn is conveniently located for visiting Penrith town, Ullswater Lake and Lowther Park.
FOOD: up to £15
Hours: lunch 12noon-2pm, dinner 6.30pm-9.30pm.
Cuisine: FRENCH / BRITISH - home-cooked meals offering excellent value for money.
Cards: Visa, Access, AmEx.
Other points: parking, children welcome, open-air dining, vegetarian meals, traditional Sunday lunch.
Directions: take the A6 from Penrith south towards Shap; turn right after Eamont Bridge.
IAN & SUE RHIND ☎(01768) 62386

## SEDBERGH • map 11D3

### THE DALESMAN COUNTRY INN
Main Street, LA10 5BN
An olde-worlde stone-built country inn, renovated by local craftsmen and situated in a village `frozen in time'. Decorated in a country style throughout, with traditional log fires, this is a popular retreat for locals and tourists alike. A nice place to `get away from it all'. Winter breaks very popular.
DOUBLE ROOM: from £20 to £30
SINGLE ROOM: from £25 to £40
FOOD: up to £15
Hours: breakfast 8.30am-9.30am, lunch 12noon-2pm, dinner 6pm-9.30pm.
Cuisine: ENGLISH - grills and steaks, gammon, local lamb chops, fresh salmon home-made Cumberland sauce, daily specials and roasts every Sunday.
Cards: Visa, Access.

Other points: licensed, Sunday lunch, children welcome, afternoon tea, vegetarian meals.
Rooms: 1 single room, 1 double room, 1 twin room, 3 double/family rooms. All en suite with TV, tea/coffee-making facilities, iron, hair dryer, toiletries. One of the family rooms is a cottage with double room and single room.
Directions: first pub on left entering Sedbergh, 5 miles from junction 37 of the M6.
BARRY & IRENE GARNETT ☎(015396) 21183

## WINDERMERE • map 11D2

### THE VILLAGE RESTAURANT
Victoria Street, LA23 1AW
Located in the old town of Windermere, this warm and friendly restaurant comes highly recommended. The extensive and varied a la carte menu is accompanied by an interesting wine list incorporating new world wines.
FOOD: from £10 to £20
Hours: dinner 6pm-10pm, open bank holidays, closed mid-November to mid-February.
Cuisine: ENGLISH / CONTINENTAL - home-cooked food with house specialities such as grilled salmon with lime, butter and hollandaise sauce, and chicken in tarragon mustard sauce.
Cards: Visa, Access.
Other points: licensed, vegetarian meals, no-smoking, baby-changing facilities.
Directions: from Kendal take the A591, turn into Windemere, restaurant on left.
DAVID & TRISH COURTMAN ☎(01539) 443429

### BECKMEAD HOUSE
5 Park Avenue, LA23 2AR
Delightful stone-built Victorian house, with a good reputation for high standards, comfort and friendliness. The breakfasts are famous. Convenient for lake, shops, restaurants and golf course.
DOUBLE ROOM: up to £20
SINGLE ROOM: up to £20
Hours: breakfast 8.30am-9am.
Cuisine: BREAKFAST
Other points: central heating, children welcome, residents' lounge, no evening meal, vegetarian meals.
Rooms: 1 single room, 2 double rooms, 1 twin room, 1 family room. All with TV, tea/coffee-making facilities.
Directions: M6 junction 36, westbound on A590 for three miles. A591 to Windermere.
MRS DOROTHY HEIGHTON ☎(015394) 42757

### GREEN GABLES GUEST HOUSE
37 Broad Street, LA23 2AB
A small, friendly guest house with very pretty bedrooms providing clean, warm, comfortable accommodation, close to local amenities, bus and railway station. Guests are assured of a warm welcome, for the Green Gables' motto is

`cleanliness, friendliness and a good hearty breakfast'.
DOUBLE ROOM: up to £20
SINGLE ROOM: up to £20
**Hours:** breakfast 8.30am, closed Christmas and New Year's day.
**Cuisine:** BREAKFAST
**Other points:** central heating, children catered for (please check age limits), residents' lounge, special breaks, no evening meal.
**Rooms:** 2 single rooms, 3 double rooms, 1 twin room, 2 family rooms. All with TV, hair dryer, tea/coffee-making facilities. Some rooms are en suite.
**Directions:** leave M6 at junction 36, A591 to Windermere. Turn left at the Windermere Hotel proceed to pedestrian crossing and turn left.
MRS SHEILA LAWLESS ☎(015394) 43886

### THE HIDEAWAY HOTEL
Phoenix Way, LA23 1DB
*A delightful Victorian stone building, The Hideaway has a reputation for good food, value and service. The easy access to the Lakes, a beautifully tended garden and well-appointed rooms keep people returning.*
DOUBLE ROOM: from £20 to £40
SINGLE ROOM: from £25 to £35
FOOD: up to £15 ☜ ≡
**Hours:** breakfast 8.30am-9.30am, dinner 7.30pm-8.30pm, open February until December.
**Cuisine:** ENGLISH / CONTINENTAL - modern English cuisine with continental influences. Menu changes daily. Hideaway crepes a speciality.
**Other points:** children welcome, afternoon tea, residents' lounge, garden, pets allowed.
**Rooms:** 3 single rooms, 6 double rooms, 4 twin rooms, 2 family rooms, all en suite and with tea/coffee-making facilities, TV, telephone, radio, alarm, hair dryer. Trouser press and room service available on request.
**Directions:** situated on Phoenix Way off Ambleside Road (A591).
MRS GORNALL & MR SUMMERLEE ☎(015394) 43070

### M & J'S FISH RESTAURANT
Birch Street, LA23 1EG
*A Swiss/Italian-style restaurant serving modern continental and speciality fish dishes, including vegetarian, vegan and childrens choices. The atmosphere is warm and friendly and attracts a mixed clientele of all ages. Situated in the centre of English Lakeland, with hiking, fishing, walking and endless other activities nearby.*
FOOD: from £15 to £20
**Hours:** 10.30am-10pm, closed Monday, Christmas day, Boxing day and New Year's day.
**Cuisine:** MODERN CONTINENTAL - speciality fish dishes plus char-grilled venison, fillet of beef and duck `duet`, vegetarian and children's dishes.
**Cards:** Visa, Access, AmEx.
**Other points:** licensed, no-smoking establishment,

patio, public telephone.
**Directions:** Windermere town centre.
MEL & JAN PARES
☎(015394) 42522

### ST JOHN'S LODGE
Lake Road, LA23 2EQ
*A small, private hotel centrally situated for touring the Lake District and only ten minutes' walk from the Lake Pier. Mini-breaks off-season. Facilities of local country sports club available to residents.*
DOUBLE ROOM: up to £25
SINGLE ROOM: up to £28
FOOD: up to £15
**Hours:** breakfast 8.15am-9am, dinner 7pm (to be ordered by 6pm), closed December and January.
**Cuisine:** ENGLISH - all dishes made from fresh, local produce. Will cater for vegetarians.
**Cards:** Visa, Access, MasterCard, Eurocard.
**Other points:** central heating, children catered for (please check for age limits), residents' lounge, residents' bar.
**Rooms:** 1 single room, 8 double rooms, 2 twin rooms, 3 family rooms. All with en suite, TV, tea/coffee-making facilities.
**Directions:** midway between Windermere village and Bowness on the A5074.
RAY & DOREEN GREGORY ☎(015394) 43078

### THORNBANK HOTEL
Thornbarrow Road, LA23 2EW
*Thornbank is a family-run hotel ideally situated in a pleasant residential area of Windermere in the beautiful Lake District, just a short distance from the lake shore. Bedrooms are fully-equipped with many modern facilities, including Sky TV, and there is a comfortable guest lounge with ample tourist information. Windermere is an excellent location for touring and exploring, with endless amenities.*
DOUBLE ROOM: up to £20
SINGLE ROOM: up to £25
FOOD: up to £15
**Hours:** breakfast 8.45am, dinner 6.45pm.
**Cuisine:** ENGLISH
**Cards:** Visa, Access, AmEx.
**Other points:** parking, children welcome, open bank holidays, no-smoking area, residents' lounge, vegetarian meals.
**Rooms:** 9 bedrooms, 4 en suite, 1 deluxe four-poster. All rooms have TV, tea/coffee-making facilities.
**Directions:** A591, turn left at Windermere Hotel towards Bowness; \ mile along is Thornbarrow Road.
MR R. & MRS P. CHARNOCK ☎(015394) 43724

---

**Join Les Routiers Discovery Club
FREE!  See page 34 for details.**

# GREATER MANCHESTER

## ALTRINCHAM • map 8A5

### WOODLAND PARK HOTEL
Wellington Road, Timperley, WA15 7RG
*The Woodland Park is a delightful family-owned
hotel, set in spacious grounds in a secluded
residential area. Brian and his attentive, courteous
staff pride themselves on personal care and
attention to detail. All the bedrooms are individually
designed and furnished, while the restaurant,
conservatory, bar and reception have all been
designed in an appealing country house style with a
warm, rustic colour scheme.*
DOUBLE ROOM: from £50
SINGLE ROOM: from £55
FOOD: from £15 to £20
**Hours:** breakfast 7am-9.30am, lunch 12noon-2pm,
dinner 7pm-10pm.
**Cuisine:** ENGLISH - mainly traditional dishes made
from fresh produce.
**Cards:** Visa, Access, Diners, AmEx.
**Other points:** parking, children welcome,
vegetarian meals, no-smoking area, residents'
lounge.
**Rooms:** 45 bedrooms. All with en suite, TV,
telephone, radio, hair dryer, tea/coffee-making
facilities.
**Directions:** M56 from Manchester Airport, exit onto
A560 to Altrincham.
MS PAT GRANGE ☎(0161) 928 8631 Fax(0161)
941 2821

## BOLTON • map 8A5

### GEORGIAN HOUSE HOTEL
Manchester Road, Blackrod, BL6 5RU
*This large Georgian building is decorated to a high
standard and provides a very comfortable stay.
Attractive meals are presented in the relaxed
atmosphere of the restaurant. With its five
conference suites and banqueting facilities, it is
ideal for either weddings or conferences. Dinner
dances on Fridays and Saturdays in the Regency
Restaurant.*
DOUBLE ROOM: from £30 to £40
SINGLE ROOM: over £50
FOOD: from £15 to £20
**Hours:** breakfast 7am-10am, bar snacks 11am-3pm,
lunch 12noon-2pm, dinner 7pm-10pm.
**Cuisine:** ENGLISH / CONTINENTAL - table d'hôte
and à la carte menu available using the best of the
local fresh produce at market and in season.
**Cards:** Visa, Access, Diners, AmEx, Switch.
**Other points:** licensed, Sunday lunch, children
welcome, afternoon tea, pets allowed, leisure
centre.
**Rooms:** 15 single rooms, 49 double rooms, 26 twin
rooms, 3 family rooms, 8 suites. All with TV, radio,
telephone, tea/coffee-making facilities, hair dryer,

satellite TV, trouser-press.
**Directions:** on the A6, 1.5 miles from M61 junction
6.
MRS DIANE NORBURY ☎(01942) 814598
Fax(01942) 813427

### WATERGATE TOLL
Watergate Drive, Over Hulton, BL5 1BU
*This attractive converted old farmhouse is a very
popular meeting point with people of all ages,
whether local or just passing through. With good
food, attentive service and a congenial atmosphere,
this is a restaurant/bar that you will want to return
to again and again.*
FOOD: up to £15    CLUB
**Hours:** meals all day (Sunday-Thursday) 11.30am-
9pm, Friday 11.30am-9.30pm, Saturday 11.30am-
10pm.
**Cuisine:** ENGLISH / INTERNATIONAL - à la carte
menu, speciality menu, bar snacks and children's
menu.
**Cards:** Visa, Access, Diners, AmEx.
**Other points:** parking, children welcome,
vegetarian meals, traditional Sunday lunch,
afternoon tea.
**Directions:** take exit 4 on M61, turn left and then
second exit off roundabout, first exit right into
Service Road.
MR M.E. DADE ☎(01204) 64989

## BURY • map 8A5

### THE BOLHOLT
Walshaw Road, BL8 1PU
*A large, extended country house set in 50 acres of
parkland and lakes. The warm and courteous
hospitality, open fires and elegant surroundings
make this hotel a joy to visit.*
DOUBLE ROOM: from £20 to £30
SINGLE ROOM: from £45 to £55
FOOD: up to £15
**Hours:** breakfast 7am 8.45am, lunch 12noon 2pm,
dinner 7pm-9.30pm.
**Cuisine:** ENGLISH - à la carte. Traditional English,
fillet steak Wellington.
**Cards:** Visa, Access, Diners, AmEx.
**Other points:** licensed, Sunday lunch, children
welcome, garden, pets allowed.
**Rooms:** 10 single rooms, 28 double rooms, 9 twin
rooms.
**Directions:** A58 from Bury towards Bolton, fork
right for Tottington, fork extreme left at Dusty Miller
Pub.
STEFAN SIKORSKI ☎(0161) 763 7007 Fax(0161)
763 1789

### ROSCO'S EATING HOUSE
173 Radcliffe Road, BL9 9LN

*Owned and run by two chefs, the atmosphere is definitely `foody'. The unassuming frontage hides a simple and welcoming restaurant which specializes in original dishes served in a distinctive style. The charcoal grill is placed so that everyone can see their steaks cooking. Booking advisable at weekends, as Rosco's is very popular with locals and other caterers - hence the late opening.*

FOOD: from £15 to £20

**Hours:** dinner Friday 6.30pm-2am, Saturday, 4.30pm-2am, Sunday 7.30pm-12midnight, Wednesday-Thursday 7.30pm-12midnight, closed Monday and Tuesday.

**Cuisine:** FRENCH / WORLD CUISINE - from simple meals costing a few pounds to original dishes with imaginative sauces freshly made to order. Large selection of fresh vegetables.

**Cards:** Visa, Access.

**Other points:** Sunday lunch, limited disabled access, children welcome, coaches by prior arrangement

**Directions:** Whitfield Road from centre, right at traffic lights near Pack Horse Pub.

STUART & JACQUELINE RUSCOE ☎(0161) 797 5404 Fax(0161) 794 6399

## HYDE • map 8A5

### NEEDHAMS FARM
Uplands Road, Werneth Low, Gee Cross, near Hyde, SK14 3AQ

*A small working farm, dating from the 16th century, which offers very comfortable accommodation and food of an excellent standard. The inspector declared it `a wonderful place to stay', and noted it was ideal for children, as there are many friendly animals on the farm. Perfect base for walking, riding and golf, with many local places of interest nearby. Highly recommended.*

DOUBLE ROOM: up to £20
SINGLE ROOM: up to £25
FOOD: up to £15

**Hours:** breakfast 6.30am-11am, dinner 7pm-9.30pm.

**Cuisine:** ENGLISH

**Cards:** Visa, Access, AmEx.

**Other points:** children welcome, special breaks, residents' lounge, cots.

**Rooms:** 1 single room, 4 double rooms, 1 triple room, 1 family room. All with TV, radio, alarm, telephone, tea/coffee-making facilities. Some rooms are en suite.

**Directions:** junction 15 on M66; off A560. Between Werneth Low Country Park and Etherow Valley.

MRS WALSH ☎(0161) 368 4610 Fax(0161) 367 9106

## MANCHESTER • map 8A5

### ELM GRANGE HOTEL
561 Wilmslow Road, Withington, M20 4GJ

*A family-run commercial hotel situated approximately 20 minutes' drive from the city centre, exhibition centre and the airport. In a main road position with a good bus service to the main shopping area, it is easily located by following the signposts to Christie Hospital, which is opposite the hotel. Good food from an extensive menu.*

DOUBLE ROOM: from £20 to £30
SINGLE ROOM: from £25 to £35
FOOD: up to £15  CLUB

**Hours:** breakfast 7.15am-9.30am.

**Cuisine:** ENGLISH

**Cards:** Visa, Access, AmEx.

**Other points:** children welcome, central heating, residents' lounge, residents' bar.

**Rooms:** 32 bedrooms. All with TV, telephone, tea/coffee-making facilities, radio, alarm, iron, video, trouser-press.

**Directions:** from A34 at West Didsbury, take B5117 to Didsbury; hotel 1 mile on right.

GORDON W. DELF ☎(0161) 445 3336 Fax(0161) 445 3336

### HOTEL CORNELIUS
175 Manchester Road, Chorlton-cum-Hardy, M16 0ED

*An Edwardian manor house with a warm, welcoming atmosphere. Its location on the B5217 about a mile outside the city centre makes it extremely popular with business people and an ideal location for seminars, working breakfasts and conferences.*

DOUBLE ROOM: from £30 to £40
FOOD: from £15 to £20

**Hours:** breakfast Monday-Friday 7am-9.30am, weekends 8am-10am, lunch and bar meals Monday-Friday 12noon-2pm, dinner and bar meals Monday-Saturday 6pm-11pm, Sunday 12noon-10pm, open bank holidays.

**Cuisine:** classic Italian dishes, pizza and pasta.

**Cards:** Access, Visa, AmEx, Diners, Switch, Delta

**Other points:** business conference and banqueting suites, bridal suite.

**Rooms:** 20 bedrooms. All en suite with tea/coffee-making facilities, satellite TV, direct dial telephone, hospitality tray, hair dryer, trouser press, room service.

**Directions:** Exit junction 7 of M63, taking A56 towards Manchester, A5067 to Trafford Bar, then B5217.

MR AND MRS O'CONNOR ☎(0161) 8629565 Fax(0161) 8629028

### THAT CAFE
1031-3 Stockport Road, Levenshulme, M19 2TB

*Situated three miles from Manchester city centre, That Café offers a good variety of both meat and vegetarian dishes. The atmosphere and decor are unique, with open fires, bric-a-brac, and 1930s and '40s music.*

FOOD: from £15 to £20

**Hours:** lunch 12.30am-3.30pm, dinner 7pm-11pm,

closed Monday evenings.
**Cuisine:** ENGLISH / CONTINENTAL - special
£14.95 table d'hôte menu, exclusive of coffee or
tea, Tuesday, Wednesday and Thursday and Friday
evenings. Daily menu change. Fresh fish. Three-
course Sunday lunch £10.95, main courses £6.95.
A la carte menu changes monthly.
**Cards:** Visa, Access, AmEx.
**Other points:** Sunday lunch, children welcome,
functions.
**Directions:** on the A6 between Manchester and
Stockport.
JOSEPH QUINN & STEPHEN KING ☎(0161) 432
4672

## RAMSBOTTOM • map 8A5

 **OLD MILL HOTEL & RESTAURANT**
Springwood, BL0 9DS
*Originally an old mill, this hotel has been
completely refurbished, achieving an attractive yet
comfortable atmosphere. With a combination of a
good choice of food and wine and attentive service,
both restaurants are well worth a visit.*
DOUBLE ROOM: from £30 to £40
FOOD: up to £15
**Hours:** breakfast 7.30am-9.30am, lunch 12noon-
2pm, dinner 6.30pm-10.30pm.
**Cuisine:** FRENCH / ITALIAN - two restaurants.
French cuisine: fish, steak, shellfish, casseroles.
Comprehensive wine list. Italian cuisine: pastas,
pizzas.
**Cards:** Visa, Access, Diners, AmEx.
**Other points:** licensed, Sunday lunch, swimming
pool, sauna, solarium, leisure centre, children
welcome, residents' lounge, garden.
**Rooms:** 12 single rooms, 12 double rooms, 12 twin
rooms. All with TV, telephone, tea/coffee-making
facilities.
**Directions:** off junction M66 with A56, situated on
A676 north of Manchester.
KAREN SACCO ☎(0170682) 2991

## ROCHDALE • map 8A5

AFTER EIGHT RESTAURANT
2 Edenfield Road, OL11 5AA
*This sumptuously decorated Victorian-style
restaurant offers a wide choice of superb dishes
from the à la carte menu. With excellent service
and a relaxing atmosphere, it is well worth a visit.*
FOOD: from £15 to £20
**Hours:** dinner from 7pm, closed first week of May.
**Cuisine:** MODERN ENGLISH / CONTINENTAL -
among the house specialities are the salmon and
asparagus parcel, baked fillet of brill, and duck
breast én croute.
**Cards:** Visa, Access, AmEx, Switch.
**Other points:** children welcome, vegetarian meals,
no-smoking in restaurant, garden.
**Directions:** on the A680 Blackburn Road, 5 minutes
from Rochdale town centre.
GEOFFREY TAYLOR ☎(01706) 46432

## WYTHENSHAWE • map 8A5

 **ROYALS HOTEL**
Altrincham Road, M22 4BJ

*On arrival you will immediately recognise that this
is a hotel which really cares about its guests. The
recently decorated bedrooms and public areas
provide a level of comfort and service which is
complemented by the small touches which make a
hotel special rather than adequate. Extremely well
situated for the motorway network and Manchester
airport. Special holiday breaks and conference
facilities available.*
DOUBLE ROOM: from £30 to £50
SINGLE ROOM: from £40 to £50
FOOD: from £10 to £20
**Hours:** breakfast 7am-9.30am, other meals from
12noon to 9.45pm. Open all year.
**Cuisine:** ENGLISH / CONTINENTAL - a widely
varied menu together with blackboard 'specials'
offering daily dishes which can be selected on a
pick and mix basis. Good wine list with wines by
the glass.
**Cards:** Visa, Access, Diners, AmEx
**Other points:** non-smoking area, licensed, central
heating, real log fires, 24 hour reception, night
porter, ironing facilities, valet/laundry service,
guests' garden, French spoken.
**Rooms:** 32 bedrooms, all with en suite facilities, TV,
direct dial telephone, tea/coffee-making facilities.
**Directions:** take exit 2 off M56 onto A560. Hotel is
2 miles from Manchester airport.
MR EBRAHAM HUKADAM
☎(0161) 998 9011 Fax(0161) 998 4641

# HUMBERSIDE

## BRIDLINGTON • map 12D6

### SEACOURT HOTEL
76 South Marine Drive, YO15 3NS

*The Seacourt Hotel stands quietly in a prime position overlooking the beautiful South Bay, with panoramic views of the old harbour, town and Flamborough Head. This is a hotel where quality abounds and is ideally situated for the many attractions which Bridlington and its surroundings have to offer. Newly opened is Annabels Restaurant which offers the finest food and wines, with the emphasis on fresh local produce. A comprehensive range of bar food is also available.*

DOUBLE ROOM: from £30 to £50
SINGLE ROOM: from £28 to £55
FOOD: from £15 to £20
**Hours:** lunch 12noon-2pm, dinner 6.30pm-10pm, open all year.
**Cuisine:** ENGLISH - table d'hôte and à la carte menus, with fish dishes, a house speciality and fresh local market produce. Children's menu.
**Cards:** Visa, Access.
**Other points:** licensed, Sunday lunch, no-smoking area, children catered for (please check for age limits), meals all day, residents' lounge, functions.
**Rooms:** 2 single rooms, 5 double rooms, 4 twin rooms, 1 family room. All with telephone, tea/coffee-making facilities, heating, satellite TV.
**Directions:** on South Marine Drive overlooking the bay.
ANNE & GEOFFREY HOLMES ☎(01262) 400872
Fax(01262 605247)

### WINSTON HOUSE HOTEL
5 South Street, YO15 3BY

*Situated near the seafront in Bridlington, this newly refurbished hotel offers guests excellent accommodation and a very good English restaurant with a continental theme. The daily-changing menu provides diners with a freshly prepared meal cooked to high standards.*

DOUBLE ROOM: up to £20
SINGLE ROOM: up to £25
FOOD: up to £15
**Hours:** breakfast 8am-8.45am, dinner 5pm-5.50pm.
**Cards:** Visa, Access.
**Other points:** children welcome, residents' lounge, no-smoking area, vegetarian meals.
**Rooms:** 2 single rooms, 10 double rooms, 2 twin rooms, 1 family room. All with satellite TV, tea/coffee-making facilities.
**Directions:** A165/A166, follow signs for South Beach; turn off seafront at lifeboat station.
DAVID & CAROL BOTHAM ☎(01262) 670216
Fax(01262) 670216

## BRIGG • map 9A3

### ARTIES MILL
Wressle Road, Castlethorpe, DN20 9LF

*This charming old windmill dates back to 1790, and the adjoining grain sheds have been converted into bars and restaurants with a pleasant and friendly atmosphere, while still retaining the fascinating mill features. Good food, comfortable accommodation and the warm friendly welcome from the proprietors combine to make this hotel `highly recommended'.*

DOUBLE ROOM: from £20 to £30
SINGLE ROOM: from £35 to £40
FOOD: up to £15    CLUB
**Hours:** breakfast 7am-9am, dinner 7pm-10pm, bar meals 11am-10pm.
**Cuisine:** ENGLISH - à la carte, table d'hôte, bar meals.
**Cards:** Visa, Access, Diners, AmEx.
**Other points:** licensed, open-air dining, Sunday lunch, children welcome, garden, functions, private dining, children welcome, cots, 24hr reception, left luggage.
**Rooms:** 8 double rooms, 17 twin rooms, 2 family rooms.
**Directions:** 1 mile from Brigg on the A18 and 5 miles from Scunthorpe.
IAN & DOREEN BRIGGS ☎(01652) 652094
Fax(01652) 657107

## CLEETHORPES • map 10A4

### AGRAH INDIAN RESTAURANT
7-9 Seaview Street, DN38 8EU

*The Agrah Indian Restaurant is decorated with brightly coloured pictures illustrating a story, and with Muslim-style wall panels. A broad clientele, including many thespians from the seasonal summer shows.*

FOOD: up to £15
**Hours:** lunch 12noon-2.30pm, dinner 6pm-12midnight.
**Cuisine:** INDIAN - Tandoori dishes.
**Cards:** Visa, Access.
**Other points:** licensed, open-air dining, Sunday lunch, children welcome.
**Directions:** Cleethorpes is four miles south of Grimsby on A46 and A16.
BASHIR MIAH ☎(01472) 698669

### STEELS CORNER HOUSE RESTAURANT
11-13 Market Street, DN35 8LY

*A popular and friendly restaurant, which continues to provide excellent value for money.*

FOOD: up to £15
**Hours:** breakfast 9am-11am, meals all day 9am-10pm.
**Cuisine:** ENGLISH - fish and chips. Grills. Business

lunches.
**Cards:** Visa, Access.
**Other points:** Sunday lunch, children welcome.
**Directions:** in the market place behind the Dolphin Hotel.
MR P. & MR K. OLIVER ☎(01472) 692644

## COTTINGHAM • map 12E6

### MANDARIN RESTAURANT
119 Hallgate, HU16 4DA
*A typically furnished Chinese-style restaurant, offering excellent cuisine in a friendly, warm atmosphere. Conveniently located. Helpful staff assist you in making a selection so that you will be sure to enjoy your meal.*
FOOD: up to £15
**Hours:** lunch 12noon-2pm, dinner 5pm-12midnight.
**Cuisine:** ORIENTAL / VEGETARIAN - Peking, Cantonese and vegetarian cuisine. Coffee specialities.
**Cards:** Visa, Access, Diners, AmEx.
**Other points:** licensed, Sunday lunch, children welcome, parking.
**Directions:** situated in Cottingham village centre.
WAI LUN CHUNG ☎(01482) 843475 Fax(01482) 875795

## HULL • map 12E6

### KINGSTOWN HOTEL
Hull Road, Hedon, HU12 8DJ
*A family-run luxury hotel with very high standards and a friendly, welcoming atmosphere. Good food excellently served in the restaurant and bar. Ideally situated for the continental ferry, rural Holderness with its seaside resorts, the historic towns of Hedon and Beverley, and the important city of Hull.*
DOUBLE ROOM: from £30 to £40
SINGLE ROOM: from £45 to £55
FOOD: from £15 to £20
**Hours:** breakfast 7am-9.30am, lunch 12noon-2.30pm, dinner 7pm-10pm.
**Cuisine:** ENGLISH - à la carte and table d'hôte menus served in the dining room and lounge bar.
**Cards:** Visa, Access, AmEx.
**Other points:** fully licensed, Sunday lunch, no-smoking area, children welcome, guide dogs, residents' lounge, conferences, baby-sitting, cots, 24hr reception, left luggage.
**Rooms:** 10 single rooms, 20 double rooms, 4 twin rooms. All with satellite TV, radio, telephone, tea/coffee-making facilities.
**Directions:** on eastern outskirts of Hull next to the roundabout at Hedon
SALLY READ ☎(01482) 890461 Fax(01482) 890713

### PEARSON PARK HOTEL
Pearson Park, HU5 2TQ
*Delightfully situated within a public ornamental park, one mile north of the city centre. Very popular with families and businessmen. The establishment has been under the same ownership for the last 30 years. Coffee-shop service weekday lunchtimes and a restaurant open in the evenings.*
DOUBLE ROOM: from £20 to £30
SINGLE ROOM: from £37 to £45
FOOD: up to £15 CLUB
**Hours:** breakfast 7.30am-9.15am, dinner 6.30pm-9pm, lunch 12.30am-2pm.
**Cuisine:** FRENCH / ENGLISH - daily specials, fresh local produce.
**Cards:** Visa, Access, Diners, AmEx.
**Other points:** Sunday lunch, children welcome, cots, 24hr reception, parking, residents' bar, residents' lounge, disabled access.
**Rooms:** 9 single rooms, 16 double rooms, 6 twin rooms, 1 family room.
**Directions:** take A1079 Beverley Road from city centre. After Mobil garage turn left onto Pearson Avenue which leads into the park.
MR & MRS D.A. ATKINSON ☎(01482) 343043 Fax(01482) 447679

## SCUNTHORPE • map 9A3

### BRIGGATE LODGE INN
Ermine Street, Broughton, DN20 0NQ
*An attractive hotel offering comfortable acommodation and fine cuisine using only the freshest of produce. Dishes may include mustard-glazed lamb chops, supreme of chicken fromage, and poached salmon steak with a lime sauce.*
DOUBLE ROOM: from £30 to £40
SINGLE ROOM: over £50
FOOD: from £20 to £25
**Hours:** breakfast 7am-10am, lunch 12noon-2pm, dinner 7pm-10pm, bar snacks 11am-11pm.
**Cuisine:** ENGLISH / FRENCH
**Cards:** Visa, Access, Diners, AmEx.
**Other points:** parking, children welcome, Sunday lunch, open bank holidays, no-smoking area, afternoon tea, Sunday dinner, disabled access, residents' lounge, vegetarian meals, garden, 27 hole championship golf course, floodlit driving range.
**Rooms:** 50 bedrooms.
**Directions:** 200 metres from junction 4 on M180. A18/A15.
MR A. MIDDLETON ☎(01652) 650770 Fax(01652) 650495

# ISLE OF MAN

## DOUGLAS • map 14E5

### INGLEWOOD HOTEL
Queens Promenade, IM2 4NF

*The Inglewood is a homely, Manx family-run hotel with a fine open outlook over the sea, sky and headlands. It is reputed for providing guests with good-quality accommodation and excellent food and service at very competitive rates. Situated close to all local amenities, the horse trams pass just outside the hotel as a means of convenient transport, and there are several lovely glens and walks within easy reach.*

DOUBLE ROOM: up to £20
SINGLE ROOM: up to £20
FOOD: up to £15

**Hours:** breakfast 8.30am-9.30am (earlier by arrangement), 6pm-7pm (later by arrangement), snacks 5pm-10pm.
**Cuisine:** BRITISH - traditional Manx cuisine using fresh farm produce.
**Other points:** children welcome, residents' lounge, no-smoking dining room, vegetarian meals (recognised by Vegetarian Society), travel arranged.
**Rooms:** 3 single rooms, 2 doubles rooms, 3 twin rooms, 13 family rooms. All with TV, hair dryer, tea/coffee-making facilities.
**Directions:** on the seafront, midway betweeen boat arrival pier and electric tram station. Horse trams pass the hotel.
BRIAN & ANNE HEAP ☎(01624) 674734
Fax(01624) 674734

### LA BRASSERIE
The Empress Hotel, Central Promenade, IM2 4RA

*An excellent restaurant situated below the Empress Hotel, serving an extensive choice of meals throughout the day. All dishes are prepared from fresh produce, well-cooked and attractively presented in generous proportions. The high-quality food is complemented by a good wine list and excellent service. Enjoy your meal in comfortable surroundings with a pleasant, relaxed atmosphere.*

DOUBLE ROOM: from £30 to £40
SINGLE ROOM: over £55
FOOD: up to £15

**Hours:** meals all day 10am-10.45pm, children's menu available until 7.30pm, open all year.
**Cuisine:** INTERNATIONAL - extensive menu, featuring fresh scallops wrapped in bacon with garlic butter, kidney and guiness pie, salmon hollandaise. Complemented by a good wine list.
**Cards:** Visa, Access, AmEx.
**Other points:** children catered for (please check for age limits), open all day, no-smoking area, afternoon tea, street parking, vegetarian meals, disabled access.
**Rooms:** 102 bedrooms. All with en suite, TV, radio, telephone, tea/coffee-making facilities, alarm.

**Directions:** directly beneath the Empress Hotel, Douglas Promenade. On seafront.
MAUREEN MCGEOWN ☎(01624) 661155
Fax(01624) 673554

### MIDLAND HOTEL
Loch Promenade, IM1 2LY

*At the Midland you can expect the personal attention of the owners, an excellent combination of good value and fine service, and comfortable accommodation. The hotel is in a perfect position, overlooking the bay and convenient for the shopping centre and the travel terminus. Visit the legendary Isle of Man and discover for yourself the many charms of this remarkable island.*

DOUBLE ROOM: up to £20
SINGLE ROOM: up to £25
FOOD: up to £15

**Hours:** breakfast 8.30am-9.15am, dinner 5.30pm, closed October until March.
**Cuisine:** BRITISH - appetizing meals available to residents.
**Cards:** Visa, Access, Diners, AmEx.
**Other points:** children welcome, residents' lounge, vegetarian meals, afternoon teas.
**Rooms:** 17 bedrooms. All with radio, alarm, iron, baby-listening device.
**Directions:** from the sea terminal, the Midland is 10 minutes' walk along the seafront.
DEREK & SYLVIA AKERMAN ☎(01624) 674990

### THE MV. "KING ORRY"-ISLE OF MAN STEAM PACKET FERRY COMPANY
Imperial Buildings, IM99 1AF

*A leisurely cruise on the "King Orry" passenger car ferry is a wonderful way to start any holiday! Enjoy the highest standards of personal care and wide range of on-board facilities which include a cinema, bars, lounges, coffee shops, children's play area and an excellent self-service restaurant. The ship provides year-round sailings between Liverpool, Heysham, Douglas.*

DOUBLE ROOM: from £30 to £40
FOOD: up to £15

**Hours:** breakfast 7.30am-11am, restaurant/bar open for lunch/bar meals 10.30am-5pm, dinner in restaurant 7.30pm-10pm (all sailings).
**Cuisine:** MODERN CONTINENTAL - Balanayre stew, vegetarian choices.
**Cards:** Visa, Access.
**Other points:** pets allowed, public telephone, residents' lounge, air conditioning, passenger lift, supervised play areas for children.
**Rooms:** 22 cabins all with tea/coffe-maker, TV, telephone. Executive lounge with Fax/phone facilities and steward service.
**Directions:** Regular sailings from Heysham and Liverpool.
MR STEPHEN QUIRKE ☎(01624) 612204

### SEFTON HOTEL
Harris Promenade, IM1 2RM

*Adjacent to the Gaiety Theatre, this hotel offers special `Island Theatre Weekends'. Whether you wish to enjoy a play or two, or simply relax, the Sefton Hotel is ideal. Good food is served in a pleasantly relaxed atmosphere. With a health club, indoor heated swimming pool and comfortable accommodation, this is just the place to return to after discovering the island. There are two bedrooms suitable for the disabled.*

DOUBLE ROOM: from £30 to £40
SINGLE ROOM: from £35 to £55
FOOD: up to £15
**Hours:** breakfast 7.30am-9.45am, lunch 12.30am-2pm, also bistro 11am-10pm, dinner 7.15pm-9.30pm, open bank holidays.
**Cuisine:** MODERN ENGLISH - dishes may include mushroom crepes with sauce mornay, grilled salmon with cucumber sauce, Manx ice cream.
**Cards:** Visa, Access, Switch.
**Other points:** licensed, poolside bar, no-smoking area, children welcome, afternoon tea, solarium, gym facilities, swimming pool, beauty therapy, sauna, coffee shop, conferences, disabled access, parking, close to island business centre and government buildings.
**Rooms:** 10 single rooms, 35 double rooms, 30 twin rooms, 5 family rooms.
**Directions:** centre of Douglas Promenade, next to the Gaiety Theatre.
CHRIS ROBERTSHAW ☎(01624) 626011
Fax(01624) 676004

## LAXEY • map 14E5

### BROWN'S CAFE & TEA ROOMS
Ham and Egg Terrace, IM4 7NY

*You are made to feel welcome from the moment you set foot inside this very special, family-run restaurant. Mrs Carey is determined that your meal will be memorable, and no effort is spared to provide all those little extra touches which mean so much. The menu is changed weekly or you can enjoy one of the celebrated `all day' breakfasts which attract diners from all over the island.*

FOOD: up to £15
**Hours:** breakfast all day. Lunch from 11.45am.
**Cuisine:** MAINLY TRADITIONAL ENGLISH - menu changes weekly.
**Other points:** parking.
**Directions:** at the start of the road to Laxey Wheel.
MRS ALISON CAREY ☎(01624) 862072
Fax(01624) 861705

## PORT ERIN • map 14E5

### THE FALCON'S NEST HOTEL
Station Road, IM9 6AF

*This attractive, family-run Georgian hotel, restored to its former elegance, provides comfort and a relaxing atmosphere, with superb quality service and cuisine to suit the most discerning visitor, whether on business or on holiday. The hotel is situated in the picturesque south-west of the island, overlooking Port Erin Bay and only two minutes' walk from the sheltered sandy beach.*

DOUBLE ROOM: from £20 to £30
FOOD: up to £15   CLUB
**Hours:** breakfast 7am-9.30am, lunch 12noon-2pm, bar meals 12noon-2pm, dinner 6pm-9pm, bar meals 6pm-7.30pm.
**Cuisine:** CONTINENTAL
**Cards:** Visa, Access, AmEx.
**Other points:** parking, children catered for (please check for age limits), pets allowed, conference facilities, residents' lounge, traditional Sunday lunch.
**Rooms:** 50 bedrooms. All with TV, telephone, radio, alarm, hair dryer, baby-listening device, tea/coffee-making facilities.
**Directions:** five miles south-west of airport, in centre of Port Erin.
ROBERT POTTS ☎(01624) 834077 Fax(01624) 835370

## RAMSEY • map 14E5

### HARBOUR BISTRO
5 East Street, IM8 1DN

*Comfortably furnished and enjoying a relaxed atmosphere, the Harbour Bistro offers an extensive menu with an emphasis on seafood. All dishes are well-cooked, attractively presented and served by helpful, friendly staff. Good wine list. Popular with locals and holiday-makers alike. The atmosphere is welcoming and relaxed.*

FOOD: up to £15
**Hours:** lunch 12noon-2pm, dinner 6.30pm-10.30pm, closed Tynwald Day, closed for 1 week in October and 2 weeks in January.
**Cuisine:** CONTINENTAL - dishes may include traditional roast duck with walnut stuffing, baked chicken breast and asparagus. Seafood specialities, and fresh lobster and Dover sole when available.
**Cards:** Visa, Access.
**Other points:** licensed, Sunday lunch, children welcome, special diets, street parking.
**Directions:** between harbour and Parliament Street.
KEN DEVANEY ☎(01624) 814182

# LANCASHIRE

### THE BROWN LEAVES COUNTRY HOTEL
Longsight Road, Copster Green, BB1 9EU
*An interesting and spacious bungalow-style hotel, where the proprietors believe in a hands-on approach. Well decorated and scrupulously clean, the hotel is ideally situated for exploring the beautiful Ribble valley, Ribchester with its Roman museum and nearby Whalley. The dining room offers good sensible home-cooking, with English roast beef a speciality.*
DOUBLE ROOM: from £20 to £30
SINGLE ROOM: from £25 to £40
FOOD: up to £15
**Hours:** breakfast 7am-9.30am, dinner (restaurant) 6.30pm-9.30pm, (bar) 6-11pm. Open all year - residents only.
**Cuisine:** traditional British-style roast beef.
**Cards:** Access,Visa,AmEx,Diners,Switch
**Other points:** parking, lounge bar, weekend breaks.
**Rooms:** 12 bedrooms en suite with tea/coffee maker, TV, alarm, hair dryer, baby listening device.
**Directions:** leave the M6 at junction 31 and proceed approximately 6 miles along the A59 towards Clitheroe.
MR A FISHER ☎(01254) 249523 Fax(01254) 245240

### MAY HOUSE RESTAURANT
208 Preston New Road, BB2 6PS
*This delightful restaurant offers diners a superb meal in a very friendly and welcoming atmosphere. Relax over an enjoyable meal with the soft tones of selected classical, jazz and easy-listening music helping to ease away the strains and pressures of the day.*
FOOD: from £15 to £30 CLUB
**Hours:** lunch 12noon-2pm, dinner 6.30pm-9.30pm (last orders).
**Cuisine:** MODERN ENGLISH/CONTINENTAL - menus change monthly.
**Cards:** Visa, Access, AmEx.
**Other points:** parking, children welcome, private room, no-smoking dining room, open-air dining, vegetarian meals.
**Directions:** exit M6 from junction 31 and take A677 towards Blackburn. The May House may be found .5 mile past The Moat House on the left.
MARK BROADBENT ☎(01254) 53160

### COASTERS BAR & DINER
Ocean Boulevard, FY4 1EZ
*An exciting restaurant reminicent of a 1920s casino. The atmosphere is always fun-filled, enhanced by the young and efficient staff. The menu is everything you would expect from a good Tex-Mex restaurant, featuring old favourites like burgers, southern fried chicken, barbecued ribs and a selection of fajitas.*
FOOD: up to £15 CLUB
**Hours:** open bank holidays.
**Cuisine:** AMERICAN / TEX-MEX - good-sized portions of favourite American-style dishes.
**Cards:** Visa, Access, Diners, AmEx.
**Other points:** parking, children welcome, no-smoking area, vegetarian meals.
**Directions:** located on Blackpool Promenade, below the tallest, fastes roller-coaster in the world.
SIMON RUSSELL ☎(01253) 401771 Fax(01253) 401098

### THE FISH INN RESTAURANT
525 Ocean Boulevard
*A traditional and popular fish restaurant, serving fresh fish daily and situated on Blackpool's South-Shore promenade on the resorts famous Pleasure Beach. The interior is furnished in the style of an ocean liner.*
FOOD: up to £15
**Hours:** meals served 12noon-late.
**Cuisine:** fresh fish
**Cards:** Visa, Access, Diners, AmEx, Switch, Eurocard.
**Directions:** situated at the Pleasure Beach's northern entrance.
MR ALAIN LEBON ☎(01253) 341033 Fax(01253) 401098

### HILL'S TUDOR ROSE HOTEL
435-7 South Promenade, FY1 6BQ
*A comfortable, medium-sized family hotel overlooking the sea and only a few minutes away from the Sandcastle. Friendly, personal service will ensure that your stay is as enjoyable as possible. The lounge bar makes a good rendezvous for a drink before dinner.*
DOUBLE ROOM: from £20 to £30
SINGLE ROOM: from £20 to £30
FOOD: up to £15
**Hours:** breakfast 8.30am-9.30am, dinner 5.30pm.
**Cuisine:** ENGLISH
**Cards:** Visa, Access, Diners, AmEx.
**Other points:** children welcome, snack lunches.
**Rooms:** 6 single rooms, 15 double rooms, 9 family rooms.
**Directions:** on the Promenade near the South Pier.
STAN HILL ☎(01253) 342656

### NEWLYN PRIVATE HOTEL
31-33 Northumberland Avenue, North Shore, FY2 9SA
*Family-run hotel noted for good food and hospitality. In quiet North Shore area, adjacent to Queens Promenade, yet close to all Blackpool's amenities. An ideal base for touring the Forest of Bowland, Lakes or Dales.*
DOUBLE ROOM: up to £20

SINGLE ROOM: up to £20
FOOD: up to £15
**Hours:** breakfast 8.30am-9am (if required earlier, continental breakfast can be served to your room), dinner 5pm.
**Cuisine:** ENGLISH
**Cards:** Visa, Access.
**Other points:** children welcome, licenced, residents' lounge.
**Rooms:** 3 single rooms, 7 double rooms, 3 twin rooms, 2 family rooms. En suite bedrooms with TV, tea/coffee-making facilities. Basic rooms with tea/coffee-making facilities.
**Directions:** off Queens Promenade.
MRS S. HARGREAVES ☎(01253) 353230
Fax(01253) 35320

 **SINGLETON LODGE COUNTRY HOUSE HOTEL**
Lodge Lane, Singleton, FY6 8LT

*An attractive red-brick Georgian vicarage, set amongst landscaped gardens offering the perfect away-from-it-all retreat with added class. Furnished throughout in classic country house style, the atmosphere is warm and friendly. The hotel's own farm-fresh produce is widely used and there is an excellent wine list. Nearby, Poulton-Le-Fylde - mentioned in the Domesday Book - is an ancient market town complete with stocks, cobbled streets and historical buildings.*
DOUBLE ROOM: from £30 to £40
SINGLE ROOM: from £40 to £50
FOOD: up to £15
**Hours:** breakfast 7.30am-9.30am, dinner 7pm-9pm, closed 3 days from Christmas day and New Year's day.
**Cuisine:** roast duckling, steak, fresh salmon.
**Cards:** Access, Visa, AmEx
**Other points:** wedding receptions, conference rooms.
**Rooms:** 10 bedrooms en suite with tea/coffee-maker, TV, telephone, radio, alarm, hair dryer, trouser press, room service to 12noon.
**Directions:** Exit M55 at junction 3, follow A585 for 3 miles, third turning on left.
ALAN & ANN SMITH ☎(01253) 883854
Fax(01253) 894432

 **SUNRAY**
42 Knowle Avenue, off Queens Promenade, FY2 9TQ
*A cheerful and comfortable guest house that has been family-run for the past 24 years under the capable hands of Mrs Jean Dodgson. With all your needs catered for by this friendly and welcoming establishment, you will find the Sunray an ideal place to stay while in the area. It provides the facilities you expect from a large hotel: direct-dial telephone, TV, hair dryer and more. Special rates can be arranged for pensioners.*
DOUBLE ROOM: from £25 to £30
SINGLE ROOM: from £25 to £30
FOOD: up to £15
**Hours:** breakfast 8.30am-9.15am, dinner 5.30pm.
**Cuisine:** ENGLISH
**Cards:** Visa, Access, AmEx.
**Other points:** children welcome, garden, pets allowed, vegetarian meals.
**Rooms:** 3 single rooms, 2 double rooms, 9 twin rooms, 2 family rooms.
**Directions:** 2 miles north of Blackpool Tower, along Promenade. Turn right at Uncle Tom's Cabin.
JEAN & JOHN DODGSON ☎(01253) 351937
Fax(01253) 593307

**WHITE TOWER RESTAURANT**
Balmoral Road, FY4 1EZ
*The White Tower Restaurant serves excellent food and wine in very pleasant, elegant surroundings. From its penthouse position, high in the exciting `Wonderful World Building', the restaurant has splendid views overlooking the Promenade and the famous Illuminations.*
FOOD: up to £15 CLUB
**Hours:** Sunday lunch 12noon-4pm, dinner 7pm-10.45pm, closed January.
**Cuisine:** CONTINENTAL - extensive à la carte menu. Dishes may include Chateaubriand, Dover sole. continental dishes. Excellent wine list.
**Cards:** Visa, Access, Diners, AmEx.
**Other points:** Sunday lunch, children welcome, guide dogs, conferences, functions.
**Directions:** M55. Yeadon Way, on Pleasure Beach.
MR MICHEAL SPENCER ☎(01253) 346710/341036 Fax(01253) 401098

## CHORLEY • map 8A4

**SHAW HILL HOTEL, GOLF & COUNTRY CLUB**
Preston Road, Whittle-le-Woods, PR6 7PP
*Set in beautiful countryside midway between Chorley and Preston, Shaw Hill is a perfect venue for golf, business seminars, weddings and private functions. Vardons Restaurant is, without doubt, one of the finest à la carte dining facilities in the north-west. The luxuriously furnished suites offer quiet and comfort, with magnificent views over the golf course and greens.*
DOUBLE ROOM: from £30 to £40
SINGLE ROOM: from £53
FOOD: from £15 to £20
**Hours:** breakfast weekdays 7am-9.30am, lunch 12noon-2pm, bar meals 11am-7pm, dinner 7pm-9.45pm.
**Cuisine:** INTERNATIONAL - fillet with truffle, pheasant with asparagus, corn-fed supreme of

chicken with scallops. Fresh fish daily.
**Cards:** Visa, Access, AmEx, Switch.
**Other points:** licensed, Sunday lunch, children welcome, pets allowed, afternoon tea, parking, residents' lounge, special breaks, own 18 hole golf course.
**Rooms:** 30 bedrooms. All en suite.
**Directions:** junction 28 of M6, follow signs for Whittle-le-Woods. Junction of M61, one mile from junction 8.
MRS TYRER ☎(01257) 269221 **Fax**(01257) 261223

## CLITHEROE • map 11E3

### BAYLEY ARMS
Hurst Green, near Whalley, BB7 9QB
*Situated in the delightful village of Hurst Green, the Bayley Arms offers warm hospitality all year round. Comfortable chairs, gleaming brass and welcoming log fires contribute to a relaxing, unhurried atmosphere.*
DOUBLE ROOM: from £20 to £30
SINGLE ROOM: from £35 to £45
FOOD: up to £15
**Hours:** breakfast 7.30am-10am, lunch 12noon-2pm, dinner 7pm-9.30pm.
**Cuisine:** ENGLISH / CONTINENTAL - imaginative chef-prepared restaurant menu and bar snacks.
**Cards:** Visa, AmEx, MasterCard.
**Other points:** licensed, Sunday lunch, open bank holidays, children welcome, cots.
**Rooms:** 5 double rooms (doubles can be let as singles), 1 twin room, 2 family rooms. All with TV, tea/coffee-making facilities.
**Directions:** in village of Hurst Green close to Stonyhurst College.
MR TAYLOR ☎(01254) 826478 **Fax**(01254) 826797

### CALF'S HEAD HOTEL
Worston, BB7 1QA
*Nestling in the historic village of Worston, the hotel offers a variety of dining locations, including a beautiful walled garden with stream and rustic bridge for warm summer days. In winter, roaring fires in the à la carte dining room or intimate Tudor Room and Bar Lounge area will melt away the chill. Private parties catered for.*
DOUBLE ROOM: from £20 to £30
FOOD: up to £15
**Hours:** breakfast 7.30am-10am, lunch 12noon-2pm, dinner 7pm-9.30pm.
**Cuisine:** ENGLISH - full à la carte menu, bar meals, Sunday 'Hot Calfery' (12noon-6pm). Barbeques on request. All food home-made using fresh, local produce.
**Cards:** Visa, Access, Diners, AmEx.
**Other points:** open-air dining, Sunday lunch, pets allowed, children welcome, weekend breaks.
**Rooms:** 1 single room, 4 double rooms, 1 twin room. All with en suite, satellite TV, telephone, tea/coffee-making facilities, baby-listening device, hair dryer, video, trouser-press.

**Directions:** situated just off A59.
MR & MRS DAVIS ☎(01200) 441218 **Fax**(01200) 441510

### THE INN AT WHITEWELL
Forest of Bowland, BB7 3AT
*A lovely riverside setting with six miles of salmon, sea-trout and trout-fishing for residents. Log fires and antique furniture create a homely atmosphere. The inn has magnificent views across the Trough of Bowland and provides an ideal location for exploring the surrounding countryside on foot.*
DOUBLE ROOM: from £30 to £40
SINGLE ROOM: from £45 to £55
FOOD: from £15 to £20 🍴
**Hours:** bar open 11am-3pm and 6pm-11pm, dinner 7.30pm-9.30pm.
**Cuisine:** ENGLISH - home-made soups. Steak, kidney and mushroom pie. Local lamb. Home-made ice cream.
**Cards:** Visa, Access, Diners, AmEx.
**Other points:** licensed, children welcome, dogs allowed.
**Directions:** follow signs to Whitewell from roundabout in Longridge centre.
RICHARD & PAM BOWMAN ☎(01200) 448222 **Fax**(01200) 448298

### SPREAD EAGLE HOTEL (SAWLEY) LTD
Sawley, BB7 4NH
*Owing to its popularity, it is advisable to book for Sunday lunch, Friday and Saturday dinner. Situated on a bend of the River Ribble, with lovely views across the river to the surrounding countryside. An excellent base from which to tour the Dales and the Lake District.*
DOUBLE ROOM: over £50
SINGLE ROOM: from £40 to £50
FOOD: from £15 to £20
**Hours:** lunch 12.30am-2pm, dinner 7pm-9pm, open all year.
**Cuisine:** ENGLISH / CONTINENTAL - à la carte menu, including beef from Aberdeen Angus stock. Regional specialities.
**Cards:** Visa, Access, Diners, AmEx.
**Other points:** licensed, Sunday lunch, children welcome.
**Rooms:** 2 single rooms, 3 double rooms, 5 twin rooms. All with TV, radio, telephone, tea/coffee-making facilities.
**Directions:** off the A59, .5 mile down the road to Sawley village.
THE TRUEMAN FAMILY ☎(01200) 441202/441406 **Fax**(01200) 441973

## DARWEN • map 11E3

### WHITEHALL HOTEL & RESTAURANT
Springbank, BB3 2JU
*A large country house, standing in its own tended grounds and pleasingly furnished throughout. It offers guests a high standard of comfort, with en*

suite rooms, indoor heated swimming pool and a highly recommended restaurant. The hotel is conveniently located for access to Ribble Valley, the Lake District and the north-west coast.
DOUBLE ROOM: from £30 to £35
SINGLE ROOM: from £45 to £55
FOOD: up to £15  CLUB
Hours: breakfast 7.30am-9.30am, lunch 12noon-2pm, dinner 7pm-10pm.
Cuisine: ENGLISH
Cards: Visa, Access, Diners, AmEx.
Other points: indoor swimming pool, sauna, solarium, snooker room.
Rooms: 15 bedrooms.
Directions: located off the A666 Bolton to Blackburn road.
MR & MRS JOSEPH & MARIE WHITEHEAD
☎(01254) 701595 Fax(01254) 773426

## ECCLESTON • map 8A4

### THE ORIGINAL FARMERS ARMS
Towngate, PR7 5QS
A country pub with an award winning restaurant. Good fresh food is served to an international standard. Friendly service combined with generous portions illustrate why the Farmers Arms enjoys such popularity. For those wishing to stay in the area, or for travellers on the M6, there are four comfortable bedrooms.
DOUBLE ROOM: up to £20
SINGLE ROOM: up to £20
FOOD: up to £15
Hours: breakfast 7am-9am, meals all day 12noon-10pm.
Cuisine: ENGLISH / INTERNATIONAL - wide choice of dishes such as home-made steak-and-kidney pie, rack of lamb and mixed grill. Plus a vast selection of home-made specials, which are written on the blackboard.
Cards: Visa, Access.
Other points: licensed, open-air dining, Sunday lunch, children welcome, beer garden, afternoon tea.
Rooms: 2 double rooms, 2 twin rooms. All with TV, radio, alarm, tea/coffee-making facilities.
Directions: B5250 west of M6 near Chorley. 2 miles from Charnock Richard service area on M6.
BARRY S. NEWTON ☎(01257) 451594
Fax(01257) 453329

## LANCASTER • map 11E3

### SPRINGFIELD HOUSE HOTEL & RESTAURANT
Wheel Lane, Pilling, PR3 6HL

A Georgian country house hotel set in extensive, attractive grounds with walled gardens and pools. The two dining rooms, The Corless Room and Miss Ciceleys, are sympathetically decorated in keeping with the 1840s style of building. Very well-cooked and presented meals offering outstanding value for money are served in a relaxed atmosphere by polite, efficient staff.
DOUBLE ROOM: from £30 to £40
SINGLE ROOM: from £25 to £35
FOOD: from £15 to £20  CLUB
Hours: lunch 12noon-2pm, dinner 7pm-9pm.
Cuisine: INTERNATIONAL - monthly changing table d'hôte menu may include trout Dundee (in a whisky and orange sauce), duckling, steak, chicken Maryland and medallions Carribean.
Cards: Visa, Access, Delta, Switch.
Other points: licensed, Sunday lunch, children welcome, pets allowed, afternoon tea, residents' lounge, garden, functions.
Rooms: 8 bedrooms.
Directions: off A588 Blackpool to Lancaster road, to the west of Pilling village.
GORDON & ELIZABETH COOKSON ☎(01253) 790301 Fax(01253) 790907

## LEYLAND • map 8A4

### RUNSHAW COLLEGE SCHOOL OF CATERING
Langdale Road, near Preston, PR5 2DQ
The Fox Holes Restaurant is part of a tertiary college, allowing students an opportunity to practise skills in food service and kitchen work.
FOOD: up to £15  CLUB
Hours: lunch 11.45am-2pm (last orders 12.45am), dinner 6.30pm-10pm (last orders 7.45pm), closed July until August, closed Saturday and Sunday.
Cuisine: ENGLISH / FRENCH / CONTINENTAL - a varied menu. Dishes include steak pie, tagliatella carbonara, champignons stroganoff, tournedos de saumon avec beurre citron.
Cards: Visa, Access, Switch, MasterCard, Eurocard.
Other points: parking, children welcome, no-smoking area, disabled access, vegetarian meals, theme events, guest chefs.
Directions: from M6 junction 28, follow signs for Leyland, take second road on left (Bent Lane). Follow to end, turn right and first left for Langdale Road.
NEIL CRUICKSHANKS ☎(01772) 642010/622677 Fax(01772) 622295

## LONGRIDGE • map 11E3

### CORPORATION ARMS
Lower Road, near Preston, PR3 2YJ
Situated in the wilds of Lancashire on the borders of the Fell Country, this pub provides a warm and friendly welcome to its customers. The food and service are excellent, making it highly recommended.
FOOD: up to £15
Hours: lunch 12.15am-2pm, dinner 7pm-9.30pm,

Sunday 12noon-9.30pm, closed Christmas day.
**Cuisine:** ENGLISH - pan-fried chicken, beef stroganoff, home-made steak, kidney and mushroom pie, stuffed mushrooms, hot chocolate fudge cake, hot sticky toffee pudding, chef specialities of the day.
**Cards:** Visa, Access, AmEx, Switch.
**Other points:** Open all day Sunday for meals.
**Directions:** on the B6245 Longridge to Blackburn road, .5 mile from Longridge centre.
MR A. GORNALL ☎(01772) 782644

## LYTHAM ST-ANNES • map 11E2

### BEDFORD HOTEL
307-311 Clifton Drive South, FY8 1HN
*Exclusive family-run hotel with an excellent reputation for comfort and cuisine. Candlelit dining in the Cartland Restaurant open to non-residents. Leisure centre with gym, sauna, solarium, jacuzzi and steam room. Situated on sunny Clifton Drive 200 yards from shops, beach and swimming pool with 4 golf courses nearby.*
DOUBLE ROOM: from £20 to £30
SINGLE ROOM: from £35
FOOD: up to £15 🍽
**Hours:** breakfast 7.30am-9.30am, lunch 12noon-5pm, dinner 6.30pm-8.30pm.
**Cuisine:** ENGLISH / CONTINENTAL
**Cards:** Visa, Access, Diners, AmEx.
**Other points:** residents' bar and lounge, afternoon tea, no-smoking area, children welcome, cots, coffee shop, vegetarian meals, lift, parking, night porter.
**Rooms:** 36 bedrooms all en suite. All with TV, telephone, tea/coffee-making facilities, radio, trouser-press, bathrobes, toiletries.
**Directions:** off M6 to M55 and Blackpool South, follow signs to St Annes.
J.P. & T. BAKER ☎(01253) 724636 Fax(01253) 729244

### CHADWICK HOTEL & LEISURE COMPLEX
South Promenade, FY8 1NP
*A modern, family-run hotel commanding lovely sea views. Spacious lounges overlook the seafront and indoor leisure pool. Other facilities include a spa bath, Turkish room, sauna, solarium, soft play adventure area and games room. The restaurant serves generous portions of very good food, and the bedrooms are comfortable and well furnished.*
DOUBLE ROOM: from £20 to £30
SINGLE ROOM: from £35 to £45
FOOD: up to £15
**Hours:** breakfast 7.30am-10am, lunch 1pm-2pm, dinner 7pm-8.30pm, bar meals 12noon-2pm, 24hr room and lounge service, open all year.
**Cuisine:** ENGLISH - traditional English cooking, local seafood specialities.
**Cards:** Visa, Access, Diners, AmEx.
**Other points:** children welcome, baby-listening device, cots, 24hr reception, foreign exchange, parking, vegetarian meals, residents' lounge,

residents' bar, disabled access, live entertainment.
**Rooms:** 72 bedrooms. All with en suite, satellite TV and movies. Some rooms have spa baths and four-poster beds.
**Directions:** off the M6 to M55, take junction 4. Turn left following signposts.
MR MILES CORBETT ☎(01253) 720061
Fax(01253) 714455

### FERNLEA HOTEL & LEISURE COMPLEX
15 South Promenade, FY8 1LU
*Situated on St Annes' South Promenade, the Fernlea is a large, comfortable, family-run hotel, with lots of fun things to do. They serve well-prepared, generous portions of food and the accommodation is of a high standard.*
DOUBLE ROOM: from £30 to £40
SINGLE ROOM: from £25 to £35
FOOD: from £15 to £20 🍽 CLUB 🍽
**Hours:** breakfast 8am-9.30am, lunch 12.30am-1.30pm, dinner 7pm-8.30pm.
**Cuisine:** ENGLISH - fixed-price four-course menu, and bar snacks at lunchtime.
**Cards:** Visa, Access, Diners, AmEx.
**Other points:** licensed, Sunday lunch, children welcome, pets allowed, swimming pool, gym facilities, solarium, squash, aerobics, sauna.
**Rooms:** 19 single rooms, 15 double rooms, 30 twin rooms, 44 family rooms, 2 suites. All with TV, radio, alarm, tea/coffee-making facilities.
**Directions:** five miles from Blackpool. Close to the pier.
TONY P. CROSTON ☎(01253) 726726

### THE LINDUM HOTEL
63-67 South Promenade, FY8 1LZ
*Open all year round, The Lindum Hotel has 80 bedrooms, all with private bath, and modern facilities. Lounge entertainment and children's parties are held regularly throughout the season. The food is all home-cooked and offers good value for money.*
DOUBLE ROOM: from £20 to £25
SINGLE ROOM: from £25 to £35
FOOD: up to £15
**Hours:** breakfast 8.30am-9.15am, Sunday lunch 12.45am-1.45pm, bar meals 12noon-2pm, dinner 6pm-7pm.
**Cuisine:** ENGLISH - dishes include sardines with saffron rice, roast beef and Yorkshire pudding, poached salmon with cucumber sauce, sticky toffee pudding.
**Cards:** Visa, Access, AmEx.
**Other points:** licensed, Sunday lunch, children welcome, pets allowed, sauna, solarium, Jacuzzi, night porter, lounge entertainment March to November, special breaks all year round.
**Rooms:** 78 bedrooms.
**Directions:** near St Annes pier, on the seafront.
LINDUM HOTEL LTD ☎(01253) 721534
Fax(01253) 721364

## MAWDESLEY • map 8A4

### ROBIN HOOD INN
Bluestone Lane, LA40 2RG

*A small family pub set in a rural area and humming with local life. Prompt friendly service and special Robin Hood dishes such as the Friar Tuck grill.*
FOOD: up to £15
**Hours:** lunch 12noon-2pm, dinner 6pm-9.30pm. All day Sunday.
**Cuisine:** ENGLISH - traditional, varied menu available in bar. Restaurant menu: steaks, fish, chicken, vegetarian dishes, large specials board.
**Cards:** Visa, Access, AmEx, Switch.
**Other points:** licensed, Sunday lunch, Sunday afternoon tea, children welcome, play area, beer garden, parking, open bank holidays.
**Directions:** take B5246 to Mawdesley. Through village, turn left.
DAVID CROPPER ☎(01704) 822275

## ORMSKIRK • map 8A4

### BEAUFORT HOTEL
High Lane, Burscough, L40 7SN

*A welcoming hotel offering excellent food and comfortable accommodation. These high standards are matched by friendly and efficient service, and the prices, especially in the restaurant, are very reasonable. Close to M6 and M58, the hotel is within easy travelling distance of Liverpool and Southport.*
DOUBLE ROOM: from £30 to £40
SINGLE ROOM: from £55
FOOD: from £15 to £20
**Hours:** breakfast 7am-9.30am, lunch 12noon-2pm, dinner 7pm-10pm.
**Cuisine:** ENGLISH / CONTINENTAL - French table d'hôte and à la carte menus.
**Cards:** Visa, Access, Diners, AmEx.
**Other points:** licensed, Sunday lunch, children welcome, pets allowed.
**Rooms:** 2 single rooms, 9 double rooms, 10 twin rooms.
**Directions:** 2 miles north of Ormskirk on A59, at corner of Pippin Street and High Lane.
TIM PENTER ☎(01704) 892655 Fax(01704) 895135

## PRESTON • map 11E3

### THE BUSHELL'S ARMS
Church Lane, Goosnargh, PR3 2BH

*A friendly village hostelry, which offers a superb variety of dishes. There is both a standard menu and a `specials' board. The ever-changing but comprehensive wine list is selected to complement the style of food. All meals are home-made and the puddings are sumptuous. Visitors can enjoy all this at very reasonable prices and relax in the friendly surroundings.*
FOOD: up to £15 CLUB
**Hours:** lunch 12noon-2.30pm, dinner 7pm-10pm,

closed occasional Mondays, closed Christmas day.
**Cuisine:** INTERNATIONAL - Dublin coddle, kefta tagine, jambalaya. Comprehensive choice of 'specials'. Changing wine list. Vegetarian meals.
**Other points:** licensed, open-air dining, Sunday lunch, no-smoking area, well behaved children welcome, beer garden.
**Directions:** M6 junction 32, north on A6 towards Garstang, turn right at lights.
DAVID BEST ☎(01772) 865235 Fax(01772) 865235

### YE HORN'S INN
Horns Lane, Goosnargh, PR3 2FJ

*This delightful oak-beamed inn offers good, home-cooked English country fare, using local farm produce. Private parties catered for. Small private rooms available. Set in rural countryside, the inn provides an ideal base from which to visit nearby beauty spots, such as Beacon Fell, The Trough of Bowland and the Hodder Valley.*
DOUBLE ROOM: over £50
SINGLE ROOM: from £40 to £50
FOOD: from £15 to £20
**Hours:** lunch 12noon-2pm, dinner 7pm-9.15pm, closed Monday lunch.
**Cuisine:** ENGLISH - home-cooking, e.g., roast duckling.
**Cards:** Visa, Access, Diners, AmEx.
**Other points:** Sunday lunch, no-smoking area, children welcome, disabled access, residents' bar, vegetarian meals.
**Rooms:** 6 twin rooms. All with TV, telephone, tea/coffee-making facilities.
**Directions:** M6 exit 36. Off the B5269 near Whittingham Hospital.
MARK WOODS & ELIZABETH JONES ☎(01772) 865230 Fax(01772) 864299

## RIBCHESTER • map 11E3

### MILES HOUSE RESTAURANT
Blackburn Road, Dutton, near Preston, PR3 3ZQ

*A traditional Ribble Valley farmhouse is home to Miles House Restaurant, a very comfortable and relaxed place to dine, whether getting together with friends or family, or enjoying a quiet evening or lunch with that special person. The atmosphere is very warm and inviting and the staff are friendly and helpful.*
FOOD: up to £15 CLUB
**Hours:** lunch 11am-3pm, dinner from 7pm, afternoon high tea 2.30pm-5pm.
**Cuisine:** ENGLISH/FRENCH - à la carte menu, featuring tempting dishes such as lobster Thermidor, halibut cooked in yoghurt and honey, served on a bed of tomato puree and grapefruit. Traditional farmhouse soup is also a speciality.
**Cards:** Visa, Access, AmEx.
**Other points:** children welcome, parking, no-smoking area, designated wildlife garden, open-air dining, vegetarian meals.
**Directions:** located .5 mile south of Ribchester,

close to the Ribble Bridge on the B6245.
MR & MRS RICHARD & CHRISTINE MARSHALL
☎(01254) 878204

## WRIGHTINGTON • map 8A4

### ⌒⌐ HIND'S HEAD HOTEL & RESTAURANT
Mossy Lea Road, WN6 9RN

*The Hind's Head is a lovely village pub, offering locals and visitors alike a comfortable and relaxed place to enjoy a good meal and a chance to sample their wide selection of fine ales, beers, wines and spirits. It is conveniently situated for visiting Wigan Pier, Camelot Theme Park and Martin Mere Wildfowl Trust.*

FOOD: up to £15  CLUB
**Hours:** lunch 12noon-2pm, dinner 6pm-9.30pm, meals all day Sunday.
**Cuisine:** ENGLISH / CONTINENTAL - an innovative menu with regularly changing specials.
**Cards:** Visa, Access, AmEx.
**Other points:** parking, children welcome, no-smoking area, open-air dining, vegetarian meals, afternoon teas, Sunday lunch.
**Directions:** leave the M6 at junction 27. Wrightington is approximately one mile to the west.
JOAN DOBSON ☎(01257) 421168

# MERSEYSIDE

## LIVERPOOL • map 8A4

### ⌒⌐ DEL SECOLO
Temple Court

*The Del Secolo is the flagship of this Italian restaurant complex. With a vast and interesting menu, an extensive range of wines and excellent service, it is no wonder that this restaurant has been acclaimed for its excellent reputation. Below the comfortable and intimate Del Secolo is the Casa Italia, a bustling pizzeria. If a choice of two styles of Italian cuisine is not enough, at the back of the Casa Italia, accessed by Temple Court, is the Villa Italia, a trattoria in true Italian style.*

FOOD: from £15 to £20 ⌐ ≡
**Hours:** lunch 12noon-2.30pm, dinner 7.30pm-10.30pm.
**Cuisine:** ITALIAN - pizza, pasta and fish dishes are the house specialities.
**Cards:** Visa, Access, Diners, AmEx.
**Other points:** children welcome, vegetarian meals, disabled access.
**Directions:** in the Cavern Quarter.
CARLO CAMPOLUCCI-BORDI ☎(0151) 236 1040
Fax(0151) 236 9985

### ⌒⌐ LA BOUFFE
48a Castle Street, L2 7LQ

*Located in the basement area of a listed building, this French-style bistro offers diners a popular place to meet, good food and a great atmosphere. There is a regular live jazz band to enhance the ambience: check for details of live music.*

FOOD: from £15 to £20 ⌐CLUB ≡
**Hours:** lunch 12noon-3pm, dinner 6.30pm-10.30pm, closed Monday evenings, Saturday lunch and all day Sunday.
**Cuisine:** CONTINENTAL - an ever changing menu, made with fresh produce. The selection of wines and sprits is of an excellent standard, perfectly complementing the imaginative menu and the fantastic cheeseboard.

**Cards:** Visa, Access, Diners, AmEx.
**Other points:** children welcome, vegetarian meals, afternoon teas, guide dogs allowed.
**Directions:** located in Liverpool City Centre.
DEBORAH HOLDEN ☎(0151) 236 3375

### ⌒⌐ MAYFLOWER RESTAURANT
48 Duke Street, L1 5AS

*A large, modern Chinese restaurant with a warm and relaxed atmosphere. The restaurant serves Pekingese, Cantonese and Schezuan dishes, including crispy fragrant duck served with pancakes. As the restaurant is open until 4am, it is ideal for anyone looking for a peaceful restaurant in which to enjoy good food, but outside the more usual opening hours.*

FOOD: up to £15
**Hours:** meals all day 12noon-4am.
**Cuisine:** PEKINGESE / CANTONESE - Peking and Cantonese cuisine, with vegetarian and seafood specialities.
**Cards:** Visa, Access, Diners, AmEx, Switch.
**Other points:** licensed, children welcome, air-conditioned, parking, disabled access.
**Directions:** two minutes from main shopping area, near Pier Head and Albert Dock.
MR SIM ☎(0151) 709 6339 Fax(0151) 7097722

## SOUTHPORT • map 8A4

### ⌂ THE AMBASSADOR PRIVATE HOTEL
13 Bath Street, PR9 0DP

*Situated in an early Victorian terrace and family-run since 1964. This small hotel offers a good standard of accommodation and is centrally situated for the main shopping areas and promenade, water sports and golf courses. The relaxed and comfortable surroundings are complemented by the friendly welcome provided by the proprietors Margaret and Harry Bennett.*

DOUBLE ROOM: from £20 to £30
SINGLE ROOM: from £20 to £30

FOOD: up to £15
**Hours:** breakfast 7.30am-9.30am, bar snacks 12.30am-2pm, dinner 6pm-7pm, bar snacks 9pm-11pm, closed Christmas and New Year.
**Cuisine:** ENGLISH - predominantly English.
**Cards:** Visa, Access.
**Other points:** no-smoking area, pets allowed, residents' lounge, parking, children welcome.
**Rooms:** 1 single room, 2 double rooms, 2 twin rooms, 3 family rooms. All with en suite, TV, radio, tea/coffee-making facilities, hair dryer.
**Directions:** from Lord Street, turn at traffic lights towards promenade, then second on the right.
MARGARET & HARRY BENNETT ☎(01704) 543998/0704 530459 **Fax**(01704) 536269

      **THE CRIMOND HOTEL**
          Knowsley Road, PR9 0HN
*A small, family-run hotel offering excellent facilities including indoor swimming pool, sauna and Jacuzzi. The good food, excellent service and comfortable accommodation combine to make this a pleasant and relaxing stay for tourists and businessmen alike. Conference facilities, including slide projector, TV and video.*
DOUBLE ROOM: from £20 to £30
SINGLE ROOM: from £35 to £45
FOOD: up to £15
**Hours:** breakfast 7.30am-9.30am, lunch 12noon-2pm, dinner 7pm-9pm.
**Cuisine:** MODERN ENGLISH - Northern lamb chops glazed with a redcurrant sauce, Aunty Neddy's special fruit meringue nests.
**Cards:** Visa, Access, Diners, AmEx.
**Other points:** no-smoking area, garden, pets allowed, conferences, functions.
**Rooms:** 4 single rooms, 4 double rooms, 2 twin rooms, 2 family rooms. All with TV, radio, telephone, tea/coffee-making facilities, hair dryer, trouser-press.
**Directions:** situated in Southport, off Park Road West. Near municipal golf links.
PAT & GEOFF RANDLE ☎(01704) 536456 **Fax**(01704) 548643

## THORNTON HOUGH • map 8B4

      **THORNTON HALL HOTEL**
          Wirral, L63 1JF

*Formerly the home of a major shipping family, Thornton Hall is a magnificent residence set in seven acres of gardens. Splendid wood carvings and panelling adorn the main staircase and many*

*rooms. The Italian Room provides a perfect setting for the hotel restaurant, with a ceiling of hand-tooled leather and mother of pearl. Suitably located in the lovely Wirral countryside. (See special feature on page 10.)*
DOUBLE ROOM: from £30 to £40
SINGLE ROOM: from £44 to £67
FOOD: from £15 to £25 **CLUB**
**Hours:** breakfast 7am-9.30am, dinner 7pm-10pm.
**Cuisine:** MODERN INTERNATIONAL - excellent choice of set and à la carte menus based on local produce and creative cooking. Comprehensive wine list complements their award-winning chef, recognized as one of the best in the north-west.
**Cards:** Visa, Access, AmEx.
**Other points:** licensed, open-air dining, Sunday lunch, children welcome, pets allowed, afternoon tea, parking, functions, special breaks, baby-listening device, baby-sitting, cots, 24hr reception, foreign exchange, left luggage.
**Rooms:** 63 bedrooms. All with TV, radio, telephone, tea/coffee-making facilities.
**Directions:** exit junction 4 of M53 and take B5151; turn off right onto B5136.
COLIN FRASER ☎(0151) 336 3938 **Fax**(0151) 336 7864

## WALLASEY • map 8A4

      **GROVE HOUSE HOTEL & RESTAURANT**
          Grove Road, Wirral, L45 3HT
*A well-appointed Victorian hotel and restaurant, situated in its own attractive gardens in a quiet residental area of Wallasey. Offering fine cuisine using a comprehensive menu, including an extensive selection of vegetarian dishes. Excellent accommodation and warm, courteous service.*
DOUBLE ROOM: from £40
SINGLE ROOM: from £40
FOOD: from £10 to £20
**Hours:** breakfast 7.30am-9.30am, lunch 12noon-2pm, dinner 7pm-9.30pm.
**Cuisine:** FRENCH / CONTINENTAL - comprehensive à la carte menu, featuring French and continental dishes.
**Cards:** Visa, Access, AmEx.
**Other points:** licensed, Sunday lunch, children welcome, garden, functions, conferences, bridal suite available.
**Rooms:** 3 single rooms, 2 twin rooms, 9 double rooms, all en suite.
**Directions:** off H53, take the A554.
MR N.J. BURN ☎(0151) 639 3947 **Fax**(0151) 639 0028

      **LEASOWE CASTLE**
          Leasowe, Moreton, L46 3RF
*This 16th century castle has been converted to accommodate an excellent restaurant with varied table d'hôte and à la carte menus. The Stables restaurant has recently opened and serves continental and English dishes in a very relaxed atmosphere. Sea views, outstanding accommodation, fine cuisine and excellent service*

---

**For Reservations & Special Offers FreeCall 0500 700 456**

combine to make Leasowe Castle a delightful place to visit.

DOUBLE ROOM: from £40 to £50
FOOD: up to £15 ☜ 🍴 CLUB
**Hours:** breakfast 7am-10am, lunch 12noon-3pm, dinner 4.30pm-11pm, dinner 7pm-10pm.
**Cuisine:** ENGLISH / CONTINENTAL - à la carte and fixed three-course menu, bar meals/snacks. A second restaurant has recently opened, serving continental and English dishes.
**Cards:** Visa, Access, Diners, AmEx.
**Other points:** licensed, Sunday lunch, no-smoking area, children welcome, garden, afternoon tea, 24hr reception, foreign exchange, residents' bar, residents' lounge, baby-listening device, baby-sitting, cots.
**Rooms:** 23 double rooms, 23 twin rooms, 3 triple rooms. All with TV, radio, alarm, telephone, tea/coffee-making facilities.
**Directions:** Wallasey is situated at the end of the M53, 3 miles from Liverpool.
MR & MRS HARDING ☎(0151) 606 9191

### 🍴 MONROES
45 Wallasey Road, L45 4NN
A bistro-style restaurant with a Marilyn Monroe theme, offering tasty and well-presented food in a happy and relaxed atmosphere. Friendly, attentive service will assist you in your choice of more than 24 steak dishes, vegetarian dishes and specials. 14-page menu and children's menu.
FOOD: up to £15 CLUB
**Hours:** dinner every night 5.30pm-10pm.
**Cuisine:** ENGLISH / INTERNATIONAL - specialities include home-made profiteroles, cheesecake and apple pie, plus vegetarian menu. Siumai, Cantonese beef balls, Texas rib starters, buffalo pie, surf'n'turf chicken, pork marsala.
**Cards:** Visa, Access, AmEx.
**Other points:** children welcome.
**Directions:** situated in Liscard, 2km north-west of Wallasey town centre.
DAVID W. CULLEN ☎(0151) 638 3633

# NORTHUMBERLAND

## ALNMOUTH • map 12A4

### 🏨 FAMOUS SCHOONER HOTEL
Northumberland Street, NE66 2RS
Listed 17th century coaching inn, situated only 100 yards from the beach, river and golf course. The Schooner is of ETB 4 Crown standard and is renowned for its superb food and extensive selection of real ales. Specializes in golf holidays.
DOUBLE ROOM: from £27 to £40
SINGLE ROOM: from £27 to £40
FOOD: up to £15 ☜ CLUB
**Hours:** breakfast 7.30am-9.30am, lunch 12noon-3pm, dinner 7pm-11pm.
**Cuisine:** ENGLISH / FRENCH - superb English and French cuisine, also a `Bistro' restaurant and conservatory. Local fresh fish a speciality.
**Cards:** Visa, Access, Diners, AmEx.
**Other points:** licensed, Sunday lunch, children welcome, garden, afternoon tea, pets allowed, squash, solarium, conservatory, conferences, free house.
**Rooms:** 25 bedrooms.
**Directions:** 100 yards from the 9-hole village golf course. 5 miles from A1, Alnwick exit. 1 mile from Alnmouth railway station (main London-Edinburgh line).
MR ORDE ☎(01665) 830216 Fax(01665) 830216

## ALNWICK • map 12A4

### 🏨 THE COTTAGE INN HOTEL
Dunstan Village, Craster, NE66 3SZ
Recently modernized, The Cottage Inn is situated in the heart of the beautiful Northumbrian countryside, just a few minutes from the sea. Craster is the ideal base for touring the wealth of nearby historic buildings, which include Alnwick Castle and Wallington House. Hosts Lawrence and Shirley Jobling offer you good food, service and an olde-worlde atmosphere.
DOUBLE ROOM: from £20 to £30
SINGLE ROOM: from £35
FOOD: up to £15 🕮
**Hours:** breakfast 8.30am-9.30am, Sunday lunch 12noon-2.30pm, bar meals 12noon-2.30pm, dinner 7pm-9.30pm, bar meals 6pm-9.30pm.
**Cuisine:** ENGLISH - à la carte, table d'hôte and extensive bar menu. Dishes may include pigeon, escalopes of venison, and monkfish in filo pastry. Vegetarian dishes.
**Cards:** Visa, Access, Switch.
**Other points:** licensed, open-air dining, Sunday lunch, no-smoking area, parking, children welcome, garden, open bank holidays, residents' bar, disabled access, listening device, cots.
**Rooms:** 2 double rooms, 8 twin rooms. All with TV, telephone, tea/coffee-making facilities.
**Directions:** 6 miles east of Alnwick and .5 mile from Craster harbour.
LAWRENCE & SHIRLEY JOBLING ☎(01665) 576658

### 🏨 HOTSPUR HOTEL
Bondgate Without, NE66 1PR
A former coaching house converted into a comfortable hotel which combines all the modern comforts with friendly and efficient service. You can also enjoy a relaxing meal in the bar or restaurant.
DOUBLE ROOM: from £25 to £30
SINGLE ROOM: from £25 to £30
FOOD: from £15 to £20
**Hours:** lunch 12noon-2pm, dinner 6pm-9pm.

**Cuisine:** ENGLISH - extensive menu.
**Cards:** Visa, Access.
**Other points:** licensed bar, restaurant and bar open to non-residents, Sunday lunch, children welcome, pets allowed, parking.
**Rooms:** 24 bedrooms all en suite with TV, telephone.
**Directions:** on B6346 just outside city wall approaching from A1.
MR PETER ROBINSON ☎(01665) 510101
Fax(01665) 505033

## BELFORD • map 12A4

 **BLUE BELL**
Market Square, NE70 7NE
*A 17th century coaching inn set in the heart of a peaceful Northumbrian village. An ideal stopover for north/south travellers or those exploring Northumbria's wonderful beaches and historic castles.*
DOUBLE ROOM: from £35 to £45
SINGLE ROOM: from £35 to £45
FOOD: from £10 to £25 CLUB
**Hours:** breakfast 8am-9.30am, lunch 12noon-2pm, dinner 7pm-9pm.
**Cuisine:** ENGLISH - fresh local produce; fish, lamb and game.
**Cards:** Visa, Access, AmEx.
**Other points:** open-air dining, Sunday lunch, children welcome, pets allowed, coaches by prior arrangement
**Rooms:** 1 single room, 8 double rooms, 8 twin rooms.
**Directions:** situated on the B6349 just off the A1.
MRS J. SHIRLEY ☎(01668) 213543 Fax(01668) 213787

## BELLINGHAM • map 11B3

 **RIVERDALE HALL HOTEL**
Bellingham, NE48 2JT
*Undoubtedly one of Northumbria's most outstanding country house hotels, having been tastefully converted from a Victorian mansion. It stands in its own large grounds on the edge of the small town of Bellingham, close to the beautiful Northumberland National Park. The elegantly furnished restaurant provides a warm, relaxed setting in which to enjoy a high standard of cuisine, including regional specialities, complemented by well-chosen wines. It is a magnet for sports and leisure enthusiasts and an ideal base from which to tour the countryside and coastline and explore the many nearby attractions. Les Routiers Newcomer of the Year 1994.*
DOUBLE ROOM: from £35 to £40
SINGLE ROOM: from £40 to £45
FOOD: from £15 to £20 CLUB
**Hours:** breakfast 7.45am-10am, lunch 12noon-2pm, dinner 6.45pm-9.30pm, bar snacks 6.45pm-9.30pm, open all year.
**Cuisine:** ENGLISH - with French influences: chicken au poivre, monkfish Thermidor, poached asparagus

glazed with cheese.
**Cards:** Visa, Access, Diners, AmEx, Switch.
**Other points:** parking, children welcome, Sunday lunch, no-smoking area, afternoon tea, Sunday dinner, residents' lounge, residents' garden, vegetarian meals, open-air dining, pets allowed.
**Rooms:** 3 single rooms, 12 double rooms, 5 family rooms.
**Directions:** situated in Bellingham on the B6320, 17 miles north of Hexham, between Hadrian's Wall and Kielder Water and Forest.
MR J COCKER ☎(01434) 220254
Fax(01434) 220457

## BERWICK-UPON-TWEED • map 16E6

 **BLACK BULL INN**
Main Street, Lowick, TD15 2UA
*A 300-year-old Northumbrian pub with good local trade and excellent visitor trade in summer. Due to this pub's popularity, the proprietors, Anne and Tom Grundy, have expanded the food side of the business to offer larger dining room facilities, where real ales are also served. Booking is advised for evenings and weekends. A cottage attached to the pub, with independent access, provides accommodation for up to six people.*
DOUBLE ROOM: from £20 to £30
SINGLE ROOM: from £25 to £35
FOOD: up to £15
**Hours:** lunch 12noon-2pm, dinner 6.30pm-9pm, closed Monday from October until Easter.
**Cuisine:** ENGLISH - well known for home-made pies and local fish. Children are welcome in the pub and dining room up till 8.30pm.
**Cards:** Visa, Access.
**Other points:** licensed, Sunday lunch, children catered for (please check for age limits), coaches by prior arrangement, limited disabled access.
**Rooms:** 2 double rooms, 1 twin room.
**Directions:** on B6353 between Coldstream and Holy Island.
ANNE & TOM GRUNDY ☎(01289) 388228

 **THE CAT INN**
Cheswick, TD15 2RL
*The Cat Inn is situated on the A1, 4 miles south of Berwick-on-Tweed, a Border town of great architectural diversity. Offering superb en suite accommodation and beautifully cooked meals, it is surrounded by open fields and is just 1.5 miles from the sea. Close to excellent golfing and fishing facilities.*
DOUBLE ROOM: up to £20
FOOD: up to £15
**Hours:** breakfast 9am-11am, closed Sunday afternoon 3pm-7pm, restaurant open all day.
**Cuisine:** ENGLISH
**Other points:** licensed.
**Directions:** on the A1, 4 miles south of Berwick-upon-Tweed.
MR W.L. KEITH ☎(01289) 387251 Fax(01289) 387251

---

## CORNHILL-ON-TWEED • map 16E6

 **TILLMOUTH PARK HOTEL**
TD12 4UU

*A country house hotel set in extensive grounds, with very comfortable surroundings, and food and accommodation of a high standard.*
DOUBLE ROOM: over £50
SINGLE ROOM: over £50
FOOD: from £20 to £25
**Hours:** breakfast 8am-9.45am, lunch 12.30am-2pm, dinner 7.30pm-9.30pm.
**Cuisine:** ENGLISH - Tweed salmon, local pheasant, Cheviot lamb.
**Cards:** Visa, Access, Diners, AmEx.
**Other points:** Sunday lunch, children welcome, pets allowed.
**Rooms:** 1 single room, 6 double rooms, 6 twin rooms, 1 family room. All with TV, radio, alarm, telephone, tea/coffee-making facilities.
**Directions:** on A698 Cornhill to Berwick-on-Tweed road. 3 miles from main A697.
CHARLES CARROLL ☎(01890) 882255
Fax(01890) 882540

## HADRIAN'S WALL • map 11B3

 **VALLUM LODGE**
Military Road, Twice Brewed, near Bardon Mill, NE47 7AN
*Vallum Lodge Hotel is situated in peaceful countryside close to Hadrian's Wall on the edge of the Northumberland National Park. A warm welcome always awaits you from resident proprietors Jack and Christine Wright. There is a particular emphasis on cleanliness, comfort, relaxation and value for money, complemented by good, freshly-prepared food and appealing, newly decorated surroundings. Licensed bar available for residents.*
DOUBLE ROOM: from £20 to £30
SINGLE ROOM: up to £25
FOOD: up to £15 ☜
**Hours:** breakfast 8am-9am, dinner 7pm-8pm, closed December until January (inclusive).
**Cuisine:** ENGLISH - fresh home-cooking.
**Cards:** Visa, Access, AmEx, Eurocard, Delta.
**Other points:** parking, no-smoking area, residents' lounge, garden, vegetarian meals.
**Rooms:** 7 bedrooms. All with radio, alarm, tea/coffee-making facilities.
**Directions:** 500 yards west of Once Brewed

National Park Visitors' Centre on B6318.
MR & MRS WRIGHT ☎(01434) 344248

## HEXHAM • map 11B3

 **BEAUMONT HOTEL**
Beaumont Street, NE46 3LT
*A busy, family-run hotel incorporating a wine bar and cocktail bar, the Park Restaurant and conference facilities. Close to the centre of this historic market town in the heart of Northumbria, the Beaumont is a popular hotel with tourists and businessmen.*
DOUBLE ROOM: from £40 to £50
SINGLE ROOM: from £45 to £55
FOOD: from £15 to £20  CLUB
**Hours:** breakfast 7.30am-9.45am, lunch 12noon-2pm, bar meals 12noon-2pm, dinner 7pm-9.45pm, closed Christmas day and New Year's day.
**Cuisine:** FRENCH - steaks, pheasant, guinea fowl, lamb.
**Cards:** Visa, Access, Diners, AmEx.
**Other points:** licensed, Sunday lunch, children welcome, lift, baby-listening device, baby-sitting, cots, 24hr reception, parking, vegetarian meals, residents' bar, residents' lounge.
**Rooms:** 6 single rooms, 11 double rooms, 5 twin rooms, 1 family room. All with TV, radio, telephone, tea/coffee-making facilities.
**Directions:** Overlooking the abbey and the park in the town centre.
MARTIN & LINDA OWEN ☎(01434) 602331
Fax(01434) 602331

 **COUNTY HOTEL**
Priestpopple, NE46 1PS
*A homely hotel, privately run by real Northumbrians who understand the meaning of real hospitality. Its old-fashioned atmosphere provides a warm, relaxing and comfortable retreat. Conveniently situated between train and bus stations.*
DOUBLE ROOM: from £20 to £30
FOOD: up to £15 ☜
**Hours:** meals all day 7.30am-10pm, lunch 12.05pm-2.15pm, dinner 7pm-9.30pm.
**Cuisine:** ENGLISH - fresh, traditional British dishes.
**Cards:** Visa, Access, AmEx.
**Other points:** licensed, Sunday lunch, children welcome, coaches by prior arrangement, children welcome, baby-listening device, cots, 24hr reception.
**Rooms:** 2 single rooms, 4 double rooms, 3 twin rooms. All TV, radio, telephone, tea/coffee-making facilities.
**Directions:** from A69, follow signs to Hexham. The hotel is on the main street.
MR KEN WATTS ☎(01434) 602030

 **LANGLEY CASTLE HOTEL**
Langley on Tyne, NE47 5LU
*Set in 10 acres of lush, mowed lawns surrounded*

*by woodland, this fascinating 14th century castle combines contemporary conveniences with authentic reminiscences of yesteryear. The food is cooked to an extremely high standard and beautifully presented, with attention to detail. The spacious surroundings and sense of history make this a glorious setting for any visit.*
DOUBLE ROOM: from £40 to £50
SINGLE ROOM: over £50
FOOD: from £15 to £20 ⌐ ⊏
**Hours:** breakfast 8am-9.30am, lunch 12noon-2pm dinner 7pm-9pm, bar meals 12noon-2pm.
**Cuisine:** FRENCH - imaginative menu, including daily specialities.
**Cards:** Visa, Access, Diners, AmEx.
**Other points:** licensed, Sunday lunch, afternoon tea, pets allowed, residents' lounge, children welcome, baby-listening device, cots.
**Rooms:** 14 double rooms, 2 twin rooms. All with TV, radio, alarm, telephone, tea/coffee-making facilities. (8 rooms in new development/conversion within the grounds.)
**Directions:** follow the A69 to Haydon Bridge, then A686 1.5 miles to Langley.
ANTON PHILLIPS ☎(01434) 688888 Fax (01434) 684019

## OTTERBURN • map 11A3

### OTTERBURN TOWER HOTEL
Otterburn, NE19 1NP
*An adapted, spacious, castellated country house in extensive grounds. Three-course menu and bar meals are offered in the traditionally furnished and wood-panelled dining room and lounges. Steeped in history - the hotel is reputedly haunted! Private fishing on 3.5 miles of the River Rede.*
DOUBLE ROOM: from £30 to £40
FOOD: up to £15    CLUB
**Hours:** open all day.
**Cuisine:** ENGLISH
**Cards:** Visa, Access, Diners, AmEx.
**Other points:** Sunday lunch, children welcome, garden.
**Directions:** the entrance to the hotel is at the junction of the A696 and B6320.
PETER HARDING ☎(01830) 520620

## SEAHOUSES • map 12A4

### BEACH HOUSE HOTEL
Seafront, NE68 7SR
*A small, friendly, family-run hotel, pleasantly situated overlooking the Farne Islands. The Beach House Hotel specializes in imaginative home-cooking and baking. Particularly suited to those looking for a quiet and comfortable holiday.*
DOUBLE ROOM: from £30 to £40
SINGLE ROOM: from £35 to £45
FOOD: from £15 to £20
**Hours:** breakfast 8.30am-9.30am, dinner 7pm-8.30pm, closed November until end March.
**Cuisine:** ENGLISH - local produce, e.g., game and fish including local kippers. Clootie dumpling.

**Cards:** Visa, Access.
**Other points:** licensed, no-smoking area, children welcome.
**Rooms:** 12 double rooms, 2 single rooms.
**Directions:** on the Seahouses to Bamburgh road.
MR & MRS F.R. CRAIGS ☎(01665) 720337 Fax (01665) 720921

### THE LODGE
146 Main Street, NE68 7UA
*The falcon sign of this small hotel makes it easy to spot. Styled along Scandinavian lines, with pine panelling and furniture throughout. Relaxing by the open fire in the convivial bar makes a perfect end to a day exploring this historic and beautiful area.*
DOUBLE ROOM: from £25 to £35
SINGLE ROOM: from £25 to £35
FOOD: from £15 to £20
**Hours:** breakfast 8.30am-9.30am, lunch 12noon-2pm, dinner 6.30pm-9.30pm.
**Cuisine:** ENGLISH / SEAFOOD - local seafood.
**Cards:** Visa, Access.
**Other points:** Sunday lunch, children catered for (please check for age limits), pets by prior arrangement, disabled access, vegetarian meals.
**Rooms:** 4 double rooms, 1 family room. All with TV, tea/coffee-making facilities.
**Directions:** on the main street in Seahouses (North Sunderland).
SELBY & JENIFER BROWN ☎(01665) 720158

## WARKWORTH • map 12A4

### THE JACKDAW RESTAURANT
34 Castle Street, NE65 0UN
*Attractive cottage-restaurant with a friendly atmosphere and home-cooking with locally purchased produce. The à la carte menu features a wide selection of traditional dishes, including mouthwatering sweets prepared daily. The menus change frequently. The fixed-price Sunday lunch is deservedly very popular.*
FOOD: up to £15 ⌐
**Hours:** lunch 12.30am-2pm, dinner 7pm-9pm, closed Sunday evening, all day Monday, Thursday evening and January until mid-February.
**Cuisine:** ENGLISH - menu changes for lunch and dinner. All dishes are home-made.
**Cards:** Visa, Access, AmEx.
**Other points:** licensed, Sunday lunch, no-smoking area, children welcome, open bank holidays, morning coffee, afternoon tea.
**Directions:** 7 miles south of Alnwick on A1068 coast road.
RUPERT & GILLIAN BELL ☎(01665) 711488

# TYNE & WEAR

## NEWCASTLE-UPON-TYNE • map 12B4

 **THE BLACK BULL**
Matfen, NE20 0RP

*Situated in the picturesque Northumbrian village of Matfen, deep in Hadrian's Wall country, this 200-year-old inn is a delight to visit, whatever the occasion. Sit outside and enjoy the scenery in summer, or experience the low beams and log fires in winter: whatever the season, you are guaranteed an intimate atmosphere and a warm welcome in this most traditional of country inns. Whether enjoying a quiet drink, staying for lunch or dinner in the à la carte restaurant or for a romantic weekend in one of the luxurious bedrooms, the Black Bull, with its view over the river and the village green, is a real find.*

DOUBLE ROOM: from £27 to £30
SINGLE ROOM: from £32
FOOD: from £15 to £20
**Hours:** breakfast 7.30am-9am (residents only), lunch 12noon-2pm, bar meals 12noon-2pm, dinner 7pm-9.30pm, bar meals 6.30pm-9pm.
**Cuisine:** ENGLISH - predominantly English, but with a wide variety of continental and vegetarian dishes and an excellent wine list.
**Cards:** Visa, Access, AmEx.
**Other points:** licensed, open-air dining, Sunday lunch, children welcome, disabled access, parking, garden, open bank holidays.
**Rooms:** 3 double rooms. All with TV, radio, tea/coffee-making facilities.
**Directions:** leave A69 at Corbridge to join B6318. 2 miles north of this road (follow signposts for Maften).
COLIN & MICHELE SCOTT ☎(01661) 886330
Fax(01661) 886330

 **THE FERNCOURT HOTEL**
34 Osborne Road, Jesmond, NE2 2AJ

*An attractive, spacious hotel, with easy access to Hadrian's Wall and other local tourist attractions. Pleasant surroundings, comfortably furnished to appeal to business executives and holiday-makers alike. Well-prepared Tex-Mex food, attractively presented in a lively atmosphere. English Tourist Board 3 Crown Commended.*

DOUBLE ROOM: from £35 to £60
SINGLE ROOM: from £25 to £50
FOOD: from £15 to £20      CLUB
**Hours:** breakfast 7am-9am, dinner (weekdays) 6.30pm-10.30pm, open all year.
**Cuisine:** TEX-MEX - large and varied menu, featuring authentic Texan and Mexican food; table d'hôte menu available weekdays.
**Cards:** Visa, Access, Diners, AmEx.
**Other points:** licensed, children welcome, vegetarian meals, pets allowed, parking.
**Rooms:** 5 single rooms, 10 double rooms, 4 twin rooms, 4 family rooms. All with TV, tea/coffee-

making facilities.
**Directions:** off the A1058, left at roundabout onto Osborne Road.
MR CLARK ☎(0191) 281 5418/281 5377
Fax(0191) 212 0783

 **SACHINS**
Forth Banks, NE1 3SG

*An authentic Punjabi restaurant in a Grade II listed building situated at the head of the Forth Banks close to the River Tyne. The menu offers a range of speciality Punjabi dishes, flavoured with the freshest of produce with the delicate aromas of herbs and spices, prepared by one of the top Punjabi chefs in Britain. The atmosphere is relaxed and comfortable.*

FOOD: from £15 to £20
**Hours:** lunch 12noon-2.15pm, dinner 6pm-11.15pm, closed Sunday.
**Cuisine:** PUNJABI - the fine menu offers a splendid array of the most exotic and enticing dishes.
**Cards:** Visa, Access, Diners, AmEx.
**Other points:** parking, children welcome, vegetarian meals, licensed.
**Directions:** easy to find behind the Central Station.
DINESH RAWLEY ☎(0191) 261 9035/232 4660

## SOUTH SHIELDS • map 12B4

 **SEA HOTEL**
Sea Road, NE33 2LD

*This busy hotel is situated on the sea front in the heart of `Catherine Cookson Country'. The hospitality, for which the region is renowned, is reflected in the friendly service.*

DOUBLE ROOM: from £30 to £40
SINGLE ROOM: over £50
FOOD: up to £15
**Hours:** breakfast 7am-9.30am, lunch 12noon-2.30pm, dinner 7pm-9.30pm.
**Cuisine:** ENGLISH - traditional English menu using local produce and a French-based à la carte menu, both offering a wide choice of dishes.
**Cards:** Visa, Access, Diners, AmEx.
**Other points:** Sunday lunch, children welcome.
**Rooms:** 14 single rooms, 12 double rooms, 7 twin rooms.
**Directions:** on the seafront at A183 and A1018 junction.
MR BASSETT & MR WATSON ☎(0191) 427 0999
Fax(0191) 4540500

## SUNDERLAND • map 12B4

 **MOWBRAY PARK HOTEL**
Borough Road, SR1 1PR

*A family-run private hotel, located within five minutes' walk of the railway station, business and shopping areas and backing onto one of Sunderland's most impressive parks. The restaurant*

offers good food, well presented and at good value for money. Ideal for either a simple business lunch or for that special occasion.
DOUBLE ROOM: from £20 to £30
SINGLE ROOM: from £30 to £40
FOOD: up to £20
**Hours:** breakfast 7am-10am, bar meals 12noon-2pm, dinner 7pm-10pm.
**Cuisine:** ENGLISH / CHINESE
**Cards:** Visa, Access, Diners, AmEx.
**Other points:** licensed, Sunday lunch, children welcome, afternoon tea, pets allowed, residents' lounge, functions, conferences.
**Rooms:** 51 bedrooms.
**Directions:** centre of Sunderland, next to Mowbray Park, town museum and library.
EDWARD HUGHES ☎(0191) 567 8221

### THE PULLMAN LODGE HOTEL
Whitburn Road, Seaburn, SR6 8AA
A real dream for railway enthusiasts, this privately-owned and personally-run modern hotel is built in unique railway style, offering the visitor every modern convenience. It is situated on one of the north-east's most unspoilt beaches, close to some of Northumbria's finest heritage sites. Enjoy a drink in the Station Bar before retreating to the well-appointed Carriage Restaurant overlooking the rugged coastline, where you can choose from an à la carte menu using only the freshest produce and cooked to perfection. The Pullman also offers a complete wedding package, along with extensive conference and private function facilities.
DOUBLE ROOM: from £20 to £30
SINGLE ROOM: from £40 to £50
FOOD: up to £15
**Hours:** breakfast 7am-10am, bar meals 12noon-10pm, dinner 7pm-10pm.
**Cuisine:** ENGLISH - a range of choices on à la

carte, table d'hôte menu and bar menu.
**Cards:** Visa, Access, Diners, AmEx.
**Other points:** parking, children welcome, large indoor children's play area, Sunday lunch, open bank holidays, weekend breaks, disabled access, pets allowed, residents' lounge, vegetarian meals.
**Rooms:** 16 twin rooms, 8 family rooms with TV, radio, alarm, telephone, tea/coffee-making facilities.
DERRICK & PAULINE HARDY ☎(0191) 529 2020 Fax(0191) 529 2077

### YORK HOUSE HOTEL
30 Park Parade, NE26 1DX
A family-run hotel offering comfort, home-cooking and good service in a friendly atmosphere. A mid-terrace Victorian building in the town centre, the hotel is ideally situated for safe, sandy beaches, parks, indoor leisure pool and the shopping centre. Much thought has been given to the comfort of their guests, whether families on holiday or business people travelling in the area.
DOUBLE ROOM: up to £20
SINGLE ROOM: from £20 to £30
FOOD: up to £15
**Hours:** breakfast 7am-9.30am, dinner 6pm-7pm.
**Cuisine:** ENGLISH
**Cards:** Visa, Access, AmEx.
**Other points:** 24hr reception, lounge, central heating, children welcome, baby-sitting, cots, disabled access.
**Rooms:** 1 single room, 3 double rooms, 2 twin rooms, 2 family rooms. All with TV, radio, alarm, telephone, tea/coffee-making facilities.
**Directions:** off A193 Park Avenue.
MICHAEL & MARISSA RUDDY ☎(0191) 252 8313 Fax(0191) 251 3953

# NORTH YORKSHIRE

### APPLETON HALL COUNTRY HOUSE HOTEL
Appleton-le-Moors, YO6 6TF
Enjoy elegance, comfort and tranquility in this delightful country house. Set in two and half acres of beautiful gardens and with lovely views over the Yorkshire Moors, the hotel is an ideal base for exploring the Moors and the Dales. Offering the very best of English cuisine and using local produce whenever posssible, their aim is to make your stay a memorable one.
DOUBLE ROOM: from £30 to £40
FOOD: from £15 to £20 ☜
**Hours:** breakfast 8.15am-9.15am, dinner 6.30pm-8.30pm, open all year.
**Cuisine:** ENGLISH
**Cards:** Visa, Access, AmEx.
**Other points:** licensed, Sunday lunch, pets allowed,

children catered for (please check for age limits), lift, parking, residents' lounge, residents' bar.
**Rooms:** 3 single rooms, 5 double rooms, 2 twin rooms. All with TV, radio, telephone, tea/coffee-making facilities. 1 double and 1 twin with private lounge.
**Directions:** less than 2 miles from the A170. Follow signs for Appleton-le-Moors.
GRAHAM & NORMA DAVIES ☎(01751) 417227/417452 Fax(01751) 417540

### KING'S ARMS HOTEL & CLUBROOM RESTAURANT
Askrigg in Wensleydale, DL8 3HQ
A Grade II listed coaching inn of atmosphere and character, which began life as the famous 18th century racing stable of John Pratt. The bars - once the tack and harness rooms - are familiar to many as

the `Drovers Arms' of Darrowby in the BBC TV series of James Herriot's All Creatures Great and Small. Famous for good food, comfort and hospitality. Casserole Award 1995, Corp D'Elite Wine List 1990, 1991.

DOUBLE ROOM: from £40 to £50
SINGLE ROOM: from £50
FOOD: from £20 to £25 🍽

**Hours:** breakfast 8.30am-9.30am, bar meals 12noon-2pm, dinner 7pm-9pm, bar meals 6.30pm-9pm.
**Cuisine:** ENGLISH / FRENCH - award winning meat, game, fresh fish and vegetarian dishes cooked to order in restaurant, grill room and bars.
**Cards:** Visa, Access, AmEx.
**Other points:** licensed, open-air dining, 4 different dining areas, Sunday lunch, no-smoking area, disabled access, children catered for (please check for age limits).
**Rooms:** 10 doubles all en suite.
**Directions:** 1 mile off the A684 at Bainbridge, in the market square in Askrigg.
LIZ & RAY HOPWOOD ☎(01969) 650258
Fax(01969) 650635

## BAINBRIDGE • map 11D3

 **RIVERDALE COUNTRY HOUSE HOTEL**
Bainbridge, Leyburn, DL8 3EW

Situated in the centre of a country village in Upper Wensleydale among hills and moors, Riverdale Country House is an ideal base for touring and walking. Area used in the filming of James Herriot's novels.

DOUBLE ROOM: from £20 to £30
SINGLE ROOM: from £25 to £35
FOOD: up to £15

**Hours:** breakfast 8.30am-9.30am, dinner 7.30pm, closed December until February.
**Cuisine:** ENGLISH
**Other points:** central heating, children welcome, residents' lounge.
**Rooms:** 6 double rooms, 4 twin rooms, 2 family rooms.
**Directions:** follow A684 to Bainbridge; the hotel overlooks the green.
MRS A. HARRISON ☎(01969) 650311

## BOROUGHBRIDGE • map 12D4

# NEWCOMER OF THE YEAR 1996

 **BLACK BULL INN**
6 St James Square, YO5 9AR

A very pretty and well maintained market town hotel offering beautifully appointed public rooms and bedrooms. After a busy day exploring this scenic corner of Yorkshire you will find that the welcoming bar and restaurant staff take care of your every need with warmth and courtesy. Very highly recommended.

DOUBLE ROOM: from £20 to £30
SINGLE ROOM: from £35
FOOD: up to £15 CLUB

**Hours:** breakfast 8am-9am, lunch 12noon-2pm, bar meals 12noon-9.30pm, dinner 6.30pm-9.30pm, open bank holidays.
**Cards:** Access, Visa, AmEx, JCB, Switch, Delta
**Rooms:** 4 double rooms en suite. All with TV, radio, alarm, television, hair dryer and tea/coffee-making facilities.
**Directions:** 5 miles north of the A59 York to Harrogate road in the centre of the town.
MARGARET CHRYSTAL & TERRY MCKENNA
☎(01423) 322413 Fax(01423) 323915

## CASTLETON • map 12C5

 **MOORLANDS HOTEL**
55 High Street, YO21 2DB

A 100-year-old stone building with modern furnishings and walls decorated with pictures by a local artist. Good traditional cuisine and à la carte menu. Located in the heart of the North Yorkshire Moors National Park.

DOUBLE ROOM: from £25 to £35
SINGLE ROOM: from £20 to £30
FOOD: from £15 to £20 CLUB

**Hours:** breakfast 8.30am-9.30am, dinner 7pm-10pm, bar snacks 10am-10pm.
**Cuisine:** ENGLISH / INTERNATIONAL
**Cards:** Visa, Access, Diners, AmEx, Switch.
**Other points:** children catered for (please check for age limits), parking, pets, garden, vegetarian meals, open-air dining, residents' lounge, residents' bar.
**Rooms:** 8 bedrooms. All with TV, tea/coffee-making facilities.
**Directions:** 4 miles south of A171 Whitby to

Middlesborough road. 15 miles west of Whitby, 40 miles north of York.
A. & A. ABRAHAMS ☎(01287) 660206
Fax (01287) 660317

## CLAPHAM • map 11D3

 **GOAT GAP INN**
LA2 8JB
*An ideal centre from which to tour the Lake District and Herriot country, this family-run inn has earned itself a proud reputation for its excellent cuisine and fine wines. The accommodation is comfortable and the atmosphere homely and unpretentious. Boasts its own helipad, all aviators welcome as are animal lovers.*
DOUBLE ROOM: from £20 to £30
SINGLE ROOM: from £30 to £40
FOOD: from £15 to £20
**Hours:** lunch 11.30am-2pm, dinner 6pm-9.30pm. Open all day Sunday.
**Cuisine:** ENGLISH/CONTINENTAL - daily changing specials, vegetarian and children's menus.
**Cards:** Visa, Access, Eurocard
**Other points:** galleried function room for buffets and banquets, garden, open-air dining, barbeque and play area, private helipad.
**Rooms:** 3 double rooms, 2 family rooms, 1 twin room; three of the rooms have four poster beds. All with TV, central heating and tea/coffee making facilities. All rooms en suite.
**Directions:** 150 yards from the A65.
MR AND MRS WILLIS ☎(01524) 241230
Fax (01524) 241230

 **NEW INN HOTEL**
LA2 8HH
*The New Inn is over 200 years old and has provided a welcome stop for visitors to the Lake District, Scotland and the Yorkshire Dales since the 18th century. This coaching inn offers a relaxing and friendly atmosphere, comfortable accommodation and well-cooked food in generous portions. Under the personal supervision of the resident proprietors.*
DOUBLE ROOM: from £20 to £30
SINGLE ROOM: from £40
FOOD: from £15 to £20   CLUB
**Hours:** breakfast 8.30am-9.30am, lunch 12noon-2pm, dinner 7pm-9pm.
**Cuisine:** ENGLISH - traditional bar meals. Table d'hote and à la carte restaurant.
**Cards:** Visa, Access, AmEx, Switch, JCB.
**Other points:** licensed, Sunday lunch, garden, afternoon tea, pets allowed, games room, real ales, children welcome, cots, residents' bar, residents' lounge, parking, vegetarian meals.
**Rooms:** 10 double rooms, 3 twin rooms. All en suite with TV, telephone, tea/coffee-making facilities. Four poster and Victorian half-tester beds.
**Directions:** situated on A65 to Lake District. Clapham is 50 miles north of the M1 and Leeds, 21 miles east of Lancaster and junction 34 of the M6.
KEITH & BARBARA MANNION ☎(015242) 51203
Fax (015242) 51496

## FAIRBURN • map 12E5

**THE BAY HORSE**
Silver Street, WF11 9JA
*The Bay Horse is near the turn-off between Ferrybridge and Selby Fork, and is easily accessible from both carriageways of the A1.*
FOOD: up to £15
**Hours:** lunch 12noon-2pm, dinner 7pm-10pm. Open all day Sunday.
**Cuisine:** ENGLISH / CONTINENTAL - dishes may include pork cordon bleu, chicken angélique, sole bonne femme.
**Cards:** Visa, Access, Diners, Switch.
**Other points:** open-air dining, Sunday lunch, children welcome, functions.
**Directions:** on the A1 northbound at the Fairburn turn-off.
J.M. & P.S. PALFREYMAN ☎(01977) 607265
Fax (01977) 670553

## FILEY • map 12D6

**THE DOWNCLIFFE HOUSE HOTEL**
The Beach, YO14 9LA
*Occupying an unrivalled position, the hotel has been newly refurbished to a high standard. All bedrooms are beautifully decorated with coordinated furniture and furnishings and have spectacular views over Filey Bay. There is also a spacious and attractive restaurant. An ideal place to stay, unwind and relax.*
DOUBLE ROOM: from £20 to £30
SINGLE ROOM: from £20 to £30
FOOD: up to £15
**Hours:** dinner 6.30pm-9pm.
**Cuisine:** varying daily specials.
**Cards:** Visa, Access, Eurocard, Delta.
**Other points:** children catered for (please check for age limits).
**Rooms:** 10 bedrooms.
**Directions:** 6 miles south of Scarborough, overlooking Filey Bay.
ELISE GARLAND ☎(01723) 513310 Fax (01723) 516141

**SEAFIELD HOTEL**
9-11 Rutland Street, YO14 9JA
*A pleasant, family-run guest house, conveniently situated for the beautiful Crescent Gardens in the traditional seaside resort of Filey. Close to the railway and bus stations. Offering good food, comfortable accommodation and a friendly `home from home' atmosphere.*
DOUBLE ROOM: up to £20
SINGLE ROOM: up to £25
FOOD: up to £15
**Hours:** breakfast 8.45am-9am, dinner 6pm.
**Cuisine:** ENGLISH
**Cards:** Visa, Access.
**Other points:** children welcome, residents' lounge, special breaks, children welcome, baby-listening device, cots, left luggage.

---

**For Reservations & Special Offers FreeCall 0500 700 456**

**Rooms:** 1 single room, 1 double room, 11 twin room, 1 family room. All with TV, tea/coffee-making facilities.
**Directions:** Rutland Street runs off The Crescent.
JILL & DON DRISCOLL ☎(01723) 513715

## GOATHLAND • map 12D5

### INN ON THE MOOR
YO22 5LZ
*Rooms are comfortably furnished and service in the restaurant is friendly, yet prompt. The Inn overlooks the Yorkshire Moors, offering the ideal opportunity to explore the countryside. Places of interest in the area include the waterfalls and the Roman Road.*
DOUBLE ROOM: from £20 to £30
SINGLE ROOM: from £28 to £48
FOOD: up to £20
**Hours:** breakfast 8.45am-9.30am, lunch 12noon-2pm, dinner 7pm-8.30pm.
**Cuisine:** ENGLISH
**Cards:** Visa, Access, AmEx.
**Other points:** licensed, Sunday lunch, children welcome, pets allowed, parking.
**Rooms:** 24 bedrooms including twin/double rooms, family suites and four-poster rooms. All with TV, telephone, tea/coffee-making facilities.
**Directions:** 9 miles from Whitby, 14 miles from Pickering.
MALCOLM SIMPSON ☎(01947) 896296
Fax(01947) 896484

## HARROGATE • map 12E4

### ABBATT & YOUNG'S HOTEL
15 York Road, HG1 2QL

*Standing within its own gardens with ample room for parking, the hotel is conveniently situated for all local amenities including the Conference Centre and Valley Gardens. The individually furnished bedrooms offer every comfort and traditional home-cooking is the basis of the frequently changing menu. An ideal base for touring this most attractive part of England.*
DOUBLE ROOM: from £20 to £30
SINGLE ROOM: from £35 to £45
FOOD: up to £15
**Hours:** breakfast 7.30am-9am Monday to Friday, 8am-9am at weekends, dinner 7pm, open bank holidays.
**Cards:** Access, Visa
**Other points:** licensed, residents' lounge, garden for guests' use, pets allowed, ironing facilities, German

spoken.
**Rooms:** 4 single rooms, 3 twin rooms, 1 double room and 1 family room, all en suite. All with TV, radio, alarm, telephone, room service, baby listening device, tea/coffee-making facilities.
**Directions:** turn off the A59 towards the town centre (Ripon Road). York Road is off Swan Road on the right before the town centre.
JAMES & KAREN AKINS ☎(01423) 567336
Fax(01423) 500042

### BRITANNIA LODGE HOTEL
16 Swan Road, HG1 2SA
*A family-run hotel in a very good position for all the attractions of Harrogate. Refurbished to a high standard, the hotel provides comfortable facilities for its guests and prides itself on personal service. Weekend/midweek breaks available at most times.*
DOUBLE ROOM: from £25 to £35
SINGLE ROOM: from £35
FOOD: up to £15
**Hours:** breakfast 7.30am-9am, dinner 6.30pm-8pm.
**Cuisine:** ENGLISH - full English breakfast. Evening menu consists of traditional Yorkshire home-cooking.
**Cards:** Visa, Access, AmEx.
**Other points:** children catered for (please check for age limits), garden
**Rooms:** 4 single rooms, 4 double rooms, 3 twin rooms, 1 family room. All with satellite TV, radio, telephone, tea/coffee-making facilities, alarm, video.
**Directions:** close to Royal Hall, Valley Gardens and exhibition complex.
P. & E.M.J. CULLING ☎(01423) 508482
Fax(01423) 526840

### GRUNDY'S RESTAURANT
21 Cheltenham Crescent, HG1 1DH
*This is an excellent restaurant serving first-class meals in comfortable surroundings. The cuisine is predominantly Modern English and all dishes are freshly cooked to order. The outstanding food is complemented by a good wine list, excellent service and a friendly, warm atmosphere. The fixed-price menu offers particularly good value for money.*
FOOD: up to £20
**Hours:** dinner 6.30pm-10pm, closed Sunday, bank holidays, 2 weeks in July/August, 2 weeks in January.
**Cuisine:** MODERN ENGLISH - menu may feature fresh wild salmon with samphire, fillet of English lamb with honey and sherry sauce. Table d'hôte and à la carte.
**Cards:** Visa, Access, AmEx, Switch.
**Other points:** licensed.
**Directions:** in town centre, approx 2 minutes' walk from Royal Hall/conference centre.
VAL & CHRIS GRUNDY ☎(01423) 502610

### KIMBERLEY HOTEL
11-19 Kings Road, HG1 5JY

Completely refurbished last year, the Kimberley Hotel is centrally located and offers the most up-to-date facilities for businessmen and families alike. The sumptuous breakfast buffet will set you up for a days sight-seeing in this stylish and historic town. End your day with a relaxing drink in the bar and allow the attentive staff make you a dinner reservation in one of many nearby restaurants.
DOUBLE ROOM: from £30 to £40
SINGLE ROOM: over £50
Hours: breakfast only 7am-10am. Closed Christmas day & Boxing day.
Cards: Access, Visa, AmEx, Diners
Other points: parking, children welcome, conference facilities.
Rooms: 7 single rooms, 23 twin rooms, 25 double rooms, 5 triple rooms, all with en suite, tea/coffee maker, TV, telephone, radio, alarm, hair dryer, baby listening device.
Directions: next to the International Conference Centre in central Harrogate.
☎(01423) 505613 Fax(01423) 530276

### THE LANGHAM HOTEL
21-27 Valley Drive, HG2 0JL
Run by three members of the Ward family, this beautiful old hotel is in the heart of Harrogate, overlooking the renowned Valley Gardens. The Langham is a friendly, comfortable establishment, offering good food, with the table d'hôte menu being of particularly good value. National parks, stately homes and golf courses are nearby.
DOUBLE ROOM: from £30 to £40
SINGLE ROOM: from £35 to £45
FOOD: from £15 to £20
Hours: dinner 7.30pm-9.30pm.
Cuisine: ENGLISH / FRENCH - traditional English and French cuisine.
Cards: Visa, Access, Diners, AmEx.
Other points: licensed, Sunday lunch, children catered for (please check for age limits), open bank holidays, vegetarian meals, residents' bar, residents' lounge.
Rooms: 50 bedrooms. All with TV, telephone, tea/coffee-making facilities.
Directions: take A1, exit onto the A59 for Harrogate. Opposite Valley Gardens.
THE WARD FAMILY ☎(01423) 502179

### SHANNON COURT HOTEL
65 Dragon Avenue, HG1 5DS
A beautiful Victorian house with character and charm, bordering on the `Stray' in High Harrogate. This family-run hotel offers its guests a warm and friendly atmosphere in pleasant surroundings, and your stay would be a happy one with Tricia and Mike on hand to welcome you. Within easy driving distance of the Yorkshire Dales and North Yorkshire Moors National Park.
DOUBLE ROOM: from £20 to £30
SINGLE ROOM: from £20 to £30
FOOD: up to £15
Hours: breakfast 8am-9am, dinner 6.30pm.

Cuisine: ENGLISH - traditional.
Cards: Visa, Access.
Other points: children welcome, residents' lounge, vegetarian meals, no-smoking area.
Rooms: 2 single rooms, 3 double rooms, 1 twin room, 2 family rooms. All with en suite, TV, tea/coffee-making facilities.
Directions: off the A59 Skipton road.
TRICIA & MIKE YOUNG ☎(01423) 509858
Fax(01423) 530606

### STUDLEY HOTEL
Swan Road, HG1 2SE
Attractively situated adjacent to the beautiful Valley Gardens but within easy walking distance of Harrogate town centre, the Studley Hotel has all amenities. All bedrooms have private facilities. Le Breton French Restaurant has a genuine charcoal grill, and in addition there is a meeting room/private party room available for up to 15 people.
DOUBLE ROOM: from £30 to £40
SINGLE ROOM: from £65
FOOD: from £15 to £20 ⬛ CLUB
Hours: breakfast 7.30am-10am, lunch 12.30am-2pm, dinner 7pm-10pm.
Cuisine: INTERNATIONAL - extensive à la carte and table d'hôte menus, including charcoal-grilled steaks, fish, chicken, seafood. Luncheon: small à la carte menu. Bar snacks available.
Cards: Visa, Access, Diners, AmEx.
Other points: licensed, Sunday lunch, pets by prior arrangement, vegetarian meals, children welcome.
Rooms: 15 single rooms, 10 double rooms, 11 twin room. All with satellite TV, radio, telephone, tea/coffee-making facilities.
Directions: adjacent to Valley Gardens.
PAT WHARLDALL ☎(01423) 560425 Fax(01423) 530967

## HELMSLEY • map 12D5

### THE FEVERSHAM ARMS HOTEL
1 High Street, YO6 5AG
Attractive, historic coaching inn, modernized but retaining its old charm, set in the North Yorkshire Moors National Park. There are 18 bedrooms including five 4-poster rooms, one suite and six ground-floor bedrooms. Tennis court, heated outdoor swimming pool (May-October) and gardens for guests' use. Golf and riding nearby. Les Routiers Cheeseboard of the Year 1994.
DOUBLE ROOM: from £30 to £40
SINGLE ROOM: from £55
FOOD: from £15 to £20 ⬛⬛⬛
Hours: breakfast 7.30am-10am, lunch 12noon-3pm, last orders 1.30pm, dinner 7pm-11pm, last orders 9.30pm.
Cuisine: ENGLISH / CONTINENTAL - fresh shellfish, game (in season), Spanish paella (if booked in advance). Wide range of continental dishes complemented by an impressive Spanish and clarets wine list.
Cards: Visa, Access, Diners, AmEx.
Other points: licensed, Sunday lunch, children

catered for (please check for age limits), special breaks, parking, vegetarian meals, residents' bar, residents' lounge, disabled access.

**Rooms:** 4 double rooms, 8 twin rooms, 5 four-poster rooms, 1 suite. All with radio, telephone, tea/coffee-making facilities, hair dryer, satellite TV, trouser-press, safe.

**Directions:** at the junction of the A170 and B1257 in Helmsley.

THE FEVERSHAM ARMS HOTEL LTD ☎(01439) 770766 Fax (01439) 770346

 **PHEASANT HOTEL**
Harome, YO6 5JG

*Near the North York Moors National Park in the charming village of Harome. The hotel was originally two blacksmiths' cottages and a shop, which have been carefully converted, with spacious rooms and much character. Many of the rooms overlook the village pond.*

DOUBLE ROOM: from £30 to £40
SINGLE ROOM: from £35 to £45
FOOD: from £15 to £20 🍽

**Hours:** breakfast 8.30am-9.30am, lunch 12noon-2pm, dinner 7.30pm-8pm, bar lunches every day, closed 1st January until 28th February.

**Cuisine:** ENGLISH - steak-and-kidney pie, fresh local meat, fish and poultry.

**Other points:** licensed, open-air dining, no-smoking area, indoor swimming pool, children catered for (please check for age limits).

**Rooms:** 2 single rooms, 5 double rooms, 12 twin rooms.

**Directions:** 3 miles from Helmsley off the A170 in the direction of Scarborough.

MR & MRS K. & MR & MRS C. BINKS ☎(01439) 771241

## KNARESBOROUGH • map 12E4

 **CARRIAGES WINE BAR & BRASSERIE**
89 High Street, HG5 0HL

*Located in a 16th century brick building in the centre of Knaresborough, Jon Holder and his partner/chef Bruce Gray are enthusiastically establishing a good reputation for their brasserie, which offers an imaginative menu complemented by an extensive wine list. Try the confit of duck, or something from the special menu board which changes regularly.*

FOOD: from £15 to £20

**Hours:** dinner (restaurant) 7pm-9.30pm, (bar area) 6pm-10pm. Closed Sundays.

**Cuisine:** starters include tataki of beef with wasbi and pickled ginger, roast goats cheese, prawn and ginger won-ton, pan fried scallop tart. Main course specialities, include confit of duck on pesto mash, tartlet of glazed vegetables with Bagna Caudia (an Italian dipping sauce) or daube of kangaroo in red wine and mushroom sauce. Extensive wine list with good value house wine.

**Other points:** licensed.

**Directions:** on the A59 York to Harrogate road in the centre of Knaresborough.

MR JON HOLDER ☎(01423) 867041

## LEEMING BAR • map 12D4

 **MOTEL LEEMING**
Great North Road,Bedale, DL8 1DT

*Motel Leeming has easy access to both carriageways of the A1 and is open and serving meals 24 hours a day.*

DOUBLE ROOM: from £20 to £30
SINGLE ROOM: from £39
FOOD: up to £15 🍽 CLUB 🛏 ≡

**Hours:** open 24 hours.

**Cuisine:** ENGLISH - farmhouse platter, cheese fritters, traditional Sunday lunch, fresh fish dishes. Award-winning cheeseboard. Only fresh produce from local suppliers is used.

**Cards:** Visa, Access, Diners, AmEx.

**Other points:** Sunday lunch, children welcome.

**Rooms:** 10 single rooms, 18 double rooms, 12 twin rooms, 4 family rooms.

**Directions:** take A1; exit at the A684. Bedale sits on the A1/A684 junction.

CARL LES ☎(01677) 422122 Fax (01677) 424507

## LEYBURN • map 12D4

**WHEATSHEAF HOTEL**
Carperby, DL8 4DF

*The Wheatsheaf Hotel is situated in one of Yorkshire's most beautiful dales, 'Wensleydale', which is 18 miles west of the A1 and 34 miles east of the M6. It is here that the famous author and veterinary spent his honeymoon, later featured in his worldwide books and films. The Wheatsheaf offers lots of old world charm, at the same time catering for the modern day traveller.*

DOUBLE ROOM: from £25 to £30
SINGLE ROOM: from £25 to £30
FOOD: up to £15

**Hours:** bar meals 12noon-2pm, dinner and bar meals 7pm-9pm.

**Cards:** Access, Visa, AmEx, Switch

**Other points:** Sir James Herriot honeymoon stay, ideal walking location.

**Rooms:** 1 single room, 7 double rooms, includin 4 four-poster rooms.

**Directions:** A1, 18 miles west of Leaming Bar and .5 mile form Aysgarth Falls.

MR & MRS MAX AND SHEILA MACKAY
☎(01969) 663216 Fax (01969) 663019

## MALTON • map 12D5

 **CORNUCOPIA**
87 Commercial Street, Norton,
YO17 9HY
*Set in the heart of the horse-racing capital of the North, the restaurant is appropriately adorned with horse-racing memorabilia. The menu is extensive and innovative, with a wine list to suit most palates. An award-winning pub and a finalist in the Steak-and-Kidney Pie Competition.*
FOOD: up to £15
**Hours:** dinner 6.30pm-10pm, lunch 12noon-2pm.
**Cuisine:** ENGLISH - halibut, salmon and prawn mornay, boned duckling, traditional Sunday lunch. Braised beef simmered in ale and herb dumplings, pork casserole and apple fritters.
**Cards:** Visa, Access.
**Other points:** licensed, open-air dining, Sunday lunch, children welcome, beer garden.
**Directions:** off the A64 in the centre of Norton.
HAROLD ST QUINTON ☎(01653) 693456

 **THE MOUNT HOTEL**
Yorkersgate, YO17 0AB
*An attractive hotel with a fascinating interior in the form of over 700 jugs and a collection of horse-racing memorabilia, Malton being a racehorse-breeding centre. Very popular with local racing folk who gather in the old-fashioned mahogany bar to enjoy the excellent home-cooking. Ideal location for touring the North Yorkshire Moors and visiting Castle Howard and Eden Camp.*
DOUBLE ROOM: from £20 to £30
FOOD: up to £15 [CLUB]
**Hours:** lunch 12noon-2pm, dinner 7pm-9pm.
**Cuisine:** BRITISH - home-cooked country fare at value-for-money prices.
**Cards:** Visa, Access.
**Other points:** street parking, children welcome, no-smoking area, afternoon tea, open all day, disabled access, vegetarian meals, air-conditioned, residents' garden.
**Rooms:** 4 single rooms, 2 double rooms, 12 twin rooms, 3 family rooms.
**Directions:** off the A64 York to Scarborough road. First hotel on left in Malton.
MR GIBSON ☎(01653) 692608 **Fax**(01653) 692608

## NORTHALLERTON • map 12D4

 **DUKE OF WELLINGTON INN**
Welbury, DL6 2SG
*A family-run, rural village inn with a warm, welcoming atmosphere enhanced by real log fires in winter. All food is fresh, well-cooked and attractively presented, and the service is warm and courteous. For a friendly, relaxed atmosphere, good food and service, the Duke of Wellington is well worth a visit. Adjoining the inn is a cottage available for holiday let.*
FOOD: up to £15

**Hours:** bar meals 12noon-2pm & 7pm-10pm, closed Monday and Tuesday lunch.
**Cuisine:** ENGLISH - traditional home-made cuisine. Dishes may include duck à l'orange, steak Diane, steak-and-kidney pie. Vegetarian dishes.
**Cards:** Visa, Access.
**Other points:** licensed, children welcome, beer garden, playland.
**Directions:** between A19 and A167. 7 miles north of Northallerton, 3 miles west of A19.
MR & MRS THOMPSON ☎(01609) 882464

## OSMOTHERLEY • map 12D5

 **THREE TUNS INN**
South End, near Northallerton, DL6 3BN
*Situated on the edge of the beautiful North Yorkshire Moors in an old village, the Three Tuns is an early 18th century inn, with a walled garden. An ideal place for a relaxing meal at good-value prices, especially after tackling one of the nearby walks: Lyke Wake, Hambleton Hobble and Cleveland Way.*
DOUBLE ROOM: from £40 to £50
FOOD: up to £15
**Hours:** lunch 12noon-2.30pm, dinner 7pm-9.30pm.
**Cuisine:** ENGLISH / FRENCH - home-cooked, using fresh produce, the speciality being seafood.
**Cards:** Visa, Access.
**Other points:** licensed, Sunday lunch, children welcome, pets allowed.
**Directions:** from north or south, take A19, turn left at sign for Northallerton/Osmotherley.
H. & J. DYSON ☎(01609) 883301

## REETH • map 12D4

**KINGS ARMS HOTEL**
High Row, near Richmond, DL11 6SY
*An 18th century listed building situated in the heart of Swaledale. Original beams and open log fires add to the cosy and friendly atmosphere of this village `local'.*
DOUBLE ROOM: from £20 to £30
SINGLE ROOM: from £20 to £25
FOOD: up to £15
**Hours:** bar meals 12noon-2pm, bar meals 6.30pm-9pm.
**Cuisine:** ENGLISH
**Other points:** licensed, open-air dining, children welcome, coaches by prior arrangement
**Rooms:** 1 double room, 1 twin room, 2 family rooms.
**Directions:** leave the A6108 at Richmond and take B6270 to Reeth.
JANE MARKHAM & ARTHUR COOK ☎(01748) 884259

## RICHMOND • map 12D4

### A66 MOTEL
Smallways, DL11 7QW

*The A66 Motel was originally a 17th century farm. Situated close to the Dales and areas of historic interest, the motel is conveniently placed for visiting this beautiful part of England.*
DOUBLE ROOM: from £22
SINGLE ROOM: from £22
FOOD: from £15 to £20
**Hours:** bar meals 12noon-2.30pm, bar meals 7pm-10.30pm, breakfast 7am-10am, lunch 12noon-2pm, dinner 7pm-10.30pm.
**Cuisine:** MODERN ENGLISH - fresh salmon salad, Aylesbury duckling, steaks with sauce Espagnole.
**Cards:** Visa, Access, Diners, AmEx.
**Other points:** licensed, Sunday lunch, children welcome, pets allowed, garden.
**Rooms:** 6 bedrooms. Some en suite.
**Directions:** on the A66, near Scotch Corner.
SONIA HALL ☎(01833) 627334 **Fax**(01833) 627334

### PEAT GATE HEAD
Low Row In Swaledale, DL11 6PP

*A 300-year-old Dales house standing in two acres of grounds with magnificent and memorable views updale to the Pennines and down to Richmond. An ideal stop for travellers to explore the bewitching countryside. All food is home-made and uses fresh, seasonal produce. Special diets, likes and dislikes are all catered for. A friendly, welcoming place to stay.*
DOUBLE ROOM: from £20 to £30
SINGLE ROOM: from £20 to £30
FOOD: from £15 to £20 ☜
**Hours:** breakfast 8.30am, dinner 7pm.
**Cuisine:** ENGLISH
**Other points:** central heating, residents' lounge, garden, vegetarian meals.
**Directions:** situated off B6270 on Langthwaite road.
ALAN EARL ☎(01748) 886388

## ROSEDALE ABBEY • map 12D5

### BLACKSMITH'S ARMS HOTEL
Hartoft End, near Pickering, YO18 8EN

*A family-run hotel at the foot of Rosedale in the North Yorkshire Moors National Park, an area renowned for its scenic beauty. The original farmhouse dates back to the 16th century and commands extensive views of the surrounding*
moors and dales. Ideal centre for touring and riding.
DOUBLE ROOM: from £40 to £50
SINGLE ROOM: from £45 to £55
FOOD: from £20 to £25
**Hours:** lunch 12noon-2pm, dinner 7pm-9pm.
**Cuisine:** FRENCH / ENGLISH - hot or cold meals available in bar, e.g., supreme of chicken filled with garlic butter. Table d'hôte, e.g., fresh local lobster.
**Cards:** Visa, Access, AmEx.
**Other points:** children welcome.
**Rooms:** 14 bedrooms.
**Directions:** set within the North Yorkshire Moors National Park.
ANTHONY & MARGARET FOOT ☎(01751) 417331

### THE MILBURN ARMS HOTEL
Near Pickering, YO18 8RA

*Set in the heart of the North Yorkshire Moors National Park, this hotel is an ideal centre for walking and touring, as many places of scenic and historical interest are within easy reach. The atmosphere is most convivial, with low beams, log fires and real ales. Award-winning cuisine.*
DOUBLE ROOM: from £30 to £40
SINGLE ROOM: from £40 to £50
FOOD: up to £25 ☜
**Hours:** breakfast 8am-9.30am, dinner 7pm-8.30pm, lunch 12noon-2pm.
**Cuisine:** ENGLISH - extensive range of bar food and full à la carte restaurant open every night.
**Cards:** Visa, Access, Diners.
**Other points:** licensed, open-air dining, Sunday lunch, children welcome, parking, vegetarian meals, no dogs.
**Rooms:** 9 double rooms, 2 twin rooms. All with TV, telephone, tea/coffee-making facilities.
**Directions:** from the A170 at Wrelton, follow the sign to Rosedale Abbey.
JACQUIE BARRIE ☎(017515) 312 **Fax**(017515) 312

## SCARBOROUGH • map 12D6

### AMBASSADOR HOTEL
Centre of the Esplanade, South Cliff, YO11 2AY

*Award-winning, charming, clifftop hotel commanding spectacular views over South Bay. Located above the Spa conference/entertainment centre. The luxurious rooms are all superbly appointed and the hotel has numerous facilites, including a tropical lounge with 35 foot heated*

*pool, sauna and solarium. This hotel is first for Yorkshire hospitality and good value, provided by professional and friendly staff.*
DOUBLE ROOM: from £20 to £30
SINGLE ROOM: from £25 to £35
FOOD: up to £15
**Hours:** breakfast 8am-9.30am, bar meals 12noon-1.30pm, dinner 6pm-7.45pm, Saturdays 6pm and 7.30pm, open Christmas and New Year.
**Cuisine:** ENGLISH - 5 course table d'hôte, 7 course candlelit dinners, à la carte meals, Yorkshire breakfasts and special diets accommodated.
**Cards:** Visa, Access, AmEx.
**Other points:** conference room, no-smoking restaurant and residents' lounge, afternoon teas, morning coffee, home-made bar lunches, bar, lift, four-poster beds, dry cleaning, disabled access, garden, disco/dances, holiday discount vouchers, theatre booking service, parking.
**Rooms:** 14 single rooms, 17 double rooms, 17 twin room, 12 family rooms. All with en suite, telephone, satellite TV, tea/coffee-making facilities, hair dryer, radio/alarm, information packs.
**Directions:** on the corner of Avenue Victoria and the Esplanade, South Cliff.
RICHARD & KATHRYN FRANK ☎(01723) 362841 Fax (01723) 362841

### ATTENBOROUGH HOTEL
28-29 Albemarle Crescent, YO11 1XX
*A welcoming hotel set in a Victorian crescent, overlooking attractive gardens. Located in the centre of town; the train and bus station are only a short distance away.*
DOUBLE ROOM: up to £20
FOOD: up to £15
**Hours:** breakfast 8.30am-9.15am, dinner 6pm.
**Cuisine:** ENGLISH - traditional English cooking with continental influence. Daily fixed menu.
**Other points:** central heating, children welcome, residents' lounge, garden, vegetarian meals.
**Directions:** A170, A171 or A165 to Scarborough. Located in centre of town.
MR & MRS J. SNOW ☎(01723) 360857

### AVONCROFT HOTEL
Crown Terrace, YO11 2BL
*A comfortable, family-run private hotel in the centre of a Georgian terrace overlooking Crown Gardens and within minutes' walk of the beach, town centre, entertainments, spa complex, road and rail terminals. There is a quiet, comfortable lounge with well-stocked bar and games room, which provide ideal meeting points. Good British tradition, comfort and hospitality.*
DOUBLE ROOM: from £20 to £30
SINGLE ROOM: from £20 to £30
FOOD: up to £15
**Hours:** breakfast 8.30am-9.15am, bar meals 11am-4pm, dinner 5.30pm-6.15pm, bar meals 7pm-11pm, closed late December until early January.
**Cuisine:** ENGLISH - a daily changing menu, prepared with fresh ingredients.

**Other points:** children welcome, open bank holidays, afternoon tea, pets allowed, residents' lounge, vegetarian meals.
**Rooms:** 34 bedrooms.
**Directions:** from town centre take A165 Filey Road across Valley Bridge; at St Andrews Church turn left into Albion Road. First left into Crown Crescent, then first right into Crown Terrace.
CHRISTINE WILDE ☎(01723) 372737 Fax (01723) 372737

### THE BLACKSMITHS ARMS INN
High Street, Cloughton, YO13 0AE
*An old country pub, with oak beams and fires, set in a village near the North Yorkshire Moors. The staff are very friendly, and the food is not only excellently cooked but also offers superb value for money. Ideal base for exploring the Moors and Whitby and for enjoying golf and pony-trekking.*
DOUBLE ROOM: from £42 to £47
SINGLE ROOM: from £25
FOOD: up to £15   CLUB
**Hours:** breakfast 9am-9.30am, lunch 12noon-2pm, dinner 7pm-10pm.
**Cuisine:** MODERN ENGLISH - house specialities include fresh poached salmon in a white wine sauce, and trout grenobloise fried with prawns, capers and lemon. Vegetarian dishes.
**Cards:** Visa, Access.
**Other points:** Sunday lunch, children welcome, open bank holidays.
**Rooms:** 6 double rooms. All with TV, tea/coffee-making facilities.
**Directions:** 5 miles north of Scarborough, on the A171 Whitby to Scarborough road.
JEAN ANN ARNALL ☎(01723) 870244

### THE COPPER HORSE
15 Main Street, Seamer, YO12 4RF
*Traditional good home-style cooking in a delightful pub atmosphere, with efficient and helpful service in comfortable surroundings. Ideally located for visiting Scarborough and touring the North Yorkshire Moors.*
FOOD: up to £15   CLUB
**Hours:** lunch 12noon, dinner 6.30pm-9.30pm, open all year.
**Cuisine:** ENGLISH - traditionally cooked food, beautifully presented. Dishes may include crispy boned half duckling, large fillet of haddock, plus steaks, grills and fish.
**Cards:** Visa, Access.
**Other points:** licensed, Sunday lunch, no-smoking area, children welcome.
**Directions:** situated off the A64 in the main street of Seamer.
MR S.T. QUINTON ☎(01723) 862029

---

### EAST AYTON LODGE COUNTRY HOTEL & RESTAURANT

Moor Lane, East Ayton, YO13 9EW

*An attractive country residence built in the early 19th century and skilfully converted to a small but luxurious hotel and restaurant. Situated three miles from Scarborough in a beautiful three-acre setting in the National Park, close to the River Derwent.*

DOUBLE ROOM: from £20 to £30

SINGLE ROOM: from £35 to £45

FOOD: from £15 to £20 `CLUB`

**Hours:** lunch 12noon-2pm, dinner 6pm-9pm.

**Cuisine:** ENGLISH / FRENCH - home-grown produce in season. Good selection of vegetarian meals.

**Cards:** Visa, Access.

**Other points:** licensed, open-air dining, Sunday lunch, children welcome, beer garden, baby-listening device, cots, 24hr reception.

**Rooms:** 13 double rooms, 3 twin rooms, 1 family room. All with TV, telephone, tea/coffee-making facilities. All rooms are let as singles when required.

**Directions:** turn left off A170 (to Scarborough) in East Ayton. Close to post office.

BRIAN GARDNER ☎(01723) 864227 Fax(01723) 862680

### THE FALCON INN

Whitby Road, Cloughton, YO13 0DY

*A select free-house on the edge of the North Yorkshire Moors, with open views of the sea. Good food served by friendly, attentive staff. Three-times winner of 'Scarborough in Bloom'. Log fires in winter.*

DOUBLE ROOM: from £20 to £30

FOOD: up to £15 `CLUB`

**Hours:** lunch 12noon-2pm, dinner 7pm-9.30pm, open all year.

**Cuisine:** ENGLISH - bar meals, with carvery on Saturday evenings, and Sunday lunchtimes in the restaurant.

**Other points:** licensed.

**Rooms:** 4 double rooms, 4 twin rooms. All with TV, tea/coffee-making facilities.

**Directions:** 9 miles from Scarborough on A171 to Whitby. Take second Ravenscar turn-off.

MR ROBERTS ☎(01723) 870717

### GOLDEN GRID FISH RESTAURANT

4 Sandside, YO11 1PE

*The restaurant is bright and cheerful, with a nautical theme throughout. The seafood is brought in daily, ensuring that your selection is always fresh. This is a very busy restaurant with high standards of food preparation and presentation.*

FOOD: up to £15 `CLUB`

**Hours:** breakfast 10.30am, full menu to 10pm, check opening December and January.

**Cuisine:** ENGLISH - an extensive menu, with fish being the speciality.

**Cards:** Visa, Access.

**Other points:** children welcome, no-smoking area, disabled access, vegetarian meals.

**Directions:** situated on the Scarborough seafront, opposite the harbour.

JOHN SENIOR ☎(01723) 360922 Fax(01723) 372715

### MANOR HEATH HOTEL

67 Northstead Manor Drive, YO12 6AF

*An attractive, well-appointed, detached hotel overlooking Peasholm Park and North Bay. Ideally situated close to all the attractions of this English seaside resort: the beach, swimming pools, Kinderland, miniature railway and Mr Marvel's Fun Park, as well as golf links, bowling and county cricket.*

DOUBLE ROOM: up to £20

SINGLE ROOM: up to £25

FOOD: up to £15

**Hours:** breakfast 9am, dinner 6pm, closed Christmas day and New Year's day.

**Cuisine:** ENGLISH

**Other points:** central heating, children welcome, TV lounge.

**Rooms:** 1 single room, 8 double rooms, 1 twin room, 4 family rooms. All with TV, tea/coffee-making facilities.

**Directions:** from Whitby, turn right just before Peasholm Park traffic lights.

MR BRIAN SMITH ☎(01723) 365720

### RED LEA HOTEL

Prince of Wales Terrace, YO11 2AJ

*One of Scarborough's most popular hotels, having undergone sympathetic conversion from six elegant Victorian houses. Located on Scarborough's fashionable South Cliff, it provides an ideal base for summer holidays, weekend breaks and conferences. Guests are assured of a warm and sincere welcome. Superb heated indoor swimming pool and fitness facilities.*

DOUBLE ROOM: from £30 to £40

SINGLE ROOM: from £30 to £40

FOOD: up to £15

**Hours:** breakfast 8.30am-9.30am, bar meals 12noon-2pm, Sunday lunch 12.30am-1.30pm, dinner 6.30pm-8pm.

**Cuisine:** ENGLISH

**Cards:** Visa, Access, AmEx.

**Other points:** licensed, children welcome, Sunday lunch, open bank holidays, no-smoking area, residents' lounge, vegetarian meals, 24hr reception, residents' bar, swimming pool, cots.

**Rooms:** 18 single rooms, 12 double rooms, 31 twin rooms, 7 family room. All with TV, radio, alarm, telephone, tea/coffee-making facilities.

**Directions:** Prince of Wales Terrace runs between the Esplanade and Filey Road.

BRUCE & VALERIE LEE ☎(01723) 362431 Fax(01723) 371230

### SOUTHLANDS HOTEL

15 West Street, South Cliff, YO11 2QW

*Southlands Hotel is ideally situated on Scarborough's select South Cliff, enjoying close proximity to the Italian Rose Gardens, Esplanade and South Bay. All bedrooms in this centrally heated hotel are well appointed, with many facilities. The Windsor Restaurant offers an à la carte and table d'hôte menu, and pre-luncheon drinks can be enjoyed in the Windsor Bar. Evening dances are held throughout the season, and in-house conference facilities can cater for 20-100 delegates.*

DOUBLE ROOM: from £30 to £40

SINGLE ROOM: from £35 to £45

FOOD: up to £15

**Hours:** breakfast 8am-9.30am, bar snacks 12noon-1.45pm, dinner 6.30pm-8.30pm.

**Cuisine:** ENGLISH

**Cards:** Visa, Access, Diners, AmEx.

**Other points:** licensed.

**Rooms:** 58 bedrooms.

**Directions:** A64, turn right at Mere to Filey road, turn left and second right.

MR & MRS H. DIXON ☎(01723) 361461 Fax(01723) 376035

### WILLOW DENE

110 Columbus Ravine, YO12 7QZ

*A family-run private hotel situated in Scarborough's prime holiday area, within minutes of all the North Bay attractions and only a short walk to the town centre. The hotel has been well maintained by the resident proprietors and offers the comforts and amenities that today's holiday-maker requires.*

DOUBLE ROOM: up to £20

SINGLE ROOM: up to £20

FOOD: up to £15

**Hours:** breakfast 9am, dinner 5.15pm.

**Cuisine:** ENGLISH - traditional English fare.

**Other points:** parking, children catered for (please check for age limits), no-smoking area, residents' lounge, vegetarian meals.

**Rooms:** 2 single rooms, 2 double rooms, 2 twin rooms, 3 family rooms. All en suite. The family rooms may be used as double rooms.

**Directions:** located near Peasholm Park, north of Scarborough town centre.

ROBERT & ELIZABETH BRIGGS ☎(01723) 365173

## STOKESLEY • map 12C5

### MILLERS RESTAURANT

9 Bridge Road, TS9 5AA

*An attractive, family-run restaurant with an excellent reputation locally. The lunchtime menu offers simpler meals at a very reasonable price. Lunch or dinner, all meals are well cooked and excellently served.*

FOOD: up to £15 ⌐ CLUB

**Hours:** lunch 12noon-2pm, dinner 7.30pm-9.30pm, last orders 9pm, closed Sunday and Monday.

**Cuisine:** FRENCH / ENGLISH - evening à la carte

menu including breast of barbarie duck aux cerises. Lighter meals served on the lunchtime menu.

**Cards:** Visa, Access, Diners, AmEx, Switch.

**Other points:** licensed, reservations, no-smoking only, street parking.

**Directions:** off Stokesley High Street (A172), by River Leven.

KATHRYN ABBOTT ☎(01642) 710880

### THE WAINSTONES HOTEL

31 High Street, Great Broughton, TS9 7EW

*A most attractive village hotel with a real `local' bar. The restaurant has a homely atmosphere and serves both à la carte and table d'hôte meals within its bright and airy setting. Great care and consideration is shown to all guests, and the accommodation is of a high standard.*

DOUBLE ROOM: from £25 to £30

SINGLE ROOM: from £49

FOOD: up to £15 ⌐

**Hours:** breakfast 7am-9.30am, lunch 12noon-2pm, bar meals 12noon-2pm, dinner 7pm-10pm, bar meals 5pm-10pm.

**Cuisine:** MODERN ENGLISH - savoury cheese fritters, medallions of pork fillet, whole leg of lamb, beef Wellington, home-made beef burgers.

**Cards:** Visa, Access, AmEx.

**Other points:** open-air dining, Sunday lunch, children welcome, conferences, guide dogs.

**Rooms:** 4 single rooms, 8 double rooms, 11 twin room. All with satellite TV, radio, telephone, tea/coffee-making facilities, heating, hair dryer.

**Directions:** situated 2 miles southeast of Stokesley on the B1257 Helmsley road.

JAMES KEITH PIGG ☎(01642) 712268 Fax(01642) 711560

## THIRSK • map 12D4

### ANGEL INN

Long Street, Topcliffe, YO3 3RW

*Dating back to the 17th century, the Angel Inn is steeped in history, being one of the main stopping points between the north and south in the days of stage coach travel. In recent years it has been tastefully extended into a charming country inn and is renowned for its warm, friendly atmosphere, excellent food and traditional Yorkshire ales. A choice of suites provide the perfect setting for private functions and conferences. Car and coach park for 150 vehicles.*

DOUBLE ROOM: from £20 to £30

SINGLE ROOM: from £30 to £35

FOOD: up to £15

**Hours:** breakfast 7am-9.15am, lunch 12noon-2.30pm, dinner 6.30pm-9.30pm.

**Cuisine:** ENGLISH / INTERNATIONAL - extensive menu choice. Specialities fresh fish and local seasonal produce.

**Cards:** Visa, Access, Switch, Delta.

**Other points:** parking, children welcome, open bank holidays, afternoon tea, residents' lounge, vegetarian meals, garden, open-air dining, fishing, conferences, functions.

**Rooms:** 2 single rooms, 8 double rooms, 4 twin rooms, 1 family room. All with satellite TV, bar, telephone, tea/coffee-making facilities.

**Directions:** on A167, just off A168. 3 miles from the A1 and A19.

TONY & TRISH ARDRON ☎(01845) 577237 Fax (01845) 578000

---

### NAG'S HEAD HOTEL & RESTAURANT
Pickhill, YO7 4JG

*There has been an inn on this site for over 200 years, providing food and rest for travellers and horses using the A1, which was then the only road connecting London and Edinburgh. Today, the Nag's Head has been upgraded to an excellent standard, with comfortable rooms, superb cuisine and a wide selection of real ales and wines. Highly recommended.*

DOUBLE ROOM: from £24 to £34
SINGLE ROOM: from £34
FOOD: from £15 to £20 ☜

**Hours:** breakfast 7am-10.30am, lunch 12noon-2pm, dinner 7pm-9.30pm, Sunday 6pm-10pm.

**Cuisine:** ENGLISH - à la carte menu: dishes include sauté of hare fillets, grilled duck breast with lime and gin sauce, pork fillet stuffed with York ham and blue Wensleydale cheese, beef steak and venison pie. Puddings include squidgy chocolate roll, banoffee pie, praline, coffee and Tia Maria pancakes. Yorkshire cheeses. Soup and sandwiches all day.

**Cards:** Visa, Access, AmEx.

**Other points:** Sunday lunch, children welcome, pets allowed, garden, conferences.

**Rooms:** 3 single rooms, 7 double rooms, 5 twin rooms. All with TV, telephone, tea/coffee-making facilities.

**Directions:** 1 mile off A1, near Thirsk.

RAYMOND & EDWARD BOYNTON ☎(01845) 567391 Fax (01845) 567212

---

### SHEPPARD'S HOTEL, RESTAURANT & BISTRO
Front Street, Sowerby, YO7 1JF

*17th century brick buildings, ideally situated in Herriot Country. Sympathetically modernized, yet retaining a comfortable, country atmosphere, which is a joy to relax and unwind in. Excellent cuisine and service amid attractive surroundings.*

DOUBLE ROOM: from £40 to £50
SINGLE ROOM: from £59
FOOD: from £15 to £25 ☜ ≣

**Hours:** breakfast 8.30am-9am, lunch 12noon-2pm, dinner 7pm-10pm, open all year.

**Cuisine:** ENGLISH / INTERNATIONAL - fresh local produce used. Restaurant and bistro.

**Cards:** Visa, Access.

**Other points:** licensed, Sunday lunch, children catered for (please check for age limits).

**Rooms:** 7 double rooms, 1 triple room. All with TV, telephone, tea/coffee-making facilities.

**Directions:** off A19, into south-west corner of Thirsk, .5 mile to Sowerby.

ROY SHEPPARD ☎(01845) 523655 Fax (01845) 524720

---

## WHITBY • map 12C5

### ANDERSONS
Silver Street, YO21 3AH

*Centrally located, this bistro is popular for either a full meal or for a snack. Often gets very full in the evenings: booking recommended. Tables in the garden in summer.*

FOOD: from £15 to £20 [CLUB]

**Hours:** lunch 11.30am-2.15pm, dinner 6.30pm-9.45pm, bar 10am-11pm.

**Cuisine:** MODERN ENGLISH - steaks with sauces, local fish dishes. Vegetarian menu available.

**Cards:** Visa, Access, Diners, AmEx.

**Other points:** open-air dining, Sunday lunch, children welcome, pets allowed.

**Directions:** Whitby is on A174 and A171; the bistro is located in the town centre.

DAVID WHISSON ☎(01947) 605383

---

### THE MAGPIE CAFE
14 Pier Road, YO21 3PU

*The McKenzie family have been serving superb fish in this historic building for nigh on 40 years. Window tables overlook the Abbey, 199 steps and picturesque harbour of Whitby. The restaurant is extremely popular with holiday-makers and locals alike. The food is always fresh and well cooked and the service friendly, quick and welcoming. Les Routiers Casserole Award 1991, 1992, 1993, 1994 and 1995.*

FOOD: up to £15 ☜

**Hours:** meals Sunday-Thursday 11.30am-6.30pm, meals Friday-Saturday 11.30am-9pm, late opening July and August 11.30am-9pm everyday, closed January and first 2 weeks in February.

**Cuisine:** ENGLISH - fresh, local fish and shellfish straight off the quayside, up to 12 varieties each day including crab, lobster and salmon. Local ham, home-made steak pie and 30 home-made desserts.

**Cards:** Visa, Access, Switch.

**Other points:** Sunday lunch, children welcome.

**Directions:** Pier Road is main road from town centre to the beach and West Pier.

I. ROBSON, A. MCKENZIE-ROBSON, S. & I. MCKENZIE ☎(01947) 602058

### SEACLIFFE HOTEL
North Promenade, West Cliff, YO21 3JX
*A friendly, family-run hotel with a restaurant which is also open to non-residents. All food is of good quality and well presented at very reasonable prices. Tastefully decorated bedrooms, some with sea views and situated close to local attractions such as Whitby Abbey, the museum and the local golf course.*
DOUBLE ROOM: from £20 to £30
SINGLE ROOM: from £30 to £50
FOOD: from £15 to £20
**Hours:** breakfast 8am-9.30am, dinner 6pm-9pm, open all year.
**Cuisine:** ENGLISH - including fresh local seafood, steaks and vegetarian dishes.
**Cards:** Visa, Access, Diners, AmEx.
**Other points:** licensed, children welcome, pets allowed, open bank holidays, residents' lounge, residents' bar, vegetarian meals, parking.
**Rooms:** 1 single room, 15 double rooms, 2 twin rooms, 2 family rooms. All with en suite, TV, radio, telephone, tea/coffee-making facilities.
**Directions:** take A171 or A174 to Whitby. Follow signs to West Cliff.
J.A. PURCELL ☎(01947) 603139 Fax(01947) 603139

### STAKESBY MANOR
Manor Close, High Stakesby, YO21 1HL
*A lovely 17th century manor house, situated on the edge of Whitby, that has been owned and controlled by two generations of the Hodgson Family. Located in a quiet area approximately one mile from town centre, golf course and beach, Stakesby Manor offers well-cooked, tasty food, friendly, attentive service and comfortable accommodation in relaxed and attractive surroundings.*
DOUBLE ROOM: from £20 to £30
SINGLE ROOM: from £35 to £45
FOOD: up to £15  CLUB
**Hours:** breakfast 8am-9am, dinner 7pm-9.30pm.
**Cuisine:** MODERN ENGLISH - three-course à la carte menu and table d'hôte, including salmon and lobster mousse, lobster cardinal, veal in leek and Stilton sauce.
**Cards:** Visa, Access, AmEx.
**Other points:** vegetarian meals, special diets, children welcome, garden, picnic lunches, functions, conferences, special breaks.
**Rooms:** 6 double rooms, 2 twin rooms. All with TV, radio, tea/coffee-making facilities.
**Directions:** off the A171.
MR & MRS HODGSON ☎(01947) 602773 Fax(01947) 602140

### TRENCHER'S RESTAURANT
New Quay Road, YO21 1DH
*A family-run seafood restaurant in the historic fishing town of Whitby. Needless to say, fresh Whitby fish and seafoods are a speciality and are cooked to a high standard. Terry and his sisters Judy*
and Nicky have received thank-you letters from as far away as Europe and the USA.
FOOD: up to £15
**Hours:** meals all day 11am-12midnight, last orders 9pm, closed January and February.
**Cuisine:** SEAFOOD - fresh local fish, salad bar, freshly cut sandwiches, home-made desserts.
**Other points:** licensed, Sunday lunch, children welcome.
**Directions:** opposite the harbour offices and quayside car park, off main A174.
TERRY, JUDY & NICKY FOSTER ☎(01947) 603212

### WHITE HOUSE HOTEL
Upgang Lane, YO21 3JJ

*The hotel is situated adjacent to Whitby Golf Course, with panoramic views of Sandsend Bay. Whitby is a charming, picturesque fishing port with a history extending back 1,000 years. An ideal location for discovering an intriguing part of Yorkshire.*
DOUBLE ROOM: from £28
SINGLE ROOM: from £28
FOOD: up to £15
**Hours:** breakfast 8.30am-10am, lunch 12noon-2pm, dinner 7pm-10pm.
**Cuisine:** ENGLISH - Yorkshire pudding with stew. `Galley' five-course dinner.
**Cards:** Visa, Access.
**Other points:** licensed, Sunday lunch, children welcome.
**Directions:** on the A174, beside Whitby Golf Course on the West Cliff.
THOMAS CAMPBELL ☎(01947) 600469 Fax(01947) 821600

## WIGGINTON • map 12E5

### JACOBEAN LODGE HOTEL
Plainville Lane, YO3 3RG
*A welcoming, 17th century converted farmhouse, set in over an acre of picturesque gardens, ideal for visitors wishing to explore the Dales, Bronte and Herriot countryside. The restaurant serves a range of traditional food and all bedrooms are spacious and well-equipped.*
DOUBLE ROOM: from £20 to £30
SINGLE ROOM: from £32
FOOD: up to £15
**Hours:** breakfast 7.30am-9.30am, lunch and bar meals 12noon-2pm, dinner and bar meals Sunday-Thursday 6.30pm-9.30pm, 6.30pm-10pm Friday and Saturday, open bank holidays.
**Cuisine:** TRADITIONAL ENGLISH - varied

vegetarian and continental choices.
**Cards:** Access, Visa, Switch
**Other points:** parking, children welcome, pets allowed, no-smoking area, outdoor dining, residents' lounge and garden, afternoon teas, Sunday lunch, conference facilities.
**Rooms:** 2 single rooms, 1 twin room, 9 double rooms, 2 family rooms all en suite with tea/coffee-maker, TV, telephone, radio, alarm, hair dryer, room service, baby listening device.
**Directions:** Situated between the B1363 York to Helmsley road, and the A19 Shipton road.
BRIAN & ELAINE GWINNETT ☎(01904) 762749 Fax(01904) 768403

## WIGGLESWORTH • map 11E3

### THE PLOUGH INN
Near Skipton, BD23 4RJ

*This lovely country hotel is situated just two miles from the A65. Boasting early 18th century origins, the Plough Inn provides excellent food and service, comfortable furnishings and good service to meet all your needs. Fine dining is offered in the bright conservatory restaurant.*
DOUBLE ROOM: from £20 to £30
SINGLE ROOM: from £25 to £35
FOOD: up to £15
**Hours:** dinner 7pm-9.45pm, lunch 12noon-2pm.
**Cuisine:** ENGLISH - seafood pancakes, whole ham shank in ginger syrup.
**Cards:** Visa, Access, Diners, AmEx.
**Other points:** licensed, Sunday lunch, children welcome.
**Rooms:** 7 double rooms, 3 twin rooms, 2 family rooms. All with TV, radio, telephone, tea/coffee-making facilities.
**Directions:** from the A65 at Long Preston, take the B6478 to Wigglesworth.
BRIAN GOODALL ☎(01729) 840243 Fax(01729) 840638

## YORK • map 12E5

### ABBOTS MEWS HOTEL
6 Marygate Lane, Bootham, YO3 7DE
*Situated in the centre of York, only minutes away from the city's historic attractions. The hotel was an original coachman's cottage with coach-house and stables, but was converted in 1976. The restaurant is renowned for its high standard of cuisine, and the service is very friendly and efficient.*
DOUBLE ROOM: from £30 to £40
SINGLE ROOM: from £40 to £50

FOOD: up to £20 CLUB
**Hours:** breakfast 7.30am-9.30am, Sunday 8.30am-10am, lunch 12noon-2pm, dinner 7pm-9.30pm.
**Cuisine:** INTERNATIONAL - specialities include sautéed medallions of beef Hongroise, chicken Madras, stir-fried beef on oyster sauce. Bar lunches are also served weekdays.
**Cards:** Visa, Access, Diners, AmEx, Switch.
**Other points:** licensed, Sunday lunch, children welcome, garden, conferences.
**Rooms:** 20 double rooms, 19 twin rooms, 11 family rooms. All with TV, radio, tea/coffee-making facilities.
**Directions:** in centre of York. Close to Museum Gardens and Bootham Bar.
MR A. LEWIS & MRS P. WATSON ☎(01904) 622395/634866 Fax(01904) 612848

### ASCOT HOUSE
80 East Parade, York, YO3 7YH
*An attractive Victorian guest house offering comfortable accommodation, a good home-cooked breakfast and a welcoming, homely atmosphere. Conveniently located for the historic town of York, York Minster, museums and the beautiful east coast.*
DOUBLE ROOM: up to £20
SINGLE ROOM: up to £20
**Hours:** breakfast 8.30am-9.30am (or on request).
**Cards:** Visa, Access, Diners.
**Other points:** parking, children welcome, sauna, residents' lounge, licensed, vegetarian meals, no evening meals.
**Rooms:** 1 single room, 8 double rooms, 3 twin rooms, 3 family rooms. 12 rooms en suite, some with four poster/canopy beds. All with TV, tea/coffee-making facilities.
**Directions:** from outer ring road follow A1036 to city centre. On reaching 30mph sign take next turn left along Heworth Road to the traffic lights. Then turn right into East Parade.
KEITH & JUNE WOOD ☎(01904) 426826 Fax(01904) 431077

### THE BLACK BULL INN
Main Street, Escrick, YO4 6JP
*This appealing cottage-style village inn close to York provides guests with comfortable accommodation in the recently refurbished bedrooms and fine food in the popular restaurant. Meals are also available in the bar, where the relaxed atmosphere provides a haven for many locals as well as passing travellers.*
DOUBLE ROOM: from £20 to £30
FOOD: from £15 to £20 CLUB
**Hours:** breakfast 7am-9am, lunch 12noon-2pm, dinner 6.30pm-10pm.
**Cuisine:** ENGLISH - traditional English cuisine, prepared and cooked to a high standard.
**Cards:** Visa, Access.
**Other points:** parking, children welcome, pets allowed, no-smoking area, vegetarian meals.
**Rooms:** 5 double rooms, 2 twin rooms, 1 family room. All with en suite, TV, radio, alarm, trouser-

press, tea/coffee-making facilities.
**Directions:** 5 miles south of York on A19 towards Selby.
HUGH & ANNE BOWMAN ☎(01904) 728245

### BYRON HOUSE HOTEL
7 Driffield Terrace, The Mount, YO2 2DD
*Byron House provides a high standard of accommodation, a friendly atmosphere, and personal service in pleasant surroundings. Good food is served in the dining room, and guests can relax in the lounge with its licensed bar and selection of wines. Within walking distance of the hotel are many attractions, including the Minster.*
DOUBLE ROOM: from £30 to £40
FOOD: from £15 to £20
**Hours:** breakfast 7.30am-9.30am, dinner 7pm, closed Christmas.
**Cuisine:** ENGLISH
**Cards:** Visa, Access, Diners, AmEx.
**Other points:** children welcome, residents' lounge, vegetarian meals, cots, left luggage, residents' bar, parking.
**Rooms:** 3 single rooms, 2 double rooms en suite, 1 twin room en suite, 4 family rooms en suite. All with TV, radio, telephone, tea/coffee-making facilities.
**Directions:** A1036, signposted York west and Racecourse. Walking distance of centre.
DICK & JEAN TYSON ☎(01904) 632525
Fax(01904) 638904

### CARLTON HOUSE HOTEL
134 The Mount, YO2 2AS
*A cosy, family-run hotel, conveniently located close to the racecourse and all city-centre amenities. A popular choice for many visitors to York and the surrounding countryside.*
DOUBLE ROOM: from £20 to £30
SINGLE ROOM: from £20 to £30
**Hours:** breakfast 7.45am-9.15am, closed Christmas.
**Cuisine:** BREAKFAST
**Other points:** central heating, children welcome, residents' lounge.
**Rooms:** 1 single room, 6 double rooms, 2 twin rooms, 4 family rooms. All en suite with TV, radio, tea/coffee-making facilities.
**Directions:** on the A1036 close to York station.
MALCOLM & LIZ GREAVES ☎(01904) 622265

### DUKE OF CONNAUGHT HOTEL
Copmanthorpe Grange, YO2 3TN
*The hotel is set in a fascinating location in York, encircled by 14th century walls, ancient streets and buildings and overlooked by the magnificent York Minster. With attractively 18th century-style furnishings and equipped with many modern facilities, guests are assured of a warm welcome and comfortable stay. There is a bright, airy lounge bar, and good access for disabled persons to all*

*ground-floor rooms. An ideal base for touring the historic city of York.*
DOUBLE ROOM: from £20 to £30
SINGLE ROOM: from £35 to £40
**Hours:** breakfast 8am-9.30am, dinner 7pm-10pm, closed Christmas.
**Cuisine:** ENGLISH
**Cards:** Visa, Access, AmEx.
**Other points:** licensed, Sunday lunch, no-smoking area, disabled access, parking, vegetarian meals, afternoon tea, residents' lounge, garden, children welcome, cots.
**Rooms:** 5 double rooms, 5 family rooms. All with TV, telephone, tea/coffee-making facilities.
**Directions:** off A64 York-Leeds road; between Appleton Roebuck and Bishopthorpe, York.
JACK HUGHES ☎(01904) 744318 Fax(01904) 774672

### THE HAZELWOOD
24-25 Portland Street, Gillygate, YO3 7EH
*Situated in the centre of town only 400 yards from York Minster yet in extremely quiet location and with its own car park. The Hazelwood is an elegant Victorian guest house with comfortable en-suite accommodation which offers excellent value. Guests can relax in the small secluded garden or in the peaceful residents' lounge where tea and coffee are always available.*
DOUBLE ROOM: from £20 to £30
SINGLE ROOM: from £20
**Hours:** breakfast 8.15am-9.15am.
**Cards:** Visa, Access, MasterCard
**Cuisine:** ENGLISH & CONTINENTAL
**Other points:** completely non-smoking, parking, small private garden, wide choice of breakfasts including vegetarian, guests' lounge with tea and coffee always available, baby-sitting service available at extra cost.
**Rooms:** 14 bedrooms, 11 en suite, all with tea/coffee maker, TV, radio, alarm, hair dryer.
**Directions:** approach city centre by A19 from the north. Turn left at lights just before city gate. Portland Street is the first on the left.
IAN & CAROLYN MCNABB ☎(01904) 626548 Fax(01904) 628032

### HEDLEY HOUSE
3 Bootham Terrace, YO3 7DH
*A Victorian residence within walking distance of the city of York. Family-run, the atmosphere is friendly and informal and complemented by good home-cooking.*
DOUBLE ROOM: from £20 to £30
SINGLE ROOM: from £25 to £35
FOOD: up to £15
**Hours:** breakfast 8am-9am, dinner 6.30pm-7pm.
**Cuisine:** ENGLISH
**Cards:** Visa, Access, AmEx.
**Other points:** children welcome, pets allowed,

residents' lounge, vegetarian meals.
**Rooms:** 15 bedrooms.
**Directions:** off the A19, third turning on left away from Bootham Bar.
GRAHAM & SUSAN HARRAND ☎(01904) 637404

 **HUDSON'S HOTEL**
60 Bootham, YO3 7BZ

*A Victorian hotel in the city centre, only minutes from Bootham Bar, the Minster and the Roman Walls. The hotel was converted from two town houses and now provides elegant accommodation and high-quality cuisine.*
DOUBLE ROOM: from £35 to £45
SINGLE ROOM: over £50
FOOD: up to £15
**Hours:** breakfast 7.30am-9.30am, lunch by prior arrangement 12noon-2pm, dinner 6.30pm-9.30pm.
**Cuisine:** ENGLISH / CONTINENTAL - extensive à la carte menu served in the Below Stairs restaurant.
**Cards:** Visa, Access, Diners, AmEx.
**Other points:** children welcome.
**Rooms:** 1 single room, 15 double rooms, 10 twin rooms, 4 family rooms. All with satellite TV, telephone, tea/coffee-making facilities.
**Directions:** very close to Bootham Bar and York Minster.
C.R. HUDSON ☎(01904) 621267 Fax(01904) 654719

☴ **KITES RESTAURANT**
13 Grape Lane, YO1 2HU

*Tucked away in a small street very close to the Minster and Stonegate. Access to the restaurant is up a narrow staircase to the second floor. All herbs come from the proprietor's own herb garden. Local produce used where possible, including a good selection of unusual cheeses from the Dales. Well-chosen but affordable wine list.*
FOOD: from £15 to £20
**Hours:** lunch Monday-Saturday 12noon-2pm, dinner 6.30pm-10.30pm, closed Sunday.
**Cuisine:** INTERNATIONAL - innovative international menu: Thai crab cakes, pan fried monkfish provencal, medallions of venison in blackcurrant and port sauce, chicken breast with Armagnac and prawns.
**Cards:** Visa, Access, Diners, AmEx.
**Other points:** bookings advisable, licensed, children welcome.
**Directions:** from Bootham Bar, follow Petergate to Low Petergate, then to Grape Lane.
MR C. WRIGHT ☎(01904) 641750 Fax(01904) 640121

 **MOUNT ROYALE**
The Mount, YO2 2DA

*Gothic in appearance but mainly William IV in style, the Mount Royale has been tastefully decorated and furnished to retain its character. The atmosphere is further enhanced by the presence of the Old English garden, which can be seen from the restaurant. A very pleasant venue in which to enjoy good food and friendly, professional service.*
DOUBLE ROOM: from £30 to £40
SINGLE ROOM: from £67 to £80
FOOD: from £25 to £30
**Hours:** breakfast 7.15am-9.30am, dinner 7pm-10.30pm.
**Cuisine:** INTERNATIONAL - including rack of lamb and duckling.
**Cards:** Visa, Access, Diners, AmEx.
**Other points:** licensed, children welcome, pets by prior arrangement, heated open air swimming pool (open summer only), trimnasium, sauna, solarium.
**Rooms:** 13 double rooms, 10 twin rooms. All with TV, radio, telephone, tea/coffee-making facilities.
**Directions:** on A1036 past racecourse, up hill to traffic lights. On right side.
STUART OXTOBY ☎(01904) 628856 Fax(01904) 611171

☴ **PLUNKETS RESTAURANT LTD**
9 High Petergate, YO1 2EN

*Plunkets is a cheerful restaurant set in a 17th century building situated near York Minster. It plays gentle jazz/disco music and is full of plants, prints and polished wooden tables.*
FOOD: up to £15
**Hours:** meals all day 12noon-11pm, closed Christmas day and New Year's day.
**Cuisine:** INTERNATIONAL - dishes include fajitas, burritos, Thai cuisine, hamburgers, steaks, home-made pies, fresh salmon fishcakes, marinated chicken breasts, salads and various vegetarian dishes.
**Cards:** Visa, Access, MasterCard.
**Other points:** licensed, Sunday lunch, children welcome.
**Directions:** located on one of York's principal streets, between the Minster and Bootham Bar.
TREVOR BARRINGTON WARD ☎(01904) 637722

☖ **RED LION MOTEL & COUNTRY INN**
Upper Poppleton, YO2 6PR

*A friendly, cheerful and welcoming country inn, offering fresh food amid pleasant surroundings. Ideally located for those who wish to tour the famous Yorkshire Dales, the Moors, or for visiting York itself and nearby Harrogate.*
DOUBLE ROOM: from £20 to £30
SINGLE ROOM: from £30 to £40
FOOD: up to £15
**Hours:** breakfast 7.30am-9am, lunch 12noon-2pm, dinner 6.30pm-9.30pm, open all year.
**Cuisine:** ENGLISH - à la carte menu. offering a choice of good home-cooked dishes, including fresh Whitby fish. Vegetarian meals also available.
**Cards:** Visa, Access, Switch, Delta.
**Other points:** licensed, open-air dining, Sunday lunch, no-smoking area, children welcome, parking, garden, open bank holidays.
**Rooms:** 8 double rooms, 2 twin rooms, 8 family rooms. All with TV, telephone, tea/coffee-making

facilities.
**Directions:** situated .5 mile from the outskirts of York on the A59.
PUBMASTER LTD ☎(01904) 781141 **Fax**(01904) 785143

---

≋ **WHITE SWAN INN & RESTAURANT**
Deighton, Escrick, YO4 6HA
*A family-run country inn, with an intimate restaurant and comfortable bar area. Offers well-prepared and presented dishes at excellent value for money, in a very pleasant, friendly atmosphere.*
FOOD: from £15 to £20    CLUB

**Hours:** Sunday lunch 12noon-2pm, bar meals 12noon-2pm, dinner 7pm-9.30pm, bar meals 7pm-9.30pm.
**Cuisine:** BRITISH - fillet of salmon in a piquant walnut sauce and half roast duckling available in restaurant. Steaks, salads, pies and special dishes of the day in the bar. Game available in season.
**Cards:** Visa, Access.
**Other points:** children welcome, open bank holidays, Sunday lunch.
**Directions:** on A19, 5 miles south of York.
MR & MRS WALKER ☎(01904) 728287

# SOUTH YORKSHIRE

## DONCASTER • map 9A2

≋ **THE REGENT HOTEL, PARADE BAR & RESTAURANT**
Regent Square, DN1 2DS
*Established under the same family ownership for 60 years, this handsome town-centre Victorian building has the unique advantage of being situated in a small Regency park on the A638. Close to Doncaster racecourse and an ideal stopping place when travelling north or south.*
DOUBLE ROOM: from £30 to £40
SINGLE ROOM: from £45 to £55
FOOD: from £15 to £20 ⌁ CLUB
**Hours:** breakfast 7.30am-9am, lunch 12noon-2pm, dinner 6pm-10pm.
**Cuisine:** INTERNATIONAL - wide choice of menus including: Evening Menu, à la carte; Bar Lunch and Evening Menu; Sunday Lunch; Vegetarian and lunchtime buffet.
**Cards:** Visa, Access, Diners, AmEx.
**Other points:** licensed, Sunday lunch, children welcome, coaches by prior arrangement.
**Rooms:** 50 bedrooms. All en suite with satellite TV, tea/coffee-making facilities, trouser-press.
**Directions:** on the main A638 road through Doncaster.
MICHAEL LONGWORTH ☎(01302) 364180

## ROTHERHAM • map 9A2

≋ **BRECON HOTEL**
Moorgate Road, S60 2AY
*A small, family-run hotel where you will find true Yorkshire hospitality. The restaurant enjoys a good reputation locally for its quality, generous portions and friendliness of service. With its good food, comfortable accommodation, welcoming service and value for money, Brecon Hotel is highly recommended.*
DOUBLE ROOM: from £20 to £30
SINGLE ROOM: from £30 to £40
FOOD: up to £15    CLUB
**Hours:** breakfast 7.30am-9.30am, lunch 12noon-

2pm, dinner 7pm-9.15pm.
**Cuisine:** ENGLISH - dishes may include beef stroganoff, roast chicken grand-mère, lamb cutlets with rosemary, salmon hollandaise. Bar meals. Traditional Sunday lunch.
**Cards:** Visa, Access, Diners, AmEx.
**Other points:** licensed, children welcome, pets allowed.
**Rooms:** 2 single rooms, 13 double rooms, 27 twin rooms.
**Directions:** off M1 junction 33. Half a mile past Rotherham General Hospital on A618.
ELIZABETH WOMBLE ☎(01709) 828811
**Fax**(01709) 820213

## SHEFFIELD • map 9A2

≋ **THE OLD SIDINGS**
91 Chesterfield Road, Dronfield, S18 6XE
*An attractive Victorian pub with railway memorabilia throughout the Waiting Room lounge and Buffet Car dining room. Within the comfortable and welcoming surroundings there is a good choice of bar meals and snacks, lunchtime and evening, in both lounge and dining room, with the emphasis on traditional, country-style, home-made fare.*
FOOD: up to £15 ⌁
**Hours:** lunch 12noon-2.30pm, dinner 6pm-9.30pm.
**Cuisine:** ENGLISH - predominantly English. House speciality: varied list of casseroles, Anne's home-made giant Yorkshire pudding, Large rump steaks. A large selection of vegetarian meals. Family budget menus and children's menu.
**Cards:** Visa, Access, Switch.
**Other points:** licensed, Sunday lunch, no-smoking area, children welcome, pets allowed, beer patio.
**Directions:** off main A61 on B6057. Next to only railway bridge in Dronfield.
WILLIAM & ANNE STANAWAY ☎(01246) 410023
**Fax**(01246) 415000

---

**For Reservations & Special Offers FreeCall 0500 700 456**

### WESTBOURNE HOUSE HOTEL
25 Westbourne Road, S10 2QQ

*A memorable, inexpensive country-house-style hotel offering a warm and friendly atmosphere, set in authentic period surroundings with beautiful gardens. The hotel is situated in a conservation area, close to the city centre and only a short walk from the universities, main hospitals and Botanical Gardens. Every room is furnished with antiques and decorated in Georgian, Victorian or Edwardian style.*

DOUBLE ROOM: from £25 to £30
SINGLE ROOM: from £30 to £48
**Hours:** breakfast 7.30am-9am.
**Cuisine:** ENGLISH / CONTINENTAL
**Cards:** Visa, Access, AmEx.
**Other points:** parking, children welcome, pets allowed, residents' lounge, garden, vegetarian breakfasts.
**Rooms:** 11 bedrooms. All with TV, radio, alarm, hair dryer, trouser-press, iron, tea/coffee-making facilities. Four rooms have four-poster or canopy beds.
**Directions:** less than a mile south-west of the city centre, off A57 to Glossop.
MARY & MICHAEL PRATT ☎(0114) 2660109
Fax(0114) 2667778

### ZING VAA RESTAURANT
55 The Moor, S1 4PF

*Genuine Cantonese dishes and atmosphere. Situated in the very heart of Sheffield's busy shopping area. Very popular with both locals, shoppers and business people. Parking is available at the rear of the restaurant.*

FOOD: from £15 to £20
**Hours:** meals all day 12noon-11.45pm, closed Christmas day.
**Cuisine:** CANTONESE / PEKINESE - Cantonese and Peking cuisine, sliced fillet with king prawns marinated and cooked in a fruity sauce, duckling dishes.
**Cards:** Visa, Access, Diners, AmEx.
**Other points:** licensed, Sunday lunch, children welcome, parking.
**Directions:** situated in the heart of Sheffield shopping centre, opposite the bandstand.
ROGER CHEUNG ☎(0114) 2722432/2756633
Fax(0114) 2729213

# WEST YORKSHIRE

## BINGLEY • map 12E4

###  FIVE RISE LOCKS HOTEL
Beck Lane, BD16 4DD

*Converted from an original Victorian mill owners residence, the hotel stands in its own mature gardens with woodland paths and far reaching views of the Aire valley. Ideally situated for exploring this beautiful part of the country, guests can be assured of a warm welcome from Mr and Mrs Oxley and their staff. The bedrooms have been individually designed and furnished and are comprehensively equipped. Public areas include games room, library and a conservatory. Well recommended.*

DOUBLE ROOM: from £20 to £30
SINGLE ROOM: from £45 to £55
FOOD: up to £15
**Cuisine:** menu changes weekly. Wine list and wines available by the glass.
**Cards:** Visa, Access.
**Other points:** resident's lounge with books, conservatory, games room, summer terrace, parking.
**Rooms:** 9 bedrooms, all en suite. All with TV, radio, telephone, trouser press, hair dryer and tea/coffee-making facilities.
**Directions:** from Bingley town centre turn up Park Road, then into Beck Lane, and the hotel is on the left.
MRS P OXLEY ☎(01274) 565296 Fax(01274) 568828

### OAKWOOD HALL HOTEL
Lady Lane, BD16 4AW

*A family-run hotel set in a quiet woodland. The decor of the hotel is of a very high standard, with furnishings of great taste. A relaxed place to visit, serving superb food with unusual starters and sweets.*

DOUBLE ROOM: from £30 to £40
SINGLE ROOM: from £45
FOOD: from £15 to £20
**Hours:** breakfast 7.30am-9.30am, lunch (except Sunday) 12noon-2pm, lunch Sunday 12.30am-2pm, dinner 7.30pm-9.30pm.
**Cuisine:** ENGLISH - à la carte menu, fixed three-course menu, bar meals and bar snacks.
**Cards:** Visa, Access, Diners, AmEx.
**Other points:** Sunday lunch, children welcome, garden, pets allowed, conferences, functions.
**Rooms:** 20 bedrooms.
**Directions:** off A650.
MRS K. BRASSINGTON ☎(01274) 564123
Fax(01274) 561477

## HALIFAX • map 12E4

###  DUKE OF YORK INN
Brighouse & Denholmegate Road, Stone Chair, HX3 7LN

*A former 17th century coaching inn, this establishment lavishly displays pots and pans from*

the ceiling. Tasty meals at value-for-money prices and a wide range of ales, spirits and malt whiskies are offered. Friendly, efficient staff help create the relaxed atmosphere, which is enjoyed by all ages.
DOUBLE ROOM: from £20 to £30
SINGLE ROOM: from £30
FOOD: up to £15
**Hours:** breakfast 7am-9am, lunch 12noon-2pm, dinner 5pm-9pm.
**Cuisine:** ENGLISH - home-cooked food, wide and varied menu. Daily specials.
**Cards:** Visa, Diners, AmEx, Switch.
**Other points:** licensed, open-air dining, Sunday lunch, children welcome.
**Rooms:** 1 single room, 7 double rooms, 2 twin rooms, 2 family rooms. All with TV, tea/coffee-making facilities, iron.
**Directions:** between Bradford and Halifax, 2 miles from M62 on main Howarth road.
STEPHEN WHITAKER ☎(01422) 202056 Fax(01422) 206618

### IMPERIAL CROWN HOTEL
42-46 Horton Street, HX1 1BR
*The hotel is under the personal supervision of the proprietors who, together with the local staff, take every care to look after their guests' comforts and needs. Within the atmosphere of informality and friendliness, the hotel provides an excellent standard of both food and accommodation. Well situated in the heart of historic Halifax. Extensive facilities for functions.*
DOUBLE ROOM: from £30 to £40
SINGLE ROOM: from £45 to £55
FOOD: from £15 to £25
**Hours:** breakfast 7am-9am, bar snacks 5pm-10pm, dinner 7pm-10pm.
**Cuisine:** FRENCH - excellent French cuisine, à la carte and table d'hôte menus.
**Cards:** Visa, Access, Diners, AmEx.
**Other points:** licensed, children welcome, residents' lounge, functions, conferences.
**Rooms:** 26 single rooms, 4 double rooms, 6 twin rooms, 2 family rooms, 1 bridal suite, 2 executive suites.
**Directions:** M62 junction 24. Directly opposite main railway station in Halifax and the Eureka Children's Museum.
C. & C.H. TURCZAK ☎(01422) 342342 Fax(01422) 349866

###  ROCK INN HOTEL & CHURCHILL'S
at Holywell Green, HX4 9BS
*Situated in a tranquil rural valley mid-way between Halifax and Huddersfield. The Rock Inn Hotel offers all the attractions of a traditional wayside inn as well as the sophistication of a first class hotel. Recently refurbished to include 2 large conservatories and patio areas. Meals are served all day, everyday. Equidistant (half a mile) to 2 superb golf courses.*
DOUBLE ROOM: from £30 to £40
SINGLE ROOM: from £40 to £70

FOOD: up to £15
**Hours:** breakfast 7am-9am, meals all day 12noon-10pm.
**Cuisine:** INTERNATIONAL - "East meets West" menu, daily blackboard specials, inn food.
**Cards:** Visa, Access, Diners, AmEx, JCB.
**Other points:** traditional Sunday lunch, children welcome, pets allowed, extensive vegetarian menu, convivial bar, disabled access.
**Rooms:** 14 double rooms (including 3 executive), 2 twin rooms, 1 triple room, 1 family room. All with satellite TV, radio, alarm, mini-bar, telephone, tea/coffee-making facilities, hair dryer, trouser-press.
**Directions:** situated 1.5 miles from junction 24 on the M62. Follow signs for Blackley then Holywell Green.
ROBERT VINSEN ☎(01422) 379721 Fax(01422) 379110

### THE TREASURE HOUSE
Newlands Gate, Warley, HX2 7SU
*Interestingly, the restaurant is four farmhouse cottages converted to become the attractive, spacious restaurant that it now is. The appealing interior provides diners with comfortable, relaxed surroundings to enjoy a fabulous meal and sample one of the many fine wines. The Treasure House is set in beautiful countryside, just 5 minutes from Halifax.*
FOOD: from £15 to £20
**Hours:** lunch 12noon-2pm, dinner 7pm-10pm, check opening times in February and March.
**Cuisine:** ENGLISH / FRENCH - regularly changing menu. Good use of fresh local produce.
**Cards:** Visa, Access, AmEx, Switch, Delta.
**Other points:** parking, children welcome, vegetarian meals, traditional Sunday lunch.
**Directions:** take the Burnley road from Halifax and turn right into Windle Royd Lane, followed by Stocks Lane, into Warley Village.
GEOFFREY & SUSAN HODGSON ☎(01422) 353278 Fax(01422) 353278

### HAWORTH • map 12E4

### OLD WHITE LION HOTEL
West Lane, BD22 8DU
*An old inn at the centre of this famous village, family-run for many years and featured in all major good-food guides. A convenient location for visitors to the Brontë Museum, parsonage and Worth Valley Steam Railway. Ideal centre for touring the Yorkshire Dales.*
DOUBLE ROOM: from £20 to £30
SINGLE ROOM: from £35 to £45
FOOD: up to £15
**Hours:** breakfast 7am-9am, lunch 11.30am-2.30pm, dinner 6.30pm-9.30pm.
**Cuisine:** ENGLISH / INTERNATIONAL - Dover sole, fillet of Old England, seafood pie, and game in season.
**Cards:** Visa, Access, Diners, AmEx.
**Other points:** Sunday lunch, children welcome, coaches by prior arrangement.

**Rooms:** 15 bedrooms. All with en suite, TV, tea/coffee-making facilities, telephone and radio. Family rooms available.
**Directions:** off M62, take A629 through Halifax and turn off before Keighley.
MR KEITH BRADFORD ☎(01535) 642313
Fax(01535) 646222

## HOLMFIRTH • map 9A1

### MELLORS
Stable Court, Huddersfield Road, HD7 1AZ
*Formerly a stable and barn Mellors Restaurant and Café Bar is located in the heart of "Summer Wine" country. Set in a courtyard it offers an imaginative selection of modern English and continental food complemented by an international wine list. The Café Bar is open daily for coffee and light lunches.*
FOOD: from £15 to £20 CLUB
**Hours:** lunch 12noon-1.30pm, dinner 6.45pm-9.30pm, closed Sunday and Monday, open bank holidays.
**Cuisine:** MODERN ENGLISH / CONTINENTAL - specializing in fresh fish and game. Vegetarian menu available. Table d'hôte menu Tuesday to Friday.
**Cards:** Visa, Access.
**Other points:** licensed, children welcome, air-conditioned, Sunday lunches, vegetarian meals.
**Directions:** off the A6024 main Huddersfield Road in Holmfirth, near the fire station.
PETER MELLOR ☎(01484) 687955

## HUDDERSFIELD • map 9A1

### ELM CREST GUEST HOTEL
2 Queens Road, HD2 2AG
*A pleasant 1860s-built house with car park and attractive conservatory. The owners, Derek and Hilary Gee, prepare and cook all meals using only fresh local produce. Ideally located near town centre and other amenities.*
DOUBLE ROOM: from £20 to £30
SINGLE ROOM: from £30 to £40
FOOD: up to £15
**Hours:** breakfast 7.30am-8.30am, lunch 12noon-2pm, dinner 7pm-9.30pm.
**Cuisine:** ENGLISH - table d'hôte menu offering a good selection of interesting dishes. Fine selection of cheeses and wines.
**Cards:** Visa, Access, Diners, AmEx.
**Other points:** garden, afternoon tea, parking, left luggage.
**Rooms:** 3 single rooms, 2 double rooms, 3 twin rooms. All with TV, radio, telephone, tea/coffee-making facilities.
**Directions:** follow A629 ring road. Over traffic lights. Centre lane for right turn. Secure parking available.
DEREK & HILARY GEE ☎(01484) 530990
Fax(01484) 516227

### HUDDERSFIELD HOTEL & ROSEMARY LANE BISTRO
HD1 1QT
*The hotel is made up of a bistro, formal hotel, pub, wine bar, all-day brasserie and night club, all under the same roof. The Brasserie is air-conditioned and serves food from 10am, closing at 11pm, seven days a week.*
DOUBLE ROOM: from £20 to £30
FOOD: up to £15
**Hours:** breakfast 7.30am-10am, brasserie 10am-11pm, lunch 12noon-2pm, dinner 7pm-11pm.
**Cuisine:** ENGLISH - grills, fish and British cooking.
**Cards:** Visa, Access, Diners, AmEx, Switch.
**Other points:** licensed, children welcome, coaches by prior arrangement.
**Rooms:** 16 single rooms, 20 double rooms, 17 twin rooms, 2 family rooms, 1 suite. All with TV, radio, alarm, telephone, tea/coffee-making facilities, heating, hair dryer, video, trouser-press.
**Directions:** off A62, on main ring road in town centre, opposite sports centre.
JOE MARSDEN ☎(01484) 512111 Fax(01484) 435262

---

### PRIX D' ELITE
### WINE OF THE YEAR 1996
### THE LODGE HOTEL
48 Birkby Lodge Road, Birkby, HD2 2BG

*A fine Victorian gentleman's residence, sympathetically restored as Huddersfield's first country house hotel and set in two acres of mature gardens. The 50-seater restaurant offers excellent and innovative cuisine using fresh seasonal foods, supplemented by an excellent wine list. An ideal venue for business luncheons, conferences, private functions and family Sunday lunch.*
DOUBLE ROOM: from £20 to £30
SINGLE ROOM: from £45 to £55
FOOD: from £15 to £20 CLUB
**Hours:** breakfast 7.30am-9.45am, lunch 12noon-2pm, dinner 7.30pm-9.45pm, closed 26th December until 28th December.
**Cuisine:** MODERN ENGLISH - fixed-price speciality menus. Dishes to choose from include pan-fried venison, sautéed pork fillet, ballantine of duck. Vegetarian menu available.
**Cards:** Visa, Access, AmEx.
**Other points:** licensed, open-air dining, Sunday lunch, no-smoking area, afternoon tea, residents' lounge, garden, parking, children welcome, baby-

listening device, cots, 24hr reception.
**Rooms:** 4 single rooms, 4 double rooms, 3 twin rooms. All with TV, radio, alarm, telephone, tea/coffee-making facilities.
**Directions:** 1 mile from Huddersfield town centre. 2 miles from M62 motorway.
GARRY & KEVIN BIRLEY ☎(01484) 431001
Fax (01484) 421590

### THREE ACRES INN & RESTAURANT
Roydhouse, Shelley, HD8 8LR
*Located in the picturesque rolling green countryside of the Pennine foothills, this 18th century coaching inn offers a comprehensive range of facilities and luxury accommodation. There are two restaurants, banqueting and conference facilities, and traditional bars, all offering a warm Yorkshire welcome.*
DOUBLE ROOM: from £20 to £30
SINGLE ROOM: from £45 to £55
FOOD: from £15 to £20
**Hours:** breakfast 7am-9am, lunch 12noon-2pm, dinner 7pm-9.45pm.
**Cuisine:** ENGLISH / EUROPEAN
**Cards:** Visa, Access, AmEx.
**Other points:** parking, children welcome, conference facilities, vegetarian meals, residents' garden.
**Rooms:** 20 bedrooms.
**Directions:** A635 or A642 off M1 or A642 from Huddersfield to Emley Moor Mast.
MR TRUELOVE & MR ORME ☎(01484) 602606
Fax (01484) 608411

### THE WHITE HOUSE
Slaithwaite, HD7 5TY
*A 200-year-old pub situated in the "Summer Wine" area with commanding views of the local countryside. The interior has been carefully restored with original flagstone floors. Noted for real ale and open fires.*
DOUBLE ROOM: up to £20
FOOD: up to £15 🍲
**Hours:** breakfast 7.30am-9am, lunch 12noon-1.45pm, dinner 6pm-9.30pm, Sunday 12noon-8.30pm.
**Cuisine:** ENGLISH - extensive menu served in the bar/restaurant with additional specialities and daily blackboard changes.
**Cards:** Visa, Access, Diners, AmEx.
**Other points:** Sunday lunch, children welcome, pets by prior arrangement.
**Rooms:** 1 single room, 6 double rooms, 1 twin room.
**Directions:** off B6107. Turn off A62 in Slaithwaite village.
MRS GILLIAN SWIFT ☎(01484) 842245
Fax (01484) 842245

## ILKLEY • map 12E4

### COW & CALF HOTEL
Ilkley Moor, LS29 8BT
*A country house on Ilkley Moor adjacent to the Cow and Calf Rocks, from which it takes its name. All bedrooms are fully en suite and offer a high standard of comfort, and well-cooked food is served lunchtime and evening. The restaurant has unrivalled views of Wharfedale, and the Moors, immortalized by the song On Ilkley Moor Baht 'at, are a mere 20 yards' walk away.*
DOUBLE ROOM: from £30 to £40
SINGLE ROOM: from £45 to £55
FOOD: up to £15    CLUB
**Hours:** breakfast 7.30am-9.30am, lunch 12noon-2pm, dinner 7.15pm-9.30pm, closed Christmas day.
**Cuisine:** MODERN ENGLISH - à la carte menu in Panorama restaurant, e.g., Panorama pâté, chicken Panorama (chicken in chef's orange-and-tarragon sauce). Fish also available.
**Cards:** Visa, Access, Diners, AmEx.
**Other points:** Sunday lunch, children welcome, parking, residents' bar, residents' lounge.
**Rooms:** 17 bedrooms. All en suite with TV, telephone, tea/coffee-making facilities.
**Directions:** located one mile off A65. Follow signs for Cow and Calf Rocks.
THE NORFOLK FAMILY ☎(01943) 607335
Fax (01943) 816022

## LEEDS • map 12E4

### AVALON GUEST HOUSE
132 Woodsley Road, LS2 9LZ
*A Victorian family house situated close to the university. Comfortable and well maintained, the Avalon Guest House has a homely atmosphere. Popular with business travellers and visitors to the university.*
DOUBLE ROOM: from £20 to £30
SINGLE ROOM: from £20 to £25
**Hours:** breakfast 7.30am-8.45am.
**Cuisine:** BREAKFAST
**Cards:** Visa.
**Other points:** garden, pets allowed, cots, baby-sitting, disabled access, central heating.
**Rooms:** 4 single rooms, 1 double room, 3 twin rooms, 2 family rooms. All with TV, tea/coffee-making facilities.
**Directions:** one mile from the city centre in the university area.
ELIZABETH DEARDEN ☎(0113) 2432848/2432545
Fax (0113) 2420649

### THE BUTLERS HOTEL
40 Cardigan Road, Headingley, LS6 3AG
*Overlooking Headingley Cricket Ground and only two minutes from the city centre, this hotel offers excellent, luxurious accommodation and a friendly, welcoming atmosphere. The superbly-appointed licensed restaurant provides a wide choice of well-cooked dishes such as entrecôte au Paivie and*

chicken chasseur. An elegant, comfortable and welcoming place to stay.
DOUBLE ROOM: from £30 to £40
SINGLE ROOM: over £55
FOOD: up to £15 🍽
Hours: breakfast 7.30am-9am, lunch 12noon-2pm, dinner 7pm-9pm, bar meals 12noon-12midnight.
Cuisine: COSMOPOLITAN
Cards: Visa, Access, Diners, AmEx.
Other points: children welcome, pets allowed, residents' lounge, afternoon tea, special breaks, vegetarian meals, baby-listening device, cots, 24hr reception, conferences, weekend breaks, parking.
Rooms: 3 single rooms, 2 double rooms, 2 twin rooms, 1 family room. All with en suite, TV, telephone.
Directions: link road between A65 Skipton and A660 Otley road. Next to Headingley Cricket Ground.
DAVID HARRY BUTLER ☎(0113) 2744755
Fax(0113) 2744755

### THE NORDIC HOTEL
18 Kelso Road, LS2 9PR
A homely Victorian hotel, tastefully decorated throughout and offering comfortable accommodation and a warm welcome. Tetley Brewery Wharf is nearby for those interested in doing a brewery tour and pub trail; or for sports fanatics, Headlingley is also very close.
DOUBLE ROOM: from £17 to £24
SINGLE ROOM: fro £25 to £35
FOOD: up to £15
Hours: breakfast 7.30am-8.30am, dinner 6pm-9pm, closed Christmas.
Cuisine: ENGLISH
Cards: Visa, Access, AmEx.
Other points: parking, children welcome, residents' lounge, no-smoking area, afternoon teas, vegetarian meals.
Rooms: 6 single rooms, 3 double rooms, 3 twin rooms, 3 triple rooms, 1 family room. All with TV, tea/coffee-making facilities.
Directions: take the A660 from Leeds city centre. Turn left into Clarendon Road at the rear of Leeds University. Kelso Road is the third turning on the right.
ALLAN & NORAH SPENCE ☎(0113) 2452357/2448261 Fax(0113) 2433009

### PINEWOOD PRIVATE HOTEL
78 Potternewton Lane, LS7 3LW
Set in a quiet residential area, the Pinewood offers a very good standard of cooking and accommodation. All food is cooked and prepared by the proprietors themselves, using fresh ingredients. Traditional standards of comfort and cleanliness are maintained at all times.
DOUBLE ROOM: from £20 to £30
SINGLE ROOM: from £25 to £35
FOOD: up to £15 🍽
Hours: breakfast weekdays 7.30am-8.30am, weekends 8.30am-9.30am, dinner 7pm.

Cuisine: MODERN ENGLISH - table d'hôte menu. Traditional home-cooking with a few surprises. Babotie, Jambalaya, chicken in lime with honey and almonds.
Cards: Visa, Access, AmEx.
Other points: licensed, weekend breaks, children welcome, residents' lounge, garden, vegetarian meals, street parking, cots, left luggage.
Rooms: 5 single rooms, 3 double rooms, 2 twin rooms. All with TV, radio, alarm, tea/coffee-making facilities.
Directions: leave Leeds on the A61 to Harrogate; approximately 2 miles from the centre on dual carriageway. Turn right at first roundabout, 600 yards on left.
CHARLES & WENDY STUBLEY ☎(0113) 2622561 Fax(0113) 2622561

## SHIPLEY • map 12E4

### THE CONNECTION
41 Westgate, BD18 3Q
A lively, family restaurant with eye-catching decor and a wide-ranging menu. Much frequented by locals and tourists alike.
FOOD: up to £15
Hours: dinner Monday-Friday 6pm-11pm, Saturday 5pm-11pm, Sunday 4pm-10pm.
Cuisine: INTERNATIONAL - hamburgers, pizzas, steaks, pancakes and chicken.
Cards: Visa, MasterCard, Switch.
Directions: on the corner of the A657 and Westgate.
S.R. JENNINGS ☎(01274) 599461

## WAKEFIELD • map 9A2

### THE CLOCK TOWER RESTAURANT
Town Hall, Wood Street, WF1 2HQ
The Town Hall was officially opened in 1880. The Clock Tower Restaurant was opened 108 years later and is located on the third floor of the Town Hall, directly under the clock tower itself. Formerly the members' dining room, the restaurant still retains the original oak panelling and carved plasterwork. The chefs pride themselves on producing and presenting interesting dishes from the regularly changing menu, using local suppliers and local produce.
FOOD: up to £15
Hours: lunch (Sunday-Friday) 12noon-2.30pm, dinner (Friday-Saturday) 7pm-11pm, closed 24th December until 31st December.
Cuisine: INTERNATIONAL - a wide selection of international meals, including traditional English, complemented by a comprehensive wine list.
Cards: Visa, Access.
Other points: children welcome, no-smoking area, vegetarian meals, traditional Sunday lunch, conference facilities.
Directions: in city centre.
MR SIMON HARTLEY ☎(01924) 295130
Fax(01924) 295293

# WALES

Although part of Britain, Wales is as different from England as France is from Spain. It has its own language, history and heritage as well as its own culture and cuisine, and it is this difference, coupled with the traditional, warm Welsh welcome, that makes any visit here such a memorable and unique experience.

Award-winning Welsh cuisine is not hard to find, and uses only the very best of local produce. Here one can expect to find on the menu, dishes such as honeyed Welsh lamb, Pembrokeshire turkey and Wye salmon, as well as a tremendous choice of cosmopolitan and continental dishes through to traditional roasts, quality home-made meals and light snacks.

We often wonder if the Welsh were thinking of Les Routiers when they composed A Welcome in the Hillsides, because there certainly is!

Accommodation ranges from welcoming hill farms with spectacular views across sea and mountains to picturesque village inns in the heart of Snowdonia, from modern hotels with full facilities to first-class country and sporting hotels.

This area also has a wealth of interesting attractions and unusual places to visit, many of them unique, such as the Italianate village of Portmerion, nestling on a secluded wooded hillside overlooking the Traeth Bach estuary, or the Centre of Alternative Technology - a 'green' village of the future in mid-Wales, where a host of environmentally friendly technologies are demonstrated.

The following counties are included in this chapter:

| | |
|---|---|
| CLWYD | GWENT |
| DYFED | POWYS |
| GLAMORGAN (MID) | |
| (SOUTH) | |
| (WEST) | |

# CLWYD

**CAFE NICOISE**
124 Abergele Road, Colwyn Bay,
LL29 7PS
*Tastefully furnished restaurant, offering traditional and modern provincial cooking. Close to beach and other attractions, including Eirias Park, Conwy Castle, Great Orme and Llandudno.*
FOOD: from £15 to £20
**Hours:** lunch 12noon-2pm, dinner 7pm-10pm, closed all day Sunday and closed for lunch Monday to Wednesday.
**Cuisine:** FRENCH - fillets of red mullet with roast peppers and basil, assiette du chef. A selection of 4 home-made desserts.
**Cards:** Visa, Access, Diners, AmEx.
**Other points:** licensed, children welcome, vegetarian meals, open bank holidays.
**Directions:** take the Old Colwyn exit from the A55. Situated on the main road through Colwyn Bay.
CARL SWIFT & LYNNE SWIFT ☎(01492) 531555

**EDELWEISS HOTEL**
Lawson Road, LL29 8HD

A 19th century country house set in its own wooded gardens and tucked away in central Colwyn Bay. Large car park, children's play area, games room and solarium. Private pathway leading to the Promenade, Eirias Park, and the sports and leisure centre.
DOUBLE ROOM: up to £20
FOOD: up to £15 🍽 CLUB
Hours: breakfast 7.45am-9.30am, lunch 12noon-2pm, dinner 6.30pm-9pm.
Cuisine: WELSH / ENGLISH - vegetarian meals, fresh vegetables, home-cut meats.
Cards: Visa, Access, Diners, AmEx.
Other points: pets allowed.
Directions: off the A55 and then the B5104.
IAN BURT ☎(01492) 532314 Fax(01492) 534707

### 🏠 NORTHWOOD HOTEL
47 Rhos Road, Rhos-on-Sea, LL28 4RS
Centrally situated in the heart of attractive Rhos-on-Sea. Excellent tradition of fine cuisine with wide choice of menu. Special diets catered for. Ground-floor bedrooms. Special mini-break rates. Easter and Christmas house parties, golfing holidays arranged.
DOUBLE ROOM: up to £20
SINGLE ROOM: up to £20
FOOD: up to £15
Hours: breakfast 8.15am-9am, dinner 6.30pm-7pm.
Cuisine: BRITISH
Cards: Visa, Access.
Other points: central heating, children welcome, pets allowed, residents' lounge, patio, residents' bar.
Rooms: 2 single rooms, 3 double rooms, 3 twin rooms, 3 family rooms. All with TV, clock/radio, tea/coffee-making facilities. All rooms are en suite.
Directions: on Rhos Road, directly off the Promenade; turn opposite Rhos-on-Sea Tourist Information Centre.
GORDON & AGNES PALLISER ☎(01492) 549931

## LLANGOLLEN • map 8B4

### 🏠 THE CHAIN BRIDGE HOTEL
Berwyn, LL20 8BS
The hotel nestles in one of the most picturesque localities in Wales, in a valley of serene and natural beauty shielded by the Berwyn and Eglwysig mountains. Situated on the banks of the River Dee, the hotel offers guests characteristic accommodation, a good restaurant with panoramic views, a cosy bar, and excellent facilities for weddings, functions and conferences.
DOUBLE ROOM: from £30 to £40
SINGLE ROOM: from £30 to £40
FOOD: up to £15 CLUB
Hours: breakfast 7.30am-9.30am, lunch 12.30am-2pm, dinner 7.30pm-9pm.
Cuisine: ENGLISH / CONTINENTAL
Cards: Visa, Access, Diners, AmEx, Switch.
Other points: parking, children welcome, pets allowed, no-smoking area, conference facilities, residents' lounge, garden, vegetarian meals, traditional Sunday lunch, afternoon teas.
Rooms: 35 bedrooms. All with TV, telephone, radio,

tea/coffee-making facilties.
Directions: 2 miles west of Llangollen, just off A5.
VICTOR BAKER ☎(01978) 860215 Fax(01978) 861841

### 🏠 GALES
18 Bridge Street, LL70 8PF
An 18th century establishment, opposite the River Dee, in the town famous for the International Eisteddfod. Over 250 wines, on- or off-sales. Limited-edition etchings and screen prints for sale. Overall winner of the Les Routiers/Mercier Wine List of the Year Award 1990.
DOUBLE ROOM: from £20 to £30
SINGLE ROOM: from £25 to £35
FOOD: up to £15 🍽 🍴
Hours: lunch 12noon-2pm, dinner 6pm-10pm, closed Sunday.
Cuisine: INTERNATIONAL - specializes in home-made soups and ice creams and offers a variety of dishes of the day.
Cards: Visa, Access, AmEx.
Other points: open-air dining, children welcome, patio.
Rooms: 10 double rooms, 5 twin rooms. All en suite.
Directions: located in the town centre.
RICHARD & GILLIE GALE ☎(01978) 860089 Fax(01978) 861313

## MOLD • map 8B4

### 🍴 CHEZ COLETTE
56 High Street, CH1 1BD
An attractive French family-run restaurant, offering fine traditional cuisine. The panelled decor is adorned with French paintings and complemented by soft background music, adding to the overall charm of this establishment, so popular with the locals. It is ideally situated for visits to the theatre and countryside walks, with the ancient parish church directly opposite.
FOOD: up to £15 🍽
Hours: lunch 11.30am-2pm, dinner 6pm-10pm, closed Sunday and Monday.
Cuisine: FRENCH - quality French provincial cuisine with table d'hôte and à la carte menus. Dishes may include mussels in garlic sauce, escargots, savoury pancake, navarin of lamb, poulet au Riesling, steak au poivre.
Cards: Visa, Access.
Other points: licensed, children welcome.
Directions: A494, A541, top of Mold High Street, opposite the parish church.
JACQUES & COLETTE DUVAUCHELLE ☎(01352) 759225

### 🍴 THE THEATR CLWYD
Rakes Lane, CH7 1YA
Combine a meal with a visit to the theatre at the only theatre-restaurant recommended by Les Routiers. The meals are well-cooked and provide

*very fair value for money - reason enough for visiting Theatr Clwyd at any time, for lunch or dinner, whether you wish to enjoy a play or just relax over a meal.*
FOOD: up to £15
**Hours:** lunch 12noon-2pm, dinner 5.30pm-10pm. Closed Sunday.
**Cuisine:** INTERNATIONAL - dishes may include tagliatelle carbonara, tarragon and lemon chicken, vegetarian chilli and trout Cleopatra. Menu changed monthly.
**Cards:** Visa, Access, Switch.
**Other points:** no-smoking area, children welcome, afternoon tea, conference and banqueting facilities available (20-350 persons).
**Directions:** situated on A494, .5 mile outside Mold town. Signposted.
MR GORDON CARSON. LEISURE CATERING SERVICES LTD ☎(01352) 759304 Fax(01352) 752302

## ST ASAPH • map 7B3

### ORIEL HOUSE HOTEL
Upper Denbigh Road, LL17 0LW
*Set in its own extensive grounds, this is a family-owned and run hotel. In these quiet, relaxed surroundings, you can enjoy well-prepared and presented meals. Comfortable accommodation and attractive decor. Good venue for wedding receptions and conferences.*
DOUBLE ROOM: from £30 to £33
SINGLE ROOM: from £40 to £47
FOOD: from £15 to £20
**Hours:** breakfast 7.15am-9.30am, lunch 11.30am-2pm, bar snacks 11am-2.30pm, dinner 7pm-9.30pm, bar snacks 6.15pm-10pm.
**Cuisine:** BRITISH - serving full à la carte menu, table d'hôte and bar snacks.
**Cards:** Visa, Access, Diners, AmEx.
**Other points:** licensed, Sunday lunch, children welcome, afternoon tea, pets allowed, garden, conferences, snooker room.
**Rooms:** 19 bedrooms. All with en suite, TV, radio, telephone, hair dryer, tea/coffee-making facilities.
**Directions:** A55 turn-off for Denbigh, left at cathedral, 1 mile on right.
MR & MRS WIGGIN & MR & MRS WOOD ☎(01745) 582716 Fax(01745) 582716

## TREFNANT • map 7B3

### BRYN GLAS HOTEL
St Asaph Road, LL16 5UD
*Set in the Vale of Clwyd, Bryn Glas is an ideal location as a base for touring the beautiful North Wales coast or just taking a relaxing break away. A home-cooked meal from the varied menu can be enjoyed in the dining room, then relax over a quiet drink in the lounge before retiring to one of the comfortable rooms for a restful night.*
DOUBLE ROOM: from £20 to £30
SINGLE ROOM: from £25 to £35
FOOD: up to £15

**Hours:** breakfast 8am-9am, lunch 12noon-2pm, dinner 6pm-7.30pm.
**Cuisine:** BRITISH
**Other points:** disabled access, children welcome, parking, pets allowed, residents' lounge, vegetarian meals, garden.
**Rooms:** 8 bedrooms. All en suite.
**Directions:** on A525, off A55 Expressway, 2.5 miles from St Asaph and the same distance from Denbigh.
MS M. TIBBETTS ☎(01745) 730868 Fax(01745) 730590

## WREXHAM • map 8B4

### TREVOR ARMS HOTEL
Marford, near Wrexham, LL12 8TA

*An old coaching inn, which maintains traditional pub hospitality together with a wide range of modern facilities and tempting menus at affordable prices. Excellent staff teamwork ensures a relaxed, no-fuss atmosphere in which to enjoy your meal. Comfortable accommodation, a safe children's play area and an outdoor barbecue. Very highly recommended by the Les Routiers inspector.*
DOUBLE ROOM: up to £20
SINGLE ROOM: from £25 to £35
FOOD: up to £15
**Hours:** breakfast 7.30am-9am, lunch 12noon-2.30pm, dinner 6pm-10pm, Sunday 7pm-10pm.
**Cuisine:** BRITISH - extensive menu available in the restaurant and bar areas. Dishes may include king scampi, sirloin steak, salmon with lemon and tarragon. Daily specials.
**Cards:** Visa, Access.
**Other points:** licensed, open-air dining, Sunday lunch, no-smoking area, playland, afternoon tea.
**Rooms:** 2 single rooms, 12 double rooms, 3 twin rooms.
**Directions:** midway between Chester and Wrexham. A short distance off A483.
MARTIN & DENISE BENNETT ☎(01244) 570436

# DYFED

## CARDIGAN • map 7E2

 **SKIPPERS**
Tresaith Beach, SA43 2JL
*Overlooking the unspoilt bay of Tresaith, this restaurant offers meals of 'outstanding quality' in a quiet, relaxed atmosphere. Efficient and friendly staff ensure an enjoyable meal. There is a definite nautical theme in the restaurant, which also has a log fire. Comfortable accommodation. Highly recommended.*
DOUBLE ROOM: from £20 to £30
FOOD: from £25 to £30 ⚓ CLUB 🍴
**Hours:** breakfast 7am-12noon, lunch 12noon-3pm, bar meals 12noon-3pm, dinner 6pm-11.30pm, last orders 9pm, closed January until Easter.
**Cuisine:** SEAFOOD / INTERNATIONAL - extensive home-made menu, which may feature oysters, fresh local crab and lobster, rack of lamb. Greek and Cypriot dishes a speciality.
**Cards:** Visa, Access.
**Other points:** licensed, open-air dining available, children welcome, afternoon tea, residents' lounge, residents' bar, vegetarian meals, pets allowed.
**Rooms:** 3 suites (6 persons), 1 twin room, 2 double rooms. Most en suite with TV, radio, alarm, tea/coffee-making facilities.
**Directions:** B4333 to Aberporth, then unclassified road to Tresaith.
IAN & JANET DARROCH ☎(01239) 810113
Fax(01239) 810176

## CARMARTHEN • map 3A3

 **THE COTHI BRIDGE HOTEL**
Pontargothi, Nantgaredig, SA32 7NG
*This family-run hotel is well located for travellers, offering good facilities and a pleasant family atmosphere. The dining room enjoys spectacular views over the river Cothi, while the bedrooms provide guests with comfortable accommodation. Many great attractions are located nearby.*
DOUBLE ROOM: from £20 to £30
SINGLE ROOM: from £25 to £35
FOOD: up to £15
**Hours:** breakfast 7.30am-9am, lunch 12noon-2pm, dinner 6pm-9.30pm.
**Cuisine:** BRITISH - freshly prepared traditional meals. Grills a speciality.
**Cards:** Visa, Access, AmEx.
**Other points:** children welcome, pets allowed, parking, residents' lounge, garden, open-air dining, vegetarian meals.
**Rooms:** 2 single rooms, 6 double rooms, 2 twin rooms, 1 triple room, 1 family room. All with TV, tea-making facilities, telephone, room service.
**Directions:** situated on the A40, half-way between Carmarthen and Llandeilo.
MRS SANDY JONES ☎(01267) 290251
Fax(01267) 290251

## FISHGUARD • map 7E1

 **ABERGWAUN HOTEL**
Market Square, SA65 9HA
*This family-run hotel offers comfort throughout. Traditional home-cooked food, made from fresh local produce, is offered in the restaurant, and the 12 bedrooms are all well appointed, to provide a `home away from home' aura. Situated in the heart of Fishguard, the hotel is a convenient stop for people on their way over to Ireland.*
DOUBLE ROOM: from £20 to £30
SINGLE ROOM: up to £25
FOOD: up to £15
**Hours:** breakfast 7.30am 9.30am, lunch
**Cuisine:** BRITISH - home-made food using fresh produce.
**Cards:** Visa, Access, Diners, AmEx, JCB.
**Other points:** children welcome, pets allowed, residents' lounge, vegetarian meals.
**Rooms:** 4 single rooms, 5 double rooms, 2 family rooms. All with TV, tea/coffee-making facilities.
**Directions:** located on the A40, in the main square of Fishguard.
MR R.L. COLLIER ☎(01348) 872077 Fax(01348) 875412

 **THE HOPE & ANCHOR INN**
Goodwick, SA64 0BP
*This small, family-run inn overlooks the harbour and is conveniently placed for both the station and the Irish ferries. There are miles of beaches nearby, with a coastal path for walkers.*
DOUBLE ROOM: up to £20
SINGLE ROOM: from £20
FOOD: up to £15
**Hours:** lunch 12noon-2.30pm, dinner 7pm-10pm.
**Cuisine:** ENGLISH / WELSH
**Other points:** open-air dining, Sunday lunch, children welcome.
**Rooms:** 3 twin rooms. All with en suite, TV.
**Directions:** at end of A40.
MR T. MCDONALD ☎(01348) 872314

## HAVERFORDWEST • map 3A2

 **THE CASTLE HOTEL**
Castle Square, SA62 2AA
*The Castle Hotel, which has recently been refurbished, is ideally situated for touring the beautiful, rugged mountains and coastline of Pembrokeshire. Comfortably and attractively furnished.*
DOUBLE ROOM: from £20 to £30
SINGLE ROOM: from £32.50 to £37.50
FOOD: up to £15 CLUB
**Hours:** breakfast 7.30am-9.30am, lunch 12noon-2.45pm, dinner 7pm-10pm, bar meals 12noon-2.45pm, 7pm-9pm, open all year.
**Cuisine:** INTERNATIONAL - bistro-style menu.

Dishes may include honey roasted chicken, pork and apricot stroganoff, nutty fettucini, rosemary lamb steak. Good selection of steaks. Vegetarian dishes.
**Cards:** Visa, Access.
**Other points:** licensed, Sunday lunch, children welcome, afternoon tea, vegetarian meals, weekend breaks.
**Rooms:** 2 single rooms, 3 double rooms, 2 twin rooms, 1 family room, plus a four poster suite. All with TV, telephone.
**Directions:** turn off left at junction of A4076 and A40 over River Cleddau.
JULIET & PHILLIP LLEWELLYN ☎(01437) 769322
Fax (01437) 769493

### THE GLEN & FIDDICH'S BRASSERIE
Merlin's Hill, SA61 2AA
*This converted Victorian house, recently refurbished attracts a mixed clientele of all ages, including families that come to sample the excellent bistro-style cooking, fine wines and ambience. A conservatory extension provides a sunny restaurant.*
FOOD: up to £15
**Hours:** lunch and bar meals 12noon-2.30pm, dinner and bar meals 6.30pm-9.30pm, open bank holidays.
**Cuisine:** seasonal cooking, with fresh fish a speciality.
**Cards:** Access,Visa
**Other points:** licensed, parking, gardens with play areas for children, baby changing facilities.
**Directions:** from the A40 take the Haverford West by-pass to Milford Haven, turning at the first roundabout towards the town centre, brasserie on left up the hill.
MR PHILIP LLEWELLYN ☎(01437) 760070
Fax (01437) 760070

### ROCH GATE MOTEL
Roch, SA62 6AF
*A modern motel, providing excellent personal service to both long- and short-term visitors. Tasty meals with an emphasis on healthy eating and comfortable accommodation. With an indoor swimming pool, family-sized Jacuzzi, solarium etc., there need never be a dull moment!*
DOUBLE ROOM: from £30 to £40
FOOD: from £15 to £20
**Hours:** breakfast 7.45am-9.30am, lunch 12noon-3pm, dinner 6pm-10pm.
**Cuisine:** CONTINENTAL - menu may feature tuna and prawn tagliatelle, cheese and walnut pasta bake, king prawns, and apple pie.
**Cards:** Visa, Access, AmEx.
**Other points:** licensed, Sunday lunch, children welcome, open bank holidays, pets allowed, sauna, gym facilities, Jacuzzi, solarium, swimming pool.
**Directions:** six miles out of Haverfordwest towards St David's.
JOHN SMITH ☎(01437) 710435

### WOLFSCASTLE COUNTRY HOTEL
Wolf's Castle, SA62 5LZ

*A country hotel where the traditional welcome of warmth, relaxation and friendliness has been maintained. Situated on a hillside amid beautiful countryside, this hotel offers a high standard of accommodation. The restaurant enjoys an enviable reputation locally for its excellent food, and imaginative bar meals are also available. A delightful hotel in which to stay or dine.*
DOUBLE ROOM: from £35 to £40
SINGLE ROOM: from £38 to £45
FOOD: from £15 to £20
**Hours:** bar meals 12noon-2pm, 7pm-9pm, breakfast 7.30am-9.30am, dinner 7pm-9pm, lunch Sunday 12noon-2pm.
**Cuisine:** BRITISH - a blend of nouvelle cuisine and home-cooking. Predominantly fresh, local produce used. Traditional Sunday lunch. Good wine list.
**Cards:** Visa, Access, AmEx, Switch, JCB.
**Other points:** licensed, Sunday lunch, children welcome, residents' lounge, log fire, functions, patio, squash.
**Rooms:** 4 single rooms, 16 double rooms, 4 twin rooms.
**Directions:** A40. 6 miles north of Haverfordwest in village of Wolf's Castle.
ANDREW STIRLING ☎(01437) 741225/741688
Fax (01437) 741383

## LITTLE HAVEN • map 3A2

### THE NEST BISTRO
12 Grove Place, near Haverfordwest, SA62 3UG
*A cosy bistro with a small cocktail bar, in an old rambling house in this unique seaside village. A wide choice of dishes such as Mexican turkey and breast of duck. Fresh local fish includes Dover sole, monkfish, stuffed fillets of lemon sole, and lobster. 100 yards from the beach and coastal path. Little Haven provides a picturesque base for touring or enjoying the many water sports.*
DOUBLE ROOM: up to £20
FOOD: up to £15
**Hours:** lunch (high season only) 12noon-2.30pm, dinner (booking advisable) 6.30pm until late, last orders 10pm, closed Monday.
**Cuisine:** ENGLISH / CONTINENTAL - an imaginative menu with all dishes home-made, featuring fresh local fish, seafood and a selection of fine steaks. Extensive wine list. Welsh cheeseboard.
**Cards:** Visa, Access.
**Other points:** licensed, children welcome, parking.

**Rooms:** 2 double rooms, 2 twin rooms.
**Directions:** off the B4341 in Broad Haven.
PAUL & MARGARET MERRICK ☎(01437) 781728

## LLANDOVERY • map 7E3

### DROVERS RESTAURANT
9 Market Square, SA20 0AB
*This attractive 18th century country-town restaurant has been tastefully modernized while retaining some of the more appealing of its original features. The comfortable bedrooms have all been lovingly decorated with period furniture. Excellent standards and cheerful, efficient service throughout make this a must when travelling in this most beautiful part of Wales.*
DOUBLE ROOM: up to £20
SINGLE ROOM: up to £20
FOOD: up to £20
**Hours:** lunch 10.30am-2.30pm, dinner 6.30pm-9.30pm, restaurant closed Sunday evening and Monday.
**Cuisine:** WELSH - an excellent choice of high-quality dishes.
**Cards:** Visa, Access, Eurocard.
**Other points:** parking, children welcome, pets allowed, vegetarian meals, traditional Sunday lunch.
**Rooms:** 2 double rooms, 1 twin room. All with TV, tea/coffee-making facilities.
**Directions:** on A40, opposite the town hall in the centre of town.
MRS BLUD ☎(01550) 721115

### THE ROYAL OAK INN
Rhandirmwyn, SA20 0NY
*A 17th century village inn with restaurant, pool room and en suite accommodation. Near Brecon Beacons, RSPB Bird Reserve, Llyn Brianne dam and reservoir, fishing, riding and fabulous scenery. Just 40 minutes from the coast and 7 miles north of Llandovery.*
DOUBLE ROOM: from £20 to £30
SINGLE ROOM: up to £25
FOOD: up to £15
**Hours:** breakfast 8am-9.30am, lunch 11.30am-3.30pm, dinner 6pm-10pm, bar meals 11.30am-3.30pm, 6pm-10.30pm.
**Cuisine:** ENGLISH - good-quality country food. Excellent-value bar meals.
**Cards:** Visa, Access.
**Other points:** licensed, Sunday lunch, children catered for (please check for age limits), pets allowed, beer garden.
**Rooms:** 2 single rooms, 1 double room, 1 twin room, 1 family room. All with TV, tea/coffee-making facilities.
**Directions:** from Llandovery, follow signs to Llyn Brianne and Rhandirmwyn.
MR & MRS L.W. ALEXANDER ☎(01550) 760201
Fax (01550) 760332

## MILFORD HAVEN • map 3A2

### BELHAVEN HOUSE HOTEL & RESTAURANT
29 Hamilton Terrace, SA73 3JJ
*A quiet hotel noted for its relaxed atmosphere. Six of the bedrooms overlook the attractive waterway. The restaurant offers a large selection of scrumptious meals to cater for most tastes.*
DOUBLE ROOM: from £20 to £30
FOOD: up to £15　CLUB
**Hours:** breakfast 6am-10.30am, lunch 12noon-2pm, dinner 6.30pm-10pm.
**Cuisine:** BRITISH / CONTINENTAL - steaks, pavlovas, vegetarian dishes. Choice of over 40 main courses.
**Cards:** Visa.
**Other points:** licensed, Sunday lunch, children welcome, afternoon tea, coaches by prior arrangement
**Rooms:** 1 single room, 1 double room, 11 twin room, 4 family rooms.
**Directions:** on the front street, overlooking the haven, just past the monument.
MR & MRS HENRICKSEN ☎(01646) 695983
Fax (01646) 690787

## NEW QUAY • map 7D2

### BLACK LION HOTEL
Glanmor Terrace, SA45 9PT
*Situated in the pretty resort of New Quay, with its sandy beach and fishing harbour, the Black Lion is a warm, friendly, family-run hotel. Most rooms are en suite, centrally heated, and have tea/coffee trays. The atmospheric old bar, dating back to 1680, has live music most weekends and bar snacks and meals available at lunchtime and evenings. Evening diners will enjoy `Dylan's' restaurant, dedicated to the poet Dylan Thomas. During the summer months, meals are also served in the beer garden, which has panoramic views over Cardigan Bay. There is also a children's play area.*
DOUBLE ROOM: from £20 to £30
SINGLE ROOM: from £25 to £35
FOOD: up to £15
**Hours:** breakfast 8.30am-10am, bar snacks 12noon-12.30am & 2.30pm-3pm, dinner 7pm-10pm, bar snacks 6pm-10pm.
**Cuisine:** BRITISH
**Other points:** parking, children welcome, no-smoking area, pets allowed, residents' lounge, vegetarian meals, open-air dining.
**Rooms:** 10 double rooms, 1 twin room.
**Directions:** at centre of town on approach to harbour and beach.
THOMAS JAMES HUNTER ☎(01545) 560209
Fax (01545) 560585

### TY HEN FARM HOTEL, COTTAGES & LEISURE CENTRE

Llwyndafydd, near New Quay, SA44 6BZ

*Situated in beautiful wooded countryside, near the spectacular Cardigan coast, this quiet stock-farm offers a choice of self-catering cottages or farm-hotel guest accommodation. Facilities in the area include riding, fishing and water sports. On-site leisure centre includes large indoor heated pool, fitness room, solarium, skittles, etc. Restaurant and bar. Smoking is restricted to cottages only. Private adult swimming lessons available.*

DOUBLE ROOM: from £20 to £30
SINGLE ROOM: up to £25
FOOD: up to £15  **CLUB**
**Hours:** breakfast 8.30am-9.30am, dinner 6.30pm-8pm.
**Cuisine:** BRITISH
**Cards:** Visa, Access, MasterCard.
**Other points:** central heating, children welcome, residents' lounge, garden, self-catering cottages, residents' bar, swimming pool, parking, disabled access.
**Rooms:** 5 bedrooms.
**Directions:** A487: follow signs to Llwyndafydd; with phone kiosk on left, go up hill approximately 1 mile, sharp right bend, then into `No Through Road' on right. Entrance is 100 yards on right.
VERONICA KFI1Y ☎(01545) 560346 **Fax**(01545) 560346

## NEWCASTLE EMLYN • map 7E2

### MAES-Y-DERW GUEST HOUSE & RESTAURANT

Cardigan Road, SA38 9RD

*It is a well-known fact that if you want to find a good restaurant, dine where the locals dine - and with its excellent reputation, Maes-y-Derw is very popular with the locals. The imposing exterior of this Victorian country house and the impressive decor, furnishings and antiques inside will impress the most discerning tastes. Here you can be assured of tasteful, comfortable accommodation, superb food and charming hospitality.*

DOUBLE ROOM: up to £20
SINGLE ROOM: up to £25
FOOD: from £15 to £20 🍽
**Hours:** breakfast 7.30am-9am, lunch 12noon-2.30pm, dinner 6.45pm-9.30pm.
**Cuisine:** FRENCH / INTERNATIONAL - very good local reputation for fresh, well-cooked food.
**Other points:** parking, children welcome, pets allowed, garden, vegetarian meals, traditional Sunday lunch, afternoon teas.
**Rooms:** 6 bedrooms. All with TV, tea/coffee-making facilities.
**Directions:** on A484 Carmarthen-Cardigan road. Between market town of Newcastle Emlyn and Cenarth Falls.
WYN & DIANE DAVIES ☎(01239) 710860 **Fax**(01239) 710860

## SAUNDERSFOOT • map 3A2

### ST BRIDES HOTEL

St Brides Hill, SA69 9NH

*Excellent location overlooking Carmarthen Bay. A very high standard is maintained in all aspects of the hotel, particularly with regard to the food and service.*

DOUBLE ROOM: from £40 to £50
SINGLE ROOM: over £55
FOOD: from £18 to £25
**Hours:** breakfast 8am-10am, lunch 12.30pm-1.30pm, dinner 7pm-9.15pm, bar 12noon-11pm.
**Cuisine:** BRITISH / CONTINENTAL - specializing in locally caught fish, lobster and crab. Flambé dishes.
**Cards:** Visa, Access, Diners, AmEx.
**Other points:** licensed, Sunday lunch, children welcome (restaurant age limit 6 years+), coaches by prior arrangement.
**Rooms:** 3 single rooms, 10 double rooms, 25 twin rooms, 5 executive suites. All with radio, bar, telephone, tea/coffee-making facilities, hair dryer, satellite TV.
**Directions:** from the A40, A477 or A476, follow signposts to Saundersfoot.
IAN BELL ☎(01834) 812304 **Fax**(01834) 813303

## ST CLEARS • map 3A2

### THE OLD MILL

LLanddowror, SA33 4HR

*A café and traditional old stone mill restaurant combined, which offers a wide range of freshly prepared meals and snacks catering for travellers and holiday makers alike. The all day breakfasts are a speciality, and vegetarians and vegans are also catered for. Jane serves her many satisfied customers with great cheerfulness and has created a bustling atmosphere akin to many of the French "Routiers" stops.*

FOOD: up to £15
**Hours:** open all day from 6.30am-6.30pm, restaurant open 7pm (reservations only), closed Christmas Day and New Year's Day.
**Cuisine:** all day breakfasts, roast lunches, home-made cakes for afternoon teas. Vegan and vegetarian dishes.
**Cards:** Visa, Access, Diners, AmEx, MasterCard.
**Other points:** 12 hours a day café, open to all; licensed, pets allowed, telephone, children

welcome, parking.
**Directions:** on the A477 trunk road 21 miles from Tembrock Dock.
MS JANE JONES ☎(01994) 230836

## ST DAVID'S • map 7E1

 **RAMSEY HOUSE**
Lower Moor, SA62 6RP

*Ramsey House offers you a unique combination of professional hotel standards of accommodation and food service, coupled with the friendly, relaxing atmosphere of a pleasant country guest house. Situated just half a mile from St David's, with its 12th century cathedral, this guest house enjoys a quiet location on the road to Porthclais and is an ideal base for touring the area. Wales Tourist Board 3 Crowns, 'Highly Commended'.*
DOUBLE ROOM: from £20 to £30
SINGLE ROOM: from £21 to £30
FOOD: up to £15 ☜ ☰
**Hours:** breakfast 8am-8.30am, dinner 7pm.
**Cuisine:** WELSH - Welsh lamb steaks with laverbread and orange, 'Dragons Eggs', salmon with cucumber sauce, Welsh venison.
**Other points:** garden, residents' lounge, pets allowed, parking, ground-floor rooms, vegetarian meals, picnic lunches, children not accepted.
**Rooms:** 4 double rooms, 3 twin rooms. All with tea/coffee-making facilities and TV.
**Directions:** from centre of St David's bear left in front of Midland Bank, signposted Porthclais. Last house on left before open country (1/2 mile).
MAC & SANDRA THOMPSON ☎(01437) 720321

 **Y GLENNYDD GUEST HOUSE**
51 Nun Street, SA62 6NU
*A cosy guest house in the charming village city of St David's. Y Glennydd aims to make each guest's stay relaxed and comfortable. A full English breakfast, dinner, picnic baskets, etc. are available. Guests will also enjoy exploring this attractive area, famous for its cathedral, coastal path and offshore islands.*
DOUBLE ROOM: up to £20
SINGLE ROOM: from £20
FOOD: up to £15 ☜
**Hours:** breakfast 8am-10am, dinner 7pm-8.30pm, closed January.
**Cuisine:** INTERNATIONAL - bistro licenced restaurant: à la carte and table d'hôte.
**Cards:** Visa, Access.
**Other points:** children welcome, residents' lounge, picnic lunches, street parking, public car park, residents' bar.

**Rooms:** 1 single room, 4 double rooms, 2 twin rooms, 3 family rooms. All with TV, tea/coffee-making facilities. Most rooms en suite.
**Directions:** A487. Nun Street is part of the one-way system from Cross Square, next door to the fire station.
TIMOTHY & TRACEY FOSTER ☎(01437) 720576
Fax(01437) 720184

## TENBY • map 3A2

 **ATLANTIC HOTEL**
Esplanade, SA70 7DU
*Fronted by magnificent gardens and with a spectacular view of the sea, this elegant Edwardian hotel fully deserves its loyal clientele. The rooms are richly furnished and fully fitted with an eye to comfort, the food is superbly prepared and presented with unobtrusive professionalism, and your every need is catered for.*
DOUBLE ROOM: from £30 to £40
SINGLE ROOM: from £45 to £55
FOOD: from £15 to £20 ☜
**Hours:** breakfast 8am-9.30am, bar meals 12noon-1.30pm, dinner 7pm-8.30pm, closed 20th December until 5th January.
**Cuisine:** WELSH / INTERNATIONAL - prepared using fresh local ingredients.
**Cards:** Visa, Access, AmEx.
**Other points:** licensed, Sunday lunch, children welcome, residents' lounge, garden.
**Rooms:** 4 single rooms, 22 double rooms, 5 twin rooms, 9 family rooms. All with TV, radio, telephone, tea/coffee-making facilities, baby-listening device, hair dryer, trouser-press.
**Directions:** follow A477 to Tenby, continue through town past 5 Arches.
DORIS & WILLIAM JAMES ☎(01834) 842881/844176 Fax(01834) 842881 ext256

☲ **FOURCROFT HOTEL**
North Beach, SA70 8AP
*Over 150 years old, the Fourcroft is situated in the most peaceful and select part of the town, with spectacular cliff-top gardens. A seafront hotel set above Tenby's Blue Flag North Beach, with magnificent views of Carmarthen Bay and Tenby Harbour.*
DOUBLE ROOM: from £30 to £40
SINGLE ROOM: from £35 to £45
FOOD: up to £15
**Hours:** meals all day 8am-12midnight.
**Cuisine:** BRITISH - Pembrokeshire turkey, honeyed Welsh lamb, local salmon, trout and plaice, interesting bar lunches.
**Cards:** Visa, Access.
**Other points:** Sunday lunch, swimming pool, leisure centre, garden, parking.
**Rooms:** 6 single rooms, 16 double rooms, 16 twin rooms, 7 family rooms. All with TV, radio, telephone, tea/coffee-making facilities.
**Directions:** fork left after 'Welcome to Tenby' sign, double back along seafront, past information office.
THE OSBORNE FAMILY ☎(01834) 842886
Fax(01834) 842888

### THE IMPERIAL HOTEL
The Paragon, SA70 7HR

*Cliff-top location overlooking the South Beach towards St Catherine's and Caldy Islands. Private steps to the beach. The Imperial offers extensive menus and a good wine list, served by courteous staff in very pleasant surroundings. Three minutes' level walk to the town centre.*

DOUBLE ROOM: from £20 to £30
SINGLE ROOM: from £25 to £35
FOOD: up to £15
**Hours:** breakfast 7.30am-9.30am, dinner 7pm-8.30pm, bar meals 11.30am-9pm.
**Cuisine:** ENGLISH - traditional English cuisine, with à la carte, table d'hôte and bar meals.
**Cards:** Visa, Access, Diners, AmEx, Switch.
**Other points:** licensed, Sunday lunch, children welcome, pets allowed, open bank holidays, functions, children welcome, baby-listening device, cots, 24hr reception, residents' lounge, residents' bar.
**Rooms:** 4 single rooms, 18 double rooms, 22 twin rooms. All with TV, radio, alarm, telephone, tea/coffee-making facilities. Executive rooms available.
**Directions:** M4, A40, A477 to Kilgetty, then A478.
JAN-ROELOF EGGENS ☎(01834) 843737
Fax (01834) 844342

# MID GLAMORGAN

## BRIDGEND • map 4B4

### ASHOKA TANDOORI
68 Nolton Street, CF31 3BP

*Situated on the main road in Bridgend, the exterior suggests a Bengali connection. A popular restaurant with a pleasantly decorated interior and unobtrusive background music.*

FOOD: from £16 to £20
**Hours:** lunch 12noon-2.30pm, dinner 5.30pm-12midnight.
**Cuisine:** INDIAN - rogon chicken special, meat masala, sag ghosht, and all popular dishes.
**Cards:** Visa, Access, Diners, AmEx.
**Other points:** open-air dining, children welcome, fully air-conditioned.
**Directions:** situated on the main road in Bridgend.
MR MISPAK MIAH ☎(01656) 793783

# SOUTH GLAMORGAN

## BARRY • map 4B4

### WALES AIRPORT HOTEL
Port Road, Rhoose, CF62 3BT

*A modern hotel which has been extended in time for the 1996 'season'. All the facilities expected of an international airport hotel are provided, and the 24 hour operation and facilities make this an ideal start point for an overseas or domestic holiday. Excellent security parking for those wishing to leave a car, with courtesy coach to the airport.*

DOUBLE ROOM: from £20 to £30
SINGLE ROOM: from £30 to £45
FOOD: from £15 to £20
**Hours:** breakfast available throughout 24 hours, lunch (bar and restaurant) 11.30am-3pm, dinner 6pm-2am. Food always available.
**Cuisine:** a wide range of meals available to travellers throughout the day.
**Cards:** Visa, Access, AmEx, Diners, Delta, Switch
**Other points:** special airport security parking with courtesy bus to airport, 24 hour food.
**Rooms:** 32 newly refurbished bedrooms all with tea/coffee-maker, TV, telephone, radio, alarm, hair dryer, room service.
**Directions:** from Cardiff West junction on the M4 follow signs to the airport - hotel is on the right within a 2 minute drive of airport.
RECEPTION ☎(01446) 710787
Fax (01446) 710856

## CARDIFF • map 4B4

### BENEDICTO'S
4 Windsor Place

*Delightfully decorated throughout, this restaurant is highly regarded in the city by local businessmen and evening theatregoers. Both the à la carte and the table d'hôte menu offer a varied selection of well-prepared meals, complemented by a good wine list.*

FOOD: from £15 to £20 CLUB
**Hours:** lunch 12noon-2.30pm, dinner 6.30pm-11.30pm, closed Sunday evenings.
**Cuisine:** INTERNATIONAL - all dishes specially prepared to order using only the freshest produce.
**Cards:** Visa, Access, Diners, AmEx.
**Other points:** children welcome, vegetarian meals, traditional Sunday lunch.
**Directions:** Windsor Place is off Queen Street in Cardiff city centre, opposite the Capital Mall.
BEN LADO ☎(01222) 371130

### THE CENTRAL HOTEL
The Monument, St Mary Street, CF1 5RH

*An imposing stone building built by the 3rd Marquis of Bute in 1887, situated in the heart of Cardiff refurbished to offer a high standard of comfort and decor. The dining room is attractively decorated with prints to create a warm atmosphere. The* comprehensive menu is complemented by a good wine list to provide the standard of cuisine expected by local and international guests.

DOUBLE ROOM: from £20 to £30
SINGLE ROOM: from £29 to £37
FOOD: up to £15
**Hours:** breakfast 7am-10am, lunch (restaurant and bar) 11.30am-3pm, dinner 7pm-10pm. Food available all day for residents.
**Cuisine:** extensive and varied à la carte menu.
**Cards:** Visa, Access, Diners, AmEx, Switch, Delta.
**Other points:** parking.
**Rooms:** 44 rooms and 2 suites all en suite with tea/coffee-maker, TV, telephone, hair dryer.
**Directions:** in Cardiff city centre.
MR DAN CLAYTON JONES ☎(01222) 396455
Fax(01222) 377559

### ◣ MARLBOROUGH GUEST HOUSE
98 Newport Road, CF2 1DG

A smart, family-run Victorian town house, well sited just 5 minutes from the city centre, theatre, castle and shops. All bedrooms are furnished to a high standard and have everything one would need for a comfortable night's stay or longer.

DOUBLE ROOM: from £20 to £30
SINGLE ROOM: from £20 to £30
FOOD: up to £15
**Hours:** breakfast 7.30am-8.30am, open bank holidays.
**Cuisine:** WELSH / INTERNATIONAL.
**Other points:** laundry service, parking.
**Rooms:** 3 single rooms (1 en suite), 2 double rooms en suite, 4 twin rooms (3 en suite) and 1 family room en suite. All with TV, hair dryer, room service and tea/coffee-making facilities.
**Directions:** exit junction 30 of M4, Cardiff city centre, A48 Newport road.
ANNETTE & PAUL HOWARD ☎(01222) 492385

### ◣ SANT-Y-NYLL
St Bride's-super-Ely, CF5 6EZ

Sant-y-Nyll House stands in its own splendid grounds surrounded by views of the picturesque

Vale of Glamorgan, yet is within easy reach of the centre of Cardiff and the airport. Mr and Mrs Renwick have furnished their house with many elegant items from their world travels creating a comfortable and relaxed atmosphere for guests. This is a unique setting for a memorable visit.

DOUBLE ROOM: up to £20
**Hours:** breakfast 7.30am-9.30am, dinner by arrangement. Open bank holidays.
**Cards:** AmEx.
**Other points:** children welcome, parking.
**Rooms:** 1 single room, 2 double rooms, 1 double room en suite, 2 twin rooms. All with TV, tea/coffee-making, hair dryer.
**Directions:** take exit 33 from the M4 onto A4232. 1st exit to to Cardiff West and 1st exit off roundabout, after 100 yards turn left to St Fagan's, through St Fagans to cross roads turn left to St Brides continue for 1 mile. 200 yards after new bridge turn right the hotel is 100 yards on left through stone pillars.
PAUL & MONICA RENWICK ☎(01446) 760209
Fax(01446) 760209

### ◣ TRAHERNE ARMS RESTAURANT
The Tumble, St Nicholas, CF5 6SA

A 400-year-old, traditional Welsh longhouse where guests can relax in comfort and enjoy excellent food and superb wines in an informal atmosphere while enjoying spectacular views of Cardiff down to the Bristol Channel. The staff are polite and very efficient.

FOOD: from £15 to £20    CLUB
**Hours:** lunch Monday to Saturday 12noon-2pm, Sunday 12noon-2.30pm, dinner Monday to Friday and Sunday 7pm-9.30pm, Saturday until 10pm, open bank holidays, closed Christmas day.
**Cuisine:** poultry, game and fish, vegetarian, daily blackboard specials, home-made cakes, sweets and pastries, traditional cream teas.
**Cards:** Visa, Switch, MasterCard, Delta.
**Other points:** licensed, parking.
**Directions:** on A48 from Cardiff to Culverhouse Cross, .5 mile towards Cowbridge.
JULIA JARVIS ☎(01222) 597707 Fax(01222) 593734

# WEST GLAMORGAN

## ABERCRAF • map 3A3

 **MAES-Y-GWERNEN**
School Road, Abercraf, Swansea Valley,
SA9 1XD

*Maes-y-Gwernen is a well-appointed licensed guest house, situated in well-kept grounds in the upper Swansea Valley village of Abercraf. The Moore family offer good food and extremely comfortable, well-equipped accommodation to both tourists and business people, at rates that represent excellent value. (See special feature on page 12.)*
DOUBLE ROOM: up to £20
SINGLE ROOM: up to £25
FOOD: up to £15
**Hours:** breakfast 7am-10am, lunch 12noon-2pm, dinner 6pm-8.30pm, open all year.
**Cuisine:** ENGLISH / FRENCH - meal times can be arranged to suit guests' requirements; everything is home-cooked on the premises, with special vegetarian menu available if required.
**Cards:** Visa, Access, AmEx.
**Other points:** parking, children welcome, pets allowed, no-smoking area, conference facilities, residents' lounge, residents' bar, garden, vegetarian meals, traditional Sunday lunch.
**Rooms:** 5 double rooms, 2 twin rooms, 1 family room. All with TV, telephone, radio, alarm, hair dryer, trouser press, tea/coffee-making facilities.
**Directions:** 12 miles north of M4 junction 45, on A4067.
ELSIE MOORE ☎(01639) 730218 Fax (01639) 730765

## GOWER • map 3A3

 **WORM'S HEAD HOTEL**
Rhossili, SA3 1PP

*Situated in a designated area of outstanding natural beauty at the westernmost tip of the Gower Peninsula, the hotel has a superb outlook over the majestic sweep of Rhossili Bay and the famous Worm's Head. The Worm's Head Hotel provides guests with well-appointed facilities in comfortable and tasteful surroundings and a very pleasant atmosphere.*
DOUBLE ROOM: from £20 to £30
SINGLE ROOM: from £30 to £35
FOOD: up to £15  CLUB
**Hours:** breakfast 8am-9.30am, lunch 12noon-2pm, bar meals 12noon-3pm, dinner 7pm-9pm, bar meals 7pm-9pm.
**Cuisine:** BRITISH - traditional home-style cooking.
**Cards:** Visa, Access, Switch.
**Other points:** parking, children welcome, pets allowed, disabled access, residents' lounge, garden, open-air dining, vegetarian meals, traditional Sunday lunch.
**Rooms:** 19 bedrooms. All with TV, tea/coffee-making facilities.
**Directions:** from Swansea, proceed along North

Gower Road, past Swansea Airport, follow signs for Oxwich Bay; Rhossili is approximately 5 miles further on.
DAVID LEGG - RHOSSILI HOTELS LTD ☎(01792) 390512 Fax (01792) 391115

## SWANSEA • map 3A3

 **CEFN-BRYN**
6 Uplands Crescent, Uplands, SA2 0PB

*Built by a mariner a century ago, a calm, quiet atmosphere prevails throughout this vast, semi-detached Victorian residence boasting some exceptional plasterwork. The rooms are comfortable and spacious all with their own en suite facilities. Ideally situated for touring Mumbles and the Gower.*
DOUBLE ROOM: from £20 to £30
SINGLE ROOM: up to £25
**Hours:** breakfast 7.30am-9am, closed Christmas and New Year.
**Cuisine:** BREAKFAST - full Welsh or continental breakfast.
**Other points:** children welcome, open bank holidays, no-smoking area, residents' lounge.
**Rooms:** 2 single rooms, 1 double room, 1 twin room, 2 family rooms. All en suite.
**Directions:** on A4118, approximately 1 mile west of city centre.
ANN TELFER ☎(01792) 466687

**THE SCHOONER**
4 Prospect Place, SA1 1QP

*Grade II listed building with wine bar, restaurant and function room. Situated in central Swansea on the fringe of the new Marina development and near the leisure centre.*
FOOD: up to £15  CLUB
**Hours:** lunch 12noon-2pm, bar meals 12noon-2pm, dinner 7pm-9.30pm, bar meals 7pm-7.30pm, closed Sunday evening.
**Cuisine:** INTERNATIONAL - fresh local produce, all home-cooked. Traditional Sunday lunches (booking advisable). Evening special menu changes monthly. Carvery meals most evenings.
**Other points:** Sunday lunch, no-smoking area, coaches by prior arrangement, vegetarian meals.
**Directions:** in the east of Swansea, close to Sainsbury's.
CHRISTINE PARKMAN ☎(01792) 649321

# GWENT

## ABERGAVENNY • map 4A4

 **THE SWAN HOTEL**
Cross Street, NP7 5ER

*The hotel is situated adjacent to the bus station and within 10 minutes' walk from the railway station. It is centrally placed in the town as well as affording easy access to the M4. Very popular because of its excellent menu and reasonable prices. Ample parking is available.*

DOUBLE ROOM: from £20 to £30
SINGLE ROOM: from £27
FOOD: up to £15
**Hours:** bar meals 12noon-2pm, dinner 7pm-9.30pm.
**Cuisine:** BRITISH - traditional home-cooking, e.g., Sunday lunch: roast beef with Yorkshire pud. Home-made pies, moussaka and fresh salads.
**Cards:** Visa, Access, AmEx.
**Other points:** Sunday lunch, children catered for (please check for age limits).
**Rooms:** 2 single rooms, 6 double rooms, 3 twin rooms. All with TV, radio, telephone, tea/coffee-making facilities.
**Directions:** next to bus station in Abergavenny.
IAN S. LITTLE ☎(01873) 852829 Fax(01873) 852829

## CHEPSTOW • map 4A5

 **THE HUNTSMAN HOTEL**
Shirenewton, Chepstow, NP6 6B4

*A small country hotel serving well-presented food in generous portions, with polite, unintrusive service. Three miles to Chepstow racecourse and golfing facilities.*

DOUBLE ROOM: up to £20
SINGLE ROOM: from £25
FOOD: up to £15
**Hours:** breakfast 7.30am-10.30am, lunch 12noon-2pm, dinner 7pm-10pm.
**Cuisine:** BRITISH / CONTINENTAL - chicken in leek and Stilton sauce, lamb griselle, breaded plaice, chicken chasseur and lasagne. All available in the restaurant or lounge bar.
**Cards:** Visa, Access, AmEx.
**Other points:** licensed, Sunday lunch, playland, pets allowed, functions.
**Rooms:** 3 single rooms, 3 double rooms, 2 twin rooms, 2 family rooms. All with TV, radio, alarm, telephone, tea/coffee-making facilities.
**Directions:** approximately 4 miles out on the B4235 Chepstow to Usk road.
MR A.C. MOLES ☎(01291) 641521/641733
Fax(01291) 641601

## CWMBRAN • map A4A

 **THE PARKWAY HOTEL & CONFERENCE CENTRE**
Cwmbran Drive, NA44 3UW

*Outstanding in all aspects, The Parkway is ideal for holiday-makers and business visitors alike. Designed on a Mediterranean theme, the hotel offers accommodation of a very high standard, first-class restaurant meals, a leisure complex, and excellent conference and banqueting facilities. Privately-owned and run, the service is excellent and a warm welcome is guaranteed. Highly recommended. Visit the Wye valley, Vale of Usk, Cardiff city and the Brecon Beacons.*

DOUBLE ROOM: over £50
SINGLE ROOM: over £50
FOOD: up to £15    CLUB
**Hours:** breakfast 7am-9.30am, lunch 12noon-2.30pm, dinner 7pm-10pm.
**Cuisine:** BRITISH / MEDITERRANEAN - extensive choice such as River Wye salmon, lemon sole Walewska, grills, tournedos Rossini. Carvery. Open-air dining in the coffee shop at lunchtimes only.
**Cards:** Visa, Access, Diners, AmEx.
**Other points:** licensed, open-air dining, Sunday lunch, children catered for (please check for age limits), garden, residents' lounge, conferences, leisure centre, baby-listening device, cots, 24hr reception.
**Rooms:** 47 double rooms, 23 twin rooms. All with TV, radio, alarm, telephone, tea/coffee-making facilities, hair dryer, trouser-press.
**Directions:** off junction 25a of the M4. Turn onto A4051 (on Cwmbran Drive). Take first roundabout third exit, then turn first right.
JOHN WOODCOCK ☎(01633) 871199
Fax(01633) 869160

## LLANTRISANT • map 4A5

 **THE GREYHOUND INN & HOTEL**
Near Usk, NP5 1LE

*The Greyhound was established as a country inn in 1845. Originally a 17th century farmhouse, with a stone stable block that has recently been converted into 10 bedrooms, all with en suite bathroom. Available in the dining room, or one of the two lounges, is a varied but inexpensive menu with an emphasis on home-cooking using traditional*

recipes. In the summer you can enjoy the beautiful surroundings in the beer garden, and in winter you can warm yourself by the real log fire. You can even shop for your country pine or antiques in the stone barn showroom.
DOUBLE ROOM: from £20 to £30
SINGLE ROOM: from £39 to £48
FOOD: up to £15
**Hours:** breakfast 7.15am-9.30am, lunch 12noon-2.15pm, dinner 6pm-10.30pm.
**Cuisine:** BRITISH - traditional home-cooking, vegetarian menu, special dishes.
**Cards:** Visa, Access.
**Other points:** parking, children welcome, garden, open-air dining, vegetarian meals, 6 real ales.
**Rooms:** 10 bedrooms. All with en suite, TV, telephone, radio, tea/coffee-making facilities.
**Directions:** take the A449 to Usk town centre. Enter the square and take the second on the left, following signs towards Llantrisant. The Greyhound may be found just over two miles down the road, on the right.
NICHOLAS DAVIES ☎(01291) 672505/673447
Fax(01291) 673255

## MONMOUTH • map 4A5

### ◢ THE CROWN AT WHITEBROOK
Whitebrook, NP5 4TX
*A small, intimate restaurant and hotel, remotely situated in beautiful scenery, five miles south of Monmouth and one mile from the River Wye. Sandra Bates specializes in creating original dishes from fresh local ingredients, and there is a good wine list. The cheerful hospitality of the proprietors and staff creates a relaxing, friendly atmosphere in which to dine or stay. Regional Newcomer of Year 1991, Prix D'Elite Wine Award 1994.*
DOUBLE ROOM: from £30 to £40
SINGLE ROOM: from £45 to £55
FOOD: from £20 to £25
**Hours:** breakfast 8am-9.30am, lunch 12noon-2pm, dinner 7pm-9pm, closed Christmas day and Boxing day.
**Cuisine:** FRENCH - specialities include quail boned and stuffed with a pork and sultana mousse. Local venison, salmon and Welsh lamb. All freshly cooked to order.
**Cards:** Visa, Access, Diners, AmEx.
**Other points:** licensed, Sunday lunch, children welcome, garden, pets allowed.
**Rooms:** 9 double rooms, 3 twin rooms.
**Directions:** off A466, 2 miles from Bigsweir Bridge. In the Whitebrook Valley.
MR ROGER BATES ☎(01600) 860254 Fax(01600) 860607

### ◢ MONMOUTH PUNCH HOUSE
Agincourt Square, NP5 3BT
*Situated in the centre of town and therefore enjoying both the local and the tourist trade. The restaurant overlooks Agincourt Square and its statues of Henry V and Charles Rolls. Throughout summer the building is festooned with hanging baskets.*
FOOD: from £15 to £20
**Hours:** bar meals 11.30am-2pm, bar meals 7pm-9pm, lunch 11.30am-2pm, dinner 7pm onwards.
**Cuisine:** BRITISH - traditional British dishes using finest, fresh local produce. Own smokery and butcher. Sunday lunch a speciality.
**Cards:** Visa, Access, AmEx.
**Other points:** open-air dining, Sunday lunch, children welcome, coaches by prior arrangement.
**Directions:** situated on the A466, in the town centre.
PEPE ☎(01600) 713855

## NEWPORT • map 4A5

### ◢ THE KNOLL GUEST HOUSE
145 Stow Hill, NP9 4FZ
*The Knoll is a homely Victorian neo-Dutch style family owned guest house situated within walking distance of Newport town centre and only minutes from the M4. Good homely cooking and comfortable bedrooms, several en suite, assure guests of a high standard of accommodation at a sensible price. Ongoing refurbishment reflects the proprietors' determination to maintain their high standards.*
DOUBLE ROOM: up to £20
SINGLE ROOM: from £22
FOOD: up to £15
**Hours:** breakfast 7am-9am, lunch 12noon-2pm, dinner 6pm-8pm. Open bank holidays.
**Cards:** None
**Other points:** licensed, residents' lounge, parking.
**Rooms:** 10 bedrooms all with TV, telephone, radio, alarm, hair dryer, trouser press, room service, baby listening device, tea/coffee-making facilities.
**Directions:** junction 27 on the M4, follow signs for Newport town centre for just under 3 miles on B4591. After 2 sets of traffic lights, The Knoll is 200 yards on the right.
GUY & LEE HEWETT ☎(01633) 263557
Fax(01633) 212168

### ◢ VILLA DINO RESTAURANT
103 Chepstow Road, Maindee, NP9 8BY
*This attractive Italian restaurant serves excellent food in a very relaxing and welcoming atmosphere. All dishes are freshly cooked to order and well presented. A small family business in a delightful Victorian setting. The service is outstanding - professional, efficient and very warm and courteous. Highly recommended: a winner of many awards.*
FOOD: from £15 to £20
**Hours:** dinner 7pm-11pm, closed Sunday.
**Cuisine:** ITALIAN - a good choice of Italian dishes. Specialities include Chateaubriand bouquetière, filetto al Stilton. Fish, veal, beef, chicken, pasta and vegetarian. Something for everyone.
**Cards:** Visa, Access, Diners, AmEx.
**Other points:** licensed, disabled access, functions.
**Directions:** on the main road from Newport to Chepstow. Five minutes to rail station and motorway.
DINO GULOTTA ☎(01633) 251267

## TINTERN • map 4A5

 **THE FOUNTAIN INN**
Trellech Grange, NP6 6QW

*A typical 17th century country inn where the food is prepared to order. The bar provides the focal point and, on a chilly day, a log fire provides a warm welcome. Real ales and whisky a speciality.*
DOUBLE ROOM: up to £20
SINGLE ROOM: up to £20
FOOD: up to £15  `CLUB`
**Hours:** lunch 12noon-3pm, Sunday 12noon-2pm, dinner 7pm-10.30pm, Sunday 7pm-9.30pm, closed

Christmas evening only.
**Cuisine:** ENGLISH - dishes include jugged hare, Tudor roast, venison, rack of lamb.
**Cards:** Visa, Access.
**Other points:** licensed, Sunday lunch, children welcome, caravan facilities.
**Rooms:** 1 single room, 2 double rooms, 5 twin rooms, 2 family rooms.
**Directions:** off A466, 2 miles from Tintern Abbey. Turn by Royal George in Tintern and bear right around ponds.
CHRIS & JUDITH RABBITS ☎(01291) 689303

# GWYNEDD

## ABERSOCH • map 7C2

 **TUDOR COURT HOTEL & RESTAURANT**
Lôn Sarn Bach, LL53 7EB

*Once the home of an old sea captain, but now extensively refurbished to provide a comfortable hotel with its own restaurant, offering fine cuisine using the best of local fresh produce. Sailing, golfing, fishing and many historical places of interest nearby. Open all Christmas and New Year. Mini-breaks and inclusive golf breaks arranged.*
DOUBLE ROOM: from £20 to £30
SINGLE ROOM: from £25 to £35
FOOD: up to £15  `CLUB`
**Hours:** breakfast 8am-9am, lunch 12.30am-2pm, dinner 6.30pm-9.30pm.
**Cuisine:** FRENCH / ENGLISH - vegetarian meals also available.
**Cards:** Visa, Access, Diners.
**Other points:** parking, children welcome, afternoon teas, no-smoking area, disabled access, pets by prior arrangement, vegetarian meals.
**Rooms:** 1 single room, 4 double rooms, 2 twin rooms, 2 family rooms.
**Directions:** from Caernarfon or Porthmadog go to Pwllheli and drive along the coast to Abersoch. The hotel is on the right-hand side of the main road through the village.
MS J. JONES ☎(01758) 713354 `Fax`(01758) 713354

**THE WHITE HOUSE HOTEL**
Abersoch, LL53 7AG

*Overlooking the picturesque harbour of Abersoch, Cardigan Bay and St Tudwal's Islands, this hotel is set back from the road in its own grounds. A warm welcome, comfortable accommodation and good food await you. The bedrooms have recently been modernized, and the elegant dining room is comfortable and spacious. A two-mile-long sandy beach is within easy walking distance.*
DOUBLE ROOM: from £30 to £40
SINGLE ROOM: from £30 to £40
FOOD: from £15 to £20
**Hours:** bar meals 6.30pm-9.30pm, dinner 7pm-9pm.

**Cuisine:** BRITISH - bar menu and à la carte restaurant menu (evenings). Fresh local produce used wherever possible. Local lobsters and crabs, Welsh lamb and beef.
**Cards:** Visa, Access, Switch.
**Other points:** licensed, children welcome, garden, pets allowed, residents' lounge, baby-sitting, cots available.
**Rooms:** 1 single room, 7 double rooms, 3 twin rooms, 1 family room. All with TV, radio, alarm, telephone, tea/coffee-making facilities.
**Directions:** A499, 7 miles from Pwllheli.
JAYNE & DAVID SMITH ☎(01758) 713427
`Fax`(01758) 713512

## AMLWCH • map 7A2

**LASTRA FARM HOTEL**
Amlwch, LL68 9TF

*Steeped in history, this delightful licensed country house hotel can accommodate any party, large or small. Situated in this most beautiful part of Wales, there is something for everyone, whether your interests lie with history or leisure activities. Lastra Farm Hotel is a great base for exploring Anglesey.*
DOUBLE ROOM: from £20 to £30
SINGLE ROOM: from £25 to £35
FOOD: up to £15  `CLUB`
**Hours:** breakfast 7.30am-9.30am, lunch 12noon-2pm, dinner 7pm-9.30pm.
**Cuisine:** BRITISH - freshly cooked British cuisine with a French influence. Game and lobster available in season.
**Cards:** Visa, Access, AmEx, Switch.
**Other points:** parking, children welcome, pets allowed, residents' lounge, garden, vegetarian meals, traditional Sunday lunch.
**Rooms:** 1 single room, 5 double rooms, 1 twin room. All with TV, telephone, radio, tea/coffee-making facilities.
**Directions:** located near the sports centre in Amlwch, northern Anglesey.
MAURICE HUTCHINSON ☎(01407) 830906
`Fax`(01407) 832552

## BALA • map 7B3

### PALÉ HALL COUNTRY HOUSE
Pale Estate, Llandderfel, LL23 7PS

This outstanding Gothic Revival style mansion was built in 1870 for a Scottish engineer who spared no expense in its construction. Now converted into a sumptuous hotel and lovingly restored to standards that echo its exterior elegance. Bedrooms are individually designed and have a spacious lounge area plus many thoughtful extras. The dining room is the focal point, specializing in the best of British and Welsh cuisine with an extensive wine list.
DOUBLE ROOM: from £40
SINGLE ROOM: over £50
FOOD: from £20 to £25 🍽
Hours: breakfast 8am-10am,lunch (restaurant & bar) 12 noon-2pm,dinner 7-9.30pm. Open all year.
Cuisine: table d' hôte and à la carte menus. Starters include sauté of chicken livers in whisky sauce and rillette of duck. Main courses include, roast rack of Welsh lamb with mustard and herb crust, roast local pheasant with crisp bacon and rich port sauce, magret of Barbary duck on a sweet onion tart.
Cards: Visa, Access, AmEx, Eurocard
Other points: parking, pets allowed (in kennels), no smoking area, conference facilities, residents' lounge and garden, outdoor dining, vegetarian meals, afternoon teas, traditional Sunday lunch.
Rooms: 17 bedrooms all with luxurious en suite facilities, tea/coffee maker, TV, telephone, hair dryer, trouser press. All rooms spacious with lounge area. 2 double room suites & 2 rooms with Jacuzzi.
Directions: travel north on A5, pass through Corwen then left onto B4401. Approximately 8.5 miles to Palé Hall.
MR AND MRS NAHED ☎(01678) 530285 Fax(01678) 530220

### PLAS COCH HOTEL
High Street, LL23 7AB
This attractive stone building, dating back to 1780, sits in the centre of Bala near Bala Lake, surrounded by Snowdonia National Park. The restaurant lends itself to traditional Welsh cooking, with an emphasis on local produce and a choice of good wines.
DOUBLE ROOM: from £30 to £40
SINGLE ROOM: from £35 to £45
FOOD: up to £15
Hours: breakfast 8am-9am, lunch 12noon-2pm, dinner 7pm-8.30pm, closed Christmas day.
Cuisine: WELSH - à la carte menu, fixed three-course menu and bar menu.

Cards: Visa, Access, Diners, AmEx.
Other points: licensed, Sunday lunch, no-smoking area, children welcome, afternoon tea, baby-listening device, cots, left luggage, residents' bar, residents' lounge, vegetarian meals, parking.
Rooms: 1 single room, 4 double rooms, 1 twin room, 4 family rooms. All with TV, radio, alarm, telephone, tea/coffee-making facilities.
Directions: Bala is on the A494, 14 miles north of Dolgellau, 10 miles south of the A5.
MR & MRS EVANS ☎(01678) 520309 Fax(01678) 521135

## BARMOUTH • map 7C3

### PANORAMA HOTEL
Panorama Road, LL42 1DG
A warm welcome awaits you at this friendly, family-run hotel, set in 2 acres of wooded grounds and overlooking the Mawddach estuary and Barmouth harbour. An excellent reputation for à la carte, table d'hôte and home-made bar meals, and a comprehensive wine list.
DOUBLE ROOM: from £20 to £30
SINGLE ROOM: from £25 to £35
FOOD: up to £15    CLUB
Hours: breakfast 8.30am-9.30am, lunch 12noon-2pm, bar meals 12noon-2pm, dinner 7pm-9pm, bar meals 7pm-9pm.
Cuisine: BRITISH - home-made food.
Cards: Visa, Access, Diners, AmEx.
Other points: open-air dining, pets allowed, children welcome, afternoon tea, vegetarian meals.
Rooms: 1 single room, 4 double rooms, 8 twin rooms, 4 family rooms.
Directions: Panorama Road is off the A496, .5 mile east of Barmouth harbour.
MR & MRS FLAVELL & MR MORGAN ☎(01341) 280550 Fax(01341) 280346

## BEDDGELERT • map 7B2

### ROYAL GOAT HOTEL
Beddgelert, LL55 4YE

This Georgian building is situated in a charming little village in the heart of the Snowdonia National Park. The Royal Goat offers traditional Welsh hospitality in great comfort and style. The combination of excellent food, accommodation and service makes this hotel a pleasure to visit. Situated in town renowned for its `Legend of Gelert', the faithful dog. Highly recommended.
DOUBLE ROOM: from £30 to £40

SINGLE ROOM: from £35 to £45
FOOD: up to £15
**Hours:** breakfast 7.45am-10am, lunch 12noon-2.30pm, dinner 7pm-10pm.
**Cuisine:** BRITISH - à la carte and fixed three-course menus. Serving fish, steak, duck and veal.
**Cards:** Visa, Access, Diners, AmEx.
**Other points:** licensed, Sunday lunch, no-smoking area, children catered for (please check for age limits), garden, afternoon tea, pets allowed, car hire, pony-trekking, baby-listening device, baby-sitting, cots, 24hr reception, residents' lounge, residents' bar.
**Rooms:** 17 double rooms, 17 twin rooms. All with TV, radio, alarm, telephone, tea/coffee-making facilities.
**Directions:** located in the town centre.
IRENIE & EVAN ROBERTS ☎(01766) 890224/890343 Fax(01766) 890422

## BETWS-Y-COED • map 7B3

### TY GWYN HOTEL
LL24 0SG
*A delightful 16th century coaching inn, which has captured the charm and character of the period with low beams, antique furnishings and tasteful decor. An idyllic setting overlooking the River Conwy in this beautiful Welsh village. Excellent home-cooking ensures a strong local following. 1987 Routiers Newcomer of the Year winner.*
DOUBLE ROOM: from £20 to £30
FOOD: up to £15
**Hours:** breakfast 8.15am-10am, lunch 12noon-2pm, bar meals 12noon-2pm, dinner 7pm-9.30pm, bar meals 7pm-9.30pm.
**Cuisine:** WELSH / CONTINENTAL - pheasant braised in a Beaujolais and wild mushroom sauce, fresh local wild salmon served with a basil and vermouth sauce, breast of chicken Rossini.
**Cards:** Visa, Access.
**Other points:** Sunday lunch, children welcome, pets allowed.
**Rooms:** 1 single room, 5 double rooms, 13 twin rooms.
**Directions:** on the A5 south of Betws-y-Coed.
JAMES & SHELAGH RATCLIFFE ☎(01690) 710383/710787

## CAERNARFON • map 7B2

### THE BLACK BOY INN
North-Gate Street, LL55 1RW
*A 15th century inn situated within the walls of Caernarfon Castle. Good sea and game fishing. Ideal for yachting on inland tidal waters. Traditional home-cooking.*
DOUBLE ROOM: up to £20
SINGLE ROOM: up to £25
FOOD: up to £15
**Hours:** lunch 12noon-2.30pm, dinner 6.30pm-9pm.
**Cuisine:** ENGLISH - traditional English cooking, e.g., roast beef, roast lamb and the trimmings. A la carte, table d'hôte menus and bar snack menu.

**Cards:** Visa, Access, Diners.
**Other points:** Sunday lunch, children welcome.
**Rooms:** 2 single rooms, 4 double rooms, 4 twin rooms, 2 family room. Most en suite.
**Directions:** located in the town centre.
MR ROBERT WILLIAMS ☎(01286) 673023

### VICTORIA HOUSE
13 Church Street, LL55 1SW
*A Victorian terraced guest house offering comfortable accommodation in delightfully furnished surroundings. Snowdonia National Park and Caernarfon Castle are close by.*
DOUBLE ROOM: up to £20
SINGLE ROOM: up to £25
**Hours:** breakfast 8am.
**Cuisine:** BREAKFAST
**Other points:** children welcome, open bank holidays, pets (by arrangement), vegetarian meals.
**Rooms:** 2 single rooms, 4 double/twin rooms, 1 family room.
**Directions:** past castle entrance, turn right at end of street.
TERENCE & JANINE SMITH ☎(01286) 673133

## CAPEL CURIG • map 7B3

### COBDEN'S HOTEL & BRASSERIE
LL24 0EE
*A 200-year-old country house hotel, set in the heart of Snowdonia. Comfortable, informal and fun; perfect for total rest and relaxation. Own 200-metre rock pool (clear running water) for swimming and fishing.*
DOUBLE ROOM: from £20 to £30
SINGLE ROOM: from £25 to £35
FOOD: up to £15
**Hours:** lunch 12noon-2pm, dinner 6.30pm-9.30pm, Sunday 7pm-9pm.
**Cuisine:** MODERN BRITISH
**Cards:** Visa, Access, AmEx.
**Other points:** licensed, Sunday lunch, children welcome, pets allowed, open bank holidays.
**Rooms:** 4 single rooms, 5 double rooms, 5 twin rooms, 2 family rooms. All with TV, tea/coffee-making facilities.
**Directions:** on A5, between Betws-y-Coed and Bangor.
THE GOODALL FAMILY ☎(01690) 720243 Fax(01690) 720354

## CONWY • map 7B3

### DEGANWY CASTLE HOTEL
Station Road, Deganwy, LL31 9DA
*Originally a cottage and over 250 years old, the Deganwy Castle Hotel offers a magnificent view of Conwy estuary and castle. A main feature is the bar, which is built from beer barrels. Tourist packages are available. The many nearby places of interest include Conwy Castle, Bodnant Gardens and the beautiful Snowdonia National Park.*
DOUBLE ROOM: from £20 to £30

SINGLE ROOM: from £20 to £30
FOOD: from £15 to £20
**Hours:** breakfast 7am-9.30am, lunch 12noon-2.30pm, dinner 7pm-9.30pm.
**Cuisine:** BRITISH / FRENCH - à la carte and table d'hôte menus, offering an extensive choice of dishes. Vegetarian dishes also available.
**Cards:** Visa, Access, Diners, AmEx.
**Other points:** licensed, open-air dining, Sunday lunch, no-smoking area, children welcome (restaurant age limit 11 years+), pets allowed, residents' lounge, garden, parking, afternoon tea.
**Directions:** proceed along A55 and take signposted turning to Deganwy.
DENNIS CHIN ☎(01492) 583555 Fax(01492) 583555

## CRICCIETH • map 7C2

### CAERWYLAN HOTEL
Beach Bank, LL52 0HW
*Caerwylan is an imposing hotel and the only one in Criccieth situated on the promenade. The lounge and several of the bedroom windows look out across the sandy beaches to the sea, or to the castle. The food is traditional Welsh. The warm welcome offered by the Davies ensures many repeat bookings.*
DOUBLE ROOM: up to £20
SINGLE ROOM: from £20
**Hours:** breakfast 8.45am-9.30am, dinner 6.45pm-7.30pm, closed mid-October until Easter.
**Cuisine:** WELSH
**Cards:** Visa, MasterCard, Delta.
**Other points:** pets allowed, children welcome, residents' lounge, TV lounge.
**Rooms:** 6 single rooms, 4 double rooms, 9 twin rooms, 7 family rooms. All with TV, radio, tea/coffee-making facilities.
**Directions:** off the A497 onto the B4411 to Criccieth. Hotel is on main promenade.
MR & MRS DAVIES ☎(01766) 522547

### GLYN Y COED HOTEL
Porthmadog Road, LL52 0HL
*A Victorian house overlooking the sea, mountains and castle. There is an attractive garden at the front with a small stream running through it. Family-run, a friendly, homely atmosphere prevails.*
DOUBLE ROOM: from £20 to £30
SINGLE ROOM: up to £25
FOOD: up to £15
**Hours:** breakfast 8.30am-9am, lunch 12.30pm-1.30pm, dinner 6pm-6.30pm, closed Christmas day and New Year's eve.
**Cuisine:** BRITISH
**Other points:** children welcome, pets allowed, residents' lounge, garden, baby-listening device, cots, 24hr reception.
**Rooms:** 2 single rooms, 3 double rooms, 2 twin room, 3 family rooms (1 ground floor bedroom). All with en suite, TV, tea/coffee-making facilities.
**Directions:** Nearest hotel to Criccieth centre on

A497 facing the sea.
MRS ANN REYNOLDS ☎(01766) 522870
Fax(01766) 523341

### THE MOELWYN RESTAURANT WITH ROOMS
Mona Terrace, LL52 0HG
*A Victorian, creeper-clad restaurant directly overlooking Cardigan Bay, with bar/lounge and well-appointed bedrooms. The restaurant serves English and French cuisine, including locally caught salmon. All food is carefully prepared and complemented by a comprehensive selection of wines. Public car park adjacent. Disabled access to restaurant only. Vegetarian menu.*
DOUBLE ROOM: from £20 to £30
SINGLE ROOM: from £20 to £30
FOOD: up to £15 ☜CLUB
**Hours:** Sunday lunch 12.30am-2pm, dinner 6.30pm-9.30pm, closed January until March.
**Cuisine:** ENGLISH / FRENCH - seafood, salmon and lamb, interesting sauces and fresh vegetables. Home-made sweets. Lobster when available.
**Cards:** Visa, Access.
**Other points:** licensed, Sunday lunch, children welcome, pets by prior arrangement.
**Rooms:** 6 en suite rooms. All with TV and tea/coffee-making facilities.
**Directions:** on the seafront.
MR & MRS PETER BOOTH ☎(01766) 522500

## DOLGELLAU • map 7C3

### CLIFTON HOUSE HOTEL
Smithfield Square, LL40 1ES

*Dating from the 18th century when it was the County Gaol, the Clifton now offers a much warmer welcome as a hotel and restaurant. Mrs Dix, the chef, makes imaginative use of fresh local produce, and all the dishes are excellently cooked. The service is `exemplary' and the warmth of the welcome is undoubtably genuine. Highly recommended for food and accommodation.*
DOUBLE ROOM: from £20 to £30
SINGLE ROOM: from £25 to £35
FOOD: from £15 to £20 ☜
**Hours:** breakfast 8am-9.30am, dinner 7pm-9.30pm, closed January.
**Cuisine:** BRITISH - interesting and varied menu featuring traditional and vegetarian dishes and using fresh, local produce.
**Cards:** Visa, Access.

**Other points:** licensed, garden, children welcome.
**Rooms:** 4 double rooms, 2 twin rooms.
**Directions:** A470. Centre of Dolgellau.
ROB & PAULINE DIX ☎(01341) 422554

### FRONOLEU FARM HOTEL & RESTAURANT
Tabor, LL40 2PS

*A 300 year old farm house sympathetically extended to blend in with its wonderful natural surroundings under the shadow of Cader Idris and over looking the magnificent Moawddach estuary. Ten comfortable bedrooms are available, six en suite and dinner is served every evening in the award winning Stable restaurant. A superb location from which to explore this beautiful area of Wales.*
DOUBLE ROOM: from £39
SINGLE ROOM: up to £20
FOOD: up to £15
**Hours:** breakfast 7am-10am, lunch (restaurant and bar) 12noon - 2.30pm, dinner (restaurant and bar) 6.30pm-10.30pm.
**Cuisine:** ENGLISH - extensive à la carte menu using only the finest cuts of Welsh beef and lamb. Game and local fish in season. Traditional roast lunch on Sunday.
**Other points:** large car park, harpist most evenings, function room available.
**Rooms:** 1 single room, 3 double rooms, plus 1 twin room, 3 double rooms and 2 family rooms en suite. All room with tea/coffee-maker, TV, hair dryer.
**Directions:** From Welshpool: at junction of A470 from Machynlleth, take road opposite Cross Foxes Inn signposted Tabor. From Dolgellau town centre follow road past hospital, proceed up hill and follow signs to restuarant.
MAGGIE & DEWI JONES ☎(01341) 422361
Fax (01341) 422361

## HARLECH • map 7C2

### CASTLE COTTAGE HOTEL & RESTAURANT
Pen Llech, LL46 2YL

*An oak-beamed dining room and bar in one of the oldest houses in Harlech. Only 300 yards from the castle. International cuisine plus modestly priced wine list. Ideally situated for the Royal St David's Golf Course and surrounding area of natural beauty.*
DOUBLE ROOM: from £20 to £30
SINGLE ROOM: up to £25
FOOD: from £15 to £20
**Hours:** Sunday lunch 12noon-2pm, dinner summer 7pm-9.30pm, winter 7pm-9pm.
**Cuisine:** INTERNATIONAL - dishes include local rack of lamb and honey and rosemary sauce. Brochette of scallops and smoked bacon, beurre blanc sauce.
**Cards:** Visa, Access, AmEx.
**Other points:** Sunday lunch, no-smoking area, children welcome.
**Rooms:** 2 single rooms, 2 double rooms, 2 twin rooms. All with en suite, radio, tea/coffee-making facilities.

**Directions:** on B4573 road to Porthmadog.
MR & MRS ROBERTS ☎(01766) 780479

### THE CASTLE HOTEL
Castle Square, LL36 2YH

*A family-run hotel open all year, offering a wide menu and warm, welcoming service. Local attractions include Harlech Castle, Cardigan Bay, a local golf club, Beddgelert copper mine and a dry ski slope. Nearby, Shell Island provides the opportunity for seal and bird spotting, and shell collecting.*
DOUBLE ROOM: from £20 to £30
SINGLE ROOM: from £28
FOOD: from £15 to £20
**Hours:** meals all day in summer 12noon-11pm, lunch 12noon-3pm, dinner 7pm-11pm, last orders 10pm.
**Cuisine:** ENGLISH - pub menu, serving a range of dishes from Dover sole and steak tartare to cow pie, lasagne and the `Kiddies Corner' selection.
**Cards:** Visa, Access.
**Other points:** licensed, Sunday lunch (in summer), no-smoking area, children welcome, pets allowed.
**Rooms:** 1 single room, 5 double rooms, 4 twin rooms. All with TV, telephone, tea/coffee-making facilities.
**Directions:** opposite the castle in the centre of Harlech, which is on the A496.
MRS T.M. SWINSCOE ☎(01766) 780529

## HOLYHEAD • map 7B2

### BULL HOTEL
London Road, Anglesey, LL65 3DP

*A pleasant, cream-painted building on the main A5 road to Holyhead. There is a large, sheltered beer garden with children's play area outside, while inside, the main, informal eating area is separate from the bar. For those wishing to linger a while, the Bull offers comfortable accommodation.*
DOUBLE ROOM: from £21 to £25
SINGLE ROOM: from £31
FOOD: up to £15    CLUB
**Hours:** breakfast 7.30am-9am, lunch 12noon-2pm, dinner 7pm-9.30pm, bar meals 12noon-9pm.
**Cuisine:** BRITISH - specials change daily.
**Cards:** Visa, Access.
**Other points:** open-air dining, Sunday lunch, pets allowed, children welcome, afternoon tea.
**Rooms:** 2 single rooms, 5 double rooms, 6 twin rooms, 2 family rooms.
**Directions:** situated 200 yards from Holyhead side traffic lights at A5025 junction.
DAVID HALL ☎(01407) 740351 Fax (O1407) 742328

---

**Join Les Routiers Discovery Club
FREE! See page 34 for details.**

---

## THE OLD RECTORY
Rhoscolyn, LL65 2DQ

*A former rectory, this fine Georgian house offers
extensive views over the sea and surrounding
countryside. Now restored, the building still retains
much of its original charm and offers guests
traditional hospitality and comfort.The dining room
overlooks the garden where a full breakfast or four-
course dinner featuring Welsh cooking can be
enjoyed. Interesting wine list. Ideal base for
exploring the coast and its many nearby attractions.*
DOUBLE ROOM: from £20 to £30
SINGLE ROOM: from £23 to £32
FOOD: up to £15
**Hours:** closed 21st December to 3rd January each
year.
**Cuisine:** traditional British cooking, casseroles, lamb
chops.
**Cards:** Connect
**Other points:** parking, children welcome, pets
allowed, no smoking area, residents'lounge and
garden.
**Rooms:** 5 rooms en suite with tea/coffee maker, TV,
radio, alarm, hair dryer, patchwork quilts.
**Directions:** Take A5 Bangor to Valley road, turn left
on to B4545 at Valley & left at four mile bridge,
signposted Rhoscolyn, proceed 2 miles along lane
to Rhoscolyn church.
MR & MRS DAVID AND LEONIE WYATT
☎(01407) 860214

### LLANBEDROG • map 7C2

#### SHIP INN
Near Pwllheli, LL53 7PE
*A public house serving very tasty food at good
prices. It also has open views on three sides, with a
protected area outside for diners. Celebrated for its
flower displays; the gardens, which are attended by
a professional gardener, give a particularly pleasant
outlook.*
FOOD: up to £15
**Hours:** lunch 12noon-3pm, dinner 6pm-9.45pm.
**Cuisine:** BRITISH - home-made pies, curries, local
crab and lobster, salads, steaks.
**Other points:** parking, children welcome, no-
smoking area, open-air dining, vegetarian meals.
**Directions:** approaching Llanbedrog from Pwllheli,
take the sharp right towards Aberdaron.
BRIAN & PATRICIA WARD ☎(01758) 740270

### LLANDUDNO • map 7B3

#### AMBASSADOR HOTEL
Promenade, LL30 2NR

*The Williams family have been in the hotel trade for
30 years and in that time have built up a regular
return business. The two sun lounges are relaxing
places to sit whatever the weather. Mini-breaks
available throughout the year.*
DOUBLE ROOM: from £20 to £30
SINGLE ROOM: from £20 to £30
FOOD: up to £15
**Hours:** breakfast 8.30am-9.15am, bar meals
12noon-1.30pm, dinner 6.30pm-7.30pm, closed
January.
**Cuisine:** BRITISH
**Cards:** Visa, AmEx
**Other points:** central heating, children welcome,
residents' lounge, lift, bar, cots, disabled access,
vegetarian meals, parking, residents' bar.
**Rooms:** 7 single rooms, 53 double/twin, 3 family
rooms. All with TV, tea/coffee-making facilities.
**Directions:** leave A55; take A470 to Llandudno.
Follow to Promenade, then turn left.
DAVID T. WILLIAMS ☎(01492) 876886
Fax(01492) 876347

#### CASANOVA ITALIAN RESTAURANT
18 Chapel Street, LL30 2SY
*Situated in the heart of town. Gingham and red
tablecloths, a cedar ceiling and lively music add to
the bustling atmosphere. A very popular restaurant:
advance booking recommended.*
FOOD: up to £15
**Hours:** dinner 6pm-10.30pm.
**Cuisine:** ITALIAN - e.g., calamari fritti, insalata
Casanova, filetto al funghi.
**Cards:** Visa, Access.
**Other points:** licensed, children welcome, street
parking.
**Directions:** off Gloddaeth Street opposite the
English Presbyterian church.
MR K.R. BOONHAM ☎(01492) 878426

#### DUNOON HOTEL
Gloddaeth Street, LL30 2DW
*Lavishly appointed with great attention to detail, the
Dunoon exudes charm and comfort. It has been in
the same family for over 40 years, which accounts
for the care shown in the elegant accommodation
and spacious restaurant. The Dunoon provides the*

*ideal place to relax and enjoy good food, a civilized ambience and splendid facilities.*
DOUBLE ROOM: from £24 to £37
SINGLE ROOM: from £32 to £37
FOOD: up to £15
**Hours:** breakfast 8.30am-10am, lunch 1pm-2pm, dinner 6.30pm-8.00pm.
**Cuisine:** BRITISH - table d'hôte, à la carte and bar meals. British cuisine specializing in fresh, local produce.
**Cards:** Visa, Access.
**Other points:** licensed, Sunday lunch, children welcome, garden, afternoon tea, pets allowed, solarium.
**Rooms:** 12 single rooms, 14 double rooms, 17 twin rooms, 12 family rooms.
**Directions:** off Mostyn Street, close to Promenade.
MR M.C. CHADDERTON ☎(01492) 860787
Fax(01492) 860787

 **EMPIRE HOTEL**
Church Walks, LL30 2HE
*A family-run hotel located near the centre of this popular holiday resort. The Empire has developed a reputation for good food served in two separate restaurants, friendly service and leisure facilities. Luxury accommodation; all rooms have Jacuzzi baths.*
DOUBLE ROOM: from £35 to £45
SINGLE ROOM: from £50 to £60
FOOD: from £15 to £20
**Hours:** bar 11am-11pm.
**Cuisine:** BRITISH - Watkins & Co. serving traditional dishes; grill room/coffee shop, fish and roasts.
**Cards:** Visa, Access, Diners, AmEx, JCB.
**Other points:** licensed, Sunday lunch, no-smoking area, children welcome, roof patio garden, swimming pool, sauna.
**Rooms:** 58 bedrooms. All en suite.
**Directions:** Church Walks leads off the Promenade.
MR & MRS MADDOCKS ☎(01492) 860555

 **GLENORMES PRIVATE HOTEL**
Central Promenade, LL30 1AR
*Former gentleman's residence situated opposite the beach. A combination of period elegance and modern comforts. "10 doors" walk to theatre/conference centre. The rooms feature antique furnishings, original fireplaces and Victorian 4 poster beds.*
DOUBLE ROOM: from £20 to £30
SINGLE ROOM: from £25 to £35
FOOD: up to £15
**Hours:** breakfst 8.30am-9am, dinner 6pm.
**Cuisine:** BRITISH - home-cooked table d'hôte menu.
**Cards:** Visa, Access.
**Other points:** parking, residents' lounge, no-smoking area, vegetarian meals, traditional Sunday lunch, restaurant age limit 17 years+.
**Rooms:** 12 bedrooms. All with en suite, TV, tea/coffee-making facilities, toiletries.
**Directions:** centre of Promenade, opposite beach.
TONY & JOANNE GIBSON ☎(01492) 876643

 **HEADLANDS HOTEL**
Hill Terrace, LL30 2LS

*Situated above the town, but only a short walk to the beach and shops, Headlands Hotel offers superb views across the bay and Conwy estuary to the mountains of Snowdonia. Friendly service and home-cooked 5-course table d'hôte dinner make this a popular choice with tourists.*
DOUBLE ROOM: from £20 to £30
SINGLE ROOM: from £25 to £35
FOOD: from £15 to £20
**Hours:** breakfast 8.30am-9.15am, bar meals 12noon-1.30pm, dinner 6.45pm-8pm, closed January and February.
**Cuisine:** BRITISH - a five-course table d'hôte menu is offered. Wide choice of dishes, using local produce, both traditional and classical. Vegetarian meals by arrangement.
**Cards:** Visa, Access, Diners, AmEx.
**Other points:** licensed, children welcome, pets by prior arrangement, bar, lounge, central heating.
**Rooms:** 4 single rooms, 8 double rooms, 3 twin rooms, 2 triple rooms. All with TV, radio, alarm, telephone, tea/coffee-making facilities.
**Directions:** at top of Hill Terrace, on the Great Orme in Llandudno.
MR & MRS WOODS ☎(01492) 877485

 **IMPERIAL HOTEL**
The Promenade, LL30 1AP
*A large hotel with many facilities including the Speakeasy Bar, based on 1920s American gangster style. Chantreys Restaurant plus Health & Fitness Centre.*
DOUBLE ROOM: from £40 to £50
SINGLE ROOM: over £50
FOOD: from £15 to £20
**Hours:** lunch 12.30am-2pm, bar meals 12noon-3pm, dinner 6.30pm-9.30pm.
**Cuisine:** INTERNATIONAL - daily table d'hôte menu and monthly speciality menu.
**Cards:** Visa, Access, Diners, AmEx.
**Other points:** Sunday lunch, children welcome, coaches by prior arrangement
**Rooms:** 20 single rooms, 27 double rooms, 49 twin rooms, 4 family rooms.
**Directions:** on the Promenade.
MR GEOFFREY LOFTHOUSE ☎(01492) 877466
Fax(01492) 878043

### THE KENSINGTON HOTEL
Central Promenade, LL30 1AT

*Situated on the main promenade, this substantial Victorian building presents an imposing facade and offers guests good value accommodation and dining. Its central position makes it ideal for just visiting Llandudno, or for exploring the beautiful countryside of Snowdonia. Mr and Mrs Beardmore are carrying out extensive refurbishment and improvemnets to give even better value in 1996.*

DOUBLE ROOM: from £30 to £40
SINGLE ROOM: from £25 to £35
FOOD: up to £15
**Hours:** breakfast 8am-9.30am, meals served all day, dinner 6pm-7pm, open bank holidays.
**Cards:** Visa, Access.
**Other points:** licensed, morning coffees, afternoon teas, parking.
**Rooms:** 10 twin rooms, 27 double rooms, all en suite. All with TV and tea/coffee-making facilities.
**Directions:** on the central promenade approximately 300 yards from the theatre.
MR STEPHEN BEARDMORE ☎(01492) 876784
Fax(01492) 874184

### RAVENHURST HOTEL
West Shore, LL30 2BB

*The Ravenhurst is situated on LLandudno's lovely West Shore, and overlooks Anglesey, the Conway estuary and the mountains of Snowdonia. The Great Orme protects the hotel from the north. At least 60% of the bookings are from returning guests. No strangers - only friends you haven't met.*

DOUBLE ROOM: from £20 to £30
FOOD: up to £15
**Hours:** breakfast 8.45am-10am (earlier on request), lunch and bar meals 12noon-2.30pm, dinner 6pm-7.45pm, closed from 30th November until 2 weeks before Easter.
**Cuisine:** BRITISH
**Cards:** Visa, Access, Diners, AmEx, Switch.
**Other points:** central heating, children welcome, 3 residents' lounges (1 no-smoking), garden, vegetarian meals.
**Rooms:** 6 single rooms, 10 twin rooms, 7 double rooms, 3 family suites. All with TV, tea/coffee-making facilities.
**Directions:** Llandudno West, on the sea front opposite boating pool.
PETER, DAVID & KATHLEEN CARRINGTON
☎(01492) 875525

### SANDRINGHAM HOTEL
West Parade, West Shore, LL30 2BD

*The bar has a definite naval flavour, with the cap bands of naval vessels and nautical seascapes on the walls. Situated in the centre of the West Shore, it is a real suntrap all day long and has unimpeded views of Anglesey and the Conwy estuary. Happy, family atmosphere.*

DOUBLE ROOM: from £20 to £30
SINGLE ROOM: from £20 to £30
FOOD: up to £15 ⌣

**Hours:** breakfast 8am-9.15am, lunch 12noon-2pm, dinner 6.30pm-8.30pm, open all year.
**Cuisine:** ENGLISH - concentration on fresh wholesome food such as home-made pies, lasagne, fish and roasts.
**Cards:** Visa, Access, Mastercard, JCB.
**Other points:** licensed, open-air dining, Sunday lunch, children welcome, residents' lounge, residents' bar.
**Rooms:** 3 single rooms, 7 double rooms, 5 twin rooms, 3 family rooms. All with telephone, tea/coffee-making facilities, heating, hair dryer, satellite TV.
**Directions:** on seafront of the quiet, sunny West Shore (not the main promenade).
MR & MRS D. KAVANAGH ☎(01492) 876513/876447 Fax(01492) 872753

### TYNEDALE PRIVATE HOTEL
Central Promenade, LL30 2XS

*Situated in a premier position opposite The Bandstand with excellent views of Llandudno Bay, a warm welcome is assured for all guests. Food is very important here and every effort is made to select the best. Guests can relax and enjoy the magnificent views from a luxurious no-smoking lounge, or retire to the Sun Lounge for peace and quiet. There are two bars and two dance floors, both air-conditioned, and comfortable accommodation with many facilities including direct dial telephones.*

DOUBLE ROOM: from £23 to £30
SINGLE ROOM: from £23 to £30
FOOD: up to £15
**Hours:** breakfast 8.15am-9.15am, bar snacks 12noon-2pm, dinner 6pm-7pm.
**Cuisine:** BRITISH
**Cards:** Visa, Access.
**Other points:** parking, children welcome, no-smoking area, disabled access, residents' lounge, vegetarian meals, sea views.
**Rooms:** 56 bedrooms.
**Directions:** on Central Promenade opposite The Bandstand.
MR MICHAEL GOODEY ☎(01492) 877426
Fax(01492) 871213

### WHITE COURT HOTEL
2 North Parade, LL30 2LP

An attractive hotel, well-situated adjacent to the pier, beach and shopping area. All bedrooms and the charming sitting room offer a very high standard of comfort, allowing guests to relax and enjoy the ambience of the hotel, which is completely non-smoking. The dining room is renowned for its good food and comprehensive wine list.
DOUBLE ROOM: from £20 to £30
SINGLE ROOM: from £30 to £40
FOOD: up to £15
**Hours:** breakfast 8am-9am, dinner 6pm-7.30pm, closed December and January.
**Cuisine:** BRITISH
**Cards:** Visa, Access.
**Other points:** children welcome, residents' lounge.
**Rooms:** 9 double rooms, 3 twin rooms, 1 family room, 1 suite. All with TV, telephone, tea/coffee-making facilities, toiletries, wine.
**Directions:** near to cenotaph, adjacent to pier, beach and shopping area.
NATASHA & STEPHEN GARLINGE ☎(01492) 876719 [Fax](01492) 871583

## PORTHMADOG • map 7C2

### BLOSSOMS RESTAURANT
Borth-y-Gêst, LL49 9TP
Overlooking the bay at Borth-y-Gêst with Snowdonia in the distance, Blossoms Restaurant is part of the `Heartbeat Wales' programme to promote healthy eating. Log fires and classical jazz or blues music set the atmosphere. It is a small restaurant, so booking is advisable.
FOOD: from £15 to £20
**Hours:** lunch (summer only) 12noon-2pm, dinner 7pm-10.30pm, closed Sunday.
**Cuisine:** MEDITERRANEAN - vegetarian dishes.
**Cards:** Visa, Access.
**Other points:** open-air dining, Sunday lunch, children welcome.
**Directions:** .5 mile from A497 in the centre of Borth-y-Gêst.
PAUL DENHAM & MEG BROOK ☎(01766) 513500

### Y LLONG - THE SHIP
Lombard Street, LL49 9AP
Built in 1824, this is the oldest public house in Porthmadog and is mentioned in many maritime books of the area. Having undergone extensive refurbishment, it still retains much of its original charm, with tiled floors, bench seats and a stone fireplace. Ideally situated for tourists and travellers. `Heartbeat Wales Award', Vegetarian Good Food Guide, Good Beer Guide (CAMRA).
FOOD: from £10 to £25
**Hours:** bar meals 12noon-2.15pm, 6.30pm-9.30pm, restaurant 5.30pm-11pm, closed Sunday.
**Cuisine:** CANTONESE / EUROPEAN - à la carte, plus extensive choice of Cantonese and Peking dishes. Daily changing specials, excellent vegetarian menu. Bar meals, snacks and traditional beers in both bars.
**Cards:** Visa, Access, Diners, AmEx.

**Other points:** licensed, no-smoking area, children catered for (restaurant only), parking, open bank holiday Sundays.
**Directions:** close to Porthmadog harbour.
ROBERT JONES & NIA JONES ☎(01766) 512990/514415

## PWLLHELI • map 7C2

### TWNTI SEAFOOD RESTAURANT
Rhydycladfy, LL53 7YH
Once the meeting place for the Monks Pilgrimage on their way to Bardsey Island, this family-run restaurant, tastefully converted from a barn, now offers real fires in winter and a warm and friendly atmosphere. It is ideally situated for visiting Caernarfon Castle, the Italianate village of Portmeirion, and the remote but beautiful wilderness of Snowdonia National Park.
FOOD: from £15 to £20
**Hours:** lunch/snacks 12noon-2pm Monday-Saturday, dinner 7pm until late Monday-Saturday.
**Cuisine:** BRITISH - à la carte menu, offering a wide choice of seafood and meat dishes, all freshly prepared and cooked daily. Also available children's menu and vegetarian meals (if given 24 hours notice).
**Cards:** Visa, Access.
**Other points:** licensed, Sunday lunch, children welcome, disabled access, open bank holidays, extensive wine list.
**Directions:** from Pwllheli, right onto A497 for Nefyn. Turn left onto the B4415, follow road for ½ mile.
KEITH JACKSON & STEPHEN WILLIAMS ☎(01758) 740929

## TAL-Y-BONT • map 7B3

### THE LODGE HOTEL
Near Conwy, LL32 8YX
An attractive and welcoming hotel and restaurant nestling in the Conwy Valley. The restaurant provides a relaxed and elegant setting in which to enjoy well-prepared traditional cuisine. Fresh local produce is used whenever possible, and most soft fruits and vegetables are grown in the hotel gardens.
DOUBLE ROOM: from £20 to £30
SINGLE ROOM: from £30 to £40
FOOD: up to £15 [CLUB]
**Hours:** breakfast 8.15am-9.30am, lunch 12noon-2pm, dinner 7pm-9pm.
**Cuisine:** BRITISH - table d'hôte and à la carte menus. Local fish specialities. Vegetarian meals are also available.
**Cards:** Visa, Access.
**Other points:** licensed, open-air dining, Sunday lunch, children welcome, pets by prior arrangement, residents' bar, parking, vegetarian meals, disabled access.
**Rooms:** 4 double rooms, 6 twin rooms. All en suite.
**Directions:** follow A55 Expressway to Conwy. At castle, turn left for the B5106.
MR & MRS BALDON ☎(01492) 660766 [Fax](01492) 660534

# POWYS

## ABERMULE • map 8D4

### DOLFORWYN HALL HOTEL
SY15 6JG

*The Hall, built in Tudor times and later extended in the Georgian era, stands in 3 acres of wooded grounds in a quiet off the road location. Privately owned and managed by Keith and Cheryl Galvin, the hotel is rapidly gaining a reputation for excellent home-cooked food and comfortable accommodation. Situated in a most historic area of Wales close to Powis Castle and Welshpool, with its large agricultural market, this is an ideal location for a relaxing break amongst beautiful surroundings.*

DOUBLE ROOM: from £20 to £30
SINGLE ROOM: from £35
FOOD: from £15 to £20
**Hours:** breakfast 7.30am-9.30am, lunch bar 12noon-2.30pm, dinner bar 6.30pm-9.30pm, dinner restaurant 6.30pm-9.30pm. Open bank holidays.
**Cards:** Visa, Access, AmEx, Switch, JCB.
**Other points:** open log fires, central heating, fully licensed, gardens, salmon fishing 10 minutes walk away, golf and pony trekking nearby, conference facilities, parking.
**Rooms:** 1 single room, 2 double rooms, 2 twin rooms, 2 family rooms. All en suite with satellite TV, room service, tea/coffee-making facilities. Hair dryer available.
**Directions:** 3.5 miles out of Newtown on the A483 towards Welshpool.
KEITH & CHERYL GALVIN ☎(01686) 630221
Fax(01686) 630360

## BRECON • map 7E3

### LA BRASERIA & RICK'S WINE BAR
1st Floor, Main Street, LD3 7LA

*An atmospheric wine bar and restaurant where the order of the day is char-grilled meals. Here you select the cut you wish to eat, and then it is cooked to your specifications before your very eyes. You only need to look at what is on offer here to see that only ingredients of the freshest and finest quality are used. This is a real find!*

FOOD: up to £15
**Hours:** dinner (Wednesday-Saturday) 6.30pm-10pm (last orders).
**Cuisine:** MEDITERRANEAN - completely new menu with a strong emphasis on fresh shellfish and seafood (daily). Commendable lobster thermidor and chinese style lobster. Mediterranean and vegetarian meals a speciality. Five weekly specials.
**Other points:** children welcome, vegetarian meals.
**Directions:** on the High Street in the centre of town.
KITY & CHARLES SMITH ☎(01874) 611313

## LLANDRINDOD WELLS • map 7D3

### THE MONTPELLIER HOTEL
Temple Street, LD1 5HW

*Set in an area of outstanding natural beauty, this family-owned, Victorian spa town hotel offers a relaxing break, quality fresh food and an international wine list. Ideal as a touring centre for exploring mid-Wales.*

DOUBLE ROOM: from £20 to £30
SINGLE ROOM: from £30 to £40
FOOD: from £15 to £20
**Hours:** lunch 12noon-2pm, dinner 7pm-10pm. Open all year.
**Cuisine:** high quality fresh food on both à la carte and table d'hôte menus. Pheasant Chasseur in season.
**Cards:** Access,Visa,Mastercard
**Other points:** parking, wedding receptions, weekend breaks.
**Rooms:** 2 single rooms, 2 twin rooms, 7 double rooms all en suite with tea/coffee-maker, TV, telephone, radio, room service. Trouser press and hair dryer available on request.
**Directions:** situated directly on A483, 5 minutes from the town centre.
MR AND MRS SPENCER-WHITE ☎(01597) 822388 Fax(01597) 822388

### SEVERN ARMS HOTEL
Penybont, LD1 5UA

*A former coaching inn, ideally situated on a popular holiday route. The inn has an olde-worlde charm with a wealth of oak beams and a log fire which burns in the bar during winter. The Severn Arms is one of the best-known unaltered coaching houses in mid-Wales, but has been modernized inside to a high standard. Reduced rates on two golf courses. Six miles of fishing available.*

DOUBLE ROOM: from £20 to £30
SINGLE ROOM: from £25 to £35
FOOD: up to £15
**Hours:** dinner 7pm-9.30pm, closed one week at Christmas.
**Cuisine:** ENGLISH - grills, roasts, home-made steak-and-kidney pie, cottage pie. Full à la carte menu and bar snacks are available seven days a week.
**Cards:** Visa, Access, Diners, AmEx.
**Other points:** licensed, Sunday lunch, children welcome, fishing, garden, caravan facilities.
**Rooms:** 3 double rooms, 1 twin room, 6 family rooms. All with en suite, TV, radio, telephone, tea/coffee-making facilities, hair dryer, trouser-press.
**Directions:** on A44, Rhayader to Leominster road.
GEOFF & TESSA LLOYD ☎(01597) 851224/851344 Fax(01597) 851693

## LLANIDLOES • map 7D3

### 🏨 UNICORN HOTEL
Long Bridge Street, SY18 6EE

*Set in an attractive terrace, this is an extremely popular and sociable hotel, both with tourists and local townsfolk. The service is efficient and helpful, complementing the welcoming atmosphere. This is an ideal base from which to tour the outstanding nearby countryside.*

DOUBLE ROOM: up to £20
SINGLE ROOM: up to £26
FOOD: up to £15     CLUB
**Hours:** breakfast 7.30am-9am, bar meals 12noon-2pm, 7pm-9pm.
**Cuisine:** ENGLISH - table d'hôte menu offering traditional English fare. Vegetarian meals are also available.
**Cards:** Visa, Access, AmEx.
**Other points:** licensed, Sunday lunch, children welcome.
**Rooms:** 5 bedrooms.
**Directions:** situated in Llanidloes town centre.
CHRISTINE & DEREK HUMPHRIES ☎(01686) 413167 Fax(01686) 413576

## LLANWDDYN • map 8C4

### 🏨 LAKE VYRNWY HOTEL
Lake Vyrnwy, SY10 0LY

*Lake Vyrnwy is everything you would expect from a unique first-class country house and sporting hotel, set in the heart of beautiful mid-Wales. The comfort of the hotel echoes the peace of the surrounding countryside and its infinite views of outstanding natural beauty. A wide range of country pursuits is available on the estate's 24,000 acres. Own country pub in grounds.*

DOUBLE ROOM: from £40 to £50
SINGLE ROOM: over £55
FOOD: from £20 to £25
**Hours:** breakfast 8.30am-9.30am, lunch 12.30am-2pm, dinner 7.30pm-9.30pm, bar meals 12.30am-2pm, 6.30pm-9pm, open all year.
**Cuisine:** BRITISH - award-winning traditional and innovative dishes. Hotel has daily changing menus, restaurant, and the estate's fish and game. Own market garden.
**Cards:** Visa, Access, Diners, AmEx.
**Other points:** licensed, Sunday lunch, no-smoking area, children welcome, pets allowed, afternoon tea, vegetarian meals, garden, residents' lounge, residents' bar.
**Rooms:** 2 single rooms, 21 double rooms, 14 twin rooms. All with TV, radio, telephone.
**Directions:** from Shrewsbury, A458 to Welshpool. Right onto B4393 to Lake Vyrnwy.
☎(01691) 870692 Fax(01691) 870259

## MACHYNLLETH • map 7C3

### 🏨 LLUGWY HALL COUNTRY HOUSE HOTEL
Pennal, SY20 9JX

*A highly recommended hotel situated in 40 acres of woodland with gardens to the bank of the river Dovey. Ideally located for coastal holidays, touring holidays and short leisure or activity breaks with easy access to many places of interest and scenic beauty within the National Park.*

DOUBLE ROOM: from £30 to £40
SINGLE ROOM: from £45 to £55
FOOD: up to £25
**Hours:** breakfast 8am-10am, lunch 12.30pm-2pm, dinner 7pm-9pm.
**Cuisine:** TRADITIONAL / MODERN - a careful selection of contemporary and traditional dishes using local seasonal produce such as Welsh lamb, Dovey salmon and shellfish.
**Cards:** Visa, Diners, AmEx, MasterCard.
**Other points:** special two day Dovey breaks including dinner and breakfast, children welcome, vegetarian meals, open air dining, light refreshments morning and afternoon, conference facilities, private trout fishing, salmon fishing, shooting arranged, pony trekking nearby, parking.
**Rooms:** 15 bedrooms. All with private facilites, TV, telephone, radio, tea/coffee-making facilities.
**Directions:** take the main A493 road from the northern end of the river bridge at Machynlleth towards Aberdovey, turn left after 1¾-2 miles where the hotel is signposted.
PAUL DAVIS ☎(01654) 791228 Fax(01654) 791231

### 🏨 THE WHITE LION COACHING INN
Heol Pentrerhedyn, SY20 2ND

*The White Lion has been welcoming guests since the early 1800s. It was one of several coaching inns in town, and retains its original oak beams, inglenook fireplace and cobbled forecourt. Regular patrons appreciate the inn for its Dyffi salmon and traditional and innovative menus. Well worth a visit.*

DOUBLE ROOM: from £20 to £30
SINGLE ROOM: from £25 to £35
FOOD: up to £15
**Hours:** lunch 12noon-2.30pm, dinner 6pm-9pm.
**Cuisine:** WELSH - traditional Welsh, including Sunday lunch. Bar meals.
**Cards:** Visa, Access.
**Other points:** licensed, Sunday lunch, children welcome, pets allowed, cots, disabled access, residents' bar, vegetarian meals.
**Rooms:** 9 bedrooms. All with TV, tea/coffee-making facilities. 6 rooms are en suite.
**Directions:** hotel is on junction of A487 and A489 by the Victorian clock.
M.K. & J.F. QUICK ☎(01654) 703455 Fax(01654) 703860

## NEWTOWN • map 8D4

### YESTERDAYS
Severn Square, SY16 2AG

*A delightful restaurant with en suite accommodation situated in Severn Square, offering a wide range of traditional fare, including seafood, poultry, grills and light snacks. Easy access to historic Powis Castle, Elan Valley and the beautiful mid-Wales countryside.*

DOUBLE ROOM: up to £20
SINGLE ROOM: from £20 to £30
FOOD: up to £15      CLUB

**Hours:** breakfast 7.30am-9.30am, lunch 12noon-2pm, dinner 6.30pm-9.30pm last orders.
**Cuisine:** ENGLISH
**Cards:** Visa, Access, AmEx, Switch.
**Other points:** children welcome, Sunday lunch, open bank holidays, disabled access, vegetarian meals, licensed.
**Rooms:** 1 double room, 1 family room. Both en suite with radio, TV, tea/coffee-making facilities, no smoking.
**Directions:** from Barclays Bank along Severn Street, 80 yards to Severn Square.
JIM & MOYRA ASTON ☎(01686) 622644

## WELSHPOOL • map 8C4

### THE LION HOTEL & RESTAURANT
Berriew, SY21 8PQ

*Situated in a quiet village on the Welsh borders surrounded by beautiful countryside, the Lion Hotel is a delightful 17th century inn. The accommodation is of a high standard, and good food is served in both the bars and restaurant.*

DOUBLE ROOM: from £40 to £50
SINGLE ROOM: from £50 to £55
FOOD: from £6 to £20      CLUB

**Hours:** breakfast 8am-9.30am, lunch 12noon-2pm, dinner 7.30pm-9pm, bar meals 12noon-2pm, 7pm-9pm, open bank holidays.
**Cuisine:** BRITISH / CONTINENTAL - English, Welsh and continental cuisine. Dishes may include fillet of smoked trout with lemon and dill dressed salad, roast duck with vermouth and cranberry sauce, fillet of Welsh venison in a sauce of redberries, port, mushrooms and onions.
**Cards:** Visa, Access, Diners, AmEx.
**Other points:** licensed, Sunday lunch, children welcome.
**Rooms:** 5 double rooms, 1 twin room, 1 family room. All with TV, tea/coffee-making facilities.
**Directions:** in village centre.
MR & MRS THOMAS ☎(01686) 640884/640452
Fax(01686) 640604

# SCOTLAND

Savour the wild beauty of the high, heather-covered mountains, sparkling blue lochs and rich green glens. Scotland is a land of legends and castles, perfected for the tourist, and Les Routiers has searched out many of the country's most excellent places to ensure that your visit to Scotland leaves a lasting memory.

There are endless traditional Scottish specialities that will get the taste buds tingling, namely Tay salmon, Highland venison, prime Galloway beef, Solway duck, Aberdeen Angus steaks, Glenturret pate, pheasant and grouse. Equally magnificent is the abundance of fresh fish and seafood: Arbroath smokies, lobster Thermidor, baked haddock, sea trout, Scotch cockles, and more.

Of course, no one could possible visit Scotland without trying one of its famous whiskies, and there is a whisky trail that one can follow, sampling the products of Scotland's greatest distilleries. Or visit Campbeltown Loch, reputed in song to consist entirely of whisky.

Scotland's turbulent history has bequeathed it a great legacy of famous monarchs and romantic palaces and castles. Les Routiers can't promise you will stay in a palace, but there are castles which carry our 'recommendation', and with it an outstanding choice of accommodation.

The following counties are included in this chapter:

| | |
|---|---|
| BORDERS | LOTHIAN |
| CENTRAL | ORKNEY & SHETLAND |
| DUMBRIES & GALLOWAY | ISLANDS |
| FIFE | STRATHCLYDE |
| GRAMPIAN | TAYSIDE |
| HIGHLANDS | WESTERN ISLES |

# *BORDERS*

## BURNMOUTH • map 16E6

### THE FLEMINGTON INN
TD14 5SL

*An attractive, well-run pub directly on the A1 in the pretty fishing village of Burnmouth. This is the `first and last' pub in Scotland. Presenting home-cooked meals made from fresh local produce at value-for-money prices, The Flemington Inn is very popular, especially with locals.*
FOOD: up to £15 🍽
**Hours:** lunch 12noon-2.15pm, Sunday 12.30am-2.15pm, dinner 6.30pm-9pm.
**Cuisine:** SCOTTISH - traditional Scottish menu with good use of local seafood.
**Other points:** licensed, parking, children catered for (children under 14 years must be off premises by 8.00pm), vegetarian meals.
**Directions:** six miles north of Berwick-upon-Tweed on A1.
MR & MRS SMILLIE ☎(018907) 81277

## GALASHIELS • map 16E5

### ABBOTSFORD ARMS HOTEL
63 Stirling Street, TO1 1BY

*A beautifully modernized family hotel 32 miles south of Edinburgh. Completely refurbished to a high standard.*
DOUBLE ROOM: from £20 to £30
SINGLE ROOM: from £25 to £35
FOOD: up to £15 🍽 CLUB
**Hours:** breakfast 8am-10am, meals all day 12noon-9pm.
**Cuisine:** SCOTTISH - steak, chicken dishes.
**Cards:** Visa, Access, Switch.
**Other points:** licensed, Sunday lunch, children welcome, coaches by prior arrangement.
**Rooms:** 3 single rooms, 4 double rooms, 5 twin rooms, 2 family rooms. All with TV, tea/coffee-making facilities.
**Directions:** in Galashiels, opposite the bus station.
MR & MRS G. SCOTT ☎(01896) 752517
Fax(01896) 750744

## HERGES
58 Island Street, TD1 1NY

*Karen and Sandy Craig offer imaginative, good-value cuisine in a very friendly and relaxed atmosphere. A former yarn brokers' store, Herges has been expertly converted to form this attractive continental-style wine bar. The service is most courteous and efficient, and all dishes are freshly cooked to a high standard.*

FOOD: up to £15
**Hours:** lunch 12noon-2.30pm, dinner 6pm-12midnight, last orders 9.30pm, open from 5pm on Sunday, closed all day Monday.
**Cuisine:** CONTINENTAL - dishes may include baked rainbow trout, roast gigot of lamb, supreme of chicken Marengo. Also lighter snacks such as filled baked potatoes and croissants.
**Cards:** Visa, Access.
**Other points:** licensed, Sunday lunch, no-smoking area, children welcome.
**Directions:** A72 to Peebles, near the B&Q superstore.
MR & MRS CRAIG ☎(01896) 750400

### HAWICK • map 11A3

## KIRKLANDS HOTEL
West Stewart Place, TD9 8BH

*A charming, small hotel pleasantly situated in the beautiful Scottish borders. Ideal base for tourists and business people. Close to many attractions. Recommended by most leading hotel guides. Weekly terms and weekend breaks available. Colour brochure and tariff on request.*

DOUBLE ROOM: from £30 to £40
SINGLE ROOM: from £40 to £50
FOOD: from £15 to £20 🍴 CLUB
**Hours:** lunch 12noon-2pm, dinner 7pm-9.30pm.
**Cuisine:** SCOTTISH / CONTINENTAL - excellent choice of Scottish and à la carte dishes. Table d'hôte and bar meals. Vegetarian dishes.
**Cards:** Visa, Access, Diners, AmEx.
**Other points:** open-air dining, no-smoking area, children welcome, beer garden, games room, library.
**Rooms:** 7 double rooms, 5 twin rooms.
**Directions:** 200 yards off the main A7, .5 mile north of Hawick High Street.
MR B. NEWLAND ☎(01450) 372263 Fax(01450) 370404

### MELROSE • map 16E5

## ABBOT'S CHOICE RESTAURANT & BORDER REIVERS INN
Main Street, Gattonside, TD6 9NB

*This newly-opened restaurant lies in the village of Gattonside, within the heart of Scott Country on a lovely stretch of the Tweed. Steaks are a speciality, morning coffee, lunches and afternoon teas are also served. Many places to visit nearby.*

FOOD: up to £15
**Hours:** open all day, 9am-midnight, open bank holidays.

**Cuisine:** Tweed salmon, steaks.
**Cards:** Visa, Access, AmEx, Diners, Switch.
**Other points:** no-smoking area, pets allowed, licensed, central heating, air conditioning, children welcome.
**Directions:** B6360, on the Galashiels to Earlstom road, 1.5 miles north of Melrose.
MR STAN POTTS ☎(01896) 823217

### PEEBLES • map 16E4

## SYMBOL OF EXCELLENCE 1996
### CRINGLETIE HOUSE HOTEL
EH45 8PL

*Cringletie is a distinguished mansion house set well back in 28 acres of gardens and woodlands. The resident proprietors provide interesting and imaginative food, with fruit and vegetables in season from the hotel's extensive kitchen garden, which is featured in The Gourmet Garden by Geraldene Holt.*

DOUBLE ROOM: from £49 to £52
SINGLE ROOM: from £52 to £65
FOOD: from £20 to £25 🍴
**Hours:** breakfast 8.15am-9.15am, lunch 1pm-1.45pm, dinner 7.30pm-8.30pm.
**Cuisine:** BRITISH - frequently-changing menu: all home-cooking. Afternoon tea including home-baking.
**Cards:** Visa, Access, AmEx.
**Other points:** Sunday lunch, no-smoking area, children welcome.
**Rooms:** 1 single room, 4 double rooms, 8 twin rooms.
**Directions:** on the Edinburgh-Peebles road (A703), 2.5 miles north of Peebles.
STANLEY & AILEEN MAGUIRE ☎(01721) 730233 Fax(01721) 730244

## PARK HOTEL
Innerleithen Road, EH45 8BA

*A friendly hotel on the outskirts of Peebles, overlooking the River Tweed. Guests can enjoy attractive gardens, well-appointed bedrooms and*

the popular hotel restaurant. When available, guests can also benefit from the facilities at the Peebles Hydro Hotel (only 700 yards away): leisure centre with pool, saunas and Jacuzzi; squash courts; tennis courts and riding.

DOUBLE ROOM: from £40 to £50
SINGLE ROOM: from £45 to £55
FOOD: from £15 to £20

**Hours:** breakfast 7.30am-10am, lunch 12noon-2pm, dinner 7pm-9pm, bar snacks 12noon-2pm, 6.30pm-9.30pm.
**Cuisine:** SCOTTISH - traditional cuisine featuring local produce such as smoked Scottish salmon and fresh local trout.
**Cards:** Visa, Access, Diners, AmEx.
**Other points:** licensed, pets allowed, garden, residents' lounge, leisure centre.
**Rooms:** 24 bedrooms. All en suite.
**Directions:** on the A72 south of Edinburgh.
LAWSON KEAY ☎(01721) 720451 Fax (01721) 723510

###  PEEBLES HOTEL HYDRO
Innerleithen Road, EH45 8LX

Few hotels offer facilities comparable to the Peebles Hydro, a resort hotel with a full range of indoor and outdoor recreation facilities. There is a superb range of top-value holiday packages all year round. Friendly staff and a warm welcome await you, and the quality of the food is excellent. Magnificent grounds of 30 acres. Sister to the Park Hotel, also in Peebles.

DOUBLE ROOM: from £40 to £50
SINGLE ROOM: over £50
FOOD: from £15 to £20

**Hours:** breakfast 8am-9.30am, lunch 12.45am-2pm, dinner 7.30pm-9pm, bar meals 12noon-3.30pm.
**Cuisine:** MODERN ENGLISH - table d'hôte dinner menu using local produce, e.g., roast leg of Border lamb with a coriander sauce. Separate vegetarian menu.
**Cards:** Visa, Access, Diners, AmEx.
**Other points:** licensed, Sunday lunch, no-smoking area, garden, leisure centre, residents' bar, residents'

lounge, swimming pool, parking.
**Rooms:** 137 bedrooms. All with TV, telephone, tea/coffee-making facilities.
**Directions:** on the A72 Peebles to Galashiels road.
MR P.J. VAN DIJK ☎(01721) 720602 Fax (01721) 722999

###  VENLAW CASTLE HOTEL
Tweedale, EH45 8QG

Venlaw Castle, on the slopes of the Moorfoot Hills yet within five minutes from the centre of Peebles, is a family-owned hotel run in the country manner with the accent on personal attention. Reputed for their good-quality home-cooked dishes, using only the freshest produce, and for providing excellent accommodation, the Cumming family's hospitality is outstanding.

DOUBLE ROOM: from £20 to £40
SINGLE ROOM: from £25 to £40
FOOD: from £15 to £20

**Cuisine:** ENGLISH - dishes include baked salmon served with hollandaise sauce, aubergine bake served with green salad. Trout, venison, fresh fish dishes, lemon sole bonne femme.
**Cards:** Visa, Access, Diners, AmEx.
**Other points:** children welcome, no-smoking area, garden, pets allowed, residents' bar, residents' lounge.
**Rooms:** 4 double rooms, 4 twin rooms, 4 family rooms.
**Directions:** A703, on the slopes of Moorfoot Hills, 5 minutes from town centre.
MR & MRS CUMMING ☎(01721) 720384

# CENTRAL

## CRIANLARICH • map 15C3

###  THE ROD & REEL
Main Street, FK20 8QN

A family-run bar and restaurant, which offers a wide choice of good food at very reasonable prices. Personally run by Elspeth and Bill Paulin, you are assured a warm welcome and friendly service.
FOOD: up to £15

**Hours:** bar meals 12noon-9pm, dinner 6pm-9pm.
**Cuisine:** BRITISH - bar meals and à la carte menu. Menus based on the use of fresh fish and local game. Good incorporation of Scottish meat for roasts and steaks, and an extensive selection of vegetarian dishes.
**Cards:** Visa, Access.

**Other points:** licensed, children welcome.
**Directions:** in the centre of Crianlarich.
ELSPETH & BILL PAULIN ☎(01838) 300271 Fax (01838) 300261

## DUNBLANE • map 15D3

###  STIRLING ARMS HOTEL
Stirling Road, FK15 9EP

Originally a 17th century coaching inn by the bridge over the Allan Water, this is a family-run hotel and restaurant. The owners pride themselves on providing comfortable accommodation and excellent food in their Oak Room Restaurant. Good value for money. History records the inn's patronage by Robert Burns and the Duke of Argyle.

DOUBLE ROOM: from £25 to £30
SINGLE ROOM: from £35 to £40
**Hours:** breakfast 8am-9am, lunch 12noon-2.30pm, dinner 6pm-9pm.
**Cuisine:** SCOTTISH - modern Scottish/continental cuisine. Specialities include Gaelic steak. Bar meals.
**Cards:** Visa, Access.
**Other points:** licensed, open-air dining, Sunday lunch, no-smoking area, children welcome, pets allowed, garden.
**Directions:** off B8033 Stirling-Perth road. Close to high street.
JANE & RICHARD CASTELOW ☎(01786) 822156 **Fax**(01786) 825300

## KILLIN • map 15C3

**CLACHAIG HOTEL**
Gray Street, Falls of Dochart, FK21 8SL
*A former 17th century coaching inn, overlooking the spectacular Falls of Dochart. The intimate and characterful restaurant offers a wide choice of quality food. Trout and salmon fishing is available on the hotel's own private stretch of the River Dochart.*
DOUBLE ROOM: up to £21
SINGLE ROOM: up to £21
FOOD: up to £15     CLUB
**Hours:** breakfast 8.15am-9.15am, lunch 12noon-2.30pm, bar meals 12noon-3.30pm, dinner 6.30pm-9.30pm, bar meals 5.30pm-9.30pm.
**Cuisine:** SCOTTISH - trout, salmon, Highland beef steaks, venison.
**Cards:** Visa, Access.
**Other points:** open-air dining, Sunday lunch, no-smoking area, disabled access, children welcome, garden, afternoon tea, pets allowed.
**Rooms:** 1 single room, 5 double rooms, 1 twin room, 2 family rooms.
**Directions:** on A827 beside Falls of Dochart.
JOHN MALLINSON ☎(01567) 820270 **Fax**(01567) 820730

## LOCHEARNHEAD • map 15C3

**LOCHEARNHEAD HOTEL**
Lochside, FK19 8PT
*This small country house beside Loch Earn forms part of a lochside water sports development, offering such sports as sailing, waterskiing and windsurfing. Coupled with the friendly atmosphere of the hotel and the superb home-cooking, this is a perfect place for water sports enthusiasts of all ages. Ideally central for golfers: access to 15 courses within the hour.*
DOUBLE ROOM: from £20 to £30
FOOD: up to £15
**Hours:** breakfast 8.30am-9.30am, lunch 11am-2.30pm, dinner 7pm-9.30pm.
**Cuisine:** FRENCH - à la carte and three-course fixed menus. French.
**Cards:** Visa, Access, Diners, AmEx.
**Other points:** licensed, open-air dining, children welcome, afternoon tea, pets allowed, garden.

**Rooms:** 1 single room, 6 double rooms, 6 twin rooms. 8 en suite. All with TV, tea/coffee-making facilities.
**Directions:** take the A84 from Stirling; turn onto the A85 to Crieff.
ANGUS CAMERON ☎(01567) 830229 **Fax**(01567) 830364

## STIRLING • map 15D3

**STIRLING MANAGEMENT CENTRE**
University of Stirling, FK9 4LA
*Conveniently located in a splendid rural setting, Stirling Management Centre is an ideal venue for business conferences and training courses. Purpose-built meeting rooms, executive accommodation, sports and leisure facilities combined with the educational resources of a progressive, modern university ensure the success of your visit here.*
DOUBLE ROOM: from £25 to £35
SINGLE ROOM: from £30 to £40
FOOD: from £15 to £20
**Hours:** breakfast 7.30am-9am, lunch 12.30am-2.30pm, dinner 6.30pm-9.00pm.
**Cuisine:** BRITISH
**Cards:** Visa, Access.
**Other points:** parking, children welcome, no-smoking area, disabled access, vegetarian meals, garden.
**Rooms:** 75 bedrooms, 1 executive suite. All with en suite.
**Directions:** from the north, follow A9; from the south, follow A74, leading to the A80/M80.
MS G. MILLER ☎(01786) 451666 **Fax**(01786) 450472

## TYNDRUM • map 15C2

**CLIFTON COFFEE HOUSE**
Tyndrum, FK20 8RY
*Spacious self-service restaurant with adjoining shops, specializing in the best Scottish dishes, whisky and confectionery. Outstanding Scottish crafts plus outdoor clothing specialists. Extensive car park and filling station facilities.*
FOOD: up to £10
**Hours:** meals every day 8.30am-5.30pm, closed January until beginning of March (carry out counter available).
**Cuisine:** SCOTTISH - home-made soups, good country cooking including game pies, hot pots and casseroles, fresh and smoked salmon and extensive salad table. Accent on fresh food served quickly but keeping a healthy option.
**Cards:** Visa, Access, Diners, AmEx, Switch.
**Other points:** Sunday lunch, no-smoking area, children welcome.
**Directions:** Tyndrum is located on the A82. The Coffee House is in the middle of the village on the roadside.
I.L. WILKIE ☎(01838) 400271 **Fax**(01838) 400330

# DUMFRIES & GALLOWAY

## ANNAN • map 11B2

 **POWFOOT GOLF HOTEL**
Links Avenue, Powfoot, DG12 5PN
*Standing beside an 18-hole golf-course with fishing nearby on the River Annan, the Golf Hotel is a tempting prospect for sporting persons. With views over the unspoilt Powfoot Bay and with the countryside and history of south-west Scotland on the doorstep, it is an excellent centre for touring. Excellent wild-fowling from September to February.*
DOUBLE ROOM: from £30 to £40
SINGLE ROOM: from £35 to £45
FOOD: up to £15    CLUB
**Hours:** breakfast 8am-9.30am, lunch 12noon-2pm, dinner 7pm-8.30pm, bar 11am-11pm, weekends 11am-12midnight.
**Cuisine:** SCOTTISH - traditional Scottish food, which is prepared where possible using local produce: for example, fresh Solway salmon, pheasant, venison, duck, prime Galloway beef.
**Cards:** Visa, Access, AmEx.
**Other points:** licensed, open-air dining, Sunday lunch, children welcome, beer garden, residents' lounge, residents' bar, foreign exchange.
**Rooms:** 1 single room, 3 double rooms, 14 twin rooms, 2 family rooms. All with TV, telephone, tea/coffee-making facilities.
**Directions:** on the B724 in Powfoot, next to the golf course.
ADAM T. GRIBBON ☎(01461) 700254
Fax(01461) 700288

## DUMFRIES • map 11B2

 **HETLAND HALL HOTEL**
Carrutherstown, DG1 4JX

*Originally built as a manor house, then converted into a boarding school, Hetland Hall is now a grand country house hotel and restaurant. Set in 45 acres of well-tended parklands with fine views over the Solway Firth. The restaurant serves an international menu in relaxed, informal surroundings. Chalet swimming pool, fitness suite and snooker are available.*
DOUBLE ROOM: from £40 to £50
SINGLE ROOM: over £50
FOOD: from £15 to £20    CLUB
**Hours:** breakfast 7.30am-9.30am, lunch 12noon-2pm, dinner 7pm-9.30pm, bar 12noon-11pm.
**Cuisine:** INTENATIONAL

**Cards:** Visa, Access, Diners, AmEx.
**Other points:** open-air dining, Sunday lunch, no-smoking area, pets allowed, children welcome (restaurant age limit 14 years+), afternoon tea, swimming pool, gym facilities, games room, residents' lounge, residents' bar, foreign exchange, disabled access, parking.
**Rooms:** 5 single rooms, 11 double rooms, 10 twin rooms. All with TV, radio, alarm, telephone, tea/coffee-making facilities, hair dryer.
**Directions:** hotel is located on the main A75, midway between Annan and Dumfries.
DAVID & MARY ALLEN ☎(01387) 840201
Fax(01387) 840211

## GATEHOUSE OF FLEET • map 11B1

 **MURRAY ARMS HOTEL**
High Street, DG7 2HY
*A warm, welcoming inn where Robert Burns wrote Scots Wha Hae. Gatehouse of Fleet is one of Scotland's scenic heritage areas, surrounded by unspoilt countryside. Residents enjoy free golf, tennis and fishing.*
DOUBLE ROOM: from £30 to £40
SINGLE ROOM: from £35 to £45
FOOD: from £15 to £20
**Hours:** meals all day 12noon-9.45pm.
**Cuisine:** SCOTTISH - Galloway beef, locally caught fish and smoked salmon, Scottish lamb, home-made soups and pâté. Vegetarian meals.
**Cards:** Visa, Access, Diners, AmEx.
**Other points:** Sunday lunch, no-smoking area, children catered for (please check for age limits), disabled access, residents' lounge, residents' bar.
**Rooms:** 1 single room, 6 double rooms, 5 twin rooms, 1 family room. All with TV, telephone, tea/coffee-making facilities.
**Directions:** off A75, 60 miles west of Carlisle between Dumfries and Stranraer.
MURRAY ARMS HOTEL LTD ☎(01557) 814207
Fax(01557) 814370

## ISLE OF WHITHORN • map 11C1

 **STEAMPACKET HOTEL**
Harbour Row, DG8 8LL
*A small, family-run hotel with a distinct nautical atmosphere where all the bedrooms overlook the harbour. Good food served in friendly, comfortable surroundings.*
DOUBLE ROOM: from £20 to £30
FOOD: from £10 to £20
**Hours:** breakfast 8am-9.30am, lunch 12noon-2pm, dinner 7pm-9.30pm.
**Cuisine:** SCOTTISH - lobster a speciality.
**Cards:** Visa, Access.
**Other points:** licensed, Sunday lunch, pets allowed.
**Rooms:** 3 double rooms, 1 twin room, 1 family room. All with TV, telephone, tea/coffee-making

facilities.
**Directions:** on quayside.
MR SCOULAR ☎(01988) 500334

## LOCKERBIE • map 11B2

 **LOCKERBIE MANOR COUNTRY HOTEL**
Boreland Road, DG11 2RG

*The Georgian mansion house retaining original Adam features, about half a mile north of Lockerbie, provides well-appointed bedrooms and comfortable public rooms. The cuisine is truly international: Eastern flavours and cooking styles blend easily with Western recipes to give a genuine East-meets-West experience that visitors will find truly unforgettable.*
DOUBLE ROOM: from £30 to £50
SINGLE ROOM: from £40 to £62
FOOD: from £15 to £20 ☜
**Hours:** breakfast 7.30am-9.30am, dinner 6.30pm-9.30pm.
**Cuisine:** INTERNATIONAL
**Cards:** Visa, Access, AmEx, MasterCard, Switch.
**Other points:** licensed, traditional Sunday lunch, children welcome, pets allowed, afternoon tea, open bank holidays, residents' lounge, garden, parking, residents' bar, vegetarian meals.
**Rooms:** 1 single, 9 doubles, 27 twin rooms. All with telephone.
**Directions:** on the A74, 25 miles north of Carlisle. Follow B723 north, turn right.
JEFFREY YEH ☎(01576) 202610 Fax(01576) 203046

## MOFFAT • map 11A2

 **BALMORAL HOTEL**
High Street, DG10 9DL
*Set in the picturesque Annan Valley, the Balmoral Hotel was once a coaching inn and frequented by Robert Burns. It is now a friendly, family-owned hotel offering comfortable accommodation, fine cuisine and welcoming, friendly service. The wide choice of dishes all offer very good value. Ideal place to relax in attractive surroundings and a warm, family atmosphere.*
DOUBLE ROOM: from £20 to £30
SINGLE ROOM: from £20 to £30
FOOD: up to £15
**Hours:** breakfast 8am-9.30am, bar meals 12noon-2pm, dinner 6pm-9.30pm, bar meals 6pm-9pm.
**Cuisine:** BRITISH / FRENCH - traditional Scottish, English and French dishes. Specialities include venison, fresh salmon, fillet steak.

**Cards:** Visa, Access.
**Other points:** licensed, Sunday lunch, children welcome, pets allowed, residents' lounge.
**Rooms:** 3 single rooms, 5 double rooms, 7 twin rooms, 1 family room. All with tea/coffee-making facilities.
**Directions:** on the A701, on the main street in Moffat.
JOHN GRAHAM ☎(01683) 220288 Fax(01683) 220451

**THE STAR HOTEL**
44 High Street, DG10 9EF
*Although this hotel is listed in the Guinness Book of Records as the narrowest detached hotel, the interior and welcome are heartwarming and wholesome. If you enjoy good food at great-value prices in splendidly comfortable surroundings, then this is the place for you.*
DOUBLE ROOM: from £20 to £30
FOOD: up to £15
**Hours:** breakfast 8am-9.30am, lunch 12noon-2.00pm, dinner 5.30pm-9pm.
**Cuisine:** BRITISH / INTERNATIONAL - wide and varied menu, daily specials.
**Cards:** Visa, Access.
**Other points:** licensed restaurant, public bar, children welcome, pets allowed, coaches by prior arrangement, functions, conferences.
**Rooms:** 4 double rooms, 2 twin rooms, 2 family rooms.
**Directions:** situated in the High Street.
MR HOUSE & MR LEIGHFIELD ☎(01683) 220156

## NEW GALLOWAY • map 11B1

**THE SMITHY**
The High Street, DG7 3RN
*As the name implies, this is a converted blacksmith's shop with a restaurant, craft shop and B&B accommodation in an attached cottage. In the summer, guests may dine outside beside the Mill Burn that flows through the property. This is the Official Tourist Information agency on behalf of the Dumfries & Galloway Tourist Board.*
DOUBLE ROOM: up to £20
SINGLE ROOM: up to £25
FOOD: up to £15
**Hours:** 1st March until Easter 10am-6pm, Easter until 31st May 10am-8pm; 1st June until 30th September 10am-9pm, 1st October until 31st October 10am-6.00pm; closed 31st October until 1st March.
**Cuisine:** SCOTTISH - home-baking and cooking, trout in wine with almonds, home-made oatcakes and cheese, range of Scottish pâtés including wild garlic, smoked salmon, venison. Children and `Grannie' portions available. A good range of Scottish wines.
**Other points:** parking, children welcome, disabled access, vegetarian meals.
**Rooms:** 1 double room, 1 twin room.
**Directions:** on the A762 to Kirkcudbright.
MR & MRS MCPHEE ☎(01644) 420269

## NEWTON STEWART • map 14C5

 **INGLENOOK BISTRO & COFFEE SHOP**
43 Main Street, Glenluce, DG8 0PP

*A small, intimate restaurant with a large inglenook fireplace. The menu offers an excellent choice of meals and snacks from 10am throughout the day until 9pm, all served within a friendly and relaxed atmosphere.*

**FOOD:** up to £15
**Hours:** meals all day 10am-9pm. Evening menu only after 6.00pm.
**Cuisine:** BRITISH - wide range of home cooked meals. Snacks and drinks available.
**Cards:** Visa, Access, Diners, AmEx, Switch.
**Other points:** Sunday lunch, children welcome, afternoon tea.
**Directions:** in Glenluce, 10 miles from Stranraer on the A75 to Dumfries.
ROY & DIANA FLETCHER ☎(01581) 300494

## THORNHILL • map 11A1

**BUCCLEUGH AND QUEENSBERRY HOTEL**
112 Drumcanrigg Street, DG3 5LU

*A family-run, comfortable hotel in the centre of Thornhill, surrounded by scenic Nithsdale. Built in 1855 by the Duke of Buccleuch, it provides a friendly, welcoming atmosphere and freshly prepared food in pleasant surroundings.*

**DOUBLE ROOM:** up to £20
**FOOD:** up to £15
**Hours:** meals all day 10am-10.30pm.
**Cuisine:** ENGLISH / CONTINENTAL
**Cards:** Visa, Access, Diners, AmEx.
**Other points:** parking, children welcome, afternoon teas, pets, residents' lounge, vegetarian meals.
**Rooms:** 12 twin rooms.
**Directions:** situated in the centre of Thornhill.
MR & MRS STACK ☎(01848) 330215

# *FIFE*

## AUCHTERMUCHTY • map 16C4

**THE FOREST HILLS HOTEL**
The Square, G11 6PT

*A traditional 18th century inn situated in the town square of the former Royal Burgh of Auchtermuchty, once a busy weaving centre. There is a comfortable oak-beamed cocktail bar with copper-topped tables and ornate fireplace, which provides a cosy and intimate atmosphere. Nearby places of interest include Falkland, with its Royal Palace, and Freuchie. Function suite for up to 80 guests.*

**DOUBLE ROOM:** from £30 to £40
**SINGLE ROOM:** up to £20
**FOOD:** up to £15     CLUB
**Hours:** breakfast 8am-9am, Sunday 9am-10am, lunch 12.30am-2pm, bar snacks 12noon-2.15pm, dinner 7pm-9.15pm, bar snacks 6pm-10pm.
**Cuisine:** BRITISH / CONTINENTAL - table d'hôte and à la carte with some flambé dishes, complemented by an interesting wine list.
**Cards:** Visa, Access, Diners, AmEx.
**Other points:** parking, children welcome, Sunday lunch, open bank holidays, afternoon tea, pets

allowed, residents' lounge, vegetarian meals, licensed, residents' bar.
**Rooms:** 2 single rooms, 3 double rooms, 3 twin rooms, 2 family rooms. All with TV, telephone, tea/coffee-making facilities, hair dryer, trouser-press.
**Directions:** 7 miles from Cupar and 6 miles from exit 8 of M90.
ERNST VAN BEUSEKOM ☎(01337) 828318
Fax(01337) 828318

## BURNTISLAND • map 16D4

**KINGSWOOD HOTEL**
Kinghorn Road, KY3 9LL

*Set in 2 acres of grounds with outstanding views across the River Forth towards Edinburgh. The hotel's ambience, tasteful furnishings and first-class cuisine all combine to make every visit an enjoyable experience.*

**DOUBLE ROOM:** from £30 to £40
**SINGLE ROOM:** from £45 to £55
**FOOD:** from £15 to £20 ☜
**Hours:** breakfast 7.30am-9am, lunch 12noon-3pm, dinner 7pm-9.30pm, bar meals 12noon-10pm.
**Cuisine:** SCOTTISH - full à la carte and table d'hôte menus available. Choices include cullen skink and fresh salmon.
**Cards:** Visa, Access, AmEx.
**Other points:** licensed, open-air dining, Sunday lunch, no-smoking area, children welcome, pets by prior arrangement.
**Rooms:** 1 single room, 3 double rooms, 5 twin rooms, 1 family room.
**Directions:** on the A92 coast road, half-way between Kinghorn and Burntisland.
RANKIN & KATHRYN BELL ☎(01592) 872329
Fax(01592) 873123

## CRAIL • map 16D5

 **MARINE HOTEL**
54 Nethergate South, KY10 3TZ
*Small family-run hotel, with eight en suite, well-appointed bedrooms, a residents' lounge and a restaurant serving à la carte and table d'hôte menus. Beautiful views of the Firth of Forth and the Isle of May can be enjoyed in the lounge bar, which has a patio leading into the garden.*
DOUBLE ROOM: from £20 to £30
SINGLE ROOM: up to £25
FOOD: up to £15 🍽
**Hours:** breakfast 8.30am-9.30am, dinner 7pm-9pm, snacks all day.
**Cuisine:** SEAFOOD - local seafood (in season).
**Cards:** Visa, Access, Diners, AmEx.
**Other points:** licensed, Sunday lunch, pets allowed, afternoon tea.
**Rooms:** 3 double rooms, 4 twin rooms, 1 family room. All with en suite, TV, tea/coffee-making facilities.
**Directions:** on junction of B940 with A917, southeast of St Andrews. Follow signs for pottery.
IAIN & AILEEN GREENLEES ☎(01333) 450207

## DUNFERMLINE • map 16D4

 **HALFWAY HOUSE HOTEL**
Kingseat, KY12 0TJ
*Scotland is renowned for its long tradition of warm hospitality, and The Halfway House Hotel is no exception. Recently redecorated, the hotel is comfortable and welcoming, and the food in the bar and restaurant is well presented and served. Nearby Loch Fitty is famous for trout fishing, golf lovers can visit St Andrews and Gleneagles, and Edinburgh is only 30 minutes away. The hotel is 2 miles from the Scottish National Water Ski Centre and 4 miles from Knockhill Motor Racing Circuit.*
DOUBLE ROOM: from £20 to £30
SINGLE ROOM: from £25 to £35
FOOD: up to £15 [CLUB]
**Hours:** breakfast 7.30am-9.30am, lunch 12noon-3.30pm, bar meals 12noon-2pm, high tea Sunday 4pm-6pm, dinner 5.30pm-9.30pm, bar meals 5.30pm-9.30pm.
**Cuisine:** SCOTTISH - specialities include salmon gravadlax and a wide range of steaks.
**Cards:** Visa, Access.
**Other points:** licensed, Sunday lunch, children welcome, residents' lounge, golf nearby, residents' bar, parking, laundry, drying room.
**Rooms:** 3 double rooms, 9 twin rooms. All with TV, telephone, tea/coffee-making facilities.
**Directions:** take M90; exit 3 for Dunfermline. Travel 100 metres to next roundabout, turn right at sign for Retail Park: Kingseat is approximately one mile.
ANN & VIC PEGG ☎(01383) 731661 [Fax](01383) 621274

## FREUCHIE • map 16D4

 **THE LOMOND HILLS HOTEL**
Parliament Square, KY7 7EY
*Set in the quiet, picturesque village in the Howe of Fife, at the foot of the Lomond hills, this is a comfortable hotel dating back to 1753 and now upgraded to a high standard. Intimate candlelit restaurant, comfortable lounges, four-poster bedrooms and a leisure centre, which is free for guests' use.*
DOUBLE ROOM: from £30 to £40
SINGLE ROOM: from £40 to £50
FOOD: from £15 to £20 🍽 [CLUB]
**Hours:** breakfast 7.30am-9am, bar snacks 12noon-2.15pm, dinner 7pm-9.15pm, bar snacks 6pm-10pm.
**Cuisine:** BRITISH / CONTINENTAL - à la carte menu, with special menu of flamed dishes.
**Cards:** Visa, Access, Diners, AmEx.
**Other points:** parking, children welcome, Sunday lunch, open bank holidays, disabled access, pets allowed, residents' lounge, vegetarian meals, garden, licensed, residents' bar, swimming pool.
**Rooms:** 2 single rooms, 8 double rooms, 10 twin rooms, 4 family rooms. All with TV, telephone, tea/coffee-making facilities.
**Directions:** in centre of Fife near Falkland, 14 miles from Kinross.
ERNST VAN BEUSEKOM ☎(01337) 857329 [Fax](01337) 857498

## GLENROTHES • map 16D4

 **TOWN HOUSE HOTEL**
1 High Street, Markinch, KY7 6DQ
*A family-run hotel bringing together traditional values and quality. Centrally situated in the Kingdom of Fife, ideal for golfing breaks. The Town House Hotel provides a warm welcome and good value for money.*
DOUBLE ROOM: from £20 to £30
SINGLE ROOM: from £30 to £40
FOOD: up to £15 🍽
**Hours:** breakfast 7am-9am, lunch 12noon-2pm, dinner 6.15pm-9.00pm.
**Cuisine:** INTERNATIONAL - dishes may include chicken stir-fry, Tay salmon fillet, chicken tikka, Chinese sweet-and-sour pork, grilled steaks, Scottish specialities.
**Cards:** Visa, Access, Diners, AmEx.
**Other points:** licensed, Sunday lunch, no-smoking area, children welcome, pets allowed, special breaks, parking.
**Rooms:** 2 single rooms, 2 double rooms. All with TV, tea/coffee-making facilities, 3 en suite, 1 with private facilities.
**Directions:** B9130, opposite railway station in Markinch.
HARRY & LESLEY BAIN ☎(01592) 758459 [Fax](01592) 741238

## ROSYTH • map 16D4

### 🛏 GLADYER INN
Heath Road, Ridley Drive, KY11 2BT

*A modern, purpose-built hotel with up-to-date facilities to match. The best of Scottish hospitality is extended to all guests whether staying overnight, dining or having a drink. Good value for money.*

DOUBLE ROOM: from £20 to £30

SINGLE ROOM: from £30 to £40

FOOD: up to £15    CLUB

**Hours:** breakfast 7am-9.30am, lunch 12noon-2pm, dinner 7pm-9.30pm, bar meals 12noon-2pm, 7pm-9.30pm.

**Cuisine:** SCOTTISH - table d'hôte menu, including traditional dishes.

**Cards:** Visa, Access, AmEx, Switch, Delta.

**Other points:** licensed, Sunday lunch, no-smoking area, children welcome, functions, pets allowed.

**Rooms:** 4 double rooms, 16 twin rooms, 1 family room. All with satellite TV, telephone, tea/coffee-making facilities.

**Directions:** from M90 junction 1 towards Kincardine Bridge, Ridley Drive on left.

JANET & JIM INNES ☎(01383) 419977 **Fax**(01383) 411728

## ST ANDREWS • map 16C5

### 🍳 THE PANCAKE PLACE
177-9 South Street, KY16 9EE

*A cheerful family restaurant serving satisfying meals at good value for money. Spacious surroundings and relaxed atmosphere. Famous golf-course, university and sea-life centre nearby. Also, beaches and cathedral ruins.*

FOOD: up to £15 🍲

**Hours:** meals all day 9.30am-5.30pm, closed Christmas 25th December, 1st January.

**Cuisine:** SCOTTISH - pancakes in traditional Scottish style, savoury and sweet. Also baked potatoes, rice and monthly specials.

**Other points:** licensed, Sunday lunch, no-smoking area, children welcome, baby-changing facilities.

**Directions:** towards the west port along South Street, near Madras College.

C.D. BURHOUSE ☎(01334) 475671

# GRAMPIAN

## ABERDEEN • map 16A6

### 🍳 BETTY BURKES
45 Langstane Place, AB1 2DJ

*Betty Burkes is a stylish and interesting bar, which has been themed as a gentlemen's club, with old portrait paintings, wood panelling and leather seats. The massive carved eagle that dominates the entrance originated in America during the War Of Independence. There are display cabinets full of old bar and glass curios. Take in the bustling, local atmosphere.*

FOOD: up to £15    CLUB

**Hours:** breakfast 10am-12noon, bar meals 12noon-9.30pm, Friday and Saturday 12noon-9pm.

**Cuisine:** ENGLISH / INTERNATIONAL - bar meals, including deep-fried mushrooms, potato skins and home-made puddings.

**Cards:** Visa, Access, AmEx, Switch.

**Other points:** children welcome, open bank holidays.

**Directions:** in city centre, close to Union Street, Aberdeen's main street.

MIKE COOK ☎(01224) 210359 **Fax**(01224) 582694

### 🛏 OLD MILL INN & RESTAURANT
South Deeside Road, Maryculter, AB1 0AX

*An historic 200-year-old mill boasting original beams and timbers and set on the banks of the famous River Dee. It has been extensively refurbished to provide a high level of comfort and personal service in a friendly, welcoming atmosphere. There are many nearby places of interest to visit, including Royal Deeside and several whisky trails.*

DOUBLE ROOM: from £20 to £30

SINGLE ROOM: from £30 to £40

FOOD: up to £15    CLUB

**Hours:** breakfast 7.30am-10am, dinner 5.30pm-10pm, lunch 12noon-2.30pm, open all day, 7.30am-11.30pm.

**Cuisine:** BRITISH / CONTINENTAL - titillate your taste-buds with the superb selection of traditional and innovative cuisine. Using only fresh, local produce, the house specialities are a must for the discerning diner. Menus change with the seasons.

**Cards:** Visa, Access, Diners, AmEx.

**Other points:** access to river fishing, golf, hill-walking, pony-trekking, parking, children welcome, Sunday lunch, open bank holidays, vegetarian meals.

**Rooms:** 1 single room, 3 double rooms, 2 twin rooms, 1 family room. All with TV, tea/coffee-making facilities.

**Directions:** from Aberdeen on south side of Dee Bridge, B9077 for 4 miles. The inn is 300 yards beyond Petercutler Bridge. Close to Story Book Glen.

VICTOR SANG ☎(01224) 733212 **Fax**(01224) 732884

### ST MAGNUS COURT HOTEL
22 Guild Street, AB1 2NF

*The St Magnus Court Hotel caters principally for the commercial sector, offering both comfortable accommodation and food well-cooked and. prepared. Pleasant, relaxed atmosphere.*

**DOUBLE ROOM:** from £20
**SINGLE ROOM:** from £30
**FOOD:** up to £15
**Hours:** breakfast 4.30am-9am, bar meals served all day, dinner 6.30pm-8pm, open bank holidays.
**Cuisine:** set menus offering traditional Scottish fare including home-made stovies.
**Cards:** Visa, Access.
**Other points:** licensed, residents' bar and lounge, central heating.
**Rooms:** 4 single rooms, 2 double rooms, 13 twin rooms, 1 family room. All with TV, telephone, tea/coffee-making facilities.
**Directions:** this commercial hotel is located in the centre of Aberdeen, directly opposite Aberdeen railway station.
CAROL EDMUNDSON ☎(01224) 589411 Fax(01224) 584352

---

### ALEXANDRA HOTEL
12 Bridge Square, AB3 6QJ

*An attractive, well-maintained exterior opens into a tastefully decorated hotel and restaurant. Table d'hôte and à la carte meals are offered with a touch of French cuisine. Close to Balmoral, Crathie church and distilleries. For anglers, there is fishing in the River Dee.*

**DOUBLE ROOM:** from £20 to £30
**FOOD:** from £21 to £25 CLUB
**Hours:** breakfast 8am-9.30am, lunch noon-2.15pm, dinner 6pm-9pm, bar 11am-midnight.
**Cuisine:** SCOTTISH / FRENCH - traditional Scottish and French: entrecôte au poivre, fillet steak Diane, trout with almonds, salmon, whole lemon sole, venison. Selection of cheese.
**Cards:** Visa, Access, Diners, AmEx.
**Other points:** licensed, central heating, children welcome, pets allowed, baby-listening device, cots, foreign exchange, left luggage, disabled access, vegetarian meals, parking.
**Rooms:** 7 bedrooms. All with en suite, TV, radio, telephone, tea/coffee-making facilities.
**Directions:** on the A93 Aberdeen to Braemar road, near the River Dee bridge.
HELEN & DAVE MACNEILL ☎(013397) 55376 Fax(013397) 55466

### AULD KIRK HOTEL
Braemar Road, AB35 5RQ

*Converted from a church to a hotel in 1990, the original structure, including the front doors, bell tower and many of the windows, have been retained. The result is fascinating and well worth a visit. The resident proprietors provide a warm*

*welcome, well-appointed accommodation all individually decorated to a high standard, good food and good value.*

**DOUBLE ROOM:** from £20 to £25
**SINGLE ROOM:** from £25 to £30
**FOOD:** from £15 to £20
**Hours:** breakfast 8.30am-9am, lunch 12noon-2pm, bar meals 11am-4pm, dinner 6.30pm-9pm, bar meals 4.30pm-9pm, open all year.
**Cuisine:** SCOTTISH - wide choice of meals from Royal Deeside salmon with hollandaise sauce to toasted sandwiches and highly recommended vegetarian food.
**Cards:** Visa, Access.
**Other points:** licensed, open-air dining, Sunday lunch, children welcome, afternoon tea, pets allowed, residents' lounge, ideal base for touring, walking and skiing.
**Rooms:** 6 bedrooms, all en suite. All with TV, hair dryer, welcome tray, direct dial telephone.
**Directions:** on main Braemar to Aberdeen road at northern end of Ballater. A93.
MONICE CHIVAS ☎(013397) 55762 Fax(013397) 55707

---

### BANCHORY LODGE HOTEL
Banchory, AB31 3HS

*At the confluence of the Feugh with the Dee, the Banchory Lodge is in a striking and historic setting, with the River Dee, a celebrated salmon river, running through the grounds. As well as salmon fishing, there is also ample opportunity for golfing, nearby forest walks and nature trails. An abundance of National Trust properties to visit nearby.*

**DOUBLE ROOM:** from £90
**SINGLE ROOM:** from £65
**FOOD:** from £25 to £30
**Hours:** bar 11am-2pm, bar 5pm-11pm, closed 12th December until 29th January.
**Cuisine:** SCOTTISH - prime Scottish beef, Dee salmon.
**Cards:** Visa, Access, AmEx.
**Other points:** children welcome, fishing, sauna.
**Rooms:** 8 double, 22 twin, 9 family rooms.
**Directions:** off the A93, 18 miles west of Aberdeen in Banchory, off Dee Street.
DUGALD JAFFRAY ☎(0330) 822625/824777 Fax(0330) 825019

---

### CALLATER LODGE HOTEL
9 Glenshee Road, AB35 5YQ

*A typical Victorian villa built from local granite and standing in one acre of mature grounds on the southern edge of Braemar. The Callater Lodge is a no-smoking establishment and the new owners Maria & Michael Franklin take care to ensure that their guests have a relaxing and enjoyable stay in comfortable accommodation. An ideal location for tourists, sportsmen, walkers and skiers, 2 self catering units also available.*

---

DOUBLE ROOM: from £20 to £30
SINGLE ROOM: from £20 to £30
FOOD: from £15 to £20
**Hours:** breakfast 8.00am-8.45am, dinner 7.30pm, open bank holidays.
**Cuisine:** BRITISH - fresh local produce is used extensively for the daily changing menu.
**Cards:** Visa, Access, Eurocard, Mastercard, Amex.
**Other points:** parking, no-smoking, pets allowed, residents' lounge, garden, licensed.
**Rooms:** 1 single, 2 double, 3 twin rooms.
**Directions:** A93 Perth to Aberdeen road, which passes through the village, 400 metres from the village centre.
MARIA & MICHAEL FRANKLIN ☎(01339) 741275
Fax (01339) 741275

## BUCKIE • map 18B5

 **MILL HOUSE HOTEL**
Tynet, AB56 2HJ
*A converted 18th-century water mill, offering all sporting and sightseeing activities. This hospitable, family-run establishment provides a relaxing atmosphere and is renowned for its excellent food and value. All 15 bedrooms are en suite with full modern facilities. Open all year.*
DOUBLE ROOM: from £20 to £30
SINGLE ROOM: from £35 to £45
FOOD: up to £15    CLUB
**Hours:** breakfast 7.45am-9.30am, lunch 12noon-2pm, dinner 7pm-9pm.
**Cuisine:** SCOTTISH - à la carte: the speciality is Scottish cuisine from local produce.
**Cards:** Visa, Access, Diners, AmEx.
**Other points:** licensed, Sunday lunch, functions, special breaks, golf packages, conferences, vegetarian meals, residents' bar, residents' lounge, disabled access, children welcome.
**Rooms:** 7 single, 3 double, 1 family, 4 twin rooms. All with TV, radio, tea/coffee-making facilities.
**Directions:** on the A98, east of Elgin. Hotel located between Buckie and Fochabers.
GILL & PHIL SILVER ☎(01542) 850233 Fax (01542) 850331

## CULLEN • map 18B5

 **THE CULLEN BAY HOTEL**
Near Buckie, AB56 2XA
*Guests will not only appreciate the good food which uses local produce, but also the spectacular views of Cullen Bay and its beautiful stretches of sand. A stylish lounge bar provides an ideal place to relax, and all bedrooms are equipped with private facilities for maximum comfort. A haven for golfers and a superb base for day tours.*
DOUBLE ROOM: from £30 to £40
SINGLE ROOM: from £30 to £40
FOOD: up to £15
**Hours:** breakfast 8am-11am, lunch and bar meals 12noon-3pm, dinner and bar meals 5pm-9.30pm, open all year.
**Cards:** Access, Visa

**Other points:** high teas, morning coffees and afternoon teas, lounge bar, garden patio with children's play area, wedding and funtions facilities.
**Rooms:** 1 single room, 5 double rooms, 6 twin rooms, all en suite, 2 family rooms. All with TV, telephone, baby-listening device, hair dryer and tea/coffee-making facilities.
**Directions:** A98, one mile west of Cullen town.
MR AND MRS EDWARDS ☎(01542) 840432
Fax (01542) 840900

## ELGIN • map 18C4

**THE TORR HOUSE HOTEL**
8 Moss Street, IV30 1LU
*A large, comfortable town house well situated in the centre of this historic area. Elgin is best known for its ruined cathedral dating from 1224 - probably one of the finest in Scotland. All guests are assured of a warm welcome and attentive service, complemented by good, sensible home-cooking at good value for money.*
DOUBLE ROOM: from £20 to £30
SINGLE ROOM: from £25 to £35
FOOD: up to £15
**Hours:** breakfast 7.30-8am, lunch (bar & restaurant) 12noon-2pm, dinner (bar & restaurant) 5.30pm-9pm. Open all year.
**Cuisine:** steaks.
**Cards:** Access, Visa, AmEx
**Other points:** parking.
**Rooms:** 8 rooms, 2 single en suite, 4 twin en suite, 1 double ensuite & 1 family. All with tea/coffee maker, TV, radio, hair dryer. 1 disabled room attached to hotel with car parking adjacent to the door.
**Directions:** in centre of town just off High Street.
MS WILMA SHERIDAN ☎(01343) 542661
Fax (01343) 548200

## INVERURIE • map 16A5

**THE LODGE HOTEL**
Old Rayne, AB52 6RY
*Situated just off the main A96 Aberdeen-Inverness road, this family-run village hotel has superb views and offers a warm and friendly welcome. With a reputation for good food and generous portions, the hotel is frequented by locals, business people and holiday-makers. Being centrally situated, the hotel is an ideal base for touring the Grampian region and for visiting the numerous castles and distilleries in the area. It also provides a welcome opportunity for the weary traveller to enjoy some peace and tranquillity.*
DOUBLE ROOM: from £20 to £30
SINGLE ROOM: from £25 to £35
FOOD: from £15 to £20
**Hours:** breakfast 8am-9am, lunch 12noon-2.30pm, dinner weekdays 7pm-8pm, weekends 7pm-9pm.
**Cuisine:** ENGLISH / CONTINENTAL - daily changing menu with a selection of 46 different soups. Fresh local produce of beef, lamb, fish, salmon and seafood. Desserts are home-made, and

the cheese platter is very good value. Special children's menu available.
**Cards:** Visa, Access, AmEx.
**Other points:** licensed, Sunday lunch, children welcome, pets allowed, vegetarian meals, residents' lounge, residents' bar.
**Rooms:** 1 single room, 1 double room, 4 twin rooms, 1 family room. All with en suite, TV, telephone, tea/coffee-making facilities, central heating, electric blankets, baby-listening facilities.
**Directions:** off the A96, 9 miles north of Inverurie, 12 miles south of Huntly.
MR & MRS NEIL ☎(01464) 851205/851636

## MACDUFF • map 18B5

### THE HIGHLAND HAVEN
Shore Street, AB44 1UB

*Commanding a superb waterfront location in Macduff, with its steep streets of quaint houses, The Highland Haven offers comfortable en suite bedrooms equipped with all modern comforts. The indoor leisure complex allows guests to relax after a strenuous days sightseeing or golfing, and prepares them to enjoy a pre-dinner drink in the cocktail bar with its superb views over Deveron Bay and the Caithness Hills.*
DOUBLE ROOM: from £20 to £30
SINGLE ROOM: from £30 to £40
FOOD: up to £20
**Hours:** breakfast 7.30am-9am, lunch restaurant and bar 12noon-2pm, dinner bar 5pm-9.30pm, dinner restaurant 7pm-9pm. Open bank holidays.
**Cuisine:** local beef and seafood.
**Cards:** Visa, Access.
**Other points:** sauna, spa, steam room, solarium, gymnasium, snooker room, conference facilities, 2 golf courses nearby, fishing and shooting can be arranged.
**Rooms:** 3 single rooms, 7 double rooms, 11 twin rooms, 3 family rooms. All en suite with TV, telephone, radio, tea/coffee-making facilities.
**Directions:** Take the A98 coastal road, the hotel overlooks the harbour entrance.
MR WILLIAM ALCOCK ☎(01261) 832408
Fax(01261) 833652

## PETERHEAD • map 18C6

### BAYVIEW HOTEL
3 St Peter Street, AB4 6RR

*Pleasant family-run hotel situated on the coastline of Scotland. Peterhead is the home of the largest fishing fleet in Europe, and during your visit you may have the opportunity to see the fish being landed. There is also a golf course nearby, and Aviemore and Inverness are just a short drive away.*
DOUBLE ROOM: from £20 to £30
SINGLE ROOM: from 25 to £35
FOOD: up to £15

**Hours:** breakfast 7am-9.30am, lunch 12noon-2pm, dinner 5pm-8.30pm.
**Cuisine:** SCOTTISH - traditional Scottish cuisine: fresh fish and seafood, chicken, beef, pork and duck.
**Cards:** Visa, Access.
**Other points:** licensed, Sunday lunch, children welcome, pets allowed.
**Rooms:** 2 single, 11 double, 4 twin rooms.
**Directions:** off the A952 between Aberdeen and Fraserburgh.
MR JAMES ELDER ☎(01779) 472523 Fax(01779) 479495

## STONEHAVEN • map 16B6

### THE TOLBOOTH RESTAURANT
Kincardine, AB3 2JU

*A building of historical interest, situated in the seaside holiday resort of Stonehaven, and offering good views across the working harbour. Excellent home-produced dishes using local produce, with the emphasis on local fish dishes. A major nearby tourist attraction is Dunotter Castle, setting for Franco Zefferelli's portrayal of Hamlet in 1990.*
FOOD: from £15 to £20
**Hours:** lunch 12noon-2pm, dinner 7pm-9pm, closed Monday, closed January.
**Cuisine:** SEAFOOD - à la carte menu. Blue fin tuna steak, red snapper ravioli, monkfish casserole, loin of venison, all home-cooked using only fresh produce.
**Cards:** Visa.
**Other points:** licensed, Sunday lunch, children welcome, vegetarian meals.
**Directions:** 15 miles south of Aberdeen. In Stonehaven, follow harbour signs.
MOYA BOTHWELL ☎(01569) 62287

# HIGHLANDS

## ALTNAHARRA • map 17A3

### ALTNAHARRA HOTEL
By Lairg, IV27 4UE

*Privately owned and managed, Altnaharra offers a warm welcome and friendly atmosphere together with good food and comfortable accommodation. With its choice of refurbished bedrooms and two annex cottages, this hotel is ideal for families or a party of enthusiastic sports persons in the area to enjoy superb salmon and sea-trout fishing. Winter and spring breaks available.*
DOUBLE ROOM: from £49
SINGLE ROOM: from £49
FOOD: from £15 to £20
**Hours:** breakfast 7.45am-9am, lunch 12noon-2pm, dinner 7.30pm-8.30pm, closed 8th October until 15th March.
**Cuisine:** SCOTTISH - prime Scottish beef and lamb, game, fresh local fish and seafood.
**Cards:** Visa, Access.
**Other points:** children welcome, garden, fishing, drying facilities, residents' lounge, residents' bar.
**Rooms:** 5 single rooms, 3 double rooms, 9 twin rooms. All with tea/coffee-making facilities.
**Directions:** off the A836 Lairg road; follow sign for Tongue.
MRS ANNE TUSCHER ☎(01549) 411222
Fax(01549) 411222

## AULTBEA • map 17B2

### AULTBEA HOTEL
IV22 2HX

*This 18th century family-run hotel is the perfect location from which to enjoy the wonders of the north-west Highlands. With exhilarating views, the hotel offers guests attractively furnished, well-appointed bedrooms, the intimate atmosphere and fine food in the Zetland Restaurant, a delightful patio and garden for dining in the warmer months, and friendly, attentive service. An attached conservatory houses the Waterside Bistro which is open all day until 9pm and offers an attractive alternative to the restaurant.*
DOUBLE ROOM: from £30 to £35
SINGLE ROOM: from £32 to £36
FOOD: from £5 to £25
**Hours:** breakfast 8am-11.30am, lunch 11am-3pm, bar meals 11am-3pm, dinner 7pm-9pm, bar meals 4.30pm-9pm.
**Cuisine:** SCOTTISH - a good selection: local seafood a speciality.
**Cards:** Visa, Access, AmEx, Switch, MasterCard, Delta, JCB
**Other points:** parking, children welcome, dogs allowed, residents' lounge, garden, open-air dining, vegetarian meals, traditional Sunday lunch, afternoon teas.
**Rooms:** 1 single room, 3 double rooms, 3 twin rooms, 1 family room. All with en suite, TV,

telephone, radio, alarm, hair dryer, trouser-press, tea/coffee-making facilities.
**Directions:** A832, on the shore of Loch Ewe.
PETER & AVRIL NIETO ☎(01445) 731201
Fax(01445) 731214

## CAWDOR • map 18C4

### CAWDOR TAVERN
The Lane, IV12 5XP

*Situated near Cawdor Castle - made famous by Shakespeare's Macbeth - you'll find Cawdor Tavern. The focal point of this charming conservation village, only 15 minutes from Inverness, the Tavern is renowned for its traditional Scottish fare. The snug lounge bar, with a welcoming log fire and old oak panelling, has a vast selection of malt whiskies to tempt the connoisseur. There is also an interesting 40-bin wine list and a superb choice of beers, including real ales and a `guest' beer. Open all year, there is a sunny patio for summer days, and children are always welcome. Run by Norman Sinclair, from the highly acclaimed Moorings Hotel in Fort William, you will see the same dedication for which The Moorings was voted `AA Hotel of the Year for Scotland' 1994.*
FOOD: from £10 to £18
**Hours:** lunch 12noon-2pm, dinner 6pm-9pm, open for morning coffee in summer.
**Cuisine:** SCOTTISH
**Cards:** Visa, Access, AmEx, MasterCard.
**Other points:** parking, children welcome, no-smoking area, open-air dining, vegetarian meals, traditional Sunday lunch.
**Directions:** .5 mile from Cawdor Castle, on B9006, off A96 Inverness to Nairn road.
NORMAN SINCLAIR ☎(01667) 404777
Fax(01667) 404777

## CROMARTY • map 18B4

### ROYAL HOTEL
Marine Terrace, IV11 8YN

*A family-run hotel with attentive staff who guard their reputation for quality food and value for money with considerable pride - the best in Scottish hospitality. Cromarty is an unspoilt fishing village on the Black Isle, where relaxation and peace are guaranteed.*
DOUBLE ROOM: from £20 to £30
SINGLE ROOM: from £25 to £35
FOOD: up to £15 🍽 CLUB
**Hours:** breakfast 8am-9.30am, lunch 12noon-2pm, dinner 7pm-8.30pm, bar meals 12noon-2pm.
**Cuisine:** SCOTTISH
**Cards:** Visa, Access, AmEx, Mastercard, Eurocard.
**Other points:** open-air dining, Sunday lunch, no-smoking area, children welcome, coaches by prior arrangement, residents' lounge, residents' bar.
**Rooms:** 3 single rooms, 5 double rooms, 2 twin rooms. All with en suite, TV, tea/coffee-making

facilities, hair dryer.
**Directions:** off the A832 in Cromarty overlooking
the beach and harbour.
JOHN & BRENDA SHEARER ☎(01381) 600217
Fax (01381) 600217

## DINGWALL • map 17C3

### THE NATIONAL HOTEL
High Street, IV15 9HA
*This Victorian hotel offers spacious accommodation,*
*warmly decorated with wood panelling and*
*comfortable furnishings, with convenient access to*
*the spectacular Highland countryside. Traditional*
*home-cooking is welcome after an invigorating day*
*spent exploring the nearby sights.*
DOUBLE ROOM: from £30 to £40
SINGLE ROOM: from £30 to £40
FOOD: up to £15
**Hours:** breakfast 7.30am-9.30am, lunch 12noon-
2.30pm, dinner 7pm-9.30pm.
**Cuisine:** SCOTTISH - traditional home-cooking.
Vegetarians catered for.
**Cards:** Visa, Access, Diners, AmEx.
**Other points:** licensed, Sunday lunch, children
welcome, afternoon tea, residents' lounge.
**Rooms:** 51 bedrooms.
**Directions:** 12 miles north of Inverness.
BERNARD & ROSEMARIE JUSTICE ☎(01349)
862166 Fax (01349) 865178

## DORNOCH • map 18B4

### MALLIN HOUSE HOTEL
Church Street, IV25 3LP
*A family-run hotel situated close to the famous golf*
*course in Dornoch. Good food and a friendly*
*atmosphere complement the high standard of*
*accommodation. Choose from the à la carte, table*
*d'hôte or bar meals menu. All dishes are freshly*
*cooked to order and attractively presented. Good*
*value for money. Especially popular with golfers*
*and anglers.*
DOUBLE ROOM: from £25 to £35
SINGLE ROOM: from £25 to £35
FOOD: from £15 to £20
**Hours:** breakfast 8.15am-9.30am, lunch 12noon-
2.15pm, dinner 6.30pm-9pm.
**Cuisine:** ENGLISH - à la carte and table d'hôte
menus. Dishes may include rack of spring lamb,
lobster Thermidor. All dishes cooked to order.
Good, imaginative bar meals.
**Cards:** Visa, Access, AmEx.
**Other points:** licensed, Sunday lunch, children
welcome, pets allowed, garden.
**Rooms:** 11 bedrooms. All en suite with colour TV,
tea/coffee-making facilities.
**Directions:** in centre of Dornoch near to the famous
golf course.
MALCOLM HOLDEN ☎(01862) 810335

## DRUMNADROCHIT • map 17C3

### LOCH NESS LODGE HOTEL
IV3 6TJ

*A comfortable and friendly Highland lodge set in 8*
*acres of woodland near Loch Ness and Urquhart*
*Castle. An ideal touring base for the Scottish*
*Highlands. Regular Scottish entertainment. Loch*
*Ness visitors' centre, giftshop, and Loch Ness*
*cruises.*
DOUBLE ROOM: from £30 to £40
SINGLE ROOM: from £40 to £60
FOOD: from £15 to £20    CLUB
**Hours:** breakfast 8am-10am, bar meals 11.30am-
6pm, 6.30pm-9.30pm.
**Cuisine:** SCOTTISH - Aberdeen Angus steaks and
fresh seafood. Carte du jour and full à la carte
menus available. Bar snacks served in the bar/coffee
shop. Children's menu. Home-baking.
**Cards:** Visa, Access, Diners, AmEx.
**Other points:** licensed, vegetarian meals, children
welcome, pets allowed, afternoon tea, coaches by
prior arrangement.
**Rooms:** 16 double rooms, 36 twin rooms, 2 triple
rooms, 1 quad room. All with TV, telephone,
tea/coffee-making facilities, hair dryer.
**Directions:** on the A831 Cannich to Inverness road.
D.W. SKINNER ☎(01456) 450342 Fax (01456)
450429

## DUNBEATH • map 18A4

### DUNBEATH HOTEL
KW6 6EB
*Situated in a quiet Highland village with views to*
*the sea, this old coaching inn, dating from around*
*1830, offers true character with modern comfort. An*
*ideal opportunity for the visitor to sample the best*
*of Highland produce, complemented by a fine wine*
*list. Caithness itself has much to offer the visitor,*
*with the Orkneys just off-shore and a wealth of*
*sporting activities available. Scottish Tourist Board 3*
*Crowns `commended'.*
DOUBLE ROOM: from £30 to £40
SINGLE ROOM: from £35 to £45
FOOD: from £15 to £20
**Hours:** breakfast 8am-9.30am, lunch 12noon-
2.30pm, bar snacks 12noon-2.30pm, dinner 7pm-
8pm, bar snacks 5pm-9pm, closed Christmas day
and 1st January until 3rd January.
**Cuisine:** SCOTTISH - venison and salmon from
local estates and seafood from northern harbours.
**Cards:** Visa, Access, Diners, AmEx.

**Other points:** licensed, Sunday lunch, no-smoking area, children welcome, pets allowed, garden, parking, cots, 24hr reception, residents' lounge, residents' bar.
**Rooms:** 4 double rooms, 2 twin rooms. All with TV, radio, tea/coffee-making facilities.
**Directions:** north on A9 from Inverness; signs to Wick/Thurso; left at roadbridge over Dunbeath Water.
NEIL & PATRICIA BUCHANAN ☎(01593) 731208
Fax(01593) 731242

## DURNESS • map 17A3

 **CAPE WRATH HOTEL**
IV27 4SW
*Originally built for the area tax official, this 200-year-old hotel is furnished in country house style, providing an ambience of comfort and relaxation. Popular with locals and tourists alike, it is an ideal location for visiting Balnakeil craft village and Smoo caves, and for exploring Cape Wrath.*
DOUBLE ROOM: from £25 to £35
SINGLE ROOM: from £25 to £35
FOOD: up to £15
**Hours:** breakfast 8.30am, dinner 7.30pm, bar meals 12noon-2pm, closed November until Easter.
**Cuisine:** INTERNATIONAL - vegetarian meals by arrangement.
**Cards:** Visa, Access.
**Other points:** room service, vegetarian meals, residents' bar, residents' lounge.
**Rooms:** 11 bedrooms.
**Directions:** on A838, 2.5 miles south of Durness.
MR J. WATSON ☎(01971) 511212

## EAST MEY • map 18A4

 **CREAG-NA-MARA**
Thurso, Caithness, KW14 8XL
*Situated close to the seashore, and overlooking the Pentland Firth and the Isle of Stroma, this small but tastefully decorated guest house offers extremely good value accommodation from which to explore this dramatic corner of Scotland. A large conservatory provides the dining area in which Mrs Kimber offers a tempting à la carte menu at a very reasonable price. Well recommended. Ideal for bird watching.*
DOUBLE ROOM: up to £20
SINGLE ROOM: up to £20
FOOD: up to £15
**Hours:** breakfast 7.30am-10am, dinner 6pm-11pm, open bank holidays.
**Cuisine:** local seafood specialities.
**Cards:** None
**Other points:** licensed, vegetarian meals, special diets accomodated, shooting and fishing by arrangement, on-site parking, pets welcome.
**Rooms:** 1 twin room en suite, 1 family room en suite, 1 double room with private bathroom. All with tea/coffee-making facilities.
**Directions:** 5 miles west of John O'Groats on the A836.
GLENYS & NORMAN KIMBER ☎(01847) 851713

## FORT AUGUSTUS • map 17C3

 **THE BRAE HOTEL**
Fort Augustus, PH32 4DG
*Originally a church manse, standing in its own landscaped grounds, this hotel offers a quiet, relaxing atmosphere with good food and drink. Some rooms offer a commanding view over the Caledonian Canal. The main nearby tourist attraction is Loch Ness and the many walks in the area.*
DOUBLE ROOM: from £20 to £30
SINGLE ROOM: from £20 to £30
FOOD: from £20 to £25 🍽
**Hours:** breakfast 8.15am-9.15am, dinner 7pm-8.30pm.
**Cuisine:** BRITISH / INTERNATIONAL - table d'hôte menu, offering an imaginative selection of both national and international dishes of a very high standard, beautifully presented.
**Cards:** Visa, Access, AmEx.
**Other points:** licensed, no-smoking dining room, vegetarian meals, special diets provided with prior notice, restaurant age limit 7 years+, residents' lounge, pets allowed, parking.
**Rooms:** 3 single rooms, 2 double rooms en suite, 3 twin rooms en suite. All with TV, tea/coffee-making facilities, most non-smoking.
**Directions:** on A82, 200 yards off main road, to the left of village.
ANDREW & MARI REIVE ☎(01320) 366289
Fax(01320) 366702

## FORT WILLIAM • map 15B2

 **GUISACHAN HOUSE**
Alma Road, PH35 6HA
*Situated in a quiet location on the hillside above the town, affording panoramic views over Loch Linnhe and the Ardgow Hills. Tastefully decorated throughout, the guest house offers fresh, modern and comfortable accommodation, good food and friendly, homely service. An ideal base when touring the area.*
DOUBLE ROOM: from £20 to £30
SINGLE ROOM: from £20 to £30
FOOD: up to £15
**Hours:** breakfast 7.45am-9am, dinner 6.30pm.
**Cuisine:** SCOTTISH - traditional home-cooking.
**Cards:** Visa, Access.
**Other points:** parking, children welcome, residents' lounge, vegetarian meals.
**Rooms:** 2 single rooms, 6 double rooms, 5 twin rooms, 4 family rooms. All with en suite, TV, tea/coffee-making facilities.
**Directions:** off Belford Road, near the swimming pool.
JOHN & ELIZABETH ROSIE ☎(01397) 703797
Fax(01397) 703797

**NEVISPORT RESTAURANT**
High Street, PH33 6EJ
*Situated in the Nevisport complex, which also includes a large mountaineering/sports shop and a*

craft and books department featuring many local crafts. Cafeteria-style system and Climbers Bar, the newest addition to the complex. Pull up a chair in front of the open fire and relax. The bar serves snacks, meals and real ales.
**FOOD:** up to £15
**Hours:** meals all day, summer from 9am-7.30pm, winter from 9am-5pm.
**Cuisine:** SCOTTISH - Scottish-influenced dishes, e.g., pan-fried Lochy trout.
**Cards:** Visa, Access, Diners, AmEx.
**Other points:** licensed, children welcome.
**Directions:** on the A82 within the Nevisport complex on the High Street.
MR CAMERON ☎(01397) 704921 Fax (01397) 705056

## GAIRLOCH • map 17B2

### BIRCHWOOD GUEST HOUSE
IV21 2AH

Beautifully situated in its own grounds amongst mature woodland and enjoying magnificent vistas from its elevated position towards Old Gairloch harbour and across to Skye and the Outer Isles. Recently refurbished to a very high standard, Birchwood offers a perfect base to explore this beautiful corner of Scotland.
**DOUBLE ROOM:** from £18 to £23
**Hours:** breakfast 8.30am-9.30am, open bank holidays, closed November to March.
**Cards:** None
**Other points:** children welcome, parking.
**Rooms:** 3 twin rooms, 2 double rooms, 1 family room, all en suite. All with tea/coffee-making facilities.
**Directions:** on the A832 - south side of the village.
MRS ELSIE RAMSAY ☎(01445) 712011

### MILLCROFT HOTEL
Strath, IV21 2BZ
Small, family-run hotel in centre of village, with magnificent views of the mountains, islands and sea. Comfortable rooms and quality cooking, with an Italian head chef. Places of interest nearby include Inverewe Gardens, Gairloch Heritage Museum and Beinn Eighe National Nature Reserve.
**DOUBLE ROOM:** from £30 to £40
**SINGLE ROOM:** from £20 to £35
**FOOD:** from £15 to £20
**Hours:** breakfast 8am-9.30am, lunch 12noon-2pm, bar meals 12noon-10pm, dinner 6pm-9pm.
**Cuisine:** SCOTTISH / ITALIAN - good choice using

local produce, i.e., fresh local salmon, venison, home-baking and home-made jams when available.
**Cards:** Visa, Access.
**Other points:** licensed, Sunday lunch, children welcome, open bank holidays.
**Directions:** take B8021 off main road, signposted Melvaig. Hotel .5 mile along.
MR G. BERNARDI ☎(01445) 712376 Fax (01445) 712091

### STEADING RESTAURANT
Achtercairn, IV21 2BP
A coffee-house/restaurant in a delightful converted 19th century farm building, which retains much of its olde-worlde atmosphere. Adjoining the award-winning Gairloch Museum of West Highland Life, it offers good food, using local fresh produce such as seafood and venison. Self-service by day and waitress service in evenings.
**FOOD:** from £15 to £20
**Hours:** meals all day 9am-9pm, closed from November until March.
**Cuisine:** SCOTTISH - fresh local seafood and venison. Home-baked cakes and scones.
**Cards:** Visa.
**Other points:** parking, children welcome, open bank holidays, afternoon tea, disabled access, vegetarian meals.
**Directions:** A832. From Inverness, 80 miles. At junction of A832 and B8031 in centre of Gairloch.
MS M. GAULT ☎(01445) 712449/712248 Fax (01445) 712551

### WHINDLEY GUEST HOUSE
Auchtercairn, IV21 2BN
A comfortable, modern guest house, with glorious views over Gairloch Bay, which offers guests fresh, home-baked bread, warm, comfortable bedrooms and a relaxing atmosphere. Ideal holiday guest house, where you can relax with breakfast in bed before your day at the golf course or on the beach, both only a few minutes' drive away. Special winter breaks featuring spinning and weaving courses.
**DOUBLE ROOM:** from £20 to £30
**Hours:** breakfast 8.30am-9.15am, lunch 12.30am-2pm, dinner 7pm-8pm.
**Cuisine:** SCOTTISH
**Other points:** children welcome, residents' lounge, vegetarian meals, special diets, picnic lunches, garden, patio.
**Directions:** uphill as you leave Gairloch on A832 towards Poolewe.
WILLIAM LESLIE HART & PAMELA NICHOLS ☎(01445) 712340

## GLENFINNAN • map 15B2

### THE PRINCES HOUSE
Glenfinnan, PH37 4LT
Originally an old staging post on the road to the Isles, this stone-built building has enormous character with a good, homely atmosphere. The

*cuisine is mostly local, using the freshest of produce, complemented by a fine wine list. Ideal location for those seeking to get away from the pressures of modern-day life.*
DOUBLE ROOM: from £30 to £40
SINGLE ROOM: from £35 to £45
FOOD: from £15 to £20
**Hours:** breakfast 8am-9am, dinner, 6.30pm-8.30pm, bar meals 12.30am-2.30pm, bar meals 5pm-9pm.
**Cuisine:** SCOTTISH - blackboard and à la carte menus, offering salmon, venison, trout and fresh shellfish.
**Cards:** Visa, Access, AmEx, Switch.
**Other points:** licensed, no-smoking rooms, open bank holidays, pets allowed, residents' lounge, afternoon tea, children catered for (please check age limits), residents' bar, vegetarian meals, parking, fishing, mountain bike hire.
**Rooms:** 5 double rooms, 2 twin rooms, 1 suite. All with TV, telephone, tea/coffee-making facilities.
**Directions:** on the main Fort William to Mallaig road in the centre of Glenfinnan.
ROBERT & CAROLE HAWKES ☎(01397) 722246
Fax(01397) 722307

## GLENMORISTON • map 15A2

 **CLUANIE INN**
IV3 6YW
*A converted coaching house, this inn offers good farmhouse cooking, comfortable accommodation and a warm welcome. With many beautiful walks through the mountains and glens, salmon and trout fishing, this is the ideal place to return to at the end of the day, with its cosy, relaxing atmosphere, fitness centre including sauna, and the very best in comfort. Highly recommended.*
DOUBLE ROOM: from £30 to £40
SINGLE ROOM: from £25 to £35
FOOD: from £15 to £20 CLUB
**Hours:** breakfast 8am-9.30am, lunch 12noon-2.30pm, dinner 6pm-9pm.
**Cuisine:** SCOTTISH - good farmhouse-style cooking.
**Cards:** Visa, Access.
**Other points:** licensed, Sunday lunch, children welcome, open bank holidays, pets allowed, garden, gym facilities, fishing.
**Rooms:** 13 bedrooms.
**Directions:** midway between Loch Ness and ferry terminal to Isle of Skye.
MR JOHN DOUGLAS CLINTON ☎(01320) 340238 Fax(01320) 340293

## GRANTOWN-ON-SPEY • map 18C4

**THE BEN MHOR HOTEL**
High Street, PH26 3EJ
*Comfortable, family-run hotel in the heart of the Spey Valley. This is an ideal spot for the holiday-maker, with an 18-hole golf course, salmon fishing, bowling green and woods nearby. Offering good food and comfortable accommodation.*
DOUBLE ROOM: from £30 to £50
SINGLE ROOM: from £20 to £30

FOOD: from £15 to £20
**Hours:** breakfast 8am-9.30am, lunch 12.30am-2pm, dinner 7pm-9pm, bar meals 5.30pm-9pm,.
**Cuisine:** BRITISH / CONTINENTAL - meals made with an emphasis on local produce whenever possible. Dishes may include salmon en croute with dill sauce, Strathspey venison.
**Cards:** Visa, Access.
**Other points:** licensed, open-air dining, Sunday lunch, children welcome, open bank holidays, afternoon tea, pets allowed, residents' bar, residents' lounge, foreign exchange, disabled access, vegetarian meals.
**Rooms:** 3 single rooms, 3 double rooms, 16 twin rooms, 2 family rooms. All with TV, radio, tea/coffee-making facilities.
**Directions:** on the main street in the town centre.
CLIVE & FIONA WILLIAMSON ☎(01479) 872056
Fax(01479) 873537

**RAVENSCOURT HOUSE HOTEL**
Seafield Avenue, PH26 3JG
*Formerly a manse, this hotel is a delightful 19th century house, now tastefully restored and retaining most of its original features. The Orangery Restaurant is designed in period style and has a cosy, intimate atmosphere. The food is excellent, using local and regional fresh Scottish produce. Comfortable accommodation and good service; great value for money.*
DOUBLE ROOM: from £30 to £40
SINGLE ROOM: from £30 to £40
FOOD: from £20 to £25
**Hours:** breakfast 8.30am-9am, lunch 12noon-2pm, dinner 7pm-9.30pm, closed January.
**Cuisine:** SCOTTISH - fine local produce with a French flair.
**Cards:** Visa, Access.
**Other points:** parking, children welcome, pets allowed, no-smoking area, residents' lounge, garden, open-air dining, vegetarian meals, afternoon teas, lunches, quiet location.
**Rooms:** 1 single room, 2 double rooms, 1 twin rooms, 2 family rooms. All with shower rooms en suite and TV, hair dryer, tea/coffee-making facilities.
**Directions:** just off the High Street, turn first left after Bank of Scotland.
CORINNE & DAVID WHALLEY ☎(01479) 872286
Fax(01479) 873260

## INVERGARRY • map 17D3

**INVERGARRY HOTEL**
PH35 4HG
*A family-run Highland hotel offering comfortable accommodation, good food, real ales and friendly service. The interior decor is in keeping with the distinctive and attractive Victorian building and provides comfortable and relaxed surroundings. Well placed to enjoy the beauty of the Scottish Highlands, fishing, golf, skiing or visits to the distilleries.*
DOUBLE ROOM: from £25 to £35
SINGLE ROOM: from £30 to £45

FOOD: from £15 to £20    `CLUB`
**Hours:** breakfast 8am-9.30am, meals all day 9am-7pm, dinner 6.30pm-8.30pm, bar meals 12noon-2pm, 6pm-9pm.
**Cuisine:** SCOTTISH / INTERNATIONAL - bar meals, self-service restaurant meals, and dinner featuring Scottish and international dishes and using fresh, predominantly local produce.
**Cards:** Visa, Access, AmEx.
**Other points:** licensed, Sunday lunch, children welcome, afternoon tea, pets allowed, residents' lounge, garden, baby-listening device, cots, foreign exchange, residents' bar, vegetarian meals, real ale.
**Rooms:** 1 single room, 5 double rooms, 4 twin rooms. All with TV, telephone, tea/coffee-making facilities.
**Directions:** from A82, take the A87 road for Kyle of Lochalsh. Hotel on the right.
Mac CALLUM FAMILY ☎(01809) 501206
`Fax`(01809) 501207

## INVERNESS • map 18C4

### BALNAIN HOUSE
40 Huntly Street, IV3 5HL
*Balnain House, the home of Highland music is a licensed cafe and exhibition centre, open all day serving good value-for-money traditional Scottish food, including haggis and neeps. In the evening it transforms into a cosy ceilidh house where some of the Highlands and Islands finest musicians can be heard.*
FOOD: up to £15
**Hours:** meals 10am-5pm, open Monday to Saturday nights throughout summer, Thursday night in winter, open bank holidays, closed Christmas day and New Year's day.
**Cuisine:** HIGHLAND HOME STYLE - haggis, smoked salmon, neeps, highland cheese and oatcakes, Clootie dumpling and custard.
**Cards:** Visa
**Other points:** licensed cafe, audio visual exhibition of Highlands and Islands music, traditional Celtic musical instruments, CDs, tapes and other gifts available from the gift shop.
**Directions:** on the south bank of the River Ness, opposite Grieg Street footbridge.
BALNAIN HOUSE TRUST ☎(01463) 715757
`Fax`(01463) 713611

### CLISHAM HOUSE
43 Fairfields Road, IV3 5QP
*Set ideally in one of Inverness's most delightful areas and within walking distance of the town centre and Eden Court Theatre, Clisham House has built a good reputation for its comfort, friendliness and true Highland hospitality. Loch Ness and Cawdor Castle are nearby.*
DOUBLE ROOM: from £20
**Hours:** breakfast 8am-10am, open bank holidays.
**Other points:** no-smoking area, residents' and television lounges, parking.
**Rooms:** 2 double rooms, 2 family rooms, all en suite. All with TV, hair dryer, tea/coffee-making

facilities.
**Directions:** ten minutes from city centre.
RHODA BEATON ☎(01463) 239965

### CULDUTHEL LODGE
14 Culduthel Road, IV2 4AG
*A Georgian building set in its own grounds and enjoying views of the River Ness. The resident owners ensure that their guests enjoy a comfortable, relaxing stay. Tastefully decorated and furnished to a very high standard. Ideal touring base.*
DOUBLE ROOM: from £30 to £40
SINGLE ROOM: from £35 to £45
FOOD: from £15 to £20 ⌐
**Hours:** breakfast 8am-9am.
**Cuisine:** SCOTTISH - table d'hôte menu changes each day, offering delicious, freshly prepared food.
**Cards:** Visa, Access.
**Other points:** pets by prior arrangement, central heating, children catered for (please check age limit), cots, left luggage.
**Rooms:** 1 single room, 9 double rooms, 2 twin rooms. All with TV, telephone, hair dryer, radio, tea/coffee-making facilities, fresh fruit, flowers, sherry, cd/cassette player, umbrella.
**Directions:** less than 1 mile from city centre. B861.
DAVID & MARION BONSOR ☎(01463) 240089
`Fax`(01463) 240089

### HAYDENS AT THE ISLANDS
11 Island Bank Road, IV2 4QN
*Pleasantly located near Loch Ness and several castles, this is a friendly establishment with a choice of three restaurants offering a full meal to a light snack. Attracts a varied clientele of locals and holiday-makers.*
FOOD: from £15 to £20
**Hours:** 12noon-10pm. Open all year.
**Cuisine:** salmon, steaks.
**Cards:** Visa, Access, Switch.
**Other points:** parking, 3 separate restaurants.
**Directions:** B862, city centre.
MRS PAT HAYDEN ☎(01463) 231833 `Fax`(01463) 236969

### HEATHMOUNT HOTEL
Kingsmill Road, IV2 3JU
*A Victorian-style building featuring ornate ceilings and decorative panels. Extremely popular local hostelry, with busy restaurant and bars. The River Ness and Inverness Castle are within easy walking distance.*
DOUBLE ROOM: from £20 to £30
SINGLE ROOM: from £30 to £40
FOOD: up to £15
**Hours:** breakfast 8am-10am, bar meals 12.15am-2.15pm, 5.45pm-9.15pm.
**Cuisine:** SCOTTISH / INTERNATIONAL - a good selection from the menu, including the Scottish speciality, haggis; also meals from the barbecue. Home-made pies, pasta and casseroles.
**Cards:** Visa, Access, Switch.

**Other points:** licensed.
**Rooms:** 5 bedrooms. All rooms en suite with TV, trouser press, tea/coffee-making facilities, hair dryers.
**Directions:** follow sign for Hilton Culcabock, left after flyover, right at roundabout, straight through traffic lights, bearing left at mini-roundabout. At next set of lights, turn right into Kingsmill Road.
MR & MRS BUXTON ☎(01463) 235877
Fax(01463) 715749

### 🏨 LOCH NESS HOUSE HOTEL
Glen Urquhart Road, IV3 6JL

*Overlooking the Caledonian Canal and the Torvean golf course, this family-owned and run hotel is ideal as a base for discovering the delights of Highland Scotland. A comfortable bar, dining room and residents' lounge await you after a day in the fresh air. Or join the locals in a ceilidh, held here most weekends. Loch Ness House is popular with locals and overseas visitors.*
DOUBLE ROOM: from £30 to £40
SINGLE ROOM: from £45 to £55
FOOD: up to £15     CLUB
**Hours:** breakfast 8am-9.30am, bar meals 12noon-2pm, dinner 7pm-9pm, bar meals 5.30pm-9pm, open all year.
**Cuisine:** SCOTTISH - à la carte and table d'hôte menus, offering traditional and new Scottish recipes, using only the freshest of local produce. Vegetarian dishes available.
**Cards:** Visa, Access, AmEx.
**Other points:** licensed, open-air dining, Sunday lunch, pets allowed, residents' lounge, garden, parking, disabled access, children welcome, baby-listening device, cots.
**Rooms:** 1 single room, 5 double rooms, 8 twin rooms, 7 triple rooms, 1 quad room. All with TV, radio, alarm, telephone, tea/coffee-making facilities.
**Directions:** 1.5 miles west of Inverness city centre on A82.
CHRISTOPHER MILROY ☎(01463) 231248
Fax(01463) 239327

ISLE OF SKYE • map 17C2

### 🏨 ATHOLL HOUSE HOTEL
IV55 8WA

*Set amongst some of Britain's wildest and truly spectacular scenery, Atholl House is an oasis of comfort and tranquility with a touch of old-fashioned Highland hospitality. Special touches in the charmingly furnished rooms include home-*

*made shortbread and there are fresh flowers everywhere. Imaginative menu includes speciality steaks.*
DOUBLE ROOM: from £20 to £30
SINGLE ROOM: from £20 to £30
FOOD: from £15 to £20     CLUB
**Hours:** breakfast 8am-9.30am, lunch 12noon-2pm, dinner 5pm-8.30pm, open bank holidays, closed January and February.
**Cuisine:** Scottish steaks, salmon.
**Cards:** Access, Visa.
**Other points:** pets allowed, licensed, residents' lounge, central heating, ironing facilities, garden for guests' use.
**Rooms:** 2 single rooms, 4 double rooms en suite, 2 twin rooms en suite, 1 family room en suite. All with TV, hair dryer, room service and tea/coffee-making facilities.
**Directions:** take A850 from Kyle of Lochalsh ferry, then left onto A863 at Sligachan.
MISS JOAN MACLEOD ☎(01470) 521219
Fax(01470) 521481

### 🍽 THE CASTLE MOIL RESTAURANT
Kyleakin, IV41 8PL

*Comfortable restaurant serving reasonably priced snacks, lunches and evening meals. Just 300 yards from Skye ferry terminal, The Castle Moil is worthy of a visit to break your journey and to enjoy a good-value meal or snack.*
FOOD: up to £15
**Hours:** breakfast all day, lunch 12noon-5pm, dinner 5pm-9.15pm, closed November to February, open bank holidays.
**Cuisine:** BRITISH / SEAFOOD - self-service during the day, table service in the evening. House speciality is seafood. Also salads, steaks, grills and all-day breakfast.
**Cards:** Visa, Access.
**Other points:** licensed, Sunday lunch, children welcome, meals all day, coaches by prior arrangement.
**Directions:** on the Skye side of the ferry.
ALEXANDER J.C. MACDIARMID ☎(01599) 534164

### 🏨 DUISDALE HOTEL
Isle Ornsay, Sleat, IV43 8QW

*Built in a Scottish hunting lodge style, this family-run hotel is set in 25 acres, overlooking the Sound of Sleat. Offering good food and comfortable accommodation, Duisdale is ideal for fishing, walking or observing the wildlife. Frequented by mixed ages, the atmosphere is quiet and peaceful.*
DOUBLE ROOM: from £38 to £45
SINGLE ROOM: from £40 to £50
FOOD: from £15 to £20
**Hours:** breakfast 8.30am-9.30am, lunch 12.30am-2pm, dinner 7.30pm-8.30pm.
**Cuisine:** SCOTTISH - dishes include platter of oak-smoked fish, casserole of venison and orange, Cloutie dumpling.
**Cards:** Visa, Access, AmEx.
**Other points:** licensed, children welcome, pets

allowed, garden, morning coffee, afternoon tea, vegetarian meals, parking, residents' bar, residents' lounge.
**Rooms:** 3 single rooms, 4 double rooms, 8 twin rooms, 2 triple rooms, 2 family rooms. All with tea/coffee-making facilities, 14 rooms are en suite.
**Directions:** from Kyleakin ferry, take A850. At Skulamus, turn left onto A851.
MARGARET COLPUS ☎(01471) 833202
Fax(01471) 833363

###  FLODIGARRY COUNTRY HOUSE HOTEL
Staffin, IV51 9HZ
*Magnificently situated with panoramic views across the sea to the Torridon mountains. Family-run, the hotel offers comfortable accommodation, Highland hospitality, and the best of traditional Scottish dishes and tempting specialities prepared from fresh local produce. The cottage next to the hotel was home to Flora MacDonald, who helped in the escape of Bonnie Prince Charlie.*
DOUBLE ROOM: from £30 to £40
SINGLE ROOM: from £30 to £40
FOOD: from £15 to £20
**Hours:** breakfast 8.30am-10.30am, Sunday lunch, 12.30am-2.30pm, bar meals 11am-10.30pm, dinner 7pm-10pm.
**Cuisine:** SCOTTISH - local salmon, lobster, langoustines and other fine fresh seafood. Highland venison and game, along with the best of other fresh Scottish fare. Restaurant and bar/conservatory menus.
**Cards:** Visa, Access, Switch.
**Other points:** licensed, open-air dining, Sunday lunch, no-smoking area, children welcome, open bank holidays, afternoon tea, pets allowed, residents' lounge, residents' bar, disabled access, vegetarian meals, parking.
**Rooms:** 4 single rooms, 10 double rooms, 7 twin rooms, 2 family rooms. All with tea/coffee-making facilities.
**Directions:** take the A855 from Portree north for Staffin (20 miles). Signposted.
ANDREW & PAMELA BUTLER ☎(01470) 552203
Fax(01470) 552301

### HOTEL EILEAN IARMAIN
Sleat, IV43 8QR

*The hotel prides itself on continuing to provide a traditional welcome with blazing log fires, and expert cooking using fresh local produce. Friendly Gaelic-speaking management and staff. Each room*

*has period furniture, offering special views of the sea and hills of Skye. All this in an idyllic and spectacular setting. Contact: Effie Kennedy (Manager).*
DOUBLE ROOM: from £40 to £50
SINGLE ROOM: over £50
FOOD: from £20 to £25
**Hours:** breakfast 8.30am-9.30am, lunch 12.30am-2pm, bar meals 12noon-2.30pm, dinner 7.30pm-9pm, bar meals 6.30pm-9.30pm, open all year.
**Cuisine:** SCOTTISH - lobsters, scallops, mussels used on a regular basis. Own oyster beds. Best local game when in season. Exciting menus with fresh local produce. Extensive wine list.
**Cards:** Visa, Access, AmEx, Eurocard.
**Other points:** Sunday lunch, restaurant no-smoking area, children welcome, stalking, shooting, fishing, entertainment,.
**Rooms:** 7 double rooms, 4 twin rooms, 1 family room. All with en suite, telephone. Non-smoking rooms available.
**Directions:** situated between Broadford and Armadale, with its ferry to Mallaig. The Skye Bridge opens end September 1995; 20 minutes from hotel.
EFFIE KENNEDY ☎(01471) 833332 Fax(01471) 833275

### KINLOCH LODGE
Sleat, IV43 8QY
*Kinloch Lodge is the home of Lord and Lady MacDonald and family, who have turned their historic home into a small, comfortable hotel. The food is superb, and Lady MacDonald's cooking and attention to detail has earned great praise from some of the best-known gourmets and food writers. An ideal spot for a quiet, relaxing holiday and to enjoy the spectacular views.*
DOUBLE ROOM: over £50
SINGLE ROOM: over £55
FOOD: from £25 to £35
**Hours:** breakfast 8.30am-9.30am, dinner 8pm, closed December until February.
**Cuisine:** MODERN ENGLISH - excellent table d'hôte menu. Main courses may include roast loin of pork with mushroom and vermouth sauce, smoked haddock roulade with scallops.
**Cards:** Visa, Access.
**Other points:** licensed, afternoon tea, children catered for (please check for age limits), pets by prior arrangement, residents' lounge, garden.
**Rooms:** 10 double/twin rooms.
**Directions:** 1 mile from A851. 6 miles south of Broadford and 8 miles north of Armadale.
LORD & LADY MACDONALD ☎(01471) 833214
Fax(01471) 833277

### ROSEDALE HOTEL
Portree, IV51 9DB
*A long established and very well appointed hotel created from a series of 19th century fishermen's dwellings with an unrivalled waterfront location in the older part of Portree. Ideally situated for exploring Skye by car.*

DOUBLE ROOM: from £30 to £40
SINGLE ROOM: from £35 to £45
FOOD: from £15 to £20
**Hours:** breakfast 8am-9.30am, dinner 7pm-8.30pm,
closed October until April.
**Cuisine:** SCOTTISH
**Cards:** Visa, Access.
**Other points:** children welcome, pets allowed,
residents' lounge, garden, bar.
**Rooms:** 5 single rooms, 5 double rooms, 13 twin
rooms. All with en suite, TV, radio, alarm,
telephone, tea/coffee-making facilities.
**Directions:** centre of village. On harbour side,
facing water.
H.M. ANDREW ☎(01478) 613131 Fax(01478)
612531

  **ROYAL HOTEL**
   Bank Street, Portree, IV51 9BU
*From Portree's Royal Hotel, the whole of Skye is on
the doorstep. With a coastline of more than 900
miles, the Isle of Skye enjoys a bountiful harvest
from the sea: prawns, lobsters, oysters and salmon.
From the hills, there is lamb or venison, and from
the rich pastures, sizzling prime steaks. Most of the
hotel's comfortably furnished bedrooms face the sea
and have stunning views, making this a popular
holiday retreat for families. Leisure and fitness
facilities available.*
DOUBLE ROOM: from £30 to £40
SINGLE ROOM: from £35 to £45
FOOD: from £15 to £20
**Hours:** breakfast 7.30am-10am, lunch 12noon-2pm,
bar snacks 12noon-2pm, dinner 7pm-9.30pm, bar
snacks 5pm-7.30pm.
**Cuisine:** SCOTTISH
**Cards:** Visa, Access.
**Other points:** hair-dresser, beautician, solarium,
parking, children welcome, no-smoking area,
disabled access, pets, residents' lounge, vegetarian
meals.
**Rooms:** 25 bedrooms.
**Directions:** off A850 to A855, .25 mile on left-hand
side, overlooking the harbour.
DAVID W. MORTON ☎(01478) 612525
Fax(01478) 613198

  **SKEABOST HOUSE HOTEL**
   Skeabost Bridge, IV51 9NP

*A former Victorian shooting lodge set in 12 acres of
secluded woodland and gardens. It is a comfortable
and relaxing, family-run hotel with three lounges,
cocktail bar and billiard room. The cuisine is
excellent, using fresh, local produce. The hotel has*

*a 9-hole golf-course and salmon and sea-trout
fishing on River Snizort - all free to guests who stay
three days or more.*
DOUBLE ROOM: from £42 to £50
SINGLE ROOM: from £41 to £48
FOOD: from £20 to £25
**Hours:** breakfast 8.30am-9.30am, lunch 12noon-
1.30pm, dinner 7pm-8.30pm, conservatory
restaurant dinner 6pm-9.30pm, closed mid-October
until April.
**Cuisine:** SCOTTISH - traditional Scottish cuisine
using fresh, local ingredients.
**Cards:** Visa, Access.
**Other points:** licensed, open-air dining, Sunday
lunch, no-smoking area, children welcome, pets
allowed, afternoon tea, fishing.
**Rooms:** 7 single rooms, 8 double rooms, 11 twin
rooms.
**Directions:** from Kyle of Lochalsh-Kyleakin ferry, 38
miles to Skeabost Bridge.
THE STUART & MCNAB FAMILIES ☎(01470)
532202 Fax(01470) 532454

  **UIG HOTEL**
   Uig, Portree, IV51 9YE

*An old coaching inn set on a hillside overlooking
Loch Snizort. It is a family-run hotel offering
excellent accommodation, good food and a warm
welcome. The hotel has its own pony-trekking and
self-catering apartments. Bargain breaks available.*
DOUBLE ROOM: from £30 to £40
SINGLE ROOM: from £30 to £40
FOOD: from £15 to £25
**Hours:** breakfast 8am-9am, lunch 12.15am-1.45pm
(buffet), dinner 7.15pm-8.15pm, closed mid-
October until end of March.
**Cuisine:** BRITISH - traditional cuisine. House
specialities are peat-smoked salmon, venison
casserole, and bread-and-butter pudding.
**Cards:** Visa, Access, Diners, AmEx, Switch.
**Other points:** licensed, no-smoking area, children
welcome, afternoon tea, pets by prior arrangement,
garden.
**Rooms:** 5 single rooms, 3 double rooms, 9 twin
rooms.
**Directions:** A856. On right-hand side of road
approaching Uig from Portree.
GRACE GRAHAM & DAVID TAYLOR ☎(01470)
542205 Fax(01470) 542308

### ULLINISH LODGE HOTEL & RESTAURANT
Struan, IV56 8FD

*An 18th century house of considerable character that has been tastefully converted to achieve a friendly, welcoming ambience. All bedrooms are comfortably furnished and have private facilities. The imaginative restaurant menu changes regularly. A beautiful setting on the shores of Loch Bracadale facing the Cuillin Hills.*

DOUBLE ROOM: from £30 to £40
SINGLE ROOM: from £40 to £45
FOOD: from £15 to £20
**Hours:** breakfast 8am-8.45am, dinner 7pm-8pm or by arrangement, bar meals 6pm-9pm, open bank holidays, closed November until end of February.
**Cuisine:** house speciality seafood dish for two, featuring lobster, local prawns, and a range of local shellfish (24 hours notice required); fine selection of wines, including an interesting range of Scottish wines, malt whiskies and liqueurs.
**Cards:**
Access,Visa,Mastercard,Eurocard,Switch,Eurocheque
**Other points:** grounds extending to 27,500 acres offering wide potential for rough shooting and fishing.
**Rooms:** 3 double rooms en suite, 1 double room with private bathroom, 2 twin rooms en suite, 2 family rooms en suite. All with TV, central heating, electric blankets and tea/coffee-making facilities.
**Directions:** 8 miles south of Dunvegan, off the A863 Sligachan to Dunvegan road. Well signposted.
MR AND MRS MULFORD ☎(01470) 572214

### KINCRAIG • map 18C4

### THE BOATHOUSE RESTAURANT
Loch Insh, PH21 1NU

*Situated on the sandy shore of Loch Insh, this restaurant is always a hub of activity because of the many sporting activities taking place, such as mountain biking, fishing, windsurfing, sailing, skiing and canoeing. This restaurant offers a warm welcome, good, well-prepared food, and value for money.*

DOUBLE ROOM: up to £20
SINGLE ROOM: up to £20
FOOD: up to £15
**Hours:** meals all day 10am-10pm, last orders 9pm.
**Cuisine:** BRITISH - home-baking, fresh salads, fondues, bar meals served all day. A la carte evening menu. Barbeques every lunchtime (July-August). Children's menu.
**Cards:** Visa, Access.
**Other points:** licensed, open-air dining, Sunday lunch, no-smoking area, children welcome, dry ski slope, winter snow skiing, water sports, fishing.
**Rooms:** 10 twin rooms, 6 family rooms en suite. Family log chalets available.
**Directions:** off A9 at Kingussie. Follow `Loch Insh Watersports' sign at Kincraig.
MR & MRS C. FRESHWATER ☎(01540) 651272
Fax(01540) 651208

### KINGUSSIE • map 18D4

### THE ROYAL HOTEL
High Street, PH21 1HX

*The Royal Hotel is in the centre of Kingussie in the beautiful Spey Valley. An ideal base for all types of outdoor activities, including skiing, and for touring the Highlands. The hotel is family-owned and run, offering good accommodation, good food and a warm welcome.*

DOUBLE ROOM: from £20 to £30
FOOD: up to £15
**Hours:** breakfast 8am-9.30am, lunch 12noon-2pm, dinner 7pm-9.30pm.
**Cuisine:** SCOTTISH - three-course lunches, four-course table d'hôte dinner, à la carte. Traditional Scottish cuisine prepared from fresh local produce.
**Cards:** Visa, Access, Diners, AmEx.
**Other points:** licensed, Sunday lunch, no-smoking area, children welcome, garden, afternoon tea, pets allowed, foreign exchange, residents' lounge, residents' bar, vegetarian meals, parking, disabled access.
**Rooms:** 52 twin rooms. All with TV, bar, telephone, tea/coffee-making facilities.
**Directions:** Kingussie is just off the A9, 40 miles from Pitlochry and Inverness.
MRS JUSTICE ☎(01540) 661898 Fax(01540) 661061

### KINLOCHLEVEN • map 17D3

### MacDONALD HOTEL
Fort William Road, PA40 4QL

*This is a small, new, comfortable hotel, built in a traditional West Highland style, where the resident proprietors and staff pride themselves on a warm welcome and personal service. Good food and accommodation offer value for money.*

DOUBLE ROOM: from £20 to £30
SINGLE ROOM: up to £35
FOOD: from £15 to £20
**Hours:** breakfast 8am-9am, bar meals 12noon-9pm, dinner 7pm-9pm, open bank holidays.
**Cuisine:** SCOTTISH - menu may feature rack of Scottish lamb glazed with honey and rosemary, medallions of local venison with a red wine sauce.
**Cards:** Visa, Access, Eurocard, MasterCard.
**Other points:** licensed, open-air dining, waterside location, cots, fishing, residents' bar, mountain bike hire, hill walking centre.
**Rooms:** 4 double rooms, 5 twin rooms, 1 triple room. All with TV, tea/coffee-making facilities.
**Directions:** going north on A82, take turning at Glencoe village.
PETER & SUSAN MACDONALD ☎(01855) 831539 Fax(01855) 831416

## KYLESKU • map 17A3

### NEWTON LODGE
IV27 4HW
A large, comfortable guest house with all modern amenities, surrounded by an inspiring panorama of mountains and lochs and over-looking a small seal colony. With a warm welcome, friendly service, good home-made food and outstanding accommodation, Newton Lodge is an ideal base for touring the beautiful Scottish countryside.
DOUBLE ROOM: from £20 to £30
SINGLE ROOM: from £25 to £35
FOOD: up to £15
Hours: breakfast 8.30am-9am, dinner 7pm-7.30pm, closed mid-October until April.
Cuisine: BRITISH - fresh fish caught on proprietor's own boat. Fresh seafood.
Cards: Visa, Access.
Other points: parking, pets allowed, residents' lounge, garden, no-smoking area, children catered for (please check for age limits).
Rooms: 4 double rooms, 3 twin rooms. All with TV, radio, alarm, hair dryer, tea/coffee-making facilities.
Directions: 1 mile south of Kylesku Bridge.
ANDREW & MYRA BRAUER ☎(01971) 502070

## LOCHCARRON • map 17C2

### ROCKVILLA HOTEL & RESTAURANT
Main Street, IV54 8YB
Situated in Lochcarron village centre, overlooking the mountains and loch beyond, this hotel provides an excellent centre from which to explore some of the most beautiful and romantic scenery in Scotland. It offers comfortable accommodation and friendly, personal service within a warm, homely atmosphere. Nearby scenic beauty spots abound, including superb views of Skye.
DOUBLE ROOM: from £20 to £30
SINGLE ROOM: from £31 to £40
FOOD: up to £15
Hours: breakfast 8am-9.15am, lunch 12noon-2pm, bar meals 12noon-2pm, dinner 6.30pm-9pm, bar meals 6pm-9pm.
Cuisine: SEAFOOD / ENGLISH - specializes in local freshly caught seafood, venison and the finest steaks. Daily changing à la carte menu, complemented by a comprehensive wine list.
Cards: Visa, Access.
Other points: licensed, Sunday lunch, no-smoking area, children welcome, parking.
Rooms: 4 bedrooms, 3 en suite.
Directions: located in the centre of the village of Lochcarron.
KENNETH & LORNA WHEELAN ☎(01520) 722379

## LOCHINVER • map 17A3

### THE ALBANNACH HOTEL
Badiddarroch, IV27 4LP
Set in mature south-facing walled gardens, this attractive 19th century house has superb sea and mountain views. Personally and informally run by the proprietors, every care is taken over your comfort and the choice and skilful preparation of the very best and freshest Highland produce.
DOUBLE ROOM: from £20 to £30
SINGLE ROOM: from £36 to £46
FOOD: from £20 to £25
Hours: breakfast 8.30am-9.30am, lunch 12.30pm-2pm, dinner 8pm. Open bank holidays.
Cuisine: game and local fish
Cards: Visa, Access.
Other points: children under 5 not admitted, mountain bike hire, parking.
Rooms: 2 double rooms, 2 twin room. All en suite with tea/coffee-making facilities.
Directions: turn right on approach to village, follow signs for Badiddarroch and Highland Stoneware .5 mile.
COLIN CRAIG & LESLEY CROSFIELD ☎(01571) 844407 Fax(01571) 844407

## NAIRN • map 18C4

### RAMLEH HOTEL & FINGAL'S RESTAURANT
Ramleh House, 2 Academy Street, IV12 4RJ
This is a family-run hotel and restaurant offering good food and comfortable accommodation. The restaurant features a new conservatory for that relaxed, friendly atmosphere. Close to the High Street, beach, two golf courses, harbour, and all amenities.
DOUBLE ROOM: from £25 to £35
SINGLE ROOM: up to £35
FOOD: from £15 to £25
Hours: breakfast 8am-9am, lunch 12noon-2pm, dinner 6.30pm-9pm.
Cuisine: EUROPEAN - a wide variety of dishes served, including fish and seafood, poultry and game, meat and also vegetarian meals. Desserts and a cheeseboard also on menu.
Cards: Visa, Access, AmEx.
Other points: licensed, children welcome, garden, residents' lounge, residents' bar.
Rooms: 3 single rooms, 2 double rooms, 4 twin rooms, 1 family room. All with TV, tea/coffee-making facilities, heating. Most rooms are en suite.
Directions: Nairn is on the A96 Aberdeen to Inverness road, 15 miles from Inverness.
GEORGE & CAROL WOODHOUSE ☎(01667) 453551 Fax(01667) 456577

## NETHY BRIDGE • map 18C4

### THE MOUNTVIEW HOTEL & HIGHLAND GAME RESTAURANT
Nethy Bridge, PH25 3EB
The hotel is situated in the beautiful Spey Valley, the centre for many attractions and central for touring the Highlands. Built in 1914 of granite and sandstone, the fully-licensed, small, family-run hotel is set in two and half acres of grounds on the edge

of the Abernethy Forest, overlooking the Cairngorm Mountains. There is a wide selection of home-made dishes from the Highland Game and bar menus (including vegetarian and children's dishes), which can be enjoyed in front of a real log fire. Attractions nearby include golf, fishing, horse-riding, mountain biking, walking, climbing, skiing, summer and winter chair lifts to the top of the Cairngorms, the Osprey Hide at RSPB Reserve Loch Garten, Strathspey Steam Railway, and many more.

DOUBLE ROOM: up to £20
SINGLE ROOM: up to £25
FOOD: up to £15    CLUB

**Hours:** breakfast 8am-9am, dinner 6pm-9pm, weekends during season, or by arrangement.
**Cuisine:** HIGHLAND GAME - à la carte menu in the restaurant and bar menu both include vegetarian and children's dishes.
**Cards:** Visa, Access.
**Other points:** licensed, open-air dining, children welcome, pets allowed, special spring, autumn and winter breaks.
**Rooms:** 7 bedrooms. All with en suite, TV, central heating. Tea/coffee-making facilities. All rooms have panoramic views.
**Directions:** take Aviemore Road off A9. Next village after Boat of Garten.
TRIXIE & STUART PARKINS ☎(01479) 821248

## NEWTONMORE • map 18D4

### BALAVIL SPORT HOTEL
Main Street, PH20 1DL

A family-run hotel situated in the centre of the village, offering a range of sporting amenities, including an indoor swimming pool. Recently renovated, the en suite bedrooms are spacious, airy and comfortable. Parties are welcomed. Good, fresh Scottish food served all day. Golf, bowling, tennis, fishing.

DOUBLE ROOM: from £25 to £35
SINGLE ROOM: from £40 to £50
FOOD: up to £15

**Hours:** breakfast 8am-9.30am, lunch 12noon-2.30pm, dinner 6.30pm-8.30pm, closed 1st January until 14th January.
**Cuisine:** SCOTTISH - home-style cooking using local Scottish produce. Includes Badenoch venison casserole, haggis, delicious pies, salmon and good home-baking.
**Cards:** Visa, Access.
**Other points:** licensed, Sunday lunch, no-smoking area, children welcome, pets allowed, parking, afternoon tea, residents' lounge, swimming pool, central heating, baby-listening device, cots, vegetarian meals, disabled access, residents' bar.
**Rooms:** 50 bedrooms. All with TV, telephone, tea/coffee-making facilities, alarm. Family rooms available, with children's discount.
**Directions:** A9, situated on the main road running through the village.
JIM & HELEN COYLE ☎(01540) 673220
Fax(01540) 673773

### LODGE HOTEL
Laggan Road, PH20 1DG

The Lodge Hotel is an attractive former shooting lodge situated in two acres of open ground surrounded by pine trees. New bedrooms and a functions suite have been skilfully added to the original building. For guests' comfort, there are two tastefully decorated lounge bars. The hotel offers a wide selection of food, from sandwiches to an appetizing à la carte menu.

DOUBLE ROOM: from £20 to £30
FOOD: up to £15

**Hours:** breakfast 8.30am-9.30am, bar meals 12noon-3pm, dinner 6pm-9.30pm, bar meals 5pm-9.30pm.
**Cuisine:** BRITISH - specialities include venison and salmon steaks.
**Cards:** Visa, Access.
**Other points:** parking, children welcome, pets allowed, garden, open-air dining, vegetarian meals, traditional Sunday lunch, afternoon teas.
**Rooms:** 4 double rooms, 30 twin rooms, 1 family room. All with en suite, TV, tea/coffee-making facilities.
**Directions:** turn left into Laggan Road at south end of Newtonmore Main Street. The hotel is 100 yards along on the right.
EILEEN REID ☎(01540) 673256 Fax(01540) 673898

### MAINS HOTEL
Main Street, PH20 1DF

A warm welcome awaits you at the Mains, a family-owned and run hotel, ideally situated in the attractive village of Newtonmore in the heart of the Spey Valley. This former coaching inn offers guests a pleasurable stay in the newly decorated bedrooms, good home-cooked food in the dining room, and polite, friendly service throughout.

DOUBLE ROOM: from £20 to £30
SINGLE ROOM: up to £25
FOOD: up to £15

**Hours:** breakfast 7.30am-9.30am, lunch 12noon-2pm, dinner 7pm-9.30pm, bar meals 12noon-9.30pm.
**Cuisine:** BRITISH - fresh home-cooked meals.
**Cards:** Visa, Access, Diners.
**Other points:** parking, children welcome, pets allowed, garden, residents' lounge, vegetarian meals.
**Rooms:** 2 single rooms, 12 double rooms, 15 twin rooms, 2 family rooms. All with en suite, TV, radio, tea/coffee-making facilities.
**Directions:** .25 mile off A9, at the fork of Main Street and Laggan Road.
MR JUSTICE ☎(01540) 673206

## POOLEWE • map 17B2

 **POOL HOUSE HOTEL**
IV22 2LE

*Across the bay from world famous Inverewe Gardens created by Osgood McKenzie, the hotel is situated in the heart of Wester Ross, at the head of Loch Ewe, and offers an exciting alternative to those seeking a base from which to explore the beauty of the Scottish Highlands. From the pleasant, candlelit restaurant, guests can watch otters, seals and cormorants feeding by day and night. The hotel has a unique, comfortable and friendly atmosphere in astonishingly beautiful surroundings. Renowned for its exceptional local fare.*

DOUBLE ROOM: from £30 to £40
FOOD: up to £15
**Hours:** breakfast 7.45am-9.15am, bar snacks 12noon-9pm, dinner 7pm-9pm.
**Cuisine:** BRITISH
**Cards:** Visa, Access.
**Other points:** licensed.
**Rooms:** 14 rooms, 13 en-suite (including 3 executive bedrooms). All with tea/coffee-making facilities, TV, telephone. Executive bedrooms £5 per person extra.
**Directions:** on main A832, on edge of River Ewe and Loch Ewe.
MR P.L. HARRISON ☎(01445) 781272 Fax(01445) 781403

## ROSEHALL • map 17B3

 **ACHNESS HOTEL**
Sutherland, IV27 4BD

*Formerly a turn-of-the-century farmhouse, the main building of the Achness Hotel is a highly successful conversion into a quadrangle, which allows parking outside the door of your room. Specially popular with holiday-makers and fishermen, the emphasis is on home-made meals, which no doubt is the reason for its popularity at lunchtimes.*

DOUBLE ROOM: from £30 to £40
SINGLE ROOM: form £35 to £45
FOOD: from £20 to £25
**Hours:** breakfast 8.30am, bar meals 12.30am-2pm, dinner 8pm, bar meals 6pm-9pm. Hotel closed Oct - Feb.
**Cuisine:** ENGLISH - fixed-price menu, with an emphasis on home-made soups and sweets.
**Cards:** Visa, Access.
**Other points:** licensed, Sunday lunch, children welcome, pets allowed, afternoon tea, residents' lounge, parking, disabled access.
**Rooms:** 3 single rooms, 2 double rooms, 7 twin rooms. All with tea/coffee-making facilities.
**Directions:** situated off the A837 in Rosehall village. Well signposted.
MR & MRS I. MUNRO ☎(01549) 441239 Fax(01549) 441324

## SCOURIE • map 17A3

 **EDDRACHILLES HOTEL**
Badcall Bay, IV27 4TH

*Eddrachilles Hotel stands in its own 320-acre estate in a magnificent situation at the head of the island-studded Badcall Bay. This is a family-run, comfortable hotel offering good food in friendly, relaxing surroundings. If you are looking for a peaceful, tranquil holiday, this hotel is well worth a visit.*

DOUBLE ROOM: from £30 to £40
SINGLE ROOM: from £45 to £55
FOOD: up to £15
**Hours:** breakfast 8am-9am, dinner 6.30pm-8.30pm.
**Cuisine:** ENGLISH - dishes include salmon pâté, pepper steak, lemon sole meunière, and desserts such as blackberry and apple pie, rhum baba and pear Belle Hélène.
**Cards:** Visa, Access.
**Other points:** licensed, children catered for (please check for age limits).
**Rooms:** 11 bedrooms.
**Directions:** on A894, approximately 6 miles north of Kylesku Bridge.
MR & MRS A.C.M. WOOD ☎(01971) 502080/502211 Fax(01971) 502477

## STRATHPEFFER • map 17C3

 **ACHILTY HOTEL**
Contin, IV14 9EG

*Beautifully restored Highland hotel with much character and spectacular mountain views. Charming bar created from old farm buildings full of unusual and interesting bric-a-brac. Ideal central location within easy travelling distance in all directions of magnificent scenery. Highly regarded restaurant featuring traditional Scottish recipes complete with welcoming, comfortable, relaxing accommodation.*

DOUBLE ROOM: from £20 to £30
SINGLE ROOM: from £20
FOOD: up to £15
**Hours:** breakfast 8am-9am, lunch 12noon-2.30pm, dinner 5.30pm-9.30pm, bar meals 12noon-2.30pm, 5.30pm-9.30pm, open all year.
**Cuisine:** BRITISH - à la carte and table d'hôte menus offering a good choice of traditional Scottish dishes using fresh local produce. Vegetarians also catered for. Bar meals also available.
**Cards:** Visa, Access.
**Other points:** licensed, open-air dining, Sunday lunch, no-smoking area, children welcome, pets allowed, afternoon tea, residents' lounge, parking, disabled access, open bank holidays, cots, fishing, vegetarian meals, residents' bar, bar meals.
**Rooms:** 3 double rooms, 5 twin rooms, 3 triple rooms, 1 quad room. All en suite with TV, tea/coffee-making facilities.
**Directions:** from Inverness, take A9, then A835 Ullapool road.
NEIL & ALISON VAUGHAN ☎(01997) 421355 Fax(01997) 421355

## TAIN • map 18B4

 **MANSFIELD HOUSE HOTEL**
Scotsburn Road, IV19 1PR
*A luxury country hotel in a Scottish Mansion house, retaining many original features such as the extensive pine panelling and ornate plaster ceilings. Offering a warm and friendly service, the hotel is an outstanding base from which to tour the Highlands of Scotland.*
DOUBLE ROOM: from £30 to £40
SINGLE ROOM: from £35 to £45
FOOD: from £15 to £20
**Hours:** breakfast 7am-9am, lunch and bar meals 12noon-2pm, bar meals 5pm-9pm, dinner 7pm-9pm, open bank holidays.
**Cuisine:** predominantly Scottish cuisine, with local seafood a speciality. Dishes may include wild Ross-shire salmon and venison from the Sutherland hills, complemented by a range of desserts, cheeses and coffees.
**Cards:** Visa, Access, AmEx.
**Other points:** chauffer service from airport or Inverness station by arrangement, foreign languages spoken, fully licensed, gardens, parking, conference facilities.
**Rooms:** 1 single room, 9 twin rooms, 2 double rooms, 3 family rooms, all en suite, 3 deluxe rooms. All with TV, radio, hair dryer, trouser press and tea/coffee-making facilities.
**Directions:** take 2nd turning off Tain by-pass towards Tain, then following signs to Tain Royal Academy, which is opposite the hotel.
MR NORMAN LAURITSEN
☎(01862) 892052 Fax(01862) 892260

**MORANGIE HOUSE HOTEL**
Morangie Road, IV19 1PY
*A fine old Victorian mansion with luxurious rooms and stained-glass windows. Professionally managed yet friendly and welcoming, and offering an extensive range of menus to suit all tastes, with food of excellent quality. Reduced-price golf to residents. Tain Museum and 14th century church nearby.*
DOUBLE ROOM: from £30 to £40
SINGLE ROOM: from £45 to £55
FOOD: up to £15
**Hours:** breakfast 7am-10am, lunch 12noon-2.30pm, dinner 7pm-10pm, bar meals 12noon-2.30pm, bar meals 5pm-10pm.
**Cuisine:** SCOTTISH / CONTINENTAL - fresh seafood is the speciality. A la carte, table d'hôte and bar menus.
**Cards:** Visa, Access, Diners, AmEx.
**Other points:** licensed, Sunday lunch, children welcome.
**Rooms:** 4 single rooms, 7 double rooms, 15 twin rooms. All with TV, telephone, tea/coffee-making facilities, hair dryer, trouser-press.
**Directions:** north on A9, take last turn-off into Tain, on right-hand side.
AVRIL & JOHN WYNNE ☎(01862) 892281
Fax(01862) 892872

## THURSO • map 18A4

**THE CASTLE ARMS HOTEL**
Mey, KW14 8XH
*A former 19th century coaching inn, situated on the John o' Groats peninsula in the north coast village of Mey and only a short distance from the Queen Mother's Highland home, the Castle of Mey. In the evenings, relax in front of the Caithness flagstone fireplace and enjoy a wee dram from a choice of fine malt whiskies. A seal colony is just one of the main nearby attractions.*
DOUBLE ROOM: from £20 to £30
SINGLE ROOM: from £30 to £40
FOOD: from £15 to £20
**Hours:** breakfast 8.30am-9.30am, lunch 12.30am-2pm, high tea 5.30pm-7pm, dinner 7pm-9pm, bar meals 5.30pm-9pm, open all year.
**Cuisine:** SCOTTISH - for dinner, a comprehensive table d'hôte menu is available, which includes locally caught fresh salmon, crab and succulent steaks. Extremely fine wine list.
**Cards:** Visa, Access, AmEx.
**Other points:** open-air dining, Sunday lunch, children welcome, pets allowed, parking, afternoon tea, cots, left luggage, residents' lounge, residents' bar.
**Rooms:** 4 double rooms, 3 twin rooms, 1 triple room. All with TV, telephone, tea/coffee-making facilities.
**Directions:** 7 miles west of John o' Groats.
MRS MORRISON ☎(01847) 851244 Fax(01847) 851244

**THE PARK HOTEL**
KW14 8RE
*A modern building, recently refurbished offering a friendly atmosphere which attracts a mixed age group. Good home cooked food. Excellent location for touring the north and as a stopover for the Orkney Islands.*
DOUBLE ROOM: from £20 to £30
SINGLE ROOM: from £20 to £30
FOOD: up to £15
**Hours:** breakfast 7.30am-9.30am, lunch and bar meals 12noon-2pm, dinner and bar meals 5pm-8pm, open bank holidays.
**Cuisine:** local fish and steaks.
**Cards:** Visa, Mastercard
**Other points:** parking.
**Rooms:** 11 twin en suite rooms. All with TV, telephone, hair dryer and tea/coffee-making facilities.
**Directions:** A882, Wick - Thurso road.
MS K HANNA & MS S CAMPBELL ☎(01847) 893251 Fax(01847) 893252

---

### THURSO COLLEGE-MORVEN BUILDING
Ormlie Road, KW14 7EE
*Set within the 1-year-old training college complex, the Flagstone Restaurant offers an excellent choice of well-presented and well-served dishes, attracting both locals and business people of all ages. Clean and comfortable facilities.*
FOOD: up to £15
**Hours:** lunch Wednesday-Friday 12.30pm-2pm (Open October-June excluding school holidays).
**Cuisine:** LOCAL PRODUCE - lamb, fish.
**Cards:** Access, Visa
**Other points:** licensed, parking.
**Directions:** outskirts of Thurso heading west on 874 Halkirk road.
MISS FREW
☎(01847) 896161 Fax(01847) 893872

## TONGUE • map 17A3

### BEN LOYAL HOTEL
Main Street, IV27 4XE
*Situated between Durness and Thurso, this small crofting village enjoys some of Scotland's most spectacular coastal and mountain scenery and wonderful, clean beaches. The warmth of welcome and the genuine friendliness of the staff and proprietors add to its reputation as a mecca for fishermen and hill-walkers and a holiday/touring centre. A true sanctuary from the stresses of urban living.*
DOUBLE ROOM: from £25 to £35
SINGLE ROOM: from £28 to £38
FOOD: from £15 to £20
**Hours:** breakfast 8am-9.15am, bar meals 12noon-2pm & 6pm-8.30pm, dinner 7pm-8pm.
**Cuisine:** SCOTTISH - traditional and modern Scottish cooking using fresh local produce.
**Cards:** Visa, Access.
**Other points:** licensed, no-smoking area, coaches by prior arrangement, vegetarian meals, cots.
**Rooms:** 3 single rooms, 4 double rooms, 5 twin rooms. All with TV, tea/coffee-making facilities.
**Directions:** at the junction of the A836 and A838 on the north Scottish coast.
MEL & PAULINE COOK ☎(01847) 611216
Fax(01847) 611212

## ULLAPOOL • map 17B3

### BRAE GUEST HOUSE
Shore Street, IV26 2UJ
*Situated on the seafront overlooking the harbour and Loch Broom, this a family-run guest house with all modern comforts to make your stay one of relaxed enjoyment. With a homely atmosphere and good, home-cooked meals, this is a good base or stopping-point for holiday-makers.*
DOUBLE ROOM: up to £20
SINGLE ROOM: up to £25
FOOD: up to £15
**Hours:** closed October until May.

**Other points:** parking, residents' lounge.
**Rooms:** 9 double rooms. All with en suite, TV, tea/coffee-making facilities.
**Directions:** A835 from the south; the white-painted Brae is the first corner building as you approach the seafront area.
ROSANNE ROSS ☎(01854) 612421

### THE HARBOUR LIGHTS HOTEL
Garve Road, IV26 2SX
*A family-run hotel and restaurant offering excellent food, a warm welcome and comfortable accommodation. The spacious lounge has a panoramic view of the harbour, Loch Broom and the surrounding hills, and the hotel is only a short walk from the centre of the old fishing port of Ullapool.*
DOUBLE ROOM: from £30 to £40
SINGLE ROOM: from £35 to £45
FOOD: from £15 to £25
**Hours:** breakfast 7.45am-9am, bar meals 12noon-2pm, Sunday lunch 12.30am-2pm, dinner 6.30pm-9pm.
**Cuisine:** BRITISH - specialities include local salmon, seafood, Scotch beef and venison, turf and surf (fillet steak, with fresh scallops, prawn tails and shellfish sauce). Bar meals available from £2 to £10.
**Cards:** Visa, Access, AmEx.
**Other points:** licensed, Sunday lunch, children welcome, garden, afternoon tea, pets allowed, residents' lounge, residents' bar.
**Rooms:** 19 bedrooms. All with TV, tea/coffee-making facilities, telephone, hair dryer.
**Directions:** on the outskirts of Ullapool.
MARILYN & DANNY GORDON ☎(01854) 612222 Fax(01854) 612222

# LOTHIAN

## DALKEITH • map 16E4

### JEWEL & ESK VALLEY COLLEGE
Newbattle Road, EH22 3AE

*A restaurant offering a wide range of outstandingly prepared, professionally served and very varied dishes. Not far from the city of Edinburgh, the restaurant's diverse clientele receives a warm welcome and excellent, efficient service.*
FOOD: from £5 to £15
**Hours:** lunch 12noon-1.45pm, dinner 7pm-9.45pm, closed bank holidays.
**Cuisine:** INTERNATIONAL - à la carte and table d'hôte menus, carvery. Lunches £4.95 for 3 courses £3.75 for 2 courses. Dinner £15-£18 Wednesdays only. Other evenings available by arrangement for minimum parties of 40.
**Cards:** Visa.
**Other points:** parking on site. Children welcome for lunch, over 12 years for dinner.
**Directions:** from the A7 take the B703, the college is near the police station.
MR GORDON HODGSON ☎(0131) 660 1010 ext. 5261 Fax(0131) 663 0271

## EDINBURGH • map 16D4

### ARTHUR'S VIEW HOTEL
10 Mayfield Gardens, EH9 2BZ

*Arthur's View offers genuine Scottish home-cooking and attractively furnished accommodation with many modern facilities. The Royal Mile with its many fascinating tourist attractions is just over a mile away.*
DOUBLE ROOM: from £40 to £50
SINGLE ROOM: from £30 to £45
FOOD: up to £15 CLUB
**Hours:** breakfast 7.30-9am, lunch 12.30pm-2pm, dinner 5.30pm-10pm.
**Cards:** Visa, Access, AmEx, MasterCard, Eurocard
**Other points:** parking.
**Rooms:** 2 single rooms, 4 twin rooms, 3 double rooms, 1 triple room, 2 family rooms all en suite with tea/coffee-making facilities, SkyTV, telephone, alarm, hair dryer, trouser press, baby listening device.
**Directions:** 1.5 miles from city centre south on A7.
ROBERT ALEXANDER BOWERS ☎(0131) 6673468 Fax(0131) 6624232

### BANGALORE TANDOORI
52 Home Street, EH3 9NA

*Situated opposite the King's Theatre, the Bangalore restaurant is ideally placed for before- or after-theatre meals. The cuisine reflects a diverse range of tastes from the Indian peninsula, flavoured with an outstanding choice of herbs and spices using the finest fresh produce. Vegetarian dishes and special 3-course lunches are available.*
FOOD: up to £15
**Hours:** lunch 12noon-2pm, dinner 5.30pm-12.30am, meals all day Friday and Saturday 12noon-1.30am.
**Cuisine:** INDIAN - all dishes are created from the finest fresh produce and freshly ground spices.
**Cards:** Visa, Access, AmEx.
**Other points:** children welcome, no-smoking area, vegetarian meals.
**Directions:** in Tollcross area, opposite King's Theatre.
MR M.R. KHAN ☎(0131) 229 1348

### FISHERS BISTRO
1 The Shore, Leith, EH6 6QW

*A popular haunt of local business people, as well as holiday-makers this smart, friendly bistro has a distinctly Continental atmosphere, serves imaginative, well-presented Scottish and French dishes and has a good range of wines. Leith Harbour and the Heritage Room are nearby.*
FOOD: from £15 to £20
**Hours:** lunch and bar meals 12noon-6pm, dinner and bar meals 6pm-10.30pm, open bank holidays, closed Christmas day and New Year's day.
**Cuisine:** SCOTTISH / FRENCH - fish, seafood.
**Cards:** Access, Visa, AmEx, Diners, Switch
**Other points:** parking.
**Directions:** in the old signal tower at the end of the shore in Leith.
MESSRS GRAEME LUMSDEN AND JAKE MILLAR ☎(0131) 5545666

### GREENSIDE HOTEL
9 Royal Terrace, EH7 5AB

*An attractive Georgian house hotel of a very high standard, decorated throughout in a tasteful classical style with spacious, comfortable accommodation. Delicious home-cooked evening meals are available to guests on request. Edinburgh Castle, Royal Mile, Carlton Hill and Princes Street are all within close proximity.*
DOUBLE ROOM: from £20 to £30
SINGLE ROOM: from £25 to £35
**Hours:** breakfast 8am-9am.
**Other points:** children welcome, residents' lounge, garden.
**Rooms:** 3 single rooms, 3 double rooms, 4 twin rooms, 4 family rooms. All with en suite, TV, radio, alarm, hair dryer, tea/coffee-making facilities.
**Directions:** turn left from Princes Street into Leith Street, pass Playhouse Theatre and turn right.
JIM HOUSTON ☎(0131) 557 0022/557 0121 Fax(0131) 557 0022

## THE HOWARD

32-36 Great King Street, EH3 6QH

*The Howard is situated in the centre of Edinburgh's Georgian New Town and comprises three listed terrace houses, skilfully joined together resulting in a unique hotel providing accommodation of exemplary quality, rich colour schemes and bold fabrics. This coupled with discreet and professional service, make The Howard the place to visit.*

DOUBLE ROOM: over £50

SINGLE ROOM: over £50

FOOD: from £20 to £30

**Hours:** breakfast 7.30am-10am, dinner 7.30pm-9.30pm.

**Cuisine:** MODERN ENGLISH / SCOTTISH

**Cards:** Visa, Access, Diners, AmEx.

**Other points:** parking, drawing room, conference and banqueting facilities.

**Rooms:** 16 bedrooms. All en suite, individually decorated and with every home comfort.

**Directions:** proceed from Princes Street down Hanover Street then Dundas Street, take the fifth turning on the right.

JONATHAN PHILLIPS ☎(0131) 557 3500 Fax (0131) 557 6515

## LANCERS BRASSERIE

5 Hamilton Place, EH3 5BA

*Lancers Brasserie has a good selection of French and Indian dishes at reasonable prices. Their warm welcome and helpful, efficient staff will make eating here a pleasurable experience.*

FOOD: from £15 to £20

**Hours:** lunch 12noon-2.30pm, dinner 5.30pm-11.30pm.

**Cuisine:** INDIAN - Bengali and North Indian dishes, kurji lamb (48 hours' notice), vegetarian thali, Lancers assorted Tandoori, selection of French dishes.

**Cards:** Visa, Access, AmEx.

**Other points:** lunch, children catered for (please check for age limits).

**Directions:** in Stockbridge area of the city.

WALI UDDIN ☎(0131) 332 3444/332 9559

## THE MAGNUM RESTAURANT & BAR

1 Albany Street, EH1 3PY

*Situated in Edinburgh'sNew Town, this is a popular retreat for local business people and visitors who can enjoy traditional fare at reasonable prices. The excellent dinner menu offers Scottish and International cuisine, complemented by a diverse luncheon menu. As well as a comprehensive wine list, the bar selection includes some 60 malt whiskies and a range of cask ales.*

FOOD: from £15 to £20

**Hours:** lunch 12noon-2.30pm, dinner 6.30pm-9.30pm, open bank holidays.

**Cuisine:** varied menus offering such dishes as fresh Scotch salmon, chicken sauté d'Anjou, steaks and the hotel's own No.1 Albany pie.

**Cards:** Access,Visa,AmEx,Diners,Mastercard,Switch

**Other points:** licensed bar open 10am-11pm, vegetarian meals, morning coffees, parties catered for.

**Directions:** on the corner of Albany Street and Dublin Street, just down from St Andrew Square and close to the city centre and Edinburgh Playhouse.

RICHARD FOX ☎(0131) 557 4366

## THE MAITLAND TOWN HOUSE HOTEL

33 Shandwick Place, EH2 4RG

*The hotel is ideally situated for the city's financial district, the new international conference centre and a multitude of diverse restaurants. For sports enthusiasts golf, fishing, riding, skiing and water sports are available by arrangement. Quality, value for money and a personal, friendly service are a priority.*

DOUBLE ROOM: from £35 to £60

SINGLE ROOM: from £55 to £65

**Hours:** breakfast only Monday-Friday 7am-9.30am, breakfast only Saturday-Sunday 8am-10am, open bank holidays.

**Cards:** Access, Visa, Diners, AmEx, Switch.

**Other points:** secretarial, fax, photocopying and PC facilities provided on request, meeting and function rooms, licensed.

**Rooms:** 14 single rooms, 17 double rooms, 39 twin rooms, 2 family rooms, all en suite, 16 double en suite executive rooms (own fax). All with TV, radio, alarm, trouser press, hair dryer and tea/coffee-making facilities, modem/fax point.

**Directions:** located in Edinburgh's west end, at the end of Princes Street.

SHANDWICK LEISURE LTD - P. ROBERTS ☎(0131) 229 1467 Fax (0131) 229 7549

## MEADOWS GUEST HOUSE

17 Glengyle Terrace, EH3 9LN

*An attractive, comfortable guest house centrally located in a residential area and within walking distance of the Castle, the Royal Mile, overlooking Park, E.I.C.C, Edinburgh University and the Royal Infirmary. Rooms are spacious, tastefully decorated and well-equipped with many modern facilities.*

DOUBLE ROOM: from £20 to £30

SINGLE ROOM: from £20 to £30

**Cards:** Visa, Access, AmEx, MasterCard.

**Other points:** pets allowed, residents' lounge, central heating, ironing facilities, electric blankets, useful visitor information, restricted car parking.

**Rooms:** 1 single room, 3 double/single rooms, 2 double/twin rooms. All with TV, radio, hair dryer, tea/coffee-making facilities.

**Directions:** Off A702, south of Princes Street, near the King's Theatre.

JON STUART ☎(0131) 229 9559 Fax (0131) 229 2226

## THE OLD BORDEAUX

47 Old Burdiehouse Road, EH17 8BJ

*The principles of good food and friendly, efficient service in comfortable surroundings can be found at* this pub on Edinburgh's southern boundary. Transformed from an original abode of exiled French silk weavers into today's warm, welcoming old-world inn, The Old Bordeaux is well worth a visit for its good food and service and very good value for money.

FOOD: up to £15 🍴

**Hours:** bar meals 10am-10pm, closed Christmas day and New Year's day.

**Cuisine:** SCOTTISH - an extensive choice of dishes such as fresh mussels, roast beef, steak pie. Daily specials include game, sea bass, salmon, salads and vegetarian meals.

**Cards:** Visa, Access, Diners, AmEx.

**Other points:** licensed, Sunday lunch, children welcome.

**Directions:** A701. Five miles south of city centre, adjacent to A720 city bypass.

LINDA & ALAN THOMSON & ADRIAN DEMPSEY ☎(0131) 664 1734 Fax (0131) 226 5936

## OSBOURNE HOTEL & SHELBOURNE LOUNGE
53-59 York Place, EH1 3JD

A city-centre hotel, ideally located near the main coach and rail stations and only a short walk from the castle, Palace, Royal Mile, Princes Street shops and gardens. The dining room offers meals to residents and groups. Visitors receive a warm welcome, and the service is polite and friendly.

DOUBLE ROOM: from £30 to £45
SINGLE ROOM: from £35 to £50
FOOD: up to £15

**Hours:** lunch 12noon-2pm, dinner 5.30pm-9pm.

**Cuisine:** CONTINENTAL - traditional pub meals.

**Cards:** Visa, Access, Diners, AmEx.

**Other points:** licensed, children welcome, pets by prior arrangement, residents' lounge, residents' bar.

**Rooms:** 13 single rooms, 12 double rooms, 12 twin rooms, 3 family rooms. All with en suite, TV, telephone, tea/coffee-making facilities.

**Directions:** in Edinburgh city centre. Follow Queen Street East onto York Place.

FEROZ WADIA ☎(0131) 556 5577 / 556 2345 Fax (0131) 556 1012

## ROYAL CIRCUS HOTEL
19-21 Royal Circus, EH3 6TL

This traditionally furnished listed building close to the city centre in a select area offers many modern facilities. At the rear is a garden, which provides for alfresco dining and drinking. Other facilities include a bistro restaurant, comfortable lounge bar and small function room. Within easy walking distance are the Castle, Royal Mile, Holyrood Palace and Botanical Gardens.

DOUBLE ROOM: from £30 to £50
SINGLE ROOM: from £25 to £40
FOOD: up to £15 CLUB

**Hours:** breakfast 7.30am-9.30am, bar lunches 12noon-2pm, bar suppers 5.30pm-9pm, dinner 5.30pm-9pm.

**Cuisine:** CONTINENTAL

**Cards:** Visa, Access, Diners, AmEx.

**Other points:** licensed.

**Rooms:** 29 bedrooms.

**Directions:** from Princes Street head down Fredrick Street and Howe Street to Royal Circus.

MR FEROZ WADIA ☎(0131) 220 5000 Fax (0131) 220 2020

## SALISBURY VIEW HOTEL
64 Dalkeith Road, EH16 5AE

A spacious, family-run Georgian hotel situated approximately 5 minutes from the city centre, its fine shopping, the Princes Street gardens and Edinburgh Castle. The hotel overlooks Holyrood Park and the Royal Commonwealth Swimming Pool. There are eight well-appointed en suite bedrooms to ensure a comfortable stay and a large private car park with security night lights for peace of mind.

DOUBLE ROOM: from £20 to £30
SINGLE ROOM: from £27 to £37
FOOD: up to £15

**Hours:** breakfast 8am-9.30am, dinner 6.30pm.

**Cuisine:** BRITISH - special diets can be catered for if notice is given.

**Cards:** Visa, Access, Diners.

**Other points:** parking, no-smoking area, residents' lounge, pets allowed, children welcome, vegetarian meals.

**Rooms:** 2 single rooms, 3 double rooms, 2 twin rooms, 1 family room. All with tea/coffee-making facilities, TV, telephone, radio.

**Directions:** located on the A7/A68, five minutes from the city centre.

KENNETH MEARCHENT ☎(0131) 667 1133 Fax (0131) 6671133

## THE TATTLER
23 Commercial Street, Leith, EH6 6JA

This 1992 winner of Les Routiers Pub of the Year and 1995 Casserole Award winner is a traditional pub and restaurant, originally four derelict shops in the heart of the historic port of Leith. Tastefully decorated in Victorian/Edwardian style, The Tattler re-creates the glory of that era and offers a taste of Scotland to tourists, businessmen and locals alike.

FOOD: from £10 to £20 🍴

**Hours:** meals all day Saturday and Sunday, lunch 12noon-2pm, dinner 6pm-10pm, bar meals 12noon-2pm, 6pm-10pm, closed Christmas day and New Year's day.

**Cuisine:** SCOTTISH - seafood, vegetarian dishes, Border lamb, steaks, roast duckling, game, roasts.

**Cards:** Visa, Access, Diners, AmEx.

**Other points:** licensed, Sunday lunch, children welcome.

**Directions:** across from the Leith shore, opposite the historic Customs House.

LINDA & ALAN THOMSON & ADRIAN DEMPSEY ☎(0131) 554 9999 Fax (0131) 226 5936

### TERRACE HOTEL
37 Royal Terrace, EH7 5AH

*This listed Georgian hotel is beautifully decorated in the style of the era. The bedrooms are large and gracious, with high ceilings and cornices. Fireplaces adorn both the bedrooms and dining room. As this hotel is centrally situated with easy access to most of Edinburgh's attractions, it is well worth a visit, with its panoramic views of the Firth of Forth.*

DOUBLE ROOM: from £20.50 to £33
SINGLE ROOM: from £23 to £34
FOOD: breakfast only
Hours: breakfast 8am-9am.
Cuisine: BREAKFAST - Scottish breakfast: choice of juices and cereals; eggs cooked to your specifications; oatcakes, porridge, kippers, toast, tea or coffee.
Cards: Visa, Access.
Other points: open bank holidays, residents' lounge, street parking, garden.
Rooms: 14 bedrooms. All with TV, tea/coffee-making facilities.
Directions: .5 mile north-east of Princes Street. Near London Road.
ANNE & MICHAEL MANN ☎(0131) 556 3423
Fax(0131) 556 2520

### TEX MEX
47 Hanover Street, EH2 2PJ

*Authentic mix of 'Cross Border' Mexican and Texan dishes, all prepared on the premises using only fresh ingredients of the highest quality. The restaurant and bar are decorated with bright colours, and subtle lighting giving the feeling of being in sunnier climes. Situated just off Princes Street, there is a constant flow of people, and the restaurant tends to get very full in the evenings. Booking is essential on Friday and Saturday nights, and advisable on other evenings.*

FOOD: up to £15    CLUB
Hours: meals all day 12noon-12midnight, closed Christmas and New Year's day.
Cuisine: MEXICAN / AMERICAN - e.g., nachos, flautas, carnitas, tortillas, burgers, home-made desserts and a wide selection of vegetarian meals. House speciality: flaming fajitas.
Cards: Visa, AmEx, MasterCard, Switch, Delta.
Other points: Sunday lunch, children welcome.
Directions: situated just off Princes Street, opposite The Mound.
DONALD & SARAH MAVOR ☎(0131) 225 1796
Fax(0131) 556 0009

### THE TOWN HOUSE
65 Gilmore Place, EH3 9NU

*Within 1 mile of the bustling city centre the house is a three storey terraced town house built in 1876 as the manse for the neighbouring church. Now modernised but tastefully decorated to retain the atmosphere of a 19th century building whilst providing comfortable accommodation. The house has parking facilities to the rear.*

DOUBLE ROOM: from £22 to £30

SINGLE ROOM: from £22 to £30
Hours: breakfast 8am-9am, open all year.
Cuisine: SCOTTISH / CONTINENTAL
Other points: central heating, no evening meal, children catered for (please check for age limits), baby-sitting, left luggage, private parking.
Rooms: 1 single room, 1 double room, 1 twin room, 1 triple room. All en suite with TV, tea/coffee-making facilities, hair dryer.
Directions: take A702 towards city centre, turn left at the King's Theatre.
MRS SUSAN VIRTUE ☎(0131) 229 1985

### VERANDAH TANDOORI RESTAURANT
17 Dalry Road, EH11 2BQ

*Winner of the Casserole Award in 1988, 1989, 1990, 1991, 1992, 1993, 1994 and 1995. The Verandah Restaurant is one of Edinburgh's most popular eating establishments, offering authentic Bangladeshi dishes. The light wicker chairs and the matching timber blinds further enhance the restaurant's already relaxed atmosphere.*

FOOD: from £15 to £20   CLUB
Hours: lunch 12noon-2.15pm, dinner 5pm-11.45pm.
Cuisine: BANGLADESHI / NORTHERN INDIAN - lamb pasanda, chicken tikka massalla, Tandoori mixed.
Cards: Visa, Access, Diners, AmEx.
Other points: Sunday lunch, children welcome.
Directions: close to Haymarket station in Edinburgh.
WALI TASAR UDDIN MBE ☎(0131) 337 5828
Fax(0131) 313 3853

## GULLANE • map 16D5

### QUEENS HOTEL
Main Street, EH31 2AS

*A family-run hotel situated in the picturesque village of Gullane. This is a welcoming and pleasant hotel with a good reputation, high standards, a relaxed atmosphere and friendly service. Golf and other packages are available.*

DOUBLE ROOM: from £30 to £40
SINGLE ROOM: from £25 to £35
FOOD: up to £15    CLUB
Hours: breakfast 7am-9am, bar meals 12noon-10pm, dinner 7pm-10pm.
Cuisine: BRITISH - dinner menu may feature beef Wellington, baked halibut, steak caprice, chicken and mushroom crepe au gratin. Bar meals available all day.
Cards: Visa, Access, Diners, AmEx.
Other points: licensed, open-air dining, Sunday lunch, children welcome, afternoon tea, residents' lounge, garden.
Rooms: 35 bedrooms. All with TV, radio, alarm, telephone, tea/coffee-making facilities.
Directions: off A1. A6137 Haddington to Aberlady, A198 to Gullane.
ANN ROBERTSON ☎(01620) 842275 Fax(01620) 842970

## LEADBURN • map 16E4

 **THE LEADBURN INN**
By Penicuik, EH46 7BE

*A country-style inn, the aptly named Carriage Restaurant is a luxurious converted railway carriage that re-creates the glory of the early trains. Only 25 minutes' drive from the centre of Edinburgh, the hotel is popular with business people, tourists and locals alike and was a winner of a Les Routiers Casserole Award in 1991.*
DOUBLE ROOM: from £25
SINGLE ROOM: from £30
FOOD: up to £15 🍽
**Hours:** breakfast by arrangement, dinner 6pm-10pm, bar meals 12noon-10pm, closed Christmas day and New Year's day.
**Cuisine:** SCOTTISH - local game and seafood are the specialities. Good value for money; extensive menu.
**Cards:** Visa, Access, Diners, AmEx.
**Other points:** licensed, Sunday lunch, open all day, children welcome, pets by prior arrangement, conservatory, residents' bar, vegetarian meals, disabled access.
**Rooms:** 2 double rooms, 2 twin rooms, 2 family rooms.
**Directions:** from Edinburgh, take the A701 to Penicuik. Continue to Leadburn.
LINDA & ALAN THOMSON & ADRIAN DEMPSEY
☎(01968) 672952

## LINLITHGOW • map 16D4

🍴 **LIVINGSTON'S RESTAURANT**
52 High Street, EH49 7AE

*This small but impressive restaurant serves oustanding meals with a highly professional, friendly service. The varied menu is accompanied by a very good cheese board and wine list, incorporating new world wines.*
FOOD: from £15 to £20
**Hours:** lunch 12noon-2.30pm, dinner 6.30pm-9.30pm, open bank holidays, closed January, closed Sundays and Mondays.
**Cuisine:** Scottish cuisine with a French flavour, with pan-fried black pudding a speciality, complimented by dishes including guinea fowl, venison and Scottish salmon.
**Cards:** Visa, Access, Mastercard, Eurocard.
**Other points:** children catered for (please check for age limits).
**Directions:** situated on Linlithgow High Street, opposite the Post Office.
☎(01506) 846565

## ROSLIN • map 16E4

 **OLD ORIGINAL ROSSLYN INN**
EH25 9LE

*This historic inn was first opened in 1827 and has remained open for business ever since. The village is in a rural area, and the inn's old-fashioned decor gives it a charming atmosphere.*
DOUBLE ROOM: up to £20
FOOD: from £15 to £20 🍽 CLUB
**Hours:** breakfast 7.30am-9.30am, lunch 12noon-2pm, dinner 6pm-10pm, Saturday and Sunday 12noon-10pm.
**Cuisine:** BRITISH - grills, daily specials such as salmon vol au vents, grilled spring lamb, walnut sundae.
**Cards:** Visa, Access, Diners, AmEx.
**Other points:** open-air dining, Sunday lunch, children welcome, coaches by prior arrangement
**Directions:** just off A701, just outside Edinburgh.
MR G.A. HARRIS ☎(0131) 440 2384

---

# For travel to France use Les Routiers Guide to France - only £7.25. Tel 0500 700 456 for your copy

---

# ORKNEY & SHETLAND ISLANDS

## KIRKWALL • map 18B6

 **ALBERT HOTEL**
Mounthoolie Lane, KW15 1JZ
*A comfortable, family-run hotel in the centre of Kirkwall. Recently refurbished, the Albert Hotel is noted for its good food made from fresh local produce. An ideal place to stay when exploring these unique islands.*
DOUBLE ROOM: from £30 to £40
SINGLE ROOM: from £40 to £50
FOOD: from £15 to £20 CLUB
**Hours:** breakfast 7.30am-9.30am, lunch 12noon-2pm, dinner 7pm-10pm, bar meals 12noon-2pm, 6pm-10pm, closed Christmas day and New Year's day.
**Cuisine:** ENGLISH / SEAFOOD - à la carte restaurant meals and bar meals made from fresh local produce. House speciality is the seafood platter and stables steak.
**Cards:** Visa, Access, AmEx, Switch, MasterCard.
**Other points:** licensed, Sunday lunch, children welcome.
**Rooms:** 9 single, 5 double, 3 twin, 2 family rooms. All with TV, telephone, tea/coffee-making facilities.
**Directions:** in centre of Kirkwall, off Junction Road. Close to harbour.
MR & MRS A. CASEY ☎(01856) 876000
Fax(01856) 875397

 **KIRKWALL HOTEL**
KW15 1LS
*Orkney's largest hotel has, in its time, played host to a number of the crown heads of Europe. This fine historic hotel, overlooking the seafront and harbour, is justifiably popular with business and tourist clientele from around the world. The completely refurbished lounge and restaurant are ideal for relaxing or enjoying the exquisite Orkney cuisine. The Kirkwall Hotel is the perfect location for those who want to `get away from it all', to discover the delights that Orkney has to offer.*
DOUBLE ROOM: from £30 to £40
SINGLE ROOM: from £45
FOOD: from £15 to £20
**Hours:** breakfast 7am-9.30am, lunch 12noon-2.30pm, dinner 6.30pm-9pm.
**Cuisine:** BRITISH - Orkney cuisine including fresh local lobster, oysters, scallops and crab. Orkney steaks.
**Other points:** children welcome, pets allowed, vegetarian meals, satellite TV, residents' bar, residents' lounge.
**Rooms:** 44 bedrooms. All with TV, telephone, tea/coffee-making facilities.
**Directions:** situated on the main town harbour.
MRS E. PIRIE ☎(01856) 872232 Fax(01856) 872812

 **LYNNFIELD HOTEL**
Holm Road, KW15 1RX
*An former distillery-owner's house, now tastefully converted into a country hotel offering comfortable accommodation and fresh local produce in a relaxed, friendly atmosphere with panoramic views over the surrounding countryside and islands. Nearby attractions include the historic burgh of Kirkwall, Stone Age village of Skara Brae and many other archeological sites.*
DOUBLE ROOM: from £30 to £40
SINGLE ROOM: from £25 to £35
FOOD: from £15 to £20
**Hours:** breakfast 7.15am-9.45am, lunch 12noon-2pm, dinner 6pm-9.30pm, open bank holidays.
**Cuisine:** house specialities of local beef and fish.
**Cards:** Visa, Access.
**Other points:** licensed, parking.
**Rooms:** 1 double room, 4 twin rooms, 3 family rooms (including 2 with four-poster beds). All en suite with TV, radio, telephone, tea/coffee making facilities.
**Directions:** one mile from Kirkwall Harbour, near the Highland Park Distillery.
MR GEORGE CUCME
☎(01856) 572505

## STROMNESS • map 18B6

**STROMNESS HOTEL**
Victoria Street, KW16 3AA
*A comfortable hotel situated in the heart of the unique fishing port of Stromness, which is also the main ferry terminal between the mainland and Orkney. The hotel overlooks the harbour and Scapa Flow, which served as the British naval base for both World Wars. All bedrooms have modern facilities, and bar lunches are served daily in the lounge bar, which enjoys panoramic views.*
DOUBLE ROOM: from £20 to £30
SINGLE ROOM: from £25 to £35
FOOD: from £15 to £20
**Hours:** bar snacks 12noon-2pm, 6.30pm-9.30pm, breakfast 7.15am-9.30am, dinner 7pm-9pm.
**Cuisine:** INTERNATIONAL
**Cards:** Visa, Access.
**Other points:** parking, children welcome, open bank holidays, pets allowed, vegetarian meals, garden.
**Rooms:** 6 single rooms, 11 double rooms, 22 twin rooms.
**Directions:** the Stromness is situated at the main pier in Stromness, on the harbour.
☎(01856) 850298 Fax(01856) 850610

# STRATHCLYDE

## ARROCHAR • map 15D2

### GREENBANK GUEST HOUSE & LICENSED RESTAURANT
G83 7AL

A small, family-run guest house and restaurant on the loch side. There is a good choice of meals available throughout the day, and the restaurant is licensed, with a selection of wines, beers and spirits. An excellent base for fishing, climbing, boating and touring. A friendly, relaxed atmosphere prevails, with fine food and accommodation at good value.

DOUBLE ROOM: up to £20
SINGLE ROOM: up to £25
FOOD: up to £15
**Hours:** meals all day 8am-9.30pm.
**Cuisine:** SCOTTISH - meals available all day. Dishes may include salmon steak, fresh-baked steak-and-kidney pie, fried Loch Fyne herring in oatmeal, curries, vegetarian dishes.
**Other points:** licensed, Sunday lunch, children welcome, pets allowed, garden, disabled access.
**Rooms:** 1 single room, 2 double rooms, 1 family room.
**Directions:** on the A83, opposite the famous Cobbler Mountain.
MR & MRS R. CLUER ☎(01301) 702305

## AYR • map 14B5

### FOUTERS BISTRO
2A Academy Street, KA7 1HS

Authentic cellar restaurant serving interesting French and British dishes using the best of local produce. Fouters Bistro is renowned for the high quality of its cuisine, steak and seafood specialities. Personally run by the proprietors. On-street parking opposite Town Hall. Holder of Les Routiers' Casserole Award 1990-1995.

FOOD: from £15 to £20
**Hours:** lunch 12noon-2pm, dinner 6.30pm-10.30pm, Sunday 7pm-10pm, closed 4 days over Christmas and 4 days over New Year.
**Cuisine:** SCOTTISH / FRENCH - fine Scottish produce cooked in the French style. Vegetarians welcomed and special diets catered for.
**Cards:** Visa, Access, Diners, AmEx.
**Other points:** children welcome.
**Directions:** opposite Town Hall, in a cobbled stone lane.
FRAN & LAURIE BLACK ☎(01292) 261391

### THE KYLESTROME HOTEL
11 Miller Road, KA7 2AX

A large stone house in Ayr, which is in the heart of Burns Country. The seafront, railway station and town centre are a short walk away, and Prestwick Airport a few minutes' drive. The stylish restaurant provides a unique atmosphere in which to enjoy fine international cuisine.

DOUBLE ROOM: from £40 to £50
SINGLE ROOM: from £40 to £50
FOOD: from £10 to £20
**Hours:** breakfast 7.30am-9.30am, lunch 12noon-2pm, bar meals 12noon-2pm, high tea 5.30pm-7pm, dinner 7pm-10pm, bar meals 5.30pm-10pm.
**Cuisine:** SCOTTISH / SEAFOOD - fresh seafood, local produce. In the bar: lamb cutlets with minted pear. In the restaurant: steak, seafood (à la carte).
**Cards:** Visa, Access, Diners, AmEx.
**Other points:** licensed, Sunday lunch, no-smoking area, children welcome, conferences.
**Rooms:** 1 single room, 7 double rooms, 12 twin rooms.
**Directions:** on a main street in Ayr, near the railway station.
☎(01292) 262474 Fax (01292) 260863

### TUDOR RESTAURANT
6-8 Beresford Terrace, KA7 2EG

Now in its 30th year of operation, the reasonably-priced lunch, high tea menus and friendly staff make the Tudor a favourite with family parties. Children may choose from their own menus.

FOOD: up to £15
**Hours:** meals all day 9am-8pm, closed Sunday except July and August.
**Cuisine:** SCOTTISH - typical lunch £4.50 & dinner £6.00 traditional Scottish high teas served with cakes and scones from own bakery.
**Other points:** no-smoking area, children welcome.
**Directions:** opposite Burn's Statue Square, off the A70 in the centre of Ayr.
KENNETH ANCELL ☎(01292) 261404

## DALMALLY • map 15C2

### GLENORCHY LODGE HOTEL
Near Oban, PA33 1AA

A small, family-run hotel in the village of Dalmally, offering warm, comfortable accommodation. Informal, lively bar and good bar meals served in generous portions. Ideal base for touring the area.
DOUBLE ROOM: from £20 to £30
FOOD: up to £15
**Hours:** breakfast 7am-9am, lunch 11am-2.30pm, dinner 5pm-9pm, closed Christmas day and New

Year's day.
**Cuisine:** SCOTTISH - traditional cuisine using fresh Scottish produce such as Highland venison in a red wine sauce, local salmon, Awe trout, steaks.
**Cards:** Visa, Access, Diners, AmEx.
**Other points:** licensed, children welcome, afternoon tea, pets allowed, residents' lounge.
**Rooms:** 1 double room, 2 triple rooms, 2 family rooms. All with TV, telephone, tea/coffee-making facilities.
**Directions:** A82 from Glasgow, A85 from Tyndrum. 16 miles Inverary, 25 miles Oban.
HECTOR & PATRICIA WHYTE ☎(01838) 200312

## DUNOON • map 15D2

### THE ARDTULLY HOTEL
297 Marine Parade, Hunter's Quay, PA23 8HN

*A family-run licensed hotel, set in its own grounds, in an elevated position affording outstanding views of the Clyde estuary and surrounding hills. The tastefully decorated rooms are well-appointed, and the high standard of friendly, polite service makes your stay unbeatable value for money.*
DOUBLE ROOM: from £20 to £30
SINGLE ROOM: from £25 to £35
FOOD: up to £15
**Hours:** breakast 8am-9am, dinner 6pm-7pm.
**Cuisine:** BRITISH / INTERNATIONAL - the

restaurant enjoys an excellent reputation and has been justifiably nominated for a `Taste of Scotland' award.
**Other points:** children catered for (please check age limits), pets allowed, parking, no-smoking area, residents' lounge.
**Rooms:** 5 double rooms, 3 twin rooms, 2 family rooms. All with TV, tea/coffee-making facilities, room-service.
**Directions:** turn right after leaving the Western Ferries terminal. The Ardtully can be found 200 yards away on the Dunoon Seafront.
JAMES & JAN THOMAS ☎(01369) 702478

### ARGYLL HOTEL
Argyll Street, PA23 7NE

*A family-run hotel centrally situated overlooking Argyll Gardens and Dunoon Pier, also with splendid views over the Firth of Clyde. The hotel offers comfortable accommodation where you can relax in a warm and friendly atmosphere and enjoy traditional fare.*
DOUBLE ROOM: from £30 to £40
SINGLE ROOM: from £30 to £40
FOOD: from £20 to £25
**Hours:** meals all day (open to non-residents) 9.30am-9pm.
**Cuisine:** BRITISH
**Cards:** Visa, Access, Switch.
**Other points:** children welcome, residents' lounge,

# ROYAL MARINE HOTEL

### And Garden Restaurant
**Marine Parade, Hunter's Quay, Dunoon, Argyll PA23 8HJ**
**Telephone: (01369) 705810  Fax: (01369) 702329**

vegetarian meals.
**Rooms:** 30 bedrooms. All with TV, radio, telephone, alarm, tea/coffee-making faiclities.
**Directions:** prominently situated in Dunoon town centre.
MR & MRS FLET¹ HER ☎(01369) 70259
Fax (01369) 704483

### ROYAL MARINE HOTEL
Marine Parade, Hunter's Quay, PA23 8HJ
*A family-run country-style mansion with restaurant situated on the sea front, offering well-presented, good food, making special use of Scottish produce, especially local fresh seafood. Friendly, attentive service and comfortable accommodation. Easy access from Glasgow when using Western Ferries, as you will disembark immediately opposite the Royal Marine Hotel.*
DOUBLE ROOM: from £20 to £30
SINGLE ROOM: from £25 to £35
FOOD: up to £15      CLUB
**Hours:** breakfast 8am-9.30am, bar meals 12noon-8.30pm, dinner 7pm-8.30pm.
**Cuisine:** BRITISH / CONTINENTAL - roast haunch of venison, haddock auld reekie, venison in red wine sauce, fillet of plaice Valkyrie, baked salmon royale.
**Cards:** Visa, Access, Switch.
**Other points:** garden, residents' lounge, games room, afternoon tea, children welcome, baby-listening device, cots, foreign exchange, residents' bar, entertainment, dinner/dances.
**Rooms:** 9 single rooms, 14 double rooms, 10 twin rooms, 2 family rooms. All with en suite, TV, telephone, tea/coffee-making facilities, radio.
**Directions:** off A815 to Dunoon. On seafront, opposite Western Ferries terminal.
MR ARNOLD & MR GREIG ☎(01369) 705810
Fax (01369) 702329

## EASDALE • map 15C1

### INSHAIG PARK HOTEL (FORMERLY THE EASDALE)
By Oban, PA34 4RF
*A fine Victorian house standing in its own grounds overlooking the sea and the islands, with truly wonderful views. This is a small, family-run, comfortable hotel in an idyllic location, with good food served by friendly, helpful staff.*
DOUBLE ROOM: from £20 to £30
SINGLE ROOM: from £25 to £35
FOOD: up to £15
**Hours:** breakfast 8.30am-9.15am, dinner 7.30pm-8.30pm.
**Cuisine:** ENGLISH
**Other points:** licensed, children welcome, garden, pets allowed.
**Rooms:** 3 double rooms, 3 twin rooms. All with TV, tea/coffee-making facilities.
**Directions:** 16 miles south of Oban on Seil Island.
B. & S. FLETCHER & G. & C. DALE ☎(01852) 300256

## GLASGOW • map 15E3

### EWINGTON HOTEL
132 Queen's Drive, G42 8QW
*Ideally situated overlooking Queen's Park in a Victorian crescent, this historic, listed terraced hotel offers accommodation of a high standard complemented by good food and an excellent wine list. For business people and tourists `the Ewington' is a friendly hotel to stay in. Golfing parties catered for. Convenient for Burrell Gallery.*
DOUBLE ROOM: from £40 to £60
SINGLE ROOM: over £70
FOOD: up to £15 ☜ ☲
**Hours:** breakfast 7am-9.30am, lunch 12.30pm, last orders 2pm, dinner from 6pm, last orders 9pm.
**Cuisine:** INTERNATIONAL / SCOTTISH - all prepared on premises from fresh produce daily, including vegetarian dishes. Excellent wine list.
**Cards:** Visa, Access, Diners, AmEx, Switch.
**Other points:** licensed, children welcome, pets allowed, afternoon tea, open all year, conferences, room service, baby-listening device, trouser press, hairdryers, residents' lounge, residents' bar, parking, vegetarian meals.
**Rooms:** 12 single rooms, 8 double rooms, 21 twin room, 1 triple room. All with TV, radio, alarm, telephone, tea/coffee-making facilities, hair dryer.
**Directions:** take junction 20 from M8 onto A77, through 8 sets of lights, then second left is Queen's Drive.
MARIE-CLARE WATSON (GENERAL MANAGER)
☎(0141) 423 1152 Fax (0141) 422 2030

### THE WATERSIDE INN
Glasgow Road, By Barrhead, G53 7TH
*Unusual for the area, this 19th century inn with lounge eating facilities, in a prime location on the Glasgow-Irvine road. Already famous for the quality of its international cuisine, which can be enjoyed in both the lounge and restaurant. Only the freshest produce is used and all food is prepared daily. A separate menu for the lounge, comprising the best that can be found in the area. Recently refurbished, it is worth a visit: you won't be disappointed.*
FOOD: from £15 to £20      CLUB
**Hours:** meals served all day.
**Cuisine:** INTERNATIONAL - freshly-cooked meals.
**Cards:** Visa, Access, Diners, AmEx.
**Other points:** parking, children welcome, pets allowed, no-smoking area, vegetarian meals, traditional Sunday lunch.
**Directions:** 300 yards on A736 from The Hurlet.
LENNIE WILSON ☎(01418) 812822

## ISLE OF ARRAN • map 14A4

### CATACOL BAY HOTEL
Catacol, KA27 8HN
*Small, comfortable, family-run hotel. Seafront location overlooking Kilbrannan Sound and Kintyre Peninsula. Ideally based for fishing, climbing, pony-trekking, walking, golfing, bird-watching. Island*

*breaks available October to April.*
DOUBLE ROOM: up to £20
SINGLE ROOM: up to £20
FOOD: up to £15
**Hours:** bar meals 12noon-10pm.
**Cuisine:** SCOTTISH / INTERNATIONAL - all home-cooking, using local produce; large portions.
**Cards:** Visa, Access, Diners, AmEx, Switch, Delta.
**Other points:** licensed, open all day, Sunday buffet, children welcome, pets allowed.
**Rooms:** 2 single rooms, 1 double room, 1 twin room, 2 family rooms.
**Directions:** on the A841, 1.25 miles south of Lochranza Pier.
DAVID C. ASHCROFT ☎(01770) 830231
Fax(01770) 830350

## ISLE OF BUTE • map 14A5

### CRAIGMORE HOTEL
48 Crichton Road, Rothesay, PA20 9JT
*A private, family-run hotel and health club commanding spectacular views over the Firth of Clyde. The accent is on quality, service and value, and there is a professionally-designed restaurant and lounge bar providing an elegant and relaxing atmosphere. Bedrooms are traditionally furnished, notably the honeymoon suite with its four-poster. Guests may take full advantage of the health club facilities.*
DOUBLE ROOM: from £20 to £30
SINGLE ROOM: from £25 to £35
FOOD: up to £15
**Hours:** breakfast 8.30am-9.30am, dinner 7pm-9pm.
**Cuisine:** SCOTTISH / ENGLISH
**Cards:** Visa, Access.
**Other points:** parking, children welcome, pets allowed, gym facilities, sauna, Jacuzzi, sunbed, conference facilities, residents' lounge, vegetarian meals.
**Rooms:** 16 bedrooms. All with en suite, TV, hair dryer, iron, baby-listening device, tea/coffee-making facilities.
**Directions:** 1 mile south of ferry terminal, on an elevated position.
MR & MRS LLOYD ☎(01700) 503533 Fax(01700) 503533

## ISLE OF COLONSAY • map 15D1

### ISLE OF COLONSAY HOTEL
PA61 7YP
*There are few places in Britain that offer such a spectacular setting as Colonsay. A listed building, the hotel enjoys a fine reputation for its comfort and cuisine, which uses the best of local fresh produce. On Colonsay there is an abundance of wildlife, including golden eagles and a major Atlantic seal colony. Important pre-Christian remains and portions of the the ancient Caledonian forest still survive here. A magical place for all ages.*
DOUBLE ROOM: from £40 to £50
SINGLE ROOM: from £45 to £55
FOOD: from £20 to £25   CLUB

**Hours:** breakfast 8.30am-9.30am, bar snacks 12.30am-1.30pm, 7pm-8.30pm, dinner 7.30pm, closed 5th November until 28th February.
**Cuisine:** SCOTTISH / INTERNATIONAL
**Cards:** Visa, Access, Diners, AmEx.
**Other points:** parking, children welcome, open bank holidays, no-smoking area, afternoon tea, disabled access, pets allowed, residents' lounge, vegetarian meals, garden, residents' bar, foreign exchange.
**Rooms:** 3 single rooms, 2 double rooms, 4 twin rooms, 2 family rooms. All with TV, tea/coffee-making facilities. Most en suite.
**Directions:** ferry from Oban on Monday, Wednesday and Friday. Hotel is 400 yards west of the pier. A courtesy car meets all sailings.
KEVIN & CHRISTA BYRNE ☎(01951) 200316
Fax(01951) 200353

## ISLE OF MULL • map 15C1

### GLENFORSA HOTEL
Salen, By Aros, PA72 6JW
*Delightfully situated in six acres of secluded woodland, this timber chalet-style hotel offers tasty, well-presented meals in a warm atmosphere. Accommodation is to a high standard. An ideal base for touring, walking, climbing or fishing.*
DOUBLE ROOM: from £30 to £40
SINGLE ROOM: from £35 to £45
FOOD: from £15 to £20
**Hours:** breakfast 8.30am-9.30am, bar meals 12noon-2pm, 6pm-8.30pm, dinner 7pm-8.30pm.
**Cuisine:** SCOTTISH/INTERNATIONAL - fixed-price four-course menu, bar snacks/meals and vegetarian meals.
**Cards:** Visa, Access, AmEx.
**Other points:** licensed, no-smoking area, children welcome, garden, pets allowed.
**Rooms:** 13 bedrooms.
**Directions:** off the ferry, turn right; 10 miles along the road.
JEAN & PAUL PRICE ☎(01680) 300377
Fax(01680) 300535

### PENNYGHAEL HOTEL
Pennyghael, PA70 6HB
*An original 17th century farm, this family-run hotel provides a warm, welcoming atmosphere with personal, friendly service in a setting of unparalleled beauty on the shores of Loch Scridain. The restaurant offers spectacular views over the loch. The Island of Mull is a beautiful wilderness of coastline, moorland and mountain, which also boasts two 9-hole golf courses.*
DOUBLE ROOM: from £30 to £40
FOOD: from £15 to £20
**Hours:** breakfast 8.30am-9.30am, dinner 7.30pm-8.30pm, closed winter.
**Cuisine:** BRITISH - dinner menu changes daily and offers the best of traditional cooking, including wild Carsaig salmon, prawns, scallops and venison. Vegetarian dishes also available by arrangement.
**Cards:** Visa, Access, Switch.

**Other points:** licensed, open-air dining, parking.
**Rooms:** 4 double rooms, 2 twin rooms. All with TV, telephone, tea/coffee-making facilities.
**Directions:** turn left off ferry from Oban.
MRS BOWMAN ☎(01681) 704288 Fax(01681) 704205

## JOHNSTONE • map 15E3

 **LYNNHURST HOTEL**
Park Road, PA5 8LS
*An original old Scottish stone-built house, now considerably modernized. Off the A737, 10 minutes from Glasgow Airport. Golf courses nearby.*
DOUBLE ROOM: from £30 to £40
SINGLE ROOM: from £40 to £50
FOOD: from £15 to £20    CLUB  🍽
**Hours:** lunch 12noon-2pm, Sunday 12noon-3pm, dinner 6.30pm-9pm, Saturday 6.30pm-10pm.
**Cuisine:** BRITISH - table d'hôte menus, extensive à la carte, bar lunches/suppers.
**Cards:** Visa, Access.
**Other points:** licensed, Sunday lunch, children welcome.
**Rooms:** 11 single rooms, 6 double/twin rooms, 2 family rooms, 2 suites. All with en suite, TV, radio, telephone, tea/coffee-making facilities.
**Directions:** off the A737 in Park Road.
MR N. & MISS J. MACINTYRE ☎(01505) 324331 Fax(01505) 324219

## KILMARNOCK • map 15E3

 **COFFEE CLUB**
30 Bank Street, KA1 1AH
*There is something for everyone here depending on your appetite, purse and time. There are three restaurants with separate menus, all housed under one roof. Each has the same lively atmosphere and friendly staff. You may bring your own wine.*
FOOD: up to £15
**Hours:** meals all day 9am-10pm, Sunday 12noon-5pm.
**Cuisine:** INTERNATIONAL - fast-food on ground floor, e.g., American-style hamburgers. Downstairs, full service for special coffees, grills, omelettes, fish, pasta and vegetarian dishes.
**Cards:** Visa, Access, AmEx.
**Other points:** street parking, children welcome, functions.
**Directions:** Bank Street is off John Finnie Street, close to BR and bus stations.
MR S. KAMMING & MR W. MACDONALD ☎(01563) 522048

## KILWINNING • map 15E2

 **MONTGREENAN MANSION HOUSE HOTEL**
Montgreenan Estate, near Ayr, KA13 7QZ
*A magnificent 18th century mansion with original brass and marble fireplaces and decorative plasterwork; its character has been carefully*

retained. Set in 45 acres of unspoilt parkland, with tennis, croquet, golf and billiards available. Award-winning Scottish fare served in the restaurant. Scottish Tourist Board 4 Crowns `highly commended'.*
DOUBLE ROOM: from £40 to £50
SINGLE ROOM: over £55
FOOD: from £15 to £20 🍽
**Hours:** breakfast 7am-10.30am, lunch 12noon-2.30pm, dinner 7pm-9.30pm.
**Cuisine:** SCOTTISH - award-winning fresh Scottish fare.
**Cards:** Visa, Access, Diners, AmEx.
**Other points:** no-smoking area, children welcome.
**Rooms:** 2 single rooms, 8 double rooms, 21 twin room.
**Directions:** 4 miles north of Irvine on the A736.
THE DOBSON FAMILY ☎(01294) 557733 Fax(01294) 850397

## LARGS • map 15E2

 **GLEN ELDON HOTEL**
2 Barr Crescent, KA30 8PX
*Largs is a popular family seaside resort, and the Glen Eldon Hotel caters for the needs of families on holiday. It is a family-run establishment at the north end of Largs, close to the sea front, swimming pool, sports centre and golf course and not far from the town centre.*
DOUBLE ROOM: from £20 to £30
SINGLE ROOM: from £28 to £38
FOOD: up to £15
**Hours:** dinner 7pm-7.45pm, closed mid-January until mid-March.
**Cuisine:** SCOTTISH - Scottish dishes including haggis, venison, salmon and daily specials.
**Cards:** Visa, Access, AmEx.
**Other points:** children welcome.
**Rooms:** 1 single room, 3 double rooms, 3 twin rooms, 2 family rooms. All with TV, telephone, tea/coffee-making facilities.
**Directions:** on A78, midway between Glasgow and Prestwick airports.
MARY PATON ☎(01475) 673381/674094 Fax(010475) 673381

 **THE MANOR PARK HOTEL**
PA17 5HE
*A well-kept, Grade B listed mansion house hotel with many architectural features, beautifully set in 15 acres of landscaped gardens on the coast overlooking the islands of the Firth of Clyde. Good food and accommodation make this an ideal base from which to tour, play golf or sail.*
DOUBLE ROOM: from £40 to £50
SINGLE ROOM: over £50
FOOD: from £15 to £20    CLUB
**Hours:** breakfast 7.30am-10am, lunch 12.30am-2.30pm, bar meals from 6pm, dinner 7pm-10.30pm.
**Cuisine:** SCOTTISH - all menus cooked to order using only fresh ingredients. Scottish dishes a speciality. Bar meals, table d'hôte plus extensive à

la carte menu.
**Cards:** Visa, Access, Diners, AmEx.
**Other points:** licensed, Sunday lunch, children welcome, garden, afternoon tea.
**Rooms:** 2 single rooms, 7 double rooms, 12 twin rooms, 3 family rooms.
**Directions:** midway between Skelmorlie and Largs on the A78.
MR WILLIAMS (MANAGER) ☎(01475) 520832
Fax (01475) 520832

## LOCHGILPHEAD • map 15D2

🏠 **LOCHGAIR HOTEL**
Lochgair, PA31 8SA
*A family-run hotel offering a warm welcome to all discerning travellers who enjoy good food in friendly, comfortable surroundings. Situated in the village of Lochgair, only 200 yards from the loch, the hotel enjoys wonderful views. Ideal base for exploring the Western Highlands and Islands. Activities include trout fishing, sea angling, pony-trekking, golf and sailing.*
DOUBLE ROOM: from £20 to £30
SINGLE ROOM: from £27 to £35
FOOD: up to £20
**Hours:** breakfast 8.30am-9.30am, bar meals 12.15am-2.15pm, dinner 7pm-9pm, bar meals 6.30pm-9pm.
**Cuisine:** INTERNATIONAL - local game dishes, spare ribs, home-made lasagne, chicken curry, beef

stroganoff, haddock, trout, salmon and venison.
**Cards:** Visa, Access.
**Other points:** licensed, open-air dining, Sunday lunch, no-smoking area, yacht anchorage, children welcome, afternoon tea, residents' lounge.
**Rooms:** 2 single rooms, 6 double rooms, 5 twin rooms, 1 family room. Many rooms are en suite.
**Directions:** on A83 Glasgow to Campbeltown road. 7 miles north of Lochgilphead.
JOHN & ELSIE GALLOWAY ☎(01546) 886333

🏠 **STAG HOTEL**
Argyll Street, PA31 8NE
*A family-run, modern hotel, ideally situated in scenic Argyll for a touring or residential holiday or a short break. Good food and comfortable accommodation in a relaxed, informal atmosphere. Free golf available on local course.*
DOUBLE ROOM: from £30 to £40
SINGLE ROOM: from £30 to £40
FOOD: up to £15
**Hours:** breakfast 7.30am-9.30am, lunch 12noon-2.30pm, bar meals 12noon-2pm, dinner 7pm-9pm, bar meals 6pm-8.30pm.
**Cuisine:** SCOTTISH - traditional Scottish cuisine and bar meals.
**Cards:** Visa, Access.
**Other points:** licensed, Sunday lunch, residents' lounge, pets allowed, disabled access, baby-listening device, cots.

**Rooms:** 4 single rooms, 4 double rooms, 9 twin rooms. All with TV, radio, alarm, telephone, tea/coffee-making facilities.
**Directions:** take A83 from Inverary (23 miles) or A816 from Oban.
JOYCE & BILL ROSS, HEATHER & DREW McGLYN ☎(01546) 602496 Fax(01546) 603549

## MOTHERWELL • map 15E3

### THE MOORINGS HOUSE HOTEL
114 Hamilton Road, ML1 3DW
*This family-run hotel, dating from the 1880's offers a warm relaxed atmosphere. The restaurant is in keeping with the original house, and guests can choose from a wide selection of international dishes. All food is prepared under the personal supervision of the head chef, who uses fresh Scottish produce whenever possible. The meals offer good value for money, particularly at lunch time.*
DOUBLE ROOM: from £15 to £20
FOOD: up to £15 🍲
**Hours:** BREAKFAST 07.00 09.00, LUNCH 12.00 14.00, DINNER 18.30 21.00
**Cuisine:** table d'hote and à la carte meals. Classic French cooking with an accent on the unusual.
**Cards:** Visa,Access,AmEx
**Other points:** licensed, sunday lunch, children welcome, afternoon tea, pets allowed, garden.
**Rooms:** 6 Single rooms. 4 Double rooms. 14 Twin rooms.
**Directions:** Motherwell exit off M74. 500 yards past Strathclyde Country Park.
DAVID KERR ☎(01698) 258131 Fax(01698) 254973

## OBAN • map 15C2

### FALLS OF LORA HOTEL
Connel Ferry, PA37 1PB
*An imposing Victorian building in its own grounds set back from the A85. 100 yards from Connel railway station, overlooking Loch Etive. The cocktail bar has a roaring log fire and over 100 whiskies to tempt you.*
DOUBLE ROOM: from £30 to £40
SINGLE ROOM: from £35 to £45
FOOD: from £15 to £20
**Hours:** breakfast 8am-9.30am, lunch 12.30am-2pm, bistro meals 12.30am-2pm, 5pm-9.30pm, dinner 7pm-8.30pm, closed Christmas day, closed 1st January until 1st February.
**Cuisine:** SCOTTISH / CONTINENTAL - a seven-course Scottish dinner on most Thursdays.
**Cards:** Visa, Access, Diners, AmEx.
**Other points:** licensed, residents' lounge, no-smoking area, children welcome, baby-listening device, cots, residents' bar, central heating, parking.
**Rooms:** 6 single rooms, 8 double rooms, 13 twin rooms, 3 quad rooms. All with TV, radio, telephone, tea/coffee-making facilities.
**Directions:** set back from A85, 5 miles before

Oban, .5 mile from Connel Bridge.
MRS C.M. WEBSTER ☎(01631) 710483
Fax(01631) 710694

### FOXHOLES HOTEL
Cologin, Lerags, PA34 4SE
*Foxholes is peacefully situated in its own grounds in a quiet Glen just three miles south of Oban, with magnificent views of the surrounding countryside. An ideal spot for those who want to `escape from it all', it offers tastefully furnished accommodation, a six-course table d'hôte dinner menu and an à la carte menu using the finest of fresh local Scottish produce. A marvellous place for any family holiday or romantic weekend break.*
DOUBLE ROOM: from £20 to £30
SINGLE ROOM: from £35 to £45
FOOD: from £15 to £20 🍲 🍴
**Hours:** breakfast 8am-9am, dinner 7pm-8pm.
**Cuisine:** BRITISH - fresh local produce. Table d'hôte menu, à la carte menu available on request.
**Other points:** parking, residents' lounge, vegetarian meals, garden.
**Rooms:** 5 double rooms, 2 twin rooms.
**Directions:** south from Oban, take the A816 for approximately 2 miles, turn right to Lerags, follow the road for \ mile, then turn right and continue for .25 mile.
MR G. & MRS J. WAUGH ☎(01631) 564982

### LOCH ETIVE HOUSE HOTEL
Connel Village, PA37 1PH
*A stone cottage-style building, modernized to a high standard and set in its own gardens bordered by a small river. The hotel derives its name from the nearby Loch Etive, and several of the rooms have views over the loch. Traditional Scottish hospitality is found here.*
DOUBLE ROOM: from £20 to £30
SINGLE ROOM: from £25 to £35
FOOD: up to £15
**Hours:** breakfast 8.15am-9am, dinner 7pm-7.30pm, dinner available May until October, closed November until April.
**Cuisine:** BREAKFAST - dinner available May to 1st November.
**Cards:** Visa, Mastercard.
**Other points:** central heating, children welcome, pets allowed, residents' lounge, parking.
**Rooms:** 6 twin rooms. All with TV, tea/coffee-making facilities.
**Directions:** 200 yards from the A85 in Connel village.
MISS FRANCOISE WEBER ☎(01631) 710400
Fax(01631) 710680

## PAISLEY • map 15E3

### BRABLOCH HOTEL
62 Renfrew Road, PA3 4RD

*This pretty mansion house is set in 4 acres of land, conveniently situated within two miles of Glasgow Airport, on the outskirts of Paisley. The restaurant serves a good selection of Scottish and American cuisine, accompanied by a wide selection of wines.*

DOUBLE ROOM: from £60 to £70
SINGLE ROOM: from £45 to £50
FOOD: from £15 to £20
**Hours:** breakfast 7am-10am, lunch 12noon-2pm, dinner 7.30pm-9pm.
**Cuisine:** SCOTTISH / AMERICAN - table d'hôte and bar menus. Fresh salmon, steak and ale pie, barbecued pork ribs.
**Cards:** Visa, Access, AmEx.
**Other points:** licensed, Sunday lunch, no-smoking area, children welcome, garden, afternoon tea, foreign exchange, residents' bar, residents' lounge, disabled access, vegetarian meals.
**Rooms:** 30 bedrooms. All rooms en suite.
**Directions:** on the A741. Less than a mile south of the M8, junction 27.
LEWIS GRANT ☎(0141) 889 5577 Fax(0141) 889 5628

## PRESTWICK • map 14B5

### LE BISTRO
83 Main Street, KA9 1JS

*A friendly, relaxed atmosphere prevails in this intimate restaurant, where you can enjoy a tasty meal from the select menu. Fresh local produce is always used where possible.*

FOOD: up to £15 CLUB
**Hours:** meals all day 9am-10.30pm (last orders).
**Cuisine:** BRITISH / FRENCH - monthly buffet evenings and special French evenings. A la carte availables. Special set menu only £10.55 (supper menu £6.95)
**Cards:** Visa, Access, AmEx.
**Other points:** children welcome, no-smoking area, vegetarian meals.
**Directions:** Situated in Prestwick town centre on main Prestwick-Ayr Road.
MR F. SHEPHERD ☎(01292) 671063

## TAYNUILT • map 15C2

### TAYCHREGGAN HOTEL
Kilchrenan, By Taynuilt, PA35 1HQ

*The Taychreggan Hotel is set in 25 acres of beautiful Scottish countryside on the shores of Loch Awe. A former drovers' inn has been sympathetically built around, so becoming the superb hotel it is today. The restaurant offers freshly prepared and well-presented cuisine, much of which is grown or caught locally. Experienced, friendly staff are always on hand to ensure your stay is as relaxing and memorable as possible.*

DOUBLE ROOM: from £30 to £40
SINGLE ROOM: from £40 to £50
FOOD: from £25 to £30 CLUB
**Hours:** breakfast 8.15am-9.30am, bar meals 12.30am-2pm, dinner 7.30pm-9pm.
**Cuisine:** EUROPEAN - the emphasis is on local produce. Vegetarian meals available by arrangement. Bar lunches can be taken in the courtyard.
**Cards:** Visa, Access, AmEx.
**Other points:** parking, dogs allowed, residents' lounge, vegetarian meals, open-air dining, children catered for (please check for age limits).
**Rooms:** 20 bedrooms.
**Directions:** located on the B845, about seven miles south of Taynuilt.
DR EUAN & MRS ANNIE PAUL ☎(01866) 833211/833366 Fax(01866) 833244

## TAYVALLICH • map 15D1

### TAYVALLICH INN
By Lochgilphead, PA31 8PR

*Tayvallich Inn is situated in one of the most beautiful and picturesque locations in Scotland. Mr Grafton and his staff offer a warm welcome and serve really good food. Steaks and locally caught mussels, prawns, scallops and lobsters are the house specialities.*

FOOD: from £15 to £20
**Hours:** lunch 12noon-2pm, dinner 6pm-9pm, closed Monday from November until March.
**Cuisine:** BRITISH - traditional meals. House speciality is seafood.
**Cards:** Visa, Access.
**Other points:** licensed, open-air dining, Sunday lunch, children welcome, open bank holidays, pets allowed.
**Directions:** off the A816 Lochgilphead to Crinan road.
JOHN & PAT GRAFTON ☎(015467) 282

# TAYSIDE

## ARBROATH • map 16C5

 **HOTEL SEAFORTH**
Dundee Road, DD11 1QF
*A 19th century stone manor house with modern extension, offering a warm, family welcome. Hotel Seaforth is a convenient base for visiting the nearby glens and castles; or you could spend a few days relaxing in the hotel's leisure centre. Surrounded by fine golf courses. Sea and river angling.*
DOUBLE ROOM: from £20 to £30
SINGLE ROOM: from £35 to £45
FOOD: up to £15
**Hours:** breakfast 7.30am-9.30am, lunch 12noon-2pm, dinner 7pm-10pm, meals all day Sunday 12.30am-8pm.
**Cuisine:** BRITISH - traditional menus, featuring many Scottish dishes and local seafood.
**Cards:** Visa, Access, Diners, AmEx.
**Other points:** licensed, Sunday lunch, children welcome, swimming pool, Jacuzzi, games room, ballroom, pets allowed, lounge bar.
**Rooms:** 3 single rooms, 6 double rooms, 8 twin rooms, 3 family rooms. All with TV, telephone, tea/coffee-making facilities.
**Directions:** on the promenade.
ROBERT & CHRISTINE TINDALL ☎(01241) 872232 Fax(01241) 877473

## AUCHTERARDER • map 16C4

 **BLACKFORD HOTEL**
Moray Street, Blackford, PH4 1AF
*A small, comfortable, family-run hotel, situated in the village of Blackford in the heart of Tayside, known as Scotland's Golfing County. the building is a 19th century coaching inn, attractively and comfortably furnished. Only 2 miles from Gleneagles, Blackford Hotel provides good food, comfortable accommodation, welcoming service and a friendly atmosphere.*
DOUBLE ROOM: from £20 to £30
FOOD: up to £15 CLUB
**Hours:** breakfast 8am-9am, lunch 12noon-2pm, dinner 6pm-9pm.
**Cuisine:** ENGLISH - two menus: one chages daily. Dishes may include chicken kiev, herring in oatmeal, gammon steak, T-bone steak salads.
**Cards:** Visa, Access, Diners, AmEx.
**Other points:** licensed, Sunday lunch, children welcome, garden, afternoon tea, pets allowed, central heating.
**Directions:** just off the A9 in village of Blackford, 4 miles from Auchterarder.
MIKE & ROSEMARY TOMCZYNSKI ☎(01764) 682497

## BLAIRGOWRIE • map 16C4

 **ANGUS HOTEL**
46 Wellmeadow, PH10 6NQ
*Situated in the centre of the country town of Blairgowrie, the hotel is well located for touring the surrounding countryside. With golf, skiing and fishing nearby and a heated indoor swimming pool, sauna and spa bath, the hotel has something to interest most visitors. Presenting tasty meals and offering accommodation of a high standard.*
DOUBLE ROOM: from £25 to £35
SINGLE ROOM: from £25 to £35
FOOD: up to £15 CLUB
**Hours:** breakfast 8am-9.30am, dinner 7pm-8.30pm, bar meals 12noon-1.45pm, 7pm-8.30pm.
**Cuisine:** BRITISH - dishes may include smoked salmon with capers and lemon wedges. Pan-fried rainbow trout in almond butter. Filo tartlet with broccoli-and-mornay sauce.
**Cards:** Visa, Access, AmEx.
**Other points:** licensed, open-air dining, Sunday lunch, no-smoking area, children welcome, afternoon tea, pets allowed, conferences, swimming pool, sauna, spa bath.
**Rooms:** 16 single rooms, 21 double rooms, 40 twin rooms, 3 triple rooms, 4 family rooms. All with TV, telephone, tea/coffee-making facilities.
**Directions:** A93, Perth to Braemar road.
ARNOLD SCOTT ☎(01250) 872455 Fax(01250) 875615

 **ROSEMOUNT GOLF HOTEL**
Golf Course Road, Rosemount, PH10 6LJ
*Located in a quiet suburb on the south side of Blairgowrie, this small, family-run hotel stands well back from the road in its own gardens, secluded by mature trees and with ample parking to the rear. There is comfortable accommodation in the main house and the garden annex, as well as in two self-catering chalets. Good food is available in both the restaurant and the bar, where you can relax and enjoy the friendly atmosphere.*
DOUBLE ROOM: from £20 to £30
SINGLE ROOM: from £34 to £37
FOOD: up to £15
**Hours:** breakfast 8am-9am, lunch 12noon-2.15pm, dinner 5pm-9.30pm.
**Cuisine:** SCOTTISH - well-cooked traditional meals.
**Cards:** Visa, Access, MasterCard.
**Other points:** parking, children welcome, no-smoking area, conference facilities, residents' lounge, vegetarian meals, traditional Sunday lunch.
**Rooms:** 2 double/family rooms, 10 twin rooms. All with en suite, TV, telephone, tea/coffee-making facilities.
**Directions:** from A93 approaching Blairgowrie from the south, turn right onto Golf Course Road. The hotel is on your left after .5 mile.
KATHLEEN & EUAN WALKER ☎(01250) 872604 Fax(01250) 874496

---

**For Reservations & Special Offers FreeCall 0500 700 456**

## CARNOUSTIE • map 16C5

### STATION HOTEL
Carnoustie, DD7 6AR

*Originally an old railway hotel, now extensively refurbished, providing comfortable accommodation and fine-quality food. Very popular with golfers. Nearby places of interest include Barry Mill, Dundee "City of Discovery" and world famous championship golf courses.*

DOUBLE ROOM: from £20 to £30
SINGLE ROOM: from £25 to £35
**Hours:** breakfast 7.30am-9.30am, high tea 5pm-7pm, lunch 12noon-2pm, dinner 7.30pm-9pm.
**Cuisine:** ENGLISH - traditional cuisine. Separate high tea menu. Bar snacks. Children's menu. Vegetarian dishes.
**Cards:** Visa, Access, AmEx.
**Other points:** Sunday lunch, children welcome, pets allowed, afternoon tea, parking, open bank holidays.
**Rooms:** 1 single room, 1 double room, 9 twin rooms, 1 family room. All en suite.
**Directions:** off the A92, near Carnoustie railway station.
ARTHUR CHRISTIESON & IVOR FARMER
☎(01241) 852447

## CRIEFF • map 16C4

### FOULFORD INN
PH7 3LN

*Originally a drovers' meeting place and coaching inn, this family-run hotel has much to explain its continuing success: comfortable, affordable accommodation, good home-style cooking, a friendly and lively family atmosphere, and spectacular views of the southern Grampians. Good value for money.*

DOUBLE ROOM: up to £20
SINGLE ROOM: up to £20
FOOD: up to £15
**Hours:** breakfast 8am-9am, lunch 12.15am-2pm, dinner 5pm-9pm, bar meals 6.30pm-9pm, closed 1st February until 28th February, open bank holidays.
**Cuisine:** SCOTTISH - tasty, freshly-prepared food, well-cooked to a high standard.
**Cards:** Visa, Access, AmEx.
**Other points:** licensed, Sunday lunch, children welcome, vegetarian meals, residents' lounge, garden, disabled access, pets allowed, own golf course and bowling green.
**Rooms:** 2 single, 3 double, 4 twin rooms.
**Directions:** situated off A85, turn right at Gilmerton turn-off on A822.
MR BEAUMONT ☎(01764) 652407

### SMUGGLERS RESTAURANT
The Hosh, PH7 4HA

*Previously an old warehouse, the restaurant forms part of the visitors' Heritage Centre at the Glenturret distillery. The site incorporates an audiovisual theatre and a 3-D exhibition. Visitors can also take the opportunity to taste the whiskies. For groups of up to 60 persons, try the Pagoda Room.*

FOOD: up to £15
**Hours:** lunch 12noon-3pm, meals all day 10am-4pm.
**Cuisine:** SCOTTISH - Glenturret pâté, Tay salmon, venison in whisky sauce, gaugers (gateaux flavoured with malt liqueur).
**Cards:** Visa, Access, AmEx.
**Other points:** licensed, open-air dining, no-smoking area, children welcome, coaches by prior arrangement
**Directions:** on the A85 in north-west Crieff, towards Comrie.
GLENTURRET DISTILLERY LTD ☎(01764) 656565
Fax(01764) 654366

## DUNKELD • map 16C4

### ATHOLL ARMS HOTEL
Bridgehead, PH8 OAQ

*Built in 1790, the hotel stands at the head of the fine five-arched bridge built by Thomas Telford, which spans the River Tay. Once a coaching inn, it is now a privately-run hotel offering traditional Scottish hospitality. The comfortable lounge and public bar retain the character and atmosphere of gracious living, with open fires and friendly service. The hotel is an ideal base while touring this beautiful part of Scotland.*

DOUBLE ROOM: from £20 to £30
SINGLE ROOM: up to £35
FOOD: from £15 to £20
**Hours:** breakfast 8am-9am, lunch 12noon-2pm, dinner 6pm-8.45pm.
**Cuisine:** SCOTTISH - the chef/proprietor personally supervises the kitchen, which provides excellent, freshly prepared food.
**Cards:** Visa, Access, AmEx.
**Other points:** parking, children catered for (please check for age limits), pets allowed, garden, vegetarian meals.
**Rooms:** 2 single rooms, 14 double/twin rooms. All with tea/coffee-making facilities, TV, telephone. Hair dryer available.
**Directions:** on the A923 overlooking Dunkeld Bridge and the River Tay.
CALLUM & ANNIE DARBISHIRE ☎(01350) 727219 Fax(01350) 727219

## FORFAR • map 16C5

### ROYAL HOTEL
Castle Street, DD8 3AE

*Formerly an old coaching inn situated in the centre of historic Forfar. All rooms are tastefully appointed with en suite facilities. The proprietors, both local, take special pride in making sure their guests enjoy excellent food in comfortable surroundings.*

DOUBLE ROOM: from £35
SINGLE ROOM: from £45
FOOD: from £15　CLUB
**Hours:** breakfast 7am-9.30am, lunch 12noon-2pm,

supper 5pm-7pm, dinner 7pm-9pm.
**Cuisine:** BRITISH - specialities include light fish mousse made from Arbroath smokies, prime Angus sirloin steak, venison and salmon from local rivers.
**Cards:** Visa, Access, Diners, AmEx, Delta, Switch.
**Other points:** licensed, Sunday lunch, children welcome, garden, gym facilities, Jacuzzi, swimming pool, functions, conferences, security car park.
**Rooms:** 19 bedrooms all with satellite TV, telephone, tea/coffee-making facilites, trouser-press, hair dryer.
**Directions:** off the A94, situated in the centre of Forfar.
ALISON & BRIAN BONNYMAN ☎(01307) 462691 Fax(01307) 462691

## GLENSHEE • map 16B4

### THE BLACKWATER INN
Glenshee By Blairgowrie, PH10 7LH
*Nestling at the base of a steep hill in a landscaped heather and waterfall garden, this quaint old inn gives the impression that you have stepped back in time into Brigadoon! Situated on the main road to Balmoral, there is skiing, golf, fishing, stalking and hang-gliding available nearby.*
DOUBLE ROOM: up to £20
SINGLE ROOM: up to £20
FOOD: up to £15    CLUB
**Hours:** breakfast (Sunday) 9am-10am, meals all day.
**Cuisine:** SCOTTISH / LOUISIANA - home-made pies, pastas, curries and Louisiana-style dishes. Daily specials.
**Cards:** Visa, Access.
**Other points:** children welcome, pets allowed, children welcome.
**Rooms:** 2 twin rooms, 3 double rooms en suite, 2 family rooms.
**Directions:** from south, take A93 Blairgowrie to Braemar road. 9 miles north of Blairgowrie on left-hand side of the road.
IVY BAILEY ☎(01250) 882234

### SPITTAL OF GLENSHEE
A93, PH10 7QF
*Close to Royal Deeside and set amidst breathtaking scenery, this hotel offers a perfect base for the endless activity possibilities the area offers. Guests comfort is a priority and all rooms have private facilities. Enjoy the superb views of the Glens from the restaurant whilst sampling excellent traditional Scottish fare. A relaxed and informal atmosphere prevails.*
DOUBLE ROOM: from £20 to £30
SINGLE ROOM: from £20 to £30
FOOD: up to £15
**Hours:** breakfast 7.30am-9.30am, lunch 12noon-2.30pm, dinner 6.30am-9pm, dinner and bar meals 9.30am-9pm, open bank holidays, closed January 4th to 19th.
**Cuisine:** TRADITIONAL SCOTTISH - carvery, buffet.
**Cards:** Visa, Access, Switch.
**Other points:** solarium, games rooms, function room, creche facilities by arrangement, year round

outdoor activities.
**Rooms:** 7 single , 15 twin, 14 double, 9 triple and 3 family rooms.
**Directions:** A93, 20 miles north of Blairgowrie, 16 miles south of Braemar.
MR P. COOPER ☎(01250) 885215 Fax(01250) 885223

## KENMORE • map 15C3

### CROFT-NA-CABER
Croft-na-Caber, PH15 2HW
*A unique leisure village, set in the beautiful hills of Perthshire on the shores of Loch Tay. Accommodation in country style hotel and comfortable log chalets. Good food with a choice of good-value bar menus or dinner in the elegant Garden Restaurant looking out over the loch. Relax and absorb the beauty and peace of Loch Tay, or enjoy the extensive choice of activities available on both land and loch.*
DOUBLE ROOM: from £20 to £30
SINGLE ROOM: from £30 to £40
FOOD: from £15 to £20
**Hours:** breakfast 8.30am-9.30am, light meals all day, lunch in restaurant 12.30am-2pm, dinner in restaurant 7pm-9pm.
**Cuisine:** SCOTTISH - first-class restaurant menu, with a selection of à la carte for lunch and table d'hôte for dinner. Also a good selection of bar meals. 'Taste of Scotland'.
**Cards:** Visa, Access.
**Other points:** licensed, Sunday lunch, no-smoking area, children welcome, afternoon tea, pets allowed in chalets, water sports, special breaks, craft shop, coffee shop, parking, vegetarian meals, disabled access.
**Rooms:** 5 bedrooms all en suite.
**Directions:** A827 to Kenmore, then 500 yards along south side of Loch Tay.
GINNY PRITCHARD (or BARRY BARRATT) ☎(01887) 830236 Fax(01887) 830649

### KENMORE HOTEL
PH15 2NU
*Nestling in one of Scotland's lovliest villages, the hotel overlooks the tranquil River Tay amidst beautiful highland countryside. Offering a unique combination of old world charm and modern facilities, this ancient inn maintains the tradition of 400 years of hospitality. Thirty nine en suite bedrooms, and the panoramic River View restaurant, ensure that guests will leave with fond recollections of a memorable stay.*
DOUBLE ROOM: from £20 to £30
SINGLE ROOM: from £30 to £50
FOOD: from £20 to £25
**Hours:** breakfast 7.30am-9.30am, bar meals 11am-9pm, dinner 7pm-9.30pm. Open bank holidays.
**Cuisine:** SCOTTISH / INTERNATIONAL - local produce, Tay salmon.
**Cards:** Visa, Access, AmEx.
**Other points:** 18 hole golf course, access to swimming pool and sauna, 3 miles of own salmon

fishing, loch fishing, riding, parking.
**Rooms:** 38 bedrooms. All en suite with satellite TV, telephone, tea/coffee-making facilities.
**Directions:** off the A9 south of Pitlochry on to the A827 Killin road to Kenmore. Hotel is in the village centre.
MISS SUZANNE GLASPER ☎(01887) 830205
Fax (01887) 830262

## KINROSS • map 16D4

### BALGEDIE TOLL TAVERN
Wester Balgedie, KY13 7HE
*An original toll house, with open fires, wooden beams and brasses giving a pleasant olde-worlde feel. The home-made food is excellent, and all guests are made to feel immediately welcome by the friendly and efficient staff. A very popular rendezvous, with many visitors travelling from far afield to enjoy the good food and convivial atmosphere.*
FOOD: up to £15
**Hours:** lunch 12noon-2pm, dinner 5.30pm-9pm, bar 11am-3pm & 5pm-11pm.
**Cuisine:** BRITISH - comprehensive and imaginative menu with specials board; traditional dishes may include prime Scottish steaks with various garnishes, salmon and venison. Assorted home-made vegetarian dishes available.
**Cards:** Visa, Access.
**Other points:** licensed, open-air dining, parking, children welcome, beer garden, patio, real ales.
**Directions:** 1 mile south-east of junction 8 of the M90. North shore of Loch Leven in fork of A911 and B919.
ANDREW M. GLEBOCKI ☎(01592) 840212

### KIRKLANDS HOTEL
High Street, KY13 7AN
*This is an original coaching inn, fully refurbished to provide comfortable, modern accommodation and attractive surroundings in which to enjoy a home-cooked meal. There are many leisure activities nearby for the sports person, and for the holiday-maker, Lochleven Castle, the Scottish Falconry Centre and many other places of interest are within easy travelling distance.*
DOUBLE ROOM: from £30 to £40
SINGLE ROOM: from £35 to £45
FOOD: up to £15
**Hours:** breakfast 7.30am-9am, bar meals 12noon-2pm, dinner 6pm-9pm.
**Cuisine:** SCOTTISH - fresh home-cooked meals.
**Other points:** parking, children welcome, no-smoking area, vegetarian meals.
**Rooms:** 3 double rooms, 5 twin rooms, 1 family room. All with en suite, TV, telephone, hair dryer, trouser-press, tea/coffee-making facilities.
**Directions:** M90 junction 6 to Kinross town centre, then turn left. The hotel is 50 yards along.
ROBERT & GAIL BOATH ☎(01577) 863313
Fax (01577) 863313

## KIRKMICHAEL • map 16B4

### THE LOG CABIN HOTEL
PH10 7NB
*A large hotel built of whole Norwegian logs, set in the hills amid a majestic pine forest. Family-run, a definite après-ski atmosphere prevails in winter. A superb four-course dinner can be enjoyed in the Edelweiss restaurant, while the Viking Bar serves a comprehensive selection of bar meals. A unique base from which to explore the Perthshire area.*
DOUBLE ROOM: from £20 to £30
SINGLE ROOM: from £25 to £35
FOOD: up to £15
**Hours:** breakfast 8.45am-9.30am, lunch 12noon-1.45pm, dinner 7.30pm-8.45pm, open all year.
**Cuisine:** BRITISH - daily specials in the bar. Table d'hôte evening menu, using fresh local produce.
**Cards:** Visa, Access, Diners, AmEx.
**Other points:** licensed, open-air dining, Sunday lunch, children and pets welcome, garden, disabled access.
**Rooms:** 5 double rooms, 4 twin rooms, 4 family rooms. All with radio, tea/coffee-making facilities.
**Directions:** off the A924. Equidistant from Pitlochry and Blairgowrie.
ALAN FINCH & DAPHNE KIRK ☎(01250) 881288
Fax (01250) 881402

## MILNATHORT • map 16D4

### THE THISTLE HOTEL
25-27 New Road, KY13 7XT
*A small, residential country inn in a rural setting, only 1.5 miles from Kinross and the M90 junction. Under the personal supervision of the managers, Mr and Mrs Quinn, The Thistle Hotel provides welcoming, friendly service and good food in the lounge bar and in the restaurant at weekends.*
DOUBLE ROOM: from £20 to £30
SINGLE ROOM: up to £25
FOOD: up to £15
**Hours:** breakfast 8am-9am, lunch 12noon-2pm, bar meals 12noon-2pm, 6pm-9pm, high tea weekends 5pm-7.30pm, dinner 6pm-9pm.
**Cuisine:** ENGLISH - specialities include steaks and home-made pâté. A la carte and bar meals. Home-made sweets, own sticky toffee pudding and apple toffee pie.
**Cards:** Visa, Access.
**Other points:** licensed, children's licence, Sunday roast beef lunch.
**Rooms:** 1 single room, 1 double en suite, 2 twin rooms, 1 family room. All with TV, tea/coffee-making facilities.
**Directions:** M90 junction 6. A91 Perth to Stirling road in Milnathort.
MR J. HARLEY ☎(01577) 863222

## MONTROSE • map 16B5

### LINKS HOTEL
Mid Links, DD10 8RL

*Recently refurbished to a high standard, the Links Hotel is located in a prime setting overlooking public gardens. The hotel is ideally suited for touring the east coast of Scotland and Grampians.*
DOUBLE ROOM: from £30 to £40
SINGLE ROOM: from £35 to £45
FOOD: up to £15
**Hours:** breakfast 7.30am-9.30am, Sunday 8am-10am, dinner and bar suppers in the conservatory 12noon-2pm, 6.30pm-9.30pm, open all year, open bank holidays.
**Cuisine:** SCOTTISH - traditional cuisine. Traditional high tea every Sunday.
**Cards:** Visa, Access, Diners, AmEx.
**Other points:** licensed, Sunday lunch, children welcome, afternoon tea, residents' lounge, baby-listening device, baby-sitting, cots, 24hr reception, foreign exchange, left luggage.
**Rooms:** 3 single rooms, 7 double rooms, 10 twin rooms. All with TV, telephone, tea/coffee-making facilities, radio, alarm.
**Directions:** 2 minutes' walk from the town centre.
MR C.W. NINTEMAN ☎(01674) 671000
Fax(01674) 672698

## PERTH • map 16C4

### ALMONDBANK INN
Almondbank, PH1 3NH

*Olde-worlde inn overlooking the River Almond in an attractive country village. Good food at very reasonable prices, friendly staff and a fun local atmosphere.*
FOOD: up to £15
**Hours:** Lunch Monday-Saturday 12noon-2.15pm, Sunday 12.30am-2.15pm, bar tea Sunday-Thursday 5pm-8.30pm, Friday and Saturday 6.30pm-10pm.
**Cuisine:** ENGLISH - all fresh ingredients used: fresh melon, prawn and cheese salad, steaks, prawn salad, plus a wide variety of special dishes.
**Cards:** Visa, Access.
**Other points:** licensed, Sunday lunch, children welcome, beer garden.
**Directions:** middle of main street of Almondbank village, about 3 miles from Perth.
MR & MRS C. LINDSAY ☎(01738) 583242

## PITLOCHRY • map 16B4

### GREEN PARK HOTEL
Clunie Bridge Road, PH16 5JY

*This is a country house hotel situated on the banks of the lovely Loch Faskally, and although secluded, it is only five minutes' walk from the centre of the town. Popular with golfers because of the nearby golf course. Other facilities include fishing, sailing, golf and walking. Casserole Award winner 1990, 1991 and 1994.*
DOUBLE ROOM: from £40 to £50

SINGLE ROOM: from £40 to £50
FOOD: from £15 to £20 🍽
**Hours:** dinner 6.30pm-8.30pm, bar meals 12noon-2.30pm, bar meals 6pm-8.30pm, closed November until mid-March.
**Cuisine:** SCOTTISH - Scottish cuisine, e.g., salmon, venison, Highland bonnets.
**Cards:** Visa, Access, Switch.
**Other points:** children welcome, no-smoking area, fishing.
**Rooms:** 2 single rooms, 12 double rooms, 23 twin rooms.
**Directions:** on the A924 in north-west Pitlochry, on the left as you leave town.
MR & MRS GRAHAM BROWN ☎(01796) 473248
Fax(01796) 473520

### PITLOCHRY FESTIVAL THEATRE
Port-na-Craig , PH16 5DR

*Not only is the Pitlochry Festival Theatre the setting for some outstanding plays and concerts, but also a magnificent riverside restaurant where visitors can enjoy a relaxed meal choosing from a range of delicious menus. Booking for dinner is essential.*
FOOD: up to £20, lunch to £13, dinner to £20
**Hours:** lunch, salad bar and snacks Monday-Saturday 12noon-2pm, dinner Monday-Saturday 6.30pm (one sitting), coffee shop Monday-Saturday 10am-11pm. losed Sunday except concert Sundays. Open bank holidays, closed 8th October until the first week of April.
**Cuisine:** poached fillet of salmon with tomato butter sauce; loin of pork with prunes and apple brandy sauce; apple, mincemeat and marzipan strudel served warm with a whisky sauce.
**Cards:** Access, Visa, Diners, AmEx, MasterCard
**Other points:** pre-booked lunches, high teas and afternoon teas available for groups. Disabled facilities, parking.
**Directions:** A9, when approaching from the south turn left at the Blair Athol Distillery.
PITLOCHRY FESTIVAL THEATRE ☎(01796) 473054 Fax(01796) 473054

### SCOTLAND'S HOTEL
Bonnethill Road, PH16 5BT

*Centrally yet quietly located in picturesque Pitlochry, this friendly, family-owned and operated hotel enjoys a good reputation for comfortable bedrooms, fine food and attentive service. A new indoor leisure club features a 12-metre swimming pool, spa bath, solarium, sauna, mini-gym and beauty salon. Complimentary mini-bus to/from the Festival Theatre, railway station and golf course.*
DOUBLE ROOM: from £40 to £50
SINGLE ROOM: from £40 to £50
FOOD: from £15 to £20
**Hours:** breakfast 7.30am-9.30am, lunch 12noon-2pm, dinner 6.30pm-8.30pm.
**Cuisine:** SCOTTISH - table d'hôte with ample choice. A la carte also available. Speciality: salmon.
**Cards:** Visa, Access, Diners, AmEx, Switch, MasterCard, Eurocard

**Other points:** licensed, parking, children welcome, garden, pets allowed, launderette, cots, bar.
**Rooms:** 13 single rooms, 1 double room, 23 twin rooms, 13 family rooms. All with TV, radio, telephone, tea/coffee-making facilities.
**Directions:** follow slip road from A9 or A924 into the centre of town. Turn off opposite Co-op, to find hotel on the right.
ERHARD J. PENKER & FAMILY ☎(01796) 472292
Fax(01796) 473284

# WESTERN ISLES

## ISLE OF BARRA • map 17D1

 **CASTLEBAY HOTEL**
Castlebay, H59 5XD
*A small, family-run hotel in the main village overlooking the harbour and the Isle of Vatersay. Comfortable accommodation and good food. While visiting here you can enjoy walking, fishing or sailing. If you would rather relax, there are plenty of beautiful, secluded, sandy beaches to choose from.*
DOUBLE ROOM: from £20 to £30
SINGLE ROOM: from £20 to £30
FOOD: up to £15
**Hours:** breakfast 7.30am-9.30am, lunch 12.30am-2pm, bar meals 11am-9pm, dinner 6pm-9pm.
**Cuisine:** ENGLISH - traditional cuisine, with an emphasis on fresh fish. Dishes may include fresh crab, scallops, cockles, mussels, steaks and vegetarian choices.
**Cards:** Visa, Access.
**Other points:** licensed, open-air dining, Sunday lunch, children welcome, afternoon tea, pets allowed, residents' lounge, residents' bar, parking.
**Rooms:** 10 twin/double rooms. All with TV, telephone, tea/coffee-making facilities.
**Directions:** in the centre of Castlebay.
MR GEORGE MACLEOD ☎(01871) 810223
Fax(01871) 810455

## ISLE OF BENBECULA • map 17C1

 **DARK ISLAND HOTEL**
Liniclate, PA88 5PJ
*Privately-owned hotel, offering comfortable, well-appointed accommodation, good food and service. Ideal holiday base, being well-situated for exploring adjacent islands: North Uist, Barra, Eriskay. Golf is available free of charge, and there is trout fishing on over 70 lochs. This is also the perfect place to stay if you are a keen archeologist or ornithologist.*
DOUBLE ROOM: from £30 to £40
FOOD: from £15 to £20 ⌐
**Hours:** bar meals 12noon, bar meals 6pm-10pm.
**Cuisine:** BRITISH - `Taste of Scotland' cuisine, specialities seafood and shellfish. Also Laird's game casserole, Ben Mor mountain haggis and shepherd's grill.
**Cards:** Visa, Access.
**Other points:** children welcome, pets allowed,

open bank holidays, residents' lounge.
**Rooms:** 8 single rooms, 22 double rooms, 13 twin rooms, 1 family room. All with TV, radio, alarm, tea/coffee-making facilities.
**Directions:** 4 miles from airport, 26 miles from ferry terminals (Loch Boisdale and Lochmaddy).
MR D.J. PETERANNA ☎(01870) 603030
Fax(01870) 602347

## ISLE OF HARRIS • map 17B1

 **THE HARRIS HOTEL**
Tarbert, Harris, HS3 3DL
*An established family-run hotel. J.M. Barrie once stayed here and etched his initials in the dining-room window. The hotel is a perfect base for touring Harris and Lewis, and people return year after year to soak up the history, peace and unspoilt beauty of these dramatic islands.*
DOUBLE ROOM: from £30 to £40
SINGLE ROOM: from £25 to £35
FOOD: CLUB
**Hours:** breakfast 8.30am-9.15am, lunch 12noon-2pm, dinner 7.30pm-9pm.
**Cuisine:** BRITISH
**Cards:** Visa, Access, MasterCard.
**Other points:** central heating, children welcome, residents' lounge, garden.
**Rooms:** 4 single room, 6 double rooms, 12 twin rooms, 2 family rooms.
**Directions:** on the A859 central to village of Tarbert.
HELEN & JOHN MORRISON ☎(0185950) 2154/2425 Fax(0185950) 2281

## NORTH UIST • map 17B1

 **LOCHMADDY HOTEL**
Lochmaddy, H56 5AA
*Having undergone extensive restoration, this family-run sporting hotel offers good-quality food and comfortable accommodation in tastefully furnished surroundings. The Lochmaddy is ideally situated for access to nearby beaches, fishing lochs, bird reserves and archeological sites.*
DOUBLE ROOM: from £28 to £36
SINGLE ROOM: from £30 to £39
FOOD: from £15 ⌐
**Hours:** breakfast 8am-9.30am, bar meals 12noon-

2pm, 5.30pm-9pm, dinner 7pm-9pm, open all year.
**Cuisine:** TRADITIONAL BRITISH - daily changing
menus offering a wide selection of local fare
including venison, salmon, scallops, king prawns,
crab, lobster etc.
**Cards:** Visa, Access, AmEx.
**Other points:** licensed, Sunday lunch, children
welcome, pets allowed, afternoon tea, garden,
residents' lounge, parking, baby-listening device,
cots, residents' bar.
**Rooms:** 8 single rooms, 4 double rooms, 3 twin
rooms. All with TV, radio, alarm, telephone,
tea/coffee-making facilities.
**Directions:** 100 yards from Lochmaddy ferry
terminal.
MR JOHN COLES ☎(01876) 500331/500332
Fax(01876) 500210

C.J.Duppa.Miller.

# IRELAND

Ireland is excellent touring country - a world where time has stood still, a wild and enchanting landscape of emerald-green, windswept moors, remote lakes, ever-changing scenery and dramatic skies.

There are now 36 Les Routiers establishments throughout Ireland. Some have won major awards for their outstanding food and accommodation, but they all offer the same unmistakeable warm friendly welcome in the true Irish spirit. In recognition of their conscientious efforts to make every visitor feel welcome, and for providing excellent quality and value, Les Routiers has given its establishments in Ireland their very own award. (See page 49 for further details.)

The scenery in Ireland is as pleasing as the Irish hospitality itself. In the north, the famous Mountains of Mourne idolized in song - with their twelve magnificent rounded summits are particularly worth seeing. The Sperrin Mountains are networked by tiny streams and roads where the walker and naturalist is often rewarded with sightings of golden plover and red grouse. The countryside is also scattered with many National Trust properties, such as Castle Coole, and Florence Court from which the yew tree originated.

Extraordinarily beautiful is the only way to describe southern Ireland. The breathtaking scenery varies immensely, from the lush, inland pastures interspersed with tiny villages, to the rugged coastal peninsulas and miles of golden, sandy beaches washed by the warm waters of the Gulf Stream. The warm coastal climate also provides some of Ireland's abundant seafood, such as mussels from West Cork and scallops from Kenmare Bay. Baked Killyleagh trout, swordfish steaks, roast monkfish, guinea fowl, game terrine and lamb kebabs are just a few of the many exquisite dishes that the visitor can expect to find on the daily menu, alongside traditional British and adventurous continental choices. Visitors seeking interesting places to visit and explore are spoilt for choice. Probably the most famous of all can be found in County Cork: Blarney Castle, with its Blarney Stone. Others regional attractions, to name but a few, include the Waterford Crystal Centre in County Waterford; Glendalough, a 6th century monastic settlement in the Wicklow Mountains; in County Cork, Fota House and Estate, Ireland's first wildlife park; the Irish Transport Museum at Killarney in County Kerry; and the Limerick City Gallery of Art.

Altogether, a charming land of equally charming people with a twinkle in their eye, who will welcome you as good friends - this is Les Routiers in Ireland.

Les Routiers establishments throughout Ireland listed in this chapter appear in the alphabetical order of their county:

| | | |
|---|---|---|
| Co. Antrim | Co. Carlow | Co. Clare |
| Co. Cork | Co. Donegal | Co. Down |
| Co. Dublin | Co. Fermanagh | Co. Galway |
| Co. Kerry | Co. Kildare | Co. Kilkenny |
| Co. Limerick | Co. Louth | Co. Mayo |
| Co. Offaly | Co. Sligo | Co. Tyrone |
| Co. Wexford | Co. Wicklow | |

## CO. ANTRIM

### BELFAST • map 13D3

**SAINTS & SCHOLARS LTD**
3 University Street, University & Malone,
BT7 1FY
*Highly popular and attractively furnished bistro-style restaurant on two floors, with a bar on each. The atmosphere is warm, welcoming and lively. Nearby places of interest include the Ulster Museum and Queens University.*
FOOD: up to £15 CLUB
**Hours:** meals all day Monday to Saturday 12noon-late, Sunday lunch 12.30pm, dinner 5.30pm-9.30pm.
**Cuisine:** INTERNATIONAL - à la carte menu, combining traditional and modern dishes, complemented by a fine wine list. Vegetarian dishes available.
**Cards:** Visa, Access, Diners, AmEx.
**Other points:** licensed, Sunday lunch, children welcome, vegetarian meals, open bank holidays, parking.
**Directions:** situated on the left, off University Road, before Queens University.
DIRK LAKEMAN ☎(01232) 325137 Fax(01232) 323240

**STORMONT HOTEL**
Upper Newtownards Road, BT4 3LP
*Superbly situated close to the city and airport and in a quiet residential area, adjacent to Stormont Castle. The hotel offers all the facilities expected by the discerning traveller including two restaurants, cocktail bar, sunken lounge area and glass roofed atrium. Excellent transport links being a mere 3 minutes from from the outer ring road linking up with the M1 to Dublin.*
DOUBLE ROOM: from £57
SINGLE ROOM: from £89
FOOD: from £15 to £20
**Hours:** breakfast 7am-10am, lunch restaurant 12.30pm-2.30pm, lunch bar 12.30pm-5pm, dinner restaurant 6.30pm-10pm, dinner bar 5pm-10pm. Open bank holidays.
**Cuisine:** FRENCH / ENGLISH - comprehensive à la carte and carte d'jour menus with a wide choice to suit all tastes. Vegetarian dishes also available.
**Cards:** Visa, Access, Diners, AmEx.
**Other points:** special weekend rates (double £26 per person, single £45 per person), weekend special break (2nights B&B + 1 dinner £80 per person), conference/banqueting facilities, access to gymnasium, tennis courts, snooker room, squash courts, indoor and outdoor bowling, outdoor playing fields, children welcome, parking.
**Rooms:** 69 double rooms, 34 twin rooms, 2 suites, 4 apartments (4 persons). All en suite with TV, telephone, radio, alarm, hair dryer, trouser press, room service, iron, tea/coffee-making facilities.
**Directions:** approximately 5 minutes drive from city centre towards Newtownards.

HASTINGS HOTELS ☎(01232) 658621 Fax(01232) 480240

---

**For ferry crossings to Liverpool / Heysham see M.V. 'King Orry' under Douglas Isle of Man page.**

---

### BUSHMILLS • map 13B3

**HILLCREST COUNTRY HOUSE & RESTAURANT**
306 Whitepark Road, BT57 8SN
*An internationally renowned, award-winning guest house, offering comfortable and well-appointed accommodation in spacious en suite rooms, all with marvellous coastal or rural views. The restaurant offers traditional menus using the finest fresh ingredients, specializing in local seafood and game. Beautifully furnished throughout, and highly recommended. Les Routiers Restaurant of the Year: Ireland 1994, Corp D'Elite Wine List 1995, All Ireland Galtee Irish Breakfast Award 1994.*
DOUBLE ROOM: from £20 to £30
SINGLE ROOM: from £25 to £35
FOOD: from £15 to £20 CLUB
**Hours:** breakfast 8.30am-9.30am, lunch 12.30am-2.30pm, dinner 5pm-9pm, closed Monday to Saturday 1st October until 31st April
**Cuisine:** BRITISH - food and service of the highest standard.
**Cards:** Visa, Access.
**Other points:** parking, children catered for (please check for age limits), Sunday lunch, no-smoking area, disabled access, residents' lounge, vegetarian meals, garden.
**Rooms:** 1 double room, 3 twin rooms.
**Directions:** one mile out of Bushmills village, on the main road to Giant's Causeway.
MR M. MCKEEVER ☎(012657) 31577 Fax(012657) 31577

### PORTRUSH • map 13B3

**CAUSEWAY COAST HOTEL & CONFERENCE CENTRE**
36 Ballyreagh Road, BT56 8LR
*Overlooking the Atlantic Ocean and hills of Donegal, this is a new, well-furnished building. The atmosphere is busy and efficient, warm and friendly, with live music. Comfortable accommodation and conference facilities are provided.*
DOUBLE ROOM: from £30 to £40
SINGLE ROOM: from £45 to £55
FOOD: up to £15
**Hours:** breakfast 7.30am-10.30am, bar snacks 12noon-2.30pm, dinner 7.30pm-9.30pm, bar snacks 5pm-9.30pm.
**Cuisine:** BRITISH
**Cards:** Visa, Access, AmEx.
**Other points:** parking, children welcome, Sunday lunch, no-smoking area, afternoon teas, disabled access, residents' lounge, vegetarian meals, evening entertainment.

---

**For Reservations & Special Offers FreeCall 0500 700 456**

**Rooms:** 21 bedrooms.
**Directions:** located on A2 coastal road between resorts of Portrush and Portstewart.
ROBERT ROONEY ☎(01265) 822435 Fax(01265) 824495

## CO. CARLOW

### LEIGHLINBRIDGE • map 19D3

🍴 **LORD BAGENAL INN**
*This famous old inn is well known for its warm welcome and comprehensive and interesting menu. Children are especially welcome, and the inn has won a "Friendly Family" symbol to emphasise this. Family Sunday lunches are a speciality and there are private rooms available for birthdays and anniversaries. The wine list is particularly impressive and features offerings from all over the world. Well recommended.*
FOOD: from £15 to £20
**Hours:** lunch restaurant and bar 12.30pm-2.30pm, dinner restaurant 6.30pm-10.15pm, dinner bar 6.30pm-10.30pm.
**Cuisine:** MODERN WITH CLASSICAL INFLUENCE - stuffed spiced shank of lamb, prawns Sicillian, poached troncon of fresh Slaney salmon, braised rabbit "hunter" style, medaillons of monkfish "Bercy".
**Cards:** Visa, Access, Diners.
**Other points:** vegetarian meals, banquet facilites car parking on site.
**Directions:** off the Dublin to Waterford road - take the exit to Leighlinbridge, N9, 8 miles fron Carlow.
MR JAMES KEHOE ☎(0503) 21668 Fax(0503) 21668

## CO. CLARE

### KILKEE • map 19D1

🏨 **HALPINS HOTEL**
Erin Street
*Overlooking old Victorian Kilkee, the tastefully refurbished Halpins Hotel offers quality, comfort and fine food. Close to Shannon Airport and Killimer car ferry, Kilkee is an excellent base when touring the West Coast. Facilities nearby include the Loop Drive, cliff walks, golf and angling. The owners offer the same quality service at Aberdeen Lodge in Dublin 4.*
DOUBLE ROOM: from £25 to £35
SINGLE ROOM: from £30 to £40
FOOD: from £15 to £20
**Hours:** breakfast 8am-10am, dinner 7pm-9.30pm, closed January until 15th March.
**Cuisine:** CONTINENTAL - fresh seafood and meat dishes.
**Cards:** Visa, Access, Diners, AmEx.
**Other points:** parking, no-smoking area, conference facilities, residents' lounge, garden, vegetarian meals, traditional Sunday lunch, afternoon teas.

**Rooms:** 2 single rooms, 3 double rooms, 3 twin rooms, 4 triple room. All en suite, with TV, telephone, radio, hair dryer, room service.
**Directions:** overlooking Kilkee Beach, 40 miles from Shannon Airport, 10 miles from Shann car ferry.
PAT HALPIN ☎(065) 56032 Fax(065) 56317

## CO. CORK

### BLARNEY • map 19E2

🏨 **THE BLARNEY PARK HOTEL**
*A modern and extremely well appointed hotel situated in the "biggest little village in Ireland". This most historic corner of Ireland offers you the opportunity to mingle with the local people or just explore the nostalgic countryside. After a busy day of sightseeing, the Blarney Park offers you a beautifully equipped bedroom to prepare for a memorable meal in The Clancarty restaurant with International cuisine complemented by a fine wine list. The swimming pool, sauna and steam room have won the national quality award for Ireland's top leisure centre.*
DOUBLE ROOM: from £30 to £50
SINGLE ROOM: from £45 to £60
FOOD: up to £15
**Hours:** breakfast 7.30am-10am, lunch 12.30pm-2.30pm, dinner 6.30pm-9.30pm.
**Cuisine:** comprehensive à la carte and table d'hôte menus offering meat, fish, poultry and vegetarian dishes. Extensive wine list.
**Cards:** Visa, Access, Diners, AmEx.
**Other points:** parking, steam room, sauna and swimming pool with National Quality Award.
**Rooms:** 22 double rooms, 16 twin rooms, 38 family rooms. All en suite with TV, telephone, radio, alarm, hair dryer, baby listening device, room service.
MR GERRY O'CONNOR ☎(021) 385281 Fax(021) 381506

### MALLOW • map 19D2

🏨 **SPRINGFORT HALL**
Mallow
*This elegant 18th century country manor house, surrounded by woodlands and landscaped gardens, makes an ideal venue for weddings, functions, conferences or just a break away from reality. Here you can relax in the spacious lounge with its open log fire, dine in the superb restaurant, or simply enjoy the comforts of the luxurious and spacious en suite bedrooms. This Grade A country house is owned and run by the Walsh family, who together with their professional and friendly staff ensure that your stay at Springfort Hall will be a memorable one.*
DOUBLE ROOM: from £30 to £40
FOOD: from £15 to £20 🍷
**Hours:** breakfast 7.30am-10am, dinner 7pm-9.30pm.
**Cuisine:** BRITISH / CONTINENTAL
**Cards:** Visa, Access, Diners, AmEx.

Other points: parking, children welcome, conference facilities, garden, vegetarian meals.
Rooms: 13 double rooms, 9 twin rooms, 2 family rooms. All with TV, telephone, radio, alarm, hair dryer, room service.
Directions: off the N20 main Cork-Limerick road.
MICHAEL & EILEEN WALSH ☎(022) 21278
Fax(022) 21557

## CO. DONEGAL

### BALLYBOFEY • map 13C1

#### JACKSON'S HOTEL
Ballybofey
*Family-run since 1945, renowned for good food, welcoming hospitality and comfortable accommodation. The new leisure centre has a 22-metre swimming pool, hairdresser, creche, etc. The hotel is situated in its own gardens on the banks of the River Finn, opposite Drumboe Woods. Local amenities include trout, salmon and pike fishing, tennis, canoeing, hill-walking, golf and horse-riding. An ideal touring base.*
DOUBLE ROOM: from £30 to £40
FOOD: up to £20
Cuisine: INTERNATIONAL
Cards: Visa, Access, Diners, AmEx.
Other points: parking, children welcome, residents' lounge, vegetarian meals, gym facilities.
Rooms: 5 single rooms, 28 double rooms, 50 twin rooms, 6 suites. All with en suite, TV, telephone, hair dryer, trouser-press, room service.
Directions: 2 hours from Belfast and 3 hours from Dublin.
MARGARET & BARRY JACKSON ☎(074) 31021
Fax(074) 31096

### LAGHEY • map 19B2

#### MOORLAND COUNTRY GUEST HOUSE
Ballinakillew Mountain
*A newly built guesthouse situated on a wild, high moor with unusual plant and animal life in an area which has been influenced by peat cutting since prehistoric times. An ideal starting point for unlimited walks, angling, sandy bathing beaches, golf and horse riding. Eight guest rooms are available together with a pleasant recreation room and sauna to recover from the exertions of the day!*
DOUBLE ROOM: from £20 to £30
SINGLE ROOM: from £15 to £25
FOOD: up to £15
Hours: breakfast 8am-11am, lunch Monday to Saturday on request, Sunday 12.30pm-3pm, dinner 6.30pm-10pm, closed bank holidays.
Cuisine: INTERNATIONAL - house speciality is "Moorland Platter", a delicious assortment of medaillons of beef, schnitzel, noisettes of lamb and a cevapcici in a red wine sauce.
Cards: Visa, Access.
Other points: recreation room, bicycles and canoes to rent, children's playground, sauna, beauty salon, high teas, parking.

Rooms: 4 twin rooms, 3 double rooms, 1 family room, all en suite. All with TV and room service.
Directions: take N15 Ballyshannon - Donegal road. Take road to Laghey and Pettigo.
☎(073) 34319

## CO. DOWN

### DUNDRUM • map 13E3

#### BUCK'S HEAD
77 Main Street, BT33 0LU
*This is a country pub, dating back to the 18th century, which has been completely renovated, and a conservatory and beer garden have been added. The conservatory will seat private parties of 20 to 40 people. The dining room is panelled in beech and cherry wood, with an open fire and an atmosphere that is conducive to casual and intimate dining. The airy, bright conservatory looks out onto a patio and beer garden. Children are welcome until 7pm.*
FOOD: from £15 to £20
Hours: lunch 12noon-2.30pm, bar meals 12noon-2.30pm, dinner 7pm-9.30pm, bar meals 5.30pm-7pm, closed Christmas day.
Cuisine: BRITISH - outstanding meals made from top-quality local ingredients and attractively presented.
Cards: Visa, Access, AmEx, MasterCard.
Other points: children welcome, open-air dining, vegetarian meals, traditional Sunday lunch.
Directions: Dundrum is located 3 miles from Newcastle on the main Belfast-Newcastle road.
MRS A.M. GRIFFITH ☎(013967) 51868
Fax(013967) 51898

### HILLSBOROUGH • map 13D3

#### THE PLOUGH INN
3 The Square, BT26 6AG
*A delightful olde-worlde licensed inn, bistro and restaurant tastefully decorated with many interesting nooks and recesses. The preparation and presentation of the food and the service of the staff are of the highest standard. A visit is highly recommended.*
FOOD: from £15 to £20
Hours: lunch 12noon-2.15pm, bar meals 5pm-7pm, dinner 6pm-9pm.
Cuisine: INTERNATIONAL - rustic home-cooking and international à la carte. Seafood and seasonal fare e.g. game and spring Irish lamb a speciality. Business lunches. Beer and herb garden. Wine bar.
Cards: Visa, Access, Diners, AmEx.
Other points: parking, conference facilities, no-smoking area, open-air dining, vegetarian meals. Special outdoor catering events arranged in summer.
Directions: follow signs to Hillsborough from the Sprucefield roundabout on the M1 Belfast to Dublin motorway.
DEREK, WILLIAM & RICHARD PATTERSON
☎(01846) 682985 Fax(01846) 682472

---

**For Reservations & Special Offers FreeCall 0500 700 456**

## KILKEEL • map 13E3

**KILMOREY ARMS HOTEL**
41-43 Greencastle Street, BT34 4BH
*Situated in County Down exactly where 'the mountains of Mourne sweep down to the sea', this is the ideal location from which to experience an incredibly beautiful part of Ireland. This family-run hotel with many modern facilities offers an unobtrusive, relaxed and friendly atmosphere, with attention to detail at all times. Surrounded by breathtaking beauty, there are miles of pathways for walkers, sports, historic houses and nearby seaside resorts to visit.*
DOUBLE ROOM: from £22
SINGLE ROOM: from £28
FOOD: up to £15
**Hours:** breakfast 7.30am-9.30am, lunch 12.30am-2.30pm, bar snacks 12noon-3pm, dinner 5.30pm-9pm, bar snacks 5pm-8pm.
**Cuisine:** INTERNATIONAL
**Cards:** Visa, Access, AmEx, Eurocard, MasterCard.
**Other points:** parking, children welcome, open bank holidays, no-smoking area, afternoon tea, disabled access, pets allowed, vegetarian meals, garden, adjoining bedrooms, disabled bedrooms, functions room (200 persons).
**Rooms:** 5 single rooms, 6 double rooms, 13 twin rooms, 3 family rooms.
**Directions:** on A2.
LINDSAY MCMURRAY & HUGH & ROBERT GIFFEN ☎(016937) 62220 Fax(016937) 65399

## KILLYLEAGH • map 14D4

**DUFFERIN ARMS**
35 High Street, BT30 9QF

*The Dufferin Arms offers a warm welcome and a friendly atmosphere for travellers and for businessmen. It is very popular and highly recommended. Ideal for visiting the many nearby attractions, including Killyleagh Castle, Strangford Lough and Delamont Country Park. Dufferin Arms also offers comfortable accommodation, self-catering apartments, and studios with a large lounge, country-style kitchen and access to barbeque and picnic table.*
DOUBLE ROOM: from £20 to £25
SINGLE ROOM: from £30
FOOD: from £15 to £20    CLUB
**Hours:** lunch 12.30am-2.30pm, Sunday brunch 12.30am-2.30pm, dinner and supper Monday-Wednesday 6pm-8.30pm, Thursday-Saturday 6pm-9.30pm.
**Cuisine:** INTERNATIONAL - à la carte menu, offering baked Killyleagh trout, char-grilled steak and lamb kebabs, all with fresh seasonal vegetables. Excellent wine list.
**Cards:** Visa, Access.
**Other points:** licensed, music, children welcome, afternoon tea, open bank holidays, vegetarian meals, activities arranged.
**Rooms:** 7 bedrooms, 3 self-catering apartments.
**Directions:** located in front of Killyleagh Castle.
MORRIS CRAWFORD & KITTY STEWART
☎(01396) 828229 Fax(01396) 828755

## LOUGHBRICKLAND • map 19B3

**ROAD CHEF**
179 Dublin Road, BT32
*This old-world restaurant offers diners attractive surroundings in which to enjoy good food, excellent service and a relaxed, homely atmosphere. All dishes from the extensive menu, catering for all tastes, are made from the freshest local produce.*
FOOD: up to £15
**Hours:** meals all day 8am-8pm, closed Christmas eve, Christmas day, Boxing day and New Year's day.
**Cuisine:** BRITISH - steaks, grills, snacks and light lunches. Good, wholesome food.
**Other points:** parking, children welcome, no-smoking area, vegetarian meals, afternoon teas, traditional Sunday lunch.
**Directions:** on main road between Belfast and Dublin, the T4 trunk road. Newry side of Loughbrickland.
FRANK DOWNEY ☎(01762) 318366

## NEWCASTLE • map 19B3

**MARIO'S RESTAURANT**
65 South Promenade, BT33 0EY
*Situated on the South Promenade, and close to the harbour, Mario Limoni and his friendly staff offer you all that is best in traditional Continental cooking complemented by fresh local seafood and a good range of steaks. Table d'hôte and à la carte menus are available supported by a very good wine list with good value red and white house wines available.*
FOOD: from £15 to £25
**Hours:** lunch and bar meals 12.30pm-2.30pm, bar meals 3pm-6pm, dinner 7pm-9pm, open bank holidays.
**Cuisine:** CONTINENTAL - wide ranging menu including many Italian specialities, seafood and steaks.
**Cards:** Visa, Access, Diners, AmEx.
**Other points:** vegetarian meals, high teas (5pm-7pm), Sunday carvery lunch, parking.
**Directions:** on the Newcastle to Kilkeel road, .5 mile from Newcastle.
MARIO LIMONI
☎(13967) 23912

## NEWTOWNARDS • map 19B3

### MING COURT
63-65 Court Street, BT23 3NX

*On the east side of Newtownards, the Ming Court offers well-presented and served traditional Cantonese cuisine amidst an efficient yet friendly atmosphere. It's popularity attracts a varied clientele of all ages.*

FOOD: up to £15   CLUB

**Hours:** lunch 12noon-2pm, dinner Monday-Friday 5.30pm-11.30pm, dinner Saturday 12noon-12midnight, dinner Sunday 12.30pm-11pm, open bank holidays.

**Cuisine:** CANTONESE - seafood, fish and lobster specialities.

**Cards:** Access, Visa, Diners

**Directions:** east side Newtownards, main route from Belfast to Portaferry, A20.

MR KWOK FUNG YAU & MISS ENG ENG TEH
☎(01247) 815073

## CO. DUBLIN

### BALLSBRIDGE • map 19C3

###  ABERDEEN LODGE
53-55 Park Avenue, Aylesbury Road, Ballsbridge, Dublin 4

*Sixteen tastefully furnished bedrooms await at this Edwardian hotel situated close to Dublin city centre. Under the proprietorship of Pat Halpin, the house was designed with space and comfort in mind, together with old-world charm and premier service.*

DOUBLE ROOM: from £30 to £40

SINGLE ROOM: from £45 to £50

FOOD: from £15 to £20

**Hours:** breakfast 7am-10am, dinner 7pm-9.30pm.

**Cuisine:** CONTINENTAL - seafood, meat and vegetarian dishes.

**Cards:** Visa, Access, Diners, AmEx.

**Other points:** parking, children welcome, no-smoking area, gym facilities, conference facilities, residents' lounge, garden, vegetarian meals, afternoon teas.

**Rooms:** 4 double rooms, 8 twin rooms, 4 family rooms. All en suite, with TV, telephone, hair dryer, trouser-press.

**Directions:** Park Avenue, off Aylesbury Road, close to the Martello Tower.

PAT HALPIN ☎(01) 2838155 Fax(01) 2837877

> **For ferry crossings to Liverpool / Heysham see M.V. 'King Orry' under Douglas Isle of Man page.**

## HOWTH • map 19C3

### HOWTH LODGE HOTEL
Howth

*Overlooking Ireland's Eye, Howth Lodge is owned and managed personally by the Hanratty family. Elegant restaurant with reputation for superb cuisine: fresh fish and charcoaled steaks a speciality. There are conference and banqueting facilities for up to 200 persons, with spectacular vistas of Claremont beach. Leisure club also available for guests' use (permission must be obtained for use of the gymnasium).*

DOUBLE ROOM: from £50 to £60

FOOD: from £17 to £22

**Hours:** breakfast 7.30am-10am, bar meals 12.30am-2pm, dinner 7pm-9.30pm, bar meals 7pm-9.30pm, closed 24th December until 27th December (inclusive).

**Cuisine:** FRENCH - using fresh local produce.

**Cards:** Visa, Access, Diners, AmEx.

**Other points:** parking, conference facilities, swimming pool, gym (only available to experienced users), sauna, steam room, Jacuzzi, vegetarian meals, traditional Sunday lunch, afternoon teas.

**Rooms:** 35 double rooms, 5 twin rooms, 6 triple rooms. All en suite, with TV, telephone, hair dryer, trouser-press, room service, tea/coffee-making facilities.

**Directions:** located on the main road from Dublin to Howth, only 12 kilometres from Dublin city centre and 9 kilometres from Dublin airport.

HANRATTY FAMILY ☎(01) 8321010 Fax(01) 322268

## CO. FERMANAGH

### ENNISKILLEN • map 13D1

### CROW'S NEST
12 High Street, BT7 4EH

*A characteristic, olde-worlde building set in the town centre offering traditional fare and efficient service amidst the comfortable, relaxed and friendly atmosphere of a family run business. Nearby places of interest, include Marble Arch Caves and Lough Erne.*

FOOD: up to £15

**Hours:** breakfast and lunch served all day, including bar meals, dinner and bar meals 6pm-late, open bank holidays.

**Cuisine:** bistro style dishes.

**Other points:** children welcome, no-smoking area, traditional Sunday lunch, vegetarian meals, afternoon teas.

**Directions:** Enniskillin town centre.

MR JAMES MCMANUS ☎(01365) 325252

### OSCARS RESTAURANT
29 Belmore Street

*A lovely little town-house restaurant situated in the centre of Enniskillen. Attractively decorated in pine, it has a friendly, fun atmosphere. Diners can choose from an extensive range of mouthwatering dishes. Nearby attractions include the Lakes of Fermanagh, Marble Arch Caves and Castle Coole.*
FOOD: up to £15 [CLUB]
**Hours:** dinner 5pm-10.30pm, closed Christmas day.
**Cuisine:** INTERNATIONAL
**Cards:** Visa, Access.
**Other points:** parking, children welcome, open bank holidays, disabled access, vegetarian meals.
**Directions:** Enniskillen town centre.
MR D. MAGEE ☎(01365) 327037

## CO. GALWAY

### CLIFDEN • map 19C1

### MALDUA GUEST HOUSE
Galway Road

*A highly acclaimed family-run guest house in the heart of Connemara. A high standard of accommodation, with all bedrooms individually designed and well appointed. Local amenities include golf course, sea angling, fishing, horse-riding, cycling, walking and historical tours. A warm welcome awaits you at Maldua.*
DOUBLE ROOM: from £20 to £30
**Hours:** breakfast 8am-9.30am, closed December.
**Cards:** Visa, Access, AmEx, Eurocard, MasterCard.
**Other points:** parking, children welcome, no-smoking area, residents' lounge, garden.
**Rooms:** 1 single room, 4 double rooms, 2 twin rooms, 2 triple rooms. All en suite, TV, telephone, radio, central heating, hair dryer, trouser-press, tea/coffee-making facilities.
**Directions:** N59 route from Galway city to Clifden.
IVOR & KATHLEEN DUANE ☎(095) 21171 [Fax](095) 21739

### LEENANE • map 19C1

### DELPHI LODGE

*Arguably Ireland's finest sporting lodge. A delightful country house in a beautiful lakeside setting surrounded by mountains providing luxurious accommodation and good home-cooking matched by a fine wine cellar. All rooms have a lake view. Nearby, the Delphi cottages combine a cosy, traditional atmosphere with 20th century comforts.*
DOUBLE ROOM: from £30 to £50
SINGLE ROOM: from £45 to £55
**Hours:** Lodge: open February 1st - September 30th. Cottages: open all year round.
**Cards:** Visa, Access.
**Other points:** Library, billiard room, children catered for (please check for age limits). The Delphi Fishery for top quality fly-fishing advance booking essential.
**Rooms:** 6 double rooms, 3 twin rooms, 2 triple rooms, all en suite.
**Directions:** north off N59, about 3 miles east of Leenane, towards Louisburgh for 6 miles. House on left in woods.
MR PETER MANTLE ☎(095) 42211 [Fax](095) 42296

### OUGHTERARD • map 19C1

### ROSS LAKE HOUSE HOTEL
Rosscahill

*Ross Lake House is a Georgian house situated at the end of a country road in a panoramic setting. The hotel is owned by Henry and Elaine Reid, and the emphasis is on quality food served in a relaxed atmosphere. An ideal base for touring Connemara, fishing on Lough Corrib or golfing at Oughterard.*
DOUBLE ROOM: from £35 to £45
SINGLE ROOM: from £45 to £60
FOOD: from £15 to £20
**Hours:** breakfast 8am-10am, dinner 7pm-9pm, closed 1st November until mid-March.
**Cuisine:** IRISH - quality ingredients used to produce quality dishes.
**Cards:** Visa, Access, Diners, AmEx.
**Other points:** parking, residents' lounge, garden, vegetarian meals.
**Rooms:** 1 single room, 12 double rooms. All with en suite, telephone, room service.
**Directions:** 14 miles from Galway city, 6 miles past Moycullen village.
HENRY & ELAINE REID ☎(091) 80109 [Fax](091) 80184

## CO. KILDARE

### NAAS • map 19C3

### JOHNSTOWN INN
Johnstown Village

*This typical Irish 'pub' is situated just 8 miles from the Curragh racecourse in the beautiful county of Kildare. Traditional music is played in the lounge every Friday, Saturday and Sunday and admission is free. Good value 'tourist' and table d' hôte menus are offered, together with a tempting wine list. 10 golf courses within easy reach, together with the Irish National Stud and museum and many other tourist attractions.*
DOUBLE ROOM: from £20 to £30
FOOD: from £15 to £20
**Hours:** lunch 12.30pm-2.30pm, bar meals 3pm-10pm, dinner 6pm-10pm, open bank holidays, closed Christmas Day.

**Cuisine:** TRADITIONAL - steaks and seafood a specialty
**Cards:** Visa, Access.
**Other points:** theme evenings, beer garden.
**Directions:** 1.5 miles from Naas (Dublin side).
MR JIM SHERIDAN ☎(045) 897547 Fax(045) 874638

## CO. KILKENNY

### KILKENNY • map 19D2

#### BUTLER HOUSE
Patrick Street
*Butler House is the dower house of Kilkenny Castle. Sweeping staircases, magnificent plastered ceilings, marble fireplaces and a walled garden are all features of this notable Georgian residence in the heart of medieval Kilkenny city. This is a room-and-breakfast experience the likes of which you are unlikely to have experienced.*
DOUBLE ROOM: from £30 to £40
SINGLE ROOM: from £41 to £50
**Hours:** breakfast 8am-10am.
**Cards:** Visa, Access, Diners, AmEx.
**Other points:** parking, children welcome, conference facilities, residents' lounge, garden.
**Rooms:** 1 single room, 3 family rooms, 2 twin rooms, 7 double rooms. All en suite, with TV, telephone, radio, hair dryer, trouser-press, tea/coffee-making facilities.
**Directions:** in the city centre, near Waterford Road.
MR ANTHONY FOLEY ☎(056) 65707/22828
Fax(056) 65626

## CO. LIMERICK

### ADARE • map 19D2

#### WOODLANDS HOUSE HOTEL
Knockanes, Adare
*Set in its own private grounds, three kilometres from Adare, Woodlands House Hotel is owned and managed by Mary and Dick Fitzgerald. A comfortable 57-bedroom hotel, offering deluxe accommodation, executive suites and conference facilities. Its excellent cuisine, using the best of Golden Vale products, makes Woodlands Hotel a popular venue for weddings, functions, Sunday lunch and candlelit dinners. Convenient for many local sporting amenities. Special group rates available.*
DOUBLE ROOM: from £20 to £30
FOOD: up to £15 ☜
**Hours:** breakfast 7.30am-10am, dinner 6.30pm-9.30pm, bar meals 12noon-10.30pm, closed 23rd December until 26th December.
**Cuisine:** IRISH - traditional dishes.
**Cards:** Visa, Access, Diners, AmEx.
**Other points:** parking, children welcome, conference facilities, garden, vegetarian meals, traditional Sunday lunch.
**Rooms:** 25 double rooms, 25 twin rooms, 3 family

rooms and 4 suites, all en suite. All with TV, telephone, radio, hair dryer, trouser-press, room service, baby-listening device, tea/coffee-making facilities.
**Directions:** off N21, 1.5 miles north of Adare; look for signposts on the right.
DICK & MARY FITZGERALD ☎(061) 396118/396553 Fax(061) 396073

### LIMERICK • map 19D2

#### HOTEL GREENHILLS
Ennis Road
*This lovely hotel situated amidst three and half acres of landscaped gardens offers 55 en suite bedrooms furnished and equipped to the highest standards. The hotel has its own lively bar, "The Jockey Club", a brasserie/grill and "The Bay Leaf" restaurant which offers top class food in intimate surroundings. An ideal touring base for the Lakes of Killarney for which a packed lunch can be provided on request. A delightful hotel which will lure you back time and again.*
DOUBLE ROOM: from £40 to £50
SINGLE ROOM: £15 single supplement
FOOD: from £85
**Hours:** breakfast 7.30am-10am, lunch (bar and restaurant) 12.30pm-2.30pm, dinner 6pm-9.30pm.
**Cuisine:** INTERNATIONAL - à la carte and table d'hôte menus, also carvery and bar snacks.
**Cards:** Visa, Access, Diners, AmEx.
**Other points:** health/leisure complex for guests' use with heated indoor pool, gardens, free parking.
**Rooms:** 55 en suite bedrooms with tea/coffee-maker, TV, telephone, radio.
**Directions:** located 5 minutes drive from Limerick city centre in the direction of Shannon airport.
MR BRYAN J. GREEN ☎061 453033
Fax061 453307

## CO. LOUTH

### DROGHEDA • map 19C3

#### BOYNE VALLEY HOTEL
Drogheda
*A gracious country house on 16 acres of beautiful gardens and woodlands beside the historic town of Drogheda, 25 miles from Dublin and 20 miles from Dublin Airport. There is a new extension with deluxe rooms. The Cellar restaurant provides a wide selection of delicious meals, and they receive a daily supply of fresh fish. Nearby are the famous prehistoric sites of Newgrange, Dowth, Knowth and the medieval abbeys of Mellifont and Monasterboice. This family-run hotel offers a warm welcome and true Irish hospitality.*
DOUBLE ROOM: from £30 to £40
FOOD: up to £15
**Hours:** breakfast 7am-11am, lunch 12.30am-2.30pm, bar meals 10am-5pm, dinner 6.30pm-10pm.
**Cuisine:** CONTINENTAL
**Cards:** Visa, Access, Diners, AmEx, MasterCard.

**Other points:** parking, children welcome, pets allowed, no-smoking area, conference facilities, residents' lounge, garden, vegetarian meals, traditional Sunday lunch, afternoon teas.
**Rooms:** 7 single rooms, 18 double rooms, 9 twin rooms, 3 family rooms. All with en suite, TV, telephone, hairdryer, room service, tea/coffee-making facilities.
**Directions:** just south of Drogheda on the N1.
MICHAEL & ROSEMARY MCNAMARA ☎(041) 37737 Fax(041) 39188

# CO. MAYO

## PONTOON • map 19B
## HOTEL OF THE YEAR 1996 - IRELAND
 **PONTOON BRIDGE HOTEL**
Pontoon

*Located on the sandy shores of Loughs Conn and Cullen, with panoramic surroundings. Excellent food and good-value wines in the Lakeside Restaurant. Nightly musical entertainment. This is Ireland's number-one angling centre for trout and salmon fishing, with guides, boats, rod hire, tackle, etc. Two- and four-day schools of fly-fishing, landscape-painting and cookery, all with professional tuition.*
DOUBLE ROOM: from £20 to £35
SINGLE ROOM: from £35
FOOD: from £20 to £25
**Hours:** breakfast 8.30am-10am, Sunday lunch 1pm-3pm, dinner 7.30pm-9.30pm, bar meals all day.
**Cuisine:** INTERNATIONAL
**Cards:** Visa, Access, Diners, AmEx.
**Other points:** parking, children welcome, pets allowed, no-smoking area, conference facilities, residents' lounge, garden, open-air dining, vegetarian meals, traditional Sunday lunch, afternoon teas.
**Rooms:** 5 single rooms, 2 double rooms, 13 twin rooms, 15 family rooms. All with en suite, TV, telephone, radio, tea/coffee-making facilities.
**Directions:** from Dublin to Lonford N4, Lonford to Foxford N5, then to Pontoon.
BRENDAN & ANN GEARY ☎(094) 56120/56688 Fax(094) 56120

# CO. OFFALY

## BIRR • map 19C2

 **COUNTY ARMS HOTEL**
Railway Road
*One of the finest examples of late Georgian architecture c.1810, its well-preserved interior features are outstanding. The atmosphere is warm, cosy and peaceful. The lavish hotel gardens and glasshouses provide fresh herbs, fruit and vegetables for the various menus available at reasonable prices. Locally available, guests can enjoy golf, horse-riding, fishing, tennis and swimming in a heated indoor pool.*
DOUBLE ROOM: from £36 to £45
SINGLE ROOM: from £39
FOOD: from £15 to £20
**Hours:** closed 24th to 27th December (inclusive).
**Cuisine:** IRISH - traditional home-cooking using fresh ingredients.
**Cards:** Visa, Access, Diners, AmEx.
**Other points:** parking, children welcome, pets allowed, conference facilities, squash courts, garden, open-air dining, vegetarian meals, traditional Sunday lunch, afternoon teas.
**Rooms:** 4 single rooms, 10 twin rooms, 4 family rooms. All with en suite, TV, telephone, room service, tea/coffee-making facilities.
**Directions:** in its own grounds in the town of Birr.
MR W LOUGHNANE ☎(0509) 20791 Fax(0509) 21234

# CO. SLIGO

## COLLOONEY • map 19B2

 **MARKREE CASTLE**
Collooney

*Charles and Mary Cooper have restored Sligo's oldest inhabited house and made it a spectacular family hotel. Home of the Cooper family since 1640 and set in the middle of a large estate, Markree boasts spectacular plasterwork and a fine Irish oak staircase, yet has all the comforts of a three-star hotel. Good food, peace and quiet, lots of space and a warm family welcome await. Riding is also available on the estate.*
DOUBLE ROOM: from £47 to £53
SINGLE ROOM: over £55
FOOD: from £20 to £25
**Hours:** breakfast 8.30am-10am, bar meals 1pm-2.30pm, dinner 7.30pm-9.30pm, closed February.
**Cuisine:** IRISH - country home-cooking.

**Cards:** Visa, Access, Diners, AmEx.
**Other points:** parking, children welcome, pets allowed, no-smoking area, conference facilities, residents' lounge, garden, vegetarian meals, traditional Sunday lunch, afternoon teas.
**Rooms:** 3 double rooms, 4 twin rooms, 7 family rooms. All with en suite, TV, telephone, hair dryer, room service, baby-listening device.
**Directions:** 1 mile east of N4, 7 miles south of Sligo town.
CHARLES & MARY COOPER ☎(071) 67800 Fax (071) 67840

## CO. TYRONE

### OMAGH • map 13D2

#### THE MELLON COUNTRY INN
134 Beltany Road, BT78 5RA
*"Mary Gray's The Restaurant" offers an extensive à la carte menu which has been developed to suit both the cosmopolitan and regular clientele, offering dishes with recipes from all over Europe and complemented by more than 100 fine wines. "Russells The Granary" is the good food pub offering budget meals in a more casual style and also also caters for `late risers', offering traditional Ulster and continental breakfasts, coffee and scones from 10.30am and meals from 12noon until 9.30pm (8.30pm Sundays). A special children's menu is also available.*
FOOD: up to £20
**Hours:** restaurant: luch 12noon-2.30pm, dinner 6.30pm-9.30pm. "Russells": breakfast 10.30am-12noon, meals served 12 noon-9.30 / 8.30pm Sundays), high teas 5.30pm-7.30pm, dinner menu from 5.30pm.
**Cuisine:** BRITISH / CONTINENTAL - à la carte and table d'hôte menus. Dishes may include lobster and fillet steak with onions, lemon and garlic, fresh duckling in a puddle of peach sauce.
**Cards:** Visa, Access, Diners, AmEx.
**Other points:** licensed, open-air dining, Sunday lunch, no-smoking area, children welcome, pets allowed, vegetarian meals, garden, afternoon tea, parking.
**Directions:** half-way between Omagh and Newtonstewart. 1 mile from the Ulster American Folk Park.
KEN RUSSELL ☎(016626) 61946 Fax (016626) 62245

## CO. WEXFORD

### ROSSLARE HARBOUR • map 19D3

#### HOTEL ROSSLARE
Rosslare Harbour
*Hotel Rosslare is the oldest hotel and catering establishment in the area and has been gracing the Rosslare Harbour skyline since 1907. It once traded under the quaint name of Pope's Tea and Boarding House. The open log fire in the lobby sets the tone*

*of welcome you will receive from your hosts, Liam and Mary Griffin. The Portholes Bar offers a lively, friendly atmosphere, and the Captain's Table Restaurant, overlooking the harbour, offers a large range of excellent seafood and meat dishes. Squash court and sauna are available free to residents.*
DOUBLE ROOM: from £30 to £40
SINGLE ROOM: from £40 to £50
FOOD: from £15 to £20
**Hours:** breakfast 7am-10am, lunch 12.30am-2.30pm, dinner 6pm-9pm.
**Cuisine:** BRITISH - seafood, grills.
**Cards:** Visa, Access, Diners, AmEx.
**Other points:** parking, children welcome, conference facilities, open-air dining, vegetarian meals, traditional Sunday lunch, afternoon teas.
**Rooms:** 11 double rooms, 5 twin rooms, 9 family rooms. All with TV, telephone, hair dryer, trouser-press, room service.
**Directions:** overlooking the harbour, third hotel on the left.
LIAM GRIFFIN ☎(053) 33110 Fax (053) 33386

### WEXFORD • map 19D3

#### SOMETHING FROM THE CELLAR
Crescent Quay, Ireland
*A modern wine bar right on Wexford quay and enjoying panoramic views. The ambience and service are welcoming and friendly, and the extensive à la carte and table d'hôte menus offer something for every taste, with seafood dishes a particular speciality. A full international wine list can be sampled by the glass or the bottle. Live grand piano music three nights a week.*
FOOD: up to £15
**Hours:** bar meals 12noon-1.30pm, lunch 12.30pm-3pm, dinner 6pm-11pm, late food until 1am.
**Cuisine:** MODERN INTERNATIONAL - dish dishes.
**Cards:** Visa, Access, Diners, AmEx.
**Other points:** live piano music Wednesday, Friday, Saturday. Private parties and conferences catered for.
**Directions:** opposite the Commodore Barry memorial, Crescent Quay.
PAT GEOGHEGAN & PETER SHIGGINS ☎(053) 22688 Fax (053) 24177

## CO. WICKLOW

### GLENDALOUGH • map 19C3

### THE GLENDALOUGH HOTEL

The family run Glendalough Hotel is situated in the heart of the beautiful wooded valley from which it takes its name. The hotel has recently been renovated and refurbished, with the interior sympathetically restored to the tasteful style expected of such a splendid early Victorian building. The Glendasan River restaurant extends from the hotel across the sparkling mountain stream after which it is named. A most tranquil and relaxing location for a holiday break.

DOUBLE ROOM: from £30 to £40
SINGLE ROOM: from £35 to £45
FOOD: from £15 to £20
**Hours:** breakfast 8am-10am, lunch and bar meals 12noon-3pm, dinner 5.30pm-9pm, bar meals 5.30pm-8pm, open bank holidays, closed mid-December to February.
**Cuisine:** EUROPEAN STYLE - good choice of appetisers and main dishes in the Glendasan River restaurant, including special childrens dishes. Gledalough Tavern offers lighter dishes and bar snacks.
**Cards:** Visa, Access, Diners, AmEx.
**Other points:** The Glendason River Restaurant, The Glendalough Tavern, The Glendalough shop, conference and business facilities, parking.
**Rooms:** 6 single rooms, 28 twin rooms, 7 double rooms, 3 family rooms, all en suite. All with satellite TV, wake up alarm, room service and telephone.
**Directions:** from Dublin N11 south to Kilmanague village, turn right for 15 miles. From Waterford/Wexford take N11 north to Arklow, then to Rathdrum and Glendalough.
MR PATRICK CASEY
☎(0404) 45135 Fax(0404) 45142

Membership Application Form
Britannia Rescue
FREEPOST
Huddersfield
HD1 1WP

**BLOCK LETTERS PLEASE**

SURNAME ------------------------ INITIALS ---------------- TITLE (Mr/Mrs/Miss/Ms) -----------

ADDRESS -------------------------------------------------------------------------------

-----------------------------------------------------------------------------------------

------------------------------- POSTCODE ---------------- TEL NO. ----------------

Cover commences from midnight of date of our receipt of this application form or later if you specify here

**COMPLETE SECTIONS A OR B AND C TOGETHER WITH METHOD OF PAYMENT DETAILS.**

**A** ANNUAL RATES applicable to 31.12.96 or later review date.

| | Single Vehicle | ✔ Tick | Two Vehicles | ✔ Tick |
|---|---|---|---|---|
| RESCUE PLUS | £30.00 | | £45.00 | |
| STANDARD | £57.25 | | £85.90 | |
| COMPREHENSIVE | £75.70 | | £116.00 | |
| DELUXE | £92.50 | | £141.50 | |
| Optional extra PERSONAL COVER (with Free Card for Spouse/Domestic Partner | | | £19.50 | |
| Annual supplement (if paying by cash, cheque, or single credit card payment) | | | £5.00 | |
| **ENTER TOTAL COST OF TICKED OPTIONS** | | | £ | |

Note: ANNUAL RATE is a single payment, providing 12 months cover.

**B** MONTHLY PREMIUMS (Direct Debit and Continuous Credit Card Authority only)

| | Single Vehicle | ✔ Tick | Two Vehicles | ✔ Tick |
|---|---|---|---|---|
| RESCUE PLUS | £2.70 | | £4.05 | |
| STANDARD | £5.75 | | £8.60 | |
| COMPREHENSIVE | £7.60 | | £11.60 | |
| DELUXE | £9.25 | | £14.15 | |
| Optional extra PERSONAL COVER (with Free Card for Spouse/Domestic Partner | | | £1.95 | |
| **ENTER TOTAL COST OF TICKED OPTIONS** | | | £ | |

Note: MONTHLY PREMIUMS are continuous payments available only by DIRECT DEBIT or Continuous Credit Card Authority until cancelled by either party and are subject to amendments from time to time. Members are given prior notice of any change of payment.

CAR GRILLE BADGE (inc. VAT and P&P) £5.50 payment by cheque only ☐ Additional vehicles - details on request.

**C** 1st CAR DETAILS

| | Reg No | Year New | Make | Model |
|---|---|---|---|---|
| 1st CAR DETAILS | | | | |
| 2nd CAR DETAILS | | | | |

The above rates include Insurance Premium Tax at the prevailing rate and are applicable only to vehicles under 2.5 tonnes / 2,540 kilos gross vehicle weight.

I wish to apply for membership of Britannia Rescue and I certify that the vehicle(s) to be covered is/are fully roadworthy and in normal use and is/are insured and kept at my home address here given. I agree to abide by the Terms and Conditions of Britannia Rescue.

ALL MEMBERS MUST SIGN.

SIGNATURE [                                    ] DATE [            ]

METHODS OF PAYMENT

1. TRANSCASH    Complete Transcash forms from the Post Office, make payable to Britannia Recovery Ltd. Girobank Account No 3006980. Please enclose receipt with application form. Standard Transcash fee will be payable.

2. CHEQUE/P.O.    Make payable to Britannia Recovery Ltd. Cheque/P.O. [            ]

3. CREDIT CARD    Please debit my ACCESS ☐ VISA ☐ (please tick)

    Card No [                        ]    Card Expiry Date [        ]

4. CONTINUOUS CREDIT CARD AUTHORITY -  Sign here only if you wish to authorise automatic renewal by credit card: I authorise Britannia Recovery Ltd. until further written notice, to charge my Access/ Visa card account with unspecified amounts in respect of my Britannia Rescue membership.

SIGNATURE [                        ]    DATE [            ]

5. DIRECT DEBIT    Please complete the direct debit mandate overleaf.

As part of our service, Britannia Rescue will send you information about valuable offers especially negotiated for members. If you prefer not to receive this information, please tick here. ☐

409

# The Direct Debit Guarantee

This Guarantee is offered by all Banks and Building Societies that take part in the Direct Debit Scheme. The efficiency and security of the Scheme is monitored and protected by your own Bank or Building Society.

If the amounts to be paid or the payment dates change, you will be told of this in advance by at least 30 days as agreed.

If an error is made by us or your Bank/Building Society, you are guaranteed a full and immediate refund from your branch of the amount paid.

You can cancel a Direct Debit at any time, by writing to your Bank or Building Society. Please also send a copy of your letter to us.

---

BRITANNIA RESCUE

## Direct Debit

## Instruction to your Bank or Building Society to pay Direct Debits.

Please fill in the whole form and send it to: Britannia Recovery Ltd, Freepost (no stamp required) Huddersfield HD1 1WP

Originators Identification Number

| 9 | 1 | 2 | 9 | 3 | 0 |

1. Names and full address of your Bank or Building Society Branch

To: The Manger

_____ Bank or Building Society

Address _____

_____ Postcode

2. Names(s) of Account holder(s)

3. Branch sort code
(from the top right hand corner of your cheque)

4. Bank or Building Society Account number

5. Britannia Recovery Ltd. reference number
(for office use only)

6. Instructions to your Bank or Building Society
Please pay Britannia Recovery Ltd. Direct Debit from the account detailed on this Instruction subject to the safeguards assured by The Direct Debit Guarantee.

Signature(s)

_____

_____ Date

Banks and Building Societies may not accept Direct Debit instructions for some types of account.

# YOUR RECOMMENDATIONS

Do you have a favourite restaurant, inn, hotel or guest house that you would like to recommend to us - or possibly a restaurant that you have visited recently and would like to see included in the *Club Bon Viveur* dining scheme?

If so, please record your recommendations on the page below, so that we can arrange for one of our inspectors to call on them. Alternatively, if you have visited a Les Routiers establishment and are dissatisfied, we would still like to receive you comments. All correspondence is treated in the strictest confidence.

You may continue on a separate piece of paper, which should be attached to this page when returning it to us.

---

Establishment Name: . . . . . . . . . . . . . . . . . . . . . . . . . . . . . . . . . . . . . . . . . . .

Address: . . . . . . . . . . . . . . . . . . . . . . . . . . . . . . . . . . . . . . . . . . . . . . . . . . . . . . .

. . . . . . . . . . . . . . . . . . . . . . . . . . . . . . . . . . . . . . . . . . . . . . . . . . . . . . . . . . . . .

. . . . . . . . . . . . . . . . . . . . . . . . . . . Post Code . . . . . . . . . . . . . . . . . . . .

Establishment type (please circle)

| **Restaurant** | **Public House** | **Hotel** |
| **Wine Bar** | **B&B** | **Other** |

Please circle:  **NOMINATION**  **COMPLAINT**

Your Comments: . . . . . . . . . . . . . . . . . . . . . . . . . . . . . . . . . . . . . . . . . . . . . . .

. . . . . . . . . . . . . . . . . . . . . . . . . . . . . . . . . . . . . . . . . . . . . . . . . . . . . . . . . . . .

. . . . . . . . . . . . . . . . . . . . . . . . . . . . . . . . . . . . . . . . . . . . . . . . . . . . . . . . . . . .

. . . . . . . . . . . . . . . . . . . . . . . . . . . . . . . . . . . . . . . . . . . . . . . . . . . . . . . . . . . .

. . . . . . . . . . . . . . . . . . . . . . . . . . . . . . . . . . . . . . . . . . . . . . . . . . . . . . . . . . . .

. . . . . . . . . . . . . . . . . . . . . . . . . . . . . . . . . . . . . . . . . . . . . . . . . . . . . . . . . . . .

. . . . . . . . . . . . . . . . . . . . . . . . . . . . . . . . . . . . . . . . . . . . . . . . . . . . . . . . . . . .

. . . . . . . . . . . . . . . . . . . . . . . . . . . . . . . . . . . . . . . . . . . . . . . . . . . . . . . . . . . .

. . . . . . . . . . . . . . . . . . . . . . . . . . . . . . . . . . . . . . . . . . . . . . . . . . . . . . . . . . . .

---

If recommending a restaurant for the *Joie de Vivre* Directory, please answer the following questions:

Type/s of cuisine: .................................................................

.................................................................

.................................................................

.................................................................

.................................................................

.................................................................

.................................................................

Average price of a meal for two (excluding drinks): £ .....................

Reason for your recommendation: ...........................................

.................................................................

.................................................................

.................................................................

.................................................................

.................................................................

.................................................................

.................................................................

Your name (Mr/Mrs/Ms/Miss): ............................................

Your address: .........................................................

.................................................................

CBV Membership number (if applicable): ..............................

Signature: ............................................................

Date: ................................................................

**Please return to: LES ROUTIERS** 25 Vanston Place, London SW6 1AZ

# INDEX OF
# LES ROUTIERS ESTABLISHMENTS

# INDEX OF TOWN NAMES

| | | | | | | |
|---|---|---|---|---|---|
| Holland Park | 81 | Kingussie | 371 | Lostwithiel | 150 |
| Holmfirth | 322 | Kinlochleven | 371 | Loughborough | 248 |
| Holton | 207 | Kinross | 394 | Loughbrickland | 402 |
| Holyhead | 342 | Kirkby Lonsdale | 280 | Louth | 251 |
| Honiton | 165 | Kirkmichael | 394 | Lulworth Cove | 184 |
| Horseheath | 101 | Kirkwall | 382 | Luton | 95 |
| Horsham | 133 | Knaresborough | 308 | Lyddington | 248 |
| Howth | 403 | Knutsford | 231 | Lydford | 168 |
| Huddersfield | 322 | Kylesku | 372 | Lyme Regis | 184 |
| Hull | 287 | | | Lymington | 194 |
| Huntingdon | 101 | **L** | | Lyndhurst | 194 |
| Hyde | 284 | Lacock | 215 | Lynmouth | 168 |
| | | Laghey | 401 | Lynton | 169 |
| **I** | | Lancaster | 293 | Lytham St Annes | 294 |
| Ickham | 110 | Land's End | 149 | | |
| Ilfracombe | 166 | Largs | 387 | **M** | |
| Ilkley | 323 | Laxey | 289 | Macclesfield | 231 |
| Ilmington | 266 | Leadburn | 381 | Macduff | 361 |
| Ilminster | 207 | Leadenhall | 83 | Machynlleth | 348 |
| Invergarry | 366 | Leadenham | 250 | Maidenhead | 143 |
| Inverness | 367 | Leatherhead | 123 | Maidstone | 110 |
| Inverurie | 360 | Ledburn | 97 | Mallow | 400 |
| Island of Sark | 222 | Ledbury | 244 | Malmesbury | 215 |
| Isle of Arran | 385 | Leeds | 323 | Malton | 309 |
| Isle of Barra | 396 | Leek | 264 | Manchester | 284 |
| Isle of Benbecula | 396 | Leeming Bar | 308 | Mansfield | 255 |
| Isle of Bute | 386 | Leenane | 404 | Marble Arch | 84 |
| Isle of Colonsay | 386 | Leicester | 247 | Margate | 110 |
| Isle of Harris | 396 | Leicester Square | 83 | Matlock | 234 |
| Isle of Mull | 386 | Leighlinbridge | 400 | Mawdesley | 295 |
| Isle of Skye | 368 | Lewes | 129 | Mayfair | 84 |
| Isle of Whithorn | 354 | Leyburn | 308 | Melmerby | 280 |
| Isles of Scilly | 149 | Leyland | 293 | Melrose | 351 |
| Ivybridge | 167 | Lichfield | 264 | Melton Mowbray | 248 |
| | | Limerick | 405 | Mere | 215 |
| **J** | | Lincoln | 250 | Mevagissey | 150 |
| Jersey | 223 | Lindfield | 133 | Mildenhall | 119 |
| Johnstone | 387 | Linlithgow | 381 | Milford Haven | 330 |
| | | Linton | 101 | Milnathort | 394 |
| **K** | | Liskeard | 149 | Milton Keynes | 97 |
| Kegworth | 234 | Little Haven | 329 | Minehead | 208 |
| Kendal | 278 | Liverpool | 296 | Moffat | 355 |
| Kenilworth | 266 | Llanbedr | 343 | Mold | 326 |
| Kenmore | 393 | Llandovery | 330 | Monmouth | 337 |
| Kensington | 81 | Llandrindod Wells | 347 | Montrose | 395 |
| Kersey | 119 | Llandudno | 343 | Moreton-in-Marsh | 240 |
| Keswick | 279 | Llangollen | 326 | Mortehoe | 170 |
| Kettering | 254 | Llanidloes | 348 | Motherwell | 389 |
| Kew | 82 | Llantrisant | 336 | Much Wenlock | 262 |
| Kilkee | 400 | Llanwddyn | 348 | Muswell Hill | 84 |
| Kilkeel | 402 | Llanymynech | 262 | Mylor Bridge | 150 |
| Kilkenny | 405 | Lochcarron | 372 | | |
| Killin | 353 | Lochearnhead | 353 | | |
| Killyleagh | 402 | Lochgilphead | 388 | **N** | |
| Kilmarnock | 387 | Lochinver | 372 | Naas | 404 |
| Kilwinning | 387 | Lockerbie | 355 | Nailsea | 141 |
| Kincraig | 371 | Long Melford | 119 | Nairn | 372 |
| King's Cross | 83 | Longham | 184 | Nantwich | 231 |
| King's Lynn | 116 | Longridge | 293 | Nethy Bridge | 372 |
| Kingsbridge | 167 | Longtown | 280 | | |
| Kingston-upon-Thames | 83 | Looe | 149 | | |

New Galloway 355
New Milton 194
New Quay 330
Newark-on-Trent 255
Newbury 144
Newcastle 402
Newcastle Emlyn 331
Newcastle-under-Lyme 265
Newcastle-upon-Tyne 302
Newlyn 151
Newport (Isle of Wight) 202
Newport 337
Newport Pagnell 97
Newquay 151
Newton Abbot 170
Newton Aycliffe 274
Newton Stewart 356
Newtonmore 373
Newtown 349
Newtownards 403
North Uist 396
Northallerton 309
Northampton 254
Norton 262
Norwich 116
Nottingham 256
Nympsfield 240

## O

Oban 389
Odiham 195
Old Dalby 248
Omagh 407
Ormskirk 295
Osmotherley 309
Oswestry 263
Otterburn 301
Oughterard 404
Oxford 259

## P

Paddington 85
Paignton 170
Paisley 390
Panborough 208
Parkend 240
Parkgate 232
Peebles 351
Penn 97
Penrith 281
Penshurst 111
Penzance 153
Perranporth 154
Pershore 244
Perth 395
Peterborough 102
Peterhead 361
Pewsey 216
Philleigh 154

Pillaton 154
Pimlico 85
Pinner 85
Pitlochry 395
Pluckley 111
Plymouth 171
Polperro 155
Pontoon 406
Poole 185
Poolewe 374
Port Erin 289
Port Isaac 155
Porthmadog 346
Portrush 399
Portsmouth 195
Preston 295
Prestwick 390
Princes Risborough 97
Putney 86
Pwllheli 346

## R

Ramsbottom 285
Ramsey 289
Ramsgate 111
Rangeworthy 142
Reading 144
Redditch 244
Reedham 116
Reeth 309
Reigate 124
Ribchester 295
Richmond (London) 86
Richmond (north Yorks) 310
Ridgmont 95
Ringwood 196
Rochdale 285
Rock 155
Rockbourne 196
Rode 208
Romsey 196
Rosedale Abbey 310
Rosehall 374
Roslin 381
Ross-on-Wye 245
Rosslare Harbour 407
Rosyth 358
Rotherham 319
Rowde 216
Royal Forest of Dean 240
Royal Leamington Spa 266
Royal Tunbridge Wells 111
Royston 107
Ruislip 87
Rusper 134
Rye 130

## S

Saffron Walden 105
Salisbury 216

Sandown 202
Saundersfoot 331
Saxmundham 120
Scarborough 310
Scourie 374
Scunthorpe 287
Seaford 130
Seahouses 301
Seaview 202
Sedbergh 281
Sevenoaks 112
Shaftesbury 187
Shaldon 172
Shanklin 203
Sheffield 319
Shepherd's Bush 87
Sherston 218
Shipley 324
Shipston-on-Stour 266
Shipton-under-Wychwood 260
Shrewsbury 263
Sidford 172
Sidmouth 172
Sittingbourne 112
Skegness 252
Sleford 252
Snettisham 116
Solihull 270
Souldern 260
South Croydon 87
South Molton 173
South Shields 302
Southampton 199
Southend-on-Sea 105
Southport 296
Southwold 120
Spalding 252
Spilsby 253
St Agnes 156
St Andrews 358
St Asaph 327
St Clears 331
St David's 332
St Helen's 204
St Ives (Cambridge) 102
St Ives (Cornwall) 156
St Just 157
St Mawes 158
Stafford 265
Staines 87
Stamford 253
Stapleton 248
Steeple Aston 260
Steppingley 95
Steyning 134
Stilton 102
Stockbridge 200
Stoke Newington 88
Stoke-sub-Hamdon 208
Stokesley 313
Stonehaven 361
Stony Stratford 98

| | | | | | | |
|---|---|---|---|---|---|---|
| Stourbridge | 270 | **W** | | **Y** | | |
| Stourpaine | 187 | Wadebridge | 159 | | | |
| Stow-on-the-Wold | 241 | Wakefield | 324 | Yeovil | 211 | |
| Stratford-upon-Avon | 267 | Wallasey | 297 | York | 316 | |
| Strathpeffer | 374 | Wandsworth | 89 | | | |
| Stromness | 382 | Warkworth | 301 | | | |
| Stroud | 241 | Warminster | 218 | | | |
| Studland | 187 | Warwick | 268 | | | |
| Sudbury | 120 | Watchet | 209 | | | |
| Sunderland | 302 | Watford | 107 | | | |
| Sutton | 88 | Watlington | 261 | | | |
| Swanage | 188 | Watton-at-Stone | 108 | | | |
| Swansea | 335 | Welford | 254 | | | |
| | | Wells | 209 | | | |
| **T** | | Wells-next-the-Sea | 117 | | | |
| Tain | 375 | Welshpool | 349 | | | |
| Tal-y-Bont | 346 | Weobley | 246 | | | |
| Taunton | 209 | West End | 89 | | | |
| Tavistock | 173 | West Hampstead | 91 | | | |
| Taynuilt | 390 | West Lulworth | 189 | | | |
| Tayvallich | 390 | West Marden | 135 | | | |
| Teddington | 88 | West Wittering | 135 | | | |
| Teignmouth | 173 | West Wycombe | 98 | | | |
| Tenby | 332 | Westminster | 91 | | | |
| Tewkesbury | 242 | Weston-super-Mare | 142 | | | |
| Thame | 260 | Westoning | 95 | | | |
| The Lizard | 158 | Wexford | 407 | | | |
| Thirsk | 313 | Weymouth | 189 | | | |
| Thornaby-on-Tees | 272 | Whatton | 257 | | | |
| Thornhill | 356 | Whitby | 314 | | | |
| Thornton Hough | 297 | Whitley Bay | 303 | | | |
| Throwleigh | 174 | Whitstable | 113 | | | |
| Thurgarton | 257 | Wigginton | 315 | | | |
| Thurso | 375 | Wigglesworth | 316 | | | |
| Tintagel | 158 | Wilton | 219 | | | |
| Tintern | 338 | Wimbledon | 92 | | | |
| Tiverton | 174 | Wimborne | 190 | | | |
| Tonbridge | 112 | Wincanton | 210 | | | |
| Tongue | 376 | Winchester | 200 | | | |
| Topsham | 175 | Windemere | 281 | | | |
| Torquay | 175 | Winterborne Zelston | 190 | | | |
| Totland Bay | 204 | Wirksworth | 235 | | | |
| Totnes | 176 | Witney | 261 | | | |
| Trefnant | 327 | Wokingham | 145 | | | |
| Tregony | 158 | Woodbridge | 120 | | | |
| Trent | 188 | Woodfalls | 201 | | | |
| Tring | 98 | Woodford Green | 92 | | | |
| Trowbridge | 218 | Woodhall Spa | 253 | | | |
| Truro | 159 | Woodstock | 261 | | | |
| Twickenham | 89 | Wool | 191 | | | |
| Tyndrum | 353 | Woolacombe | 176 | | | |
| | | Woolverton | 211 | | | |
| **U** | | Worcester | 246 | | | |
| Ullapool | 376 | Worksop | 257 | | | |
| Uppingham | 249 | Worthing | 135 | | | |
| | | Wrentham | 121 | | | |
| **V** | | Wrexham | 327 | | | |
| Ventnor | 204 | Wrightington | 296 | | | |
| Victoria | 89 | Wythenshawe | 285 | | | |

For Reservations & Special Offers FreeCall 0500 700 456

# NOTES

# NOTES

# NOTES